CALIFORNIA World History

Ancient Civilizations

myWorld INTERACTIVE

TEACHER EDITION

Pearson

Boston, Massachusetts Chandler, Arizona
Glenview, Illinois New York, New York

Cover: Jon Bower at Apexphotos/Moment Open/Getty Images; lv: MBI/Alamy Stock Photo

Pearson

ISBN-13: 978-0-32-895880-1
ISBN-10: 0-32-895880-8
3 17

AUTHORS, CONSULTANTS, PARTNERS

Program Authors

Frank Karpiel
teaches at the Citadel Military College in South Carolina and earned his Ph.D. degree in history from the University of Hawaii. His focus of study is world history and how cross-cultural interactions shape present-day human society.

George F. Sabato
is a Past President of the California Council for the Social Studies.

Michael Yell
is a Past President of the National Council for the Social Studies.

Program Consultants

ELL Consultant
Jim Cummins Ph.D.
Professor Emeritus, Department of Curriculum, Teaching, and Learning
University of Toronto
Toronto, Canada

Differentiated Instruction Consultant
Marianne Sender
In-Class Resource Teacher
Renaissance @ Rand Middle School
Montclair, New Jersey

Reading Consultant
Elfrieda H. Hiebert Ph.D.
Founder, President and CEO of TextProject, Inc.
University of California, Santa Cruz

Inquiry and C3 Consultant
Dr. Kathy Swan
Professor of Curriculum and Instruction
University of Kentucky
Lexington, Kentucky

Program Partners

NBC Learn, the educational arm of NBC News, develops original stories for use in the classroom and makes archival NBC news stories, images, and primary source documents available on demand to teachers, students, and parents. NBC Learn partnered with Pearson to produce the topic opening videos that support this program.

Campaign for the Civic Mission of Schools is a coalition of over 70 national civic learning, education, civic engagement, and business groups committed to improving the quality and quantity of civic learning in American schools.

Constitutional Rights Foundation is a nonprofit, nonpartisan, community-based organization focused on educating students about the importance of civic participation in a democratic society. The Constitutional Rights Foundation is the lead contributor to the development of the Civic Discussion Quests for this program.

REVIEWERS

Pearson would like to extend a special thank you to all of the California teachers who helped guide the development of this program. We gratefully acknowledge your efforts to realize Next Generation Social Studies teaching and learning that will prepare American students for college, careers, and active citizenship.

Program Reviewers

Warren J. Blumenfeld, Ed.D.
Former Associate Professor, Iowa State University, School of Education
South Hadley, Massachusetts

Barbara B. Brown
African Studies Center
Boston University
Boston, Massachusetts

J.P. Dessel
Department of History
University of Tennessee
Knoxville, Tennessee

J. Michael Francis
Department of History
University of North Florida
Jacksonville, Florida

Judy E. Gaughan
Department of History
Colorado State University
Fort Collins, Colorado

Huping Ling
Department of History
Truman State University
Kirksville, Missouri

Gordon Newby
Department of Middle Eastern and South Asian Studies
Emory University
Atlanta, Georgia

Thomas J. Sanders
Department of History
United States Naval Academy
Annapolis, Maryland

David Webster
Department of Anthropology
Pennsylvania State University
University Park, Pennsylvania

California Teacher Reviewers

Jeff Caron
Bellflower USD
Bellflower, California

Ruth Castro
Inglewood USD
Inglewood, California

Dan Fong
Bellflower USD
Bellflower, California

Stephanie Fortunato
Inglewood USD
Inglewood, California

Christina Hernandez
Chula Vista ESD
Chula Vista, California

Jennifer Mazurie
Bellflower USD
Bellflower, California

Steve Rowe
Inglewood USD
Inglewood, California

Anthony Zambelli
San Diego Center for Economic Education
San Diego, California

Welcome to Your Program

Built in partnership with California educators, ***California History-Social Science myWorld Interactive*** applies the latest **research and technology** to effectively engage students in social studies through **civic involvement** and literacy. Students will learn about their world while covering the core history-social science standards. A highly **flexible** blend of print and digital materials **maximizes** student learning and classroom time.

Program Organization

A research-based, student-centered instructional model with a four-part structure enhances teaching and learning. Students will interact with the content by Connecting, Investigating, Synthesizing, and Demonstrating their understanding.

The Student Edition begins with several pages where students explore the guiding questions found in the California History-Social Science Framework. Each Topic begins with a listing of **digital resources** that are available throughout the topic as well as an exploration of the topic's **Essential Question**. As students dive into the topic content, they are provided with a map, timeline and a few biographies to set the context of the topic by exploring **Who**, **What**, **Where**, and **When**.

CONTENT. INQUIRY. LITERACY. CITIZENSHIP. This program is written entirely to the California State Standards and the 2016 California History-Social Science Framework.

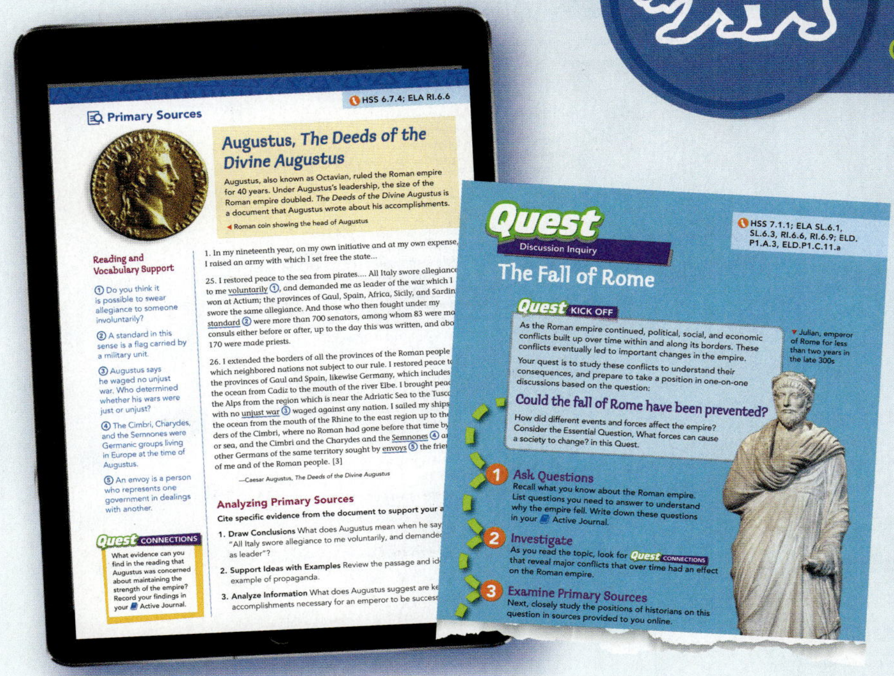

The **Quest Inquiry Activity** is an inquiry project that takes place over the course of the entire topic. Students are presented with a question or problem, and throughout the chapter they conduct research, read the text, analyze primary sources, and answer the question or problem. The Quest culminates at the end of the topic, where students apply their knowledge and demonstrate their understanding in a final project: essay, discussion, presentation, or informed action activity. Quests may be assigned as an individual activity or as group work.

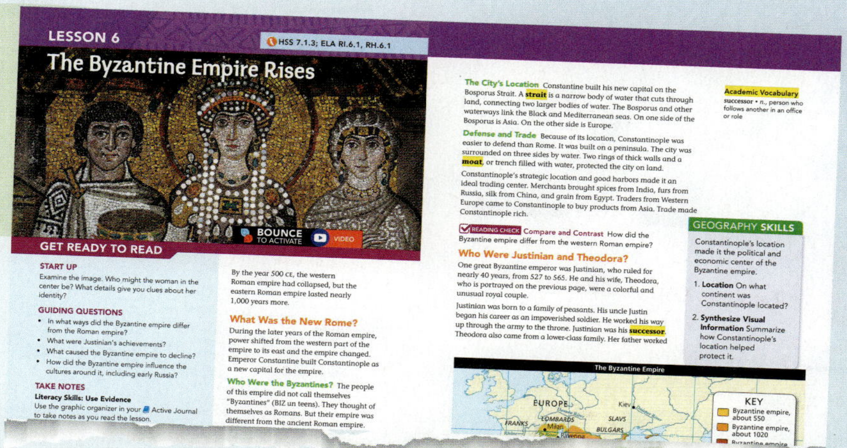

Literacy support is built into the text with **Get Ready to Read** sections, **Lesson Narratives**, **Reading Checks,** vocabulary and word skills, writing projects, support for English Language Development (ELD), and online Interactivities.

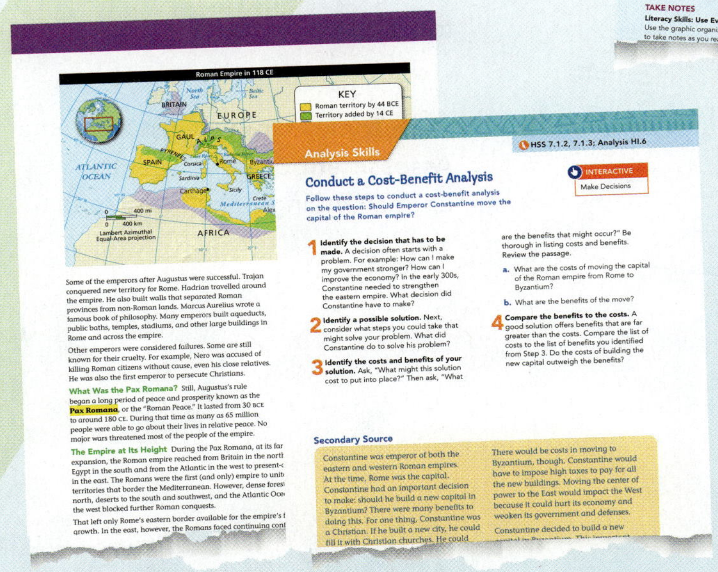

Geography skills are embedded in each lesson in the form of maps and critical thinking and analysis questions. The **Analysis Skills** features provide students with the opportunity to practice and apply important critical thinking skills.

Program Organization

Primary Sources are embedded throughout the narrative to give voice to both the famous and ordinary people of history. The text narrative is rich with **Biography Features** of leaders and ordinary people whose actions and decisions made history.

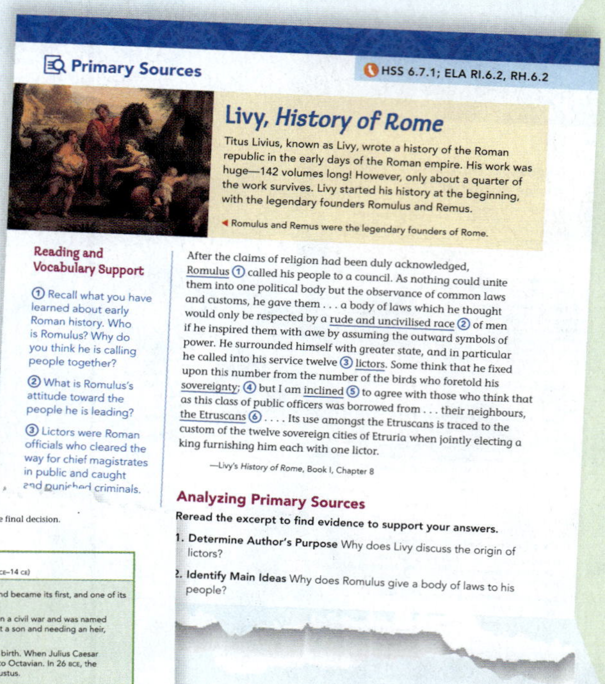
Primary Sources

HSS 6.7.1; ELA RI.6.2, RH.6.2

Livy, History of Rome

Titus Livius, known as Livy, wrote a history of the Roman republic in the early days of the Roman empire. His work was huge—142 volumes long! However, only about a quarter of the work survives. Livy started his history at the beginning, with the legendary founders Romulus and Remus.

◀ Romulus and Remus were the legendary founders of Rome.

Reading and Vocabulary Support

① Recall what you have learned about early Roman history. Who is Romulus? Why do you think he is calling people together?

② What is Romulus's attitude toward the people he is leading?

③ Lictors were Roman officials who cleared the way for chief magistrates in public and caught and punished criminals.

After the claims of religion had been duly acknowledged, Romulus ① called his people to a council. As nothing could unite them into one political body but the observance of common laws and customs, he gave them . . . a body of laws which he thought would only be respected by a rude and uncivilised race ② of men if he inspired them with awe by assuming the outward symbols of power. He surrounded himself with greater state, and in particular he called into his service twelve ③ lictors. Some think that he fixed upon this number from the number of the birds who foretold his sovereignty; ④ but I am inclined ⑤ to agree with those who think that as this class of public officers was borrowed from . . . their neighbours, the Etruscans ⑥ . . . . Its use amongst the Etruscans is traced to the custom of the twelve sovereign cities of Etruria when jointly electing a king furnishing him each with one lictor.

—Livy's History of Rome, Book I, Chapter 8

Analyzing Primary Sources

Reread the excerpt to find evidence to support your answers.

1. Determine Author's Purpose Why does Livy discuss the origin of lictors?
2. Identify Main Ideas Why does Romulus give a body of laws to his people?

Sometimes the Roman army made the final decision.

BIOGRAPHY
5 Things to Know About
AUGUSTUS
Roman Emperor (c. 62 BCE–14 CE)

- He founded the Roman empire and became its first, and one of its greatest, emperors.
- His great-uncle, Julius Caesar, won a civil war and was named Rome's dictator in 46 BCE. Without a son and needing an heir, Caesar adopted Octavian.
- Augustus was named Octavius at birth. When Julius Caesar adopted him, his name changed to Octavian. In 26 BCE, the Roman Senate renamed him Augustus.
- After Caesar was murdered in 44 BCE, Augustus formed alliances and fought bloody battles to win control of the empire.
- He persuaded the senate that he ruled according to the traditions of the republic. In fact, he held all power. His long reign as emperor was prosperous and peaceful.

Critical Thinking What methods did Augustus use to gain total power over Rome?

316 Lesson 8.1 • The Roman Empire Begins

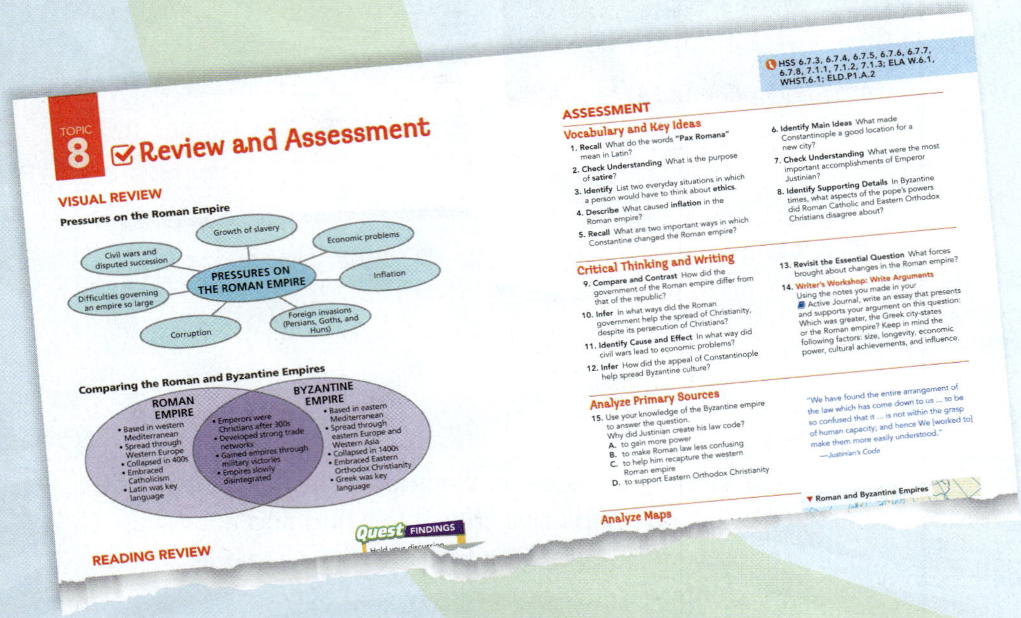
TOPIC 8 Review and Assessment

VISUAL REVIEW

Pressures on the Roman Empire

Comparing the Roman and Byzantine Empires

READING REVIEW

Quest FINDINGS

HSS 6.7.3, 6.7.4, 6.7.5, 6.7.6, 6.7.7, 6.7.8, 7.1.1, 7.1.2, 7.1.3; ELA W.6.1, WHST.6.1; ELD.P1.A.2

ASSESSMENT

Vocabulary and Key Ideas

1. Recall What do the words "Pax Romana" mean in Latin?
2. Check Understanding What is the purpose of satire?
3. Identify List two everyday situations in which a person would have to think about ethics.
4. Describe What caused inflation in the Roman empire?
5. Recall What are two important ways in which Constantine changed the Roman empire?
6. Identify Main Ideas What made Constantinople a good location for a new city?
7. Check Understanding What were the most important accomplishments of Emperor Justinian?
8. Identify Supporting Details In Byzantine times, what aspects of the pope's powers did Roman Catholic and Eastern Orthodox Christians disagree about?

Critical Thinking and Writing

9. Compare and Contrast How did the government of the Roman empire differ from that of the republic?
10. Infer In what ways did the Roman government help the spread of Christianity, despite its persecution of Christians?
11. Identify Cause and Effect In what way did civil wars lead to economic problems?
12. Infer How did the appeal of Constantinople help spread Byzantine culture?
13. Revisit the Essential Question What forces brought about changes in the Roman empire?
14. Writer's Workshop: Write Arguments Using the notes you made in your Active Journal, write an essay that presents and supports your argument on this question: Which was greater, the Greek city-states or the Roman empire? Keep in mind the following factors: size, longevity, economic power, cultural achievements, and influence.

Analyze Primary Sources

15. Use your knowledge of the Byzantine empire to answer the question. Why did Justinian create his law code?
    A. to gain more power
    B. to make Roman law less confusing
    C. to help him recapture the western Roman empire
    D. to support Eastern Orthodox Christianity

"We have found the entire arrangement of the law which has come down to us ... to be so confused that it ... is not within the grasp of human capacity; and hence We [worked to] make them more easily understood."
—Justinian's Code

Analyze Maps

▼ Roman and Byzantine Empires

The **Visual Review** at the end of each topic summarizes key content using charts, graphs, and tables. These aids are designed to provide quick review tools for students.

Each Topic culminates in a summative **Assessment** of the student's understanding of key concepts.

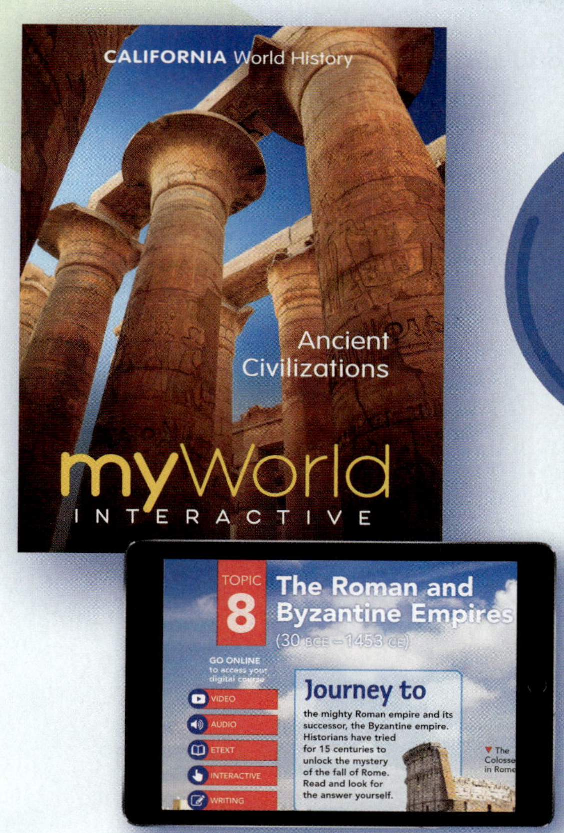

Flexible Print and Digital Program

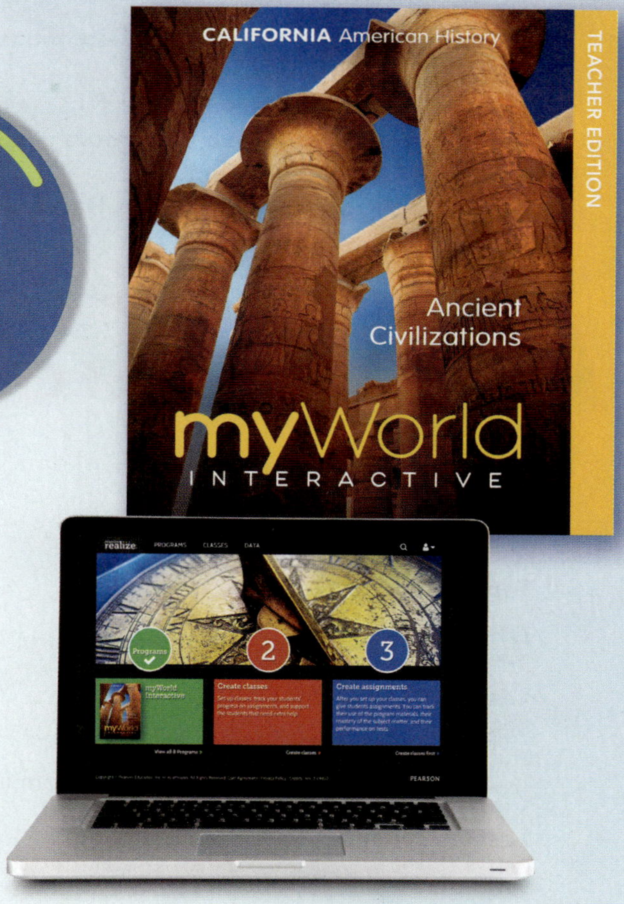

Student Components

Student Edition Hard Cover: Includes all core content lessons, skill lessons, and primary source features.

Active Journal: Consumable notebook including support for completing the "Quest" inquiry/activity strand, close reading support, and vocabulary practice.

Online Student Resources PEARSON realize™: Full Digital Course for each grade with Interactivities and links to the Student eText for narrative content.

Teacher Components

Teacher Guide: Print Teacher Edition with full lesson support and integrated ELD support. Aligns to California State Standards and the 2016 California History-Social Science Framework.

Active Journal Answer Key: Answer key for the student Active Journal.

Online Teacher Resources PEARSON realize™: Digital course with Interactivities and links to the eText for narrative content. Includes Teacher Resources and blackline masters for additional support with ELL strategies, close reading, and skills instruction.

CONTENTS

TOPIC 1

HSS 6.1.1, 6.1.2, 6.1.3, 6.2.1, 6.2.2, 6.2.9, 7.7.1, 7.7.2, 7.7.4, 7.7.5

Origins of Civilization (Prehistory–4000 BCE)

TOPIC 2

HSS 6.2.1, 6.2.2, 6.2.3, 6.2.4, 6.2.9, 6.3.1, 6.3.2, 6.3.3, 6.3.4, 6.3.5

Civilizations and Peoples of the Fertile Crescent (3400 BCE–70 CE)

TOPIC 3

HSS 6.2.1, 6.2.2, 6.2.3, 6.2.5, 6.2.6, 6.2.7, 6.2.8, 6.2.9

Ancient Egypt and Kush (3000 BCE–600 BCE)

CONTENTS

TOPIC 4 HSS 6.5.1, 6.5.2, 6.5.3, 6.5.4, 6.5.5, 6.5.6, 6.5.7

Early Civilizations of India (3100 BCE–540 CE)

TOPIC 5

HSS 6.2.9, 6.6.1, 6.6.2, 6.6.3, 6.6.4, 6.6.5, 6.6.6, 6.6.7, 6.6.8

Early Civilization of China (1700 BCE–220 CE)

TOPIC 6

HSS 6.4.1, 6.4.2, 6.4.3, 6.4.4, 6.4.6, 6.4.7, 6.4.8

Ancient Greece (2000 BCE–300 BCE)

TOPIC 7 HSS 6.7, 6.7.1, 6.7.2, 6.7.3, 6.7.4
The Roman Republic (800 BCE–30 BCE)

ACCESS MORE ONLINE
videos, audio, etext, interactivities, games, worksheets, and more!

TOPIC 8

HSS 6.7.3, 6.7.4, 6.7.5, 6.7.6, 6.7.8, 7.1.1, 7.1.2, 7.1.3

The Roman and Byzantine Empires (30 BCE–1453 CE)

DIGITAL RESOURCES

Core Concepts

These digital lessons introduce key concepts for all of the social sciences and personal finance.

Culture
Economics
Geography
Government and Civics
History
Personal Finance

Topic Videos NBC LEARN

Begin each topic with a front seat view of history.

TOPIC 1
Çatalhöyük: Life in an Ancient Settlement

TOPIC 2
The Code of Hammurabi

TOPIC 3
In the Artifact Lab

TOPIC 4
Indian Classical Dance in the Modern World

TOPIC 5
Shi Huangdi, First Emperor of Unified China

TOPIC 6
Pericles and the Golden Age of Athens

TOPIC 7
Cicero and the Roman Republic

TOPIC 8
Augustus and the Pax Romana

Lesson Videos

Preview key ideas from the lesson in these videos.

TOPIC 1
Lesson 1 Unearthing Evidence of the Earliest Humans
Lesson 2 How Hunter-Gatherers Lived
Lesson 3 Migrating and Adapting to New Environments
Lesson 4 The Birth of Farming
Lesson 5 The Growth of Cities
Lesson 6 Features of Mayan Civilization

TOPIC 2
Lesson 1 Adapting to Life in Mesopotamia
Lesson 2 Hammurabi's Code
Lesson 3 The Assyrian and Persian Empires
Lesson 4 The Alphabet
Lesson 5 The Origins of Judaism
Lesson 6 The Central Beliefs of Judaism
Lesson 7 Israel and the Jewish Diaspora

TOPIC 3
Lesson 1 Pharaohs of Ancient Egypt
Lesson 2 The Legacy of Ancient Egypt
Lesson 3 Trade Between Egypt and Kush

TOPIC 4
Lesson 1 Indus Valley Achievements
Lesson 2 The Caste System
Lesson 3 Hindu Traditions and Practices
Lesson 4 Teachings and Spread of Buddhism
Lesson 5 Chandraputra Maurya's Rule
Lesson 6 The Life of Ashoka
Lesson 7 The Golden Age of the Gupta

TOPIC 5
Lesson 1 The Influence of Geography on China
Lesson 2 The Dynastic Cycle and the Mandate of Heaven
Lesson 3 How Confucius's Life Shaped His View of Government
Lesson 4 Comparing Legalism and Confucianism
Lesson 5 The Bureaucratic Structure of the Han Government
Lesson 6 The Economy of China Under the Han

TOPIC 6
Lesson 1 Impact of Geography on Early Greece
Lesson 2 The Athenian Concept of Citizenship
Lesson 3 Growing Up Spartan
Lesson 4 Men, Women, and Children in Ancient Greece
Lesson 5 Causes and Effects of the Persian Wars
Lesson 6 Greek Mythology
Lesson 7 Socrates and Plato
Lesson 8 Cultural Exchange in the Hellenistic Age

TOPIC 7

Lesson 1 Rome's Founding and Early Days
Lesson 2 Citizenship in Rome
Lesson 3 Roman Society
Lesson 4 Why did the Roman Republic End?

TOPIC 8

Lesson 1 Trade in the Roman Empire
Lesson 2 Reasons for the Spread of Christianity
Lesson 3 The New Testament
Lesson 4 Rome's Cultural Gifts
Lesson 5 Why Did the Roman Empire End?
Lesson 6 The Byzantine Empire's Place in History
Lesson 7 Byzantine Culture

Interactive Primary Sources

Go to the original sources to hear voices from the time.

TOPIC 2

Lesson 2 Code of Hammurabi
Lesson 7 Psalm 23

TOPIC 4

Lesson 3 *The Bhagavad-Gita*
Lesson 6 Asoka, Edicts

TOPIC 5

Lesson 3 Confucius, *Analects*
Lesson 3 Laozi, *The Dao de Jing*

TOPIC 6

Lesson 5 Herodotus, *The Persian Wars*
Lesson 6 Euripides, *Medea*
Lesson 7 Aristotle, *Politics*
Lesson 7 Plato, *The Republic*

TOPIC 8

Lesson 3 Paul, First Letter to the Corinthians

Interactive Biographies

Read about the people who made history.

TOPIC 2

Lesson 2 Hammurabi
Lesson 7 David
Lesson 7 Yohan ben Zaccai

TOPIC 4

Lesson 6 Asoka

TOPIC 5

Lesson 3 Confucius
Lesson 4 Shi Huangdi

TOPIC 6

Lesson 7 Hypatia
Lesson 8 Alexander the Great

TOPIC 7

Lesson 4 Julius Caesar

TOPIC 8

Lesson 1 Augustus
Lesson 5 Constantine
Lesson 6 Justinian I

DIGITAL RESOURCES

21st Century Skills Tutorials

Learn, practice, and apply important skills using these online tutorials.

Analyze Cause and Effect
Analyze Data and Models
Analyze Images
Analyze Media Content
Analyze Political Cartoons
Analyze Primary and Secondary Sources
Ask Questions
Avoid Plagiarism
Being an Informed Citizen
Categorize
Compare and Contrast
Compare Viewpoints
Compromise
Consider and Counter Opposing Arguments
Create Charts and Maps
Create Databases
Create a Research Hypothesis
Develop a Clear Thesis
Develop Cultural Awareness
Distinguish Between Fact and Opinion
Draw Conclusions
Draw Inferences
Evaluate Existing Arguments
Evaluate Web Sites
Generalize
Generate New Ideas
Give an Effective Presentation
Identify Bias
Identify Evidence
Identify Main Ideas and Details
Identify Trends
Innovate
Interpret Sources
Make Decisions
Make a Difference
Make Predictions
Organize Your Ideas
Participate in a Discussion or Debate
Paying Taxes
Political Participation
Publish Your Work
Read Charts, Graphs, and Tables
Read Physical Maps
Read Special Purpose Maps
Search for Information on the Internet
Serving on a Jury Sequence
Set a Purpose for Reading
Share Responsibility
Solve Problems
Summarize
Support Ideas With Evidence
Synthesize
Take Effective Notes
Use Content Clues
Use Parts of a Map
Voting
Work in Teams
Write an Essay
Write a Journal Entry

Interactivities

Explore maps one layer at a time to see how events unfolded over time, go on a gallery walk to examine artifacts and primary sources, analyze data, and explore key historical sites and objects in 3-D!

INTERACTIVE MAPS

Fossil Finds in Africa Topic 1 Topic Map
Migrations of Homo Sapiens Topic 1 Lesson 2
River Valley Civilizations Topic 1 Lesson 5
Mayan Civilization Topic 1 Lesson 6
Early Civilizations of the Fertile Crescent Topic 2 Topic Map
Sumer and the Fertile Crescent Topic 2 Lesson 1
Assyrian and Persian Empires Topic 2 Lesson 3
The Exodus in Jewish Tradition Topic 2 Lesson 5
The Ancient Nile Valley Topic 3 Topic Map
Egyptian Religion Topic 3 Lesson 1
Indian Subcontinent: Physical Features Topic 4 Topic Map
The Origins and Spread of Buddhism Topic 4 Lesson 4
Geography of China Topic 5 Topic Map
Ancient Chinese Dynasties Topic 5 Lesson 5
Geography of Greece Topic 6 Topic Map
The Journey of Odysseus Topic 6 Lesson 1
Expansion and Trade in the Greek World Topic 6 Lesson 4
Persian Wars Topic 6 Lesson 5
Culture of the Developing Roman Republic Topic 7 Topic Map

Interactivities (continued)

Growth of the Roman Republic, 500 B.C. to 44 B.C. Topic 7 Lesson 1
The Roman World Topic 8 Topic Map
Invasions of the Roman Empire Topic 8 Lesson 5
The Byzantine Empire Topic 8 Lesson 6

INTERACTIVE CHARTS

Akkadian and Babylonian Empires Topic 2 Lesson 2
Technology of the Indus Civilization Topic 4 Lesson 1
Confucianism and Daoism Topic 5 Lesson 3
Greek Philosophers Topic 6 Lesson 7

INTERACTIVE GALLERIES

Piecing the Past Together Topic 1 Lesson 1
Paleolithic Cave Art Topic 1 Lesson 3
Otzi—the Neolithic Ice Man Topic 1 Lesson 4
Significance of Major Jewish Holidays Topic 2 Lesson 6
Origins of Judaism Topic 2 Lesson 7
Village Life in India Topic 4 Lesson 5
The Gupta Empire Topic 4 Lesson 7
Chinese Writing Topic 5 Lesson 1
Terra Cotta Army of Shi Huangdi Topic 5 Lesson 4
Silk Making in Ancient China Topic 5 Lesson 6
Athenian Democracy Topic 6 Lesson 2
Art and Architecture of Ancient Greece Topic 6 Lesson 6
Alexander the Great's Conquests and Contributions Topic 6 Lesson 8
Who Was Julius Caesar? Topic 7 Lesson 4
Early Christian Symbols Topic 8 Lesson 2
Christianity Today Topic 8 Lesson 3
Hagia Sophia Topic 8 Lesson 7

INTERACTIVE TIMELINES

Development of the Modern Latin Alphabet Topic 2 Lesson 4
Asoka's Life Topic 4 Lesson 6
Roman Rulers Who Made History Topic 8 Lesson 1

INTERACTIVE ILLUSTRATIONS

Vedic Era Gods Topic 4 Lesson 2
The Dynastic Cycle Topic 5 Lesson 2
Comparing Sparta and Athens Topic 6 Lesson 3

INTERACTIVE 3D MODELS

Egyptian Pyramids Topic 3 Lesson 2
Hindu Temple Topic 4 Lesson 3
Roman Villa Topic 7 Lesson 3
Pantheon Topic 8 Lesson 4

INTERACTIVE SIMULATIONS

Ancient Egypt and Kush Topic 3 Lesson 3
The Roman Republic Topic 7 Lesson 2

Maps

The World: Political
The World: Physical
The United States: Political
The United States: Physical
North and South America: Political
North and South America: Physical
Europe: Political
Europe: Physical
Africa: Political
Africa: Physical
Asia: Political
Asia: Physical
Australia, New Zealand, and Oceania: Political-Physical
The Arctic: Physical
Antarctica: Physical
California: Political
California: Physical

SPECIAL FEATURES

Quest

Ask questions, explore sources, and cite evidence to support your view!

PROJECT-BASED LEARNING INQUIRY

DISCUSSION INQUIRY

DOCUMENT-BASED WRITING INQUIRY

Primary Sources

Excerpts from original sources allow you to witness history.

Primary Source Quotations

Quotations in the text bring history to life.

Primary Source Quotations (continued)

SPECIAL FEATURES

Analysis Skills

Practice key skills.

Biographies

Read about the people who made history.

Charts, Graphs, Tables, and Infographics

Find these charts, graphs, and tables in your text. It's all about the data!

Charts, Graphs, Tables, and Infographics (continued)

Timelines

When did this happen? Find out with these timelines.

SPECIAL FEATURES

Maps

Where did this happen? Find out with these maps.

Maps (continued)

TOPIC 8

ATLAS

CALIFORNIA HISTORY AND SOCIAL SCIENCE STANDARDS ROAD MAP

Use this chart to pace instruction and monitor progress towards mastery of the History-Social Science Content Standards for California Public Schools and the Historical and Social Sciences Analysis Skills standards.

	TOPIC 1 24 days								TOPIC 2 26 days							TOPIC 3 16 days		
HISTORY-SOCIAL SCIENCE CONTENT STANDARDS	EH	CI	1	2	3	4	5	6	1	2	3	4	5	6	7	1	2	3
6.1 Students describe what is known through archaeological studies of the early physical and cultural development of humankind from the Paleolithic era to the agricultural revolution.																		
6.1.1 Describe the hunter-gatherer societies, including the development of tools and the use of fire.			•	•														
6.1.2 Identify the locations of human communities that populated the major regions of the world and describe how humans adapted to a variety of environments.			•	•														
6.1.3 Discuss the climatic changes and human modifications of the physical environment that gave rise to the domestication of plants and animals and new sources of clothing and shelter.					•	•												
6.2 Students analyze the geographic, political, economic, religious, and social structures of the early civilizations of Mesopotamia, Egypt, and Kush.																		
6.2.1 Locate and describe the major river systems and discuss the physical settings that supported permanent settlement and early civilizations.							•		•							•		
6.2.2 Trace the development of agricultural techniques that permitted the production of economic surplus and the emergence of cities as centers of culture and power.						•	•		•					•		•		
6.2.3 Understand the relationship between religion and the social and political order in Mesopotamia and Egypt.									•		•					•		
6.2.4 Know the significance of Hammurabi's Code.										•								
6.2.5 Discuss the main features of Egyptian art and architecture.																	•	
6.2.6 Describe the role of Egyptian trade in the eastern Mediterranean and Nile valley.																		•
6.2.7 Understand the significance of Queen Hatshepsut and Ramses the Great.																•		
6.2.8 Identify the location of the Kush civilization and describe its political, commercial, and cultural relations with Egypt.																		•
6.2.9 Trace the evolution of language and its written forms.				•				•	•	•		•					•	
6.3 Students analyze the geographic, political, economic, religious, and social structures of the Ancient Hebrews.																		
6.3.1 Describe the origins and significance of Judaism as the first monotheistic religion based on the concept of one God who sets down moral laws for humanity.													•	•	•			

KEY: • =Standard Covered EH=ELA Handbook CI=Course Introduction

TOPIC 4 26 days							TOPIC 5 21 days						TOPIC 6 26 days								TOPIC 7 15 days				TOPIC 8 26 days						
1	2	3	4	5	6	7	1	2	3	4	5	6	1	2	3	4	5	6	7	8	1	2	3	4	1	2	3	4	5	6	7
							•																								

CA H-SS STANDARDS ROAD MAP (continued)

	TOPIC 1 24 days								TOPIC 2 26 days							TOPIC 3 16 days		
HISTORY-SOCIAL SCIENCE CONTENT STANDARDS	EH	CI	1	2	3	4	5	6	1	2	3	4	5	6	7	1	2	3
6.3.2 Identify the sources of the ethical teachings and central beliefs of Judaism (the Hebrew Bible, the Commentaries): belief in God, observance of law, practice of the concepts of righteousness and justice, and importance of study; and describe how the ideas of the Hebrew traditions are reflected in the moral and ethical traditions of Western civilization.													•	•	•			
6.3.3 Explain the significance of Abraham, Moses, Naomi, Ruth, David, and Yohanan ben Zaccai in the development of the Jewish religion.													•	•	•			
6.3.4 Discuss the locations of the settlements and movements of Hebrew peoples, including the Exodus and their movement to and from Egypt, and outline the significance of the Exodus to the Jewish and other people.													•		•			
6.3.5 Discuss how Judaism survived and developed despite the continuing dispersion of much of the Jewish population from Jerusalem and the rest of Israel after the destruction of the second Temple in A.D. 70.															•			
6.4 Students analyze the geographic, political, economic, religious, and social structures of the early civilizations of Ancient Greece.																		
6.4.1 Discuss the connections between geography and the development of city-states in the region of the Aegean Sea, including patterns of trade and commerce among Greek city-states and within the wider Mediterranean region.																		
6.4.2 Trace the transition from tyranny and oligarchy to early democratic forms of government and back to dictatorship in ancient Greece, including the significance of the invention of the idea of citizenship (e.g., from Pericles' Funeral Oration).																		
6.4.3 State the key differences between Athenian, or direct, democracy and representative democracy.																		
6.4.4 Explain the significance of Greek mythology to the everyday life of people in the region and how Greek literature continues to permeate our literature and language today, drawing from Greek mythology and epics, such as Homer's Iliad and Odyssey, and from Aesop's Fables.																		
6.4.5 Outline the founding, expansion, and political organization of the Persian Empire.											•							
6.4.6 Compare and contrast life in Athens and Sparta, with emphasis on their roles in the Persian and Peloponnesian Wars.																		
6.4.7 Trace the rise of Alexander the Great and the spread of Greek culture eastward and into Egypt.																		
6.4.8 Describe the enduring contributions of important Greek figures in the arts and sciences (e.g., Hypatia, Socrates, Plato, Aristotle, Euclid, Thucydides).																		

KEY: • =Standard Covered EH=ELA Handbook CI=Course Introduction

TOPIC 4 26 days							TOPIC 5 21 days						TOPIC 6 26 days								TOPIC 7 15 days				TOPIC 8 26 days						
1	2	3	4	5	6	7	1	2	3	4	5	6	1	2	3	4	5	6	7	8	1	2	3	4	1	2	3	4	5	6	7
													•			•															
														•			•														
														•																	
													•					•													
															•		•														
																				•											
																			•												

CA H-SS STANDARDS ROAD MAP (continued)

	TOPIC 1 24 days								TOPIC 2 26 days							TOPIC 3 16 days		
HISTORY-SOCIAL SCIENCE CONTENT STANDARDS	EH	CI	1	2	3	4	5	6	1	2	3	4	5	6	7	1	2	3
6.5 Students analyze the geographic, political, economic, religious, and social structures of the early civilizations of India.																		
6.5.1 Locate and describe the major river system and discuss the physical setting that sup-ported the rise of this civilization.																		
6.5.2 Discuss the significance of the Aryan invasions.																		
6.5.3 Explain the major beliefs and practices of Brahmanism in India and how they evolved into early Hinduism.																		
6.5.4 Outline the social structure of the caste system.																		
6.5.5 Know the life and moral teachings of Buddha and how Buddhism spread in India, Ceylon, and Central Asia.																		
6.5.6 Describe the growth of the Maurya empire and the political and moral achievements of the emperor Asoka.																		
6.5.7 Discuss important aesthetic and intellectual traditions (e.g., Sanskrit literature, including the Bhagavad Gita; medicine; metallurgy; and mathematics, including Hindu-Arabic numerals and the zero).																		
6.6 Students analyze the geographic, political, economic, religious, and social structures of the early civilizations of China.																		
6.6.1 Locate and describe the origins of Chinese civilization in the Huang-He Valley during the Shang Dynasty.																		
6.6.2 Explain the geographic features of China that made governance and the spread of ideas and goods difficult and served to isolate the country from the rest of the world.																		
6.6.3 Know about the life of Confucius and the fundamental teachings of Confucianism and Taoism.																		
6.6.4 Identify the political and cultural problems prevalent in the time of Confucius and how he sought to solve them.																		
6.6.5 List the policies and achievements of the emperor Shi Huangdi in unifying northern China under the Qin Dynasty.																		
6.6.6 Detail the political contributions of the Han Dynasty to the development of the imperial bureaucratic state and the expansion of the empire.																		
6.6.7 Cite the significance of the trans-Eurasian "silk roads" in the period of the Han Dynasty and Roman Empire and their locations.																		
6.6.8 Describe the diffusion of Buddhism northward to China during the Han Dynasty.																		

KEY: • =Standard Covered EH=ELA Handbook CI=Course Introduction

TOPIC 4 26 days							TOPIC 5 21 days						TOPIC 6 26 days								TOPIC 7 15 days				TOPIC 8 26 days						
1	2	3	4	5	6	7	1	2	3	4	5	6	1	2	3	4	5	6	7	8	1	2	3	4	1	2	3	4	5	6	7
•																															
	•																														
		•																													
	•																														
			•																												
				•	•																										
	•	•				•																									
							•	•																							
							•	•																							
									•																						
									•			•																			
										•																					
											•																				
											•																				
											•																				

CA H-SS STANDARDS ROAD MAP (continued)

	TOPIC 1 24 days								TOPIC 2 26 days							TOPIC 3 16 days		
HISTORY-SOCIAL SCIENCE CONTENT STANDARDS	EH	CI	1	2	3	4	5	6	1	2	3	4	5	6	7	1	2	3
6.7 Students analyze the geographic, political, economic, religious, and social structures during the development of Rome.																		
6.7.1 Identify the location and describe the rise of the Roman Republic, including the importance of such mythical and historical figures as Aeneas, Romulus and Remus, Cincinnatus, Julius Caesar, and Cicero.																		
6.7.2 Describe the government of the Roman Republic and its significance (e.g., written constitution and tripartite government, checks and balances, civic duty).																		
6.7.3 Identify the location of and the political and geographic reasons for the growth of Roman territories and expansion of the empire, including how the empire fostered economic growth through the use of currency and trade routes.																		
6.7.4 Discuss the influence of Julius Caesar and Augustus in Rome's transition from republic to empire.																		
6.7.5 Trace the migration of Jews around the Mediterranean region and the effects of their conflict with the Romans, including the Romans' restrictions on their right to live in Jerusalem.																		
6.7.6 Note the origins of Christianity in the Jewish Messianic prophecies, the life and teachings of Jesus of Nazareth as described in the New Testament, and the contribution of St. Paul the Apostle to the definition and spread of Christian beliefs (e.g., belief in the Trinity, resurrection, salvation).																		
6.7.7 Describe the circumstances that led to the spread of Christianity in Europe and other Roman territories.																		
6.7.8 Discuss the legacies of Roman art and architecture, technology and science, literature, language, and law.																		
7.1 Students analyze the causes and effects of the vast expansion and ultimate disintegration of the Roman Empire.																		
7.1.1 Study the early strengths and lasting contributions of Rome (e.g., significance of Roman citizenship; rights under Roman law; Roman art, architecture, engineering, and philosophy; preservation and transmission of Christianity) and its ultimate internal weaknesses (e.g., rise of autonomous military powers within the empire, undermining of citizenship by the growth of corruption and slavery, lack of education, and distribution of news).																		
7.1.2 Discuss the geographic borders of the empire at its height and the factors that threatened its territorial cohesion.																		
7.1.3 Describe the establishment by Constantine of the new capital in Constantinople and the development of the Byzantine Empire, with an emphasis on the consequences of the development of two distinct European civilizations, Eastern Orthodox and Roman Catholic, and their two distinct views on church-state relations.																		

KEY: • =Standard Covered EH=ELA Handbook CI=Course Introduction

TOPIC 4 26 days							TOPIC 5 21 days						TOPIC 6 26 days								TOPIC 7 15 days				TOPIC 8 26 days						
1	2	3	4	5	6	7	1	2	3	4	5	6	1	2	3	4	5	6	7	8	1	2	3	4	1	2	3	4	5	6	7
																					•	•	•	•							
																						•									
																								•	•						
																								•	•						
																										•					
																										•	•				
																										•		•			
																									•			•			
																									•	•		•	•		
																									•			•	•		
																														•	•

CA H-SS STANDARDS ROAD MAP (continued)

	TOPIC 1 24 days								TOPIC 2 26 days							TOPIC 3 16 days		
HISTORY-SOCIAL SCIENCE CONTENT STANDARDS	EH	CI	1	2	3	4	5	6	1	2	3	4	5	6	7	1	2	3
7.7 Students compare and contrast the geographic, political, economic, religious, and social structures of the Meso-American and Andean civilizations.																		
7.7.1 Study the locations, landforms, and climates of Mexico, Central America, and South America and their effects on Mayan, Aztec, and Incan economies, trade, and development of urban societies.								•										
7.7.2 Study the roles of people in each society, including class structures, family life, war-fare, religious beliefs and practices, and slavery.								•										
7.7.3 Explain how and where each empire arose and how the Aztec and Incan empires were defeated by the Spanish.								•										
7.7.4 Describe the artistic and oral traditions and architecture in the three civilizations.								•										
7.7.5 Describe the Meso-American achievements in astronomy and mathematics, including the development of the calendar and the Meso-American knowledge of seasonal changes to the civilizations' agricultural systems.								•										
HISTORY AND SOCIAL-SCIENCES ANALYSIS SKILLS	EH	CI	1	2	3	4	5	6	1	2	3	4	5	6	7	1	2	3
Analysis CST.1 Students explain how major events are related to one another in time.				•														
Analysis CST.2 Students construct various time lines of key events, people, and periods of the historical era they are studying.															•			
Analysis CST.3 Students use a variety of maps and documents to identify physical and cultural features of neighborhoods, cities, states, and countries and to explain the historical migration of people, expansion and disintegration of empires, and the growth of economic systems.																•		
Analysis HI.1 Students explain the central issues and problems from the past, placing people and events in a matrix of time and place.																		
Analysis HI.2 Students understand and distinguish cause, effect, sequence, and correlation in historical events, including the long-and short-term causal relations.									•									
Analysis HI.3 Students explain the sources of historical continuity and how the combination of ideas and events explains the emergence of new patterns.																		
Analysis HI.4 Students recognize the role of chance, oversight, and error in history.											•							
Analysis HI.5 Students recognize that interpretations of history are subject to change as new information is uncovered.																		

KEY: • =Standard Covered EH=ELA Handbook CI=Course Introduction

TOPIC 4 26 days							TOPIC 5 21 days						TOPIC 6 26 days								TOPIC 7 15 days				TOPIC 8 26 days						
1	2	3	4	5	6	7	1	2	3	4	5	6	1	2	3	4	5	6	7	8	1	2	3	4	1	2	3	4	5	6	7

1	2	3	4	5	6	7	1	2	3	4	5	6	1	2	3	4	5	6	7	8	1	2	3	4	1	2	3	4	5	6	7
						•																									
																									•						
																								•							
												•														•					
																			•												

CA H-SS STANDARDS ROAD MAP (continued)

	TOPIC 1 24 days								TOPIC 2 26 days							TOPIC 3 16 days		
HISTORICAL AND SOCIAL SCIENCES ANALYSIS SKILLS	EH	CI	1	2	3	4	5	6	1	2	3	4	5	6	7	1	2	3
Analysis HI.6 Students interpret basic indicators of economic performance and conduct cost-benefit analyses of economic and political issues.																		
Analysis REP.1 Students frame questions that can be answered by historical study and research.																		•
Analysis REP.2 Students distinguish fact from opinion in historical narratives and stories.																		
Analysis REP.3 Students distinguish relevant from irrelevant information, essential from incidental information, and verifiable from unverifiable information in historical narratives and stories.			•														•	
Analysis REP.4 Students assess the credibility of primary and secondary sources and draw sound conclusions from them.																		
Analysis REP.5 Students detect the different historical points of view on historical events and determine the context in which the historical statements were made (the questions asked, sources used, author's perspectives).																		

KEY: • =Standard Covered EH=ELA Handbook CI=Course Introduction

TOPIC 4 26 days							TOPIC 5 21 days						TOPIC 6 26 days								TOPIC 7 15 days				TOPIC 8 26 days						
1	2	3	4	5	6	7	1	2	3	4	5	6	1	2	3	4	5	6	7	8	1	2	3	4	1	2	3	4	5	6	7
																							•							•	
								•																							
														•																	
				•						•																					
	•																•														

CALIFORNIA COMMON CORE ENGLISH LANGUAGE ARTS STANDARDS FOR HISTORY AND SOCIAL-SCIENCE

World History: Ancient Civilizations helps students learn and practice skills laid out in the California Common Core State Standards for English Language Arts and California Common Core Standards for History/Social Studies.

CALIFORNIA COMMON CORE STATE STANDARDS FOR ENGLISH LANGUAGE ARTS	WHERE ALIGNED
Reading Standards for Informational Text, Grade 6	
RI.6.1 Cite textual evidence to support analysis of what the text says explicitly as well as inferences drawn from the text.	Topic 1 Lesson 6 Literacy Skill; Topic 3 Quest; Topic 5 Quest; Topic 5 Lesson 4 Literacy Skill; Topic 5 Analysis Skill Distinguish Fact from Opinion; Topic 5 Analysis Skill Draw Sound Conclusions from Sources; Topic 6 Lesson 4 Literacy Skill; Topic 7 Quest; Topic 8 Lesson 6 Literacy Skill
RI.6.2 Determine a central idea of a text and how it is conveyed through particular details; provide a summary of the text distinct from personal opinions or judgments.	Topic 1 Lesson 1 Literacy Skill; Topic 1 Primary Source *The Epic of Gilgamesh*; Topic 3 Lesson 1 Literacy Skill; Topic 3 Lesson 3 Literacy Skill; Topic 4 Lesson 1 Literacy Skill; Topic 5 Quest; Topic 5 Lesson 2 Literacy Skill; Topic 6 Primary Source Pericles, Funeral Oration; Topic 7 Primary Source Livy, *History of Rome*
RI.6.3 Analyze in detail how a key individual, event, or idea is introduced, illustrated, and elaborated in a text (e.g., through examples or anecdotes).	Topic 1 Primary Source *The Epic of Gilgamesh*; Topic 2 Primary Source 23rd Psalm; Topic 3 Quest; Topic 3 Primary Source The Victory of Ramses II Over the Hittites; Topic 4 Primary Source *The Ramayana*; Topic 5 Quest; Topic 5 Primary Source Confucius, *The Analects*
RI.6.4 Determine the meaning of words and phrases as they are used in a text, including figurative, connotative, and technical meanings. (See grade 6 Language standards 4–6 for additional expectations.)	Topic 1 Primary Source *The Epic of Gilgamesh*; Topic 2 Primary Source 23rd Psalm; Topic 3 Quest; Topic 3 Primary Source The Victory of Ramses II Over the Hittites; Topic 4 Primary Source *The Ramayana*; Topic 5 Primary Source Sun Tzu, *The Art of War*; Topic 5 Analysis Skill Draw Sound Conlcusions from Sources
RI.6.5 Analyze how a particular sentence, paragraph, chapter, or section fits into the overall structure of a text and contributes to the development of the ideas. a. Analyze the use of text features (e.g., graphics, headers, captions) in popular media.	Topic 4 Primary Source *The Ramayana*; Topic 8 Lesson 3 Literacy Skill; Topic 8 Lesson 5 Literacy Skill
RI.6.6 Determine an author's point of view or purpose in a text and explain how it is conveyed in the text.	Topic 2 Primary Source Contracts in Ancient Mesopotamia; Topic 3 Quest; Topic 4 Analysis Skills Detect Historical Points of View; Topic 8 Quest; Topic 8 Primary Source The Gospel of Matthew, The Sermon on the Mount
RI.6.7 Integrate information presented in different media or formats (e.g., visually, quantitatively) as well as in words to develop a coherent understanding of a topic or issue.	Topic 4 Analysis Skill Interpret Thematic Maps; Topic 6 Lesson 6 Literacy Skill
RI.6.8 Trace and evaluate the argument and specific claims in a text, distinguishing claims that are supported by reasons and evidence from claims that are not.	Topic 1 Analysis Skill Distinguish Essential from Incidental Information; Topic 2 Quest; Topic 3 Analysis Skills Distinguish Verifiable from Unverifiable Information; Topic 4 Analysis Skill Assess Credibility of a Source; Topic 8 Quest

CALIFORNIA COMMON CORE STATE STANDARDS FOR ENGLISH LANGUAGE ARTS	WHERE ALIGNED
RI.6.9 Compare and contrast one author's presentation of events with that of another (e.g., a memoir written by and a biography on the same person).	Topic 6, Analysis Skill: Compare Different Points of View; Topic 8 Quest
RI.6.10 By the end of the year, read and comprehend literary nonfiction in the grades 6–8 text complexity band proficiently, with scaffolding as needed at the high end of the range.	Topic Quest 2, Topic Quest 3, Topic Quest 5, Topic Quest 7, Topic Quest 8
Writing Standards, Grade 6	
W.6.1 Write arguments to support claims with clear reasons and relevant evidence. a. Introduce claim(s) and organize the reasons and evidence clearly. b. Support claim(s) with clear reasons and relevant evidence, using credible sources and demonstrating an understanding of the topic or text. c. Use words, phrases, and clauses to clarify the relationships among claim(s) and reasons. d. Establish and maintain a formal style.	Topic 5 Writing Workshop; Topic 8 Writing Workshop
W.6.2 Write informative/explanatory texts to examine a topic and convey ideas, concepts, and information through the selection, organization, and analysis of relevant content. a. Introduce a topic or thesis statement; organize ideas, concepts, and information, using strategies such as definition, classification, comparison/contrast, and cause/effect; include formatting (e.g., headings), graphics (e.g., charts, tables), and multimedia when useful to aiding comprehension. b. Develop the topic with relevant facts, definitions, concrete details, quotations, or other information and examples. c. Use appropriate transitions to clarify the relationships among ideas and concepts. d. Use precise language and domain-specific vocabulary to inform about or explain the topic. e. Establish and maintain a formal style. f. Provide a concluding statement or section that follows from the information or explanation presented.	Topic 3 Writing Workshop; Topic 5 Quest; Topic 6 Quest; Topic 6 Writing Workshop
W.6.3 Write narratives to develop real or imagined experiences or events using effective technique, relevant descriptive details, and well-structured event sequences. a. Engage and orient the reader by establishing a context and introducing a narrator and/or characters; organize an event sequence that unfolds naturally and logically. b. Use narrative techniques, such as dialogue, pacing, and description, to develop experiences, events, and/or characters. c. Use a variety of transition words, phrases, and clauses to convey sequence and signal shifts from one time frame or setting to another. d. Use precise words and phrases, relevant descriptive details, and sensory language to convey experiences and events. e. Provide a conclusion that follows from the narrated experiences or events.	Topic 1 Writing Workshop; Topic 2 Writing Workshop; Topic 3 Quest
W.6.4 Produce clear and coherent writing in which the development, organization, and style are appropriate to task, purpose, and audience. (Grade-specific expectations for writing types are defined in standards 1–3 above.)	Topic 1 Writing Workshop; Topic 4 Writing Workshop; Topic 5 Quest; Topic 5 Writing Workshop
W.6.5 With some guidance and support from peers and adults, develop and strengthen writing as needed by planning, revising, editing, rewriting, or trying a new approach. (Editing for conventions should demonstrate command of Language standards 1–3 up to and including grade 6.)	Topic 1 Writing Workshop; Topic 3 Quest; Topic 4 Writing Workshop

CALIFORNIA COMMON CORE ENGLISH LANGUAGE ARTS STANDARDS FOR HISTORY AND SOCIAL-SCIENCE

CALIFORNIA COMMON CORE STATE STANDARDS FOR ENGLISH LANGUAGE ARTS	WHERE ALIGNED
W.6.6 Use technology, including the Internet, to produce and publish writing as well as to interact and collaborate with others; demonstrate sufficient command of keyboarding skills to type a minimum of three pages in a single sitting.	Topic 6 Quest
W.6.7 Conduct short research projects to answer a question, drawing on several sources and refocusing the inquiry when appropriate.	Topic 1 Quest; Topic 4 Writing Workshop; Topic 6 Project Quest
W.6.8 Gather relevant information from multiple print and digital sources; assess the credibility of each source; and quote or paraphrase the data and conclusions of others while avoiding plagiarism and providing basic bibliographic information for sources.	Topic 1 Quest; Topic 4 Writing Workshop; Topic 4 Assess Credibility of a Source; Topic 6 Project Quest
W.6.9 Draw evidence from literary or informational texts to support analysis, reflection, and research. a. Apply grade 6 Reading standards to literature (e.g., "Compare and contrast texts in different forms or genres [e.g., stories and poems; historical novels and fantasy stories] in terms of their approaches to similar themes and topics"). b. Apply grade 6 Reading standards to literary nonfiction (e.g., "Trace and evaluate the argument and specific claims in a text, distinguishing claims that are supported by reasons and evidence from claims that are not").	Topic 1 Quest; Topic 4 Writing Workshop; Topic 6 Project Quest
W.6.10 Write routinely over extended time frames (time for research, reflection, and revision) and shorter time frames (a single sitting or a day or two) for a range of discipline-specific tasks, purposes, and audiences.	Topic 3 Quest; Topic 5 Quest; Topic 7 Quest
Speaking and Listening Standards, Grade 6	
SL.6.1 Engage effectively in a range of collaborative discussions (one-on-one, in groups, and teacher-led) with diverse partners on grade 6 topics, texts, and issues, building on others' ideas and expressing their own clearly. a. Come to discussions prepared, having read or studied required material; explicitly draw on that preparation by referring to evidence on the topic, text, or issue to probe and reflect on ideas under discussion. b. Follow rules for collegial discussions, set specific goals and deadlines, and define individual roles as needed. c. Pose and respond to specific questions with elaboration and detail by making comments that contribute to the topic, text, or issue under discussion. d. Review the key ideas expressed and demonstrate understanding of multiple perspectives through reflection and paraphrasing.	Topic 2 Quest; Topic 8 Quest
SL.6.2 Interpret information presented in diverse media and formats (e.g., visually, quantitatively, orally) and explain how it contributes to a topic, text, or issue under study.	Topic 1 Quest; Topic 4 Quest; Topic 4 Writing Workshop; Topic 6 Quest; Topic 7 Writing Workshop
SL.6.3 Delineate a speaker's argument and specific claims, distinguishing claims that are supported by reasons and evidence from claims that are not.	Topic 8 Quest
SL.6.4 Present claims and findings (e.g., argument, narrative, informative, response to literature presentations), sequencing ideas logically and using pertinent descriptions, facts, and details and nonverbal elements to accentuate main ideas or themes; use appropriate eye contact, adequate volume, and clear pronunciation. a. Plan and deliver an informative/explanatory presentation that: develops a topic with relevant facts, definitions, and concrete details; uses appropriate transitions to clarify relationships; uses precise language and domain specific vocabulary; and provides a strong conclusion.	Topic 1 Quest; Topic 2 Quest; Topic 6 Quest; Topic 8 Quest

CALIFORNIA COMMON CORE STATE STANDARDS FOR ENGLISH LANGUAGE ARTS	WHERE ALIGNED
SL.6.5 Include multimedia components (e.g., graphics, images, music, sound) and visual displays in presentations to clarify information.	Topic 1 Quest; Topic 4 Quest; Topic 6 Quest
SL.6.6 Adapt speech to a variety of contexts and tasks, demonstrating command of formal English when indicated or appropriate. (See grade 6 Language standards 1 and 3 for specific expectations.)	Topic 1 Quest; Topic 2 Quest; Topic 6 Quest; Topic 8 Quest
CALIFORNIA COMMON CORE STANDARDS FOR HISTORY/ SOCIAL STUDIES	**WHERE ALIGNED**
Reading	
RH.1 Cite specific textual evidence to support analysis of primary and secondary sources.	Topic 1 Lesson 6 Literacy Skill; Topic 3 Quest; Topic 5 Quest; Topic 5 Lesson 4 Literacy Skill; Topic 5 Analysis Skill Distinguish Fact from Opinion; Topic 5 Analysis Skill Draw Sound Conclusions from Sources; Topic 6 Lesson 4 Literacy Skill; Topic 7 Quest; Topic 8 Lesson 6 Literacy Skill
RH.2 Determine the central ideas or information of a primary or secondary source; provide an accurate summary of the source distinct from prior knowledge or opinions.	Topic 1 Lesson 1 Literacy Skill; Topic 1 Primary Source *The Epic of Gilgamesh*; Topic 3 Lesson 1 Literacy Skill; Topic 3 Lesson 3 Literacy Skill; Topic 4 Lesson 1 Literacy Skill; Topic 5 Quest; Topic 5 Lesson 2 Literacy Skill; Topic 6 Primary Source Pericles, Funeral Oration; Topic 7 Primary Source Livy, *History of Rome*
RH.3 Identify key steps in a text's description of a process related to history/social studies (e.g., how a bill becomes law, how interest rates are raised or lowered).	Topic 4, Lesson 4, Chart, p. 161
RH.4 Determine the meaning of words and phrases as they are used in a text, including vocabulary specific to domains related to history/social studies.	Topic 1 Primary Source *The Epic of Gilgamesh*; Topic 2 Primary Source 23rd Psalm; Topic 3 Quest; Topic 3 Primary Source The Victory of Ramses II Over the Hittites; Topic 4 Primary Source *The Ramayana*; Topic 5 Primary Source Sun Tzu, *The Art of War*; Topic 5 Analysis Skill Draw Sound Conlcusions from Sources
RH.5 Describe how a text presents information (e.g., sequentially, comparatively, causally).	Topic 2 Analysis Skill Distinguish Cause and Effect; Topic 7 Analysis Skill Analyze Sequence, Causation and Correlation;Topic 7 Lesson 1 Literacy Skill; Topic 8 Lesson 3 Literacy Skill
RH.6 Identify aspects of a text that reveal an author's point of view or purpose (e.g., loaded language, inclusion or avoidance of particular facts).	Topic 2 Primary Source Contracts in Ancient Mesopotamia; Topic 3 Quest; Topic 4 Analysis Skills Detect Historical Points of View; Topic 8 Quest; Topic 8 Primary Source The Gospel of Matthew, The Sermon on the Mount
RH.7 Integrate visual information (e.g., in charts, graphs, photographs, videos, or maps) with other information in print and digital texts.	Topic 4 Analysis Skill Interpret Thematic Maps; Topic 6 Lesson 6 Literacy Skill
RH.8 Distinguish among fact, opinion, and reasoned judgment in a text.	Topic 5 Analysis Skill Distinguish Fact and Opinion; 21st Century Skills Tutorial: Distinguish Fact From Opinion; 21st Century Skills Tutorial: Identify Bias
RH.9 Analyze the relationship between a primary and secondary source on the same topic.	Topic 3 Quest; Topic 5 Quest; Topic 7 Quest
RH.10 By the end of grade 8, read and comprehend history/social studies texts in the grades 6–8 text complexity band independently and proficiently.	Topic Quest 2; Topic Quest 3; Topic Quest 3; Topic Quest 5; Topic Quest 7; Topic Quest 8

CALIFORNIA COMMON CORE ENGLISH LANGUAGE ARTS STANDARDS FOR HISTORY AND SOCIAL-SCIENCE

CALIFORNIA COMMON CORE STANDARDS FOR HISTORY/ SOCIAL STUDIES	WHERE ALIGNED
Writing	
WHST.1 Write arguments focused on discipline-specific content. a. Introduce claim(s) about a topic or issue, acknowledge and distinguish the claim(s)from alternate or opposing claims, and organize the reasons and evidence logically. b. Support claim(s) with logical reasoning and relevant, accurate data and evidence that demonstrate an understanding of the topic or text, using credible sources. c. Use words, phrases, and clauses to create cohesion and clarify the relationships among claim(s), counterclaims, reasons, and evidence. d. Establish and maintain a formal style. e. Provide a concluding statement or section that follows from and supports the argument presented.	Topic 5 Writing Workshop; Topic 8 Writing Workshop
WHST.2 Write informative/explanatory texts, including the narration of historical events, scientific procedures/experiments, or technical processes. a. Introduce a topic clearly, previewing what is to follow; organize ideas, concepts, and information into broader categories as appropriate to achieving purpose; include formatting (e.g., headings), graphics (e.g., charts, tables), and multimedia when useful to aiding comprehension. b. Develop the topic with relevant, well-chosen facts, definitions, concrete details, quotations, or other information and examples. c. Use appropriate and varied transitions to create cohesion and clarify the relationships among ideas and concepts. d. Use precise language and domain-specific vocabulary to inform about or explain the topic. e. Establish and maintain a formal style and objective tone. f. Provide a concluding statement or section that follows from and supports the information or explanation presented.	Topic 3 Quest; Topic 3 Writing Workshop; Topic 5 Quest; Topic 6 Quest; Topic 6 Writing Workshop
WHST.3 (See note; not applicable as a separate requirement) Note: Students' narrative skills continue to grow in these grades. The Standards require that students be able to incorporate narrative elements effectively into arguments and informative/explanatory texts. In history/social studies, students must be able to incorporate narrative accounts into their analyses of individuals or events of historical import. In science and technical subjects, students must be able to write precise enough descriptions of the step-by-step procedures they use in their investigations or technical work that others can replicate them and (possibly) reach the same results.	Topic 1 Writing Workshop; Topic 2 Writing Workshop;
WHST.4 Produce clear and coherent writing in which the development, organization, and style are appropriate to task, purpose, and audience.	Topic 1 Writing Workshop; Topic 4 Writing Workshop; Topic 5 Quest; Topic 5 Writing Workshop
WHST.5 With some guidance and support from peers and adults, develop and strengthen writing as needed by planning, revising, editing, rewriting, or trying a new approach, focusing on how well purpose and audience have been addressed.	Topic 1 Writing Workshop; Topic 3 Quest; Topic 4 Writing Workshop;
WHST.6 Use technology, including the Internet, to produce and publish writing and present the relationships between information and ideas clearly and efficiently.	Topic 6 Quest

CALIFORNIA COMMON CORE STANDARDS FOR HISTORY/ SOCIAL STUDIES	WHERE ALIGNED
WHST.7 Conduct short research projects to answer a question (including a self-generated question), drawing on several sources and generating additional related, focused questions that allow for multiple avenues of exploration.	Topic 1 Quest; Topic 4 Writing Workshop; Topic 6 Project Quest
WHST.8 Gather relevant information from multiple print and digital sources (primary and secondary), using search terms effectively; assess the credibility and accuracy of each source; and quote or paraphrase the data and conclusions of others while avoiding plagiarism and following a standard format for citation.	Topic 1 Quest; Topic 4 Quest; Topic 4 Writing Workshop; Topic 4 Assess Credibility of a Source; Topic 6 Project Quest; Topic 7 Writing Workshop
WHST.9 Draw evidence from informational texts to support analysis reflection, and research.	Topic 1 Quest; Topic 4 Writing Workshop; Topic 6 Project Quest
WHST.10 Write routinely over extended time frames (time for reflection and revision) and shorter time frames (a single sitting or a day or two) for a range of discipline-specific tasks, purposes, and audiences.	Topic 3 Quest; Topic 5 Quest; Topic 7 Quest

CALIFORNIA ENGLISH LANGUAGE DEVELOPMENT STANDARDS FOR WORLD HISTORY: ANCIENT CIVILIZATIONS

World History: Ancient Civilizations provides support for students who are learning English at the three levels set out in the California English Language Development Standards for Grade 6.

	CALIFORNIA ENGLISH LANGUAGE DEVELOPMENT STANDARDS			WHERE ALIGNED
	Emerging	**Expanding**	**Bridging**	
ELD.PI.A.1	**Exchanging information/ideas** Engage in conversational exchanges and express ideas on familiar topics by asking and answering yes-no and wh-questions and responding using simple phrases.	**Exchanging information/ideas** Contribute to class, group, and partner discussions by following turn-taking rules, asking relevant questions, affirming others, adding relevant information, and paraphrasing key ideas.	**Exchanging information/ideas** Contribute to class, group, and partner discussions by following turn-taking rules, asking relevant questions, affirming others, adding relevant information and evidence, paraphrasing key ideas, building on responses, and providing useful feedback.	Teacher Edition and English Language Development worksheet: Topic 1, Lesson 1; Topic 3, Lesson 1
ELD.PI.A.2	**Interacting via written English** Engage in short written exchanges with peers and collaborate on simple written texts on familiar topics, using technology when appropriate.	**Interacting via written English** Engage in longer written exchanges with peers and collaborate on more detailed written texts on a variety of topics, using technology when appropriate.	**Interacting via written English** Engage in extended written exchanges with peers and collaborate on complex written texts on a variety of topics, using technology when appropriate.	Teacher Edition and English Language Development worksheet: Topic 1, Lesson 2; Topic 3, Lesson 2 Quest:Topic 4; Writing Workshop: Topics 2, 4, 7, 8
ELD.PI.A.3	**Supporting opinions and persuading others** Negotiate with or persuade others in conversations (e.g., to gain and hold the floor or ask for clarification) using basic learned phrases (e.g., I think . . . , Would you please repeat that?), as well as open responses.	**Supporting opinions and persuading others** Negotiate with or persuade others in conversations (e.g., to provide counterarguments) using an expanded set of learned phrases (I agree with X, but . . .), as well as open responses.	**Supporting opinions and persuading others** Negotiate with or persuade others in conversations using appropriate register (e.g., to reflect on multiple perspectives) using a variety of learned phrases, indirect reported speech (e.g., I heard you say X, and Gabriel just pointed out Y), as well as open responses.	Teacher Edition and English Language Development worksheet: Topic 1, Lesson 3; Topic 3, Lesson 3 Quest: Topics 2, 8
ELD.PI.A.4	**Adapting language choices** Adjust language choices according to social setting (e.g., classroom, break time) and audience (e.g., peers, teacher).	**Adapting language choices** Adjust language choices according to purpose (e.g., explaining, persuading, entertaining), task, and audience.	**Adapting language choices** Adjust language choices according to task (e.g., facilitating a science experiment, providing peer feedback on a writing assignment), purpose, task, and audience.	Teacher Edition and English Language Development worksheet: Topic 1, Lesson 4; Topic 5, Lesson 6

	CALIFORNIA ENGLISH LANGUAGE DEVELOPMENT STANDARDS			WHERE ALIGNED
	Emerging	**Expanding**	**Bridging**	
ELD.PI.B.5	**Listening actively** Demonstrate active listening in oral presentation activities by asking and answering basic questions, with prompting and substantial support.	**Listening actively** Demonstrate active listening in oral presentation activities by asking and answering detailed questions, with occasional prompting and moderate support.	**Listening actively** Demonstrate active listening in oral presentation activities by asking and answering detailed questions, with minimal prompting and support.	Teacher Edition and English Language Development worksheet: Topic 1, Lesson 5; Topic 6, Lesson 1
ELD.PI.B.6.a	**Reading/viewing closely** Explain ideas, phenomena, processes, and text relationships (e.g., compare/contrast, cause/effect, problem/solution)based on close reading of a variety of grade-level texts and viewing of based on close reading of a variety of grade-level texts and viewing of multimedia, with substantial support.	**Reading/viewing closely** Explain ideas, phenomena, processes, and text relationships (e.g., compare/contrast, cause/effect, problem/solution) based on close reading of a variety of grade-level texts and viewing of multimedia, with moderate support.	**Reading/viewing closely** Explain ideas, phenomena, processes, and text relationships (e.g., compare/contrast, cause/effect, problem/solution) based on close reading of a variety of grade-level texts and viewing of multimedia, with light support.	Teacher Edition and English Language Development worksheet: Topic 1, Lesson 6; Topic 6, Lesson 2
ELD.PI.B.6.b	**Reading/viewing closely** Express inferences and conclusions drawn based on close reading of grade-level texts and viewing of multimedia using some frequently used verbs (e.g., shows that, based on).	**Reading/viewing closely** Express inferences and conclusions drawn based on close reading of grade-level texts and viewing of multimedia using a variety of verbs (e.g., suggests that, leads to).	**Reading/viewing closely** Express inferences and conclusions drawn based on close reading of grade-level texts and viewing of multimedia using a variety of precise academic verbs (e.g., indicates that, influences).	Teacher Edition and English Language Development worksheet: Topic 2, Lesson 1; Topic 6, Lesson 3
ELD.PI.B.6.c	**Reading/viewing closely** Use knowledge of morphology (e.g., affixes, roots, and base words), context, reference materials, and visual cues to determine the meaning of unknown and multiple-meaning words on familiar topics.	**Reading/viewing closely** Use knowledge of morphology (e.g., affixes, roots, and base words), context, reference materials, and visual cues to determine the meaning of unknown and multiple-meaning words on familiar and new topics.	**Reading/viewing closely** Use knowledge of morphology (e.g., affixes, roots, and base words), context, reference materials, and visual cues to determine the meaning, including figurative and connotative meanings, of unknown and multiple-meaning words on a variety of new topics.	Teacher Edition and English Language Development worksheet: Topic 2, Lesson 2; Topic 6, Lesson 4
ELD.PI.B.7	**Evaluating language choices** Explain how well writers and speakers use language to support ideas and arguments with detailed evidence (e.g., identifying the precise vocabulary used to present evidence, or the phrasing used to signal a shift in meaning) with substantial support.	**Evaluating language choices** Explain how well writers and speakers use specific language to present ideas or support arguments and provide detailed evidence (e.g., showing the clarity of the phrasing used to present an argument) with moderate support.	**Evaluating language choices** Explain how well writers and speakers use specific language resources to present ideas or support arguments and provide detailed evidence (e.g., identifying the specific language used to present ideas and claims that are well supported and distinguishing them from those that are not) with light support.	Teacher Edition and English Language Development worksheet: Topic 2, Lesson 3; Topic 6, Lesson 5

CALIFORNIA ENGLISH LANGUAGE DEVELOPMENT STANDARDS FOR WORLD HISTORY GRADE 6 (continued)

	CALIFORNIA ENGLISH LANGUAGE DEVELOPMENT STANDARDS			WHERE ALIGNED
	Emerging	Expanding	Bridging	
ELD.PI.B.8	**Analyzing language choices** Explain how phrasing or different common words with similar meaning (e.g., choosing to use the word cheap versus the phrase a good saver) produce different effects on the audience.	**Analyzing language choices** Explain how phrasing, different words with similar meaning (e.g., describing a character as stingy versus economical), or figurative language (e.g., The room was like a dank cave, littered with food wrappers, soda cans, and piles of laundry) produce shades of meaning and different effects on the audience.	**Analyzing language choices** Explain how phrasing, different words with similar meaning (e.g., stingy, economical, frugal, thrifty), or figurative language (e.g., The room was depressed and gloomy. The room was like a dank cave, littered with food wrappers, soda cans, and piles of laundry) produce shades of meaning, nuances, and different effects on the audience.	Teacher Edition and English Language Development worksheet: Topic 2, Lesson 4; Topic 6, Lesson 6
ELD.PI.C.9	**Presenting** Plan and deliver brief oral presentations on a variety of topics and content areas.	**Presenting** Plan and deliver longer oral presentations on a variety of topics and content areas, using details and evidence to support ideas.	**Presenting** Plan and deliver longer oral presentations on a variety of topics and content areas, using reasoning and evidence to support ideas, as well as growing understanding of register.	Teacher Edition and English Language Development worksheet: Topic 2, Lesson 5; Topic 6, Lesson 7
ELD.PI.C.10.a	**Writing** Write short literary and informational texts (e.g., an argument for protecting the rain forests) collaboratively (e.g., with peers) and independently.	**Writing** Write longer literary and informational texts (e.g., an argument for protecting the rain forests) collaboratively (e.g., with peers) and independently using appropriate text organization.	**Writing** Write longer and more detailed literary and informational texts (e.g., an argument for protecting the rain forests) collaboratively (e.g., with peers) and independently using appropriate text organization and growing understanding of register.	Teacher Edition and English Language Development worksheet: Topic 2, Lesson 6; Topic 6, Lesson 8 Quest: Topics 5, 7
ELD.PI.C.10.b	**Writing** Write brief summaries of texts and experiences using complete sentences and key words (e.g., from notes or graphic organizers).	**Writing** Write brief summaries of texts and experiences using complete sentences and key words (e.g., from notes or graphic organizers).	**Writing** Write clear and coherent summaries of texts and experiences using complete and concise sentences and key words (e.g., from notes or graphic organizers).	Teacher Edition and English Language Development worksheet: Topic 2, Lesson 7; Topic 7, Lesson 1
ELD.PI.C.11.a	**Justifying/arguing** Justify opinions by providing some textual evidence (e.g., quoting from the text) or relevant background knowledge, with substantial support.	**Justifying/arguing** Justify opinions or persuade others by providing relevant textual evidence (e.g., quoting from the text or referring to what the text says) or relevant background knowledge, with moderate support.	**Justifying/arguing** Justify opinions or persuade others by providing detailed and relevant textual evidence (e.g., quoting from the text evidence (e.g., quoting from the text directly or referring to specific textual evidence) or relevant background knowledge, with light support.	Teacher Edition and English Language Development worksheet: Topic 4, Lesson 1; Topic 7, Lesson 2 Quest: Topic 8

	CALIFORNIA ENGLISHLANGUAGE DEVELOPMENT STANDARDS			WHERE ALIGNED
	Emerging	**Expanding**	**Bridging**	
ELD.PI.C.11.b	**Justifying/arguing** Express attitude and opinions or temper statements with some basic modal expressions (e.g., can, has to).	**Justifying/arguing** Express attitude and opinions or temper statements with a variety of familiar modal expressions (e.g., maybe/ probably, can/could, must).	**Justifying/arguing** Express attitude and opinions or temper statements with nuanced modal expressions (e.g., probably/certainly/ definitely, should/would, might) and phrasing (e.g., In my opinion).	Teacher Edition and English Language Development worksheet: Topic 4, Lesson 2; Topic 7, Lesson 3
ELD.PI.C.12.a	**Selecting language resources** Use a select number of general academic words (e.g., author, chart) and domain-specific words (e.g., scene, cell, fraction) to create some precision while speaking and writing.	**Selecting language resources** Use a growing set of academic words (e.g., author, chart, global, affect), domain-specific words (e.g., scene, setting, plot, point of view, fraction, cell membrane, democracy), synonyms, and antonyms to create precision and shades of meaning while speaking and writing.	**Selecting language resources** Use an expanded set of general academic words (e.g., affect, evidence, demonstrate, reluctantly), domain-specific words (e.g., scene, setting, plot, point of view, fraction, cell membrane, democracy), synonyms, antonyms, and figurative language to create precision and shades of meaning while speaking and writing.	Teacher Edition and English Language Development worksheet: Topic 4, Lesson 3; Topic 7, Lesson 4
ELD.PI.C.12.b	**Selecting language resources** Use knowledge of morphology to appropriately select affixes in basic ways (e.g., She likes X).	**Selecting language resources** Use knowledge of morphology to appropriately select affixes in a growing number of ways to manipulate language (e.g., She likes X. That's impossible).	**Selecting language resources** Use knowledge of morphology to appropriately select affixes in a variety of ways to manipulate language (e.g., changing observe → observation, reluctant → reluctantly, produce → production, and so on).	Teacher Edition and English Language Development worksheet: Topic 4, Lesson 4; Topic 8, Lesson 1
ELD.PII.A.1	**Understanding text structure** Apply basic understanding of how different text types are organized to express ideas (e.g., how a narrative is organized sequentially with predictable stages versus how arguments are organized around ideas) to comprehending texts and writing basic texts.	**Understanding text structure** Apply growing understanding of how different text types are organized to express ideas (e.g., how a narrative is organized sequentially with predictable stages versus how arguments are structured logically around reasons and evidence) to comprehending texts and writing texts with increasing cohesion.	**Understanding text structure** Apply increasing understanding of how different text types are organized to express ideas (e.g., how a historical account is organized chronologically versus how arguments are structured logically around reasons and evidence) to comprehending texts and writing cohesive texts.	Teacher Edition and English Language Development worksheet: Topic 4, Lesson 5; Topic 8, Lesson 2

CALIFORNIA ENGLISH LANGUAGE DEVELOPMENT STANDARDS FOR WORLD HISTORY GRADE 6 (continued)

	CALIFORNIA ENGLISH LANGUAGE DEVELOPMENT STANDARDS			WHERE ALIGNED
	Emerging	**Expanding**	**Bridging**	
ELD.PII.A.2.a	**Understanding cohesion** Apply basic understanding of language resources for referring the reader back or forward in text (e.g., how pronouns refer back to nouns in text) to comprehending texts and writing basic texts.	**Understanding cohesion** Apply growing understanding of language resources for referring the reader back or forward in text (e.g., how pronouns or synonyms refer back to nouns in text) to comprehending texts and writing texts with increasing cohesion.	**Understanding cohesion** Apply increasing understanding of language resources for referring the reader back or forward in text (e.g., how pronouns, synonyms, or nominalizations refer back to nouns in text) to comprehending texts and writing cohesive texts.	Teacher Edition and English Language Development worksheet: Topic 4, Lesson 6; Topic 8, Lesson 3
ELD.PII.A.2.b	**Understanding cohesion** Apply basic understanding of how ideas, events, or reasons are linked throughout a text using a select set of everyday connecting words or phrases (e.g., first/next, at the beginning) to comprehending texts and writing basic texts.	**Understanding cohesion** Apply growing understanding of how ideas, events, or reasons are linked throughout a text using a variety of connecting words or phrases (e.g., for example, in the first place, as a result, on the other hand) to comprehending texts and writing texts with increasing cohesion.	**Understanding cohesion** Apply increasing understanding of how ideas, events, or reasons are linked throughout a text using an increasing variety of academic connecting and transitional words or phrases (e.g., consequently, specifically, however, moreover) to comprehending texts and writing cohesive texts.	Teacher Edition and English Language Development worksheet: Topic 4, Lesson 7; Topic 8, Lesson 4
ELD.PII.B.3	**Using verbs and verb phrases** Use a variety of verb types (e.g., doing, saying, being/having, thinking/feeling), tenses (e.g., present, past, future, simple, progressive) appropriate to the text type and discipline (e.g., simple past and past progressive for recounting an experience) on familiar topics.	**Using verbs and verb phrases** Use various verb types (e.g., doing, saying, being/having, thinking/feeling, reporting), tenses (e.g., present, past, future, simple, progressive, perfect) appropriate to the task, text type, and discipline (e.g., simple present for literary analysis) on an increasing variety of topics.	**Using verbs and verb phrases** Use various verb types (e.g., doing, saying, being/having, thinking/feeling, reporting), tenses (e.g., present, past, future, simple, progressive, perfect) appropriate to the task, text type, and discipline (e.g., the present perfect to describe previously made claims or conclusions) on a variety of topics.	Teacher Edition and English Language Development worksheet: Topic 5, Lesson 1; Topic 8, Lesson 5
ELD.PII.B.4	**Using nouns and noun phrases** Expand noun phrases in simple ways (e.g., adding a sensory adjective to a noun) in order to enrich the meaning of sentences and add details about ideas, people, things, and the like.	**Using nouns and noun phrases** Expand noun phrases in a variety of ways (e.g., adding comparative/ superlative adjectives to noun phrases or simple clause embedding) in order to enrich the meaning of sentences and add details about ideas, people, things, and the like.	**Using nouns and noun phrases** Expand noun phrases in an increasing variety of ways (e.g., adding comparative/superlative and general academic adjectives to noun phrases or more complex clause embedding) in order to enrich the meaning of sentences and add details about ideas, people, things, and the like.	Teacher Edition and English Language Development worksheet: Topic 5, Lesson 2; Topic 8, Lesson 6

	CALIFORNIA ENGLISHLANGUAGE DEVELOPMENT STANDARDS			WHERE ALIGNED
	Emerging	**Expanding**	**Bridging**	
ELD.PII.B.5	**Modifying to add details** Expand sentences with simple adverbials (e.g., adverbs, adverb phrases, prepositional phrases) to provide details (e.g., time, manner, place, cause) about a familiar activity or process.	**Modifying to add details** Expand sentences with an increasing variety of adverbials (e.g., adverbs, adverb phrases, prepositional phrases) to provide details (e.g., time, manner, place, cause) about a familiar or new activity or process.	**Modifying to add details** Expand sentences with an increasing variety of adverbials (e.g., adverbs, adverb phrases and clauses, prepositional phrases) to provide details (e.g., time, manner, place, cause) about a variety of familiar and new activities and processes.	Teacher Edition and English Language Development worksheet: Topic 5, Lesson 3; Topic 8, Lesson 7
ELD.PII.C.6	**Connecting ideas** Combine clauses in a few basic ways to make connections between and join ideas (e.g., creating compound sentences using and, but, so).	**Connecting ideas** Combine clauses in an increasing variety of ways (e.g., creating compound and complex sentences) to make connections between and join ideas, for example, to express a reason (e.g., He stayed at home on Sunday to study for Monday's exam) or to make a concession (e.g., She studied all night even though she wasn't feeling well).	**Connecting ideas** Combine clauses in a wide variety of ways (e.g., creating compound and complex sentences) to make connections between and join ideas, for example, to express a reason (e.g., He stayed at home on Sunday because he had an exam on Monday), to make a concession (e.g., She studied all night even though she wasn't feeling well), or to link two ideas that happen at the same time (e.g., The students worked in groups while their teacher walked around the room).	Teacher Edition and English Language Development worksheet: Topic 5, Lesson 4
ELD.PII.C.7	**Condensing ideas** Condense ideas in simple ways (e.g., by compounding verbs, adding prepositional phrases, or through simple embedded clauses or other ways of condensing as in, This is a story about a girl. The girl changed the world. → This is a story about a girl who changed the world) to create precise and detailed sentences.	**Condensing ideas** Condense ideas in an increasing variety of ways (e.g., through various types of embedded clauses and other ways of condensing, as in, Organic vegetables are food. They're made without chemical fertilizers. They're made without chemical insecticides) → Organic vegetables are foods that are made without chemical fertilizers or insecticides) to create precise and detailed sentences.	**Condensing ideas** Condense ideas in a variety of ways (e.g., through various types of embedded clauses, ways of condensing, and nominalization as in, They destroyed the rain forest. Lots of animals died → The destruction of the rain forest led to the death of many animals) to create precise and detailed sentences.	Teacher Edition and English Language Development worksheet: Topic 5, Lesson 5

CREATING AN ACTIVE CLASSROOM

This California Social Studies program places a strong emphasis on **inquiry** through the Quests. There are three types of Quests: Document-Based Writing Inquiry, Project-Based Learning Inquiry, and Discussion Inquiry.

Each inquiry type requires students to formulate and express their own arguments based on evidence. To support this learning approach, the program integrates **Active Classroom strategies** throughout each topic. These strategies encourage students to begin building their own arguments and collecting evidence about the past and present in every lesson.

You can use these strategies to help students participate in their own learning as you call upon them to **draw**, **write**, **speak**, **decide**.

Look for the **Active Classroom** logo in the Teacher Edition for suggestions of where to use the strategies described below.

Active Classroom Strategies

Activity Name	How to Activate
Quickdraw	• Pair students and give them 30 seconds to share what they know about a concept or Key Term by creating a symbol or drawing.
Graffiti Concepts	• Ask students to reflect on the meaning of a concept or idea and create a visual image and/or written phrase that represents that concept. Allow approximately three to five minutes. • Next ask students to post their "graffiti" on the board or on chart paper and ask students to look at all the various responses. • Next discuss similarities and differences in the responses as a group.
Word Wall	• Ask students to choose one of the Key Terms for the lesson and create a visual image with a text definition. Allow approximately three to five minutes. • Ask students to post their words on the board or on chart paper and ask students to look at all the various responses. • Discuss similarities and differences in the responses as a group. • Pick a few favorites and post them on the class "Word Wall" for the year.
Cartoon It	• Ask students to make a quick drawing of one compelling image from this lesson on a piece of paper. • Next ask students to turn their drawing into a political cartoon that illustrates a key concept or main idea from the lesson by adding a text caption or text "bubbles." • Ask students to share their cartoons with a partner or within small groups.
Wallpaper	• Ask students to review information they have learned in a topic and design a piece of "wallpaper" that encapsulates key learnings. • Then have students post their wallpaper and take a "gallery" walk, noting what others have written and illustrated in their samples.

Active Classroom Strategies

Activity Name	How to Activate
Quick Write	• Ask students to write what they know about a key idea or term in 30 seconds.
Make Headlines	• Have students write a headline that captures the key idea in a map, photo, timeline, or reading. • Ask students to share their headline with a partner.
Circle Write	• Break into groups and provide a writing prompt or key question. • Have students write as much as they can in response to the question or prompt for one minute. • Next have students give their response to the person on their right. That person should improve or elaborate on the response where the other person left off. • Continue to pass each response to the right until the original response comes back to the first person. • Each group then reviews all the responses and decides which is the best composition and shares that with the larger group.
Write 1-Get 3 (or Write 5-Get 4)	• Ask a question with multiple answers, such as: What are four key characteristics of ________ (a dictator)? What are the five key causes of ________? • Have students write down one response and then go around the room asking for three other responses. If they think a response is correct, ask them to write it down. • Have students keep asking and writing until they have three more responses on their page. • Have students share and discuss responses with the class.
Sticky Notes	• Ask students to spend three minutes jotting down their response to a critical thinking question on a sticky note. • Ask students to work in pairs and share their responses. • Next ask students to post their sticky notes on the board or on chart paper and read all the notes. • Discuss similarities and differences in the responses as a group.
Connect Two	• Select 10 to 12 words or phrases you think are important for students to know prior to reading a selection. • List the words and phrases on the board. • Ask students to "Connect Two" or choose two words they think might belong together, and state the reason. "I would connect ________ and ________ because ________." Consider posting their Connect Two statements on the board. • As students read the text they should look for evidence to support or refute their Connect Two statements.
Conversation With History	• Ask students to choose one of the people mentioned or pictured in the text and write down a question they would like to ask that person if they could. • Next ask students to write what they think that person would say in response and then what they would say in response to that.

Active Classroom Strategies

Activity Name	How to Activate
Walking Tour	• Post passages from a reading around the room. • Ask small groups to tour the room and discuss each passage. • Summarize each passage as a class. • Alternatively, assign each small group to a passage and have them summarize that passage for the rest of the class.
Audio Tour	• Ask students to work in pairs. Have the first student give the second a verbal "tour" of a map, graph, or infographic. • Have the second student give the first an explanation of what the graphic shows.
My Metaphor	• Post the following metaphor on the board: This (map, timeline, image, primary source) shows that ________ is like ________ because ________________. • Ask students to fill in the metaphor prompt based on their understanding of the source.
Act It Out	• Choose an image in the lesson and ask students to think about one of the following questions as appropriate to the image: What may have happened next in this image? What may have happened just before this image? What do you think the people in this image are thinking? What do you think the people in this image are saying to each other?
If Photos/Images/ Art Could Talk	• Ask the following questions about an image in the course: What do you think the person in this photo would say if they could talk? What's your evidence?
See-Think-Wonder	• Ask students to work in pairs. • Ask them to look at an image, map, or graph and answer these questions: What do you see? What does that make you think? What are you wondering about now that you've seen this? • Have students share their answers with the class.
A Closer Look	• Project a map or image on the board and divide it into four numbered quadrants. • Have students count off from 1 to 4 into four small groups. Have each group look closely at the part of the image in their quadrant. • Have each small group report on what they observed and learned as a result of their focus on this part of the image.

Active Classroom Strategies

<table>
<tr><th>Activity Name</th><th>How to Activate</th></tr>
<tr><td>Take a Stand</td><td><ul><li>Ask students to take a stand on a yes-or-no or agree/disagree critical thinking question.</li><li>Ask students to divide into two groups based on their answer and move to separate areas of the classroom.</li><li>Ask students to talk with each other to compare their reasons for answering yes or no.</li><li>Ask a representative from each side to present and defend the group's point of view.</li><li>Note: you can adapt this activity to have students take their place on a continuum line from 1 to 10 depending on how strongly they agree or disagree.</li></ul></td></tr>
<tr><td>Rank It</td><td><ul><li>List a group of items/concepts/steps/causes/events on the board.</li><li>Ask students to rank the items/steps . . . according to X criteria (which is most important, which had the greatest impact . . . most influential, essential, changed, affected).</li><li>Ask students to provide a justification for the ranking decisions they made.</li><li>Then ask students to work in pairs to share their rankings and justifications.</li><li>Poll the class to see if there is agreement on the ranking.</li></ul>OR<ul><li>Place stickies on the board with key events from the lesson or topic.</li><li>Break students into small groups and ask each group to go up and choose the sticky that they think describes the most significant event.</li><li>Ask the group to discuss among themselves why they think it is most significant.</li><li>Ask one person from each group to explain why the group chose that event.</li></ul></td></tr>
<tr><td>Sequence It</td><td><ul><li>Place key events from a lesson or topic on sticky notes on the board.</li><li>Ask students to place the events in chronological order.</li><li>You could do this activity with multiple groups in different parts of the classroom.</li></ul></td></tr>
<tr><td>PMI Plus/Minus/ Interesting</td><td><ul><li>Place students in groups and give each group a three-column organizer with headings Plus/Minus/Interesting for recording responses.</li><li>Ask students to analyze a text or examine an issue and then answer these three questions in their organizer:</li></ul><ol><li>What was positive about this text/issue?</li><li>What was negative about this text/issue?</li><li>What was interesting about this text/issue?</li></ol></td></tr>
</table>

THE CULTURALLY RESPONSIVE CLASSROOM

myWorld Interactive **includes many materials in the Teacher's Edition and student materials to help you build a culturally sensitive classroom. By following the suggestions here, and by calling out acts of intolerance when they are observed, school leaders can promote a school culture of acceptance and respect.**

California is extremely diverse, as you know. In its public schools, more that 20 percent of children are English Learners, speaking languages at home that represent all parts of the world. Nearly 60 percent of California students qualify for free or reduced lunch, a reflection of poverty in the home. And, while data is not available, it is likely that LGBTQ children attend all or most California schools.

It is important to note that these categories of language proficiency, ethnic background, level of poverty, and sexual identification are not mutually exclusive. A child may be poor and Hispanic, or black and gay, or an English Learner and Pakistani.

Your own classroom probably reflects at least some aspects of this diversity.

This is both a great opportunity and a challenge. The children in the classroom each bring a unique set of experiences and outlooks. These differences should be honored and celebrated. The children can learn from each other, sharing their perspectives. It is a teacher's responsibility to make the classroom safe for that sharing.

Steps you as a teacher can take

1 Check for Unconscious Bias Consider unconscious bias. Everyone has ideas and ways of speaking that they use in their everyday activities and speech. But sometimes these ways of thinking and speaking can inadvertently express bias. And because children look up to their teachers as role models, they can be very sensitive to a teacher's behavior. So unconscious bias may be hurtful despite the best intentions.

For example, a teacher may assume boys will want to do certain activities and girls will want to do others. Or maybe a teacher notices misbehavior among students of one ethnic group more often than he or she notices it among others. Or a teacher may call on certain students more than others.

2 Create a Culture of Inclusion Look around the classroom. Does the classroom represent the students in the class? Consider the pictures hung on the wall: are there children of many ethnic and racial groups represented? Think about the classroom library: does it have books on topics that will engage children with many different interests and from different backgrounds? Teachers can make inclusiveness a daily priority.

3 Words and Connections Matter A teacher should be thoughtful about how he or she talks with children. At the beginning of the year, she can learn every child's name and how to pronounce it correctly. This will make each student feel acknowledged and respected. She can try to avoid bias words that hurt, by learning the words that don't. For example, in some communities, *trans, gay, American Indian*, and *African American* are used and accepted. A teacher should find out what is right for his or her community. And early in the year, the teacher can take the time to get to know each student. Awareness of their special interests and personal stories can go a long way to building trust in a classroom.

4 Make Space for Student Voices If children feel safe, they will express their interests and worries. There may be a subject they heard adults talking about that they didn't fully understand, but made them worry. Or it may be an upsetting incident that took place outside of school. Teachers should be ready to hear these concerns and make space in the lesson to talk about them together.

5 Honor Multiple Viewpoints Help the children listen to and respect multiple viewpoints. Identify a difficult issue bubbling up in the school or community. Try assigning children to take one side or the other about the issue. They can explain their thinking and give reasons for their point of view. Then ask them to take the opposite perspective. This will help children see that there is merit to arguments other than their own.

6 Be a Role Model Children who are different may experience bullying, and they may not want to talk about it. But teachers and other school leaders can set a tone that does not tolerate bullying for any reason.

7 Resources Find out about resources that can help. Here are a few:

- **stopbullying.gov/resources:** a website sponsored by the US Department of Health and Human Services that offers resources and suggestions for parents, teachers, and community leaders.
- **Edutopia.org:** a website with articles and resources related to diversity and to bullying prevention, along with many other education topics.
- **GLSEN.org:** a national organization with many local branches that focuses on LGBTQ issues in K-12 education.
- **www.tolerance.org:** a site where teachers can find free resources for teaching and learning about diversity.

COURSE INTRODUCTION

CONNECT

Explore the Guiding Question

World History and Geography: Ancient Civilizations covers the period from the earliest humans through the Roman Empire. To help the students make sense of such a vast amount of information, the California Framework lists four thematic questions around which the historical narrative can be organized. The Course Introduction gives you specific examples of and applications for those four questions that you can highlight as you teach the course.

Draw Conclusions What might cause people to migrate *away* from an environment? *(Sample answers: It might be too dry for agriculture. A natural disaster might destroy a settlement.)* What might cause people *to* migrate to an environment? *(Sample answers: It might have fertile land or useful resources.)*

Identify Cause and Effect What are some ways that environmental factors affect the ways people live? *(Sample answer: People must adapt their housing, clothing, and farming techniques to climate and environment.)*

Humans Begin to Farm

Have students examine the image of the ruins of the ancient settlement of Céide Fields, Ireland, which has the oldest known system of farm fields. Ask a volunteer to read the caption.

Draw Conclusions What advantages does this site have that makes it suitable for a settlement? *(Sample answer: It has stone for building. It is near the sea for fishing.)*

Cite Evidence What disadvantage might it have for farming? Cite evidence from the photograph. *(The soil is full of stones that would have to be cleared away.)*

See Also For other examples of how the environment influenced ancient the development of societies, refer students to:

- Topic 2, Lesson 1
- Topic 5, Lesson 1

COURSE INTRODUCTION

Questions from the History-Social Science Framework for California Public Schools to guide your study of World History and Geography: Ancient Civilizations

In your journey through world history this year, you will be visiting many different regions of the world across a period of more than 1,000 years. At the same time, you will see certain themes come up again and again. The following Guiding Questions will help you focus on how changes in the world helped societies form and develop in ancient civilizations.

GUIDING QUESTIONS

How did the environment influence human migration, ancient ways of life, and the development of societies?

For millions of years, humans and their ancestors survived in the same way. They hunted large animals for their meat and gathered small wild plants to eat. Changes in the environment influenced humans to change their ways of survival, caused them to migrate in large groups to other parts of the planet, and enabled them to develop and organize the first societies. Here are three examples of how the environment influenced humans to change their ways of living.

Humans Begin to Farm

Around 10,000 years ago, temperatures rose and glaciers that had covered much of the earth melted. Many animals that people had hunted died out. Some people observed that seeds scattered on the ground grew into new plants. This was the beginning of farming.

See Topic 1, Lesson 3, to learn more about how environmental changes led to an agricultural revolution.

HISTORICAL BACKGROUND

Çatalhüyük As far back as 8,700 years ago, humans were learning to adapt to their environment to create a more stable, richer life for themselves. Near the city of Kona, Turkey, is a major stone-age site known as Çatalhüyük, which is believed to have been inhabited from about 6700 to 5650 BCE. The people there cultivated grains, oil-producing seeds, and nuts, and they also kept animals. They lived in rectangular houses made of sun-dried brick, each of which had a hearth, an oven, and platforms for sleeping and sitting. The settlement also had religious shrines that were elaborately decorated with sculptures made from bone or stone and colored murals.

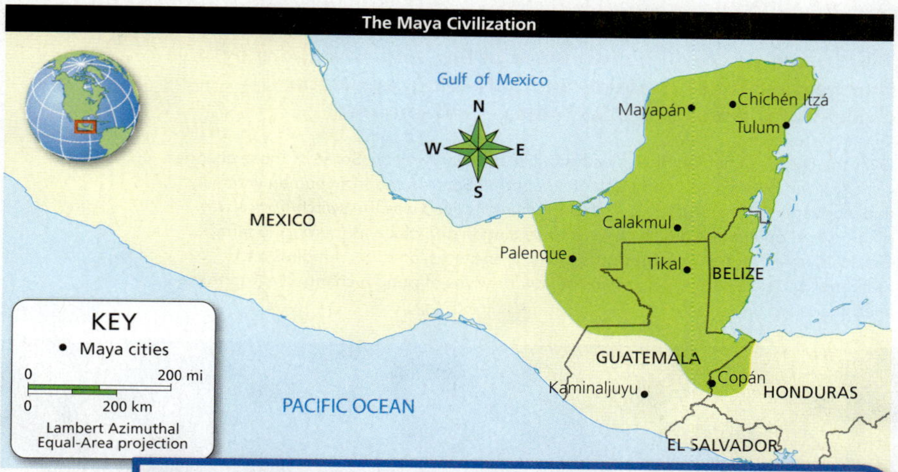

Rich Volcanic Soil Helps the Mayan Civilization Grow

The environment in Mesoamerica gave the Maya many resources. Volcanic ash in the highlands made the soil fertile. Heavy rainfall in the lowlands supported a tropical forest rich in plant and animal life. Good soil and many trade goods helped the Maya prosper.

See Topic 1, Lesson 6, to see how the environment helped the Maya build an advanced civilization.

Phoenicians Develop Trade and Find New Areas to Settle

The Phoenicians lived on the shores of the Mediterranean Sea. Their forested, mountainous land was not well suited for farming, so they became sailors. They traded goods—including cloth they manufactured and colored with purple dye made from sea snails—with other communities as they traveled.

See Topic 2, Lesson 4, to learn more about how the Phoenicians built a culture based on the sea.

Connecting to the Guiding Question

1. What is an environment? Identify two ways the environments described in these examples affected the people who lived in them.
2. From the examples given here, identify two ways that ancient peoples used what they found in their environment to their advantage.
3. Identify one way that people today are directly affected by their environment. How can our environment help us progress? How can it harm us?

Rich Volcanic Soil Helps the Mayan Civilization Grow

Have students study the map of the Maya civilization. As a volunteer to read the caption.

Analyze Maps How might having a long coastline have helped the Maya? *(Sample answer: They were probably able to catch fish and other seafood.)*

Draw Conclusions Notice the number of cities on the map. What conclusion can you draw about the Maya from this detail? *(Sample answers: They had a large population. They must have had a sophisticated society with a system of government.)*

See Also For other examples of how the environment help groups build an advanced civilization, refer students to:

- Topic 3, Lesson 1
- Topic 4, Lesson 1

Phoenicians Develop Trade and Find New Areas to Settle

Have students examine the photograph of the Phoenician coastline. Ask a volunteer to read the caption.

Identify Cause and Effect Why was the Phoenicians' environment poorly suited for farming? *(The land was covered by forests and mountains.)*

Solve Problems How did the Phoenicians turn their reliance on the sea into an advantage? *(Sample answers: They sailed over the sea to trade goods with other societies. They made a valuable product—purple dye—from sea snails.)*

See Also For other examples of people who relied on trade to provide what their environment lacked, refer students to:

- Topic 3, Lesson 3
- Topic 6, Lesson 1

CONNECTING TO THE GUIDING QUESTION

1. An environment is the surroundings in which a person or group lives. The fertile soil of the Mayas' environment allowed them to grow many crops and prosper. In contrast, the Phoenicians' environment was not good for farming so they turned to trade.
2. Sample answers: Ancient people observed that scattered seeds grew into plants, so they learned how to farm. The Phoenicians figured out how to use sea snails to make a valuable dye.
3. Sample answers: Today, people can be affected by drought or blizzards. Our environment can help us progress by providing resources like precious metals. It can harm us if drought or severe weather occur.

Explore the Guiding Question

Point out that several aspects of human life changed in ancient times. The first aspect was the source of humanity's food supply, which farming made more dependable. The next aspect was the size and complexity of human communities, which kept increasing. These two factors contributed to a third change: the ability of people to work at a wider variety of jobs.

Draw Conclusions What are the disadvantages of relying entirely on the hunting of animals and the gathering of nuts, seeds, and berries for food? *(Sample answer: There would be times when people couldn't find animals to hunt or foods to gather. Hunger would be a frequent occurrence.)*

Make Generalizations Why does the development of farming cause people to settle in one place? *(They must live where their fields are so they can tend their crops.)*

Uruk, the World's First City

Have students study the image of the buildings. Ask a volunteer to read the caption.

Draw Conclusions Why do you think farming villages eventually grew into cities? *(Sample answers: People gathered in cities for safety or to be able to trade with each other.)*

Categorize What kinds of jobs do you think people did in a city such as Uruk? *(Sample answers: builders, merchants, record keepers, guards, rulers, religious leaders)*

See Also For other examples of early cities, refer students to:

- Topic 2, Lesson 1
- Topic 3, Lesson 1

What were the early human ways of life, and how did they change over time? (hunting and gathering, agriculture, civilizations, urban societies, states, and empires)

Over the course of human history, ways of life changed greatly. Some of these changes were spurred by events outside of human control. Some came from human creativity and innovation. A major change in the way humans lived was the switch from a way of life based on hunting and gathering to settling in one place as a group to farm. Gradually small settlements grew into cities, then states, and then empires and civilizations. Here are three examples of how the lives of people changed along these lines in ancient times.

Uruk, the World's First City

The growth of agriculture led humans to settle together and live in one place, a shift from the nomadic lifestyle of the hunter-gatherers that had prevailed for millions of years. In the Middle East, simple farming villages eventually grew into the world's first cities. Historians believe that Uruk was the world's first city, founded 6,000 to 7,000 years ago. The 40,000 people who lived there built large public buildings and had an organized government.

See Topic 1, Lesson 4, to learn more about Uruk, the world's first city.

CI 2 Course Introduction

HISTORICAL BACKGROUND

Technology and Cities To make it possible for large numbers of people to live together in one place, humans had to come up with technological solutions to certain problems:

- Cities require shipments of food from the surrounding countryside. To make this possible, people had to develop roads and invent the wheel.
- People need a regular supply of fresh water. Many communities could not exist without canals or pipes to carry water to every part of the city.
- The invention of rafts, dugouts, and eventually boats made it possible to use waterways for transport.

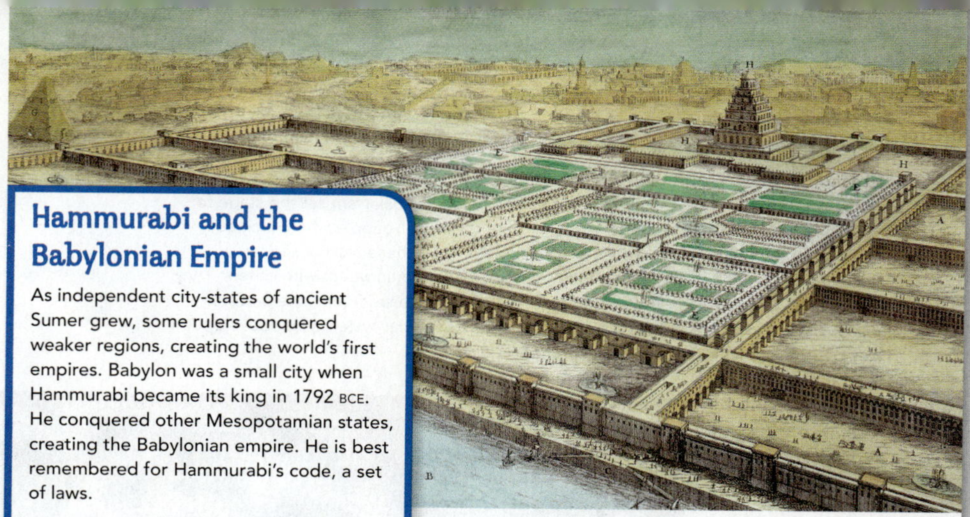

Hammurabi and the Babylonian Empire

As independent city-states of ancient Sumer grew, some rulers conquered weaker regions, creating the world's first empires. Babylon was a small city when Hammurabi became its king in 1792 BCE. He conquered other Mesopotamian states, creating the Babylonian empire. He is best remembered for Hammurabi's code, a set of laws.

See Topic 2, Lesson 2, to explore the impact of Hammurabi's code.

Egypt: One of the World's First Great Civilizations

Like the Fertile Crescent of Mesopotamia, Egypt was home to one of the world's first great civilizations. The Nile River enabled Egyptians to grow a surplus of crops, which helped their civilization grow. Plentiful crops supported a growing population and trade that added to their wealth. Egypt's cities supported a diverse range of skilled workers. This diversity helped to create a social order shaped like a pyramid.

See Topic 3, Lesson 1, to learn more about the ancient civilization of Egypt.

Connecting to the Guiding Question

1. What do we mean when we talk about cities, empires, and civilizations? How do these concepts relate to each other? How do these three examples explore those concepts?
2. Are there empires and civilizations today? How are modern societies organized? Give two examples.

CONNECTING TO THE GUIDING QUESTION

1. Sample answers: A city is a large community with a system of government and a variety of skilled workers. An empire is a government that rules more than one country or region. A civilization is a complex society that has made cultural achievements. A society must have cities to become a civilization. Empires are large units of government but are not needed for a society to become a civilization.

2. Sample: Yes, there are civilizations today. For example, the United States and China are both distinct civilizations. Many modern societies are organized into representative governments, such as that of the United States and Great Britain. Many modern societies are organized into class systems, which have divisions.

Hammurabi and the Babylonian Empire

Have students study the image of Babylon. Ask for a volunteer to read the caption.

Infer Why might an empire need a written code of laws? *(Sample answer: Because of their size, empires cannot assume that everyone shares the same ideas about laws or will understand what the ruler wants. A written code helps make sure all parts of the empire are ruled the same way.)*

Analyze Visual Information Notice the pyramid-shaped building in the illustration. What type of building do you think it was? *(Sample answers: It was most likely a temple or a government building.)*

See Also For other examples of ancient empires, refer students to:

- Topic 5, Lesson 4
- Topic 8, Lesson 1

Egypt: One of the World's First Great Civilizations

Have students study the diagram of Egypt's social pyramid. Ask for a volunteer to read the caption.

Analyze Visual Information How did the upper classes of Egyptian society compare in size to the lower classes? *(The upper classes have much fewer people.)*

Synthesize If Egypt's farmers had not been able to grow surplus crops, would Egypt have had a diverse range of skilled workers? Explain. *(No, it wouldn't. If each farmer grew only enough for his or her own family, then almost everyone would have had to farm or people would have starved.)*

See Also For other examples of great ancient civilizations, refer students to:

- Topic 4, Lesson 7
- Topic 6, Lesson 7

Explore the Guiding Question

Remind students that religious and philosophical systems usually provide guidance about the difference between right and wrong and often teach people how to treat each other.

Connect How do standards of right and wrong help people to live in society? *(Sample answer: If people in a society share standards of right and wrong, they are more likely to live in harmony because they will consider similar actions to be appropriate.)*

Support Ideas with Examples What is an example of a way that religions help people to understand how the universe works? *(Sample answers: Many religions have stories about how the world began. Many religions teach that God is the supreme power in the universe.)*

The Birth and Growth of Hinduism in india

Have students study the painting of a leader teaching holy law. Ask a volunteer to read the caption.

Connect What concepts of Hinduism are similar to the teachings of other religions? *(Sample answers: the idea of one spiritual power, the question of what happens after we die)*

Summarize What major religious change did India undergo from the writing of the Vedas to about 500 BCE? *(The Vedas offer ways to please many Gods. By 500 BCE, Indians began to embrace the idea of a single spiritual power that resides in all things.)*

See Also For other examples of how religions developed, refer students to:

- Topic 2, Lesson 5
- Topic 8, Lesson 2

How did the major religious and philosophical systems (Judaism, Greek thought, Hinduism, Buddhism, Confucianism) support individuals, rulers, and societies?

Early religions and philosophies such as Hinduism and Confucianism set the stage for later spiritual systems. These ideas spread among groups of people when societies traded and when states were joined together as empires. These religious ideas supported people in their efforts to find ways to cooperate and compete with others. They also helped people fulfill their desire to understand how the world and the universe worked. Here are three examples of religious or philosophical systems that developed in ancient societies.

The Birth and Growth of Hinduism in India

The Vedas, India's oldest religious texts, contain hymns and rituals to please many Gods. Around 500 BCE, Indians began to embrace the concept of *Brahman,* a single spiritual power that resided in all things. Others asked important questions such as: Why are we born? How should we live? What happens to us when we die? Hinduism evolved from efforts to answer these questions. It has been the main religion of India for the past 2,000 years. The word *Hinduism* means, "the religion of the people of India."

See Topic 4, Lesson 3, to explore the birth and development of Hinduism in India.

CURRICULUM CONNECTION: VISUAL AND PERFORMING ARTS

Statues of the Buddha Statues of the Buddha often employ many symbols meant to convey information to followers of that faith. For example, the Buddha is often shown with very long earlobes. This is a reminder that he was originally a prince who wore heavy earrings, a practice he gave up when he left his privileged life. The gestures that the statue makes can also be symbolic. If the statue sits cross-legged with both hands palm upward, one lying on top of the other, that indicates meditation. If the statue sits with one hand resting on the lap palm upward, that is a gesture of enlightenment. If the statue stands with one hand held palm outward, that is a gesture of reassurance to the Buddha's followers.

Greek Religion and Mythology

Although the Greek city-states often fought one another, most Greeks worshipped the same group of gods and goddesses, whom they believed looked and acted like human beings. Greeks expressed their religious beliefs in their mythology. Some myths explained natural phenomena, others taught moral lessons. In this way, Greeks tried to make sense of the natural world.

See Topic 6, Lesson 6, to understand more about how religion and mythology supported the lives of the ancient Greeks.

Belief Systems in Ancient China

Three main belief systems shaped Chinese culture. Daoism emphasized a close relationship with nature. Buddhism, based on the teaching of Indian spiritual leader Siddhartha Gautama, teaches that the suffering of life can be relieved through enlightenment. Confucianism, a system of moral behavior, influenced the nature of Chinese government.

See Topic 5, Lesson 3, to understand how these ways of thought supported the lives of the people of ancient China. See Topic 4, Lesson 4 to learn more about Buddhism and Topic 2, Lesson 6 to learn more about the belief system of the Hebrew people.

Connecting to the Guiding Question

1. What do the religious systems described have in common? How do they differ in their efforts to support the ancient people who practiced them? Use two examples from these pages to explain your answer.
2. In general, how did individuals, rulers, and societies benefit from a shared religious or philosophical system?

CONNECTING TO THE GUIDING QUESTIONS

1. Sample answer: They all tackle questions related to the meaning of life. Some, such as the ancient Vedic writings, focused more on humanity's relationship with the Gods. Others, such as Confucianism, focused more on how humans should live in society.

2. Sample answer: They benefited from having a common understanding of what was important and how people should treat each other. This gave them a basis for trying to do the right them and for evaluating what behaviors would help society to run more smoothly.

Greek Religion and Mythology

Have students examine the photograph of the figures on ancient Greek pottery. Ask a volunteer to read the caption.

Infer How would believing in the same gods help unify the Greeks in different city-states? *(Sample answer: They would share the same understanding about what the gods expected of humans and the same ideas about how the world works.)*

Connect What did ancient religion have in common with modern-day science? *(Sample answer: Both are attempts to understand natural phenomena.)*

See Also For other examples of religions that relied on mythology, refer students to:

- Topic 2, Lesson 1
- Topic 3, Lesson 1

Belief Systems in Ancient China

Have students examine the statue of Confucius. Ask for a volunteer to read the caption.

Apply Concepts Which of the three belief systems of ancient China would most likely appeal to a writer who composes poems about mountains and forests? Why? *(Sample answer: Daoism because it emphasizes a close relationship with nature)*

Synthesize Why would the Chinese government be especially interested in a system of moral behavior like Confucianism? *(Sample answer: Some of the tasks of government are to pass good laws and to convince people to obey the law.)*

See Also For other examples of philosophies, refer students to:

- Topic 6, Lesson 7
- Topic 8, Lesson 4

Explore the Guiding Question

Point out to students that people often trade things to gain more of what they want. For example, two friends having lunch together might agree to trade half a hamburger for a slice of pizza so that each person can have both of their favorite foods instead of eating just one. Societies do much the same thing but on a much larger scale.

Summarize How does trade increase interaction between societies? *(Sample answer: When people from two societies trade, they have to meet and communicate with each other. Over time, they may learn more about each other than just information about products.)*

Draw Conclusions How can empire building cause unrelated cultures to come into contact with each other? *(Sample answer: An empire brings different countries or regions under one government. Cultures that were formally independent will share rulers as a result, and this may lead to increased interactions among them.)*

Egypt and Kush

Have students study the mural showing princes from Kush bringing gold to Egypt. Ask a volunteer to read the caption.

Support Ideas with Examples Give an example of mutually beneficial trade that might have taken place between Egypt and Kush. *(Sample answer: Egypt traded grain to Kush for iron.)*

Draw Conclusions Why do you think Egypt and Kush went from conducting peaceful trade to trying conquer each other? *(Sample answer: First, Egypt decided it wanted to control all the wealth the two nations had access to, and then Kush decided the same thing.)*

See Also For other examples of trade causing cultures to interact, refer students to:

- Topic 4, Lesson 1
- Topic 6, Lesson 4

How did societies interact with each other? How did connections between societies increase over time?

Since the first city-states formed and became stable enough for people to travel in search of things they lacked or wanted more of, societies have interacted with each other. Groups of people traded goods with each other. Stronger powers conquered their neighbors to create empires. Here are three examples of how societies interacted with each other in various ways.

Egypt and Kush

South of Egypt, farther up the Nile River was a land that Egyptians called Kush. It extended from present-day southern Egypt to northern Sudan. Trade was important to Egypt and Kush. Egypt had a surplus of crops because of its fertile land. Kush had less agriculture but had other resources, such as wood from their forests and iron from their mines, to offer. They also had gold and made cloth to sell. Kush was in closer contact than Egypt was with the peoples of Africa. They provided Egyptians with a link to those peoples in terms of trade. Egypt conquered Kush at one point to gain control over their riches. Then in the mid-700s BCE, Kush conquered Egypt and controlled it for almost 100 years.

See Topic 3, Lesson 3, to learn more about how the peoples of Egypt and Kush interacted.

HISTORICAL BACKGROUND NOTE

Egypt and Punt Kush was not the only region in Africa to trade with Egypt. Egyptian pharaohs are known to have sent expeditions to a land called Punt, which is located along the coast of what are now Ethiopia and Djibouti. The most famous of these was sent by Queen Hatshepsut, one of the few women to reign as pharaoh. Her emissaries brought back gold, ebony, ivory, myrrh, cinnamon, trees, and even live animals to Egypt. This expedition was considered such an achievement that Hatshepsut made sure it was recorded in detail on her mortuary temple.

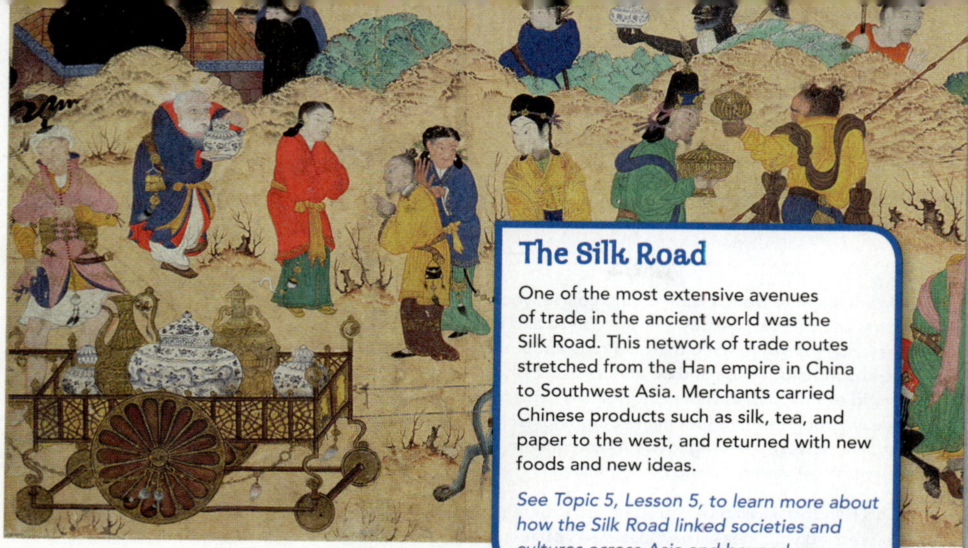

The Silk Road

One of the most extensive avenues of trade in the ancient world was the Silk Road. This network of trade routes stretched from the Han empire in China to Southwest Asia. Merchants carried Chinese products such as silk, tea, and paper to the west, and returned with new foods and new ideas.

See Topic 5, Lesson 5, to learn more about how the Silk Road linked societies and cultures across Asia and beyond.

The Roman Empire

By 100 CE, the two dominant empires of the ancient world were the Han empire in China and the Roman empire in the Mediterranean region. From their homeland on the Italian peninsula, the Romans conquered lands in Europe, North Africa, and southwestern Asia. Goods and ideas traveled along Roman trade routes. Roman governors enforced and spread Roman ideas about law. Interactions between the Romans and the Jewish people influenced the development of a new religion, Christianity.

See Topic 8, Lesson 1, to learn how the "Roman Peace" encouraged interaction among different peoples.

Connecting to the Guiding Question

1. What caused societies to trade with one another? What did societies gain by conquering others?
2. In what ways do nations interact with each other today?

CONNECTING TO THE GUIDING QUESTION

1. Sample answer: Societies traded with one another to gain products and resources they did not have in their own region. Through conquest, societies gained control over the land, resources, and wealth-producing enterprises of other countries or regions.

2. Sample answers: Today, nations interact with each other through trade, negotiation, diplomacy, alliances, public statements, and to a lesser extent, conquest.

The Silk Road

Have students study the painting of a scene along the Silk Road. Ask for a volunteer to read the caption.

Analyze Visual Information What products do you see being traded or transported in this image? *(Sample answers: pottery, brass vessels)*

Cite Evidence What evidence does the painting show of interaction among different cultures? *(Sample answer: It shows people with different skin colors. It shows people with different styles of dress.)*

See Also For other examples of trade spreading culture, refer students to:

- Topic 2, Lesson 4
- Topic 7, Lesson 1

The Roman Empire

Have students study the image of the Roman coin. Ask for a volunteer to read the caption.

Draw Conclusions How do you think conquered peoples felt about being forced to obey Roman law? *(Sample answers: They might have resented giving up their own law codes. They might have liked having a systematic code of law because it was fair.)*

Hypothesize Do you think conquered peoples ever influence their rulers? Explain. *(Sample answer: Yes, culture probably spreads both ways when rulers and conquered people interact. If the conquered group has an attractive idea or product, the conqueror will most likely adopt it.)*

See Also For other examples of empires that brought about cultural interaction, refer students to:

- Topic 2, Lesson 3
- Topic 6, Lesson 8

CALIFORNIA ENGLISH–LANGUAGE ARTS HANDBOOK

Use this English–Language Arts Handbook to help your students use social studies content to strengthen their reading, writing, and speaking and listening skills. This handbook has three sections.

READING

The READING section offers instruction in how to:

- Analyze Informational Text
- Evaluate Arguments
- Analyze Visuals
- Analyze Primary and Secondary Sources
- Support Analyses With Evidence

WRITING

The WRITING section offers instruction in how to:

- Use the Writing Process
- Write an Argument
- Write Informative or Explanatory Essays
- Write Narrative Essays
- Find and Use Credible Sources
- Write Research Papers

SPEAKING and LISTENING

The SPEAKING AND LISTENING section offers instruction in how to:

- Discuss Ideas
- Give Effective Presentations
- Use Effective Listening

SKILLS ASSESSMENT

Use the Course Pretest to assess your students' skills at the beginning of the course. The results will help you focus your skills instruction throughout the year.

This program has a collection of 21st Century Skills Tutorials online, each of which include a video that models the skill, a Quick Reference that lists and explains the steps, and a brief assessment. Use these as remediation or to deepen the quick instruction given in this handbook.

CALIFORNIA ENGLISH-LANGUAGE ARTS HANDBOOK

As you explore world history in this course, you will read informational texts and primary sources. For this course and in other courses and beyond, you will need to think critically about the texts you read to absorb information and be able to express your thoughts about world events, past and present. You will need to communicate your ideas through writing (summaries, arguments, informative essays, and narratives), speaking (debates and one-on-one and small group discussions), and by giving presentations.

This Handbook will give you some tools for reading critically and expressing your ideas. The Quests and other activities in this program give you opportunities to write and speak about your ideas and create projects that will help you practice these skills.

INTERACTIVE

The 21st Century Skills Tutorials, found on Realize, support many of the skills discussed here. Go online to find a Quick Reference, video of the skill being modeled, and more.

DIFFERENTIATED INSTRUCTION

Below Level You will find tips for differentiated instruction of English Language Arts skills with your social studies content throughout this handbook. Begin this instruction by reviewing with students the differences and similarities between Reading, Writing, and Speaking and Listening.

Display a Venn diagram with four overlapping circles labeled Reading, Writing, Speaking, and Listening. In the center overlap, write the word Language. In the overlap between Reading and Writing, write the label Written Language. In the overlap between Speaking and Listening, write the label Spoken Language. Invite students to mime or act out the acts of Reading, Writing, Speaking, and Listening.

READING

Analyze Informational Text

ELA RI.6.2, 6.4–5; RH.6.2, 6.4–5; ELD PI.B.8, PII.A.1

Reading nonfiction texts, like a magazine article or your textbook, is not the same as reading a fictional story or novel. The purpose of reading nonfiction is to acquire new information. It's something that you, and the adults around you, do all the time.

Process What You Read When you read informational text, it helps to know what to look for and what questions to ask yourself as you read. Use the chart below as a guide when you read.

	Look for	Questions to Ask	For More Help
Central Ideas and Details	• Central ideas or claims • Supporting details or evidence	• What is the subject or main point of this text? • What details support the main point? • What inferences do you need to make? • How does the author develop a few central ideas throughout a text?	**Skills Tutorial** • Identify Main Ideas and Details • Draw Inferences • Summarize **Analysis Skill** Identify Central Issues and Problems
Word Choice	• Unfamiliar words and phrases • Words and phrases that produce a certain effect on a reader	• What inferences about word meaning can you make from the context? • What tone and mood are created by word choice? • What alternate word choices might the author have made?	**Skills Tutorial** • Draw Inferences
Text Structure	• Ways the author has organized the text • Ways sentences and paragraphs work together to build ideas • Clue words signaling a particular structure	• Does the text have a specific structure? • For instance, is it structured by sequence or chronology? By comparisons and contrasts? By causes and effects?	**Skills Tutorial** • Identify Evidence • Analyze Cause and Effect • Sequence • Compare and Contrast

INTEGRATED ENGLISH LANGUAGE DEVELOPMENT

Emerging Display the word *informational*. Draw a line under or circle the word *inform* within the word *informational* and then underline or circle the word *information* within the word *informational*. Explain that to *inform* means to provide facts or data or *information* about a topic or event and *informational* text is something you can read to get information.

Expanding Elicit the idea that in reading informational text, students will want to look for the central ideas and details the writer offers so they can understand the information the writer is providing. Discuss the terms *evidence*, *cause and effect*, *sequence*, and *compare and contrast* and how each structure could be used to organize text.

ELA RI.6.2, 6.4–5; RH.6.2, 6.4–5; ELD PI.B.8, PII.A.1

READING

Analyze Informational Text

LEARN

Invite a student to explain the term *Informational Text.* Ask volunteers to offer examples of informational text that they have encountered in their daily lives. Students may mention instructions for operating a device, directions for traveling from one place to another, or news articles on a website or in a magazine that provide information about an event or situation. Point out that their textbook (whether printed or online) is also informational text.

Preview the Process What You Read chart with students, and then play the first video.

INTERACTIVE

Project the Identify Main Ideas and Details video in the 21st Century Skills Tutorial. Use the Quick Reference and Assessment to provide additional instruction in this skill. You may also use the other skill tutorials listed in the chart to help your students begin to develop skills to analyze informational text.

PRACTICE

Students will practice analyzing informational text throughout their study of world history. Have them start by identifying central ideas and details in the example text Writing Has Changed the World in the next handbook lesson.

ASSESS

To assess this skill, have students identify the main ideas of the text under the heading "Studying Early Humans" in Lesson 1 of Topic 1.

ELA RI.6.8, RH.6.8; ELD PI.B.7, PII.A.1

Evaluate Arguments

LEARN

Invite a student to explain the term argument. Ask students to explain what is needed for a good argument; then play the video.

INTERACTIVE

Project the Evaluate Existing Arguments video in the 21st Century Skills Tutorial. Use the Quick Reference and Assessment to provide additional instruction in this skill. You may also use the Consider and Counter Opposing Arguments and Support Ideas With Evidence tutorials to support instruction of this skill.

PRACTICE

Have students practice the skill by reading the model text. Ask: What is the writer's claim in Writing Has Changed the World? *(Over time, writing has grown in importance.)* How does the author support this claim? *(The writer supports their claim with several examples from ancient societies, such as the Sumerians.)*

ASSESS

To assess this skill, have students identify the claim and evidence in the text under the heading "Who Were the Neanderthals?" at the beginning of Lesson 2 in Topic 1.

Evaluate Arguments

ELA RI.6.8, RH.6.8; ELD PI.B.7, PII.A.1

One important reason to read and understand informational text is so you can recognize and evaluate written arguments. An argument is a logical way of presenting a belief, conclusion, or stance. A good argument is supported with reasoning and evidence and will often address opposing claims. Study the model below to see how the writer developed an argument about the impact of writing on the world.

Writing Has Changed the World

Here the writer clearly states the claim.

At one time, knowledge was shared by word of mouth. By 3000 BCE, however, ancient peoples had created systems of writing. Over time, writing has grown in importance.

The writer uses this example to support one of the claims.

At first, writing was a practical way to record information. The Sumerians began writing to keep track of grain production. In time, people found additional uses for writing. Scholars began to write about mathematics and science. They created calendars and wrote about their history. Much of what we know about the Sumerians, Egyptians, and Mayans comes from their writings.

The claim is supported by an example from the Babylonian empire.

Perhaps most importantly, writing has been used to unite people. For example, Hammurabi had his law code written in stone. It was displayed throughout the Babylonian empire. All the people knew the laws. For the first time, an entire empire was united by the written word.

The writer finishes by summarizing the impact of writing on our lives today.

People today find it hard to imagine a world without writing. Print and online sources provide a steady stream of written words. It began as a way to count bushels of grain, but now it's our greatest source of knowledge.

INTERACTIVE

Go online for these interactive skills tutorials:
- Evaluate Arguments
- Consider and Counter Opposing Arguments
- Support Ideas with Evidence

ELA 2 California English-Language Arts Handbook

INTEGRATED ENGLISH LANGUAGE DEVELOPMENT

Emerging Discuss the different definitions of the word *argument*. Explain that an argument can be a disagreement or a quarrel; it can also be a statement that is backed up with evidence. Have students use both definitions of argument in sentences.

Expanding Have students point in the text to evidence that the writer uses to support their point.

Analyze Visuals

ELA RI.6.7, RH.6.7

Another key component of understanding informational texts is being able to understand any visuals that go with written text, like the maps, graphs, charts, and photos. Study the chart and the example to help you analyze some common types of visuals in your social studies text.

	Look for	For More Help
Maps	• Read the title. • Read the key. • Study the locator globe, scale bar, and compass rose. • Apply the key and labels to the map.	**Skills Tutorial** • Use Parts of a Map • Read Physical Maps • Read Political Maps • Read Special-Purpose Maps
Graphs and Tables	• Read the title. • Use labels and key. • Look for patterns or changes over time.	**Skills Tutorial** • Read Charts, Graphs, and Tables • Create Charts and Maps
Photographs	• Identify the content. • Note emotions. • Read captions or credits. • Study the image's purpose. • Consider context. • Respond.	**Skills Tutorial** • Analyze Images • Analyze Political Cartoons

Origins of Arabic Numerals

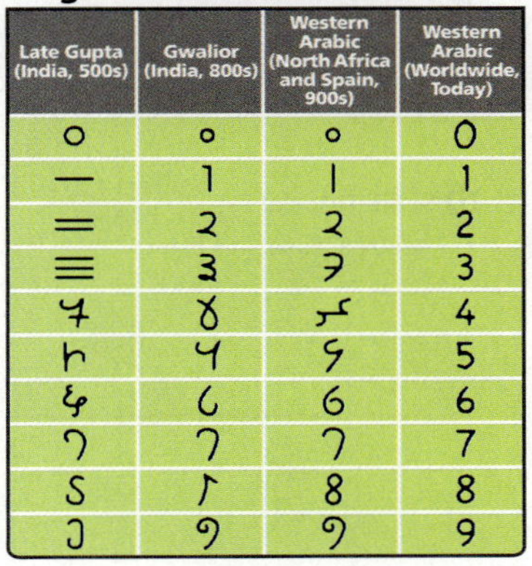

1. What is the title of the chart?
2. Read the labels. What does the first column on the left show?
3. Which numbers seem to be the most consistent through all four written languages?
4. What evidence supports your conclusion?

DIFFERENTIATED INSTRUCTION

Below Level Display the Origins of Arabic Numerals chart on a board or wall. Circle and label the parts of the chart, including the title and labels.

Advanced Have students discuss the advantages of using visuals with written information. How can visuals help a reader understand the content?

ELA RI.6.7, RH.6.7

Analyze Visuals

LEARN

Invite volunteers to define the terms map, graph, table, and photograph. Encourage students to skim the text and find examples of each type of visual. Point out the parts of the visual such as the title, caption, labels and key.

Preview the Analyze Visuals chart and then play the video.

INTERACTIVE

Project the Read Charts, Graphs, and Tables video in the 21st Century Skills Tutorial. Use the Quick Reference and Assessment to provide additional instruction in this skill. You may also use the skills tutorials listed in the chart to provide additional instruction for other types of visuals.

PRACTICE

Have students practice the skill by answering the questions about the chart (*The title of the chart is "Origins of Arabic Numerals"; the column on the left shows numerals used in the Late Gupta period in India; the most consistent numbers seem to be 7 and 9; that conclusion is supported by the appearance of the numerals in the chart.*)

ASSESS

Have students practice analyzing visuals by looking at the map "Origins of Agriculture" in Topic 1, Lesson 4.

ELA RI.6.3–4, 6.6, 6.9; RH.6.4, 6.6, 6.9; ELD PI.B.7, PI.B.8, PII.A.2

Analyze Primary and Secondary Sources

LEARN

Invite a student to define the terms primary source and secondary source. Make a list on the board of examples of primary and secondary sources.

Preview the chart and then play the video.

INTERACTIVE

Project the Analyze Primary and Secondary Sources video in the 21st Century Skills Tutorial. Use the Quick Reference and Assessment to provide additional instruction in this skill. You may also use the other skills tutorials listed in the chart to help students learn more about analyzing primary and secondary sources.

PRACTICE

Have students practice the skill by working in small groups to analyze the source on Shi Huangdi. Encourage students use the questions in the chart (where applicable) as they read this source.

What was the author's purpose in writing this inscription? *(The author was likely writing the inscription for Shi Huangdi to honor him.)* What would influence the author's point of view? *(The author's point of view might have been very positive to avoid angering Shi Huangdi.)* How would this point of view affect the information included in the inscription? *(The author might avoid including any facts or using any words that imply that any of Shi Huangdi's actions were negative.)*

Analyze Primary and Secondary Sources

ELA RI.6.3–4, 6.6, 6.9; RH.6.4, 6.6. 6.9; ELD PI.B.7, PI.B.8, PII.A.2

A primary source is information from someone who saw or was part of what is being described. A secondary source is information recorded later by someone who was not part of the event. You will encounter many primary and secondary sources throughout your textbook and in Quests and other activities. Study these questions and the model primary sources that follows to help you unlock the meaning of these sources.

	Questions to Ask	For More Help
Determine the Author's Purpose	• Is the source written mainly to convey information, like a textbook? • Or, is its purpose to persuade you to think a certain way, like an opinion piece in a newspaper?	**Skills Tutorial** • Analyze Primary and Secondary Sources • Analyze Media Content • Draw Inferences
Determine the Author's Point of View	• What is the author's point of view? • Is the author's point of view shaped by subjective influences such as feelings, prejudices, experiences? • Is the author's point of view shaped by his or her field of study?	**Skills Tutorial** • Analyze Primary and Secondary Sources • Compare Viewpoints
Compare Viewpoints	• How is the author's point of view different from that of other authors' writing on the same subject? • Does the author avoid including certain facts that would change his or her point of view?	**Skills Tutorial** • Compare Viewpoints
Analyze Word Choice	• Does the author use words in a neutral, factual way? • Does the author use loaded words that try to persuade the reader to think a certain way?	**Skills Tutorial** • Identify Bias
Analyze Interactions	• How have individuals, events, and ideas influenced each other? • What connecting words signal these interactions (*next, for example, consequently, however,* etc.)?	**Skills Tutorial** • Analyze Cause and Effect

DIFFERENTIATED INSTRUCTION

Below Level To help students understand the differences between primary and secondary sources, list the key characteristics of each on the board before asking students to name examples of each.

Advanced Have students evaluate the advantages and disadvantages of various types of primary and secondary sources in the study of history. How do they help a historian to better understand a topic? How are they limited in their usefulness?

Primary Sources Model Shi Huangdi founded the Qin dynasty. His rule was marked by great accomplishments as well as strict and sometimes cruel actions. This excerpt describes Shi Huangdi's rule. Study the excerpt and call-outs to help you better understand the author's purpose, word choices, and point of view.

Shi Huangdi Memorial Inscription

A new age is inaugurated by the Emperor;
Rules and measures are rectified, . . .
Human affairs are made clear
And there is harmony between fathers and sons.
The Emperor in his [wise ways], [kindness], and justice
Has made all laws and principles [understandable].

He set forth to pacify the east,
To inspect officers and men;
This great task accomplished
He visited the coast.
Great are the Emperor's achievements,
Men attend diligently to basic tasks,
Farming is encouraged, . . .

All the common people prosper;
All men under the sky
Toil with a single purpose;
Tools and measures are made uniform,
The written script is standardized,
Wherever the sun and moon shine. . . .

—*The Records of the Grand Historian*, Sima Qian.

The adjectives are all positive and suggest that Emperor Shi Huangdi was a good emperor.

This inscription was ordered by Shi Huangdi, so the writer probably needed to make the descriptions positive.

The author only refers to Shi Huangdi's positive actions and not his more controversial ones.

Sima Qian lived about 100 years after the life of Shi Huangdi. He is quoting from a marker put up during Shi Huangdi's time.

ASSESS

To assess this skill, have students work in small groups to analyze the Primary Source: *Epic of Gilgamesh* that follows Lesson 1 in Topic 1.

INTEGRATED ENGLISH LANGUAGE DEVELOPMENT

Emerging Ask students questions to help them understand the sources on Shi Huangdi such as, who set forth to pacify the east? And Who made uniform coins?

Expanding Ask students questions to help them understand the sources on Shi Huangdi such as, What are some of the positive words the inscription uses to describe Shi Huangdi?

ELA RI.6.1; RH.6.1; ELD PI.B.7

Support Your Analyses with Evidence

LEARN

Invite a student to define the terms *assertion*, *claim* and *evidence*. Ask students to offer assertions about everyday life that they can back up with evidence. Discuss why it is important to look for evidence for a claim rather than merely accepting a claim as fact and why it is important to support one's own claims with evidence.

Preview the chart and then play the video.

INTERACTIVE

Project the Identify Evidence video in the 21st Century Skills Tutorial. Use the Quick Reference and Assessment to provide additional instruction in this skill. You may also use the Support Ideas With Evidence tutorial to help students master this skill.

PRACTICE

Have students practice the skill by examining claims and evidence in the Model Secondary Source on the town of Jericho. *(The claim is that Jericho was a busy town, evidence provided is that the available food supply supported a population of some three thousand people; and that traders made Jericho busy.)*

ASSESS

To assess this skill, have students identify evidence supporting the competing claims mentioned in the text under the heading "What Do We Know About Early Migration?" in Lesson 2 of Topic 1.

Support Your Analyses with Evidence

ELA RI.6.1; RH.6.1; ELD PI.B.7

Historians and other writers make assertions, or claims, about events. Before accepting a claim as fact, however, look carefully at the evidence the author provides. Study the chart and the model secondary source to learn more about how to use evidence to support your ideas.

	Look for	Questions to Ask	For More Help
Support Your Analyses With Evidence	• The subject of the passage • Any assertion or claim that something is true • Appropriate evidence to support the claim • How well the evidence supports the claim, either explicitly or by inference	• What is the passage about? • Are there claims that something is true? • If so, what language supports the claim? • Does the evidence support the claim? • Did the author convince you that the claim was correct?	**Skills Tutorial** • Identify Evidence • Support Ideas with Evidence

Model Secondary Source Look for evidence in this model passage. Do you think the main point is supported by the evidence?

The subject of a passage is usually stated toward the beginning of the passage. This passage's subject is about how Jericho was a busy town.

These sentences show how Jericho's food surplus allowed Jericho to support many people.

This sentence provides evidence that trade made Jericho busy.

The ancient town of Jericho lies near the Dead Sea. In 8000 BCE, Jericho was a hub of activity. The surrounding fields yielded huge crops of wheat and barley. The nearby wilderness provided a good supply of meat. Gazelles and ibexes were plentiful. With this agricultural surplus, Jericho was able to support a population of up to three thousand people.

Traders did a brisk business in Jericho. People came from near and far to trade salt, obsidian, and semiprecious stones.

Jericho was well protected against attack. There was a high stone wall around the town. There was also a broad ditch and watchtower almost 30 feet high.

DIFFERENTIATED INSTRUCTION

Below Level Students who are below level may benefit from marking up the text. Since students cannot usually write in texts, or the text may be online, students may need to use alternative methods to mark up a text. Items such as sticky notes or wiki-sticks can help students focus on areas of a text and are easily removable once a lesson is complete.

WRITING

Using the Writing Process

ELA W.6.4–6, WHST.6.4–6; ELD PI.A.4, C.10

A systematic approach—including planning, drafting, revising, editing, rewriting, and proofreading—will help strengthen your writing.

Prewriting: Plan Your Essay

1. **Choose a topic.** Often your teacher will provide you with a topic. Sometimes, you will be able to choose your own. In that case, select a topic that you care about and that you think will interest others.
2. **Narrow your focus.** Most writers begin with too broad a topic. For example, you might decide to write about the Renaissance. You will need to focus on a single artist or discovery.
3. **Gather information.** Collect facts and details for your essay. Research any points you want to include that you are unsure about.
4. **Organize your ideas.** Writers often create an outline to plan their essay. You need not create a formal outline, but you should jot down your main ideas, the details that support them, and the order in which you will present your ideas. A graphic organizer can help you organize ideas. Here is one for a paper on arts in ancient Greece:

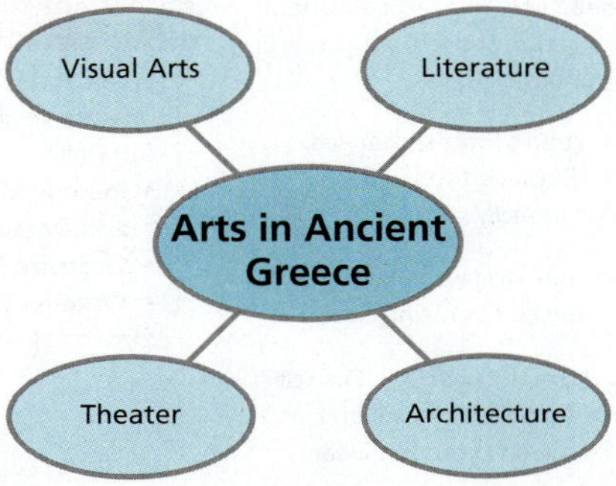

5. **Write a thesis statement.** A thesis statement focuses your ideas into a sentence or two and tells readers what the essay is about.

Drafting

1. **Maintain a clear focus.** If you find that your writing is starting to get off track, go back to your thesis statement.
2. **Elaborate for interest and emphasis.** Give details and specific examples about each point in your essay to help the reader understand the issue.
3. **Provide evidence.** Evidence is key to convincing an audience. Provide factual, concrete evidence to back up your ideas and assertions.

ELA W.6.4–6, WHST.6.4–6; ELD PI.A.4, C.10

WRITING

Using the Writing Process

LEARN

Invite a student to list the steps of the writing process. Ask students to offer examples of times that they have used the writing process in the past. What type of writing assignments have they completed?

Encourage students to reflect on how their writing changed throughout the writing process and then play the video.

INTERACTIVE

Project the Write an Essay video in the 21st Century Skills Tutorial. Use the Quick Reference and Assessment to provide additional instruction in this skill. You may also use the skill tutorials for Identify Main Ideas and Details and Organize Your Ideas to help students understand the writing process.

PRACTICE

Have students practice the skill by examining the steps of the writing process. Read each step one by one and ask students questions to gauge their understanding of the material

Prewriting: What steps are parts of prewriting? Why is it important to organize your ideas before beginning to draft your essay?

Drafting: What should you consider while drafting your essay?

DIFFERENTIATED INSTRUCTION

Below Level Before students complete each part of a writing assignment, have them review the step in the writing process. For example, review the prewriting step before asking students to prewrite for an essay. Then, review drafting before students begin to draft.

Making a model assignment together with the class can help students to better grasp the writing process. Together with students, complete the steps of the writing process, modeling the results on chart paper. This model can serve as an example for students as they complete the writing process for various assignments throughout the course.

Revising, Editing, and Rewriting: What should you think about while revising and editing your writing? Why is it important to proofread your writing yourself instead of relying on a spell-checker?

ASSESS

Each topic in this course provides an opportunity to practice writing in the Writing Workshop. The Quest often involves writing as well. Assign the Writing Workshop for some topics to assess students' skills as they work through the course. The Active Journal provides scaffolding for the writing tasks and the Active Journal Answer Key has rubrics for each type of essay.

Revising, Editing, and Rewriting

1. **Add transition words.** Make cause-and-effect relationships clear with words such as *because*, *as a result*, and so on. To compare or contrast ideas, use linking words, such as *similarly*, *both*, and *equally* or *in contrast*, *instead*, and *yet*. Use words such as *first*, *second*, *next*, and *finally* to help readers follow steps in a sequence. Look at the following examples. In the revised version, a reader knows the correct order in which to perform the steps.

First Draft	Revision
Historians form an educated guess called a hypothesis. They test that hypothesis with further research.	<u>Next</u>, historians form an educated guess called a hypothesis. <u>Then</u>, they test that hypothesis with further research.

2. **Focus on how well you have addressed your purpose.** Be sure that your essay addresses your purpose for writing. For a problem-solution essay, that means anticipating opposing arguments and responding to them. For a cause-and-effect essay, stress the way one event leads to the next.
3. **Focus on your audience.** Check that you have not left out any steps in your essay and that your audience can follow your thinking. Make sure that your writing will hold your audience's interest.
4. **Review organization.** Confirm that your ideas flow in a logical order. Write your main points on sticky notes. Reorganize these until you are satisfied that the order best strengthens your essay.
5. **Revise sentences and words.** Use both short and long sentences. Scan for vague words, such as *good* or *nice*. Replace them with specific and vibrant words, such as *helpful* or *friendly*.
6. **Peer review.** Ask a peer—a friend or classmate—to read your draft. Is it clear? Can your reader follow your ideas? Revise confusing sections.

INTERACTIVE

Go online for these interactive skills tutorials:
- Identify Main Ideas and Details
- Organize Your Ideas
- Write an Essay

Proofread Always proofread for spelling and grammar errors. Do not simply rely on spellchecking apps or programs. A spellchecker won't catch the difference between *see* and *sea* or between *deer* and *dear*.

Use Technology

Here are a few ideas:
- ✓ Use a word processing program to plan and write your essay.
- ✓ Use the Internet for research (see guidelines later in this Handbook).
- ✓ Use email and other online tools to collaborate with classmates.
- ✓ Create informative charts, graphs, and diagrams for presentations.
- ✓ Share your writing with others through a blog or website.

ELA 8 California English-Language Arts Handbook

DIFFERENTIATED INSTRUCTION

Above Level If students are above level in writing, they may have already completed many of the steps of the revision process while writing their drafts. They may be resistant to additional revision. Encourage students to consider additional ways to improve their writing during the revision process. For example, challenging a student to make their writing more succinct can encourage them to consider how to use words to make the most impact on their writing.

Write an Argument

ELA W.6.1, WHST.6.1; ELD PI.C.10, 11

In addition to evaluating other writers' arguments, you also need to be able to express arguments of your own, in writing and speaking. An argumentative, or persuasive, essay sets forth a belief or stand on an issue. A well-written argument may convince the reader, change the reader's mind, or motivate the reader to take a certain action.

In this program, you'll practice writing arguments in some Document-Based Inquiry Quests and Writing Workshops, with support in your **Active Journal**. Use the checklist to help you write a convincing argument.

An Effective Argument Includes
✓ a precise claim
✓ consideration of alternate claims, or opposing positions, and a discussion of their strengths and weaknesses
✓ logical organization that makes clear connections among claim, reasons, and evidence
✓ valid reasoning and evidence, using credible sources and accurate data
✓ a concluding statement or section that follows from and supports the argument
✓ formal and objective language and tone
✓ error-free grammar, including accurate use of transitions

INTERACTIVE

For more help, go online for these interactive skills tutorials:

- Evaluate Arguments
- Consider and Counter Opposing Arguments
- Support Ideas with Evidence

INTEGRATED ENGLISH LANGUAGE DEVELOPMENT

Emerging Write the following two sentences on the board. *I eat breakfast before school. I can eat breakfast before school.* Discuss how adding *can* changes the meaning of the sentence.

Remind students that they will be writing about things that took place in the past. Ask students to change the above sentences into the past tense. (*eat* to *ate* and *can* to *could*)

Expanding Write the following two sentences on the board. *Shi Huangdi was a cruel ruler. Shi Huangdi was* probably *a cruel ruler*. Discuss with students how adding the word *probably* changes the strength of the argument.

Explore how to use other words and phrases such as *maybe, has to, must,* and *can/could.*

ELA W.6.1, WHST.6.1; ELD PI.C.10, 11

Write an Argument

LEARN

Invite a volunteer to define the terms *argument* and *persuasive writing*. Ask students to offer examples of times that they have done persuasive writing. What were they trying to persuade the reader to think or do? How did they try to persuade the reader that their argument was correct?

Students may have done persuasive writing in Language Arts, such as writing a letter to a parent asking for something or trying to persuade a government official to take action on a particular topic. Connect students' experiences with persuasive writing in Language Arts with persuasive writing in Social Studies by exploring the similarities and differences between the two.

Preview the elements of an effective argument listed in the table and then play the video.

INTERACTIVE

Project the Support Ideas with Evidence video in the 21st Century Skills Tutorial. Use the Quick Reference and Assessment to provide additional instruction in this skill. You may also use the skill tutorials Evaluate Existing Arguments and Consider and Counter Opposing Arguments to help students learn more about arguments.

PRACTICE

Have students practice the skill by reviewing the graphic "An Effective Argument Includes." Ask: How does considering opposing positions help strengthen your argument? Why is it important to use credible sources in your argument? How does using formal and objective language make your argument stronger?

ASSESS

To assess this skill, have students complete the Writing Workshop assignments for Topics 5 and 8.

ELA W.6.2.a–f; WHST.6–8.2.a–f; ELD PI.C.10, 12, PII.A.1

Write Informative or Explanatory Essays

LEARN

Invite a volunteer to define the terms *informative* and *explanatory*. Ask students to offer examples of times that they have done informative writing. What were the topics? How did they make their writing stronger?

Preview the pieces of an Effective Informative or Explanatory Essay then play the video.

INTERACTIVE

Project the Organize Your Ideas video in the 21st Century Skills Tutorial. Use the Quick Reference and Assessment to provide additional instruction in this skill. You may also use the other videos listed on the student text to help students with steps in this process.

PRACTICE

Have students prepare to practice the skill by reviewing pieces of an Effective Informative/ Explanatory Essay. Ask: What is the purpose of a thesis statement? How might you organize your essay? What can you use to support or expand on a topic or point?

ASSESS

To assess this skill, have students complete the Writing Workshop assignments in Topics 3 and 6.

Write Informative or Explanatory Essays

ELA W.6.2, WHST.6.2; ELD PI.C.10, 12 PII.A.1

Informative/explanatory texts present facts, data, and other evidence to give information about a topic. Readers turn to these texts when they wish to learn about a specific idea, concept, or subject area, or if they want to learn how to do something.

An Effective Informative/Explanatory Essay Includes

- ✓ a thesis statement that introduces the concept or subject
- ✓ an organization (such as definition, classification, comparison/contrast, cause/effect) that presents information in a clear manner
- ✓ headings (if desired) to separate sections of the essay
- ✓ definitions, quotations, and/or graphics that support the thesis
- ✓ relevant facts, examples, and details that expand upon a topic
- ✓ clear transitions that link sections of the essay
- ✓ precise words and technical vocabulary where appropriate
- ✓ formal and objective language and tone
- ✓ a conclusion that supports information given and provides fresh insights

Suppose you are writing an essay describing the development of civilization in ancient Egypt. You might start by creating a flowchart. You would then fill it in with facts, descriptions, and examples.

Your thesis statement might be "The Nile's fertile soil allowed the people of Egypt to gradually develop a complex civilization."

Your organization might be:

I The Nile A. Water B. Rich soil **II Agricultural Surplus** A. New farming technologies B. Effects of agricultural surplus	OR	**III Development of New Jobs** A. Government B. Artisans **IV Towns into Cities** A. Why people settled in towns B. City life

INTERACTIVE

Go online for these interactive skills tutorials:

- Organize Your Ideas
- Compare and Contrast
- Analyze Cause and Effect
- Develop a Clear Thesis
- Draw Conclusions
- Support Ideas with Evidence

INTEGRATED ENGLISH LANGUAGE DEVELOPMENT

Emerging Explain to students that they will be learning some new vocabulary that is specific to Social Studies classes. Have students flip to Topic 3 and examine the terms for the lessons. Discuss with students what terms they might use to make an essay on the development of civilization in Ancient Egypt more specific.

As the class progresses, allow students to refer to a word wall of academic and domain-specific language when completing writing assignments.

Expanding Discuss with students how the use of synonyms can make writing more specific and precise. Write the following sentence on the board: Farming succeeded along the Nile River. Ask students to discuss synonyms they could use to make the sentence stronger.

Write Narrative Essays

ELA W.6.3.a–e; ELD PI.C.10, 12, PII.A.1

A narrative is any type of writing that tells a story. Narrative writing conveys an experience, either real or imaginary, and uses time order to provide structure. Usually its purpose is to entertain, but it can also instruct, persuade, or inform.

An Effective Narrative Includes
✓ an engaging beginning in which characters and setting are established
✓ a well-structured, logical sequence of events
✓ narrative techniques, such as dialogue and description
✓ a variety of transition words and phrases to convey sequence and signal shifts from one time frame or setting to another
✓ precise words and phrases, relevant descriptive details, and sensory language that brings the characters and setting to life
✓ a conclusion that follows naturally from the story's experiences or events

Model Narrative This passage is a fictional letter from a young woman in Rome to her aunt. Notice how it begins by establishing the setting as Rome at the time of the Vandals invasion. Note that the writer also offers details on how the invasion of the Vandals is affecting her life.

Dear Aunt Lavinia,

Everyone is telling me not to be afraid, but I think they are foolish. The Vandals are at the gates of Rome, threatening to enter at any minute. We hear stories of death and destruction wherever the invading armies go. They have already sacked many villages. Food is becoming more scarce because they have ripped up the fields. There remains only the grain stored in our warehouse. Mother and Father are not sure that the Emperor's armies can protect us. They have packed a box with our most precious things so we can move quickly. Please be ready to receive us, if we can get away from here with our lives.

Your loving niece, Portia

INTERACTIVE

For more help, go online for these interactive skills tutorials:
- Sequence
- Draw Conclusions
- Write an Essay
- Write a Journal Entry

DIFFERENTIATED INSTRUCTION

Below Level Use a Venn diagram to help students compare and contrast narrative writing in Language Arts versus Social Studies. If possible, have a sample narrative from a Language Arts class to allow students to compare the two.

Advanced Ask students to examine Portia's letter and revise it to make it stronger. Have students consult Topic 8 Lesson 5 for additional information on the decline of the Roman Empire. Students should use the elements of an effective narrative to help them create a stronger letter.

ELA W.6.3; ELD PI.C.10, 12, PII.A.1

Write Narrative Essays

LEARN

Invite a volunteer to define the term *narrative*. Ask students to offer examples of times that they have done narrative writing. What did they write about? How did they make their writing stronger?

Students may have done narrative writing in a Language Arts class. Discuss the similarities and differences between narrative writing in Language Arts and narrative writing in Social Studies. For example, any narrative writing done in social studies would be based on the historical period being studied. Students would need to combine accurate facts with creative imaginings of how people would respond to historical events and conditions.

Preview the elements of an effective narrative; then play the video.

INTERACTIVE

Project the Write a Journal Entry video in the 21st Century Skills Tutorial. Use the Quick Reference and Assessment to provide additional instruction in this skill. You may also use the other skills tutorials listed in the student text to help students with this type of writing.

PRACTICE

Have students prepare to practice the skill. Ask: What should be included in a narrative's beginning? How might dialogue and description strengthen a narrative? What are some examples of sensory language that might bring a historical setting to life?

ASSESS

Have students read Portia's letter. Students should discuss how the letter is or is not an effective narrative, using the criteria of an effective narrative listed above. To assess this skill, have students complete the Writing Workshop assignments for Topics 1 and 2.

ELA W.6.8; WHST.6–8.8

Find and Use Credible Sources

LEARN

Invite a student to define the term *source*. Ask students to recall times that they searched for sources for a project or paper. What challenges did they have? How did they know if they had a source with good information?

If possible, display an online source that is clearly not credible and ask students to point out concerns they might have with the source.

Have students preview the headings of each section then play the video.

INTERACTIVE

Project the Evaluate Web Sites video in the 21st Century Skills Tutorial. Use the Quick Reference and Assessment to provide additional instruction in this skill. You may also use the other skills tutorials listed in the student text to help students master other aspects of finding and using sources.

PRACTICE

Have students practice the skill by reading and discussing the information about finding and using credible sources. Ask: What are some types of sources you can use in a research project? Why is it important to evaluate sources you find?

Find and Use Credible Sources

ELA W.6.8, WHST.6.8

You will often need to conduct research using library and media sources to gain more knowledge about a topic. Not all of the information that you find, however, will be useful—or reliable. Strong research skills will help you find accurate information about your topic.

Using Print and Digital Sources An effective research project combines information from multiple sources. Plan to include a variety of these resources:

- **Primary and Secondary Sources:** Use both primary sources (such as interviews or newspaper articles) and secondary sources (such as encyclopedia entries or historians' accounts).
- **Print and Digital Resources:** The Internet allows fast access to data, but print resources are often edited more carefully. Plan to include both print and digital resources in order to guarantee that your work is accurate.
- **Media Resources:** You can find valuable information in media resources such as documentaries, television programs, podcasts, and museum exhibitions.
- **Original Research:** Depending on your topic, you may wish to conduct original research, such as interviews or surveys of people in your community.

Evaluating Sources It is important to evaluate the credibility and accuracy of any information you find. Ask yourself questions such as these to evaluate sources:

- **Authority:** Is the author well known? What are the author's credentials? Does the source include references to other reliable sources? Does the author's tone win your confidence? Why or why not?
- **Bias:** Does the author have any obvious biases? What is the author's purpose for writing? Who is the target audience?
- **Currency:** When was the work created? Has it been revised? Is there more current information available?

Did you know?

Beware of online encyclopedias. They can be a good starting place for information, but their contributors are not required to fact-check their submissions.

Using Search Terms Finding information on the Internet is easy, but it can be a challenge to find facts that are useful and trustworthy. If you type a word or phrase into a search engine, you will probably get hundreds of results.

However, those results are not guaranteed to be relevant or accurate. These strategies can help:

- Create a list of keywords before you begin using a search engine.
- Enter six to eight keywords.
- Choose unique nouns. Most search engines ignore articles and prepositions.
- Use adjectives to specify a category. For example, you might enter "ancient Rome" instead of "Rome."
- Use quotation marks to focus a search. Place a phrase in quotation marks to find pages that include exactly that phrase.
- Spell carefully. Many search engines correct spelling automatically, but they cannot catch every spelling error.
- Scan search results before you click them. The first result isn't always the most useful. Read the text before make a choice.

Avoiding Plagiarism When you conduct research, you must give credit for any ideas or opinions that are not your own. Presenting someone else's ideas, research, or opinion as your own—even if you have phrased it in different words—is plagiarism. Plagiarism is the equivalent of stealing. Be sure to record your sources accurately so you can identify them later. When photocopying from a source, include the copyright information. Include the web addresses from online sources.

Quoting and Paraphrasing When including ideas from research into your writing, you will need to decide whether to quote directly or paraphrase. You must cite your sources for both quotations and paraphrases. A **direct quotation** uses the author's exact words when they are particularly well-chosen. Include complete quotations, without deleting or changing words. Enclose direct quotations in quotation marks. A **paraphrase** restates an author's ideas in your own words. Be careful to paraphrase accurately. A good paraphrase does more than simply rearrange an author's phrases, or replace a few words with synonyms.

Formats for Citing Sources When you cite a source, you acknowledge where you found your information and give readers the details necessary for locating the source themselves. Always prepare a reference list at the end of a research paper to provide full information on your sources in a list of sources called a bibliography.

INTERACTIVE

For more help, find these interactive skills tutorials on your Realize course:

- Search for Information on the Internet
- Evaluate Web Sites
- Take Effective Notes
- Avoid Plagiarism

Did you know?

A citation for a book should look like this: Pyles, Thomas. *The Origins and Development of the English Language*. 2nd ed. New York: Harcourt, 1971. Print. A citation for a website should include this information: Romey, Kristin. "Face of 9,500-Year-Old Man Revealed for First Time." *National Geographic*, Jan. 2017. *news. nationalgeographic.com* Web. 20 Jan. 2017.

How can you make your internet searches more successful? What steps can you take to avoid plagiarism? What is the difference between a quote and a paraphrase? Why is it important to cite both?

ASSESS

Have students work in groups to conduct a web search on ancient Rome. Students should identify three credible sources and one source that is not credible. Ask students to defend their choices by writing an annotated bibliography or making a presentation.

INTEGRATED ENGLISH LANGUAGE DEVELOPMENT

Emerging and Expanding Pair emerging and expanding students with more fluent readers. Have pairs evaluate the sources together. Ask more fluent readers to explain some of the more nuanced language in the source to less fluent readers.

You can also scaffold the project for emerging and expanding students by giving them a set of pre-selected web sites to search within when completing a research project.

ELA W.6.7, 6.9; WHST.6.7, 6.9; ELD PI.C.10.a

Write Research Papers

LEARN

Invite volunteers to recall what the class has already learned about the writing process and finding and using credible sources.

Preview the three tips for writing research papers and then play the video.

INTERACTIVE

Project the Create a Research Hypothesis video in the 21st Century Skills Tutorial. Use the Quick Reference and Assessment to provide additional instruction in this skill. You may also use the skills tutorials Ask Questions and Synthesize to help students with this skill.

PRACTICE

Have students prepare to practice the skill by reading the three tips for writing research papers. Ask: How might you make the topic of Ancient Egypt more narrow? How do research questions help you search for information?

ASSESS

Have students skim a lesson from the text and develop a possible topic of research. Then divide students into pairs. Have pairs evaluate their topics and determine whether they are too narrow, too broad, or just right. To assess the skill, have students complete the Writing Workshop assignments for Topics 4 and 7.

Write Research Papers

ELA W.7.7, 7.9 WHST.6.7, 6.9; ELD PI.C.10.a

You will often need to conduct research in the library or on the Internet for a project or essay. In this program, you will conduct research for Quest projects and some Writing Workshop assignments. Before you begin, review the information in Use the Writing Process as well as in Find and Use Credible Sources. Then follow these additional tips to help you make the most of your research.

1. Narrow or Broaden Your Topic Choose a topic that is narrow enough to cover completely. If you can name your topic in just one or two words, it is probably too broad. For example, a topic such as ancient Egypt would be too broad. When you begin to research, pay attention to the amount of information available. If there is way too much information when you begin your research on your topic, narrow your focus.

You might need to broaden a topic if there is not enough information available. A topic is too narrow when it can be thoroughly presented in less space than the required size of your assignment. It might also be too narrow if you can find little or no information in library and media sources. Broaden your topic by including other related ideas.

2. Generate Research Questions Use research questions to focus your inquiry. For example, instead of simply hunting for information about Augustus, you might ask, "Why are people still interested in Augustus?" or "How might the history of Rome have been different if Augustus had not ruled?" As you research your topic, continue to ask yourself questions. Follow your new questions in order to explore your topic further. Refocus your research questions as you learn more about your topic.

3. Synthesize Your Sources Effective research writing is more than just a list of facts and details. Good research synthesizes—gathers, orders, and interprets—those elements. These strategies will help you synthesize effectively:

- Review your notes. Look for connections and patterns among the details you have collected.
- Organize notes or notecards to help you plan how you will combine details.
- Pay close attention to details that emphasize the same main idea.
- Also look for details that challenge each other. For many topics, there is no single correct opinion. You might decide to conduct additional research to help you decide which side of the issue has more support.

INTERACTIVE

For more help, go online for these interactive skills tutorials:
- Ask Questions
- Create a Research Hypothesis
- Synthesize

DIFFERENTIATED INSTRUCTION

Below Level Offer students a set of topics such as *the Shang Dynasty* or *what did Confucius eat for breakfast*? Ask students whether the topics need narrowing or broadening. Then have students revise the topics to make them more appropriate.

Have students practice generating research questions. Have students reread the article on the town of Jericho and come up with research questions on Jericho.

Advanced Advanced students may be ready to delve into narrower topics and more detailed sources. Introduce advanced students to online libraries of primary sources as well as articles by historians. Some are available online at no charge, others may be available through your school or public library.

SPEAKING AND LISTENING

Discuss Your Ideas

ELA SL.6.1.a–d; ELD P1.A.1, 3, C.11.a–b

A group discussion is an informal meeting of people that is used to openly discuss ideas, readings, and issues. You can express your views and hear those of others. In this program, you'll participate in Discussion Inquiry Quests and many one-to-one, group, and teacher-led discussions. You'll work with different partners on many topics and issues. Use the Keys to Effective Discussions to help you be an active participant in lively discussions.

Keys to Effective Discussions
✓ Come to discussions prepared, having studied the required material and/or read relevant background information.
✓ Build on others' ideas and express your own ideas clearly.
✓ Be sure that your comments directly contribute to the topic, text, or issue under discussion.
✓ Give specific evidence for the points you wish to make.
✓ Follow rules for civic discussions, including letting everyone have a chance to speak and listening carefully to others' points of view.
✓ Pose and respond to specific questions and issues with elaboration and details.
✓ Be prepared to demonstrate your understanding of the different perspectives people have put forth during the discussion.
✓ Acknowledge the views of others respectfully, but ask questions that challenge the accuracy, logic, or relevance of those views.

INTERACTIVE

Go online for these interactive skills tutorials:

- Participate in a Discussion or Debate
- Support Ideas with Evidence
- Work in Teams

ELA SL.6.1.a–d; ELD P1.A.1, 3, C.11.a–b

SPEAKING AND LISTENING

Discuss Your Ideas

LEARN

Invite a volunteer to define the term *discussion*. Ask students to share examples of discussions they have participated in or witnessed in the past.

Review the table and then play the video.

INTERACTIVE

Project the Participate in a Discussion or Debate video in the 21st Century Skills Tutorial. Use the Quick Reference and Assessment to provide additional instruction in this skill. You may also use additional videos as you assess your students' mastery of the ELA skills and standards in this handbook.

PRACTICE

Have students prepare to practice the skill by reviewing the chart. Ask: Why is it important to prepare for a discussion? What rules should you follow for a discussion? How should you respond to others' views?

ASSESS

Have students discuss whether Shi Huangdi was a good emperor, based on the information given in the Primary and Secondary sources of the Writing Handbook. To assess this skill, assign the Quests for Topics 2 and 8, which are Discussion Inquiries.

DIFFERENTIATED INSTRUCTION

Advanced Have students view or listen to several discussions of current events, ideally some that were effective and some that were not. Have students evaluate the effectiveness of the discussions, pointing out their strengths and weaknesses.

INTEGRATED ENGLISH LANGUAGE DEVELOPMENT

Emerging and Expanding Group emerging and expanding students with more fluent students to have smaller discussions on Shi Huangdi rather than participating in a class-wide discussion.

ELA SL. 6.4–6; ELD P1.A.4, C.9

Give an Effective Presentation

LEARN

Invite a student to define the term *presentation*. Ask students to offer examples of times that they have been asked to give presentations in the past.

Preview the chart and then play the video.

INTERACTIVE

Project the Give an Effective Presentation video in the 21st Century Skills Tutorial. Use the Quick Reference and Assessment to provide additional instruction in this skill. You may also use additional videos as you assess your students' mastery of the ELA skills and standards in this handbook.

PRACTICE

Have students practice the skill by examining the chart. Ask: Why is it important to practice a presentation? How does clear pronunciation help a presentation to be effective? How do transitions help a presentation?

ASSESS

Have students work in groups to create and give brief presentations on the characteristics of a good presentation. To assess this skill, have students complete the Quests for Topics 1 and 6, which are Project-Based Learning Inquiries that involve presenting the final project.

Give an Effective Presentation

ELA SL. 6.4–6; ELD P1.A.4, C.9

Many of the Quests in this program will require you to give a presentation to your teacher and classmates, and sometimes even to a wider audience. These presentations will be good practice for the presentations you will need to give in school and in professional settings. You can speak confidently if you prepare carefully and follow this checklist.

Keys to Effective Presentations
✓ Prepare your presentation in advance and practice it in order to gain comfort and confidence.
✓ Present your claims and findings in a logical sequence so that your audience can easily follow your train of thought.
✓ Use relevant descriptions, facts, and specific details.
✓ Consider using nonverbal elements such as hand gestures and pauses to emphasize main ideas or themes.
✓ Use appropriate eye contact, adequate volume, and clear pronunciation.
✓ Use appropriate transitions (*for example, first, second, third*) to clarify relationships.
✓ Use precise language and vocabulary that is specific to your topic.
✓ Provide a strong conclusion.
✓ Adapt your wording to your purpose and audience. Use formal English for most presentations, but try to sound natural and relaxed.
✓ Include multimedia components such as you see in the chart to clarify information.

Maps	Graphs/Charts/ Diagrams	Illustrations/Photos	Audio/Video
Clarify historical or geographical information	Show complex information and data in an easy-to-understand format	Illustrate objects, scenes, or other details	Bring the subject to life and engage audiences

INTERACTIVE

Go online for these interactive skills tutorials:
- Give an Effective Presentation
- Create Charts and Maps
- Support Ideas with Evidence

ELA 16 California English-Language Arts Handbook

DIFFERENTIATED INSTRUCTION

Below Level Break down the steps of creating a presentation for students, such as choosing a topic, gathering information, organizing information, etc. Point out to students that a presentation requires planning and preparation just as an essay does.

Effective Listening

ELA SL.6.2–3; ELD P1.B.5

Active listening is a key component of the communication process. Like all communication, it requires your engaged participation. Follow the "Keys to Effective Listening" to get the most out of discussions, presentations by others, lectures by your teacher, and any time you engage in listening.

Keys to Effective Listening
✓ Look at and listen to the speaker. Think about what you hear and see. Which ideas are emphasized or repeated? What gestures or expressions suggest strong feelings?
✓ Listen carefully to information presented in different media and formats—including videos, lectures, speeches, and discussions—so you can explain how the information you learn contributes to the topic or issue you are studying.
✓ Listen for the speaker's argument and specific claims so that you can distinguish claims that are supported by reasons and evidence from claims that are not.
✓ Listen to fit the situation. Active listening involves matching your listening to the situation. Listen critically to a speech given by a candidate for office. Listen with kindness to the feelings of a friend. Listen appreciatively to a musical performance.

INTERACTIVE

For more help, go online for these interactive skills tutorials:

- Identify Bias
- Identify Evidence
- Distinguish Between Fact and Opinion
- Evaluate Existing Arguments

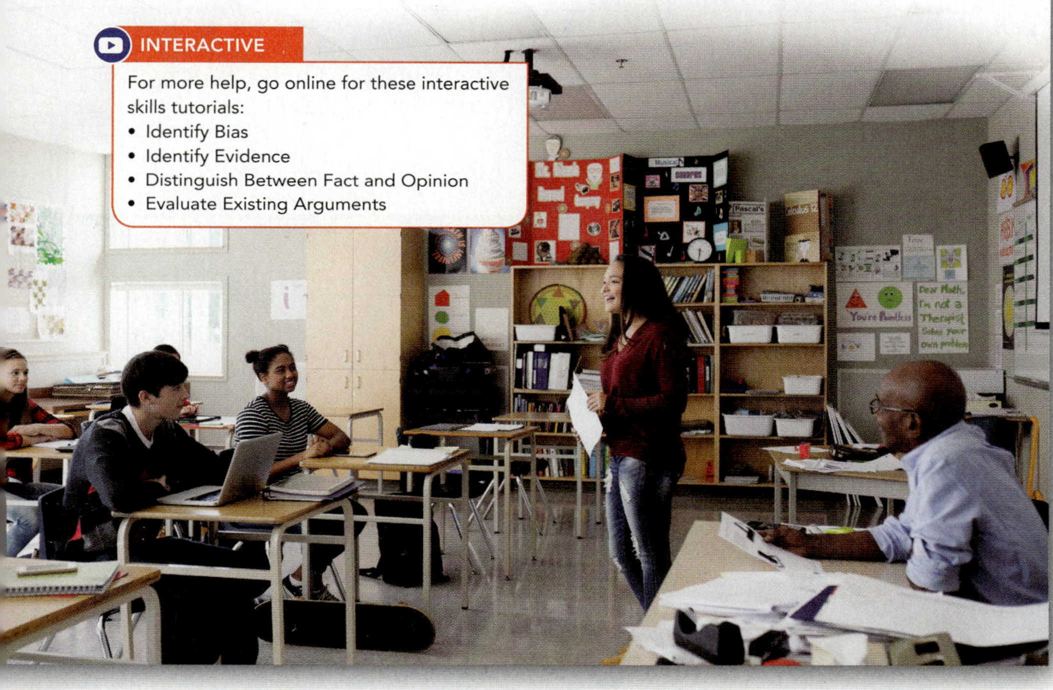

ELA SL.6.2–3; ELD P1.B.5

Effective Listening

LEARN

Invite students to list words that describe an effective listener. Encourage students to think of words that describe how a listener looks and sounds. Invite students to share how they feel when others are actively listening to them.

Preview the Keys to Effective Listening table then play the video.

INTERACTIVE

Project the Identify Bias video in the 21st Century Skills Tutorial. Use the Quick Reference and Assessment to provide additional instruction in this skill. You may also use additional videos as you assess your students' mastery of the ELA skills and standards in this handbook.

PRACTICE

To have students practice the skill, divide students into pairs and have them each respond to the question: Why is it important to learn about the past? Have the partner practice effective listening to their classmate.

ASSESS

To assess this skill, have students work in groups to create a poster on effective listening. Display the poster in the classroom for reference throughout the year.

DIFFERENTIATED INSTRUCTION

Below Level As you discuss words describing an active listener, write the words on the board. Group related words together to help students create associations between the words.

TOPIC 1

Topic-at-a-Glance

Origins of Civilization

(Prehistory–4,000 BCE)

Pacing: Approximately 19 periods, 9.5 blocks	Resources: Student Edition	Resources: Active Journal	Resources: Online	Pacing	California Standards
CONNECT					
NBC LEARN VIDEO The Archaeology of Food in Neolithic Turkey			video	10 min.	HSS.6.1.2
ESSENTIAL QUESTION ACTIVITY How Much Does Geography Shape People's Lives?		✓	interactive	10 min.	HSS.6.1.2
OVERVIEW ACTIVITY: TIMELINE AND MAP Origins of Civilization (Prehistory–4,000 BCE)		✓	interactive	10 min.	HSS.6.1.1–3
Quest KICK OFF: Ask Questions	✓	✓		20 min.	HSS 6.1.2; Analysis REP.3; ELA W.6.7–9, SL.6.4–6, WHST.6.7–9; ELD.PI.C.9
INVESTIGATE					
LESSONS 1–5 and Case Study	See Lesson-at-a-Glance pages				
Quest INVESTIGATE: Quest Connections	✓	✓		20 min.	See Quest Kick Off
SYNTHESIZE					
WRITING WORKSHOP Write a Narrative Essay		✓	interactive	30 min.	ELD.P1.A.2, P1.C.10.a
TOPIC MINI-GAMES Origins of Civilization (Prehistory–4,000 BCE)			game	10 min.	HSS 6.1.1–3, 6.2.1, 6.2.2, 6.2.9, 7.7.1–5
Quest SOURCES: Conduct Research			book	30 min.	See Quest Kick Off
DEMONSTRATE					
TOPIC REVIEW AND ASSESSMENT Origins of Civilization (Prehistory–4,000 BCE)	✓		book	20 min.	
TOPIC TEST	✓		test	30 min.	
Quest FINDINGS: Design a Village	✓	✓	book	30 min.	See Quest Kick Off

Quest

Each Quest is designed to reinforce the topic content through an inquiry arc that students work on throughout the Topic. This Topic's Quest, Design a Village, is a Project-Based Learning Inquiry in which students design a Neolithic village and create a diagram that shows how it works.

Active Journal Resources

- Ask Questions
- Quest Connections
- Conduct Research
- Design Your Village

Quest Sources Online

- Project Contract
- Project Tracker
- Team Assessment
- Rubric for Design Your Village

Additional Resources

Support for Struggling Readers

- Reading Support, Teacher Resources
- Lesson Summaries, Teacher Resources
- English Language Development, Teacher Resources

Suggested Resources

- *DK Eyewitness Books: Early Humans*
- *Painters of the Caves*, Patricia Lauber
- *National Geographic Investigates: Ancient Maya: Archeology Unlocks the Secrets of the Maya's Past*, Nathaniel Harris
- *Laetoli Footprints, PBS Learning Media*
- *Mummies Alive: How Neolithic Mountain Climbers Geared Up*, Smithsonian Channel

Beyond the Classroom

Use Online and Library Media Centers

Use a media center to gain online access to the resources of distant museums, such as the University of California Museum of Paleontology, the "Unearthed: Ancient Life in Boulder Valley" exhibit of the University of Colorado Museum, and the exhibit "Maya: Heart of Sky, Heart of Earth" at the San Diego Museum of Man. Interactive online exhibits such as Virtually the Ice Age, an educational resource developed by Creswell Crags Museum & Heritage Centre in conjunction with the British Museum, allows students to understand more about how stone age people lived and about how scientists are learning about them today. Science journalist Richard Milton has created an interactive site called Museum of the Stone Age. By clicking their way through the floor plan of a virtual museum, students can learn to distinguish Stone Age tools and understand how they were made.

Objectives

Objective 1: Explain how scientists use fossils and artifacts to draw conclusions about early humans.

Objective 2: Discuss how archaeological evidence indicates that human life began in Africa.

Objective 3: Explain how people lived by the gathering and hunting way of life.

Objective 4: Identify the new skills that hunter-gatherer societies developed in order to survive.

The Distant Past

	Resources			Pacing	California Standards
	Student Edition	Active Journal	Online	approx. 4 periods, 2 blocks	
CONNECT					
VIDEO Unearthing Evidence of the Earliest Humans			▶	5 min.	HSS 6.1.1
START UP ACTIVITY Get Ready to Read	✓	✓	📖	5 min.	HSS 6.1.1
TAKE NOTES AND PRACTICE VOCABULARY		✓			
INVESTIGATE					
READ Lesson 1: The Distant Past	✓	✓	📖	30 min.	HSS 6.1.1; ELA RI.6.2
INTERACTIVE GALLERY Piecing Together the Past			👆	10 min.	HSS 6.1.1
PRIMARY SOURCES *Epic of Gilgamesh*	✓		📖	40 min.	ELA RI.6.2-4
ANALYSIS SKILLS Distinguish Essential from Incidental Information	✓		📖	30 min.	Analysis REP.3
21ST CENTURY SKILLS TUTORIAL Categorize			▶	10 min.	Analysis REP.3
READING SUPPORT			📄		
SYNTHESIZE					
WRITING WORKSHOP Introduce Characters	✓	✓	📖	10 min.	ELA W.6.3–6.5; ELD P1.A.2, ELD.P1.C.10.a
LESSON SUMMARY			📄		
DEMONSTRATE					
LESSON QUIZ			☑	10 min.	HSS 6.1.1

Objectives

Objective 1: Discuss how we know the characteristics of modern humans and Neanderthals.

Objective 2: Explain why modern humans succeeded.

Objective 3: Summarize how and why modern humans succeeded and populated most regions of the world.

Objective 4: Analyze how the environment influenced the migrations of early humans.

Objective 5: Identify how early humans adapted to new environments and climate changes.

Humans Spread Out

	Resources			Pacing	
	Student Edition	Active Journal	Online	approx. 3 periods, 1.5 blocks	California Standards
CONNECT					
VIDEO How Hunter Gathers Lived			✓	5 min.	HSS 6.1.2, 6.2.9
START UP ACTIVITY Get Ready to Read	✓	✓	✓	5 min.	HSS 6.1.2, 6.2.9
TAKE NOTES AND PRACTICE VOCABULARY		✓			
INVESTIGATE					
READ Lesson 2: Humans Spread Out	✓	✓	✓	40 min.	HSS 6.1.2, 6.2.9
INTERACTIVE MAP Migrations of *Homo sapiens*			✓	10 min.	HSS 6.1.2
ANALYSIS SKILLS Relate Events in Time	✓		✓	30 min.	Analysis CST.1
21ST CENTURY SKILLS TUTORIAL Sequence			✓	10 min.	Analysis CST.1
READING SUPPORT			✓		
SYNTHESIZE					
WRITING WORKSHOP Establish Setting	✓	✓	✓	10 min.	ELA W.6.3–6.5; ELD.P1.A.2, ELD.P1.C.10.a
LESSON SUMMARY			✓		
DEMONSTRATE					
LESSON QUIZ			✓	10 min.	HSS 6.1.2, 6.2.9

Developing Complex Cultures

Objectives

Objective 1: Discuss what the existing evidence reveals about how human societies became more complex.

Objective 2: Explain how humans learned to modify their environment.

Objective 3: Analyze why some humans developed agriculture while others lived as herders.

	Resources: Student Edition	Resources: Active Journal	Resources: Online	Pacing (approx. 2 periods, 1 block)	California Standards
CONNECT					
VIDEO Migrating and Adapting to New Environments			●	5 min.	HSS 6.1.3
START UP ACTIVITY Get Ready to Read	✓	✓	●	5 min.	HSS 6.1.3
TAKE NOTES AND PRACTICE VOCABULARY		✓			
INVESTIGATE					
READ Lesson 3: Developing Complex Cultures	✓	✓	●	40 min.	HSS 6.1.3
INTERACTIVE GALLERY Paleolithic Cave Art			●	10 min.	HSS 6.1.3
QUICK ACTIVITY Explore Cave Paintings		✓			
READING SUPPORT			●		
SYNTHESIZE					
WRITING WORKSHOP Introduce Characters	✓	✓	●	10 min.	ELA W.6.3–6.5; ELD.P1.A.2, ELD.P1.C.10.a
LESSON SUMMARY			●		
DEMONSTRATE					
LESSON QUIZ			●	10 min.	HSS 6.1.3

New Ways of Life

Objectives

Objective 1: Explain how farming helped people develop specialized skills.

Objective 2: Describe how farming villages developed into cities.

Objective 3: Identify the effects of these new ways of life.

	Resources: Student Edition	Resources: Active Journal	Resources: Online	Pacing (approx. 2 periods, 1 block)	California Standards
CONNECT					
VIDEO The Birth of Farming			✓ (video)	5 min.	HSS 6.1.3, 6.2.2
START UP ACTIVITY Get Ready to Read	✓	✓	✓ (book)	5 min.	HSS 6.1.3
TAKE NOTES AND PRACTICE VOCABULARY		✓			
INVESTIGATE					
READ Lesson 4: New Ways of Life	✓	✓	✓ (book)	40 min.	HSS 6.1.3, 6.2.2
INTERACTIVE GALLERY Otzi the Neolithic Ice Man			✓ (interactive)	10 min.	HSS 6.1.3, 6.2.2
QUICK ACTIVITY: Explore Ancient Inventions			✓		
READING SUPPORT			✓ (document)		
SYNTHESIZE					
WRITING WORKSHOP Organize Sequence of Events	✓	✓	✓ (book)	10 min.	ELA W.6.3–6.5; ELD.P1.A.2, ELD.P1.C.10.a
LESSON SUMMARY			✓ (document)		
DEMONSTRATE					
LESSON QUIZ			✓ (quiz)	10 min.	HSS 6.1.3, 6.2.2

The Rise of Civilizations

	Resources: Student Edition	Resources: Active Journal	Resources: Online	Pacing (approx. 2 periods, 1 block)	California Standards
CONNECT					
VIDEO The Growth of Cities			Video	5 min.	HSS 6.2.1, 6.2.9
START UP ACTIVITY Get Ready to Read	✓	✓	Interactive reading	5 min.	HSS 6.2.1, 6.2.9
TAKE NOTES AND PRACTICE VOCABULARY		✓			
INVESTIGATE					
READ Lesson 5: The Rise of Civilizations	✓	✓	Interactive reading	40 min.	HSS 6.2.1, 6.2.9
INTERACTIVE MAP River Valley Civilizations			Interactive	10 min.	HSS 6.2.1, 6.2.9
READING SUPPORT			Document		
SYNTHESIZE					
WRITING WORKSHOP Use Descriptive Details and Sensory Language	✓	✓	Interactive reading	10 min.	ELA W.6.3-6.5; ELD.P1.A.2, ELD.P1.C.10.a
LESSON SUMMARY			Document		
DEMONSTRATE					
LESSON QUIZ			Quiz	10 min.	HSS 6.2.1, 6.2.9

Objectives

Objective 1: Describe the environmental factors that helped civilizations grow.

Objective 2: Analyze the impact that civilizations and complex urban societies had on the surrounding environment.

Objective 3: Discuss how and why cities gave rise to the world's first civilizations.

Objective 4: Identify the features that all early civilizations have in common.

Case Study: The Mayan Civilization

Objectives

Objective 1: Describe how the geography of Mesoamerica influenced the development of Mayan culture.

Objective 2: Identify the features of civilization that the Maya developed in Mesoamerica.

Objective 3: Summarize the unique achievements of the Maya.

Objective 4: Discuss how the Mayan civilization gained power over other peoples and territories.

	Resources: Student Edition	Resources: Active Journal	Resources: Online	Pacing (approx. 2 periods, 1 block)	California Standards
CONNECT					
VIDEO Features of Mayan Civilization			✓	5 min.	HSS 6.2.9, 7.7.1, 7.7.2, 7.7.3, 7.7.4, 7.7.5
START UP ACTIVITY Get Ready to Read	✓	✓	✓	5 min.	HSS 6.2.9, 7.7.1, 7.7.2, 7.7.3, 7.7.4, 7.7.5
TAKE NOTES AND PRACTICE VOCABULARY		✓			
INVESTIGATE					
READ Lesson 6: Case Study: The Mayan Civilization	✓	✓	✓	40 min.	HSS 6.2.9, 7.7.1, 7.7.2, 7.7.3, 7.7.4, 7.7.5
INTERACTIVE GALLERY Features of Mayan Civilization			✓	10 min.	HSS 6.2.9, 7.7.1, 7.7.2, 7.7.3, 7.7.4, 7.7.5
READING SUPPORT			✓		
SYNTHESIZE					
WRITING WORKSHOP Use Narrative Techniques	✓	✓	✓	10 min.	ELA W.6.3-6.5; ELD.P1.A.2, ELD.P1.C.10.a
LESSON SUMMARY			✓		
DEMONSTRATE					
LESSON QUIZ			✓	10 min.	HSS 6.2.9, 7.7.1, 7.7.2, 7.7.3, 7.7.4, 7.7.5

TOPIC 1 Origins of Civilization (Prehistory–4,000 BCE)

HSS 6.1.1, 6.1.2, 6.1.3, 6.2.1, 6.2.2, 6.2.9, 7.7.1, 7.7.2, 7.7.3, 7.7.4, 7.7.5

CONNECT

Introduction

The exact origin of early humans is lost in the mists of prehistory. The only concrete evidence that can be used to make inferences about the ways early humans developed and lived is through the physical evidence left behind. Archaeologists have been at work for many decades unearthing hominin and early human remains and artifacts, piecing together our knowledge of our distant past.

Activate Prior Knowledge

Ask students what they know about early humans. Have volunteers offer details about what they may have seen in museums or in TV documentaries about the origins and activities of early humans. Ask students if they can think of how scientists find out about prehistory without written records. *(Possible answer: Scientists have to search for bones, ruins of buildings, and objects people left behind like tools and weapons.)*

Explore the Essential Question

Project the Essential Question activity from the course. Have a volunteer read the question, "How much does geography shape people's lives?" As students consider the Essential Question, remind them that early people in most cases faced a harsh environment and had to figure out ways to adapt. Discuss the key role of tool-making and fire to human survival.

ACTIVE JOURNAL

Essential Question Have students begin to explore the Essential Question in their Active Journals.

Classify Make a list of the difficulties that early humans had to overcome to survive. Then have students rank these difficulties according to how many students mentioned each one.

TOPIC 1

Origins of Civilization (Prehistory–4000 BCE)

GO ONLINE to access your digital course

VIDEO
AUDIO
ETEXT
INTERACTIVE
WRITING
GAMES
WORKSHEET
ASSESSMENT

Think about a time

when the first direct human ancestors appeared on Earth. You might be very surprised at how harsh their lives were. However, they, and the peoples who followed, had something in common with the way modern humans live. Like we do, these early human ancestors used the environment to improve their lives.

Explore The Essential Question

How much does geography shape people's lives?

Early humans used the natural environment to adapt to a harsh world. How did early people discover ways to make life easier?

Unlock the Essential Question in your Active Journal.

2

ANALYZE VISUALS

Ask students to speculate about the structures shown in photograph. Explain that the picture shows the ruins of a 5,000-year-old public bath in the ancient Indus Valley civilization at Mohenjo-daro in current-day Pakistan. Mention to students that this great bath is considered the earliest public water tank in the ancient world. It was made water-tight by applying a tar-like wax covering over the stones and was probably used for religious purposes in cleansing ceremonies. Ask: What does the structure indicate about this civilization's knowledge of building techniques? *(that they were very advanced)*

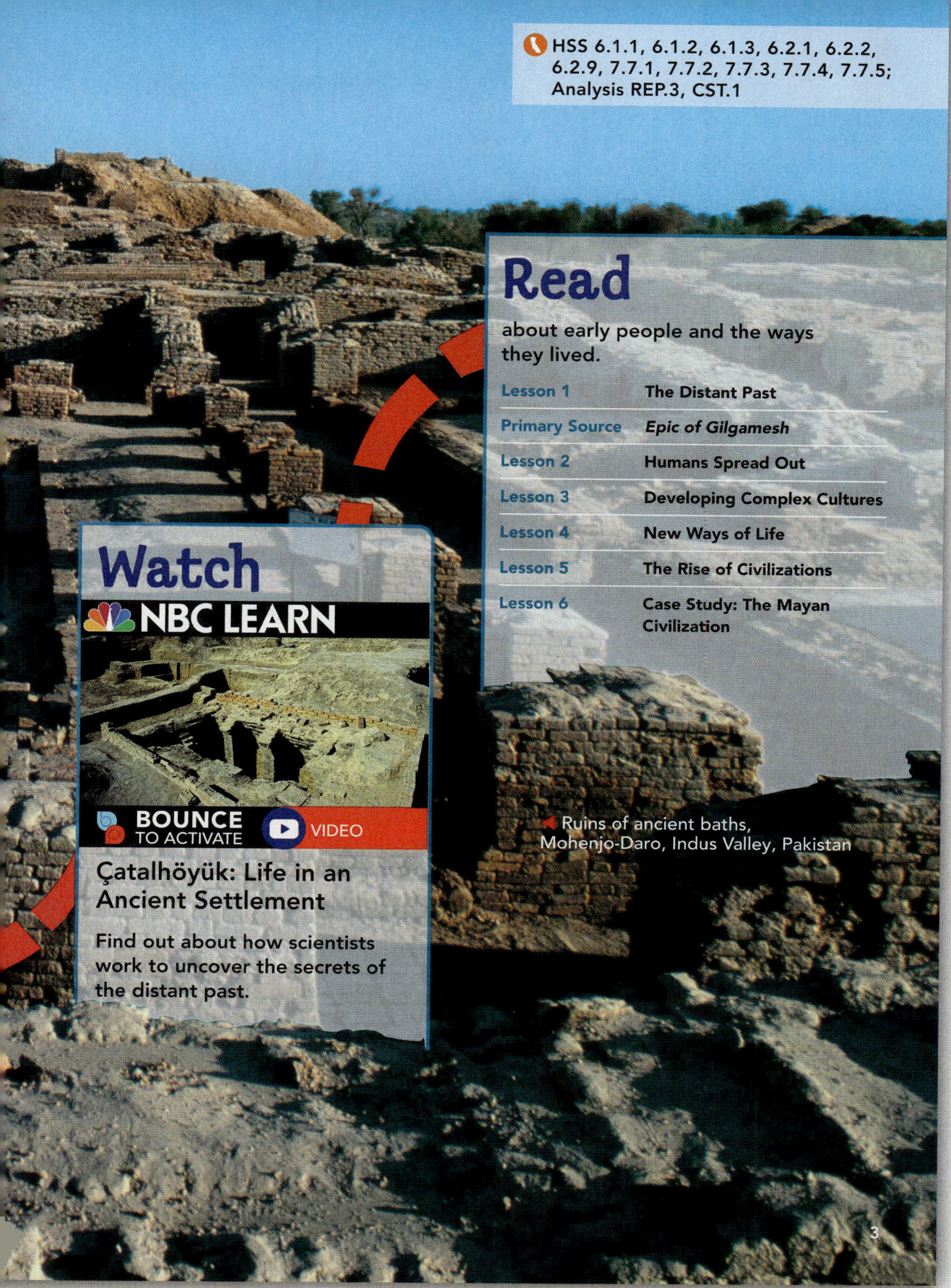
HSS 6.1.1, 6.1.2, 6.1.3, 6.2.1, 6.2.2, 6.2.9, 7.7.1, 7.7.2, 7.7.3, 7.7.4, 7.7.5; Analysis REP.3, CST.1

Read

about early people and the ways they lived.

Lesson 1	The Distant Past
Primary Source	*Epic of Gilgamesh*
Lesson 2	Humans Spread Out
Lesson 3	Developing Complex Cultures
Lesson 4	New Ways of Life
Lesson 5	The Rise of Civilizations
Lesson 6	Case Study: The Mayan Civilization

Watch

NBC LEARN

BOUNCE TO ACTIVATE VIDEO

Çatalhöyük: Life in an Ancient Settlement

Find out about how scientists work to uncover the secrets of the distant past.

Ruins of ancient baths, Mohenjo-Daro, Indus Valley, Pakistan

3

RECOGNIZE CULTURAL AND EXPERIENTIAL BACKGROUNDS

Make use of your knowledge of students' lives to make connections between their own experiences, backgrounds, and interests and the content of this topic. If you have students whose ethnic heritage is related to the content of this topic, make an effort to emphasize the contributions and achievements of this society and how it has enriched the world.

If appropriate, allow students the opportunity to share cultural, ethnic, or linguistic traditions and knowledge from their experiences.

If students have family experiences (such as travel to or family members who have lived in the region being studied), allow them to share relevant stories.

Watch

VIDEO — NBC LEARN VIDEO

Project the Topic Opener video showing an archaeologist working in the ancient city of Çatalhöyük.

Check Understanding Why does Professor Twiss study animal bones? (to help understand what people ate and what animals they raised.)

Hypothesize What aspects in addition to animal bones do you think archaeologists study? *(Possible answers: remains of buildings to see where people lived, tools and weapons that have lasted, human bones.)*

Read

Share these lesson previews with students.

Lesson 1: Archaeologists have discovered a great deal about hominins, our earliest ancestors, as well as how early humans survived as hunter-gatherers.

Primary Source: The Epic of Gilgamesh recounts the story of the legendary king of the ancient city of Uruk who heroically killed the monster Huwawa.

Lesson 2: Early humans probably migrated over thousands of years from Africa into Europe, Asia, and other parts of the world as they adapted to new environments.

Lesson 3: Over the course of tens of thousands of years, humans learned to domesticate plants and animals and developed complex cultures.

Lesson 4: As farming advanced, people settled into permanent villages and food surpluses increased. These changes led to the rise of the first cities.

Lesson 5: As civilizations developed, cities became larger and people engaged in more job specialization, trade, public works, art, and architecture.

Lesson 6: The Maya formed an early civilization in Mesoamerica, where they built great cities, developed advanced farming techniques, used trade routes, learned mathematics and astronomy, and created impressive art and architecture.

TOPIC 1

6.1.1, 6.1.2, 6.1.3, 6.2.1, 6.2.2, 6.2.9, 7.7.1, 7.7.2, 7.7.3, 7.7.4, 7.7.5

What Happened and When?

Have students examine the timeline. Ask: What do the broken lines on the timeline indicate? *(extremely long periods of time)* According to the timeline, how many years separate the last Ice Age and when people began to grow food? *(about 2,000)* Ask: How long was the last Ice Age? *(58,000 years)* Ask: What is the purpose of this timeline? *(To show how much time is considered a part of prehistory.)*

ACTIVE JOURNAL

Timeline Skills Students can also use the Timeline Skills activity in their Active Journals to record information about the history of early people as they read the topic. During their reading, they should add the dates of at least three events they think are important. After completing the topic, have students write a paragraph identifying the dates they added and explaining why each is significant.

INTERACTIVE TIMELINE

Display the topic Interactive Timeline for the class. Use the interactivity to learn more about early human history. Have volunteers read entries.

Discuss Ask: What can you conclude about early people at the end of the Ice Age? *(Not too long afterwards in terms of human history, they began to learn how to farm. This skill led to the growth of villages and cities.)*

TOPIC 1

Origins of Civilization

(Prehistory–4000 BCE)

Learn more about human beginnings and the world's first civilizations by making your own map and timeline in your Active Journal.

INTERACTIVE

Topic Map

Where did the first human ancestors live?

Scientists believe that the first human ancestors, or hominins, lived in Africa. Locate Hadar, where bones of a hominin named Lucy were found in 1974.

INTERACTIVE

Topic Timeline

What happened and when?

Basic stone tools...hunting and gathering for food...farming...the birth of villages and cities. Explore the timeline to see what was happening during our earliest history.

2.5 million years ago Hominins in Africa make stone tools.

230,000 years ago Neanderthals appear in Europe.

70,000 years ago Last ice age begins.

TOPIC EVENTS

2 million years ago | 300,000 years ago | 200,000 years ago | 100,000 years ago

1.9 million years ago hominins migrate to Eurasia.

200,000 years ago *Homo sapiens* appear in Africa.

4 TOPIC 1 • Origins of Civilization

DIFFERENTIATED INSTRUCTION

Special Education Prepare index cards for each of the dates and events on the timeline. Pass out the index cards to students and form a "living timeline." Remind students that BCE dates go backward in time, with the greatest number on the left, if the timeline is read from left to right.

Below Level Project the Sequence video in the 21st Century Skills Tutorial. Use the Quick Reference and Assessment to provide additional instruction on this skill.

Advanced Have students research additional information about other important events that occurred between the end of the Ice Age and the beginning if the Common Era. For example, the beginning of the Iron Age or the rise of Kush.

HSS 6.1.1, 6.1.2, 6.1.3, 6.2.1, 6.2.2, 6.2.9, 7.7.1, 7.7.2, 7.7.3, 7.7.4, 7.7.5

Who will you meet?

Mary Leakey, an archaeologist who made an important discovery

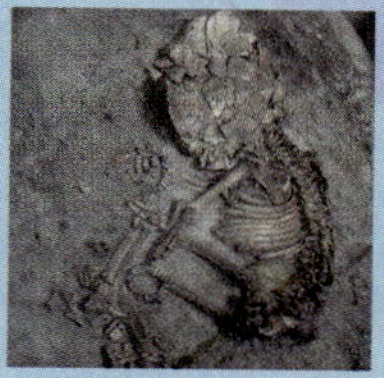

Child from a Stone Age burial

The people of Uruk, the world's first city

6,000-7,000 years ago Uruk, the world's first city, in Southwest Asia, is established.

8,500 years ago Oldest known farming village in Turkey appears.

12,000 years ago Last ice age ends.

20,000 years ago | 15,000 years ago | 10,000 years ago | 5,000 years ago

10,000 years ago People begin to grow food; Neolithic agricultural revolution begins.

5

RECENT SCHOLARSHIP

Mural in Çatalhöyük Scientists have differing interpretations of a mural painted on the walls of a structure in the Neolithic settlement of Çatalhöyük in present-day Turkey. The mural shows a series of rectangles with a shape above that resembles two triangles fused together. Some scientists believe that the rectangles are purely ornamental and that the shape represents a stretched-out leopard skin. However, other scientists believe that the rectangles are actually a map of Çatalhöyük and the shape above represents Mount Hasan, a volcano with two peaks about 90 miles away from the settlement. Rock samples taken from Mount Hasan in 2013 show that the volcano erupted around 6900 BCE, around the time the mural was painted. With this information, scientists believe that the mural may depict the eruption of Mount Hasan and its significance to the people of Çatalhöyük.

Where Did the First Human Ancestors Live?

In 2003, the oldest remains of early humans were excavated in Ethiopia about 100 miles or so northeast of the capital city of Addis Ababa. These fossils date back about 160,000 years and include nearly complete skulls, including one of a child. These fossils are now considered the oldest early human remains with features almost identical to modern humans.

ACTIVE JOURNAL

Map Skills Have students use the Map Skills activity in their Active Journals to fill in an outline map of East Africa with the labels of key places.

Analyze Maps How do you think geography influenced the lives of early humans? *(They had to learn to adapt to geographical conditions. For example, if the climate was very hot, they might sleep at midday to conserve energy. They also needed to learn to use their environment to suit their needs, such as creating tools from stone.)* How might the geography of East Africa have benefited early humans? *(The climate was temperate, the landscape made it easy to hunt, and geographical and natural features provided shelter.)*

Who Will You Meet?

Preview the images under the heading. Then have students read the captions beneath the images. Conduct a poll to find out which person interests students the most. Record the results on the board. Have students discuss why they are interested in each figure. *(Sample answer: Mary Leakey is the most interesting because she was a scientist who made a major discovery.)*

TOPIC 1

HSS 6.2.1; ELA W.6.7–9, SL.6.4–6, WHST.6.7–9; ELD.PI.C.9

Quest
Project-Based Learning Inquiry

Design a Village

Quest Kick Off

In this Quest, students will use the student edition, other sources, and their Active Journals to plan and create a drawing of a Neolithic village.

1 Ask Questions

Launch the Quest by discussing the Guiding Question as a class, "What was it like to live in an ancient village?" Have students generate the questions they will need to have answered to accomplish the Quest in their Journals.

2 Investigate

As they read the lessons, remind students to look for and respond to the three Quest Connections in the student text, which provide clues to their Quest. They should also identify and record two connections of their own.
Suggestion: If students are struggling identifying their own connections, suggest they think about the daily activities that villagers would likely have to perform in a Neolithic village.

3 Conduct Research

Find and Use Evidence As students complete the topic, have them identify sources they can draw on to complete their Quest. Remind students to find a variety of reliable sources that support their plans for their village. Direct them to their Active Journals for help working with their team and finding good sources.
Suggestion: If students need help with this step, refer them to the Analysis Skill following Lesson 1, Distinguish Essential From Incidental Information.

4 Design Your Village

When students complete the topic, have them return to the Quest, which can be used as a performance-based authentic assessment. To complete the Quest, they should (1) plan what they want to include in their drawing; (2) make a sketch of their village; (3) share their sketch with others; (4) revise their sketch to a create a final drawing; and (5) present and explain their drawing.

Analysis REP.3; HSS 6.2.1; ELA W.6.7–9, SL.6.4–6, WHST.6.7–9; ELD.PI.C.9

Quest
Project-Based Learning Inquiry

Design a Village

Quest KICK OFF

About 8,000 years ago, people were living in a time of great change. Humans were beginning to farm and were settling in the first villages.

What was it like to live in an ancient village?

How did early humans and the Neolithic people who followed them live? Explore the Essential Question "How much does geography shape people's lives?" in this Quest.

1 Ask Questions

Thousands of years ago, human societies were very different from those that followed. Get started on your Quest by making a list of questions you want to ask about how people lived in the distant past. Write the questions in your Active Journal.

2 Investigate

As you read the lessons in this topic, look for Quest CONNECTIONS that provide information about the way people lived long ago. Capture notes in your Active Journal.

3 Conduct Research

Next, find valid primary sources of information about life during the Neolithic Era on your own. Capture notes in your Active Journal.

Quest FINDINGS

4 Design Your Village

As society became more complex, Neolithic people formed villages. At the end of the topic you'll design a Neolithic village and create a drawing of how your village will look. When you complete your drawing, you will present it to the class in an oral presentation. Get help for creating your village in your Active Journal.

▲ Remains of Skara Brae, a Neolithic village in Scotland

DIFFERENTIATED INSTRUCTION

Below Level After students present and explain their drawings, discuss the parts of the village that students think would be most important to villagers.
Advanced Have students research the archeological plans for ancient Neolithic villages such as Dimini in ancient Greece or Skara Brae in ancient Scotland.

INTEGRATED ENGLISH LANGUAGE DEVELOPMENT

Emerging Have students draw an aerial version of their Neolithic village. Explain that they will draw a picture of the village from a point of view of how it would look from overhead. Then have them write one or two word labels next to parts of the village. Have students identify and use words and phrases from the lesson and their research that explain parts of the village.

LESSON 1

HSS 6.1.1; ELA RI.6.2

The Distant Past

BOUNCE TO ACTIVATE

VIDEO

GET READY TO READ

START UP

What does this photo tell you about how people gather information from the distant past?

GUIDING QUESTIONS

- How do scientists use fossils and artifacts to draw conclusions about early humans?
- How does archaeological evidence indicate that human life began in Africa?
- How did people live by the gathering and hunting way of life?

TAKE NOTES

Literacy Skills: Identify Main Ideas

Use the graphic organizer in your Active Journal to take notes as you read the lesson.

PRACTICE VOCABULARY

Use the vocabulary activity in your Active Journal to practice the vocabulary words.

Vocabulary		Academic Vocabulary
anthropology	artifact	evidence
archaeologist	hunter-gatherer	conclude
prehistory	culture	
fossil		
geologist		

We are all interested in people. But certain people, called anthropologists, have made a science out of studying people. **Anthropology** is the study of how human beings behave, how they act together, where they came from, and what makes one group of people different from another.

In this lesson, we will look at the work of a particular group of anthropologists known as archaeologists. **Archaeologists** study human life in the past by examining the things that people left behind.

Studying Early Humans

Until about 5,000 years ago, people had no way to write things down. To study **prehistory**, or the time before written records, archaeologists look for the places where people may have lived.

What Are Fossils? To learn about the earliest humans, archaeologists depend mainly on fossils. **Fossils** are hardened remains or imprints of living things that existed long ago. These remains may include plants, feathers, bones, and even footprints.

PRACTICE VOCABULARY

To help students integrate new vocabulary, group the terms and introduce them. Explain that an *archaeologist* studies life in the past, whereas a *geologist* studies physical materials such as soil and rock. *Anthropology* is the study of how humans behave. *Prehistory* is the time before written records, whereas a *fossil* is the hardened remains of a living thing and an *artifact* refers to an object made by people. *Culture* refers to shared beliefs, social practices, and characteristics shared by a group of people.

Point out the academic vocabulary in the margin. Provide sample sentences that clarify meaning.

evidence: The evidence shows that the defendant is guilty of the crime.

conclude: The jurors' job is to conclude if a person is guilty.

HSS 6.1.1; ELA RI.6.2

The Distant Past

CONNECT

GET READY TO READ

ETEXT START UP

Project the Start Up Activity. As students enter the classroom and get settled, ask them to examine the photograph, which shows young archaeologists looking for fossils and artifacts at an excavation.

Draw Conclusions Have students draw conclusions about how archaeologists work based on the photograph. *(Sample response: They use very fine tools to carefully dig and scrape away dirt and dust. This suggests that most objects they find are small and delicate. Finding artifacts can be physically challenging and awkward.)*

Discuss Remind students that scientists must rely only on the physical evidence that past societies have left behind, so uncovering new evidence is important.

After completing the Start Up Activity, project the Lesson Opener or direct students to their textbooks. Preview the lesson by working through the Get Ready to Read items with the class. Remind students to pay close attention to the Guiding Questions as they read the lesson.

ACTIVE JOURNAL

Take Notes Have students focus on Main Ideas and Details as they use the lesson literacy skills graphic organizer in their Active Journals to take notes as they read the lesson.

Practice Vocabulary Have students complete the activity in their Active Journals to build their vocabulary.

VIDEO VIDEO

Assign the lesson video as homework.

WORKSHEET

TEACHER RESOURCES

Have students who need additional support use the following worksheets from the Teacher Resources on the course:

- **Reading Support**
- **English Language Development**
- **Lesson Summary**

INVESTIGATE

Studying Early Humans

Discuss why it is difficult to study the history of early people before the invention of writing.

Compare and Contrast Direct students' attention to the first paragraph below the heading Studying Early Humans. Ask: How is **prehistory** different from history? *(Prehistory occurs before written records. History has written records.)*

Identify Details What are some examples of **fossil** remains? *(parts of plants, feathers, bones)*

Identify Main Ideas What do all **fossils** have in common? *(They come from living things that existed long ago.)*

INTERACTIVE

INTERACTIVE GALLERY

Piecing Together the Past

Display the Interactive Gallery: Piecing Together the Past for the class. Click through the images and call on volunteers to read the accompanying text aloud. Ask: What challenges do you think scientists had as they excavated and washed the bones? *(Possible response: Scientists had to be careful not to damage the bones. The bones may have been brittle and delicate.)*

INTERACTIVE

Piecing the Past Together

Fossils form in several ways. For example, after a living thing dies, it may quickly become covered by sand or mud. Once covered, the soft parts of the plant or animal rot away. The harder parts, such as bones, teeth, or woody stems, last much longer. Over many years, minerals from the soil slowly replace this once-living material. What remains is a rocklike copy of the original.

How Are Ancient Remains Dated? Archaeologists use several methods for determining the ages of fossils and other prehistoric objects. In this work, they get valuable information from **geologists**, scientists who study the physical materials of Earth itself, such as soil and rocks.

One dating method is to compare objects found in similar layers of rock or soil. Objects found in lower layers are generally older than those found in upper layers. Archaeologists may also compare an object with a similar fossil or artifact whose age is already known.

Radioactive dating is another method for determining the age of objects up to about 50,000 years old. Living things contain radioactive elements that decay, or break down, over time. By measuring the radioactive material in bones and other materials that were once alive, scientists can tell when an object was formed.

In recent years, scientists have developed other methods to study fossils. They use DNA to compare human remains from the past with people living today. Genetic evidence has uncovered new information about how people changed and how they moved from place to place.

Why Do Scientists Look for Artifacts? Human ancestors, called hominins, lived millions of years ago. To study prehistoric people who lived more recently, archaeologists look for old settlements, such as villages or campsites. Such sites often lie buried beneath layers of soil.

Approximate Ages of Human Ancestor Remains in East Africa

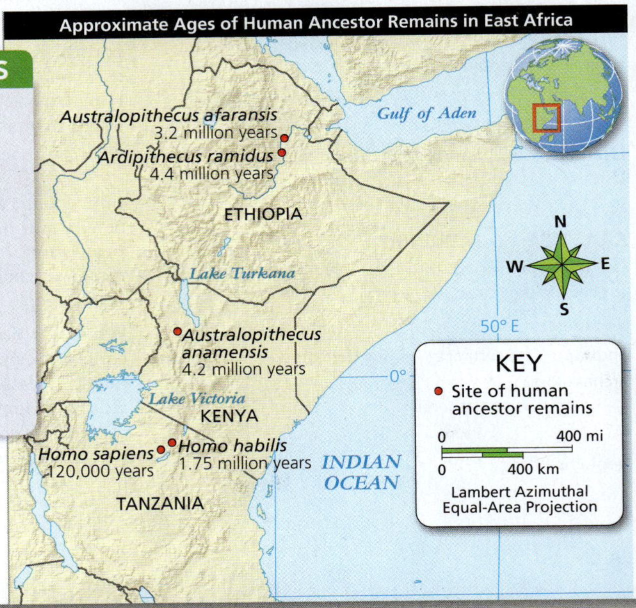

GEOGRAPHY **SKILLS**

Archaeologists have made major archaeological discoveries in Africa.

1. **Region** In what part of Africa did most fossil finds occur?
2. **Human-Environment Interaction** What environmental factors may have led to the development of early humans in East Africa?

8 Lesson 1.1

DIFFERENTIATED INSTRUCTION

Advanced Have students research an archeological site of their choosing and draw a diagram of the site. Students should be sure to note where particular artifacts or fossils were discovered.

Below Level Ask students to imagine an archeological dig of their own home or community many centuries in the future. Have students make a list of items that might be found. Then have students list items they think might be found in an archeological dig of a prehistorical settlement.

Special Education Ask students to think about why archeologists and anthropologists are interested in learning about the past. Have students discuss their answers with a partner.

Archaeologists must carefully excavate, or uncover, these sites to learn about the people who once lived there.

As archaeologists dig up a site, they look for artifacts such as tools, pottery, or weapons. **Artifacts** are anything made and used by humans. These scientists then try to identify patterns, examining what artifacts are found together in the same spot. Artifacts found in an ancient campsite can help archaeologists understand how the people who once camped there hunted for food or what they ate.

READING CHECK **Use Evidence** What types of objects do archaeologists study to learn about the past?

Where Did Human Ancestors Live?

Where did human ancestors first appear on Earth? For a long time, scientists could not agree on an answer.

Then, in 1960, British archaeologists Mary and Louis Leakey discovered a piece of a human-like skull at Olduvai Gorge in East Africa. The Leakeys called their find *Homo habilis* ("handy man") because **evidence** showed that these early human ancestors made and used tools. Tests showed that the *Homo habilis* fossils were at least 1.75 million years old. From that point on, the search for the origins of humankind has largely focused on Africa.

African Beginnings On November 30, 1974, American anthropologist Donald Johanson made a discovery that helped shape how scientists view early human history. For three years, Johanson had been searching for evidence of human ancestors in Ethiopia, a country in East Africa. Johanson later recalled,

▲ Mary Leakey at work in Tanzania, Africa

Primary Source

On this November morning, it was about noon, I was heading back to my Land Rover to drive back to camp. And I happened to look over my right shoulder. And as I did so, I saw a fragment of a bone which I recognized as coming from the elbow region in a skeleton. . . . There was a piece of a leg, there was a piece of a pelvis, there was a piece of a jaw, there was a piece of a skull. And I realized almost instantaneously that we had part of a skeleton.

—Donald C. Johanson, Academy of Achievement interview, 1991

Academic Vocabulary
evidence • *n.*, something that can be used as proof

ACTIVE CLASSROOM

After viewing the Interactive Gallery: Piecing Together the Past, use the Make Headlines strategy. Students should write a headline that describes the findings in the Interactive Gallery and their importance to anthropology. Have students compare headlines with a partner.

Where Did Human Ancestors Live?

Discuss the hominin remains found in Africa and how these led to theories about where human beings originated.

Identify Details How old was the skull Mary and Louis Leakey found in Olduvai Gorge? *(It was at least 1.75 million years old.)*

Check Understanding Why did the Leakeys call their find *Homo habilis*? *(Homo habilis means "handy man." There was evidence that the hominin they found made and used tools.)*

Summarize What did scientists conclude from finding the skull? *(that scientists interested in human origins should focus their attention on East Africa)*

BACKGROUND NOTE

Olduvai Gorge The geography at Olduvai Gorge made it easier for Mary and Louis Leakey to make their discovery. An ancient river had carved out the land so that seven layers—or "beds"—of geological strata were visible. The skull of *Homo habilis* was discovered in Bed 1, which is the oldest part of Olduvai Gorge. Bed 1 is about 197 feet deep and filled with volcanic ash and lava flows that helped preserve the skull. It took about three weeks of careful digging to find the roughly 400 pieces that comprised the discovered skull. In all, scientists working at the site have discovered more than 60 individuals including three types of ancient human ancestors—*Australopithecus boisei, Homo habilis,* and *Homo erectus.*

ANSWERS

Region *East Africa*

Human-Environment Interaction *Possible response: a favorable climate and accessible food sources*

Use Evidence *Archaeologists study fossils of bones and other ancient remains and artifacts such as tools, pottery, weapons, or other human-made objects to learn about the past.*

Compare and Contrast In what ways was Donald Johanson's discovery of Lucy different from the Leakeys' discovery at Olduvai Gorge? *(The Leakeys discovered a skull and other artifacts, whereas Johanson discovered many pieces of the same skeleton. Johanson's skeleton was about 3.2 million years old, almost 1.5 million years older than the Leakeys' discovery.)*

Compare and Contrast How does Tim White's Ardi differ from that of Johanson's Lucy? *(Ardi was taller and heavier than Lucy and walked more slowly and awkwardly. Ardi was also about 1.2 million years older than Lucy.)*

Synthesize How might walking have contributed to the evolution of pre-humans from Ardi to Lucy? *(Walking probably burned more calories and resulted in stronger leg and back muscles, eventually making Lucy smaller, lighter, and more upright and mobile.)*

Summarize What does Michel Brunet believe about the location of the first humans? *(He believes that humans may have originated in central Africa, not East Africa, and that they are much older than previously believed.)*

Cite Evidence What evidence does Brunet have to support his claim? *(His evidence is the discovery of a skull nearly 7 million years old in Chad.)*

After two weeks of careful searching, Johanson and his team had uncovered hundreds of pieces of bone. They decided that all the bones belonged to one individual because they did not find two examples of any one type of bone. They determined that she was a 3.5-foot-tall female. Johanson named her "Lucy" after a song by the Beatles.

Johanson's team found some 40 percent of Lucy's skeleton. The bones of her legs, pelvis, ankle, and spine suggest that, like us, she walked upright on two legs. However, she lived 3.2 million years ago.

Since then, even older fossils have been found in Africa. In 1992, American anthropologist Tim White found remains of hominins who lived in Ethiopia at least 4.4 million years ago. Beginning with a single tooth, White's team uncovered more fragments. Finally, in 2009, White unveiled a nearly complete skeleton of a female that he named "Ardi." More than a million years older than Lucy, Ardi was taller and heavier. She probably walked upright, but slowly and awkwardly.

Academic Vocabulary
conclude • *v.*, to decide as a result of thinking or reasoning

What Is the "Oldest One"?

Many scientists believe that the oldest humans began to develop, or evolve, from their great ape cousins about 5-7 million years ago. This process is what's known as evolution. Discoveries such as Lucy and Ardi have also led most scientists to **conclude** that humankind began in East Africa about 4.5 million years ago.

Analyze Images A scientist cleans the rib of a long extinct elephant. **Infer** Why is it easier to find ancient animal bones than the bones of human ancestors?

French scientist Michel Brunet is one of a group of scientists that believes that human life started elsewhere in Africa. In 2001, Brunet found a humanlike skull in the country of Chad. Tests showed the skull to be nearly 7 million years old. That makes it, says Brunet, "the oldest one."

Brunet's discovery has raised questions. Chad is in central Africa. Did humankind begin there rather than in East Africa? The skull Brunet found is older than other human fossils discovered so far. Is humankind older than scientists once thought?

Scientists will continue to look for answers to questions like these. Meanwhile, the search continues. "This is the beginning of the story," says Brunet of his work in Chad, "just the beginning."

READING CHECK **Identify Main Ideas** Why do most scientists believe that human life began in Africa?

INTEGRATED ENGLISH LANGUAGE DEVELOPMENT

Collaborative Explain that using comparative and superlative adjectives adds clarity and descriptiveness to both written and spoken language. Review the function of adjectives, comparative adjectives, and superlative adjectives, and prompt students to practice speaking using terms from the text (old, older, oldest) as well as other sets of adjectives, with the goal of increasing their accuracy and ease.

Emerging Briefly summarize information presented in the text about the skull Michel Brunet found in Chad. Ask students to say a sentence about the subject, using the word "old," "older," or "oldest."

Expanding Ask: What is the oldest human fossil described in the text? What fossils is it older than? Have pairs of students make up sentences to answer this question.

ANSWERS

Infer *Many more animals than humans existed.*

Identify Main Ideas *Most scientists believe that human life began in Africa because of the fossils of human ancestors that have been discovered there.*

How Did Hunter-Gatherers Live?

Early humans were **hunter-gatherers**, which means that they lived by hunting small animals and gathering plants. They also probably scavenged for food left by predators. They formed societies and developed ways to improve their chances for survival.

Archaeologists know very little about how early hunter-gatherers such as Lucy lived. But they do know that their lives were often harsh. Many groups appeared for a time and died out. To survive and grow, early humans developed technology, tools, and skills to meet their needs.

How Were the First Tools Made? About 2.5 million years ago, early humans learned how to make tools out of stone. This technology was so important to human survival that archaeologists call this period the Paleolithic Era, or the Old Stone Age. The Paleolithic Era ended about 2,500 to 10,000 years ago.

Over time, toolmakers become more skillful, making thinner and sharper stone blades. Some blades were used to tip spears and arrows. Toolmakers also began making weapons from bones and antlers. As their skills and weapons improved, Paleolithic hunters were able to turn from hunting small animals to hunting larger animals such as deer.

How Did Fire Affect Human Development? Around 800,000 years ago, people also learned how to use fire. With fire, people could have light on dark nights, cook meat and plants, and use flames to aid in hunting and to scare off dangerous animals. Making fire also had important long-term effects such as enabling people to live in places where it otherwise would have been too cold for people to survive.

Analyze Images This painting of a bull was found in a cave in Lascaux, France, and dates from the Paleolithic Era. **Draw Conclusions** How do you think ancient artists chose which subjects to paint?

Did you know?

Many of the artifacts found in North America are cutting tools and arrowheads made of flint.

ELD.PII.A.1

Bridging Ask pairs of students to discuss what discoveries described in the text have helped scientists understand when and where humankind began. Encourage each partner to use a variety of comparative and superlative adjectives during the discussion by including each type at least once.

WORKSHEET **TEACHER RESOURCES**

For additional IELD support addressing the standard, have students complete the Lesson ELD activity from the Teacher Resources found on the course.

How Did Hunter-Gatherers Live?

Discuss how hunter-gatherers survived by using tools and fire.

Identify Main Ideas What activities did **hunter-gatherers** engage in that improved their chances of survival? *(They hunted smaller animals, gathered edible plants, and formed groups.)*

Identify Details What is one unique way that early humans solved problems? *(They invented technology.)*

Identify Main Ideas Why is the Paleolithic era named for stone? *(It is the period in which humans learned to make stone tools.)*

Hypothesize What is one way that stone tools might have made the lives of early humans easier? *(Sample response: Scraping flesh from an animal skin could allow early humans to make clothing and stay warm.)*

Summarize How did Stone Age tools change over time? *(Blades became thinner and sharper. Tools were made from different materials.)*

Draw Conclusions How might improving tools change hunting practices for early humans? Explain. *(Sample response: As tools improved, early humans could hunt more effectively. For example, they could hunt larger animals because they had spears and arrows that could kill from a distance.)*

ELD TIP English learners may not understand the use of a hyphen in a term such as hunter-gatherers. Explain that in English a hyphen is sometimes put between to words to indicate that a person has two identities or jobs that are equally important and possibly related (such as "singer-songwriter"). Discuss how hunter-gatherers survived. Then ask students to think of other examples of words that might make sense as a term when joined with a hyphen.

ANSWERS

Based on the painting, they likely chose scenes and objects from their daily lives, such as these animals.

HSS 6.1.1; ELA RI.6.2; ELD.PI.A.2, ELD.PI.C.10.a

Analyze Text What does the Primary Source mean by "The control of fire was presumably the first great step in man's [freedom] from the bondage of his environment"? *(It means that they could keep warm in cold locations, they could cook meats and plants, and they could complete tasks at night.)*

SYNTHESIZE

Assess and Reteach Have students use a Think-Pair-Share strategy to complete Lesson Check questions 1–5. Review their responses. If they had any incorrect answers, use the Guiding Questions to discuss the lesson's main ideas, focusing on the ideas they struggled with.

ACTIVE JOURNAL

Writing Workshop Have students complete the Lesson 1 Writing Task in their Active Journals. Students will write a few sentences about a member of a hunter-gatherer group for their end-of-topic essay.

DEMONSTRATE

ASSESSMENT **ONLINE LESSON QUIZ**

Assign the Online Lesson Quiz for this lesson if you haven't already done so. Students will be offered automatic remediation or enrichment based on their score.

DISCUSSION **DISCUSSION BOARD**

Post this question to the class on the Discussion Board:

Analyze What role has archaeology played in helping us understand our early ancestors? *(Sample response: Archaeologists have discovered information about the physical characteristics of early humans, the type of activities they engaged in, and the tools they made.)*

ANSWERS

Identify Cause and Effect *They developed stone tools and learned how to use fire. They lived in small hunter-gatherer bands, moving frequently.*

Did you know?

Hunter-gathers still live in regions of the world where it is hard to grow food. They live in South America, Africa, Asia, and Australia.

Here, a British archaeologist explains why learning to control fire was an important step in human development.

Primary Source

The control of fire was presumably the first great step in man's [freedom] from the bondage of his environment . . . . [Mankind] is no longer restricted in his movement to a limited range of climates, and his activities need not be entirely determined by the sun's light. But in mastery of fire man was controlling a mighty physical force.

—V. Gordon Childe, *Man Makes Himself*

What Was Life Like for Hunter-Gatherers? **Culture** includes the many different elements that make up the way of life of a people. These include social and family organization, beliefs and values, technology, shelter and clothing, common activities, storytelling, rituals, and art.

Stone age hunter-gatherers lived in small groups, or bands. After gathering as much food as they could in one area, they moved on. They built temporary huts out of branches or made tents of animal skins. Bands stayed small so they could move easily. A typical band included ten or twelve adults and their children.

Men generally did the hunting, but they also gathered other food. Women usually gathered fruit, grains, seeds, nuts, eggs, and honey. They caught small animals and may have picked herbs for medicine.

READING CHECK **Identify Cause and Effect** How did people survive during the Paleolithic Era?

Lesson Check

HSS 6.1.1; ELA RI.6.2; ELD.PI.A.2, ELD.PI.C.10.a

Practice Vocabulary

1. How do scientists date **fossils** and **artifacts**?
2. What **technology** was used during the Paleolithic Era?

Critical Thinking and Writing

3. **Summarize** How do archaeologists look for evidence about early people?
4. **Infer** Why do you think scientists are trying to find out more about how and where early humans lived?
5. **Identify Cause and Effect** Why was the ability to control fire a significant advancement for humans?
6. **Writing Workshop: Introduce Characters** Imagine you are traveling through different periods of human history. Your first stop is the Paleolithic Era. Write a few sentences in your Active Journal about how a member of a hunter-gatherer group lived and the person's role in the wandering band.

LESSON CHECK

1. examining strata, radioactive dating, and physical or chemical DNA tests **DOK1**
2. stone tools and fire **DOK1**
3. They find places where early people may have lived and then dig for artifacts. **DOK2**
4. Possible answer: Understanding past human life teaches us where we came from. **DOK3**
5. Fire allowed people to control the environment. **DOK2**
6. Students should explain how the character lived based on the description of hunter-gatherer societies. **DOK4**

ELA RI.6.2–4

Primary Sources

The Epic of Gilgamesh

Nearly 3,000 years ago, a writer inscribed clay tablets like the one shown here with a legend about Gilgamesh, the legendary king of Uruk—here called *Erech.* As you've learned, Uruk was the world's first city. The Epic of Gilgamesh tells the story of Gilgamesh—Gish, in this reading—and his friend Enkidu, who work together to defeat a monster named Huwawa. Here Gish announces his daring plan.

▶ text on a clay tablet

I will lure him to the cedar forest,
Like a strong offspring of Erech.
I will let the land hear [that]
I am determined to lure (him) in the cedar [forest].
A name I will establish. (1)

The elders (2) of Erech of the plazas brought word to Gish:
"Though art young, O Gish, and thy heart carries thee away. (3)
Thou dost not know what thou proposes to do.
We hear that Huwawa is enraged.

* * *

"Huwawa, whose roar is a deluge, (4)
whose mouth is fire, whose breath is death.
Why does thou desire to do this?"

* * *

Gish heard the report of his counselors. (5)
He saw and cried out to [his] friend:
"Now, my friend, thus [I speak]
I fear him, but [I will go to the cedar forest]."

—*The Epic of Gilgamesh*, translated by Morris Jastrow, Jr. and Albert T. Clay

Reading and Vocabulary Support

(1) What do you think it means when Gilgamesh says "A name I will establish"?

(2) An *elder* is an older and wiser person.

(3) What do you think the elders mean when they say to Gilgamesh "your heart carries you away"?

(4) A *deluge* in this sense means something that overwhelms and overpowers a person.

(5) A *counselor* is a person who provides advice.

Analyzing Primary Sources

Cite specific evidence from the document to support your answers.

1. **Draw Conclusions** What kind of name do you think Gilgamesh believes he will establish for himself by carrying out his plan?
2. **Generate Explanations** Gilgamesh says that he fears Huwawa. Why do you think he admits this fact?
3. **Summarize** Write a brief summary that explores the central ideas of this excerpt.

ANALYZING PRIMARY SOURCES

1. Gilgamesh thinks he will be called a hero by carrying out his plan. **DOK3**
2. Possible answer: Gilgamesh admits his fear to show that he is like other men who can do brave things despite their fears. **DOK3**
3. Possible answer: In this excerpt, Gilgamesh announces that he will go into the cedar forest and kill the monster Huwawa. **DOK3**

ELA RI.6.2–4

Primary Sources

The Epic of Gilgamesh

Read aloud the explanatory note about the source. Direct students' attention to the photograph on the page. Ask: What does the image suggest about the way *The Epic of Gilgamesh* was recorded? *(It was recorded by pressing symbols into wet clay.)*

GUIDING READING

Read aloud the first stanza of the poem without stopping. Then reread the stanza, pausing to let students answer the numbered questions. Do the same for the other stanzas. Use the questions in the text to prompt students' analysis of the primary source.

Reading and Vocabulary Support Answers

1. *He means that he will do something that will make him famous.*

3. *They mean that Gish is letting his youthful strong feelings get the better of him.*

GUIDED ANALYSIS

After completing the poem, discuss what this primary source reveals about the beliefs of the people of Uruk. What does it suggest about how much they value bravery and heroism?

Interpret Sources What point is the poet making in the third stanza? *(The elders are explaining to Gish why Huwawa is so dangerous.)* How does Gish respond to the advice of the elders? *(He listens to what they say, acknowledges his fear, but says he will go into the cedar forest to find the monster anyway.)*

To assess understanding, have students respond to the Analyzing Primary Sources questions in writing.

Analysis REP.3

Analysis Skills

Distinguish Essential From Incidental Information

LEARN

Preview the steps in the student text with students and then play the video.

VIDEO **21ST CENTURY SKILLS**

Project the Categorize video in the 21st Century Skills Tutorial. Use the Quick Reference and Assessment to provide additional instruction in the skill.

PRACTICE

Have students practice the skill of distinguishing essential from incidental information using text from the secondary source. Follow the steps on the student page, providing instruction and then asking students the questions.

As an alternative, have students work in pairs or small groups to respond to the questions and activities mentioned in the four steps of the text. Then invite the groups to state their findings to the class. Discuss strategies that students use to categorize information as essential or incidental.

ASSESS

To assess this skill, have students identify essential from incidental information from another source that you find online.

ANSWERS

1. a. Students should note that they should concentrate on finding essential information.
b. Sample answers: What animals did Neolithic people domesticate? How did farming change people's lives?
c. domestication

2. Sources might include scholarly books or articles. Online research should be limited to well-documented .edu or .org websites.

3. Possible response: Information and data from archeological research about ancient peoples and the places where they lived would be most helpful in doing research.

4. Information about animals and animal sources of food would be incidental.

Distinguish Essential from Incidental Information

INTERACTIVE
Categorize

Use the secondary source and these steps to distinguish essential from incidental information.

1 **Identify a focus or topic.** Set a purpose for your research.

a. What exactly are you trying to find out?

b. What key question are you trying to answer?

c. What idea or event are you trying to understand?

2 **Locate your sources.** The sources you choose will depend on your focus and topic. What sources might you use if you were researching the domestication of grains during the Neolithic Age?

3 **Identify information that is essential to your topic.** Based on your focus:

a. What information will help you achieve your goal?

b. What kinds of data will answer questions or increase your understanding?

4 **Identify information that is incidental to your topic.** Remember the focus you have set for your research. Information that is not related to this focus is incidental. Take a look at the excerpt from the text below. If you were conducting research on only the plants that were domesticated by early humans, what information in the excerpt would be incidental to your focus?

Secondary Source

Domesticated crops, such as wheat, rice, or maize, became a nutritious and reliable source of food. These grains were chief food sources for entire societies. Animals were a source of food. People ate their meat, but also the eggs, milk, and honey they produced. Horses and oxen helped them work the fields. The fur of sheep and llamas was used to make clothing.

Domesticated animals, such as horses, sheep, and cattle, were easier to control than their wild counterparts. Some people lived in places where growing food was difficult. They traveled to different places with their animals so that they would have grasslands to eat from. The people herding the animals would use them for food and clothing. This way of life was called pastoral nomadism.

At first, wild and domesticated breeds were similar. But over time, people selected the seeds of the plants that produced the best crops. Domesticated plants began to produce more abundant food that was larger, easier to cook, and tastier. A domesticated tomato is the size of an orange, but a wild tomato is the size of a cherry. By contrast, some breeds of domesticated goats, pigs, and cattle are smaller than their wild ancestors. Smaller animals may have been easier to manage.

DIFFERENTIATED INSTRUCTION

Below Level Before practicing the skill, call on students to define essential and incidental information. *(Essential means "absolutely necessary or very important." Incidental means "less important or secondary.")*

INTEGRATED ENGLISH LANGUAGE DEVELOPMENT

Bridging Have students turn to a partner and talk about what "domesticated" means. Then have them discuss how people made certain types of wild animals and plants "domesticated." Have them talk about why early humans did this, and what domesticated plants and animals we have today. Provide students with historical context as needed.

LESSON 2 HSS 6.1.2, 6.2.9

Humans Spread Out

GET READY TO READ

START UP

What questions would you ask the people who once lived in this settlement located on the French coast?

GUIDING QUESTIONS

- How and why did modern humans succeed and populate most regions of the world?
- How did the environment influence the migrations of early humans?
- How did early humans adapt to new environments and climate changes?

TAKE NOTES

Literacy Skills: Analyze Cause and Effect

Use the graphic organizer in your Active Journal to take notes as you read the lesson.

PRACTICE VOCABULARY

Use the vocabulary activity in your Active Journal to practice the vocabulary words.

Vocabulary	Academic Vocabulary
migration	complex
environment	network
adapt	

Over time, new species of hominins arose. In this lesson, you will read about these human ancestors and the ways they were different from those who came before them.

What Were Later Stone Age Peoples Like?

Toward the end of the Paleolithic Era, two groups of larger-brained hominins appeared. Both groups had more developed technologies than earlier peoples. However, only one of these groups would survive past the Stone Age.

Who Were the Neanderthals? A group known as Neanderthals appeared in Europe and parts of Asia about 230,000 years ago. Their name comes from the Neander Valley in present-day Germany, where their fossil remains were first found. Fossils of a close relative of the Neanderthals, called the Denisovans, have been found in Asia.

Some archaeologists believe that the Neanderthals were the first hominins to bury their dead. Remains of flowers and other objects in burial sites may be evidence

Lesson 1.2 • Humans Spread Out 15

PRACTICE VOCABULARY

Help students integrate new vocabulary by making connections among words. *Migration* occurs when a group people or animals leave one area to live in another. Explain that Stone Age people had to *adapt* to a new *environment* as they moved from place to place.

Point out the academic vocabulary in the margin. Provide sample sentences that clarify meaning.

complex: The jigsaw puzzle had a thousand pieces and was much too **complex** for a five-year old to put together.

networks: The family was very large and had **networks** that kept in touch with all of them throughout the year.

HSS 6.1.2, 6.2.9

Humans Spread Out

CONNECT

GET READY TO READ

ETEXT START UP

Project the Start Up Activity. As students enter the classroom and get settled, ask them to examine the photograph, which shows the remains of a Neolithic settlement on the coast of France.

Infer Ask students to consider what construction methods the people who built this site might have used. Then ask them to consider any similarities and differences between ancient methods and construction methods used today. Divide students into small groups to discuss their responses.

Discuss Explain that most scientists agree that our ancestors migrated from Africa to populate much of the rest of the world. Discuss different world environments and how these early groups of migrants might have adapted to them.

After completing the Start Up Activity, project the Lesson Opener or direct students to their textbooks. Preview the lesson by working through the Get Ready to Read items with the class. Remind students to pay close attention to the Guiding Questions as they read the lesson.

ACTIVE JOURNAL

Take Notes Have students focus on Cause and Effect as they use the lesson literacy skills graphic organizer in their Active Journals to take notes as they read the lesson.

Practice Vocabulary Have students complete the activity in their Active Journals to build their vocabulary.

VIDEO VIDEO

Assign the lesson video as homework.

WORKSHEET **TEACHER RESOURCES**

Have students who need additional support use the following worksheets from the Teacher Resources on the course:

- **Reading Support**
- **English Language Development**
- **Lesson Summary**

INVESTIGATE

What Were Later Stone Age People Like?

Discuss the different types of hominins identified in the previous lesson. Ask students to speculate what they think might have happened to these hominins as time passed.

Compare and Contrast How did human ancestors change toward the end of the Paleolithic era? *(They had larger brains and a more developed culture.)*

Identify Details How long ago did Neanderthals live? Where did they live? *(About 230,000 years ago; they were discovered in the Neander Valley of Germany in Europe and in parts of Asia.)*

Summarize How did Neanderthals treat their dead? *(They buried them, sometime with simple rituals and with flowers and other objects.)*

Compare and Contrast What characteristics of culture did both Neanderthals and *Homo sapiens* share in common? *(Both groups made tools, used fire, hunted animals, and gathered plants.)*

Cause and Effect Why would the development of complex language give *Homo sapiens* an advantage as hunters? *(It would allow them to organize a hunt and communicate as they hunted.)*

ANSWERS

Compare *The Neanderthal skull seems larger and heavier than the Homo sapiens skull.*

Identify Supporting Details *complex language*

that Neanderthals carefully buried bodies and may have believed in life after death. Other archaeologists, however, disagree. Even if Neanderthals did bury their dead, their burial practices were much simpler than those of later people.

When Did Modern Humans Appear? About 200,000 years ago, the last new group of humans appeared. The scientific name of this group is *Homo sapiens*, which means "wise people." *Homo sapiens* were the first modern humans—or people like us.

These people were like Neanderthals in some ways. Both groups made tools, used fire, and hunted animals. But modern humans were taller, lighter, and less muscular.

Although at one time it was thought that Neanderthals could only make noises resembling a frog's croak, we know from fossil finds that Neanderthals could speak and form words. About 70,000 years ago, however, *Homo sapiens* developed a powerful new skill—**complex** language. Having a shared language gave *Homo sapiens* a great advantage in the struggle to survive. They could organize a hunt, warn of danger, and pass knowledge and skills on to their young.

Academic Vocabulary
complex • *adj.*, having many related parts; not simple

The ability to use complex language, think, and cooperate with other people helped *Homo sapiens* develop new skills and teach them to each other. As a result, they could survive harsh conditions and live in new places. These traits also made it possible for them to defend against threats.

For thousands of years, Neanderthals and modern humans lived near each other, but the Neanderthals eventually disappeared. Although the two groups intermingled, some archaeologists believe they fought with the newcomers and lost. Whatever the cause, there is no fossil evidence of Neanderthals in Europe after about 28,000 years ago.

READING CHECK **Identify Supporting Details** What skill gave modern humans an advantage over Neanderthals?

Analyze Visuals This photograph shows a Neanderthal skull on the left and a Homo sapiens skull on the right. **Compare** What differences do you notice between the two skulls?

16 Lesson 1.2 • Humans Spread Out

INTEGRATED ENGLISH LANGUAGE DEVELOPMENT

Collaborative Use "What Were Later Stone Age Peoples Like?" to help students understand the concept of comparing and contrasting in both written and spoken language. Review the meaning of the terms "compare" and "contrast" and prompt students to discuss these concepts using terms from the text, with the goal of increasing their speaking and writing skills.

Emerging Put students in pairs or groups. Briefly summarize information presented in the text about Neanderthals and *Homo sapiens*. Ask students to collaborate in writing down one fact about each group that uses information from your summary.

Expanding Ask: What could *Homo sapiens* do that Neanderthals could not? Have pairs of students write the question and their answers to it together.

Migrations of *Homo Sapiens*

GEOGRAPHY SKILLS

Early humans are thought to have migrated throughout the world roughly according to the routes shown on this map.

1. **Region** At what point on this map did human migration begin?
2. **Movement** Based on this map, describe the movement of early people from their starting point in Africa.

What Do We Know About Early Human Migration?

Most archaeologists agree that *Homo sapiens* have walked on Earth for only about 200,000 years. But they do not agree on where modern humans came from or how they spread. Scientists have studied both fossils and genetic information, or the physical qualities that living things pass from one generation to the next. They have developed two main theories, or possible explanations, about the movement of early humans.

Migration from Africa Most scientists think that *Homo sapiens,* like other early humans, originated in Africa. From there, *Homo sapiens* began a long **migration** to other regions of the world. A migration occurs when people leave their homeland to live somewhere else. Scientists who support the "out of Africa" theory suggest that as modern humans migrated from Africa to new places, they gradually replaced the older groups who were already living there.

Some scientists argue that large-brained humans developed separately in many different parts of the world and they eventually mixed together. However, most scientists disagree with this theory.

New Evidence For years, there was little fossil evidence to support either theory. Then in 2007, scientists analyzed a fossil skull that had been found in South Africa. Tests showed that it was about 36,000 years old, the same as skulls found in Europe from the same period. This similarity suggests that humans were already in their modern form when they migrated from Africa.

INTERACTIVE

Migrations of *Homo sapiens*

ELD.PII.A.2

Bridging Ask pairs of students to write questions about Neanderthals and *Homo sapiens* on paper and hand them to the other student. Then have them write their answers on the paper underneath the other student's question. Encourage each partner to mention more than one characteristic or ability of each group.

WORKSHEET **TEACHER RESOURCES**

For additional IELD support addressing the standard, have students complete the Lesson ELD activity from the Teacher Resources found on the course.

What Do We Know About Early Human Migration?

Discuss what routes humans took as they migrated throughout the world and what the experience of these journeys might have been like.

Sequence About when did *Homo sapiens* begin to walk on Earth? *(about 200,000 years ago)*

Identify Details What have scientists studied to find out where modern humans originally came from? *(They have studied fossils and genetic information.)*

Identify Main Ideas What is the "Out of Africa" theory? *(Early humans originated in Africa. They spread through migrations all over the world and replaced older populations.)*

INTERACTIVE **INTERACTIVE MAP**

Migrations of *Homo sapiens*

Display the Interactive Map: *Migrations of* Homo sapiens for the class. Click through the hot spots to see how *Homo sapiens* migrated across Earth.

ACTIVE CLASSROOM

After viewing the Hot Spot Map: Migration of *Homo sapiens*, use a Sequence It strategy. Give students pieces of paper that list each location shown on the Hot Spot Map. Then have students arrange themselves in the order that *Homo sapiens* arrived in each location.

ANSWERS

Region *East Africa*

Movement *People went from East Africa through Asia, across to North America, and south to South America.*

Find Evidence How did the discovery in 2007 of the skull from South Africa support the "Out of Africa" theory? *(Tests showed that the skull was about 36,000 years old, which is about the same age as skulls found in Europe. This suggests that humans were already in their modern form when they migrated to Europe.)*

How Did Humans Adapt to Varied Environments?

Discuss how environmental changes affected early human societies.

Identify Details What were some main ways that humans had to adapt to new environments? *(Sample answer: They had to identify plants that were safe to eat, ways to hunt new animals, and materials for tools and shelter.)*

Infer Why were these adaptations necessary? *(Sample answer: Eating the wrong plants can make people sick or die. Failing to catch animals can leave people hungry or starving to death. Tools make survival tasks easier to accomplish. Shelter keeps people safe from weather.)*

Identify Details What happened to Earth's climate shortly after modern humans appeared? *(The last great Ice Age began.)*

Identify Main Ideas What is the main idea of the Infographic? *(to show how early humans were able to survive.)*

Identify Cause and Effect How did expanding glaciers affect climate? *(Rainfall decreased, grasslands became deserts, and sea levels dropped to expose new land.)*

Summarize What are three things that early humans did to stay warm as the climate grew colder? *(They made clothing from animal skins, built stronger and warmer shelters, and kept fires burning day and night.)*

ANSWERS

Demonstrate Reasoned Judgement *Possible answer: Shelter was the most important because people needed protection.*

Ask Questions *Possible answers: Could* Homo sapiens *have developed in several areas of the world at once? Why did* Homo sapiens *develop in Africa? Why did* Homo sapiens *begin to migrate?*

Did you know?

Humans used both a land bridge and boats to reach Australia.

In 2008, scientists completed a genetic study of nearly a thousand people around the globe. Scientists found the greatest genetic variety in communities closest to Africa. This finding supports the idea that, as people migrated away from Africa, groups branched off to populate new areas. The new evidence gives a boost to the "out of Africa" theory. Still, many questions about human migration remain unanswered.

Wherever *Homo sapiens* first appeared, they eventually spread across Earth. By about 30,000 years ago, these modern humans were living in Africa, Asia, Europe, and Australia. About 15,000-18,000 years ago, humans entered North America by crossing a land bridge from Asia. Evidence suggests that modern humans were living as far south as central Chile in South America by about 12,500 years ago.

READING CHECK **Ask Questions** What questions do you think still remain about human migration?

How Did Humans Adapt to Varied Environments?

As modern humans migrated, they settled in a variety of **environments**, or surroundings. With each move, people had to **adapt**, or change their way of life, to suit their new environment. They had to find out which plants could be eaten, hunt different animals and to find new materials for tools and shelters.

How Did the Climate Change? Over time, people also had to adapt to changes in the world's climate. During the past two million years the Earth has experienced four long ice ages. The last great Ice Age began about 70,000 years ago, soon after modern humans appeared.

Analyze Diagrams Many factors helped early humans to survive. **Demonstrate Reasoned Judgment** Which of the key factors for human survival shown do you think was the most important? Choose one and explain your reasoning.

DIFFERENTIATED INSTRUCTION

Advanced Have students research current theories about climate change. Then, have them write a paragraph or two proposing ways that people might have to alter their lifestyles to survive and be comfortable in the future due to a changing climate.

Below Level Ask students to think about how they adapt to changing seasons and different weather conditions. Then, have them draw upon their answers to make inferences about how ancient people adapted to a changing climate. Have students write a paragraph explaining ways they think ancient people altered their way of life due to a changing climate.

Special Education Let students draw a picture for their response rather than write a paragraph.

During the last Ice Age, thick sheets of ice, called glaciers, spread across large regions of Earth. Glaciers covered the northern parts of Europe, Asia, and North America. Parts of the Southern Hemisphere were also under ice. Moving glaciers created many of the world's mountains, lakes, and rivers.

With so much of Earth's water frozen in the glaciers, rainfall decreased. Areas that had once been grasslands became deserts. Sea levels dropped, exposing "land bridges" where ocean waters had once been. Because of these changes, many animals had to migrate to find food. The people who depended on those animals had to follow the herds.

▲ Woolly mammoth skull

How Did Humans Stay Warm? As winters grew longer, people learned to use whatever materials they could find to build warm shelters. In Eastern Europe, for example, people built huts out of mammoth bones. Mammoths were huge furry animals, related to elephants, that lived during the Ice Age. Hunters covered these huts with animal skins and kept fires burning in their hearths day and night.

Why Did People Form Larger Communities? Some groups adapted to change by forming larger communities. In larger groups, hunters could work together to kill animals such as mammoths. They could also better defend their communities from attack by other nomadic groups.

Growing communities might be organized into groups of families with a common ancestor. A group would be made up of perhaps 25 to 50 people. Group leaders took on decision-making roles, such as organizing hunts. Everywhere human society developed, **networks** of groups or families played a vital role in creating strong communities.

In time, Stone Age communities began to trade with one another for special stones or shells. They likely also traded information about finding food during hard times.

Academic Vocabulary
network • *n.* a closely interconnected group of people or things

READING CHECK **Identify Supporting Details** What did humans do to survive in different environments?

Lesson Check

HSS 6.1.2, 6.2.9; ELD.PI.A.2, ELD.PI.C.10.a

Practice Vocabulary

1. What are some of the things that make up a person's **environment**?
2. What did humans do to **adapt** after moving to new environments?

Critical Thinking and Writing

3. **Compare and Contrast** How did Neanderthals and *Homo sapiens* differ from earlier people?
4. **Understand Effects** How did the development of language help humans survive harsh conditions and live in new places?
5. **Draw Conclusions** Why did early humans migrate?
6. **Understand Effects** How did forming larger communities help people survive?
7. **Writing Workshop: Establish Setting** In your Active Journal, explain how the hunter-gatherer in your story is adapting to a changing climate.

LESSON CHECK

1. climate, plants, and animals **DOK1**
2. They found out which plants they could eat and found new materials for tools and shelters. **DOK2**
3. They had larger brains and more developed social structures. **DOK2**
4. They were able to cooperate with each other and teach new skills to one another. **DOK2**
5. Climate change may have forced people to move in search of food or certain areas may have become over-populated. Perhaps people also migrated because they were curious about new places. **DOK3**
6. Larger communities could hunt larger animals and more easily protect themselves from attack. **DOK3**
7. Students should write about the materials that hunter-gatherers used to stay warm and build shelters.

HSS 6.1.2, 6.2.9; ELD.PI.A.2, ELD.PI.C.10.a

SYNTHESIZE

Assess and Reteach Have students work with a partner and quiz each other with Lesson Check questions 1–6. Review their responses. If they had any incorrect answers, use the Guiding Questions to discuss the lesson's main ideas, focusing on the ideas they struggled with.

ACTIVE JOURNAL

Writing Workshop Have students complete the Lesson 2 Writing Task in their Active Journals. Students should add to their portrait of a hunter-gatherer by explaining how their character would adapt to a changing environment. As they move through the topic, students will revisit their statements, revising as needed.

DEMONSTRATE

ASSESSMENT **ONLINE LESSON QUIZ**

Assign the Online Lesson Quiz for this lesson if you haven't already done so. Students will be offered automatic remediation or enrichment based on their score.

DISCUSSION **DISCUSSION BOARD**

Post this question to the class on the Discussion Board:

Analyze What are some of the environmental reasons a group of people might migrate to a new area? *(Sample answer: The land on which they live no longer provides enough food for the population. There are severe weather and climate problems such as drought or flooding. They want to escape overcrowding or disease.)*

ANSWERS

Identify Supporting Details *They learned to hunt different animals and to find new materials for tools and shelters.*

Analysis CST.1

Analysis Skills
Relate Events in Time

LEARN
Preview the steps in the student text with students, and then play the video.

VIDEO **21ST CENTURY SKILLS**

Project the Sequence video in the 21st Century Skills Tutorial. Use the Quick Reference and Assessment to provide additional instruction in this skill.

PRACTICE
Have students practice the skill of relating events in time using the secondary source text and the timeline. Follow the steps on the student page, providing instruction and then asking students the questions.

As an alternative, have students work in pairs or small groups to respond to the questions and activities in steps 1–3 of the text. Then invite the groups to share their findings with the class. Discuss sequencing strategies that students use.

ASSESS
To assess this skill, have students identify sequence and relate events in time from another passage in the text or that you find online.

ANSWERS
1. The timeline covers the period that stretches from 13,000 years ago to 9,000 years ago.
2. During, over time, as time passed, when, still
3. Possible answers: when, later. When the Ice Age ended, the mastodon became extinct. About a thousand years later, the ground sloth became extinct.

Relate Events in Time

Use the sources and these steps to relate events in time.

INTERACTIVE Sequence

1 **Identify key events and topics.** Set a purpose for your research by listing the time period, people, or events you are focusing on. For example, the excerpt from the text covers a time period that stretches from two million years ago to 70,000 years ago. What period does the timeline cover?

2 **Look for clues about time.** Important clues include information about dates and times of key events. For example, the excerpt uses the phrase "over time," which suggests that a long period of time is going to be discussed. What other words or phrases indicate that events are happening in sequence?

3 **Look for clues about relationships.** Besides dates and times, a variety of words can signal how key events are related in time. Examples include words such as *before, after, during,* or *while.* The excerpt says many creatures that lived *during* the last Ice Age have gone extinct.

a. What are two other words that suggest how events are related in time?

b. Use those words to summarize the information in the timeline.

Secondary Source

Many of the creatures who roamed the planet during the Ice Age have become extinct. Large mammals, such as mastodons, ground sloths, and sabercats, died off and disappeared from the earth. Some animals, however, managed to adapt over time. For example, the first jaguars hunted and ate very large prey. As time passed and the number of large prey animals dwindled, jaguars began to eat smaller animals. Making this change enabled jaguars to survive as a species when the large prey animals they had once depended on went extinct. As a result, jaguars are still found in the wild today.

Ice Age Events in Years Ago

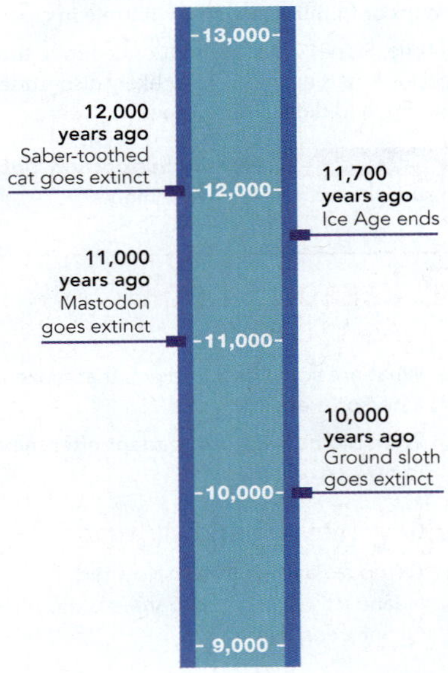

DIFFERENTIATED INSTRUCTION
Below Level Before practicing the skill, call on students to define sequence. *(Sequence refers to "the order in which events happen.")*

INTEGRATED ENGLISH LANGUAGE DEVELOPMENT
Expanding Have students work with a partner to write short sentences about the ways the jaguar adapted over time. Provide students with guidance as needed. Then have students discuss why some large mammals did not survive the Ice Age.

HSS 6.1.3

Developing Complex Cultures

BOUNCE TO ACTIVATE

VIDEO

GET READY TO READ

START UP

This image shows a reproduction of a cave painting from about 20,000 years ago. Why are people today interested in these ancient paintings?

GUIDING QUESTIONS

- What evidence reveals how human societies became more complex?
- How did humans learn to modify their environment?
- Why did some people develop agriculture while others lived as herders?

TAKE NOTES

Literacy Skills: Sequence

Use the graphic organizer in your Active Journal to take notes as you read the lesson.

PRACTICE VOCABULARY

Use the vocabulary activity in your Active Journal to practice the vocabulary words.

Vocabulary	Academic Vocabulary
populate	potential
animism	reliable
domesticate	
revolution	
nomad	

Over millions of years, many groups of early humans appeared and then died out. *Homo sapiens*, or modern humans, were the last of these groups to appear. As you will read, scientists still have much to learn about the development of the first modern humans. But one fact is clear: These large-brained "wise people" were often on the move. Over many thousands of years, they spread out to **populate**, or become inhabitants of, almost every land area of the world.

When Did People Start to Create Art?

Over the course of the Ice Age, the culture of Paleolithic communities became more and more complex. One of the most important signs of a complex culture is the existence of artwork such as paintings and statues.

What Can We Learn from Ancient Cave Paintings? In 1940, four French teenagers and their dog made a remarkable discovery. The boys were exploring a cave near Lascaux in southern France. By the dim light of their lamps, they were amazed

PRACTICE VOCABULARY

Help students integrate new vocabulary by explaining connections among words and key ideas in the lesson. For example, explain that early people believed in *animism*, the idea that the world around them was filled with spirits. Explain that when early people learned to *domesticate* plants and animals, they had much more food. The shift from hunting for food to farming created a *revolution*, a complete change in living for early people.

Point out the academic vocabulary in the margin. Provide sample sentences that clarify meaning.

potential: No one doubts that she has the potential to be a great leader.

reliable: The family was looking to hire a reliable dog walker.

HSS 6.1.3

Developing Complex Cultures

CONNECT

GET READY TO READ

ETEXT **START UP**

Project the Start Up Activity. As students enter the classroom and get settled, ask them to examine the photograph, which shows a man examining a cave painting.

Draw Conclusions Have students first describe what they see in the cave painting and then draw conclusions about the painter's purpose. Ask: What do you see in the cave painting? *(An animal with four legs, likely a horse.)* What do you think the painter was trying to communicate? *(Possible response: The painter was trying to show a herd of wild horses that roamed nearby.)*

Discuss Point out that ancient peoples gradually learned a skill so important that it revolutionized how people lived. Ask students if they can guess what that skill might be. *(farming)*

After completing the Start Up Activity, project the Lesson Opener or direct students to their textbooks. Preview the lesson by working through the Get Ready to Read items with the class. Remind students to pay close attention to the Guiding Questions as they read the lesson.

ACTIVE JOURNAL

Take Notes Have students focus on Sequence as they use the lesson literacy skills graphic organizer in their Active Journals to take notes as they read the lesson.

Practice Vocabulary Have students complete the activity in their Active Journals to build their vocabulary.

VIDEO **VIDEO**

Assign the lesson video as homework.

WORKSHEET **TEACHER RESOURCES**

Have students who need additional support use the following worksheets from the Teacher Resources on the course:

- **Reading Support**
- **English Language Development**
- **Lesson Summary**

INVESTIGATE

When Did People Start to Create Art?

Discuss the idea of a culture becoming more complex over long periods of time. Ask students to speculate about ways that human culture might have changed during the last Ice Age.

Identify Details What did French teenagers discover in a cave near Lascaux? *(They found paintings on the walls of the cave.)*

Draw Conclusions What do cave and rock paintings tell us about life in the Ice Age? *(Sample answer: They tell us that Ice Age humans made art. This means they had the time, motivation, and skills to make art.)*

Make Connections In what way is Ice Age art similar to art today? *(Sample answer: Both are products of human imagination and skill.)*

Analyze Primary Sources How does the author feel after returning to the surface after viewing some cave paintings? *(He feels in awe of the people who created the paintings and their will to create art.)*

ELD TIP Academic vocabulary is particularly challenging for English learners. Do a close read of the Primary Source quote about the mark of human genius, explaining any vocabulary they are not familiar with.

ANSWERS

Draw Conclusions *Early artists had the skill to depict recognizable animals and convey a sense that the animals are in motion.*

Analyze Images This Neolithic cave painting of animals was found in Laas Geel, Somalia. **Draw Conclusions** What can you conclude about the skill of early artists from this painting?

to see that the walls were covered with paintings of horses, bison, bulls, and other prehistoric animals. Other paintings in the cave showed human figures or abstract designs.

Scientists later determined that the Lascaux cave paintings dated back about 16,000 years, to the time of the last Ice Age. Some images were carved into the stone, but most were painted. The artists made pigments by grinding up minerals of various colors.

Even older cave paintings have been found elsewhere in France, as well as in Spain. Examples of cave and rock art have also been discovered in many other parts of the world where early people lived. For example, the rock paintings shown at the beginning of this chapter are from the Sahara, a vast desert in North Africa.

Stone Age artists also carved small statues. Like the cave paintings, many of these carvings represent animals. Others depict pregnant women.

What Does Stone Age Art Tell Us? Early works of art such as these show that Stone Age people were capable of complex thoughts and actions. After visiting one French cave, an archaeologist commented,

Academic Vocabulary
potential • *n.*, possibility to grow and change in the future

Primary Source

The mark of human genius is here, full-blown, with its immense and eternal mystery, and with all its potential for hope in the success of the adventure of modern man. We become modest in these surroundings; a great feeling of timelessness [comes] from them. When we return to the surface, we can't help but question the motivations that lie behind the creation of all those frescoes. To imagine the unimaginable. In any case, in contemplating them we feel the presence ... of an intense, enormous will to create.

—Robert Begouën, *The Cave of Chauvet-Pont-d'Arc*

CURRICULUM CONNECTION: ART

Cave Paintings at Altamira One of the earliest discoveries of cave art was in 1879 at Altamira, Spain. Today, we know that these paintings were made 25,000 to 35,000 years ago. At the time of their discovery, however, many archaeologists believed that the paintings were fake—a hoax created by a modern artist. Some said the art was too good and could not have been made by humans in the Paleolithic Era. Others said that humans of that era lacked the abstract thinking to draw images of people or animals. It was only when other cave art was discovered in the 1890s that the cave paintings at Altamira were accepted as authentic.

We do not know the exact reasons Stone Age people created these works of art. Perhaps hunter-gatherers believed that creating an image of an animal would give them power over that animal during the hunt. Statues of pregnant women may have been intended to bring good luck to women about to give birth.

INTERACTIVE

Paleolithic Cave Art

READING CHECK **Draw Inferences** What subjects did Stone Age people show in their art? Why might Stone Age artists have chosen to show animals, human figures, and abstract designs?

What Do We Know About Stone Age Religion?

Quick Activity

Explore ancient cave paintings in your Active Journal.

Cave paintings and other art provide strong evidence that the cultures of Stone Age people became more complex over time. Another sign of a more complex culture is the development of religious beliefs and practices. Many of these practices involve death and burial.

How Did Early People Bury Their Dead? Scientists have found much evidence to show that Ice Age people buried their dead. One grave found in present-day Russia contained the bodies of two children, a boy about 13 years old and a girl about 8 years old. Both children were covered with thousands of ivory beads. On his chest, the boy wore an ivory pendant carved in the shape of an animal. The girl wore a bead cap and an ivory pin at her throat.

What Were Some Early Religious Practices? Discoveries such as cave paintings, statues, and burial sites may suggest how early humans reacted to what they thought were mysterious and powerful forces. These rituals and symbols were an important part of early culture. They go beyond survival, and express deeper meanings of the natural and social world.

The evidence suggests that these early people believed that the natural world was filled with spirits, a belief known as **animism**. To early humans, there were spirits in the animals they hunted. There were also spirits in the trees, rocks, water, and weather around them. Prehistoric people may have painted pictures of animals, such as bison or deer, to honor the spirits of those animals and to ask forgiveness for having to kill them.

READING CHECK **Identify Implied Main Ideas** What did the development of religious practices suggest about the relationship early humans had with the natural and social world?

Analyze Images This child was carefully buried with jewelry made of bones and precious stones. **Infer** What does this burial suggest about the culture of the people who buried him?

What Do We Know About Stone Age Religion?

Discuss how religion played a role in the lives of prehistoric people.

Identify Details What burial practices did Ice Age people perform? *(They buried people with valuable objects such as ivory beads and jewelry.)*

Identify Main Ideas What do prehistoric burial sites suggest about human culture of that era? *(They suggest that humans had ideas about birth and death, which indicate the beginnings of religion.)*

Summarize In what important ways did human culture change during the Paleolithic Era? *(Sample answer: It spread to many parts of the world and adapted to many environments. Language and the use of tools developed. Abstract ideas such as art and religion appeared.)*

INTERACTIVE **INTERACTIVE GALLERY**

Paleolithic Cave Art

Display the Interactive Gallery: Paleolithic Cave Art for the class. Ask: What do you think Paleolithic people were trying to communicate with this art?

DIFFERENTIATED INSTRUCTION

Advanced With a partner, have students research examples of Neolithic art. Individually, have students write out a brief interpretation of each piece of art they found. Then have students compare their interpretations with their partners.

Below Level Show students several examples of contemporary visual communication, such as abstract paintings, computer-generated graphics, photographs, or advertisements. Discuss what the creators of these graphics were trying to communicate. Then discuss the motivations of ancient people for creating art.

Special Education Provide an oral description of the images presented to the class for students with visual impairments. Then have students share their own interpretations of the meaning behind the visuals.

ANSWERS

Infer *It suggests that people valued life and perhaps that they believed in an afterlife.*

Draw Inferences *They depicted the things around them but were also interested in making interesting and beautiful things.*

Identify Implied Main Ideas *It suggested that humans had developed a deeper connection with the natural and social world, and that they were interested in more than just survival.*

ACTIVE CLASSROOM

After viewing the Paleolithic Cave Art Interactive, use a Quickdraw strategy. Have students create a drawing in 30 seconds that communicates something about the lives of Paleolithic people. Then have students compare drawings with a partner.

ACTIVE JOURNAL

Quick Activity Remind students to pay attention to details in the cave paintings such as color, content, and relationship between items.

When Did People Start to Farm?

Discuss how changes in climate affected the ways people acquired food.

Identify Main Ideas What was the biggest change of the Neolithic Era? *(People learned to farm.)*

Draw Conclusions Why do you think this change was so important? *(Sample answer: With farming, people could stop moving all the time in search of animals and plants. They could form permanent communities.)*

Identify Cause and Effect How did Earth's climate, land, and water change at the end of the last Ice Age? *(Temperatures increased and rainfall patterns changed. Glaciers began to shrink, causing ocean levels to rise. Plants and animals adapted to these changes or died out.)*

ACTIVE JOURNAL

Quest Connection Direct students to the Quest Connections page in their Active Journal. Students should consider how the things shown in the photo, such as the stones and the water, could be useful to people living there.

When Did People Start to Farm?

By the end of the Paleolithic Era, human beings occupied many regions of the world. They had developed complex spoken language, learned to make a variety of tools and weapons, and adapted to different environments. Yet, in many important ways, their lives had not changed. They still lived in relatively small groups as hunter-gatherers, following the herds of animals that they depended on for survival.

Then, beginning as much as 18,000 years ago, humans gradually began to learn a new skill that over time changed how they would live. By around 10,000-9,000 years ago, some communities were relying on farming for food. This development marked the end of the Paleolithic Era and the beginning of what we call the Neolithic Era, or New Stone Age. (The prefix neo- means "new".) Around this time, temperatures increased and rainfall patterns changed. Glaciers that had covered so much of Earth began to shrink. As the ice from the glaciers melted, ocean levels rose.

Most plants and animals adapted to these changes. Fir trees, which could survive cold weather, spread north into once-icy regions.

Some large Ice Age animals, however, did not adapt to a warmer world, and many species died out. People who had hunted some of these animals for food had to find something else to eat. Some people adapted to these changes by searching for new sources of food. They found smaller animals to hunt. People living near rivers or lakes began to depend more on fishing.

Quest CONNECTIONS

Study the photo. What does it suggest about what makes a good location for a village? Record your answer in your Active Journal.

▲ Céide Fields, Ireland, is the site of a Neolithic settlement. It is about six and a half thousand years old and one of the oldest known system of fields used for farming in the world.

INTEGRATED ENGLISH LANGUAGE DEVELOPMENT

Collaborative Explain that some basic phrases can be used to support your opinions and persuade others. Demonstrate ways to "gain and hold the floor" in a conversation, ask for clarification, and make a point. Prompt students to practice these techniques.

Emerging Briefly summarize information presented in the text about how domesticated plants and animals changed people's lives. Ask students to talk to each other about their opinions about the topic. Remind them to use phrases like "May I speak?" to enter the conversation and "Would you repeat that?" if they did not understand another student.

Expanding Ask: What was more important to humanity, domesticating plants or animals? Have pairs of students practice discussing this, using sets of learned phrases such as

How Did People First Modify the Environment? Others learned to modify or change their environment so that it would provide more food. For example, people cleared trees and bushes by setting them on fire. The grasses that grew back attracted grazing animals such as deer. People may also have noticed that, if seeds were scattered on the ground, new plants grew there the next year. This discovery led them to find ways to encourage the growth of wild food plants.

How Did Domesticated Plants and Animals Change People's Lives? Over time, people learned to domesticate plants and animals, especially those that they used for food. To **domesticate** means to change the growth of plants or behavior of animals in ways that are useful for humans. Widespread domestication marked the birth of farming. The shift from hunting to farming was so important that historians call it the Neolithic Agricultural Revolution. A **revolution** is a complete change in ways of thinking, working, or living.

Even before the Agricultural Revolution, wild wolves developed into dogs, which humans then domesticated. Dogs provided help in the hunt, as well as companionship and protection.

Domesticated plants, or crops, became a **reliable** source of food. Grains such as wheat, rice, or maize became chief food sources for entire societies. Many animals also provided food—not only meat, but eggs, milk, and even honey. Horses and oxen became work animals. Sheep and llamas had coats of hair that were used to make clothing.

Domesticated animals, such as horses, sheep, and cattle, were easier to control. People who lived in places where growing food was difficult traveled to different places with their animals. By moving to new areas, the animals would find new grasslands to eat from. The people herding, or guiding, the animals would use them for food and clothing. This way of life was called pastoral nomadism. **Nomads** are people who move from place to place with their herds.

Analyze Images
Ancient people learned to domesticate wolves 20,000 to 15,000 years ago. **Compare** How does the wolf on the left differ from the herding dog on the right?

Academic Vocabulary
reliable • *adj.*, dependable, steady, not risky

Identify Details What were two things that early people did to modify their environment? *(People cleared the land of vegetation and discovered ways to plant seeds for food.)*

Analyze What important scientific observation did Neolithic people make about their environment? *(People observed that plants grew near where seeds had fallen earlier.)*

Identify Cause and Effect How did **domesticating** plants and animals change the food supply for humans? *(It increased the food supply significantly and made it more reliable.)*

Compare and Contrast What were some differences between wild and **domesticated** plants and animals? *(Sample answer: Domesticated plants produce more food than wild plants and may produce bigger or better fruits, grains, and vegetables. Domesticated animals are often smaller than wild animals of the same type and, therefore, are easier to tend.)*

Identify Details What new tools helped farmers to clear land and harvest grains? *(the axe and the sickle)*

Draw Conclusions Why do historians label eras of history according to the names of materials found in nature? *(The names of eras reflect the materials humans used in that time period to make tools.)*

ELD.PII.A.3

"I agree with that but…" to persuade each other of their points of view.

Bridging Ask pairs of students to discuss whether they think domesticating plants or animals was more important to humanity. Have them model indirect reported speech, i.e., "I heard an expert say that…".

WORKSHEET **TEACHER RESOURCES**

For additional IELD support addressing the standard, have students complete the Lesson ELD activity from the Teacher Resources found on the course.

ANSWERS

Compare *The wolf is a wild animal; the herding dog is a domestic animal that has been trained to work for people.*

HSS 6.1.3; ELD.PI.A.2, ELD.PI.C.10.a

SYNTHESIZE

Assess and Reteach Have students use a Think-Pair-Share strategy to complete Lesson Check questions 1–6. Review their responses. If they had any incorrect answers, use the Guiding Questions to discuss the lesson's main ideas, focusing on the ideas they struggled with.

ACTIVE JOURNAL

Writing Workshop Have students complete the Lesson 3 Writing Task in their Active Journals. Students should focus on the different activities of early humans who were involved with **domesticated** plants and animals and those who were herders. As they move through the topic, students will revisit their statements, revising as needed.

DEMONSTRATE

ASSESSMENT **ONLINE LESSON QUIZ**

Assign the Online Lesson Quiz for this lesson if you haven't already done so. Students will be offered automatic remediation or enrichment based on their score.

DISCUSSION **DISCUSSION BOARD**

Post this question to the class on the Discussion Board:

Analyze What are two ways that the **domestication** of dogs might have helped Neolithic people survive? *(Sample response: Dogs could help people as they hunted other animals. Dogs could alert people to approaching animals or human enemies and fight them off. Dogs could be used to herd other domesticated animals such as sheep.)*

ANSWERS

Analyze Cause and Effect *Once early farmers understood that they could cultivate plants, they needed tools to help them grow more and healthier plants. As they learned more about how to farm, they would have created better and more kinds of tools.*

▲ These Neolithic stone farm tools are about 10,000 years old. On the left is a hoe. On the right is a plow blade.

At first, there was little difference between wild and domesticated breeds. But over time, people selected the seeds of the plants that produced the best crops to sow again. As a result, domesticated plants began to produce more abundant food that tasted better, were larger, and easier to cook. A wild tomato, for example, is the size of a cherry, but a domesticated tomato is the size of an orange. By contrast, some breeds of domesticated goats, pigs, and cattle are smaller than their wild ancestors. Smaller animals may have been easier to manage.

What New Tools Did People Make? Farmers invented new tools. They used axes to cut down trees for farmland and sickles to harvest grain. The grain was then ground into flour with grinding stones or hand mills.

All of these tools were at first made out of stone. Later people mined for bronze and iron and learned how to smelt, or use heat, to remove metals from a mineral. They used these metals to create more efficient tools. That is why historians refer to different stages of early history as the Stone Age, the Bronze Age, and the Iron Age.

READING CHECK **Analyze Cause and Effect** Why might learning to farm have led early farmers to create new tools?

Lesson Check

HSS 6.1.3; ELD.PI.A.2, ELD.PI.C.10.a

Practice Vocabulary

1. What is a belief in **animism**?
2. Why do historians say the ability to **domesticate** plants and animals was a **revolution**?

Critical Thinking and Writing

3. **Understand Effects** What are two signs that people who lived during the Ice Age developed more complex cultures?
4. **Draw Inferences** What skills and tools would be needed to make cave paintings? What does this suggest about the people who created them?
5. **Identify Supporting Details** What did animals do to improve life for humans?
6. **Identify Cause and Effect** Why did some people choose pastoral nomadism as a way of life?
7. **Writing Workshop: Introduce Characters** You're now visiting the Neolithic Era. Write one or two sentences in your Active Journal about an early man or woman who worked with domesticated plants and animals. Write another sentence or two about a herder (pastoral nomad).

LESSON CHECK

1. Animism is the belief that the natural world is filled with spirits. **DOK1**
2. It led to a complete change in the way many humans lived. **DOK1**
3. They created works of art and developed religion. **DOK2**
4. tools to grind and mix minerals for paint colors, to apply the paint, and to see in dark caves; They must have been skilled to use the materials at hand. **DOK3**
5. Animals provided food, clothing, and companionship and could be trained to herd. **DOK3**
6. They lived in places where growing food was difficult. **DOK2**
7. Students should write about the farmer's use of domesticated plants and animals and the pastoral nomad's way of life. **DOK4**

New Ways of Life

GET READY TO READ

START UP

What are these ancient Egyptians doing? What does this activity suggest about their way of life?

GUIDING QUESTIONS

- How did farming enable people to settle in one place and develop specialized skills?
- How did farming villages develop into cities?
- What were the effects of these new ways of life?

TAKE NOTES

Literacy Skills: Analyze Cause and Effect
Use the graphic organizer in your Active Journal to take notes as you read the lesson.

PRACTICE VOCABULARY

Use the vocabulary activity in your Active Journal to take practice the vocabulary.

Vocabulary	Academic Vocabulary
surplus	benefit
specialization	accumulate
economy	

People of the Paleolithic Era, or Old Stone Age, lived as hunter-gatherers. They could not have imagined many of the things that we now take for granted. People often had to follow herds of animals, so they were unable to settle for long in one place. People could own few possessions—only what they could easily carry. Food supplies were uncertain. Life for many was short and dangerous.

In time, most hunter-gatherers stopped wandering in search of food and settled in one place. Life was still difficult, and survival was still the main concern. But with people staying in one place, the world began to take on many features we recognize today.

Where Did Farming Begin and How Did It Spread?

No one knows for sure where people first began to plant seeds for food. Still, archaeologists have found evidence to suggest where farming began and how it spread. They have also learned something about the way people lived in early farming communities.

PRACTICE VOCABULARY

Help students integrate new vocabulary by explaining connections among words and key ideas in the lesson. For example, say that over time farming and herding methods improved and early farmers began to grow a *surplus* of food—more food than each family needed. *Surplus* food made it possible for people to engage in *specialization*, as they performed tasks other than farming. *Surplus* food and *specialization* help to grow an *economy*, or system used to produce and distribute goods and services.

Point out the academic vocabulary in the margin. Provide sample sentences that clarify meaning.

benefits: There are many benefits to eating good food and exercising.

accumulate: The family accumulated wealth through their investments.

HSS 6.1.3, 6.2.2

New Ways of Life

CONNECT

GET READY TO READ

ETEXT START UP

Project the Start Up Activity. As students enter the classroom and get seated, ask them to examine the drawing, which shows ancient people working in grain fields.

Compare and Contrast In small groups, have students discuss how life for ancient people was different before and after farming. Ask: How do you think the lives of these farmers would have been different if they were hunter-gatherers? *(Sample response: They would have likely been nomadic as hunter-gatherers. They probably live near their crops in a permanent settlement.)* What do you think led to the beginning of farming? *(Sample response: People might have observed that seeds fall from plants and grow into new plants.)*

Discuss Remind students that agriculture is one of the distinguishing features of human development. Farming techniques generated a stable food supply, which allowed people more time to pursue other activities.

After completing the Start Up Activity, project the Lesson Opener or direct students to their textbooks. Preview the lesson by working through the Get Ready to Read items with the class. Remind students to pay close attention to the Guiding Questions as they read the lesson.

ACTIVE JOURNAL

Take Notes Have students focus on Cause and Effect as they use the lesson literacy skills graphic organizer in their Active Journals to take notes as they read the lesson.

Practice Vocabulary Have students complete the activity in their Active Journals to build their vocabulary.

VIDEO VIDEO

Assign the lesson video as homework.

WORKSHEET **TEACHER RESOURCES**

Have students who need additional support use the following worksheets from the Teacher Resources on the course:

- **Reading Support**
- **English Language Development**
- **Lesson Summary**

INVESTIGATE

Where Did Farming Begin and How Did It Spread?

Discuss the importance of farming to modern life. Ask students to speculate about ways that life might be different if each person had to grow his or her own food.

Identify Main Ideas Where do historians think agriculture began? *(southwestern Asia)*

Identify Evidence What evidence do historians use to support their belief in the origins of agriculture? *(Sample answer: Domesticated and wild wheat seed found in the area are similar. This means that the domesticated types came naturally from that area.)*

ELD TIP Have English learners look at the graphic about the history of domestication to practice understanding the concepts of "before" and "after." Ask questions such as "Were horses domesticated before or after goats were?", etc.

Identify Main Ideas What are the main costs and benefits of farming? *(Costs include the time and energy needed for planting or herding, the uncertainty of success due to weather or disease, and the danger of attack. Benefits include food surpluses, smaller land needs, and the chance to build permanent homes.)*

ANSWERS

Sequence *Assuming dogs were domesticated 20,000 years ago, it took about another 15,000 years.*

Academic Vocabulary
benefit • *n.*, gain; favorable result

Where Were the First Centers of Agriculture? Most historians believe that about 10,000 years ago southwestern Asia became the first center of agriculture. There, scientists have unearthed seeds from domesticated wheat plants that were buried long ago. The seeds are similar to wild varieties of wheat that still grow in the area.

Farming may then have spread from southwestern Asia westward into Africa. It may also have spread northward into Europe and eastward into the Indus River valley of South Asia.

Other centers of agriculture appeared independently in different areas of the world. In southwestern Asia, for example, farming began when people started to plant wheat and barley. In the southern part of present-day China, farming began with the domestication of rice. Farther to the north, a grain called millet was the first crop to be domesticated.

In Central and South America, people learned to grow potatoes, beans, and squash. In Africa, farming began with crops such as sorghum and yams.

What Were the Costs and Benefits of Farming? In every place that agriculture developed, the transition from hunting and gathering to farming took place gradually, over a long period of time. Each way of life had costs as well as **benefits**.

Some of the costs of shifting to agriculture were clear. First, planting crops and herding, or bringing together, animals took a great deal of time and energy. Second, farming was uncertain. If a year's crop failed due to bad weather or disease, a family might starve. Third, farming could be dangerous. Evidence suggests that bands of nomads sometimes attacked farmers and stole their food.

Analyze Diagrams Domestication started with dogs. Other animals and fruits, vegetables, and grains followed. **Sequence** How many years did it take before horses and cats were domesticated?

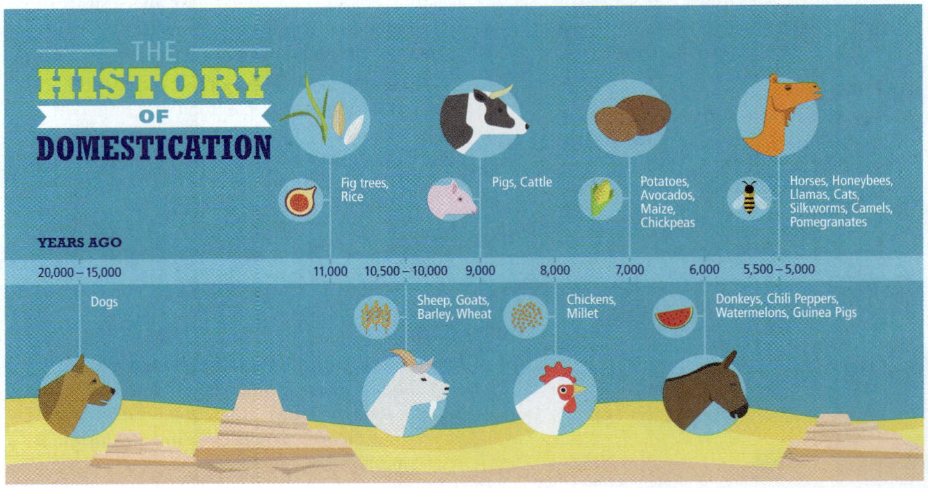

CURRICULUM CONNECTIONS: SCIENCE

Plant Domestication To draw a connection with what students are learning in their science classrooms, explain that the earliest examples of plant domestication came from southwest Asia near present-day Syria about 12,000 years ago. Scientists have identified grains of rye from the period that have the same genetic make-up as present-day rye seeds. Other cereal grains such as wheat, barley, oats, and millet were commonly domesticated in Mesopotamia at the time, and seeds quickly spread over the next 2,000 years throughout the Middle East, Europe, and Asia, as well as in North and South America.

GEOGRAPHY SKILLS

Agriculture most likely originated in many regions.

1. **Interaction** What were some early crops grown in South America? In West Africa?
2. **Region** Identify a crop that was grown in more than one part of the world.

Agriculture also offered many benefits. Farming produced more food and required less land than hunting and gathering. An early farm family might need only six to seven acres of land to raise enough wheat or maize to feed themselves for a year. In contrast, a hunter-gatherer family needed about 20,000 acres on which to find enough food for a year.

As a result of agriculture, more people were able to build permanent homes and farming villages. Farming also provided new sources of material for clothing. (Later in this section, you will read more about the new types of shelter and clothing that were invented during the Neolithic Era.)

Some groups tried farming for a time and then returned to hunting and gathering. But in the end, most people chose to remain farmers.

READING CHECK **Summarize** Where did farming begin and how did it spread?

How Did Farming Change Human Culture?

The first effect of farming was on people's food supply. But over time, the Neolithic Agricultural Revolution transformed every part of human culture.

What New Kinds of Shelter Did People Build? Farmers found ways to build permanent shelters. People used a mixture of mud and straw to form walls. The sun baked and hardened the mixture. People made roofs by placing poles and branches across the tops of walls and covering them with mud.

INTERACTIVE

Otzi the Neolithic Ice Man

DIFFERENTIATED INSTRUCTION

Advanced Have students research the history of farming in the United States and how the business of agriculture has evolved over the centuries. Have students create a timeline to display their findings.

Below Level Ask students to consider a pet they have or that they have encountered at a friend or family member's house. Have students write a brief paragraph describing the pet and how it benefits its owners. Keeping contemporary pets in mind, ask students to write several more sentences about how ancient people may have benefited from domesticating animals.

Special Education Remind students that some people with special physical or emotional needs use a support animal for help, such as a seeing eye dog for the blind. Ask students to share ways that domesticated animals help people with special needs today.

How Did Farming Change Human Culture?

Discuss how farming affected early societies.

Identify Cause and Effect How did farming change peoples' shelters? (*Sample answer: People needed permanent homes and experimented with materials to build stable structures.*)

INTERACTIVE **INTERACTIVE GALLERY**

Otzi the Neolithic Ice Man

Display the Interactive Gallery: Otzi the Neolithic Ice Man. Ask: Why did artists make Otzi look older in his reproduction? (*He likely looked older than his age due to harsh living conditions.*) What can you infer about what Otzi was doing before he died? (*Otzi was likely fighting or fleeing from attack due to this arrow wound and the blow to his head.*)

ACTIVE CLASSROOM

After viewing the Interactive Gallery: Otzi the Neolithic Ice Man, use a Conversation with Otzi strategy. Have students write down two or three questions that they would like to ask Otzi if they were able to speak with him. Invite volunteers to share their questions with the class.

ANSWERS

Interaction (*South America: squash, beans, cotton; West Africa: millet, rice*)

Region (*millet, wheat, cotton, or rice*)

Summarize *Farming began in southwestern Asia and spread outward from that region. It also arose independently in other parts of the world.*

Lesson 1.4 • New Ways of Life 29

Identify Details How were houses in Çatalhöyük built? How did people enter them? *(Sample answer: The walls were made of mud and straw, and roofs were made of wood and reeds plastered with mud. Houses were close together and entered through the roofs.)*

Draw Conclusions Why do you think the interior walls of houses in Çatalhöyük were filled with art such as mural paintings, reliefs, and sculptures? *(Sample answer: Art was an important impulse among early people and probably reflected their social and religious beliefs.)*

Identify Main Ideas What was the biggest change that farming caused in the way Neolithic people dressed? *(Hunter-gatherers made their clothing from animal skins and fur. With farming, cotton, flax, and other fibers were used to weave cloth that could be easily sewn.)*

Identify Cause and Effect What effect did surplus food have on Neolithic communities? *(Surplus food supported an increase in population and resulted in larger farming villages.)*

Identify Details What are some examples of new **specialization** in the Neolithic Era? *(Toolmakers turned stone into tools, such as axes and knives; potters made clay bowls; weavers made cloth.)*

ACTIVE JOURNAL

Quick Activity Divide students into pairs to discuss one of the inventions listed in the activity and its effects.

ACTIVE JOURNAL

Quest Connection Tell students to think about how life and daily activities could influence the design of their village based on the quotation.

Quick Activity

Explore ancient innovations, including farming, in your Active Journal.

Quest CONNECTIONS

Based on the primary source, what was life like in a Neolithic village? Record your findings in your Active Journal.

One of the oldest known farming settlements in the world is a village called Çatalhöyük (chah tahl hyoo yook). It stood in present-day Turkey more than 8,000 years ago.

At its height, up to six thousand people may have lived in Çatalhöyük. The environment provided sources of water and building materials. A British archaeologist described the two-story homes that made up the settlement:

Primary Source

> The houses of Çatalhöyük were so tightly packed together that there were few or no streets. Access to interior spaces was across roofs—which had been made of wood and reeds plastered with mud—and down stairs. People buried their dead beneath the floors. Above all, the interiors were rich with artwork—mural paintings, reliefs, and sculptures, including images of women that some interpreted as evidence for a cult of a mother goddess.
>
> —Ian Hodder, "This Old House"

Each home had its own kitchen and food storage area. The people grew grains and raised flocks of sheep and goats.

▲ Spinning yarn from wool the way it would have been done in ancient times

How Did Farming Change Clothing? Agriculture also changed the way that people dressed. For hunter-gatherers, the most important materials for clothing were animal hides and furs. Farming provided new materials that were lighter and easier to work with. From Egypt and India to the Americas, farmers domesticated the cotton plant. They learned to weave cloth from the plant fibers. Another plant, flax, became a source of linen.

Domesticated animals such as sheep and yaks also provided clothing materials. People used wool and other animal hair to form yarn or thread. In China, people later learned to breed silkworms.

What Were the Effects of Food Surpluses? As crops and herds improved, the amount of food that farmers could produce each year increased. Some families were able to raise a **surplus**, or more than they needed to feed themselves. Surplus food could support a growing population. The size of farming villages thus increased.

INTEGRATED ENGLISH LANGUAGE DEVELOPMENT

Collaborative Explain that we use language differently for different purposes, such as explaining something, persuading someone to agree with us, or entertaining them. Have students think about the different ways they would speak or say things to a friend, to a parent, or to their teacher. Engage the class in a discussion about different techniques they use when speaking at school or at home.

Emerging Read the section "Where Did Farming Begin and How Did It Spread?" aloud. Ask students to make a statement about something they learned from the text in the way they would express it to a teacher or principal. Then ask them to express the same idea the way they would to a younger sibling at home.

Expanding Have students work together in pairs. Have one student take an idea from the text and try to

When there was a surplus of food, not everyone in a village needed to farm. Some people could specialize. **Specialization** occurs when people spend most of their time working at a single job or craft. They could then trade the goods they made for the surplus food grown by farmers. Skilled toolmakers turned stone into polished axes and knives. Potters shaped clay into bowls. Weavers wove sheep's wool into cloth. A few people also became skilled at metalworking. Early metalworkers heated ore to extract, or remove, such metals as copper and tin.

How Did Farming Change Social Organization?

Early farming communities remained small. Like hunting, farming required close cooperation among members of the community. Heads of families consulted to make important decisions. They might discuss when to plant and harvest crops, what to do with food surpluses, or how to protect the community from outside dangers.

Archaeologists have uncovered the remains of several Neolithic villages, such as Skara Brae in Scotland. In these villages, all homes were more or less the same size. Some historians believe this means that great differences in social standing did not yet exist.

Still, having a permanent place to live meant that people could own more possessions. Early farmers filled their homes with furniture, tools, clay pots, and other goods. These items would have been too heavy to move from one campsite to another. Over time, some families **accumulated** more food and possessions than others. Food surplus sometimes led to conflict, however, as some groups wanted to expand their supplies at the expense of others. Some people hired guards to protect their wealth.

As surpluses increased and people began to specialize, greater social differences emerged. As evidence of this inequality, scientists have unearthed graves with jewelry and other fine materials while other graves have none of these things.

READING CHECK **Identify Cause and Effect** How did farming lead to specialization?

Analyze Images This gold stag was crafted by an artist in Çatalhöyük. **Infer** What does it suggest about the skills of ancient craftspeople?

How Did the First Cities Begin?

The world's first cities began as farming villages in the Middle East. As the villages grew, they began to trade with one another. Trade, like farming, became an important source of wealth.

The City of Uruk Many historians consider Uruk to be the world's first city. It is thought to have been founded 6,000 to 7,000 years ago. Uruk was different from Çatalhöyük and older farming villages. One difference was Uruk's size. Çatalhöyük covered about 32 acres and was home to no more than 6,000 people. When Uruk was at its height, more than 40,000 people lived there. Uruk covered an area of nearly 1,000 acres and had houses, gardens, and large public buildings such as temples.

Academic Vocabulary
accumulate • *v.*, collect or attain a large amount of something

ELD.PII.A.4

persuade the other student of an opinion about it. Then have the other student tell an idea to the first student the way they would explain it if the other student did not understand that part of the text.

Bridging Have pairs of students work together. After reading the topic, have each student write two or three short paragraphs about how the spread of farming affected humans. Have students exchange papers with partners and read each other's work. Then have them give verbal feedback to each other.

WORKSHEET **TEACHER RESOURCES**

For additional IELD support addressing the standard, have students complete the Lesson ELD activity from the Teacher Resources found on the course.

Analyze How did government take shape in Neolithic villages? *(Heads of families began to consult with each other and make decisions for the benefit of the community.)*

Infer What do some scientists infer about the social structure of Neolithic villages from the evidence that all homes were the same size? *(This evidence indicates that great differences in social standing did not yet exist among Neolithic people.)*

Identify Details What types of useful objects did early farmers fill their homes with? *(furniture, tools, clay pots)*

Draw Conclusions How did permanent settlements lead to social differences in the Neolithic Era? *(As people began to live in permanent homes, they could begin to accumulate possessions. Over time, those who had more would eventually have higher social standing.)*

How Did the First Cities Begin?

Discuss the ways in which early cities were more complex than smaller settlements.

Identify Main Ideas According to historians, why is Uruk important? *(Many historians consider Uruk the world's first city.)*

Compare and Contrast How was Uruk different from Çatalhöyük? *(Uruk was bigger and more populous than Çatalhöyük. Uruk had a more elaborate government than Çatalhöyük.)*

Compare and Contrast How were the economies of Uruk and Çatalhöyük similar and different? *(Çatalhöyük had a simple economy based mainly on farming. Uruk had a complex economy that included farming as well as trade.)*

Identify Cause and Effect Why did new people move to Uruk? *(The city was wealthy and had jobs to offer. It was also the source of many goods that people wanted to buy.)*

Identify Details How did the city of Uruk protect itself from raiders? *(It built a high thick wall that stretched for six miles around the city.)*

ANSWERS

Infer *They were skilled at making complex, stylized, and beautiful objects.*

Identify Cause and Effect *Farming provided surplus food so that others could do specialized jobs.*

HSS 6.1.3, 6.2.2; ELD.PI.A.2, ELD.PI.C.10.a

ACTIVE JOURNAL

Quest Connection Remind students that they could use the photo of the Neolithic village as inspiration when they design their villages.

SYNTHESIZE

Assess and Reteach Have students work with a partner and quiz each other using Lesson Check questions 1–5. Review their responses. If they had any incorrect answers, use the Guiding Questions to discuss the lesson's main ideas, focusing on the ideas they struggled with.

ACTIVE JOURNAL

Writing Workshop Have students complete the Lesson 4 Writing Task in their Active Journals. Students should make a chronological list or sequence of events they plan to include in their narratives.

DEMONSTRATE

ASSESSMENT **ONLINE LESSON QUIZ**

Assign the Online Lesson Quiz for this lesson if you haven't already done so. Students will be offered automatic remediation or enrichment based on their score.

DISCUSSION **DISCUSSION BOARD**

Post this question to the class on the Discussion Board:

Analyze Which characteristics of early cities do you consider most important? *(Student responses may include the size and diversity of a city's population, its government, its buildings, and its trade with other people.)*

ANSWERS

Compare and Contrast *In small villages, people acted and made decisions according to ancient customs and a council settled disputes. Uruk was much larger, so it had a strong, well-organized government with lots of power.*

▲ A reconstructed Neolithic settlement in the eastern Mediterranean

Quest CONNECTIONS

Based on the photo, what conclusions can you draw about life in a Neolithic village? Record your findings in your Active Journal.

Another difference was Uruk's form of government. Villages such as Çatalhöyük had little need for complex government. People acted and made decisions according to ancient village customs. A village council settled most disputes. A city such as Uruk was too large to manage that way. Uruk had a strong, well-organized government. The city's first rulers were probably temple priests. Later, powerful military leaders ruled Uruk as kings. These rulers had far more power than a village council did.

How Did Cities Become Centers of Wealth? A city such as Uruk also had a more complex economy than did early farming villages. An **economy** is the system that a community uses to produce and distribute goods and services.

In the earliest human communities, each group produced those goods and services that were necessary for its survival. The group produced these goods and services by hunting and gathering. The goods and services were then shared by the members of the community.

Çatalhöyük's economy was based mainly on farming. By contrast, Uruk's more complex economy was based on both farming and trade. Workshops that produced all kinds of goods lined the city's streets. Traders from Uruk traveled widely. Archaeologists have found pottery and other trade goods from Uruk in many places in the Middle East.

The wealth of Uruk and other early cities attracted many newcomers. People began to move from the countryside into the cities. Many early cities built walls to protect themselves from raiders. Uruk, for example, was surrounded by a thick wall that stretched for 6 miles around the city. This wall was a sign that Uruk was a wealthy city worth protecting.

READING CHECK **Compare and Contrast** How did the government of Uruk differ from that in villages such as Çatalhöyük?

Lesson Check

HSS 6.1.3, 6.2.2; ELD.PI.A.2, ELD.PI.C.10.a

Practice Vocabulary

1. How did a **surplus** of food affect the size of the population?
2. How was Uruk's **economy** different from the economy of Çatalhöyük?

Critical Thinking and Writing

3. **Identify Implied Main Ideas** How did farming change the kinds of communities people lived in?
4. **Draw Conclusions** What are some of the benefits and drawbacks of job specialization?
5. **Infer** Why do you think people in early cities began to trade with other cities?
6. **Writing Workshop: Organize Sequence of Events** Make an ordered list in your Active Journal to show what happens to your characters in your narrative essay. You will use this sequence of events when you write your narrative essay at the end of the Topic.

LESSON CHECK

1. It helped the population grow. **DOK1**
2. Çatalhöyük's economy was based mainly on farming, Uruk's economy was based on both farming and trade. **DOK1**
3. Because they could grow food, people settled and built more permanent homes. **DOK2**
4. Sample benefit: Society can form a more developed culture; Sample drawback: Individuals don't learn certain skills. **DOK3**
5. Trading allowed people to get goods they might not be able to produce. They also acquired wealth by selling surplus food. **DOK3**
6. Students should create a sequence of events for their narratives. **DOK3**

LESSON 5 HSS 6.2.1, 6.2.9

The Rise of Civilizations

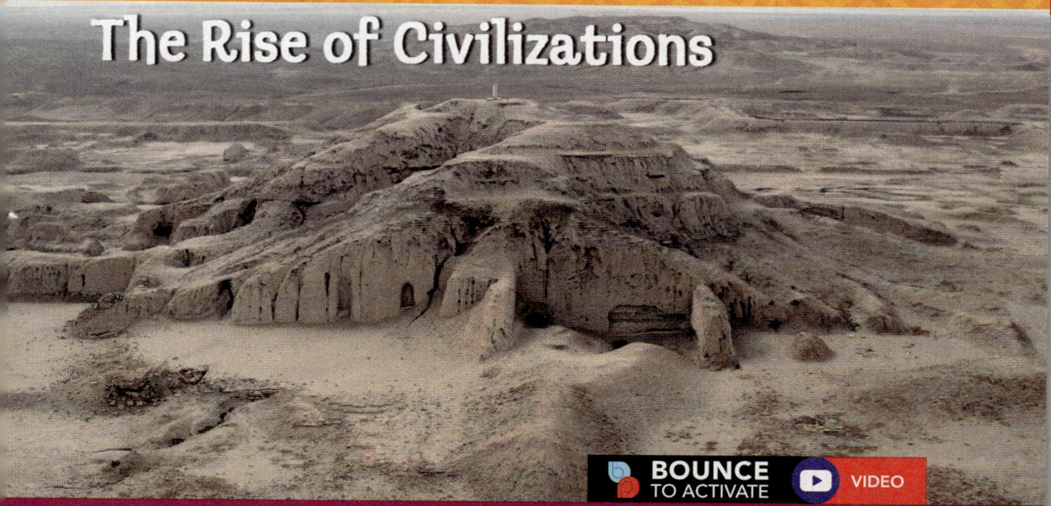

BOUNCE TO ACTIVATE VIDEO

GET READY TO READ

START UP

Examine the photo of the ruins of the ancient city of Uruk. What does it tell you about the society that was centered there?

GUIDING QUESTIONS

- What environmental factors helped civilizations grow?
- What impact did civilizations and complex urban societies have on the surrounding environment?
- How and why did cities give rise to the world's first civilizations?
- What features did all early civilizations have in common?

TAKE NOTES

Literacy Skills: Summarize

Use the graphic organizer in your Active Journal to take notes as you read the lesson.

PRACTICE VOCABULARY

Use the vocabulary activity in your Active Journal to practice the vocabulary words.

Vocabulary		Academic Vocabulary
civilization	religion	manage
resource	social class	specialization

As farming spread, many small settlements appeared. In time, some villages grew into cities. In this lesson, you will read about the rise of early civilizations.

How Did Cities Lead to Civilizations?

As early cities grew in size and power, some of them became centers of civilizations. A **civilization** is a complex society that has cities, a well-organized government, and workers with specialized job skills. The word *civilization* comes from the Latin word *civis*, meaning "resident of a city."

What Resources Were Important? The rise of early civilizations depended on the creation of a food surplus. Creating that surplus, in turn, depended on the ability of people to manage their resources well. A **resource** is a supply of something that can be used as needed.

The most important resources that people needed were fertile soil, fresh water, and seeds. However, these resources were worth

Lesson 1.5 • The Rise of Civilizations 33

PRACTICE VOCABULARY

Help students integrate new vocabulary by explaining connections among words and key ideas in the lesson. For example, tell students that *civilizations*—complex societies with cities, governments, and specialized workers—have risen all over the world throughout history. Early civilizations depended on natural *resources* such as fertile land and water. The people belonged to different *social classes*—for example, kings and priests were part of the ruling class. Another common feature that arose in early civilizations is the belief in *religion*, or shared spiritual ideas.

Point out the academic vocabulary in the margin. Provide sample sentences that clarify meaning.

manage: Despite the obstacles, she managed to succeed.

specialization: She studied for many years to obtain a specialization in forensic anthropology.

HSS 6.2.1, 6.2.9

The Rise of Civilizations

CONNECT

GET READY TO READ

ETEXT START UP

Project the Start Up Activity. As students enter the classroom and get settled, ask them to examine the photograph, which shows ancient ruins of Uruk.

Infer Have students write a few sentences in which they imagine what life was like living in Uruk. Then have students compare their sentences with a partner and discuss any differences in their assumptions.

Discuss Remind students that large buildings are one of the distinguishing features of early civilizations. The skills and tools needed to construct such architecture are highly complex and provide insights into the knowledge and skills of the ancient people of Uruk.

After completing the Start Up Activity, project the Lesson Opener or direct students to their textbooks. Preview the lesson by working through the Get Ready to Read items with the class. Remind students to pay close attention to the Guiding Questions as they read the lesson.

ACTIVE JOURNAL

Take Notes Have students focus on Summarizing as they use the lesson literacy skills graphic organizer in their Active Journals to take notes as they read the lesson.

Practice Vocabulary Have students complete the activity in their Active Journals to build their vocabulary.

VIDEO VIDEO

Assign the lesson video as homework.

WORKSHEET **TEACHER RESOURCES**

Have students who need additional support use the following worksheets from the Teacher Resources on the course:

- **Reading Support**
- **English Language Development**
- **Lesson Summary**

INVESTIGATE

How Did Cities Lead to Civilizations?

Discuss how resources helped cities grow and more complex cultures to develop.

Identify Main Ideas What is a **civilization**? *(a society that has cities, a well-organized government, and workers with specialized job skills)*

Identify Cause and Effect Why was **resource** management important to creating food surpluses? *(Sample answer: People had to organize their supplies and labor in order to produce the most food possible from the available resources.)*

Identify Main Ideas Why were river valleys good locations for permanent settlements and the rise of civilizations? *(After the rivers flooded each year, a fresh layer of fertile soil was left on top that farmers could use to grow crops.)*

Compare and Contrast How were the early Greek and Maya civilizations different from other early civilizations? *(Neither the Greek nor Maya civilizations started in river valleys.)*

What Are the Features of Civilizations?

Discuss how government, religion, and cultural elements, such as art and architecture, contributed to early civilizations.

ANSWERS

Understand Effects *Early civilizations arose in river valleys because these locations offered fertile land for agriculture and a reliable source of water.*

▲ Statue of a man from about 3500-3300 BCE found in Uruk, Iraq

little if people could not provide the labor and tools needed to produce enough food. Managing these resources well required a level of planning and organization that marked a new stage in human society.

Where Were Early Civilizations? Like the earliest villages, the earliest civilization also appeared in southwestern Asia, in the city-state of Sumer. In time, other civilizations appeared in different parts of the world.

Four of these early civilizations developed in the fertile valleys surrounding major rivers: the Nile in northeastern Africa; the Tigris and Euphrates in the southwest Asian area of Mesopotamia; the Indus in South Asia; and the Huang River in China.

River valleys provided a good setting for permanent settlements. Each year, the rivers rose and flooded the nearby land. When the floodwaters went down, a fresh layer of fertile soil remained that farmers could use to grow crops.

Not all early civilizations began in river valleys. Greek civilization, for example, emerged on a rocky peninsula in southeastern Europe and a series of islands in the eastern Mediterranean Sea. Civilizations also changed their surrounding environment. Farmers near rivers built irrigation systems. Civilizations in the Americas cut down trees and burned them to create farmland. People cleared land to build houses, temples, and markets.

READING CHECK **Understand Effects** Why did many early civilizations arise in river valleys?

INTERACTIVE

River Valley Civilizations

What Are the Features of Civilizations?

The civilizations that arose in different parts of the world differed in many ways. Still, all of them had certain things in common. Most early civilizations shared eight basic features: cities; organized governments; established religion; job specialization; social classes; public works; arts and architecture; and a system of writing.

Cities The first of these features was cities. Early cities emerged near farming centers. As food surpluses led to rapid population growth, villages grew into cities and cities grew into civilizations. They served as centers of religion, government, and culture. A few ancient population centers, such as Damascus, Syria, are still major cities today.

INTEGRATED ENGLISH LANGUAGE DEVELOPMENT

Interpretive Explain that listening is an active skill. It is important to develop good listening skills to get the most out of oral presentations such as a teacher giving a lesson, or a fellow student giving an oral presentation or report to the class. Tell students that learning to ask and answer good questions about an oral presentation is an important part of making listening skills work even better. Recognizing presentation techniques such as repetition and slight varying of ideas to make a point is important in listening, too.

Emerging Reread the primary source quote in the lesson, "Penitential Psalms," aloud for students. Have students ask questions about the meaning of the text, prompting them to ask about certain ideas in the text you feel are most important and proving substantial support of their comprehension.

Organized Government The second feature of early civilizations was a well-organized government. One role of government is **managing** society's resources so that people get those things they need to survive. A strong government can also form and train an army to defend a society from attack or to expand its borders.

Academic Vocabulary
manage • *v.*, to direct; have control over

As populations grew, government became more difficult. Powerful rulers called warlords took control of tribes in larger areas and formed governments headed by kings or queens. They relied on large numbers of public officials who handled different duties.

Established Religion A third common feature of a civilization was an established **religion**, or a set of shared spiritual beliefs. Everyone generally followed the same beliefs and practices. Religion was often linked to government. Rulers of early civilizations usually claimed that their right to rule came from the gods. In China, for example, emperors were called "Sons of Heaven."

In most early civilizations, people believed in many gods and goddesses that controlled most events in their lives. People feared their gods, but also hoped that the gods would protect them from harm.

Analyze Diagrams Although civilizations arose in different parts of the world, they shared these eight characteristics. *Demonstrate Reasoned Judgment* What feature do you think was the most important to a successful civilization? Why?

Identify Details In what way was **religion** often connected to government in early civilizations? *(Rulers of early civilizations often claimed they were gods or their right to rule came from the gods.)*

Draw Conclusions How might organized **religion** have unified early communities? *(People shared the same ideas about religion so they felt connected to each other and to a larger community.)*

ELD TIP Have groups of English learners and native English speakers look at the graphic "Eight Features of Civilization." Have each one take a turn reading the text about one of the features aloud. Make sure English learners understand the meanings of more difficult key words from the topic such as civilization, architecture, and specialization.

INTERACTIVE **INTERACTIVE MAP**

River Valley Civilizations

Display the Interactive Map: River Valley Civilizations and click through each of the four civilizations. Ask: What do all of these civilizations have in common? *(The river valleys provided fertile soil for farming.)*

ACTIVE CLASSROOM

After viewing the Interactive Map: River Valley Civilizations, use a Closer Look strategy. Divide the class into four groups and assign each group one of the river valley civilizations shown on the map. Ask students to look closely at the physical geography of each civilization and describe what they see.

ELD.PI.A.5

Expanding Read "Penitential Psalms," aloud. Ask: "Who is the speaker addressing? Is it one person? Is it a god or a goddess? Encourage students to ask detailed questions with moderate support from you.

Bridging Have pairs of students work together. Have one read "Penitential Psalms," aloud to the other. Then have students take turns asking and answering questions.

WORKSHEET **TEACHER RESOURCES**

For additional IELD support addressing the standard, have students complete the Lesson ELD activity from the Teacher Resources found on the course.

ANSWERS

Demonstrate Reasoned Judgment *Sample answer: Well-organized government because it made the other features possible through organization and central control.*

Analyze Primary Sources To whom is the prayer directed? *(to a god and goddess)*

Infer In the Primary Source, what effect is the repetition of words and phrases intended to have on the reader or speaker of this prayer? *(Sample answer: The repetition helps the reader or speaker remember the prayer and emotionally relate to its message.)*

Identify Main Ideas What do you think the main idea of the prayer is? *(Sample response: People can do wrong without knowing it and need to ask for forgiveness.)*

Identify Cause and Effect Why was job **specialization** important for early civilizations? *(Job specialization allowed a community to produce the tools and talents necessary to expand and support its needs.)*

Summarize What are the three different **social classes in** early civilizations? *(the priests and rulers of the upper class; the farmers, merchants, and skilled workers of the middle class; and the slaves of the lower class)*

Infer Why do you think art increased as civilizations grew larger and more powerful? *(As civilizations grew, they had more specialized workers, better tools, and more time to create works of art.)*

ANSWERS

Each person is doing a different job in making pottery.

Academic Vocabulary

specialization • *n.*, act of concentrating on a limited number of goods or activities

To keep their gods and goddesses happy, priests offered sacrifices and led prayers. This prayer is from the civilization of ancient Sumer:

Primary Source

May the known and unknown god be pacified!

May the known and unknown goddess be pacified!

The sin which I have committed I know not. . . .

My god, my sins are seven times seven; forgive my sins!

My goddess, my sins are seven times seven; forgive my sins!

—"Penitential Psalms," translated by Robert F. Harper

From earliest times, religion included beliefs about life after death. People also looked to their religion for rules about how to treat one another and how to live moral lives.

Job Specialization Job specialization was a fourth feature that was common to civilizations. Most people in early civilizations were farmers. They produced enough food to support many kinds of specialized workers. Skilled craftworkers specialized in producing goods. Traders and merchants specialized in buying and selling goods. Job **specialization** allowed people to develop the many skills and talents needed to create and maintain a civilization.

Analyze Images In this painting from about 1425 BCE, Egyptians are shaping metal storage vessels. **Identify Main Ideas** How does this painting show job specialization?

Social Classes A fifth feature of early civilizations was a system of social classes. **Social classes** are groups of people that occupy different ranks or levels in society. Class structures resembled pyramids, with the smallest number of people at the top and the largest number at the bottom.

The highest social class in most early societies was made up of priests and rulers. The people at these ranks had the most power and wealth.

The social classes in the middle included farmers, merchants, and skilled workers. Members of these classes varied in wealth and status from one society to another. In many societies, slaves made up the lowest class. Slaves were often prisoners captured in war or poor people who sold themselves to pay their debts.

Public Works Public works were a sixth feature of civilizations. Governments organized workers to build large-scale projects such as roads, water systems, city walls, and granaries where food was stored after harvesting. Building these public works was costly,

DIFFERENTIATED INSTRUCTION

Advanced Ask students to analyze the idea of social hierarchy, considering examples in ancient times as well as contemporary examples. In small groups, have students debate the benefits and drawbacks of social hierarchies on a society.

Below Level Have students design and draw a diagram that shows a social hierarchy in ancient times. Then have students describe their diagram to a partner.

Special Education Students with small motor difficulties may struggle to draw a diagram. Have these students list social hierarchies in order from top to bottom and describe each one.

time-consuming, and often dangerous. Often, workers were injured or killed. Still, public works benefited the society as a whole.

Arts and Architecture Architecture was closely related to public works. Early people built and decorated magnificent temples, tombs, and palaces. Many of these buildings served a public function, but they were also objects of beauty.

Early civilizations developed other forms of art as well. In this chapter, you can see a number of examples of statues and paintings that date back thousands of years. Skilled craftworkers also produced fine luxury items for the upper classes, such as gold jewelry and perfume boxes. Music and literature, too, enriched the lives of early people and became a mark of advanced civilization.

System of Writing The final common feature of many civilizations was a system of writing. Forms of writing varied, from picture writing to symbols representing sounds and letters.

In some early societies, writing was first developed mainly to record numbers, such as the amount of grain harvested. Eventually, however, people used writing to preserve all kinds of information. They recorded laws, wrote down prayers to the gods, and described the mighty deeds of rulers.

Historians have learned much about the early civilizations that left behind written records. With the development of writing, we pass from prehistory to recorded history.

▲ Ancient Chinese writing, etched into bone

READING CHECK **Identify Main Ideas** What are the eight basic features of civilization?

Lesson Check

HSS 6.2.1, 6.2.9; ELD.PI.A.2, ELD.PI.C.10.a

Practice Vocabulary

1. Choose one of the eight features of **civilization** and explain how it still exists in our civilization today.
2. What social classes were common in most early civilizations?

Critical Thinking and Writing

3. **Infer** What would happen to a civilization if it ran out of resources?
4. **Identify Supporting** Details What are public works? Give two examples.
5. **Synthesize** How was job specialization linked to the emergence of social classes?
6. **Writing Workshop: Use Descriptive Details and Sensory Language** Write notes in your Active Journal about descriptive details and sensory language that you can use in the narrative essay you will write at the end of the Topic.

LESSON CHECK

1. Sample response: We still have public works, as seen in our roads, bridges, dams, and water and sewer systems today. **DOK3**
2. rulers and priests, merchants, farmers and skilled workers, slaves **DOK1**
3. It would eventually die out. **DOK2**
4. Public works are large building projects that benefit society as a whole, such as roads, water systems, city walls, and granaries. **DOK1**
5. Class was determined by the kind of work someone did. In hunter-gatherer societies, there were few people and everyone performed the same actions, so social classes did not emerge. **DOK4**
6. Students should list details that make their characters' activities vivid and interesting. They should express those details using language that appeals to the five senses. **DOK4**

HSS 6.2.1, 6.2.9; ELD.PI.A.2, ELD.PI.C.10.a

SYNTHESIZE

Assess and Reteach Have students use a Think-Pair-Share strategy to complete Lesson Check questions 1–5. Review their responses. If they had any incorrect answers, use the Guiding Questions to discuss the lesson's main ideas, focusing on the ideas they struggled with.

ACTIVE JOURNAL

Writing Workshop Have students complete the Lesson 5 Writing Task in their Active Journals. Encourage students to brainstorm descriptive phrases and sensory language that is related to the narrative they are writing.

DEMONSTRATE

ASSESSMENT **ONLINE LESSON QUIZ**

Assign the Online Lesson Quiz for this lesson if you haven't already done so. Students will be offered automatic remediation or enrichment based on their score.

DISCUSSION **DISCUSSION BOARD**

Post this question to the class on the Discussion Board:

Analyze What are some examples of public works of art or architecture in our community? *(Student responses may include references to public buildings such as courthouses, museums, and outdoor sculpture.)*

ANSWERS

Identify Main Ideas *cities, organized governments, established religion, job specialization, social classes, public works, arts and architecture, system of writing*

HSS 6.2.9, 7.7.1, 7.7.2, 7.7.3, 7.7.4, 7.7.5; ELA RI.6.1

Case Study: The Mayan Civilization

CONNECT

GET READY TO READ

ETEXT **START UP**

Project the Start Up Activity. As students enter the classroom and get settled, ask them to examine the photograph, which shows a step pyramid at Chichén Itzá, a Mayan city in present-day Mexico.

Infer Have students make inferences about how the Maya used this pyramid. *(Possible response: They might have used it for religious or civic ceremonies.)*

Discuss Explain that monumental public buildings erected by the Maya are unique features of early Mesoamerican civilization. The skills and tools needed to construct stepped pyramids, temples, and palaces are very complex and give historians important insights into the knowledge and skills of the ancient Maya.

After completing the Start Up Activity, project the Lesson Opener or direct students to their textbooks. Preview the lesson by working through the Get Ready to Read items with the class. Remind students to pay close attention to the Guiding Questions as they read the lesson.

ACTIVE JOURNAL

Take Notes Have students focus on Using Evidence as they complete the lesson literacy skills graphic organizer in their Active Journals while reading the lesson.

Practice Vocabulary Have students complete the activity in their Active Journals to build their vocabulary.

VIDEO **VIDEO**

Assign the lesson video as homework.

LESSON 6

HSS 6.2.9, 7.7.1, 7.7.2, 7.7.3, 7.7.4, 7.7.5; ELA RI.6

Case Study: The Mayan Civilization

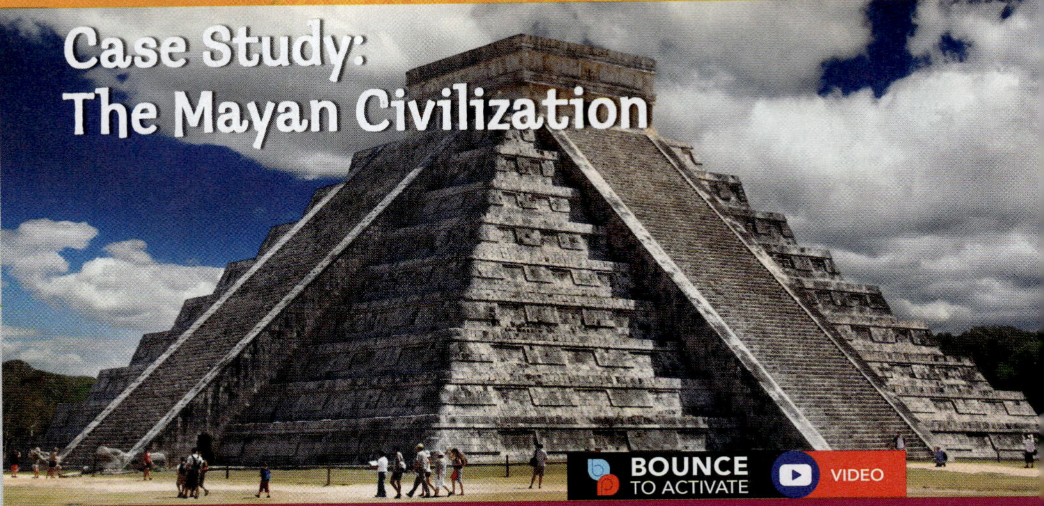

BOUNCE TO ACTIVATE · VIDEO

GET READY TO READ

START UP

Examine the photo of the Maya pyramid. How does it compare to other pyramids you might have seen?

GUIDING QUESTIONS

- How did the geography of Mesoamerica influence the development of Maya culture?
- What features of civilization did the Maya develop in Mesoamerica?
- What were the unique achievements of the Maya?

TAKE NOTES

Literacy Skills: Use Evidence

Use the graphic organizer in your Active Journal to take notes as you read your lesson.

PRACTICE VOCABULARY

Use the vocabulary activity in your Active Journal to practice the vocabulary.

Vocabulary		Academic Vocabulary
obsidian	hieroglyphic	dense
quetzal	observatory	economy
drought		

The oldest civilizations in the Americas formed in an area called Mesoamerica. Mesoamerica extends south from central Mexico into northern Central America. Several advanced cultures, including the Olmec (OHL mek), the Zapotec (ZAH poh tek), and the Maya (MY uh), developed there. The Olmec lived in the tropical forests and learned to grow corn, beans, and other crops. As they produced more food, their population grew and cities arose. The Olmec set a pattern for future civilizations, including the Maya, in Mesoamerica.

Geography of Mesoamerica

In the part of Mesoamerica that gave rise to the first civilizations, highlands cover the south and lowlands lie to the north. The highlands have warm temperatures year round and rain from April to October. The lowlands have a hot, wet climate.

Ash from volcanoes in the highlands produced rich soils. Volcanoes also produced **obsidian**, or volcanic glass, used to make sharp blades for spears and arrows.

38 Lesson 1.6 • Case Study: The Mayan Civilization

PRACTICE VOCABULARY

Help students integrate new vocabulary by explaining connections among words and key ideas in the lesson. Tell students that the Maya used hard volcanic glass called *obsidian* to make blades. They traded brightly colored feathers from a bird called the *quetzal*. Mayan culture had a complex *hieroglyphic* writing system that used pictures to represent words, ideas, or sounds. The Maya built *observatories* to study the sky. Maya cities collapsed possibly due to a long *drought*, when almost no rain fell.

Point out the academic vocabulary in the margin. Provide sample sentences that clarify meaning.

dense: The forest is so dense that it is difficult to find an easy path to walk through it.

economy: The American economy has continued to grow as unemployment has dropped.

Heavy rainfall in parts of the hot lowlands supports a **dense** tropical forest. The soil in the tropical forests was fertile and could produce abundant crops. The forests also produced valuable resources, including plant foods and animals hunted for their meat, skin, or feathers.

Academic Vocabulary
dense • *adj.*, tightly packed; very thick

READING CHECK **Identify Implied Main Ideas** How would the geography of Mesoamerica have supported farming and hunting?

Features of Mayan Civilization

The Maya lived in what are today Honduras, Guatemala, Belize, and the Yucatán Peninsula in Mexico. Between about 200 and 900 CE, the Maya built great cities and made advances in writing, mathematics, and astronomy. Helped by rich farmland and widespread trade, the Maya developed a powerful and wealthy civilization.

What Do We Know About Mayan Cities? Archaeologists have learned much about the Maya by studying Mayan cities such as Tikal (tee KAHL), Palenque (pah LENK ay), Calakmul (ka lak MOOL) and Copán (koh PAHN). These cities resembled huge royal courts or households. They had hundreds of buildings, including stone pyramids, temples, and palaces. In Mayan cities, large, paved plazas were gathering places. Causeways, or raised roads, connected these plazas.

Most Maya, however, did not live in the center of a city. Instead, most lived in farming villages surrounding a city.

GEOGRAPHY SKILLS

The Mayan civilization grew up in the region of modern Mexico called the Yucatán Peninsula.

1. **Region** Which Mayan city was in the highlands?
2. **Location** Using the scale bar, find how far this city lay from the Caribbean coast.

The Maya Civilization

BACKGROUND NOTE

Origins of Maya Civilization For several decades, scientists have been split between two theories about the origins of the classic Maya civilization. One theory argues that the Maya civilization was directly descended from the earlier "mother culture" of the Olmecs. A newer theory suggests that the Maya and Olmec civilizations developed separately from each other, although there were influences that flowed each way from one culture to the other. According to Dr. Takeshi Inomata, an expert in Maya civilization, recent archaeological work at Ceibal in northern Guatemala indicates that it is "more likely that there was a broad history of interactions across these regions, and through these interactions, a new form of society developed."

WORKSHEET **TEACHER RESOURCES**

Have students who need additional support use the following worksheets from the Teacher Resources on the course:

- **Reading Support**
- **English Language Development**
- **Lesson Summary**

INVESTIGATE

Geography of Mesoamerica

Discuss how the physical geography of Mesoamerica affected the Mayan people and their culture.

Compare and Contrast What are the two main geographic areas of Mesoamerica and how are they different? *(The highlands cover the southern area of Mesoamerica. This area has warm temperatures, a long rainy season, and rich soil. The lowlands cover the northern area of Mesoamerica, where the temperatures are hot and heavy rains occur throughout the year.)*

Identify Details What hard stone was used to make blades in Mesoamerica? *(obsidian)*

Features of Maya Civilization

Discuss what life was like in Maya cities.

Synthesize How have archaeologists gained knowledge about the Maya? *(by excavating and exploring the ruins of Maya cities)*

Hypothesize Why did Maya cities have large plazas? *(to allow large numbers of people to gather, perhaps for worship.)*

ANSWERS

Region *Copán*

Location *about 75 miles*

Identify Implied Main Ideas *Rich soils in the highlands would have supported farming. The dense tropical forest in the lowlands provided habitats for animals, which would have supported hunting.*

Summarize How was Maya society organized? *(There were three main social groups: the noble ruling class; the middle class of merchants, soldiers, and skilled craft workers; and the commoners that worked in the fields and on the construction of buildings.)*

Identify Details What was the basic social unit in Maya society? *(The basic social unit was the extended family consisting of an older couple, their children, and their grandchildren.)*

Identify Details What natural resources did the Maya trade? *(food, cotton, cacao beans, obsidian, jade, feathers, salt, dried fish, and pearls)*

Infer Why was trade important to the Maya? *(Trade allowed people in Maya cities to obtain items that they could not find or produce on their own.)*

Identify Main Ideas Where were the centers of government in Maya civilizations? *(in the large cities, which were independent city-states)*

Infer How might having many kings affect the region where the Maya lived? *(Having many kings might cause uncertainty and chaos because there was no central government.)*

ACTIVE CLASSROOM

After looking at the image of the Maya clay figure, use a See-Think-Wonder strategy. Ask students to write down what they see, what it makes them think, and what they wonder about the figure. Invite volunteers to share their responses with the class.

▲ Maya clay figure

What Was Maya Society Like? The Maya had wealthy and complex societies. The three main groups were nobles, a middle class, and commoners.

The nobles were people born into powerful families. They ruled Maya cities, kept order, defended their territory, and performed religious rituals.

Most Maya were commoners who raised crops. Men worked in the fields and on the village buildings. Women raised children, tended gardens and farm animals, and cooked food.

Lower-ranking lords and higher-ranking commoners formed a kind of middle class. Minor officials, soldiers, and scribes were also part of this group, along with skilled craftworkers who served the nobles.

The basic social unit in Maya society was the extended family. Extended families often included an older couple, their children, and their grandchildren. Extended families often lived in a group of simple houses around a central patio.

On days of major ceremonies, people gathered in cities for religious festivals. There, they saw great stone pyramids and temples and the palaces of the nobles.

How Did the Maya Farm? Nobles controlled large farm plots. Most families also had small plots of their own, where they grew fruit, beans and other vegetables, and raised turkeys and ducks. The production of food was at the center of the Maya **economy**.

The Maya used slash-and-burn agriculture in the heavily forested lowlands. Near their cities, they also fertilized fields so that they could use them year after year. On the Yucatán Peninsula there are few rivers, so the Maya got their water from deep pits in the ground. They also built cisterns, or tanks, to hold rainwater.

The Maya Trade Network Traveling merchants linked Maya cities together in a large trade network. Merchants traveled on footpaths or by canoe along the coast. Traders from farming villages traded food, cotton, and cacao beans, used to make chocolate. Those from the highlands traded obsidian, jade, and feathers from the **quetzal**, a colorful tropical bird. Traders from the coast brought salt, dried fish, and pearls.

Academic Vocabulary
economy • *n.*, the system by which a country's people make a living

What Was Maya Government Like? The Maya region contained dozens of independent city-states. Each Maya city-state had its own king. Usually, the kingship passed from a father to his son. Nobles helped run the government. Maya kings increased their power through warfare. Maya cities went to war to take captives. They also fought over control of trade routes and land.

INTEGRATED ENGLISH LANGUAGE DEVELOPMENT

Interpretive Tell students that reading a text closely can help them understand and explain relationships such as cause and effect, compare and contrast, and problem and solution. Close reading means paying close attention to the ideas in a text, pausing to ask questions about ideas and words that are unclear.

Emerging Briefly summarize information presented in the text. Ask students to find an example of compare/contrast, cause/effect or problem/solution. (For example, How did the Maya build their temples and pyramids without cattle, wheeled vehicles, or metal tools? or What caused the fall of the Maya?) Give students substantial support with other books and Internet resources if necessary.

Expanding Briefly summarize information presented in the text. Ask students to find an example of compare/contrast,

How Did the Maya Worship? The Maya were a deeply religious people who worshiped many gods. Most of these gods represented forces of nature, such as rain and lightning. Forces of nature often play a part in Maya myths, such as this creation myth:

Primary Source

> First the earth was formed, the mountains and the valleys; the currents of water were divided, the rivulets [streams] were running freely between the hills, and the water was separated when the mountains appeared.
>
> —From *Popol Vuh: Sacred Book of the Ancient Quiché Maya*, translated by Delia Goetz and Sylvanus G. Morley

The Maya believed that their priests and kings could communicate with the gods through religious rituals. Priests and kings performed many of these rituals in temples atop pyramids. Temples were built on pyramids so that they could be closer to the gods in heaven. Also, the towering pyramids were meant to show the power of the priests and kings.

Many Maya nobles were priests, and it is thought that many kings served as priests before becoming king. Commoners feared displeasing priests or kings because they believed that their leaders could call on the gods to punish them.

Warfare Warfare was part of Maya life. Powerful rulers raised large armies and fought other cities. One goal of warfare was to take prisoners. Farmers and workers who were captured in battle became slaves, or captive workers. High-ranking prisoners were sacrificed to the gods.

What Caused the Fall of the Maya? After about 750 CE, many great Maya cities fell into ruin. Warfare was one cause. Drought may also have caused food shortages. **Drought** is a prolonged period of little or no rainfall.

Smaller Maya cities lasted another 600 years in the northern Yucatán Peninsula. These Maya traded with peoples such as the Aztecs. The Spanish conquered the Maya in the early 1500s, but the Maya people and language survive to this day.

READING CHECK **Draw Conclusions** Why did the Maya become powerful?

Analyze Images This carving shows the Maya ruler Lord Bird Jaguar. **Compare** What characteristics does this carving have in common with the clay figure on the previous page?

Identify Details What did the gods that the Maya worshiped usually represent? *(forces of nature, such as rain and lightning)*

Infer Why did the Maya revere and fear their priests and nobles? *(They believed that priests and nobles were able to communicate with the gods through religious rituals and could ask the gods to punish them.)*

Identify Main Ideas According to scientists and historians, why did many of the great cities of the Maya fall into ruin about CE 750? *(because of warfare and possibly food shortages caused by drought)*

Make Connections How is the Maya creation myth like those of other ancient people? *(Most creation stories begin with the formation of Earth and its land and water.)*

ELD.PII.B.6.a

cause/effect or problem/solution. Give students support as requested.

Bridging Ask pairs of students to find an example of compare/contrast, cause/effect or problem/solution. Have one student explain his or her idea to the other.

WORKSHEET **TEACHER RESOURCES**

For additional IELD support addressing the standard, have students complete the Lesson ELD activity from the Teacher Resources found on the course.

ANSWERS

Compare *Sample answer: Both are imposing figures with large features; both show intricate patterns.*

Draw Conclusions *They were able to increase their wealth by growing a surplus and through trade. They also waged war with other regions.*

What Were the Achievements of the Maya?

Discuss how writing, math, astronomy, and art affected the Maya civilization.

Identify Details What types of astronomical events were the Maya able to predict? *(eclipses of the sun and moon)*

Synthesize How did astronomy help the Maya create calendars? *(By tracing the movement of the sun, moon, planets, and stars, the Maya could keep close track of the passage of time.)*

Compare and Contrast How were Maya mathematics more advanced than European mathematics of the same time period? *(Maya mathematics included a symbol for zero.)*

Infer Why did the Maya build temples of stone rather than of wood? *(Sample answer: They wanted their temples to last a long time, and wood would quickly rot in a rainy climate.)*

INTERACTIVE **INTERACTIVE GALLERY**

Features of Maya Civilization

Display the Interactive Gallery: Features of Maya Civilization for the class. Click through each item and ask students to think about what makes each item significant to Maya culture.

ANSWERS

Make Generalizations *Writing systems help people communicate.*

Identify Supporting Details *Calendars allowed the Maya to plan seasonal farming tasks, as well as plan religious festivals and keep track of historical dates.*

INTERACTIVE

Features of Maya Civilization

What Were the Achievements of the Maya?

The Maya and other Mesoamerican cultures made many important achievements. They developed a complex writing system, created impressive works of art, and made important discoveries in astronomy and mathematics. Many of these achievements influenced other civilizations of Mesoamerica. Maya culture has also had a lasting influence on the cultures of Mexico and Central America.

Why Was Writing Important to the Maya? The Maya had a rich oral tradition. The Popul Vuh means "Book of the People" and contains poems and stories that describe Maya beliefs and way of life. The Maya also developed the most advanced writing system in the ancient Americas. This system used hieroglyphics. A **hieroglyphic**—also known as a glyph—is a symbol that stands for a word, idea, or sound. The Maya could combine 800 individual glyphs to form any word in their language. Writing enabled the Maya to preserve information that would otherwise be lost.

Maya books recorded Maya learning and beliefs. The Spanish destroyed most of them, but scholars have learned much from the few that survive. Carved glyphs have also been preserved on stone monuments called stelae.

Astronomy and Mathematics The Maya were excellent astronomers. Although they had no telescopes, they plotted the movements of the sun, moon, and planets. They used this information to predict events such as eclipses of the sun and moon.

Maya astronomers developed a complex system of calendars. They used a 260-day religious calendar and a 365-day solar calendar. The Maya used these calendars to plan religious festivals and seasonal farming tasks. They also used a 394-year calendar for historical dates.

Analyze Images The Maya preserved their culture through oral tradition and a system of writing. **Make Generalizations** How do writing systems help civilizations grow and advance?

DIFFERENTIATED INSTRUCTION

Advanced Have students invent and draw their own hieroglyphics. Remind students that the images can represent words, ideas, or sounds. Then have students share the symbols they created with the class, explaining why they drew them as they did.

Below Level Have students research Maya hieroglyphics with a partner. Then have each student use the hieroglyphics they researched to create a message for their partner. Have students switch messages and decode what their partner wrote.

Special Education Allow students who have difficulty speaking to write out their translations rather than saying them aloud.

Mathematics in Maya Society The Maya also developed an advanced system of numerals. This system, unlike that of Europeans at the time, included a numeral for zero. Zeros made calculation easier.

What Was Impressive About Maya Architecture and Art? The Maya created impressive architecture and art. All Maya cities contained pyramids, temples, and palaces. Pyramids, the largest buildings, rose hundreds of feet into the air. Some were built for holding sacrificial rituals and were meant to be climbed. All had temples at the top.

The Maya also built **observatories**, or buildings for observing the sky. Maya astronomers used observatories to follow the paths of the sun, moon, and other objects in the sky.

Almost all the bulk of a big Mayan building like a temple, palace, or observatory consisted of small stones, rubble, and earth that was carried in baskets or by hand. This core material was then covered by a thin skin of well-shaped stone.

Today, most Maya buildings are just plain, gray stone structures. But when they were built, they had elaborate decorations. Sculptures of kings, gods, jaguars, and other figures lined the walls. The buildings were also painted bright blue, green, yellow, and red.

Maya artists painted colorful murals on the walls of temples and palaces. Artists also created fine pottery. They crafted jewelry and masks from jade and pearls. Historians appreciate the art of the Maya stelae. These stone slabs are carved with writing about Maya history. They are monuments to the glory of Maya civilization.

▲ Maya astronomers used this observatory to view objects in the sky.

READING CHECK **Identify Supporting Details** Why was the development of calendars an important achievement?

Lesson Check

HSS 6.2.9, 7.7.1-5; ELA RI.6.1; ELD.PI.C.10.a

Practice Vocabulary

1. How might **drought** have affected the Maya?
2. What are **observatories**, and how did the Maya use them?

Critical Thinking and Writing

3. **Cite Evidence** Describe some of the major accomplishments of the Maya.
4. **Summarize** How did the environment of the Maya affect their culture?
5. **Infer** How did Maya architecture reflect Maya religious beliefs?
6. **Writing Workshop: Use Narrative Techniques** Write a few sentences in your Active Journal to identify and record some narrative techniques you can use to tell your story. You will use these narrative techniques when you write your narrative at the end of the Topic.

LESSON CHECK

1. It might have caused food shortages that helped bring down Maya cities. **DOK3**
2. buildings used to watch objects in the sky; to predict events like eclipses and to create their calendars **DOK2**
3. complex calendars, a writing system, the idea of zero, and impressive stone buildings **DOK2**
4. Their environment favored farming; it also produced resources such as obsidian that favored trade. **DOK3**
5. They believed temples at the top would be closer to the gods. **DOK2**
6. Students might use narrative techniques such as flashbacks or foreshadowing to build suspense. They might also wish to use techniques such as simile or metaphor. **DOK4**

HSS 6.2.9, 7.7.1, 7.7.2, 7.7.3, 7.7.4, 7.7.5; ELA RI.6.1; ELD.PI.C.10.a

SYNTHESIZE

Assess and Reteach Have students use a Think-Pair-Share strategy to complete Lesson Check questions 1–5. Review their responses. If they had any incorrect answers, use the Guiding Questions to discuss the lesson's main ideas, focusing on the ideas they struggled with.

ACTIVE JOURNAL

Writing Workshop Have students complete the Lesson 6 Writing Task in their Active Journals. Encourage students to brainstorm narrative techniques they have learned about in their Language Arts classes and to use these techniques in their essays.

DEMONSTRATE

ASSESSMENT **ONLINE LESSON QUIZ**

Assign the Online Lesson Quiz for this lesson if you haven't already done so. Students will be offered automatic remediation or enrichment based on their score.

DISCUSSION **DISCUSSION BOARD**

Post this question to the class on the Discussion Board:

Make Connections What are two ways in which the interests of modern civilization are similar to those of the Maya? *(Student responses may include references to contemporary interest in astronomy, monumental buildings, road building, and the improvement of agricultural methods.)*

HSS 6.1.1, 6.1.2, 6.1.3, 6.2.1, 6.2.2, 6.2.9, 7.7.1, 7.7.2, 7.7.3, 7.7.4, 7.7.5; ELA W.6.3–6.5; ELD.PI.A.2; ELD.PI.C.10.a

Review and Assessment

VISUAL REVIEW

Direct students' attention to the "Neanderthals and Early Humans" chart. For each point listed, call on volunteers to provide details that they recall from their reading.

Direct students' attention to the "Hunting, Gathering, and Farming" flowchart. Discuss as a class how the flowchart is organized with the top box being the first event and the subsequent events following below in chronological order. Then focus on the key events listed in the flowchart.

READING REVIEW

WORKSHEET **TEACHER RESOURCES**

Have students who need additional support read the Lesson Summaries, available in Teacher Resources on the Realize Course.

GAMES **TOPIC MINI-GAMES**

For additional vocabulary practice, students can go online to access the Topic Mini-Games in Realize.

TOPIC 1

Review and Assessment

VISUAL REVIEW

Neanderthals and Early Humans

Neanderthals	Homo Sapiens
• Were first to bury their dead • May have believed in life after death • Hunted animals • Could form language • Used tools and fire	• Had larger brains than predecessors • Could form complex language • Cooperated with each other • Hunted animals • Used tools and fire

Hunting, Gathering, and Farming

THE NEOLITHIC REVOLUTION

↓

Until about 10,000 years ago, humans survived by hunting and gathering.

↓

Then, over time, people learned to domesticate plants and animals.

↓

Centers of agriculture formed, leading to the development of cities.

READING REVIEW

Use the Take Notes and Practice Vocabulary activities in your Active Journal to review the topic.

INTERACTIVE

Practice vocabulary using the Topic Mini-Games.

Quest FINDINGS

Design Your Village

Get help for designing your Neolithic village in your Active Journal.

Quest FINDINGS

Design a Village

Have students complete their Topic Quests by creating a drawing of their own Neolithic village. Remind students to follow these steps: (1) plan what they want to include in their drawing; (2) make a sketch of their village; (3) share their sketch with others; (4) revise their sketch to create a final drawing; and (5) present and explain their drawing.

ANSWERS

Vocabulary and Key Ideas

1. Archaeologists study the fossils and artifacts that people left behind. Geologists study soil and rocks to help determine the age of fossils and artifacts. **DOK1**
2. They traveled from place to place hunting small animals and gathering plants for food. **DOK1**
3. Possible answer: They used material like mammoth bones and hides to make warmer shelters and clothing. **DOK1**
4. It was the time in history when people first learned to farm and to domesticate plants and animals. **DOK2**
5. Improved skills and crops increased the amount of food farmers could produce. Sometimes they raised more than they needed to use. **DOK3**

HSS 6.1.1, 6.1.2, 6.1.3, 6.2.1, 6.2.2, 6.2.9, 7.7.1, 7.7.2, 7.7.3, 7.7.4, 7.7.5; ELA W.6.3-6.5; ELD.PI.A.2, ELD.PI.C.10.a

ASSESSMENT

Vocabulary and Key Ideas

1. **Explain** How do **archaeologists** and **geologists** help us learn about the past?
2. **Describe** How did **hunter-gatherers** of the Paleolithic Era survive?
3. **Describe** How did people **adapt** to changing climate conditions during the last Ice Age?
4. **Summarize** What was the Neolithic Agricultural **Revolution**?
5. **Explain** How did farming lead to food **surpluses**?
6. **Explain** In early civilizations, how was government connected to religion?
7. **Define** What is a **hieroglyphic**?

Critical Thinking and Writing

8. **Compare and Contrast** How were Stone Age people different and similar to us?
9. **Infer** What do you think happens to species that fail to adapt?
10. **Analyze Cause and Effect** How did farming lead to the development of social classes?
11. **Analyze Cause and Effect** Do you think there could have been civilization without the development of agriculture? Explain.
12. **Revisit the Essential Question** Does geography really shape people's lives? Explain.
13. **Writing Workshop: Write a Narrative Essay** Use the notes you made in your Active Journal to write a narrative essay in which you travel through time to see how hunter-gatherers, early farmers, and pastoral nomads lived.

Analyze Primary Sources

14. According to the primary source, animals were domesticated in certain ways in order to
   A. be larger.
   B. have keener senses.
   C. be more useful to people.
   D. survive better in the wild.

"Chickens were selected to be larger, wild cattle (aurochs) to be smaller. . . . Most domestic animals . . . have smaller brains and less acute sense organs than do their wild ancestors. Good brains and keen eyes are essential to survival in the wild, but represent a . . . waste of energy in the barnyard, as far as humans are concerned."

—Jared Diamond, *Nature*, August 8, 2002

Analyze Maps

Use the map at right to answer the following questions.

15. Which letter represents Mesopotamia? Which rivers was it settled near?
16. Which letter represents the Indus Valley? Which continent is it on?
17. Which letter represents Egypt? Which body of water does the Nile River flow into?

Early Civilizations

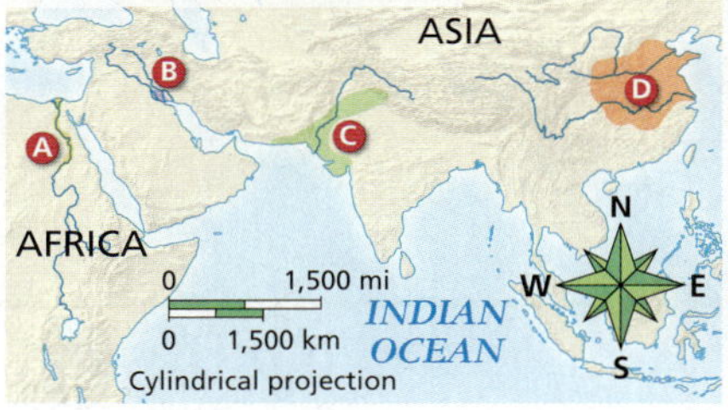

6. Many early rulers claimed that their power to rule came from the gods. **DOK1**
7. a symbol that stands for a word, idea, or sound **DOK1**

Critical Thinking and Writing

8. Sample answer: Stone Age people had a less complex culture and lived in smaller communities. Like us, they wanted to survive, wondered about life after death, and created art. **DOK3**
9. They go extinct. **DOK2**
10. Staying in one place allowed people to have more possessions than they could carry. Owning more possessions than other people might become one sign of higher social class. **DOK3**
11. Students should recognize that civilization depended on the growth of cities that could support larger populations. This would not be possible if agriculture had not allowed people to create permanent settlements. **DOK3**
12. Sample answer: It is clear that geographical factors played a large role in the development of human beings. Where humans lived helped influence the technologies and skills they developed. Changes in climate and other factors forced humans to adapt in ways that greatly influenced the development of the species. Geographical factors also affected where humans settled and where agriculture first developed. **DOK4**
13. Students' stories should include all the elements of a narrative essay and thoroughly describe the different ways that hunter-gatherers, farmers, and pastoral nomads lived. **DOK4**

Analyze Primary Sources

14. C **DOK3**

Analyze Maps

15. B, Tigris and Eurphrates **DOK1**
16. C, Asia **DOK1**
17. A, Mediterranean Sea **DOK1**

ASSESSMENT **TOPIC TEST**

For summative assessment, assign the Topic Test in Realize.

Civilizations and Peoples of the Fertile Crescent

Pacing: Approximately 26 periods, 13 blocks	Resources: Student Edition	Resources: Active Journal	Resources: Online	Pacing	California Standards
CONNECT					
NBC LEARN VIDEO The Code of Hammurabi			✓	10 min.	HSS 6.2.4
ESSENTIAL QUESTION ACTIVITY How Do Societies Preserve Order?		✓	✓	10 min.	HSS 6.2.3, 6.2.4
OVERVIEW ACTIVITY: TIMELINE & MAP Civilizations and Peoples of the Fertile Crescent		✓	✓	10 min.	HSS 6.2.1, 6.2.2, 6.2.3
Quest KICK OFF: Ask Questions	✓	✓		20 min.	HSS 6.2.3, 6.2.4; ELA SL.6.1; ELD.P1.A.3, P1.C.11.a
INVESTIGATE					
LESSONS 1–7	See Lesson-at-a-Glance pages				
Quest INVESTIGATE: Quest Connections	✓	✓		20 min.	See Quest Kick Off
SYNTHESIZE					
WRITING WORKSHOP Write a Narrative Essay		✓	✓	30 min.	ELD.P1.A.2, P1.C.10.a
TOPIC MINI-GAMES Civilizations and Peoples of the Fertile Crescent			✓	10 min.	HSS 6.2.1, 6.2.2, 6.2.3, 6.2.4; ELA SL.6.1; ELD.P1.A.3, P1.C.10.a, P1.C.11.a
Quest SOURCES: Examine Primary Sources			✓	30 min.	See Quest Kick Off
DEMONSTRATE					
TOPIC REVIEW AND ASSESSMENT Civilizations and Peoples of the Fertile Crescent	✓		✓	20 min.	
TOPIC TEST Civilizations and Peoples of the Fertile Crescent			✓	30 min.	
Quest FINDIINGS Discussion!	✓	✓	✓	30 min.	See Quest Kick Off

Quest

Each Quest is designed to reinforce the topic content through an inquiry arc that students work on throughout the topic. This topic's Quest, Debate Punishments for Crimes, is a Discussion Inquiry in which students debate whether harsh punishments are necessary for a safe society.

Active Journal Resources

- Ask Questions
- Quest Connections
- Examine Primary Sources
- Discuss!

Quest Sources Online

- Forbes's Testimony (2007)
- Yates's Testimony (2010)
- Mauer's Testimony (2007)
- "Reconsidering Mandatory Minimum Sentences" (2014)
- Rules for Civic Discussion
- Rubric for Civic Discussion

Additional Resources

Support for Struggling Readers

- Reading Support, Teacher Resources
- Lesson Summaries, Teacher Resources
- English Language Development Teacher Resources

Suggested Resources

- *Hammurabi*, Judith Levin
- *Hammurabi: Babylonian Ruler*, Christine Mayfield
- *The Ancient Near Eastern World*, Amanda H. Podany and Marni McGee
- *Ancient Mesopotamia (DVD)*, Phoenix Learning Group
- *Exodus*, Brian Wildsmith

Beyond the Classroom

Use Online and Library Media Centers

Use a media center to gain online access to the resources of distant museums, such as the Metropolitan Museum of Art, the Louvre, or the British Museum, or educational institutions that specialize in the region, such as the Oriental Institute at the University of Chicago. Virtual tours are available of museums or archaeological sites, such as the Virtual Museum of Iraq available on the University of Chicago website. These experiences can help students grasp the cultural achievements of the people of Mesopotamia.

LESSON 1 | Lesson-at-a-Glance

Civilization Emerges in Mesopotamia

	Resources: Student Edition	Resources: Active Journal	Resources: Online	Pacing (approx. 5 periods, 2.5 blocks)	California Standards
CONNECT					
VIDEO Adapting to Life in Mesopotamia			✓	5 min.	HSS 6.2.1, 6.2.2
START UP ACTIVITY Get Ready to Read	✓	✓	✓	5 min.	HSS 6.2.2
TAKE NOTES AND PRACTICE VOCABULARY		✓			
INVESTIGATE					
READ Lesson 1: Civilization Emerges in Mesopotamia	✓	✓	✓	80 min.	HSS 6.2.1, 6.2.2, 6.2.3, 6.2.9; ELA RI.6.2
INTERACTIVE MAP Sumer and the Fertile Crescent			✓	10 min.	HSS 6.2.3
PRIMARY SOURCES Contracts in Ancient Mesopotamia	✓		✓	40 min.	ELA RI.6.6
ANALYSIS SKILLS Distinguish Cause and Effect	✓		✓	30 min.	HSS 6.2.2, Analysis HI.2
21ST CENTURY SKILLS TUTORIAL Analyze Cause and Effect			✓	10 min.	Analysis HI.2
READING SUPPORT			✓		
SYNTHESIZE					
WRITING WORKSHOP Introduce Your Character	✓	✓	✓	10 min.	ELD.P1.A.2, P1.C.10.a
LESSON SUMMARY			✓		
DEMONSTRATE					
LESSON QUIZ			✓	10 min.	HSS 6.2.1, 6.2.2, 6.2.3, 6.2.9

Objectives

Objective 1: Explain how civilization developed in Mesopotamia and how fertile land supported this development.

Objective 2: Analyze the impact that civilization in Mesopotamia had on the surrounding environment.

Objective 3: Explain why priests and kings held great power in the city-states of Sumer.

Objective 4: Identify the achievements of the Sumerians in technology, writing, and the arts.

The First Empires

Objectives

Objective 1: Explain how Sargon formed the world's first empire in Mesopotamia.

Objective 2: Understand how people's lives changed when the Babylonian empire conquered Sumer.

Objective 3: Describe the lasting impact of the Babylonian emperor Hammurabi's legal code.

	Resources			Pacing	California Standards
	Student Edition	Active Journal	Online	approx. 2 periods, 1 block	
CONNECT					
VIDEO Hammurabi's Code			✓ (video)	5 min.	HSS 6.2.4
START UP ACTIVITY Get Ready to Read	✓	✓	✓ (book)	5 min.	HSS 6.2.2
TAKE NOTES AND PRACTICE VOCABULARY		✓			
INVESTIGATE					
READ Lesson 2: The First Empires	✓	✓	✓ (book)	35 min.	HSS 6.2.4
QUICK ACTIVITY An Eye for an Eye?		✓			HSS 6.2.4
INTERACTIVE CHART Akkadian and Babylonian Empires			✓ (interactive)	10 min.	HSS 6.2.4
INTERACTIVE PRIMARY SOURCE Hammurabi's Code			✓ (interactive)	5 min.	HSS 6.2.4
READING SUPPORT			✓ (document)		
SYNTHESIZE					
WRITING WORKSHOP Introduce Other Characters	✓	✓	✓ (book)	10 min.	ELD.P1.A.2, P1.C.10.a
LESSON SUMMARY			✓ (document)		
DEMONSTRATE					
LESSON QUIZ			✓ (quiz)	10 min.	HSS 6.2.4

The Assyrian and Persian Empires

Objectives

Objective 1: Explain how Assyrian armies conquered their vast empire.

Objective 2: Analyze how the Persian empire balanced local self-government with central power.

Objective 3: Describe how the cultures of Mesopotamia created a rich cultural tradition.

	Resources: Student Edition	Resources: Active Journal	Resources: Online	Pacing (approx. 3 periods, 1.5 blocks)	California Standards
CONNECT					
VIDEO The Assyrian and Persian Empires			✓	5 min.	HSS 6.2.3, 6.4.5
START UP ACTIVITY Get Ready to Read	✓	✓	✓	5 min.	HSS 6.2.3
TAKE NOTES AND PRACTICE VOCABULARY		✓			
INVESTIGATE					
READ Lesson 3: The Assyrian and Persian Empires	✓	✓	✓	40 min.	HSS 6.2.3, 6.4.5
INTERACTIVE GALLERY Assyrian and Persian Empires			✓	10 min.	HSS 6.2.3, 6.4.5
ANALYSIS SKILLS Recognize the Role of Chance, Error, and Oversight	✓		✓	30 min.	HSS 6.4.5, Analysis HI.4
21ST CENTURY SKILLS TUTORIAL Analyze Primary and Secondary Sources			✓	10 min.	Analysis HI.4
READING SUPPORT			✓		
SYNTHESIZE					
WRITING WORKSHOP Establish Setting	✓	✓	✓	10 min.	ELD.P1.A.2, P1.C.10.a
LESSON SUMMARY			✓		
DEMONSTRATE					
LESSON QUIZ			✓	10 min.	HSS 6.2.3

Objectives

Objective 1: Analyze how contact, trade and other links grew among the societies of Mesopotamia and the eastern Mediterranean.

Objective 2: Describe how the Phoenicians spread their culture over a wide area.

Objective 3: Explain the important contribution Phoenicians made to the development of writing.

The Phoenicians

	Resources: Student Edition	Resources: Active Journal	Resources: Online	Pacing (approx. 2 periods, 1 block)	California Standards
CONNECT					
VIDEO The Alphabet			✓	5 min.	HSS 6.2.9
START UP ACTIVITY Get Ready to Read	✓	✓	✓	5 min.	HSS 6.2.1
TAKE NOTES AND PRACTICE VOCABULARY		✓			
INVESTIGATE					
READ Lesson 4: The Phoenicians	✓	✓	✓	40 min.	HSS 6.2.9
QUICK ACTIVITY The Power of Invention		✓			HSS 6.2.9
INTERACTIVE TIMELINE Development of the Modern Latin Alphabet			✓	10 min.	HSS 6.2.9
READING SUPPORT			✓		
SYNTHESIZE					
WRITING WORKSHOP Organize Sequence of Events	✓	✓	✓	10 min.	ELD.P1.A.2, P1.C.10.a
LESSON SUMMARY			✓		
DEMONSTRATE					
LESSON QUIZ			✓	10 min.	HSS 6.2.9

TOPIC 2

Origins of Judaism

Objectives

Objective 1: Explain how the Israelites' belief in one God developed into a religion known as Judaism.

Objective 2: Describe how the environment shaped the Jewish religion.

Objective 3: Understand why Abraham and Moses are important figures in Judaism.

	Resources: Student Edition	Resources: Active Journal	Resources: Online	Pacing (approx. 3 periods, 1.5 blocks)	California Standards
CONNECT					
VIDEO The Origins of Judaism			Video	5 min.	HSS 6.3.1
START UP ACTIVITY Get Ready to Read	✓	✓	eText	5 min.	HSS 6.3.2
TAKE NOTES AND PRACTICE VOCABULARY		✓			
INVESTIGATE					
READ Lesson 5: Origins of Judaism	✓	✓	eText	35 min.	HSS 6.3.1, 6.3.3, 6.3.4
INTERACTIVE MAP The Exodus in Jewish Tradition			Interactive	10 min.	HSS 6.3.3, 6.3.4
PRIMARY SOURCES Psalm 23			eText	40 min.	HSS 6.3.3; ELA RI.6.3, RI.6.4
INTERACTIVE PRIMARY SOURCE Psalm 23	✓		Interactive	5 min.	HSS 6.3.3; ELA RI.6.3, RI.6.4
READING SUPPORT			Document		
SYNTHESIZE					
WRITING WORKSHOP Organize Sequence of Events	✓	✓	eText	10 min.	ELD.P1.A.2, P1.C.10.a
LESSON SUMMARY			Document		
DEMONSTRATE					
LESSON QUIZ			Quiz	10 min.	HSS 6.3.1, 6.3.3, 6.3.4

Beliefs of Judaism

Objectives

Objective 1: Explain the importance of the Hebrew Bible and the Commentaries in Judaism.

Objective 2: Discuss why the Jewish people give special importance to study and law.

Objective 3: Explain the ethical teachings and central beliefs of Judaism, including the importance of righteousness and justice.

Objective 4: Describe what the Jewish people believe about the importance of righteousness and justice.

	Resources			Pacing	
	Student Edition	Active Journal	Online	approx. 2 periods, 1 block	California Standards
CONNECT					
VIDEO The Central Beliefs of Judaism			✓	5 min.	HSS 6.3.2
START UP ACTIVITY Get Ready to Read	✓	✓	✓	5 min.	HSS 6.3.2
TAKE NOTES AND PRACTICE VOCABULARY		✓			
INVESTIGATE					
READ Lesson 6: Beliefs of Judaism	✓	✓	✓	40 min.	HSS 6.3.2
INTERACTIVE GALLERY Significance of Major Jewish Holidays			✓	10 min.	HSS 6.3.2
READING SUPPORT			✓		
SYNTHESIZE					
WRITING WORKSHOP Use Narrative Techniques	✓	✓	✓	10 min.	ELD.P1.A.2, P1.C.10.a
LESSON SUMMARY			✓		
DEMONSTRATE					
LESSON QUIZ			✓	10 min.	HSS 6.3.2

TOPIC 2

Early History of the Jewish People

Objectives

Objective 1: Understand how early Judaism supported individuals, rulers, and societies.

Objective 2: Describe how Jewish communities spread to many different parts of the ancient world.

Objective 3: Analyze how the religious and ethical teachings of Judaism are reflected in society today.

	Resources: Student Edition	Resources: Active Journal	Resources: Online	Pacing (approx. 5 periods, 2.5 blocks)	California Standards
CONNECT					
VIDEO Israel and the Jewish Diaspora			✓	5 min.	HSS 6.3.5
START UP ACTIVITY Get Ready to Read	✓	✓	✓	5 min.	HSS 6.3.2, 6.3.5
TAKE NOTES AND PRACTICE VOCABULARY		✓			
INVESTIGATE					
READ Lesson 7: Early History of the Jewish People	✓	✓	✓	120 min.	HSS 6.3.2, 6.3.3, 6.3.5
INTERACTIVE GALLERY Origins of Judaism			✓	10 min.	HSS 6.3.1
ANALYSIS SKILLS Construct a Timeline	✓		✓	30 min.	Analysis CST.2
21ST CENTURY SKILLS TUTORIAL Sequence			✓	10 min.	Analysis CST.2
READING SUPPORT			✓		
SYNTHESIZE					
WRITING WORKSHOP Use Descriptive Details and Sensory Language	✓	✓	✓	10 min.	ELD.P1.A.2, P1.C.10.a
LESSON SUMMARY			✓		
DEMONSTRATE					
LESSON QUIZ			✓	10 min.	HSS 6.3.2, 6.3.3, 6.3.5

PEARSON realize™

Use the suite of online resources to

Enrich your instruction with topic and lesson videos and interactivities.

VIDEO

Help struggling learners with tools built into the eText, reading support worksheets, lesson summaries, English Language Development exercisess and more.

ETEXT

WORKSHEET

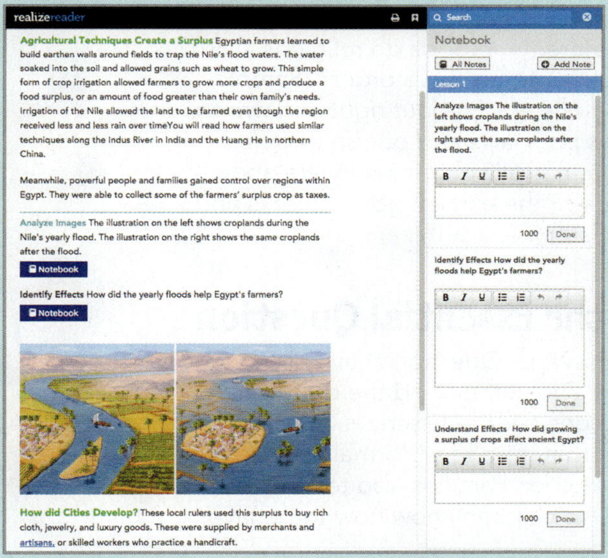

Assess and monitor student progress with automatic answer reporting for lesson prompts, lesson quizzes with remediation, and topic-level assessments.

ETEXT

ASSESSMENT

GAMES

TOPIC 2

Civilizations and Peoples of the Fertile Crescent

(3400 BCE–70 CE)

HSS 6.2.1, 6.2.2, 6.2.3, 6.2.4, 6.2.9, 6.3.1, 6.3.2, 6.3.3, 6.3.4, 6.3.5, 6.4.5; Analysis CST.2, HI.2, HI.4

CONNECT

Introduction

More than 5,000 years ago, people learned to farm in a region called the Fertile Crescent. Having plenty of food led to population growth and the rise of cities. Some of those cities grew powerful enough to conquer others, and the world's first empires were born. These early civilizations left a legacy of inventions, ideas, and religious beliefs that still influence us.

Activate Prior Knowledge

Remind students that both religions and governments act to keep order in society. Ask: What different methods do religions and governments use to preserve order? *(Sample answer: Religions teach about right and wrong. Governments pass laws and punish people who break them.)* Tell students they are about to study some of the earliest governments and religions in history.

Explore the Essential Question

Project the Essential Question activity from the course. Have a volunteer read the question. As students consider the Essential Question, remind them that it isn't just formal institutions that promote order. Families also teach manners and customs so children know how to behave.

ACTIVE JOURNAL

Essential Question Have students begin to explore the Essential Question in their Active Journals.

Draw Conclusions Ask students to think of some laws that an early agricultural society might need. *(Sample answers: They might need laws against stealing property or harming animals or dishonesty in trading.)* Have them record their ideas in their journals to refer to as they read the topic.

TOPIC 2

Civilizations and Peoples of the Fertile Crescent

(3400 BCE–70 CE)

GO ONLINE to access your digital course

- VIDEO
- AUDIO
- ETEXT
- INTERACTIVE
- WRITING
- GAMES
- WORKSHEET
- ASSESSMENT

Over 5,000 years ago

civilization began between two rivers in the Middle East, a region known as the **FERTILE CRESCENT**. Great empires and kingdoms came and went—and laid some of the foundations of society as we know it today.

Explore The Essential Question

How do societies preserve order?

The world's first empires and the world's first religion based on one God sprung up in the Fertile Crescent. How did geography, religion, and culture influence the ways in which societies in this region developed?

Unlock the Essential Question in your Active Journal.

46

ANALYZE VISUALS

Ask students to closely examine the photograph of ruins. Was this most likely a small village or large city? *(Sample answer: It was a large city because this seems to have been an impressive building.)* Ask: What would a society need to build something like this? *(Sample answers: The society would need to understand math and engineering. The society would need access to stone. The society would have to be able to organize workers.)*

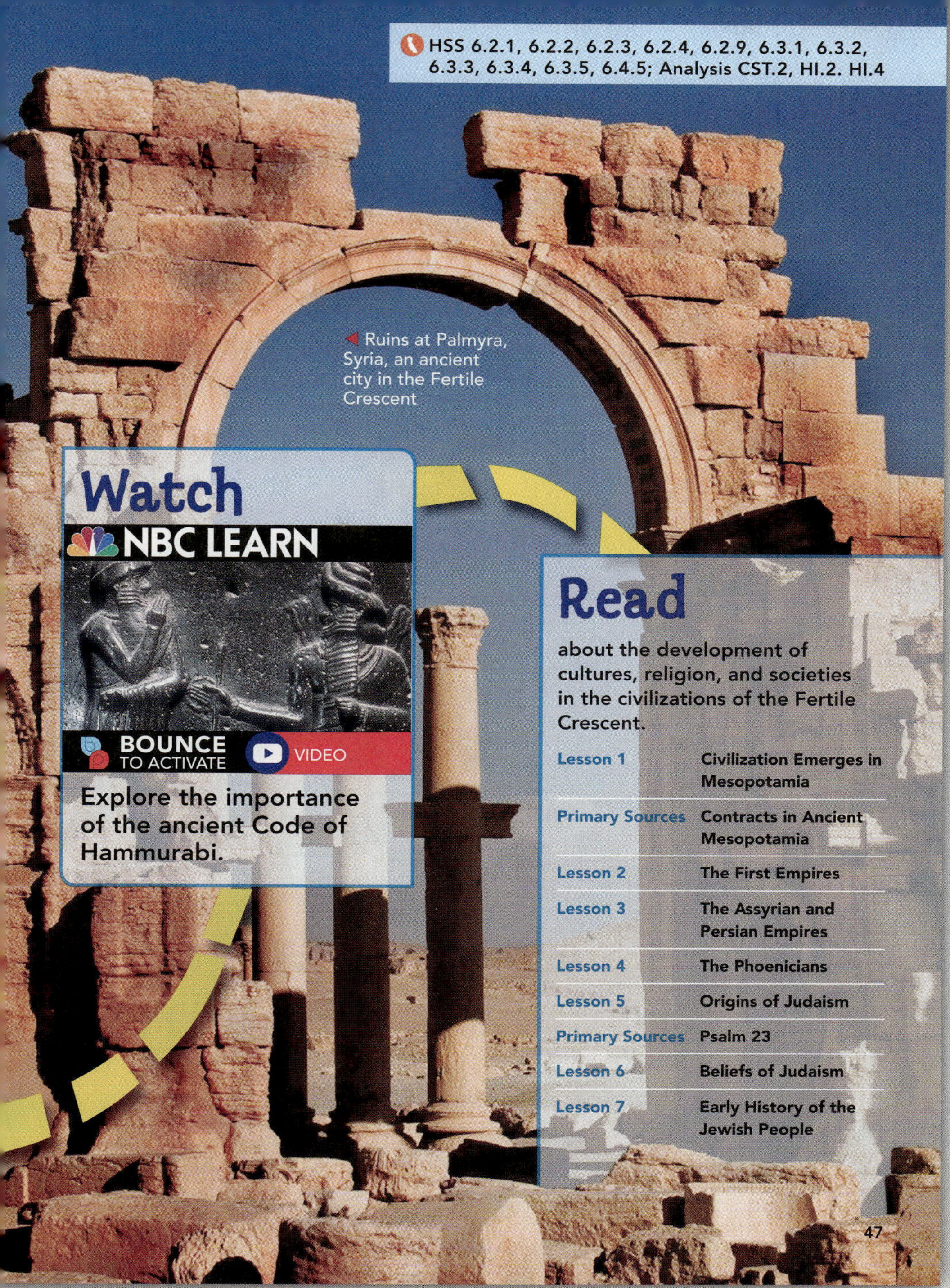

RECOGNIZE CULTURAL AND EXPERIENTIAL BACKGROUNDS

Make use of your knowledge of students' lives to make connections between their own experiences, backgrounds, and interests and the content of this topic. If you have students whose ethnic heritage is related to the content of this topic, make an effort to emphasize the contributions and achievements of this society and how it has enriched the world.

If appropriate, allow the students the opportunity to share cultural, ethnic, or linguistic traditions and knowledge from their experiences.

If students have family experiences (such as travel to or family members who have lived in the region being studied), allow them to share relevant stories.

Watch

VIDEO NBC LEARN VIDEO

Project the Topic Opener video about the Code of Hammurabi. After viewing the video, ask students to respond to the following questions:

Connect Which laws seem similar to laws that exist today? *(Sample answers: death penalty for killing, laws that regulate minimum wage)*

Make Generalizations What word would you use to describe the law code overall? *(Sample answers: harsh, fair, strict)*

Read

Share these lesson previews with students.

Lesson 1: The development of farming led to the rise of cities and the first civilization.

Primary Sources: Contracts reveal details about business dealings in ancient Mesopotamia.

Lesson 2: The Akkadians and the Babylonians developed the first empires in history.

Lesson 3: The Assyrians built a military empire. The Persian rulers used many techniques to unify a diverse empire.

Lesson 4: The Phoenicians were bold traders who influenced world history by developing the first alphabet.

Lesson 5: Judaism developed among the descendants of Abraham, who later went to Egypt and were enslaved. A prophet named Moses led them out of slavery back to their homeland.

Primary Sources: Psalm 23 provides insight into the beliefs of Judaism.

Lesson 6: Judaism is based on a sacred book called the Hebrew Bible and on teachings and commentaries. Jews believe in one God and in the importance of righteousness, justice, and the law.

Lesson 7: The ancient Jews established the kingdom of Israel, which eventually split in two. Both kingdoms were conquered by foreign powers and people dispersed to different regions.

TOPIC 2

HSS 6.2.1, 6.2.2, 6.2.3, 6.2.4, 6.2.9, 6.3.1, 6.3.2, 6.3.3, 6.3.4, 6.3.5, 6.4.5

What Happened and When?

Have students examine the timeline. Ask: How many years are shown on the timeline? *(4,000 years)* Ask: When did the first city-states form? *(about 3400 BCE)* Judging from the timeline, what did Hammurabi and Cyrus the Great have in common? *(Both ruled Babylon.)*

ACTIVE JOURNAL

Timeline Skills Students can also use the Timeline Skills activity in their Active Journals to record information about the history of the Fertile Crescent as they read the topic. During their reading, they should add the dates of at least three events they think are important. After completing the topic, have students write a paragraph identifying the dates they added and explaining why each is significant.

INTERACTIVE — INTERACTIVE TIMELINE

Display the Interactive Topic Timeline for the class. Have volunteers read entries.

Discuss Ask: What is the first empire listed on this interactive timeline, and who was its ruler? *(The first empire was the Akkadian empire ruled by Sargon.)*

TOPIC 2

Civilizations and Peoples of the Fertile Crescent

(3400 BCE–70 CE)

Learn more about the Fertile Crescent and early civilizations by making your own map and timeline in your Active Journal.

INTERACTIVE — Topic Map

Where is the Fertile Crescent?

The Fertile Crescent extends from the Persian Gulf to the Mediterranean Sea. As its name states, it is both fertile and crescent-shaped. The fertile soil of this part of the world gave rise to the first civilizations.

INTERACTIVE — Topic Timeline

What happened and when?

Agricultural inventions ... new civilizations ... enormous empires ... and the beginning of Judaism. Explore the timeline to see how civilization began to unfold.

TOPIC EVENTS

3400 BCE Sumerian city-states form.

2334 BCE Sargon unites Mesopotamia under Akkadian empire.

1792-1750 BCE Hammurabi rules over the Babylonian empire.

4000 BCE — 3000 BCE — 2000 BCE

WORLD EVENTS

3100 BCE First pharaoh unites Egypt.

1800 BCE Shang kingdom founded in China.

48 TOPIC 2 • Civilizations and Peoples of the Fertile Crescent

DIFFERENTIATED INSTRUCTION

Special Education Point out that this timeline covers 4,000 years, divided into 1,000-year increments. Because it covers such a long period, students will learn about the rise and fall of several empires.

Below Level Make sure that students understand that the Fertile Crescent is not the name of a political state. It is a geographic region where many political states existed over time.

Advanced Suggest that students choose one of the empires listed on the timeline and do research to create a timeline of three to five additional events that occurred during that empire.

HSS 6.2.1, 6.2.2, 6.2.3, 6.2.4, 6.2.9, 6.3.1, 6.3.2, 6.3.3, 6.3.4, 6.3.5, 6.4.5

Who will you meet?

Hammurabi, a king of Babylon

Cyrus the Great, a powerful leader

Ruth, a central figure in the Bible's book of Ruth

1200s BCE Moses leads Exodus (traditional date).

720s BCE Assyria conquers Israel.

586 BCE Babylonians conquer Judah.

539 BCE Cyrus the Great captures Babylon.

70 CE Second Temple destroyed.

1000 BCE

1 CE

1200 BCE Olmec civilization begins in modern Mexico.

400 BCE Buddhism becomes widespread in northern India.

49

RECENT SCHOLARSHIP

In the 1980s, Dr. Irving Finkel, a curator of Mesopotamian artifacts at the British Museum, was given an ancient clay tablet that sheds light on the biblical story of Noah, who is said to have built an ark to save his family and a collection of animals from a catastrophic flood. Finkel spent years trying to decipher the tablet, which contained a version of a Babylonian flood story similar to the story of Noah. He eventually figured out that it contained precise instructions for building an ark from wooden ribs, about 332 miles of rope, and hot bitumen for waterproofing. The most surprising detail? The ark was round, not rectangular as has usually been supposed.

Where Is the Fertile Crescent?

Direct students' attention to the map of North Africa and Southwest Asia in the student text. Make sure they identify the Fertile Crescent. Ask: Where are the two ends of the Fertile Crescent? *(Persian Gulf and Mediterranean Sea)* Ask: What geographic feature is noticeable within the Fertile Crescent? *(Sample answer: two rivers)*

ACTIVE JOURNAL

Map Skills Have students use the Map Skills activity in their Active Journals to fill in an outline map of the region with the labels of key geographic and political features.

Analyze Maps In which direction did the Tigris and Euphrates rivers flow? Explain. *(Sample answer: They flowed southeast and emptied into the Persian Gulf.)*

INTERACTIVE — INTERACTIVE MAP

Display the Interactive Topic Map for the class. Work through the maps to learn more about the early civilizations of the Fertile Crescent. Have volunteers read the captions on each layer. Ask: Which of the empires shown extended well beyond the Fertile Crescent? *(Persia)*

Who Will You Meet?

Many students access historical materials best through the stories of the people who made them. Preview these key people that students will encounter in the topic. Read the short description of each, and then conduct a poll asking students which figure they are most interested in. Record the results on the board. Then ask volunteers why they are interested in a particular figure. *(Accept reasonable responses. Students may say that they are curious about Hammurabi because of his law code; that they want to know whether Cyrus was a military leader; or that they want to know why a woman who looks like a farm worker is important.)*

TOPIC 2

HSS 6.2.3, 6.2.4; ELA SL.6.1; ELD.P1.A.3, P1.C.11.a

Quest Discussion Inquiry

Debate Punishments for Crimes

Quest Kick Off

In this Quest, students will use the student text, other sources, and the Active Journal to hold a discussion about whether harsh punishments are necessary to keep society safe.

1 Ask Questions

Launch the Quest by discussing the Guiding Question as a class. Have students generate the questions they will need to have answered to accomplish the Quest in their Journals.
Suggestion: If students need help with the Ask Question step, refer them to the Analysis Skills feature following Lesson 1, Distinguish Cause and Effect. Have them consider how to pose questions that focus on the effects of certain punishments.

2 Investigate

As they read the lessons, remind students to look for and respond to the three Quest Connections in the student text that provide clues to their Quest. They should also identify and record two connections of their own.
Suggestion: If students are struggling to identify their own connections, suggest that they look for words and phrases that indicate passages where laws and punishments are being discussed.

3 Examine Primary Sources

As students complete the topic, distribute the Quest Primary Sources for this topic.

Analyze Documents Have students process the primary sources in their Active Journals, focusing on identifying information related to the Guiding Question in preparation for holding a discussion on the use of harsh punishments.

4 Discuss!

When students complete the topic, have them return to the Quest, which can be used as a performance-based authentic assessment. To complete their Quests, they should use their knowledge of ancient law codes and evidence from sources to make convincing arguments as they discuss the question.

Quest Discussion Inquiry

HSS 6.2.3, 6.2.4; ELA SL.6.1; ELD.P1.A.3, P1.C.11.a

Debate Punishments for Crimes

Quest KICK OFF

You are a legal advisor to the president of the United States! The president wants your advice on mandatory minimum sentences. These are sentences a judge must use when someone is convicted of a crime. You need to help answer one of the most important questions of justice in history:

Are harsh punishments necessary for a safe society?

Explore the Essential Question "How do societies preserve order?" in this Quest.

1 Ask Questions

Get started by making a list of questions about how the ancient Babylonians viewed criminal punishments. Write the questions in your Active Journal.

2 Investigate

As you read the lessons in this topic, look for Quest CONNECTIONS that provide information about different ways groups tried to create order. Collect examples in your Active Journal.

3 Examine Primary Sources

Next, explore a set of sources. They will support differing viewpoints about whether harsh punishments are necessary in today's world. Capture notes in your Active Journal.

4 Discuss!

After you collect your clues and examine the sources, prepare to discuss this question: **Are harsh punishments necessary for a safe society?** You will use your knowledge of ancient law codes as well as evidence from sources to make convincing arguments to answer the question.

50 TOPIC 2 • Civilizations and Peoples of the Fertile Crescent

DIFFERENTIATED INSTRUCTION

Below Level Ask students if they have ever heard the statement *The punishment should fit the crime.* Hold a class discussion about what they think this means.
Advanced Suggest that students review the Eighth Amendment, which prohibits "cruel and unusual punishment." They may want to do research to learn what types of punishments are prohibited in the U.S.

INTEGRATED ENGLISH LANGUAGE DEVELOPMENT

Emerging Support emerging students by asking them Wh- questions, such as What is a an example of a law? What is an example of a crime? What punishments do people get for breaking the law or committing a crime?

LESSON 1

HSS 6.2.1, 6.2.2, 6.2.3, 6.2.9; ELA RI.6.2

Civilization Emerges In Mesopotamia

BOUNCE TO ACTIVATE

VIDEO

GET READY TO READ

START UP

Study the Standard of Ur, which is a small box covered with mosaics. What can you conclude about daily life in Mesopotamia from this box?

GUIDING QUESTIONS

- How did civilizations develop in Mesopotamia and how did the fertile land support this development?
- What impact did civilization in Mesopotamia have on the surrounding environment?
- Why did priests and kings hold great power in the city-states of Sumer?
- What were the achievements of the Sumerians in technology, writing, and the arts?

TAKE NOTES

Literacy Skills: Identify Main Idea and Details

Use the graphic organizer in your Active Journal to take notes as you read the lesson.

PRACTICE VOCABULARY

Use the vocabulary activity in your Active Journal to practice the vocabulary words.

Vocabulary		Academic Vocabulary
Fertile Crescent	barter	distinct
Mesopotamia	polytheism	prosper
irrigate	ziggurat	
city-state	cuneiform	

The **Fertile Crescent** is a region of the Middle East that stretches in a large, crescent-shaped curve from the Persian Gulf to the Mediterranean Sea. The Fertile Crescent includes **Mesopotamia** (mes uh puh TAY mee uh), a wide, flat plain in present-day Iraq. This plain lies between two great rivers, the Tigris (TY gris) and the Euphrates (yoo FRAY teez). In fact, *Mesopotamia* means "land between the rivers" in Greek. Here, thousands of years ago, the world's first civilization began to form. This was the civilization of Sumer (SOO mur).

How Was Agriculture Important in Mesopotamia?

As its name suggests, the Fertile Crescent's soil is rich and fertile. Some of the most productive land in the region is in Mesopotamia. This rich soil allowed Sumerian farmers to grow many grains and vegetables. They also raised sheep, goats, and cattle.

Geography of Mesopotamia Northern Mesopotamia includes the foothills of the Taurus and Zagros mountain chains. To the south, these foothills flatten into plains that stretch southeast toward the Persian Gulf.

Lesson 2.1 51

PRACTICE VOCABULARY

To help students integrate new vocabulary, explain that the *Fertile Crescent* and *Mesopotamia* are both regions in the Middle East. A *city-state* is an independent state that includes a city and its surrounding lands. *Polytheism* is the worship of many gods, while a *ziggurat* was a special kind of temple in Mesopotamia. To *irrigate* is to carry water to crops, while *cuneiform* was the writing system of ancient Sumer.

Reinforce the terms during the lesson using the teaching notes.

Point out the academic vocabulary in the lesson margins. Provide sample sentences that clarify meaning.

distinct: Those flowers have a distinct odor that makes them easy to identify.

prosper: A strong economy can help cities grow and prosper.

HSS 6.2.1, 6.2.2, 6.2.3, 6.2.9; ELA RI.6.2

Civilization Emerges in Mesopotamia

CONNECT

GET READY TO READ

ETEXT — START UP

Project the Start Up Activity. As students enter the classroom and get settled, ask them to examine the photograph of the mosaic showing life in early Mesopotamia. The box has mosaics on two sides, one depicting peacetime and one depicting war.

Draw Conclusions Have students draw conclusions about Mesopotamian life based on this image. *(Sample answers: They grew crops and raised animals. Food production was a key to society. Many people were involved in producing food.)* Have them share their conclusions

Discuss Explain that in this topic, students will learn the importance of rivers to ancient civilizations. Ask: Why do you think people depended on rivers? *(Sample answers: to obtain water for farming, to fish, or to travel by boat)*

After completing the Start UP activity, project the Lesson Opener or direct students to their textbooks. Preview the lesson by working through the Get Ready to Read items with the class. Remind students to pay close attention to the Guiding Questions as they read the lesson.

ACTIVE JOURNAL

Take Notes Have students use the lesson literacy skills graphic organizer in their Active Journals to take notes as they read the lesson.

Practice Vocabulary Have students complete the activity in their Active Journals to build their vocabulary.

VIDEO — VIDEO

Assign the lesson video as homework.

WORKSHEET **TEACHER RESOURCES**

Have students who need additional support use the following worksheets from the Teacher Resources on the course:

- **Reading Support**
- **English Language Development**
- **Lesson Summary**

INVESTIGATE

How Was Agriculture Important in Mesopotamia?

Discuss how Mesopotamians used their natural environment and technology to farm.

Categorize How could the floods of Tigris and Euphrates rivers be both helpful and harmful? *(They could be helpful by providing water and good soil. They could be harmful if high floods caused damage.)*

INTERACTIVE **INTERACTIVE MAP**

Sumer and the Fertile Crescent

Display the map of Sumer and the **Fertile Crescent.** Click each hotspot. Ask volunteers to read labels. Ask: Where were most of the **city-states** located? *(Sample answer: on the lower, or southeastern, portion of the rivers)*

ACTIVE CLASSROOM

Use the My Metaphor strategy. Give students this prompt: "This map shows that **Mesopotamia** is like _____ because _____________." Ask volunteers to share their metaphors.

Southern Mesopotamia is a hot, dry region with little rainfall. At first glance, the land looks like a desert. But the soils are not desert soils. In fact, they are rich with nutrients.

INTERACTIVE
Sumer and the Fertile Crescent

The southern part of Mesopotamia owes its good soil to the Tigris and Euphrates rivers. These rivers begin in the mountains of southeastern Turkey and flow south and east, through present-day Iraq. The rivers carry fine, fertile soil called silt down from the mountains. Each spring, the rivers flood their banks, spreading floodwaters and silt across the plain. When the floods end, they leave behind a fresh layer of moist, fertile earth that is perfect for growing crops.

But Mesopotamia's geography also gave Sumerian farmers many challenges. The heavy spring floods could wash away crops and even whole villages. During the summer, the hot sun baked the ground rock hard. With little rain for months, plants died.

GEOGRAPHY SKILLS

A series of early civilizations beginning with Sumer arose in Mesopotamia, the region between the Tigris and Euphrates rivers.

1. **Interaction** What natural features may have limited the expansion of these civilizations?
2. **Contrast** How was the Fertile Crescent different from neighboring areas?

Farming the Land Despite these challenges, the Sumerians used technology to turn Mesopotamia into productive farmland. Remember that technology is the practical application of knowledge to accomplish a task.

The Sumerians used technology to **irrigate**, or supply water to, their crops. They dug many miles of irrigation canals to bring water from the rivers to their fields. With irrigation, people transformed their environment so that crops could still get water during the hot, dry summer. People began settling in new areas where irrigation made growing crops possible, turning land into fields and building homes.

Fertile Crescent 3000 BCE

CURRICULUM CONNECTION: ENVIRONMENTAL EDUCATION

California Education and the Environment Initiative This topic links with the California Curriculum Unit 6.2.1 River Systems and Ancient Peoples. That unit includes the Mesopotamian flood myth from *The Epic of Gilgamesh*, information about Hammurabi's Code, information about the cities of Ur and Uruk, and useful vocabulary words. The unit may be found at http://www.californiaeei.org/curriculum/.

Sumerians also developed a new way of planting crops. Earlier farmers used a wooden plow pulled by oxen when planting. The plow cut a long furrow, or trench, in the soil. Then the farmers dropped seeds into the furrow. But Sumerian farmers developed a seed funnel that they attached to their plows. As the plow moved forward, seeds automatically dropped from the funnel into the soil. This made planting faster and easier.

READING CHECK **Predict** Predict how irrigation in Mesopotamia led to the development of cities.

Analyze Images Walls and buildings of ancient Mesopotamia were made of mud bricks baked dry. **Synthesize Visual Information** How do these structures show the skill of Mesopotamian builders?

City-States of Sumer

Better agricultural techniques helped the Sumerians produce more food. With a dependable food supply, the population began to grow. Around 3400 BCE, cities started to form in southern Mesopotamia. These cities depended on nearby rivers for irrigation to grow crops to support the growing populations. Other major civilizations, such as the Harappa along the Indus River and the Chinese along the Huang River, formed in river valleys for the same reason.

Cities Emerge The first Mesopotamian city was Uruk. Uruk had a population of more than 40,000 people. Other early cities were Ur, Lagash, and Nippur. Some cities grew large and powerful. They became the world's first city-states. A **city-state** is an independent state that includes a city and its surrounding territory. Each Sumerian city-state had its own government and laws, and each had its own main god. Cities had walls and densely packed houses.

Trade Each city-state was a center of trade. Southern Mesopotamia had fertile soil, but it had little wood or stone and no metal ores. Sumerians traveled far to find these important resources. Most trade was done by barter. **Barter** is a trading system in which people exchange goods directly without using money.

Early traders often used the rivers and major canals to transport their goods. They loaded goods onto barges, or large rafts. Workers on land used ropes to pull the barges along the water.

As they had done with agriculture, the Sumerians used new technologies to make trade easier. For example, the Sumerians invented the wheel, which they used on their carts. Many historians include the wheel as one of the most important discoveries of all time. Sumerians also used sails on their boats. With wheeled carts and sailboats, they could more easily transport barley, wheat, dates, and cloth to faraway lands. They could also bring home trade goods like lumber, metals, and precious stones.

City-States of Sumer

Discuss how increases in the food supply led to population growth and the rise of cities.

Identify Cause and Effect What caused Sumer's population to grow? *(A dependable food supply enabled it to grow.)*

Infer Why do you think most trade was done by **barter**? *(Sample answers: A city-state's money was probably not usable outside its own borders, or perhaps money had not been invented yet.)*

Identify Cause and Effect What advances made widespread trade possible? *(The sail and the wheel improved travel, which made it possible to trade with people farther away.)*

CURRICULUM CONNECTION: ECONOMICS

Barter Even in today's economy, many people trade goods and services without using money. People may barter directly with one another. They may also use a barter exchange or barter club. The Internet has provided many outlets for barter. With certain exceptions, the U.S. government still requires people to report the fair market value of their barter for tax purposes.

ANSWERS

Interaction *The Syrian and Arabian deserts, the Zagros Mountains*

Contrast *It had two major rivers.*

Predict *Irrigation allowed people to grow crops in areas where they previously could not. People began settling in these areas, and these settlements continued to grow and become powerful cities because the farmers could provide food for everyone there.*

Synthesize Visual Information *Sample answer: The images show that Mesopotamian builders could construct buildings that have lasted thousands of years.*

Summarize Who made up the three classes in Sumer? *(The ruling family, high priests, and leading officials made up the highest class; priests, merchants, scribes, and artisans made up the next highest class; peasant farmers made up the second to lowest class; and the lowest class was made up of enslaved workers.)*

What Role Did Religion Have in Sumerian Society?

Discuss the characteristics and importance of Sumerian religion.

Draw Conclusions What is one reason Sumerians looked to the gods for answers? *(Sample answer: They could not control the weather, so they hoped their gods could do it for them.)*

Infer Why do you think the Sumerians built their **ziggurats** so high? *(Sample answer: They were trying to reach up to their gods.)*

ELD TIP Form students into groups to discuss the Sumerian Social Hierarchy diagram. Ask questions such as *What does it mean to be at the top of the pyramid? Why is the top of the pyramid smaller than the bottom? Why are slaves on the bottom?*

Sumerian Social Hierarchy

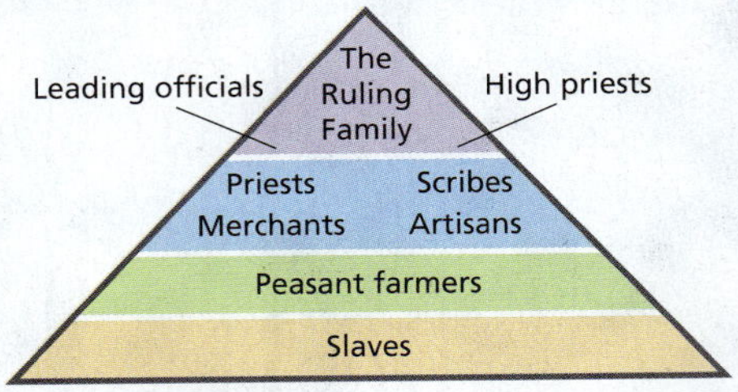

Analyze Diagrams
Sumerian civilization saw the formation of the first social classes. **Use Evidence** What does the chart indicate about how Sumerian society supported itself?

Social Classes The Sumerians developed a social order with three classes. People of each class had **distinct** roles within Sumerian society. The upper class included the ruler, his top officials, powerful priests, wealthy merchants, and owners of large plots of land. Farmers and skilled workers made up the middle class. The lowest class was mostly enslaved peoples. The city-states' governments and Sumerian religious beliefs, which were firmly connected, helped support this social order.

The rise of social classes was a new development for human societies. Men generally had a higher social position than women, but women in the higher class could gain power. Some could be priestesses, for example, and when kings emerged, their wives had some power.

READING CHECK **Understand Effects** Why did Sumer, Harappa, and the Chinese civilization all form in river valleys?

What Role Did Religion Have in Sumerian Society?

Like most ancient peoples, the Sumerians practiced **polytheism**, the belief in more than one god. Sumerians believed these gods controlled every aspect of life, including rain, wind, and other elements of nature. Some gods represented agriculture or other activities.

Sumerians believed that the gods behaved much like people. They thought that the gods ate, drank, slept, and married. However, Sumerians also believed that the gods lived forever and had great power. If the gods were happy with people's prayers and offerings, they might bring good fortune to the city. If not, they might bring war, floods, or other disasters. As a result, Sumerians felt that they needed to keep the gods happy in order for their cities to grow and **prosper**.

Academic Vocabulary
distinct • *adj.*, separate, different
prosper • *v.*, to gain in wealth

Sumerians believed that only priests knew how to communicate with the gods. They depended on priests to tell them what the gods wanted. As a result, priests had an important role in Sumerian society. Their connection with the gods brought peace and social order.

In larger Sumerian cities, temples were pyramid-shaped brick towers known as **ziggurats** (ZIG OO rats). The largest ziggurats were seven stories tall. They rose upward in steps, with each level smaller than the one below. Some were filled with beautiful paintings and statues.

The area around a temple often included farmland controlled by the temple. Priests kept goods belonging to temples in large storehouses.

READING CHECK **Draw Conclusions** Why did Sumerians believe the success of their society depended on their priests?

ANSWERS

Use Evidence *Sumerian society supported itself with agriculture and trade.*

Understand Effects *They were able to make use of the river to irrigate crops to support growing populations.*

Draw Conclusions *Sumerians believed that only priests knew how to communicate with the gods. They believed they needed the priests so they would know how to please the gods.*

INTEGRATED ENGLISH LANGUAGE DEVELOPMENT

Interpretive Students use How Was Agriculture Important in Mesopotamia? to draw logical conclusions about how the geography and weather of Mesopotamia, farming, and the development of technology led to the settlement of the Fertile Crescent.

Emerging As students read, ask questions such as *What challenges did farmers face in order to grow crops?, What technology did they use to farm their land?*, and *What happened when they started using the technology?*

Expanding Have students work in groups. They should ask and answer questions that help them draw conclusions about the connections between the geography, weather, farming, technology, and the settlement of the Fertile Crescent. Show them how to use arrows to illustrate how their ideas connect.

What Was the Sumerian Writing System Like?

Sumerian priests needed a system to keep track of their stored goods. At first they drew pictographs on clay. Pictographs are simple pictures that represent objects. To record the number of fish given to a temple, for example, Sumerian priests drew a fish. Then they added marks to represent the number of fish. In time, this way of keeping records developed into the world's first system of writing.

Cuneiform By 3100 BCE, Sumerian priests had created a new writing system called cuneiform. **Cuneiform** is a system of writing that uses triangular-shaped symbols to stand for words, ideas, or sounds.

Cuneiform involved pressing wedge-shaped marks into clay tablets. By combining the marks in different ways, Sumerians could create thousands of symbols.

Epic of Gilgamesh Cuneiform was originally used to record sales, taxes, and agreements. Later, Sumerians began to use writing for more than record keeping. The *Epic of Gilgamesh*, which was written in cuneiform on 12 clay tablets, told the story of a hero.

The stories about Gilgamesh are myths, or made-up tales of gods and heroes. However, some scholars believe that Gilgamesh may have been a real king. These scholars think that he ruled the Sumerian city-state of Uruk sometime after 3000 BCE.

READING CHECK **Identify Main Ideas** How did the use of Sumerian writing change over time?

Did you know?

The largest surviving ziggurat measures 335 feet (102 meters) on each side and is estimated to have been over 150 feet (45 meters) tall.

Analyze Images The Ziggurat of Ur is an ancient temple built by Sumerians to honor their moon god, Nanna. **Use Visual Information** How might the height of a ziggurat have affected Sumerian people?

ELD.PI.B.6.b

Bridging Have students work in groups. They should ask and answer questions that help them draw conclusions about the connections between the geography, weather, agriculture, technology, and settlement of the Fertile Crescent. Show them how to connect their ideas using phrases such as *because of, for that reason,* and *since.*

WORKSHEET **TEACHER RESOURCES**

For additional IELD support addressing this standard, have students complete the Lesson ELD activity from the Teacher Resources found on the course.

What Was the Sumerian Writing System Like?

Discuss how the need for record keeping led to the development of cuneiform.

Synthesize How was the development of writing a result of improvements in agriculture? *(Improvements in agriculture led to surplus food. As a result, Sumerians needed a way to keep track of their stored goods, so they developed a system of writing.)*

Distinguish In what way was **cuneiform** more sophisticated than the use of pictographs? *(The wedgelike marks that made up cuneiform could represent words, ideas, or sounds, while pictographs represented only objects.)*

Compare Points of View What different points of view do scholars hold about the *Epic of Gilgamesh*? *(Some think that it is just a myth, while others believe that Gilgamesh was a real king of Uruk.)*

ANSWERS

Identify Main Ideas *At first, Sumerian writing was used for record keeping, but later it was used to record many things, including myths.*

Use Visual Information *Sample answers: It might have made them proud of their civilization; it might have made them feel their own insignificance.*

How Did Sumerian Government Work?

Discuss the roles that military leaders, kings, and priests played in Sumerian government.

Sequence Who originally ruled the city-states, and who ruled after them? *(First priests ruled, and then kings.)*

Identify Patterns Did priests and kings have a supportive relationship or a relationship full of conflict? Explain. *(It was supportive. Priests supported the kings by declaring the gods had chosen them. The kings supported the priests by respecting their rights and powers.)*

Hypothesize What is the advantage of having a written law code? *(Sample answer: The laws remain the same all the time for everyone. There are fewer disputes because the laws are clear to all.)*

Sumerian Achievements

Discuss the advances in technology made by Sumerians.

Summarize What were the Sumerians' main achievements? *(They used irrigation, invented the seed plow and cuneiform, found ways to divide time that we still use today, and developed bronze, which was harder than copper.)*

Identify Cause and Effect How did the Sumerians' achievements spread to other lands? *(Sumerian achievements spread through trade.)*

Analyze Information Cuneiform developed over time from a simple system for record keeping into a system of writing. **Understand Effects** How did cuneiform writing allow Sumerians to communicate more effectively?

How Did Sumerian Government Work?

The first leaders of Sumerian city-states were priests, not kings. But when conflicts arose among city-states, the way cities were ruled began to change.

Development of Kingship As city-states grew, people in different cities began to argue with one another over the control of land and water. These conflicts sometimes led to war.

In times of war, priests helped choose the best person to lead the city-state into battle. After the war was over, this leader was expected to give up his power and return to normal life. But some of these military leaders kept control of the city-states even after war ended. These military leaders became the first kings.

Kings and Priests To stay in power, kings needed the support of the priests. So kings were careful to respect the priests' rights and powers. In turn, priests declared that the gods had sent the king to rule the city. This idea that kings were chosen by the gods became common in Sumer. Together, kings and priests created religious ceremonies that supported royal power.

Sumerian kings eventually took over many jobs the priests once did. They hired workers to build new canals, temples, and roads. Each king also served as the city's chief lawmaker and judge.

Written Laws Some rulers collected city laws into a law code, or a written set of laws. The earliest known law code was issued around 2100 BCE by Ur-Nammu (uhr NAHM OO), the king of Ur. The Ur-Nammu law code included laws about marriage, slavery, and causing harm to other people.

ANSWERS

Understand Effects *Cuneiform allowed Sumerians to record information for future use or for people who were not present.*
Sequence *Leaders were brought in to head city-states in time of war, but when the war ended, they kept power and began taking over many of the jobs the priests had.*

Infer *the wealthy upper class; only they could afford materials and skills to have it made.*

Understand Effects *Bronze could be used to make stronger, better weapons. Cities with bronze weapons were more powerful than cities without bronze weapons.*

DIFFERENTIATED INSTRUCTION

Special Education To help students differentiate between city-states and modern states, review how large modern cities usually have a core surrounded by residential neighborhoods, surrounded by agricultural areas. Explain that an ancient city-state would include all these regions, and that the agricultural areas would ship their crops to the central city.

Below Level Have students work in pairs to create a flow chart that shows how the growth of city-states led to war and how war led to the rise of kings.

Advanced Suggest that students create a "contract" between a king and a high priest, outlining what each one's rights and powers are and explaining what each must do to support the other.

One law read, "If a man knocks out the eye of another man, he shall weigh out half a mina of silver." (A mina is a unit of weight that varied over time but was approximately one pound.)

READING CHECK **Sequence** What steps led to kings replacing priests as rulers of Sumerian city-states?

Sumerian Achievements

Under the rule of priests and kings, Sumerians produced many advances in technology. You have already read about the Sumerians' improvements to farming, such as their use of irrigation and the invention of the seed plow. You have read about their development of cuneiform, which allowed them to keep records. Innovations like the wheel and the sail improved transportation.

The Sumerians also made advances in mathematics and astronomy. Dividing an hour into 60 minutes and a minute into 60 seconds began with the Sumerians. They also divided the year into 12 months of 30 days each, much as we do today. Through trade, many of these Sumerian advances spread to other lands.

Another important advance in technology was the development of bronze. The Sumerians were one of the first cultures to make bronze, which is made by mixing copper and tin. Bronze is a harder metal than copper, so it is better for making tools and weapons. Bronze weapons would later play an important role in the growth of cities into large, powerful states.

Analyze Information
The bull's head decorating a harp shows the skill of Sumerian craft workers. **Infer** Which level of Sumerian society do you think this instrument was meant for? Why?

READING CHECK **Understand Effects** How did the invention of bronze lead to cities becoming large, powerful states?

Lesson Check

HSS 6.2.1, 6.2.2, 6.2.3, 6.2.9; ELD.P1.A.2, P1.C.10.a

Practice Vocabulary

1. How did **city-states** develop?
2. How did **cuneiform** develop?

Critical Thinking and Writing

3. **Use Evidence** How did the priests and kings of Sumer support one another?
4. **Understand Effects** Name two technological advances of the Sumerians and explain why these advances helped Sumeria become more prosperous and powerful.
5. **Draw Conclusions** How did irrigation affect Sumer?
6. **Writing Workshop: Introduce Characters** Imagine you are a person living in ancient Mesopotamia. Write a few sentences in your Active Journal that describe who you are and what your role is in society. You will use this information for a narrative essay you will write at the end of this topic.

HSS 6.2.1, 6.2.2, 6.2.3, 6.2.9; ELD.P1.A.2, P1.C.10.a

SYNTHESIZE

Assess and Reteach Have students use a Think-Pair-Share strategy to complete Lesson Check questions 1–5. Review their responses. If they had any incorrect answers, use the guiding questions to discuss the lesson's main ideas, focusing on the ideas they struggled with.

ACTIVE JOURNAL

Writing Workshop Have students complete the Lesson 1 Writing Task in their Active Journals. Students will write a few sentences introducing the character that they will use in their narrative essay. As they move through the topic, students will revisit their character introduction, adding details as needed.

DEMONSTRATE

ASSESSMENT **ONLINE LESSON QUIZ**

Assign the Online Lesson Quiz for this lesson. Students will get automatic remediation or enrichment based on their score.

DISCUSSION **DISCUSSION BOARD**

Post this question to the class on the Discussion Board:

Summarize How did civilization develop in **Mesopotamia**? *(People began to farm in the land between the rivers because floods provided water and fertile land. Developments in technology such as irrigation and the seed funnel helped them grow surplus crops. This caused the population to grow and cities to develop.)*

LESSON CHECK

1. City-states developed in places where food was abundant due to irrigation. As more people came to an area, it grew into a large and powerful city that became a city-state, governing itself. **DOK1**
2. Priests needed a way to keep track of their stored goods, so they began using pictographs. Over time, the symbols they used developed into cuneiform. **DOK1**
3. Priests supported the king by claiming the gods had sent him to rule. The king upheld the priests' rights and powers to stay in the gods' favor. **DOK3**
4. Sample answers: The seed funnel helped farmers plant more efficiently. The invention of bronze made for better tools and weapons. **DOK2**
5. Irrigation allowed desert areas to be farmed, which increased the food supply and helped the population grow. **DOK3**
6. Answers will vary. Students should identify the role and social position of their character based on the description of different social classes and their activities. **DOK4**

ELA RI.6.6

Primary Sources

Contracts in Ancient Mesopotamia

Read aloud the explanatory note about the source. Direct students' attention to the image of the clay tablet. Ask: What do you notice about the inscription on the tablet? *(Sample answer: It seems to show a type of map and quite of bit of cuneiform writing.)*

GUIDED READING

Read aloud all the passages without stopping. Then reread the passage, pausing after each paragraph to let students answer the numbered questions. Use the questions in the text to prompt students' analysis of the primary source.

Reading and Vocabulary Support Answers

3. *People only had one name so they had to be identified by who their parents were.*

4. *The sellers will have to pay the buyer.*

GUIDED ANALYSIS

After completing the reading, discuss what this primary source reveals about contracts in Mesopotamia.

Analyze Information Judging from the second and third contracts, how did ancient Mesopotamians identify their years? *(They counted the number of years the current monarch had been ruling.)*

Infer Why was it important to guarantee that the emerald would not fall out of the ring? *(Sample answer: Emeralds are valuable, so its loss would reduce the value of the ring and also damage the ring's appearance.)*

To assess understanding, have students respond to the Analyzing Primary Sources questions in writing.

ACTIVE JOURNAL

Quest Connection After answering the questions, have students respond to the Quest Connection question in their Active Journals.

ELA RI.6.6

Primary Sources

Contracts in Ancient Mesopotamia

As civilizations developed in ancient Mesopotamia, so did laws that governed daily life. Contracts, or agreements, from ancient Mesopotamia give us a glimpse into what daily life was like for people living there. The contracts shown here were all signed by the parties involved in the contract.

◄ Cuneiform tablet from 1500 BCE

Reading and Vocabulary Support

① *Shekel, talent,* and *qa* were units of measurement in ancient Mesopotamia.

② Tammuz was a month in ancient Mesopotamia. Other dates are linked to years in the reigns of different kings.

③ Relationships of persons to parents were often given in contracts to identify the people agreeing to the contract. What does this tell you about names in ancient Mesopotamia?

④ What will happen if the emerald falls out of the ring before 20 years have passed?

Quest CONNECTIONS

Read and think about these contracts. How would agreements like these contribute to social order? Record your findings in your Active Journal.

Akhibte has taken the house of Mashqu from Mashqu, the owner, on a lease for one year. He will pay one shekel ① of silver, the rent of one year. On the fifth of Tammuz ② he takes possession. Date: the fifth of Tammuz, the year of the wall of Kar-Shamash.

One talent one qa of dates from the woman Nukaibu daughter of Tabishna, ③ and the woman Khamaza, daughter of ___, to the woman Aqubatum, daughter of Aradya. In the month Siman they will deliver one talent one qa of dates. Date: adar the sixth, thirty-second year of Darius, King of Babylon and countries.

Bela-akha-iddin and Bel-shunu, sons of Bel-___ and Khatin, son of Bazuzu, spoke unto Bel-shum-iddin, son of Murashu, saying: "As to the ring in which an emerald has been set in gold, we guarantee that for twenty years the emerald will not fall from the gold ring. If the emerald falls from the gold ring before the expiration of twenty years, Bel-akha-iddin, Bel-shunu, (and) Kathin will pay to Bel-shum-iddin ten manas of silver." ④ Date: Nippur. Elul eighth, the thirty-fifth year of Artaxerxes.

Analyzing Primary Sources

Cite specific evidence from the contracts to support your answers.

1. **Infer** What role did women have in society according to the contracts?
2. **Compare and Contrast** How is the third contract different from the first two contracts? How does this difference make that contract stronger than the other two contracts?
3. **Compare Authors' Points of View** What was each person in each of these agreements trying to achieve by having a contract?

58 Primary Sources • Contracts in Ancient Mesopotamia

ANALYZING PRIMARY SOURCES

1. Sample response: They could make contracts just like men. The second contract is only between women regarding the delivery of an amount of dates.
2. Sample response: It includes information about what will happen if the guarantee is not met. The makers of the ring will pay the buyers. It makes the contract stronger because there is a consequence attached if the contract is not fulfilled.
3. Sample Response: In each agreement, each person wants to make sure the other person will keep his or her promise either to provide or pay for a good or service.

Analysis HI.2 HSS 6.2.2

Distinguish Cause and Effect

Use the graphic organizer and follow these steps to distinguish cause and effect.

INTERACTIVE
Analyze Cause and Effect

1 **Identify the key event.** Understanding causes and effects is a matter of finding factors that led to something happening. Those factors are the causes. The event or development they led to is the effect. The Sumerian invention of the wheel was a cause. Greater ease in moving goods was its effect that was also a cause, as it resulted in increased trade.

a. What is the central event or development that is the focus of this graphic organizer?

b. Is it a cause, an effect, or both?

2 **Study earlier events or conditions as possible causes.** A cause of the key event must happen before the key event. Look for earlier events by asking, Why did the key event happen? or What led to the key event? You may also find such clue words as *because* and *the reason that*, which suggest that one thing caused another. Bear in mind that key events often have more than one cause.

a. What physical feature contributed to there being a surplus of food?

b. What human factor contributed to there being a surplus of food?

3 **Study later events or conditions as possible effects.** Effects must follow the key event. They may include short-term effects or longer lasting ones. To find later events, ask What did the key event lead to? or What was a result of the key event? You may also find clue words or phrases, such as *brought about*, *led to*, *as a result*, or *therefore*. Look at the graphic organizer.

a. What were the effects of having a surplus of food?

b. Which of these was a long-term effect?

c. How did that effect come about?

Causes and Effects of the Rise of Sumerian City-States

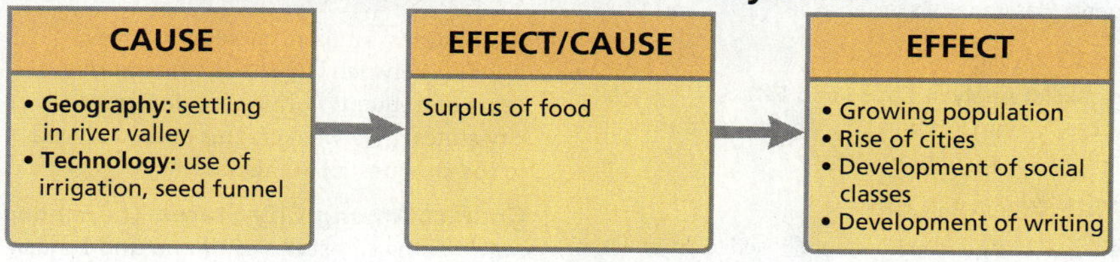

Analysis HI.2; HSS 6.2.2

Analysis Skills
Distinguish Cause and Effect

LEARN

Preview the steps in the student text with students, and then play the video.

VIDEO **21ST CENTURY SKILLS**

Project the Analyze Cause and Effect video in the 21st Century Skills Tutorial. Use the Quick Reference and Assessment to provide additional instruction on this skill.

PRACTICE

Have students practice the skill using the graphic organizer on the student page, providing the instruction and then asking students the questions.

As an alternative, you could form students into pairs or groups to perform the activity. Then invite the groups to describe the cause-and-effect relationships they found to the class.

ASSESS

To assess this skill, have students reread the section "When Did People Start to Farm?" in Lesson 3 of the previous topic. Ask them to create a cause-and-effect chart based on the material in this section.

DIFFERENTIATED INSTRUCTION

Below Level Remind students that there can be short-term effects and long-term effects of events. For example, the immediate effect of the annual flooding of the Tigris and Euphrates rivers was to bring water and fertile soil to the region. The long-term effect was to promote the development of agriculture.

INTEGRATED ENGLISH LANGUAGE DEVELOPMENT

Bridging Give students a list of verbs such as *led to*, *caused*, and *made* to help them express the cause-and-effect relationships.

ANSWERS

1. a. the surplus of food
b. It is both.

2. a. settling in a river valley
b. development of new technology, including the use of irrigation and seed funnels

3. a. growing population; rise of cities; development of social classes; development of writing
b. Rise of cities was a long-term effect.
c. Population growth led to the rise of cities, as people concentrated in one place.

HSS 6.2.4

The First Empires

CONNECT

GET READY TO READ

ETEXT **START UP**

Project the Start Up Activity. As students enter the classroom and get settled, ask them to examine the illustration of the city of Babylon. Ask them what details stand out in the image.

Formulate Questions Have students record two questions that they have about daily life in the city. *(Sample answers: What activities took place in the green parklike spaces? Was the tall structure at the back a religious or government building? Did rich people or poor people live in the central part of the city?)* Then have them share their questions with another student, either in class or through a chat or blog.

Discuss Explain that as conflict among the city-states continued, strong rulers decided to try to conquer the whole region.

After completing the Start UP activity, project the Lesson Opener or direct students to their textbooks. Preview the lesson by working through the Get Ready to Read items with the class. Remind students to pay close attention to the Guiding Questions as they read the lesson.

ACTIVE JOURNAL

Take Notes Have students use the lesson literacy skills graphic organizer in their Active Journals to take notes as they read the lesson.

Practice Vocabulary Have students complete the activity in their Active Journals to build their vocabulary.

VIDEO **VIDEO**

Assign the lesson video as homework.

LESSON 2 HSS 6.2.4

The First Empires

GET READY TO READ

START UP

Examine the image of the city of Babylon. Write two questions about what everyday life was like in the city.

GUIDING QUESTIONS

- How did Sargon form the world's first empire in Mesopotamia?
- How did people's lives change when the Babylonian empire conquered Sumer?
- What was the lasting impact of the Babylonian emperor Hammurabi's legal code?

TAKE NOTES

Literacy Skills: Analyze Cause and Effect

Use the graphic organizer in your Active Journal to take notes as you read the lesson.

PRACTICE VOCABULARY

Use the vocabulary activity in your Active Journal to practice the vocabulary words.

Vocabulary		Academic Vocabulary
empire	Hammurabi's Code	abundant
ally	rule of law	govern
cultural trait		

As the independent city-states of Sumer grew in size, power, and wealth, they became rivals. They each wanted to gain control over more resources. As a result, they often came into conflict. For hundreds of years, the city-states fought among themselves. In time, strong rulers conquered the whole region, creating the world's first empires. An **empire** is a state containing several countries or territories.

The Conquest of Sumer

As Sumerian kings struggled for power, fighting between city-states was common. Years of frequent fighting made Sumerian city-states grow weaker. This eventually led to the conquest of Sumer.

Conflict Among City-States The fighting between the city-states of Umma and Lagash is one example of the widespread conflict in Sumer. For many years, Umma and Lagash and their allies fought to control a fertile region on their shared border. An **ally** is an independent state that works with other states to achieve a shared military or political goal.

60 Lesson 2.2 • The First Empires

PRACTICE VOCABULARY

To help students integrate new vocabulary, explain that an *empire* is a state that rules several territories. Empires sometimes seek *allies*, or other independent states that will help them achieve a goal. A *cultural trait* is an idea or custom that is common to a culture. *Rule of law means* that everyone must obey the laws. *Hammurabi's Code* is a set of laws developed in the Babylonian empire. Reinforce the terms during the lesson using the teaching notes.

Point out the academic vocabulary in the lesson margins. Provide sample sentences that clarify meaning.

abundant: The harvest was good, so food was abundant.

govern: The president governed the country.

Around 2450 BCE, armies from Umma and Lagash met in a major battle. Soldiers used bronze axes and long spears with sharp metal points. Thousands of troops died in the fighting before Lagash won the battle. To celebrate their victory, Lagash soldiers looted and burned Umma. They captured prisoners from Umma to be sold as slaves.

It took years for Umma to recover from the defeat. Around 2375 BCE, a powerful king of Umma finally defeated Lagash and several other Sumerian city-states. His rule soon came to an end, however.

How Did Sargon Build an Empire? While the Sumerian city-states struggled for power, a new society arose in Mesopotamia. The Akkadian people lived to the northwest of Sumer, but they were not related to Sumerians. Akkadians spoke a different language and had different customs.

During the 2300s BCE, an Akkadian man named Sargon became king of the Sumerian city-state of Kish. He changed the language used by the government to Akkadian. Under Sargon's rule, the Akkadian army conquered other Mesopotamian city-states. He placed loyal Akkadians in important government and religious positions. For example, he chose his daughter to be a high priestess in the city-state of Ur. These moves helped him solidify his power. Then Sargon united much of Mesopotamia under his rule, creating the world's first empire, which is called the Akkadian empire.

Akkadian Culture The Akkadians and Sumerians shared some cultural traits. A **cultural trait** is an idea or way of doing things that is common in a certain culture. For example, the Akkadians and Sumerians had similar religious practices, and both societies used the cuneiform system of writing.

As Sargon's troops moved throughout the Fertile Crescent, they brought their cultural traits with them. Furthermore, Akkadians began to trade with people as far away as the Indus Valley in modern day Pakistan. While the Fertile Crescent provided **abundant** crops, it had few trees and did not provide any minerals. Trading to the east and west, Akkadians obtained wood, copper, silver, and precious stones like red carnelian and blue lapis lazuli. Through trade, Akkadian and Sumerian culture spread to other regions and was adopted by other peoples.

How Did the Akkadian Empire End? To control such a large empire, Sargon appointed local rulers. Each local ruler served as king of the land he oversaw. Sargon was able to control the Akkadian empire for more than 50 years.

After Sargon's death in 2279 BCE, the Akkadian empire faced a growing number of rebellions and invasions. Within 100 years, the empire had collapsed. Warriors from the Zagros Mountains, east of the Tigris River, eventually took control of the region.

INTERACTIVE
Akkadian and Babylonian Empires

▲ Sargon, builder of the world's first empire

Academic Vocabulary
abundant • *adj.*, plentiful

WORKSHEET TEACHER RESOURCES

Have students who need additional support use the following worksheets:

- **Reading Support**
- **English Language Development**
- **Lesson Summary**

INVESTIGATE

The Conquest of Sumer

Discuss how Sargon conquered Sumer and built an empire.

Distinguish Cause and Effect Identify the cause and effect of the conflict between Umma and Lagash. *(Cause: The city-states fought to control fertile land on their shared border. Effect: Umma was defeated.)*

Connect How was Sargon able to rule such a vast **empire**? *(He appointed local rulers to serve as kings of their various lands.)*

INTERACTIVE INTERACTIVE CHART

Akkadian and Babylonian Empires

Display the Interactive Chart: Akkadian and Babylonian Empires. Have volunteers sort the tiles into the correct boxes. Ask: Why was the Akkadian ruler called an emperor? *(Sample answer: He had great power and ruled over an empire.)*

ACTIVE CLASSROOM

Use the Opinion Line strategy. Ask students to form an opinion line based on which empire they would rather have lived in, with strongly want to be Akkadian and strongly want to be Babylonian on either side of the room.

DIFFERENTIATED INSTRUCTION

Special Education Students may know the term *code* only in the sense of a cipher, which might lead to confusion in this lesson. Introduce them to the broader sense of the term. A *code* is usually a system: a code of laws, a code of conduct, or a code of symbols used to hide a message.

Below Level Suggest that students use the 5 Ws to record details about Hammurabi's Code: *What* is Hammurabi's Code? *Who* compiled it? *When* were the laws written? *Why* was the code compiled? *Where* was it compiled?

Advanced Suggest that groups of students do Internet research to learn what similarities exist between Hammurabi's Code and Old Testament laws. They can make a poster listing laws that are similar in each and display it in class.

Sequence What events happened in Sumer from about 2100 BCE to about 2000 BCE? *(Ur-Nammu, ruler of Ur, reunited Sumer; Ur prospered for about 100 years; then an uprising of rebels destroyed Ur and ended Ur's rule over Sumer.)*

The Babylonian Empire

Discuss how Babylon grew from a small city to an empire.

Cite Evidence What can you conclude about Hammurabi's character from the way he built his **empire**? Cite details that demonstrate his character. *(Sample answer: He was careful and organized. He solidified his power and built an army before attacking other city-states.)*

Compare and Contrast How was Hammurabi's method of ruling similar to Sargon's? *(Both gave power to rulers who controlled distant cities.)*

INTERACTIVE **PRIMARY SOURCE**

Have students go online to analyze the Code of Hammurabi Interactive Primary Source.

Then ask: What can you conclude about Babylonian society from these laws? *(Possible answer: (Babylonian society was complex, and people experienced many of the issues we experience today, including robberies, lawsuits, floods and droughts, inheritance issues, and poor workmanship. It is also clear that slavery was a common practice in Babylonian society.)*

Analyze Images This carving honors the Akkadian king Naram-Sin's victory over enemies. **Identify Supporting Details** What details in the carving glorify the king?

Around 2100 BCE, Sumer was united again, this time by Ur-Nammu, the ruler of Ur. Ur-Nammu issued the world's first known law code. Ur prospered for about 100 years under Ur-Nammu and later rulers. Then, an uprising of rebels from the east managed to destroy Ur and capture its ruler. This ended Ur's rule over Sumer. Once again, the Sumerian city-states fought over power.

READING CHECK **Identify Cause and Effect** How did Sargon strengthen his power?

The Babylonian Empire

After the destruction of Ur, many groups invaded Sumer. One of them, the Amorites, came from northern Mesopotamia. The Amorites took control of several Sumerian cities, including Babylon (BAB uh lahn). At the time, Babylon was a small, unimportant city on the Euphrates River near present-day Baghdad, Iraq. But under a king named Hammurabi (hah muh RAH bee), Babylon became the center of a new Mesopotamian empire.

The Empire Forms Around 1792 BCE, Hammurabi became king of Babylon. For 30 years, he solidified his power and built up his army. Then he launched a series of attacks against other Mesopotamian city-states. Within a few years he had united southern Mesopotamia into what we now call the Old Babylonian (bab uh LOH nee uhn) empire, which is also called Babylonia.

Hammurabi was an excellent military leader, and he was also a skilled ruler. Like Sargon, after Hammurabi built his empire he had to create a government strong enough to hold it together. He sent his own governors, tax collectors, and judges to rule distant cities. He spread out his well-trained troops over the empire. Hammurabi also oversaw a number of public building projects and encouraged the growth of trade with other lands.

The Significance of Hammurabi's Code Today, Hammurabi is best remembered for his creation of **Hammurabi's Code**, a set of laws that governed life in the Babylonian empire. Many of these laws had existed since Sumerian times, but Hammurabi wanted to make sure everyone in Babylonia knew the laws they were expected to live by. In the introduction to his code, Hammurabi wrote that he wanted to

INTEGRATED ENGLISH LANGUAGE DEVELOPMENT

Interpretive Students identify the correct meaning of multiple-meaning words.

Emerging As students read, they underline *ruler, power, building, set, order,* and *key*. Then they choose the definition of the words as used in the passage from two definitions (e.g., *key*: "important" and "something that opens a lock").

Expanding As students read, they underline *ruler, power, building, set, order,* and *key*. Then they match the words as they are used in the passage with the correct definition. Have students use the definition to rewrite each sentence.

Bridging Students work in pairs and use a dictionary to look up *ruler, power, building, set, order,* and *key*. They find and copy the definition that best

ANSWERS

Identify Cause and Effect *Sargon appointed Akkadians to important government and religious positions because they were loyal to him, so they would help him solidify his power and unite the empire.*

Identify Supporting Details *Sample answer: He is bigger than other figures. He is shown standing on his enemies.*

Primary Source

bring about the rule of righteousness in the land, to destroy the wicked and the evil-doers; so that the strong should not harm the weak—so that I should . . . further the well-being of mankind.

—Hammurabi's Code

Hammurabi's Code includes nearly 300 laws. Some laws have to do with crimes such as robbery and murder. The code states specific punishments for these crimes. For example, one law reads, "If a man put out the eye of another man, his eye shall be put out." Although such punishments may sound cruel by modern standards, they did encourage social order.

Other laws in Hammurabi's Code dealt with private matters such as business contracts, taxes, marriage, and divorce. Many of these laws treated various groups of people differently. For example, the penalty for harming someone of the same rank in society was greater than the penalty for harming someone of lower rank, such as an enslaved person.

Hammurabi's Code was more detailed than Ur-Nammu's law code. In fact, it was the first major attempt to organize and write down all the laws that **governed** a society. It established the **rule of law**, or the idea that all members of a society must obey the law. This idea is a key part of modern democratic principles.

Quick Activity

Explore Hammurabi's Code and make your own modern laws in your Active Journal.

Academic Vocabulary

govern • *v.*, to control or strongly influence

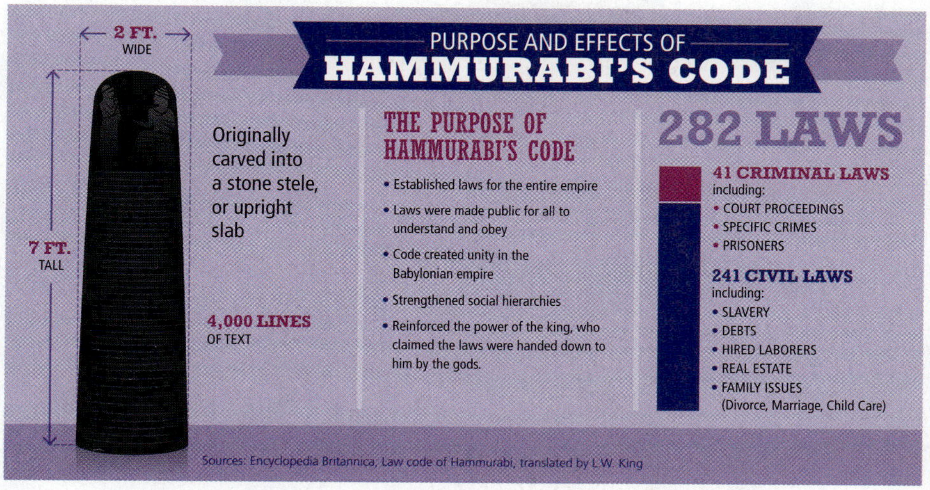

Analyze Diagrams The purpose of Hammurabi's Code was to create common rules for the diverse people of the society. **Identify Main Ideas** Why was it important that Hammurabi's Code was written down?

ELD.PI.B.6.c

matches the meaning of the words as they are used in the passage.

WORKSHEET **TEACHER RESOURCES**

For additional IELD support addressing these standards, have students complete the Lesson IELD activity from the Teacher Resources found on the course.

ACTIVE JOURNAL

Quick Activity Have students work in pairs to make their own code of laws and record it in their Active Journals. Have pairs share their ideas in class, and if you have time, compile a class code of laws.

ELD TIP Give students time to think about the task and the language they'll use before they share their ideas with their partners or hear their partners' answers.

Draw Conclusions Do you think the Babylonians found the laws in **Hammurabi's Code** shocking or cruel? *(Sample answer: No, it was based on laws they already had and knew.)*

Support Ideas with Examples Have students read the primary source. How do you think Hammurabi's Code helped to "further the well-being of mankind"? *(Sample answer: By providing a system of laws, Hammurabi's Code was meant to give people a safe, orderly place to live.)*

Connect How is a law code related to **rule of law**? *(Sample answer: Having a written law code means that society's expectations are clearly recorded, and no one has an excuse not to obey or to impose laws arbitrarily.)*

Infer What enabled Sumer's influence to survive after the Babylonian **empire** collapsed? *(Sample answer: Through trade, many people from other places had learned about Sumerian achievements and they took that knowledge back to their homelands where it survived.)*

ANSWERS

Identify Main Ideas *Sample answer: It was important to write down laws to make sure they were applied consistently and to pass them down to future generations.*

HSS 6.2.4; ELD.P1.A.2, P1.C.10.a

SYNTHESIZE

Assess and Reteach Have students work in groups to complete Lesson Check questions 1–7. Use the guiding questions to review any ideas they struggled with.

ACTIVE JOURNAL

Writing Workshop Have students complete the Lesson 2 Writing Task in their Active Journals. Students will identify other people from Mesopotamian society to be characters in their narrative.

DEMONSTRATE

ASSESSMENT **ONLINE LESSON QUIZ**

Assign the Online Lesson Quiz for this lesson if you haven't already done so.

DISCUSSION **DISCUSSION BOARD**

Post this question to the class on the Discussion Board:

Identify Cause and Effect How did **Hammurabi's Code** shape modern governments? *(It established the rule of law, a principle in modern democracies.)*

ANSWERS

Infer *They were skillful craftspeople who could creatively depict what they saw.*

Draw Conclusions *It established the idea that all members of society must obey the law.*

Analyze Images An artist gave this decorative cup the form of a sheep. **Infer** What can you conclude about the artists of this period from this object?

Life in the Babylonian Empire Hammurabi's Code and other Babylonian writings give historians a great deal of information about life in Babylonia. People's lives changed when states and empires took over. There were greater social differences. Now there were kings, priests, and government officials. But still most people were very poor. They were farmers, artisans, or slaves. Many people's lives revolved around agriculture. Food had to be grown and distributed. Irrigation canals had to be kept clear of silt. Wool had to be collected and woven into textiles, or cloth.

In the cities, some people used new technologies to make tools, weapons, pottery, perfumes, and medicines. Babylonian artists were known for their stone and bronze sculptures. They also used gold and precious stones to make jewelry. All the goods were traded within the empire and with other lands.

Legacy of Sumer Sumerian culture stayed alive in Babylonia, just as it had in the Akkadian empire under Sargon. But Hammurabi's empire eventually collapsed after his death in 1750 BCE. In the years that followed, the once-great civilization of Sumer slowly faded away.

Sumer's influence, however, did not disappear. The many peoples who had come into contact with Sumerian civilization adopted ideas and customs from it. In this way, Sumerian advances lived on.

READING CHECK **Draw Conclusions** Why was Hammurabi's Code important?

Lesson Check

HSS 6.2.4; ELD.P1.A.2, P1.C.10.a

Practice Vocabulary

1. What Sumerian **cultural traits** did Akkadians share?
2. How did Sargon create Mesopotamia's first **empire**?
3. What is the **rule of law** and why is it important?

Critical Thinking and Writing

4. **Explain** How did Sargon and Hammurabi keep control of large empires?
5. **Identify Main Ideas** Why was trade with other societies important to the Akkadian and Babylonian empires?
6. **Draw Inferences** How did the geography of Mesopotamia help spread Sumerian advances?
7. **Compare and Contrast** the roles of farmers, artisans, and slaves to the roles of rulers and other government officials in the Akkadian and Babylonian empires.
8. **Writing Workshop: Introduce Characters** In your Active Journal, identify other people from Mesopotamian society that your character would interact with. Explain what these other characters do and how they know your character.

LESSON CHECK

1. Akkadians shared Sumerian religious practices and cuneiform. **DOK1**
2. Sargon created the first Mesopotamian empire, the Akkadian empire, by conquering Mesopotamian city-states and uniting them under his rule. **DOK1**
3. It is the idea that all members of society must obey the law. It is important because it means no one is above the law. **DOK1**
4. They appointed local rulers who governed each region. **DOK1**
5. People of the Fertile Crescent could produce their own food but did not have access to wood or minerals such as silver. **DOK1**
6. Mesopotamia's location between the Tigris and Euphrates, nearness to the Mediterranean, and lack of mountains encouraged trade, which spread Sumerian advances. **DOK2**
7. Farmers, artisans, and slaves did jobs such as growing food and crops and making wool into textiles. They had little power. Kings and priests contributed to society by making laws and governing. They had the most power. **DOK3**
8. Students should identify the other people and explain their relationship to the main character. **DOK4**

LESSON 3

HSS 6.2.3, 6.4.5

The Assyrian and Persian Empires

GET READY TO READ

START UP

Examine the carving of Assyrian fighters. What can you conclude about Assyrian warfare from this image?

GUIDING QUESTIONS

- How did Assyrian armies conquer their vast empire?
- How did the Persian empire balance local self-government with central power?
- How did the cultures of Mesopotamia create a rich cultural tradition?

TAKE NOTES

Literacy Skills: Summarize

Use the graphic organizer in your Active Journal to take notes as you read the lesson.

PRACTICE VOCABULARY

Use the vocabulary activity in your Active Journal to practice the vocabulary words.

Vocabulary		Academic Vocabulary
cavalry	currency	elite
standing army	stele	reform
tribute		

Invaders swept into Mesopotamia after Hammurabi's death in 1750 BCE. Hundreds of years passed before the Assyrians, a people of northern Mesopotamia, united the region again. In time, the Assyrian empire gave way to the powerful Persian empire.

How Did the Assyrian and Neo-Babylonian Empires Develop?

Assyria (uh SEER ee uh) lay north of Babylon, along the Tigris River. Like much of Mesopotamia, it fell under the influence of Sumer. Later, Assyria was part of the Akkadian and Babylonian empires.

Why Was Assyria Known as a Military State? After Babylonia fell, the Assyrians fought against a steady stream of invaders. Some of them conquered Assyria, but for long periods the Assyrians stayed free.

Assyria's armies included some of the world's earliest **cavalry**, or soldiers who fight while riding horses. Assyrians used iron weapons and tools, which were stronger than the bronze ones.

PRACTICE VOCABULARY

To help students integrate new vocabulary, group related terms. A *cavalry* is an army that fights on horseback, while a *standing army* is a permanent army. *Currency* refers to money, while *tribute* is payment that a conquered people pays to their conquerors. A *stele* is a carved stone slab or pillar that stands upright. Reinforce the terms during the lesson using the teaching notes.

Point out the academic vocabulary in the lesson margins. Provide sample sentences that clarify meaning.

elite: Elite athletes make up the championship basketball team.

reform: A country can reform its economy by improving its finances.

HSS 6.2.3, 6.4.5

The Assyrian and Persian Empires

CONNECT

GET READY TO READ

ETEXT START UP

Project the Start Up Activity. As students enter the classroom and get settled, ask them to examine the carving of Assyrian warriors.

Draw Conclusions Have students record at least two conclusions they can make based on the carving about Assyrian warriors. *(Sample answers: The army used chariots. The* soldiers *used armor.)* Then have them share their ideas with another student, either in class or through a chat or blog.

Discuss Remind students that the development of bronze helped the Sumerians defeat their enemies. Note that they will learn about the Assyrians' technological innovations.

After completing the Start UP activity, project the Lesson Opener or direct students to their textbooks. Preview the lesson by working through the Get Ready to Read items with the class. Remind students to pay close attention to the Guiding Questions as they read the lesson.

ACTIVE JOURNAL

Take Notes Have students use the lesson literacy skills graphic organizer in their Active Journals to take notes as they read the lesson.

Practice Vocabulary Have students complete the activity in their Active Journals to build their vocabulary.

VIDEO VIDEO

Assign the lesson video as homework.

WORKSHEET **TEACHER RESOURCES**

Have students who need additional support use the following worksheets from the Teacher Resources on the course:

- **Reading Support**
- **English Language Development**
- **Lesson Summary**

INVESTIGATE

How Did the Assyrian and Neo-Babylonian Empires Develop?

Discuss how the Assyrians and Babylonians built and controlled empires.

Identify Cause and Effect How did the Assyrians become powerful warriors? *(Frequent fighting with their enemies led them to become fierce warriors.)*

Solve Problems How did the Assyrians try to solve the problem of ruling a large empire? *(They divided the empire into about 70 provinces, each ruled by a governor who reported directly to the Assyrian ruler.)*

Draw Conclusions How did Nebuchadnezzar strengthen Babylon's defenses? *(Sample answer: He built great walls and gates.)*

How Did the Persian Empire Rise?

Discuss how the Persians built the largest empire the world had seen.

Support Ideas With Evidence What evidence supports the idea that the Persians built a great empire? *(It covered more territory than any earlier empire. It also lasted more than a thousand years.)*

ANSWERS

Identify Supporting Details *Governors reported directly to the Assyrian king, so he could stay in control of even remote areas.*

Infer *Sample answer: They used both spears and bows and arrows.*

Did you know?

The Hanging Gardens of Babylon were so impressive that they were judged to be one of the seven wonders of the ancient world. Archaeologists have not yet found the site of this wondrous structure, however.

The Assyrians built up a strong military state by the mid-800s BCE. Within 200 years, they turned that state into an empire. By the mid-600s BCE, the Assyrian empire stretched north from the Persian Gulf across the entire Fertile Crescent and southwest into Egypt.

Political Order in the Empire Like Sargon and Hammurabi, Assyrian rulers found that controlling a large empire was difficult. The Assyrians divided the empire into about 70 smaller units of government called provinces. They assigned a governor to each province. Each governor reported directly to the Assyrian ruler. This helped the ruler keep control of distant lands.

An Assyrian ruler named Ashurbanipal (osh ur BANH ee pol) made the city of Nineveh his capital. There, he built a library and filled it with cuneiform tablets. They were mainly texts and letters from Sumer and Babylonia on subjects such as law, literature, mathematics, and science. Some 20,000 of these tablets survive today.

How Was Babylon Restored? After Ashurbanipal's death, civil war and enemy attacks weakened the Assyrian empire. In 604 BCE, Nebuchadnezzar (neb yuh kud NEZ ur) II became king of Babylon. He expanded his power as far west as Egypt. He also captured Jerusalem, destroyed the Jewish Temple, and exiled many Jews to Babylon. Nebuchadnezzar's empire is known as the Neo-Babylonian empire. Nebuchadnezzar spent much money building great walls, gates, and temples. His most famous project was the Hanging Gardens of Babylon. The Hanging Gardens were elaborate gardens built on a series of stone terraces.

Analyze Images These archers decorated the palace of a Persian emperor. **Infer** What can you conclude about the Persian armies from this image?

READING CHECK **Identify Supporting Details** How did the structure of Assyrian government help kings run their empire?

How Did the Persian Empire Rise?

Babylon's thick walls and strong gates were not able to keep out new conquerors. In 539 BCE, Babylon and the rest of Mesopotamia fell under the control of the powerful Persian empire. That empire soon became the largest the world had ever seen. Although the names of the Persian empire changed over time depending on who was ruling, the empire itself stayed in existence for over a thousand years. It dominated much of southwestern Asia and sometimes even Egypt between 500 BCE and 630 CE. It had great political and cultural influence over western Asia during these centuries.

DIFFERENTIATED INSTRUCTION

Special Education To help students understand the difficulties of controlling a large empire, ask them to think about the difference between one adult trying to control two children in a public place and one adult trying control a large group of children. Have them discuss the kinds of problems that occur with larger groups. Help them anticipate similar problems that might occur in a large empire, such as poor communication, insufficient rulers, or disobedience.

Below Level Have students skim through the section noting images, headings, and boldfaced terms. Ask them to explain what this preview demonstrates about life in the Assyrian and Persian empires.

Advanced Have students conduct research into what kind of rulers the Assyrian and Persian emperors were. Have them create a graphic organizer, such as a Venn diagram, to summarize the information.

Assyrian and Persian Empires, 934–300 BCE

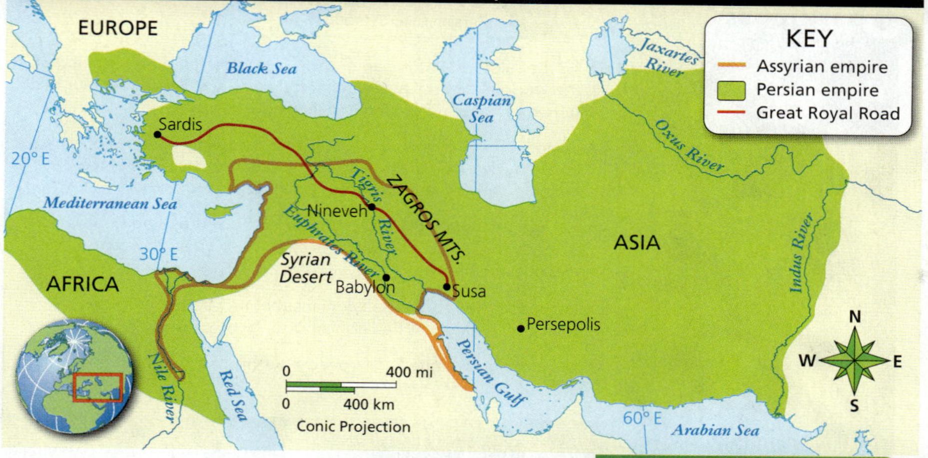

Cyrus the Great Persia formed to the east of Mesopotamia, in what is now Iran. For years, the Persians had been ruled by their neighbors to the north, a people called the Medes. But in 550 BCE, Cyrus the Great led the Persians to victory over the Medes. By conquering the Medes, the Persians won an empire.

Cyrus fought to create an even larger empire. He began in Asia Minor, in what is now Turkey, fighting the kingdom of Lydia. He defeated Lydia's rich king, Croesus (KREE sus). Then Cyrus pushed south into Ionia, a region settled by Greeks. One by one, he conquered Ionia's city-states. Later, Cyrus expanded Persia's border in the east, toward India.

Persia's rapid growth was due to its large and highly skilled standing army. A **standing army** is a permanent army of professional soldiers. The core of this army was a force of 10,000 **elite** soldiers known as the "Immortals."

Conquest of Babylon Cyrus and the Persian army captured Babylon in 539 BCE. Under his rule, Babylon grew into the wealthiest province of the Persian empire. In general, Cyrus treated the Babylonians and other conquered peoples well. He allowed them to keep their own customs and religions rather than forcing them to adopt Persian ways. For example, when Cyrus conquered Babylon he allowed the Jewish people to return to Jerusalem and rebuild their Temple.

Further Development Cyrus died in a battle in 530 BCE. His son Cambyses (kam BY seez) II continued his father's dream of increasing the size of the Persian empire. First, Cambyses invaded northeast Africa and conquered Egypt. From there, he traveled south to try to capture Kush, but failed.

GEOGRAPHY SKILLS

The Assyrian empire began from a base in northern Mesopotamia. The Persian empire originated further east.

1. **Region** Which empire mainly occupied the Fertile Crescent?
2. **Use Visual Information** What did the Great Royal Road connect?

Academic Vocabulary
elite • *adj.*, representing the best

INTERACTIVE
Assyrian and Persian Empires

Sequence Events How did Cyrus the Great win and then expand his empire? *(First, he defeated the Medes, who ruled Persia. This won the Persians an empire. Then he began to conquer other neighboring territories, such as Lydia and Ionia.)*

Draw Conclusions Why is it an advantage for an empire to have a **standing army**? *(Sample answer: Having a permanent army allows the soldiers to constantly improve their fighting skills.)*

Infer Why do you think Cyrus allowed conquered peoples to keep their own customs and religions? *(Sample answer: to make them more content and reduce the chance of uprisings)*

INTERACTIVE **INTERACTIVE GALLERY**

Assyrian and Persian Empires

Display the Interactive Gallery: Assyrian and Persian Empires. Click on each image and ask volunteers to read the captions. Ask: What did you learn about their technology? *(Sample answer: The Assyrians developed iron weapons.)* Ask: What did you learn about the ways they unified their empires? *(Sample answers: The Persians built the Royal Road.)*

HISTORY BACKGROUND

Royal City Archaeologists have uncovered an ancient city named Pasargadae, which Cyrus turned into his royal capital city. The remains of extensive grounds have revealed the ruins of two palaces, formal gardens, and smaller open-sided pavilions. The gardens were divided into four equal parts, possibly to symbolize the "four quarters" of the world that Cyrus claimed to rule. The gardens were watered by nearly one mile of stone conduit. At intervals, square basins carved from a single rock were used to store water for the plants.

ACTIVE CLASSROOM

Use the Take a Stand strategy. Ask students whether they would have preferred to live in the Assyrian or Persian empire. Have them move to different sides of the room based on their answers. Groups should discuss reasons for their choice and appoint a representative to share them with the class.

ANSWERS

Region *the Assyrian empire*

Use Visual Information *the cities Sardis, Nineveh, and Susa*

Draw Conclusions After students have read 5 Things to Know About Cyrus the Great, ask: What do you think is the cleverest decision that Cyrus made? Why? *(Sample answer: The cleverest decision was terrorizing Lydian horses with the smell of camels because it gave him a victory without a lot of fighting.)*

Cause and Effect What was the result of the invasion of Kush by Cambyses? *(It ended in disaster; Persian soldiers did not have enough food and many died of starvation.)*

Persia's Government and Religion

Discuss how the Persians used government and religion to unify their empire.

Summarize How did the Persians keep their vast empire together? *(They balanced local and central power.)*

Infer What is the purpose of demanding tribute of conquered peoples? *(Sample answers: It helps the empire's finances; it reminds the conquered peoples that they are ruled by someone stronger.)*

ACTIVE JOURNAL

Quest Connection As students read the text on these two pages, direct them to the Quest Connections pages in their Active Journals. Make sure that students connect the topic of punishments to the idea of Persian policies.

ELD TIP Pair emerging and expanding students with fluent speakers to read How Did the Persian Empire Rise? Have students use the map on the previous page to trace Cyrus' exploits.

ANSWERS

Critical Thinking *He greatly expanded the Persian empire.*

Identify Implied Main Ideas *Persia extended over a large area, lasted in different forms for more than a thousand years, and influenced Asia politically and culturally.*

BIOGRAPHY
5 Things to Know About CYRUS THE GREAT
Persian ruler 590/580–c. 529 BCE

- As the ruler of the Persian empire, Cyrus declared himself king of the world in 539 BCE and within fifty years, the Persian empire had grown to cover nearly three million square miles.
- Using his knowledge that horses are frightened by the smell of camels, he swiftly defeated the Lydian army and doubled the size of the Persian empire simply by terrorizing the Lydian horses with camels.
- He had his troops dig trenches overnight to drain the Euphrates River to thigh level, allowing his soldiers to cross and capture the city of Babylon.
- He proclaimed to the Babylonians that he had been chosen by Marduk, the highest Babylonian god, to be their ruler.
- His empire continued to expand after his death, lasting more than a thousand years.

Critical Thinking What did Cyrus do that convinced Persians to call him "the Great"?

Cambyses marched the Persian army through the desert with little food or other supplies. Soon his men were forced to kill and eat their pack animals. Many Persians died of starvation.

After Cambyses died, Darius (duh RY us) took the Persian throne by force. Under his rule, Persia grew even larger, and Darius became known as Darius the Great. He extended Persian rule east to the Indus Valley. In the west, the Persian army defeated Thrace, which was the first Persian victory in Europe. But later campaigns against Greece ended in Persia's defeat at the Battle of Marathon.

Quest CONNECTIONS How did Cyrus and other Persian rulers try to establish social order? Record your thoughts in your Active Journal.

READING CHECK **Identify Implied Main Ideas** Why was the Persian empire important to the history of southwest Asia?

Persia's Government and Religion

The vast Persian empire included peoples with many different cultures. Persian rulers had to find a way to unify the empire. They might have tried to force people to follow the same customs and same laws. The Persians took a different approach, however.

Local Self-Government Darius created a political structure that gave local people some control over their own government. Darius divided his empire into satrapies, or provinces, and chose a leader for each one. Darius allowed them to keep their local laws and traditions and make many of their own decisions.

Academic Vocabulary
reform • *v.*, to improve

Central Control Darius also **reformed** the empire's central, or overall, government. First, he improved its finances. Conquered peoples had always sent tribute to the Persian ruler. **Tribute** is payment made to show loyalty to a stronger power, but the amount of tribute was often set by the ruler.

INTEGRATED ENGLISH LANGUAGE DEVELOPMENT

Interpretive Use Persia's Government and Religion to encourage students to exchange ideas about Darius's reforms.

Emerging Read the text aloud, pausing at the end of the first paragraph. Ask, *Did the Persian rulers force everyone to follow the same laws? Which word tells you that they didn't?*

Expanding Group students to use textual evidence to provide four examples of how Darius's reforms made life fairer, trade easier, and communication faster among Persian provinces.

Before Darius, Persian rulers often showed no concern for what a region could really afford to pay. Darius created a fairer system in which each province paid according to its wealth.

Next, Darius created a common currency. **Currency** is money that is used as a medium of exchange, usually bills or coins. Darius introduced gold coins—printed with an image of himself—that would be accepted across the Persian empire as payment for goods. The currency helped unify the Persian economy by making it easier for distant provinces to trade with one another.

New Roads Darius used some of Persia's great wealth to build roads across the empire. Trade goods and tribute traveled on these roads. So did armies, government officials, and royal messengers.

The Persians set up postal stations along the 1,500-mile-long Great Royal Road. Messengers on horseback brought messages from one station to the next. It took three months for a message to travel from one end of the road to another. Still, the Persian system was the fastest communication system in the ancient world. The Greek historian Herodotus wrote:

Primary Source

Nothing mortal travels so fast as these Persian messengers. . . . [T]hese men will not be hindered from accomplishing at their best speed the distance which they have to go, either by snow, or rain, or heat, or by the darkness of night.

—from *The Persian Wars* by Herodotus, translated by George Rawlinson

Analyze Images This sculpture from a Persian capital shows conquered peoples carrying tribute. **Draw Conclusions** Why would a Persian ruler want to show a scene like this?

Religion In ancient times, most people worshiped many gods. But beginning around 600 BCE, a Persian man known as Zoroaster (zoh roh AS tur) taught that there is one supreme god, Ahura Mazda, who has an evil opponent. Over time, Zoroaster's beliefs developed into the religion Zoroastrianism. Zoroastrianism eventually became the official religion of the empire, although conquered people could worship their own gods.

The sacred text of Zoroastrianism is the Avesta, which includes prayers, hymns, and other writings. Zoroastrianism's central belief is that the universe is in a state of struggle between the forces of good and evil. Zoroastrians believe that people have an important role to play in this conflict by working for good. They also believe in the existence of an afterlife. Historians think that these teachings later influenced Judaism, Christianity, and Islam.

READING CHECK **Identify Supporting Details** How did Darius change the Persian empire?

Identify Cause and Effect What effect did creating a common **currency** have on Darius's empire? *(It helped unify the Persian economy by making it easier for distant provinces to trade with one another.)*

Identify Cause and Effect What effect did the roads that Darius built have on the empire? *(They improved trade, and they allowed armies, officials, and messengers to move quickly from one place to another.)*

Connect Which beliefs of Zoroastrianism may have influenced later religions? *(Sample answer: There is a struggle between good and evil, and there is an afterlife.)*

Arts of Mesopotamia

Discuss what the arts of Mesopotamia reveal about culture there.

Compare and Contrast How were Sumerian sculptures different from those in the past? *(Sumerian sculptures were more realistic.)*

ELD.PI.B.7

Bridging Form students into groups. Have them discuss the various ways Darius unified Persia. Remind students to use specific language and detailed evidence from the text to describe the reforms.

WORKSHEET **TEACHER RESOURCES**

For additional IELD support addressing these standards, have students complete the Lesson ELD activity from the Teacher Resources found on the course.

ANSWERS

Draw Conclusions *A scene like this demonstrates a Persian ruler's great power.*

Identify Supporting Details *Darius reformed the empire's finances, gave local rulers control of individual territories, and supported trade and his rule by building a road system.*

HSS 6.2.3, 6.4.5; ELD.P1.A.2, P1.C.10.a

SYNTHESIZE

Assess and Reteach Have students work in groups to complete Lesson Check questions 1–5, and then used a Numbered Heads Together strategy to have them share their responses. If they had any incorrect answers, use the guiding questions to discuss the lesson's main ideas, focusing on the ideas they struggled with.

ACTIVE JOURNAL

Writing Workshop Have students complete the Lesson 3 Writing Task in their Active Journals. Students will establish a setting for their narratives. As they move through the topic, students will revisit their descriptions of the setting, revising them as needed.

DEMONSTRATE

ASSESSMENT **ONLINE LESSON QUIZ**

Assign the Online Lesson Quiz for this lesson if you haven't already done so. Students will be offered automatic remediation or enrichment based on their score.

DISCUSSION **DISCUSSION BOARD**

Post this question to the class on the Discussion Board:

Summarize How did the Persian empire balance local self-government with central power? *(Local people had some control over their own governments and they were allowed to keep some local laws, traditions, and religious practices. However, they had to pay tribute to the empire and use the same currency as the rest of the empire. In addition, Darius chose the leader of each province.)*

ANSWERS

Use Visual Information *Sample answer: a human, a bird, and a horse*

Identify Implied Main Ideas *Sample answer: It suggests that the Persians had a lot to keep track of and were engaged in a great deal of commerce.*

Analyze Images Creatures like this decorated many Assyrian palaces. **Use Visual Information** What three types of beings make up this imaginary creature?

Arts of Mesopotamia

Unlike art produced by earlier world cultures, the arts of ancient Mesopotamia give us a glimpse of daily life, as you saw on the Standard of Ur. They show people engaged in different activities.

Seals The Sumerians often used carved stone seals to identify the owner of an object, especially before the development of cuneiform writing. A seal left the owner's personal mark—such as an animal or a geometric shape—stamped in clay. For example, a sack containing trade goods might be tied closed with a string. Then the owner would cover the knot with wet clay and stamp the clay with the seal.

Some seals were shaped like cylinders, or tubes. When rolled over wet clay, the seals left the image of an entire scene.

Sculptures Sumerians also carved statues of people that, for the first time in history, looked like real humans. Other peoples created a form of sculpture known as relief. In relief sculpture the scene sticks out from the surface of the base material.

Many relief sculptures were carved on steles (STEE lee). A **stele** is a carved stone slab or pillar that stands on end. A famous example is the stele of Hammurabi. At the top of this stele is a relief showing Hammurabi and the Babylonian god Shamash. Below the relief is Hammurabi's Code, carved in cuneiform.

The Assyrians created large, colorful reliefs on the sides of buildings. They decorated structures with colorful tiles and bricks that formed elaborate patterns and images of real and imagined animals. Assyrians also decorated walls with cone-shaped pieces of baked clay painted in white, black, and red.

READING CHECK **Identify Implied Main Ideas** What did the use of stone seals suggest about daily life?

Lesson Check

HSS 6.2.3; ELD.P1.A.2, P1.C.10.a

Practice Vocabulary

1. What was the effect of having a **standing army** on Persia's growth?
2. How did the use of **currency** unify Persia's economy?

Critical Thinking and Writing

3. **Summarize** How did the Assyrians create an empire?
4. **Synthesize Visual Information** What subject do most of the images in this lesson have in common? What does this subject suggest about the societies that created these works of art?
5. **Identify Implied Main Ideas** How did the way the Persian government handled religion throughout the empire help preserve social and political order?
6. **Writing Workshop: Establish Setting** Write a few sentences in your Active Journal to describe the setting where your character lives in Mesopotamia. You will use this information in the narrative essay you will write at the end of this topic.

70 Lesson 2.3 • The Assyrian and Persian Empires

LESSON CHECK

1. It helped Persia to grow rapidly because it made conquering other people more efficient. **DOK1**
2. It made it easier for distant provinces to trade with one another. **DOK1**
3. They used iron weapons to expand a military state into an empire. **DOK2**
4. Most of the images show the army or conquered peoples. This reveals that the societies in this lesson all focused war and conquest. **DOK4**
5. They treated conquered peoples well, allowing them to often keep their religions and have some control over their government. This led the people to be content under Persian rule, so they did not try to break the empire apart. **DOK2**
6. Students should define a setting consistent with the character and social role they have chosen, which may be a revision to the initial one they chose in Lesson 1. **DOK4**

Recognize the Role of Chance, Error, and Oversight

Use the primary source and follow these steps to recognize the role of chance, oversight, and error.

INTERACTIVE

Analyze Primary and Secondary Sources

1 Identify the topic. When studying an event, begin by focusing on what the passage is about. For example, is the passage about a military campaign or the rise of a new leader? Where did the event happen? Who were the key figures? Read the passage from *The History of Herodotus.*

a. What is the passage about?

b. Where did the event happen, and who were the key figures?

2 Identify the goal or expected outcome. Ask, What is the leader trying to accomplish? What is likely to happen if everything goes as planned?

a. In this passage, what is the leader trying to accomplish?

b. What challenges is he likely to encounter if his plan does not go as he thought it would?

3 Identify any unexpected outcomes. As you consider the event or time period, ask, Did events happen as expected? Did something go wrong? Did key people achieve their stated goals?

a. Consider what the leader's goals were in the passage. Did he achieve his goals? Explain why or why not.

b. What problem did his soldiers face?

4 Analyze the cause of the unexpected outcomes. Look for explanations for unexpected outcomes. Did something that nobody could have predicted go wrong—a storm or illness, for example? Did a person make a key mistake? Did someone forget some key steps?

a. Analyze the passage. What went wrong?

b. Could the outcome have been prevented? If so, how?

Primary Source

"Cambyses ... set out on his march against the Kush without making any provision for the feeding of his army .... Like a senseless madman ... he began his march. Before he had traveled one-fifth of the distance, all the army's food was gone. The men were forced to eat the pack animals, which were soon gone also. If at this time, Cambyses ... had confessed himself in the wrong, and led his army back, he would have done the wisest thing that he could ... but ... he ... continued to march forward. So long as the earth gave them anything, the soldiers lived by eating the grass and herbs. But when they came to the bare sand, a portion of them were guilty of a horrid deed. By tens they cast lots for a man, who was slain to be the food of the others. When Cambyses heard of these doings ... he gave up his attack on Kush ...."

—from *The History of Herodotus*, Book 3, 440 BCE

Analysis HI.4

Analysis Skills
Recognize the Role of Chance, Error, and Oversight

LEARN

Preview the steps in the student text with students, and then play the video.

VIDEO **21ST CENTURY SKILLS**

Project the Analyze Primary and Secondary Sources video in the 21st Century Skills Tutorial. Use the Quick Reference and Assessment to provide additional instruction on this skill.

PRACTICE

Have students practice the skill using the primary source on the student page, providing the instruction and then asking students the questions.

As an alternative, you could form students into pairs or groups to perform the activity. Then invite the groups to identify the expected and unexpected outcomes and to offer any explanations they came up with for the unexpected outcomes.

ASSESS

To assess this skill, have students read the first two paragraphs under the heading What Was the Exodus? in Lesson 5 of this topic. Ask: Why did Jacob's family move to Egypt? *(to avoid famine)* What did they expect the outcome to be? *(to find grain)* What was the unexpected outcome? *(slavery)*

ANSWERS

1. a. Cambyses's campaign against Kush
b. The event happened between Persia and Kush. The key figure was Cambyses.

2. a. Cambyses wants to conquer Kush.
b. He will face the challenge of withdrawing his troops over a great distance.

3. a. Cambyses did not achieve his goals because his soldiers lacked food.
b. They did not have enough food.

4. a. Cambyses's army lacked food, and he had to end his campaign against Kush.
b. Cambyses could have planned better to have enough food for his soldiers.

DIFFERENTIATED INSTRUCTION

Advanced Ask students to research the reason rabbits were introduced into Australia in the 1800s and to find out the unexpected outcome of that decision. Give them a choice of writing a paragraph or drawing a cartoon to share their findings.

INTEGRATED ENGLISH LANGUAGE DEVELOPMENT

Emerging Support emerging students by simplifying the steps into a flow chart with four boxes. For the first box, ask students *Who is this about? Where are they going?* For the second box, ask *What does he want to happen?* For the third box ask, *What problems did they have?* For the last box, ask *What happened? Why?* Fill in the box as students answer.

HSS 6.2.9

The Phoenicians

CONNECT

GET READY TO READ

ETEXT **START UP**

Project the Start Up Activity. As students enter the classroom and get settled, ask them to examine the photograph of lands that were once part of Phoenicia.

Describe Have students record a description of a human activity that they think might have taken place in the scene in the photograph. *(Sample answer: With a coastal location, the Phoenicians might have been involved in fishing or trade by sea.)* Then have them share their descriptions with another student, either in class or through a chat or blog.

Discuss Remind students that they have learned about ancient societies that traded along rivers. The Phoenicians traded by sailing across the sea.

After completing the Start Up Activity, project the Lesson Opener or direct students to their textbooks. Preview the lesson by working through the Get Ready to Read items with the class. Remind students to pay close attention to the Guiding Questions as they read the lesson.

ACTIVE JOURNAL

Take Notes Have students use the lesson literacy skills graphic organizer in their Active Journals to take notes as they read the lesson.

Practice Vocabulary Have students complete the activity in their Active Journals to build their vocabulary.

VIDEO **VIDEO**

Assign the lesson video as homework.

LESSON 4

HSS 6.2.9

The Phoenicians

BOUNCE TO ACTIVATE

VIDEO

GET READY TO READ

START UP

Look at this land that was once part of Phoenicia. How might people have adapted to this land?

GUIDING QUESTIONS

- How did contact, trade, and other links grow among the societies of Mesopotamia and the eastern Mediterranean?
- How did the Phoenicians spread their culture over a wide area?
- What important contribution did the Phoenicians make to the development of writing?

TAKE NOTES

Literacy Skills: Summarize

Use the graphic organizer in your Active Journal to take notes as you read the lesson.

PRACTICE VOCABULARY

Use the vocabulary activity in your Active Journal to practice the vocabulary words.

Vocabulary		Academic Vocabulary
import	cultural diffusion	assembly
export	alphabet	profit
navigation		
colony		

The Mediterranean Sea forms the western boundary of the Fertile Crescent. The Phoenician (fuh NISH un) civilization began here, on a thin strip of land along the Mediterranean coast, in what is now Lebanon. Like Sumer, Phoenicia consisted of city-states. Although Phoenicia was small in size, it had an important influence on the region's history.

Who Were the Phoenicians?

The Phoenicians were fearless sailors who guided ships full of trade goods through ocean waters. For hundreds of years, they dominated sea trade across the Mediterranean, just as the earlier Greek Minoan people had done.

Origins Phoenician society developed from the earlier Canaanites (KAY nun ites). The Canaanites were a people who lived in parts of what are now Israel, Jordan, Lebanon, and Syria. Nearby Egypt had a strong influence on Canaan. In fact, Egypt controlled parts of Canaan off and on from around 1500 BCE to 1150 BCE.

PRACTICE VOCABULARY

To help students integrate new vocabulary, help them to understand that an *import* is a product that people buy and bring into a country. An *export* is a product that they sell to someone outside their country. *Navigation* refers to the art of steering a ship. A *colony* is an area settled and ruled by a distant country. Reinforce the terms during the lesson using the teaching notes.

Point out the academic vocabulary in the lesson margins. Provide sample sentences that clarify meaning.

assembly: The assembly gathered to make new laws for the state.

profit: We will profit from the garage sale.

Phoenician society began to emerge after Egyptian rule ended. The independent Phoenician city-states soon prospered. In general, the rulers of Phoenician city-states were priest-kings who shared power with leading merchant families and a citizen **assembly**.

Academic Vocabulary
assembly • *n.*, group organized for a purpose

Farming and Manufacturing Geography greatly influenced Phoenicia's development. The Lebanon Mountains formed Phoenicia's eastern border. These heavily forested mountains sloped down close to the Mediterranean coast, leaving little flat land for farming.

Phoenicians manufactured a number of goods. Weavers created cloth that they colored with a rare purple dye made from tiny sea snails. They sold this purple cloth for high prices. Skilled Phoenician craftsworkers made pottery and glass and metal objects. They also used trees to make wood furniture.

Phoenician Traders Phoenicia had few natural resources of its own, so the Phoenicians traded with other cultures for resources and goods. Phoenician traders brought back many imports. An **import** is a good or service sold within a country that is produced in another country. Most Phoenician imports were raw materials, including gold, silver, tin, copper, iron, ivory, and precious stones.

Phoenician craftsworkers used these raw materials to make bronze and silver bowls, iron tools and weapons, and gold jewelry. Traders shipped these goods—as well as pine and cedar logs, wine, olive oil, salt, fish, and other goods—as exports to ports across the Mediterranean. An **export** is a good or service produced within a country and sold outside the country's borders.

READING CHECK **Identify Cause and Effect** Why did the Phoenicians trade?

GEOGRAPHY SKILLS

The Phoenicians sailed across the Mediterranean Sea and then explored lands to the north and south.

1. **Region** Where were most Phoenician colonies located?
2. **Analyze Maps** What information on the map supports the claim that the Phoenicians were skilled sailors?

Phoenician Colonies and Trade Routes, About 700 B.C

WORKSHEET **TEACHER RESOURCES**

Have students who need additional support use the following worksheets from the Teacher Resources on the course:

- **Reading Support**
- **English Language Development**
- **Lesson Summary**

INVESTIGATE

Who Were the Phoenicians?

Discuss that the Phoenicians turned to trade because they had little land suitable for farming.

Summarize Describe the Phoenician people. *(They developed from the earlier Canaanites. They were fearless sailors who dominated trade throughout the Mediterranean region.)*

Identify Cause and Effect How did geography influence Phoenicia's development? *(Heavily forested mountains left little land for farming, so the Phoenicians were forced to take to the sea.)*

Cite Evidence How do Phoenicia's **exports** demonstrate that they made use of the resources they had? *(They had a lot of forests, so they exported logs. They also exported products from the sea, such as fish and a cloth dyed with a rare purple dye made from sea snails.)*

INTEGRATED ENGLISH LANGUAGE DEVELOPMENT

Interpretive Use Who Were the Phoenicians? to help students grasp how similar words or phrases affect meaning.

Emerging Use synonyms to help students with difficult words and phrases. Ask: *How did the land of Phoenicia slant from the eastern mountains toward the shore? Where was it higher and where was it lower?*

Expanding Use synonyms to help students with domain-specific words. To help with the words *import* and *export*, ask, *What did Phoenicia bring from other countries? What did Phoenicians sell to other countries?*

Bridging Use descriptive words in the text to help students understand connotations. Ask: *Why were Phoenicians able to sell the purple cloth for high prices? What does the word precious tell you about the value of the imported stones?*

ANSWERS

Identify Cause and Effect *They had few natural resources of their own.*

Region *Most Phoenician colonies were located on coastlines in the western Mediterranean.*

Analyze Maps *Sample answer: Some of the routes veer away from the coastlines and cross open water.*

How Did Phoenicians Use the Sea?

Discuss how the Phoenicians extended trade routes farther and farther away from Phoenicia and also set up colonies.

Summarize What methods did the Phoenicians use for **navigation**? *(They developed a thorough knowledge of wind patterns and ocean currents.)*

Infer Why do you think so many people consider the Phoenicians great sailors? *(Sample answer: They built large trading ships and used navigation to sail great distances.)*

Paraphrase Ask students to read the primary source and then restate it in their own words. *(Sample answer: Phoenicians knew that silver was valuable, but the people they bought it from did not. The Phoenicians carried the silver to Greece and Asia and sold it for a great profit.)*

Identify Cause and Effect How did establishing colonies help the Phoenicians? *(Colonies gave Phoenicians a place to get supplies or to trade with other people.)*

ELD TIP Pair students of different levels to read the Primary Source on this page. Have the pairs ask and answer questions about words that may be unfamiliar. Then have them craft a sentence that explains the main idea of the selection.

▲ Ruins of the Phoenician colony of Carthage in North Africa

How Did Phoenicians Use the Sea?

Phoenicia's location was ideal for trade. It lay on the western edge of Asia, within sailing distance of Europe and Africa. Several overland trade routes from the east ended in Phoenicia. As a result, many peoples came to depend on the Phoenicians to ship their trade goods across the Mediterranean Sea.

Navigation Because of Phoenicia's location between the Mediterranean and the Lebanon Mountains, Phoenicians turned to the sea to trade. They became experts at **navigation**, or the art of steering a ship from place to place. Phoenician sailors developed a thorough knowledge of wind patterns and ocean currents. At first, the Phoenicians sailed and traded among nearby lands. Later, they took their ships to new areas.

Exploring Unknown Waters From Phoenicia, the Phoenicians sailed south and west past Egypt and along the North African coast. Others traveled north and west past the Balkan and Italian peninsulas. They explored the Mediterranean islands of Sicily and Sardinia. In time, the Phoenicians reached the Iberian Peninsula, at the western end of the Mediterranean Sea. Today this land includes Spain and Portugal.

After passing the southern tip of Iberia, Phoenician sailors left the Mediterranean for the Atlantic Ocean. Some sailed north along the Iberian coast, and a few traveled all the way to Britain. Others headed south to West Africa.

Phoenician sailors showed great courage by sailing far into unknown waters. But why did they keep traveling ever farther from home? Some historians think that the Phoenicians were driven to find precious metals. Indeed, the Phoenicians traded for silver in Iberia and gold in West Africa. An ancient Greek historian described how Phoenicians **profited** from the silver trade:

Academic Vocabulary
profit • *v.*, to make a gain

Primary Source

Now the natives were ignorant of the use of the silver, and the Phoenicians . . . purchased the silver in exchange for other [goods] of little if any worth. And this was the reason why the Phoenicians, as they transported this silver to Greece and Asia and to all other peoples, acquired great wealth.

—Diodorus Siculus, *Library of History*

ELD.PI.B.8

WORKSHEET **TEACHER RESOURCES**

For additional IELD support addressing these standards, have students complete the Lesson ELD activity from the Teacher Resources found on the course.

Colonies and City-States Phoenician sailors found many sheltered harbors along the Mediterranean coast. At first these places served as trading stations where ships stopped to pick up water, food, and other supplies. Those areas with fertile land or other resources attracted farmers and other settlers. Those settlements grew into colonies. A **colony** is an area ruled by a distant country. When Phoenicia came under attack by Assyrians and others starting in the 800s BCE, many Phoenicians left Phoenicia. They migrated to their colonies for safety.

A few Phoenician colonies developed into wealthy city-states. One was Carthage, on the North African coast. Carthage eventually became rich and powerful, setting up its own colonies and fighting three wars against the powerful Romans. In the last of these wars, the Romans destroyed Carthage. Over time, the Roman empire took over all of the Phoenician city-states and colonies.

READING CHECK **Identify Cause and Effect** Why did the Phoenicians form colonies?

What Is the Cultural Legacy of the Phoenicians?

Phoenicia did not survive, but some of its achievements did last. Greece and Rome absorbed parts of Phoenician culture through cultural diffusion. **Cultural diffusion** is the spreading of cultural traits from one region to another. The Phoenicians' legacy included the spread of its culture and a new way of writing.

Links to Other Societies Through trade, the Phoenicians linked the diverse peoples and cultures around the Mediterranean region and beyond. In the process, Phoenicians helped ideas spread. They passed parts of their culture on to the Greeks. For example, the Greeks used the Phoenician standard of weights and measures. Greek culture later spread throughout the entire Mediterranean region, and its influence continues today.

INTERACTIVE
Development of the Modern Latin Alphabet

Development of the Alphabet

COMPARISON OF WRITING SYSTEMS

Phoenician	Early Greek	Early Latin	Modern English Capitals
𐤀	ᗅ	ᐱ	A
𐤁	8	B	B
𐤂	⅂	<	C
𐤃	Δ	D	D

Analyze Charts As other peoples adopted the Phoenician alphabet, they changed the letter forms. **Analyze Information** How was the alphabet used today in English influenced by the Phoenicians?

What Is the Cultural Legacy of the Phoenicians?

Discuss how Phoenician culture, particularly its alphabet, affected later cultures.

Connect What brought about the **cultural diffusion** of Phoenician culture? *(trade)*

INTERACTIVE **INTERACTIVE GALLERY**

Development of the Modern Latin Alphabet

Display the gallery of the development of the modern Latin alphabet. Click on each image, and ask volunteers to read the captions. Ask: In what way was the Phoenician alphabet different from ours? *(Sample answer: It had fewer letters.)*

ACTIVE CLASSROOM

Use the Sticky Notes strategy. Suggest that students write an English word using the Phoenician alphabet on a sticky note. Point out that there are no vowels, so they will have to omit those. Have pairs exchange notes and write what they think the English word is below the original. Display all the notes in class on a piece of chart paper.

DIFFERENTIATED INSTRUCTION

Special Education When discussing Phoenician navigation, have students turn back to the map of Phoenician trade routes and trace the routes with a finger. Point out how close most of the routes were to the coastline. Explain that the Phoenicians lived before scientific instruments like compasses and GPS. Staying close to land helped them keep track of where they were.

Below Level Have students reread the description of how Phoenician trade routes expanded over time. Then have them review the map on the previous page and explain how they think the Phoenicians chose the locations of their colonies.

Advanced Have pairs of students write a dialogue in which they are Phoenician sailors debating whether to sail further than they have ever gone before. Each participant should take a different position and give reasons for his or her stance.

ANSWERS

Identify Cause and Effect *At first, Phoenicians used places as trading stations but liked the fertile land they found and settled there.*

Analyze Information *The Phoenician alphabet developed into the Greek alphabet, then the Latin alphabet, and finally into our modern alphabet.*

Compare and Contrast *The Phoenician alphabet used a few letters to represent sounds. Cuneiform used many symbols to represent whole words or syllables.*

HSS 6.2.9; ELD.P1.A.2, P1.C.10.a

ACTIVE JOURNAL

Quick Activity Divide students into pairs and have them discuss how a single invention can have a major effect on people's lives and then record their ideas in their Active Journals.

SYNTHESIZE

Assess and Reteach Have students use a Think-Pair-Share strategy to complete Lesson Check questions 1–5. Use the guiding questions to discuss any ideas they struggled with.

ACTIVE JOURNAL

Writing Workshop Have students complete the Lesson 4 Writing Task in their Active Journals. Students will list a sequence of events for their narrative. As they move through the topic, students will revisit this list and revise it as needed.

DEMONSTRATE

ASSESSMENT **ONLINE LESSON QUIZ**

Assign the Online Lesson Quiz for this lesson if you haven't already done so. Students will be offered automatic remediation or enrichment based on their score.

DISCUSSION **DISCUSSION BOARD**

Post this question to the class on the Discussion Board:

Infer Why was the Phoenician writing system their most lasting contribution? *(The Phoenician alphabet stood for sounds, not ideas or words. This made it possible to write with a small number of symbols and it evolved into the modern alphabet.)*

Quick Activity

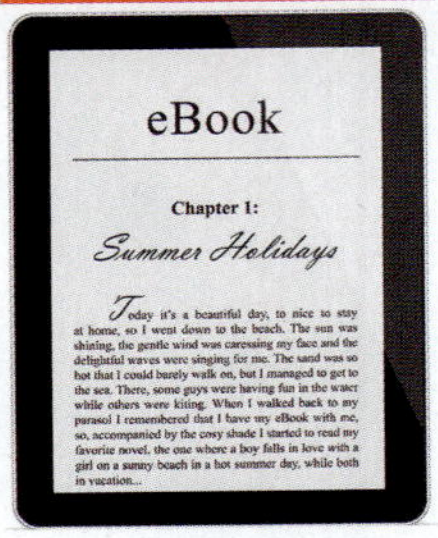

Explore how a single invention can have a huge effect on how people live in your Active Journal.

The Alphabet The Greeks also adopted the Phoenician way of writing. Before the Phoenicians, the main writing system in the ancient Near East was cuneiform. In cuneiform, symbols represent syllables or whole words. In order to be able to write, a person had to learn and remember hundreds of symbols.

The Phoenicians developed an alphabet. An **alphabet** is a small set of letters or symbols, each of which stands for a single sound. The Phoenician alphabet had 22 symbols. Each symbol stood for a consonant sound. This new approach to writing was a major improvement over cuneiform. Now, instead of having to memorize hundreds of different symbols, a person only had to know 22 symbols in order to write. This alphabet made writing much easier to learn, making it possible for more people to learn how to write.

People who traded with the Phoenicians learned their alphabet in order to communicate with them. By 750 BCE, the Greeks had begun using the Phoenician alphabet. Around 500 BCE, the Greeks added letters to represent vowels. They also gave the letters names. The word *alphabet* comes from the first two letters in the Greek alphabet—alpha and beta.

Around 100 BCE, the Romans adopted the Greek alphabet. The Romans changed some letters. The result was an alphabet that looks much like ours today. The Romans carried their culture across much of Europe and into other lands. Their language and system of writing was adopted in those lands. Through that process, it passed into widespread use. While it is the Roman form of writing that became the alphabet used to write English, that writing system had its origins in ancient Phoenicia.

READING CHECK **Compare and Contrast** How was Phoenician writing different from cuneiform?

Lesson Check

HSS 6.2.9

Practice Vocabulary

1. How did the Phoenicians turn **imports** from other cultures into **exports**?
2. How was the Phoenician **alphabet** similar to the alphabet we use today?

Critical Thinking and Writing

3. **Understand Effects** How is the Greek adoption of the Phoenician way of writing an example of cultural diffusion?
4. **Generate Explanations** Explain how the evolution of language impacted the number of people who could read and write in each of the societies—Phoenician, Greek, and Roman.
5. **Summarize** How did the Phoenicia's location allow Phoenicians to more easily make contact with other cultures?
6. **Writing Workshop: Organize Sequence of Events** Make an ordered list of events in your Active Journal to show what happens to your character in your narrative essay. You will use this sequence of events when you write your narrative essay at the end of this topic.

LESSON CHECK

1. They used the raw materials they imported to make metal items, iron tools, and weapons that they sold to people in other countries. **DOK1**
2. It consists of a relatively small number of letters, each of which stands for a single sound. **DOK2**
3. Cultural diffusion is the spreading of cultural traits, and one of the cultural traits of the Phoenicians was their way of writing. **DOK2**
4. Sample response: In each society, more and more people could read and write than in the last society because with each society, the alphabet and system of writing became easier to use. **DOK3**
5. Phoenicia bordered the Mediterranean, which allowed Phoenicians to easily travel to other lands by sailing. **DOK2**
6. Students should develop ideas related to daily tasks they want to include in their narratives. **DOK4**

76 Lesson 2.4 • The Phoenicians

Origins of Judaism

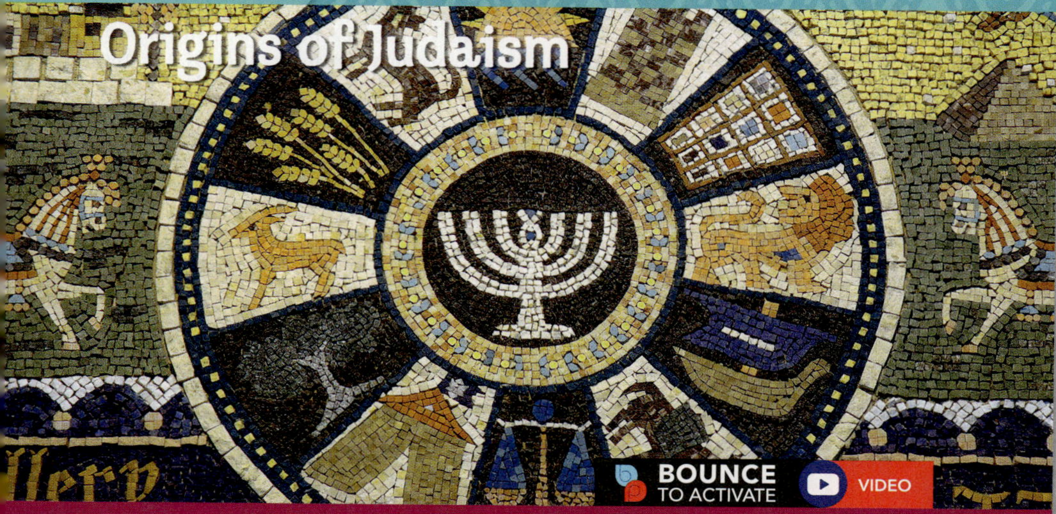

BOUNCE TO ACTIVATE VIDEO

GET READY TO READ

START UP

Examine the mosaic, which shows the symbols of the 12 tribes of Israel. Choose two of the symbols and write about what you think they might represent.

GUIDING QUESTIONS

- How did the Israelites' belief in one God develop into Judaism?
- How did the environment shape Jewish religion?
- Why are Abraham and Moses important figures in Judaism?

TAKE NOTES

Literacy Skills: Summarize

Use the graphic organizer in your Active Journal to take notes as you read the lesson.

PRACTICE VOCABULARY

Use the vocabulary activity in your Active Journal to practice the vocabulary words.

Vocabulary		Academic Vocabulary
monotheism	Exodus	eventually
ethics	commandment	compel
Torah		
covenant		

Judaism first developed as a religion more than 3,000 years ago in the Fertile Crescent. It was the world's first religion based on one God who set down laws about right and wrong. Judaism has helped shape the religions of Christianity and Islam, as well as modern ideas about law and human rights.

The Early Israelites and the Worship of One God

The Israelites were related to other peoples of the Fertile Crescent, but they developed a unique culture. Although their neighbors worshiped many gods, the Israelites practiced **monotheism**, or the belief that there is only one God. They believed that God created each person in God's image.

The Israelites also had important beliefs about the proper way for people to live. They believed that God called on them to act based on **ethics**, or ideas of right and wrong. Their teachings and practices became known as Judaism, the religion of the Jewish people. Judaism is one of the world's oldest religions.

PRACTICE VOCABULARY

To help students integrate new vocabulary, explain that all these terms relate to the religion of Judaism. *Monotheism* is the belief that there is only one God. *Ethics* are ideas of right and wrong, while a *commandment* is an order to do something. The *Torah* is the first five books of the Hebrew Bible. A *covenant* is a binding agreement. The *Exodus* was the escape of the Israelites from slavery in Egypt. Reinforce the terms during the lesson using the teaching notes.

Point out the academic vocabulary in the lesson margins. Provide sample sentences that clarify meaning.

eventually: We waited a long time, but eventually we got a seat in the movie theater.

compel: My brother doesn't want to go inside, so I will have to compel him with a gentle push.

HSS 6.3.1, 6.3.3, 6.3.4

Origins of Judaism

CONNECT

GET READY TO READ

ETEXT START UP

Project the Start Up Activity. As students enter the classroom and get settled, ask them to examine the mosaic showing symbols of the 12 tribes of Israel.

Hypothesize Have students choose two of the symbols and write about what they might represent. *(Sample answers: The lion might represent kingship. The ship might represent trade.)* Then have them share their ideas with another student, either in class or through a chat or blog.

Discuss Explain to students that today, several major religions believe in one God. When Judaism began, however, most peoples believed in many gods.

After completing the Start Up activity, project the Lesson Opener or direct students to their textbooks. Preview the lesson by working through the Get Ready to Read items with the class. Remind students to pay close attention to the Guiding Questions as they read the lesson.

ACTIVE JOURNAL

Take Notes Have students use the lesson literacy skills graphic organizer in their Active Journals to take notes as they read the lesson.

Practice Vocabulary Have students complete the activity in their Active Journals to build their vocabulary.

VIDEO

Assign the lesson video as homework.

WORKSHEET **TEACHER RESOURCES**

Have students who need additional support use the following worksheets from the Teacher Resources on the course:

- **Reading Support**
- **English Language Development**
- **Lesson Summary**

INVESTIGATE

The Early Israelites and the Worship of One God

Discuss how the Israelites came to believe in one God with whom they had a special relationship.

Contrast How was the religion of the Israelites different from the religion of their neighbors? *(The Israelites believed that there is only one God, and each person is created in God's image. Their neighbors worshiped many gods.)*

Synthesize How was the Israelites' idea about **ethics** related to their ideas about God? *(Sample answer: They believed that God called on them to act ethically.)*

Summarize What was the **covenant** between God and Abraham? *(Abraham would obey God and travel to the land of Canaan, which God would give to Abraham and his descendants. God would be their God for all ages.)*

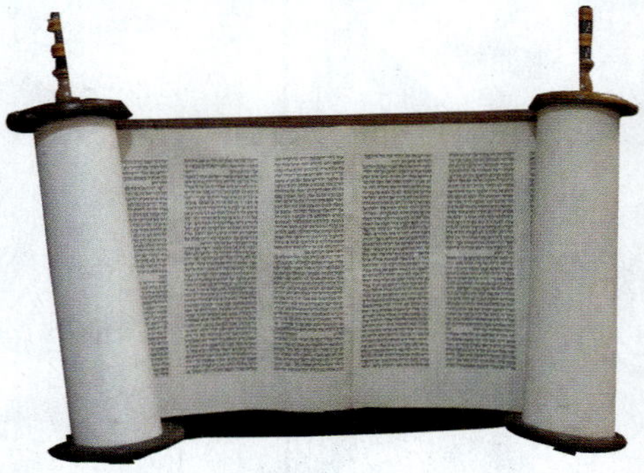

Analyze Images The scroll contains the Torah. **Identify Main Ideas** Why is the Torah important to Judaism?

What Are the Origins of Judaism? Most of what Jews believe about the origins of their religion comes from the Torah (TOH ruh). The **Torah** consists of the first five books of the Hebrew Bible. (These are also the first five books of the Christian Old Testament, which has all of the books of the Hebrew Bible.) The archaeology and history of Egypt and Mesopotamia also help us understand the world of the Torah.

Abraham's Covenant The Torah tells about a man named Abraham, who may have lived about 1700 BCE. He herded animals near Ur in Mesopotamia.

According to the Torah, God told Abraham to leave Ur and travel with his family to Canaan (KAY nun) on the coast of the Mediterranean Sea. The Torah says that God then made a **covenant**, or binding agreement, with Abraham. The land of Canaan would belong to Abraham's descendants, so it became known as the Promised Land.

Primary Source

> *I will maintain My covenant between Me and you, and your offspring to come, as an everlasting covenant throughout the ages, to be God to you and your offspring to come.*
>
> —Genesis 17:7

The Patriarchs The Torah says that Abraham led his people to Canaan. Abraham, his son Isaac, and Isaac's son Jacob are known as the patriarchs, or the forefathers of the Jewish people.

According to the Torah, Abraham's grandson Jacob had twelve sons. Each of Jacob's sons became the ancestor of at least one large group of related families called a tribe. Jacob was later renamed Israel. The twelve tribes descended from Jacob became known as the Israelites.

Academic Vocabulary
eventually • *adj.*, after a time

Scholars believe that the stories of the patriarchs were passed along by word of mouth for hundreds of years. **Eventually**, they were written down in Genesis (JEH nuh sihs), the first book of the Torah.

READING CHECK **Identify Implied Main Ideas** Why does the Torah contain many references to herding?

What Was the Exodus?

The last chapters of Genesis describe a famine in Canaan. Because Egypt had great supplies of grain, according to the Torah, Jacob's family moved there.

78 Lesson 2.5 • Origins of Judaism

INTEGRATED ENGLISH LANGUAGE DEVELOPMENT

Productive Students use Abraham's Covenant and What Was the Exodus? to give presentations about the travels of Abraham, Jacob, and Moses.

Emerging Read the text aloud, pausing to point out the routes on the map. Pair students, and have students take turns telling about Abraham's and then Moses' journey using the map Lands of the Hebrew Bible for assistance.

Expanding Using the text to support their ideas, have students prepare and present oral presentations describing the travels of the Patriarchs and Moses during the Exodus.

Bridging Using the text for details, reasons, and evidence, have students prepare and present formal presentations describing the beliefs and travels of the Patriarchs and Moses during the Exodus.

ANSWERS

Identify Main Ideas *The Torah contains the story of the origin of Judaism.*

Identify Implied Main Ideas *The Torah reflects the way of life of Abraham and his descendants.*

The Book of Exodus (EKS uh duhs) comes after Genesis in the Torah. According to Exodus, as the number of Jacob's descendants grew, a new pharaoh, or king of Egypt, became mistrustful of them. Exodus describes how the pharaoh enslaved and mistreated the Israelites. According to the Torah, the pharaoh **compelled** the Israelites to do harsh work.

Academic Vocabulary
compel • *v.*, force

Moses Exodus states that Moses was an Israelite who was adopted by the pharaoh's family. According to Exodus, God appeared to Moses and told him to rescue his people. Moses asked the pharaoh to let him lead the Israelites out of Egypt, but the pharaoh refused.

Exodus describes terrible hardships that God brought to Egypt because of the Pharaoh's refusal. The last and worst punishment was the death of every firstborn son of the Egyptians. Moses told the Israelites that God would let their sons live if they marked their doorways with the blood of a lamb.

INTERACTIVE
The Exodus in Jewish Tradition

Finally, the pharaoh allowed the Israelites to leave Egypt. Moses led the Israelites to the Sinai (SY ny) Peninsula, out of the pharaoh's reach. The escape of the Israelites from slavery in Egypt is called the **Exodus**. Each year, Jews celebrate Passover to commemorate the journey from slavery in Egypt to freedom.

The Desert Experience Many biblical scholars believe, the Exodus occurred during the 1200s BCE. According to the Torah, after the Israelites left Egypt, they lived in the Sinai Desert for 40 years. During this time, God prepared them for life in the Promised Land, then called Canaan. They received a series of instructions from God. They also learned ways to worship God and created important religious objects.

GEOGRAPHY SKILLS

The ancient history of the Israelites took place in the Fertile Crescent and Mesopotamia.

1. **Movement** Why would Egypt be more appealing to the ancient Israelites in time of drought than Mesopotamia?
2. **Identify Multiple Causes** What made Canaan attractive as a place to live?

Lands of the Hebrew Bible, About 1700–1200s BCE

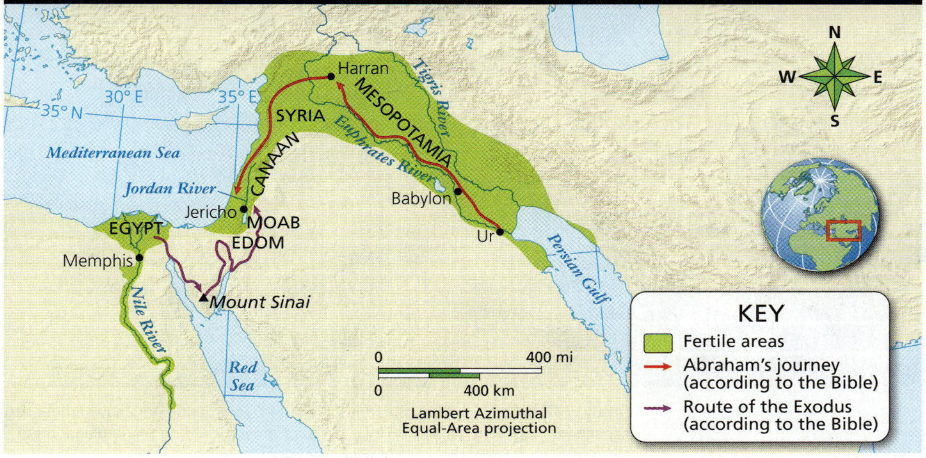

ELD.PI.C.9

WORKSHEET **TEACHER RESOURCES**

For additional IELD support addressing these standards, have students complete the Lesson IELD activity from the Teacher Resources found on the course.

What Was the Exodus?

Discuss how Moses led the Israelites out of slavery in Egypt.

Draw Conclusions Why did the Egyptians enslave and mistreat the Israelites? *(They became mistrustful of the Israelites.)*

Summarize What happened to the Israelites in the desert? *(They lived there for 40 years, received God's instructions, created religious objects, battled other peoples, and came to believe that God would provide for them.)*

INTERACTIVE **INTERACTIVE MAP**

The Exodus in Jewish Tradition

Display the Interactive Map: The Exodus in Jewish Tradition. Click on each of the hotspots, and ask volunteers to read the captions. Ask: What arm of the Red Sea did the Israelites cross? *(Gulf of Suez)* Ask: How was Canaan different from the land the Israelites traveled through? *(Sample answers: It was not a desert.)*

ACTIVE CLASSROOM

Use the Make Headlines strategy. Have students write a headline that captures one event depicted on the Exodus map. The headline should capture the most important aspect of that event. Students should then pass their headlines to a partner for review and make any revisions as necessary.

ANSWERS

Movement *Sample answer: The area along the Nile was fertile.*

Identify Multiple Causes *Sample answer: It had fertile land along a river, and was near the Mediterranean Sea, which might promote fishing or trade with the Phoenicians.*

What Are the Ten Commandments?

Discuss how Moses gave the Ten Commandments to the Israelites as described in the Hebrew Bible.

Connect How did Judaism affect Christianity? *(Sample answers: Christians also believe in the Ten Commandments. Christians also see the Exodus as a lesson that God will protect and support them.)*

Return to the Promised Land

Discuss how, according to the Hebrew Bible, the Israelites took possession of the land when they reached Canaan.

Identify Cause and Effect Why did Moses not enter the Promised Land? *(He died first.)*

Cite Evidence Why was Joshua qualified to lead the Israelites after Moses? *(He commanded the Israelites when they were attacked just after leaving Egypt.)*

Infer How did the Israelites keep their identity? *(They always returned to the Torah and their belief in only one God.)*

ELD TIP Students may not recognize the meaning of "bear false witness" in the eighth commandment. From TV shows, they may be familiar with the idea of a witness as someone who speaks about something that happened.

On the journey through the desert to Canaan, according to the Torah, the Israelites faced harsh conditions. Occasionally, the Israelites battled other peoples. Some Israelites questioned the leadership of Moses or of God. However, they came to believe that if they obeyed God's commands, God would provide for them. The Torah states that during their journey, God even provided them with water and food.

READING CHECK **Identify Main Ideas** Why do Jews celebrate Passover?

What Are the Ten Commandments?

The Book of Exodus says that during the Israelites' journey, they stopped at the foot of Mount Sinai. Moses went up the mountain to meet with God. The Torah tells how at Sinai God gave Moses the Torah, which forms the foundation of Judaism. The Torah includes laws, among them those known today as the Ten Commandments. A **commandment** is an order to do something. The Torah contains many other laws, but the Ten Commandments are the most important.

The accounts of Exodus and the Ten Commandments are important to Jews, Christians, and others. For them, the lesson of Exodus is that if people believe in God and obey God's laws, God will protect them and support them.

READING CHECK **Identify Main Ideas** What do Jews believe about personal responsibility?

The Ten Commandments

The Ten Commandments helped shape American laws and people's ideas about right and wrong.

COMMANDMENT	EXPLANATION
1st You shall have no other gods besides Me.	to recognize God as the one and only God
2nd You shall not swear falsely by the name of the Lord your God.	to speak the truth; seen today in legal oaths
3rd Remember the Sabbath day and keep it holy.	to dedicate one day to worship
4th Honor your father and your mother.	to respect and love one's parents
5th You shall not murder.	to avoid killing others; seen today in laws about murder
6th You shall not commit adultery.	to ensure faithfulness to one's spouse; seen today in divorce laws
7th You shall not steal.	to prevent taking another person's belongings
8th You shall not bear false witness against your neighbor.	to prevent lying; seen today by laws against testifying falsely in a court of law
9th You shall not covet your neighbor's house.	to prevent wanting other people's possessions
10th You shall not covet your neighbor's wife.	to help ensure that families are not broken up

Analyze Charts Over time, the ideas in the Ten Commandments have influenced aspects of modern legal and political systems. **Infer** Based on the explanation of the ninth commandment, what does *covet* mean?

ANSWERS

Identify Main Ideas *They celebrate Passover to commemorate God's freeing the Israelites from slavery in Egypt.*

Identify Main Ideas *They believe that every individual has the responsibility to do what is right.*

Infer *Sample answer: It means wanting something that someone else has.*

Draw Conclusions *Moses rescued the Israelites from slavery in Egypt, presented them with the Ten Commandments, and led them toward the Promised Land.*

DIFFERENTIATED INSTRUCTION

Special Education Explain to students that the term *commandment* is related to the word *command*. The most common situation in which the word *command* is used is in the military. Explain that the Ten Commandments are religious laws, and that the Israelites were expected to obey them without question, just as soldiers must obey orders.

Below Level Explain that some of the Ten Commandments have to do with a person's relationship with God and some with a relationships with others. Ask them to sort the commandments into those two categories.

Advanced Have pairs think how to apply at least three commandments to our high-tech world. "Thou shalt not bear false witness against thy neighbor" could become "Don't lie about people on Facebook."

Return to the Promised Land

After the Israelites received the laws from Moses, according to the Torah, they continued to the Promised Land. Moses saw Canaan from a mountain, but he died without entering the Promised Land. His deputy, Joshua, took his place as the leader of the Israelites. According to the Hebrew Bible, Joshua commanded the Israelites when they were attacked just after leaving Egypt. He also accompanied Moses to the foot of Mount Sinai.

According to the Book of Joshua in the Bible, the Israelites entered Canaan from the east under Joshua's leadership. One of the first cities they conquered was the high-walled city of Jericho (JEHR ih koh). After the defeat of Jericho, the Israelites went on to conquer several other kingdoms in Canaan.

Then each of the tribes descended from Jacob's sons settled in a different area. The tribes of Judah, Simeon, and Benjamin settled in the south. The other tribes settled in lands to the north. They herded their animals and farmed by making terraces on hillsides.

According to the Hebrew Bible, the Israelites maintained their identity. They sometimes strayed from God's commandments, but they always returned to the teachings of the Torah, including the belief in only one God.

▲ A Jewish family celebrates Passover.

Did you know?

The ancient settlement of Jericho might be the lowest town in the world. It sits 825 feet (251 m) below sea level.

READING CHECK **Draw Conclusions** How was Moses important to the development of the Jewish religion?

Lesson Check

HSS 6.3.1, 6.3.3, 6.3.4; ELD.P1.A.2, P1.C.10.a

Practice Vocabulary

1. Explain the relationship between Judaism and **monotheism**.
2. Use the words **commandment** and **ethics** in a sentence about Judaism.

Critical Thinking and Writing

3. **Draw Conclusions** Explain the connection, according to the Hebrew Bible, between Abraham's covenant with God and the Israelites' belief about Canaan.
4. **Identify Main Ideas** What was the lesson of the Exodus, according to the Torah?
5. **Sequence** What did the Israelites do after they reached Canaan?
6. **Understand Effects** Explain how religion helped shape the culture of the ancient Israelites, as presented in the Hebrew Bible.
7. **Writing Workshop: Revise Your Sequence of Events** Revise the sequence of events you prepared in your Active Journal to show what happens to your character in your narrative essay. You will use this sequence of events when you write your narrative essay at the end of the topic.

HSS 6.3.1, 6.3.3, 6.3.4; ELD.P1.A.2, P1.C.10.a

SYNTHESIZE

Assess and Reteach Have students work in discussion groups to complete Lesson Check questions 1–6. Review their responses. If they had any incorrect answers, use the guiding questions to discuss the lesson's main ideas, focusing on the ideas they struggled with.

ACTIVE JOURNAL

Writing Workshop Have students complete the Lesson 5 Writing Task in their Active Journals. Students will refine their sequence of events.

DEMONSTRATE

ASSESSMENT **ONLINE LESSON QUIZ**

Assign the Online Lesson Quiz for this lesson if you haven't already done so. Students will be offered automatic remediation or enrichment based on their score.

DISCUSSION **DISCUSSION BOARD**

Post this question to the class on the Discussion Board:

Summarize What roles did Abraham and Moses play in the origins of Judaism? *(The Israelites are descended from Abraham, who had a covenant with God and moved to the Promised Land at God's command. Moses led the Israelites out of slavery in Egypt, gave them the Ten Commandments, and led them back to the Promised Land.)*

LESSON CHECK

1. Judaism holds that there is only one God, which is the definition of monotheism. **DOK1**
2. Sample answer: The Ten Commandments form a basis for Jewish ethics and behavior. **DOK1**
3. According to the Hebrew Bible, God promised to give the land of Canaan to Abraham's descendants. **DOK3**
4. God would provide for the Israelites and their descendants if they obeyed God's law. **DOK1**
5. They conquered those who already lived there. Then they settled on the land. **DOK2**
6. Sample answer: Religion guided how they lived their daily lives. They strived to do what their religious laws told them was right. **DOK2**
7. Students should develop a sequence of the daily tasks that they are thinking of including in their narratives. **DOK4**

HSS 6.3.3; ELA RI.6.3, RI.6.4

Primary Sources

Psalm 23

Read aloud the explanatory note about the source. Direct students' attention to the image. Many of the psalms are attributed to King David, who began life not as a noble but as an ordinary boy who tended his father's flocks of sheep. The Bible records that he played a harp. Ask: What details of this image show that it is intended to represent David? *(Sample answer: crown, harp)*

GUIDED READING

Read aloud the excerpt without stopping. Then reread the passage, pausing after each stanza to let students answer the numbered questions. Use the questions in the text to prompt students' analysis of the primary source.

Reading and Vocabulary Support Answers

3. *Sample response: The LORD provides comfort and peace—"still waters," "green pastures." The LORD provides guidance—"He leads me"—and protection—"I fear no harm / for You are with me." The speaker explains that the presence of the LORD's provides "comfort" as well.*

4. *In spreading a table, the LORD provides a safe and protected place for the Israelites, despite the adversities they face. The table provides them with food and a sense of belonging. Even among their enemies, Israelites experience the LORD's plenty, represented by the abundant drink.*

GUIDED ANALYSIS

After completing the reading, discuss what this primary source reveals about Jewish beliefs.

Infer Why do you think David describes God as a shepherd rather than a king? *(Sample answer: He wanted to convey that God provides personal, direct care for his people.)*

Draw Conclusions How might the shepherd's rod and staff be comforting to the flock? *(Sample answer: The shepherd uses them to chase predators away from the sheep.)*

To check understanding, have students write answers to the Analyzing Primary Sources questions.

Primary Sources

HSS 6.3.3; ELA RI.6.3, RI.6.4

Psalm 23

While living in Canaan, Abraham and his people herded sheep and other animals. Later, they raised crops. The Torah makes many references to herding flocks or to farming. Psalm 23 is an example. The Psalms are a collection of 150 religious hymns in the Hebrew Bible. These songs reflect the Israelites' belief in God as the powerful savior of Israel. Many of the psalms praise the faithfulness of God to each of his people. In Psalm 23, the speaker describes his faith in God's protection and celebrates the Israelites' sense of a special relationship with a loving God using a herding metaphor.

◂ King David, author of Psalm 23 according to the Hebrew Bible

The LORD is my shepherd, I lack nothing;

He makes me lie down in green pastures;
He leads me to still waters;

He renews (1) my life;
He guides me in right paths as befits His name.

Though I walk through the valley of the shadow of death,
I fear no harm,
for You are with me;
Your rod and Your staff (2)—they comfort me. (3)

You spread a table before me in the full view of my enemies; (4)
You anoint (5) my head with oil; my drink is abundant.

Only goodness and steadfast love shall
pursue me all the days of my life,
and I shall dwell in the house of the LORD for many long years.

Reading and Vocabulary Support

(1) *Renew* means to return to a former condition.

(2) A staff is a walking stick.

(3) What does the psalm say the Lord provides to the Israelites? What phrases serve as clues?

(4) What do you think it means that the Lord "spread[s] a table" for the Israelites "in the full view of [their] enemies"?

(5) To *anoint* means to rub oil into a part of the body as part of a religious ceremony.

Analyzing Primary Sources

Cite specific evidence from the document to support your answers.

1. **Demonstrate Reasoned Judgment** Given the Israelites' belief in a covenant, does comparing God to a shepherd makes sense?
2. **Analyze Style and Rhetoric** What is the tone of this psalm? How does this tone reflect the relationship the Israelites had with God?
3. **Vocabulary: Analyze Word Choices** What might the poem's speaker hope to convey by using so many metaphors?

ANALYZING PRIMARY SOURCES

1. Sample response: A shepherd watches out for his flock. This is similar to God saying that he will look after the Israelites, who are his "chosen people."

2. Sample response: The tone is peaceful and calm. This emphasizes the great appreciation the speaker has for God and all that God provides. The speaker also sounds empowered.

3. Sample response: Metaphors make the psalm stronger and more compelling. For example, the psalm compares God to a shepherd and compares life to a valley of the shadow of death. Examples help readers picture God's guidance in dark times. The metaphors indicate what kind of figure God is and characterize the relationship God has with the Israelites.

Beliefs of Judaism

BOUNCE TO ACTIVATE VIDEO

GET READY TO READ

START UP

Examine the photo of a synagogue service. What aspects of a traditional service may be portrayed here?

GUIDING QUESTIONS

- What is the importance of the Hebrew Bible and the commentaries in Judaism?
- Why do the Jewish people give special importance to study and law?
- What are the ethical teachings and central beliefs of Judaism, including those about righteousness and justice?

TAKE NOTES

Literary Skills: Analyze Cause and Effect

Use the graphic organizer in your Active Journal to take notes as you read the lesson.

PRACTICE VOCABULARY

Use the vocabulary activity in your Active Journal to practice the vocabulary words.

Vocabulary		Academic Vocabulary
prophet	righteousness	commentary
rabbi	justice	individual
Talmud	Sabbath	

God's covenant with the Israelites and God's commandments for God's people are described in the Torah. They form the basis for the Jewish religion and its teachings. These teachings mainly have to do with how people should relate to God and to one another.

The Hebrew Bible

The written tradition is very important in Judaism. Jews greatly value scholarship and learning. In fact, Jews are often called "People of the Book." The Torah and the larger Hebrew Bible are Jewish sacred writings and are the source of Jewish teachings. The Hebrew Bible is also known as the Tanakh in Hebrew.

To Jews the Hebrew Bible is not just a history of their ancestors. They believe it reveals God's will as carried out in human events. This shared account unites Jews all over the world with a common set of teachings. The Hebrew Bible also forms the basis for the Christian Old Testament, which includes the books of the Hebrew Bible, but in a different order.

PRACTICE VOCABULARY

To help students integrate new vocabulary, point out the proper nouns. Explain that *Scriptures* are sacred writings, the *Sabbath* is a weekly day of rest, and the *Talmud* is a book of teachings and commentaries. Then explain that a *prophet* is a person who is believed to be God's messenger, while a *rabbi* is a religious teacher. Judaism is very concerned with *righteousness*, or ethical living, and *justice*, fair treatment for everyone.

Reinforce the terms during the lesson using the teaching notes.

Point out the academic vocabulary in the lesson margins. Provide sample sentences that clarify meaning.

commentary: Jamal read his friend's commentary on the movie before deciding to watch it.

individual: Sarah counted the individual pennies to find out how many there were.

HSS 6.3.2

Beliefs of Judaism

CONNECT

GET READY TO READ

ETEXT **START UP**

Project the Start Up Activity. As students enter the classroom and get settled, ask them to examine the photograph of a Jewish service. Explain that the place of worship is called a synagogue.

Connect Have students record their ideas about what aspects of a traditional service can be seen in the photograph. *(Possible answers: several worshippers reverence for the Torah scroll; people holding books that may be the Hebrew Bible)* Then have them share their ideas with another student.

Discuss Remind students that Judaism is much older than Christianity. Explain that in this lesson they will learn some of the ways Jews have kept their faith alive.

After completing the Start Up Activity, project the Lesson Opener or direct students to their textbooks. Preview the lesson by working through the Get Ready to Read items with the class. Remind students to pay close attention to the Guiding Questions as they read the lesson.

ACTIVE JOURNAL

Take Notes Have students use the lesson literacy skills graphic organizer in their Active Journals to take notes as they read the lesson.

Practice Vocabulary Have students complete the activity in their Active Journals to build their vocabulary.

VIDEO **VIDEO**

Assign the lesson video as homework.

WORKSHEET **TEACHER RESOURCES**

Have students who need additional support use the following worksheets from the Teacher Resources on the course:

- **Reading Support**
- **English Language Development**
- **Lesson Summary**

INVESTIGATE

The Hebrew Bible

Discuss that the Hebrew Bible is the holy book of Judaism, and explain what it contains.

Infer In what way does the Hebrew Bible unite Jews worldwide? *(It gives them a common set of teachings, history, and body of law.)*

Contrast What is the difference between the Christian Old Testament and the Hebrew Bible? *(The Christian Old Testament includes the books of the Hebrew Bible but in a different order.)*

Contrast What is the difference between the **Prophets** and the Writings? *(The Prophets contain words from people who reminded the Jewish people to follow God. The Writings contain wise sayings and stories about heroes.)*

ELD TIP Homophones can be confusing for English learners. Remind students of the verb *profit*, from Lesson 4. Explain to students that although the noun *prophet* has the same pronunciation, it has a completely different meaning. A prophet was a messenger of God. Ask students, *How did prophets deliver God's messages?*

ANSWERS

Cite Evidence *Sample answer: He is using a pointer to make sure he reads each word.*

Analyze Images A Jewish boy reads from the Torah during his bar mitzvah, a ritual that marks his coming of age. The ceremony for girls is called a bat mitzvah. **Cite Evidence** What detail in the photograph shows the boy is reading the text with great care?

The Hebrew Bible describes events believed to have happened hundreds of years before the Bible was put into writing. The books of the Hebrew Bible are divided into three sections.

The Torah As you have learned, the first five books of the Hebrew Bible are called the Torah. The Torah begins by telling the story of God's creation of the world and the first people. It tells of a man named Noah who escaped a great flood on an ark, or boat. It tells of the life of Abraham and God's covenant with him.

The Torah then focuses on Abraham's son Isaac, his grandson Jacob, and Jacob's descendants, the Israelites. The Torah follows their journey from Egypt back to the Promised Land. The Torah is also called the Law of Moses because of the many rules and laws it contains.

The Prophets The next section of the Hebrew Bible is called the Prophets. This section contains books by or about Jewish prophets. A **prophet** is a person believed to be chosen by God as a messenger to bring truth to the people. The prophets were preachers, poets, and reformers. They reminded people to obey God's laws. In so doing, they told people how they should relate to God, to other people, to the land in which they lived, and even to themselves.

The Prophets traces the history of Judaism and the Jewish people. Beginning with the Book of Joshua, this section continues the story of the Israelites from the Torah, describing their arrival in the Promised Land. Other books deal with the creation of the kingdom of Israel.

The Writings The last section of the Hebrew Bible is the Writings. This section includes great Hebrew literature such as the Psalms (sahmz). Psalms are poems or songs offering praises or prayers to God.

HISTORY BACKGROUND

Biblical Prophets The prophets mentioned in the Bible include Isaiah, Jeremiah, Ezekiel, Hosea, Joel, Amos, Obadiah, Jonah, Micah, Nahum, Habakkuk, Zephaniah, Haggai, Zechariah, and Malachi.

Isaiah is the longest book of the prophets. About half of Isaiah warns the Israelite leaders to act with justice. The second half was written during the Babylonian Exile and offers hope that the Israelites will return to their homeland. The Book of Obadiah is the shortest book of the prophets and the shortest in the Hebrew Bible. It warns the Edomite people that they will suffer punishment for attacking the Jews and states that the Jewish people will survive.

The Writings also include the Book of Proverbs. It contains wise sayings. Many give advice to young people, such as this example:

Primary Source

> Do not envy a lawless man, Or choose any of his ways.
>
> —Proverbs 3:31

Other Writings tell about heroes such as Esther, Ruth, and Job (johb). The Writings also contain books, such as Chronicles, that provide a history of the early Jewish people.

READING CHECK **Summarize** What is contained in the Torah?

What Is the Importance of Law and Learning?

The Hebrew Bible and **commentaries** on the Bible are vitally important to Jews. They are important because they are the source of Jews' most important teachings, including teachings about ethics.

Academic Vocabulary
commentary • *n.*, a set of comments or a recorded discussion about something

Laws, the Talmud, and Commentaries Respect for God's laws is basic to Judaism. The great leader Moses is known to Jews as "Moses our teacher." The Torah contains many laws in addition to the Ten Commandments. Many of these laws give directions for religious rituals. Others describe how to have a fair society, how to help those in need, and even how to protect the health of the community through cleanliness and sanitation.

Many centuries after the time of Moses, prominent Jewish **rabbis** (RAB yz), or religious teachers, recorded oral laws that they believed had come down from the teachings of Moses. Other rabbis discussed how laws should be interpreted in different situations. Eventually, they wrote down their commentaries, or discussions, about the laws. The **Talmud** (TAHL mood), a text finished around 600 CE, is a collection of oral teachings and commentaries about the Hebrew Bible and Jewish law. Jews still study and discuss it.

Analyze Images This illustrated manuscript is from a book of Jewish laws written by a scholar of the 1300s. **Cite Evidence** Based on the image, what ceremony is the focus of the laws shown on this page?

The Need to Study The Hebrew Bible and the Talmud are central to Jewish teaching and practice. As a result, Jews value the study of these religious texts. Jewish scholars still write commentaries on the Hebrew Bible and Talmud today.

The Hebrew Bible is mostly written in the Hebrew language. As a result, many Jews people try to learn to read Hebrew. Some also learn Aramaic, the language of most of the Talmud.

READING CHECK **Identify Cause and Effect** Why do Jews value the Hebrew Bible and Talmud?

What Is the Importance of Law and Learning?

Discuss how Judaism places great emphasis on respecting God's law and studying the Scriptures.

Contrast What is the difference between the Torah and the **Talmud**? *(The Torah is the first five books of the Bible. The Talmud is a collection of teachings and commentaries about the Hebrew Bible and Jewish law.)*

Categorize What are two types of discussions found in the **Talmud**? *(There are records of oral teachings about Jewish law and commentaries about or interpretations of the laws.)*

Infer What types of things are important for devout Jews to study? *(They study the languages, their religious laws, and the interpretations of those laws.)*

DIFFERENTIATED INSTRUCTION

Special Education To help students understand the idea of commentaries, explain that whenever someone describes what something means—either orally or in writing—that is a commentary. Ask them to name commentaries they are familiar with. *(Sample answers: movie reviews, discussions of the strategy used in a sporting event)*

Below Level Have pairs of students reread the section titled Laws, the Talmud, and Commentaries. Tell them to list all the words and phrases that help them understand the purpose of commentaries. *(Sample answers: teachings, interpreted, different situations.)*

Advanced Suggest students write a commentary about a school rule. They can discuss why the rule was passed, its effect on how school is run, and whether people completely understand the rule.

ANSWERS

Summarize *The Torah is the first five books of the Hebrew Bible. It tells the stories of God's creation of the world, of Noah, of Abraham, and of the Exodus from Egypt to the Promised Land. it contains the Ten Commandments and many other rules and laws.*

Cite Evidence *Sample answer: It focuses on marriage because of the couple holding hands.*

Identify Cause and Effect *They are valued because they are the source of the Jewish people's most important teachings.*

What Are the Basic Teachings of Judaism?

Discuss how Judaism emphasizes monotheism, righteousness, justice, the law, and love for others.

Contrast How was the Israelites' idea of God different from that of other peoples? *(Most religions believed gods lived in certain places and could be represented physically. The Israelites believed their one God was invisible and everywhere.)*

INTERACTIVE **INTERACTIVE GALLERY**

Significance of Major Jewish Holidays

Display the Interactive Gallery: Significance of Major Jewish Holidays Click on each image, and ask for volunteers to read the captions. Ask: Which holiday allows Jews a chance to repent of the things they have done wrong? *(Sample answer: Yom Kippur)*

ACTIVE CLASSROOM

Use the If Images Could Talk strategy. Choose an image from the gallery and ask: "What do you think the person [insert identifying detail] in this image would say if they could talk? What's your evidence?"

ACTIVE JOURNAL

Quest Connection As students read the text, direct them to the Quest Connections pages in their Active Journals. Make sure they understand how basic teachings of Judaism support social order through laws about behavior.

ANSWERS

Identify Main Ideas *Sample answer: All the other teachings are based on the idea that there is only one God who sets down rules for how to live.*

Analyze Charts Several beliefs are central to the teachings of Judaism. **Identify Main Ideas** Why does the belief in ethical monotheism come first?

INTERACTIVE
Significance of Major Jewish Holidays

What Are the Basic Teachings of Judaism?

The idea of God in Judaism was unique in the ancient world. In other early religions, people worshiped many gods. They had images of these gods made of wood, stone, pottery, or metal. People believed that each god lived in a certain place. In contrast, the God of the Israelites did not live in stones, rocks, or the sea. God did not take a human or an animal form. God was invisible, and yet God was everywhere.

Primary Source

> Am I only a God near at hand —says the LORD— And not a God far away? If a man enters a hiding place, Do I not see him? —says the LORD— For I fill both heaven and earth —declares the LORD.
>
> —Jeremiah 23:23–24

Quest CONNECTIONS
How do the basic teachings of Judaism support social order? Record your thoughts in your Active Journal.

Ethical Monotheism According to the Hebrew Bible, in the Sinai Desert the Israelites made a covenant with God to follow a code of laws, including the Ten Commandments. Along with the Ten Commandments, Jewish people follow other teachings from the Torah, as interpreted by the Talmud and other commentaries. Many of these teachings have to do with ethics.

Ethical monotheism is probably the most important teaching of Judaism. This is the idea that there is one God who sets down ethical rules, or rules about right and wrong. Being faithful to God means following these rules.

INTEGRATED ENGLISH LANGUAGE DEVELOPMENT

Productive Students use concepts learned in What Are the Basic Teachings of Judaism? to write informational texts.

Emerging Read the text aloud, assisting students with difficult concepts. Then, pair students to write three sentences about equality and women's rights according to Jewish belief.

Expanding Have students read individually. Then pair students to organize and write informational texts explaining three Jewish beliefs.

Bridging Have students independently organize and write a formal informational text about three of the key teachings of Judaism.

Righteousness and Justice Ethical monotheism calls on Jews to know the difference between right and wrong. For them, actions should be based on righteousness and justice. **Righteousness** is acting or living in a way that is ethically right and obeys God's laws.

As you have learned, Jews maintain that each person has value and worth because he or she is created in the image of God. Along with **individual** worth comes individual responsibility to God. Each individual has the responsibility to act righteously in God's eyes.

Righteousness was a key concern of the prophets. For example, they reminded people that they needed to be honest and kind to each other. They criticized rulers who were cruel to the poor and weak. They urged people to work for **justice**—fairness or fair treatment—for everyone. Jewish teachers also expected everyone to help those in need.

Observance of Law The laws and other rules that Jews follow are seen as part of the Jewish people's covenant with God. According to the Torah, God had a special relationship with the Israelites. In return, the Israelites believed that they had a responsibility to obey God's laws and commandments.

The Jewish idea of individual responsibility means that these laws and commandments apply equally to every Jewish person. This means that God's laws apply equally to leaders such as Moses and to the ordinary people who follow them. This idea of equality in the eyes of God helped shape modern systems of law.

Women in Ancient Judaism In ancient Judaism, as in most ancient religions and cultures, men had the most power. Women rarely owned property, although they did have the right to buy and sell land. Jewish law gave women other important rights and protections, including the right to be consulted about whom they would marry and the right to take cases to court.

Academic Vocabulary
individual • *adj.*, having to do with a single person or thing

◀ A woman rabbi

Summarize How has Judaism shaped modern law? *(The idea of equality before the law is derived from Jewish law.)*

Support Ideas with Examples What are some practical ways that Jews live out the commandment to love others? *(Jews have participated in efforts to fight discrimination, and many Jews give to charity.)*

Connect Why do Jewish people feel connected to the land of Israel? *(Judaism began there, and Jews believe it is the land God promised to Abraham and his descendants.)*

ELD.PI.C.10a

WORKSHEET **TEACHER RESOURCES**

For additional IELD support addressing these standards, have students complete the Lesson IELD activity from the Teacher Resources found on the course.

ANSWERS

Cite Evidence *They are donating food.*

Summarize *It is the belief in one God who calls on the people to obey moral laws and practice ethics.*

HSS 6.3.2; ELD.P1.A.2, P1.C.10.a

SYNTHESIZE

Assess and Reteach Have students work with a partner to complete Lesson Check questions 1–6. Review their responses. If they had any incorrect answers, use the guiding questions to discuss the lesson's main ideas, focusing on the ideas they struggled with.

ACTIVE JOURNAL

Writing Workshop Have students complete the Lesson 6 Writing Task in their Active Journals. Students will identify narrative techniques that they can use to write their stories. As they move through the topic, students will revisit their list of techniques, adding to it as needed.

DEMONSTRATE

ASSESSMENT **ONLINE LESSON QUIZ**

Assign the Online Lesson Quiz for this lesson if you haven't already done so.

DISCUSSION **DISCUSSION BOARD**

Post this question to the class on the Discussion Board:

Summarize Why do Jews give special importance to study and law? *(Because God expects people to live ethical, moral lives, it is important to obey God's law. To obey it, one must know it and understand it, which is why study is so important.)*

Analyze Images Many Jews make donations and volunteer time to assist the needy. **Cite Evidence** How are these people contributing to charity?

Love for Others The Hebrew Bible commands, "Love your fellow [human being] as yourself." Jews are required to help others. As a result, Jews have been involved in many efforts to fight discrimination. Jews also give to charities in response to this teaching. These ideas have influenced modern thinking about basic human rights.

Other Key Teachings Another important Jewish teaching is to observe the **Sabbath**, or a weekly day of rest. This belief is basic to Judaism and is found in the Ten Commandments. For Jews, the Sabbath is the seventh day of the week, or Saturday. According to Jewish teachings, this should be a day free from work. Many nations have adopted the practice of having a weekly day of rest.

Jewish teaching also stresses the importance of study and prayer. You have learned about the importance of studying the Torah and Hebrew Bible and commentaries on them, such as the Talmud. Jews also value prayer as a way of communicating with God.

The Jewish people's ties to the Land of Israel are also central to Judaism. This is the land that was promised to Abraham, according to the Torah. It includes the modern state of Israel. Many Jews feel a deep connection to this land because of its place in the Jewish sacred writings and Jewish history.

READING CHECK **Summarize** What is ethical monotheism?

Lesson Check

HSS 6.3.2; ELD.P1.A.2, P1.C.10.a

Practice Vocabulary

1. What is a **prophet**, and what kind of writings are found in the collection of books called the Prophets?
2. What is the relationship between the **Talmud** and the Hebrew Bible? What do they say about Jewish ideas of **righteousness** and **justice**?
3. Why do you think observation of the **Sabbath** is an important Jewish teaching?

Critical Thinking and Writing

4. **Classify and Categorize** What are the three main parts of the Hebrew Bible and how do they differ?
5. **Draw Conclusions** Why is studying the Hebrew Bible and commentaries such as the Talmud so important to Jews?
6. **Cite Evidence** How are God's covenants with the Jewish people related to Jewish teachings about ethics and justice?
7. **Writing Workshop: Use Narrative Techniques** Write a few sentences in your Active Journal to identify and record some narrative techniques you can use to tell your story. You will use these narrative techniques when you write your narrative at the end of the topic.

88 Lesson 2.6 • Beliefs of Judaism

LESSON CHECK

1. A prophet is someone believed to be chosen by God to be a messenger to bring truth to the people. The Prophets contain history, preaching, poetry, and calls for reform. **DOK1**
2. These works emphasize individual responsibility and living a righteous and just life. **DOK2**
3. Sample answer: The Sabbath is a weekly day of rest when people can reflect on their lives and faith apart from the demands of work. **DOK2**
4. The Torah is the first five books, focusing on the early Israelites and God's laws. The Prophets are by or about Jewish prophets and describe the history of the Israelites. The Writings contain wise sayings, books with stories of heroes, and more of the early history of the Jewish people. **DOK2**
5. These works provide Jews with sacred rules for living. **DOK3**
6. Jews believe they have made covenants with God to follow God's laws and to behave ethically and justly. **DOK3**
7. Students might use techniques to build suspense, to use flashbacks or foreshadowing, or to mark transitions from one part of the story to another. **DOK4**

LESSON 7

HSS 6.3.2, 6.3.3, 6.3.5

Early History of the Jewish People

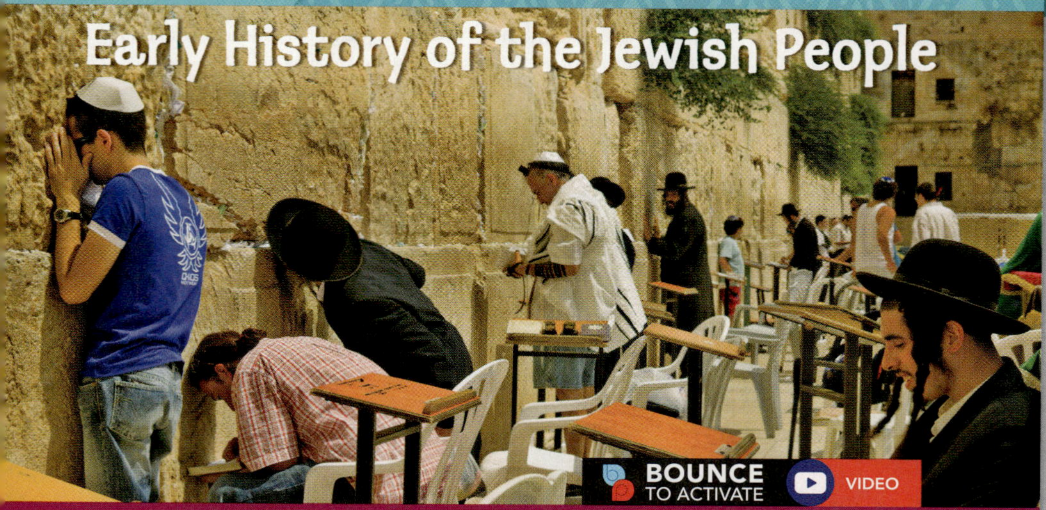

BOUNCE TO ACTIVATE

VIDEO

GET READY TO READ

START UP

Examine the photo of Jews praying at the Western Wall today. What do you think this place means to the Jewish people?

GUIDING QUESTIONS

- How did the environment and history shape Jewish religion and practices over time?
- How did early Judaism support individuals, rulers, and societies?
- Why did Jewish communities spread to many different parts of the ancient world?
- How are the religious and ethical teachings of Judaism reflected in society today?

TAKE NOTES

Literary Skills: Sequence

Use the graphic organizer in your Active Journal to take notes as you read the lesson.

PRACTICE VOCABULARY

Use the vocabulary activity in your Active Journal to practice the vocabulary words.

Vocabulary		Academic Vocabulary
judge	Diaspora	commission
exile	synagogue	reject

After the Israelites settled in the Land of Israel, they lived as a group of separate tribes before joining to form a kingdom. After about 70 years the kingdom split, and the Israelites were later conquered by foreign empires. The descendants of the Israelites, known as Jews, later spread to many parts of the world.

The Kingdom of Israel

Most of what we know of early Jewish history comes from the Hebrew Bible. Archaeologists also have found evidence for some of the events mentioned in the Hebrew Bible before about 900 BCE. After that date, there is even more evidence from other written sources and from archaeology for events mentioned in the Hebrew Bible.

The Time of the Judges The Hebrew Bible states that Joshua led the Israelites in the conquest of Canaan. After Joshua died, the Israelites remained a group of tribes without a common government. They faced a number of conflicts with other peoples.

PRACTICE VOCABULARY

To help students integrate new vocabulary, explain that a *judge* was a leader who helped the Israelites defend their land. When stronger empires conquered their kingdoms, the Jews experienced *exile*, or separation from one's homeland, and the *Diaspora*, which refers to Jewish communities living outside their homeland. Because of this, Jews had to worship away from Jerusalem in meeting places called *synagogues*. Reinforce the terms during the lesson using the teaching notes.

Point out the academic vocabulary in the lesson margins. Provide sample sentences that clarify meaning.

commision: The celebrity commissioned a painting of his family for his new home.

reject: The prisoner will lose her case if the court rejects her argument.

HSS 6.3.2, 6.3.3, 6.3.5

Early History of the Jewish People

CONNECT

GET READY TO READ

ETEXT **START UP**

Project the Start Up Activity. As students enter the classroom and get settled, ask them to examine the photograph of Jews praying at the Western Wall, which is the only remaining part of the Jewish Temple that used to stand in Jerusalem.

Infer Have students describe what they think this structure means to Jewish people today, judging from what they see in the photograph. *(Sample answers: It is a holy site. It reminds them of past glories.)* Then have them share their thoughts with another student, either in class or through a chat or blog.

Discuss Remind students that they just read about how the Israelites returned to the Promised Land. Ask them what kinds of things people do after they settle a land. *(Sample answers: build houses, set up a government)*

After completing the Start Up Activity, project the Lesson Opener or direct students to their textbooks. Preview the lesson by working through the Get Ready to Read items with the class. Remind students to pay close attention to the Guiding Questions as they read the lesson.

ACTIVE JOURNAL

Take Notes Have students use the lesson literacy skills graphic organizer in their Active Journals to take notes as they read the lesson.

Practice Vocabulary Have students complete the activity in their Active Journals to build their vocabulary.

VIDEO **VIDEO**

Assign the lesson video as homework.

WORKSHEET **TEACHER RESOURCES**

Have students who need additional support use the following worksheets.

- **Reading Support**
- **English Language Development**
- **Lesson Summary**

INVESTIGATE

The Kingdom of Israel

Discuss how the Israelites formed a kingdom and what happened to it.

Infer After students read the 5 Things to Know About Ruth, ask: Why do you think Ruth's story is important enough to include in the Bible? *(Sample answer: She is an example of love and loyalty.)*

INTERACTIVE **INTERACTIVE GALLERY**

Origins of Judaism

Display Origins of Judaism. Click on each image. Ask: What does the image of Jerusalem show about how the Israelites had changed? *(They had changed from a herding people to a people who also had sophisticated cities.)*

ACTIVE CLASSROOM

Use the Rank It strategy. Ask student groups to choose the event that they think is the most significant and explain their reasons.

ANSWERS

Critical Thinking *Sample answer: "Wherever you will go, I will go" can be seen as pledge of devotion.*

INTERACTIVE
Origins of Judaism

In times of distress, the Israelites often rallied around leaders called judges. As used in the Hebrew Bible, a **judge** was a leader who rallied the Israelites to defend their land. Judges were often warriors or prophets. They did not pass leadership to their descendants.

Deborah and Ruth Some women became well known during the time of the judges. The prophet Deborah, who inspired an army to win a great battle, was the only female judge. Other well-known women are Ruth and Naomi. When her husband died, Ruth followed her mother-in-law Naomi back to Israel. She accepted Naomi's religion and joined the tribe of Judah. It was dangerous at the time for Naomi and Ruth to be without male protection, but Naomi was determined to return. Her dedication to the Jewish home and Ruth's loyalty make them significant. The time of the judges ended when the warrior Saul became the first king of Israel.

David and Solomon The Hebrew Bible states that one of Saul's best fighters was David, a young shepherd and musician. David became the next king. Some archaeologists and historians date that to about 1000 BCE. He captured the city of Jerusalem and made it his capital. He extended the kingdom's borders. David is believed to have written beautiful psalms—poems or songs in the Bible—such as this one:

Academic Vocabulary
commission • *v.*, to order the creation of

Primary Source

> The LORD is my shepherd, I lack nothing; . . .
> Though I walk through the valley of the shadow of death, I fear no harm, for You are with me; Your rod and Your staff—they comfort me.
>
> —Psalm 23:1, 4

BIOGRAPHY
5 Things to Know About
Ruth
Biblical figure c. 1100–1000 BCE

- Ruth was from Moab and was not a Jew, but was married to the Jewish son of Naomi for ten years before he died.
- Naomi begged for her to return to Moab, but Ruth would not leave her mother-in-law alone. Leaving her own parents, she followed Naomi to Bethlehem.
- In telling Naomi her plan to return with her to Bethlehem, Ruth said, "Wherever you go, I will go," which is often used during wedding services as an example of love and dedication.
- With Naomi's help, Ruth marries a prosperous relative of Naomi named Boaz, who was impressed by Ruth's loyalty to Naomi.
- Ruth is one of the few women with a book named after them in the Hebrew Bible. Her story became the Book of Ruth.

Critical Thinking Why do you think Ruth's words are used in wedding ceremonies today?

DIFFERENTIATED INSTRUCTION

Special Education Allow students with language difficulties to create simple drawings to represent the following sequence of events (or one of the events): rule by judges; rule by kings; a divided kingdom; conquest of both kingdoms by stronger empires; return of some Jews to Judah.

Below Level Have students work in pairs to create a sequence chart or timeline of the major events between the Jews' arrival in the Promised Land and the Babylonian captivity.

Advanced Have students research one of the following topics and report back to the class about how it fits with the events in this lesson: Ruth's relationship to the line of kings; the role of either the prophet Daniel or the prophet Ezekiel during the Babylon captivity; or the role Nehemiah played after the Jews returned to Jerusalem.

David's son Solomon ruled after him. He **commissioned** the great First Temple in Jerusalem. According to tradition, Solomon wrote many of the wise sayings in the Hebrew Bible's Book of Proverbs.

The Kingdom Divides The kingdom of Israel split in two after Solomon died, around 900 BCE. Solomon's descendants ruled the kingdom of Judah in the south. From the name *Judah*, the religion of the Israelites became known as Judaism. The descendants of the Israelites became known as Jews.

A rival, or competing, kingdom in the north kept the name of the Kingdom of Israel. About 722 BCE, the Assyrian Empire conquered Israel. The Assyrians were brutal. Thousands of Israelites were sent to distant parts of the empire. Other Israelites fled south to Judah.

One hundred years later, the city-state of Babylon rebelled against Assyria and began the Neo-Babylonian empire. Babylon's greatest emperor, Nebuchadnezzar (neb yuh kud NEZ ur) conquered Judah. About 587 BCE, the Babylonians destroyed Jerusalem, including Solomon's Temple.

The Babylonian Captivity The Babylonians took thousands of Jews from Judah to faraway Babylon. Many Jewish prophets urged the Jews to obey the Torah while living in exile. **Exile** means separation from one's homeland. According to the Hebrew Bible, some Jews, such as Daniel, became important people in Babylon. Many Jews wished to return to their homeland.

Cyrus the Great, king of the Persians, conquered the Babylonian empire. The Persian empire now controlled most of Southwest Asia. In 538 BCE, Cyrus allowed the Jewish people to go home. Many did return to Judah. Jewish leaders began to build the Second Temple in Jerusalem. They completed the Second Temple in 515 BCE. They later rebuilt the walls of Jerusalem.

READING CHECK **Identify Supporting Details** What are some of the accomplishments that David is known for in Judaism?

Israel Under King David, 966 BCE

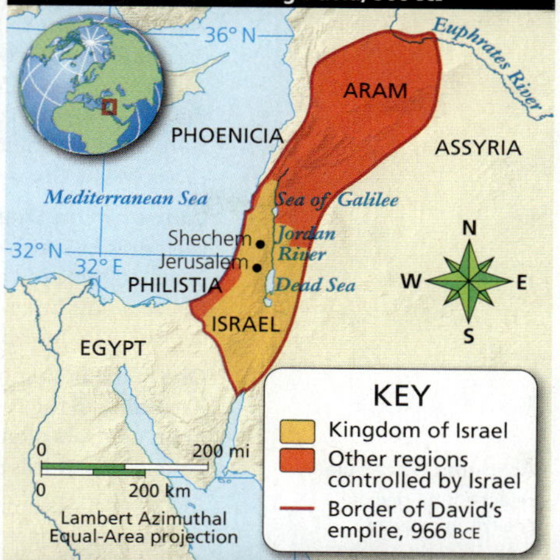

Israel and Judah, About 900–722 BCE

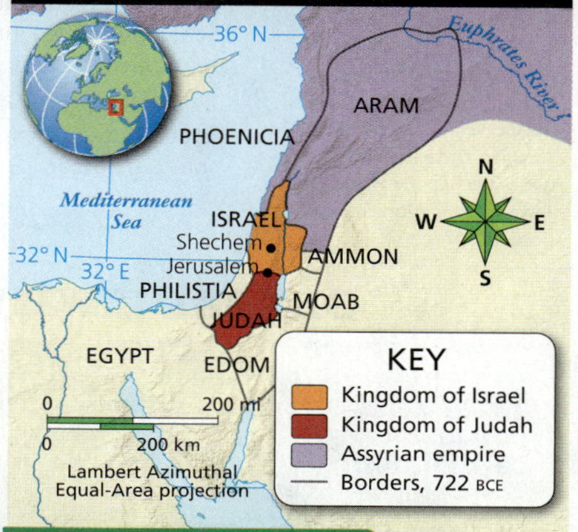

GEOGRAPHY SKILLS

The united kingdom of Israel ruled by David and Solomon (*top*) was larger than the two divided kingdoms.

1. **Location** Which of the divided kingdoms had easy access to the sea?
2. **Draw Conclusions** Which kingdom was under greater threat from a foreign power? Why?

Cause and Effect What happened to the united kingdom of Israel? *(The kingdom split into two parts: Israel in the north, Judah in the south.)*

Sequence Which Israelite kingdom was the first to be conquered? *(Israel)*

Synthesize How did Cyrus the Great help the Jews? *(He allowed them to return home from Babylon and rebuild their temple.)*

HISTORY BACKGROUND

Cyrus the Reformer Jewish people remember Cyrus the Great as the Persian ruler who allowed the Jews to return to Jerusalem. His reputation as a just leader is boosted by a document he left behind—a clay cylinder covered with cuneiform writing. In 1879, an archaeologist discovered the cylinder in the foundation wall of ancient Babylon. It mentions reforms Cyrus began when he became ruler. The cylinder, called the Cyrus Cylinder, is sometimes called the first charter of human rights. Cyrus says, "I collected together all of their people and returned them to their settlements." For many Jewish people, this phrase is linked to Cyrus's permission for the exiled Jews in Babylon to return to Jerusalem and rebuild the Temple, as told in the Book of Ezra and in the very last passage of the Hebrew Bible, in 2 Chronicles.

ANSWERS

Identify Supporting Details *David was king. He captured the city of Jerusalem and made it the Jewish capital. He expanded the kingdom and is believed to have written psalms.*

Location *Israel*

Draw Conclusions *Israel was, because the Assyrian Empire lay on its borders.*

What Was the Diaspora?

Discuss how the Jews became scattered outside Israel and how that affected Judaism.

Summarize Which lands did the Persian empire cover? *(The Land of Israel, Egypt, Asia Minor, Mesopotamia, Iran, and parts of Central Asia)*

Identify Cause and Effect What event ended the Persian empire? *(Alexander the Great conquered it.)*

Sequence What happened to the Jews after Alexander died? *(They moved into all the areas Alexander had conquered, as well as Arabia and Africa.)*

ELD TIP To help students understand the Infographic, use simple questions to scaffold the question for emerging students. Ask, *Were there more Jewish people in Israel in 1950 or today? Were there more Jewish people in the Diaspora in 1950 or today?*

What Was the Diaspora?

The Babylonian Exile was a turning point in Jewish history. Communities of Jews now lived throughout the Babylonian empire, which stretched across the Fertile Crescent. These communities outside the Land of Israel came to be known as the **Diaspora** (dy AS puh ruh), or communities of Jews living outside of their ancient homeland. *Diaspora* is a Greek word meaning dispersion, or scattering.

Lands of the Diaspora After the Persians conquered Babylon, their empire spread across all of Southwest Asia. The Persian empire included the Land of Israel, but it also included Egypt, Asia Minor (present day Turkey), Mesopotamia, what is now Iran, and parts of central Asia. Jewish people spread across these regions.

One of the best-known Jewish people in the Persian empire was Esther. According to the Hebrew Bible, she married the Persian emperor. One of his advisors planned to kill all the Jews. Esther convinced the Persian king to **reject** this plan.

Academic Vocabulary
reject • *v.*, to decide against, turn away

In 330 BCE, Alexander the Great, from present-day Greece, conquered the Persian empire. After his death, Greek empires ruled the Land of Israel, the rest of Southwest Asia, Egypt, and parts of southern Europe. In the years that followed, Jewish people settled in all of these regions. Some also settled far to the south, in Arabia and Africa. Others settled to the east in many parts of Asia.

By this time, millions of Jews lived inside and outside of the Land of Israel. Nonetheless, Jews everywhere still looked to Jerusalem as their spiritual home.

Analyze Diagrams Israel has the world's largest Jewish population. But a majority of Jews live in the Diaspora, or outside Israel. **Analyze Data** In what two ways has the world's Jewish population changed since 1950?

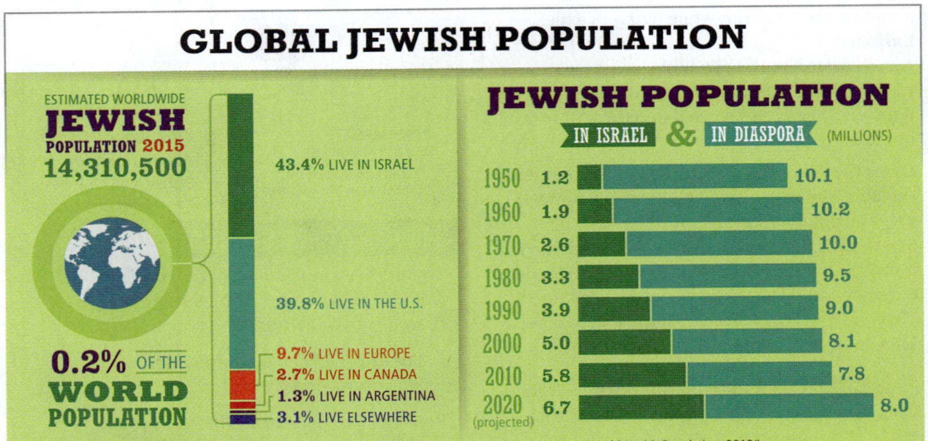

Sources: DellaPergola, *World Jewish Population, 2015*; Pew Research Center; University of Connecticut, "World Jewish Population, 2012"; Rabinovich and Reinharz, *Israel in the Middle East*, 2008.

INTEGRATED ENGLISH LANGUAGE DEVELOPMENT

Productive Use What Was the Diaspora? to help students take notes and write summaries about how Judaism has spread and changed.

Emerging Read the text aloud, pausing to allow students to write brief notes about each paragraph. Pair students, and have them to compare notes and use their notes to write several short sentences summarizing how Judaism has changed in the Diaspora.

Expanding Encourage students to note key words and ideas as they individually read the text. Pair students to compare notes, selecting only the most important ideas. Have students work collaboratively to write details to include in concise summaries about of how Judaism spread and changed in the Diaspora.

ANSWERS

Analyze Data *The population in Israel has grown, and the population in the Diaspora has decreased.*

New Ways to Worship The Diaspora brought changes in the way Jews worshiped. Many Jews lived too far from Jerusalem to return for worship.

Previously, most Jews could worship at the Temple in Jerusalem. Because of the Diaspora, however, Jews had to practice their faith wherever they were living.

Some Jews had already been used to gathering in a **synagogue**, or meeting place. There they could pray and discuss the Torah and Hebrew Bible. Often, someone who knew the Torah well became the group's rabbi, or teacher. In the Diaspora, synagogues became even more important.

Greek Rule After the Babylonian Exile ended, Jews in Israel tried hard to follow their religion. But that was difficult because they faced harsh and unfair treatment by rulers of the Greek Empires.

Jews rebelled against harsh Greek rule. During the 100s BCE, a family known as the Maccabees rebelled and won independence from Greek rulers who tried to ban important parts of Judaism. The Jewish holiday of Hanukkah celebrates the victory of the Maccabees, freedom of religion, and reclaiming of the Temple.

Roman Rule In 6 CE, the Land of Israel became part of the Roman Empire. By this time, it was called Judaea, or later "land of the Jews." Roman disrespect toward Judaism led Jews to rebel against Rome. In response, in 70 CE, the Romans destroyed Jerusalem, including the Second Temple.

The Romans also killed or enslaved thousands of Jews. Thousands more fled to other lands. During the war, a teacher from the Second Temple named Yohanan ben Zaccai (YOH hah nahn ben ZAH keye) secretly visited the Roman commander. He received permission to set up a center for Jewish scholars in another part of Judaea. The Temple was gone, but learning survived and remained important to Jews.

After another Jewish rebellion, the Romans changed the name of the province in 135 CE to Palaestina, later shortened to Palestine, after the ancient Israelites' enemies the Philistines. The Romans required provinces to pay tributes and taxes to support the rulers and the empire.

Judaism Changes and Develops The religious practices of early Judaism changed as a result of interactions with other societies. The Torah and Jewish law needed interpretation as society changed. For many centuries, details of the interpretation of the laws of the written Torah had been passed down orally from teacher to student. These explanations were called the Oral Torah. Jewish leaders feared that the Oral Torah would be lost in the Diaspora, and that direct passing down of the law might become impossible or unreliable. Because of that, within a few hundred

Analyze Images Jewish families takes part in religious services in a modern synagogue. **Identify Main Ideas** What development gave rise to the practice of worshiping in a synagogue?

Summarize Describe how the **Diaspora** changed the way Jews worship. *(They met and studied at synagogues rather than the Temple in Jerusalem.)*

Identify Cause and Effect How did some Jews react to harsh Greek rule? *(They rebelled.)*

Connect How is the victory of the Maccabees commemorated today? *(It is commemorated in the holiday of Hanukkah.)*

Summarize How did Jewish learning survive during and after the war with Rome? *(Yohanan ben Zaccai received permission to set up a center for jewish scholars in another part of Judaea.)*

Identify Patterns What did Jewish leaders do to keep their laws from changing too much as Jews interacted with other societies? Explain how this compares to the way other societies preserved their culture. *(Jewish leaders set down the Torah in writing. Keeping written records is one of the most common ways that societies try to preserve their culture.)*

ELD.P1.C.10.b

Bridging Encourage students to note key words and ideas as they read the text. Pair students to compare notes. Then have students write clear and coherent summaries of how Judaism spread and changed in the Diaspora.

WORKSHEET **TEACHER RESOURCES**

For additional IELD support addressing these standards, have students complete the Lesson ELD activity from the Teacher Resources found on the course.

ANSWERS

Identify Main Ideas *The Diaspora gave rise to worshiping in synagogues.*

Explain Central Issues From the Past Why did Jewish leaders decide to change Judaism from a focus on worship in the Temple to a focus on the Torah and Jewish teachings? *(The change enabled the religion to survive after Jews were scattered around the world.)*

Judaism's Support for Society

Discuss how Judaism has influenced world civilization as a whole.

Connect What major religious concept did Judaism introduce to society? *(monotheism)*

Categorize What social justice issues are included in the Hebrew Bible? *(It includes guidelines for responding to poverty, famine, and injustice; it emphasizes respecting human life, giving generously, caring for strangers and refugees, and respecting property.)*

years after the destruction of the Second Temple, the Oral Torah was set down in writing, which later formed the core of the Talmud.

The preservation of those texts and laws, and of ethical and ritual requirements, was key to the development of Judaism as a religion. Judaism survived outside the homeland by focusing on the Torah and Jewish teachings, and by maintaining its strong religious and historic connection to the Land of Israel. This Judaism, in which traditions could be handed down through the generations in writing, became known as Rabbinic Judaism. Its practices no longer centered on the Temple. But Judaism's main teachings remained unchanged.

READING CHECK **Understand Effects** How did Yohanan ben Zaccai help the Jewish religion to continue during the war against the Romans?

Judaism's Support for Society

Judaism is given credit for introducing monotheism to society. Beyond monotheism, Judaism's contributions have affected every part of our society. Biblical teachings and laws in both the Written and Oral Torahs have shaped not only early Jewish society, but civilization as a whole. The early Noahide Laws (described in the Oral Torah as given to the Biblical figure of Noah, generations before Abraham) are seven laws that Jews believe apply to society as a whole. They contain some of the elements of the Ten Commandments: to not deny or curse God and to not murder, steal, or engage in improper relationships.

How Does Judaism Help Ensure Social Justice? The Ten Commandments and later teachings contain laws about honoring parents, a day of rest, and justice. The guidelines for social justice, and for rulers and leaders, supported the needs of society and its members. The Hebrew Bible contains guidance and laws that detail how people

Analyze Images The Second Temple is thought to have looked something like this. **Synthesize Visual Information** How would the setting and the Temple itself inspire worshipers?

CURRICULUM CONNECTION: ENVIRONMENTAL EDUCATION

The practice of using crop rotation, introduced in the Torah, to allow some fields to lie fallow is particularly useful in dry regions. The fallow field is usually plowed and tilled but not planted. Rather it lies unused for a growing season. This practice allows any precipitation that falls to seep into the soil and remain stored for the following growing season. It is important for the farmer to prevent weeds from taking over the field during the fallow period.

Modern practices have improved the fallow system. Now farmers often use chisels or other tools that loosen the soil but allow straw from the previous crop to remain on the surface. The straw helps hold in moisture, prevent wind erosion, and deter the growth of weeds.

ANSWERS

Synthesize Visual Information *Sample answer: The setting and Temple would inspire worshipers to remember the history of the Jewish people.*

Understand Effects *He obtained permission from the Roman commander to set up a center for Jewish scholars in another part of Judaea. There, they could continue to learn.*

Religious Holidays in the Jewish Tradition Today

Day	Early Practice	Today
Sabbath	"Remember the Sabbath day, to keep it holy." Exodus 20:7	Jews who accidentally break the rule of the Sabbath are to perform prayers and observances focused on making the Sabbath a positive spiritual experience.
Rosh Hashanah	"And in the seventh month, on the first of the month, it shall be declared a holiday for you, a day of sounding a teruah [blast of a shofar, or ram's horn] for you." Numbers 29:1	The shofar is blown during synagogue services for Rosh Hashanah.
Passover	In the Temple period, Passover originally occurred on the celebration of the barley harvest.	Passover is a week of remembrance of the Exodus. Its main event is the seder, a ritual meal. Its foods symbolize the simple meal that marked the Israelites' escape from slavery.

Analyze Charts Jewish religious practice has changed somewhat over time, as shown by the changes with these holidays. **Draw Conclusions** How are the holidays connected to the Hebrew Bible and the history of the Israelites?

should respond to poverty, famine, and injustice. It teaches that one must, above all, respect human life and give generously to the needy. Individuals and society must care for strangers and refugees, respect others' rights and property, and honor parents and respect marriage.

The concept of justice and equality under the law is contained in what may be the earliest legal system, with lower courts for simple disputes, and high courts that examine and rule on the difficult cases. The idea of making amends with money for crimes and debts took the place of a death penalty. Protection from those who would take the law into their own hands was guaranteed by setting up asylum cities in ancient Israel where those who were accused of killing others could safely await trial.

Laws Supporting Animal Rights and the Environment The Written and Oral Torahs also support the needs of animals and the environment. The Torah and Talmud provide instructions on animal rights and humane treatment. The Torah also includes environmental protections. These include introducing the practice of crop rotation to leave fields uncultivated during some seasons. This practice is useful because it helps maintain the nutrients in soil that keep the land fertile. Another protection for the environment found in the Torah is the obligation to not destroy or waste resources.

READING CHECK **Identify Main Ideas** List three teachings of Judaism and explain why they are important today.

Analyze Information What guidelines did the Hebrew Bible give for structuring a court system? *(Lower courts handled simple disputes, and high courts examined and ruled on difficult cases.)*

What Is the Legacy of Judaism?

Discuss how Judaism continues to influence the modern world.

Connect Which two religions share with Judaism a belief in only one God? *(Christianity and Islam)*

Summarize What are three values of Judeo-Christian tradition that have influenced modern democracies? *(The equal importance of every individual, individual freedom and responsibility, emphasis on justice and human rights, equality before the law)*

COMMON MISCONCEPTIONS

The Ten Commandments The Ten Commandments remain important to Jews, Catholics, and Protestants today, but they differ for each group. Both Jews and Catholics have "I am the Lord thy God" as the first commandment. Protestants start with "Thou shalt have no other gods before me," which is the second commandment for Jews and Catholics. Protestants list "Thou shalt not make unto thee any graven images" as the second commandment. Jews combine that with the second commandment. Catholics do not list it at all. Commandments 4–9 are the same for Jews and Protestants; Catholics have the same commandments numbered 3–8. The last two Catholic commandments are "Thou shalt not covet thy neighbor's wife" and "Thou shalt not covet thy neighbor's goods." Jews and Protestants have those combined into commandment number 10.

ANSWERS

Draw Conclusions *Many of the holidays, such as Purim and Passover, commemorate events from the history of the Jews as recorded in the Hebrew Bible.*

Identify Main Ideas *Sample answer: Respect for human life is an important teaching because in our society we sometimes encounter prejudice and even people who will kill others. Public education is an important teaching because the idea that everyone has access to free public education is the backbone of the U.S. education system. Protecting the environment is important as we face climate change, pollution, and dependence on fossil fuels.*

Summarize *It is a set of values that Christians and Jews share.*

HSS 6.3.2, 6.3.3, 6.3.5; ELD.P1.A.2, P1.C.10.a

SYNTHESIZE

Assess and Reteach Have students use a Jigsaw strategy to complete Lesson Check questions 1–6. Review their responses. If they had any incorrect answers, use the guiding questions to discuss the lesson's main ideas, focusing on the ideas they struggled with.

ACTIVE JOURNAL

Writing Workshop Have students complete the Lesson 7 Writing Task in their Active Journals. Students will identify descriptive and sensory details they can use in their narrative. As they complete the topic, students may revisit their list, revising it as needed.

DEMONSTRATE

ASSESSMENT **ONLINE LESSON QUIZ**

Assign the Online Lesson Quiz for this lesson if you haven't already done so. Students will be offered automatic remediation or enrichment based on their score.

DISCUSSION **DISCUSSION BOARD**

Post this question to the class on the Discussion Board:

Summarize Why did Jewish communities spread to many different parts of the ancient world? *(Many ancient empires conquered the Jews' homeland, often forcing them into exile. Over time, Jewish communities existed in much of the ancient world.)*

▲ Rabbi Yitzhak Yosef (left) shakes hands with Pope Francis in Jerusalem. Jews and Christians share many traditions.

What Is the Legacy of Judaism?

Today, nearly 14 million Jews live throughout the world. A large majority of the world's Jews live in either the United States or Israel.

Judaism's legacies, or the concepts and values it has given the world, include teachings about one supreme, invisible God who created everything. Christians and Muslims, like Jews, honor Abraham as a founding figure and Moses as a messenger of God. They both share with Jews the belief in a single God. The ethical teachings of Judaism have influenced spiritual leaders in all parts of the world.

The Hebrew Bible is another legacy of Judaism. Its poetic language makes it a classic of world literature, as do its dramatic stories of unforgettable figures such as Moses, David, and Esther.

One of the greatest legacies of Judaism is the set of values that have been incorporated into what many call the Judeo-Christian tradition. These moral and ethical values form a basis for modern democratic societies such as the United States. They relate to such ideas as the worth of the individual and the importance of moral behavior. Examples include the equal importance of every individual, individual freedom and responsibility, community responsibility, and the importance of human rights and justice.

READING CHECK **Summarize** What is the Judeo-Christian tradition?

Lesson Check

HSS 6.3.2, 6.3.3, 6.3.5; ELD.P1.A.2, P1.C.10.a

Practice Vocabulary

1. Who were the **judges**, and what role did they play in the lives of the Israelites?
2. What were the Jews who were in **exile** in Babylonia able to do with their sacred texts for the first time?
3. How were **synagogues** important to Jews in the Diaspora?

Critical Thinking and Writing

4. **Support Ideas with Evidence** Why are Naomi and Ruth significant figures?
5. **Draw Conclusions** How did the position of the Land of Israel, in a region conquered by several ancient empires, affect Jewish history?
6. **Understand Effects** Describe some of the ways in which Judaism has influenced modern democratic societies.
7. **Writing Workshop: Use Descriptive Details and Sensory Language** Write notes in your Active Journal about descriptive details and sensory language that you can use in the narrative essay you will write at the end of the topic.

96 Lesson 2.7 • Early History of the Jewish People

LESSON CHECK

1. The judges were warriors and prophets who led the Israelites in defending their land. **DOK1**
2. They were able to write them down and organize them. **DOK1**
3. They became places of worship because the Jews were too far away from their Temple. **DOK1**
4. She accepted Judaism and joined the tribe of Judah even though she wasn't Jewish to support her mother-in-law. **DOK3**
5. Its vulnerable location resulted in the land being invaded often, with the people forced to move elsewhere. **DOK3**
6. It emphasizes individual respect, responsibility, and equality before the law. **DOK2**
7. Students should find details that make the characters' activities vivid and interesting. They can also express those details using sensory language. **DOK4**

Analysis CST.2

INTERACTIVE
Sequence

Construct a Timeline

Use the secondary source and follow these steps to construct a timeline.

1 **Identify the time span.** To organize information in a timeline, identify the earliest date and the latest date at which key events or periods occurred.

a. In the passage, what was the date of the first event?

b. What was the date of the last event?

2 **Identify your timeline's beginning and end points.** Begin the timeline at a date just before the oldest date in your list of events or periods. At the end of the timeline, place a date just after the last date in your list of events or periods.

3 **Divide the timeline into equal time spans.** Calculate the length of your timeline from start to finish. Then, divide that time period into equal segments. Mark each segment on the timeline and label it.

4 **Place items along the timeline.** Write down key events and their dates where they fall along the timeline. For time spans, place them at the point they begin. Make sure to arrange all items in sequence. Be sure to include all of the dates mentioned in the passage.

Secondary Source

"The time of the judges ended when the judges chose Saul to become the first king of Israel in 1021 BCE. He remained king for the next 20 years and is known for defending Israel against its enemies. David, who was considered one of Saul's best fighters, became the next king of Israel around 1000 BCE. David captured Jerusalem and made it the capital city. David's son Solomon followed in his father's footsteps, becoming king in 967 BCE. He extended the kingdom and built the First Temple in Jerusalem. After Solomon died around 900 BCE, the kingdom of Israel split. Solomon's descendants ruled the kingdom of Judah, in the south. The kingdom in the north kept the name of Israel. It stood until about 722 BCE when it was conquered by the Assyrian empire. Many Israelites fled south to Judah to avoid capture by the Assyrians."

Analysis CST.2

Analysis Skills
Construct a Timeline

LEARN

Preview the steps in the student text with students, and then play the video.

VIDEO **21ST CENTURY SKILLS**

Project the Sequence video in the 21st Century Skills Tutorial. Use the Quick Reference and Assessment to provide additional instruction on this skill.

PRACTICE

Have students practice the skill using the secondary source on the student page, providing the instruction and then asking students the questions.

As an alternative, you could form students into pairs or groups to perform the activity. Then invite the groups to identify events, place them in sequence, and create a timeline.

ASSESS

To assess this skill, have students read the section under the heading "How Did the Persian Empire Rise?" in Topic 2, Lesson 3. Ask them to list the dates they find in that section and use them to create a timeline.

DIFFERENTIATED INSTRUCTION

Below Level Remind students that in the period marked BCE, dates get smaller as time passes. They should put the larger dates on the left side of their timeline and smaller dates on the right.

INTEGRATED ENGLISH LANGUAGE DEVELOPMENT

Emerging Support emerging students by breaking the secondary source into manageable sentences containing one event each and writing each sentence on a file card. Hand each student one event. Have each student read his or her sentence. Then have student place the sentence into chronological order on a desk.

ANSWERS

1. a. 1021 BCE
   b. 722 BCE
2. Students' timelines should be from 1100 BCE to 700 BCE.
3. Students' timelines should be divided into 100-year segments.
4. Students' timelines should include the following dates: 1021 BCE: Saul becomes first king of Israel. 1000 BCE: David becomes king of Israel. 967 BCE: Solomon becomes king of Israel. 900 BCE: Solomon dies, and kingdom of Israel splits. 722 BCE: Assyrian empire conquers northern kingdom.

HSS 6.2.1, 6.2.2, 6.2.3, 6.2.4, 6.2.9, 6.3.1, 6.3.2, 6.3.3, 6.3.4, 6.4.5; ELA W.6.3; ELD. P1.A.2, P1.C.10.a

Review and Assessment

VISUAL REVIEW

Direct students' attention to the "Achievements of Mesopotamian Civilization and Empires" flowchart. As a class, review the achievements that are listed for each culture or empire.

Direct students' attention to "Early History of Judaism and the Israelites" table. Ask volunteers to read the entries for each column.

READING REVIEW

WORKSHEET **TEACHER RESOURCES**

Have students who need additional support read the Lesson Summaries available in Teacher Resources on the Realize course.

GAMES **TOPIC MINI-GAMES**

For additional vocabulary practice, students can go online to access the Topic Mini-Games in Realize.

Quest FINDINGS

Discuss! Have students complete their Topic Quests by using the notes in their Active Journals to hold a discussion on the question "Are harsh punishments necessary for a safe society?" Remind students to use their knowledge of ancient law and evidence from sources to make convincing arguments.

TOPIC 2

Review and Assessment

VISUAL REVIEW

Achievements of Mesopotamian Civilizations and Empires

Sumerian City-States (c. 3500 BCE–2350 BCE)	Akkadian Empire (c. 2334–c. 2154 BCE)	Babylonian Empire (c. 1850 BCE–1595 BCE)
• Irrigation • Cities • Cuneiform • Bronze	• World's first empire • Trade and spread of culture	• Rule of law • Hammurabi's Code • Advances in technology

Assyrian Empire (934 BCE–627 BCE)	Neo-Babylonian Empire (626 BCE–539 BCE)	Persian Empire (539 BCE–330 BCE)
• First cavalry • Iron technology • Library	• Nebuchadnezzar • Hanging gardens • Other structures	• Standing army • Roads • Local control • Common currency

Early History of Judaism and the Israelites

Early Israelites	Jewish Beliefs
• Worship of one God	• Ethical monotheism
• God's covenant with Abraham	• Observance of law
• Torah	• Love for others
• Exodus and return to Promised Land	• Observance of Sabbath
• Ten Commandments	• Study and prayer
• Prophets, kings	• Connection to land of Israel

READING REVIEW

Use the Take Notes and Practice Vocabulary activities in your Active Journal to review this topic.

INTERACTIVE

Practice vocabulary using the Topic Mini-Games.

Quest FINDINGS

Have Your Discussion About Preserving Order

Use your notes and your sources to make your arguments. Refer to your Active Journal.

ANSWERS

1. It established a system that spelled out the rules that applied to all members of society. **DOK2**
2. It became the world's first system of writing. **DOK3**
3. Sample answer: Writing systems spread. Stories such as the flood narrative spread. Technology such as irrigation spread. **DOK2**
4. Sample answer. Priests gave their support to kings by saying the gods chose them to rule, and kings did not interfere with the power of priests. **DOK2**
5. The Exodus was the departure of the Israelites from slavery in Egypt. The Diaspora was the dispersal of the Jewish people because of conquests by more powerful empires. **DOK1**
6. The Torah teaches that people should love God and one another and forms the basis for Jewish ethics. **DOK2**

HSS 6.2.1, 6.2.2, 6.2.3, 6.2.4, 6.2.9, 6.3.1, 6.3.2, 6.3.3, 6.3.4, 6.3.5; ELA W.6.3; ELD.P1.A.2, P1.C.10.a

ASSESSMENT

Vocabulary and Key Ideas

1. **Check Understanding** How did Hammurabi's Code establish the **rule of law**?
2. **Draw Conclusions** Why was **cuneiform** important?
3. **Describe** Give three examples of **cultural diffusion** in the Fertile Crescent.
4. **Identify Main Ideas** How were religion and government related in these societies?
5. **Define** What were the **Exodus** and the **Diaspora**?
6. **Identify Main Ideas** What is the connection between the **Torah** and Jewish **ethics**?

Critical Thinking and Writing

7. **Draw Inferences** Why do you think the Phoenicians were better than other civilizations at ocean navigation and trade?
8. **Draw Conclusions** Why did the Phoenician alphabet make writing easier and more efficient than cuneiform?
9. **Analyze Cause and Effect** Why was Sumerians' use of farming technology essential to the development of cities as centers of culture and power?
10. **Draw Inferences** How did the Jews' interactions with other groups affect Judaism?
11. **Revisit the Essential Question** How did the societies of the Fertile Crescent preserve order?
12. **Writing Workshop: Write a Narrative Essay** Using the notes you made in your Active Journal to write a narrative essay in which you are a person living in ancient Mesopotamia describing your daily life.

Analyze Primary Sources

13. What was Hammurabi's main reason for publishing his code of laws?
    A. improve trade
    B. end wicked behavior and protect the weak
    C. expand Babylonian territory
    D. show Babylonia's greatness

"[T]hen [the gods] Anu and Bel called by name me, Hammurabi, the exalted prince, who feared God, to bring about the rule of righteousness in the land, to destroy the wicked and the evil-doers; so that the strong should not harm the weak; . . . to further the well-being of mankind."

—*Introduction to Hammurabi's Code, about 1780 BCE*

Analyze Maps

14. Compare and contrast the size and location of the Babylonian empire and Phoenicia.
15. How do you think the location of rivers in the Fertile Crescent influenced the founding and growth of Sumer?
16. Which is the largest empire shown on the map?
17. Where on this map were the Promised Land and the first kingdom of Israel?

Peoples of the Fertile Crescent

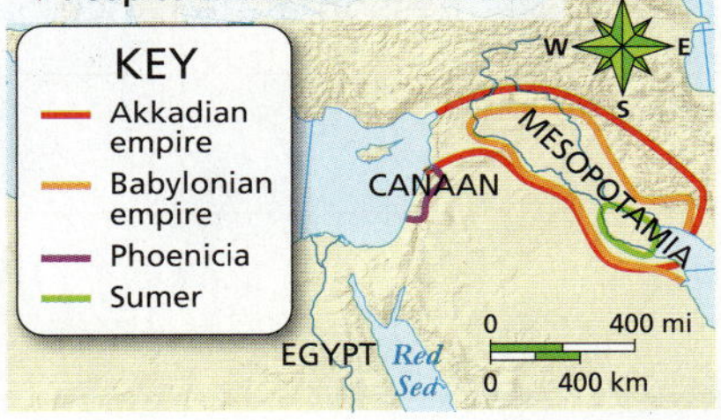

11. Sample answer: The societies of the Fertile Crescent developed laws such as Hammurabi's Code and the Jewish Torah. Leaders of empires divided their empires into smaller units, allowing those smaller units to be governed individually. Some gave local people some more control over their local governments. Others sent troops out across their empires and sent governors, tax collectors, and judges to rule distant cities. **DOK2**
12. Sample answer: For a farmer in ancient Mesopotamia, daily life follows the needs of the farm. We rise with the sun and have a bite to eat before walking to our fields. We spend the day looking over our crops, removing weeds. getting rid of pests, and making sure that the plants are well watered. This work continues until dark, when we return home for a meal and some time with the family before going to sleep. The next day, the work begins again. **DOK4**
13. B **DOK2**
14. The Babylonian empire was much larger than Phoenicia; Babylonia included much of Mesopotamia, while Phoenicia occupied a small area along the Mediterranean coast. **DOK3**
15. Sample answer: The rivers provided water for growing crops; they also provided routes for travel and trade. **DOK2**
16. Akkadian empire **DOK1**
17. Canaan **DOK1**

7. Sample answer: They lived near the sea. Their location helped them to become fearless sailors who developed sailing techniques and traded with other lands for much-needed resources. **DOK2**
8. The Phoenician alphabet had fewer characters, which represented sounds. Therefore, it was easier to learn. **DOK3**
9. By using irrigation, the Sumerians could grow surplus food, which led to a growth in population, the formation of cities and the government needed to run them, specialization, and trade. **DOK2**
10. Sample answer: It led to the Torah becoming a written document so it could be preserved from outside influence. **DOK2**

ASSESSMENT **TOPIC TEST**

For summative assessment, assign the Topic Test in Realize.

TOPIC 3

Ancient Egypt and Kush

Pacing: Approximately 16 periods, 8 blocks	Resources: Student Edition	Resources: Active Journal	Resources: Online	Pacing	California Standards
CONNECT					
NBC LEARN VIDEO Uncovering Mummies' Secrets in the Artifact Lab			✓	10 min.	HSS 6.2.7
ESSENTIAL QUESTION ACTIVITY What makes a great leader?		✓	✓	10 min.	HSS 6.2.3, 6.2.7
INTERACTIVE MAP Ancient Egypt and Kush		✓	✓	10 min.	HSS 6.2.1
Quest KICK OFF: Ask Questions	✓	✓		20 min.	HSS 6.2.3, 6.2.7
INVESTIGATE					
LESSONS 1–3	See Lesson-at-a-Glance pages				
Quest INVESTIGATE: Quest Connections	✓	✓		20 min.	HSS 6.2.3, 6.2.7
SYNTHESIZE					
WRITING WORKSHOP Write an Explanatory Essay		✓	✓	30 min.	HSS 6.2.1
TOPIC MINI-GAMES Ancient Egypt and Kush			✓	10 min.	HSS 6.2.1, 6.2.2, 6.2.3, 6.2.5, 6.2.6, 6.2.7, 6.2.8, 6.2.9
Quest SOURCES: Examine Sources			✓	30 min.	HSS 6.2.3, 6.2.7
DEMONSTRATE					
TOPIC REVIEW AND ASSESSMENT Ancient Egypt and Kush	✓		✓	20 min.	
TOPIC TEST Ancient Egypt and Kush			✓	30 min.	
Quest FINDINGS: Write Your Inscription	✓	✓	✓	30 min.	HSS 6.2.3, 6.2.7

Quest

Each Quest is designed to reinforce the topic content through an inquiry arc that students work on throughout the topic. This topic's Quest, Pharaoh-in-Training, is an opportunity for students to write an inscription for a monument to a great pharaoh and answer the question: What do you need to learn to become a great pharaoh?

Active Journal Resources

- Ask Questions
- Investigate
- Examine Primary Sources
- Write Your Monument Inscription

Quest Resources Online

- Hymn to the Nile
- Discovering King Tut's Tomb
- Edwin Smith Surgical Papyrus
- Judgment of the Dead
- Luxury Products Imported by Egypt
- Rubric for an Explanatory Essay

Additional Resources

Support for Struggling Readers

- Reading Support, Teacher Resources
- Lesson Summaries, Teacher Resources
- English Language Development, Teacher Resources

Suggested Resources

- *Ancient Egypt* by Lisa J. Amstutz
- *Egyptian Myths* by Jacqueline Morley
- *Egypt's Golden Empire* (PBS Documentary, 2005)
- *National Geographic: Into the Great Pyramid* (Documentary, 2003)

Beyond the Classroom

Use Online and Library Media Centers

Use a media center to gain online access to the resources of distant museums, such as the Metropolitan Museum of Art or the British Museum, or educational institutions that specialize in the region, such as the Penn Museum. Virtual tours are available of museums or archaeological sites, such as UCLA's: Digital Karnak or the PBS Nova: Explore Ancient Egypt site. These experiences can help students grasp the scale, antiquity, and engineering achievement of the structures made by people of ancient Egypt and Nubia.

TOPIC 3

Egypt Under the Pharaohs

Objectives

Objective 1: Explain how Egypt's unique geography helped its civilization grow.

Objective 2: Describe how a complex society developed in Egypt.

Objective 3: Analyze how pharaohs changed Egypt.

Objective 4: List ways that religion affected the lives of ancient Egyptians.

	Resources			Pacing	California Standards
CONNECT	Student Edition	Active Journal	Online	approx. 6 periods, 3 blocks	
VIDEO Pharaohs of Ancient Egypt			(video)	5 min.	HSS 6.2.1–3, 6.2.7
START UP ACTIVITY Get Ready to Read	✓	✓	(book)	5 min.	HSS 6.2.3
TAKE NOTES AND PRACTICE VOCABULARY		✓			
INVESTIGATE					
READ Lesson 1: Egypt Under the Pharaohs	✓	✓	(book)	120 min.	HSS 6.2.1–3, 6.2.7; ELA RI.6.2
QUICK ACTIVITY How did Ancient Egyptians View Their Pharaohs?		✓			
INTERACTIVE GALLERY Egyptian Religion			(interactive)	10 min.	HSS 6.2.6
PRIMARY SOURCES The Victory of Ramses II	✓		(book)	40 min.	HSS 6.2.7
ANALYSIS SKILLS Identify Physical and Cultural Features	✓		(book)	30 min.	Analysis CST.3
21ST CENTURY SKILLS TUTORIAL Read Special-Purpose Maps	✓		(video)	10 min.	Analysis CST.3
READING SUPPORT			(document)		
SYNTHESIZE					
WRITING WORKSHOP Develop a Clear Thesis	✓	✓	(book)	10 min.	HSS 6.2.1; ELD.PI.C.10a
LESSON SUMMARY			(document)		
DEMONSTRATE					
LESSON QUIZ			(quiz)	10 min.	HSS 6.2.1–3, 6.2.7

Objectives

Objective 1: Describe the impact of writing on Egypt.

Objective 2: Identify the main features of Egyptian architecture and art.

Objective 3: Analyze the effects of advancements in science, mathematics, and technology on Egyptian society.

Achievements of Egyptian Civilization

	Resources			Pacing	
CONNECT	Student Edition	Active Journal	Online	approx. 3 periods, 1.5 blocks	California Standards
VIDEO The Legacy of Ancient Egypt			▶	5 min.	HSS 6.2.9
START UP ACTIVITY Get Ready to Read	✓	✓	📖	5 min.	HSS 6.2.6
TAKE NOTES AND PRACTICE VOCABULARY		✓			
INVESTIGATE					
READ Lesson 2: Achievements of Egyptian Civilization	✓	✓	📖	40 min.	HSS 6.2.5, 6.2.9; ELA RI.6.1
QUICK ACTIVITY How Did They Do It?		✓			
INTERACTIVE 3D MODEL Egyptian Pyramids			☝	10 min.	HSS 6.2.6
ANALYSIS SKILLS Distinguish Verifiable from Unverifiable Information	✓		📖	30 min.	Analysis REP.3
21ST CENTURY SKILLS TUTORIAL Distinguish Fact and Opinion			▶	10 min.	Analysis REP.3
READING SUPPORT			📄		
SYNTHESIZE					
WRITING WORKSHOP Support Thesis with Details	✓	✓	📖	10 min.	HSS 6.2.1; ELD.PI.C.10a
LESSON SUMMARY			📄		
DEMONSTRATE					
LESSON QUIZ			☑	10 min.	HSS 6.2.5, 6.2.9

Egypt and Kush

Objectives

Objective 1: Explain how trade linked Egypt and neighboring lands.

Objective 2: Analyze how the location of Kush helped its civilization grow.

Objective 3: Summarize Kush's achievements.

	Resources: Student Edition	Resources: Active Journal	Resources: Online	Pacing (approx. 3 periods, 1.5 blocks)	California Standards
CONNECT					
VIDEO Trade Between Egypt and Kush			Video	5 min.	HSS 6.2.6, 6.2.8
START UP ACTIVITY Get Ready to Read	✓	✓	eText	5 min.	HSS 6.2.6
TAKE NOTES AND PRACTICE VOCABULARY		✓			
INVESTIGATE					
READ Lesson 3: Egypt and Kush	✓	✓	eText	40 min.	HSS 6.2.6, 6.2.8, 6.2.9; ELA RI.6.1
INTERACTIVE SIMULATION Ancient Egypt and Kush Trade			Interactive	10 min.	HSS 6.2.6
ANALYSIS SKILLS Frame Questions	✓		eText	30 min.	Analysis REP.1
21ST CENTURY SKILLS TUTORIAL Ask Questions	✓		Video	10 min.	Analysis REP.1
READING SUPPORT			Document		
SYNTHESIZE					
WRITING WORKSHOP Update Your Thesis	✓	✓	eText	10 min.	HSS 6.2.1; ELD.PI.C.10a
LESSON SUMMARY			Document		
DEMONSTRATE					
LESSON QUIZ			Quiz	10 min.	HSS 6.2.6, 6.2.8, 6.2.9

PEARSON realize™

Use the suite of online resources to

Enrich your instruction with topic and lesson videos and interactivities.

VIDEO

Help struggling learners with tools built into the eText, reading support worksheets, lesson summaries, English Language Development exercises and more.

ETEXT

WORKSHEET

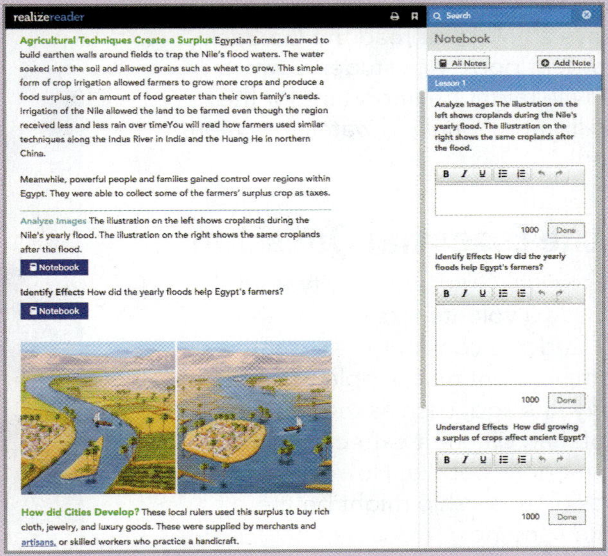

Assess and monitor student progress with automatic answer reporting for lesson prompts, lesson quizzes with remediation, and topic-level assessments.

ETEXT

ASSESSMENT

GAMES

TOPIC 3

Ancient Egypt and Kush

(3000 BCE–600 BCE)

HSS 6.2.1, 6.2.2, 6.2.3, 6.2.5, 6.2.6, 6.2.7, 6.2.8, 6.2.9

CONNECT

Introduction

As in Mesopotamia, Egyptian civilization developed along a river valley. The annual flooding of the Nile River provided water and fertile soil that allowed farmers to produce a food surplus. This surplus supported a complex society made up of slaves, farmers, artisans, merchants, soldiers, and priests, topped by a powerful monarch known as a pharaoh. Through trade and conquest, Egyptian civilization spread its influence through parts of Africa, Asia, and the Mediterranean world.

Activate Prior Knowledge

Ask students what they know about Egypt and Kush. Have a volunteer read the Go Back text in the student book. Ask students why a river like the Nile might be important for the growth of civilization. *(drinking water, irrigation, transportation)*

Explore the Essential Question

Project the Essential Question activity from the course. Have a volunteer read the question. As students consider the Essential Question, remind them that people who lived thousands of years ago, such as the people of ancient Egypt, had different expectations of leaders than modern people. However, some characteristics of leadership might be the same both then and now.

ACTIVE JOURNAL

Essential Question Have students begin to explore the Essential Question in their Active Journals.

Classify Make a list of the leadership qualities that students have identified as the most important. Rank them according to how many students identified a particular quality as the most important. If there is a tie, conduct a poll.

TOPIC 3

Ancient Egypt and Kush (3000 BCE–600 BCE)

GO ONLINE to access your digital course

VIDEO
AUDIO
ETEXT
INTERACTIVE
WRITING
GAMES
WORKSHEET
ASSESSMENT

Go back over 5,000 years

to ANCIENT EGYPT AND KUSH. Why? To check out the pyramids and mummies, of course! You will also see how Egypt and its neighbor Kush show us how geography—in this case the Nile River—can be essential to the growth of a civilization.

Explore The Essential Question

What makes a great leader?

Egypt and Kush were ruled by kings known as pharaohs. How did the pharaohs help build Egypt into one of the world's greatest ancient civilizations?

Unlock the Essential Question in your Active Journal.

100

ANALYZE VISUALS

Ask students to identify the structures shown in the photo. Point out the Sphinx to students. Explain that the Sphinx represents the Egyptian sun god Ra but that it had the face of a pharaoh Khafre, who had it built along with his pyramids. Ask: Why did Egypt's rulers, the pharaohs, build the pyramids? *(as tombs)* Explain that Khafre's pyramid was built more than 4,500 years ago. Ask: How could these structures remain standing after so many years? *(They were made of stone. They are in a very dry climate.)* Explain that building the pyramids involved tens of thousands of workers over many years. The sides have consistent, straight angles. The massive stones had to be moved a great distance and were carefully placed to create the structures. The construction of the pyramids demonstrates the Egyptians' mastery of engineering.

HSS 6.2.1, 6.2.2, 6.2.3, 6.2.5, 6.2.6, 6.2.7, 6.2.8, 6.2.9; Analysis CST.3, REP.1, REP.3

Read

about the complex culture that created the pyramids, the Sphinx, and thousands of mummies.

Watch

NBC LEARN

BOUNCE TO ACTIVATE VIDEO

Uncovering Mummies' Secrets in the Artifact Lab

Unravel the mysteries of some of Egypt's most powerful pharaohs.

The Great Sphinx at Giza, Egypt

101

RECOGNIZE CULTURAL AND EXPERIENTIAL BACKGROUNDS

Make use of your knowledge of students' lives to make connections between their own experiences, backgrounds, and interests and the content of the topic. If you have students whose ethnic heritage is related to the content of the topic, make an effort to emphasize the contributions and achievements of this society and how it has enriched the world.

If appropriate, allow students the opportunity to share cultural, ethnic, or linguistic traditions and knowledge from their experiences.

If students have family experiences (such as travel to or family members who have lived in the region being studied), allow them to share relevant stories.

Watch

VIDEO NBC LEARN VIDEO

Project the Topic Opener video showing laboratory work on a mummy. After viewing the video, ask students to respond to the following questions:

Check Understanding Why did the Egyptians make mummies? *(so people would be remembered and as a result continue to live in the afterlife)*

Hypothesize What challenges do you think scientists have in trying to preserve objects from ancient cultures such as Egypt? *(Possible answers: Objects are very frail and could disintegrate with too much handling; remains might be so deteriorated that no one would know how they really looked.)*

Read

Share these lesson previews with students.

Lesson 1: Born of the Nile River, Egypt developed a complex society ruled by god-pharaohs, a system that endured through many dynasties.

Primary Sources: Egyptian pharaoh Ramses II fights a famous battle.

Lesson 2: Over 3,000 years, Egyptian culture produced lasting monuments, devised a complex system of writing, and made discoveries in math and science.

Lesson 3: Egypt and Kush were rivals and neighbors who shared the Nile River. The river became a highway along which the two peoples shared cultures.

TOPIC 3

HSS 6.2.1, 6.2.2, 6.2.3, 6.2.5, 6.2.6, 6.2.7, 6.2.8, 6.2.9

What Happened and When?

Have students examine the timeline. Ask: How many years are shown on the timeline? *(4,000)* Ask: How much time separates the first and last events from Egypt's history shown on the timeline? *(2,757)* Ask: How much time elapsed between the first event in Egypt and the first event in Sumer? *(about 100 years)* Ask: How much time elapsed between the first event in Egypt and the first event in China? *(about 1,000 years)*

ACTIVE JOURNAL

Timeline Skills Students can also use the Timeline Skills activity in their Active Journals to record information about the history of events in ancient Egypt as they read the topic. During their reading, they should add the dates of at least three events they think are important. After completing the topic, have students write a brief description of the significance of each event they added.

INTERACTIVE — INTERACTIVE TIMELINE

Display the Interactive Topic Timeline for the class. Have volunteers read entries to learn more about ancient Egypt.

Discuss Ask students: What can you conclude about ancient Egyptian society from the great length of its history? *(Sample answers: Egyptian society was very stable; Egypt had few threats from external enemies.)*

TOPIC 3

Ancient Egypt and Kush

(3000 BCE–600 BCE)

Learn more about ancient Egypt and Kush by making your own map and timeline in your Active Journal.

INTERACTIVE
Topic Map

Where were ancient Egypt and Kush?

These ancient kingdoms were located in the northeast corner of Africa, to the west of ancient Mesopotamia. Locate the Nile and its delta on the map in the circle.

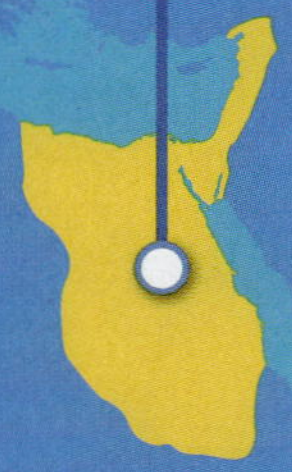

INTERACTIVE
Topic Timeline

What happened and when?

Huge stone pyramids built without modern machines . . . riches beyond imagining . . . . Explore the timeline to see some of what was happening in Egypt and Kush and in the rest of the world.

TOPIC EVENTS

About 3100 BCE Egypt's first pharaoh unites Upper and Lower Egypt.

About 2450 BCE The Great Pyramid of Giza is built.

4000 BCE — **3000 BCE**

WORLD EVENTS

About 3000 BCE The Sumerians invent a written language.

2100 BCE Xia Dynasty rises in China.

DIFFERENTIATED INSTRUCTION

Special Education Give students an event from the Topic portion of the timeline written on an index card with the date included. Then have them form a living timeline with the events in order.

Below Level Project the Sequence video in the 21st Century Skills Tutorial. Use the Quick Reference and Assessment to provide additional instruction on this skill.

Advanced Challenge students to conduct research to find three additional events from 4,000 BCE to 1 BCE. For example, they could find out about events that occurred in North and South America during this period.

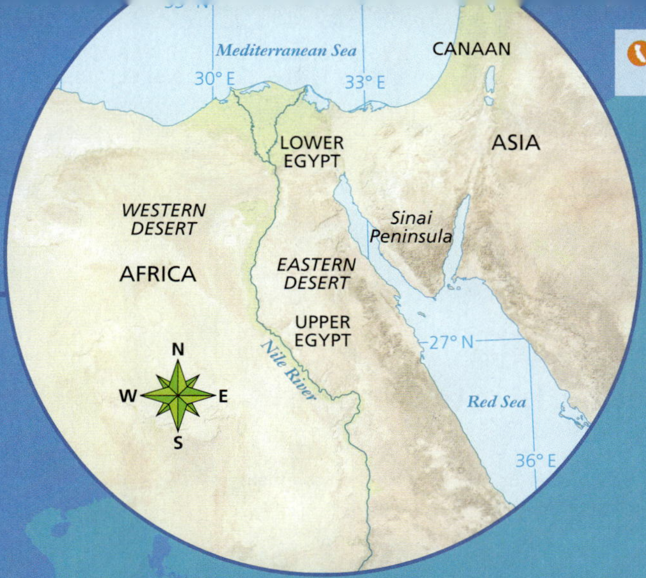

HSS 6.2.1, 6.2.2, 6.2.3, 6.2.5, 6.2.6, 6.2.7, 6.2.8, 6.2.9

Who will you meet?

Hatshepsut, the woman who was pharaoh

Tutankhamen, whose magnificent tomb glittered with gold

Ramses II, the conqueror

1473 BCE Hatshepsut becomes pharaoh.

About 1333 BCE Tutankhamen becomes pharaoh.

1279 BCE Ramses II becomes pharaoh.

730 BCE A Nubian pharaoh conquers Egypt.

343 BCE Persian invaders defeat the last Egyptian pharaoh.

2000 BCE | 1000 BCE | 1 BCE

About 1700 BCE Hammurabi writes early set of laws.

750 BCE City-states begin to rise in Greece.

103

COMMON MISCONCEPTIONS

BCE and CE, B.C. and A.D. Years and Centuries The timeline on these pages shows dates BCE, or "before the common era," and CE meaning "common era." In many books, the date B.C., meaning "before Christ," is used instead of BCE. When B.C. is used, then A.D., Latin for "anno Domini" meaning "in the year of Our Lord" is used instead of CE.

The B.C. and A.D. dates were first used in Europe in the year A.D. 525. This system is based on the assumption that Jesus Christ was born in the year A.D. 1. No matter which time tags are used, neither system has a year 0. So, dates move from 1 BCE to 1 CE, or from 1 B.C. to A.D. 1.

The first century B.C. or BCE refers to the years 100 B.C. to 1 B.C. or 100 BCE to 1 BCE. The first centuries A.D. or CE refer to the years A.D. 1 to A.D. 100 or 1 CE to 100 CE. Under both systems, each century begins in the year that end with the digits "01."

Where Were Ancient Egypt and Kush?

Direct students' attention to the outline map of Africa in the student text. Then have them look at the inset map. Ask: Where is Egypt located? *(in the northeast corner of Africa)* Ask: How would you describe Egypt's land? *(There are two huge deserts separated by a long thin strip of fertile land along the length of the Nile River and its delta.)*

ACTIVE JOURNAL

Map Skills Have students use the Map Skills activity in their Active Journals. They will fill in an outline map of Egypt and Kush with the labels of key geographic and political features.

Analyze Maps Ask: How do you think the geography would have affected where people settled in Egypt? *(They probably settled along the Nile River because they could grow crops there.)* Ask: What effects would the deserts have had on the political development of Egypt? *(The deserts probably served as barriers to invasions.)*

INTERACTIVE — INTERACTIVE MAP

Display the Interactive Topic Map. Work through the layers of maps, having volunteers read each caption.

Discuss Ask students: Egypt is at a crossroads that links Asia, Africa, and Europe. What effect might a mighty empire like ancient Egypt have had on the surrounding areas. (Sample response: Egypt probably influenced people in surrounding areas. They may have even conquered some of them.)

Who Will You Meet?

Many students access historical materials best through the stories of the people who lived during this time. Preview the key people that students will encounter in the topic. Read the short description of each, and then conduct a poll asking students which figure they are most interested in. Record the results on the board. Then ask volunteers why they are interested in a particular figure. *(Accept reasonable responses. Students may mention an interest in Hatshepsut's accomplishments; that they have heard of Tutankhamen; or that Ramses II's conquests may make him a particularly important ruler.)*

TOPIC 3

HSS 6.2.3, 6.2.7; ELA W.6-5; RI.6.1, RI.6.3-4, RI.6.6; ELD.PI.C.9

Quest
Document-Based Writing Inquiry

Become a Pharaoh-in-Training

Quest Kick Off

In this Quest, students will use the student text, other sources, and their Active Journals to write an inscription for a monument to their rule as pharaoh.

1 Ask Questions

Launch the Quest by discussing the Guiding Questions as a class. Have students generate the questions they will need to have answered to accomplish the Quest in their Active Journals. **Suggestion:** If students need help with the Ask Questions step, refer them to the Analysis Skills feature following Lesson 3, Frame Questions.

2 Investigate

As they read the lessons, remind students to look for and respond to the three Quest Connections in the student text that provide clues to their Quest. They should also identify and record two connections of their own. **Suggestion:** If students are struggling to identify their own connections, suggest they think about the impact of particular pharaohs on art, religion, the economy, and Egypt's place in the world.

3 Examine Primary Sources

As students complete the topic, distribute the Quest Primary Sources for this topic.

Analyze Documents Have students process the primary sources in their Active Journals, focusing on identifying information related to the Guiding Question in preparation for writing their inscriptions.

4 Write Your Monument Inscription

When students complete the topic, have them return to the Quest, which can be used as a performance-based authentic assessment. To complete the Quest, they should follow the steps of (1) prewriting, (2) drafting their inscriptions, (3) sharing with a partner, (4) revising the draft based on feedback, and (5) presenting the final product. **DOK4**

Quest
Document-Based Writing Inquiry

HSS 6.2.3, 6.2.7; ELA W.6.5, RI.6.1, RI.6.3–4, RI.6.6; ELD.PI.C.9

One of Hatshepsut's obelisks

Become a Pharaoh-in-Training

Quest KICK OFF

The year is **1000 BCE**. Your uncle has died suddenly and you have been crowned Pharaoh of Ancient Egypt!

What do you need to learn to become a great pharaoh?

How did the pharaohs rule ancient Egypt? Explore the Essential Question "What makes a great leader?" in this Quest.

1 Ask Questions

Being a pharaoh is a big job. Get started now by making a list of questions about how best to rule. Write the questions in your Active Journal.

2 Investigate

As you read the lessons in this topic, look for Quest CONNECTIONS that provide information on how Egypt's pharaohs built a highly accomplished civilization. Capture notes in your Active Journal.

3 Examine Primary Sources

Next explore a set of primary and secondary sources from Ancient Egypt. They'll help you learn even more about how to be a great pharaoh. Capture notes in your Active Journal.

Quest FINDINGS

4 Write Your Monument Inscription

The pharaohs of ancient Egypt captured records of their great deeds on monuments throughout Egypt. At the end of the topic you'll write a message to appear on a monument built in your honor. The message will celebrate all of your great deeds as pharaoh. Get help for writing your message in your Active Journal.

DIFFERENTIATED INSTRUCTION

Below Level If time allows, have students present their inscriptions orally to the rest of the class. Discuss the achievements that students think would make pharaohs the most proud.
Advanced Have students choose a pharaonic name and learn how to write it in hieroglyphics.

INTEGRATED ENGLISH LANGUAGE DEVELOPMENT

Emerging Instead of writing a monument message, encourage English learners to draw pictures to symbolize their great deeds as pharaohs.

HSS 6.2.1, 6.2.2, 6.2.3, 6.2.7; ELA RI.6.2

Egypt Under the Pharaohs

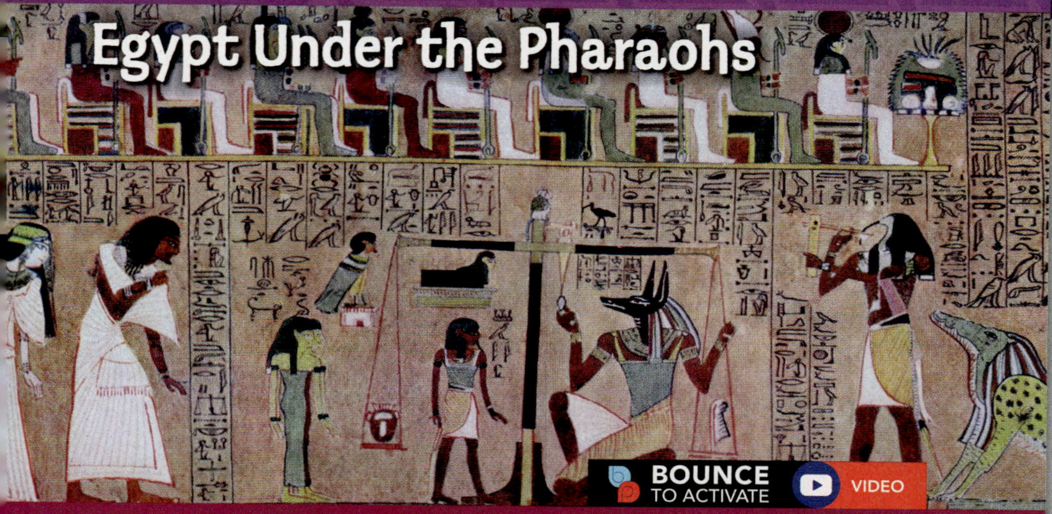

GET READY TO READ

START UP

Examine the Egyptian tomb painting. Notice the symbols, objects, and the clothing and interactions of the people and gods. Write three questions you have about ancient Egypt based on the painting.

GUIDING QUESTIONS

- How did Egypt's unique geography help its civilization grow?
- How did a complex society develop in Egypt?
- How did pharaohs change Egypt?
- How did religion affect the lives of ancient Egyptians?

TAKE NOTES

Literacy Skill: Main Ideas and Details Use the graphic organizer in your Active Journal to take notes as you read the lesson.

PRACTICE VOCABULARY

Use the vocabulary activity in your Active Journal to practice the vocabulary words.

Vocabulary		Academic Vocabulary
cataract	dynasty	environmental
delta	bureaucracy	devotion
artisan	mummy	
pharaoh		

Like the Fertile Crescent of Mesopotamia, Egypt was home to one of the world's first great civilizations. As in the Fertile Crescent, Egypt's civilization developed in a river valley with rich soil. However, Egypt's geography and culture differed in many ways from those of the Fertile Crescent.

The Nile River Valley

The ancient Egyptians treasured the Nile River. They knew that without the Nile, their land would be nothing but a sun-baked desert of bright blue skies and dry sand.

The World's Longest River The Nile is the world's longest river. It begins in East Africa and flows about 3,500 miles north to the Mediterranean Sea.

This great river has two main sources—the White Nile and the Blue Nile. The White Nile flows from Lake Victoria. The Blue Nile rushes down from the highlands of present-day Ethiopia. The two rivers meet in present-day Sudan. In ancient times, northern Sudan was known as Nubia, or Kush.

PRACTICE VOCABULARY

To help students integrate new vocabulary, group the terms into pairs. Explain that both *cataracts* and *deltas* are connected to rivers. Say that an *artisan* is a craftperson and *bureaucracy* is a system of government workers. Explain that a *pharaoh* is a king and a *mummy* is the preserved body of a dead person. Reinforce the terms during the lesson using the teaching notes.

Point out the academic vocabulary in the margin. Provide sample sentences that clarify meaning.

environmental: Environmental regulations protect communities by limiting pollution.

devotion: She performed rituals to show devotion to her religion.

HSS 6.2.1, 6.2.2, 6.2.3, 6.2.7; ELA RI.6.2; ELD.PI.C.10.a

Egypt Under the Pharaohs

CONNECT

GET READY TO READ

ETEXT START UP

Project the Start Up Activity. As they enter the classroom and get settled, ask students to examine the tomb painting, which comes from the tomb of pharaoh Horemheb and features some of Egypt's gods and goddesses, including Hathor (on the left with circular headdress).

Formulate Questions Have students record three questions that they have about ancient Egypt based on the tomb painting. *(Sample answers: Why did ancient Egyptians decorate tombs? What symbols are in the painting? Who ruled ancient Egypt?)* Then have them share their questions with another student, either in class or through a chat or blog.

Discuss Remind students that religion and beliefs concerning an afterlife can form a fundamental part of a people's culture.

After completing the Start Up activity, project the Lesson Opener or direct students to their textbooks. Preview the lesson by working through the Get Ready to Read items with the class. Remind students to pay close attention to the Guiding Questions as they read the lesson.

ACTIVE JOURNAL

Take Notes Have students use the lesson literacy skill graphic organizer in their Active Journals to take notes as they read the lesson.

Practice Vocabulary Have students complete the activity in their Active Journals to build their vocabulary.

VIDEO VIDEO

Assign the lesson video as homework.

WORKSHEET **TEACHER RESOURCES**

Have students who need additional support use the following worksheets from the Teacher Resources on the course:

- **Reading Support**
- **English Language Development**
- **Lesson Summary**

INVESTIGATE

The Nile River Valley

Discuss the importance of geography in the development of the river valley civilization in Egypt.

Identify Details Direct students' attention to the labels showing the regions of ancient Egypt on the map. Ask: What is the region upstream from the Mediterranean? *(Upper Egypt)* Why is this region called "upper" Egypt? *(because it is upriver, toward the river's source rather than its mouth)*

Synthesize How did the Nile influence life in ancient Egypt? *(It allowed people to have rich farmland and forced them to work together to control the waters.)*

Contrast Explain that **cataracts** and **deltas** are not found in all rivers but are present in the Nile. Ask: How do **cataracts** differ from waterfalls? *(Cataracts are rocky areas where water flows rapidly; waterfalls are one location where water falls from higher to lower ground.)* How is a delta different from the mouth of a river? *(A delta is an area of land formed at the mouth of a river; it is not the mouth itself.)*

ANSWERS

Interaction *Most Egyptians probably lived along the Nile River or in the Nile Delta because that is where they could grow crops.*

Infer *The Nile River probably made trade between different parts of Egypt easier, and its mouth on the Mediterranean Sea helped connect the interior of Egypt with distant lands.*

Summarize *The Nile begins in East Africa and flows north through Egypt to the Mediterranean Sea. It was important to ancient Egypt because it provided water in the desert and made farming possible.*

The Nile River Valley

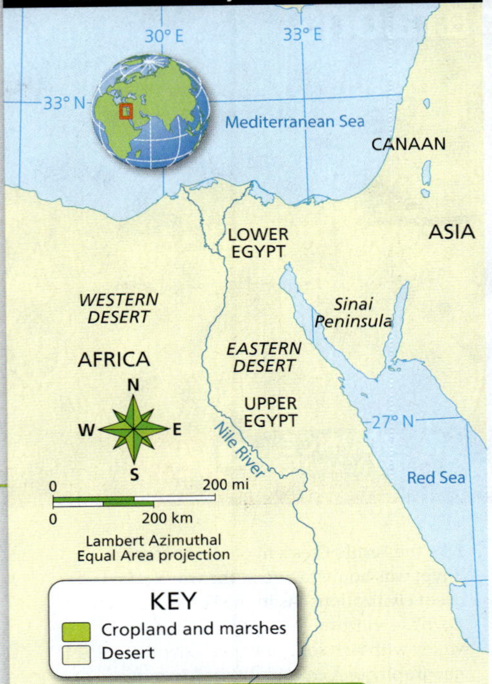

GEOGRAPHY SKILLS

Egyptian civilization developed in the Nile River valley in northeastern Africa.

1. **Interaction** Where do you think most Egyptians lived, and why?
2. **Infer** How might the Nile have affected trade in ancient Egypt?

In Kush and Egypt, the Nile flows through the Sahara, a vast desert that stretches across most of northern Africa. Before reaching Egypt, the river in ancient times roared through six **cataracts**, or groups of rocky rapids. The rocky cataracts made it impossible for people to travel by ship upstream from Egypt.

Upper and Lower Egypt Below the cataracts, the Nile flows through a narrow valley lined with cliffs. This region is known as Upper Egypt because it is upstream from the Mediterranean Sea.

The river carries silt—fine mineral particles that can form fertile soil—from its sources in East Africa. Near the end of its journey, the Nile slows down and fans out into many streams and marshy areas. As it slows, the river drops its silt. Over thousands of years, this silt has built up to form a large river delta. A **delta** is an area of sediment—soil or minerals carried by water—deposited at the mouth of a river. The Nile delta forms the region known as Lower Egypt.

Floods and the Black Land A narrow strip of fertile soil lines both banks of the Nile and covers its delta. This rich, dark soil was so important to the Egyptians that they called their country *Kemet*, which means "the Black Land."

The yearly flooding of the Nile created the Black Land. Each summer, heavy rainfall in East Africa poured into the Nile's sources. Flood waters surged through Egypt. When the flood waters drained away, they left behind a layer of fresh soil.

However, the Nile floods were unpredictable. If too much water came, the floods could be a natural disaster that swept away soil. If too little water came, Egypt could suffer a drought, or a shortage of water. Droughts could bring hunger by causing crops to fail.

On either side of the Black Land lay vast deserts. Egyptians called these deserts "the Red Land." Unlike the Black Land, the Red Land was a deadly place of hot, burning sands.

READING CHECK **Summarize** Describe the Nile and its importance to ancient Egypt.

HISTORY BACKGROUND

The Nile Today In 1970, Egypt constructed the Aswan High Dam about 400 miles south of Cairo. It blocked the Nile and created Lake Nasser, named for a former president of Egypt, Gamal Abdel Nasser. The dam produces about 15 percent of modern Egypt's electricity. The dam has stopped the yearly floods of the Nile. Instead, water is released all year long, making it possible to farm even during dry times. The dam has had several negative effects, however. Silt is trapped behind the dam and is no longer carried downriver, meaning the soil is not replenished. As a result, farmers must use expensive artificial fertilizers to keep the soil good for growing.

How Did Egyptian Civilization Develop?

More than 7,000 years ago, people began growing grains in the fertile soil left behind by the Nile floods. Over time, Egypt's farmers were able to grow more and more food. This food supported a growing population.

Agricultural Techniques Create a Surplus Egyptian farmers learned to build earthen walls around fields to trap the Nile's flood waters. The water soaked into the soil and allowed grains such as wheat to grow. This simple form of crop irrigation allowed farmers to grow more crops and produce a food surplus, or an amount of food greater than their own family's needs. Irrigation of the Nile allowed the land to be farmed even though the region received less and less rain over time. Later, you will read how farmers used similar techniques along the Indus River in India and the Huang He in northern China.

Meanwhile, powerful people and families gained control over regions within Egypt. They were able to collect some of the farmers' surplus crop as taxes.

How Did Cities Develop? These local rulers used this surplus to buy rich cloth, jewelry, and luxury goods. These were supplied by merchants and **artisans**, or skilled workers who practice a handicraft.

Farmers' production of a surplus supported these artisans. Some became full-time artisans, such as weavers or potters. Artisans and merchants began to settle around the homes of local rulers. In time, these settlements grew into cities.

Egypt's cities brought together wealthy and skilled people. They became centers of culture and power. Skilled architects built impressive buildings. Artists created great works of art to decorate them. Egyptian cities grew to be large and powerful, like those in Sumer.

READING CHECK **Understand Effects** How did growing a surplus of crops affect ancient Egypt?

Did you know?

Without the Nile, Egyptian cities would never have developed. Beyond the Nile valley lay a deadly landscape of hot burning sand that the Egyptians called "the Red Land."

Analyze Images The illustration on the left shows croplands during the Nile's yearly flood. The illustration on the right shows the same croplands after the flood. **Identify Effects** How did the yearly floods help Egypt's farmers?

How Did Egyptian Civilization Develop?

Discuss the importance of the Nile for farming and trading and the development of a strong Egyptian civilization.

Summarize How did technology aid Egypt's food production? *(Simple earth walls were developed to hold the Nile's waters and keep soil moist. This allowed farming to be productive.)*

Synthesize How did increased food production allow some people to become merchants or **artisans**? *(Because not everyone had to produce food, some people could engage in other activities such as handicrafts.)*

COMMON MISCONCEPTIONS

Geography The Nile may be the world's longest river, but it is far from the world's largest river in terms of its annual discharge, or flow. The Amazon River of South America carries almost 100 times as much water as the Nile River. Even the Columbia River in the northwestern United States carries more than five times as much water as the Nile, although the Columbia is only about one third as long as the Nile.

The explanation for the Nile's relatively low flow is that, unlike rivers in rainy regions, the Nile travels for much of its length through deserts. This makes the relatively low flow of the Nile all the more precious, because it brings water to otherwise dry lands.

ANSWERS

Identify Effects *The Nile's yearly floods helped farmers by leaving rich soil on its banks that they could use to grow crops.*

Understand Effects *Food surpluses enabled some people to perform work other than farming because they didn't have to concentrate exclusively on producing food.*

The Kingdoms of Egypt

Discuss the history of Egypt's **dynasties** and its governmental structure headed by a pharaoh atop a centralized bureaucracy.

Sequence In what order did Egypt's kingdom's arise? *(The Old Kingdom came first, then the Middle Kingdom, and finally the New Kingdom.)*

Summarize How did Middle Kingdom **pharaohs** control the Nile's floods? *(They built canals that drained flood waters and irrigated new farmland.)*

Describe Old Kingdom **pharaohs** set up **bureaucracies** to help administer a strong, organized central government. Describe the government **bureaucracy** of ancient Egypt. *(It was a monarchy with the pharaoh at the top, a chief administrator called a vizier who led various departments, and scribes who were below the vizier and carried out the vizier's directives.)*

▲ The pharaoh Tutankhamen ruled for nine short years during the New Kingdom era.

The Kingdoms of Egypt

During the 3000s BCE, two kingdoms developed in Egypt. The kings of Upper Egypt wore white crowns. The kings of Lower Egypt wore red crowns.

Uniting Egypt You might remember that the city-states of Sumer never united under one kingdom. However, Egypt's two kingdoms did unite. Legends say that Narmer brought them together in about 3000 BCE. This made him the first **pharaoh**, or king, of a united Egypt. He wore a double crown of red and white and founded Egypt's earliest dynasty. A **dynasty** is a ruling family.

Normally, control passed between members of a dynasty. Sometimes, however, a new dynasty gained power. Historians divide Egypt's history into periods based on kingdoms and dynasties.

The Old and Middle Kingdoms Historians call the period from about 2686 to 2125 BCE the Old Kingdom. Like later kingdoms, the Old Kingdom was a period of prosperity, political strength, and cultural achievement. After a period of civil wars, the Middle Kingdom began. It lasted from about 2055 to 1650 BCE. Pharaohs of the Middle Kingdom dealt with one of Egypt's major **environmental** challenges—the Nile floods. As the Sumerians had done in Mesopotamia, the pharaohs built a system of canals that could drain dangerous flood waters and irrigate new farmland.

Academic Vocabulary
environmental • *adj.*, having to do with natural surroundings

High Point and Decline The New Kingdom followed more civil wars and invasions. The New Kingdom lasted from about 1550 to 1070 BCE. New Kingdom pharaohs conquered lands in Asia and Africa. This was the high point of ancient Egyptian power and prosperity.

However, the New Kingdom eventually declined and broke apart. Egypt faced foreign invasions. One late dynasty gained power only with the help of the Assyrians. Still later, Egypt was conquered by the Persian empire. In 332 BCE, the Greek army of Alexander the Great conquered Egypt.

The Political Order in Egypt The pharaoh relied on a **bureaucracy**, or a system of offices and officials that handle the business of government. The head of Egypt's bureaucracy was an official called the vizier. The bureaucracy collected taxes from farmers. Farmers paid these taxes mainly in the form of surplus crops.

The bureaucracy took some of this surplus for itself. It distributed the rest to priests, to the pharaoh, and to artisans and merchants who worked for the pharaoh. Egypt's bureaucracy and system of taxation were a model for later governments, including those of today.

READING CHECK **Categorize** Name one accomplishment of pharaohs of the Middle and New Kingdoms.

ANSWERS

Categorize *Sample answer: Pharaohs of the Middle Kingdom built canals to control Nile floods; pharaohs of the New Kingdom conquered lands in Asia and Africa, adding to Egypt's size and wealth.*

INTEGRATED ENGLISH LANGUAGE DEVELOPMENT

Collaborative Use How was Egyptian Society Organized? to help students grasp the structure of Egyptian society, by exchanging ideas.

Emerging Read the text aloud, pausing from time to time to ask students yes/no questions or questions beginning with *wh-* words, such as *Who was at the top of Egyptian society? Or What groups made up the lowest and largest level of Egyptian society?*

Expanding Form students into groups. Have them discuss the organization of Egyptian society by taking turns asking each other relevant questions and responding with accurate information that paraphrases key ideas.

Bridging Form students into groups. Have group members discuss the organization of Egyptian society by taking turns asking each other relevant questions and responding with accurate

108 Lesson 3.1 • Egypt Under the Pharaohs

How was Egyptian Society Organized?

To control Egypt, pharaohs needed the loyalty and labor of the people. Egypt's social order provided both.

Egyptian society was shaped like a pyramid. The pharaoh was at the top of that pyramid. Egyptians believed that gods controlled everything. The pharaoh controlled Egypt, so people saw him as a god-king who deserved loyalty.

Just below the pharaoh were nobles, priests, and officials. They helped the pharaoh govern Egypt. Scribes kept records for Egypt's bureaucracy.

Merchants and artisans made up a middle level. Painters, stonecutters, and builders spent their lives working on temples and tombs.

Farmers were lower on the social pyramid. By far, most of the people of ancient Egypt were farmers. During the growing season, farmers raised Egypt's food. For the rest of the year, many were required to work as laborers on the pharaoh's building projects. Most did so willingly out of religious **devotion**. They believed that if they helped the god-king, they would be rewarded after death.

Slaves were at the bottom of the social pyramid. Many were prisoners of war or debtors who were freed from slavery after serving for a period of time. Slaves were the property of their owners and had to do forced labor.

Academic Vocabulary
devotion • *n.*, dedication, loyalty

Quest CONNECTIONS
Look at the diagram. How did each of these groups contribute to Egypt's greatness? As a pharaoh, how can you earn their loyalty? Record your findings in your Active Journal.

READING CHECK **Identify Main Ideas** Describe how Egyptian society functioned.

Analyze Diagrams To control Egypt, pharaohs needed the loyalty and labor of the people. Egypt's social order provided both. **Draw Conclusions** What does the widening nature of the pyramid suggest about the number of people who belonged to each level of society?

How Was Egyptian Society Organized?

Discuss the importance of an organized social hierarchy in early civilizations. Point out that in ancient Egypt, as in all early civilizations, farming was the basis of the economy. Therefore, peasant farmers made up the largest part of the population.

Analyze Diagrams Direct students to the diagram. Ask: Which levels in the social pyramid were responsible for governing Egypt? *(The top three, which included: pharaoh; nobles, priests, officials; scribes)*

Synthesize What does the much greater relative size of the lowest class tell you about the need for laborers in Egyptian society? *(Many workers were needed for such activities as building pyramids and other monuments and working in the fields.)*

Compare and Contrast How was life for farmers in ancient Egypt alike and different from life for slaves? *(Both occupied the lowest level of the social pyramid, and both were required to give their labor for free to others. Farmers' labor obligation, however, was temporary and often a sign of their religious devotion.)*

ACTIVE JOURNAL
Quest Connection As students read the text and analyze the chart, direct them to the Quest Connections pages in their Active Journals. Make sure that students understand how this diagram helps them with their Quest.

ELD.PI.A.1

information that paraphrases key ideas. Encourage group members to give feedback to each other and to build responses that other members provide.

WORKSHEET **TEACHER RESOURCES**
For additional IELD support addressing the standard, have students complete the Lesson ELD activity from the Teacher Resources found on the course.

ANSWERS

Identify Main Ideas *Egyptian society functioned by encouraging all social levels to work to support the pharaoh, who was seen as a god, maintaining the religion.*

Draw Conclusions *Sample answer: The people below the pharaoh did the work needed to support Egyptian society by growing food, making products, trading goods, writing texts, defending the land, and maintaining the religion. There were more people of lower status than of higher status.*

Egyptian Religion

Discuss the religious beliefs of the ancient Egyptians and the role religion played in their lives.

Draw Conclusions Why was preservation of the body consistent with a belief in the afterlife? *(Ancient Egyptians believed that the spirit would need to inhabit the body in the afterlife.)*

Make Connections How were the religious beliefs of the ancient Sumerians similar to those of the ancient Egyptians? *(Both peoples were polytheists, believers in many gods.)*

Draw Conclusions Why do you think Amon-Re and Osiris were important gods for Egyptians? *(Both gods represented overcoming death.)*

Identify Details What was the purpose of making a **mummy** of a person's body after death? *(Bodies needed to be preserved in order for the spirit to inhabit them after death.)*

INTERACTIVE **INTERACTIVE GALLERY**

Egyptian Religion Gallery

Display the Interactive Gallery: Egyptian Religion for the class. Ask students to think about how the Egyptians used these religious artifacts and how their religious practices are similar to and different from various religious practices that are common today.

ACTIVE CLASSROOM

Use the See-Think-Wonder strategy. After looking through the images in the Egyptian Religion Gallery, have students work in pairs. Then ask them: What do you see? What does that make you think? What are you wondering about?

▲ After death, a person's body was cleaned, bathed with chemicals, and wrapped in linen bandages to preserve it, making a mummy.

Egyptian Religion

Religion played an important role in the life of the people of Egypt. They believed that their gods controlled everything from the flooding of the Nile River to the death of a child. Their gods could be kind or dangerous. To please the gods, Egyptians built them temples and offered prayers and gifts.

Many Gods Like the Sumerians, ancient Egyptians were polytheists. They worshiped hundreds of gods. Many were associated with animals. Statues or other works of art often show a god with the head or body of a lion, a crocodile, or some other creature. Egyptians believed that gods shared the qualities of these animals, such as their strength, speed, or bad temper.

One of the most important gods was Amon-Re, the sun god. Egyptians believed that Amon-Re made a daily journey across the sky. Each night, he died in the west as the land grew dark. Each morning, he was reborn in the east as the sun rose.

Osiris was the god of the underworld, or the world of the dead. According to Egyptian legend, Osiris was killed and chopped into pieces by a rival god named Seth. Isis, the wife of Osiris, was the mother goddess of Egypt. She moved heaven and earth to help her husband. Isis found the pieces of Osiris's body and brought her husband back to life.

Isis represented love, caring, and protection. Egyptians looked to Isis for protection in both life and death.

Horus was the son of Isis and Osiris. Egyptian legends tell of great battles between Horus and Seth. When Horus defeated Seth, he united the two lands of Egypt. As a result, every pharaoh was thought to be Horus in human form.

Religion and Society The belief that the pharaoh was a god on Earth contributed to the power of the pharaoh. People obeyed the pharaoh and his officials for fear of angering a god. Priests were also powerful, because Egyptians thought priests could help a person gain favor with the gods. The priests of the Temple of Amon-Re in the city of Thebes were especially powerful.

Preparing for the Afterlife Egyptians believed that they, like Osiris, could overcome death. Life on Earth could lead to an afterlife, or life after death. However, this required preparation.

The first way to prepare for the afterlife was to live a good life. Egyptians believed that Osiris decided who would have an afterlife. Those who had lived good lives would be allowed to live forever, but the sinful would be destroyed.

DIFFERENTIATED INSTRUCTION

Special Education Connect the reading to students' experiences by asking them to compare the role of pharaoh to the role of the American President. Emphasize the differences between the two roles.

Below Level Have students review the main ideas from Egyptian Religion and Two Great Rulers in conversation pairings.

Advanced Have students read the Story of Osiris paragraph again, then research and write a description of another Egyptian myth.

Preserving the Dead The second way that Egyptians prepared for the afterlife was by preserving their bodies after death. Egyptians believed that their spirit would need to recognize their preserved body and use it as a home.

Poor people were buried in the desert, where the hot, dry sand quickly dried out their bodies. Wealthy Egyptians had their bodies made into mummies. A **mummy** is a body preserved by a special process. The knowledge of this process was one of ancient Egypt's great achievements. From mummies, scientists have learned much about life and death in ancient Egypt.

INTERACTIVE
Egyptian religion gallery

READING CHECK **Identify Cause and Effect**
What role did the afterlife play in the lives of ancient Egyptians?

Great Rulers

Hatshepsut, Ramses II, and Thutmose III were powerful New Kingdom pharaohs who shaped Egypt's history.

Hatshepsut Hatshepsut was one of the few women to rule Egypt. She was the daughter of one pharaoh and the wife of another. When her husband died, he left a son, named Thutmose III, who was too young to rule. So Hatshepsut decided to make herself Egypt's new pharaoh.

Some Egyptians did not want to bow to a woman. To gain their support, Hatshepsut carried out all of the rituals expected of a king. Her statues showed her dressed as a king. She even wore the false beard that was a

Quick Activity
Explore the impact of Egypt's pharaohs in your Active Journal.

BIOGRAPHY
5 Things to Know About
RAMSES II
Egyptian Pharaoh (c.1303–1213 BCE)

- He became pharaoh when he was very young and ruled for 66 years, the second-longest reign in Egyptian history.
- In addition to ruling as pharaoh, Ramses also led the Egyptian army and conquered a large amount of territory.
- Ramses won his greatest fame in the Battle of Kadesh, where he fought off a surprise attack by a much larger Hittite force.
- He brought tremendous wealth to Egypt and built many temples.
- When Ramses died at over 90 years of age, he was beloved throughout Egypt.

Critical Thinking What qualities of leadership do you think Ramses II had to make him successful?

Great Rulers

In its long history, ancient Egypt had hundreds of **pharaohs**. Discuss three of the greatest, Hatshepsut, Thutmose III, and Ramses II, who employed different means to rule.

Infer What were some of Hatshepsut's accomplishments? *(She increased Egypt's wealth through trade.)*

Identify Details Where did Thutmose III conquer land? *(Africa, Palestine, Syria, and the Fertile Crescent)*

Compare and Contrast How were the reigns of Hatshepsut and Ramses II different from each other? *(Hatshepsut peacefully extended Egyptian influence through trade. Ramses extended Egyptian power through war.)*

Summarize What was the outcome of Ramses' conflicts with the Hittites? *(After much loss of life and a period of war, Ramses made peace with the Hittites.)*

ACTIVE JOURNAL

Quick Activity Remind students that the images reflected the pharaoh's values and how he or she wanted to be presented to the people. Have each group write their interpretations in their Active Journals. During the discussion, ask groups with differing interpretations of the images to explain why they interpreted them as they did.

ELD TIP For the Quick Activity, pair emerging and expanding students with fluent speakers, calling on those speakers to ask the questions and encouraging English language learners to respond.

CURRICULUM CONNECTION: SCIENCE

Egyptian Medicine Egyptians learned a great deal about human anatomy through the practice of mummification. Egyptians also practiced medicine that was advanced for its time. Several papyrus texts preserve Egyptian medical knowledge. Research shows that most of the remedies from these texts could still be considered correct treatments. Egyptian doctors had a variety of specialties, just like doctors today. Some Egyptian doctors specialized in treating disorders of the mouth. Others specialized in disorders of the eyes. Still others specialized in digestive ailments. Unlike modern physicians, many Egyptian doctors were also priests who sometimes tried to cure disease using supernatural means through rituals or chanting. Egyptian doctors developed knowledge that later influenced Greek and Roman doctors, and even modern doctors today.

ANSWERS

Identify Cause and Effect *Egyptians believed they could overcome death in the afterlife, but they had to prepare for it.*

Critical Thinking *Possible response: Ramses's military victories showed his strength, courage, and devotion to the Egyptian people.*

HSS 6.2.1, 6.2.2, 6.2.3, 6.2.7; ELA RI.6.2; ELD.PI.C.10.a

SYNTHESIZE

Assess and Reteach Have students use a Think-Pair-Share strategy to complete Lesson Check questions 1–5. Review their responses. If they had any incorrect answers, use the Guiding Questions to discuss the lesson's main ideas, focusing on the ideas they struggled with.

ACTIVE JOURNAL

Writing Workshop Have students complete the Lesson 1 Writing Task in their Active Journals. Students will form a clear thesis for their end-of-topic essay. Effective thesis statements should clearly state a valid main point about the effects of the region's geography on ancient Egyptians. As they move through the topic, students will revisit their statements, revising as needed.

DEMONSTRATE

ASSESSMENT **ONLINE LESSON QUIZ**

Assign the Online Lesson Quiz for this lesson if you haven't already done so. Students will be offered automatic remediation or enrichment based on their score.

DISCUSSION **DISCUSSION BOARD**

Post this question to the class on the Discussion Board:

Analyze What was more important to Egypt, the Nile River or the **pharaohs**? *(Sample response: The Nile River made the development of Egyptian civilization possible. Its floods enriched Egypt's farmland, producing surpluses that freed some people to become artisans, warriors, and even pharaohs. The Nile River was more important because it enabled the pharaohs to rule a flourishing civilization.)*

ANSWERS

Draw Conclusions *Hatshepsut ruled peacefully and brought prosperity. Ramses II conquered new lands, bringing Egypt new wealth.*

▲ Hatshepsut ruled as Pharaoh for more than 20 years. **Draw Conclusions** Based on this statue, how do you think the Egyptian people felt about Hatshepsut?

traditional symbol of the pharaoh's strength and power. Most Egyptians came to accept Hapshetsut's rule.

Primary Source

"[T]he god's wife Hatshepsut executed the affairs of the Two Lands according to her counsels. Egypt worked for her, head bowed . . ."

— A government official during Hatshepsut's reign, from "The 18th Dynasty Before the Amarna Period," by Betsy M. Bryan, in *The Oxford History of Ancient Egypt*

Hatshepsut's rule was peaceful. Hatshepsut built Egypt's wealth and power through trade. She sent traders by sea to a land called Punt in East Africa. They returned with precious wood, ivory, gold, and perfumes. Hatshepsut recorded the story of their journey on the stone walls of an enormous temple that she built.

Thutmose III When Hatshepsut died, Thutmose III became ruler of Egypt. Unlike Hatshepsut, he used war to strengthen and expand the empire. He conquered land in Africa, Palestine, Syria, and the Fertile Crescent. His conquests gave Egypt more wealth, power, and prestige.

Ramses II Ramses II, who ruled about 150 years after Thutmose III, also used war to build Egypt's wealth and power. He spent the first half of his time as pharaoh fighting in Canaan and Syria, in the Fertile Crescent. In 1275 BCE, Ramses II led his army against the powerful Hittites. The two armies fought in Kadesh in present-day Syria. Ramses II lost many soldiers to the Hittites in the battle of Kadesh. He later made peace with the Hittites by agreeing on a border. Ramses II was a great builder. He built more monuments than any other pharaoh.

READING CHECK **Identify Supporting Details** What actions showed that Hatshepsut, Thutmose III, and Ramses II were great rulers?

Lesson Check

HSS 6.2.1, 6.2.2, 6.2.3; ELA RI.6.2; ELD.PI.C.10.a

Practice Vocabulary

1. What role did **pharaohs, artisans**, and the **bureaucracy** play in ancient Egypt?
2. How is the creation of **mummies** related to Egypt's dynasties?

Critical Thinking and Writing

3. **Explain** How did the Nile contribute to the growth of ancient Egyptian culture?
4. **Compare and Contrast** Compare and contrast the ways in which farmers and scribes contributed to ancient Egyptian civilization.
5. **Identify Central Ideas** What role did pharaohs play in ancient Egypt's religion?
6. **Writing Workshop: Develop a Clear Thesis** Write a sentence in your Active Journal that expresses the effects of geography on Egypt. This sentence will become the thesis statement for an essay you will write at the end of the topic.

LESSON CHECK

1. Sample response: Pharaohs led Egyptian society. Artisans made necessary goods. The bureaucracy supported the pharaoh and ran the government. **DOK1**
2. After death, the pharaohs of Egypt were made into mummies to preserve them for the afterlife. **DOK1**
3. Because of the Nile's floods, farmers could grow surpluses. As a result, other members of society could specialize in other jobs. **DOK3**
4. Farmers provided food for scribes. Scribes kept records, collected taxes, and supervised projects. All served the pharaoh. **DOK3**
5. Pharaohs were seen as gods, so people obeyed them. **DOK1**
6. Sample answer: The Nile River was central to life in ancient Egypt. **DOK4**

Primary Sources

HSS 6.2.7; ELA RI.6.3–4, RH.6.1

The Victory of Ramses II

Around 1273 BCE, Egyptian forces under Pharaoh Ramses II battled the Hittites for control of the city of Kadesh in Syria. In one of the largest chariot battles in history, Ramses fought his way out of a Hittite ambush.

▶ Ramses II is the largest figure in this painting.

Then the king he lashed each horse, . . .
Then he looked behind, and found
That the foe were all around,
Two thousand and five hundred of their chariots of war;
And the flower of the Hittites, and their helpers in a ring. . . .

Then spake Pharaoh, and he cried:
"Father Ammon, ① where are you?
I have built for you tall gates and wondrous works beside the Nile . . . .
It is I who sent for you,
The ships upon the sea,
To pour into your coffers ② the wealth of foreign trade . . . .
To you my cry I send,
Unto earth's extremest end,
Saying 'Help me, father Ammon, against the Hittite horde.' ③

Then my voice it found an echo in Hermonthis' ④ temple-hall,
Ammon heard it, and he came unto my call;
And for joy I gave a shout,
From behind, his voice cried out,

"I have hastened to you, Ramses Miamun,
Behold! I stand with you,
Behold! 'tis I am he,
Own father thine, the great god Ra, the sun.
Lo! mine hand with then shall fight. . . ." ⑤

—From *The Poem of Pen-ta-ur*

Reading and Vocabulary Support

① Recall what you have learned about Egyptian religion. Who is Amon, or Amon-Re? Why do you think Ramses is crying out to Amon?

② A coffer is a box that holds money.

③ What request does Ramses make to Amon? Why does he think he deserves Amon's help?

④ Hermonthis was an important city in Egypt.

⑤ According to this poem, how does Amon respond to the pharoah's request?

Analyzing Primary Sources

Cite specific evidence from the document to support your answers.

1. **Determine Author's Purpose** Why do you think Ramses wanted this poem inscribed on temples?
2. **Use Evidence** Would you consider this poem a reliable source of information? Explain.

Quest CONNECTIONS

Based on the poem, how does Ramses want to be remembered? Record your findings in your Active Journal.

ANALYZING PRIMARY SOURCES

1. Possible answer: to show Egyptians his great power **DOK3**
2. Possible answer: In showing the importance of Amon-Re to pharaohs, it is probably reliable. However, its exaggerated description of the battle is probably not reliable. **DOK4**

HSS 6.2.7; ELA RI.6.3-4, RH.6.1

Primary Sources

The Victory of Ramses II

Read aloud the explanatory note about the source. Direct students' attention to the illustration on the page. Ask: What does the illustration show? *(Ramses defeating the Hittites)*

GUIDED READING

Read aloud the first stanza of the poem without stopping. Then reread the stanza, pausing to let students answer the numbered questions. Do the same for the other stanzas. Use the questions in the text to prompt students' analysis of the primary source.

Reading and Vocabulary Support Answers

1. *the Egyptian sun god; Ramses is asking the god for help*

3. *He asks for Amon's help against the Hittite army. He thinks he deserves the god's support because he is Amon's son and because he has honored him with monuments and wealth gained through trade.*

5. *by joining him in the fight*

GUIDED ANALYSIS

After completing the poem, discuss what this primary source reveals about the beliefs of ancient Egyptians and the role of pharaohs in Egyptian society and religion.

Interpret What point is Ramses making with his statements in lines 3–6 of the second stanza? *(He is trying to show his complete devotion to Amon-Re.)* Why is he making this claim? *(to convince Amon-Re to help him)*

To assess understanding, have students respond to the Analyzing Primary Sources questions in writing.

ACTIVE JOURNAL

Quest Connection After answering the questions, have students respond to the Quest Connection question in their Active Journals.

Analysis CST.3

Analysis Skills
Identify Physical and Cultural Features

LEARN

Preview the steps in the student text with the students, and then play the video.

VIDEO **21ST CENTURY SKILLS**

Project the Read Special-Purpose Maps video in the 21st Century Skills Tutorial. Use the Quick Reference and Assessment to provide additional instruction in this skill.

PRACTICE

Have students practice the skill using the map and photograph on the student page. Follow the steps on the student page, providing instruction and then asking students the questions.

As an alternative, have students work in pairs or small groups to perform the activity. Then invite the groups to state their findings to the class. Discuss the different features that students identify and how the text and photograph information link to the map.

ASSESS

To assess this skill, have students identify physical and cultural features using maps and images from the previous topic, Civilizations and Peoples of the Fertile Crescent.

ANSWERS

1. a. The photograph shows that the Valley of the Kings was a very rocky, very dry area.
   b. The map indicates the rockiness of the area with shading that suggests mountains. The light brown color indicates that much of the area was a dry desert.
2. The main cultural feature of ancient Egypt is the various tombs, which were all buildings.
3. Possible answer: The Valley of the Kings was not located closer to the Nile because the land nearest the Nile had fertile soil needed for farming.

Analysis CST.3

Identify Physical and Cultural Features

Use the sources below as you follow these steps to identify physical and cultural features.

INTERACTIVE
Read Special-Purpose Maps

1 Identify physical features. Physical features include bodies of water, coastlines, mountains, valleys, and deserts.

a. What does the photograph show you about the physical features of the land where the Valley of the Kings is located?

b. How does the map show this same information?

2 Identify cultural features. Cultural features are features created by people, such as cities borders, buildings, roads, railroads, or canals. What is the main cultural feature of ancient Egypt shown on the map?

3 Relate physical and cultural features. Cultural features are often related to physical features. For example, a river (physical feature) can form a border between two countries (cultural feature). The natural landscape may determine where a city is built. Based on the photo and map, why do you think the Valley of the Kings was not located closer to the Nile?

Primary Source

▲ Many of the most powerful pharaohs and nobles of ancient Egypt are buried in the Valley of the Kings.

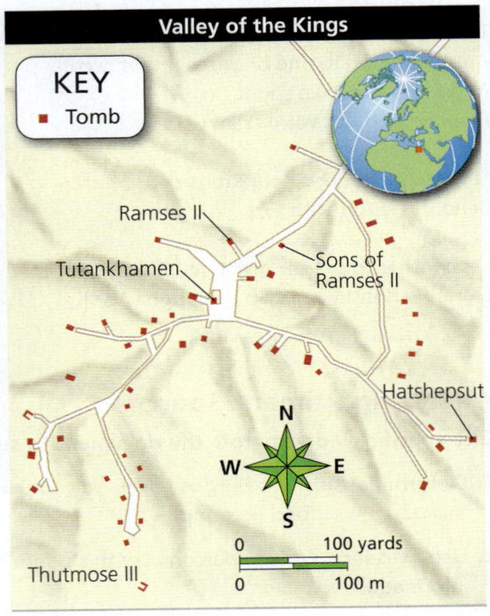

DIFFERENTIATED INSTRUCTION

Below Level Before practicing the skill, call on students to define physical and cultural features. *(Physical features are natural characteristics of an area such as landforms, bodies of water, natural resources, or types of vegetation. Cultural features are made by humans, such as cities, buildings, or roads.)*

INTEGRATED ENGLISH LANGUAGE DEVELOPMENT

Emerging Support emerging students by asking yes-no questions, such as, *Is a mountain a physical feature? What about the rocky background shown in the photograph?*

LESSON 2

HSS 6.2.5, 6.2.9

Achievements of Egyptian Civilization

GET READY TO READ

START UP

Notice the size and scale of the pillars in the photo. How do you think the ancient Egyptians achieved great feats of architecture without the technology we have today?

GUIDING QUESTIONS

- What was the impact of writing on Egypt?
- What were the main features of Egyptian architecture and art?
- How did advancements in science, mathematics, and technology affect Egyptian society?

TAKE NOTES

Literacy Skills: Summarize

Use the graphic organizer in your Active Journal to take notes as you read the lesson.

PRACTICE VOCABULARY

Use the vocabulary activity in your Active Journal to practice the vocabulary words.

Vocabulary		Academic Vocabulary
hieroglyphic	anatomy	survive
papyrus		construct
pyramid		
sculpture		

Like the Sumerians, the ancient Egyptians were great inventors. In writing, literature, art, architecture, mathematics, and science, the Egyptians made advances that paved the way for later civilizations.

Writing and Literature

The ancient Egyptians developed one of the world's first writing systems. Egyptian writing preserved some of the world's oldest records and works of literature.

What was Hieroglyphic Writing?

Ancient Egyptians developed early forms of writing by 3200 BCE. At around the same time, Sumerians in Mesopotamia were developing their own system of writing. Scholars aren't sure who developed writing first. They also don't know if one group borrowed the idea of writing from the other, or if each people came up with the idea separately.

Egyptian writing used hieroglyphics. A **hieroglyphic** is a drawing or symbol that represents a word or a sound.

PRACTICE VOCABULARY

To help students integrate new vocabulary, group the terms into pairs and introduce each word. Explain that *hieroglyphic* and *papyrus* are both connected to writing. Say that a *pyramid* is a building made of stone and ancient *statues* are carved from stone. Explain that *anatomy* refers to the body structure of a person or animal. Reinforce the terms during the lesson using the teaching notes.

Point out the academic vocabulary in the margin. Provide sample sentences that clarify meaning.

survive: Although the desert is hot and dry, many animals have developed ways to survive there.

construct: Builders do a lot of planning before they can construct a skyscraper.

HSS 6.2.5, 6.2.9; ELA RI.6.1; ELD.PI.C.10a

Achievements of Egyptian Civilization

CONNECT

GET READY TO READ

ETEXT **START UP**

Project the Start Up Activity. As students enter the classroom and get settled, ask them to look at the picture of the ruins, which are from the Egyptian Karnak Temple complex. The complex was built more than 2,000 years ago as part of the monumental city of Thebes.

Infer How do you think the ancient Egyptians achieved great feats of architecture without the technology we have today? *(Sample response: Building times probably spanned decades and they used thousands of workers instead of machines.)*

Discuss Remind students that art, literature, science, and mathematics are all hallmarks of a complex civilization.

After completing the Start Up activity, project the Lesson Opener or direct students to their textbooks. Preview the lesson by working through the Get Ready to Read items with the class. Remind students to pay close attention to the Guiding Questions as they read the lesson.

ACTIVE JOURNAL

Take Notes Have students use the literacy skills graphic organizer in their Active Journals to take notes as they read the lesson.

Practice Vocabulary Have students complete the activity in their Active Journals to build their vocabulary.

VIDEO **VIDEO**

Assign the lesson video as homework.

WORKSHEET **TEACHER RESOURCES**

Have students who need additional support use the following worksheets from the Teacher Resources on the course:

- **Reading Support**
- **English Language Development**
- **Lesson Summary**

INVESTIGATE

Writing and Literature

Discuss the importance of writing in the development of a complex civilization. Explain that historians often use the development of writing as a marker dividing prehistory from history.

Summarize What is a **hieroglyphic**? *(a drawing or symbol that represents a word or sound)*

Main Idea Why were scribes valued in Egyptian society? *(Scribes knew how to read and write.)*

Compare and Contrast Why was **papyrus** easier than clay to use for writing? *(It was easier to write with ink than press letters into wet clay, and it was lighter than clay to transport.)*

Connect Why are **papyrus** documents from ancient Egypt important to historians today? *(These documents give us details about the knowledge and beliefs of ancient Egyptians.)*

Synthesize How might the invention of **hieroglyphic** writing and **papyrus** have affected the development of Egyptian literature? *(These inventions made it possible to share a variety of texts of varying lengths.)*

ANSWERS

Use Visual Information *In an alphabet, symbols represent sounds. Some heiroglyphics represent sounds, but others represent whole words.*

Understand Effects *It allowed Egyptians to share and preserve knowledge.*

Analyze Images Scholars have studied hieroglyphics to learn how the ancient Egyptians lived. **Use Visual Information** List the hieroglyphs you recognize. How is writing with symbols different from using an alphabet?

Mesopotamian cuneiform and Egyptian hieroglyphics shared some similarities. Both systems of writing used signs that represented sounds, or phonemes, and other signs—logograms—that represented the meanings of words or phrases.

Most ancient Egyptians did not know how to write. Scribes, or officials who knew how to write, were valued for their knowledge. With writing, Egyptians could share and preserve knowledge. This ability made its complex civilization and advanced technology possible.

The Importance of Papyrus Egyptians invented a material very similar to paper. This material is called **papyrus** (puh PY rus) and was made from the papyrus reed that grew along the Nile. Our word *paper* comes from the word *papyrus*. Scribes wrote in ink on papyrus sheets. This was much easier than pressing letters into wet clay as the Sumerians did. Papyrus sheets were also easier to transport than pieces of clay.

Papyrus sheets had another important quality. They could last a very long time in the dry environment of Egypt. Many documents written on papyrus—including medical books, calendars, stories, poems, and prayers—have **survived** to the present. Wall paintings may show us how Egyptians lived; however, written records give us a fuller sense of what was in their hearts and minds.

Egyptian Literature Ancient Egyptian literature included teachings, stories, poems, religious texts, and histories. Egyptian literature was written on sheets of papyrus, carved on stone monuments, and painted on the coffins of mummies.

One famous text, *The Book of the Dead,* is a guide to the afterlife for dead souls. *The Tale of Sinuhe* tells the tale of an Egyptian official. Hearing that the pharaoh has been killed, he flees Egypt out of fear that he will be blamed for the crime:

Primary Source

> "My heart staggered, my arms spread out; trembling fell on every limb. I removed myself, leaping, to look for a hiding place."
>
> —From *The Tale of Sinuhe*, translated by R. B. Parkinson

Academic Vocabulary
survive • *v.,* to last, to continue to live

READING CHECK **Understand Effects** How did writing make Egypt's complex civilization and technology possible?

INTEGRATED ENGLISH LANGUAGE DEVELOPMENT

Collaborative Use Science and Mathematics to help students comprehend the achievements of ancient Egyptians in these two areas of knowledge. Encourage students to write to exchange their ideas.

Emerging Read the text aloud and periodically stop to ask students to write down the achievements of ancient Egyptians in science and mathematics.

Expanding Divide students into groups. Have them write the achievements of ancient Egyptians in science and mathematics by taking turns asking each other questions.

Bridging As students work in groups identifying and writing the achievements of ancient Egyptians in science and mathematics, have these students give feedback to others and

Architecture and Art

The Egyptians created temples for their gods and tombs for their pharaohs. The temple complex at Karnak contains the ruins of the world's largest temples, built with massive blocks of stone. These great buildings, and the art they contain, continue to inspire artists to this day.

Why did the Egyptians Build Pyramids? Tombs of early rulers were underground chambers, or rooms. The burial chamber contained items that the ruler might want in the afterlife.

An architect named Imhotep designed a new kind of tomb for his pharaoh, with six stone mounds, one on top of the other. The result is known as a step pyramid. Later architects made the sides smoother to create a true **pyramid,** or structure with triangular sides.

During the Old Kingdom, three enormous pyramids were built at Giza for King Khufu, his son Khafre, and his grandson Menkaure. The largest is the Great Pyramid of Khufu. For nearly 4,000 years, this pyramid was the world's tallest building. Nearby stands the Sphinx, a famous statue. The Sphinx guarded the road to Khafre's pyramid.

When they were built, these pyramids were the largest structures on Earth. They were a great achievement. They show Egyptians' command of mathematics and advanced building techniques.

Building the pyramids also required the labor of thousands of workers. Workers cut and placed the huge stones by hand. Scholars once thought that slaves had built the pyramids. They now think that many workers were farmers.

The great age of pyramid building ended about 2200 BCE. Pharaohs who ruled after that time carved massive tombs from the cliffs at the edge of the Nile Valley. Egypt's massive tombs and temples show that Egyptians valued monuments to the gods, including pharaohs.

INTERACTIVE
Egyptian Pyramids

Quick Activity

Explore how the ancient Egyptians moved the stone blocks that created the pyramids in your Active Journal.

Quest CONNECTIONS

What were Egyptian pharaohs trying to accomplish by building pyramids? Record your findings in your Active Journal.

Analyze Images The Great Pyramid of Giza is considered on of the seven wonders of the ancient world. **Infer** Why is the Great Pyramid of Giza called a "wonder."

ELD.PII.A.2.b

help build on their responses with additional information from the text.

WORKSHEET **TEACHER RESOURCES**

For additional IELD support addressing the standard, have students complete the Lesson IELD activity from the Teacher Resources found on the course.

Architecture and Art

Discuss the importance of architecture and art to all civilizations, ancient and modern.

Infer Why do you think the pharaohs built large tombs such as the **pyramids**? *(They wanted to display their own power and importance.)*

Synthesize Building **pyramids** took many workers a long time. What does this suggest about teamwork in ancient Egypt? *(Teamwork was valued and successful.)*

INTERACTIVE **INTERACTIVE 3-D MODEL**

Egyptian Pyramids

Display the Interactive 3-D Model: Egyptian Pyramids for the class. Have students examine the diagram of the interior of the pyramid. Ask: Why do you think the chambers were in the center of the pyramid? *(Sample response: The pharaoh's mummy and belongings would be safest there.)* Then move on to the gallery to learn more about Egyptian funerary practices.

ACTIVE JOURNAL

Quick Activity Have students work in small groups to discuss the drawing showing workers moving giant stones to build the pyramids. Then have groups complete the Team Challenge.

ACTIVE JOURNAL

Quest Connection Have students respond to the Quest Connection question in their Active Journals.

ANSWERS

Infer *It is a huge, imposing structure that was built without modern technology.*

ACTIVE CLASSROOM

Use the Quickdraw strategy. After students examine the 3-D Model: Egyptian Pyramids, give them 30 seconds to draw a diagram of the pyramid. Remind students to consider features on the interior and exterior of the pyramid. Then have them compare drawings with a partner and note the features that each student included.

Summarize Why did the artists of ancient Egypt create paintings and **sculptures** showing people at work and play? *(The paintings and sculptures were made so that the person buried in the tomb would have all the objects and pleasures needed for the afterlife.)*

Science and Mathematics

Discuss some of the achievements of the ancient Egyptians in science, mathematics, medicine and technology.

Identify Central Ideas Why did the ancient Egyptians develop a solar calendar? *(They wanted to help farmers by keeping the calendar linked to the seasons.)*

Cite Evidence How does the construction of the pyramids prove the Egyptians were experts at mathematics? *(Knowledge of mathematics helped the Egyptians build the pyramids so precisely.)*

Draw Conclusions Why would irrigation systems be needed to bring water from the Nile? *(These systems would bring water to farther areas for farming, relieve excessive flooding, and provide more water for agriculture during dry periods of the year.)*

Make Connections How did mummification affect Egyptian knowledge of **anatomy** and medicine? *(Egyptians learned about the body through mummification and used this knowledge to improve medical treatments.)*

ANSWERS

Draw Conclusions *The pharaoh might want the statue in the afterlife.*

Draw Conclusions *When they were built, the pyramids were the largest structures on Earth and showed that the Egyptians had a command of mathematics and advanced building techniques. Egyptian artists were very skilled.*

▲ Statue from the tomb of the Pharaoh Tutankhamun.

Painting and Sculpture Egyptians were skilled artists and builders. Much of what we know about life in Egypt comes from paintings on the walls of tombs that show Egyptians at work and at play; their purpose was not decoration. The paintings were created to provide the person buried in the tomb with all of the objects and pleasures shown on the walls.

Egyptian artists also created wonderful sculptures. A **sculpture** is a statue or other free-standing piece of art made of clay, stone, or other materials. Colossal statues of gods stood in temples. Egyptians placed smaller statues of people in tombs along with their mummies. If a mummy was destroyed, the statue could replace it as a home for the dead person's spirit.

READING CHECK **Draw Conclusions** Why do people still admire the pyramids and art the Egyptians created?

Science and Mathematics

The Egyptians made many great discoveries in science, mathematics, and technology. Later civilizations built on these discoveries.

The Egyptian Calendar Like most early peoples, prehistoric Egyptians probably measured time by the cycles of the moon. The result would have been a lunar, or moon-based, year of about 354 days.

Over the years, the seasons would run ahead of such a calendar, since the seasons follow a solar, or sun-based, year of 365.2422 days. The ancient Egyptians wanted to keep the calendar linked to the seasons to help farmers plan when to plant and harvest crops. They watched for a bright star called Sirius which would appear above the horizon before sunrise about the same time of year as the Nile floods. Sometimes the first appearance of Sirius came too close to the end of the lunar year, so the Egyptians added an extra month to that year to catch up to the seasons.

However, this meant that each year had a different number of days. That made record keeping and planning difficult. So the ancient Egyptians developed a solar calendar with exactly 365 days. They used this calendar for official record keeping.

The seasons still slowly shifted through this solar calendar, too, so the ancient Greeks added leap years when they ruled Egypt in the 200s BCE. Our modern calendar was modeled after this solar calendar.

Mathematics The ancient Egyptians developed a solid understanding of mathematics. Their ability to **construct** the great pyramids proves their command of arithmetic, or addition, subtraction, multiplication, and division. It also shows their skill in geometry, or the measurement of dimensions.

Academic Vocabulary
construct • *v.*, to build or put together

DIFFERENTIATED INSTRUCTION

Special Education Connect the reading to students' experiences by asking them to compare the Great Pyramids to modern buildings and monuments.

Below Level Have students work in groups of three to review the main ideas from the three key sections of the lesson: Writing and Literature, Architecture and Art, and Science and Mathematics. Encourage one student in each group to take the lead on one of the three topics.

Advanced Have students read about *The Tale of Sinuhe* online and then write or reenact part of the story to share with other students.

Science, Technology, and Medicine Ancient Egyptians also made advances in science, technology, and medicine. As you have learned, the Egyptians knew that the star Sirius first appeared in the early morning sky at the same time of year as the Nile flood. This was part of their advanced knowledge of astronomy—the study of the stars and other objects in the sky.

The construction of the great pyramids shows the ancient Egyptians' mastery of engineering. No other civilization had been able to plan and build structures so large or so perfectly shaped.

The ancient Egyptians also made many of the earliest discoveries in chemistry. These discoveries led to many new inventions. These included the earliest forms of glass, mortar for setting stones and bricks, and many kinds of cosmetics.

The great pyramids were not the only example of Egyptian engineering. To bring the water of the Nile River to their fields, the ancient Egyptians developed complex systems of irrigation, or ways of watering land.

The Egyptians had the most advanced medical knowledge of their time. From their work with mummies, for example, they learned much about human anatomy. **Anatomy** is the study of the structure of the body and its organs. The ancient Egyptians were skilled surgeons. Egyptian doctors also studied diseases and developed effective medicines to treat or cure them.

READING CHECK **Summarize** What were three Egyptian achievements in science and mathematics?

Analyze Images This waterwheel in the Nile delta is similar to the irrigation systems that may have been used by ancient Egyptians. **Infer** How do you think advances in irrigation helped ancient Egyptian society to prosper?

Lesson Check

HSS 6.2.5, 6.2.9; ELA RI.6.1; ELD.PI.C.10a

Practice Vocabulary

1. How did Egyptians' use of **hieroglyphics** and **papyrus** help advance their society?
2. Why were the Egyptians able to build the **pyramids**?

Critical Thinking and Writing

3. **Infer** If papyrus couldn't last a long time in Egypt's dry environment, how would that have affected our understanding of ancient Egyptian society?
4. **Use Evidence** Why are the pyramids considered one of ancient Egypt's greatest achievements?
5. **Identify Supporting Details** How did the Egyptians' knowledge of astronomy help them farm?
6. **Writing Workshop: Support Thesis with Details** Refer to the thesis statement you wrote in Lesson 1. What details from Lessons 1 and 2 support your point? Write them in an outline in your Active Journal.

LESSON CHECK

1. They made it possible for the Egyptians to share knowledge and create literature. **DOK1**
2. The Egyptians were skilled at geometry and engineering. **DOK1**
3. We wouldn't know as much because the written records give us a sense of what was in the hearts and minds of the Egyptian people. **DOK2**
4. They were the largest structures on Earth and required vast organization, labor, and supplies. **DOK3**
5. The Egyptians understood that Sirius appeared above the horizon before sunrise about the same time of year as the Nile floods. **DOK1**
6. Students should include details from Lessons 1 and 2 that support their theses. **DOK3**

HSS 6.2.5, 6.2.9; ELA RI.6.1; ELD.PI.C.10a

SYNTHESIZE

Assess and Reteach Have students use a Numbered Heads strategy to complete Lesson Check questions 1–5. Review their responses. If they had any incorrect answers, use the Guiding Questions to discuss the lesson's main ideas, focusing on the ideas they struggled with.

ACTIVE JOURNAL

Writing Workshop Have students complete the Lesson 2 Writing Task in their Active Journals. Students will add details to support the thesis for their end-of-topic essay. Details should directly relate to their thesis statements.

ELD TIP For the Active Journal Writing Workshop, provide English learners with an example of strong details. they can use as a guide.

DEMONSTRATE

ASSESSMENT **ONLINE LESSON QUIZ**

Assign the Online Lesson Quiz for this lesson if you haven't already done so. Students will be offered automatic remediation or enrichment based on their score.

DISCUSSION **DISCUSSION BOARD**

Post this question to the class on the Discussion Board:

Analyze What achievement of the ancient Egyptian civilization do you think was the most important? Explain why. *(Possible response: A writing system was important because it allowed ideas to be communicated across time and locations.)*

ANSWERS

Infer *Irrigation made farming possible in drier areas, which gave the Egyptians a reliable food source.*

Summarize *The Egyptians created a calendar, developed an irrigation system, and were skilled in mathematics, chemistry, engineering, astronomy, and medicine.*

Analysis REP.3

Analysis Skills
Distinguish Verifiable from Unverifiable Information

LEARN

Preview the steps in the student text, and then play the video.

VIDEO **21ST CENTURY SKILLS**

Project the Distinguish Between Fact and Opinion video in the 21st Century Skills Tutorial. Use the Quick Reference and Assessment to provide additional instruction on this skill.

PRACTICE

Have students practice the skill of identifying verifiable and unverifiable information by reading the secondary source and examining the photograph on the student page. Work with students through the steps listed on the page, providing instruction and then asking students the questions.

As an alternative, have students work in pairs or small groups to perform the activity. Then invite students to share examples of verifiable information that they found in the secondary source. Have students discuss whether or not they agree.

ASSESS

To assess this skill, have students identify verifiable and unverifiable information using a section of text from the previous topic, Civilizations and Peoples of the Fertile Crescent.

ANSWERS

1. All the statements that make up the text are verifiable to varying degrees.
2. Make sure students locate an appropriate website with the suffix .gov, .org, or .edu.
3. **a.** "Scribes probably found it much easier... [than pressing] letters into wet clay as Sumerians did." **b.** "Easier" is a relative term. We cannot say for sure what people long ago might have thought without evidence.

Distinguish Verifiable from Unverifiable Information

INTERACTIVE
Distinguish Between Fact and Opinion

Use the secondary source as you follow these steps to distinguish verifiable information from unverifiable information.

1 Identify statements that could be verified. Historical sources may contain facts, or statements that can be proved to be true. Look at the secondary source from the lesson. How many factual statements—statements that you could prove to be true—does it include?

2 Determine how you might verify these statements. Find ways to verify each statement. For example, you could compare a statement to a reliable online source. Reliable sources often end in .gov, .org, or .edu. Go online and find a reliable source to verify the statement that Egyptians invented papyrus.

3 Identify statements that cannot be verified. It is not possible to verify something like a person's opinion. It is also not possible to prove that tall tales or myths about events from an ancient time are true. Remember, though, that statements can be valuable even though they are not verifiable.

a. Which sentence in the secondary source might be difficult to verify?

b. What makes it difficult to verify?

Secondary Source

Egyptians invented a material very similar to paper. This material, papyrus, was made from the papyrus reed that grew along the Nile. Our word *paper* comes from the word *papyrus*. Scribes wrote in ink on papyrus sheets. Scribes probably found it much easier to write this way than to press letters into wet clay as the Sumerians did. Papyrus sheets were also less heavy to transport than pieces of clay.

Primary Source

▲ Egyptians formed papyrus by pressing together and drying the tissue of papyrus plants.

DIFFERENTIATED INSTRUCTION

Below Level Before practicing this skill, call on students to define verifiable and unverifiable information. *(Verifiable information involves facts that can be proved to be true based on reliable sources. Unverifiable information includes statements of opinion, judgments, or beliefs that cannot be proved true.)*

INTEGRATED ENGLISH LANGUAGE DEVELOPMENT

Emerging Support English learners by defining the term *factual statements*. Then encourage students to underline the factual statements in the secondary source to keep track of which statements should be verified.

LESSON 3

HSS 6.2.6, 6.2.8, 6.2.9; ELA RI.6.2

Egypt and Kush

GET READY TO READ

START UP

Examine the photo of Kush pyramids. How do they compare to Egyptian pyramids?

GUIDING QUESTIONS

- How did trade link Egypt and neighboring lands?
- How did its location help civilization in Kush grow?
- What were Kush's achievements?

TAKE NOTES

Literacy Skill: Main Ideas and Details Use the graphic organizer in your Active Journal to take notes as you read the lesson.

PRACTICE VOCABULARY

Use the vocabulary activity in your Active Journal to practice the vocabulary words.

Vocabulary	Academic Vocabulary
commerce	rely
ivory	generate
ebony	
interdependence	
Meroitic script	

South of Egypt, farther up the Nile River, was a land that the Egyptians called Kush. Another name for this region is Nubia. Nubia extends from present-day southern Egypt into northern Sudan. Trade brought Egypt and Kush together.

Why was Trade Important for Egypt and Kush?

Egypt was rich in sunshine and fertile soil, but it lacked the forests, minerals, horses, and other useful natural resources found in Kush and other countries. The people of ancient Egypt had to get these resources through trade, or commerce, with neighboring countries. **Commerce** is the buying and selling of goods and services.

As their country grew in wealth, Egyptians also wanted to buy luxury goods from other lands. Luxury goods are expensive goods that are not needed, but that make life more enjoyable. Egyptian luxury goods included precious stones and perfumes. Trade gave Egypt access to goods it would not otherwise have.

PRACTICE VOCABULARY

Ask students to fill in the correct content vocabulary terms to complete the following sentences: The buying and selling of goods and services is called *(commerce)*. Two luxury items that ancient Egyptians bought in Kush were *(ivory)* and *(ebony)*. Egypt wanted Kush's gold, and Kush wanted Egypt's grain so *(interdependence)* between the two kingdoms grew. The Kushites created one of the world's oldest alphabets called *(Meroitic script)*.

Reinforce the terms during the lesson using the teaching notes.

Point out the academic vocabulary in the margin. Provide sample sentences that clarify meaning.

rely: I can rely on my older brother to help me with my math homework.

generate: The new power plant will generate five times as much electricity as the old one.

HSS 6.2.6, 6.2.8, 6.2.9; ELA RI.6.1; ELD.PI.C.10.a

Egypt and Kush

CONNECT

GET READY TO READ

ETEXT **START UP**

Project the Start Up Activity. As students enter the classroom and get seated, have them look at the photograph of Kush pyramids. Explain that the photograph shows pyramids and other tombs from Meroë, once the capital of the Kingdom of Kush. The tombs were often filled with valuable objects such as horse riding equipment, furniture, tools, and even makeup.

Compare and Contrast Have students make a list of the similarities and differences between the Kushite and Egyptian pyramids. Reminds students to consider the physical characteristics of the pyramids as well as what the pyramids might symbolize to each civilization.

Discuss Explain to students that the ancient civilization of Kush was located on the Nile River south of Egypt. Remind students that two civilizations that are located near each other often share parts of their cultures.

After completing the Start Up activity, project the Lesson Opener or direct students to their textbooks. Preview the lesson by working through the Get Ready to Read items with the class. Remind students to pay close attention to the Guiding Questions as they read the lesson.

ACTIVE JOURNAL

Take Notes Have students use the literacy skills graphic organizer in their Active Journals to take notes as they read the lesson.

Practice Vocabulary Have students complete the activity in their Active Journals to build their vocabulary.

VIDEO **VIDEO**

Assign the lesson video as homework.

INVESTIGATE

Why Was Trade Important for Egypt and Kush?

Explain how trade helps provide a nation with goods and services that it does not have but needs or wants. Provide modern-day examples such as Japan having few crops but lots of electronic products it can trade with the world.

INTERACTIVE **INTERACTIVE SIMULATION**

Ancient Egypt and Kush Trade

Display the Interactive Map: Ancient Egypt and Kush Trade Simulation for the class. Have volunteers read each option and then poll the class before choosing one. If the choice leads to a negative outcome, try again. After completing the simulation, ask: How does the simulation demonstrate the **interdependence** between Egypt and Kush? *(Egypt relied on Kush for iron and gold, while Kush relied on Egypt for grain. Each traded for what it lacked.)*

ACTIVE CLASSROOM

Use the simulation about Egypt and Kush to explore the importance of trade between the two countries. Have students work in small groups to discuss the choices involved in each decision-making step as they work their way through the simulation.

ANSWERS

Movement *Mediterranean Sea, Red Sea, Gulf of Aden*

Infer *the lack of water, food, and shelter in the desert*

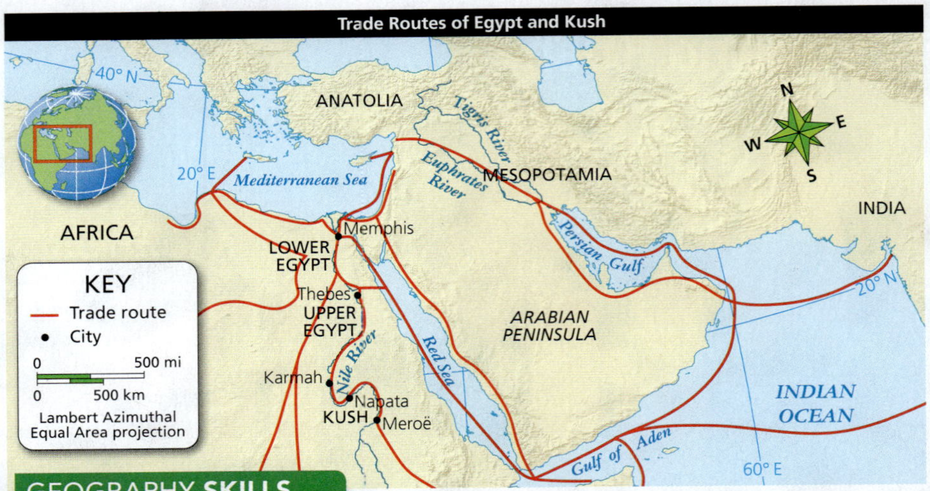

GEOGRAPHY SKILLS

Egypt traded with its neighbors in Africa and the Middle East.

1. **Movement** Which seas did traders cross to reach Egypt?
2. **Infer** Considering the lands around the Nile Valley, what challenges might land trade routes have posed?

Trade in the Eastern Mediterranean The pharaohs sent merchants and officials to other lands to promote trade. As early as the Old Kingdom, a pharaoh named Snefru promoted trade with lands on the eastern Mediterranean Sea.

The area of modern Lebanon in the eastern Mediterranean had forests that Egypt lacked. The Egyptians crossed the Red Sea because they were eager to buy its cedar wood. In other Mediterranean lands, they bought olive oil and metals such as tin and copper. Rulers in Egypt, Mesopotamia, Syria, and Anatolia sent diplomats from one region to another. The movement of government officials and luxury goods among these royal courts formed the world's first trading community.

Egypt strengthened its relationships with other lands in other ways. New Kingdom pharaohs made peace by signing treaties with former enemies such as the Babylonians, the Syrians, and the Hittites. Pharaohs sometimes married princesses from the places they made peace with. As a result, trade with these lands flourished.

Trade in the Nile Valley Snefru also boosted trade between Egypt and Kush. Under later dynasties, trade between Egypt and Kush increased.

INTERACTIVE
Ancient Egypt and Kush trade simulation

The most valuable goods that Egyptians bought in Kush were gold and elephant tusks, which were a source of **ivory**, a hard white material made from these tusks. They also bought incense and a dark, black wood called **ebony**. In return, the Egyptians sold grain, cloth, papyrus, glass, and jewelry.

INTEGRATED ENGLISH LANGUAGE DEVELOPMENT

Collaborative Use How Did Kush Develop? to help students express opinions about the similarities and differences between Egypt and Kush.

Emerging Read the text aloud, stopping periodically to rephrase key content in accessible language. Ask students simple opinion questions, such as, Why would you rather live in ancient Egypt? Why would you prefer to live in ancient Kush?

Expanding Read the text aloud, stopping periodically to define any challenging vocabulary. Then guide a discussion about where students would prefer to live, either ancient Egypt or ancient Kush. Support students as they use learned phrases, such as *I agree with your idea, but ____.*

Bridging After students read the text, divide them into groups and instruct students to share which civilization they

Egypt **relied** on Kush's gold, and Kush relied on Egypt's grain. Trade created **interdependence**, or dependence by each country or group on the other.

Trade brought the Kushites into closer contact with ancient Egypt. Over time, the Kushites adopted elements of Egyptian culture, including Egyptian religion.

READING CHECK **Use Evidence** Why did Egyptians want to trade with Kush?

Academic Vocabulary

rely • *v.*, to produce, create

generate • *v.*, to depend, trust

How did Kush Develop?

Like Egypt, Kush had an ancient culture. Kush's geography was similar to Egypt's in some ways and different in others.

How Did Geography Affect Kush? Kush lay in the upper Nile Valley, where rainfall was higher than in Egypt and land for farming and raising cattle stretched beyond the river banks. Like Egypt, however, Kush's farmers depended on the Nile and its annual floods. Their farming methods **generated** a surplus, though a smaller one than Egypt's. This surplus supported cities with artisans and merchants.

However, the Nile's cataracts lay within Kush. While Egyptians used boats, cataracts made it impossible to travel very far by boat in Kush. Instead, people had to travel on foot through the rugged desert.

Another difference from Egypt was that the Kushites had much less land to farm. As a result, the Kushites were sometimes short of food. This made them eager to trade gold, iron, and other products for Egypt's grain.

Kush was also in closer contact than Egypt with the peoples of Africa south of the Sahara. The Kushites traded goods and ideas with these peoples just as they did with the Egyptians.

How Do We Know About Kush? Scholars have used both historical records and archaeological evidence to learn about Kush. Written records in Egypt document trade with Kush. They also describe a powerful kingdom in Kush modeled on the kingdom of Egypt.

Some of the evidence of trade with Egypt comes from archaeology. Archaeologists have also found that the Kushites and Egyptians both saw kings as gods. This idea was common in Africa and may have come to Egypt through Kush.

READING CHECK **Identify Supporting Details** How did Kush's geography affect its relationship with Egypt?

Analyze Images Kush princes and their servants bring gold to Egypt. **Infer** What do you think princes from Kush hoped to receive in return for the gold they brought to Egypt?

Identify Main Ideas Why would Egypt and Kush be willing to depend on each other's trade goods? *(Each had something the other could not produce, so they were willing to become interdependent.)*

Identify Details What important good did Egypt buy from Lebanon? *(wood)*

Understand Cause and Effect How did trade with Egypt affect Kush? *(The Kushites adopted some Egyptian ideas and ways of doing things, including Egyptian religion.)*

How Did Kush Develop?

Discuss how geography affected the development of Kush.

Compare and Contrast How was the geography of Kush like that of Egypt? *(Both lay along the Nile, received little rainfall, and depended on the river flood. In addition, their area for settlement was limited by deserts.)*

Compare and Contrast How was Kush's geography different from Egypt's? *(Cataracts in Kush made the Nile unusable for transportation.)*

Identify Main Ideas How do scholars know about Kush? *(through archaeological evidence and Egyptian written documents)*

ELD.PI.A.3

would prefer to live in and why. Encourage students to carefully listen and reflect on the opinions of others during the discussion.

WORKSHEET **TEACHER RESOURCES**

For additional IELD support addressing the standard, have students complete the Lesson IELD activity from the Teacher Resources found on the course.

ANSWERS

Infer *The princes probably wanted to receive grain because Egypt had more food than Kush.*

Use Evidence *To obtain goods they could not produce themselves*

Identify Supporting Details *Kush could not grow as much food as Egypt because it did not receive as much water from the Nile during flooding. This made the Kush interdependent on Egypt for food.*

Kush and Egypt

Discuss the importance of trade in precious metals and luxury goods to both Kush and Egypt.

Identify Main Ideas How did gold from Kush help the Egyptians trade with other parts of the ancient world? *(Gold was valued everywhere, so more gold made it easier for the Egyptians to trade for wood and other resources from other civilizations.)*

Identify Details What kinds of tribute did Kushites have to pay the pharaoh after Egypt conquered Kush? *(gold, cattle, ivory, and ostrich feathers)*

Summarize How did the Kush leader Piye conquer Egypt? *(Piye expanded the Kush empire by conquering one Egyptian city after another.)*

Interpret Why is the text of the primary source an appropriate inscription for a monument to Piye, or Piankhi? *(The text celebrates Piye's conquering of Egypt [the Northland] and his rule over Thebes.)*

Identify Main Ideas Why did Kush's control of Egypt end? *(Kush went to war with Assyria, which defeated them and drove them out of Egypt.)*

ELD TIP Remind English learners that in a quotation, ellipses indicate words that have been omitted, and the words in the brackets are words that have been added to help make sense of the quotation.

Analyze Images Egyptians used Kush gold to make jewelry. **Infer** Why might Egypt have relied on Kush gold to make jewelry?

Kush and Egypt

Through trade, the Egyptians discovered that Kush was rich in resources, including gold. The Egyptians realized that the more gold they had, the more wood and other resources they could buy from the eastern Mediterranean.

Egypt Conquers Kush Egypt conquered most of Kush for a time during the Middle Kingdom, and then again during the New Kingdom. The conquered Kushites had to pay tribute to the pharaoh. One year's tribute to the pharaoh Thutmose III included hundreds of pounds of gold, cattle, ivory, and ostrich feathers from Kush. Kush also gave Egypt enslaved people as part of its tribute.

After the rule of Ramses II, Egypt weakened, and the New Kingdom ended. Rival leaders in different cities fought for control of Egypt. Meanwhile, Kush became an independent kingdom ruled by Kushite kings.

Kush Conquers Egypt In the mid-700s BCE, a Kushite king conquered the Egyptian city of Thebes. The next ruler of Kush, a king named Piye (PEE yeh), or Piankhi, expanded the Kushite empire by conquering one Egyptian city after another. Finally, Piye declared himself pharaoh of a united Egypt and Kush.

Primary Source

"O mighty, mighty Ruler, Piankhi, O mighty Ruler, [you come] having gained the dominion of the Northland. . . . [You are] unto eternity, [your] might endure[s], O Ruler, beloved of Thebes."

—Inscription from the victory monument of Piye, translated by James Henry Breasted

Pharaohs from Kush ruled Egypt for almost a hundred years. Kushite rulers promoted the traditional Egyptian ways that they had learned under earlier pharaohs. They built temples to honor Kushite and Egyptian gods. At the same time, the Kushites created painted pottery and other distinctive works of art.

The rulers from Kush might have ruled Egypt longer if they had not tried to expand their power. They went to war with the Assyrians, skillful warriors who had recently conquered the Fertile Crescent. Assyrian troops invaded Egypt around 665 BCE. After losing many battles, the Kushites retreated from Egypt back to Kush.

READING CHECK **Identify Cause and Effect** Why did Egypt conquer Kush?

DIFFERENTIATED INSTRUCTION

Special Education Remind students that people today still wear gold jewelry. Have students locate a picture of a piece of gold jewelry from a magazine and describe it to a partner.

Below Level Have students state in their own words the reasons Egypt conquered Kush, including the tribute that the Kush had to pay each year.

Advanced Have students work in small groups to prepare a scene in which they are travelers who have come upon the monument to Piye. Have the students perform their scene including a dramatic reading of the monument inscription from the Primary Source.

ANSWERS

Infer *Gold is soft and easy to shape and decorate into luxury objects such as bracelets and necklaces. Egyptian jewelry was sought after by wealthy Egyptians and foreigners.*

Identify Cause and Effect *Egypt wanted control over the riches found in Kush.*

What Were Kush's Accomplishments?

Kush remained a highly developed civilization for almost a thousand years after it lost Egypt. It developed its own system of writing, economy, and government.

Did you know?
The modern country of Sudan includes most of former Kush.

Independent Kush In 591 BCE, the Egyptians destroyed Napata, the capital of Kush. The Kushites moved their capital south to the city of Meroë (MEHR oh ee), which was easier to defend.

Meroë was also located near iron deposits and on a trade route from Central Africa. This region received more rain than did most of Kush. This rain supported the growth of wood that the Kushites could burn to smelt, or melt out, iron from a rock called iron ore.

The Kushites turned Meroë into Africa's first ironworking center. Kush's iron tools and weapons were much stronger than Egypt's soft bronze tools. The Kushites continued to make jewelry and other beautiful objects from their gold.

The Kushites built hundreds of pyramids at Napata and Meroë. These pyramids were built at a steep angle. The pyramids held the tombs of the kings and the queen-mothers of Kush.

The queen-mothers of Kush are also known by their Roman name—*candaces*. Candaces remained powerful, sometimes more powerful than kings, throughout the history of Kush.

The Kushites created the **Meroitic script**, one of the world's first alphabets. Scholars have learned to read this alphabet but still don't understand the words of the Meroitic language written in it.

Analyze Images
Civilizations in Africa and the Fertile Crescent developed different writing systems that used either pictures, symbols, or marks to communicate ideas. **Synthesize Visual Information** Describe the differences between the three forms of writing.

Comparing Writing Systems

Hieroglyphs (Egypt)	Meroitic script (Meroë)	Cuneiform (Mesopotamia)

• Pictures of objects (hieroglyphs) to represent both letters and words	• Symbols to represent letters	• Wedge-shaped marks at first to form pictures; later to represent concepts
• Written on papyrus or carved in stone	• Written on papyrus or parchment or carved in stone	• Marks made in clay
• Developed over 5,000 years ago	• Developed over 2,100 years ago	• Developed over 5,000 years ago

RECENT SCHOLARSHIP

The Meroitic language was spoken in the area around Meroë, the capital of Kush, from about 300 BCE to about 400 CE. The language had two written forms, one based on hieroglyphics and the other based on a form of cursive writing, or script. Scholars have learned to read aloud the Meroitic script, but the language itself cannot be understood because no bilingual text that might serve as a translation has ever been found. When scholars finally understand the meaning behind the Meroitic script, their knowledge of Kush and its culture will be greatly expanded.

What Were Kush's Accomplishments?

Discuss the importance of architecture, writing, ironwork, and trade to the development of civilization in Kush.

Generate Explanations Why was it significant that Meroë was located on trade routes and near iron deposits? *(Its location and its resources such as wood and iron allowed Meroë to become wealthy and powerful through trade.)*

Compare and Contrast How were the pyramids the Kushites built different from Egyptian pyramids? *(Kushite pyramids had steeper sides.)*

Identify Main Ideas What purpose did the Kushite pyramids serve? *(They were tombs of the kings and queen-mothers of Kush.)*

Identify Supporting Details Where did Kush's ebony come from? *(West Africa)*

Identify Cause and Effect What effect did war with the Roman empire have on Kush? *(War with Rome weakened Kush.)*

Draw Conclusions According to the text, what was the main way Kush was linked to other countries? *(Kush was linked to other countries primarily through trade.)*

ANSWERS

Synthesize Visual Information *The Egyptian writing system at the left was composed mostly of pictograms; the Kush writing system in the middle was composed of different shaped lines; and the Mesopotamian writing system was composed of abstract shapes and lines.*

HSS 6.2.6, 6.2.8, 6.2.9; ELA RI.6.1; ELD.PI.C.10.a

SYNTHESIZE

Assess and Reteach Invite students to work in pairs or small groups to answer the Lesson Check questions 1–5. Review their responses. If they got any incorrect, use the Guiding Questions to discuss the lesson's main ideas, focusing on particular ideas they struggled with.

ACTIVE JOURNAL

Writing Workshop Have students complete the Lesson 3 Writing Task in their Active Journals. Students will update the thesis they wrote in Lesson 1. Remind students to consider new facts they learned in Lessons 2 and 3 as they update their theses.

DEMONSTRATE

ASSESSMENT **ONLINE LESSON QUIZ**

Assign the Online Lesson Quiz for this lesson if you haven't already done so. Students will be offered automatic remediation or enrichment based on their score.

DISCUSSION **DISCUSSION BOARD**

Post this question to the class on the Discussion Board:

Analyze Which achievement of the Kush civilization had the greatest effect on later history? Why? *(Sample answer: Learning to smelt iron ore to make tools and weapons had the greatest effect on later history. Stronger, more effective tools improved farming and architecture.)*

Analyze Images The abundant iron in Kush was used to make tools, weapons, and objects like this silver libation bowl found in the tomb of Netaklabah-Amon. **Infer** Why is iron a good material to use for making tools and weapons?

Kush's Links to Africa and the World Kush played an important role in ancient Africa. The kingdom may have controlled an area larger than the Egyptian empire. Kush had advanced ironworking technology. The Kushites traded iron goods, cloth, and gold with other African peoples. In return, the Kushites bought ebony and ivory from East and Central Africa. The Kushites also sold slaves from other parts of Africa to the Egyptians.

The Kushites also traded with Greek and Roman Egypt. Kushites sold ebony, ivory, gold, and iron goods and bought grains and cloth in Egypt. The Kushites used irrigation to grow more food for their busy cities, but they still had to trade to meet some of their need for food.

The ancient Greeks and Romans knew the Kushites for their metalworking skills, and they valued Kushite iron tools and weapons. Ports on the Red Sea allowed the Kushites to trade with countries as far away as India.

By the 200s CE, war with the Roman empire, which controlled Egypt, had weakened Kush. Meanwhile, desert peoples raided Kush's cities and disrupted its trade. Finally, in the 300s, Kush was conquered by the kingdom of Axum, centered in the present-day country of Ethiopia to the southeast.

Throughout its history, Kush had linked Africa south of the Sahara with other ancient civilizations. The Kushites created patterns of trade and farming that continued after the conquest by Axum. These traditions have continued in the region to this day.

READING CHECK **Understand Effects** What was the impact of Kush moving its capital to Meroë?

Lesson Check

HSS 6.2.6, 6.2.8, 6.2.9; ELA RI.6.1; ELD.PI.C.10.a

Practice Vocabulary

1. Describe the way **interdependence** had an affect on **commerce** in ancient Egypt.
2. What was different about Kush's **Meroitic script**?

Critical Thinking and Writing

3. **Understand Effects** How did trade cause culture and ideas to spread between Egypt and Kush?
4. **Draw Conclusions** How did trade benefit both Egypt and Kush?
5. **Infer** Why might the Kushites have depended more heavily on trade than the Egyptians?
6. **Writing Workshop: Update Your Thesis** Add details from Lesson 3 to your outline. Examine your outline for details that do not support your thesis. If necessary, update your thesis in your Active Journal to reflect the details in your outline.

ANSWERS

Infer *Iron was stronger than other kinds of metal; therefore, tools made from iron would last longer and could be used more effectively.*

Understand Effects *Meroë was easier to defend. It provided more water for farming, growing trees, and melting iron ore.*

LESSON CHECK

1. Egypt's interdependence through trade and commerce helped its economy. **DOK2**
2. It was a true alphabet. Its characters stood for sounds rather than ideas. **DOK2**
3. Trade brought the Kushites and Egyptians into closer contact with each other. **DOK2**
4. Both used trade to gain wealth and to obtain goods they could not produce locally. **DOK3**
5. The Kushites relied on trade for food, whereas the Egyptians did not. **DOK3**
6. Students should include relevant details and update their theses as necessary. **DOK1**

Analysis REP.1

Frame Questions

INTERACTIVE
Ask Questions

Use the primary and secondary sources as you follow these steps to frame questions.

1 **Identify your focus.** When studying a primary or secondary source about a place or event, begin by focusing on what the passage is about and what you are trying to learn. Use the "5WH" technique—ask "Who? What? Where? When? Why? and How?"—to help you. Based on the sources, what are some questions you might ask about the kingdom of Kush?

2 **Identify the information provided.** As you review sources, ask, "Which of my questions are answered by these sources?" Which of your questions about Kush are answered by the primary and secondary sources that appear here?

3 **Frame remaining questions.** Now think about what you still need to learn after you study your sources.

a. Which questions about Kush remain to be answered?

b. Which of your 5WH questions are not answered by the excerpt and photo?

4 **Plan your research.** Use your list of unanswered questions to decide how you will seek answers. Ask yourself, "What kinds of sources would help me answer these questions?"

Secondary Source

Kush had a long history of trade and other contacts with Egypt. But in the mid-700s BCE, a Kushite king conquered the Egyptian city of Thebes. The next king of Kush, Piye, expanded the Kushite empire by conquering one Egyptian city after another. Finally, Piye declared himself pharoah of a united Egypt and Kush.

Kush ruled Egypt for almost one hundred years. Kushite rulers promoted the traditional Egyptian ways that they had learned under earlier Pharoahs. They built temples to honor both Kushite and Egyptian gods. But the rulers of Kush could not maintain their power.

Primary Source

▲ These ruins of Kush pyramids can be found in present-day Sudan.

DIFFERENTIATED INSTRUCTION

Below Level Before practicing this skill, call on students to identify the words that form the 5WH strategy. *(Who? What? Where? When? Why? and How?)*

INTEGRATED ENGLISH LANGUAGE DEVELOPMENT

Emerging Support emerging English learners by providing them with 5WH questions that help them identify their focus, such as *What is the relationship between Egypt and Kush?*

Analysis REP.1

Analysis Skills
Frame Questions

LEARN

Preview the steps in the student text, and then play the video.

VIDEO **21ST CENTURY SKILLS**

Project the Ask Questions video in the 21st Century Skills Tutorial. Use the Quick Reference and Assessment to provide additional instruction on this skill.

PRACTICE

Have students practice the skill of framing questions by reading the sources on the student page. Follow the steps on the student page, providing the instruction and then asking students the questions.

As an alternative, you could form students into pairs or groups to perform the activity. Then invite students to share their questions based on the secondary source. Have students discuss which 5WH question is being used in each question.

ASSESS

To assess this skill, have students frame questions about the text and photographs from the previous topic, Civilizations and Peoples of the Fertile Crescent.

ANSWERS

1. Sample answers: Where was Kush located relative to Egypt? Who was the most powerful leader in the history of Kush? Why were pyramids in Kush different from those in Egypt?
2. Have students number their questions and make notes about whether the sources answer each question.
3. Possible answer: The question, "Why were pyramids in Kush different from Egypt?" is not answered in the text.
4. Possible answer: Online sources ending in .gov, .org, or .edu would be the most reliable for answering the question.

HSS 6.2.1, 6.2.2, 6.2.3, 6.2.5, 6.2.6, 6.2.7, 6.2.8, 6.2.9; ELA W.6.2; WHST.6.2; ELD. PI.A.2, PI.C.10.a

Review and Assessment

VISUAL REVIEW

Direct students' attention to the "Achievements of Egypt and Kush" chart. For each point listed, call on volunteers to explain how the achievement contributed to the development of Egypt or Kush.

Direct students' attention to the "Comparing Egypt and Kush" Venn diagram. Discuss as a class how the physical or human geography of Egypt and Kush contributed to each unique characteristic. Then focus on the characteristics shared by both regions.

READING REVIEW

WORKSHEET **TEACHER RESOURCES**

Have students who need additional support read the Lesson Summaries, available in Teacher Resources on the Realize Course.

GAMES **TOPIC MINI-GAMES**

For additional vocabulary practice, students can go online to access the Topic Mini-Games in Realize.

TOPIC 3

Review and Assessment

VISUAL REVIEW

Achievements of Egypt and Kush

Egypt	Kush
• Organized bureaucracy and taxation system • Strong pharaohs • Papyrus and hieroglyphic writing • Massive building projects • Calendar; scientific, and medical advances	• Vast trading network • Strong pharaohs • Meroitic script writing system one of world's first alphabets • Massive building projects • Ironworking center and skilled metal workers

Comparing Egypt and Kush

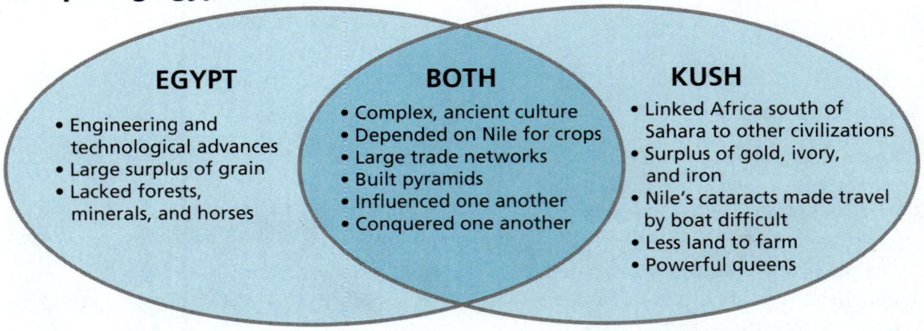

READING REVIEW

Use the Take Notes and Practice Vocabulary activities in your Active Journal to help you to review the topic.

INTERACTIVE

Practice vocabulary using the Topic Mini-Games.

Quest FINDINGS

Write your Monument Inscription

Get help for writing your message in your Active Journal.

ANSWERS

Vocabulary and Key Ideas

1. They are areas of rocky rapids that make travel by boat impossible. **DOK1**
2. Artisans were skilled handworkers who created handicrafts and luxury items. **DOK1**
3. Possible answer: The bureaucracy enabled Egypt's government to control different aspects of life across Egypt. **DOK1**
4. They enabled record keeping to take place and allowed knowledge to be passed from generation to generation. **DOK3**
5. Possible answer: pyramids and other engineering achievements; two calendars **DOK3**
6. Each had goods the other wanted or needed, and the two civilizations depended on each other to supply these goods. **DOK3**

Quest FINDINGS

Create Your Inscription

Have students complete their topic Quest by writing an inscription in their Active Journal. Remind students to follow the writing process steps: (1) prewrite; (2) draft; (3) share; (4) revise; and (5) present. **DOK4**

HSS 6.2.1, 6.2.2, 6.2.3, 6.2.5, 6.2.6, 6.2.7, 6.2.8, 6.2.9; ELA W.6.2, WHST.6.2; ELD.PI.A.2, PI.C.10.a

ASSESSMENT

Vocabulary and Key Ideas

1. **Define** What are the **cataracts** of the Nile?
2. **Describe** What did **artisans** in ancient Egypt and Kush do?
3. **Describe** Use the word **bureaucracy** in a sentence describing ancient Egyptian government.
4. **Recall** Why were **papyrus** and **hieroglyphics** important in ancient Egypt?
5. **Identify** Which achievements show Egyptians' mathematical abilities?
6. **Explain** Why is the relationship between Egypt and Nubia described as one of interdependence?
7. **Define** What is Meroitic script?

Critical Thinking and Writing

8. **Understand Central Ideas** Why did the ancient Egyptians want to control the Nile's flood waters?
9. **Cite Evidence** How did Hatshepsut build Egypt's wealth and power?
10. **Classify and Categorize** How were Mesopotamian cuneiform and Egyptian hieroglyphics similar?
11. **Compare and Contrast** How were the civilizations of ancient Egypt and Kush both similar and different?
12. **Revisit the Essential Question** Were Egyptian pharaohs great leaders? Explain.
13. **Writer's Workshop: Write an Explanatory Essay** Using the outline you created your Active Journal, answer the following question in a three-paragraph explanatory essay: How did geography affect the lives of ancient Egyptians and Kushites?

Analyze Primary Sources

14. For whom is the source below likely written?
    A. a king or pharaoh
    B. a young person
    C. a fisherman
    D. a sandalmaker

"The sandal maker is utterly wretched . . . I mention to you also the fisherman. He is more miserable than one of any other profession. . . . See, there is no office free from supervisors, except the scribe's. He is the supervisor! But if you understand writings, then it will be better for you than the professions which I have set before you."

—from *The Literature of the Ancient Egyptians*, standardized by Adolf Erman

Analyze Maps

Use the map at right to answer the following questions.

15. Which letter represents Lower Egypt? Why is this area known as Lower Egypt?
16. Which letter represents the Red Sea? Which continents does this sea separate?
17. Which letter represents the Mediterranean Sea? Which continent lies north of the Mediterranean Sea?

▼ Ancient Egypt and Kush

Review and Assessment 129

7. It is one of the oldest alphabets, used by the Kushites. **DOK1**

Critical Thinking and Writing

8. They wanted to reduce damage and be able to direct water to places that most needed it. **DOK1**
9. She sent traders to East Africa. They returned with wood, ivory, gold, and perfumes. **DOK1**
10. Both systems of writing used signs that represented sounds, and other signs that represented the meanings of words or phrases. **DOK3**
11. Both had similar ideas about kingship, built pyramids, depended on the Nile, and worshiped many different gods. Kush had closer links to other parts of Africa, better ironworking skills, and created its own alphabet. **DOK3**
12. Possible answer: Yes, they were great leaders because they made Egypt wealthy and powerful and built impressive structures. **DOK4**
13. Answers will vary, but they should discuss the influence of the Nile River and the desert conditions of Kush and Egypt. **DOK4**
14. B. **DOK3**
15. D. It's called Lower Egypt because it's at the mouth of the Nile River. **DOK2**
16. A. It separates Africa and Asia. **DOK1**
17. B. Europe **DOK1**

ASSESSMENT **TOPIC TEST**

For summative assessment, assign the Topic Test in Realize.

Early Civilizations of India

(3100 BCE–540 CE)

Pacing: Approximately 26 periods, 13 blocks	Resources: Student Edition	Resources: Active Journal	Resources: Online	Pacing	California Standards
CONNECT					
NBC LEARN VIDEO Indian Classical Dance in the Modern World			✓ (video)	10 min.	HSS 6.5.7
ESSENTIAL QUESTION ACTIVITY What Makes a Culture Endure?		✓	✓ (interactive)	10 min.	HSS 6.5.1, 6.5.2
OVERVIEW ACTIVITY: TIMELINE & MAP Early Civilizations of India		✓	✓ (interactive)	10 min.	HSS 6.5.1
Quest KICK OFF: Ask Questions	✓	✓		20 min.	HSS 6.5.7; Analysis REP.4; ELA W.6.7–9, WHST.6.7–9; ELD. P1.A.2, P1.C.9
INVESTIGATE					
LESSONS 1–7	See Lesson-at-a-Glance pages				
Quest INVESTIGATE: Quest Connections	✓	✓		20 min.	See Quest Kick Off
SYNTHESIZE					
WRITING WORKSHOP Write a Research Paper		✓	✓ (interactive)	30 min.	HSS 6.5.7; ELD.P1.A.2, P1.C.10.a; ELA W.6.4-5, 7–8; WHST.6.7–9
TOPIC MINI-GAMES Early Civilizations of India			✓ (interactive)	20 min.	HSS 6.5.1, 6.5.2, 6.5.3, 6.5.4, 6.5.5, 6.5.6, 6.5.7
Quest SOURCES: Conduct Research			✓ (interactive)	30 min.	See Quest Kick Off
DEMONSTRATE					
TOPIC REVIEW AND ASSESSMENT Early Civilizations of India	✓		✓ (interactive)	20 min.	
TOPIC TEST Early Civilizations of India			✓ (interactive)	30 min.	
Quest FINDINGS: Create a Travel Brochure	✓	✓	✓ (interactive)	30 min.	See Quest Kick Off

Quest

Each Quest is designed to reinforce the topic content through an inquiry arc that students work on throughout the topic. This topic's Quest is to Conduct Research to create a travel brochure for a trip to India. Students conduct research to learn more about the history and culture of India and then decide where people should visit.

Active Journal Resources

- Ask Questions
- Quest Connections
- Conduct Research
- Create a Travel Brochure

Quest Resources Online

- Project Contract
- Project Tracker
- Team Assessment
- Rubric for a Travel Brochure

Additional Resources

Support for Struggling Readers

- Reading Support, Teacher Resources
- Lesson Summaries, Teacher Resources
- English Language Development, Teacher Resources

Suggested Resources

- *Buddhism (World Religions)*, Don Nardo
- *Becoming Buddha: The Story of Siddhartha*, Whitney Stewart
- *Hanuman*, Erik Jendresen
- *Life in the Ancient Indus River Valley*, by Hazel Richardson
- *Science in Ancient India*, by Melissa Stewart
- *The Story of India* (PBS documentary, 2009

Beyond the Classroom

Use Online and Library Media Centers

Use a media center to gain online access to the resources of distant museums, such as the British Museum's *Ancient India* website, which offers online cultural, historical, and geographic exhibits. The Indian Government grants one-stop online access to 10 Indian museums, virtual exhibits, and other features on its *Museums of India* website. Specialist websites such as the online *RBI Monetary Museum*, hosted by the Reserve Bank of India, also provide insight into everyday life in ancient India. These experiences can help students grasp the scale and achievement ancient peoples and understand their customs and ways of life.

The Indus Valley Civilization

Objectives

Objective 1: Analyze how the environment influenced the Indus Valley civilization.

Objective 2: Describe the achievements of the Indus Valley civilization.

Objective 3: Explain why the Indus Valley civilization's politics, religion, and history remain a mystery.

	Resources: Student Edition	Resources: Active Journal	Resources: Online	Pacing (approx. 2 periods, 1 block)	California Standards
CONNECT					
VIDEO Indus Valley Achievements			✓	5 min.	HSS 6.5.1
START UP ACTIVITY Get Ready to Read	✓	✓	✓	5 min.	HSS 6.5.1
TAKE NOTES AND PRACTICE VOCABULARY		✓			
INVESTIGATE					
READ Lesson 1: The Indus Valley Civilization	✓	✓	✓	40 min.	HSS 6.5.1; ELA RI.6.2; ELD.PI.C.11a
QUICK ACTIVITY Museum Gallery		✓			
INTERACTIVE 3D Model Technology of the Indus Civilization			✓	10 min.	HSS 6.5.1
READING SUPPORT			✓		
SYNTHESIZE					
WRITING WORKSHOP Generate Questions to Focus Research	✓	✓	✓	10 min.	HSS 6.5.1; ELD. P1.A.2, P1.C.10.a
LESSON SUMMARY			✓		
DEMONSTRATE					
LESSON QUIZ			✓	10 min.	HSS 6.5.1

India's Vedic Age

Objectives

Objective 1: Summarize how connections between the Indian subcontinent and other regions increased during the Vedic period.

Objective 2: Discuss what the sacred hymns known as the Vedas teach us about religion and customs in ancient India.

Objective 3: Describe how the caste system that emerged in India divided groups based on birth and occupation.

	Resources: Student Edition	Resources: Active Journal	Resources: Online	Pacing (approx. 3 periods, 1.5 blocks)	California Standards
CONNECT					
VIDEO The Caste System			✓ (video)	5 min.	HSS 6.5.2, 6.5.4, 6.5.7
START UP ACTIVITY Get Ready to Read	✓	✓	✓ (book)	5 min.	
TAKE NOTES AND PRACTICE VOCABULARY		✓			
INVESTIGATE					
READ Lesson 2: India's Vedic Age	✓	✓	✓ (book)	40 min.	HSS 6.5.2, 6.5.4, 6.5.7; ELA SL.7.2, RH.7.7; ELD.PI.C.11b
INTERACTIVE GALLERY Vedic Era Gods		✓	✓ (interactive)	10 min.	HSS 6.5.1
ANALYSIS SKILLS Detect Historical Points of View	✓		✓ (book)	30 min.	HSS 6.5.2; Analysis REP.3; ELA RI.6.6
21ST CENTURY SKILLS TUTORIAL Compare Viewpoints			✓ (video)	10 min.	Analysis REP.3
READING SUPPORT			✓ (document)		
SYNTHESIZE					
WRITING WORKSHOP Generate Questions to Focus Research	✓		✓ (book)	10 min.	ELD.P1.A.2, P1.C.10.a
LESSON SUMMARY			✓ (document)		
DEMONSTRATE					
LESSON QUIZ			✓ (quiz)	10 min.	HSS 6.5.2, 6.5.7

TOPIC 4

Origins and Beliefs of Hinduism

	Resources: Student Edition	Resources: Active Journal	Resources: Online	Pacing (approx. 4.5 periods, 2.25 blocks)	California Standards
CONNECT					
VIDEO Hindu Traditions and Practices			●	5 min.	HSS 6.5.3, 6.5.7
START UP ACTIVITY Get Ready to Read	✓	✓	●	5 min.	
TAKE NOTES AND PRACTICE VOCABULARY		✓			
INVESTIGATE					
READ Lesson 3: Origins and Beliefs of Hinduism	✓	✓	●	95 min.	HSS 6.5.3, 6.5.7
QUICK ACTIVITY Rewriting Poetry		✓			
INTERACTIVE 3D MODEL Hindu Temple			●	10 min.	HSS 6.5.3
PRIMARY SOURCES The *Ramayana*	✓		●	40 min.	HSS 6.5.3, 6.5.7; ELA RI.6.3–5
INTERACTIVE PRIMARY SOURCES The *Bhagavad-Gita*			●	5 min.	HSS 6.5.3, 6.5.7; ELA RI.6.3–5
READING SUPPORT			●		
SYNTHESIZE					
WRITING WORKSHOP Find and Use Credible Sources	✓	✓	●	10 min.	HSS 6.5.3, 6.5.7; ELD.P1.A.2, P1.C.10.a
LESSON SUMMARY			●		
DEMONSTRATE					
LESSON QUIZ			●	10 min.	HSS 6.5.3, 6.5.7

Objectives

Objective 1: Describe how Hinduism grew out of the Vedas.

Objective 2: Describe what Hindus believe about Brahman.

Objective 3: Explain how Hinduism supported people and society in ancient India.

Objective 4: Summarize how Hinduism spread and what its lasting impact has been.

Origins and Beliefs of Buddhism

	Resources: Student Edition	Resources: Active Journal	Resources: Online	Pacing (approx. 4 periods, 2 blocks)	California Standards
CONNECT					
VIDEO Teachings and Spread of Buddhism			✓	5 min.	HSS 6.5.5
START UP ACTIVITY Get Ready to Read	✓	✓	✓	5 min.	HSS 6.5.5
TAKE NOTES AND PRACTICE VOCABULARY		✓			
INVESTIGATE					
READ Lesson 4: Origins and Beliefs of Buddhism	✓	✓	✓	80 min.	HSS 6.5.5
INTERACTIVE MAP The Origins and Beliefs of Buddhism			✓	10 min.	HSS 6.5.5
PRIMARY SOURCES *The Life or Legend of Gaudama*	✓		✓	40 min.	HSS 6.5.5; ELA RI.6.2-4, 6
READING SUPPORT			✓		
SYNTHESIZE					
WRITING WORKSHOP Support Ideas with Evidence	✓	✓	✓	10 min.	HSS 6.5.5; ELD. P1.A.2, P1.C.10.a
LESSON SUMMARY			✓		
DEMONSTRATE					
LESSON QUIZ			✓	10 min.	HSS 6.5.5

Objectives

Objective 1: Explain why the Buddha gave up a life of luxury and how he found enlightenment.

Objective 2: Discuss why Buddhists follow the eight-step path.

Objective 3: Describe how Buddhism supported those who followed the teaching of the Buddha.

Objective 4: Analyze how Buddhism spread.

The Maurya Empire Begins

Objectives

Objective 1: Describe how Chandragupta used military strategy to unite much of India for the first time.

Objective 2: Summarize how Chandragupta developed a bureaucracy, a tax system, and a system of spies to help rule his empire.

	Resources: Student Edition	Resources: Active Journal	Resources: Online	Pacing (approx. 3 periods, 1.5 blocks)	California Standards
CONNECT					
VIDEO Chandragupta Maurya's Rule			✓	5 min.	HSS 6.5.6
START UP ACTIVITY Get Ready to Read	✓	✓	✓	5 min.	HSS 6.5.6
TAKE NOTES AND PRACTICE VOCABULARY		✓			
INVESTIGATE					
READ Lesson 5: The Maurya Empire Begins	✓	✓	✓	40 min.	HSS 6.5.6
INTERACTIVE GALLERY Village Life in India			✓	10 min.	HSS 6.5
ANALYSIS SKILLS Assess Credibility of a Source	✓		✓	30 min.	HSS 6.5.6; Analysis REP.4; ELA W.6.8
21ST CENTURY SKILLS TUTORIAL Analyze Primary and Secondary Sources			✓	10 min.	HSS 6.5.6; Analysis REP.4; ELA W.6.8
READING SUPPORT			✓		
SYNTHESIZE					
WRITING WORKSHOP Cite Sources	✓	✓	✓	10 min.	HSS 6.5.6; ELD. P1.A.2, P1.C.10.a
LESSON SUMMARY			✓		
DEMONSTRATE					
LESSON QUIZ			✓	10 min.	HSS 6.5.6

Asoka's Rule

	Student Edition (Resources)	Active Journal (Resources)	Online (Resources)	Pacing approx. 2 periods, 1 block	California Standards
CONNECT					
VIDEO The Life of Ashoka			▶	5 min.	HSS 6.5.6
START UP ACTIVITY Get Ready to Read	✓	✓	📖	5 min.	HSS 6.5.6; ELD.II.B.2.a
TAKE NOTES AND PRACTICE VOCABULARY		✓			
INVESTIGATE					
READ Lesson 6: Asoka's Rule	✓	✓	📖	35 min.	HSS 6.5.6; ELD.PII.A.2a
INTERACTIVE TIMELINE Asoka's Life			👆	10 min.	HSS 6.5.6
INTERACTIVE PRIMARY SOURCES Edicts, Asoka			👆	5 min.	HSS 6.5.6; ELA RI.6.3–5
READING SUPPORT			📄		
SYNTHESIZE					
WRITING WORKSHOP Develop a Clear Thesis	✓	✓	📖	10 min.	HSS 6.5.6; ELD. P1.A.2, P1.C.10.a
LESSON SUMMARY			📄		
DEMONSTRATE					
LESSON QUIZ			☑	10 min.	HSS 6.5.6

Objectives

Objective 1: Explain why the emperor Asoka turned from war to peace.

Objective 2: Describe how Asoka promoted the growth of Buddhism and encouraged morality among his subjects.

Objective 3: Discuss how Buddhism supported Asoka's hopes for his empire.

TOPIC 4

The Gupta Empire

Objectives

Objective 1: Describe how the Gupta dynasty created the second major Indian empire.

Objective 2: Analyze how India made advances in the arts, science, and mathematics, including our modern system of numerals, during Gupta rule.

	Resources: Student Edition	Resources: Active Journal	Resources: Online	Pacing approx. 3 periods, 1.5 blocks	California Standards
CONNECT					
VIDEO The Golden Age of the Gupta			✓	5 min.	HSS 6.5.7
START UP ACTIVITY Get Ready to Read	✓	✓	✓	5 min.	HSS 6.5.7
TAKE NOTES AND PRACTICE VOCABULARY		✓			
INVESTIGATE					
READ The Gupta Empire	✓	✓	✓	40 min.	HSS 6.5.7; ELD. PII.A.2b
INTERACTIVE GALLERY A Golden Age in the Arts			✓	10 min.	HSS 6.5.7
ANALYSIS SKILLS Interpret Thematic Maps	✓	✓	✓	30 min.	HSS 6.5.5; Analysis CST.3; ELA RI.6.7
21ST CENTURY SKILLS TUTORIAL Read Special Purpose Maps			✓	10 min.	HSS 6.5.5; Analysis CST.3
READING SUPPORT			✓		
SYNTHESIZE					
WRITING WORKSHOP Write an Introduction	✓	✓	✓	10 min.	HSS 6.5.7; ELD. P1.A.2, P1.C.10.a
LESSON SUMMARY			✓		
DEMONSTRATE					
LESSON QUIZ			✓	10 min.	HSS 6.5.7

PEARSON realize™

Use the suite of online resources to

Enrich your instruction with topic and lesson videos and interactivities.

VIDEO

Assess and monitor student progress with automatic answer reporting for lesson prompts, lesson quizzes with remediation, and topic-level assessments.

ETEXT

ASSESSMENT

GAMES

Help struggling learners with tools built into the eText, reading support worksheets, lesson summaries, English Language Development exercises and more.

ETEXT

WORKSHEET

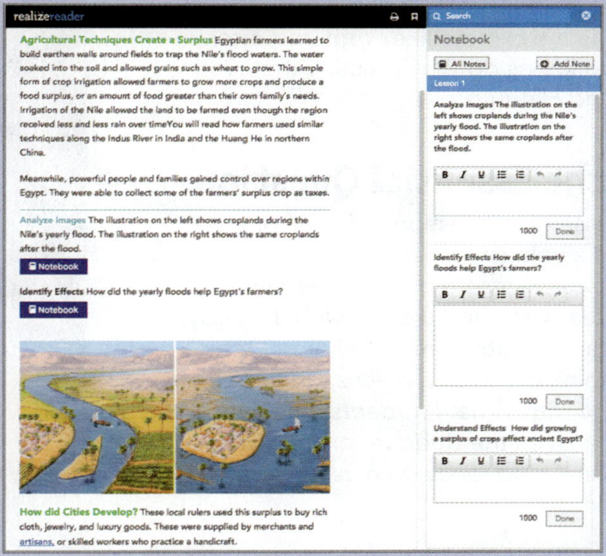

TOPIC 4

Early Civilizations of India (3100 BCE–540 CE)

HSS 6.5.1, 6.5.2, 6.5.3, 6.5.4, 6.5.5, 6.5.6, 6.5.7; Analysis CST.3, REP.4, REP.5

CONNECT

Introduction

At about the same time as the Egyptians were establishing their civilization on the Nile, another group of people also settled by a river. The Indus Valley in western India was home to a society that grew, developed, and then mysteriously disappeared. But other groups followed, founding religions, empires, and a society that still exists today.

Activate Prior Knowledge

Ask students to share what they know from TV shows, movies, or books about India; for instance, what do people traditionally wear in India, what do they eat, what animals live there? What is the climate like? *(hot and often rainy)* What religions do they practice there? *(Buddhism and Hinduism)*

Explore the Essential Question

Project the Essential Question activity from the course. Have a volunteer read the question. Discuss what elements from the ancient cultures they have already studied are still with us today, for example art, architecture, or religion. Ask students to think of people, places, or ideas they associate with India. *(Students may mention people such as the Buddha, places such as the Taj Mahal, and ideas such as nirvana and enlightenment.)*

ACTIVE JOURNAL

Essential Question Have students begin to explore the Essential Question in their Active Journals.

Make Generalizations Thousands of years from now, what do you think will have lasted from our civilization? *(Sample answers: art, architecture, everyday objects)*

TOPIC 4

Early Civilizations of India (3100 BCE–540 CE)

GO ONLINE to access your digital course

VIDEO
AUDIO
ETEXT
INTERACTIVE
WRITING
GAMES
WORKSHEET
ASSESSMENT

India's Early Civilizations

The early civilizations of India were nothing short of surprising. Emperors built vast empires. Two of the world's major religions developed in the region and spread throughout Asia and the rest of the world.

Explore The Essential Question

What makes a culture endure?

Indian cultural traditions created important thinkers and teachers, who founded schools of thought and religions that still endure today. How did this happen in an era of turmoil and conquest?

Unlock the Essential Question in your Active Journal.

130

ANALYZE VISUALS

Ask students what they think this building is. *(A temple, specifically a famous Hindu temple honoring the God Shiva.)* Shiva is the Hindu creator God. The temple is meant to bring Hindus closer to Shiva and to give them a place to perform the rituals, such as praying and burning incense. The temple is an example of two enduring aspects of culture: religion and architecture. Ask: Why do people make beautiful and elaborate buildings and art to honor their religion? *(to honor their God, to help people remember the importance of their religion)* Point out the tall tower. Ask: Why did the architect put it there? *(Most religions picture their gods as living above the sky. The tower is "reaching" to heaven.)*

HSS 6.5.1, 6.5.2, 6.5.3, 6.5.4, 6.5.5, 6.5.6, 6.5.7; Analysis CST.3, REP.4, REP.5

Read

about the empires of ancient India and their complex cultures.

Watch

NBC LEARN

BOUNCE TO ACTIVATE VIDEO

Indian Classical Dance in the Modern World

Learn about Indian arts that endure today.

▲ Brihadisvara Temple and Chandikesvara shrine, Tanjore, Tamil Nadu, India

RECOGNIZE CULTURAL AND EXPERIENTIAL BACKGROUNDS

Make use of your knowledge of students' lives to make connections between their own experiences, backgrounds, and Interests and the content of this Topic. If you have students whose ethnic heritage is related to the content of this Topic, make an effort to emphasize the contributions and achievements of this society and how it has enriched the world.

If appropriate, allow the students the opportunity to share cultural, ethnic, or linguistic traditions and knowledge from their experiences. If students have family experiences (such as travel to or family members who have lived in the region being studied), allow them to share relevant stories.

Watch

VIDEO NBC LEARN VIDEO

Project the topic opener video *Indian Classical Dance in the Modern World*, which shows traditional Indian dance and its origins. Ask: What is the purpose of the hand and eye movements used in the dance? *(to tell a story)*

Check Understanding Why does Sonali teach Indian American girls traditional dancing? *(to connect them to their ancient culture)*

Hypothesize Have students suggest other ways the girls might connect to their culture. *(sample answers: cooking, storytelling, religious practice)*

Read

Share these lesson previews with students.

Lesson 1 The Indus Valley Civilization
By the Indus River, people created a complex culture that later vanished.

Lesson 2 India's Vedic Age
Hinduism developed during the Vedic Age, along with a lasting literature and the beginnings of a social structure.

Lesson 3 Origins and Beliefs of Hinduism
Hindus live their lives based on beliefs such as reincarnation and karma.

Primary Sources: The *Ramayana*
This epic poem is the story of the noble hero Rama and his many adventures.

Lesson 4 Origins and Beliefs of Buddhism
Buddhism was born in India and is now practiced around the world.

Primary Sources: *The Life or Legend of Gaudama*
Stories from the Buddha's life help explain his teachings.

Lesson 5: Chandragupta oversaw the spread of the huge Maurya Empire.

Lesson 6: Asoka's conversion to Buddhism turned him from a warrior to a caring leader concerned for the welfare of his people.

Lesson 7: Chandra Gupta reunited India in an empire known for its artistic achievements.

TOPIC 4

HSS 6.5.1, 6.5.2, 6.5.3, 6.5.4, 6.5.5, 6.5.6, 6.5.7; Analysis CST.3, REP.4, REP.5

What Happened and When?

Have students examine the timeline. Ask: How many years are shown on the timeline? *(4,000)* Ask: How long did the Indus Valley civilization last? *(about 700 years)* Ask: About when did Buddhism and Classical Hinduism develop? *(around 500s BCE)* Which Indian empire extended into the Common Era? *(Gupta)*

ACTIVE JOURNAL

Timeline Skills Students can also use the Timeline Skills activity in their Active Journals to locate and add events.

INTERACTIVE **INTERACTIVE TIMELINE**

Display the topic Interactive Topic Timeline for the class. Have volunteers read the entries. Discuss with students how long Indian civilizations lasted compared with the others they have studied—Egypt and Mesopotamian.

Analyze Timelines What other civilizations were developing at the same time as the Maurya and Gupta Empires in India? *(Chinese, Greek, and Roman)*

TOPIC 4

Early Civilizations of India (3100 BCE–540 CE)

Learn more about ancient India by making your own map and timeline in your Active Journal.

INTERACTIVE
Topic Map

Where was ancient India?

These ancient civilizations and empires were located on the Indian subcontinent, which today includes India, Pakistan, Bangladesh, Nepal, Bhutan, Afghanistan, and Sri Lanka.

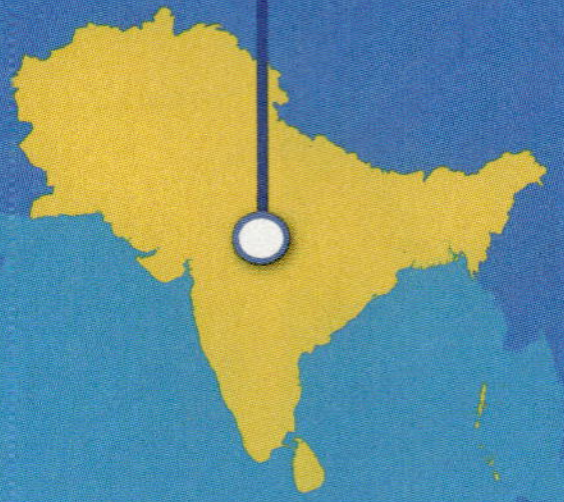

INTERACTIVE
Topic Timeline

What happened and when?

You may think that most innovation has happened in the last hundred years. You'd be wrong. Thousands of years ago, civilizations were growing, changing, and making new discoveries. Explore the timeline to see what was happening in ancient India and around the world.

TOPIC EVENTS

- 2600 BCE Indus Saraswati civilization reaches its peak.
- 1900 BCE Indus Saraswati civilization begins to break down.
- 1600 BCE Vedic period emerges.

3000 BCE | 2500 BCE | 2000 BCE | 1500 BCE

WORLD EVENTS

- 2630 BCE The first pyramid is built in Egypt.
- 2000 BCE The Middle Bronze Age begins.
- 1600 BCE Mycenaean culture develops in Greece.

132 TOPIC 4 • Early Civilizations of India

DIFFERENTIATED INSTRUCTION

Special Education Have students stand up and form a map of India with some students representing the mountains, some the rivers, and some the oceans. Point out the continent's triangular shape.

Below Level Place a large paper outline map of India on an easel or on the board (or have students draw one depending on ability). While students look at map in the book ask: Who can draw in the Himalaya mountains? Provide a pencil for a student to draw in the mountains. Others may come up and add or erase to correct the map. Repeat with rivers, plateau, ocean and other features.

Advanced Have students skim the topic to find out the durations of the Indian civilizations cited on the timeline. Then have them create a bar graph comparing the durations.

HSS 6.5.1, 6.5.2, 6.5.3, 6.5.4, 6.5.5, 6.5.6, 6.5.7; Analysis CST.3, REP.4, REP.5

Who will you meet?

Siddhartha Gautama, the Buddha

Chandragupta Maurya, who united India

Asoka, a powerful emperor who gave up war and chose peace.

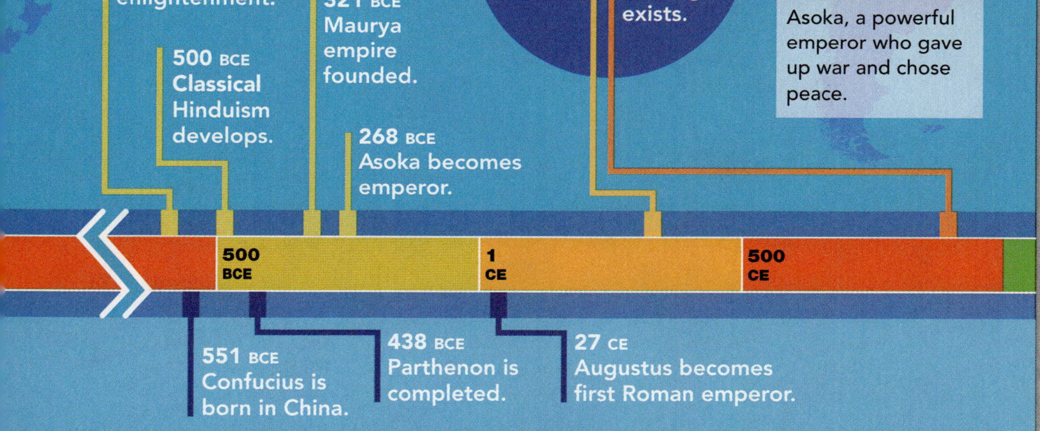

133

COMMON MISCONCEPTIONS

Indus Valley Accomplishments
Students may think that people who lived so far away and so far in the past must have been primitive and unintelligent. The idea that our own time is superior to any other is a common, but mistaken idea.

The Indian civilizations had cities, writing, and technology. Evidence shows the people of these civilizations laid out their cities in precise geometric patterns. Elaborate temple-like buildings show signs of organized religion and skill in architecture. They traded with other groups, created literature and art, and understood mathematics. They used accurate weights and measures. Smart human beings have been making and using new discoveries for thousands of years.

Where Was Ancient India?

Direct students' attention to the map of India. Ask: Where was ancient India? *(on the Indian subcontinent).* Ask: What surrounds India? *(mountains and oceans)* A *subcontinent* is a large landmass cut off from the neighboring land. Ask: What makes India a subcontinent? *(the Himalaya mountains)*

ACTIVE JOURNAL

Map Skills Have students use the Map Skills activity in their Active Journals to locate and name the important land features of the Indian subcontinent.

Analyze Maps Ask: Where are the rivers located? *(in the north)* Ask: Why do you think the rivers are important? *(Like most ancient civilizations, the Indian civilizations formed near rivers.)*

INTERACTIVE — INTERACTIVE MAP

Display the Interactive Topic Map. Work through the map to learn more about the geography of South Asia. Note that the first civilizations in India were in the northwest corner of the subcontinent. Discuss how the locations of these civilizations compare with those of other river civilizations they have studied.

Draw Conclusions Ask: How do you think the rivers and mountains affected the development of Indian civilizations? *(The rivers provided water and opened them to trade from the south. The mountains cut them off from the land to the north.*

Who Will You Meet?

Many students access historical materials best through the stories of the people who made them. Preview these key people that students will encounter in the topic. Read the short description of each, and then conduct a poll asking students which figure they are most interested in. Record the results on the board. Then ask volunteers why they are interested in a particular figure. *(Sample answers: the Buddha, because he taught people how to find peace; Chandragupta Maurya, because he ruled a huge empire. Asoka; because he gave up war for peace.)*

TOPIC 4

HSS 6.5.7; Analysis REP.4; ELA W.7–9. WHST.6.7–9; ELD.P1.A.2, P1.C.9

Quest
Project-Based Learning Inquiry

A Trip Through India

Quest Kick Off

In this Quest, students will use the student edition, other sources, and their Active Journals to create a travel brochure about the land, people, and culture of India.

1 Ask Questions

Launch the Quest by discussing the Guiding Question as a class. Have students generate questions in their Journals they will need to answer to accomplish the Quest.

2 Investigate

As they read the lessons, remind students to look for and respond to the Quest Connections in the student text that provide clues to their Quest. They should also identify and record two connections of their own.

Suggestion: If students are struggling to identify their own connections, suggest they think about the civilizations of ancient India and what evidence of those civilizations and their cultures can still be seen in India today.

3 Conduct Research

Find and Use Evidence As students complete the topic, have them identify sources they can draw on to complete their Quest. Remind students to find a variety of reliable sources that support their travel brochure. Direct them to their Active Journals for help working with their team and finding good sources.

Suggestion: If students need help with the Conduct Research step, refer them to the Analysis Skills feature following Lesson 5, Assess Credibility of a Source.

4 Create a Travel Brochure

When students complete the topic, have them return to the Quest, which can be used as a performance-based authentic assessment. To complete the Quest, they should (1) choose pictures and illustrations, (2) write a draft, (3) design a layout for the text and illustrations, (4) share with a partner, (5) revise the draft based on feedback, and (6) publish the brochure. **DOK4**

Quest
Project-Based Learning Inquiry

HSS 6.5.7; Analysis REP.4; ELA W.7–9, WHST.6.7–9; ELD.P1.A.2, P1.C.9

A Trip Through India

Quest KICK OFF

You have the amazing opportunity to lead a tour group to India. You get to plan the entire trip!

Where should you visit?

What cultural experiences should not be missed on a visit to India? Explore the essential question "What makes a culture endure?" in this Quest.

1 Ask Questions

India is a large country with a complex history. There are many reasons to visit. Write a list of questions you think someone visiting India for the first time may have about India. Write the questions in your Active Journal.

2 Investigate

As you read this topic, look for Quest CONNECTIONS that provide information on different sites in India. Capture notes in your Active Journal.

3 Conduct Research

Next, do more research about places to visit and things to do in India. Take notes in your Active Journal and describe their historic and cultural significance.

Quest FINDINGS

4 Create a Travel Brochure

People look at brochures to plan travel. At the end of the topic, you'll create a brochure of historical and cultural things to do and see in India. Your brochure should include a travel schedule with information about each of the sites you'll visit. Get help for creating your travel brochure in your Active Journal.

▲ On a trip to India you might see Indians celebrating their culture during one of many festivals.

DIFFERENTIATED INSTRUCTION

Below Level Help students to select pictures by writing questions on the board: What place is this? What details tell you where it is? What does it tell us about India? Model the process by projecting a picture. Have them jot down notes to use to write the brochure. Students who need further help may be paired with more advanced classmates.

INTEGRATED ENGLISH LANGUAGE DEVELOPMENT

Emerging Instead of writing a full travel brochure, encourage English learners to find photos of historical places and cultural activities in India. For each photo, have students write a short caption.

LESSON 1

HSS 6.5.1; ELA RI.6.2

The Indus Valley Civilization

GET READY TO READ

START UP

Examine the photo of the Indus River. What can you predict about the Indus Valley civilization based on what you know about the development of other ancient civilizations in river valleys?

GUIDING QUESTIONS

- How did the environment influence the Indus Valley civilization?
- What were the achievements of the Indus Valley civilization?
- Why do the Indus Valley civilization politics, religion, and history remain a mystery?

TAKE NOTES

Literacy Skills: Identify Main Idea and Details

Use the graphic organizer in your Active Journal to take notes as you read the lesson.

PRACTICE VOCABULARY

Use the vocabulary activity in your Active Journal to practice the vocabulary words.

Vocabulary		Academic Vocabulary
subcontinent	granary	achievement
river system	citadel	evidence
monsoon		

The first civilizations arose near rivers. One such civilization was in South Asia. Its people farmed along the Indus River. Farmers grew plenty of food, and populations grew. In time, some of the people settled in towns and cities and formed governments.

What Is the Indian Subcontinent?

Geographers divide the continent of Asia into regions. One of those regions is South Asia. It looks like a huge triangle jutting out into the Indian Ocean. Today, it includes the countries of India, Pakistan, Bangladesh, Sri Lanka, Maldives, Nepal, and Bhutan. India is by far the biggest country in the region.

For much of its history, all of South Asia was known simply as India. It is still called the Indian subcontinent. A **subcontinent** is a large landmass that is set apart from the rest of the continent. The Indian subcontinent stretches almost 2,000 miles from north to south. In some places, it is nearly as wide from east to west. The subcontinent is separated from the rest of Asia by the towering Himalayas and Hindu Kush, two mountain ranges to the north.

HSS 6.5.1; ELA RI.6.2

The Indus Valley Civilization

CONNECT

GET READY TO READ

ETEXT START UP

Project the Start Up Activity. As students enter the classroom and get seated, ask them to examine the photo of the Indus River. Remind them of the other river valley civilizations they have studied.

Make Predictions Ask students to make predictions about the Indus Valley civilization based on their previous knowledge. *(Sample answers: The people would be farmers. They would develop trade.)*

Distinguish If you were a farmer new to the Indus Valley, at what place in the picture would you start your farm? Why? *(Sample answer: the area that is flatter because it would be easier to plow)*

After completing the Start Up activity, project the Lesson Opener or direct students to their textbooks. Preview the lesson by working through the Get Ready to Read items with the class. Remind students to pay close attention to the Guiding Questions as they read the lesson.

ACTIVE JOURNAL

Take Notes Have students use the lesson literacy skills graphic organizer in their Active Journals to take notes as they read the lesson.

Practice Vocabulary Have students complete the activity in their Active Journals to build their vocabulary.

VIDEO VIDEO

Assign the lesson video as homework.

PRACTICE VOCABULARY

Have students use the correct vocabulary term or terms to complete the following sentences: Because it is separated from Asia by the Himalaya mountains, India is called a (subcontinent). The Indus people built a (citadel) to protect themselves. Farmers store crops in a (granary). In the Indian climate, the (monsoon) provides water for crops. The water that supplies the Indus Valley is a (river system). Reinforce the terms during the lesson using the teaching notes.

Have students locate and pronounce the academic vocabulary in the lesson margins. Provide sample sentences that clarify meaning.

achievement: Winning an athletic competition is quite an achievement.

evidence: The evidence proves the suspect committed the crime.

WORKSHEET **TEACHER RESOURCES**

Have students who need additional support use the following worksheets from the Teacher Resources on the course:

- **Reading Support**
- **English Language Development**
- **Lesson Summary**

INVESTIGATE

What Is the Indian Subcontinent?

In order for a civilization to grow, its farmers must able to produce surplus food. Because the Indus Valley was so fertile, they developed an advanced civilization with technology, art, and architecture.

Summarize What were two of the Indus civilization's achievements and how did they benefit the people? *(Sample answers: Mounds of earth protected them from floods. Brick sewers kept the city clean. Weights and measures made trade possible.)*

Identify Draw students' attention to the Indus Valley on the map (in the northwest of the subcontinent). Ask: What kind of land lies to the southeast of the river valley? *(a desert)*

Explain How does this fact explain the importance of the monsoon? *(With a desert so near, the valley could dry out quickly without the monsoon rains, and the people could starve.)* What advantage did living near mountains give the valley people? *(Melting snow provided water for the river.)*

ANSWERS

Region *the Himalayas and the Hindu Kush mountain ranges*

Infer *Sample answer: They most likely settled along the coasts and rivers and in the lower elevations.*

Identify Main Ideas *They provided water for growing crops, which led to a surplus of food.*

The Indian Subcontinent: Physical Geography

GEOGRAPHY SKILLS

The Indian subcontinent is separated from the rest of Asia by seas and mountains.

1. **Region** What are the names of the physical features of South Asia that make the region a subcontinent?
2. **Infer** In what parts of the subcontinent did the people of ancient India most likely settle?

River Systems The Indus River flows across the northwestern part of the subcontinent. The Indus forms part of a **river system**, or a main river and all of the other rivers and streams that drain into it. Another river, which is dry, but flowed parallel to the Indus, was the Saraswati. Recently, archaeologists have found almost 600 towns and villages buried in sand along course of this now dry river.

India's first civilization grew around the valleys of the Indus and Saraswati rivers. This civilization developed in an area that is dry most of the year. When the river flooded, it left behind very rich soil. River water let farmers harvest plentiful crops. These crops fed the cities of the civilization.

To the east, the Ganges River flows more than 1,500 miles across the northern part of the subcontinent. Its floods created a huge, fertile plain. After the Indus Saraswati civilization died out, the Ganges Plain became the center of Indian civilization.

INTERACTIVE

Technology of the Indus Valley

Climate Much of the Indian subcontinent has a tropical climate. Seasonal winds, known as **monsoons**, help shape life in this region. In the winter, dry monsoon winds blow from the land to the sea. Little rain falls. In the summer, wet winds from the ocean blow onto the land. They bring rain, which provides water for crops and a welcome break from the intense heat.

For much of its history, Indian agriculture depended on the summer monsoon. If the rains came on time, all was well. If the rains came late or not at all, crops died and people could starve.

READING CHECK **Identify Main Ideas** How did rivers and monsoons support the development of India's first civilizations?

CURRICULUM CONNECTIONS: ENGLISH/LANGUAGE ARTS

Monsoon Poetry The monsoon has inspired many songs and poems. They are sung at festivals to welcome the much-needed rains. This is from an ancient Tamil poem: "While sacred lightnings flash from every point… While the sore sorrow of the fervent heat hides itself… it sounds forth in mighty grace as a drum… and the tender drops of sweet unfailing grace distill."

CURRICULUM CONNECTIONS: SCIENCE

Monsoon India's October and November are characterized by the northeast, or retreating, monsoon, which brings mild, dry air to most of the country but rain to the south. During the southwest monsoon, rainfall is unpredictable and intense. Meteorologists try to determine when the rains will arrive—usually early June—to help farmers know when to plant crops.

136 Lesson 4.1 • The Indus Valley Civilization

Indus Valley Civilization

Farmers began growing crops in hills near the Indus river system around 7000 BCE. With a steady food supply, the population grew. After 3000 BCE, cities began to develop on the broad plains of the Indus Valley. By about 2500 BCE, these cities were the centers of the advanced Indus Valley civilization. However, by around 1700 BCE, the civilization had largely disappeared.

Archaeologists have discovered most of what we know about the Indus Valley civilization. In the 1920s, they discovered the ruins of two great cities: Harappa and Mohenjo-Daro. Since then, archaeologists have found more than a thousand other towns and villages from this civilization.

Technology Indus Valley cities were well planned and organized. The people of the Indus Valley built thick walls around their cities. They also built huge raised mounds of earth and brick in their cities. During times of flooding, these mounds remained above water.

Many houses in these cities had a bathroom and toilet. Wastewater from houses flowed into brick-lined sewage channels. These were the world's first citywide sewer systems. A trash chute in many houses led to a bin in the street.

Many of the **achievements** of the Indus Valley people showed an advanced knowledge of mathematics. Their cities were built with wide, straight streets in a grid pattern. They had an advanced system of weights and measurements using multiples of ten, like the modern metric system.

Farming The dry region of northerwest India could not always depend on the monsoon rains. Therefore, farmers built irrigation channels and ditches. These brought river water to the wheat and barley fields. Some

Quick Activity

Explore artifacts of the Indus Valley civilization in your Active Journal.

Academic Vocabulary
achievement • *n.*, accomplishment that requires effort or skill

▼ Mohenjo-Daro, the largest of the Indus Valley civilization's cities, grew because farmers produced a surplus of food.

INTERACTIVE CHART

Technology of the Indus Civilization

Display the Interactive Chart: Technology of the Indus Civilization for the class. Working as a class, complete the chart by having a volunteer place each tile and then identifying which category it belongs in.

ACTIVE CLASSROOM

Act It Out Divide the class into groups and send the groups to different areas of the room. Assign each group the objects or practices on one of the tiles. Have the groups work together to act out a scene in which the object is used or the practice carried out.

Indus Valley Civilization

Discuss how the environment of the Indus Valley influenced the lives of its people.

ACTIVE JOURNAL

Quick Activity Have students work in pairs to use their Active Journals to explore artifacts of the Indus Valley civilization. Then invite them to share the results with the class.

ELD TIP For the Quick Activity, pair emerging or expanding students with fluent speakers to state their opinions about the artifacts. Rather than asking students to share with the entire class, invite them to share with another pair of students.

DIFFERENTIATED INSTRUCTION

Below Level On a map of India have students draw wavy lines to represent the winds from northeast mountains and the southeast ocean. Discuss the importance of the wet wind and the dangers of the dry wind.

Advanced In groups, have students look up the weather science behind the monsoon (air masses moved to collide by pressure, temperature, humidity and other factors). They will create an oral presentation with charts explaining how monsoons are formed and why they do not always bring rain.

Special Education Ask students what the weather is like in the summer and the winter. Contrast monsoon weather with your local climate. Talk about dry weather, rain, wind, and sun.

Check Understanding Discuss how the Indus Valley river system facilitated trade with other river valley civilizations. Ask: With which cultures did the Indus Valley trade? *(Egypt and Mesopotamia)* Ask: What made trade possible? *(river and sea transportation)*

Steps in a Process Ask students to describe the process by which the river valley societies reached the stage of trading with each other. *(Farms produced surplus food; cities produced surplus products; people developed trade to use their surplus to acquire things they couldn't produce themselves.)*

scholars think that these farmers stored their surplus crops in a **granary**, or special building used to hold grain. They may have been the first farmers to grow cotton for making cloth.

Farmers also raised cattle, sheep, goats, and chickens for food. They used oxen, or cattle, to pull carts. Animals seem to have been important to the Indus people. They carved wooden animals and painted pictures of animals on pottery.

Trade The Indus Valley environment was rich in resources for trade. Indus Valley jewelers made beautiful jewelry from precious stones. Traders sold this jewelry as far away as Mesopotamia, where they could travel by sea. Traders sold cotton cloth woven in the Indus Valley. They also sold teak, a valuable wood from a tree that grows in India. Indus Valley cities prospered from trade.

Indus Valley traders used stone seals with writing to identify their goods. They stamped their seals on soft clay squares attached to their goods. Accurate weights and measures helped promote trade.

Sumerian writers mentioned trade with people who probably came from the Indus Valley. Trade spread ideas between these two civilizations.

READING CHECK **Identify Main Ideas** How did the environment contribute to the development of the Indus Valley civilization?

GEOGRAPHY SKILLS

The Indus Valley civilization was connected to Egypt and Mesopotamia by a network of overland and sea routes.

1. **Movement** How did Mesopotamian traders get to the Indus Valley by water?
2. **Use Visual Evidence** Why were there no trade routes from the Indus Valley that headed to the east?

Indus Trade Routes

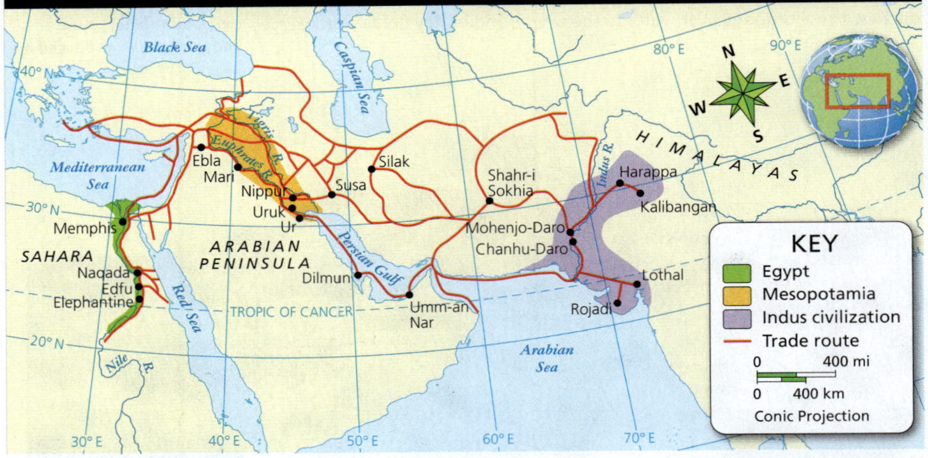

ANSWERS

Movement *by travelling through the Persian Gulf and Arabian Sea by ship*

Use Visual Evidence *Sample response: The Himalayas most likely blocked eastern trade routes.*

Identify Main Ideas *Sample response: The environment of the Indus River valley provided water to irrigate farmland. Successful farming led to a surplus of crops that helped the civilizations grow. The fertile environment also produced resources that the civilizations could trade.*

INTEGRATED ENGLISH LANGUAGE DEVELOPMENT

Productive Read the section Government and Religion aloud. Write these expressions on the board: *I think that . . . In my opinion, . . . I believe that . . .* Pair students with fluent speakers to share opinions about what kind of government the Indus Valley people had using those expressions.

Emerging Read the section Government and Religion aloud. Provide students with these expressions: *I think that . . . In my opinion, . . .* In pairs, have students use evidence in the text and the expressions to share opinions about the kind of government the Indus Valley people had.

Expanding Pair students to share opinions one of the following aspects of Indus Valley civilization: forms of government, religion, or writing. Have students use evidence in the text to support their opinions.

What Mysteries Surround the Indus Valley Civilization?

Artifacts and ruins of many buildings have been found in the Indus Valley. They provide a lot of information. But scholars still have many questions about this ancient civilization. They want to know more about its rulers, religion, and writing. They wonder about the reasons why it disappeared and where its people went.

Analyze Images Traders from the Indus Valley used seals like these. **Use Visual Information** What do you think the animal symbols meant?

Government and Religion

Clearly, the people of the Indus Valley were well organized. Their cities show a surprising level of planning. They all used a common system of weights and measures. These facts suggest that the Indus Valley people had a strong central government. Yet no royal statues or tombs have been found. This makes it seem unlikely that kings ruled the Indus Valley. Based on the available evidence, it just isn't possible to know for sure what kind of government the Indus Valley had.

Most cities had a huge **citadel**, or fortified area. The walled citadel was built on a raised platform of earth and brick that could have protected it from floodwaters or attackers. Scholars are not sure, but the citadel may have been a center of government, a place to lead religious ceremonies, or both.

Religion is another part of the Indus Valley civilization about which little is known. Scholars have found no direct evidence of temples and no clear sign of activity led by religious leaders.

However, some Indus Valley statues and small carvings have features that seem to show practices of Hinduism, a religion that developed later in this region. Some of the artifacts share characteristics of statues of Hindu Gods, though the connection is still debated. Also, some Indus Valley carvings look like people meditating or offering a formal greeting, important practices in Hinduism today.

Writing Scholars have not yet discovered how to read the symbols found on the stone seals and pottery of the Indus Valley. There are too few examples of each symbol to be sure of its meaning. Most experts think that these marks are a form of writing. However, they do not know if these markings are names, records of sales, or something else.

ELD.PI.C.11a

Bridging Pair students to share opinions about forms of government, religion, or writing in Indus Valley society. Have each student use evidence in the text to persuade his or her partner to agree with each opinion.

WORKSHEET **TEACHER RESOURCES**

For additional IELD support addressing these standards, have students complete the Lesson ELD activity from the Teacher Resources found on the course.

Apply Concepts Draw students' attention to the trade route map. Ask: What physical barriers would the Indus Saraswati merchants have to overcome to trade with Egypt? *(mountains, oceans, alternating between land and sea travel)* Ask: How might their technology have helped them overcome these barriers? *(Sample answer: Accurate measures and building skills could be used to make ships and wagons.)*

What Mysteries Surround the Indus Valley Civilization?

Around 1700 BCE the Indus Saraswati civilization began to fade. Eventually, the cities were abandoned. No one knows exactly why this happened.

Analyze Images Have students write details about each artifact, what each artifact tells them about life in ancient India, and one question about each artifact. Invite them to share what they wrote with the class.

ANSWERS

Use Visual Information *Answers will vary, may include that they symbolize the region from which the traders came or that each symbol identified a specific trader.*

HSS 6.5.1; ELA RI.6.2; ELD.P1.A.2, P1.C.10.a

SYNTHESIZE

Assess and Reteach Divide students into groups of three or four to cooperate to complete the Lesson Check questions 1–5. When they have finished, invite students to share their answers with the class. Review their responses. If they got any incorrect, use the Guiding Questions to discuss the lesson's main ideas, emphasizing the concepts students did not understand.

ACTIVE JOURNAL

Writing Workshop Have students complete the Lesson 1 Writing Task in their Active Journals. Students will write three or four questions about Indus Valley technology. Solicit questions from students about the assignment and monitor their progress, as some students may have trouble formulating their thoughts into questions.

DEMONSTRATE

ASSESSMENT **ONLINE LESSON QUIZ**

Assign the Online Lesson Quiz for this lesson if you haven't already done so. Students will be offered automatic remediation or enrichment based on their score.

DISCUSSION **DISCUSSION BOARD**

Post this question to the class on the Discussion Board.

Integrate Information Which theory about what happened to the Indus Valley civilization is best supported by the evidence? *(Sample answer: Drought, because India has often suffered from drought.)*

ANSWERS

Identify Cause and Effect *Sample response: There are many ideas that are related to the environment. They include disease, lack of forest cover, overgrazing by cattle, a salt buildup in the soil, a major earthquake, and climate changes resulting in drought.*

▲ One explanation for the disappearance of the Indus civilization is a long-term drought. Droughts still challenge the Indian subcontinent.

Why Did the Indus Civilization Disappear? The greatest mystery is what caused this civilization to disappear. Sometime before 1700 BCE, the Indus Valley people began to abandon their cities. The civilization declined rapidly after that. No one knows why.

There are many possible explanations. Some **evidence** suggests that standing water in drains may have bred mosquitos that spread disease and weakened Indus Valley populations. Indus Valley people may also have stripped forests of trees, leaving them without wood for building or fuel. A lack of forest cover could have caused severe floods that damaged Indus Valley cities. Their cattle may have overgrazed the land, leaving bare soil. Smaller herds could have led to starvation. Salt could also have built up in the soil, making it difficult to grow crops. Another possibility is that a major earthquake wiped out the population.

Some historians think that climate change may have brought an end to the civilization. Years of drought could have dried up the rivers and made it impossible to feed city dwellers. The most widespread theory says that many people finally moved away towards the Ganges, where the rains were more regular.

Academic Vocabulary
evidence • *n.*, information used to prove something

READING CHECK **Identify Cause and Effect** Different possibilities exist for why the Indus civilization disappeared. Which of these were related to environmental changes?

Lesson Check

HSS 6.5.1; ELA RI.6.2; ELD.P1.A.2, P1.C.10.a

Practice Vocabulary

1. Explain why India is called a **subcontinent**.
2. How was a **granary** used?

Critical Thinking and Writing

3. **Identify Main Ideas** How did ancient farmers use the water of the Indus river system to help grow crops?
4. **Classify and Categorize** What were some innovations of the Indus Valley civilization?
5. **Compare and Contrast** What are some similarities and differences between the Indus Valley civilization and other ancient river valley civilizations?
6. **Writing Workshop: Generate Questions to Focus Research** Write three to four questions in your Active Journal about technological innovations in ancient India. These questions will help you focus your research on the topic of technological innovations in ancient India for a research paper you will write at the end of the topic.

LESSON CHECK

1. It is a large landmass set apart from the main continent of Asia. **DOK1**
2. to store surplus grain **DOK1**
3. The floods deposited rich soil; farmers made irrigation channels to water their fields. **DOK1**
4. They had houses with bathrooms and trash chutes and a sewage system. They created an advanced system of weights and measures. **DOK2**
5. All grew near rivers, used irrigation for farming, and built cities. The Indus Valley had a larger river and well-planned cities, but no tombs for their leaders. No one has deciphered their writing yet. **DOK3**
6. Students should write three to four questions on technological innovations. **DOK3**

140 Lesson 4.1 • The Indus Valley Civilization

HSS 6.5.2, 6.5.4, 6.5.7

India's Vedic Age

BOUNCE TO ACTIVATE
VIDEO

GET READY TO READ

START UP

Examine the carving of the god Indra atop a mythical beast. What details do you notice?

GUIDING QUESTIONS

- During the Vedic period, how did connections between the Indian subcontinent and other regions increase?
- What do the sacred hymns known as the Vedas teach us about religion and customs in ancient India?
- How did the varnas and jatis develop into the caste system?

TAKE NOTES

Literacy Skills: Summarize

Use the graphic organizer in your Active Journal to take notes as you read the lesson.

PRACTICE VOCABULARY

Use the vocabulary activity in your Active Journal to practice the vocabulary words.

Vocabulary		Academic Vocabulary
Veda	varna	migrate
caste	jati	status

After 2000 BCE, another group of people lived in the Indus Saraswati region. They called themselves Aryans Scholars often refer to them as Indo-Aryans. These peoples may have brought with them beliefs and practices that mixed with local groups. This idea is based on the fact they spoke Sanskrit, an Indo-Aryan language. Sanskrit is also the language in which the ancient Indo-Aryans composed religious hymns and poetry. These hymns are known as Vedas and are the reason this period of history is called the Vedic Age.

Who Were the Indo-Aryans and How Did They Live?

Historians have taken different views on the origins of the Indo-Aryans. In the past, historians accepted the Aryan Invasion Theory. This theory held that the Indo-Aryans were nomadic warriors who crossed the mountains into India. They used horse-drawn chariots and iron weapons to defeat the local people. This theory has proven to be false, however.

PRACTICE VOCABULARY

Write each word on the board and explain it. Have students repeat each word. Ask for or provide a comparison for each to something students already know: The Vedas are (Indo-Aryan holy books). Another term for caste is (social group). A varna is a group based on (skill). A jati is a group based on (occupation).

Have students locate and pronounce the academic vocabulary in the lesson margins. Provide sample sentences that clarify meaning.

migrate: Groups of people migrate because they cannot live well where they are.

status: Officers have higher status than the soldiers they command.

HSS 6.5.2, 6.5.4, 6.5.7

India's Vedic Age

CONNECT

GET READY TO READ

ETEXT START UP

Project the Start Up Activity. As students enter the classroom and are seated, ask them to examine the photo of the God Indra carved into the wall of a temple and identify the details they notice.

Use Evidence Have students record the details they notice. *(Possible answers: The God is seated and may be smiling. He wears a hat or helmet. He is on top of a platform that sits on the head of a creature with a large head. There are many decorations.)* Have students share their findings with classmates.

Infer Ask students what clues about the Vedic religion they see in the photo. Ask: What did people value? *(art, craftsmanship, worship)*

After completing the Start Up activity, project the Lesson Opener or direct students to their textbooks. Preview the lesson by working through the Get Ready to Read items with the class. Remind students to pay close attention to the Guiding Questions as they read the lesson.

ACTIVE JOURNAL

Take Notes Have students use the lesson literacy skills graphic organizer in their Active Journals to take notes as they read the lesson.

Practice Vocabulary Have students complete the activity in their Active Journals to build their vocabulary.

VIDEO VIDEO

Assign the lesson video as homework.

WORKSHEET **TEACHER RESOURCES**

Have students who need additional support use the following worksheets from the Teacher Resources on the course:

- **Reading Support**
- **English Language Development**
- **Lesson Summary**

INVESTIGATE

Who Were the Indo-Aryans and How Did They Live?

Discuss the theories about the presence of Indo-Aryans in India.

Locate Direct students' attention to the map showing the route probably taken by the Indo-Aryans to get to India. Ask: What barrier did they need to cross? *(the Hindu Kush mountains)*

Infer Ask: What would they need to cross the mountains? *(Sample answers: courage, physical strength, warm clothes, possibly tools or horses)* Ask: How could these assets help them connect with other cultures later on? *(Sample answers: They were good travelers—strong, adaptable, adventurous.)*

ANSWERS

Movement *Sample response: Nomadic herders would want to migrate to the area if they could find more or better grazing for their cattle.*

Draw Conclusions *in the fertile valleys and along the rivers or northern India*

Others have argued that the Aryans were India's original inhabitants. They say that if the Indo-Aryans came from a region outside of India, the Vedas would refer to it. The Vedas, however, do not make any mention of such a place.

More recently, scholars suggest a third theory, which suggests Indo-Aryans were originally from what is now Afghanistan and Central Asia. Over many centuries, they **migrated** into India with their livestock, mixed with local people and adopted local beliefs. Local people adopted the Indo-Aryan language. Over time, people across a large part of the Indian subcontinent came to see themselves as Indo-Aryans.

Academic Vocabulary
migrate • *v.*, to move from one region to another in order to live there

GEOGRAPHY SKILLS

Recent theories suggest that the Indo-Aryans migrated into South Asia through passes in the mountains of the Hindu Kush.

1. **Movement** Why would nomads raising cattle on dry grasslands want to migrate into South Asia?
2. **Draw Conclusions** Where in India do you think the Indo-Aryans settled?

What are the Vedas? The Indo-Aryans composed the Vedas. There are four Vedas: the Rig-Veda, Sama-Veda, Yajur-Veda, and Atharva-Veda. Each **Veda** is a collection of hundreds, and even thousands, of sacred hymns.

Ancient Indians, usually priests, memorized and sang or chanted these verses during ceremonies. The Vedas called upon people to make offerings to their gods. Typical offerings might be barley, butter, or milk.

For a thousand years, Indians passed the Vedas down by word of mouth. They sang or chanted them in Sanskrit, which is a distant relative of English. Today, Sanskrit remains a language of sacred literature. Sanskrit is the ancestor of many modern Indian languages, including Hindi and Urdu. Eventually, Indians began to collect the Vedas and put them into writing.

The oldest of the Vedas is the Rig Veda. It includes about 10,000 hymns. One passage, "The truth is one; the wise call it by many names," is considered a key part of Hindu philosophy. Most of

Indo-Aryan Migration

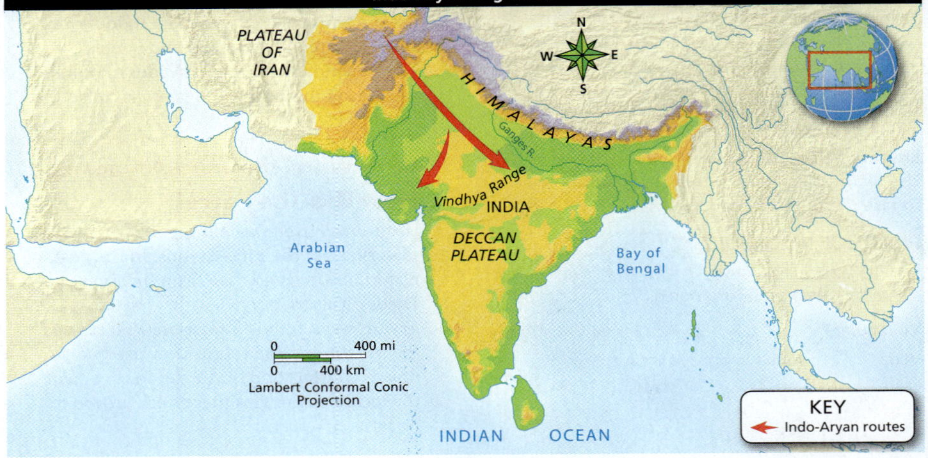

INTEGRATED ENGLISH LANGUAGE DEVELOPMENT

Productive Students express opinions after reading Who Were the Indo-Aryans and How Did They Live?

Emerging Read the text aloud, writing the three theories of Indo-Aryan origins on the board. Model ways to express opinions: *Maybe they . . . It is possible that they . . .* Pair students to express their own views using those expressions.

Expanding Model the following expressions, and discuss differences in certainty: *Maybe the Indo-Aryans were original inhabitants. They probably were nomads. They must not have been invaders.* Pair students to express opinions on Indo-Aryan origins using *maybe*, *probably*, or *must*.

Bridging Pair students to express opinions on Indo-Aryan origins. Write the following words on the board:

the hymns also praise various Gods and Goddesses representing natural forces such as the sky, sun, and fire. These deities are viewed as different forms of a single, divine absolute. Another Veda is dedicated to an earth Goddess. She is praised for her bounty. The Vedas are considered to have influenced and and contributed to the development of Hinduism, and are still used in some Hindu rituals today.

How Did the Indo-Aryans Live? The Rig-Veda and the other sacred texts provide a record not only of the Vedic religion, but also of the people themselves. Most of what we know about Indo-Aryan life on the Indian subcontinent during this period comes from the Vedas.

Though scholars do not know the origins of Indo-Aryans, the Vedas show that they lived as herders. They raised cattle, horses, goats, and sheep. Cattle held special importance for them since the herds provided both food and clothing. Early on, ancient Indians measured their wealth by the size of their cattle herds.

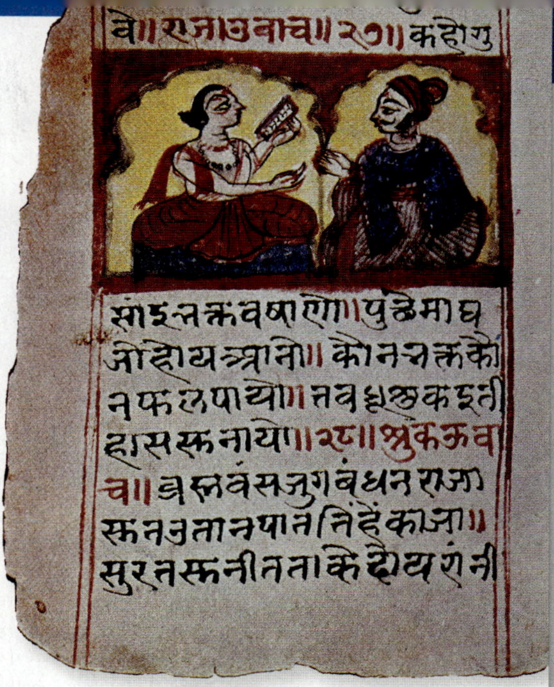

▲ Page of Sanskrit from the Rig-Veda, or "Knowledge of the Hymns of Praise"

The Vedas also mention that the Aryans practiced agriculture, and grew several different crops including barley, wheat, and lentils. The Rig-Veda mentions water channels dug from the banks of the Saraswati and other rivers to irrigate these crops. Milk and its products were a very important part of their diet. As the Indo-Aryans began to focus more on growing crops, however, they gave up dairy farming as their main source of food.

The Vedas show that the Indo-Aryans found joy in their day-to-day lives. They loved music and dancing. They held chariot races and enjoyed gambling. They also questioned the meaning of life and existence through their texts. The following passage from a hymn in the Rig-Veda describes the connection between the human body and a divine power:

Primary Source

The human body is the temple of God. One who kindles the light of awareness within gets true light. The sacred flame of your inner shrine is constantly bright. The experience of unity is the fulfillment of human endeavors. The mysteries of life are revealed.

—Rig-Veda

INTERACTIVE

Vedic Gods

INTERACTIVE **INTERACTIVE GALLERY**

Vedic Era Gods

Display the Interactive Gallery: Vedic Era Gods for the class. Click the images of the Gods to show their connection to later Hinduism. Have volunteers read the entries. Ask student pairs to take turns describing the traits of each God.

ACTIVE CLASSROOM

Have students spend three minutes jotting down their response to this question on a sticky note: Why do you think these aspects of nature of human life were so important to the Indo-Aryans?

Interpret Ask a volunteer to read aloud the quotation from the Rig-Veda on the page. Ask: Based on this passage, what was important to the Indo-Aryans? *(Possible answers: unity, understanding the mysteries of life, feeling a sacred connection to the Gods.)*

ELD.PI.C.11b

probably, might, certainly, could, and definitely. Have students temper their statements by using one of those words to express differing levels of certainly as they express their ideas.

WORKSHEET **TEACHER RESOURCES**

For additional IELD support addressing these standards, have students complete the Lesson ELD activity from the Teacher Resources found on the course.

Compare and Contrast How was Indo-Aryan society organized politically? *(into a dozen kingdoms and republics)* Discuss as a class how this is similar to or different from the history of civilizations that have already been studied.

Identify Main Ideas How did southern India differ from other areas? *(Societies in the southern part of India has their own culture and spoke Tamil and other languages. When Sanskrit-speaking people settled there, the groups created new customs blending both cultures.)*

The Caste System

The caste system organizes people by their occupations. Ask: In what other ways can groups of people be organized? *(by education, income, religion, where they live)* Ask: How does the **caste** system work? *(Caste influenced specific rules of behavior for people, such as where they lived, how they earned a living, whom they could eat with, and whom they could marry.)*

Analyze Images Look at the photograph on the page. Ask: What is the occupation of these men? *(herders)* Ask: To what caste would they belong under the caste system? *(Sudra)* Ask: What advantage might there be in belonging to the Sudra caste? *(People all have similar jobs, they know, understand, and can help one another.)*

ELD TIP Pair emerging and expanding students with fluent speakers to discuss ideas about how the caste system developed, expressing the probability that their explanation is correct.

Analyze Images The early Indo-Aryans tended flocks of livestock, much like these modern Indian goat herders. **Draw Conclusions** Why did the Indo-Aryans stop living as nomads and begin settling down in villages?

The Growth of Vedic Civilization Over many hundreds of years, Vedic civilization slowly spread eastward across the humid and fertile Ganges Plain. The Indo-Aryans carved farms and villages from the forests. Some villages grew into towns and cities.

At first, communities were divided into clans, or groups of people who believe that they share a common ancestor. Each clan had a chief.

Later, clans joined together to form republics. Leaders made decisions in an assembly, but over time powerful leaders gained control and made themselves kings. By 500 BCE, more than a dozen kingdoms and republics covered northern, western, and central India.

As Vedic civilization grew, societies in the southern part of India also developed their own culture. People in this part spoke languages like Tamil, which had no similarity to Sanskrit. Over time, Sanskrit-speaking people eventually mingled with these groups, creating new customs based on a mixture of the different groups.

READING CHECK **Summarize** What is the importance of Sanskrit?

The Caste System

In ancient Indian society, a system of social classes based on birth developed. These evolved over many centuries, and eventually became known as the caste system. They became closely linked to Indian notions of a proper society. While the social groupings might not have begun this way, over time, they became associated with Indian notions of purity. Today, **caste** is a fixed social class into which a person is born.

Over many centuries in India and other parts of the Indian subcontinent, caste became a prominent part of people's lives. One's caste influenced specific rules of behavior, such as where people lived, how they earned a living, whom they could eat with, and whom they could marry.

144 Lesson 4.2 • India's Vedic Age

DIFFERENTIATED INSTRUCTION

Below Level Ask students to create a web diagram with "Indo-Aryans" in the center oval and in the outer ovals, descriptive phrases about the Vedas, Indo-Aryan daily life, farming, the spread of their culture, and the caste system.

Advanced research varni and jati in the Vedic age and present a short oral report to the class.

Special Education To help students understand lesson content, write the following categories on the board and ask students to say one idea about each: herders, farmers, religion in early India.

ANSWERS

Draw Conclusions *Sample response: They began to focus more on growing crops so they settled in one place.*

Summarize *Sanskrit was the language of the Vedic culture and a distant relative of English.*

How Was Caste Determined? Most scholars agree that the caste system did not emerge until much later in Indian history, but its roots are in ancient India, when two social groupings emerged. The Vedas identify four **varnas**, or groupings based on one's skill. The varnas were Brahmins, who were known as priests and teachers; Ksathriyas, or the rulers and warriors; Vaishyas, who were landowners, bankers, and merchants; and Sudras, who did farm work and other manual work.

Another grouping was by occupation. The term for an occupation-based caste is **jati**, meaning "birth group." Some scholars think that these castes began as extended families who may have had a family business or occupation. Today, many people refer to jati when they are referring to caste. All across South Asia, thousands of jatis developed, each with its own rules and restrictions.

By 500 CE or so, another group outside of the jatis emerged. They were known as Untouchables, and later Dalits, who did work considered impure and had a low social **status**. These inequalities did not derive from Hindu teachings, but over time, many Indians of all faiths came to identify with one caste or another.

Academic Vocabulary
status • *adj.*, position in society

How Did the Caste System Develop? Scholars are not sure how the caste system developed. They aren't sure whether the status-based varnas or the occupation-based jatis developed first. Most say the fixed nature of caste might be a more recent development in Indian history.

At first, caste may have been mainly based on a person's occupation or family membership. Children might have been able to move into a different caste than their parents. In fact, the evidence suggests that families could sometimes move from one varna to another. Hindu sages like Valmiki and Vyasa were not Brahmins, while some who were born into Vaisya or Sudra families became warriors.

Over hundreds of years, castes seem to have become more rigid. By the time the Portuguese arrived in India in the 15th century, many people across the Indian subcontinent identified with a caste. Each caste was

The Caste System

Caste	Occupation Groups
Brahmins	Priests
Kshatriyas	Rulers and warriors
Vaishyas	Landowners, bankers, and merchants
Sudras	Farmers, laborers, and servants
Dalits	People who performed dirty jobs

Analyze Charts The caste system grouped ancient Indians into an occupation-based caste called jati and a religious status caste called varna. **Summarize** What did these types of groupings have in common?

Compare and Contrast How did **varnas** differ from **jatis**? *(Possible answers: Varnas were based on broad skills; jatis were based on specific occupations and includes many rules and regulations for each. There were only five varnas including Dalits but there were thousands of jatis.)*

Analyze Charts Direct students to examine the chart called "The Caste System." Ask: Why do you think priests are placed above rulers in the **caste** system? *(Priests are believed to be in contact with the Gods, and Gods are greater than human beings.)*

Infer Have volunteers read aloud the section, "How Did the Caste System Develop?" Ask, why is the origin of this system so unclear? *(Possible answers: It began a long time ago, so its origins are difficult to see clearly. It is something that developed slowly across society rather than being imposed by a ruler, so its origins are difficult to pin down.)*

Compare and Contrast How was the caste system different in the 15th century than it had been earlier? *(It was more rigid by then.)* How is it different now than it was in the 15th century? *(Possible answers: Many Hindus in India and the United States no longer identify themselves with a caste. Discrimination based on caste is illegal in India now. People's jobs no longer depend on their caste.)*

HISTORY BACKGROUND

Ancient Indian Texts The Vedas and other Sanskrit literature were written over hundreds of years. While Sanskrit texts, both religious and secular, continued to be produced during the following empires, texts in Old Tamil, an even older language, also began to appear around 300 BCE.

ANSWERS

Summarize *Both are based on how or in what way people work.*

HSS 6.5.2, 6.5.4, 6.5.7; ELD.P1.A.2, P1.C.10.a

SYNTHESIZE

Have students work in pairs to complete the Lesson Check questions 1–5. When they are finished have them share their answers with the class. Review their responses. If they got any incorrect, use the Guiding Questions to discuss the lesson's main ideas, emphasizing the concepts students did not understand.

ACTIVE JOURNAL

Writing Workshop Have students complete the Lesson 2 Writing Task in their Active Journals. Students will write two more questions about Indus Valley technology. Solicit questions from students about the assignment and monitor their progress, as some students may have trouble formulating their thoughts into questions.

DEMONSTRATE

ASSESSMENT **ONLINE LESSON QUIZ**

Assign the Online Lesson Quiz for this lesson if you haven't already done so. Students will be offered automatic remediation or enrichment based on their score.

DISCUSSION **DISCUSSION BOARD**

Post this question to the class on the Discussion Board.

Integrate Information Why might the caste system have become rigid over time? *(Sample answers: It may have been easier to keep order if social classes were fixed. Some people may have felt more secure knowing their place in society.)*

Analyze Images Meira Kumar, a Dalit, was elected India's first woman parliamentary speaker. **Draw Conclusions** What was the significance of her election?

given a particular status. People were born into a caste and could not leave it. Though Hindu leaders preached against the fixed nature of the caste system, many Hindus in the Indian subcontinent eventually accepted caste as a part of daily life.

In time, the caste system became the basis for India's social structure. By 1900, almost everyone in the Indian subcontinent identified with a caste, though some groups, such as Muslims, Christians, and Sikhs, did not have as many caste rules as Hindus did. The system brought both costs and benefits. For instance, the system limited people's individual freedom. The patterns of their lives were fixed at birth.

However, some believe that the caste system helped India develop. They feel that it brought stability to Indian society. Indian goods became famous because caste members perfected their skills. The system also allowed different groups to follow their own beliefs.

In India today, the law forbids caste discrimination. Many Hindus in India and the United States do not identify themselves with a caste. People's jobs no longer depend on their caste alone. Brahmins or Kshatriyas may work with their hands. Dalits may work as professionals.

READING CHECK **Summarize** What was the caste system?

Lesson Check

HSS 6.5.2, 6.5.4, 6.5.7; ELD.P1.A.2, P1.C.10.a

Practice Vocabulary

1. Explain why the **Vedas** are important.
2. Explain the meaning of the term ***caste*** in Indian history.

Critical Thinking and Writing

3. **Identify Evidence** What evidence would offer proof for the different theories about the origins of the Indo-Aryans?
4. **Compare and Contrast** What are the similarities and differences between jati and varna?
5. **Support Ideas with Evidence** Why can Sanskrit be described as an important Indo-Aryan tradition?
6. **Writing Workshop: Generate Questions to Focus Research** Write two questions in your Active Journal to focus your research for the research paper you will write about technological innovations in ancient India at the end of the topic.

146 Lesson 4.2 • India's Vedic Age

ANSWERS

Draw Conclusions *Sample response: Kumar was a Dalit, a member of a very low status group. Her election suggests that India's caste system has weakened and people are able to move up and succeed no matter what their caste.*

Summarize *The caste system is an Indian system of social classes based on birth.*

LESSON CHECK

1. They provide a record of Indo-Aryan life and beliefs; they are still read today. **DOK2**
2. It is a social class into which a person is born. **DOK1**
3. Sample responses: writings depicting Indo-Aryan migration; Indo-artifacts in Afghanistan or Central Asia **DOK3**
4. Both are social groupings. Hundreds of jatis are grouped by occupation. Four varnas are grouped by skills. **DOK2**
5. Sanskrit is the language of the Vedas, first as an oral tradition and later written down. It is the ancestor of many modern Indian languages. **DOK3**
6. Students should write additional questions in their Active Journals related to technological innovations. **DOK3**

HSS 6.5.2; Analysis REP.5; ELA RI.6.6

Detect Historical Points of View

INTERACTIVE
Compare Viewpoints

Use the secondary source and follow these steps to detect historical points of view.

1 Identify the topic or issue. What is the author writing about?

- **a.** What is the overall topic that the author is addressing?
- **b.** What is his point of view about the subject?
- **c.** What might be an opposing point of view to this one?

2 Determine the author's position on the topic or issue. What is the author's position? Often, an author will state his or her overall point of view in a topic sentence. What is the author's position on the subject? Are there topic sentences or summary statements that state his point of view? What are they?

3 Identify important background information about the passage. Identifying the author's background and the time and place in which the author lived can help you analyze a historical point of view.

- **a.** What information is given about the author's area of research? Is he an expert on the topic?
- **b.** When was the passage written? Does that affect the argument? How?

4 Analyze the possible impact of historical background on the author's beliefs. People's beliefs and opinions may be influenced by the context in which the author is writing. The context is what is happening in the world around the author. Ask, "How might the context have affected this author?"

Secondary Source

Several species of *Equus*, including the true horse, existed in the Indus-Sarasvati civilization, probably in small numbers. Some of them may have entered India over a much longer time span than is usually granted, in the course of the Indus-Sarasvati civilization's interactions with neighbouring areas, but certainly not through any Aryan invasion or migration. There was no epoch exhibiting a sudden, first-time introduction of the animal.

—Michel Danino, quoted in *Archaeology Online* in "The Horse and the Aryan Debate by Michel Danino."

DIFFERENTIATED INSTRUCTION

Below Level Prepare the class by asking questions, such as these: What is an opinion? *(one person's idea about a subject)* What makes one opinion more correct than another? *(the person knows a lot about the subject)* Read the secondary source. As a class review the steps and answer the questions.

INTEGRATED ENGLISH LANGUAGE DEVELOPMENT

Emerging Support emerging students by breaking the texts into chunks. Then, ask simple questions, such as, What is the passage about? *(the presence of horses in India and how that is connected to the arrival of Indo-Aryans)* What does Michel Danino believe? *(Horses were in the region before Indo-Aryans arrived, so they could not have introduced horses suddenly.)*

HSS 6.5.2; Analysis REP.5; ELA RI.6.6

Analysis Skills
Detect Historical Points of View

LEARN

Preview the steps in the student text with students, and then play the video.

VIDEO **21ST CENTURY SKILLS**

Project the Read Compare Viewpoints video in the 21st Century Skills Tutorial. Use the Quick Reference and Assessment to provide additional instruction in the skill.

PRACTICE

Tell students they are going to read a secondary source about the introduction of the horse in the Indus civilization, called Indus-Sarasvati in this source. Have them Think-Pair-Share to answer the questions, working together to resolve any differences. Review students' answers as a class.

ASSESS

To assess this skill, have students state the author's main point in his own words.

ANSWERS

1. a. the existence of horses in the Indus-Sarasvati civilization
b. The Indus-Sarasvati had several species of horses
c. Sample answer: The Indus civilization did not have horses.

2. He thinks horses were present in this civilization and not introduced later.

3. a. Danino's area of research is not stated, but he seems to offer evidence.
b. The date of the source is unknown; possibly research since then has uncovered clearer evidence.

4. Sample answer: Danino writes in the context of whether the Indo-Aryans migrated into India. His point of view is influenced by that debate.

HSS 6.5.3, 6.5.7

Origins and Beliefs of Hinduism

CONNECT

GET READY TO READ

ETEXT **START UP**

Project the Start Up Activity. As students enter the classroom and are seated, ask them to examine the photo of the Hindu temple.

Identify Ask students to describe what they see *(bright colors, elaborate arches, towers)*

Infer Ask: Why do you think the builders decorated the temple with such bright colors and intricate architecture? *(to honor their Gods/religion, to impress people with its beauty)*

After completing the Start Up activity, project the Lesson Opener or direct students to their textbooks. Preview the lesson by working through the Get Ready to Read items with the class. Remind students to pay close attention to the Guiding Questions as they read the lesson.

ACTIVE JOURNAL

Take Notes Have students use the lesson literacy skills graphic organizer in their Active Journals to take notes as they read the lesson.

Practice Vocabulary Have students complete the activity in their Active Journals to build their vocabulary.

VIDEO **VIDEO**

Assign the lesson video as homework.

LESSON 3

HSS 6.5.3, 6.5.7

Origins and Beliefs of Hinduism

GET READY TO READ

START UP

Examine the photo of the Hindu temple. What does it suggest to you about Hinduism?

GUIDING QUESTIONS

- How did Hinduism grow out of the Vedas?
- How did Hinduism support people and society in ancient India?
- How did Hinduism spread and what has been its lasting impact?

TAKE NOTES

Literacy Skills: Sequence

Use the graphic organizer in your Active Journal to take notes as you read the lesson.

PRACTICE VOCABULARY

Use the vocabulary activity in your Active Journal to practice the vocabulary words.

Vocabulary		Academic Vocabulary
Brahmanism	karma	issue
guru	dharma	devote
Brahman	ahimsa	
reincarnation	moksha	

Hinduism is one of the oldest religions in the world and the third largest, with about 1 billion followers. It began in India during the Vedic age, growing slowly and changing into a more popular Hinduism. It is the majority religion of India, Nepal, and Mauritius, and has existed in countries like Indonesia, Vietnam, Cambodia, and Thailand for many centuries.

What Are the Roots of Hinduism?

For thousands of years, Hinduism has been the main religion of India and widely practiced in South and Southeast Asia. Hinduism is based on the word *Hindu*, which is what early Persian traders called the people they encountered in India.

Vedic Age Beliefs and Practices As you have learned, the Vedas are the subcontinent's oldest known religious texts. They were memorized and passed on by word of mouth. They were later written down, though the oral tradition remained important.

PRACTICE VOCABULARY

Since most of the vocabulary words will be unfamiliar to students, write them on the board and explain them one at a time. Ask students to repeat them aloud. Help students' understanding by classifying or associating each word: Brahmanism/religion, guru/Brahman, karma/reincarnation, dharma/ahimsa, moksha/afterlife. Reinforce the terms during the lesson using the teaching notes.

Have students locate and pronounce the academic vocabulary in the lesson margins. Provide sample sentences that clarify meaning.

issue: Discuss the issues before making a decision.

devote: He devotes a lot of time to reading.

The Vedas contain hymns to many Gods and Goddesses. They also describe religious rituals, including offerings of food to specific Gods such as Agni, the God of fire, or Vayu, the God of the wind. These Gods later became part of popular Hinduism, taking lesser roles as other deities such as Vishnu, Shiva, and Devi became more widely worshipped.

What Was Early Hinduism Like? During the Vedic Age, early Hinduism, also known by some scholars as Brahmanism, was a religion based on rituals, particularly sacrifices to the gods. The term Brahmanism referred to Brahman, the all-powerful deity that Hindus worship. Much of the ritual authority was given to priests, or Brahmins, though recall that varnas might not have been fixed at that time. Scholars say that non-Brahmin sages also had influence during this period. However, because early Hinduism relied on ritual, it was limited to priests.

READING CHECK **Understand Effects** How is Hinduism related to the Vedas?

How Did Classical Hinduism Develop?

Beginning about or before 500 BCE, Hindu beliefs began to change. Some thinkers moved away from ritual and more openly embraced the concept of Brahman, a single spiritual power that existed beyond the gods of the Vedas and resided in all things. Other people began asking questions such as: Why are we born? How should we live? What happens to us when we die? Hinduism evolved from Indians' efforts to answer these difficult questions.

Did you know?

Early travelers to the Indus Valley, beginning with the Greeks and Persians, spoke of its inhabitants as "Hindu" (Greek: *'indoi'*).

Analyze Images A leader teaches holy law in this painting from the 1800s. **Recognize Multiple Causes** What role did gurus have in developing Hinduism?

CURRICULUM CONNECTION: ENGLISH/LANGUAGE ARTS

Sanskrit Sanskrit is part of the Indo-European language family of languages, a family that includes English as well as Latin and Greek. According to linguists, the earliest Indo-European language first divided into separate languages about 4500 BCE. Some words across the Indo-European languages are still similar. For example, the Sanskrit word *pitar* relates to *pater* in Latin and Greek, *vater* in German, and *father* in English.

WORKSHEET **TEACHER RESOURCES**

Have students who need additional support use the following worksheets from the Teacher Resources on the course:

- **Reading Support**
- **English Language Development**
- **Lesson Summary**

INVESTIGATE

What Are the Roots of Hinduism?

Hinduism developed from the religion of the Vedic age, called by some **Brahmanism**. There are many other gods in Hinduism, but Brahman is considered the universal life force.

Identify Ask: How was religious life organized in early Hinduism? *(rituals, particularly sacrifices to the Gods)*

Formulate Questions Ask: What questions would you ask a believer in Hinduism? *(Do you have a special day of worship? What is it like inside a temple? Have you read any of the Hindu religious texts? What part did you like best?)*

How Did Classical Hinduism Develop?

Hinduism began to change in response to what are called universal questions like these: Why do humans exist? What is out purpose in life? What happens when we die? Discuss how most religions address these issues in some form.

ANSWERS

Understand Effects *The Vedas contain hymns to Gods and Goddesses and rituals that are also part of Hinduism.*

Recognize Multiple Causes *The gurus were teachers who contemplated Hindu concepts and spread understanding of those ideas among their students.*

Contrast Ask: In what way were the new ideas in Hinduism different from early Hinduism? *(Some thinkers moved toward the concept of Brahman, a single spiritual power; people began asking spiritual questions about life and death.)*

Draw Conclusions Ask: Why are the most important Hindu scriptures written in verse? *(Sample answers: Verse was the style of ancient authors. Verse makes it easier for people to remember the moral teachings of Hindu literature.)*

Contrast Ask: What is the difference between the Upanishads and the Vedas? *(Only priests were allowed to read the Vedas. Anyone could read the Upanishads.)* Ask: Why is this difference important? *(People are more likely to understand moral teachings that they can read and think about for themselves.)*

ACTIVE JOURNAL

Quick Activity Have students work in pairs to complete the Hindu Poetry activity in their Journals. Then have each pair share their results with another pair.

INTERACTIVE PRIMARY SOURCE

Have students go online to analyze the excerpt from the *Bhagavad-Gita*.

Ask students why they think the author structured the selection as a dialogue. *(Possible answers: because a dialogue between two characters is more interesting than an essay; because some of the questions might be questions that listeners and readers have themselves.)*

ANSWERS

Identify Main Ideas *The Bhagavad-Gita is one of the most important Hindu scriptures and explores such central Hindu beliefs as the soul and life.*

Summarize *Both are epic poems with dramatic stories that contain religious ideas and explain how people should live.*

Analyze Images An illustration from the *Bhagavad-Gita* shows Krishna and Radha, who often symbolize the love of Brahman for humans. **Identify Main Ideas** Why is the *Bhagavad-Gita* important to Hindus?

New Teachings To find those answers, thinkers and teachers known as **gurus** left their homes to live in the forest, to think, and to talk about religious ideas. In a sense, these gurus and their students were founders of modern Hinduism. The ideas of these teachers were passed down orally at first. Later, they were written down.

Their ideas survive in writings known as the Upanishads (OO PAN uh shadz). The Upanishads made connections between heavenly forces and people's lives. Alongside the Vedas, the Upanishads became Hindu holy scriptures. The oldest Upanishads date to around 800 or 700 BCE. Indian thinkers continued to produce them for several hundred years.

The Upanishads helped connect people to Hinduism. These sacred writings dealt with questions of life and death or right and wrong that concern all people. These teachings are a key piece of Hinduism as it is practiced today.

Quick Activity

Explore Hindu poetry in your Active Journal.

Epic Poems Two epic poems also emerged during this period, and are revered by Hindus and non-Hindus all over the world. An epic poem is a long story of heroes told in verse. Both of these poems took shape during the period when classical Hinduism emerged. These epics are the *Ramayana* and the *Mahabharata*. They helped explain religious ideals and how people should live their lives. These epic poems are the *Ramayana* (rah MAH yuh nuh) and the *Mahabharata* (muh hah BAH rah tuh). They helped explain religious ideals and how people should live their lives.

The *Ramayana* is the story of a king named Rama and his beautiful wife, Sita. Sita is kidnapped by the demon king Ravana. His niece, the demon Trijata, protects Sita. Aided by his brother Lakshman and the monkey God Hanuman, Rama eventually rescues Sita. This epic emphasizes the importance of dharma, or righteous action.

The *Mahabharata* may be the world's longest poem. It is 200,000 lines long. It tells the story of two families at war for control of a kingdom. Like the *Ramayana,* it deals with moral **issues**. These include the conflict between loyalty to family and duty.

Academic Vocabulary
issue • *n.*, problem or subject to be discussed or decided

The most widely read section of the *Mahabharata* is the *Bhagavad-Gita* (BUG uh vud GEE tuh). This means "Song of the Lord." Some scholars

INTEGRATED ENGLISH LANGUAGE INSTRUCTION

Productive Use How Did Classical Hinduism Develop? and What Are Hindus' Beliefs About God? to help students understand and use academic expressions and domain-specific words.

Emerging Read Epic Poems aloud, pausing to discuss academic and domain-specific vocabulary. Explain that events in a story are called the *plot* and that the problem in a story is called conflict. Ask students, *What is the plot of the* Ramayana? *What is the story's conflict?*

Expanding Discuss the language arts terms plot, conflict, and theme. Then, pair students to discuss the plots, conflicts, and themes in the two Hindu epics.

consider the *Bhagavad-Gita* to be Hinduism's most important religious text, and its impact goes beyond Hinduism. It has influenced world leaders like Mahatma Gandhi and Nelson Mandela, and has been translated into hundreds of languages across the world.

This text deals with key Hindu beliefs. These beliefs have to do with the nature of the soul and its relationship to God, and different ways to live a good life. These ways are called yoga.

INTERACTIVE
Hindu Temple 3D model

READING CHECK **Summarize** Explain the significance of the *Mahabharata* and *Ramayana*.

What Are Hindus' Beliefs About God?

Hinduism is like a great river. Over thousands of years, many beliefs and traditions have flowed into it. As a result, Hindus may have different practices, but they share certain basic beliefs.

The Upanishads contain two beliefs that lie at the heart of Hinduism. The first is that there is one supreme cosmic consciousness, spiritual force, or God known as **Brahman**. The Upanishads teach that all of the Gods that Indians worship are forms of Brahman. Brahman, they say, is the source of all things.

Many Hindus worship individual Gods or Goddesses as forms of Brahman. Some Hindus worship Brahman as Vishnu. Others worship Brahman as Shiva. Still others worship Brahman as the Goddesses Shakti or Sarasvati, the Goddess of learning These Gods and Goddesses may have other named forms. For example, the God Krishna is a form of Vishnu.

The second core Hindu belief is that every person is born with a soul, which is also a form of Brahman. According to the Upanishads:

Primary Source

This soul of mine within the heart is smaller than a grain of rice.... This soul of mine within the heart is greater than the earth,... greater than the sky.... This soul of mine within the heart, this is Brahman.

—*The Thirteen Principal Upanishads*

READING CHECK **Summarize** What do Hindus believe about Brahman and the soul?

Analyze Images This statue of Shiva overlooks the Arabian Sea in western India. **Use Visual Evidence** How does this statue show the importance of Shiva to Hindus?

What Are Hindus' Beliefs About God?

Hindus believe in one universal life force, Brahman, although they may worship individual Gods or Goddesses that are forms of Brahman.

Categorize Is the Hindu religion monotheistic? *(Sample answers: Yes, because in the end everything is part of a single life force.)*

INTERACTIVE **INTERACTIVE 3-D MODEL**

Hindu Temple 3D Model

Display the 3D Model: Hindu Temple for the class. Click through the hotspots, emphasizing the purpose of each one and discussing how each relates to Hindu belief.

ACTIVE CLASSROOM

Use the Conversation with History activity. Tell students to imagine that they are having a conversation with a Hindu worshipper in the temple beginning with a question they'd like to ask and creating the conversation that might follow.

ELD.PI.C.12a

Bridging Discuss the figurative language used to describe the development of Hinduism. Ask students, How are Hinduism and rivers similar? Why does the author use this comparison? In pairs, have students read the Primary Source and discuss the meaning behind the figurative language describing the soul.

WORKSHEET **TEACHER RESOURCES**

For additional IELD support addressing these standards, have students complete the Lesson ELD activity from the Teacher Resources found on the course.

ANSWERS

Use Visual Evidence *Sample response: The statue has four arms and carries a number of symbolic objects that are important to Hindus.*

Summarize *Sample response: They believe the different Gods and one's soul are all a form of the supreme God, Brahman.*

What Do Hindus Believe About Life?

Hinduism prescribes how humans should live the right kind of life.

Identify Central Ideas Read the Primary Source on the page. Ask: How does the author describe the soul? *(as small as a grain of rice, yet as big as the earth and sky).* Ask: What part of Hindu belief does that description explain? *(that each individual soul is part of one great soul—Brahman)* Ask: What literary device does the author use to describe the soul? *(metaphor)*

Apply Concepts How are dharma, karma, and moksha interrelated? *(If a person fulfills his dharma—or duty—in earthly life, he will build up karma –or merit—for moksha—the final liberation from reincarnation.)*

Distinguish Direct student's attention to the primary source quote on this page. Ask: How does it explain reincarnation? *(It is like taking off old clothes and putting on new ones.)* Ask: Does the quote show reincarnation as positive or negative? *(positive)* Ask: What does quote imply about karma? *(that it will be good)*

Summarize Have students work in small groups to write a summary of what Hindus believe about God, how to live life, and the afterlife. Have them read their summaries to the class. Discuss and correct mistaken ideas. *(Summaries should include and connect the concepts of reincarnation, karma, dharma, Brahman, and moksha.)*

ELD TIP Have emerging and bridging students work together to sharpen understanding of domain-specific vocabulary such as *ritual, devotion,* and *meditation* Students could use a concept web or other graphic organizer to define the terms and give examples or other information about each one.

ANSWERS

Identify Cause and Effect *Sample answer: Dharma means doing what is right, which includes doing no harm to any living being (ahimsa). When people adhere to this principle, they help one another. Also, people can trust each other not to steal from them, hurt them, or commit other crimes against them.*

What Do Hindus Believe About Life?

Hindu scriptures such as the Upanishads and the *Bhagavad-Gita* also teach important Hindu beliefs about life.

Reincarnation and Karma Hinduism teaches that when people die, most will undergo reincarnation. **Reincarnation** is the rebirth of a soul in a new body.

In the *Bhagavad-Gita,* the god Krishna explains the process of reincarnation to Arjuna, the hero of the *Mahabharata:*

Primary Source

> As a man discards worn-out clothes to put on new and different ones, so the embodied self (soul) discards its worn-out bodies to take on other new ones.
>
> —*Bhagavad-Gita*

The law of karma determines how a person is reborn. **Karma** is the effect of a person's actions in this and in previous lives. Hindus believe that bad karma—evil deeds—will bring more suffering in a next life, while good karma can lead to a clearer path to liberation.

What Are Hinduism's Four Goals? Hindus believe that people have four basic goals in life. People should pursue all four, but not everyone achieves all of these goals in one lifetime.

The first goal is doing what is right. For Hindus, **dharma** is a person's duty or what is right. Dharma includes the duties that come with one's age or position in life. Dharma also includes the rule of **ahimsa**, or avoiding doing harm to any living thing, truthfulness, and moderation and self-control. Following dharma brings good karma. Violating dharma brings bad karma.

The second goal is striving for well-being, or earning a livelihood with dignity. This goal can involve making a good living and raising a family. It can involve starting or running an honest business. However, Hindus say, material well-being by itself does not bring true happiness.

Analyze Images A dharma wheel symbolizes the Hindu belief in a cycle of birth, life, and death and the concept of doing right. **Identify Cause and Effect** How would dharma have a positive influence on Indian society?

HISTORY BACKGROUND

In paintings and sculpture several Hindu Gods are shown as having many arms. One of these is Shiva, the God who destroys in order to transform. Shiva is one of the most important gods in Hinduism. He is often pictured as a dancer, and the position of each arm has special meaning. In one hand he holds a drum, which symbolizes creation. From another hand flashes the flame of destruction. A third hand gestures in protection of the faithful, and the fourth hand, along with an upraised foot, symbolize release from the illusion of life.

The third goal is pleasure. This includes eating good food or taking a hot bath. However, seeking nothing but pleasure, can leave a person feeling empty.

The final goal is **moksha**, or liberation from reincarnation. When this happens, many Hindus believe a person's soul becomes one with Brahman, while others believe the soul lives close to Brahman forever. For Hindus, the purpose of life is to achieve moksha. A soul that achieves moksha lives forever in a state of joy.

▲ A Hindu woman worships at a temple shrine.

What Are the Paths to Moksha? Hinduism lays out four main paths to moksha. These paths are all forms of yoga, defined as a way of seeking moksha. These paths are the way of knowledge, the way of works, the way of devotion, and the way of meditation.

For a person following the way of knowledge, moksha comes with a true understanding of one's soul and its oneness with Brahman—or God. The Upanishads say that such understanding does not come easily.

The way of works means carrying out the religious rituals and duties that will improve one's karma. To follow the way of works, Hindus must carry out duties within their family. They also offer prayers and food to the gods. Those who do good deeds without expecting any reward are especially praised.

The way of devotion is also known as the path of love. People on this path **devote** themselves to loving God. For most Hindus, following the path of love means worshiping one of the Hindu Gods or Goddesses. These Gods and Goddesses have human forms and personalities, as well as those of animals and nature.

Academic Vocabulary
devote • *v.*, to set aside for a purpose

The way of devotion takes many forms. People on this path may present offerings to their God at a temple. They may travel to sites sacred to their God. In all of these ways, Hindus try to move closer to God in their hearts.

The path of meditation teaches that the mind can be disciplined with the help of spiritual practices like yoga meditation. Such a mind turns away from desires and towards Brahman.

READING CHECK **Draw Inferences** Explain Hinduism's four goals in your own words.

What Is the Impact of Hinduism?

More than a billion people live in India today. About 80 percent of them follow Hinduism. The rest follow other religions. Hindus also live and worship in many places outside of India. The spread of Hinduism has had a lasting impact on India and on the world.

The Spread of Hinduism Long ago, the people of India lived under many separate rulers, spoke different languages, and worshipped different gods. Yet most Indians practiced Hinduism, supported by Hinduism's shared values of devotion and following dharma.

Draw Conclusions Ask, how would the variety of paths to moksha help Hinduism appeal to more people? *(Possible answer: It allows people to find a way of worship or practice that suits them.)*

Recognize Cause and Effects Ask, how does one achieve moksha through the way of knowledge? *(Study leads to a true understanding of one's soul and its oneness with Brahman.)*

Summarize What actions do Hindus take if they follow the way of works? *(They carry out religious rituals and duties that will improve karma.)*

What Is the Impact of Hinduism?

Hinduism, while still primarily centered in India, has spread around the world as Indians have migrated to other countries.

Identify Ask: What are two reasons why so many of the Indian people accepted Hinduism? *(It could be combined with other religions. It did not demand attendance at regular worship services.)*

DIFFERENTIATED INSTRUCTION

Special Education Explain the key beliefs of Hinduism one at a time. For example, Brahman, the great soul that contains many small souls, or reincarnation, one person living many different lives. As a class submit ideas for a diagram that illustrates that belief, such as a big circle with smaller circles inside, or a group of ascending stick figures. Have students draw the diagram.

Below Level Have students write three questions about Hindu beliefs on a piece of paper. They will exchange papers with a partner. Each will answer the other's questions.

Advanced Students will create a diagram, chart, or graphic organizer that arranges and explains Hindu beliefs.

ANSWERS

Draw Inferences *doing what is right and avoiding doing harm; striving for well-being and earning a livelihood with dignity; pleasure; achieving moksha, or liberation from reincarnation and freedom from want, fear, and pain.*

Map Activity Draw students' attention to the map of the spread of Hinduism on this page. Ask students to explain the map key and to summarize the information shown on the map. *(The key shows the regions to which Hinduism spread by various dates. By 500 BCE, Hinduism had spread across central and northern India and into parts of modern Pakistan, Nepal, and Bangladesh. 500 years later, it had spread south, and to the north and northeast. In another 600 years, it spread to the southeast as far as Malaysia.)*

Analyze Visuals Draw students' attention to the picture of the Hindu festival on the next page. Ask: What adjectives describe the picture? *(sample answers: colorful, crowded, artistic, urban)* Ask: What details do you notice about the photograph? *(Sample answers: It looks very festive. There are balloons and bright colors. The floats look like tents.)* Discuss with students whether they would like to go to the festival and why.

ANSWERS

Movement *It expanded eastward and to the south.*

Synthesize Visual Information *It probably expanded by sea because the countries to which it spread are most easily or only accessible by sea.*

Several things helped the growth of Hinduism in India. One was Hinduism's flexibility. Because Hinduism views all gods as forms of a single, supreme God, it can accept the worship of new gods. People did not have to give up their old religion when they became Hindus. Instead, Hinduism adopted their traditions and gods or viewed their gods as forms of existing Hindu gods.

Hinduism also did not require regular attendance at religious services. Instead, Hindus could pray or make offerings to the gods at a local temple during special celebrations or whenever it was convenient. They could also pray or make offerings at shrines in their homes. A shrine is a place of worship that is often dedicated to a sacred object or being. So no matter where Indians went, they could easily practice their religion.

While Hinduism is the only major world religion in which God is thought of as having a female as well as a male form, women were often not treated as equals in the Indian subcontinent. This often went against core Hindu teachings about equality of genders. Women had rights to their own personal wealth, but in most cases, had fewer property rights than men. This was similar to other ancient societies. Women could also participate in religious ceremonies, and there were some women who became Hindu sages. But most often, women were not treated as equals.

GEOGRAPHY **SKILLS**

Hinduism began in India and spread into other parts of Asia.

1. **Movement** In which direction did Hinduism expand between 1 CE and 1100 CE?
2. **Synthesize Visual Information** Based on the map, do you think Hinduism expanded during that time mainly by land or mainly by sea? Explain.

Spread of Hinduism

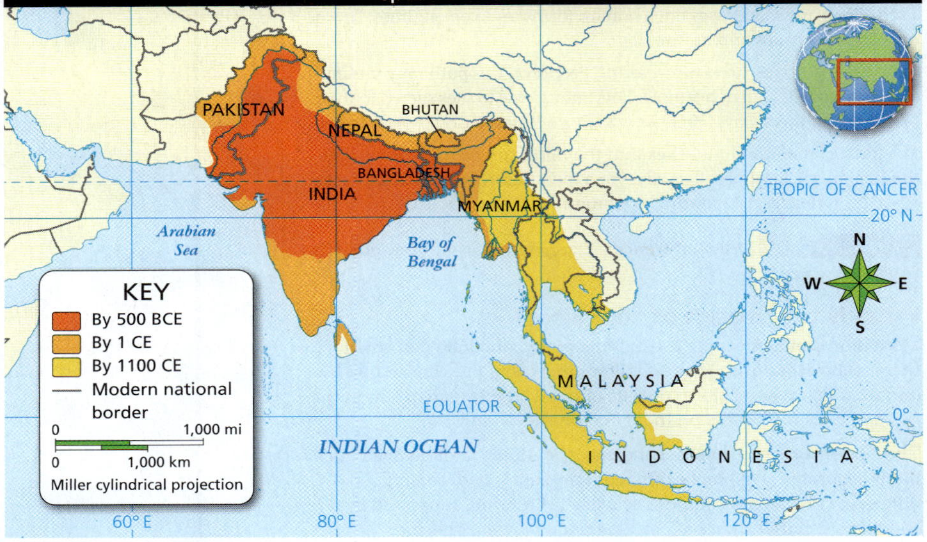

HISTORY BACKGROUND

Diwali One of the most famous Hindu festivals is Diwali, also known as the Festival of Lights. It is a five-day festival held during the new moon in October and November. Diwali signifies the renewal of life and light over darkness and ignorance. Oil lamps are lit, homes are decorated, and fireworks exploded. It is common to exchange gifts and sweets and wear new clothes during the festival.

Over time, Hinduism spread to other lands. For more than a thousand years after 1 CE, Indian traders and priests carried Hinduism to Southeast Asia. Hinduism left a lasting influence on Thailand and Indonesia, where the *Ramayana* remains popular. Today, most people on the Indonesian island of Bali are Hindus.

Indians also took Hinduism with them when they moved across the seas. Many migrated to Great Britain, the United States, and Canada. More than two million Hindus now live in the United States.

Hindu Traditions Today Hindus live in some 150 countries, but most Hindus still live in India. Hindu traditions remain an important part of Indian life. Hindu festivals draw huge crowds. One festival takes place on the Ganges River. It is one of India's holiest sites. Every year, millions of Indians line the banks of the Ganges and bathe in its waters. They believe that those waters can wash away bad karma and cure disease.

Hinduism's openness to all religions has shaped India's political system. It guarantees religious freedom.

Hinduism has also influenced India's art and literature. Beautiful carvings of Gods and Goddesses decorate Hindu temples. The temples are places of worship, but they also serve as centers of art, music, and dance.

The *Mahabharata* and the *Ramayana* were India's first great literature. They have inspired other literature for hundreds of years. In India, comic books and movies still retell the stories of these epic poems today.

READING CHECK **Draw Conclusions** Why do you think Hinduism is still practiced throughout the world?

▲ Parade in Venice, California, celebrating the Hindu Festival of Chariots

Lesson Check

HSS 6.5.3, 6.5.7; ELD.P1.A.2, P1.C.10.a

Practice Vocabulary

1. Describe how **gurus** helped Hinduism to grow.
2. Use the terms *Brahman*, *karma*, and *moksha* to describe Hindu beliefs.

Critical Thinking and Writing

3. **Identify Implied Main Ideas** How did the Upanishads and the Hindu epic poems contribute to the growth of Hinduism?
4. **Analyze Cause and Effect** Why might a Hindu offer food or flowers to a God such as Shiva?
5. **Draw Conclusions** Why is the *Bhagavad-Gita* considered by some scholars to be the most important text of Hinduism?
6. **Writing Workshop: Find and Use Credible Sources** Find credible sources for your research paper on technological innovations in ancient India. Begin reading these sources and taking notes in your Active Journal.

LESSON CHECK

1. Gurus helped people consider ideas and questions about life and death covered in the Upanishads. **DOK1**
2. Sample response: With good karma, Hindus show devotion to Brahman and grow closer to moksha. **DOK1**
3. Unlike the Vedas, the Upanishads could be read and understood by all people. **DOK2**
4. Such actions reflect the devotion path to moksha. **DOK2**
5. It deals with key Hindu beliefs about the nature of the soul, life, and the Gods and Hindu practices. **DOK3**
6. Students should choose reliable, objective, credible sources and take notes for their papers. They will complete their notes in the next lesson. **DOK3**

HSS 6.5.3, 6.5.7; ELD.P1.A.2, P1.C.10.a

SYNTHESIZE

Assess and Reteach Divide students into groups of three or four to cooperate to complete the Lesson Check questions 1–5. When they have finished, invite students to share their answers with the class. Review their responses. If they got any incorrect, use the Guiding Questions to discuss the lesson's main ideas, emphasizing the concepts students did not understand.

ACTIVE JOURNAL

Writing Workshop Have students complete the Lesson 3 Writing Task in their Active Journals. Students will search for credible sources for their research paper on technological innovations in ancient India. Assist them as needed.

DEMONSTRATE

ASSESSMENT **ONLINE LESSON QUIZ**

Assign the Online Lesson Quiz for this lesson if you haven't already done so. Students will be offered automatic remediation or enrichment based on their score.

DISCUSSION **DISCUSSION BOARD**

Post this question to the class on the Discussion Board.

Which of the four paths to moksha do you think would work best for you? *(Sample answers: the way of works because it is the most practical, the way of knowledge for someone who likes to read)*

ANSWERS

Draw Conclusions *Sample answer: Hinduism is still practiced today because Indians have scattered throughout the world and brought their religion with them.*

Lesson 4.3 • Origins and Beliefs of Hinduism 155

HSS 6.5.3, 6.5.7; ELA RI.6.3–5

Primary Sources

The Ramayana

Read students the introductory note at the top of the page, including the picture caption. Explain that this is an illustration from the *Ramayana* and shows several scenes. Tell students Rama is depicted with blue skin. Ask students to locate and describe Rama and the king *(on the throne)*.

GUIDED READING

Read—or have several fluent students read—the excerpt from the *Ramayana*. Use the Reading and Vocabulary Support questions in the text to prompt students' analysis of the primary source.

Reading and Vocabulary Support Answers

2. *Sample answer: The quote "My heart is burning indeed with one sorrowful feeling that king himself has not directly informed me about Bharata's coronation" indicates Rama is sad that the king did not tell Rama directly about Bharat's coronation.*

4. *Sample answer: because Rama is going to go to the forest and live there for 14 years*

GUIDED ANALYSIS

Remind students of the purpose of the *Ramayana*: to show a hero who embodies all the qualities that Hinduism values, such as loyalty and respect.

Connect In the story, Rama's rightful throne is taken from him. How would you expect an ordinary person to react to this? *(Sample answer: with anger and jealousy)* How does Rama react? *(with patience and grace)* Why does he react in this unusual way? *(because he shows the ideal virtues)*

To assess understanding, have students respond to the Analyzing Primary Sources questions in writing.

Primary Sources

HSS 6.5.3, 6.5.7; ELA RI.6.3–5

The Ramayana

The *Ramayana*, an epic poem, tells the story of Rama's quest. The *Ramayana* is often used to instruct people on how to live a morally perfect life. Kaikeyi is Rama's stepmother and Bharata is Kaikeyi's son. Kaikeyi has just told Rama that Bharata will become king instead of him.

◄ Kaikeyi tells Rama he will not be king.

Reading and Vocabulary Support

① *Inviolable* means sacred or holy.

② What is Rama sad about in this part of the poem?

③ Kings and queens are crowned during a *coronation* ceremony.

④ Why do you think the king is crying and unable to speak to Rama?

⑤ *Maternal* means related through a mother.

Rama the annihilator of enemies heard those harsh and deadly words but was unruffled. He spoke these words to Kaikeyi: "Let it be, as you said it. I shall fulfill the king's promise, go to the forest from here to reside there, wearing braided hair and covered with a hide. But I want to know why the king, the inviolable ① and the subduer of enemies, is not greeting me today as before. Oh, queen! you need not be indignant. I am telling before you that I shall go to the forest, wearing rags and braided hair. Become delighted as well. How can I not do faithfully an action dear to my father, as commanded by him as well-wisher, venerable man, as person with right conduct and as king. My heart is burning indeed with one sorrowful ② feeling that king himself has not directly informed me about Bharata's coronation ③. Without being asked, I myself would have gladly offered even Sita with kingdom, even my life, loved ones and wealth. Being directed by [the] king, who is my father himself, how much more should I tell that I can give everything to Bharata, duly obeying father's promise to fulfill your beloved desire. That is why, you console him. Why indeed the king is thus slowly shedding tears, with eyes gazed upon the floor? ④ Let messengers go now itself on fleet horses to bring Bharata from maternal ⑤ uncle's house as per orders of the king. I am glad that he would certainly go and urged him to make haste at once. Immediately, I shall go to live in forest of Dandaka for fourteen years, without reflecting on whether my father's words are right or wrong."

Analyzing Primary Sources

Cite evidence from the poem to support your answers.

1. **Analyze Information** What is Rama's dharma in the passage according to Rama?
2. **Cite Evidence** What can you conclude about Kaikeyi's role in Bharata being made king instead of Rama? Cite evidence from the passage.
3. **Analyze Style and Rhetoric** What are Rama's first words in the passage? How do they set the tone for his response to the news about Bharata?

ANALYZING PRIMARY SOURCES

1. His dharma is to follow his father's orders and not question whether they are right or wrong. **DOK3**
2. She may have played a role in getting the king to give the throne to her son instead of Rama and may not like Rama since she is said to speak "harsh and deadly words" to him at the beginning of the passage. **DOK3**
3. His first words are "Let it be as you said it." This statement sets his tone of complete acceptance of the decision. **DOK3**

156 Primary Sources • The Ramayana

LESSON 4 HSS 6.5.5

Origins and Beliefs of Buddhism

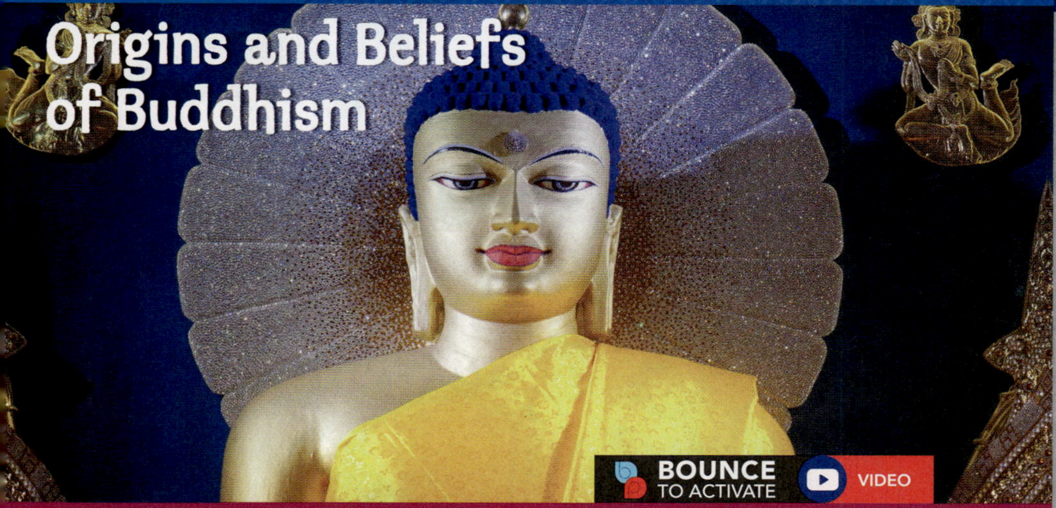

BOUNCE TO ACTIVATE | VIDEO

GET READY TO READ

START UP

Look at the statue of Buddha. What do you think the Buddha meant to his followers in ancient India?

GUIDING QUESTIONS

- Why did the Buddha give up a life of luxury, and how did he find enlightenment?
- Why do Buddhists follow the eight-step path?
- How did Buddhism support those who followed the teaching of the Buddha?
- How did Buddhism spread?

TAKE NOTES

Literacy Skills: Compare and Contrast

Use the graphic organizer in your Active Journal to take notes as you read the lesson.

PRACTICE VOCABULARY

Use the vocabulary activity in your Active Journal to practice the vocabulary words.

Vocabulary		Academic Vocabulary
meditate	Theravada Buddhism	consequences
enlightenment	Mahayana Buddhism	widespread
nirvana		
monastery		

At the end of the Vedic period, around 600 BCE, many Indians left their homes and families to become wandering teachers of new philosophies of life. Two well-known teachers were Siddhartha Gautama (sid DAHR tuh GOW tuh muh), and Mahavira (muh hahVEE ruh). Siddhartha became known as the Buddha (BOO duh). Buddhism is a religion based on the teachings of the Buddha. We call his followers Buddhists. Mahavira was the founder of Jainism. Both faiths arose in ancient India and, like Hinduism, spread elsewhere.

The Life of the Buddha

Scholars know few hard facts about the Buddha. The story of his life comes mainly from Buddhist texts. Those texts include the teachings of the Buddha, which his followers memorized and passed down by word of mouth. But they also include many legends.

A Pampered Youth Siddhartha Gautama was probably born during the 500s BCE in what is now Nepal. A Hindu prince, he was raised in wealth and luxury. According to legend, Siddhartha's mother had a dream.

HSS 6.5.5

Origins and Beliefs of Buddhism

CONNECT

GET READY TO READ

ETEXT START UP

Project the Start Up Activity. As students enter the classroom and are seated, ask them to examine the photo of the Buddha statue and reflect on the meaning of the Buddha to followers.

Hypothesize Ask students to describe the expression on the Buddha's face. *(Possible answers: happy, calm, untroubled)* Ask: What do you think makes him so calm? *(Possible answer: thinking good thoughts, helping others, finding peace)*

After completing the Start Up activity, project the Lesson Opener or direct students to their textbooks. Preview the lesson by working through the Get Ready to Read items with the class. Remind students to pay close attention to the Guiding Questions as they read the lesson.

ACTIVE JOURNAL

Take Notes Have students use the literacy skills graphic organizer in their Active Journals to take notes as they read the lesson.

Practice Vocabulary Have students complete the activity in their Active Journals to build their vocabulary.

VIDEO VIDEO

Assign the lesson video as homework.

PRACTICE VOCABULARY

Since the vocabulary words pertaining to Buddhism may be unfamiliar to students, write them on the board, and model the pronunciation of each. Ask students to repeat them aloud. Explain each word, using sample sentences such as these: *Believers in Theravada Buddhism concentrate on the Buddha's wisdom. Believers in Mahayana Buddhism imitate his compassion for others. Nirvana is the Buddhist version of moksha.*

Have students locate and pronounce the academic vocabulary in the lesson margins. Provide sample sentences that clarify meaning.

consequence: If you break the law, you must suffer the consequences.

widespread: That new style of phone has become widespread.

WORKSHEET **TEACHER RESOURCES**

Have students who need additional support use the following worksheets from the Teacher Resources on the course:

- **Reading Support**
- **English Language Development**
- **Lesson Summary**

INVESTIGATE

The Life of the Buddha

Siddhartha Gautama gave up the life of a pampered prince and through meditation he became enlightened. He then began to teach others. Discuss the progression of Gautama's life from pampered aristocrat to humble teacher.

Contrast Ask: What was Gautama's life like in the beginning? How did it change once he left home? Contrast the two. *(He was protected from the realities of life and lived in great luxury. He gave up all his wealth, wore poor clothes and devoted himself to meditation. He became enlightened.)*

Identify Cause and Effect Ask: Why did Gautama leave his comfortable life and become poor? What did he gain by doing so? *(He saw great suffering in the world and wanted to do something about it. He gained peace, enlightenment, and the joy of helping others.)*

▲ Young Prince Siddhartha shows off his archery skills, thus pleasing his father.

She dreamed that an elephant came to her from heaven. Based on the dream, a prophet predicted that the child would grow up to be a holy man. This disturbed Siddhartha's father. He wanted his son to be a ruler.

To keep Siddhartha from becoming a holy man, his father shielded him from everything unpleasant or disturbing. The prince never saw anyone who was poor, sad, or sick. When he rode out of the palace in his chariot, guards traveled ahead of him to clear beggars and sick people from the streets.

Buddhist tradition says that one day when Siddhartha was about 29, he rode out of the palace without any guards. During that ride, Siddhartha saw an old, bent, toothless man leaning on a stick. On a second ride, Siddhartha saw a man shrunken by disease. On a third, the prince saw a dead man. Siddhartha was shocked. He realized that he, too, faced old age, sickness, and death.

A few days later, Siddhartha rode out of the palace again. He came upon a fourth sight, a wandering holy man. The holy man was homeless and owned nothing. Still, he seemed content. Siddhartha decided to search for the same sense of peace that the holy man showed.

A Search for Truth That night, Siddhartha cut his hair and traded his rich clothing for the simple robe of a religious seeker. He set out to find the truth about life, suffering, and death.

Siddhartha began his search by studying with Hindu gurus. They taught him that life was a cycle of birth, death, and rebirth. Then he joined a band of religious ascetics. Ascetics deny themselves physical comforts to seek a spiritual goal.

RECENT SCHOLARSHIP

Traditionally, the date of Buddha's birth was placed in the 400s BCE in Lumbini, Nepal, a place marked by a Buddhist temple. Archaeologists on a 2013 dig, however, discovered that under the temple is a Buddhist tree shrine that carbon dating places in the 700s BCE. This means that the date of Buddha's birth could be 300 years earlier than originally thought.

HISTORY BACKGROUND

The Bodhi Tree The Bodhi Tree, under which Siddhartha Gautama reached enlightenment, was damaged by invaders soon after his death. To preserve the tree, Buddhist monks planted a cutting from it. That cutting thrived and has become one of the world's oldest trees. Monks have carried branches from it all over the world, and today many Buddhist temples have a Bodhi tree nearby.

For five years, Siddhartha wore scratchy clothes and fasted, or went without food, for long periods. He lost weight and became very weak. After six years of self-denial, he realized that going to such extremes was not the path to truth.

Finding Enlightenment Siddhartha renewed his search. One day Siddhartha sat down under a fig tree to meditate. To **meditate** means to calm or clear the mind, often by focusing on a single object. The fig tree would come to be known as the Bodhi Tree, or Tree of Knowledge.

According to legend, Siddhartha meditated under the tree for 49 days and nights. During this time, he came to understand the cycle of birth, death, and rebirth. Finally, Siddhartha reached an awareness that freed him from his ties to the world. He entered a new life free of suffering. He had, at last, achieved **enlightenment**—a state of perfect wisdom. Siddhartha had become the Buddha, which means "the Enlightened One."

According to Buddhist texts, the Buddha had freed himself from the "wheel of existence." He could have enjoyed freedom from the world's suffering. Instead, he went back into the world to teach others what he had learned.

For the next 45 years, the Buddha traveled across India sharing his message. He attracted many followers and students. He trained some of them to be teachers and religious leaders.

The Buddha died at about the age of 80. According to legend, his dying words to his followers were these:

Primary Source

This is my last advice to you. All . . . things in the world are changeable. They are not lasting. Work hard to gain your own salvation.

—Rev. Siridhamma, *Life of the Buddha*

READING CHECK **Identify Cause and Effect** How did Siddhartha achieve enlightenment?

Analyze Images The Buddha meditates beneath the Bodhi Tree. **Use Evidence** What details in the painting point to the Buddha having reached a state of peace and enlightenment?

Paraphrase Call students' attention to the Primary Source at the bottom of the page. Invite a volunteer to read it aloud; then have students turn to a classmate and paraphrase it. Clarify any misunderstandings before continuing. Ask: In what way does this quote reflect the Buddha's teaching about **enlightenment**? *(The idea that nothing is lasting reflects the teaching that reality is an illusion. Working hard for salvation implies seeking the Eightfold Path to achieve nirvana.)*

Infer Ask: In what way was the Buddha's **enlightenment** unique? *(Enlightenment means the ability to leave behind the physical world. Though he had that ability, the Buddha chose to stay in the world to lead others to the path of enlightenment.)*

INTEGRATED ENGLISH LANGUAGE DEVELOPMENT — ELD.PII.A.1

Productive Use The Life of the Buddha to write sentences and discuss the sequence of events in Buddha's life that led to enlightenment.

Emerging Read the text aloud, pausing to list events in the Buddha's life. Have students use past tense verbs to discuss the Buddha's life. Point out the *-ed* at the end of regular past tense verbs.

Expanding Discuss events in the Buddha's life, pointing out how disturbing sights changed his way of thinking.

Bridging Group students. Have one group talk about the Buddha's awareness of suffering and the other group talk about his understanding of the cycle of life.

ANSWERS

Use Evidence *His posture, facial expression, and hand gesture suggest peace, as do the light behind and above his head and the quietly grazing deer.*

Identify Cause and Effect *He meditated under a tree for 49 days and nights and learned to understand the cycle of birth, death, and rebirth, finally reaching an awareness that freed him from ties to the world.*

What Are Buddhist Beliefs?

The Buddha's teachings include guidelines for living a good life: The Eightfold Path and the Four Noble Truths.

Identify Ask: What beliefs did Buddhism carry over from Hinduism? *(karma and its consequences, reincarnation, reunion with the infinite–nirvana/moksha)*

Interpret Ask: Why do you think the Buddha settled on desire as the primary cause of suffering? *(Sample answers: Desires cause suffering when they are disappointed. Sometimes we want things that are bad for us.)*

Compare The Greeks believed in "The Golden Mean," or never going to extremes in life. What part of Buddhist belief is similar to this philosophy? *(the Middle Way)*

ELD TIP Have students continue working on expressing ideas using the past tense by identifying uses of the regular past tense in the first three paragraphs under the heading "What Are Buddhist Beliefs?" (Examples are *accepted*, *believed*, *moved*, and *supported*. Have them write original sentences about the Buddha using one of those verbs in the past tense.

Analyze Images A Buddhist nun walks out of a temple in Kathmandu, Nepal. **Infer** What does this image suggest about Buddhism today?

What Are Buddhist Beliefs?

Buddhists believe that when the Buddha gained enlightenment, he had a flash of insight. He understood why people suffer. He also saw how people could escape the cycle of death and rebirth.

The Buddha accepted the Hindu idea of karma—the idea that a person's actions have **consequences** in this or in future lives. However, the Buddha did not accept the Hindu idea of a permanent soul. He believed that a "self" might be reborn in a new body, but he thought that the "self" was an illusion. He believed that it would disappear and cease to exist when a person achieved enlightenment.

The Buddha moved even further away from other Hindu beliefs. For example, the Buddha did not believe in the existence of any god. He also did not accept specific varna roles. The Buddha believed that good and bad actions were more important than social roles. Like Hinduism, however, his teachings supported a moral and ethical society.

The Middle Way The Buddha had lived in luxury, as a wealthy prince. He had also lived in poverty, as an ascetic. One was "a life given to pleasures." The other was a life of suffering. Neither way of life had led him to enlightenment. To gain enlightenment, the Buddha advised people to follow a Middle Way. Buddhism supports individuals in their quest to find enlightenment through the Middle Way and other teachings. Following the Middle Way meant accepting four truths.

The Four Noble Truths These Four Noble Truths were among the insights the Buddha had when he achieved enlightenment under the Bodhi Tree.

The First Noble Truth is that all of life involves suffering. Birth, sickness, old age, and death bring suffering.

The Second Noble Truth is that wanting or desiring things for oneself causes suffering. Not all desires are bad. It is not wrong to desire the happiness of others. However, selfish desires lead to suffering.

The Third Noble Truth is that people can end their suffering. The way to do this is to give up all selfish desires.

The Fourth Noble Truth is that there is a way to overcome selfish desires. The way to overcome those desires is to follow the Eightfold Path.

The Eightfold Path was another of the Buddha's insights. By following this path, he believed, people could end their desires and suffering. The Buddha taught that this path was open to anyone. People of any caste could follow it.

Academic Vocabulary
consequences • *n.*, result of an action, effect

WORKSHEET **TEACHER RESOURCES**

For additional IELD support addressing these standards, have students complete the Lesson ELD activity from the Teacher Resources found on the course.

ANSWERS

Infer *Sample answer: Young women are devoting themselves to Buddhism and becoming nuns.*

The Eightfold Path The Eightfold Path takes its name from its eight steps. These steps lead to Three Qualities.

The first two steps are Right Belief and Right Purpose. They involve preparing one's mind for spiritual growth. These steps produce the first of the Three Qualities, wisdom.

The next three steps are Right Speech, Right Conduct, and Right Livelihood (or profession). These steps call for taking charge of one's behavior. These steps produce the quality of morality, or right action.

The last three steps train the mind to gain enlightenment. The third quality produced is the same as the eighth step—meditation.

Reaching Nirvana The goal of a person who follows the Eightfold Path is to reach nirvana. **Nirvana** is a state of blissful peace without desire or suffering. Those who reach nirvana are at peace with themselves. They are also freed from having to go through reincarnation. A person can reach nirvana without dying but will not be reborn after dying.

Some Buddhists believe that nirvana always brings enlightenment. Others believe that enlightenment only sometimes follows nirvana.

READING CHECK **Compare and Contrast** How were the Buddha's beliefs different from Hindu beliefs?

Analyze Charts The Eightfold Path is the way to end suffering, according to Buddha. **Identify Supporting Details** How might the steps on this path help Buddhists overcome selfish desires?

THE EIGHTFOLD PATH

The First Two Steps involve preparing one's mind for a new way of life.	1. Right Belief	The first step is belief and understanding of the Four Noble Truths.
	2. Right Purpose	The second step is to make spiritual growth the purpose of one's life.
The Next Three Steps involve taking charge of one's behavior.	3. Right Speech	The third task is to become aware of what one says. This means avoiding lies in statements that hurt others.
	4. Right Conduct	The next task is to understand one's behavior and to work to improve it. Right conduct means not killing, stealing, lying, or hurting others.
	5. Right Livelihood	This involves choosing a livelihood, or profession, that supports one's spiritual growth. A person should earn a living in a way that does not harm other living things.
The Last Three Steps help train the mind to gain enlightenment.	6. Right Effort	The sixth step involves making an effort to avoid bad thoughts and to hold only good thoughts in one's mind.
	7. Right Mindfulness	Mindful means becoming aware of what one thinks and feels. A person with right mindfulness controls his or her thoughts and emotions.
	8. Right Meditation	The last step is to practice meditation that can lead to enlightenment. Buddhists say that those who complete this step will experience a new reality.

Analyze Charts Direct students' attention to the chart at the bottom of the page. Ask students to choose one of the eight steps and write an example of how that step could apply to real life. *(Sample answer: Right Livelihood – a person chooses a job that benefits others instead of one that primarily makes money)* They will share their examples with the class.

Identify Steps in a Process Ask: Which step of the Eightfold Path do you think is most important? Why? Encourage students to choose different steps. *(Sample answers: Right Mindfulness, because controlling thoughts leads to controlling one's behavior. Right Purpose because your purpose affects everything you do in life.)*

DIFFERENTIATED INSTRUCTION

Below Level Write these sentences on the board to help students use comparing and contrasting to understand concepts: Buddhism and Hinduism are similar because they both ___________. They are different because Buddhism ___________ and Hinduism ___________. For lower level students, fill in the blanks as a class. Have higher level students copy the sentences and write in the blanks.

Advanced Have students create a skit for each step and then explain how their skit demonstrates one or more of the Four Noble Truths.

Special Education As a class, create eight sentences, each explaining a step in the Eightfold Path. Have pairs of students draw and caption a picture that illustrates one step. Display the pictures in order.

ANSWERS

Identify Supporting Details *Each step in the Eightfold Path focuses on performing good actions and thinking good thoughts.*

Compare and Contrast *The Buddha did not believe in the existence of any god. He also did not accept specific varna roles. He believed that the good and bad actions of people were more important than caste. He also believed in following what he called the Middle Way, the Four Noble Truths, and the Eightfold Path.*

How Did Buddhism Spread?

Buddhism spread primarily through monks who devoted themselves to the Buddha's teachings.

Compare and Contrast Ask: What teachings does **Theravada Buddhism** emphasize? *(the Buddha's wisdom and the personal goal of nirvana)* Ask: What does **Mahayana Buddhism** emphasize? *(sharing enlightenment and compassion with others)* Discuss possible reasons why these two branches separated.

INTERACTIVE **INTERACTIVE MAP**

Origins and Beliefs of Buddhism

Display the Interactive Map: Origins and Beliefs of Buddhism. Click on the red circles and have volunteers read the entries to learn more about how Buddhism began, developed, and spread.

ACTIVE CLASSROOM

Use the Make Headlines activity. The Buddha has come to town to spread his teachings. Have students write headlines for this event.

ELD TIP For the Make Headlines activity, pair English learners with fluent speakers. Support comprehension by restating any unfamiliar language using basic, known words.

What Is Jainism?

Mahavira, the founder of Jainism, taught at about the same time as the Buddha. Followers of Jainism believe in ahimsa.

Interpret Ask students to define and give examples of ***ahimsa***. *(nonviolence to all life, such as refusing to kill animals for food and releasing an insect outdoors instead of killing it)*

How Did Buddhism Spread?

For hundreds of years, the Buddha's followers memorized his teachings. After many years, they wrote those teachings down. Those written teachings make up the sacred scriptures of Buddhism today. Different branches of Buddhism accept different collections of these scriptures. However, all Buddhists accept the Four Noble Truths and the Eightfold Path.

INTERACTIVE

Origins and Beliefs of Buddhism

Monasteries and Missionaries As the Buddha preached, he gained many followers. At first they followed him from place to place. After a while, the Buddha found places for them to stay during the rainy season. These became Buddhist **monasteries**, or religious communities. The most devoted Buddhists lived in monasteries. There they had time to study and meditate.

The Buddha urged his followers to carry his teachings to all corners of Earth. A person who spreads religious ideas is a missionary. Buddhist missionaries carried Buddhism across India and to Sri Lanka, then throughout Asia. Some traveled north to Central Asia. Then missionaries followed trade routes east into China. From China, Buddhism spread to Korea and Japan. Buddhism arrived later in Tibet.

What Are the Two Branches of Buddhism? As Buddhism spread, its followers split into two major branches, or sects. The two branches share basic beliefs, but they see the Buddha's life and teachings differently.

One branch is **Theravada Buddhism** (thehr uh VAH duh). This sect focuses on the wisdom of the Buddha. Members think that the Buddha's greatest achievement was his enlightenment and entry into nirvana.

Mahayana Buddhism (mah huh YAH nuh) is the other branch. It focuses on the Buddha's compassion. For its members, the Buddha's greatest achievement was returning from nirvana to share his wisdom out of compassion for others.

Analyze Images The Paro Taktsang Buddhist monastery in Bhutan is also called "Tiger's Nest." It was built alongside a rocky cliff 3,000 feet above the Paro valley. **Identify Main Ideas** What is the purpose of a monastery?

COMMON MISCONCEPTIONS

Students may have heard of Buddhist practices such as meditation and may consider Buddhists strange and otherworldly. But parts of Buddhism are common to most religions—leaders who humbly teach believers, rules for right living, a connection to an eternal afterlife, compassion for others, and so forth. If someone in the class is a Buddhist, allow him or her to tell the class about Buddhism in daily life.

The Legacy of Buddhism Today, there are about 400 million Buddhists throughout the world. Most live in Asia. Theravada Buddhism is the main religion of Sri Lanka, Myanmar (or Burma), Thailand, and Cambodia. Mahayana Buddhism is **widespread** in Bhutan, Vietnam, China and Taiwan, Mongolia, the Koreas, and Japan.

More than two million Buddhists live in the United States. Few Buddhists remain in India, but the Buddha's teachings made a lasting impact on Hinduism.

Buddhism has inspired beautiful art and architecture. It has been a source of wisdom even for some non-Buddhists.

READING CHECK **Identify Main Ideas** How did Buddhism spread in India and Sri Lanka, and later across Asia?

▲ Women from the Jain community attend a prayer meeting for world peace.

What Is Jainism?

Mahavira, another successful wandering teacher around the same time as Siddhartha, was a teacher of Jainism. Jainism and Buddhism developed at the same time. A main characteristic of Jainism was the idea of **ahimsa**, which is nonviolence to all life. As such, Jainism encourages vegetarianism. The path to enlightenment in Jainism comes through nonviolence. Jainism continues to play a role in India today. Mohandas Gandhi, a well-known peace activist in India in the first half of the twentieth century, practiced nonviolent protest. He protested against British rule in India.

Academic Vocabulary
widespread • *adj.*, common, spread across a large area

READING CHECK **Identify Supporting Details** Why did people who followed Jainism practice *ahimsa*?

Lesson Check

HSS 6.5.5; ELD.P1.A.2, P1.C.10.a

Practice Vocabulary

1. Explain the meaning of the term **nirvana** for Buddhism.
2. Describe the difference between **Theravada Buddhism** and **Mahayana Buddhism.**

Critical Thinking and Writing

3. **Infer** How does Buddhism support individuals who want to achieve enlightenment?
4. **Synthesize** What are Buddhism's moral teachings, or teachings about right and wrong?
5. **Analyze Information** What role did missionaries play in Buddhism in India, Sri Lanka, and Central Asia?
6. **Writing Workshop: Support Ideas with Evidence** Use your sources to complete gathering credible evidence to support your ideas about technological innovation in ancient India by taking notes in your Active Journal.

HSS 6.5.5; ELD.P1.A.2, P1.C.10.a

SYNTHESIZE

Assess and Reteach Have students use a Numbered Heads strategy to complete the Lesson Check questions 1–5. Review their responses. If they got any incorrect, use the Guiding Questions to discuss the lesson's main ideas, emphasizing the concepts students did not understand.

ACTIVE JOURNAL

Writing Workshop Have students complete the Lesson 4 Writing Task in their Active Journals. Students will finish gathering credible evidence to support their ideas on technological innovation in ancient India.

DEMONSTRATE

ASSESSMENT **ONLINE LESSON QUIZ**

Assign the Online Lesson Quiz for this lesson if you haven't already done so. Students will be offered automatic remediation or enrichment based on their score.

DISCUSSION **DISCUSSION BOARD**

Post this question to the class on the Discussion Board:

Apply Concepts Buddhists believe that the source of suffering is selfish desire. How does the Eightfold Path help believers overcome these desires? *(The steps gradually make believers mindful of their actions and motives until they gain control of their consciousness.)*

LESSON CHECK

1. Nirvana is a state of blissful peace achieved through enlightenment. **DOK1**
2. Theravada Buddhism focuses on the Buddha's wisdom, Mahayana Buddhism on his compassion. **DOK1**
3. It provides the Eightfold Path and the four Noble Truths. **DOK2**
4. Buddhism teaches that it is wrong to lie, speak hurtful words, steal, or harm living things. **DOK3**
5. They traveled to spread Buddhism. They built monasteries. **DOK2**
6. Students should complete their research on technological innovation in ancient India to use for their research papers. **DOK4**

ANSWERS

Identify Main Ideas *Monasteries provide a place for monks to live while they devote themselves to studying the Buddha's teachings.*

Identify Main Ideas *The Buddha encouraged people to spread Buddhism all over the world. After he died, missionaries traveled to do so.*

Identify Supporting Details *They believed ahimsa was the path to enlightenment.*

HSS 6.5.5; ELA RI.6.2–4, 6

Primary Sources

The Life or Legend of Gaudama

Ask a student to read the text beside the image of the Buddha. Ask students to speculate on the relationship between this picture and the passage the text introduces. *(Sample answer: The statue shows a young man sitting, just as Siddartha was sitting in this passage.)*

GUIDED READING

Read the excerpt from *The Life or Legend of Gaudama.* Use the Reading and Vocabulary Support questions to prompt students' analysis of the primary source.

Reading and Vocabulary Support Answers

3. *The whole passage suggests that humans are trapped or caught in misunderstanding and suffering.*

5. *The idea that he can help others makes the Buddha happy because he is so good-hearted.*

GUIDED ANALYSIS

Review with students the Four Noble Truths. Note the phrases the passage that connect to this belief, such as "endless miseries" and the "dark abyss of ignorance" (suffering) and "the web of passions" (desire).

Draw Conclusions Ask: Considering how the Buddha came to enlightenment, why do you think he taught that God is not necessary? *(He had come to enlightenment through his own efforts and believed others could do the same.)*

To assess understanding, have students respond to the Analyzing Primary Sources questions in writing.

ACTIVE JOURNAL

Quest Connection Have students respond to the Quest Connection question in their Active Journals. Ask students to explain what decision the question refers to. If they do not recognize that it is the decision described in the Primary Source passage, guide them to that realization.

Primary Sources

HSS 6.5.5; ELA RI.6.2–4, 6

The Life or Legend of Gaudama

The Life or Legend of Gaudama is a Burmese text that tells the story of the Buddha's life and relates his teachings. The early section discusses his birth and his growing desire to gain spiritual wisdom. In the passage prior to this excerpt, the young Siddartha sits under a tree to meditate.

◀ A sculpture of the enlightened Buddha

Reading and Vocabulary Support

① *Contemplation* means to think deeply about.

② A *vortex* is a whirlpool, a swirling body of water.

③ What does this phrase suggest?

④ *Benevolent* means kind or caring.

⑤ Why does this thought delight the Buddha?

"Buddha continued to remain . . . in a cross-legged position, with a mind absorbed into contemplation ① during seven days. Mental exertion and labor were at an end. Truth, in its [bright] beauty, encompassed his mind and shed over it the purest rays. Placed in that [shining] center, [Buddha] saw all beings entangled in the web of passions, . . . whirling in the vortex ② of endless miseries, . . . sunk into the dark abyss of ignorance, the wretched victims of an illusory, unsubstantial, and unreal world. He said then to himself,: 'In all the worlds, there is no one but me who know how to break through the web of passions, . . . to save them from the whirlpool of miseries, . . . to [drive away] the mist of ignorance by the light of truth, to teach all intelligent beings, the unreality and non-existence of this world, and thereby to lead them to the true state of [enlightenment].' ③ Having thus [expressed] the feelings of compassion that pressed on his benevolent ④ heart, [Buddha] . . . delighted in contemplating the great number of beings who would avail themselves of his preachings, and labor to free themselves from the slavery of passions." ⑤

Quest CONNECTIONS

Based on the text, what does the Buddha decide to do? How do you think that affected ancient India and the culture of present-day India? Record your findings in your Active Journal.

Analyzing Primary Sources

Cite evidence from the text to support your answers.

1. **Analyze Information** How does the Buddha come to view the world as a result of his meditation?
2. **Cite Evidence** What constitutes enlightenment, according to the Buddha?
3. **Determine Author's Point of View** What attitude does the author of this text show toward the Buddha?

164 Primary Sources • The Life or Legend of Gaudama

ANALYZING PRIMARY SOURCES

1. The Buddha sees the world as a place of misery and suffering and as being unreal. **DOK3**

2. Enlightenment involves breaking out of the trap of passion, escaping from human miseries, overcoming ignorance by seeing the truth, and recognizing the unreality and non-existence of this world. **DOK3**

3. Possible response: The author sees the Buddha as wise and admirable. He not only gains enlightenment, but his first thought on doing so is to help others reach that state as well and thus end their suffering. **DOK3**

LESSON 5

HSS 6.5.6

The Maurya Empire Begins

GET READY TO READ

START UP

Examine the statue of Chandragupta Maurya. Write two things you think may have been true about Chandragupta and his rule based on how he is portrayed.

GUIDING QUESTIONS

- How did Chandragupta use military strategy to unite much of India for the first time?
- How did Chandragupta develop a bureaucracy, a tax system, and a system of spies to help rule his empire?

TAKE NOTES

Literacy Skills: Analyze Cause and Effect

Use the graphic organizer in your Active Journal to take notes as you read the lesson.

PRACTICE VOCABULARY

Use the vocabulary activity in your Active Journal to practice the vocabulary words.

Vocabulary	Academic Vocabulary
strategy	mission
province	welfare
bureaucracy	
subject	

By the end of the Vedic age, many kingdoms and chiefdoms covered India. The strongest of the kingdoms was Magadha (MUH guh duh). Around 321 BCE, a rebel army overthrew the king of Magadha. The leader of the rebels was a young man named Chandragupta Maurya (chun druh GOOP tuh MOWR yuh).

How Did Chandragupta Unite India?

Most of what we know about Chandragupta's life comes from ancient writings and legends. Some legends say that he was born into Magadha's royal family but was left with poor farmers when he was young. Historians may never know the real story.

Seizing Power As a young man, Chandragupta depended on the advice of an older, educated Brahmin named Kautilya (kow TIL yuh). Legends say that Kautilya searched for a leader to drive Greek invaders out of northwestern India. In one story, Kautilya saw Chandragupta playing as a boy and knew that he could be trained as a leader.

PRACTICE VOCABULARY

To help students integrate new vocabulary, explain that all these terms relate to building or governing an empire. A *strategy* is a long-term plan for achieving a goal. A *province* is a region of an empire that has its own government. A *bureaucracy* is a system of offices that carries out government rules and regulations. *Subjects* are people who live under the rule of an emperor. Reinforce the terms during the lesson using the teaching notes.

Point out the academic vocabulary in the lesson margins. Provide sample sentences that clarify meaning.

mission: During vacation, my family departed on our mission to experience the best amusement parks in the state.

welfare: Adding entrance ramps to buildings increased the welfare of people in wheelchairs.

HSS 6.5.6

The Maurya Empire Begins

CONNECT

GET READY TO READ

ETEXT START UP

Project the Start Up Activity. As students enter the classroom and get settled, ask them to examine the statue of Chandragupta Maurya.

Hypothesize Have students jot down the leadership qualities they think are portrayed in the statue of Chandragupta. *(Sample answers: Chandragupta is proud, strong, fearless, watchful.)* Then have them share their ideas with another student, either in class or through a chat or blog.

Discuss Begin a discussion with students about the skills and knowledge that the leader of a large country needs. Elicit from students a list of these traits based on what they know about American presidents or governors.

After completing the Start Up activity, project the Lesson Opener or direct students to their textbooks. Preview the lesson by working through the Get Ready to Read items with the class. Remind students to pay close attention to the Guiding Questions as they read the lesson.

ACTIVE JOURNAL

Take Notes Have students use the lesson literacy skills graphic organizer in their Active Journals to take notes as they read the lesson.

Practice Vocabulary Have students complete the activity in their Active Journals to build their vocabulary.

VIDEO VIDEO

Assign the lesson video as homework.

WORKSHEET **TEACHER RESOURCES**

Have students who need additional support use the following worksheets from the Teacher Resources on the course:

- **Reading Support**
- **English Language Development**
- **Lesson Summary**

INVESTIGATE

How Did Chandragupta Unite India?

Discuss how the Maurya Empire came to dominate.

Analyze Maps Have students locate the kingdom of Magadha on the map. Ask: Why would gaining power over Magadha be important? *(Sample answers: It was a large and powerful kingdom in the Ganges River Valley; its location seems good for trade.)*

Summarize Ask: What are some legends describing Chandragupta's origins? *(He was born into a royal family but was left with poor farmers. He was trained by an educated Brahmin named Kautilya who saw signs that he could become a leader.)*

Synthesize Ask: How would a leader plan a strategy? *(The leader would choose a large goal, and outline a series of steps to achieve it.)*

Kautilya helped Chandragupta raise an army and develop a strategy to gain power. A **strategy** is a long-term plan for achieving a goal. Their strategy was to take control of the northwest from the Greeks and then attack Magadha from the northwest.

Success on the Battlefield Kautilya trained his pupil well to become a brilliant military leader. Chandragupta armed his men with powerful weapons, including the Indian bow. This bow was as tall as a man. Its arrows could pierce a strong shield.

A story says that Chandragupta saw a mother scold her child for starting to eat from the center of the plate. She said the center is too hot. So Chandragupta weakened Magadha by attacking its borders, then moved in to take its capital city.

After Chandragupta conquered Magadha, he attacked other kingdoms. By 305 BCE, he ruled much of the Indian subcontinent. After Chandragupta forced the Greeks out of northwestern India, his Maurya empire stretched from the Bay of Bengal to present-day Afghanistan. For the first time, one state controlled all of northern India.

READING CHECK **Draw Conclusions** How did Chandragupta start the Maurya empire and make it grow?

GEOGRAPHY SKILLS

At its height, the Maurya empire controlled almost the entire Indian subcontinent.

1. **Place** On which river was Pataliputra located?
2. **Infer** In which kingdom —Magadha, Kalinga, or Bactria—did Chandragupta fight the Greeks?

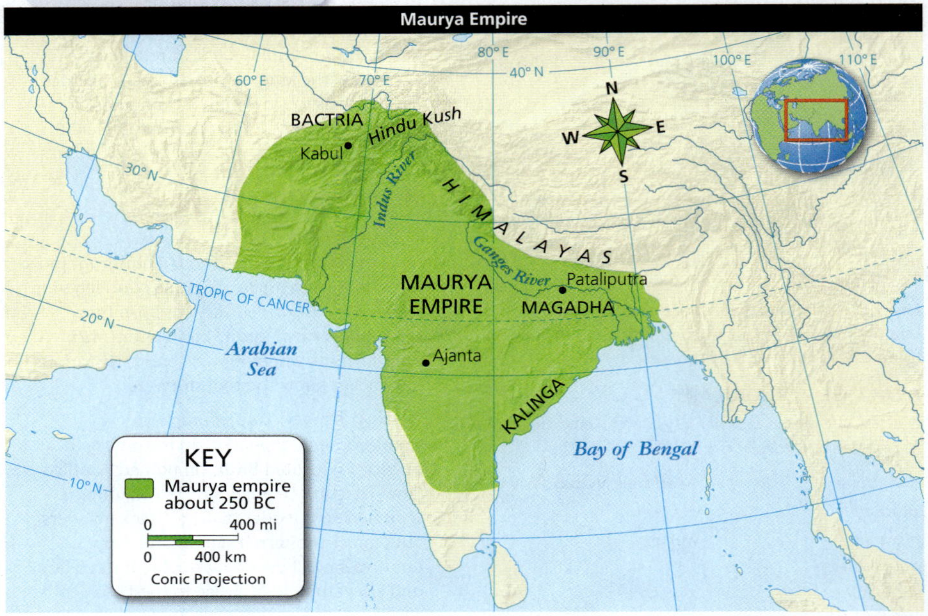

INTEGRATED ENGLISH LANGUAGE DEVELOPMENT

Structure Cohesive Texts Use How Did Chandragupta Unite India? as a model of narrative writing. Then have students retell the story in writing.

Emerging Read the text aloud, pausing to list events. Explain that this narrative tells a story in order of events. Have students write a short narrative of Chandragupta's life using the words *first*, *then*, and *after*.

Expanding After students read the text, ask Is this a narrative or a persuasive text? *(narrative)* Ask, how does the writer tell the story? *(relating a sequence of events)* Have students retell Chandragupta's narrative in chronological sequence.

Bridging Write these text structures on the board: narrative, comparison/contrast, persuasive. When students finish

ANSWERS

Place *The Ganges*

Infer *Bactria*

Draw Conclusions *He was a brilliant military leader. He developed strategies to conquer other parts of India and had success with his powerful weapons.*

166 Lesson 4.5 • The Maurya Empire Begins

How Did Chandragupta Rule an Empire?

As emperor, Chandragupta faced the same problem as other empire builders: How could he rule over a large area with many different needs and traditions?

Building a Government Chandragupta solved this problem by dividing his empire into four regions. He divided each region into smaller provinces A **province** is a region with its own government.

The emperor also set up a **bureaucracy**, or a system of offices that carries out government rules and regulations. He patterned his government after that of the Persian empire. Appointed officials in each region, province, and village carried out the emperor's orders. In this way, he was able to control every village in his empire.

Chandragupta also set up a tax system. Tax workers collected 25 percent of the crops raised by farmers. They also collected a sales tax on goods. Chandragupta used the taxes to pay government workers. He used them to support a large army and his own costly lifestyle as well.

This system gave the Maurya empire an efficient government. However, its strength depended on the power and authority of the ruler. The government was only as strong as the emperor.

Connections to Other Regions The Maurya empire also maintained strong connections to other regions. Chandragupta was friendly with a Greek kingdom to the west, though relations were not good at first. After conquering northwestern India, Chandragupta sent troops west of the Indus River. They clashed with the forces of Seleucus, a Greek general who ruled Persia. Rather than engaging in an all-out war, the two rulers settled their differences. They agreed on a peace treaty. Seleucus gave up control of some lands west of the Indus. Chandragupta, in exchange, sent Seleucus 500 elephants.

This was the beginning of relationships with many neighbors to the empire. These governments often sent envoys to each other. An envoy is a messenger or representative. An envoy is usually sent on **missions** concerning relations between governments.

Subjects and Spies Chandragupta ruled a vast empire, but he lived in constant fear of his enemies. He had servants taste his food for poison. He slept in a different bed every night.

To ease his fears, Chandragupta had specially trained female warriors guard his palace. He set up a huge spy network to watch his **subjects**, or people under his rule. He even hired spies to watch other spies. The emperor set aside time every day to receive reports from his spies.

Analyze Images Chandragupta issued gold coins with his image on them. **Infer** How could placing his image on coins help Chandragupta rule his empire?

INTERACTIVE
Village Life in India

Academic Vocabulary
mission • *n.*, journey with a purpose

ELD.PII.A.1

reading, ask, What type of writing is this? *(narrative)* Ask, To write a narrative, do you need to write a sequence of events or to use reasons? Have students retell Chandragupta's story in chronological order.

WORKSHEET **TEACHER RESOURCES**

For additional IELD support addressing these standards, have students complete the Lesson ELD activity from the Teacher Resources found on the course.

How Did Chandragupta Rule an Empire?

Discuss how Chandragupta ruled this large area with its many needs and traditions.

Describe How did Chandragupta control the empire? *(He divided it into four regions subdivided into smaller provinces. A bureaucracy of appointed officials in each region, province, and village carried out his orders.)*

Compare Ask: What type of taxes supported Chandragupta's government? *(The government collected 25 percent of crops plus a sales tax.)* Ask: How were these taxes similar to modern taxes? *(Local, state, and national governments tax income. Many states have sales taxes.)*

INTERACTIVE **INTERACTIVE GALLERY**

Village Life in India

Display the Interactive Gallery: Village Life in India. Click through the pairs of images to show the continuity of Indian village life past and present.

ACTIVE CLASSROOM

Have students draw their own village life pairings. They might draw a picture of their ancestors in front of their houses and contrast it with their families in front of their own homes.

ELD TIP Write two sentences on the board: *Chandragupta is the subject of this lesson. Chandragupta used spies to watch his subjects.* Elicit from students the different meanings of the word *subject* in use.

ANSWERS

Infer *Having his image on coins let all of Chandragupta's subjects know who their ruler was.*

HSS 6.5.6; ELD.P1.A.2, P1.C.10.a

SYNTHESIZE

Assess and Reteach Have students complete Lesson Check questions 1–5 individually. Review their responses using an Idea Wave strategy. If they had any incorrect answers, use the Guiding Questions to discuss the lesson's main ideas, focusing on the ideas they struggled with.

ACTIVE JOURNAL

Writing Workshop Have students complete the Lesson 5 Writing Task in their Active Journals. Students will cite their sources for the research paper.

DEMONSTRATE

ASSESSMENT **ONLINE LESSON QUIZ**

Assign the Online Lesson Quiz for this lesson if you haven't already done so. Students will be offered automatic remediation or enrichment based on their score.

DISCUSSION **DISCUSSION BOARD**

Post this question to the class on the Discussion Board:

Summarize How did Chandragupta Maurya unify and rule India? *(He conquered other kingdoms. He divided the empire into smaller regions and provinces to make it easier to govern. He established a bureaucracy that carried out his orders. He had spies watching his subjects. The subjects had no right to privacy or freedom of speech.)*

▲ Portrait of Chandragupta

Chandragupta's subjects had no right to privacy or freedom of speech.

Some members of the empire had absolutely no freedom of any kind. Slavery existed in Maurya India. Most slaves were prisoners of war or people who could not pay what they owed. Laws protected slaves from harsh treatment in India, unlike in other countries.

Kautilya's Advice Many of Chandragupta's ideas about ruling came from his advisor Kautilya. Kautilya was the author of a book called the *Arthashastra*. The book gives advice on how to be a good ruler. "The primary duty of a king," the *Arthashastra* says, "is the protection of his subjects." He went on to give more detail about what he saw as a ruler's responsibility:

Primary Source

> In the happiness of his subjects lies the king's happiness. In the welfare of his subjects, his welfare. A king's good is not that which pleases him, but that which pleases his subjects.
>
> —Kautilya, *Arthashastra*

On the other hand, the *Arthashastra* also advises the ruler to do whatever is necessary to keep power. Kautilya says that people cannot be trusted, and he urges severe punishments for crimes.

Academic Vocabulary
welfare • *n.*, well-being, comfort, prosperity

READING CHECK **Identify Cause and Effect** What did Mauryan rulers do to maintain connections with other nearby governments?

Lesson Check

HSS 6.5.6; ELD.P1.A.2, P1.C.10.a

Practice Vocabulary

1. Use the terms **bureaucracy** and **subject** to describe Maurya government.
2. How did **strategy** help Chandragupta Maurya's rise to power?

Critical Thinking and Writing

3. **Identify Main Ideas** How did Chandragupta Maurya conquer Magadha?
4. **Use Evidence** How did a bureaucracy help the Maurya emperors rule?
5. **Draw Conclusions** What was the relationship between the Maurya government and the people it governed?
6. **Writing Workshop: Cite Sources** Cite sources for your research paper in your Active Journal. You will write your research paper at the end of the topic.

LESSON CHECK

1. Sample response: Chandragupta set up three levels of bureaucracy to control his subjects. **DOK1**
2. He developed a plan to gain control of the northwest from the Greeks and then move to attack Magadha, and then he carried out that plan. **DOK1**
3. He first attacked its borders before taking its capital. **DOK2**
4. Appointed officials in each region, province, and village carried out the emperor's orders. **DOK2**
5. Maurya emperors ruled their subjects, who had little say in the government. **DOK3**
6. Students should cite their sources accurately and in the required format. They should be aware of the dangers of plagiarism. **DOK4**

ANSWERS

Identify Cause and Effect *They sent envoys to other governments on missions concerning relations between them.*

HSS 6.5.6; Analysis REP.4
ELA W.6.8

Assess Credibility of a Source

Use the primary source and follow these steps to assess credibility of a source.

INTERACTIVE
Analyze Primary and Secondary Sources

1 Identify who created the source and when it was created. Read the passage. Determine who wrote it. The information may or may not state when it was created. Use information about the source to determine when it was created. What can you conclude from this source about when it was created?

2 Identify the topic. What is the creator of the source writing about? Sometimes the subject will be named directly and other times it will be implied. Does this source tell who or what it is about specifically? Who or what is the topic of this source?

3 Identify the facts, opinions, and possible inaccuracies or biases. What facts are present? Are any important ones left out? What opinions are stated? You can look for words that show a strongly favorable or unfavorable view of the topic. Does the author takes a balanced approach to the subject? Is more than one point of view given about the subject? Read the passage again.

a. State the facts included in this source.

b. Is there any reason to doubt Megasthenes' description of these facts?

c. Does Megasthenes seem to have an opinion about the subject of the passage? If so, what is his opinion?

d. What evidence does Megasthenes give in the passage that supports this opinion?

4 Assess the credibility of the source. Compare the source to other sources on the same subject. Evaluate the facts included, the fairness of their presentation, and the opinions or points of view. A source that seems heavily biased or incomplete may not be a reliable source. A primary source is generally more reliable than a secondary source because the person actually witnessed the event.

a. Is Megasthenes a primary or a secondary source?

b. Does Megasthenes have a strong opinion? If so, what is it?

c. Do you think this is a credible source? Why or why not?

Primary Source

"Outside the gates of the palace stand the bodyguards and the rest of the soldiers. . . . Nor does the king sleep during the day, and at night he is forced at various hours to change his bed because of those plotting against him. . . . When he leaves to hunt, he is thickly surrounded by a circle of women, and on the outside by spear-carrying bodyguards. The road is fenced off with ropes, and to anyone who passes within the ropes as far as the women death is the penalty."

—Megasthenes, a Greek ambassador to Chandragupta's court at Pataliputra

DIFFERENTIATED INSTRUCTION

Below Level Before practicing the skill, tell students that *credible* means "believable." Elicit from students characteristics of believable and unbelievable sources. (believable: fact-based, clear description, plain language; unbelievable: made-up, superlative descriptions) Ask students to give examples of both kinds of sources. They can use examples from their experience or ones they make up.

INTEGRATED ENGLISH LANGUAGE DEVELOPMENT

Emerging To help students understand the scenes described in the primary source, break the description into three parts. Assign one part to each of three groups of students. Then, have each group act out the scene described. Simplify the questions in the steps if necessary to help students assess the source's credibility.

HSS 6.5.6; Analysis REP.4; ELA W.6.8

Analysis Skills
Assess Credibility of a Source

LEARN

Preview the steps in the student text with students, and then play the video.

VIDEO **21st CENTURY SKILLS**

Project the Analyze Primary and Secondary Sources video in the 21st Century Skills Tutorial. Use the Quick Reference and Assessment to provide additional instruction in the skill.

PRACTICE

Have students practice the skill using the text on the student page alone or working in pairs. When they are finished, discuss the details they used to determine the credibility of the source.

ASSESS

To assess this skill, have students review the section "How Did Chandragupta Rule an Empire" in Lesson 5. Direct them to identify details that help them assess the credibility of this source.

ANSWERS

1. It was written by Megasthenes, a Greek ambassador to Chandragupta's court, so he was able to see or hear about the things he describes.
2. The writer describes security around Chandragupta.
3. a. The palace is guarded. The king changes beds throughout the night. When he hunts, he's closely guarded, and separated from strangers by ropes.
   b. There seems to be no reason to doubt the description.
   c. Megasthenes seems to accept that the king's fears are reasonable.
   d. Megasthenes says that there are people plotting against the king.
4. a. primary
   b. Megasthenes seems to accept that the threats against the king are real.
   c. Sample answer: I think this is credible because it was written by a witness and is based on facts.

HSS 6.5.6

Asoka's Rule

CONNECT

GET READY TO READ

ETEXT **START UP**

Project the Start Up Activity. As students enter the classroom and get settled, ask them to examine the painting of Asoka.

Use Visual Information Have students record their impressions of Asoka and his rule based on this image. *(Possible answer: He looks peaceful and thoughtful; he was probably a just and compassionate ruler.)*

Discuss Explain that empires of the ancient world were not always at war. Depending on its ruler, an empire could be more concerned with improving the welfare of its people than increasing its size. Ask what projects a ruler concerned with improving people's lives would work on. *(Sample responses: educating more people, increasing trade, inventing new technologies)*

After completing the Start Up activity, project the Lesson Opener or direct students to their textbooks. Preview the lesson by working through the Get Ready to Read items with the class. Remind students to pay close attention to the Guiding Questions as they read the lesson.

ACTIVE JOURNAL

Take Notes Have students use the literacy skills graphic organizer in their Active Journals to take notes as they read the lesson.

Practice Vocabulary Have students complete the activity in their Active Journals to build their vocabulary.

VIDEO **VIDEO**

Assign the lesson video as homework.

LESSON 6 HSS 6.5.6

Asoka's Rule

BOUNCE TO ACTIVATE VIDEO

GET READY TO READ

START UP

Examine the painting of Asoka as a Buddhist. What does it tell you about the kind of ruler Asoka was?

GUIDING QUESTIONS

- Why did the emperor Asoka turn from war to peace?
- How did Asoka promote the growth of Buddhism and encourage morality among his subjects?
- How did Buddhism support Asoka's hopes for his empire?

TAKE NOTES

Literacy Skills: Sequence

Use the graphic organizer in your Active Journal to take notes as you read the lesson.

PRACTICE VOCABULARY

Use the vocabulary activity in your Active Journal to practice the vocabulary words.

Vocabulary	Academic Vocabulary
tolerance	eventually
stupa	

170 Lesson 4.6 • Asoka's Rule

Power in the Maurya empire passed from grandfather, to father, to son. Chandragupta's son, Bindusara, expanded the empire farther across India. When his son, Asoka, gained power, at first he waged war. Then he turned to peace.

Why Did Asoka Turn to Peace?

As Chandragupta grew older, he became a Jain—a follower of Jainism (JY niz um). Like Buddhists, Jains aim for enlightenment. However, they accept the reality of the soul like Hindus. According to legend, Chandragupta gave up being emperor to enter a Jain monastery.

Asoka Rises to Power Asoka was one of Bindusara's seven sons. Legends say that Bindusara did not like him. As soon as Asoka was old enough to hold a job, Bindusara sent him away to be the ruler of a faraway province.

PRACTICE VOCABULARY

To help students integrate new vocabulary, explain that these terms relate to the way Asoka tried to rule his empire. *Tolerance* is a willingness to respect different beliefs and customs, which Asoka used to rule the diverse empire. A *stupa* is a Buddhist burial mound. Asoka became a follower of Buddhism and supported construction of Buddhist buildings and mounds.

Reinforce the terms during the lesson using the teaching notes.

Have students locate and pronounce the academic vocabulary in the lesson margins. Provide sample sentences that clarify meaning.

eventually: We planted a tiny oak sapling in the hope that it will eventually become a giant tree.

When Bindusara died, there was a struggle for the Maurya throne. One legend says that Asoka killed his own brothers in order to become emperor. After four years of fighting, Asoka became the third Maurya emperor.

Asoka spent the next eight years strengthening his hold on power. Then, he went to war again. His target was the kingdom of Kalinga, which had resisted conquest. The war between Maurya and Kalinga was long and terrible. **Eventually**, Asoka conquered Kalinga, but at a terrible cost. Thousands of soldiers died. Another 150,000 people were captured and sent to other parts of the empire.

Academic Vocabulary
eventually • *adv.*, after a long time

Asoka was shocked by the suffering caused by the war. "The slaughter, death, and carrying away of captive people," he later wrote, "is a matter of profound sorrow and regret to His Sacred Majesty."

New Rules for the Empire The suffering that Asoka saw during the war made him think hard about how he wanted to rule. Asoka began trying to follow Buddhist values. He turned away from violence.

Supported with Buddhist ideals, Asoka replaced rule by force with rule based on dharma, or moral law. His rule of moral law included three principles. The first was the principle of ahimsa, or the belief that one should not hurt any living thing. Asoka gave up hunting and banned the cruel treatment of animals.

INTERACTIVE
Asoka's Life

The second principle was tolerance. **Tolerance** is a willingness to respect different beliefs and customs. Asoka was a Buddhist, but he respected Hinduism, Jainism, and other religions.

The third principle was the people's well-being. Asoka believed that a ruler must be careful to rule his people well. As a result, Asoka made many decisions to make his empire a better place to live.

BIOGRAPHY
5 Things to Know About
ASOKA MAURYA
Emperor

- Asoka reportedly studied Buddhism at a Buddhist monastery while recovering from his wounds from the conquering of Kalinga.
- Asoka built hospitals for animals as well as hospitals for people.
- Mahinda, who was either a son or brother of Asoka, was the first Buddhist monk on the island of Sri Lanka.
- Asoka created a special group of high officers who went out into communities to encourage dharma work.
- Asoka built many stupas, which were Buddhist commemorative burial mounds.

Critical Thinking Explain how one of Asoka's actions directly reflected one or more of his three principles of moral law.

INVESTIGATE

Why Did Asoka Turn to Peace?

Discuss how Chandragupta's grandson, Asoka, changed the focus of the Maurya Empire.

Hypothesize Ask: What was Asoka like when he first became emperor? *(Sample answer: He was ruthless.)* Ask: Why would his experience during war cause him to preach **tolerance**? *(Sample answer: Experiencing so much death and destruction would shock a person into changing outlooks.)*

Infer After reading the biography, ask students to infer how Asoka's change affected the empire. *(Possible answer: People had to begin living according to dharma.)*

INTERACTIVE **INTERACTIVE CHART**

Asoka's Life

Display the Interactive Chart: Asoka's Life for the class. Drag and drop events onto the timeline of Asoka's life.

ACTIVE CLASSROOM

Use a Quick Write, allowing students 30 seconds to write a headline that captures the most important aspect of Asoka's life. Then have them review their headlines in pairs.

ELD TIP Pair developing students with fluent speakers, and provide pairs with other words and expressions similar to *eventually: ultimately, sooner or later.* Have students sort the expressions according to formality.

ANSWERS

Critical Thinking *Sample answer: Building hospitals for animals as well as people reflects both ahimsa and the people's well-being.*

INTEGRATED ENGLISH LANGUAGE DEVELOPMENT

Structure Cohesive Texts Use Why Did Asoka Turn to Peace? to help students understand how ideas are linked throughout a text. Then encourage students to use similar techniques in their own speaking and writing as they answer questions.

Emerging Read the text aloud, pausing to clarify ideas and track events. Point out how the use of *he* and *they* to refer to Chandragupta and Jains in the first paragraph. Ask students to spot other pronoun references in the passage.

Expanding Read Buddhism Expands aloud. Ask, In the second sentence, who does his refer to? *(Asoka)* Why does the writer say *the religion* instead of repeating Buddhism? *(to avoid repetition)*

Bridging Read Asoka's Stone Pillars and Buddhism Expands aloud. Ask,

(Continued on the next page.)

Compare Ask: To what modern object can Asoka's pillars be compared? Explain. *(They can be compared to roadside billboards. Both provide messages to travelers on the road.)*

Identify Cause and Effect Ask: What was the main cause of Buddhism's expansion and the construction of monasteries and **stupas**? *(As a Buddhist, Asoka supported its expansion, which gave the religion prestige.)*

INTERACTIVE **PRIMARY SOURCES**

Have students go online to analyze Asoka's Edicts. Then have volunteers paraphrase each statement in their own words. *(Sample answer: "The faiths of others all deserve to be honored... By acting otherwise, one injures one's own faith." can be restated as "If one is intolerant of another's religion, it reflects badly on one's own religion.")*

ACTIVE JOURNAL

Quest Connection As students read the text and analyze the photograph, direct them to the Quest Connections pages in their Active Journals. Make sure that students understand how this photograph helps them with their Quest.

What Was Asoka's Legacy?

Invite students to speculate about whether Asoka's legacy affected people in India after his rule ended.

▲ Ceremonies celebrating the introduction of Buddhism to Sri Lanka

Quest CONNECTIONS

Look at the ceremony at the Buddhist monastery in Sri Lanka. What could visitors learn about Buddhism today from visiting such a monastery? Explore more about these monasteries and record your findings in your Active Journal.

Asoka's Stone Pillars To share his ideas, Asoka had stone pillars, or columns, set up across his empire. Each pillar rose 40 feet into the air and weighed 50 tons. Some of Asoka's stone pillars are still standing today.

These pillars were not just decorative. Asoka had messages carved into the polished pillars. In some of these messages, he assured his subjects that he was focused on their well-being. He apologized for making war on Kalinga, and he explained his new goals. He urged people to respect their parents and to be generous to other people. He urged respect for all religions. Most of all, Asoka encouraged people to live moral lives.

Buddhism Expands While Asoka respected all religions, he became a follower of Buddhism. His support for Buddhism helped the religion spread. With Asoka's backing, Buddhists were able to build monasteries and shrines throughout India. They also built **stupas**, Buddhist commemorative burial mounds, that still exist.

Buddhists also sent missionaries to neighboring countries, such as Sri Lanka. The support of the powerful Maurya emperor gave the religion prestige. This encouraged other rulers to adopt it.

READING CHECK **Understand Effects** How did each of the three principles of Asoka's rule of law improve life for his people?

INTEGRATED ENGLISH LANGUAGE DEVELOPMENT continued ELD.PII.A.2a

In the second paragraph, why does the writer say "these pillars" rather than "Asoka's stone pillars"? *(Their being stone was already stated.)* After reading the last paragraph, ask, What does *it* refer to? (Buddhism) Why does the writer use the word? *(to avoid repetition)*

WORKSHEET **TEACHER RESOURCES**

For additional IELD support addressing these standards, have students complete the Lesson ELD activity from the Teacher Resources found on the course.

What Was Asoka's Legacy?

Asoka ruled India for nearly 40 years. During that time, he did much to improve life for his people. He set up hospitals and dug wells. He built an excellent road system.

The roads promoted trade within the empire. They also increased trade with neighboring lands, such as the Greek-controlled kingdoms of southwest Asia.

The longest of these roads—the Royal Road—stretched more than a thousand miles across northern India. Trees along the road provided shade for travelers. Rest houses offered food and shelter.

As a result of Asoka's efforts, India prospered. The country was at peace. There was little crime. People could leave their homes unguarded and travel the country without fear.

Asoka died in 232 BCE. After his death, the Maurya empire struggled. The emperors that followed Asoka were weak. As you have read, the Maurya government depended completely on the emperor's ability to make good decisions and command loyalty. As emperors lost control of parts of the empire, they lost support. In 185 BCE, the last Maurya ruler was murdered. After 136 years, the Maurya empire had come to an end.

▼ Stupa in Sanchi, India

READING CHECK **Use Evidence** Which of Asoka's achievements do you think was his greatest? Why?

Lesson Check

HSS 6.5.6; ELD.P1.A.2, P1.C.10.a

Practice Vocabulary

1. Use the term **tolerance** to describe the rule of Asoka.

Critical Thinking and Writing

2. **Analyze Information** What role did the stone pillars Asoka created play in his rule?
3. **Draw Conclusions** How did Asoka incorporate the well-being of his people into activities such as trade along the Royal Road?
4. **Understand Effects** How did Asoka's rule promote Buddhism?
5. **Writing Workshop: Develop a Clear Thesis** Think about the information you have collected on technological innovations in ancient India for your research paper. What conclusions can you draw about how technology was used, the process by which it was developed, or the areas of life affected by new technology? Write a clear thesis on the subject in your Active Journal.

LESSON CHECK

1. Asoka promoted tolerance of all religions, which led to peace and prosperity. **DOK2**
2. They enabled him to communicate with his people and promote moral law. He used the messages on the pillars to urge people to live better lives. **DOK2**
3. He built the road with features to help travelers, such as trees to provide shade and rest houses offering food and shelter. **DOK2**
4. He gave the religion prestige, which encouraged other rulers to adopt it. **DOK2**
5. Students should organize their information and develop a thesis stating how technological innovations were developed and used and how they changed people's lives in ancient India. **DOK4**

HSS 6.5.6; ELD.P1.A.2, P1.C.10.a

SYNTHESIZE

Assess and Reteach Have students use the Give One, Get One strategy to complete Lesson Check questions 1–4. Review their responses. If they had any incorrect answers, use the Guiding Questions to discuss the lesson's main ideas, focusing on the ideas they struggled with.

ACTIVE JOURNAL

Writing Workshop Have students complete the Lesson 6 Writing Task in their Active Journals. Students will draw conclusions and develop a thesis statement for their research papers.

DEMONSTRATE

ASSESSMENT **ONLINE LESSON QUIZ**

Assign the Online Lesson Quiz for this lesson if you haven't already done so. Students will be offered automatic remediation or enrichment based on their score.

DISCUSSION **DISCUSSION BOARD**

Post this question to the class on the Discussion Board:

Distinguish Cause and Effect How did Buddhism help Asoka reach his goals? *Sample answer: Because Buddhism emphasized doing no harm, tolerance, and well-being, when people adhered to its principles, his empire was more peaceful and law-abiding; this made it easier and less expensive to govern. It also became more prosperous.)*

ANSWERS

Understand Effects *Ahimsa protected people from harm. Tolerance allowed people religious freedom. Well-being made sure his people were cared for.*

Use Evidence *Sample answer: The ways Asoka improved his people's lives were his greatest achievement because they had the greatest impact. His people were happy and healthy, so India prospered.*

HSS.6.5.7

The Gupta Empire

CONNECT

GET READY TO READ

ETEXT **START UP**

Project the Start Up Activity. As students enter the classroom and get settled, ask them to examine the photograph of modern Indian dancers performing a traditional dance.

Draw Conclusions Have students write about why ancient practices like these dances are still being followed today. *(Possible answers: They become cherished traditions. People still draw value and pleasure from them.)*

Discuss Remind students that some of the modern world's most important concepts and practices rely on a foundation of thought that may be hundreds and even thousands of years old.

After completing the Start Up activity, project the Lesson Opener or direct students to their textbooks. Preview the lesson by working through the Get Ready to Read items with the class. Remind students to pay close attention to the Guiding Questions as they read the lesson.

ACTIVE JOURNAL

Take Notes Have students use the literacy skills graphic organizer in their Active Journals to take notes as they read the lesson.

Practice Vocabulary Have students complete the activity in their Active Journals to build their vocabulary.

VIDEO **VIDEO**

Assign the lesson video as homework.

The Gupta Empire

BOUNCE TO ACTIVATE VIDEO

GET READY TO READ

START UP

Look at the photo of modern Indian dancers performing a traditional dance. Why might ancient arts still be practiced in India today?

GUIDING QUESTIONS

- How did the Gupta dynasty created the second major Indian empire?
- During Gupta rule, how did India make advances in the arts, science, and mathematics, including our modern system of numerals?

TAKE NOTES

Literacy Skills: Summarize

Use the graphic organizer in your Active Journal to take notes as you read the lesson.

PRACTICE VOCABULARY

Use the vocabulary activity in your Active Journal to practice the vocabulary words.

Vocabulary	Academic Vocabulary
citizenship	drama
numeral	extract
decimal system	
metallurgy	

After the collapse of the Maurya empire, India broke into many small kingdoms. Armies from the north and west invaded India repeatedly. Meanwhile, trade brought Indians into contact with China, Southeast Asia, and the Roman empire. Invaders and traders brought new ideas from the ancient Greeks and other peoples. Indians built on these ideas to make their own advances in art, literature, math, and science.

A New Empire in India

About 500 years after the Mauryas, the Gupta dynasty reunited northern India. Chandra Gupta I, the first Gupta ruler, may have been named after the founder of the Maurya empire, Chandragupta. Like the first Maurya emperor, Chandra Gupta I dreamed of building an empire. He gained power over a kingdom in the Ganges Basin and ruled from about 320 CE to 335 CE. He expanded his territory across the Ganges Basin through alliances and wars of conquest.

PRACTICE VOCABULARY

To help students integrate new vocabulary, explain that these terms name concepts and things that can be traced to the Gupta Empire. *Citizenship* is a human status with political rights and obligations. A *numeral* is a symbol that represents a number. The *decimal system* is a counting system based on units of ten. *Metallurgy* is a science dealing with extracting metal from ore and using it to create objects. Reinforce the terms during the lesson using the teaching notes.

Have students locate and pronounce the academic vocabulary in the lesson margins. Provide sample sentences that clarify meaning.

drama: Julio prefers watching dramas to reading novels because he enjoys the acting.

extract: Miners extracted gold from deep within the ground.

Chandra Gupta's son, Samudra Gupta, conquered most of the remaining small kingdoms of northern India, calling himself the "Exterminator of Kings." Samudra Gupta also conquered lands to the south and west.

Under Samudra's son, Chandra Gupta II, the Gupta empire reached its greatest size. He conquered areas along the west coast. Then, like Asoka, he tried to bring peace and prosperity to India. Unlike the Mauryas, the Guptas did not try to rule their entire empire directly. Instead, they left most decisions in the hands of local leaders. Governors controlled provinces. Village and city councils made decisions at the local level.

In each village, the leading families sent representatives to the council. In the cities, guilds, or groups of merchants or craftsmen working in the same line of business, sent representatives to the city council. People living in the Maurya empire were subjects, with a duty to obey. The people of the Gupta empire were also subjects, but some also had a kind of **citizenship**, or a status with political rights and obligations.

A Buddhist monk from China named Fa Xian (fah shen) visited India under the Guptas. He wrote:

Did you know?

The name Gupta is a common last name in India today. It means *ruler* or *protector.*

Primary Source

The people are numerous and happy. . . . If they want to go, they go. If they want to stay, they stay. The king governs without . . . corporal [physical] punishments[.]

—Fa Xian, *A Record of the Buddhistic Kingdoms*

Gupta Empire

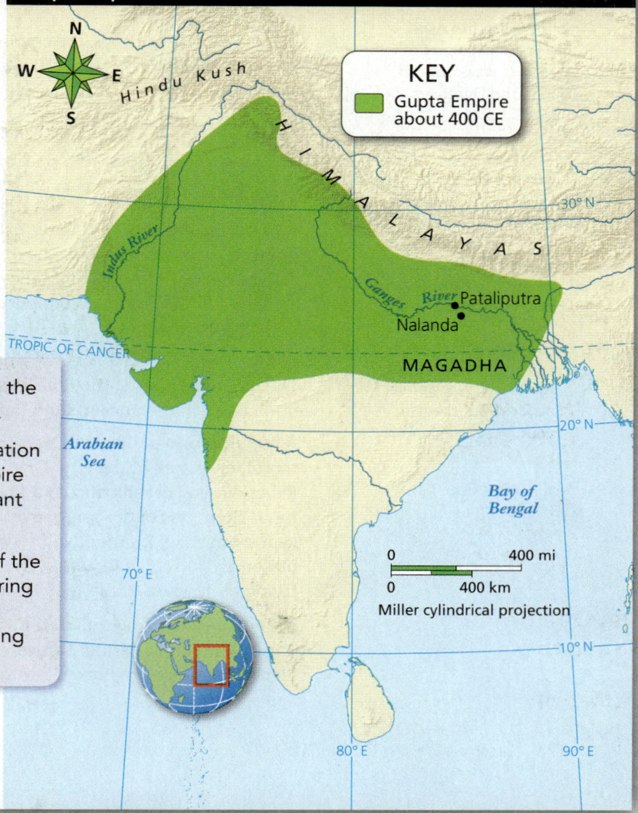

GEOGRAPHY SKILLS

The Gupta empire stretched from the Arabian Sea to the Bay of Bengal.

1. **Movement** How might the location and expanse of the Gupta empire have promoted trade with distant lands?
2. **Sequence** Place these events of the Gupta empire in order: conquering of northern kingdoms; allowing local decision making; conquering areas along the west coast.

WORKSHEET **TEACHER RESOURCES**

Have students who need additional support use the following worksheets from the Teacher Resources on the course:

- **Reading Support**
- **English Language Development**
- **Lesson Summary**

INVESTIGATE

A New Empire in India

Discuss how, after a centuries of unrest, a new dynasty reunited northern India, paving the way for advances in arts, sciences, and mathematics.

Summarize Ask: What happened to India after the collapse of the Maurya empire? *(It broke into small kingdoms, and armies invaded repeatedly. Trade brought contact with the Romans, China, and Southeast Asia, which brought new ideas.)*

Compare and Contrast Ask: How did the Guptas' and the Mauryas' approach to governing differ? *(The Guptas allowed their subjects to have rights of citizenship, whereas the Mauryas controlled everything from the top.)*

Identify Ask: Under which ruler did the Gupta empire reach its greatest size? *(Chandra Gupta II)*

INTEGRATED ENGLISH LANGUAGE DEVELOPMENT

Structuring Cohesive Texts Use A New Empire in India to help students write comparisons of Indian empires.

Entering Read the text aloud, pausing to note differences between the two dynasties. Have students write three differences between the dynasties using *but, however,* and *in contrast.*

Expanding As students read, have them take notes on similarities and differences between the two dynasties. When finished, pair students to write a paragraph comparing and contrasting the dynasties, using words such as *like, unlike, similarly, on the other hand,* and *although.*

Bridging After students read independently, pair them to compare notes about the two dynasties. Then, have each student write a paragraph comparing and contrasting the two

(*Continued on the next page.*)

ANSWERS

Movement *The empire stretched across India from the Arabian Sea to the Bay of Bengal, so its traders could access sea routes to distant ports east and west.*

Sequence *expanding across the Ganges Basin; conquering northern kingdoms; conquering areas along the west coast; allowing local decision making*

What Was Gupta Culture Like?

The arts flourished during the Gupta period and their influence has lasted into the present day.

Summarize Ask: What three forms of literature flourished around the time of the Guptas? *(plays, poetry, fables)*

Identify Ask: Who was considered the greatest writer during the Gupta reign? *(Kalidasa)*

Describe Ask: What other fables do you know, and what are their morals? *(Sample answers: "The Tortoise and the Hare"—slow and steady wins the race; "The Three Little Pigs"—hard work pays off in the end)*

Identify Ask: What board game was invented in India? *(chess)*

Draw Conclusions During the Gupta empire, dance was entertainment as well as part of religious ceremonies. Ask: What entertaining traits would you expect to see in the dances? *(colorful costumes, elaborate movements, striking facial expressions, strong symbolism)*

ACTIVE JOURNAL

Quest Connection As students read and analyze the text, direct them to the Quest Connections pages in their Active Journals. Make sure that students understand how works of Indian art such as this helps them in their Quest.

ANSWERS

Sequence *Chandra Gupta I expanded across northern India through war and alliances after he took over a kingdom in the Ganges Basin. Then his son, Samudra Gupta, conquered the remaining small kingdoms of northern India. Finally, Chandra Gupta II tried to bring peace and prosperity.*

▲ Murals in the Ajanta caves are examples of Buddhist art produced during the Gupta empire.

Under later Gupta rulers, the empire faced new invaders from the west. Parts of the empire broke away. The last Gupta ruler died around the year 540.

READING CHECK **Sequence** How did the Gupta empire develop from a warring empire to a peaceful land?

Quest CONNECTIONS

Travelers to India want to see the art created during the Gupta Era. Think about why travelers would want to see a painting such as these murals in the Ajanta caves. Capture notes about them in your Active Journal.

What Was Gupta Culture Like?

Around the time of the Guptas, artists produced great literature, painting, and architecture. The art and literature of the Gupta period still influence Indian culture today. Much of this art was religious. While Buddhism remained important under the Guptas, the Guptas favored Hinduism.

A Flowering of Literature Under Gupta rule, literature flourished. The greatest writer of the time was the poet Kalidasa, who wrote plays and poetry in the ancient language of Sanskrit.

A popular form of literature was the fable. A fable is a short story with a moral, or lesson, at the end. One Indian fable describes two frogs that fell into a pail of milk and could not jump out. They swam for a long time. Then, one of the frogs gave up hope and drowned. The other frog kept swimming. Eventually, the swimming frog churned the milk into butter and was able to jump out easily. The lesson of this fable is to keep trying even when things look hopeless.

Music, Dance, and Entertainment Music and dance thrived during the Gupta period. Dancers created works based on Hindu literature. Musicians played stringed instruments and drums.

INTEGRATED ENGLISH LANGUAGE DEVELOPMENT continued ELD.PII.A.2b

dynasties, using words such as *like, unlike, similarly, whereas, in contrast,* and *on the other hand.*

WORKSHEET **TEACHER RESOURCES**

For additional IELD support addressing these standards, have students complete the Lesson ELD activity from the Teacher Resources found on the course.

Some forms of Indian **drama** combined stories, dance, and music. Performers with elaborate makeup and costumes told stories through song and dance.

The game of chess was invented under the Guptas. From India, the game moved along trade routes both east, into other parts of Asia, and west, into the Middle East and Europe.

Architecture and Painting Hindus and Buddhists built many temples and monasteries during this time. Stonecutters carved some temple buildings from rock. Architects also built impressive free-standing temples and monasteries. Both rock-carved and free-standing temples show good engineering skills.

Just after the Gupta period, Indians carved temples and monasteries into the rocks of cliffs. In central India, the rock-cut shrines of Ellora contain brilliant sculptures and paintings.

Academic Vocabulary
drama • *n.*, plays or performances that tell stories

INTERACTIVE
A Golden Age in the Arts

READING CHECK **Compare and Contrast** How did a fable differ from poems or plays in the Gupta empire?

Mathematics and Science

During the Gupta period, trade and invasion brought the learning of Greece and Persia to India. Indian scholars drew on this learning to make advances of their own in mathematics and science.

The Decimal System Indian mathematicians developed the concept of zero as a number and as a **numeral**, or a symbol used to represent a number. Probably the greatest advance was the **decimal system**, a counting system based on units of ten. Together these advances were the basis for what we know as the Hindu-Arabic, or Arabic, numerals, in use worldwide today.

A New World of Mathematics Combining a decimal system with a numeral for zero transformed mathematics. With the new Indian system of numerals, multiplication and division became much easier. This new system opened the way for other advances in mathematics, such as algebra.

Aryabhata (ahr yuh BUH tuh) was an important Indian astronomer

Origins of Arabic Numerals

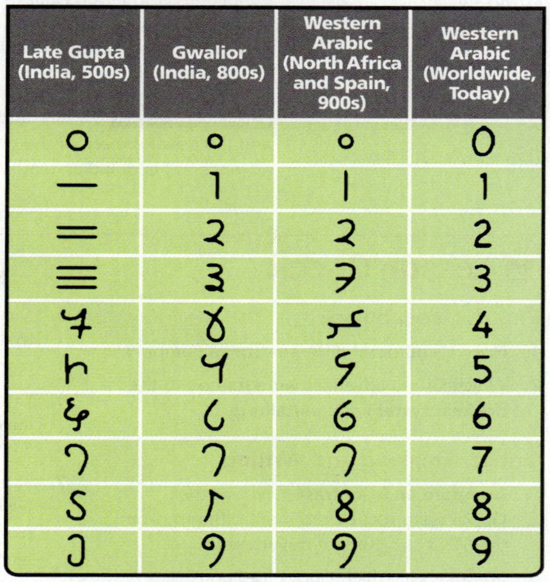

Analyze Charts Gupta mathematicians developed numerals 1,500 years ago that evolved into the shapes we use today. **Identify Main Ideas** Which numeral especially transformed mathematics? Why?

INTERACTIVE **INTERACTIVE GALLERY**

A Golden Age in the Arts

Display the Interactive Gallery: A Golden Age in the Arts for the class to show some of the great cultural achievements of the Gupta era. Click through the images, discussing each one.

ACTIVE CLASSROOM

Use the Closer Look activity. Project each image, and use a whiteboard tool to divide it into four numbered quadrants. Have students count off 1 to 4 and examine their quadrants. Have them share their observations and insights in a class discussion.

Mathematics and Science

Gupta thinkers made lasting contributions to mathematics and science.

Synthesize Ask: How does the concept of zero affect understanding of the real world? *(People can express quantities having opposite directions or values: for example, elevations above and below sea level and temperatures above and below zero.)*

CURRICULUM CONNECTION: VISUAL AND PERFORMING ARTS

Indian Dance and Music One form of Indian dance is called Bharata Natyam. It is named for the sage Bharat, with whom an Indian God is said to have shared the secrets of dance. His name is a combination of the abbreviations for *Bhava* (expressions), *Raga* (melody), and *Tala* (rhythm)—the three basic parts of the dance. It takes years to learn the 120 basic positions of Bharata Natyam. Thousands of variations on the basic moves can tell an infinite number of stories. Most of the dance takes place in one spot, as the dancer constantly bends her knees, moves her feet to complicated rhythms, and uses hand movements to tell a story. A single female dancer performs the dance in a performance that lasts two hours with no rest. She is accompanied by two musicians, one playing drums to provide the rhythm, and a singer. The Bharata Natyam was originally a temple dance, and the dance presents Hindu themes and concepts.

ANSWERS

Compare and Contrast *A fable has a moral whereas a play or poem does not necessarily have a moral.*

Identify Main Ideas *Sample answer: The numeral zero especially transformed mathematics. It allowed the concept of negative numbers. It helped make multiplication and division faster.*

HSS 6.5.7; ELD.P1.A.2, P1.C.10.a

SYNTHESIZE

Assess and Reteach Have students use a Think-Pair-Share strategy to complete Lesson Check questions 1–6. Review their responses. If they had any incorrect answers, use the guiding questions to discuss the lesson's main ideas, focusing on the ideas they struggled with.

ACTIVE JOURNAL

Writing Workshop Have students complete the Lesson 7 Writing Task in their Active Journals. Students will draft an introductory paragraph that explains their conclusion about the topic and previews how the topic will be discussed.

DEMONSTRATE

ASSESSMENT **ONLINE LESSON QUIZ**

Assign the Online Lesson Quiz for this lesson. Students will be offered automatic remediation or enrichment based on their score.

DISCUSSION **DISCUSSION BOARD**

Post this question to the class on the Discussion Board:

Summarize What were the most important Indian contributions to the world during the Gupta empire? *(Sample answer: Indian mathematicians invented zero and the decimal system. Indian writers crafted drama, fables, and poetry that is still performed. Indian scientists made discoveries about the universe and medicine. Indian artisans made advancements in metalwork.)*

ANSWERS

Understand Effects *They completely changed the way mathematical operations were done. Multiplication and division became much easier, which led to even greater advancements in math, such as algebra.*

Analyze Images Eighteenth century sundial in Jaipur, India, built in the style used by Indian astronomers

and mathematician. In 499 CE, Aryabhata wrote a mathematics book on arithmetic, algebra, and trigonometry.

Hundreds of years later, mathematicians in Europe relied on Aryabhata's work to calculate the area of triangles and the volume of spheres.

Astronomy Aryabhata was the first astronomer to state that the Earth rotates, or spins, on its axis to create day and night. He discovered that eclipses were caused by the motion of Earth and the moon. Aryabhata also discovered that the moon shines because it reflects sunlight.

Medicine Indian doctors made progress in medical science as well. They developed a system of medicine known as Ayurveda. Ancient Ayurvedic medical textbooks describe many different diseases and how to treat medical problems. They also explain how to make hundreds of medicines from plants, animal parts, and minerals.

Academic Vocabulary
extract • *v.*, remove, draw out

Metallurgy Gupta artisans also made progress in **metallurgy**, the science that deals with **extracting** metal from ore and using it to create useful objects. The Iron Pillar of Delhi is a famous example of their skill in producing metal compounds of great quality. This 23-foot-high column was made from a single piece of iron. It has stood outside for more than 1,500 years without turning to rust.

READING CHECK **Understand Effects** Why are the decimal system and the development of the concept of zero considered the greatest advancements of Indian mathematicians?

Lesson Check

HSS 6.5.7; ELD.P1.A.2, P1.C.10.a

Practice Vocabulary

1. How is a **numeral** different from a number?
2. Which Gupta advances were related to the **decimal system** and **metallurgy**?

Critical Thinking and Writing

3. **Compare and Contrast** How was the Gupta system of government different from the Maurya system of government?
4. **Summarize** Which Gupta traditions continue to influence the art of India today?
5. **Cite Evidence** How do historians know that metal workers in the Gupta empire made great progress in metallurgy?
6. **Cite Evidence** What proof do historians have of how medicine was practiced in the Gupta empire?
7. **Writing Workshop: Write an Introduction** Write an introductory paragraph for your research paper on technological innovation in ancient India in your Active Journal. Explain what you concluded from your research and how you are going to show it in the body of the paper.

LESSON CHECK

1. A numeral is a symbol used to represent a number. **DOK2**
2. numeral zero; metals that did not rust **DOK2**
3. Maurya emperors used an elaborate bureaucracy to rule subjects. Gupta emperors left many government decisions in the hands of locals. **DOK3**
4. Traditions in dance, music, architecture, and sculpture **DOK3**
5. The Iron Pillar of Delhi Delhi was made in Gupta times from one piece of iron and has not rusted despite being 1,500 years old. **DOK3**
6. ancient medical textbooks that describe many different diseases and treatments **DOK3**
7. Students' introductions should state their thesis and set the essay's organization. **DOK4**

HSS 6.5.5; Analysis CST.3; ELA RI.6.7

Interpret Thematic Maps

Follow these steps to review the ways to analyze a thematic map.

INTERACTIVE

Read Special Purpose Maps

1 Identify the topic of the thematic map. A thematic map shows information about an area. The map title indicates the type of map and its topic. The key also gives information.

a. What is the title of this map? What does it tell you about the map?

b. What does the key to this map tell you about the information the map shows?

c. How can you use the key to help you find specific information on the map?

2 Determine the place on the map. Map titles indicate the map's region. When it does not, use the map or nearby text to understand what area is being shown.

a. Does the title indicate the region?

b. What information tells you the place or places shown on the map?

3 Determine the time shown on the map. Look for dates in the map title or key. If no dates are shown, look for clues in the title and key. Look also at information around the map to find clues about the time. Read the text that accompanies the map. What information lets you know the period?

4 Explain what the map shows. Use the key to understand colors and symbols.

a. What does the shaded area show?

b. Where did Buddhism start?

Secondary Source

The Buddha urged his followers to carry his teachings to all corners of Earth. A person who spreads religious ideas is a missionary. Buddhist missionaries carried Buddhism across India and to Sri Lanka, then throughout Asia. Some traveled north to Central Asia. Then missionaries followed trade routes east into China. Buddhism spread to Korea and Japan. Buddhism arrived later in Tibet.

The Spread of Buddhism

DIFFERENTIATED INSTRUCTION

Below Level Tell students that the arrows show the general directions in which Buddhism spread from its origins. Liken the spreading influence of the missionaries to what happens when a river overflows its banks: the water spreads out and touches all points near its path, just as teachings of missionaries spread out and touch many people near their path.

INTEGRATED ENGLISH LANGUAGE INSTRUCTION

Emerging To help students understand map terminology, have a volunteer point to the title, key, and nearby text (secondary source). As you read the Secondary Source aloud, have students use a pointer to follow Buddhism's spread on the map.

HSS 6.5.5; Analysis CST.3; ELA RI.6.7

Analysis Skills

Interpret Thematic Maps

VIDEO **21ST CENTURY SKILLS**

Project the Compare Viewpoints video in the 21st Century Skills Tutorial. Use the Quick Reference and Assessment to provide additional instruction in the skill.

LEARN

Ask a volunteer to read each step aloud and clarify any misunderstandings that arise. Then play the video.

PRACTICE

Have students practice the skill using the map and text on the page. Reread each step, and allow students time to answer before reviewing answers as the class.

ASSESS

To assess this skill, have students apply the skill to the trade route map in Lesson 1 or the maps of the Maurya and Gupta empires in Lessons 5 and 7.

ANSWERS

1. a. The title is "The Spread of Buddhism." It indicates the map will show how the religion spread.
b. The key indicates the map shows where Buddhism originated and the routes along which it spread to other regions.
c. The information in the key explains what the markings on the map mean.

2. a. The title does not state the region.
b. The locator map indicates that the places on the map are in Asia, and the labels identify specific places.

3. There are no dates on the map. The text accompanying the map discusses what the Buddha urged his followers to do, which means the map's time period is during and after the Buddha's life—around the fifth century BCE.

4. a. where Buddhism originated
b. Buddhism started in eastern India, near Nepal.

HSS 6.5.1, 6.5.2, 6.5.3, 6.5.4, 6.5.5, 6.5.6, 6.5.7; ELA W.6.4–5, 7–8; WHST.6.7–9; ELD.P1.A.2, P1.C.10.a

Review and Assessment

VISUAL REVIEW

Direct students' attention to the "Comparing Hinduism and Buddhism" Venn diagram. Discuss as a class how each religion shaped its followers' outlook on the world. Then focus on the characteristics shared by both religions.

Direct students' attention to the "Early Indian Civilizations and Empires" flow chart. As a class, discuss each civilization or empire, and then ask students to summarize key characteristics of each in their own words.

READING REVIEW

WORKSHEET **TEACHER RESOURCES**

Have students who need additional support read the Lesson Summaries available in Teacher Resources on the Realize Course.

GAMES **TOPIC MINI-GAMES**

For additional vocabulary practice, students can go online to access the Topic Mini-Games in Realize.

Quest FINDINGS

Make Your Travel Brochure

Have students complete their Topic Quests by creating their travel brochure in their Active Journals. Remind students to follow the writing process steps: (1) prewrite; (2) draft; (3) share; (4) revise; and (5) present. **DOK4**

TOPIC 4

Review and Assessment

VISUAL REVIEW

Comparing Hinduism and Buddhism

HINDUISM
- Epic poems
- Upanishads sacred writings
- Worship of many Gods
- Belief in a supreme spiritual force
- Four goals

SIMILARITIES
- Began in India
- Belief in karma
- Belief in reincarnation
- Spread throughout the world

BUDDHISM
- Begun by Siddhartha Gautama (the Buddha)
- No gods
- The Middle Way
- Four Noble Truths
- Eightfold Path

Early Indian Civilizations and Empires

Indus Saraswati	→	Vedic Kingdoms	→	Maurya Empire	→	Gupta Empire
• Built cities in a grid pattern • Established system of weights and measurements		• Compiled the Vedas and the Upanishads • Spoke Sanskrit • Spread Hinduism		• Organized efficient government • Established trade with other regions • Built roads and hospitals		• Wrote Sanskrit literature • Made advances in medicine, metallurgy, and mathematics

READING REVIEW

Use the Take Notes and Practice Vocabulary activities in your Active Journal to review the topic.

INTERACTIVE

Practice vocabulary using the Topic Mini-Games.

Quest FINDINGS

Make Your Travel Brochure

Get help for making your travel brochure in your Active Journal.

180 Topic 4 • Early Civilizations of India

ANSWERS

1. He divided the empire into four regions, and then divided each region into smaller provinces. A bureaucracy of appointed officials in each region, province, and village carried out the emperor's orders. **DOK1**
2. They sent representatives to village or city councils and so helped govern. They could enter or leave their region without punishment. **DOK1**
3. Citadels were walled, fortified areas built on raised platforms. They were possible centers of government or religion. **DOK2**
4. The Kshatriyas had a great deal of power, second only to the Brahmins. The two groups had different roles also. Kshatriyas governed and fought battles; the Vaishyas owned land and ran banks and stores but were not involved with governing. **DOK2**
5. Dharma is a person's duty to do what is right. What is right includes ahimsa, or not harming any living thing. **DOK2**
6. The monsoons brought the rain that allowed people to grow food. **DOK1**
7. Kautilya's strategy was to protect the subjects of the empire, but he believed they could not be trusted. Asoka's strategy was to make the empire a better place to live. **DOK2**

HSS 6.5.1, 6.5.2, 6.5.3, 6.5.4, 6.5.5, 6.5.6, 6.5.7; ELA W.6.4-5, 7.7–8; WHST.6.7–9; ELD.P1.A.2, P1.C.10.a

ASSESSMENT

Vocabulary and Key Ideas

1. **Describe** How did Chandragupta's **bureaucracy** work?
2. **Check Understanding** What **citizenship** rights did people have in the Gupta empire?
3. **Describe** Describe the **citadels** of the Indus Saraswati civilization and their possible function.
4. **Identify Main Ideas** How was life for **Kshatriyas** different from life for **Vaishyas**?
5. **Identify Supporting Details** How are **dharma** and **ahimsa** related in Hinduism?
6. **Recall** How did early Indian civilizations depend on **monsoons**?
7. **Describe** Kautilya's **strategy** for governing and how it differed from Asoka's strategy.

Critical Thinking and Writing

8. **Identify Main Ideas** Why are important aspects of the rise and decline of the Indus Saraswati civilization so mysterious?
9. **Infer** What are the main paths to moksha in Hinduism, and how might the acceptance of these paths have contributed to the spread of Hinduism?
10. **Compare and Contrast** How is Buddhism similar to and different from Hinduism?
11. **Infer** Why would discoveries in metallurgy be important to a civilization?
12. **Revisit the Essential Question** How have cultures of ancient India endured to today?
13. **Writing Workshop: Write a Research Paper** Using the notes you have made and the sources you have found, write a research paper on technological innovations in ancient India.

Analyze Primary Sources

14. For whom is the source below likely written?

"In the happiness of his subjects lies the king's happiness. In the welfare of his subjects, his welfare. A king's good is not that which pleases him, but that which pleases his subjects."

—*Kautilya, Arthashastra*

Analyze Maps

Use the map to answer the following questions.

15. Which of these empires was most likely significantly stronger than its neighbors? Why?
16. Why might both empires have wanted access to both the Arabian Sea and the Bay of Bengal?
17. How is the location of these two empires related to the geography of the Indian subcontinent?

▼ Ancient India

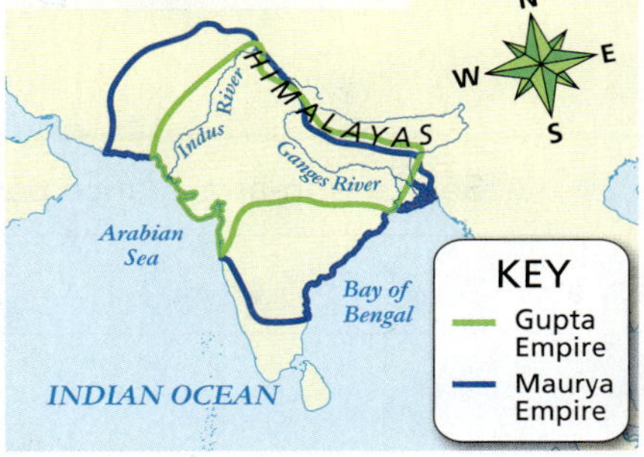

Review and Assessment 181

8. Sample response: The system of writing is not understood, so whatever records they kept cannot be read. In addition, scholars do not understand what factor or factors caused the decline of that civilization. **DOK3**

9. The four paths are the way of knowledge, the way of works, the way of devotion, and the way of meditation. The acceptance of four paths made it possible for people to find a way to adhere to Hinduism that suited them, making it easier for more people to accept the religion. **DOK3**

10. Sample response: Both religions began in ancient India and spread. Both reflect belief in karma, reincarnation, and leading a moral life. Hinduism has many Gods and Goddesses and recognizes four ways of achieving moksha, or liberation from reincarnation. Buddhism does not include a belief in specific gods and seeks enlightenment. **DOK3**

11. Sample response: Discoveries in metallurgy lead to improvements in metals, which result in stronger, safer, and longer lasting buildings and tools. **DOK3**

12. Sample response: Many aspects of ancient Indian culture can still be seen today. The most important enduring legacies are the religions, like Hinduism, Buddhism, and Jainism, which began in ancient India and still have millions of followers. Ancient structures like temples, religious statues, and the stone columns of Asoka still stand. The stories of the *Ramayana* and *Mahabharata* still inspire people today, as do ancient sculpture, paintings, and dance forms. **DOK3**

13. Students should write their research paper describing technological innovations in India. **DOK4**

14. an emperor **DOK3**

15. The Maurya empire was probably stronger than its neighbors because it was larger, which indicates it had conquered more rival powers. **DOK3**

16. to enable trade to both the east and the west **DOK3**

17. Both empires included the major river valleys of the Indus and Ganges Rivers, which have fertile soil that can support crop production and a growing population. **DOK3**

ASSESSMENT **TOPIC TEST**

For summative assessment, assign the Topic Test in Realize.

Early Civilizations of China
(1700 BCE–220 BCE)

Pacing: Approximately 21 periods, 10.5 blocks	Resources: Student Edition	Resources: Active Journal	Resources: Online	Pacing	California Standards
CONNECT					
NBC LEARN VIDEO Shi Huangdi, First Emperor of United China			Video	10 min.	HSS 6.2.9, 6.6.1–8; Analysis REP.2, REP.4, HI.3
ESSENTIAL QUESTION ACTIVITY How do Societies Preserve Order?		✓	Interactive	10 min.	HSS 6.2.9, 6.6.1–8; Analysis REP.2, REP.4, HI.3
OVERVIEW ACTIVITY: TIMELINE & MAP Early Civilizations of China (1700 BCE–220 BCE)		✓	Interactive	10 min.	HSS 6.2.9, 6.6.1–8; Analysis REP.2, REP.4, HI.3
Quest KICK OFF: Ask Questions	✓	✓		20 min.	HSS 6.6.5; ELA W.6.2, W.6.4, RI.6.1–3, RH.6.2, WHST.6.4; ELD PI.C.10.a
INVESTIGATE					
LESSONS 1–6	See Lesson-at-a-Glance pages				
Quest INVESTIGATE: Quest Connections	✓	✓		20 min.	See Quest Kick Off
SYNTHESIZE					
WRITING WORKSHOP Write an Argumentative Essay		✓	eText	30 min.	HSS 6.2.9, 6.6.1–8; ELD.PI.C.10.a
TOPIC MINI-GAMES Early Civilizations of China (1700 BCE–220 BCE)			Game	10 min.	HSS 6.2.9, 6.6.1–8
Quest SOURCES: Examine Primary Sources		✓	eText	30 min.	See Quest Kick Off
DEMONSTRATE					
TOPIC REVIEW AND ASSESSMENT Early Civilizations of China (1700 BCE–220 BCE)	✓		eText	20 min.	
TOPIC TEST Early Civilizations of China (1700 BCE–220 BCE)			Assessment	30 min.	
Quest FINDINGS: Write Your Obituary	✓	✓	eText	30 min.	See Quest Kick Off

Quest

Each Quest is designed to reinforce the Topic content through an inquiry arc that students work on throughout the Topic. This Topic's Quest, Evaluating a Leader's Legacy, is a Document-Based Writing Inquiry in which students write an obituary that sums up the life and leadership of Shi Huangdi.

Active Journal Resources

- Ask Questions
- Quest Connections
- Examine Primary Sources
- Write Your Obituary

Quest Sources Online

- Project Contract
- Project Tracker
- Team Assessment
- Rubric for Writing an Obituary

Additional Resources

Support for Struggling Readers

- Reading Support, Teacher Resources
- Lesson Summaries, Teacher Resources
- English Language Development, Teacher Resources

Suggested Resources

- *Confucius: The Golden Rule*, by Russell Freedman
- *The Emperor's Silent Army: Terracotta Warriors of Ancient China*, by Jane O'Connor
- *The Gods and Goddesses of Ancient China*, by Leonard Everett Fisher
- *The Great Wall of China*, by Leonard Everett Fisher

Beyond the Classroom

Use Online and Library Media Centers

Search the online library media center for images of and videos about ancient China and museums with materials related to ancient China.

The following California museums have collections or materials related to the early civilizations of China:

Asian Art Museum, San Francisco, CA

Los Angeles County Museum of Art, Los Angeles, CA

USC Pacific Asia Museum, Pasadena, CA

The Huntington Library, Art Collections, and Botanical Gardens, San Marino, CA

TOPIC
5

The Huang Valley

	Resources: Student Edition	Resources: Active Journal	Resources: Online	Pacing approx. 2 periods, 1 block	California Standards
CONNECT					
VIDEO The Influence of Geography on China			✓	5 min.	HSS 6.2.9, 6.6.1, 6.6.2
START UP ACTIVITY Get Ready to Read	✓	✓	✓	5 min.	HSS 6.2.9, 6.6.1, 6.6.2
TAKE NOTES AND PRACTICE VOCABULARY		✓			
INVESTIGATE					
READ Lesson 1: The Huang Valley	✓	✓	✓	40 min.	HSS 6.2.9, 6.6.1, 6.6.2
INTERACTIVE GALLERY Chinese Writing			✓	10 min.	HSS 6.2.9, 6.6.1, 6.6.2
READING SUPPORT			✓		
SYNTHESIZE					
WRITING WORKSHOP Introduce Claims	✓	✓	✓	10 min.	HSS 6.2.9. 6.6.1, 6.6.2; ELD.PI.C.10.a
LESSON SUMMARY			✓		
DEMONSTRATE					
LESSON QUIZ			✓	10 min.	HSS 6.2.9. 6.6.1, 6.6.2

Objectives

Objective 1: Identify how location and environment influenced the development of civilization in China.

Objective 2: Describe why Chinese society emerged along the Huang River

Objective 3: Summarize the major achievements of the Shang dynasty.

Objective 4: Compare and contrast the Chinese system of writing with that of modern English.

The Zhou Dynasty

Objectives

Objective 1: Explain how the Zhou dynasty gained power.

Objective 2: Discuss how the idea of the Mandate of Heaven explained the rise and fall of dynasties.

Objective 3: Summarize the successes and failures of the Zhou dynasty.

Objective 4: Compare and contrast the Zhou and Shang dynasties.

	Resources: Student Edition	Resources: Active Journal	Resources: Online	Pacing (approx. 4 periods, 2 blocks)	California Standards
CONNECT					
VIDEO The Dynastic Cycle and the Mandate of Heaven			✓	5 min.	HSS 6.6.2
START UP ACTIVITY Get Ready to Read	✓	✓	✓	5 min.	HSS 6.6.2
TAKE NOTES AND PRACTICE VOCABULARY		✓			
INVESTIGATE					
READ Lesson 2: The Zhou Dynasty	✓	✓	✓	40 min.	HSS 6.6.2
QUICK ACTIVITY Letter to the People		✓			
INTERACTIVE CHART The Dynastic Cycle			✓	10 min.	HSS 6.6.2
PRIMARY SOURCES Sun Tzu, *The Art of War*	✓		✓	40 min.	ELA RI.6.4, RH.6.4
ANALYSIS SKILLS Distinguish Fact from Opinion	✓		✓	30 min.	Analysis REP.2; ELA RH.6.1
21ST CENTURY SKILLS TUTORIAL Distinguish Between Facts and Opinions			✓	10 min.	Analysis REP.2
READING SUPPORT			✓		
SYNTHESIZE					
WRITING WORKSHOP Support Claims	✓	✓	✓	10 min.	HSS 6.6.2; ELD.PI.C.10.a
LESSON SUMMARY			✓		
DEMONSTRATE					
LESSON QUIZ			✓	10 min.	HSS 6.6.2

Chinese Belief Systems

	Resources: Student Edition	Resources: Active Journal	Resources: Online	Pacing (approx. 3 periods, 1.5 blocks)	California Standards
CONNECT					
VIDEO How Confucius's Life Shaped His View of Government			✓ (video)	5 min.	HSS 6.6.3, 6.6.4
START UP ACTIVITY Get Ready to Read	✓	✓	✓ (book)	5 min.	HSS 6.6.3, 6.6.4
TAKE NOTES AND PRACTICE VOCABULARY		✓			
INVESTIGATE					
READ Lesson 3: Chinese Belief Systems	✓	✓	✓ (book)	40 min.	HSS 6.6.3, 6.6.4
INTERACTIVE CHART Confucianism and Daoism			✓ (interactive)	10 min.	HSS 6.6.3, 6.6.4
QUICK ACTIVITY How Do Ideas Change Lives?		✓			
PRIMARY SOURCES Confucius, the *Analects*	✓		✓ (book)	40 min.	HSS 6.6.3, 6.6.4; ELA RI.6.3
READING SUPPORT			✓ (document)		
SYNTHESIZE					
WRITING WORKSHOP Support Claims	✓	✓	✓ (book)	10 min.	HSS 6.6.3, 6.6.4; ELD.PI.C.10.a
LESSON SUMMARY			✓ (document)		
DEMONSTRATE					
LESSON QUIZ			✓ (quiz)	10 min.	HSS 6.6.3, 6.6.4

Objectives

Objective 1: Analyze the role that belief in spirits and reverence for ancestors played in early Chinese religion.

Objective 2: Explain how the philosophical system of Confucianism supported individuals, rulers, and societies.

Objective 3: Summarize the values that Daoism affirmed.

Objective 4: Describe how Confucianism and Daoism developed different solutions to the chaos of the Warring States period.

The Unification of China

Objectives

Objective 1: Discuss the steps that Shi Huangdi took to unite China.

Objective 2: Explain why Shi's centralized government was so powerful.

Objective 3: Describe how Legalist principles shaped the Qin dynasty.

Objective 4: Identify one cause of the fall of the Qin dynasty.

	Resources: Student Edition	Resources: Active Journal	Resources: Online	Pacing (approx. 3 periods, 1.5 blocks)	California Standards
CONNECT					
VIDEO Comparing Legalism and Confucianism			Video	5 min.	HSS 6.6.5; ELA RI.6.1
START UP ACTIVITY Get Ready to Read	✓	✓	eText	5 min.	HSS 6.6.5; ELA RI.6.1
TAKE NOTES AND PRACTICE VOCABULARY		✓			
INVESTIGATE					
READ Lesson 4: The Unification of China	✓	✓	eText	40 min.	HSS 6.6.5
INTERACTIVE GALLERY Terra Cotta Army of Shi Huangdi			Interactive	10 min.	HSS 6.6.5
ANALYSIS SKILLS Draw Sound Conclusions from Sources	✓		eText	30 min.	HSS 6.6.5; Analysis REP.4; ELA RI.6.1, RI.6.3
21ST CENTURY SKILLS TUTORIAL Draw Conclusions			Video	10 min.	Analysis REP.4
READING SUPPORT			Document		
SYNTHESIZE					
WRITING WORKSHOP Use Credible Sources	✓	✓	eText	10 min.	HSS 6.6.5; ELD.PI.C.10.a
LESSON SUMMARY			Document		
DEMONSTRATE					
LESSON QUIZ			Quiz	10 min.	HSS 6.6.5

The Han Dynasty Expands

Objectives

Objective 1: Describe the social customs and government policies that helped China to unify into a single state under the Han dynasty.

Objective 2: Analyze the role that Confucianism played in the development of the civil service.

Objective 3: Explain how the establishment of the Silk Road increased trade, the spread of Buddhism, and the connections between China and other regions of Afro-Eurasia.

Objective 4: Compare and contrast the Han and Qin dynasties.

	Resources			Pacing	
CONNECT	Student Edition	Active Journal	Online	approx. 2 periods, 1 block	California Standards
VIDEO The Bureaucratic Structure of the Han Government			Online (video)	5 min.	HSS 6.6.6, 6.6.7, 6.6.8
START UP ACTIVITY Get Ready to Read	✓	✓	Online (book)	5 min.	HSS 6.6.6, 6.6.7, 6.6.8
TAKE NOTES AND PRACTICE VOCABULARY		✓			
INVESTIGATE					
READ Lesson 5: The Han Dynasty Expands	✓	✓	Online (book)	40 min.	HSS 6.6.6, 6.6.7, 6.6.8
INTERACTIVE CHART Ancient Chinese Dynasties			Online (interactive)	10 min.	HSS 6.6.6, 6.6.7, 6.6.8
READING SUPPORT			Online (document)		
SYNTHESIZE					
WRITING WORKSHOP Shape Tone	✓	✓	Online (book)	10 min.	HSS 6.6.6, 6.6.7, 6.6.8; ELD.PI.C.10.a
LESSON SUMMARY			Online (document)		
DEMONSTRATE					
LESSON QUIZ			Online (quiz)	10 min.	HSS 6.6.6, 6.6.7, 6.6.8

Han Society and Achievements

Objectives

Objective 1: Identify how Confucian teachings about relationships shaped Han society.

Objective 2: Analyze why China's economy was strong under the Han.

Objective 3: Summarize the major achievements of Han China in the arts, science, and technology.

Objective 4: Explain the importance of the invention of paper.

	Resources: Student Edition	Resources: Active Journal	Resources: Online	Pacing (approx. 3 periods, 1.5 blocks)	California Standards
CONNECT					
VIDEO China's Economy Under the Han			✓	5 min.	HSS 6.6.4, 6.6.6
START UP ACTIVITY Get Ready to Read	✓	✓	✓	5 min.	HSS 6.6.4, 6.6.6
TAKE NOTES AND PRACTICE VOCABULARY		✓			
INVESTIGATE					
READ Lesson 6: Han Society and Achievements	✓	✓	✓	40 min.	HSS 6.6.4, 6.6.6
INTERACTIVE GALLERY Silk Making in Ancient China			✓	10 min.	HSS 6.6.4, 6.6.6
ANALYSIS SKILLS Identify Sources of Continuity	✓		✓	30 min.	HSS 6.6.3; Analysis HI.3
21ST CENTURY SKILLS TUTORIAL Develop Cultural Awareness			✓	10 min.	Analysis HI.3
READING SUPPORT			✓		
SYNTHESIZE					
WRITING WORKSHOP Write a Conclusion	✓	✓	✓	10 min.	HSS 6.6.4, 6.6.6; ELD.PI.C.10.a
LESSON SUMMARY			✓		
DEMONSTRATE					
LESSON QUIZ			✓	10 min.	HSS 6.6.4, 6.6.6

TOPIC 5 Early Civilizations of China

(1700 BCE–220 CE)

HSS 6.2.9, 6.6.1, 6.6.2, 6.6.3, 6.6.4, 6.6.5, 6.6.6, 6.6.7, 6.6.8; Analysis REP.2, REP.4, HI.3

CONNECT

Introduction

As in Egypt and the Fertile Crescent, civilization in China developed along rivers. Unlike Egypt and the Fertile Crescent, deserts and mountains isolated China from much of the rest of the world. Tucked away from other regions, China developed a textured culture that in some ways was more advanced than those in distant places.

Activate Prior Knowledge

Ask students what they know about early Chinese civilization. Have a volunteer read the It began at the edge text in the student book. Explain that ancient China gave the world ideas people still live by today and created paper, silk, coins, the seismometer, and the wheelbarrow.

Explore the Essential Question

Project the Essential Question activity from the course. Have a volunteer read the question. As students consider the Essential Question, have them offer their initial thoughts about how societies preserve order.

ACTIVE JOURNAL

Essential Question Have students begin to explore the Essential Question in their Active Journals.

Apply Concepts Is it easier to preserve order in a small, tightly knit country or a large empire? Why? *(Sample response: It's easier in a small country. A large empire has more people living over a greater area, and there may be cultural differences among its people, all of which make it harder to preserve order.)*

TOPIC 5 Early Civilizations of China (1700 BCE–220 CE)

GO ONLINE to access your digital course

VIDEO
AUDIO
ETEXT
INTERACTIVE
WRITING
GAMES
WORKSHEET
ASSESSMENT

It began at the edge of a great river over 7,000 years ago. Sounds familiar, right? Like other early civilizations, the EARLY CIVILIZATIONS OF CHINA depended on rivers to grow and thrive. In time, China emerged as a great empire with a rich and complex history and culture.

Explore The Essential Question

How do societies preserve order?

Over its rich history, ancient China experienced many changes in its ruling dynasties and in the religious and cultural practices of its people.

Different rulers and religions struggled with the challenge of maintaining order in what became a great empire.

Unlock the Essential Question in your Active Journal.

182

ANALYZE VISUALS

Discuss the photo. Explain that these terra cotta figures were discovered by farmers digging in a field near the ancient city of Xi'an. The life-sized clay figures were buried with the tomb of China's first emperor, Shi Huangdi. The faces of the figures are all different, which suggests that many people posed for the artists who sculpted the "army." Ask: What does this enormous example of ancient art tell us about the emperor? *(Possible responses: He was very wealthy and powerful. He thought the army would protect him in the afterlife.)*

HSS 6.2.9, 6.6.1, 6.6.2, 6.6.3, 6.6.4, 6.6.5, 6.6.6, 6.6.7, 6.6.8; Analysis REP.2, REP.4, HI.3

◀ Emperor Shi Huangdi's tomb, containing thousands of life-sized terra cotta soldiers

Watch

NBC LEARN

BOUNCE TO ACTIVATE | VIDEO

Shi Huangdi, First Emperor of Unified China

Learn about the controversial figure who unified China under his firm command.

Read

about the beginnings and rise of an empire of great cultural, scientific, and cultural achievement.

RECOGNIZE CULTURAL AND EXPERIENTIAL BACKGROUNDS

Make use of your knowledge of students' lives to make connections between their experiences, backgrounds, and interests and the content of this topic. If you have students whose ethnic heritage is related to the content of this topic, make an effort to emphasize the contributions and achievements of this culture, and this period, and how they have enriched the world.

If appropriate, allow students the opportunity to share cultural, ethnic, or linguistic traditions and knowledge from their experiences.

If students have family experiences (such as travel to or family members who have lived in China), allow them to share relevant stories.

Watch

VIDEO | NBC LEARN VIDEO

Project the Topic Opener video about Shi Huangdi and the unification of China.

Identify Central Ideas Why was Shi Huangdi a severe ruler? *(He felt it was the best way to bring order to his empire.)*

Check Understanding What were some positive effects of Shi Huangdi's rule? *(He introduced standardized weights and measures, a universal currency, and uniformity in Chinese writing.)* What were some of his negative effects? *(He violently suppressed all dissent.)*

Read

Share these lesson previews with students.

Lesson 1: Chinese civilization rose in the Huang Valley and grew to dominate a large part of the region.

Lesson 2: Around 1050 BCE, the Zhou overthrew the Shang and began a new 800-year dynasty.

Primary Sources: Sun Tzu writes on military strategy.

Lesson 3: Isolated by geography, China had a unique culture with two important belief systems, Confucianism and Daoism.

Primary Sources: Confucius develops a doctrine to restore harmony.

Lesson 4: China was unified by the kingdom of Qin. Shi Huangdi became the emperor.

Lesson 5: Han emperors created one of the most influential Chinese dynasties.

Lesson 6: The Han dynasty was a time of innovation and economic development.

TOPIC 5

HSS 6.2.9, 6.6.1, 6.6.2, 6.6.3, 6.6.4, 6.6.5, 6.6.6, 6.6.7, 6.6.8

What Happened and When?

Have students examine the timeline. Ask: How many years are shown on the timeline? *(about 5,000)* Ask: What happened in another part of the world 200 years after the Shang kingdom was founded? *(Aryans began to compose Vedas.)* Ask: What happened in another part of the world around the same time the Zhou dynasty began? *(The Assyrian empire began.)*

ACTIVE JOURNAL

Timeline Skills Students can also use the Timeline Skills activity in their Active Journals to record information about and better understand this time period. As they read the topic, they should add the dates of at least three events they think are important. After completing the topic, have students review their timelines and write a paragraph identifying the dates they added and explaining why each is significant.

INTERACTIVE

INTERACTIVE TIMELINE

Display the Interactive Topic Timeline for the class. Have volunteers read the entries. Ask: How long did the Shang dynasty exist before writing developed? *(400 years)*

Evaluate Sources Which empire predates the Han dynasty by about 700 years? *(the Assyrian empire)*

TOPIC 5

Early Civilizations of China (1700 BCE – 220 BCE)

Learn more about the early civilizations of China by making your own map and timeline in your Active Journal.

INTERACTIVE
Topic Map

Where did ancient Chinese civilization begin?

Ancient China was born in the valleys of great rivers, the Huang and Chang. The early civilization grew up in these valleys and in the broad area between the vast deserts and towering mountains that helped cut off China from the rest of the world.

INTERACTIVE
Topic Timeline

What happened and when?

Great dynasties are founded ... brilliant philosophers are born. Explore the timeline to see some of what was happening in China and in the rest of the world.

About 1400 BCE The Shang begin writing oracle bones.

1800 BCE Shang kingdom founded; Shang artisans make bronze tools.

5000 BCE Farmers settle villages along the Huang River.

TOPIC EVENTS

5000 BCE | 2000 BCE

WORLD EVENTS

1600 BCE Aryans begin to compose Vedas.

DIFFERENTIATED INSTRUCTION

Special Education Say aloud, in random order, the periods shown on the timeline (5000 BCE; 1000 BCE, etc.) Have students point to the part of the timeline that corresponds to each period.

Below Level Have students match the dynasties shown on the map with their entries on the timeline.

Advanced Have students choose an entry on the timeline and do research to learn more about it. Ask students to share their findings with the class.

HSS 6.2.9, 6.6.1, 6.6.2, 6.6.3, 6.6.4, 6.6.5, 6.6.6, 6.6.7, 6.6.8

Who will you meet?

King Wu, first Zhou king

Confucius, a philosopher whose teachings changed the course of Chinese history

Shi Huangdi, first emperor to unify China

- 1050 BCE The Zhou Dynasty begins.
- 551 BCE Confucius is born.
- 475 BCE The Warring States period begins.
- 206 BCE Han Dynasty begins.
- 221 BCE Qin Dynasty begins.
- 103 BCE Trade begins on Silk Road.

1000 BCE — 1 CE

- 934 BCE Assyrian empire begins.
- 700 BCE Greek colonies spread.
- 44 BCE Julius Caesar becomes dictator of Rome.

185

HISTORY BACKGROUND

Dragon Bones Scholars have long known about the Shang dynasty from the written records of the Zhou. It was not until 1899, however, that archaeological evidence proved that the Shang existed. That year, Chinese scholars noticed that pharmacists were selling "dragon bones" with ancient inscriptions. These "dragon bones" were actually oracle bones.

The scholars traced the origins of the oracle bones to a place near the Huang River in Henan province. The place was excavated and found to be the site of Anyang, the last Shang capital. Foundations and stone pillars of Shang palaces, upper-class homes, storage pits, and workshops were discovered in 1928.

Where Did Ancient Chinese Civilization Begin?

Direct students' attention to the map of China. Ask: Which dynasty controlled the most territory? *(Han)* What does that suggest? *(Ancient China was at its height during the Han dynasty.)*

ACTIVE JOURNAL

Map Skills Have students use the Map Skills activity in their Active Journals to fill in an outline map of modern China, showing its borders and labeling its neighboring countries.

INTERACTIVE — INTERACTIVE MAP

Display the Interactive Topic Map for the class. Work through the map with students to learn more about the geography of China.

Analyze Maps What geographic features are related to China's isolation? *(Gobi Desert; Plateau of Tibet; Himalayas)* What geographic features suggest a way China could have had contact with the outside world? *(East China Sea; South China Sea; Pacific Ocean)*

Who Will You Meet?

Preview the key people that students will encounter in the topic. Read the short description of each, and then conduct a poll asking students who they are most interested in. Record the results on the board. *(Students may say they are interested in* King Wu *because he was the first Zhou king; they are interested in* Confucius *because they have heard of him; they are interested in* Shi Huangdi *because he unified China.)*

TOPIC 5

HSS 6.6.5; ELA W.6.2, W.6.4, RI.6.1–3, RH.6.2, WHST.6.4; ELD.P1.A.2, PI.C.10.a

Quest

Document-Based Writing Inquiry

Evaluating a Leader's Legacy

Quest Kick Off

In this Quest, students will use the student edition, other sources, and their Active Journals to write an obituary for Shi Huangdi.

1 Ask Questions

Launch the Quest by discussing the Guiding Question as a class. Then have students generate in their Journals the questions they will need to answer to accomplish the Quest.
Suggestion: If students need help with asking questions, refer them to the Analysis Skills feature following Lesson 4, Draw Sound Conclusions from Sources.

2 Investigate

As they read the lessons, remind students to look for and respond to the three Quest Connections in the student text that provide clues to their Quest. They should also identify and record two connections of their own.
Suggestion: Help students identify their own connections by having them think about what they would write about the life of a leader living today.

3 Examine Primary Sources

As students complete the topic, distribute the Quest Primary Sources for this topic.

Analyze Documents Have students process the primary sources in their Active Journals, focusing on identifying information related to the Guiding Question.

4 Write Your Obituary

When students complete the topic, have them return to the Quest, which can be used as a performance-based authentic assessment. To complete their Quests, they should follow the steps of (1) prewriting, (2) drafting their obituaries, (3) sharing with a partner, (4) revising the draft based on feedback, and (5) presenting the final product. **DOK4**

HSS 6.6.5; ELA W.6.2, W.6.4, RI.6.1–3, RH.6.2, WHST.6.4; ELD.PI.A.2, PI.C.10.a

Quest

Document-Based Writing Inquiry

Evaluating a Leader's Legacy

Quest KICK OFF

The year is 210 BCE. The great Shi Huangdi has died, and you have been given the job of writing his obituary.

How do you sum up the life of a great but harsh leader?

What challenges did Shi Huangdi face, and how did he meet them? Explore the Essential Question "How do societies preserve order?" in this Quest.

1 Ask Questions

The life and rule of Shi Huangdi was successful—but controversial. What questions do you have about the challenges he faced and the decisions he made? Write your questions in your Active Journal.

2 Investigate

As you read the lessons in this topic, look for Quest CONNECTIONS that provide information about the rule of Shi Huangdi and how he united China. Capture your notes in your Active Journal.

3 Examine Primary Sources

Next explore a set of primary sources from Qin China. They'll help you learn more about the rule of Shi Huangdi. Capture your notes in your Active Journal.

Quest FINDINGS

4 Write Your Obituary

An obituary sums up the achievements and highlights of a person's life. At the end of this topic, you'll write an obituary for the leader who first unified all of China—sometimes though controversial means. Your obituary will help summarize this ruler's life—the good, the bad, and the ugly. Get help for writing your obituary in your Active Journal.

▲ Statue of Emperor Shi Huangdi

DIFFERENTIATED INSTRUCTION

Below Level Help students focus their response to the Quest question by having them write answers to these questions: How old are you? Where were you born? Where do you live now? Explain that these are the types of facts they would include if they were summing up their own life.

INTEGRATED ENGLISH LANGUAGE DEVELOPMENT

Emerging Instead of requiring students to write an obituary, encourage students to create annotated illustrations showing the achievements of Shi Huangdi.

LESSON 1

HSS 6.2.9, 6.6.1, 6.6.2

The Huang Valley

BOUNCE TO ACTIVATE

VIDEO

GET READY TO READ

START UP

Write two predictions about how the geographic features you see in this picture of the Huang Valley might have influenced the development of Chinese civilization.

GUIDING QUESTIONS

- How did location and the environment influence the development of civilization in China?
- Why did Chinese society emerge along the Huang River?
- What were the major achievements of the Shang dynasty?

TAKE NOTES

Literacy Skills: Summarize

Use the graphic organizer in your Active Journal to take notes as you read the lesson.

PRACTICE VOCABULARY

Use the vocabulary activity in your Active Journal to practice the vocabulary words.

Vocabulary		Academic Vocabulary
loess	pictograph	interpret
dike	logograph	challenge
oracle bone		

Chinese civilization arose along the Huang (hwong) River, also called the Yellow River. By around 5000 BCE, farmers had settled in a number of villages in this river valley. Over time, powerful rulers united these villages to create large kingdoms. Among these, the Shang kingdom rose to become the most influential.

Geography of China

Today, the country of China is a huge land, similar in size to the United States. Much of China is covered by rugged mountains and vast deserts. Despite the challenges of the geography, early people found the resources they needed along China's river valleys.

River Systems Rivers helped China's development, just as they aided the development of civilizations in Mesopotamia, Egypt, and India. China has two main rivers: the Huang and the Chang (chahng). They provide water for farming. People move goods along these waterways. Both rivers begin in the mountains of western China.

The Chang, also called the Yangtze River, is China's longest river. But the Huang River

HSS 6.2.9, 6.6.1, 6.6.2

The Huang Valley

CONNECT

GET READY TO READ

ETEXT START UP

Project the Start Up Activity. As students enter the classroom and get settled, have them study the photograph. Explain that this photo shows the Huang Valley, birthplace of Chinese civilization.

Make Predictions Write two predictions about how the geographic features you see in this picture might have influenced the development of Chinese civilization. *(Sample response: River travel became important; towns were isolated from one another.)*

Draw Conclusions What do you notice about these mountains? *(They are sharp and jagged.)* What does that suggest? *(It might have been especially difficult to cross them.)*

After completing the Start Up activity, project the Lesson Opener or direct students to their textbooks. Preview the lesson by working through the Get Ready to Read items with the class. Remind students to pay close attention to the Guiding Questions as they read the lesson.

ACTIVE JOURNAL

Take Notes Have students use the lesson literacy skills graphic organizer in their Active Journals to take notes as they read the lesson.

Practice Vocabulary Have students complete the activity in their Active Journals to build their vocabulary.

VIDEO VIDEO

Assign the lesson video as homework.

PRACTICE VOCABULARY

To help students integrate new vocabulary, group the terms and introduce them. Explain that *loess* (a dustlike material that can form soil) and *dike* are related because they are found along the Huang River. Ask students what other words are like *loess*. *(dirt, earth, sand)* Explain that *oracle bones, pictograph*, and *logograph* are related because they refer to Chinese writing. Ask students if they can think of similar words. *(alphabet, hieroglyphics)*

Have students locate and pronounce the academic vocabulary in the lesson margins. Provide sample sentences that clarify meaning.

interpret: Language scholars interpret picture writing.

challenge: Learning a new language is a challenge.

WORKSHEET **TEACHER RESOURCES**

Have students who need additional support use the following worksheets from the Teacher Resources on the course:

- **Reading Support**
- **English Language Development**
- **Lesson Summary**

INVESTIGATE

Geography of China

Discuss the impact of geography on the development of civilization in China. What geographic features were especially significant?

Identify Cause and Effect Why did the first settlements in China develop on the North China Plain? *(The fertile soil deposited by the Huang River was well suited for agriculture.)*

Identify Cause and Effect How did geography slow the spread of information and ideas in China? *(Geography made travel difficult, so ideas and information took longer to reach people.)*

Identify Central Ideas What was the single biggest impact of geography on China? *(It isolated China from other civilizations.)*

ANSWERS

1. **Region** *the Huang and the Chang*
2. **Recognize Multiple Causes** *the Gobi and Taklimakan deserts, the Plateau of Tibet, and the Himalaya Mountains*

Identify Cause and Effect *Most people settled in the fertile river valleys in the northern plains. China's vast area and challenging terrain, such as mountain ranges and deserts, affected the movement of information and goods within and beyond China.*

Did you know?

The Chang River is China's longest river. It is almost twice as long as the Missouri River, the longest river in the United States.

was especially important to China's early history. It flows east to the Yellow Sea and crosses the flat North China Plain. Winds from the Gobi Desert blow loess (LOH es) onto the Huang River valley. **Loess** is a fine, dustlike material that can form soil. The Huang River cuts through deep deposits of loess and picks it up. The loess makes the river muddy and turns it yellow. The name of the Huang River comes from this mud. In Chinese, *huang* means yellow.

When the river overflows its banks, it deposits the loess on the surrounding plain. The floods can be unpredictable. However, this fertile soil makes the North China Plain well suited for agriculture. Even with simple tools, ancient farmers could easily plant their crops in the soft soil. Here, people created the first large settlements in China.

GEOGRAPHY SKILLS

Ancient Chinese civilization developed in the North China Plain and was affected by other geographical features.

1. **Region** What two rivers flow through the North China Plain?
2. **Recognize Multiple Causes** What multiple geographic land features might have caused ancient China to be isolated from other civilizations?

How Did Isolation Affect China's Development?

China is nearly surrounded by physical barriers. Two great deserts, the Taklimakan (tah kluh muh KAHN) and the Gobi, lie to the north and west of China. The towering Himalayas form a wall between China and India. To the south lie more mountains, and to the east the Pacific Ocean.

China's geography slowed the spread of information and ideas, which made governing the vast land difficult. It was difficult for ideas and goods to travel between China and other civilizations. Some early innovations, such as the domesticated horse, may have come to China from western Asia. However, ancient China was largely cut off from other civilizations.

READING CHECK **Cause and Effect** What geographic features affected settlement patterns and government in early China?

China: Physical Geography

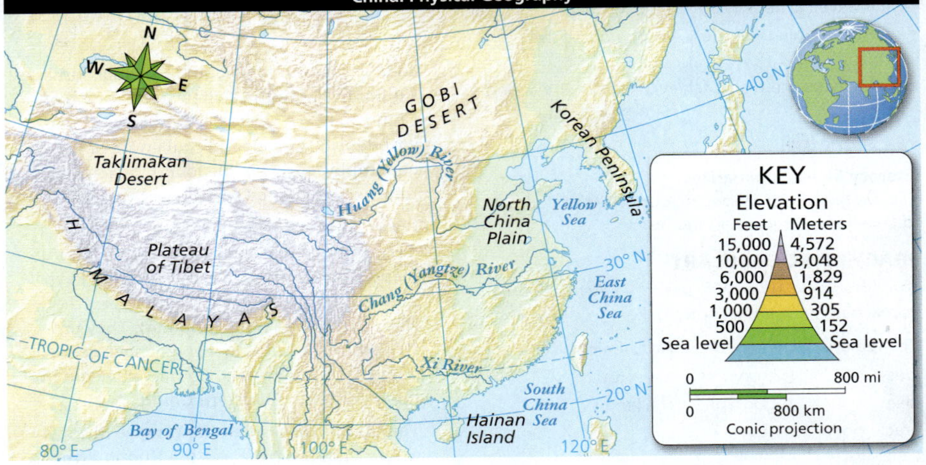

INTEGRATED ENGLISH LANGUAGE DEVELOPMENT

Productive Read The Shang Dynasty aloud with students to help them understand the rise and significance of the first Chinese dynasty.

Emerging Have students answer who, what, when, where questions such as: When did the Shang dynasty form? or How did the Shang try to control the river floods? Check for proper use of past tense.

Expanding Have students answer the question: What was the purpose of oracle bones in the Shang culture? Check for proper use of past tense.

Bridging Students answer the question: What were the accomplishments of the Shang Dynasty? Check for proper use of past tense.

The Shang Dynasty

From the early settlements along the Huang River, the Shang kingdom rose to dominate a large part of the region. The language and culture of the Shang would have a lasting influence on China.

The Shang Rise Farming villages grew along the Huang River. The people used stone tools and made pottery and silk cloth. Some of these villages had chiefs, or rulers, who organized workers and commanded warriors. Strong chiefs led their warriors to take control of nearby villages, creating small kingdoms.

Around 1700 BCE, one of those kingdoms began to expand. A ruler from this kingdom founded the Shang dynasty. A dynasty is a ruling family that holds power for many years. This dynasty lasted some 600 years. It is the earliest dynasty for which we have a written record.

How Did the Shang Government Rule? Strong rulers ran the government. The Shang kept power within the family. Rule passed from brother to brother and from the youngest brother to his oldest son.

The Shang leaders organized groups of farmers to clear and prepare new land. The result was larger harvests. With extra food, Shang rulers could support many soldiers. They attacked neighboring lands and expanded their territory. Soldiers fought with bows, lances, and bronze axes. Some rode into battle in chariots.

Shang rulers used their wealth to build a number of large walled cities. They also tried to control the floods along the Huang River. They built **dikes**, or walls to hold back water.

Writing The earliest written records from China are **oracle bones** from the Shang dynasty. Oracle bones are animal bones or turtle shells carved with written characters that the Shang kings used to try to tell the future.

Questions were written on the bone, which was then heated until it cracked. The king or a priest would **interpret** the cracks to get an answer. No one knows exactly how the cracks were read.

At times, the Chinese also used oracle bones to record important events related to their questions. From these written records, scholars have learned much about ancient China and its rulers.

The Shang did not use an alphabet for their written words, which are called characters. Instead, some characters were **pictographs**; that is, pictures that represent words or ideas. Other characters were a combination of symbols. Some symbols stood for the meaning of the word while others represented the sound.

▲ Religious leaders would carve outcomes on bones or shells like this one, then crack it and interpret the cracks for the king.

Academic Vocabulary
interpret • *v.*, to explain, give the meaning of

INTERACTIVE
Chinese Writing

The Shang Dynasty

Discuss the rise of the Shang dynasty. What were its major accomplishments?

Identify Cause and Effect How did Shang rulers grow stronger? *(They organized farmers to grow extra food so they could feed soldiers and expand territory.)*

Identify Central Ideas What did Shang leaders do to strengthen and protect their territory? *(They built walled cities and built dikes to control flooding along the Huang River.)*

Explain What were **oracle bones** used for? *(to try to tell the future; to record important events)*

ELD TIP Ask students to tell what they see on the image of the oracle bone and relate it to the caption and the text.

INTERACTIVE **INTERACTIVE GALLERY**

Chinese Writing

Display the Interactive Gallery: Chinese Writing for the class. Click through the interactive. Discuss how combining characters leads to new words.

ACTIVE CLASSROOM

Use the Connect strategy. Have students choose two English words and show how they could be combined to form a third word or new idea. Ask volunteers to share their responses with the class.

Compare and Contrast What's the main difference between Chinese characters and an alphabet? *(Each Chinese character represents a complete word or phrase. In an alphabet, written characters represent sounds.)*

ELD.PII.B.3

WORKSHEET

For additional IELD support addressing the standard, have students complete the Lesson ELD activity from the Teacher Resources found on the course.

CURRICULUM CONNECTION: ENVIRONMENTAL EDUCATION

In China, dam building began in 240 BCE, when a dam was built across the Jing River. Modern China's biggest dam is the Three Gorges Dam on the Yangtze River. It is about 7,660 feet long and about 607 feet high. Construction began in 1994. When the dam was completed in 2006, it was the largest dam in the world. As of 2012, it was the world's biggest producer of hydroelectric power.

HSS 6.2.9, 6.6.1, 6.6.2; ELD.P1.C.10.a

SYNTHESIZE

Assess and Reteach Have students complete Lesson Check questions 1–4 individually. Review their responses using an Idea Wave strategy. If they had any incorrect answers, use the guiding questions to discuss the lesson's main ideas, focusing on the ideas they struggled with.

ACTIVE JOURNAL

Writing Workshop Have students complete the Lesson 1 Writing Task in their Active Journals. Students will write a sentence about the values necessary for successful leadership. This will be the basis for an argumentative essay they will write at the end of the topic.

DEMONSTRATE

ASSESSMENT **ONLINE LESSON QUIZ**

Assign the Online Lesson Quiz for this lesson if you haven't already done so. Students will be offered automatic remediation or enrichment based on their score.

DISCUSSION **DISCUSSION BOARD**

Post this question to the class on the Discussion Board:

Identify Cause and Effect What might cause a dynasty to fall? *(Sample answer: A dynasty might fall when people who are more powerful defeat it. Famine, natural disaster, or other economic dislocations can weaken the hold of a government or dynasty on its people, allowing another group to rise to power.)*

ANSWERS

Infer *Bronze was probably too rare and expensive for everyday use.*

Summarize *A strong kingdom emerged from the many farming villages along the Huang River. This became the Shang dynasty.*

Analyze Images Shang dynasty artisans were skilled in creating detailed objects in bronze and jade. This was a ceremonial bronze axe head. **Infer** Why do you think ancient Chinese ceremonial objects were made of bronze, but everyday objects were not?

By 1300 BCE, the Shang had a fully developed writing system. Many ancient characters became the writing Chinese people use today. The sound changed, but their meaning can still be understood.

Chinese characters use a logographic script. A **logograph** is a written character that represents a complete word or phrase. By contrast, in an alphabet such as the one used in the United States, written characters represent sounds. Chinese writing requires more memorization because it has thousands of characters , making it a **challenge** to learn.

Still, this system is useful in a country where people speak many languages. Spoken Chinese is different across the country, but all Chinese speakers use the same characters. In a sense, Chinese characters are like numbers. A number has the same meaning in many languages even if the spoken word used for that number is different in each of those languages.

Bronze Metalworking Shang artisans created pottery and jade carvings, but they are best known for their bronze metalworking. These objects included finely decorated pots, cups, and weapons.

Most tools used on a daily basis were not made out of bronze. The Shang used the expensive, beautiful bronzes in religious ceremonies. Human and animal sacrifices were prepared with bronze blades. They also offered food and wine to their gods and ancestors in the hope that these spirits would help them.

Academic Vocabulary
challenge • *n.*, something that is difficult or demanding to do

READING CHECK **Summarize** How and from where did the Shang dynasty develop?

Lesson Check

HSS 6.2.9. 6.6.1, 6.6.2; ELD.PI.C.10.a

Practice Vocabulary

1. What is **loess**?
2. Use the terms ***oracle bones***, ***pictograph***, and ***logograph*** to describe the Chinese language.

Critical Thinking and Writing

3. **Identify Cause and Effect** How did the geography of the Huang River valley affect the lives of the Chinese who settled there?
4. **Draw Conclusions** How did organization allow the leaders of the Shang dynasty to increase their power?
5. **Writing Workshop: Introduce Claims** Examine what values you think made the Shang dynasty successful. Write a sentence in your Active Journal that states what values you think a government needs in order to successfully lead. This will become the basis for an argumentative essay that you will write at the end of this topic.

LESSON CHECK

1. a fine, dustlike material that can form soil **DOK1**
2. Sample response: The earliest written Chinese records are oracle bones carved with logographs and pictographs. **DOK1**
3. The Huang River held loess from the Gobi Desert, which it deposited on the North China Plain when it overflowed its banks. Deposits of loess created fertile soil for growing food. **DOK2**
4. The Shangs' organization of farmers led to large harvests. Extra food allowed the Shang to support an army to conquer neighboring lands. **DOK3**
5. Sentences should state the values students think a government needs to lead successfully. **DOK4**

LESSON 2

HSS 6.6.1, 6.6.2; ELA RI.6.2

The Zhou Dynasty

BOUNCE TO ACTIVATE

VIDEO

GET READY TO READ

START UP

Examine the illustration of Zhou emperor Mu Wang riding in his chariot. Write three questions you have about Zhou rulers based on the picture.

GUIDING QUESTIONS

- How did the Zhou dynasty gain power?
- How did the idea of the Mandate of Heaven explain the rise and fall of dynasties?
- What were the successes and failures of the Zhou?

TAKE NOTES

Literacy Skills: Identify Main Ideas

Use the graphic organizer in your Active Journal to take notes as you read the lesson.

PRACTICE VOCABULARY

Use the vocabulary activity in your Active Journal to practice the vocabulary words.

Vocabulary	Academic Vocabulary
Mandate of Heaven	survived
warlord	minor
chaos	

Around 1050 BCE, a group called the Zhou (joh) attacked the Shang kingdom from the west. They overthrew the Shang ruler and established a new dynasty. The Zhou dynasty ruled for about 800 years. For much of the second half of its rule, however, the Zhou struggled to keep its large kingdom united. The widespread use of iron had much to do with the Zhou dynasty falling. Iron became readily available, and even the peasants had access to iron tools and weapons. With iron weapons readily available to the masses, the result was wars and upheavals.

Rise and Fall of the Zhou

Most of what is known about the fall of the Shang comes from sources written during the Zhou. According to these sources, the Zhou gained power because the Shang kings had grown corrupt. The last Shang king governed badly. He cared only about his own enjoyment, and many people came to resent him. When the Zhou attacked the Shang, many Shang warriors refused to fight. They surrendered and accepted the Zhou king as their new ruler.

Lesson 5.2 • The Zhou Dynasty 191

PRACTICE VOCABULARY

To help students integrate new vocabulary, introduce the terms. Explain that the Zhou believed they had heaven's support to rule, or the *Mandate of Heaven*. Explain that *warlords* are military rulers of small states. Ask students: What other kinds of rulers do you know? *(queens, presidents)* Explain that *chaos* is total disorder. Ask: What might cause chaos? *(war, a natural disaster)*

Have students locate and pronounce the academic vocabulary in the lesson margins. Provide sample sentences that clarify meaning.

survived: People who have survived a disaster are fortunate.

minor: A minor character in a play has few lines.

HSS 6.6.1, 6.6.2; ELA RI.6.2

The Zhou Dynasty

CONNECT

GET READY TO READ

ETEXT START UP

Project the Start Up Activity. As students enter the classroom and get settled, have them study the image of Zhou emperor Mu Wang riding in his chariot.

Formulate Questions Write three questions you have about Zhou rulers based on the picture. *(Possible responses: Did all Zhou rulers travel with only a few soldiers? Did all Zhou rulers travel with attendants?)*

Evaluate Sources Mu Wang is traveling with very few soldiers. What does that suggest? *(Sample responses: He felt safe. He was well liked. He had few enemies.)*

After completing the Start Up activity, project the Lesson Opener or direct students to their textbooks. Preview the lesson by working through the Get Ready to Read items with the class. Remind students to pay close attention to the Guiding Questions as they read the lesson.

ACTIVE JOURNAL

Take Notes Have students use the lesson literacy skills graphic organizer in their Active Journals to take notes as they read the lesson.

Practice Vocabulary Have students complete the activity in their Active Journals to build their vocabulary.

VIDEO VIDEO

Assign the lesson video as homework.

INVESTIGATE

Rise and Fall of the Zhou

Discuss the Zhou dynasty. How did it rise to power? What was the **Mandate of Heaven**?

Identify Cause and Effect How did the Shang dynasty bring about its own downfall? *(Shang kings became corrupt and their people came to resent them; when the Zhou attacked, people easily accepted them as their new rulers.)*

Apply Concepts How did the **Mandate of Heaven** lead to good leadership? *(It encouraged leaders to act virtuously, care for their people, and stop corruption.)*

Apply Concepts How did the **Mandate of Heaven** lead to unjust leadership? *(A leader could seize control by force. If he succeeded, he could claim that heaven supported his actions.)*

Draw Conclusions How does the primary source illustrate the **Mandate of Heaven**? *(It says the Zhou kings treated their subjects well, so Heaven gave them "the decree to rule.")*

ACTIVE JOURNAL

Quick Activity Have students complete the Quick Activity in their Active Journal. Ask volunteers to share their responses with the class.

ELD TIP For the Quick Activity, encourage emerging and expanding students to use annotated images to complete the activity.

ANSWERS

1. Locate *It encompassed the land between the Huang and Chang rivers and was bordered on the east by the Yellow Sea. The area between Huang and Chang Rivers provided fertile soil for agriculture.*

2. Infer *The Gobi Desert prevented westward expansion.*

GEOGRAPHY SKILLS

This map shows the locations of Shang and Zhou civilizations.

1. **Locate** Where was the Shang dynasty located? Why was it located there?
2. **Infer** What do you think prevented Shang and Zhou civilizations from expanding further west?

The Right to Rule After taking power, the Zhou leaders declared that their success proved that they had heaven's support. In their view, heaven was the highest force of nature that gave dynasties the right to rule. They called this right to rule the **Mandate of Heaven**. If a dynasty failed to act properly, it lost this right. This mandate would then pass to a new dynasty. The Mandate of Heaven permitted a leader to seize control by force, if necessary. Victory served as proof that heaven supported the change in leadership.

The concept of the Mandate of Heaven became a tradition of Chinese government. Under this tradition, the ruler was called the Son of Heaven. If he acted virtuously, there would be harmony between heaven and earth. Emperors were supposed to care for their people and stop corruption. Uprisings and natural disasters were seen as possible omens that the current dynasty had lost the Mandate of Heaven and its right to stay in power.

One ancient Chinese source, the *Book of History*, explains why the Zhou kings received and kept the Mandate of Heaven:

Quick Activity

As a new Zhou ruler, use your Active Journal to convince your subjects you have the Mandate of Heaven.

Primary Source

> . . . our kings of Zhou treated the people well . . . and presided over services to spirits and to Heaven. Heaven therefore instructed the Zhou kings, chose them . . . and gave them the decree to rule.
>
> —*Book of History*

INTEGRATED ENGLISH LANGUAGE DEVELOPMENT

Productive Use the text under the heading Zhou Society to help students understand characteristics of the Zhou dynasty.

Emerging Have students write simple sentences about Zhou society. Encourage students to use adjectives to make noun phrases more complex.

Expanding Have students write a paragraph describing one aspect of Zhou society. Encourage students to make their sentences more complex by adding adjectives and simple descriptive clauses.

Bridging Have students write a paragraph describing one aspect of Zhou society. Encourage students to make their sentences more complex by adding academic vocabulary.

Governing the Zhou Through conquest, the Zhou expanded its lands. At its height, the Zhou ruled a territory that reached to the Chang River. This large kingdom included many different cultures. To keep control, the king placed family members in charge of individual regions or states. As with the Shang, some of China's geographical features slowed travel and communication, making governing from a central location difficult. Over time, the ties between the Zhou king and local nobles weakened.

In 771 BCE, a group of nobles joined with nomadic invaders to try to overthrow the king. With the help of other nobles, the Zhou **survived** this attack. But the power of the Zhou king decreased. From that point on, the Zhou kings were weak and dependent on the nobles who had helped them to stay in power.

States that had once been tied to the Zhou grew more independent. Fighting broke out between **warlords**. Warlords are military rulers of small states. Although these warlords claimed loyalty to the king, they often really sought power for themselves. Many increased their military might by learning to make iron weapons.

The Warring States Period Eventually, **minor** battles escalated into full-scale warfare. China entered an era of **chaos**—total disorder and confusion. This era, from about 475 to 221 BCE, became known as the Warring States period. Brutal and destructive conflict marked the period. Battles ravaged the countryside. Millions of people died.

Stronger states conquered weaker ones. Over time, a few large states emerged. Loyalty to the Zhou dynasty disappeared. In 256 BCE, the last Zhou ruler was overthrown. Fighting continued for years, however, before a new dynasty managed to unite China.

READING CHECK **Identify Central Ideas** What made governing the Zhou kingdom difficult?

Zhou Society

The Zhou adopted much of Shang culture. They followed the same basic laws, wore similar clothing, and spoke the same language. They produced bronze art that rivaled that of the Shang. However, great changes also occurred in the Zhou dynasty. For example, the Zhou kings gave up the practice of human sacrifice and stopped using oracle bones.

Structure of Society The Zhou kings, just as the Shang rulers before them, occupied the center of government. The Zhou, however, gave more power to individual states and the nobles who led them. Those states set up their own walled capital cities, from which they controlled the lands of lesser nobles. The nobles were expected to serve the king and raise armies to support him.

INTERACTIVE
The Dynastic Cycle

Academic Vocabulary
survive • *v.*, to last, to continue to live
minor • *adj.*, not serious, not important

Analyze Images This image shows Zhou Emperor Yeo Wang using gunpowder to frighten his enemy. **Use Visual Information** What do other details from this image you tell about how battles were fought at the time of the Zhou?

Describe Explain why Zhou kings placed family members in charge of individual regions or states. *(They felt family members would be more loyal than local nobles.)*

Zhou Society

Discuss Zhou government. How did the dynasty start to decline? What was Zhou society like?

Compare and Contrast How was Zhou society different from Shang society? *(There was no human sacrifice; oracle bones were not used; individual states and their ruling nobles had more power.)*

INTERACTIVE **INTERACTIVE CHART**

The Dynastic Cycle

Display the Interactive Chart: The Dynastic Cycle for the class in order to learn more about China's dynastic cycle. Ask: Why is the rise and fall of dynasties described as a cycle? *(It is a predictable set of periods that follow a cyclical pattern.)*

ACTIVE CLASSROOM

Use the Make Headlines strategy. Have students choose a hotspot on the chart and write a newspaper headline related to the development in that hotspot. Ask volunteers to share their headlines with the class.

ELD.PII.B.4

the word *minor*, and simple descriptive clauses to add information to their paragraphs.

WORKSHEET **TEACHER RESOURCES**

For additional IELD support addressing the standard, have students complete the Lesson ELD activity from the Teacher Resources found on the course.

ANSWERS

Use Visual Information *Soldiers fought from horseback and used long spears.*

Identify Central Ideas *Zhou conquests led to extensive territory that included many different cultures. Over time, the ties between the Zhou king and local nobles weakened.*

HSS 6.6.1, 6.6.2; ELD.PI.C.10.a

SYNTHESIZE

Assess and Reteach Have students use a Think-Pair-Share strategy to complete Lesson Check questions 1–5. Review their responses. If responses are incorrect, use the Guiding Questions to discuss the lesson's main ideas, focusing on the ideas that are causing difficulty.

ACTIVE JOURNAL

Writing Workshop Have students complete the Lesson 2 Writing Task in their Active Journals. Students will list values of the Shang and Zhou societies that they think helped these governments to lead effectively.

DEMONSTRATE

ASSESSMENT **ONLINE LESSON QUIZ**

Assign the Online Lesson Quiz for this lesson if you haven't already done so. Students will be offered automatic remediation or enrichment based on their score.

DISCUSSION **DISCUSSION BOARD**

Post this question to the class on the Discussion Board:

Synthesize Which dynasty had a more advanced culture, the Shang or the Zhou? Why? *(Sample response: the Zhou, because they eliminated human sacrifice and treated the people well)*

Analyze Images Zhou coins were made in many shapes including knives and spades, and some had holes so they could be carried on a string. **Compare and Contrast** How are Zhou coins like and unlike the coins we use today?

The majority of Zhou people, as in most ancient societies, were peasants. They farmed the land and served as soldiers. There were also a small number of merchants, artisans, and slaves. People were sold into slavery as punishment for crimes and to pay debts.

Family Relationships The ancient Chinese put a high value on family. Society demanded that individuals show loyalty to their family. Older family members had more power and privileges than younger ones. As in most ancient societies, men had higher status than women.

Economy and Technology During the Zhou, there were many technological advances. For weapons, one important invention was the crossbow. Artisans learned to make iron, which is stronger than bronze. The Zhou used iron to make weapons.

Innovations also helped strengthen the Zhou economy. Iron was used to make stronger, more effective farm tools. Crop yield also increased as the Zhou used irrigation and fertilizer for more of their farmland. The Zhou built a network of roads, which helped travel and trade. A number of new cities sprang up.

Coins were also used for the first time in the Zhou dynasty. Coins made trade across the large Zhou empire easier.

Cultural Life The Zhou dynasty was a time of great creative energy. As the leaders of the Warring States vied for influence, they supported poets and artists. They looked for wise men to help them to rule. The writings of thinkers from this time became the foundation of much of Chinese thought for centuries.

READING CHECK **Understand Effects** How did technological advances strengthen Zhou society?

Lesson Check

HSS 6.6.1, 6.6.2; ELD.PI.C.10.a

Practice Vocabulary

1. What is a **warlord**?
2. Use the term ***chaos*** to write a sentence about the Warring States period.

Critical Thinking and Writing

3. **Compare and Contrast** How was the Zhou dynasty similar to and different from the Shang dynasty?
4. **Draw Conclusions** How did China's geography make it difficult for the Zhou kings to keep their large kingdom united?
5. **Infer** How did the invention of coins help make trade easier?
6. **Writing Workshop: Support Claims** What values did Shang and Zhou societies have that you think helped their governments to lead effectively? Write down examples in your Active Journal that support your claim.

LESSON CHECK

1. A warlord is a military ruler of a small state. **DOK1**
2. Sample response: When a government is weak, chaos is likely. **DOK1**
3. Similarities: same basic laws, similar clothing, same language, bronze art; Differences: no human sacrifice or oracle bones **DOK2**
4. The vast Zhou territory included mountainous regions and deserts that made travel and communication difficult. **DOK3**
5. Coins were easy to carry and had the same value everywhere. **DOK3**
6. Responses will be the societal values that students think helped these governments to lead effectively. **DOK4**

ANSWERS

Compare and Contrast *Possible responses—Like: They are easily carried and have value. Unlike: They are not round.*

Understand Effects *The Zhou made crossbows and iron, which contributed to success in warfare. The introduction of irrigation and fertilizer increased crop yields.*

ELA RI.6.4, RH.6.4

Primary Sources

Sun Tzu, *The Art of War*

The Art of War is a classic text on military strategy, written by Sun Tzu during the Warring States period. According to legend, a Chinese king named Helu (514–496 BCE) had a small army of 30,000, but was facing an invasion by an army of more than 300,000. To survive and prevail, he turned to Sun Tzu to train his army in the art of war and deception.

▶ Sun Tzu

All warfare is based on deception.

Hence, when able to attack, we must seem unable; when using our forces, we must seem inactive; when we are near, we must make the enemy believe we are far away; when far away, we must make him believe we are near.

Hold out baits (1) to entice the enemy. Feign (2) disorder, and crush him.

If he is secure at all points, be prepared for him. If he is in superior strength, evade (3) him.

If your opponent is of choleric temper, (4) seek to irritate him. Pretend to be weak, that he may grow arrogant.

If he is taking his ease, give him no rest. If his forces are united, separate them.

Attack him where he is unprepared, appear where you are not expected.

These military devices, leading to victory, must not be divulged (5) beforehand.

—Sun Tzu, *The Art of War*

Reading and Vocabulary Support

(1) People often use worms as bait to lure fish. What type of bait might an army use to entice an enemy?

(2) To feign is to pretend. What would an army look like if it feigned disorder?

(3) When you evade people, you avoid or escape them.

(4) A person with a choleric temper is proud, impatient, and short-tempered.

(5) Why would it be important not to divulge, or reveal, these military tactics?

Analyzing Primary Sources

Cite specific evidence from the document to support your answers.

1. **Explain an Argument** Soldiers are taught to stand tall and strong and to always be ready for action. Why then does Sun Tzu advise them to pretend to be inactive, disorganized, or weak?
2. **Generate Explanations** *The Art of War* has been studied for more than 1,000 years and by armies around the world. What makes these deceptive strategies so effective?

ANALYZING PRIMARY SOURCES

1. Sun Tzu advises these behaviors as a way of giving one's enemy a false impression, luring the enemy into a false sense of confidence and thus allowing you to surprise and defeat them. **DOK2**
2. Possible response: These strategies are effective because they employ logic and psychology. One example of using these strategies today is pretending to have weapons that may or may not exist. **DOK3**

ELA RI.6.4, RH.6.4

Primary Sources

Sun Tzu, *The Art of War*

Read aloud the explanatory note about the source. Direct students' attention to the illustration on the page. Ask: What impression do you think the artist was trying to convey about Sun Tzu? *(Possible response: The artist portrayed Sun Tzu with a pleasant but serious expression.)*

GUIDED READING

Read aloud or ask volunteers to read aloud the text. Use the Reading and Vocabulary Support notes to deepen students' understanding of the primary source.

Reading and Vocabulary Support Answers

1. *the appearance of weakness or small numbers*

2. *Soldiers might pretend to retreat in panic.*

5. *By not revealing these tactics, you can catch the enemy by surprise.*

GUIDED ANALYSIS

After completing the text, discuss why its title includes the phrase "the art of deception."

Infer What does Sun Tzu mean when he says "all warfare is based on deception"? *(Sun Tzu means that opposing forces always try to use both strength and psychology to win conflicts.)* Why is deception such an effective military strategy? *(It enables an army to surprise an enemy; it enables an army to defeat a larger, better-equipped force.)*

To assess understanding, have students respond to the Analyzing Primary Sources questions in writing.

Analysis REP.2; ELA RH.6.1

Analysis Skills
Distinguish Fact from Opinion

LEARN
Preview the steps in the student text with students, and then play the video.

VIDEO **21ST CENTURY SKILLS**

Project the Distinguish Between Fact and Opinion video in the 21st Century Skills Tutorial. Use the Quick Reference and Assessment to provide additional instruction in the skill.

PRACTICE
Have students practice the skill using the text on the student page. When students are finished, discuss their responses as a class.

As an alternative, you could form students into pairs or groups to perform the activity.

ASSESS
To assess this skill, have students review the *Book of History* primary source in Lesson 2. Have students identify facts and opinions. Also have them identify which opinions can be supported by facts and how they would find information that supports them.

ANSWERS
1. a. He overthrew the government of Shang, delivered the count of Qi from prison, raised a tumulus over the grave of Bi Gan,dispersed the treasures of the Lu Dai, and distributed the grain of Zhu Jiao.
   b. They can be proved.
2. Web sites; books or articles about King Wu; other primary sources
3. a. All the people joyfully submitted. He gave offices only to the worthy, and jobs only to the able. He had only to let his robes fall down, fold his hands, and the kingdom was orderly ruled.
   b. They cannot be proved.
4. primary sources like official records that have accounts of the king being truthful

Analysis REP.2; ELA RH.6.1

Distinguish Fact from Opinion
Follow these steps to distinguish fact from opinion.

INTERACTIVE
Distinguish Between Fact and Opinion

1 **Identify the facts.** A fact is something that can be proved to be true. A fact often provides information such as *who, what, where, when,* or *how*. The source is from *The Book of History*, and it describes the actions of the first Zhou ruler, King Wu, who ruled from approximately 1046 to 1043 BCE.

a. What are some facts you find in this passage?

b. How do you know they are facts?

2 **Confirm that the facts can be verified.** Use reliable sources to confirm the accuracy of any facts. These include strong online sources, such as sites ending in *.gov*, *.edu*, or *.org*. Print sources from the library can also confirm facts. In the case of this excerpt, historical records about King Wu could be used. Where are some places you would look to verify the facts you found in the primary source?

3 **Identify the opinions.** An opinion is a personal belief or judgment. Opinions cannot be proved to be either true or false. Writers may introduce opinions using the words *I think, I feel*, or *I believe*. Other clues that indicate something may be an opinion are words that describe qualities such as *honorable, attractive,* or *generous*.

a. What are some examples of opinions in this passage?

b. How do you know they are opinions?

4 **Evaluate opinions.** While opinions are not true or false, some are stronger than others. A strong opinion is supported by facts. For example, the opinion that people submitted joyfully to the king's rule could be supported with facts about the absence of conflict or opposition during his reign. What facts would be needed to support the opinion that the king showed that he was truthful?

Primary Source

He overthrew the existing government of Shang, and made it resume its old course. He delivered the count of Qi from prison, and raised a tumulus [earthen mound] over the grave of Bi Gan. He bowed in his carriage at the gate of Shang Yong's village. He dispersed the treasures of the Lu Dai, and distributed the grain of Zhu Jiao, thus conferring great gifts throughout the empire, and all the people joyfully submitted. He arranged the orders of nobility into five. . . . He gave offices only to the worthy, and jobs only to the able. He attached great importance to the people being taught the duties of the five relations of society. . . . He showed that he was truthful, and proved that he was righteous. He honored virtue, and rewarded merit. Then he had only to let his robes fall down, fold his hands, and the kingdom was orderly ruled.

—Shu Jhing, *Book of History*, Chapter 21

196 Analysis Skills • Distinguish Fact from Opinion

DIFFERENTIATED INSTRUCTION
Advanced Have students write a paragraph with five sentences, all of which are opinions. Then have them write each sentence separately, listing the facts that support the opinion.

INTEGRATED ENGLISH LANGUAGE DEVELOPMENT
Emerging Create several short sentences from the content of the Primary Source. Have students identify which sentences are facts and which are opinions.

HSS 6.6.3, 6.6.4

Chinese Belief Systems

BOUNCE TO ACTIVATE | VIDEO

GET READY TO READ

START UP

Study the photograph of the Daoist monastery. Why do you think it was built in this location? Write one prediction about how the monastery's location might influence people who lived or visited there.

GUIDING QUESTIONS

- What role did belief in spirits and reverence for ancestors play in early Chinese religion?
- How did the philosophical system of Confucianism support individuals, rulers, and societies?
- What values did Daoism affirm?

TAKE NOTES

Literacy Skills: Compare and Contrast

Use the graphic organizer in your Active Journal to take notes as you read the lesson.

PRACTICE VOCABULARY

Use the vocabulary activity in your Active Journal to practice the vocabulary words.

Vocabulary	Academic Vocabulary
philosophy	income
filial piety	stable

Isolated by its geography, ancient China had a unique culture. Two important belief systems, Confucianism and Daoism, developed during the Zhou. Each is a **philosophy**, that is, a set of beliefs about the world and how to live. These philosophies influenced all aspects of society. Religious practices, such as the worship of certain gods, became connected to these philosophies. Today, Daoist and Confucian temples are found across China. Before these philosophies appeared, the Chinese followed ancient spiritual traditions.

Spiritual Traditions

Some ancient Chinese viewed Earth as a flat square. Heaven stretched above. Both heaven and Earth were populated by a variety of spirits.

Many Spirits The ancient Chinese viewed heaven as the home of the spirits of the sun, moon, stars, and storms. On Earth, spirits lived in hills, rivers, rocks, and seas. These spirits ruled the daily lives of people.

PRACTICE VOCABULARY

To help students integrate new vocabulary, group the terms and introduce them. Explain that *philosophy* (a set of beliefs) and *filial piety* (the devotion of children to their parents) are related because filial piety is part of Chinese beliefs. Ask students what other sets of beliefs they know of *(religion, capitalism, communism, socialism).*

Have students locate and pronounce the academic vocabulary in the lesson margins. Provide sample sentences that clarify meaning.

income: A job provides a person with income that he or she uses to pay bills.

stable: In a stable society, there is little conflict.

HSS 6.6.3, 6.6.4

Chinese Belief Systems

CONNECT

GET READY TO READ

ETEXT — START UP

Project the Start Up Activity. As students enter the classroom and get settled, have them study the image. Explain that it shows a Daoist monastery.

Make Predictions Why do you think the monastery was built in this location? *(It was built here so it would be away from the rest of the world.)* What prediction could you make about the people who came here? *(They would probably be very dedicated because it appears to be very difficult to reach.)*

Draw Conclusions Why would people in a monastery want to be away from the rest of the world? *(Isolation would help them focus on their religious practices.)*

After completing the Start Up activity, project the Lesson Opener or direct students to their textbooks. Preview the lesson by working through the Get Ready to Read items with the class. Remind students to pay close attention to the Guiding Questions as they read the lesson.

ACTIVE JOURNAL

Take Notes Have students use the lesson literacy skills graphic organizer in their Active Journals to take notes as they read the lesson.

Practice Vocabulary Have students complete the activity in their Active Journals to build their vocabulary.

VIDEO — VIDEO

Assign the lesson video as homework.

WORKSHEET **TEACHER RESOURCES**

Have students who need additional support use the following worksheets from the Teacher Resources on the course:

- **Reading Support**
- **English Language Development**
- **Lesson Summary**

INVESTIGATE

Spiritual Traditions

Discuss Chinese spiritual traditions. How are these traditions in evidence today?

Identify Supporting Details Why do Chinese festivals include firecrackers? *(The noise is supposed to frighten away evil spirits.)*

Identify Main Ideas What role did ancestor worship play in Chinese religious traditions? *(Sample response: The ancient Chinese believed that the spirits of deceased ancestors remained part of the family. If honored, they would protect and guide the family.)*

Life and Teachings of Confucius

Discuss the life and teachings of Confucius. What were his Five Relationships?

Describe What injustices did Confucius witness in his government job? *(Officials often did not enforce the law. Some took bribes. Peasants starved while rulers taxed them to pay for wars.)*

Recall How did these injustices violate the Mandate of Heaven? *(Leaders were supposed to act virtuously, care for their people, and stop corruption.)*

ANSWERS

Formulate Questions *Sample response: What other powers did the Kitchen God have? How many gods and spirits did the Chinese believe in?*

Identify Central Ideas *They believed that ancestors protected and guided the living. Ancestor spirits who were not honored could cause people trouble.*

Analyze Images According to Chinese tradition, the Kitchen God is a friendly spirit who lives in a family's kitchen. **Formulate Questions** What else do you want to know about the Kitchen God and the role of spirits in the lives of ancient Chinese? What questions could you ask to help you find out more?

Good spirits made crops grow, kept sailors safe, and brought happiness. Harmful spirits might harm travelers at night or hide in a house, bringing bad luck. During festivals, people used loud sounds to frighten evil spirits away.

Honoring Ancestors The most important spirits to many ancient Chinese were those of their ancestors. They believed that family members lived on after death in the spirit world and remained part of the family. If family members took care of their ancestors, then the ancestors would protect and guide the living. Ancestor spirits who were not honored could cause people trouble.

Over the centuries, the Chinese developed many rituals to honor their ancestors. Families had shrines with tablets inscribed with ancestors' names. They set out food for their ancestors on special occasions to welcome them home. After paper money came into use, they burned fake "spirit" money to give the ancestors **income** in the afterlife. Practices of honoring the dead are often called ancestor veneration. Many rituals related to ancestor veneration are performed at holidays and funerals in China today.

READING CHECK **Identify Central Ideas** Why was it important to the ancient Chinese to honor their ancestors?

Life and Teachings of Confucius

Confucianism, the teachings of the thinker Confucius, is one of the most important philosophies that developed in China. Confucius lived just before the Warring States period. He and later thinkers at the end of the Zhou dynasty looked for solutions to China's problems. Among these thinkers, Confucius had the greatest effect on Chinese culture. He is known as the "First Teacher" and is honored for his great wisdom.

Life of a Philosopher Confucius was born into a poor family in 551 BCE. He held several low-level government jobs that allowed him to see greed and cruelty. Officials often did not enforce the law. Some took bribes, or illegal payments, to do favors for the rich. Peasants starved while rulers taxed them to pay for wars.

Confucius believed that the cause of disorder was that the Chinese had turned away from the traditional roles and values of the early Zhou. Only a return to those ideals could bring order to China. Confucius made his life's work teaching the wise ways of the ancestors.

Confucius started his own school. Students of Confucius collected his teachings and wisdom in a book called the *Analects*.

Academic Vocabulary
income *n.*, payments of money

INTEGRATED ENGLISH LANGUAGE DEVELOPMENT

Productive Use the text under the heading Life and Teachings of Confucius to help students better describe the actions and beliefs of Confucius.

Emerging Have students write simple sentences about Confucius. Encourage students to use adverbs to better describe the verbs in their sentences.

Expanding Have students write a paragraph describing an important belief of Confucius. Encourage students to make their sentences more complex by adding adverbs and prepositional phrases.

Bridging Have students write a paragraph describing an important belief

Though Confucius never achieved great wealth or influence in his lifetime, his students spread his teachings. In later centuries, the *Analects* became central to political and ethical thought across China and East Asia. Chinese students still memorize passages from it today.

What Were the Five Confucian Relationships? The heart of Confucianism lay in a vision of a **stable**, orderly society based on five relationships: (1) ruler and subject, (2) father and son, (3) husband and wife, (4) older and younger brothers, and (5) two friends.

Especially important was the relationship between father and son, or parents and their children. Elders care for and teach younger family members. In return, children respect and obey their elders. The devotion of children to their parents is called **filial piety**. Confucians referred to this as "the source of all virtues."

The relationship between parents and children was the model for the other four relationships. The person of higher status in each of the five relationships should respect the senior person. Confucius believed order and harmony would come to society once all people acted according to their roles.

Teaching by Example Confucius believed that the best way for a ruler to lead people was by setting a good example. He taught:

Primary Source

> If they people are led by laws . . . they will try to avoid the punishment but have no sense of shame. If they are led by virtue . . . they will have the sense of shame and will become good.
>
> —Confucius, *Analects*

Academic Vocabulary
stable • *adj.*, able to last, not likely to fall apart

Did you know?
Under Confucianism, women were instructed to play subordinate roles to fathers, husbands, and brothers. Despite this, some Chinese women produced Confucian literary works.

Analyze Charts Confucius stressed the importance of five basic relationships that shape behavior. Most relationships are between family members who are different ages or status. **Use Visual Information** According to Confucius, which is the only relationship that is between equals?

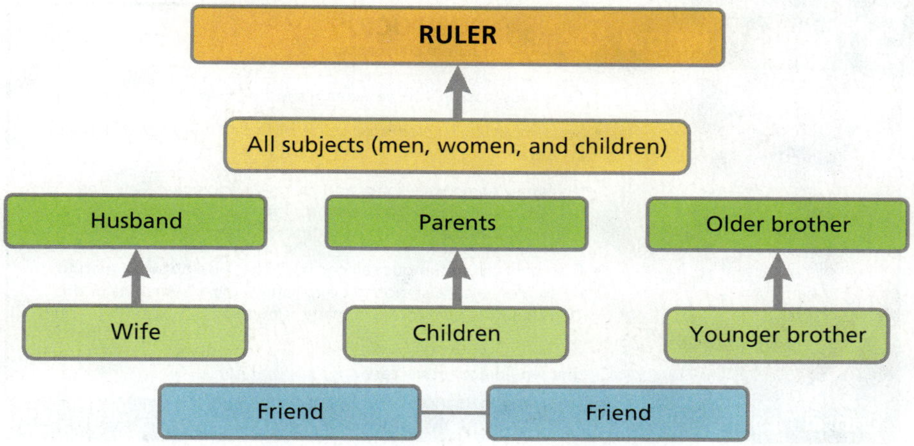

Apply Concepts How is **filial piety** the model for four of the five Confucian Relationships? *(It establishes respect for people.)*

Distinguish How does **filial piety** apply to the ruler-subject relationship? *(The ruler is the father; the subjects are children who respect the parent.)*

Draw Conclusions How might living according to the Five Relationships of Confucius result in a stable society? *(If all people were respectful to one another, there would be no conflict.)* How might wives and younger brothers have regarded their roles? *(They might have resented their subordinate positions.)*

Identify Main Ideas Read the primary source quotation aloud. Ask: What is the main point of the statement in the primary source? *(People who behave properly simply to obey laws are just avoiding punishment rather than really being virtuous; those who live virtuously are genuinely good people who would be ashamed to do wrong.)*

ELD TIP Pair emerging and expanding students to discuss whether most people do good because they are afraid of punishment or because they would be ashamed to do wrong.

ELD.PII.B.5

of Confucius. Encourage students to make their sentences more complex by adding adverbs, clauses, and prepositional phrases.

WORKSHEET **TEACHER RESOURCES**

For additional IELD support addressing the standard, have students complete the Lesson ELD activity from the Teacher Resources found on the course.

ANSWERS

Use Visual Information *two friends*

Beliefs of Daoism

Discuss Daoism and its roots in ancient Chinese beliefs.

Check Understanding According to Daoism, what is the key to harmony in the universe? *(balance between yin and yang)*

Apply Concepts How would living according to Daoism result in a stable society? *(The people would not compete with each other, and the ruler would take little action, so society would remain in balance.)*

INTERACTIVE **INTERACTIVE CHART**

Confucianism and Daoism

Display the Interactive Chart: Confucianism and Daoism for the class.

Ask a volunteer to read the instructions. Then have volunteers match each quotation or idea to the correct philosophy.

ACTIVE CLASSROOM

Use the Wallpaper strategy. Have students design a piece of "word wallpaper" that rephrases one of the concepts on the chart in their own words. Post the wallpaper and have students take a gallery walk to see what others have written.

INTERACTIVE

Confucianism and Daoism

Confucius believed that the chün-tzu, or "gentleman," must set the moral example for others by being kind and benevolent. He also stressed that traditional rituals and education supported social order.

READING CHECK **Explain** What is the most important virtue in Confucianism?

Beliefs of Daoism

Another group of thinkers saw the disorder during the Zhou dynasty and responded differently. Their reaction led to the development of Daoism. Daoism is an ancient Chinese way of life that emphasizes a simple and natural existence. It is a philosophy of following the Dao (dow); that is, the natural way of the universe.

The Legend of Laozi According to legend, a man named Laozi (LOW dzuh) founded Daoism. Laozi is known as a sage, or wise person. He is said to have written down his beliefs in a book called the *Dao De Jing* (DOW deh jing).

Historians do not know whether Laozi actually lived. They believe that the *Dao De Jing* was probably written by many people. It is a small book, made up mostly of poems. People throughout the world still read the *Dao De Jing* for its wisdom.

Yin and Yang Daoism reflects ancient Chinese beliefs about the world such as the quiet order in the changing seasons and the violence of nature in floods and storms.

Daoists believed that two great forces called yin and yang were at work in nature. They are opposites. Yin is female, dark, cool, and quiet. Yang is male, bright, warm, and active. Chinese thinkers believed balance between yin and yang was key to harmony in the universe.

BIOGRAPHY

5 Things to Know About CONFUCIUS

Chinese philosopher

- Confucius was only three when his father died.
- September 28 is celebrated as his birthday. It is an official holiday in Taiwan.
- His family name was Kong, and his given name was Qui. The name Confucius is not a meaningful term in Chinese. It was coined in Europe around the eighteenth century.
- One of his most famous sayings is, "What I do not wish men to do to me, I also wish not to do to [other] men." Versions of this "Golden Rule" are found in many cultures.
- At the age of 56, Confucius left China to find another feudal state that would accept his services.

Critical Thinking Why do you think Confucius left China?

DIFFERENTIATED INSTRUCTION

Special Education Tell students to imagine two scenarios: I don't like to be yelled at, but I yell at other people. / I don't like to be lied to, so I never lie to others. After each statement, ask if Confucius would agree with it. Have students explain their answers.

Below Level One of Confucius's ideas expresses what we have come to call the Golden Rule. Ask students to write a sentence stating the Golden Rule in their own words.

Advanced Have students learn more about Confucius and his ideas by doing research online or at the library. Ask students to write a brief report containing information that is not in the text. Have students present their reports to the class.

ANSWERS

Explain *filial piety*

Critical Thinking *He probably felt his ideas were not valued.*

The Dao Daoists saw the Dao, which means "the way" or "the path," as the source of yin and yang. The Dao is mysterious and impossible to define clearly. However, Daoists felt people should try to understand the Dao. Often, they saw evidence of the Dao in natural things, like water:

Primary Source

There is nothing in the world more soft and weak than water, and yet for attacking things that are firm and strong, nothing is better than it . . .

—Laozi, *Dao De Jing*

▲ This symbol represents yin and yang.

Water, through patient effort over time, is even stronger than rock. By acting like water, people are following the Dao.

People can upset order with their actions. Order comes when people keep to a simple life, instead of competing for wealth and power. Daoists believed a good leader took little action, leaving people to live a simple life. Daoists were not concerned with the morals, rituals, and learning that the Confucians valued. Also unlike Confucians, Daoists believed in the possibility of life after death or even immortality.

Most Chinese thinkers studied and used ideas from both philosophies. Throughout Chinese history, Confucianism and Daoism influenced Chinese culture even as new ideas came from abroad.

Quick Activity

Examine how the ideas of Confucius and Laozi from ancient China shape lives in your Active Journal.

READING CHECK **Compare and Contrast** What is one difference between Confucianism and Daoism?

Lesson Check

HSS 6.6.3, 6.6.4; ELD.PI.C.10.a

Practice Vocabulary

1. What is a **philosophy**?
2. Use the term ***filial piety*** to describe the ideas of Confucius.

Critical Thinking

3. **Draw Conclusions** What role did ancestors play in ancient Chinese religion?
4. **Summarize** How would you summarize the main teachings of Confucius?
5. **Solve Problem** How did Confucianism and Daoism develop different solutions to the chaos of the Warring States period?
6. **Writing Workshop: Support Claims** Write a list in your Active Journal of beliefs that Confucius and Daoists had about what values help governments to lead effectively. Identify which values support your claim and which oppose it.

LESSON CHECK

1. A philosophy is a set of beliefs about the world and how to live. **DOK1**
2. Sample response: Filial piety was the model of respect and proper behavior for society. **DOK1**
3. If family members took care of their ancestors, the ancestors would protect and guide the living. **DOK2**
4. An orderly society is based on the relationships between ruler and subject, father and son, husband and wife, older and younger brothers, and two friends. **DOK2**
5. Confucianism: Chaos would end if rulers governed well and justly. Daoism: Chaos would end if people lived simply and followed the Dao. **DOK2**
6. Responses will identify which support the student's claim and which oppose it. **DOK3**

HSS 6.6.3, 6.6.4; ELD.PI.C.10.a

SYNTHESIZE

Assess and Reteach Have students use a Numbered Heads strategy to complete Lesson Check questions 1–5. Review their responses. If they had any incorrect answers, use the Guiding Questions to discuss the lesson's main ideas, focusing on the ideas they struggled with.

ACTIVE JOURNAL

Writing Workshop Have students complete the Lesson 3 Writing Task in their Active Journals. Students will list claims made by Confucius and Daoists about which values help governments to lead effectively, and then identify which support their claim and which oppose it.

DEMONSTRATE

ASSESSMENT **ONLINE LESSON QUIZ**

Assign the Online Lesson Quiz for this lesson if you haven't already done so. Students will be offered automatic remediation or enrichment based on their score.

DISCUSSION **DISCUSSION BOARD**

Post this question to the class on the Discussion Board:

Synthesize Which philosophy do you think is more likely to lead to an ordered society—Confucianism or Daoism? Why? *(Sample response: Confucianism—if there is mutual respect, most of society's problems will no longer exist)*

ACTIVE JOURNAL

Quick Activity Have students complete the Quick Activity in their Active Journal.

ANSWERS

Compare and Contrast *Daoists believe in a simple life and are not concerned with the morals, rituals, and learning that Confucians value.*

HSS 6.6.3, 6.6.4; ELA RI.6.3

Primary Sources

Confucius, The Analects

Read aloud the explanatory note about the source. Direct students' attention to the illustration on the page. Ask: Based on this image, what impression of Confucius was the sculptor trying to convey? *(Possible response: The sculptor probably wanted to show that Confucius was a benign and happy person.)*

GUIDED READING

Read aloud or ask volunteers to read aloud the text. Use the Reading and Vocabulary Support notes to deepen students' understanding of the primary source.

Reading and Vocabulary Support Answers

3. *Do not behave in a way that is improper; do not listen to, say, or do anything that violates the rules of society.*

5. *He means treat people respectfully.*

GUIDED ANALYSIS

After completing the text, discuss why this work is called rules to live by.

Infer If someone followed these rules, how would he or she behave? *(He or she would always be polite, respectful, good to others, and never do anything wrong or hurtful.)* If everyone in a society followed these rules, what kind of society would they have? *(a society, in which there was no crime or conflict.)*

To assess understanding, have students respond to the Analyze Primary Sources questions in writing.

ACTIVE JOURNAL

Quest Connection After students work through the primary source, direct them to the Quest Connection pages in their Active Journals. Have students record their thoughts about Shi Huangdi in light of the teachings of Confucius.

HSS 6.6.3, 6.6.4; ELA RI.6.3

Primary Sources

Confucius, *The Analects*

Confucius lived at a time of conflict and change. He developed a doctrine that he hoped leaders would adopt to restore harmony. Although leaders of his time refused to practice his ideas, Confucius became a revered teacher whose ideas have inspired followers for thousands of years.

◀ Statue of Confucius

Yen Yuan asked about perfect virtue ①.

The Master said, "To subdue one's self and return to propriety ②, is perfect virtue. If a man can for one day subdue himself and return to propriety, all under heaven will ascribe perfect virtue to him. . . .

Yen Yuan said, "I beg to ask the steps of that process." The Master replied, "Look not at what is contrary to propriety; listen not to what is contrary to propriety; speak not what is contrary to propriety; make no movement which is contrary to propriety. ③ Yen Yuan then said, "Though I am deficient ④ in intelligence and vigor, I will make it my business to practice this lesson."

Chung-kung asked about perfect virtue. The Master said, "It is, when you go abroad, to behave to every one as if you were receiving a great guest; to employ the people as if you were assisting at a great sacrifice ⑤; not to do to others as you would not wish done to yourself; to have no murmuring against you in the country, and none in the family. Chung-kung said, "Though I am deficient in intelligence and vigor, I will make it my business to practice this lesson."

—*The Analects of Confucius*

Reading and Vocabulary Support

① *Virtue* means goodness, or the quality of being good to others.

② The word *propriety* means the proper way to behave.

③ How would you summarize the steps of the process of a "return to propriety" described by the Master?

④ To be deficient means to be in short supply of something.

⑤ Sacrifices are very important rituals. When Confucius says to treat others as if assisting at a great sacrifice, what do you think he means?

Quest CONNECTIONS

Based on Confucius teaching of perfect virtue and propriety, does Shi Huangdi meet the standard of the right way to govern a state? Record your findings in your Active Journal.

Analyzing Primary Sources

Cite specific evidence from the document to support your answers.

1. **Determine Author's Point of View** Confucius suggests that all under heaven would consider a person to have perfect virtue if he or she could master correct behavior for a full day. What does Confucius suggest about the difficulty of mastering this behavior?
2. **Infer** Do you think the students really consider themselves unintelligent and lacking in vigor, as they state in the passage? What do these words suggest about the Confucian attitude toward modesty?
3. If both the leaders and the citizens of a state were to adopt these behaviors, how could these principles lead to harmony among people?

ANALYZING PRIMARY SOURCES

1. It is very difficult; most people can't live this way for even a day. **DOK3**

2. No, the students are being humble. The words suggest that Confucius valued modesty. **DOK3**

3. If leaders and citizens of the state all behaved properly and practiced modesty, there would be no conflict among people. **DOK3**

LESSON 4

HSS 6.6.5; ELA RI.6.1

The Unification of China

GET READY TO READ

START UP

Look closely at the photograph of the Great Wall, then preview the lesson. Write down several facts you already know about the Great Wall.

GUIDING QUESTIONS

- What steps did Shi Huangdi take to unite China?
- Why was Shi's centralized government so powerful?
- How did Legalist principles shape the Qin dynasty?

TAKE NOTES

Literacy Skills: Use Evidence

Use the graphic organizer in your Active Journal to take notes as you read the lesson.

PRACTICE VOCABULARY

Use the vocabulary activity in your Active Journal to practice the vocabulary words.

Vocabulary	Academic Vocabulary
Great Wall	uniform
standardize	collapse
Legalism	
censor	

The Warring States period came to an end when the kingdom of Qin (chin) unified China. King Zheng (jung) of Qin, who became the First Emperor, is remembered as a leader determined to build a great empire. Although his dynasty lost power soon after his death, later dynasties built upon his methods for ruling a large empire.

Unity Under the Qin

Qin was a mountainous kingdom located in northwestern China. Beyond Qin lay the foreign lands of Central Asia. The Qin rulers built a strong kingdom with an efficient government. By the late Zhou dynasty, Qin was the strongest kingdom in western China. Still, King Zheng, who came to power in 247 BCE, thirsted for more power.

How Were the Warring States United? Under King Zheng's leadership, Qin brought down rival kingdoms. In 221 BCE, Qin forces defeated their last enemy and united China, yet many challenges remained. Languages and customs varied.

PRACTICE VOCABULARY

To help students integrate new vocabulary, group the terms and introduce them. Explain that *Great Wall* and *Legalism* are related because they both refer to efforts of Shi Huangdi to protect and unify China. Explain that *standardize* and *censor* are related for the same reason. Shi Huangdi standardized weights and measures, and censored books he did not want people to read.

Have students locate and pronounce the academic vocabulary in the lesson margins. Provide sample sentences that clarify meaning.

currency: Coins and paper bills are currency.

legendary: King Arthur was a legendary hero.

HSS 6.6.5; ELA RI.6.1

The Unification of China

CONNECT

GET READY TO READ

ETEXT — START UP

Project the Start Up Activity. As students enter the classroom and get settled, have them study the photo. Explain that this is a photo of the Great Wall of China.

Recall Write down several facts you already know or can observe about the Great Wall. *(Students may have observed that the wall is a vast structure that stretches into the horizon through mountains and valleys; it is very high; there are guard towers at regular intervals.)*

Draw Conclusions What element of the wall makes it an effective defense barrier? *(Soldiers can stand on top of it and fire down on an enemy.)*

After completing the Start Up activity, project the Lesson Opener or direct students to their textbooks. Preview the lesson by working through the Get Ready to Read items with the class. Remind students to pay close attention to the Guiding Questions as they read the lesson.

ACTIVE JOURNAL

Take Notes Have students use the lesson literacy skills graphic organizer in their Active Journals to take notes as they read the lesson.

Practice Vocabulary Have students complete the activity in their Active Journals to build their vocabulary.

VIDEO — VIDEO

Assign the lesson video as homework.

INVESTIGATE

Unity Under the Qin

Discuss the rise of the Qin dynasty. How did Shi Huangdi unify and protect China? How was a united China organized?

Identify Implied Ideas Why was the **Great Wall** built only along China's northern border? *(It was meant to defend China against invaders from the north. China wasn't threatened on its southern border, and it was bordered by the ocean in the east.)*

Identify Central Ideas How did **standardization** unify China? *(It established a single language, made travel and trade easier, and gave people a single currency.)*

INTERACTIVE **INTERACTIVE GALLERY**

Terra Cotta Army of Shi Huangdi

Display the Interactive Gallery: Terra Cotta Army of Shi Huangdi for the class. Click through the images to find out more about Shi Huangdi and ancient China. Discuss the images with students. Ask: What does the terra cotta army tell us about Shi Huangdi? *(Possible responses: He was vastly powerful, and he wanted this to be evident to anyone who saw his grave; he believed that the army would protect him in the afterlife.)*

ACTIVE CLASSROOM

Use the See-Think-Wonder strategy. Have students choose one of the images in the gallery and write the answers to the following questions: What do you see? What does that make you think? What are you wondering about now that you've seen this? Ask volunteers to share their responses with the class.

Rebellion was always a danger, as was invasion by nomads from north and west of China. The king needed to make the Chinese into one people ruled by one government.

Who Was the First Emperor? The Qin ruler decided that "king" was too small a title for the leader of such a vast empire. He thus declared himself to be Shi Huangdi, or "First Emperor." The word "Huangdi" was tied to the gods and rulers of China's past. Shi Huangdi unified China from the Yellow River to the Yangtzee River.

How Was the Empire Defended? Before the Qin unification, the many Chinese kingdoms built walls to protect themselves from other kingdoms. Shi Huangdi had these walls torn down to make rebellion more difficult. Without these walls, local leaders could not defend their territory and break away from Qin rule.

INTERACTIVE
Terra Cotta Army of Shi Huangdi

The First Emperor also began work on one of the largest public works projects in history—the **Great Wall**, a long wall running east and west along his empire's northern border to defend the empire from nomads living to the north.

▲ Shi Huangdi had workers build an enormous tomb filled with thousands of statues of soldiers, like the one above. He may have believed this terra cotta army would protect him in the afterlife.

The wall went up quickly. Already, there were shorter walls along the border. Workers connected these old walls together, making a huge stone barrier. Building the wall was hard and dangerous. Many died while working on the wall. These workers included the many prisoners and citizens Hangdi uprooted from their homes to work on various projects.

The Great Wall did not always keep nomads out. Determined invaders were able to get around it. Still, the emperors of dynasties that followed the Qin also relied on the wall as a way to protect their northern border. Later emperors made the wall stronger, adding towers in key locations along its length.

Uniform Standards Shi Huangdi knew he needed to standardize many aspects of daily life in order to unify China's economy and culture. To **standardize** is to set rules that make things more similar. Anyone who did not follow the standards was punished as a traitor.

Perhaps most importantly, the Qin government established a single written language with standard characters. These characters are the basis of the written language in China today.

Transportation was also standardized. The government established a standard length for the axles of all vehicles. As a result, all ruts made in Chinese roads by the wheels of carts would be the same width. This made travel between different areas easier. The Qin government also created a uniform set of weights and measures for use in trade. It made uniform coins to be used as currency across China.

INTEGRATED ENGLISH LANGUAGE DEVELOPMENT

Collaborative Use the text under the heading How Were the Warring States United to help students create more complex sentences about the unification of the Warring States.

Emerging Have students write compound sentences about how Shi Huangdi unified the Warring States.

Expanding Have students write a paragraph summarizing how Shi Huangdi unified the Warring States. Then ask students exchange their paragraphs with a partner to revise. Encourage students to connect ideas to one another by creating compound and complex sentences. Offer students a word bank to use including words such as *because, even though, while,* and *before.*

Bridging Have students write a paragraph summarizing how Shi Huangdi unified the Warring States. Have students exchange their paragraphs

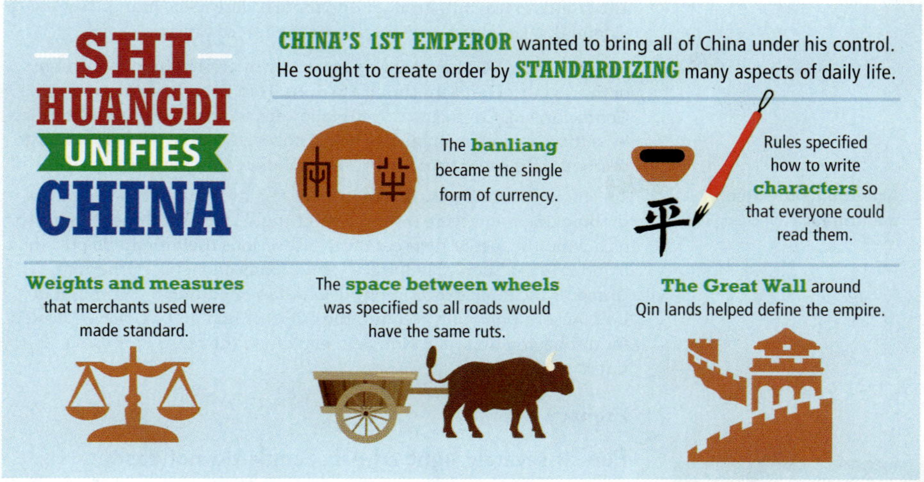

How Was the Empire Organized? Shi Huangdi introduced the concept of centralization, or a central governing system. He organized China into 36 provinces. Each province was divided into counties. County leaders were responsible to the heads of provinces. Province heads reported to the central government which, in turn, reported to the emperor. The emperor dismissed any official who failed to carry out his policies.

To prevent rebellion, Shi Huangdi forced thousands of noble families to move to the capital. There, government spies could watch over them.

READING CHECK **Explain** Why did Shi Huangdi call himself the First Emperor?

Rule of the First Emperor

Shi Huangdi is remembered as a cruel leader. He believed strict rules were necessary to end the chaos in China. The laws he created helped unite the empire, but his harsh rule was also one cause of the fall of the Qin dynasty. Although he built roads, dikes, and palaces, he forced tens of thousands of people to leave their homes to work on these projects.

A Legalist Government In the late Zhou, the Qin rulers brought in advisors from other kingdoms to help make Qin stronger. Shang Yang (shahng yahng) was one important advisor. He belonged to a school of thought called Legalism. According to **Legalism**, a strong leader and a strong legal system are needed to create social order.

Following Shang Yang's advice, the Qin kings took more direct control over the common people. Heavy taxes and required labor service increased the wealth of the Qin kings.

Analyze Charts The chart shows ways Shi Huangdi standardized certain aspects of Chinese life. **Generate Explanations** How do you think having the same currency and weights and measures helped to unify the empire?

Quest CONNECTIONS

Why did Shi Huangdi make great efforts to standardize and centralize so many aspects of Chinese life? Record your findings in your Active Journal.

ELD.PII.C.6

with a partner to revise. Encourage students to connect ideas to one another by creating compound and complex sentences.

WORKSHEET **TEACHER RESOURCES**

For additional IELD support addressing the standard, have students complete the Lesson ELD activity from the Teacher Resources found on the course.

Summarize How did Shi Huangdi organize the government to give the emperor more control? *(He divided China into provinces, and provinces into counties. County leaders reported to province leaders, who reported to the central government led by the emperor.)*

Identify Central Ideas Why was centralization an effective way to govern China? *(Instead of governing a vast territory, officials ruled smaller regions that were more easily controlled.)*

ACTIVE JOURNAL

Quest Connections Direct students to the Quest Connections pages in their Active Journals. Have them record their thoughts about Shi Huangdi's efforts to organize the empire. After students complete this activity, tell them to consider how they can use their response when they complete their Quest.

ELD TIP For the Quest Connections, have students create annotated illustrations of ways that Shi Huangdi standardized Chinese life.

Rule of the First Emperor

Apply Concepts Do you agree with **Legalism**? Why or why not? *(Possible response: I agree with it because without strong laws society might fall apart. However, laws should not be too harsh.)*

ANSWERS

Generate Explanations *It made trade easier and helped people feel they were all part of the same kingdom.*

Explain *King was too small a title for the leader of a vast empire.*

Apply Concepts Do you agree that people must be forced to be good? Why or why not? *(Possible response: I don't agree. Most people are good and don't have to be forced to behave correctly.)*

Apply Concepts Do you agree with the statement in the primary source that "light crimes" should be punished severely? Why or why not? *(Possible response: I don't agree. A light crime should receive a lighter punishment. Any punishment should fit the crime.)*

Draw Conclusions Why do you think Shi Huangdi made it a crime to praise past rulers? *(If people praised past rulers, they might start to think Shi Huangdi was not as good as they were.)*

Synthesize How did Shi Huangdi help cause the downfall of his government? *(The penalty for failure was so severe that when Chen Sheng saw he was about to fail he had nothing to lose by rebelling. Resentment of harsh laws led others to join him.)*

The kingdom became stronger and more orderly. Shi Huangdi set out to extend this Legalist government over the rest of China.

Harsh Laws Shi Huangdi was especially interested in the teachings of the Legalist Han Feizi (hahn FEY zuh). Han Feizi did not agree with Confucianism. Confucius and his followers believed people could be led by setting a good example. Han Feizi believed people must be forced to be good. This could be done by making and enforcing strict laws.

Academic Vocabulary
uniform • *adj.*, unchanging; fixed

Shi Huangdi made a **uniform** legal code across his empire. Penalties for breaking a law were severe. A thief could face punishment as harsh as having the feet or nose cut off. A less serious theft might be punished by hard labor, such as helping to build roads and walls. Other punishments included execution by beheading or cutting the criminal in half. According to one account, the emperor had 460 scholars executed for disobeying an order. Han Feizi explained the reason for these harsh punishments:

Did you know?
Shi Huangdi appointed inspectors, who were actually more like spies, to check on local officials and tax collectors to make sure they were carrying out his laws.

Primary Source

Punish severely light crimes. People do not easily commit serious crimes. But light offenses [crimes] are easily abandoned by people. . . . Now, if small offenses do not arise, big crimes will not come. And thus people will commit no crimes and disorder will not arise.

—Han Feizi

BIOGRAPHY
5 Things to Know About
SHI HUANGDI
Chinese Emperor (259 BCE–210 BCE)

- Shi Huangdi was only 13 years old when he took the throne.
- He standardized Chinese writing and built much of the Great Wall of China.
- Later Confucian scholars condemned Shi Huangdi for his harsh rule and for burning Confucian texts.
- He was guarded in death by 6,000 life-sized terra cotta guards in a secret tomb.
- His empire fell less than four years after his death.

Draw Conclusions Why did Shi Huangdi's empire fall less than four years after his death? What does that tell you about the state of China at the time?

206 Lesson 5.4 • The Unification of China

DIFFERENTIATED INSTRUCTION

Special Education Write a word using a mix of English letters and symbols. Discuss why this word is impossible to read. Then, write the word using English letters. Guide students to understand that they can read the second word because the writing is standardized.

Below Level Ask students how they would feel if they had to use a different system of writing. Discuss how the people of China might have felt when Shi Huangdi standardized Chinese writing.

Advanced Have students do research and stage a debate for the class about standardized writing. One side can argue the benefits of introducing standardized writing. The other side can argue the disadvantages, such as loss of cultural heritage.

ANSWERS

Draw Conclusions *People in China were very unhappy if they wanted change so quickly.*

Thought Control The First Emperor also tried to control Chinese thought. He decided to **censor**, or ban, ideas he found dangerous or offensive. Censorship took many forms. Debate about the government was banned. People were not allowed to praise past rulers or criticize the present one. The emperor ordered the burning of all books that did not support his policies.

The Fall of the Qin Dynasty These policies were not popular, but they did help create a single nation from China's diverse regions. The First Emperor believed that his dynasty would last forever, but it **collapsed** about three years after his death.

The Qin Dynasty was undone by its unbending enforcement of its harsh laws. A rebellion was sparked by a soldier named Chen Sheng, who led a band of men north to guard China's border. Along the way, heavy rains delayed the band. Chen knew that the penalty for arriving late would be severe. So he and his men decided that they had nothing to lose by rebelling.

As news of Chen's uprising spread, thousands rose up to support him. Qin generals tried to put down the uprisings, but the rebellions spread rapidly. Knowing the punishments for failure, some generals joined the rebellions. The rebels joined together long enough to overthrow the Qin, but then began fighting amongst themselves. China again slid into chaos.

Analyze Images Scholars who disobeyed Shi Huangdi were buried alive. He also had many books burned, but preserved those about agriculture and medicine. **Draw Conclusions** Why do you think these books were not burned?

READING CHECK **Describe** How did Shi Huangdi try to stop people from criticizing him?

Academic Vocabulary
collapse • *v.*, to break down or fall down

Lesson Check

HSS 6.6.5; ELD.PI.C.10.a

Practice Vocabulary

1. Use the terms ***standardize*** and ***censor*** to describe how Shi Huangdi united his empire.
2. Why did Shi Huangdi build the **Great Wall**?

Critica Thinking and Writing

3. **Compare and Contrast** How is Legalism different from Confucianism?
4. **Analyze Cause and Effect** Why did Shi Huangdi create harsh laws?
5. **Identify Cause and Effect** What was one cause of the fall of the Qin dynasty?
6. **Writing Workshop: Use Credible Sources** Where can you find credible sources of information to support your argument? Research at a library and on reputable websites or use the primary and secondary sources in this book. Make sure to consider the point of view of each source and remain alert for bias. Take notes from your sources in your Active Journal.

HSS 6.6.5; ELD.P1.C.10.a

SYNTHESIZE

Assess and Reteach Have students use the Give One, Get One strategy to complete Lesson Check questions 1–5. Review their responses. If they had any incorrect answers, use the Guiding Questions to discuss the lesson's main ideas, focusing on the ideas they struggled with.

ACTIVE JOURNAL

Writing Workshop Have students complete the Lesson 4 Writing Task in their Active Journals. Students will locate credible sources of information to support their argument.

DEMONSTRATE

ASSESSMENT **ONLINE LESSON QUIZ**

Assign the Online Lesson Quiz for this lesson if you haven't already done so. Students will be offered automatic remediation or enrichment based on their score.

DISCUSSION **DISCUSSION BOARD**

Post this question to the class on the Discussion Board:

Summarize Shi Huangdi was a harsh ruler, but he unified China. Were harsh laws an acceptable way to unify a nation? Why or why not? *(Sample response: No. Harsh punishments are a poor way to unify an empire.)*

LESSON CHECK

1. Sample response: People were forced to use standardized coins, which made it easier to conduct business throughout the empire. Ideas that could harm Qin rule were censored. **DOK1**
2. to prevent attacks from northern nomads **DOK1**
3. Legalism taught that laws and punishments were the key to social order. Confucianism taught that practicing filial piety and having respect for authority resulted in social order and that rulers should lead by example. **DOK2**
4. He believed harsh laws were necessary to end chaos in society. **DOK2**
5. harshness of laws **DOK2**
6. Responses will be a list of credible sources of information that support the student's argument. **DOK4**

ANSWERS

Draw Conclusions *The information in those books could help China.*

Describe *He banned debate about government and executed scholars who disobeyed his policies.*

HSS 6.6.5; Analysis REP.4; ELA RI.6.1, RI.6.3

Analysis Skills

Draw Sound Conclusions from Sources

LEARN

Preview the steps in the student text with students, and then play the video.

VIDEO **21ST CENTURY SKILLS**

Project the Draw Conclusions video in the 21st Century Skills Tutorial. Use the Quick Reference and Assessment to provide additional instruction in the skill.

PRACTICE

Have students practice the skill using the text on the student page. When students are finished, discuss their responses as a class.

ASSESS

To assess this skill, have students apply these steps to the primary source on the Lesson 2 Analysis Skills page.

ACTIVE JOURNAL

Quest Connections Direct students to the Quest Connections pages in their Active Journals. After students complete this activity, tell them to consider how they can use their response when they complete their Quest.

ANSWERS

1. a. All information that the Qin do not approve of will be destroyed.
   b. All historical records but those of Qin should be burned. Only court scholars can keep literature, historical records, or philosophical writings.
2. Why is this being suggested?
3. He was ruthless enough to find the suggestion acceptable.
4. a. Sample response: He was a harsh ruler who permitted no opposition.
   b. Yes. He would consider historical records or writings to be opposition.
   c. The Primary Source confirmed that Shi Huangdi was a ruthless autocrat.

HSS 6.6.5 Analysis REP.4; ELA RI.6.1, RI.6.3

Draw Sound Conclusions from Sources

Follow these steps to learn how to draw sound conclusions from sources.

INTERACTIVE Draw Conclusions

1 **Study the facts and main ideas in a source.** This primary source came from the prime minister, Li Si to the Qin emperor, Shi Huangdi.

a. What seems to be the main idea of this passage?

b. What facts or evidence does the author include to support the main idea?

2 **Formulate questions about the source.** Asking questions about the source can help you uncover its purpose and meaning. For example, with this source you might ask, "What is Li Si proposing about books of poetry, history, and philosophy?" What is another question you could ask about the purpose or meaning of the source?

3 **Draw conclusions from the source.** This source provides some insight in the rule of Shi Huangdi and the methods he used. What can you conclude about Shi Huangdi based on this passage?

4 **Test any conclusions for soundness.** Ask, "Do the facts in the source support my conclusions?"

a. What have you learned about Shi Huangdi?

b. Does what you learned match the conclusions you have drawn from the source?

c. Do you need to adjust your conclusion based on what you learned?

Primary Source

I humbly propose that all historical records but those of Qin be burned. If anyone who is not a court scholar dares to keep the ancient poems, historical records, or writings of the hundred schools of philosophy, these books shall be confiscated and burned by the provincial governor and army commander. Those who in conversation dare to quote the old poems and records should be publicly executed; those who use old precedents to oppose the new order should have their families wiped out; and officers who know of such cases but fail to report them shall be punished in the same way. If thirty days after the issuing of this order, the owners of these books still have not destroyed them, they shall have their faces tattooed and be condemned to hard labor at the Great Wall. The only books which need not be destroyed are those dealing with medicine, divination, and agriculture.

— Sima Qian, *Records of the Grand Historian*

Quest CONNECTIONS

What does this excerpt from Sima Qian tell you about how Shi Huangdi faced challenges during his rule? Record your findings in your Active Journal.

DIFFERENTIATED INSTRUCTION

Special Education To help students understand the concept of drawing conclusions, ask the following questions: What would you think if you saw someone carrying a shovel while it was snowing? What would you think if you saw someone holding keys as they approached a door? Explain that each answer is a conclusion they reached based on what they saw.

INTEGRATED ENGLISH LANGUAGE DEVELOPMENT

Emerging Ask students simple yes-and-no questions such as "Did the author want to burn books?" and "Did the author want to send people who kept their books to prison?"

LESSON 5

HSS 6.6.6, 6.6.7, 6.6.8

The Han Dynasty Expands

BOUNCE TO ACTIVATE VIDEO

GET READY TO READ

START UP

Look at the photograph of this scene along the Silk Road. Write down several facts you know or questions that you have about the Silk Road.

GUIDING QUESTIONS

- What social customs and government policies helped China unify under the Han?
- What role did Confucianism play in the development of the civil service?
- How did the Silk Road increase trade, the spread of Buddhism, and connections between China and other regions of Afroeurasia?

TAKE NOTES

Literacy Skills: Analyze Cause and Effect

Use the graphic organizer in your Active Journal to take notes as you read the lesson.

PRACTICE VOCABULARY

Use the vocabulary activity in your Active Journal to practice the vocabulary words.

Vocabulary		Academic Vocabulary
official	envoy	assigned
civil service	cuisine	obtained
Silk Road		

Besides founding China's first empire, Shi Huangdi also laid the foundation for a system of government to rule a large empire. The next ruling family was the Han. The Han emperors built on the successes of the Qin to create one of the most influential dynasties in Chinese history.

How Did the Han Govern China?

The fighting that toppled the Qin dynasty lasted for several years. Finally, a rebel general named Liu Bang (LYOH bahng) gained control of China. In 206 BCE, he founded the Han dynasty. The Han ruled China for about 400 years. Today, the largest ethnic group in China still call themselves the "Han." Later dynasties were established that were governed by Confucian principles using scholar-officials. Maintaining the philosophy laid out in the Mandate of Heaven was crucial to following Confucian principles.

Reuniting and Expanding China The first Han emperor came from a poor family. His success was, in part, due to his ability to surround himself with capable advisors.

PRACTICE VOCABULARY

To help students integrate new vocabulary, group the terms and introduce them. Explain that *official*, *envoy*, and *civil service* all refer to people who work in government. Ask what similar words students might know. *(mayor, senator, ambassador, representative)* Explain that in this lesson *Silk Road* (a trade route) and *cuisine* (a cooking style) are related because Chinese cuisine was influenced by goods traded on the Silk Road.

Have students locate and pronounce the academic vocabulary in the lesson margins. Provide sample sentences that clarify meaning.

assigned: In a group project, people are assigned specific tasks.

obtained: Knowledge is obtained through study.

HSS 6.6.6, 6.6.7, 6.6.8

The Han Dynasty Expands

CONNECT

GET READY TO READ

ETEXT **START UP**

Project the Start Up Activity. As students enter the classroom and get settled, have them study the image. Explain that this image shows a scene on the Silk Road a network of trade routes connecting China with Central and Southwest Asia.

Frame Questions Write down three questions that you have about the Silk Road. *(Sample response: What was the Silk Road? Where was it? Who used it?)*

Evaluate Sources What is your impression of the Silk Road? *(It was a place of great activity.)*

After completing the Start Up activity, project the Lesson Opener or direct students to their textbooks. Preview the lesson by working through the Get Ready to Read items with the class. Remind students to pay close attention to the Guiding Questions as they read the lesson.

ACTIVE JOURNAL

Take Notes Have students use the lesson literacy skills graphic organizer in their Active Journals to take notes as they read the lesson.

Practice Vocabulary Have students complete the activity in their Active Journals to build their vocabulary.

VIDEO **VIDEO**

Assign the lesson video as homework.

WORKSHEET **TEACHER RESOURCES**

Have students who need additional support use the following worksheets from the Teacher Resources on the course:

- **Reading Support**
- **English Language Development**
- **Lesson Summary**

INVESTIGATE

How Did the Han Govern China?

Discuss the Han dynasty. What were its achievements? Why did it decline?

Identify Central Ideas Why were the Han so willing to rule differently from the Qin? *(They knew that the Qin lost power because of their cruel policies.)*

Interpret Why did the Han emperors keep many Qin laws and policies? *(Standardization had helped China. They kept laws that helped, and ended policies that hurt China.)*

Summarize What was the Han emperors' main strategy for maintaining power? *(They kept local leaders too weak to challenge their authority.)*

ELD TIP Have students create annotated illustrations of ways that the Han emperors learned from the rule of Shi Huangdi.

Analyze Images Han Emperor Wudi rides in a chariot as he prepares to exit his walled palace. **Draw Conclusions** What can you infer about life in a Han palace, based on the picture? Cite evidence to support your conclusion.

As emperor, he consulted with a Confucian scholar who pointed out that the Qin lost power because of cruel policies. The emperor encouraged learning, lowered taxes, and ended many of the Qin's harsh rules.

Confucian scholars throughout the Han gave practical advice and encouraged rulers to set an example of mercy and proper behavior. Han emperors kept many of the Qin laws and policies to standardize Chinese life, but avoided the harsh rule that had caused unrest.

The Han not only stayed in power, they expanded China's territory. Much of this expansion took place under the fifth Han emperor, Wudi (woo dee). Remembered as one of the country's greatest emperors, Wudi ruled for more than 50 years. Wudi sent his armies west to conquer lands far into Central Asia. He extended his empire north to the Korean peninsula and south into what is now Vietnam.

Han Government Han emperors followed the example of the Qin by creating a strong central government. In this way, they avoided the problem of disunity that the Zhou dynasty had faced. As the Zhou dynasty had expanded, local noblemen became more powerful than the Zhou king. The Han emperors tried to make sure that local leaders remained too weak to challenge their authority. When the Han emperors conquered new lands, they administered this land directly rather than giving it to a nobleman.

The Han government was organized like a pyramid. The broad base of the pyramid was made up of China's many towns and villages. At the top of the pyramid were the emperor and his chief advisors. Many layers of government lay between. At each level, **officials**, that is, people **assigned** to a position in the government, took orders from those above them and gave orders to those below them.

Academic Vocabulary
assign • *v.*, to give as a job or task

How Did Civil Service Strengthen the Han Government? The strength of the Han government lay in its civil service. A **civil service** is a system of government employees mainly selected for their skills and knowledge. In the first 200 years of Han rule, the civil service grew to more than 130,000 officials.

Positions in the civil service were not hereditary; that is, they were not passed down from father to son. Officials were appointed to their positions. Han emperors asked their officials to recommend people for the civil service. From those recommendations, the emperors selected officials from across the empire.

ANSWERS

Draw Conclusions *Life in a Han palace was luxurious and serene. The women are well dressed and everyone seems to be very calm.*

INTEGRATED ENGLISH LANGUAGE DEVELOPMENT

Collaborative Use the text under the heading How did the Han Govern China? to help students condense ideas about the Han dynasty into precise and detailed sentences.

Emerging Have students write sentences using prepositional phrases about the organization of the Han government.

Expanding Have students write a paragraph summarizing how the civil service worked under the Han. Have students exchange their paragraphs with a partner to revise. Encourage students to condense ideas into more detailed and succinct sentences. Offer students a word bank to use, including words such as *who, that,* and *led to.*

Bridging Have students write a paragraph summarizing how the civil service worked under the Han. Encourage students to condense ideas into more

Emperor Wudi also created exams to find talented people for the civil service. These exams were based on the ideas of Confucius. In later dynasties, the exam system would become even more important for selecting officials.

INTERACTIVE
Ancient Chinese Dynasties

Han officials enjoyed high salaries and a life of comfort and influence. They wore special clothes that indicated their rank. They collected taxes, organized labor, and enforced laws. They could even force people to move. If there were too many people in one area, officials could relocate them to lands with fewer people.

The Han emperors placed limits on the powers of officials. For example, officials were not allowed to serve in their home districts. This prevented them from organizing against the emperor with family and friends. The emperors knew that to rule successfully, they needed their officials' loyalty.

Decline of the Han At its height, the Han dynasty ruled some 60 million people. It ruled China for over 400 years. Then, like other powerful empires, it went into a decline. Once again, the central government weakened and warlords competed for power. China was plunged into disunity for several centuries. Still, the idea of a unified China never died. Future dynasties eventually emerged, modeling themselves on the Han.

READING CHECK **Identify** Name one achievement of Wudi.

The Silk Road

One of the most lasting contributions of the Han dynasty was establishment of the Silk Road. The **Silk Road** is a network of trade routes that crossed Asia, connecting China to Central

GEOGRAPHY SKILLS

The Silk Road stretched from China to the Mediterranean with trade routes by both land and sea.

1. **Movement** Name the locations of two different routes Chinese travelers could take to get to Rome.
2. **Use Visual Information** Based on the map, how do you think the growth of the Han dynasty was impacted by trade on the Silk Road?

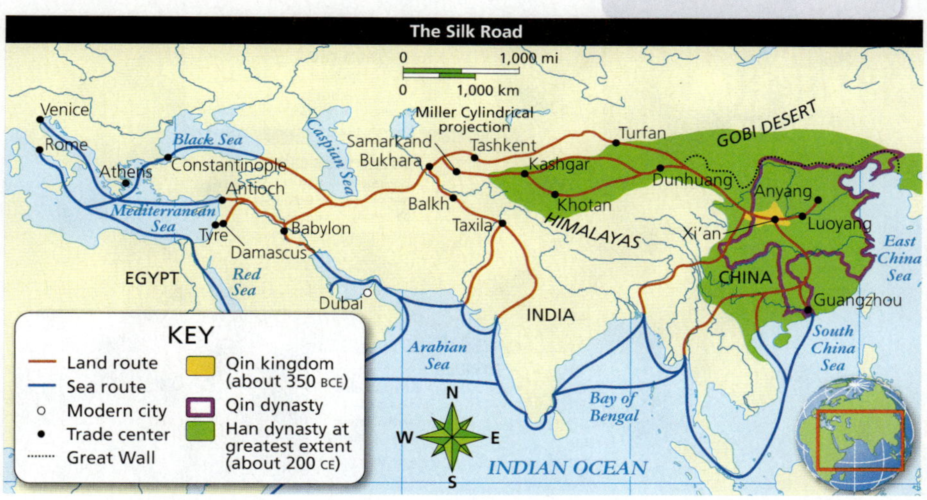

Identify Supporting Details What were two strengths of the Han civil service system? *(Positions were not passed down from father to son; exams were required to obtain positions.)*

Draw Conclusions Why were these strengths? *(They ensured that qualified people became government officials.)*

Identify Main Ideas Why did Han emperors place restrictions on government officials? *(to prevent them from becoming too powerful and perhaps plotting against the emperor.)*

Draw Conclusions Though the Han went into decline, future dynasties modeled themselves on the Han. What does that suggest? *(They were greatly admired.)*

INTERACTIVE **INTERACTIVE MAP**

Ancient Chinese Dynasties

Display the Interactive Map: Ancient Chinese Dynasties for the class. Ask a volunteer to read the Introduction and Instructions. Have volunteers read the information for each dynasty. Ask: What historical pattern do you see? *(the cycle of dynasties)*

ACTIVE CLASSROOM

Use the Quick Write strategy. Have students select one of the dynasties on the chart. Give them 30 seconds to write their overall impression of that dynasty. Ask volunteers to share their responses.

ANSWERS

1. Movement *land route west across Asia; sea route west across the South China Sea and the Indian Ocean*

2. Use Visual Information *The Han dynasty probably grew in a westward direction to have more of the Silk Road in its territory.*

Identify *Possible responses: conquests of lands west, north, and south; strong central government; civil service exams*

ELD.PII.C.7

detailed and succinct sentences. Have students exchange paragraphs with a partner to revise.

WORKSHEET **TEACHER RESOURCES**

For additional IELD support addressing the standard, have students complete the Lesson ELD activity from the Teacher Resources found on the course.

The Silk Road

Discuss the **Silk Road**. Why was it so important to China and the rest of the world?

Identify Cause and Effect Why might it be said that the **Silk Road** was established "by accident"? *(The Chinese first traveled to Central Asia to seek an ally, not to trade.)*

Synthesize What advantage did the Chinese have in the **Silk Road** trade? *(They were the only ones who knew how to make silk.)* Why do you think they guarded the secret of silk-making so closely? *(Sample response: As long as they controlled silk production, they would have a valuable good to trade with other peoples.)*

Describe Describe the flow of ideas east and west along the Silk Road. *(Possible response: Buddhism traveled east to China; Confucianism and Daoism traveled west from China.)*

Did you know?

The Silk Road was not a road. It was a network of many routes over land and water that connected Asia with Europe and Africa.

and Southwest Asia. Trade routes across Central Asia had existed before the Han, but during the reign of Wudi, contact between China and regions to the west increased. Merchants made their fortunes along the Silk Road, but it was also a path for the spread of ideas.

The Journey of Zhang Qian At first, the Chinese traveled to Central Asia not to trade, but to seek an ally in their fight against a fierce group of nomads, the Xiongnu (shong noo). Emperor Wudi heard of a people from Central Asia called the Yuezhi (yooeh jur) who were also enemies of the Xiongnu. Wudi hoped the Yuezhi would help fight the Xiongnu. He asked for a volunteer to find the Yuezhi. Zhang Qian (jahng chyen) stepped up to take on this challenge.

Zhang set out to the west. He was captured by the Xiongnu and held prisoner for ten years. He escaped and found the Yuezhi, but could not persuade them to ally with the Han against the Xiongnu.

Still, Wudi was interested in Zhang's account of his travels. Zhang described exotic lands where horses sweat blood and "the inhabitants ride elephants when they go into battle." Wudi and later Han emperors sent **envoys**, that is, representatives of the emperor, to create relations with kingdoms to the west. The Han also sent troops to the west. With the Han army protecting the region, trade flourished. Merchants could trade with less fear of being attacked by bandits.

Analyze Diagrams More than just goods were exchanged along the Silk Road. **Recognize Multiple Causes** What are two reasons why you think ideas like religion and philosophy traveled in both directions along the Silk Road?

A Major Trade Route The name "Silk Road" comes from China's most important export: silk. It is made from the cocoon of a caterpillar called the silk worm. It is strong, soft, and can be dyed many colors. Only the Chinese knew how to make silk. They guarded this secret closely. It was illegal to export silk worms. However, toward the end of the second century BCE, the Han Dynasty began to exchange

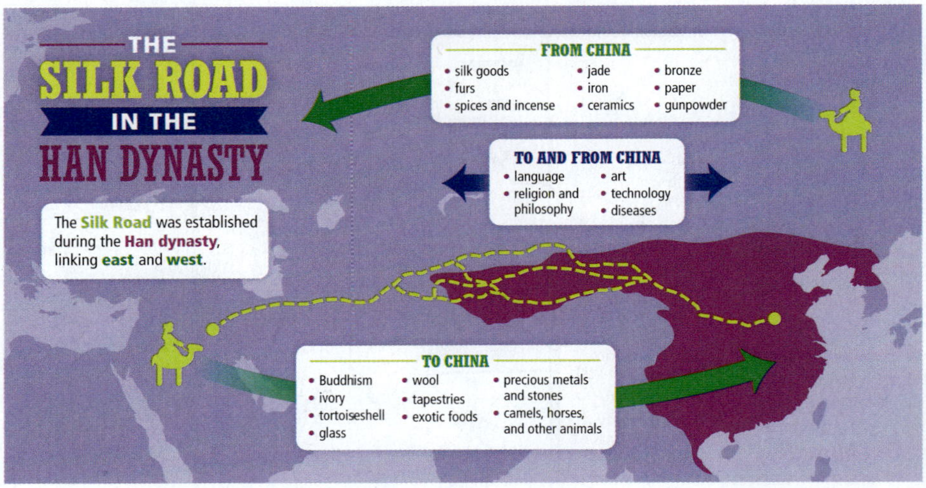

DIFFERENTIATED INSTRUCTION

Special Education Provide students with a large map of the Silk Road and sticky notes identifying goods exchanged in the Silk Road trade. Have students place each note on the source of each good.

Below Level Have students use the map to trace a route on the Silk Road and identify geographic features along that route.

Advanced Have students do research and write a report on how silk is made. Has silk-making changed since the Han dynasty? In what ways? Ask volunteers to share their information with the class.

ANSWERS

Recognize Multiple Causes *Merchants from both directions brought new ideas as well as goods. The West was open to Chinese philosophies; China was open to new religions.*

ambassadors with other Asian and African states. Chinese ambassadors and merchants gave gifts of silk cloth to Persia, Kush, and the Maurya empire of India. As a result, other central Asian states began to trade regularly with Chinese merchants.

The Chinese exchanged silk and other luxury goods for a wide range of products. The Chinese particularly valued the strong horses of central Asia. The Silk Road also enriched Chinese **cuisine**; that is, the style of cooking. Grapes, sesame, and onion were all brought into China along the Silk Road. The emperor also **obtained** rare animals, such as elephants, lions, and ostriches, from abroad. In addition to the Silk Road, Chinese merchants also traded along seas that ran along the coast of Asia from China to the Red Sea.

Exchanges of Ideas The Silk Road was a path for the exchange of ideas. Chinese inventions, such as paper, spread west along the Silk Road.

Foreign ideas, such as Buddhism, entered China during the Han along these trade routes. The religion of Buddhism started in India and spread into Central Asia. The Chinese, then, learned about this religion from Buddhists in Central Asia. Over time, Buddhism became very popular in China. After the Han, Chinese Buddhists traveled to India to study the religion. Chinese Buddhists also brought new ideas and practices to the religion.

Along with Confucianism and Daoism, Buddhism is one of the most influential belief systems in China. Chinese scholars mixed ideas from the three belief systems in their writings and art.

▲ Buddhist temples and images of the Buddha can be found across China today. Many combine Indian, central Asian, and Chinese artistic influences.

Academic Vocabulary

obtain • *v.*, to get or to receive something

READING CHECK **Identify Cause and Effect** How did the Silk Road benefit China?

Lesson Check

HSS 6.6.6, 6.6.7, 6.6.8; ELD.PI.C.10.a

Practice Vocabulary

1. Use the terms ***official*** and ***civil service*** to describe the government of the Han.
2. What was the **Silk Road**?

Critical Thinking and Writing

3. **Compare and Contrast** How was the Han dynasty similar to and different from the Qin dynasty?
4. **Classify and Categorize** How did Emperor Wudi organize the Han government to make it stronger?
5. **Understand Effects** How did the Silk Road lead to the spread of Buddhism into China?
6. **Writing Workshop: Shape Tone** Draft your argument in your Active Journal. Then evaluate your argument. Is your claim effectively presented in a clear and logical manner? Does the tone of your argument help you to make a strong argument? Identify places in your argument where you can use strong verbs and supporting evidence to more strongly make your point.

LESSON CHECK

1. Han officials reported to the central government. An educated civil service strengthened Han government.
2. It was a network of trade routes connecting China to Central and Southwest Asia. **DOK1**
3. Similar: The Han continued standardization and centralization. Different: The Han ended the Qin's harsh rules and lowered taxes. **DOK2**
4. He had civil service positions appointed rather than passed down from father to son; he created exams to find talented people. **DOK2**
5. Buddhism started in India and spread into Central Asia. From there, it spread to China over the Silk Road. **DOK2**
6. Students will draft their argument, evaluate it, and revise for tone. **DOK4**

HSS 6.6.6, 6.6.7, 6.6.8; ELD.P1.C.10.a

SYNTHESIZE

Assess and Reteach Have students use a Think-Pair-Share strategy to complete Lesson Check questions 1–5. Review their responses. If responses are incorrect, use the Guiding Questions to discuss the lesson's main ideas, focusing on the ideas that are causing difficulty.

ACTIVE JOURNAL

Writing Workshop Have students complete the Lesson 5 Writing Task in their Active Journals. Students will draft their argument, evaluate it, and revise or strengthen its tone if necessary.

DEMONSTRATE

ASSESSMENT **ONLINE LESSON QUIZ**

Assign the Online Lesson Quiz for this lesson if you haven't already done so. Students will be offered automatic remediation or enrichment based on their score.

DISCUSSION **DISCUSSION BOARD**

Post this question to the class on the Discussion Board:

Synthesize It might be said that the Han was the most advanced dynasty. Do you agree? Why or why not? *(Sample response: I agree. The Han built on the accomplishments of past dynasties and avoided their mistakes; China prospered under the Han.)*

ANSWERS

Identify Cause and Effect *It brought new goods and ideas into China; trade enriched China.*

HSS 6.6.4, 6.6.6

Han Society and Achievements

CONNECT

GET READY TO READ

ETEXT **START UP**

Project the Start Up Activity. As students enter the classroom and get settled, have them study the photograph.

Draw Conclusions What does this picture of a Chinese garden tell you about how the Chinese came to value the natural world? *(Possible response: They came to value nature's balance and harmony.)*

Evaluate Sources What other impression do you have of this garden? *(Possible response: It appears to be a calm, quiet place.)*

After completing the Start Up activity, project the Lesson Opener or direct students to their textbooks. Preview the lesson by working through the Get Ready to Read items with the class. Remind students to pay close attention to the Guiding Questions as they read the lesson.

ACTIVE JOURNAL

Take Notes Have students use the lesson literacy skills graphic organizer in their Active Journals to take notes as they read the lesson.

Practice Vocabulary Have students complete the activity in their Active Journals to build their vocabulary.

VIDEO **VIDEO**

Assign the lesson video as homework.

HSS 6.6.4, 6.6.6

Han Society and Achievements

GET READY TO READ

START UP

Many modern Chinese ideas, such as garden design, were influenced by Han ideas. What does this picture of a Chinese garden tell you about how the Chinese came to value the natural world?

GUIDING QUESTIONS

- How did Confucian teachings about relationships shape Han society?
- Why was China's economy strong under the Han?
- What were the major achievements of Han China in the arts, science, and technology?

TAKE NOTES

Literacy Skills: Summarize

Use the graphic organizer in your Active Journal to take notes as you read the lesson.

PRACTICE VOCABULARY

Use the vocabulary activity in your Active Journal to practice the vocabulary words.

Vocabulary		Academic Vocabulary
monopoly	acupuncture	exempt
calligraphy	seismometer	benefit
lacquer		

The Han dynasty was a time of innovation and economic development. The production of many goods increased and trade flourished. More people worked as craftsmen and merchants. Many important inventions also date to this dynasty.

Han Society

Han China was a mixture of peoples and cultures, but the country became more unified during this dynasty. Han emperors continued many of the Qin policies that standardized life in China, such as using a common currency. Shared values also bound the people together.

The Social Order China's social order was based on Confucian values. Confucius and his followers valued mental work more than physical labor. Scholars, therefore, were highly respected. Farmers were also highly respected because they produced the most important and basic goods: food and cloth. Artisans were valued for their skill and hard work.

PRACTICE VOCABULARY

To help students integrate new vocabulary, group the terms and introduce them. Explain that *calligraphy* (the art of beautiful writing) and *lacquer* (a protective coating) are related because they both have to do with Chinese arts. Explain that *acupuncture* (a therapy that uses needles to cure sickness and stop pain) and *seismometer* (an instrument that detects earthquakes) are both Chinese scientific accomplishments.

Have students locate and pronounce the academic vocabulary in the lesson margins. Provide sample sentences that clarify meaning.

exempt: Organizations that are exempt from taxes do not have to pay them.

benefit: Ocean breezes are among the benefits of living at the seashore.

214 Lesson 5.6 • Han Society and Achievements

Confucius and many other early Chinese thinkers had little respect for merchants because merchants do not produce anything. As a result, merchants fell lower in the social order. The government placed restrictions on merchants. They were not allowed to wear fine clothing or own land. Their children could not become officials. Still, many merchants became wealthy and powerful. They lived comfortable lives despite the lack of respect for trade.

At the bottom of the social order were a small number of slaves. When someone committed a serious crime, family members might be punished with slavery. Other people were sold into slavery when their families fell deep into debt.

Family Life Confucian teachings about family loyalty and respect for elders were key values. During the Han, ancestor worship continued. People made offerings to show respect and gain support from their ancestors.

Also, the Han legal code enforced Confucian values. Parents could report children who did not behave with filial piety. Adult children would be punished harshly. Younger children, though, were usually **exempt** from punishment.

The Role of Women The status of women was generally lower than that of men. Most worked in the home, weaving and caring for their children and elderly family members.

One exceptional woman was Ban Zhao (bahn jow). Unlike most Han women, she received a good education. Ban became a historian in the royal court. She wrote that young women deserved an education, yet she also accepted the higher status of men in society.

Primary Source

If a wife does not serve her husband, then the proper relationship between men and women . . . [is] neglected and destroyed.

—Ban Zhao, *Lessons for Women*

READING CHECK **Cite Evidence** What evidence supports the generalization that merchants held a low place in Chinese society?

Academic Vocabulary
exempt • *adj.*, to be free from a punishment or duty

Analyze Images This image recreates what a pottery workshop may have looked like at the time of the Han. **Synthesize Visual Information** What can you tell about the work and lives of Han artisans from this picture?

DIFFERENTIATED INSTRUCTION

Special Education Read together the section The Social Order in the textbook. Give students a sheet of paper showing a pyramid, and sticky notes identifying people in Han society. Have students place the sticky notes correctly on the pyramid.

Below Level Have students create a chart showing the responsibilities and limitations of women in the Han dynasty versus women in the United States today.

Advanced Have students research traditional stories about Chinese filial piety and share them with the class.

WORKSHEET **TEACHER RESOURCES**

Have students who need additional support use the following worksheets from the Teacher Resources on the course:

- **Reading Support**
- **English Language Development**
- **Lesson Summary**

INVESTIGATE

Han Society

Discuss Han society. How was the family viewed? How were women viewed?

Identify Central Ideas Who were the most valued members of Han society? *(scholars, farmers, and artisans)*

Identify Central Ideas Why were these people highly valued? *(The social order was based on Confucian values. Confucianism valued mental work, so scholars were highly respected. Farmers were respected because they produced food and cloth. Artisans were valued for their skill and hard work.)*

Identify Central Ideas Why were merchants not valued members of Han society? *(Merchants do not produce anything.)*

Compare and Contrast Why is Ban Zhao considered to be an exceptional woman? *(She received a good education and became a historian in the royal court in a society that relegated women to the home and domestic tasks.)*

Identify Central Ideas As "exceptional" as she was, in what way was Ban Zhao a product of her times? *(She accepted and embraced the idea that a wife must serve her husband.)*

ANSWERS

Synthesize Visual Information *Han artisans did a lot of work by hand and mass-produced objects.*

Cite Evidence *Merchants were not allowed to wear fine clothing or to own land. Their children could not become officials.*

Economic Life

Discuss the Han economy. Why did the government want to control production and prices? How did they do this?

Cite Evidence What evidence suggests that Wudi was a more effective ruler than Shi Huangdi? *(Under his rule, China prospered.)*

Identify Central Ideas Why did Wudi create state **monopolies**? *(He used the profits to pay for his military activities; they helped keep important producers and merchants from becoming too powerful.)*

Identify Central Ideas Why did Han emperors try to control food prices? *(They wanted to avoid high prices and food shortages when harvests were bad.)*

INTERACTIVE **INTERACTIVE GALLERY**

Silkmaking in Ancient China

Display the Interactive Gallery: Silkmaking in Ancient China for the class. Ask a volunteer to read the Introduction. Ask: Is the process of making silk more or less complicated than you thought it was? *(Possible response: It is more complicated because securing the raw materials for making silk is more time-consuming than acquiring wool or cotton.)*

ACTIVE CLASSROOM

Use the My Simile strategy. Have students choose an image from the gallery and use it to complete the following prompt: This ________ is like ________ because ________. Ask volunteers to share their similes with the class.

ANSWERS

Synthesize Visual Information *Silk was produced by women using simple tools.*

Analyze Images
This image shows a method of ancient Chinese silk production. **Synthesize Visual Information** What does this image tell you about how ancient Chinese silk was produced and who produced it?

Economic Life

China under the Han was peaceful compared to the chaotic Warring States period. The Han emperors lowered the high taxes that Shi Huangdi had collected. China prospered in this more stable time.

Agriculture Farmers were the backbone of China's economy. They made up about 90 percent of the population. As one Han emperor said,

Primary Source

> Agriculture is the foundation of the world. No duty is greater.
>
> —Emperor Wen, *Hanshu*

Most farms in Han China were small. Farmers grew wheat, millet, barley, beans, and rice. Farmers with more land might also grow fruit or bamboo. Farming families often made their own cloth.

Silk production was especially important as trade along the Silk Road increased. On small farms, the women of the family tended silkworms and wove silk. In wealthy households, the women hired workers to help make silk. Workshops in cities also employed many weavers. Workshops bought silk thread from farms. They specialized in making the most expensive, high-quality cloth.

Industry Industries, such as iron production, also became important. Iron was useful for making tools and weapons. Salt mining was another key industry.

These industries became so important that one Han emperor, Wudi, turned them into state monopolies. A **monopoly** is when a single group controls the production of a good or service.

The monopolies brought in money. Profits from selling iron and salt helped support Wudi's military adventures.

Controlling Production and Prices Wudi's monopoly was also a way to try to keep important producers and merchants from becoming too powerful. Some producers of salt and iron had become very wealthy. They bought huge areas of land and employed large numbers of people. The Han emperors worried that these producers could become so influential that they could challenge the emperor's power. The emperors also worried that too many farmers were leaving their fields to work for these producers. Without enough farmers, China might face food shortages.

INTERACTIVE
Silkmaking in Ancient China

INTEGRATED ENGLISH LANGUAGE DEVELOPMENT

Collaborative Use the text under the heading Economic Life to help students understand the economic conditions during the Han dynasty.

Emerging Read the text aloud, pausing from time to time to ask students yes/no questions or questions that begin with *wh-* words, such as *What type of crops did farmers grow?* or *Why did Emperor Wudi control prices of some products?*

Expanding Organize students into groups. Have groups discuss economic conditions during the Han dynasty by taking turns asking each other relevant questions and responding with accurate information that paraphrases key ideas.

Bridging Organize students into groups. Have them discuss economic conditions during the Han dynasty by taking turns asking each other relevant questions and responding with accurate

The Han emperors also made policies to try to control prices. For example, in years when crops were good, the government bought up the extra grain. In years when the harvest was bad, the grain harvest decreased and grain became expensive. The government then sold back the stored grain to keep prices lower and avoid a shortage.

Despite the **benefits** of these policies, there were many problems. Some officials tried to make money by selling stored goods at high prices. Also, there were complaints that iron tools produced by the government monopoly were poor quality. Many emperors after Wudi either changed or gave up these policies.

Academic Vocabulary
benefit • *n.*, something good or helpful

READING CHECK **Explain** Why did Wudi take control of the iron and salt industries?

Han Achievements

The prosperity of Han China helped support many cultural achievements. Artists, writers, and musicians created works of beauty. Scientists and inventors also made important advances.

China's Traditional Arts The traditional arts of China include painting, sculpture, and poetry. Han artists painted colorful murals. Sculptors created beautiful works in stone, clay, and bronze. Poets wrote about the Chinese countryside.

Because Confucius believed that music was good for the spirit, Han rulers created an official Bureau of Music. Musicians played drums, bells, flutes, and harps. Music and dancing were common at public festivals and ceremonies.

Two other traditional arts were garden design and **calligraphy**, the art of beautiful writing. Calligraphers expressed emotions in the way they painted Chinese characters. Garden designers carefully arranged plants, rocks, and water to resemble scenes in nature.

Perhaps the greatest craft of the Han period was lacquerware. **Lacquer** is a protective coating made from the sap of a special tree. Han artists brushed it on wood or metal objects to create a hard finish. The process required many layers of lacquer and many hours of work. When color was added, the lacquerware seemed to glow.

Advances in Science Han China is also known for scientific advances. Astronomers studied the sky and made precise calculations of the length of the solar year.

Analyze Images This example of Han dynasty lacquerware is a vessel painted with a cloud design. **Infer** Based on the detail and design, what can you infer about the skill Chinese artisans must have needed in order to create such a piece?

Han Achievements

Discuss Han achievements. What were the artistic accomplishments of the Han? What were their scientific accomplishments?

Synthesize Identify two reasons the arts and crafts flourished under the Han. *(The prosperity of Han China helped support the arts. Confucianism valued artisans.)*

Apply Concepts Confucius believed that music was good for the spirit. Do you agree? Why or why not? *(Sample response: I agree, because when I listen to music I feel good.)*

Summarize What were some Han advances in science? *(Astronomers calculated the length of the solar year; doctors developed herbal medicines and acupuncture; inventors created the seismometer, the wheelbarrow, and paper.)*

ELD.PI.A.4

information that paraphrases key ideas. Encourage group members to give feedback to each other and to build on responses that other members provide.

WORKSHEET **TEACHER RESOURCES**

For additional IELD support addressing the standard, have students complete the Lesson ELD activity from the Teacher Resources found on the course.

ANSWERS

Explain *He wanted to prevent salt and iron producers and merchants from becoming so wealthy and powerful that they would threaten his power.*

Infer *Chinese artisans had great skill and probably used precise tools.*

HSS 6.6.4, 6.6.6; ELD.P1.C.10.a

SYNTHESIZE

Assess and Reteach Have students complete Lesson Check questions 1–5 individually. Review their responses using an Idea Wave strategy. If they had any incorrect answers, use the Guiding Questions to discuss the lesson's main ideas, focusing on the ideas they struggled with.

ACTIVE JOURNAL

Writing Workshop Have students complete the Lesson 6 Writing Task in their Active Journals. Students will write a conclusion to their argument. The conclusion should restate their claim.

DEMONSTRATE

ASSESSMENT **ONLINE LESSON QUIZ**

Assign the Online Lesson Quiz for this lesson if you haven't already done so. Students will be offered automatic remediation or enrichment based on their score.

DISCUSSION **DISCUSSION BOARD**

Post this question to the class on the Discussion Board:

Synthesize What do you think was the most significant Han achievement? Why? *(Sample response: paper, because it completely changed the world.)*

Analyze Images In this seismometer, earthquake tremors cause a pendulum to open the jaw of the dragon, which drops a ball into the mouth of the toad below. **Generate Explanations** Why must it have been important to the early Chinese people to detect and measure earthquakes?

Han doctors made progress in medicine. They studied ancient texts on medicine and developed new theories to explain and treat illness. Herbal medicines were one important treatment. Another was **acupuncture**, a therapy that uses needles to cure sickness and stop pain.

Chinese Inventions Han inventors produced important new tools. One was the **seismometer**, a tool to detect earthquakes. The seismometer was a metal jar that dropped small balls when a tremor from an earthquake was felt.

Another invention was the wheelbarrow. This human-powered cart appeared in China about 100 BCE. It was so useful for moving heavy loads that it was called the "wooden ox."

Perhaps the most important innovation of the Han was paper. Early paper was made from rags and bark. Paper was probably not widely used at first. Documents continued to be written on more durable wood and silk. In later dynasties, printing on paper became a way to make cheap books. More people could afford books, and new ideas spread quickly.

READING CHECK **Make Connections** What kinds of workers might have found the wheelbarrow useful?

Lesson Check

HSS 6.6.4, 6.6.6; ELD.PI.C.10.a

Practice Vocabulary

1. What is a **monopoly**?
2. Use the terms ***acupuncture*** and ***seismometer*** to describe the achievements of the Han dynasty.

Critical Thinking and Writing

3. **Understand Effects** How did Confucian beliefs affect the structure of Han society?
4. **Identify Cause and Effect** How do you think the relative peacefulness of the Han era is related to its successful economy?
5. **Identify Implied Main Ideas** What do the achievements of Han society say about its success as a dynasty?
6. **Summarize Writing Workshop: Write a Conclusion** Write a concluding sentence in your Active Journal. Your conclusion should restate your claim about what values a government needs to successfully lead.

ANSWERS

Generate Explanations *Knowing earthquake-prone areas guided decisions on where to build.*

Make Connections *farmers, construction workers, people delivering goods*

LESSON CHECK

1. A monopoly is a single company or group that controls the production of goods or a service. **DOK1**
2. Han doctors used herbal medicines and acupuncture to treat illness and pain. Han scientists created the seismometer to detect earthquakes. **DOK1**
3. Confucian beliefs placed scholars, farmers, and artisans at the top of society; they placed merchants at the bottom. **DOK2**
4. The relative peacefulness allowed trade to flourish without disruption by war. **DOK2**
5. Han achievements show that the dynasty was very successful.
6. Students will write a conclusion to their argument about what values a government needs to successfully lead. **DOK4**

HSS 6.6.3 Analysis HI.3

Identify Sources of Continuity

Follow these steps to learn to identify the sources of continuity in a society.

INTERACTIVE

Develop Cultural Awareness

1 Gather information about the society. Look at a variety of resources to learn about life in the society that you are studying. Examine the primary and secondary sources below. What is the subject of these sources?

2 Identify possible sources of continuity in the society. Look for information about the society's government, values, family life, economy, religion, philosophy, language, and culture.

a. What do the sources below have to say about Chinese family life?

b. What else do the sources say about Chinese values?

3 Determine which sources of continuity are important in the society. Think about what these sources are saying about the treatment of parents, elders, and people of authority. What sources of continuity do you observe? You may want to take notes about each one.

4 Summarize what you discover. Use the information you have learned to make a general statement. What are the sources of continuity in Chinese society?

Primary Source

"They are few who, being filial and fraternal [devoted to their parents], are fond of offending against their superiors. There have been none, who, not liking to offend against their superiors, have been fond of stirring up confusion."

— *The Analects of Confucius*

Secondary Source

This passage from the Analects of Confucius reflects a key aspect of the great philosopher's system. It helps explain why even today Chinese children grow up with a deep respect for authority starting with their relationship with parents, then teachers, and later with employers and government officials. While in many countries students are encouraged to debate ideas with their teachers, in China it is dishonorable to disagree with a teacher. In fact, the Chinese word for teacher, *laoshi,* meaning "old master," conveys the deep respect people have for their teachers. Elderly people in China are esteemed, too. A person's 60th birthday is one of the most festive celebrations of a person's life.

HSS 6.6.3; Analysis HI.3

Analysis Skills
Identify Sources of Continuity

LEARN

Preview the steps in the student text with students, and then play the video.

VIDEO **21ST CENTURY SKILLS**

Project the Develop Cultural Awareness video in the 21st Century Skills Tutorial. Use the Quick Reference and Assessment to provide additional instruction in the skill.

PRACTICE

Have students practice the skill using the text on the student page. When students are finished, discuss their responses as a class.

As an alternative, you could form students into pairs or groups to perform the activity.

ASSESS

To assess this skill, have students apply these steps to the section Han Achievements in Lesson 6.

DIFFERENTIATED INSTRUCTION

Below Level To help students understand the idea of continuity, describe things you do in the classroom to establish continuity in your instruction (pointing out you're continuing a lesson from yesterday; reminding them they've already studied a topic you're revisiting). Explain that if they celebrate a holiday with their family each year, that, too, is continuity.

INTEGRATED ENGLISH LANGUAGE DEVELOPMENT

Emerging Ask simple yes and no questions such as "Were Chinese children taught to respect authority?" or "Is a person's 20th birthday one of the most important in a person's life?"

ANSWERS

1. devotion to parents; Chinese respect for authority

2. a. Parents and older relatives are highly respected.

b. It is important to be well behaved and respectful of society, and to respect authority and the elderly.

3. ancient writings; family, teachers, government; language

4. The sources of continuity in Chinese society are traditional philosophies and beliefs, family, teachers, government, and language.

HSS 6.2.9, 6.6.1, 6.6.2, 6.6.3, 6.6.4, 6.6.5, 6.6.6, 6.6.7, 6.6.8; ELA W.6.1, W.6.4, WHST.6.1, WHST.6.4; ELD.PI.C.10.a

Review and Assessment

VISUAL REVIEW

Direct students' attention to the "Early Chinese Dynasties" chart. As a class, review the information about each dynasty.

Direct students' attention to the "Development of Government in China" diagram. As a class, discuss how government developed in China under each dynasty or in each period.

READING REVIEW

WORKSHEET **TEACHER RESOURCES**

Have students who need additional support read the Lesson Summary, available in Teacher Resources on the Realize course.

GAMES **TOPIC MINI-GAMES**

For additional vocabulary practice, students can go online to access the Topic Mini-Games in Realize.

Quest FINDINGS

Write Your Obituary

Have students complete their Topic Quests by writing the obituary in their Active Journals. Remind students to follow these writing process steps: (1) prewrite; (2) draft and review; (3) revise; (4) present. **DOK4**

TOPIC 5

Review and Assessment

VISUAL REVIEW

Early Chinese Dynasties

Zhou Dynasty	Qin Dynasty	Han Dynasty
• Ruled by "Mandate of Heaven" • Expanded lands under Zhou control • Developed iron tools and weapons, irrigation and fertilizer, and system of roads	• First emperor Shi Huangdi–unified China • Established uniform standards for all China • Ruled with brutal control of thought, behavior • Rejected Confucianism in favor of Legalism	• Expanded Chinese territory • Organized government based on Confucian ideals, strengthened civil service • Started the Silk Road

Development of Government in China

The Shang
Established family control over government, with power passed from brother to brother, then to oldest son

The Zhou
Claimed "Mandate of Heaven" to rule, which required rulers to act in a virtuous way

Warring States period
Warlords fought for power in a declining Zhou dynasty

Shi Huangdi and the Qin
Used Legalism to control a vast empire

The Han
Established a vast civil service based on Confucian ideas to aid in government

READING REVIEW

Use the Take Notes and Practice Vocabulary activities in your Active Journal to help you to review the topic.

INTERACTIVE

Practice vocabulary using the Topic Mini-Games.

Quest FINDINGS

Get help for writing Shi Huangdi's obituary in your Active Journal.

220 Topic 5 • Early Civilizations of China

ANSWERS

1. Rulers had to act virtuously and serve the needs of the people. **DOK1**
2. from 475 BCE to 221 BCE; battles raged and millions died. **DOK1**
3. Confucius was concerned about corrupt officials and those who did not enforce the law justly. **DOK1**
4. Lead a simple life; keep a balance between yin and yang to achieve harmony in the universe. **DOK2**
5. His harsh rules did not inspire loyalty, so his soldiers revolted when the Qin were attacked. **DOK1**
6. The Han created a civil service to collect taxes, organize labor, and enforce laws. Officials did not serve in their home districts, which kept them loyal to the emperor. **DOK1**
7. In his more than 50-year rule, he expanded the empire, established a civil service, and created prosperity. **DOK1**

ASSESSMENT

HSS 6.2.9, 6.6.1, 6.6.2, 6.6.3, 6.6.4, 6.6.5, 6.6.6, 6.6.7, 6.6.8; ELA W.6.1, W.6.4, WHST.6.1, WHST.6.4; ELD.P1.C.10.a

Vocabulary and Key Ideas

1. **Discuss** According to Chinese beliefs, how did rulers have to act in order to keep the **Mandate of Heaven?**
2. **Explain** When was the Warring States period and what happened during this time?
3. **Recall** What problems did Confucius address in Chinese society?
4. **Summarize** What are the basic ideas of Daoism?
5. **Explain** Why did Shi Huangdi's harsh rules lead to the fall of the Qin dynasty?
6. **Describe** Describe the civil service created during the Han dynasty.
7. **Recall** Why is Wudi considered a great ruler?
8. **Summarize** How did the Chinese begin trading along the **Silk Road?**

Critical Thinking and Writing

9. **Identify Cause and Effect** What is one political effect of the geography of China?
10. **Core Concepts: Citizenship** Confucius compares the role of the king to the role of a father. Do you agree that the role of a leader is similar to a parent? Explain why or why not?
11. **Analyze Cause and Effects** What effect did Shi Huangdi's policies have on the culture and government of China?
12. **Compare Viewpoints** Why might a Confucian scholar and a Legalist scholar have different viewpoints about censorship?
13. **Revisit the Essential Question** What were some of the different ways Chinese rulers maintained order in ancient China?
14. **Writing Workshop: Write an Argument** Using the notes and draft in your Active Journal, write an argumentative essay on the following topic: Which ancient Chinese values or belief system helped produce the most effective government in ancient China?

Analyze Primary Sources

15. According to the source below, what does wisdom result in?
   A. unhappiness
   B. harmonious relationships
   C. remedies
   D. simple happiness

"Forget about knowledge and wisdom,
and people will be a hundred times better off.
Throw away charity and righteousness,
and people will return to brotherly love.
Throw away profit and greed,
and there won't be any more thieves.
Renounce knowledge and your problems
will end."

—*Dao De Jing*

Analyze Maps

Use the map at right to answer the following questions.

16. What does the red line represent?
17. What rivers did the Zhou civilization form around?
18. What geographic feature lay to the north of the Zhou civilization?

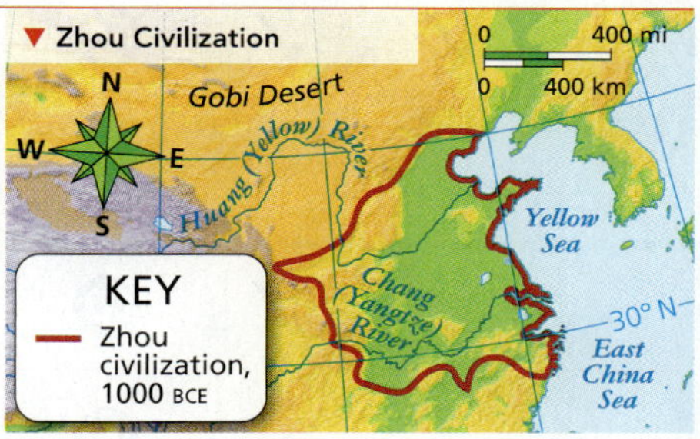

Review and Assessment 221

8. Zhang Qian traveled west to find allies for the Han. When Zhang returned, he described what he had seen. The Han began to trade silk for western goods along the routes known as the Silk Road. **DOK1**
9. Mountains, deserts, and oceans isolated China, resulting in a unique culture. **DOK2**
10. Sample responses: Yes, like a parent, a leader must both care for and discipline the people. No, a leader must treat people as equals. **DOK4**
11. Shi Huangdi's standardization of language, currency, weights and measures, and transportation unified China. The centralized government imposed harsh rules and censorship. **DOK2**
12. A Confucian scholar would disapprove of censorship, believing that educated people benefited the country. A Legalist scholar would approve of censorship, believing that people needed laws and enforcement, not education and philosophy. **DOK3**
13. Some rulers used harsh laws and censorship; others created large bureaucracies to maintain order. **DOK2**
14. Responses will be an argumentative essay that makes and supports a claim about which values governments needed to lead successfully. **DOK4**
15. D **DOK3**
16. the geographic area of the Zhou civilization **DOK1**
17. the Huang and the Chang Rivers **DOK1**
18. the Gobi Desert **DOK1**

ASSESSMENT **TOPIC TEST**

For summative assessment, assign the Topic Test in Realize.

TOPIC 6

Topic-at-a-Glance

Ancient Greece

Pacing: approx. 26 periods, 13 blocks	Resources: Student Edition	Resources: Active Journal	Resources: Online	Pacing	California Standards
CONNECT					
NBC LEARN VIDEO Pericles, the Golden Age of Athens			●	10 min.	HSS 6.4.1, 6.4.2, 6.4.3, 6.4.4, 6.4.6, 6.4.7, 6.4.8
ESSENTIAL QUESTION ACTIVITY What is the Best Form of Government?		✓	●	10 min.	HSS 6.4.1, 6.4.2, 6.4.3, 6.4.4, 6.4.6, 6.4.7, 6.4.8
OVERVIEW ACTIVITY: TIMELINE AND MAP Ancient Greece		✓	●	10 min.	HSS 6.4.1, 6.4.2, 6.4.3, 6.4.4, 6.4.6, 6.4.7, 6.4.8
Quest **KICK OFF:** Ask Questions	✓	✓		20 min.	HSS 6.4; ELA W.6.7–9, WHST.6.7–9, SL.6.4–6
INVESTIGATE					
LESSONS 1–8	See Lesson-at-a-Glance pages				
Quest **INVESTIGATE:** Quest Connections	✓	✓	●	20 min.	See Quest Kick Off.
SYNTHESIZE					
WRITING WORKSHOP Write an Explanatory Essay		✓	●	30 min.	ELA W.6.2, WHST.6.2
TOPIC MINI-GAMES Ancient Greece			●	10 min.	HSS 6.4.1–4, 6.4.6–8; ELA W.6.2, WHST.6.2
Quest **SOURCES:** Conduct Research			●	30 min.	See Quest Kick Off.
DEMONSTRATE					
TOPIC REVIEW AND ASSESSMENT Ancient Greece	✓		●	20 min.	
TOPIC TEST Ancient Greece	✓		●	30 min.	
Quest **FINDINGS:** Create a News Magazine	✓	✓	●	30 min.	See Quest Kick Off.

Quest

Each Quest is designed to reinforce the topic content through an inquiry arc that students work on throughout the topic. This topic's Quest, The Influence of Ancient Greece, is a Document-Based Learning Inquiry in which students work as a team to create a television news magazine about ancient Greek culture.

Active Journal Resources

- Ask Questions
- Quest Connections
- Conduct Research
- Create Your Television News Magazine

Quest Resources Online

- Project Contract
- Project Tracker
- Team Assessment
- Rubric for a Television News Magazine

Additional Resources

Support for Struggling Readers:

- Reading Support, Teacher Resources
- Lesson Summaries, Teacher Resources
- English Language Development, Teacher Resources

Suggested Resources:

- *Black Ships Before Troy: The Story of the Iliad*, by Rosemary Sutcliff
- *Odysseus*, by Geraldine McCaughrean
- *Parthenon*, by Lynn Curlee
- *Science in Ancient Greece*, by Kathlyn Gay

Beyond the Classroom

Use Local Resources

Invite professors at local colleges who teach courses on ancient Greece or Greek civilization to come in and speak to the students.

The following California museums have collections or materials related to ancient Greece:

The Getty Villa, Los Angeles, CA

San Francisco State University Museum Collection, San Francisco, CA

The Phoebe A. Hearst Museum of Anthropology, University of California, Berkeley, CA

TOPIC 6

Objectives

Objective 1: Explain how physical geography helped shape the development of Greek societies.

Objective 2: Describe how the Minoans and Mycenaeans influenced Greek culture.

Objective 3: Discuss how city-states developed and how they interacted with one another.

The Early Years of Greek Civilization

	Resources: Student Edition	Resources: Active Journal	Resources: Online	Pacing (approx. 2 periods, 1 block)	California Standards
CONNECT					
VIDEO Impact of Geography on Ancient Greece			✓ (video)	5 min.	HSS 6.4.1
START UP ACTIVITY Get Ready to Read	✓	✓	✓ (book)	5 min.	HSS 6.4.1
TAKE NOTES AND PRACTICE VOCABULARY		✓			
INVESTIGATE					
READ Lesson 1 The Early Years of Greek Civilization	✓	✓	✓ (book)	40 min.	HSS 6.4.1
INTERACTIVE MAP The Journey of Odysseus			✓ (interactive)	10 min.	HSS 6.4.4
READING SUPPORT			✓ (interactive)		
SYNTHESIZE					
WRITING WORKSHOP Consider Your Purpose	✓	✓	✓ (book)	10 min.	HSS 6.4.1; ELD.PI.C.10.a
LESSON SUMMARY			✓ (interactive)		
DEMONSTRATE					
LESSON QUIZ			✓ (interactive)	10 min.	HSS 6.4.1

Objectives

Objective 1: Describe the political forms that Greek city-states experimented with.

Objective 2: Explain how Athenian democracy worked.

Objective 3: Summarize the achievements and limitations of Athenian democracy.

Democracy in Athens

	Resources: Student Edition	Resources: Active Journal	Resources: Online	Pacing (approx. 4 periods, 2 blocks)	California Standards
CONNECT					
VIDEO The Athenian Concept of Citizenship			(video)	5 min.	HSS 6.4.2, 6.4.3
START UP ACTIVITY Get Ready to Read	✓	✓	(book)	5 min.	HSS 6.4.2, 6.4.3
TAKE NOTES AND PRACTICE VOCABULARY		✓			
INVESTIGATE					
READ Lesson 2: Democracy in Athens	✓	✓	(book)	40 min.	HSS 6.4.2, 6.4.3
INTERACTIVE GALLERY Athenian Democracy			(interactive)	10 min.	HSS 6.4.2, 6.4.3
PRIMARY SOURCES Pericles' Funeral Oration	✓		(interactive)	40 min.	HSS 6.4.2; ELA RI.6.2, RH.6.1–2
ANALYSIS SKILLS Distinguish Relevant from Irrelevant Information	✓		(interactive)	30 min.	Analysis RE.3
21ST CENTURY SKILLS TUTORIAL Identify Evidence	✓		(interactive)	10 min.	Analysis RE.3
READING SUPPORT			(interactive)		
SYNTHESIZE					
WRITING WORKSHOP Pick an Organizing Strategy	✓	✓	(book)	10 min.	HSS 6.4.2, 6.4.3; ELD.PI.C.10.a
LESSON SUMMARY			(interactive)		
DEMONSTRATE					
LESSON QUIZ			(interactive)	10 min.	HSS 6.4.2, 6.4.3

TOPIC 6

Oligarchy in Sparta

Objectives

Objective 1: Summarize the type of government that developed in Sparta.

Objective 2: Describe what life was like in Sparta.

Objective 3: Explain how Sparta differed from Athens.

	Resources: Student Edition	Resources: Active Journal	Resources: Online	Pacing (approx. 2 periods, 1 block)	California Standards
CONNECT					
VIDEO Growing Up Spartan			✓ (video)	5 min.	HSS 6.4.6
START UP ACTIVITY Get Ready to Read	✓	✓	✓ (eText)	5 min.	HSS 6.4.6
TAKE NOTES AND PRACTICE VOCABULARY		✓			
INVESTIGATE					
READ Lesson 3: Oligarchy in Sparta	✓	✓	✓ (eText)	40 min.	HSS 6.4.6
QUICK ACTIVITY Contrasting Primary Sources		✓			Analysis RE.5; ELA RI.6.9
INTERACTIVE CHART Comparing Sparta and Athens			✓ (interactive)	10 min.	HSS 6.4.6
READING SUPPORT			✓ (interactive)		
SYNTHESIZE					
WRITING WORKSHOP Develop a Clear Thesis	✓	✓	✓ (eText)	10 min.	HSS 6.4.6; ELD.PI.C.10.a
LESSON SUMMARY			✓ (interactive)		
DEMONSTRATE					
LESSON QUIZ			✓ (interactive)	10 min.	HSS6.4.6

Ancient Greek Society and Economic Expansion

Objectives

Objective 1: Describe the roles and rights of women in the Greek city-states.

Objective 2: Explain how Greek society was organized.

Objective 3: Discuss why the Greeks expanded through trade, conquest, and colonization.

Objective 4: Analyze how the Greeks' expansion affected connections within the ancient world.

	Resources: Student Edition	Resources: Active Journal	Resources: Online	Pacing (approx. 2 periods, 1 block)	California Standards
CONNECT					
VIDEO Men, Women, and Children in Ancient Greece			video	5 min.	HSS 6.4.1
START UP ACTIVITY Get Ready to Read	✓	✓	eText	5 min.	HSS 6.4.1; ELA RI.6.1
TAKE NOTES AND PRACTICE VOCABULARY		✓			
INVESTIGATE					
READ Lesson 4: Ancient Greek Society and Economic Expansion	✓	✓	eText	40 min.	HSS 6.4.1; ELA RI.6.1
INTERACTIVE MAP Alexander the Great's Conquests and Contributions			interactive	10 min.	HSS 6.4.1, 6.4.7
READING SUPPORT			interactive		
SYNTHESIZE					
WRITING WORKSHOP Support Thesis with Details	✓	✓	eText	10 min.	ELA W.6.2.a–e; ELD.PI.C.10.a
LESSON SUMMARY			interactive		
DEMONSTRATE					
LESSON QUIZ			interactive	10 min.	HSS 6.4.1

TOPIC 6

Warfare in Ancient Greece

Objectives

Objective 1: Explain how the Greek city-states defeated the Persian empire.

Objective 2: Identify the role taken by Athens after the Persian Wars.

Objective 3: Summarize the causes and effects of the Peloponnesian War.

	Resources: Student Edition	Resources: Active Journal	Resources: Online	Pacing (approx. 3 periods, 1.5 blocks)	California Standards
CONNECT					
VIDEO Causes and Effects of the Persian Wars			✓	5 min.	HSS 6.4.2, 6.4.4
START UP ACTIVITY Get Ready to Read	✓	✓	✓	5 min.	HSS 6.4.2, 6.4.4, 6.4.6
TAKE NOTES AND PRACTICE VOCABULARY		✓			
INVESTIGATE					
READ Lesson 5: Warfare in Ancient Greece	✓	✓	✓	30 min.	HSS 6.4.2, 6.4.6
INTERACTIVE MAP Persian Wars, 490 BCE–479 BCE			✓	10 min.	HSS 6.4.6
INTERACTIVE PRIMARY SOURCE Herodotus, *The Persian Wars*			✓	10 min.	HSS 6.4.6
ANALYSIS SKILLS Compare Different Points of View	✓		✓	30 min.	HSS 6.4.4; ELA RI.6.9
21ST CENTURY SKILLS TUTORIAL Compare Viewpoints	✓		✓	10 min.	ELA RI.6.9
READING SUPPORT			✓		
SYNTHESIZE					
WRITING WORKSHOP Update Your Thesis	✓	✓	✓	10 min.	HSS 6.4.2, 6.4.4; ELD.PI.C.10.a
LESSON SUMMARY			✓		
DEMONSTRATE					
LESSON QUIZ			✓	10 min.	HSS 6.4.2, 6.4.6

Ancient Greek Beliefs and Arts

Objectives

Objective 1: Analyze the effect of Greek religion and mythology on individuals and society.

Objective 2: Identify the what ways Greek art and architecture have remained influential today.

Objective 3: Discuss how Greek literature continues to permeate our literature and language today.

	Resources: Student Edition	Resources: Active Journal	Resources: Online	Pacing approx. 3 periods, 1.5 blocks	California Standards
CONNECT					
VIDEO Greek Mythology			Video	5 min.	HSS 6.4.4, 6.4.8
START UP ACTIVITY Get Ready to Read	✓	✓	eText	5 min.	HSS 6.4.4, 6.4.8; ELA RI.6.7
TAKE NOTES AND PRACTICE VOCABULARY		✓			
INVESTIGATE					
READ Lesson 6: Ancient Greek Beliefs and Arts	✓	✓	eText	40 min.	HSS 6.4.4, 6.4.8; ELA RI.6.7
INTERACTIVE GALLERY Art and Architecture in Ancient Greece			Interactive	10 min.	HSS 6.4.8
QUICK ACTIVITY Create a Comic Strip		✓			HSS 6.4.4
PRIMARY SOURCES Homer's the *Odyssey*	✓		Interactive	40 min.	HSS 6.4.4; ELA RH.6.1, 6.3
READING SUPPORT			Interactive		
SYNTHESIZE					
WRITING WORKSHOP Support Thesis with Details	✓	✓	eText	10 min.	HSS 6.4.4, 6.4.8; ELD.PI.C.10.a
LESSON SUMMARY			Interactive		
DEMONSTRATE					
LESSON QUIZ			Interactive	10 min.	HSS 6.4.4, 6.4.8

TOPIC 6

Ancient Greek Learning

Objectives

Objective 1: Identify the enduring contributions Greek scholars made to philosophy and history.

Objective 2: Describe the scientific and medical discoveries made by the ancient Greeks.

Objective 3: Explain how Greek thought affected individuals, states, and societies.

	Resources: Student Edition	Resources: Active Journal	Resources: Online	Pacing (approx. 4 periods, 2 blocks)	California Standards
CONNECT					
VIDEO Socrates and Plato			✓	5 min.	HSS 6.4.8
START UP ACTIVITY Get Ready to Read	✓	✓	✓	5 min.	HSS 6.4.8
TAKE NOTES AND PRACTICE VOCABULARY		✓			
INVESTIGATE					
READ Lessson 6: Ancient Greek Learning	✓	✓	✓	70 min.	HSS 6.4.8
INTERACTIVE CHART Understanding Greek Philosophers			✓	10 min.	HSS 6.4.8
INTERACTIVE BIOGRAPHY Hypatia			✓	10 min.	HSS 6.4.8
ANALYSIS SKILLS Update an Interpretation	✓		✓	30 min.	Analysis HI.5
21ST CENTURY SKILLS TUTORIAL Synthesize	✓		✓	10 min.	Analysis HI.5
READING SUPPORT			✓		
SYNTHESIZE					
WRITING WORKSHOP Draft Your Esssay	✓	✓	✓	10 min.	HSS 6.4.8; ELD.PI.C.10.a
LESSON SUMMARY			✓		
DEMONSTRATE					
LESSON QUIZ			✓	10 min.	HSS 6.4.8

Alexander and the Hellenistic World

Objectives

Objective 1: Explain how Macedonian rulers defeated the Greek city-states.

Objective 2: Describe the ways in which Alexander's conquests affected connections between cultures in the ancient world.

Objective 3: Discuss how Hellenistic learning expanded the impact of Greek culture.

	Resources			Pacing	
CONNECT	Student Edition	Active Journal	Online	approx. 2 periods, 1 block	California Standards
VIDEO Cultural Exchange in the Hellenistic Age			Video	5 min.	HSS 6.4.7, 6.4.8
START UP ACTIVITY Get Ready to Read	✓	✓	eText	5 min.	HSS 6.4.7, 6.4.8
TAKE NOTES AND PRACTICE VOCABULARY		✓			
INVESTIGATE					
READ Lesson 7: Alexander and the Hellenstic World	✓	✓	eText	30 min.	HSS 6.4.7, 6.4.8
INTERACTIVE GALLERY Alexander the Great's Conquests and Contributions			Interactive	10 min.	HSS 6.4.7, 6.4.8
INTERACTIVE BIOGRAPHY Alexander			Interactive	10 min.	HSS 6.4.7
READING SUPPORT			Interactive		
SYNTHESIZE					
WRITING WORKSHOP Revise	✓	✓	eText	10 min.	HSS 6.4.7, 6.4.8; ELD.PI.C.10.a
LESSON SUMMARY			Interactive		
DEMONSTRATE					
LESSON QUIZ			Interactive	10 min.	HSS 6.4.7, 6.4.8

TOPIC 6
Ancient Greece
1750 BCE–133 BCE

HSS 6.4.1, 6.4.2, 6.4.3, 6.4.4, 6.4.6, 6.4.7, 6.4.8; Analysis RE.3, RE.5, HI.5

CONNECT

Introduction

The Greeks followed in the footsteps of older societies in Mesopotamia and Egypt in some respects, but established a powerful culture that had a lasting impact on the world. Greek culture laid the foundation for Western civilization by introducing ideas that still influence us today in such areas as drama, philosophy, art, and political science. When we talk about democracy or celebrate the Olympic Games, we're engaging with the culture of the ancient Greeks.

Activate Prior Knowledge

Ask students what they know about Ancient Greece. Have a volunteer read the Go Back paragraph in the student text. Explain that *democracy* comes from two Greek words: *demos* (people) and *kratiae* (rule). Ask students how this relates to democracy as we know it today. *(In a democracy, people elect their leaders, who in turn answer to the people.)*

Explore the Essential Question

Project the Essential Question activity from the course. Have a volunteer read the question. As students consider the Essential Question, have them think about the different types of governments people create.

ACTIVE JOURNAL

Essential Question Have students begin to explore the Essential Question in their Active Journals.

Apply Concepts What type of government would you most want to live under? Why? *(Accept all reasonable responses. Sample response: I would want to live in a democracy because people elect their leaders and have many other freedoms. In other forms of government, people might not have complete freedom.)*

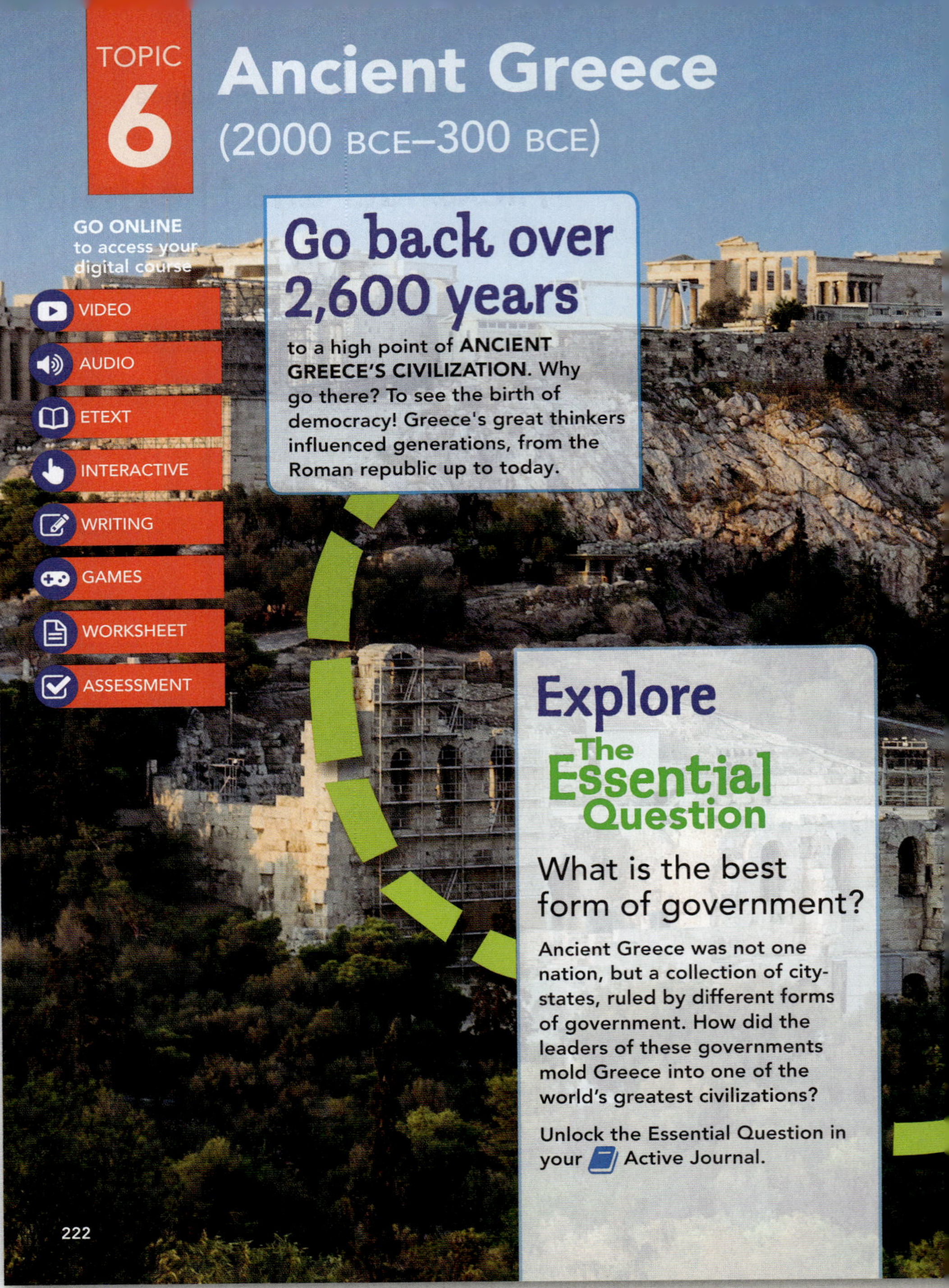
TOPIC 6

Ancient Greece

(2000 BCE–300 BCE)

GO ONLINE to access your digital course

VIDEO
AUDIO
ETEXT
INTERACTIVE
WRITING
GAMES
WORKSHEET
ASSESSMENT

Go back over 2,600 years

to a high point of ANCIENT GREECE'S CIVILIZATION. Why go there? To see the birth of democracy! Greece's great thinkers influenced generations, from the Roman republic up to today.

Explore The Essential Question

What is the best form of government?

Ancient Greece was not one nation, but a collection of city-states, ruled by different forms of government. How did the leaders of these governments mold Greece into one of the world's greatest civilizations?

Unlock the Essential Question in your Active Journal.

222

ANALYZE VISUALS

Discuss the photo. Ask: What's your immediate impression of this culture? Why? *(Sample response: It is a well-developed culture because the city seems to be well planned.)* Ask: The building in the center of the photo is a temple. What does that suggest about religion in ancient Greek culture? Why? *(Religion was very important in this culture; the temple is the biggest building in the picture and is located high above the other buildings.)*

HSS 6.4.1, 6.4.2, 6.4.3, 6.4.4, 6.4.6, 6.4.7, 6.4.8; Analysis RE.3, RE.5, HI.5

Read

about the culture, science, and various forms of government that made ancient Greece the birthplace of Western civilization.

Watch

NBC LEARN

BOUNCE TO ACTIVATE VIDEO

Pericles, the Golden Age of Athens

Learn how Pericles ruled over the Golden Age of Athens.

▲ The Acropolis of Athens, Greece

223

RECOGNIZE CULTURAL AND EXPERIENTIAL BACKGROUNDS

Make use of your knowledge of students' lives to make connections between their own experiences, backgrounds, and interests and the content of this topic. If you have students whose ethnic heritage is related to the content of this topic, make an effort to emphasize the contributions and achievements of this society and how it has enriched the world.

If appropriate, allow the students the opportunity to share cultural, ethnic, or linguistic traditions and knowledge from their experiences.

If students have family experiences (such as travel to or family members who have lived in the region being studied), allow them to share relevant stories.

Watch

VIDEO NBC LEARN VIDEO

Project the Topic Video about Pericles and the Golden Age of Athens. After viewing the video, ask students to respond to this question:

Check Understanding Why was Pericles such an important figure in the development of Athens? *(He oversaw the construction of the city's great buildings and initiated democratic reforms.)*

Read

Share these lesson previews with students.

Lesson 1: Geography helped foster the city-states in which Greek culture developed.

Lesson 2: Athens developed democracy (rule by the people).

Primary Sources: Pericles describes Athens' democracy in his speech to honor fallen soldiers.

Lesson 3: Sparta, a military state, was ruled by an oligarchy (rule by a small group).

Lesson 4: Women's rights varied, depending on their city-state. Daily life was shaped by a class system.

Lesson 5: Greeks united to fight Persia but then fought one another once more.

Lesson 6: Greeks valued religion, sports, the arts, and literature.

Primary Sources: This excerpt introduces Odysseus, the hero of Homer's *Odyssey*.

Lesson 7: Ancient Greece became a great center of learning.

Lesson 8: Philip of Macedonia and his son Alexander conquered Greece. Alexander then extended the Greek empire through Europe, Asia and Africa

TOPIC 6

HSS 6.4.1, 6.4.2, 6.4.3, 6.4.4, 6.4.6, 6.4.7, 6.4.8

What Happened and When?

Have students examine the timeline. Ask: How many years are shown on the timeline? *(600)* Ask: What was happening in other parts of the world at about the same time democracy was developing in Athens? *(Persia was conquering Egypt.)* Ask: Which part of the timeline shows a period of warfare in Greece? *(400s BCE)* Ask: What event on the timeline indicates that Greece has been conquered? *(Alexander the Great invades Asia.)*

ACTIVE JOURNAL

Timeline Skills Students can also use the Timeline Skills activity in their Active Journals to record information about and better understand the development of ancient Greece. As they read the topic, they should add the dates of at least three events they think are important. After completing the topic, have students review their timelines and write a paragraph identifying the dates they added and explaining why each is significant.

INTERACTIVE — INTERACTIVE TIMELINE

Display the Interactive Topic Timeline for the class. Have volunteers read the entries.

Explain Historical Continuity About how long did the independent Greek city-states last before they were conquered? *(415 years.)*

TOPIC 6

Ancient Greece

(2000 BCE–300 BCE)

Learn more about the development of ancient Greece by making your own map and timeline in your Active Journal.

INTERACTIVE — Topic Map

Where was ancient Greece?

Ancient Greece was centered on the Balkan Peninsula in the Mediterranean Sea in Europe.

INTERACTIVE — Topic Timeline

What happened and when?

Epic battles...thinkers with immortal ideas... Explore the timeline to see some of what was happening in ancient Greece and in the rest of the world.

TOPIC EVENTS

750 BCE New city-states appear in Greece.

508 BCE Democracy develops in Athens.

800 BCE | 700 BCE | 600 BCE

WORLD EVENTS

650 BCE Ironworking begins in China.

525 BCE Persia conquers Egypt.

DIFFERENTIATED INSTRUCTION

Special Education Draw students' attention to the picture of Pericles and explain that he died in 429 BCE. Have students indicate this event on the timeline.

Below Level Have students working in pairs take turns saying one of the intervals shown on the timeline (700 BCE; 500 BCE). The other student points to the part of the timeline that corresponds to the period.

Advanced Have students pick three events on the timeline and do research to find a fact for each event. Ask students to share their facts with the class.

HSS 6.4.1, 6.4.2, 6.4.3, 6.4.4, 6.4.6, 6.4.7, 6.4.8

Who will you meet?

Pericles, the great Athenian statesman

Socrates, the ancient philosopher

Hypatia, a Hellenistic mathematician, philosopher, and astronomer

490 BCE Battle of Marathon is fought.

431 BCE Peloponnesian War begins.

399 BCE Socrates is sentenced to death.

334 BCE Alexander the Great invades Asia.

500 BCE | 400 BCE | 300 BCE | 200 BCE

500 BCE Hinduism develops.

400 BCE Buddhism begins to spread.

225

COMMON MISCONCEPTIONS

Divided They Remained Students may think that the Greeks considered themselves "Greek" first. In fact, the deep and true loyalty of these people was to their city-states, or polis, rather than to a larger Greek or Hellenic state. They did share the same language and religion, and they all admired Homer. On the other hand, the governments and economies of the city-states varied dramatically. As a result, the city-states were separate, autonomous, and independent from one another, and they differed in character. On occasion, they united against a common enemy, notably the Persians. More often, however, their differences lead to confict—sometimes disastrous—among the city—states.

Where Was Ancient Greece?

Direct students' attention to the map of ancient Greece in the student text. Ask: Where is Greece located? *(Possible Responses: in Europe; on the Mediterranean Sea; north of Africa, west of Asia)* Ask: In which part of Greece is Athens located? *(eastern Greece)* Ask: Where in Greece is Sparta located? *(southern Greece, on the Peloponnesian Peninsula)* Ask: What other Greek city states do you see on the map? *(Olympia; Mycenae)*

ACTIVE JOURNAL

Map Skills Have students use the Map Skills activity in their Active Journals to fill in an outline map of ancient Greece, labeling city-states and bodies of water.

Analyze Maps How do you think the geography of Greece, especially its coasts and islands, influenced ancient Greek development and culture? Why? *(Since many city-states were on or near the sea, trade with other city-states and with other regions was commonplace. This led to an exchange of ideas as well as goods.)*

INTERACTIVE | INTERACTIVE MAP

Display the Interactive topic map for the class. Have a volunteer read the instructions. Then work with students to drag the labels to the correct locations on the map. Ask students what they know about Mt. Olympus. *(Some students may recognize Mt. Olympus as the "home" of the gods of ancient Greece.)*

Who Will You Meet?

Preview the key people that students will encounter in the topic. Read the short description of each, and then conduct a poll asking students who they are most interested in. Record the results on the board. *(Accept reasonable responses. Students may say they are interested in Pericles because he was a great statesman; they are interested in Socrates because they have heard of him and want to learn more about him; they are interested in Hypatia because she was a woman of accomplishment living in a world dominated by men.)*

TOPIC 6

HSS.6.4, Analysis HI-3; ELA W.6.7–9, WHST.6.7–9, SL.6.4–6

Quest Project-Based Learning Inquiry

Create a News Magazine

Quest Kick Off

In this Quest, students will use the student edition, other sources, and their Active Journals to create a news magazine about ancient Greece.

1 Ask Questions

Launch the Quest by discussing the Guiding Question as a class. Have students write in their Journals as they generate the questions they will need to answer in order to complete the Quest.

Suggestion: If students need help with Asking Questions, refer them to the Analysis Skills feature following Lesson 2, Distinguish Relevant from Irrelevant Information.

2 Investigate

As they read the lessons, remind students to look for and respond to the Quest Connections in the student text that provide clues to their Quest. They should also identify and record two connections of their own

Suggestion: If students are struggling with identifying their own connections, suggest they look for familiar words with Greek roots *(polis; demos; cracy; logy)*.

3 Conduct Research

Remind students to find a variety of reliable sources. Direct them to take notes in their Active Journals.

4 Create Your News Magazine

When students complete the topic, have them return to the Quest, which can be used as a performance-based authentic assessment. To complete the Quest, they should write, produce, and perform a news magazine. **DOK4**

HSS 6.4; ELD.PI.C.9; ELA W.6.7–9, WHST.6.7–9, SL.6.4–6

Quest Project-Based Learning Inquiry

The Influence of Ancient Greece

Quest KICK OFF

It's the year 30 BCE, and the golden age of ancient Greece is drawing to a close, leaving behind a rich, living legacy of ideas. Your quest, as part of a team, is to create a television news magazine about ancient Greece based on the question:

Why has ancient Greece's culture endured?

How did one of the forms of government developed in ancient Greece leave a lasting legacy? Explore the Essential Question "What is the best form of government?" in this Quest.

Athena, the Greek goddess of wisdom and war

1 Ask Questions

First, you'll need to research the five story segments that will combine to form your news magazine. Begin by making a list of the questions you need to answer in your news magazine. Write these questions in your Active Journal.

2 Investigate

As you read the lessons in the Topic, look for Quest CONNECTIONS that show how ancient Greece still influences life today in government and politics. Record notes in your Active Journal.

3 Conduct Research

Next, begin researching aspects of ancient Greece, using print and online sources. Capture notes in your Active Journal.

Quest FINDINGS

4 Create Your News Magazine

Next, work with your team to fully research, write, and produce the news magazine, either recorded or performed live for your class. Each team member will research and write one segment. Get help for this task in your Active Journal.

DIFFERENTIATED INSTRUCTION

Below Level Help students focus their response to the Quest question by having them write brief responses to these questions: Why is democracy practiced today? What is the connection between democracy and ancient Greece?

INTEGRATED ENGLISH LANGUAGE DEVELOPMENT

Expanding Students can read sections of their writing to each other and then ask the other students questions about what they just heard. The second student should be prepared to answer the questions.

The Early Years of Greek Civilization

GET READY TO READ

START UP

The photograph shows part of the coastline of Greece. What challenges might people living here face?

GUIDING QUESTIONS

- How did physical geography help shape the development of Greek societies?
- How did the Minoans and Mycenaeans influence Greek culture?
- How did city-states develop, and how did they interact with one another?

TAKE NOTES

Literacy Skills: Analyze Cause and Effect

Use the graphic organizer in your Active Journal to take notes as you read the lesson.

PRACTICE VOCABULARY

Use the vocabulary activity in your Active Journal to practice the vocabulary words.

Vocabulary		Academic Vocabulary
polis	politics	eventual
citizen	aristocracy	exclude
acropolis		

The ancient Greece world was spread across the coasts and islands of the Mediterranean Sea. Greeks interacted with older societies in Mesopotamia and Egypt and built on the accomplishments of those civilizations. At the same time, the Greeks developed their own unique ways of living. The Greeks made contributions to art, drama, philosophy, and political science. Greek culture helped form Western civilization—the civilization of Europe and the Americas. The Greeks gave us words and concepts such as *democracy, geometry,* and *politics*. How did the Greeks come to have so much influence on our world?

How Did Geography Shape the Greek World?

In ancient times, there was no country called Greece. Instead, there were communities of Greek speakers scattered across the islands and coasts of the Mediterranean Sea. This early Greek world lay on the fringe of two continents—Europe and Asia. Travelers and traders passed through the region exchanging goods, ideas, and customs.

PRACTICE VOCABULARY

To help students integrate new vocabulary, group the terms and introduce them. Explain that *polis* and *politics* are related because the word *polis* (city-state) led to the word *politics* (the practice of government). Ask students to explain how *acropolis* is part of this word grouping. *(Acropolis (high hill) is refers to a place in a city-state.)* Explain that *citizen* and *aristocracy* are related because members of the aristocracy were citizens of their city-state.

Have students locate and pronounce the academic vocabulary in the lesson margins. Provide sample sentences that clarify meaning.

eventual: Direct democracy in Athens led to the eventual development of representative democracy.

exclude: Athenian democracy was known to exclude women, slaves, and foreigners from citizenship.

HSS 6.4.1

The Early Years of Greek Civilization

CONNECT

GET READY TO READ

ETEXT START UP

Project the Start Up Activity. As students enter the classroom and get seated, have them study the photograph. of the Greek coastline.

Draw Conclusions Ask: What challenges might people living here face? *(Possible responses: living on a mountainous terrain; lack of farmable land; separation from other communities.)*

Make Generalizations Based on the photo, have students draw three conclusions about daily life in ancient Greece. *(Sample response: Fishing was important. Sailing and trading were major occupations. Communication between city-states might have been slow.)* Have students share their answers with the class.

After completing the Start Up activity, project the Lesson Opener or direct students to their textbooks. Preview the lesson by working through the Get Ready to Read items with the class. Remind students to pay close attention to the Guiding Questions as they read the lesson.

ACTIVE JOURNAL

Take Notes Have students use the lesson literacy skill graphic organizer in their Active Journals to take notes as they read the lesson.

Practice Vocabulary Have students complete the activity in their Active Journals to build their vocabulary.

VIDEO VIDEO

Assign the lesson video as homework.

WORKSHEET **TEACHER RESOURCES**

Have students who need additional support use the following worksheets from the Teacher Resources on the course:

- **Reading Support**
- **English Language Development**
- **Lesson Summary**

INVESTIGATE

How Did Geography Shape the Greek World?

Discuss how Greece's geography and location shaped ancient Greece and its culture. What affect did climate have?

Identify Cause and Effect How did mountain ranges affect Greece's development? *(They isolated the city-states, which developed independently and did not unite under one government.)*

Identify Central Ideas How did being near the sea affect development of Greek civilization? *(The Greeks became sailors and merchants, leading to contact with older, more developed cultures in North Africa and Asia.)*

Identify Cause and Effect How did Greece's climate affect its development? *(Grain did not grow well in the dry summers, so the Greeks had to get grain elsewhere; olives and grapes thrived, so olive oil and wine became important trade goods.)*

ANSWERS

Location *Asia lies to the east, Africa to the south.*

Analyze Cause and Effect *The location gave Greeks access to trade routes and cultural contacts with other parts of the world. The sea provided food for Greece, where there was little farmland. The map shows that Greek communities were isolated from each other by mountain ranges and the sea.*

GEOGRAPHY SKILLS

Ancient Greek civilization developed among the islands clustered around the Aegean, Mediterranean, and Ionian Seas.

1. **Location** What continents lie to the east and south of Greece?
2. **Analyze Cause and Effect** What effect did Greece's location near so many seas have on the Greek way of life? What information in the text does the appearance of Greece's islands support?

Where is Greece? Modern Greece occupies a large peninsula that juts into the Mediterranean Sea. A peninsula is a land area surrounded by water on three sides. A number of other peninsulas also extend from the peninsula of mainland Greece. The largest of them, in southern Greece, is called the Peloponnesian (pel uh puh NEE shun) Peninsula.

About 2000 BCE, Greek-speaking peoples entered these lands from the north. They settled on mainland Greece. A mainland is an area of land that is part of a continent. Greek speakers also settled on the islands of the Aegean (ee JEE un) Sea.

Mainland Greece is divided by mountain ranges. Between these ranges lie narrow valleys and small plains. The mountains were good for grazing sheep and goats, but they were too steep and rocky for farming. Less than one quarter of the land could be used to grow crops. The only fertile land was in the lowland valleys and plains. Here people settled in farming communities.

The mountains isolated these lowland communities, so a fiercely independent spirit developed among the Greeks. They never attempted to unite under a single government. In fact, Greek cities were often at war with one another.

Surrounded by the Sea Although mountain ranges isolated communities, the sea brought contact with the wider world. The Greeks became skillful sailors and merchants. Greek fishing and trading ships crisscrossed the waters of the Mediterranean Sea to the south, the Aegean Sea to the east, and the Ionian (eye OH nee un) Sea to the west. This led to contact with the older, more complex cultures of North Africa and Asia.

INTEGRATED ENGLISH LANGUAGE DEVELOPMENT

Listening Explain that active listening means paying careful attention to a speaker. Read a paragraph from the text and then prompt students to ask questions about it.

Emerging Read Emergence of City States from later in the lesson aloud to students. Ask students about the three kinds of inhabitants of the polis in ancient Greece. Ask what the three separate classes could do and not do. Allow them to ask questions and give them substantial prompting and support.

Expanding Read Politics in the Polis from later in the lesson aloud to students. Ask what made citizens unique in the Greek city states. Allow students to ask questions and give them occasional prompting and moderate support.

Bridging Have students work in pairs. Have one student read Politics in the

A Mediterranean Climate Greece has a Mediterranean climate, with mild, wet winters and hot, dry summers. The lack of rain made it difficult to grow shallow-rooted crops such as grains, which need frequent watering. So the mainland Greeks were always searching for foreign sources of grain. On the other hand, the Mediterranean climate was ideal for growing deep-rooted plants such as olive trees and grape vines. Olive oil and wine became important trade goods and brought in wealth.

READING CHECK **Identify Cause and Effect** How did physical geography shape Greek culture?

Who Influenced the Early Greeks?

The early Greeks were influenced by an early civilization—the Minoans. Minoan culture developed on Crete, an island south of mainland Greece. It spread across the Aegean islands and influenced mainland Greece around 2000 BCE.

The Minoans Minoan civilization was highly advanced. The Minoans had a writing system and built huge stone palaces with running water, like the one at Knossos (NAH sus). They traded goods throughout the Mediterranean. Around 1450 BCE, Minoan palaces and towns were mysteriously destroyed. Most historians believe that mainland Greeks were responsible.

The Mycenaeans The Minoans influenced a civilization that developed among Greek speakers on mainland Greece. This civilization, known as Mycena (my suh NEE uh), developed around 1600 BCE. Each Mycenaean town was governed by a monarchy, a government headed by a king. Mycenaean rulers lived in stone fortresses on hilltops overlooking their towns.

The Mycenaeans made fine bronze weapons and pottery. They traded these goods for copper, ivory, and luxury goods from other lands. Mycenaeans sometimes raided other peoples and one another for gold and other goods.

Eventually, the Mycenaean kingdoms grew weak. Then, around 1100 BCE, this civilization was destroyed by newcomers from the north known as Dorians.

The Dark Age With the fall of the Mycenaeans, Greek culture declined. People lost the ability to read and write. The following period, which lasted roughly from 1100 to 750, has been called a dark age. During these centuries, mainland Greeks migrated across the Aegean, settling the islands and the west coast of Anatolia, an area that became known as Ionia (eye OH nee a).

Analyze Images Ruins from a Minoan palace at Knossos still stand. **Identify Supporting Details** What is impressive about this palace?

Who Influenced the Early Greeks?

Discuss Minoan civilization and how it influenced later Greek culture. Also discuss the ebb and flow of different cultures in the region.

Identify Patterns What is one thing that Minoan and Mycenaean civilizations had in common? *(Possible answers: Both civilizations developed a system of writing. Their rulers lived in large stone fortresses or palaces. Both civilizations fell to outside invaders.)*

Explain Historical Continuity Why was the legend of the Trojan War an important part of Ionian culture? *(To the Greeks in Ionia, who were living through a dark age, the Mycenaeans represented a heroic past. Stories about the Trojan War helped keep that heroic past alive for Ionian Greeks.)*

ELD.P1.B.5

Polis from later in the lesson aloud to the other. Have one ask the other questions about the inhabitants of the city-states. When they have finished, ask what made citizens unique in the Greek city-states.

WORKSHEET **TEACHER RESOURCES**

For additional IELD support addressing the standard, have students complete the Lesson ELD activity from the Teacher Resources found on the course.

ANSWERS

Identify Cause and Effect *Mountain ranges isolated Greek communities, encouraging an independent spirit, while the sea brought them into contact with other cultures.*

Identify Supporting Details *The layout of the ruins suggests that they are part of a larger complex of buildings. The stairway on the right appears to have given access to an upper floor or chamber. It is impressive to consider that it is more than 3,000 years old.*

The Trojan War

Discuss the Trojan War. How did the Trojan War influence later Greek culture?

Connect How did Homer's *Iliad* and the *Odyssey* shape Greek culture? *(The values expressed in these works (bravery, strength, honor) became part of Greek identity; the ancient Greeks tried to live up to these ideals.)*

INTERACTIVE **INTERACTIVE MAP**

The Journey of Odysseus

Interactive Instruction Display the Interactive Map: The Journey of Odysseus. Click through the interactive to learn more about Odysseus's journey. Ask: How does Odysseus overcome the many challenges he faces? *(through a combination of perseverence, courage, and cleverness)*

ACTIVE CLASSROOM

Use the Conversation with Mythology strategy. Have students imagine they are having a conversation with Odysseus. Students should write down a question they'd like to ask, then write how Odysseus would respond. Ask volunteers to share their conversation with the class.

ANSWERS

Identify Supporting Details *The Minoans had a writing system and running water. The Mycenaeans made fine bronze weapons and pottery.*

Draw Conclusions *The story is memorable because it demonstrates the enormous power of curiosity.*

Identify Supporting Details *He kept alive the golden age of that civilization through his stories about victory in their war with Troy.*

Analyze Images Trojans celebrate the gift of the wooden horse in this scene from a recent movie. **Draw Conclusions** What about the story of the Trojan horse do you think interests audiences so many years later?

The Greeks in Ionia brought their culture with them through several waves of migration. They never forgot the "heroic age" of the Mycenaeans. They told stories and sang songs of the world that existed before the dark age. One of these stories was about the Trojan War.

READING CHECK **Identify Supporting Details** How were the Minoans and Mycenaeans advanced cultures?

The Trojan War

In the legend of the Trojan War, warriors from Mycenaean kingdoms sailed across the Aegean to attack Troy, a city in Anatolia, also called Asia minor (now the country of Turkey). The ten-year-long conflict ended when the Greeks tricked the Trojans into accepting a "gift" of a large wooden horse. Greeks hiding in the horse crept out and opened the city gates. The Greek army entered and burned Troy to the ground.

For centuries, the stories of the Trojan War were recited or sung, as the Greeks could no longer read or write. Then, in the 700s, the Greeks developed an alphabet based on the Phoenician alphabet. According to tradition, a poet named Homer shaped the stories of the Trojan War into a long epic poem, the *Iliad*. The poem was eventually written down.

Academic Vocabulary
eventual • *adj.*, final

The *Iliad* tells of events during the war, but stops before the Greeks' **eventual** victory. Homer's *Odyssey* is another epic poem, which describes the adventures of the hero Odysseus on his journey home after the war. Both the *Iliad* and the *Odyssey* imagined a Mycenaean world of fearless warriors.

The *Iliad* and the *Odyssey* shaped Greek culture. Students learned the verses by heart. The values expressed in these poems became part of Greek identity, including bravery, strength, and honor. In the *Iliad*, the warrior Achilles speaks to his troops before battle:

Primary Source

> "Every man make up his mind to fight And move on his enemy! Strong as I am, It's hard for me to face so many men And fight with all at once. . . . And yet I will!"
>
> —Homer, the *Iliad*

The ancient Greeks tried to live up to the ideals of the poems' warriors, who sought glory through courageous feats.

INTERACTIVE
The Journey of Odysseus

READING CHECK **Identify Supporting Details** How did Homer preserve the memory of Mycenaean civilization?

230 Lesson 6.1 • The Early Years of Greek Civilization

HISTORY BACKGROUND

The Trojan War In Greek mythology, the Trojan War started because of Helen of Troy. She was the most beautiful woman in the world, and men from all over Greece wanted to marry her. She married Menelaus, a Spartan king, but ran off with Paris, the son of the king of Troy. Menelaus called on other Greek leaders to help him get Helen back, and his brother Agamemnon (the king of Argos) led the Greek forces against Troy.

In Homer's telling, the Greek gods are deeply involved with the events of the war. They behave much like humans, with passions, rivlalries and jealousies, helping favored heroes and punishing those who offend them.

Emergence of City-States

By the time Homer's epics were composed, each Greek community had begun to organize itself into a **polis**, or city-state. The city-state became one of the most important features of Greek culture. The Greeks created such city-states everywhere they settled, mostly along the coast.

Geography played an important role in the emergence of the city-state. Greek cities were cut off from one another by mountains and water. The remoteness of these cities did not allow for a huge empire to be grow as in Egypt or Persia. Instead, the cities flourished on their own, each establishing its own system of commerce, government, and culture. The seas allowed city-states to trade their unique products with one another and the outside world.

What was the Polis? A polis was more than just a city. It was a community with its own government. The government of a polis ruled a wide area that included not only the city but its surrounding villages and countryside as well.

Each Greek city-state usually had a marketplace and government center. Here members of the city-state who had legal rights—the **citizens**—would meet to make laws and discuss issues affecting the entire community.

The area and population of a polis were generally small. All the citizens of the polis could gather to make decisions as a single group.

The Acropolis: "The High City" A typical polis was usually built on two levels. On a high hill stood the **acropolis** (uh KRAH puh lis), a word meaning "high city." Public buildings and marble temples were located in this area. The acropolis also served as a fortress in times of danger. On lower ground, below the hill, lay people's homes, shops, and farms. In Athens, the lower city included the agora, or marketplace. There people gathered to discuss public affairs.

Analyze Images The ruins of the Parthenon, an ancient temple, sit on the acropolis of Athens, high above the modern city. **Use Visual Information** How does this view of Athens help you understand the idea of an acropolis?

Draw Conclusions In the centuries before the *Iliad* and the *Odyssey* were written down, the poems were recited many times. What might have happened to the poems over the centuries? *(They probably were changed and embellished and became different from the original versions.)*

Infer The *Iliad* is the version of the events of the Trojan war that has come down through history. Is Homer's account likely accurate in all its details? Why or why not? *(Sample response: It is probably not completely accurate. It existed long before it was written down, and it was written from the Greek point of view.)*

ELD TIP Refer English learners to the image of the Trojan Horse. Remind them that the Greeks used the horse to trick the Trojans. Explain that "Trojan Horse" is an English idiom that refers to a gift that secretly delivers something that will be harmful to the recipient. Ask students if they can think of any other idioms.

Emergence of City-States

Discuss the development of city-states. How were they organized and governed? What was their place in Greek culture?

Check Understanding How was a city-state more than just a city? *(Each city-state had its own system of commerce, government, and culture, and controlled the surrounding villages and countryside.)*

DIFFERENTIATED INSTRUCTION

Special Education Students with learning disabilities might have problems absorbing the details of the text image. Point out the Parthenon and ask students to answer these questions: Where is the building? *(on a hill)* How does it compare in size to the other buildings? *(It is much larger.)* Why would people feel safe in the building in time of danger? *(It was so high above the city that they could see an enemy approaching.)*

Below Level Have students study the photo in the student text. Ask them to point out the Parthenon. Have them identify the part of the city where the agora would probably have been.

Advanced Have students gather additional online or print information about the key parts of a polis: the acropolis and the agora. Ask students to share their information with the class.

ANSWERS

Use Visual Information *The Acropolis was the dominant feature of the city as befitted its great religious and civic importance. It was a vast structure compared to the buildings below.*

HSS 6.4.1; ELD.P1.A.2, ELD.P1.C.10.a

SYNTHESIZE

Assess and Reteach Have students use a Think-Pair-Share strategy to complete Lesson Check questions 1–4. Review their responses. If responses are incorrect, use the Guiding Questions to discuss the lesson's main ideas, focusing on the ideas that are causing difficulty.

ACTIVE JOURNAL

Writing Workshop Have students complete the Lesson 1 Writing Task in their Active Journals. Students should recognize that they are writing the essay to explain ideas in the topic to to their teacher, showing that they understand those ideas themselves.

DEMONSTRATE

ASSESSMENT **ONLINE LESSON QUIZ**

Assign the Online Lesson Quiz for this lesson if you haven't already done so. Students will be offered automatic remediation or enrichment based on their score.

DISCUSSION **DISCUSSION BOARD**

Post this question to the class on the Discussion Board:

Understand Effects How might Greece have developed differently if it had different geography? *(If there were no mountain ranges in Greece, the city-states would not have been as isolated and the Greeks might have established a unified state under one government.)*

▲ Bronze discs used in Athens for voting

Politics in the Polis The word *polis* gave rise to the term **politics**, the art and practice of government. Each city-state had a different kind of government. Some city-states were monarchies, ruled by a king. In early times the polis was governed by an **aristocracy**, a hereditary class of rulers. Aristocracy meant "rule by the best people."

But in some city-states an extraordinary thing happened—the citizens began governing themselves. Rule by citizens made such Greek city-states unique. By contrast, in most of the world, priests and kings held all the political power.

Even though self-government was a feature of most city-states, not everyone was allowed to participate in making decisions. Women, slaves, and foreigners were all **excluded** from the process. The polis had three kinds of inhabitants: citizens (who could vote), women and free foreigners (who could not vote), and slaves, who had few rights at all.

Academic Vocabulary
exclude • *v.*, to shut out, keep from participating

"The Framework of Greek Life" Citizens felt strong pride and loyalty toward their polis. Greeks believed that a good citizen should always be willing to sacrifice for his city. He should be prepared to die for his polis, if necessary.

As one historian wrote, "The polis was the framework of Greek life." Greeks identified with their city. If their polis was a success, so were they. Throughout the history of ancient Greece, the polis played a key role in Greek life.

READING CHECK **Identify Supporting Details** Why was a Greek person's polis important to his or her identity?

Lesson Check

Practice Vocabulary

1. How did **citizens** take part in the running of their **polis**?
2. What role did the **aristocracy** play in **politics**?

Critical Thinking and Writing

3. **Synthesize** What changes took place in the Greek world during the dark age?

HSS 6.4.1; ELD.PI.C.10.a

4. **Compare and Contrast** Compare the advantages and disadvantages of Greece's physical geography for settlers.
5. **Writing Workshop: Consider Your Purpose** You will write an explanatory essay exploring why independent Greek city-states rose, peaked, and ultimately, fell. Who is your audience for this essay? How will that affect how you write it? Consult your Active Journal for help.

LESSON CHECK

1. Citizens were able to govern themselves because they had the right to vote in their polis. **DOK1**
2. At first, the aristocracy dominated politics in Greece, but, slowly, citizens gained more power. **DOK1**
3. People lost the ability to read and write. People also migrated from Greece to Anatolia. **DOK2**
4. Greece's geography isolated people as they settled in valleys and on islands. However, geography allowed city-states to emerge independently from one another. Each had its own system of government and its own culture. Isolation also fostered endless rivalries that led to war. **DOK3**
5. Students should indicate that they understand the purpose and audience of the essay they will write. **DOK3**

ANSWERS

Identify Supporting Details *Greeks felt pride in their cities and felt like successes if their city-state did well.*

LESSON 2

HSS 6.4.2, 6.4.3

Democracy in Athens

BOUNCE TO ACTIVATE

VIDEO

GET READY TO READ

START UP

Look at the picture of the agora in Athens, the open marketplace where people could gather. How do meeting places like this help new ideas develop and grow?

GUIDING QUESTIONS

- What political forms did Greek city-states experiment with?
- How did Athenian democracy work?
- What were the benefits and limitations of the democracy practiced in Athens?

TAKE NOTES

Literacy Skills: Summarize

Use the graphic organizer in your Active Journal to take notes as you read the lesson.

PRACTICE VOCABULARY

Use the vocabulary activity in your Active Journal to practice the vocabulary words.

Vocabulary		Academic Vocabulary
oligarchy	citizenship	maintain
phalanx	direct democracy	lecturer
tyranny	representative democracy	
democracy		

One night in 508 BCE, the sounds of a power struggle echoed through the streets of Athens. Isagoras, the city's leading judge, was trying to crush a movement for democracy. He had invited warriors from the city-state of Sparta to help him defeat this dangerous new trend. He forced the popular leader Cleisthenes (KLYS thuh neez) to flee the city. Isagoras also exiled 700 families who supported democratic reform.

But now some Athenians were fighting back. The Spartans were excellent soldiers, but they were overwhelmed by the Athenian people. After the Spartans surrendered, Cleisthenes returned, and Athens continued building its democracy.

Experimenting with Forms of Government

Isagoras and the Spartans were trying to keep government in the hands of the aristocrats, a type of government the Greeks called an **oligarchy** (AHL ih gahr kee). In an oligarchy, political power is held by a small group of people.

PRACTICE VOCABULARY

To help students integrate new vocabulary, group the terms and introduce them. Explain that *oligarchy* (rule by the few), *tyranny* (rule by an oppressive power), *and democracy* are all forms of government. Explain that *direct democracy* and *representative democracy* are two forms of democracy. Ask students to describe the difference between the two. Discuss the responses and clarify students' understanding if necessary.

Have students locate and pronounce the academic vocabulary in the lesson margins. Provide sample sentences that clarify meaning.

maintain: In order to maintain a healthy democracy, citizens must vote.

lecturer: In Athens, people who were being educated learned about a subject from a lecturer.

HSS 6.4.2, 6.4.3

Democracy in Athens

CONNECT

GET READY TO READ

ETEXT **START UP**

Project the Start Up Activity. As students enter the classroom and get seated, ask them to study the image. Explain that this is a representation of the agora in Athens.

Infer How do meeting places like this help new ideas develop and grow? *(Possible response: In a place such as this, one can meet people from other places and exchange ideas.)*

Discuss Explain that even today many cities have public gathering places, such as parks or squares. Discuss how such places give power to citizens, by allowing them to collect and join forces.

After completing the Start Up activity, project the Lesson Opener or direct students to their textbooks. Preview the lesson by working through the Get Ready to Read items with the class. Remind students to pay close attention to the Guiding Questions as they read the lesson.

ACTIVE JOURNAL

Take Notes Have students use the lesson literacy skill graphic organizer in their Active Journals to take notes as they read the lesson.

Practice Vocabulary Have students complete the activity in their Active Journals to build their vocabulary.

VIDEO **VIDEO**

Assign the lesson video as homework.

WORKSHEET **TEACHER RESOURCES**

Have students who need additional support use the following worksheets from the Teacher Resources on the course:

- **Reading Support**
- **English Language Development**
- **Lesson Summary**

INVESTIGATE

Experimenting with Forms of Government

Discuss oligarchies in the city-states. Have students consider how the introduction of the phalanx might have eventually led to democracy.

Distinguish Cause and Effect What was the connection between the introduction of the phalanx and the beginning of democracy? *(The phalanx allowed men who could not afford horses and armor to the army. City-states' dependence on the phalanx gave political power to more people, paving the way for government by the people rather than the aristocracy.)*

Describe How did tyranny develop without the use of military force? *(Tyrants won popular support by promising land and other benefits to their followers.)*

Analyze Images The phalanx was a formation of soldiers that might be as deep as eight lines. **Draw Conclusions** How might such a battle formation create a spirit of equality?

Academic Vocabulary

maintain • *v.*, to keep and support

Oligarchies Oligarchies were usually headed by a council of leaders who belonged to the aristocracy. One of these aristocratic leaders was a lawgiver named Draco. He created a legal code that specified harsh punishments for all offenses, from serious to minor crimes. Today, people still use the word *draconian* to describe laws that seem unnecessarily harsh or severe.

A Military Tactic Changes Government

In many city-states, power began to shift into the hands of more people. This process may have been sparked by a change in the way Greek armies were organized. In earlier times, the outcome of battles depended on fights between individual aristocratic warriors. Around 700 BCE, a new military formation called the phalanx was introduced. The **phalanx** was a formation of heavily armed foot soldiers who moved together as a unit. Before battle, these citizen-soldiers lined up to form a row of overlapping shields. Each man's shield helped protect his neighbor. He held the shield with his left arm. In his right hand he held a spear or sword.

As foot soldiers, fighters in a phalanx did not need to be rich enough to buy and **maintain** a horse. More men could afford the necessary weapons and armor. As city-states came to depend on the phalanx formation for defense, citizen-soldiers may have gained more political power. Some historians believe this gave more men a voice in government. Aristocratic leaders risked losing the support of their army if they did not consider the interests of these men.

Each city-state set up a different form of government. With so many city-states, great political variety characterized the Greek world.

Tyrannies At first tyrants, or strong leaders, emerged to champion the interests of ordinary citizens. Tyrants were usually members of the aristocracy. But by promising land and other benefits to the poor, they won popular support. Then they were able to set up a **tyranny**, or government run by a strong ruler.

Tyrants did not allow others to play a significant role in government. Nevertheless, Greek tyrants were not always bad rulers. In some city-states, they governed fairly and worked to improve life for ordinary people.

Many tyrants, however, found that they could not fulfill their promises. Other tyrants ruled harshly. Eventually, other forms of government replaced tyrannies.

READING CHECK **Compare and Contrast** How are oligarchies and tyrannies different?

INTEGRATED ENGLISH LANGUAGE DEVELOPMENT

Reading Have students read along silently while you read Experimenting With Forms of Government aloud to them.

Emerging Point out the word *phalanx* and make sure students understand its meaning. Refer them to the image of the phalanx. Ask them to explain in their own words how the individual members of the phalanx protected each other.

Expanding Have students look again at the image. Discuss the overlapping shields and the lances. Remind students that soldiers had to buy their own weapons and armor. Ask whether these soldiers needed horses. Discuss why joining a phalanx allowed men who did not have much money to become soldiers.

ANSWERS

Draw Conclusions *Each soldier's shield helped protect his neighbor, making everyone equal and dependent on one another.*

Compare and Contrast *In an oligarchy, power is held by a small group of people. Under tyranny, the government is run by one strong ruler.*

The World's First Democracy

Most city-states adopted tyranny, but some moved toward rule by the many. The Greeks called this form of government **democracy**, which means "rule by the people." In these new democracies, large numbers of men participated in civic affairs.

When Did Democracy in Athens Begin? In the year 594 BCE, the aristocrats of Athens chose Solon to lead the polis. Solon ended the practice of selling into slavery poor people who could not pay their debts. He also gave some non-aristocratic men the right to vote for officials. These measures set Athens on the path to democracy.

Later Reforms In 508 BCE, a leader named Cleisthenes made several reforms that reduced the power of the rich. By increasing the number of citizens who could vote, he brought in many new voters from the lower classes. Cleisthenes also increased the power of the assembly, which included all male citizens. The assembly met to discuss political issues and make decisions for the city-state.

Another major reform took place in 461 BCE. In that year, Athens created citizen juries. A jury is a group of people who hear evidence and decide a court case. The new system put legal decisions in the hands of the people.

The Age of Pericles More reforms followed in the 450s BCE under Pericles. His first major change was to pay citizens for participating in jury service and in other civic duties. These payments helped poor people to take part in government. These reforms created the world's first democracy. Athenians were proud of what they had achieved.

One factor that encouraged democracy in Athens was the idea of citizenship. **Citizenship** is membership in a community. Elsewhere in the ancient world, people lived as subjects of a ruler whom they were expected to obey without question. In contrast, the Greeks gave ordinary people the right to help make government decisions.

Education's Role in Democracy Education helped promote the growth of democracy in Athens. The education students received was designed to produce well-rounded citizens.

Although some girls could probably read and write, most education was reserved for boys. They attended school from the age of seven and studied literature, physical education, and music.

By the 420s BCE, there was also higher education. Commonly, a **lecturer** taught students subjects such as mathematics and public speaking.

READING CHECK **Identify Main Ideas** What important political development occurred in Athens?

Academic Vocabulary

lecturer • *n.*, person who gives an informative talk to students

▼ Athenian leader Solon ended the practice of enslaving people who could not pay debts.

The World's First Democracy

Discuss the development of democracy in Athens. What role did **citizenship** play? What role did education play?

Identify Cause and Effect In what ways did Solon's reforms promote early **democracy** in Athens? *(By ending the practice of selling into slavery poor people who could not pay their debts and by giving non-aristocratic men the right to vote for officials, Solon gave non-aristocrats a greater role in society.)*

Explain Historical Continuity In what ways did the reforms embraced under Cleisthenes continue the development of **democracy**? *(Increasing the number of citizens who could vote introduced new voters from the lower classes. Increasing the power of the assembly gave Athenians more say in their city's government. Citizen juries put legal decisions in the hands of the people.)*

Compare and Contrast How did the concept of **citizenship** make Athens different from other places in the ancient world? *(People who lacked the rights of citizens lived under a ruler they had to always obey. In Athens, citizenship gave people the right to help make government decisions and decide the laws under which they would live.)*

Identify Central Ideas How did Athenians use education to **maintain** their **democracy**? *(Education produced citizens who were prepared to take an active part in their government.)*

ELD.PI.B.6.a

Bridging Ask pairs of students read Experimenting With Forms of Government. Ask the pairs of students to discuss how the invention of the phalanx in warfare resulted in a larger army. Ask how being part of a large group gave more men a voice in government. Discuss how large groups can affect governments today.

WORKSHEET **TEACHER RESOURCES**

For additional IELD support addressing the standard, have students complete the Lesson ELD activity from the Teacher Resources found on the course.

ANSWERS

Identify Main Ideas *The world's first democracy developed in Athens.*

How Did Athenian Democracy Work?

Athenian democracy depended on the active citizen involvement.

Identify Main Ideas What were some of the limitations of Athenian democracy? *(Women could not vote or hold office; foreigners had no voice in government; slaves had no rights.)*

INTERACTIVE **INTERACTIVE GALLERY**

Athenian Democracy

Interactive Instruction Display the Interactive gallery: Athenian Democracy for the class. Ask a volunteer to read the explanatory text. Then, click through the images and ask volunteers to read the captions. Ask: What duty do U.S. citizens have that is identical to the duty of citizens of Athens? *(the duty to vote)*

ACTIVE CLASSROOM

Use the Make Headlines strategy. Have students choose an image in the gallery and write a newspaper headline related to it. Encourage students to be creative. Ask volunteers to share their headlines with the class.

ACTIVE JOURNAL

Quest Connections Direct students to the Quest Connections pages in their Active Journals. After students complete this activity, tell them to consider how they can use their response when they complete their Quest.

ANSWERS

Draw Inferences *Without a group that filtered bills submitted to the assembly, there would have been no way to accomplish the necessary work.*

INTERACTIVE
Athenian Democracy

How Did Athenian Democracy Work?

Political reforms produced a golden age of democracy in Athens. Citizens ran all parts of the government. The most important were the assembly, the council, and the courts.

The Business of Government The main political body of Athens was the assembly, which all free adult male citizens had the right to attend. Meetings took place 40 times a year. Everyone who attended the assembly had the right to speak, from the poorest farmer to the richest aristocrat.

A 500-person council, known as the boule, was the second key component of the Athenian government. The council helped decide which issues should come before the assembly. Members of the council were chosen by lot, or at random, from among the citizens. As a result, every male citizen had a chance of serving on the council.

The Courts The government's third key component was the court system. Athens had many different courts, each of which decided different types of cases. Juries made up of citizens served in the courts, deciding cases by majority vote.

Juries in Athens were much larger than modern juries. Many people, from several hundred to several thousand, might serve on a single jury! Additional laws were passed to discourage bribery.

As democracy grew stronger in Athens, older governmental bodies lost power. For example, the Areopagus (ar ee OP uh gus), a council of advisers who decided some court cases, lost all its functions except the right to judge murder cases.

Quest CONNECTIONS

Look at the diagram of Athenian democracy. In what ways did Athenian democracy influence the U.S. government? Record your findings in your Active Journal.

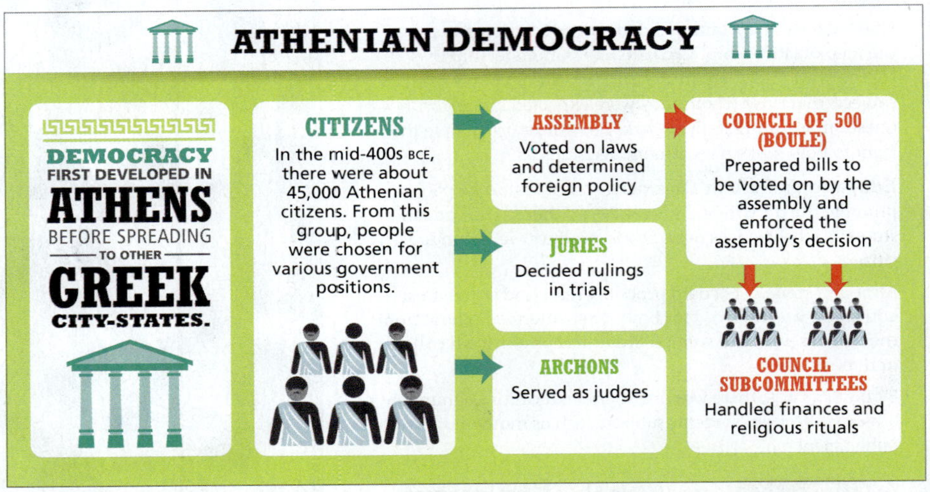

Analyze Diagrams The Athenian assembly was open to all male citizens. **Draw Inferences** Why do you think the boule and its subcommittees were created?

DIFFERENTIATED INSTRUCTION

Special Education Discuss with students how Athenian democracy worked. Have them point to each box in the diagram. Read and discuss the importance of each part of the government. Relate each function of the Athenian government with aspects of the United States government with which they are familiar.

Below Level Refer students to description of the boule. Ask students why it is necessary to have someone decide what is important and what is not.

Advanced Have students do research online or in the library and create a chart comparing the way the legislature of the United States government works with the way the Athenian government functioned. Have students share their charts with the class.

Did Athenian Democracy Have Limitations? Athens was not completely democratic. Women could not vote or hold office. Foreigners, even if they came from another Greek city-state, could not be citizens and had no voice in the government. Slaves had no rights.

Athens, then, did not have rule by all the people. Compared to most places in the ancient world, however, Athens included far more people in government.

Analyze Images Greek men used stones to vote. Here, two men vote under the watchful eye of the Greek goddess Athena. **Draw Conclusions** What does artwork showing a goddess watching over voting tell you about Athenians' views on the practice?

Direct and Representative Democracy: The Differences

Athenian democracy depended on active citizen involvement. A political system in which citizens participate directly in decision making is called a **direct democracy**. Direct democracy worked in Athens because the population of the city-state was small and because of the commitment and hard work of its citizens.

Direct democracy is less practical in large countries like the United States. In countries spread over a wide area of land, citizens live too far apart to meet. In addition, nations like the United States have so many citizens that Athenian-style assemblies would be too big.

For this reason, most democracies today are representative democracies. In a **representative democracy**, citizens elect others to represent them in government. These representatives then make the decisions and pass laws on behalf of all the people. Despite the differences, modern democracies share the Athenian ideal of rule by the people.

READING CHECK **Identify Supporting Details** How did the assembly provide Athenians with a direct role in government decisions?

Lesson Check

HSS 6.4.2, 6.4.3; ELD.PI.C.10.a

Practice Vocabulary

1. How did the **phalanx** help encourage **democracy** in Athens?
2. How do an **oligarchy** and **tyranny** differ?
3. What are the differences between **representative democracy** and **direct democracy**?

Critical Thinking and Writing

4. **Draw Conclusions** Why did the use of the phalanx affect politics?
5. **Compare and Contrast** How is the modern democracy of the United States different from Athenian democracy?
6. **Writing Workshop: Pick an Organizing Strategy** How did Athens' government contribute to its rise? Start thinking about how you might organize your essay. Take notes in your Active Journal.

LESSON CHECK

1. Because soldiers in a phalanx did not need a lot of money to fight, more men became soldiers. Their increased importance gave them a greater voice in government. **DOK2**
2. In an oligarchy, a small group of people rules. In a tyranny, there is one strong leader. **DOK1**
3. Direct democracy: each citizen participates directly. Representative democracy: citizens elect people to represent them. **DOK2**
4. As their numbers increased, citizen-soldiers became powerful. **DOK3**
5. In the representative democracy of the United States, women can vote. In the direct democracy of Athens, only men could vote. **DOK2**
6. Students will choose an organizing structure. **DOK2**

HSS 6.4.2, 6.4.3; ELD.P1.C.10.a

SYNTHESIZE

Assess and Reteach Have students complete Lesson Check questions 1–5 individually. Remind students to use details from the text to support their answers. Review their responses using an Idea Wave strategy.

If any are incorrect, use the Guiding Questions to discuss the lesson's main ideas, focusing on the ideas that are causing difficulty.

ACTIVE JOURNAL

Writing Workshop Have students complete the Lesson 2 Writing Task in their Active Journals. Students will answer the question, start thinking about how they will organize their essay, and make appropriate notes in their Active Journal.

DEMONSTRATE

ASSESSMENT **ONLINE LESSON QUIZ**

Assign the Online Lesson Quiz for this lesson if you haven't already done so. Students will be offered automatic remediation or enrichment based on their score.

DISCUSSION **DISCUSSION BOARD**

Post this question to the class on the Discussion Board:

Analyze How was the selection of the members of Athens' council extremely democratic? *(Members of the council were chosen at random, by lot, so every male citizen had a chance of serving on the council.)* What would have made Athens even more democratic? *(Women could have been given citizenship. Enslaved people could have been freed and been allowed to vote.)*

ANSWERS

Draw Conclusions *Athenians looked upon voting with religious reverence.*

Identify Supporting Details *It voted on laws, made foreign policy, and had members that served in the boule.*

HSS 6.4.2; ELA RI.6.2, RH.6.1–2

Primary Sources

Pericles' Funeral Oration

Read aloud the explanatory note about the source. Direct students' attention to the image on the page. Ask: What does this show? *(a statue of Pericles)* What is on the figure's head? *(some sort of war helmet)* Why would it have been appropriate for Pericles to wear a war helmet while he gave the speech excerpted here? *(Pericles led Athens during the first Peloponnesian War; this speech was given in honor of Athenians who died in that war.)*

GUIDED READING

Read aloud or ask volunteers to read aloud the text. Use the Reading and Vocabulary Support notes to deepen students' understanding of the primary source.

Reading and Vocabulary Support Answer

1. *the ability to serve the state*
2. *envying others for what they have and judging others for how they live and behave*

GUIDED ANALYSIS

After completing the text, discuss what this primary source reveals about life in Athens and how Athenians felt about living in a democracy.

Interpret Sources What point is Pericles making about Athens in the first sentence? *(Athens does not follow in the footsteps of other city-states; others follow Athens' lead.)* What point is Pericles making in the second paragraph? *(Having the freedoms of democracy doesn't mean Athens has no laws; the city has many laws, which its citizens obey, making Athens a very orderly city.)* What does Pericles mean when he talks about laws that "although unwritten...cannot be broken without acknowledged disgrace"? *(Some things should be done—or not done—whether or not a law says so. He's referring to ethical behavior.)*

To assess understanding, have students respond to the Analyze Primary Sources questions in writing.

Primary Source

HSS 6.4.2; ELA RI.6.2, RH.6.1–2

Pericles, Funeral Oration

In the years after the Persian Wars, Pericles guided Athens to a golden age, when the economy thrived and the government became more democratic. At the end of the first Peloponnesian War (431–404 BCE), Pericles gave a famous speech that Thucydides recounted. It was a funeral oration Pericles gave at a public funeral for the war dead where he compares Athens to Sparta.

◀ A statue of Pericles

Reading and Vocabulary Support

① According to Pericles, what determines a man's ability to advance in Athenian society?

② What do you think Pericles meant by "jealous surveillance"?

③ A magistrate is a judge or high government official.

④ *Elegance* means richness.

Our constitution does not copy the laws of neighboring states; we are rather a pattern to others than imitators ourselves. Its administration favours the many instead of the few; this is why it is called a democracy. If we look to the laws, they afford equal justice to all in their private differences; if no social standing, advancement in public life falls to reputation for capacity, class considerations not being allowed to interfere with merit; nor again does poverty bar the way, if a man is able to serve the state, he is not hindered by the obscurity of his condition. ① The freedom which we enjoy in our government extends also to our ordinary life. There, far from exercising a jealous surveillance ② over each other, we do not feel called upon to be angry with our neighbor for doing what he likes, or even to indulge in those injurious looks which cannot fail to be offensive, although they inflict no positive penalty. But all this ease in our private relations does not make us lawless as citizens. Against this fear is our chief safeguard, teaching us to obey the magistrates ③ and the laws, particularly such as regard the protection of the injured, whether they are actually on the statute book, or belong to that code which, although unwritten, yet cannot be broken without acknowledged disgrace.

Further, we provide plenty of means for the mind to refresh itself from business. We celebrate games and sacrifices all the year round, and the elegance ④ of our private establishments forms a daily source of pleasure. . . .

—From *The History of the Peloponnesian War, Book 2,* by Thucydides

Analyzing Primary Sources

Cite specific evidence from the document to support your answers.

1. **Determine Author's Purpose** After reading this document, what do you think is Pericles' point of view regarding Athenian society?
2. **Determine Central Ideas** What are some of the main ideas expressed by Pericles in this document?

ANALYZING PRIMARY SOURCES

1. Students should cite specific examples that indicate that Pericles believes Athenian society is superior. **DOK2**
2. Citizens are an important part of democracy. Because of its society, Athens is a center for international trade. Athens is also a nation of laws. **DOK2**

INTEGRATED ENGLISH LANGUAGE DEVELOPMENT

Bridging Have students turn to a partner to determine the meaning of the primary source quotation. Provide students with historical context as needed. Then have students discuss what Pericles felt was special about Athens.

Analysis RE.3

Distinguish Relevant from Irrelevant Information

INTERACTIVE
Identify Evidence

Follow these steps to distinguish relevant from irrelevant information.

1 **Identify your focus or topic.** By clearly defining your topic, you can better determine which pieces of information will be relevant or irrelevant. If you were preparing a report on Pericles' character, what types of information would you look for to support your points?

2 **Locate sources and read about the topic.** Based on the topic you identified, select a number of sources that will likely offer information on this topic. You may find sources online or in your school's media center.

a. What is the source of the passage below?

b. What other types of sources might offer relevant information about Pericles' character?

3 **Identify the information that is relevant to your topic.** Scan your sources to find passages that may relate to your topic. Then, read these passages closely to determine whether or not they provide relevant information.

a. What is one piece of relevant information found in this passage?

b. What does this information tell you about Pericles' character?

4 **Identify the information that is irrelevant to your topic.** Irrelevant information, such as anecdotes, may be interesting, but it is not central to the topic. Give one detail from the passage that is irrelevant to the topic.

Primary Source

The Character of Pericles

"Pericles was born into the best families of Athens, both on his father's and mother's side. He received a good education from his teachers, including the philosopher Zeno....One day, Pericles was in the marketplace of Athens doing business. All day long some noisy pest followed him around, yelling at him and calling him names. He even followed Pericles home. Throughout the ordeal, Pericles stayed calm. It was dark by the time Pericles arrived home. So he gave orders for one of his servants to take a torch and guide this pest safely back to wherever he lived. Some people said that Pericles was only trying to fool the public with a false front of virtue. But Zeno replied that if Pericles were faking virtue, they should do the same."

—from Plutarch's *Lives*

DIFFERENTIATED INSTRUCTION

Below Level To help students understand the difference between relevant and irrelevant information, have students working in pairs imagine they are writing a report on airplanes. Have each student write four facts about airplanes (two facts that are relevant and two that are irrelevant). Have students exchange papers and label each fact as relevant or irrelevant.

INTEGRATED ENGLISH LANGUAGE DEVELOPMENT

Bridging Have students turn to a partner to determine the meaning of the primary source quotation. Provide students with historical context as needed. Then have students discuss how Pericles found a solution to the problem of the noisy pest.

Analysis RE.3

Analysis Skills
Distinguish Relevant from Irrelevant information

LEARN

Preview the steps in the student text with students. If appropriate, review the difference between *relevant* and *irrelevant*. Then, play the video.

VIDEO **21ST CENTURY SKILLS**

Project the Identify Evidence video in the 21st Century Skills Tutorial. Use the Quick Reference and Assessment to provide additional instruction in the skill.

PRACTICE

Have students name other sources they think might have relevant information on the topic of Pericles' character. Have students practice the skill using the text on the student page. When students are finished, discuss their responses as a class.

As an alternative, you could form students into pairs or groups to perform the activity. Then, invite the groups to share their responses with the class.

APPLY

To apply this skill, have students distinguish relevant from irrelevant information using the quote from Herodotus in Lesson 5 of this topic.

ANSWERS

1. information about his behavior or opinions of other respected Athenians
2. a. Plutarch's *Lives*
   b. Pericles' speeches, historians' accounts
3. a. Pericles saw to the safety of his critic.
   b. He practiced the virtue he preached.
4. Possible responses: He was born into a good family; he received a good education.

HSS 6.4.6

Oligarchy in Sparta

CONNECT

GET READY TO READ

ETEXT START UP

Project the Start Up Activity. As students enter the classroom and get settled, have them study the photograph. Explain that the image shows the Spartan king Leonidas.

Interpret What does the image of Leonidas tell you about the role of warfare in Spartan society? *(Sample response: Military might was the highest value.)*

Cite Evidence What led you to that conclusion? *(Leonidas is shown in full battle armor; this indicates that able fighters were highly valued in Sparta.)*

After completing the Start Up activity, project the Lesson Opener or direct students to their textbooks. Preview the lesson by working through the Get Ready to Read items with the class. Remind students to pay close attention to the Guiding Questions as they read the lesson.

ACTIVE JOURNAL

Take Notes Have students use the lesson literacy skill graphic organizer in their Active Journals to take notes as they read the lesson.

Practice Vocabulary Have students complete the activity in their Active Journals to build their vocabulary.

ELD TIP Academic vocabulary and subject matter vocabulary is particularly challenging for English learners. Review terms such as *authority, military, citizen, helot,* and *ephor* to assess students' comprehension.

VIDEO VIDEO

Assign the lesson video as homework.

LESSON 3

HSS 6.4.6

Oligarchy in Sparta

GET READY TO READ

START UP

What does the image of Spartan king Leonidas tell you about the role of warfare in Spartan society?

GUIDING QUESTIONS

- What type of government developed in Sparta?
- What was life like in Sparta?
- How did Sparta differ from Athens?

TAKE NOTES

Literacy Skills: Compare and Contrast

Use the graphic organizer in your Active Journal to take notes as you read the lesson.

PRACTICE VOCABULARY

Use the vocabulary activity in your Active Journal to practice the vocabulary words.

Vocabulary	Academic Vocabulary
ephor	authority
helot	innovation
military state	
barracks	

Life was simple in Sparta. Most decisions were made for you. If you were a Spartan boy, the state would take you from your family at the age of seven. You would spend more than 20 years training for and serving in the professional army. If you were a girl, you would be raised for the sole purpose of bearing strong children for the state.

The Spartan State: A Contrast to Athens

Other Greeks regarded Sparta with a mix of fear and admiration. In contrast to democratic Athens, Sparta felt like an army camp, its male citizens obligated to full-time military training. Its government was an odd mixture of monarchy, oligarchy, and democracy. People in city-states such as Athens were amused by Sparta's strange customs. They were also frightened by its growing power.

Government in Sparta Sparta was a city-state on the Peloponnesian Peninsula. The center of Sparta was inland, so Sparta was not a sea power. Neither was it a democracy.

PRACTICE VOCABULARY

To help students integrate new vocabulary, group the terms and introduce them. Point out that an *ephor* (a member of the Spartan assembly) and a *helot* (a forced laborer) represent levels of Spartan society. Ask students to identify similar levels of Athenian society. (*citizen; slave*) Explain that *military state* and *barracks* are related because they both relate to soldiers and warfare. Reinforce the terms during the lesson using the teaching notes.

Have students locate and pronounce the academic vocabulary in the lesson margins. Provide sample sentences that clarify meaning.

authority: In Sparta, obedience to authority was extremely important.

innovation: People who do not like change are resistant to innovation.

Sparta was ruled by two kings who served as military leaders. The kings headed Sparta's governing body, the council of elders. The council included 28 men over the age of 60. This oligarchy was the true government of Sparta.

Sparta did have a democratic assembly made up of some free adult males, but it had only about 9,000 citizens, compared to about 45,000 in Athens. The Spartan assembly also had far less power than the Athenian assembly. It could pass laws, but the council had to approve them.

However, the Spartan assembly did have one important power. It elected five ephors. An **ephor** (EH for) was responsible for the day-to-day operation of the government. The five ephors made sure that the kings and the council acted within the limits of Spartan law. Ephors could remove a king who broke the law.

Military Conquests Without the resources and trading opportunities of the sea, Sparta turned to conquest to meet its growing needs.

The Spartans conquered the neighboring city-state of Messenia. Some conquered Messenians became a kind of slave called a **helot** (HEL ut). The helots belonged not to individual Spartans but to the polis as a whole. They were forced to farm the land and turn over half the food they raised to Sparta. Helots were treated harshly.

The helots produced enough food to support the Spartans. As a result, the Spartans did not have to farm for a living. Spartan men were free to become professional warriors.

The Helot Revolts In the early 400s BCE, the helots launched a violent revolt. Although the Spartans put down the revolt, they lived in fear of further unrest. The helots outnumbered them.

The Spartans faced a choice. They could give up control of the helots and the food they produced, or they could strengthen their control by turning Sparta into a military state. A **military state** is a society organized for the purpose of waging war.

The Spartans chose the second option. Not only did they create a military society, they also tried to control the helots through terror. Every year, the ephors declared war on the helots. This gave any Spartan the right to kill any helot without fear of punishment. At the same time, secret police watched over the helots.

READING CHECK **Draw Conclusions** What did the existence of helots say about life in Sparta?

GEOGRAPHY SKILLS

Helots revolted in Messenia, next to Sparta.

1. **Place** What is Sparta's location relative to the sea?
2. **Draw Conclusions** Why might Messenia's location have made it a valuable region for Sparta to control?

Sparta and Helot Revolts

WORKSHEET **TEACHER RESOURCES**

Have students who need additional support use the following worksheets from the Teacher Resources on the course:

- **Reading Support**
- **English Language Development**
- **Lesson Summary**

INVESTIGATE

The Spartan State: A Contrast to Athens

Discuss Spartan culture. How was it different from Athens? How did the **helot** revolts affect Sparta?

Contrast What was the main difference between Athens and Sparta? *(Athens was a democracy; Sparta was an oligarchy that tightly controlled its society.)*

Identify Cause and Effect Why did Sparta rely on conquests to meet its needs? *(Its distance from the sea denied it the resources and trading opportunities of a coastal state.)*

Explain Historical Continuity Why did Sparta become a **military state**? *(After the helot revolt, the Spartans realized they were vulnerable to the more numerous helots. As a military state, Sparta could control the helots through oppression and terror.)*

ANSWERS

Place *about 25 miles*

Draw Conclusions *Messenia gave Sparta access to the Ionian Sea and control of the entire southern peninsula.*

Draw Conclusions *The helots were treated as unpaid farm laborers. This demonstrated the Spartans' indifference to human rights.*

INTEGRATED ENGLISH LANGUAGE DEVELOPMENT

Interpretive Tell students that an inference is something that can be understood without being stated directly. Tell students that they make inferences when they read. Ask what they could infer if a paragraph discussed all the armor worn by Spartans. Would they infer that the Spartans spent a lot of time fighting?

Emerging Read aloud the section Military Training in Sparta. Ask students to make inferences about what was most important to Spartan men. Model the pattern "This fact shows that..." for students and have them use it when expressing their ideas.

Expanding Ask students to make inferences about why Spartan men who failed the military test were treated by the others as "inferiors" for the rest of their lives. Model the pattern, "This

(*Continued on the next page.*)

Military Training in Sparta

Discuss Spartan military training and how it shaped Spartan culture. Also discuss the status of women.

Integrate Information Would you have wanted to live in Sparta? Why or why not? *(In favor: Students might approve of Spartan values; might appreciate the status of women. Against: Spartan culture was too strict and warlike; people had no say in government.)*

ACTIVE JOURNAL

Quick Activity After students read the material in their Active Journals, have them respond to the prompt. Ask volunteers to share their responses with the class.

INTERACTIVE

INTERACTIVE CHART

Comparing Sparta and Athens

Interactive Instruction Display the Interactive chart: Comparing Sparta and Athens for the class. Ask a volunteer to read the text on each tile and then place it in Sparta or Athens. Discuss why each tile belongs where it does.

ACTIVE CLASSROOM

Use the Write 1 – Get 3 strategy. Divide the class into "Sparta" and "Athens." Ask: "What are four words or phrases that describe your city-state?" Have students fold a piece of paper into quarters, write one response in the first box, and pass the paper to another student in their city-state, until four responses have been written. Have groups share responses with the class.

▲ A Spartan helmet, armor, and shield

Military Training in Sparta

Because of their history of conquest and their need to control the helots, Spartans valued military discipline. Even today, the adjective *spartan* means "highly disciplined or lacking in comfort." Unlike Athenians, Spartans did not value luxury goods or beautiful buildings.

Education in Sparta With the helots working the fields, Spartan males had plenty of time to train for military service. At seven, they were taken away from their homes to live together in **barracks**, or military housing.

Spartan boys did not receive a well-rounded education. They spent most of their time exercising, hunting, and training. They were taught to obey orders rather than to think for themselves. As Greek writer Plutarch wrote, "All their education was directed toward prompt obedience to **authority**, stout endurance of hardship, and victory or death in battle."

At the age of 18, young men began a two-year program of military training. During this time the trainees could marry, but they were allowed little time for a life at home. Even after the age of 30, when they left the army, they spent most of their time with other men.

Academic Vocabulary
authority • *n.*, people in power

Spartan Social Classes When they left the school system, Spartan men faced another test. In order to become full citizens, they had to gain entry to a men's club of soldiers. If they failed, they became "inferiors" who would never gain citizenship and would live as outcasts.

Men who won election to a men's club became known as "equals." They had full citizen rights. This included membership in the assembly and the right to a piece of state-owned land worked by helots. At age 60, an equal became a candidate for election to the council of elders.

Women's Unique Role in Sparta Spartan women were raised to be strong and vigorous. They participated in sports. By staying fit, they could have healthy babies who would grow into good soldiers.

Spartan women had a good deal of freedom and responsibility because their husbands spent almost their entire lives away at military camp. Spartan women were responsible for raising future soldiers for the state, so they had greater independence than women had in other Greek city-states.

Quick Activity
Compare Pericles's view of Sparta with those of another Athenian, Xenophon, in your Active Journal.

Comparing Sparta and Athens The discipline and training of Spartan life created a powerful army and a stable government. But Spartan society feared individual differences and change. The Spartans valued people who fit in, not those who stood out.

Unlike the Spartans, the Athenians valued individual expression and new ideas. Athenian democracy evolved over time. Sparta's rigid oligarchy and society changed very little. These differences led the

INTEGRATED ENGLISH LANGUAGE DEVELOPMENT continued ELD.PI.6.b

fact suggests that…" for students and have them use it when expressing their ideas.

Bridging Ask pairs of students to work together. Ask students to make inferences about why Spartans decided to get the food they lacked by conquering others, while Athenians did so by trading with other societies. Model the pattern, "This fact suggests that…" for students and have them use it when expressing their ideas.

WORKSHEET

TEACHER RESOURCES

For additional IELD support addressing these standards, have students complete the Lesson ELD activity from the Teacher Resources found on the course.

Governments of Athens and Sparta

Athens	Sparta
• Main political body is a large assembly • Members of smaller council chosen at random to serve one-year terms • Assemblies made up of free males • Large citizen-juries run court system	• Government led by two kings • Smaller and less powerful assembly than in Athens • Councils made up of free adult males • Council members elected for life • *Ephors* monitor both kings and council

Greek historian Thucydides to describe the Athenians as "addicted to **innovation**." In contrast, he viewed the Spartans as having "a genius for keeping what you have got." The opposing values of Athens and Sparta helped create tensions between the two city-states.

Economically, Sparta and Athens were very different. Because of their lack of natural resources, neither city-state was able to produce enough food to feed its growing population. Athens, however, had vast amounts of silver and relied on trade to obtain food for its citizens. Sparta relied on conquest and slave labor in the conquered territories to obtain its food. When food was scarce, the Athenians traded with others to get what they needed, while the Spartans conquered more territory.

Athenian leader Pericles believed that Athenian democracy was far superior than life in Sparta. Pericles was the leader of Athens during the Peloponnesian War against Sparta (431-404 BCE). He tried to raise morale by contrasting the two cities in his famous funeral oration.

READING CHECK **Identify Cause and Effect** How did Sparta's rigid society affect the lives of women?

Analyze Charts The Athenian and Spartan governments differed significantly. **Summarize** What is the main difference between the two?

Academic Vocabulary
innovation • *n.*, new ways of doing things

INTERACTIVE
Comparing Sparta and Athens

Lesson Check

HSS 6.4.6; ELD.PI.C.10.a

Practice Vocabulary

1. What role did an **ephor** play in Spartan government?
2. What is the purpose of **barracks**?
3. What is a **military state** like?

Critical Thinking and Writing

4. **Make Inferences** Why did Sparta become a military society?
5. **Compare Viewpoints** What might have bothered Spartans and Athenians about each other's society?
6. **Writing Workshop: Develop a Clear Thesis** How did Spartans develop their society? Begin to draft a thesis statement about the rise and peak of Greek city-states in your Active Journal.

LESSON CHECK

1. Ephors helped to keep the king and the council within the law. **DOK1**
2. to serve as military housing **DOK1**
3. A military state is a society in which life is organized around preparing for war. **DOK1**
4. Sparta became a military society in order to maintain its control over the helots and to gain resources through conquest. **DOK2**
5. Their values were different: Sparta was conservative and military; Athens was progressive and artistic. Politically, economically, and culturally, they had little in common. **DOK3**
6. Students will begin to draft a thesis statement based on the lesson content. **DOK3**

HSS 6.4.6; ELD.P1.C.10.a

SYNTHESIZE

Assess and Reteach Have students use a Numbered Heads strategy to complete Lesson Check questions 1–5. Remind students to use details from the text to support their answers. Ask volunteers to share their answers with the class.

If responses are incorrect, use the Guiding Questions to discuss the lesson's main ideas, focusing on areas of difficulty.

ACTIVE JOURNAL

Writing Workshop Have students complete the Lesson 3 Writing Task in their Active Journals. Students will respond to the question about Spartan society and begin to draft a thesis statement about the development of Greek society.

DEMONSTRATE

ASSESSMENT **ONLINE LESSON QUIZ**

Assign the Online Lesson Quiz for this lesson if you haven't already done so. Students will be offered automatic remediation or enrichment based on their score.

DISCUSSION **DISCUSSION BOARD**

Post this question to the class on the Discussion Board:

Apply Concepts Which city-state, Athens or Sparta, was better organized for long-term survival? Why? *(Accept all reasonable responses. Athens: better organized because it was a more open and adaptive society. Sparta: better organized because of its military power.)*

ANSWERS

Summarize *The main difference is who had the power in government—citizens in Athens and kings and ephors in Sparta.*

Identify Cause and Effect *Men were forced to live away from home, so women assumed their responsibilities as well as rights and freedoms they would not have enjoyed in other societies.*

HSS 6.4.1; ELA RI.6.1

Ancient Greek Society and Economic Expansion

CONNECT

GET READY TO READ

ETEXT **START UP**

Project the Start Up Activity. As students enter the classroom and get settled, have them study the photograph.

Interpret What does the image show about trade and economy in ancient Greece? Have students write their responses in their Active Journals. Ask volunteers to share their responses with the class. *(Possible responses: Sea trade was flourishing; the Greeks developed large fleets.)*

After completing the Start Up activity, project the Lesson Opener or direct students to their textbooks. Preview the lesson by working through the Get Ready to Read items with the class. Remind students to pay close attention to the Guiding Questions as they read the lesson.

ACTIVE JOURNAL

Take Notes Have students use the lesson literacy skill graphic organizer in their Active Journals to take notes as they read the lesson.

Practice Vocabulary Have students complete the activity in their Active Journals to build their vocabulary.

VIDEO **VIDEO**

Assign the lesson video as homework.

LESSON 4 HSS 6.4.1; ELA RI.6.1

Ancient Greek Society and Economic Expansion

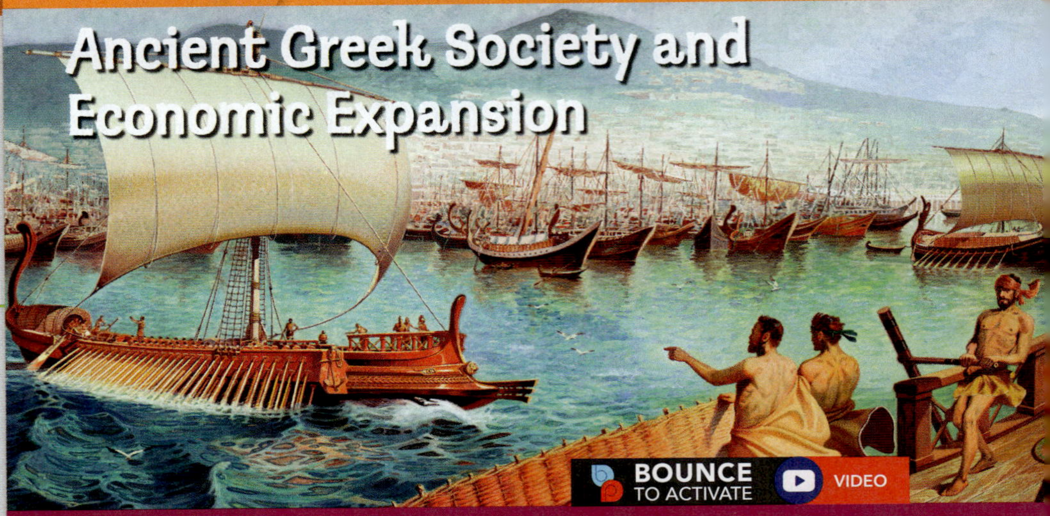

GET READY TO READ

START UP

Study the image and briefly describe what it shows about trade and the economy in ancient Greece.

GUIDING QUESTIONS

- What roles and rights did women have in the Greek city-states?
- How was Greek society organized?
- Why did the Greeks expand through trade, conquest, and colonization?
- How did the Greeks' expansion affect connections within the ancient world?

TAKE NOTES

Literacy Skills: Use Evidence

Use the graphic organizer in your Active Journal to take notes as you read the lesson.

PRACTICE VOCABULARY

Use the vocabulary activity in your Active Journal to practice the vocabulary words.

Vocabulary	Academic Vocabulary
tenant farmer	obtain
metic	symbolize
slavery	

A Greek traveler in ancient times would have felt at home in any Greek port city. Greeks spoke the same language and worshiped many of the same gods.

However, our ancient traveler might also have been startled at the differences between city-states. He or she would have observed a variety of governments, economies, and ways of organizing society.

What Was the Role of Women in Ancient Greece?

In the Greek world, women had different rights and roles, depending on the city-state. In Sparta, they had a good deal of freedom. However, in city-states such as Athens, they had few rights.

Family Life The typical Greek family consisted of husband, wife,and children. As head of the house, the man had control over his family. Poorer women worked outdoors on farms or sold goods in markets. But in city-states like Athens, women from richer families were expected to stay at home while the men took part in public life. Although

244 Lesson 6.4

PRACTICE VOCABULARY

To help students integrate new vocabulary, group the terms and introduce them. Explain that *tenant farmer* and *metic* (a resident alien) are related because they both refer to a person's place in Greek society. Similarly, *slavery* refers to the condition of people in another part of Greek society. Ask students to identify other segments of Greek society. (*aristocrat; citizen*)

Have students locate and pronounce the academic vocabulary in the lesson margins. Provide sample sentences that clarify meaning.

obtain: When Sparta needed more food, it would obtain it by conquering more territory.

symbolize: The Statue of Liberty has come to symbolize freedom.

women did play public roles in religious ceremonies, for the most part their lives were restricted. The Greek philosopher Xenophon described Greek gender roles:

Primary Source

"The gods have ordered and the law approves that men and women should each follow their own capacity. It is not so good for a woman to be out of doors as in. And it is more dishonorable for a man to stay indoors than to attend to his affairs outside."

—Xenophon, *Economics*

In most Greek homes, women supervised the household, raised the children, kept track of money and spending, and managed the slaves. Many Greek women made most or all of the clothing family members needed. They had to spin wool or flax into yarn, weave fabric, and sew or knit the clothes. Greek women also supervised the preparation of meals.

Spartan Women In Sparta, women enjoyed more rights and freedoms than did women in other city-states. Spartan women could sell their property. Like their brothers, Spartan girls were educated and trained in sports. Such Spartan customs shocked the Greeks of other city-states.

READING CHECK **Compare and Contrast** How did the lives of women in Athens and Sparta differ?

What Were the Social Divisions in Greek Society?

Ancient Greek society had a complex class system, with rich landowners at the top and slaves at the bottom. Between these two extremes were ranked the small landowners, merchants and artisans, and the landless poor of Greek society.

The Aristocracy Early city-states were controlled by aristocrats or kings. Some aristocrats claimed descent from kings or gods. They believed this gave them the right to hold political power. Their wealth came from owning large plots of land, where they raised crops and livestock. Slaves did most of the work on these estates. This left aristocrats with free time for politics and leisure activities.

Analyze Images Pottery shows a scene of women collecting water at a tap. **Identify Main Ideas** How does this piece of art reflect one of the roles women had in ancient Greece?

WORKSHEET **TEACHER RESOURCES**

Have students who need additional support use the following worksheets from the Teacher Resources on the course:

- **Reading Support**
- **English Language Development**
- **Lesson Summary**

INVESTIGATE

What Was the Role of Women in Ancient Greece?

Discuss the role of women in ancient Greece. How did it differ from city-state to city-state?

Apply Concepts Why did Sparta's customs regarding the treatment of women shock the Greeks of other city-states? *(In other city-states, women did not have as much freedom as they had in Sparta.)*

Contrast How did rich Athenian women's lives compare to poor Athenian women's lives? *(Poor Athenian women left the home to work on farms or sell goods at markets, while rich women were encouraged to stay at home as much as possible.)*

DIFFERENTIATED INSTRUCTION

Special Education Have students study the image of the women fetching water. Ask students how they obtain water at home. Discuss what things modern people have that people did not have in ancient Greece. Discuss why life might have been more difficult for women in ancient Greece.

Below Level Read the primary source quotation with the students. Ask them if they agree with what Xenophon wrote. Have student volunteers tell what they would say to Xenophon if he were present in the classroom.

Advanced Have students work in a group to create a chart showing the advantages and disadvantages of being a woman in Athens, Sparta, and in the modern United States. Have students share their chart with the class.

ANSWERS

Identify Main Ideas *It shows women doing the household task of collecting water.*

Compare and Contrast *The lives of Athenian women were restricted to the home, while Spartan women received schooling and athletic training and enjoyed property rights.*

What Were the Social Divisions in Greek Society?

Discuss the social divisions in Greek society. What rights did the people in each division have? What rights were they denied?

Identify Central Ideas What was the main difference between citizens and non-citizens? *(Citizens were completely free and had the right to participate in government. Non-citizens had limited rights; the lower they were in Greek society the fewer rights they had.)*

Integrate Information If you were living in ancient Greece and were not an aristocrat, but you could choose your place in society, what would you choose to be? Why? *(Accept all reasonable responses. Sample response: I would choose to be a citizen of a polis because I would be free and have many rights.)*

Evaluate What was the aristocrats' claim to power? *(They said they were descended from kings or gods.)* What was the real basis for their power? *(They were wealthy and controlled large plots of land.)*

ELD TIP Have English learners look at the graphic chart about Ancient Greek Society. Ask them yes/no questions to see if they understand the stratifications of class in that society, such as," Were small farmers free?" "Were women citizens?" and so forth.

Citizens and Noncitizens Society was divided between citizens (who were all adult males) and noncitizens, whose rights were limited. All citizens had the right to vote.

Farmers who owned large areas of land enjoyed a relatively high status, or rank in society. Although such landowners were rich, they made up only a minority of citizens. Many more citizens were small farmers—farmers who owned smaller plots of land. Small farmers rarely had enough land to raise livestock or produce a food surplus. On a lower social scale were tenant farmers. A **tenant farmer** was someone who paid rent, either in money or crops, to grow crops on another person's land. These tenant farmers were called *thetes*.

Merchants and artisans were often resident aliens. One of these resident aliens, called a **metic**, might be a Greek from another city-state or someone who was not Greek. Metics were noncitizens. Although they were free, they enjoyed fewer rights than the native-born men of the polis.

Slavery in Ancient Greece The lowest class in Greek society was made up of enslaved people. **Slavery** is the ownership and control of other people as property.

Enslaved people became slaves in various ways. Most were prisoners of war. Others were bought from slave traders or sold into slavery by their families. Sometimes parents who could not care for their children abandoned them. These children often become slaves. Many enslaved people in Greek city-states came from other lands. Some slaves were Greeks themselves.

Analyze Diagrams Identify the different social divisions in Greek society, using the images in the diagram.
Classify and Categorize Which three groups shown could take part in government?

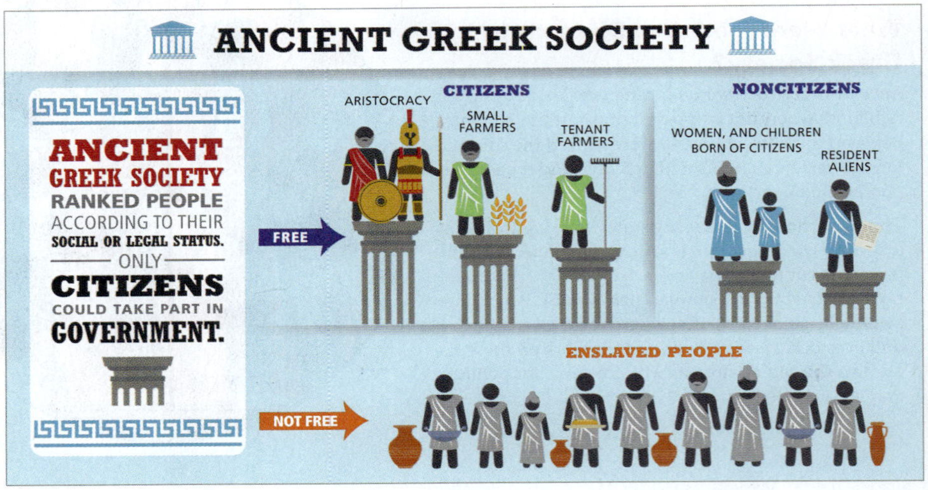

INTEGRATED ENGLISH LANGUAGE DEVELOPMENT

Interpretive Explain that there are many ways of learning the meaning of words. Context is one. Knowing about affixes is another. Write some simple words familiar to the class that have prefixes or suffixes (i.e., disagree, commitment) and ask students to explain their meanings to you.

Emerging Have students read the subsection Conquest silently. Ask them to look at the sentence with the word *obtained* in it. Ask what information in the sentence or those around it helps explain what the word means.

Expanding Read the subsection Colonization with students aloud. Have students read the sentence with the word *symbolize*. Ask students if they see an affix in the word. Ask students to think of other verbs that end in *-ize*. If they can't think of any, suggest *colonize*. Point out that sometimes

ANSWERS

Classify and Categorize *aristocracy, small farmers, and tenant farmers*

By the 500s BCE, slavery was widespread in Greece. In some city-states, enslaved people made up one third of the population. Slaves did many jobs in Greek society. Household slaves cooked, cleaned, and took care of children. Some enslaved people were teachers. Others worked on farms, ships, or in mines. Their labor helped the Greek economy grow.

Some slaves were treated kindly. A few were even freed. But slaves had no legal rights and could be punished harshly by their owners. Enslaved people were sometimes worked to death under cruel conditions.

Use Visual Information In a scene from the *Odyssey*, enslaved women do work for Odysseus's wife, Penelope. **Use Visual Information** What kind of jobs did these women have?

READING CHECK **Identify Supporting Details** What were some social divisions in ancient Greece?

The Greek Economy

As you have read, the Greeks lacked good farmland and some basic resources. When the population of Greek city-states increased, the Greeks had to find ways of feeding their people.

Conquest Some city-states **obtained** more land and resources by conquering their neighbors. Sparta, located inland on the Peloponnesian Peninsula, decided not to depend on trade for growth. Spartan troops conquered the neighboring city-state of Messenia and turned its conquered people into non-free laborers. The Messenians were forced to raise crops for the Spartans.

Academic Vocabulary
obtained • *v.*, gained

This captive workforce freed Spartan men from their farming chores. So the Spartans were able to form a professional army that was the most feared in Greece. By the mid-500s BCE, Sparta controlled most of the Peloponnesian Peninsula.

Colonization Migration—moving to a new area—was another solution to the population problem. Beginning in the 700s BCE, new waves of Greek colonists sailed off to find new places to settle. Leaving home was not an easy decision. Colonists faced danger and uncertainty on the voyage and the challenge of building new homes. As historian Donald Kagan notes, "Only powerful pressures like overpopulation and land hunger" drove people to take such risks.

The ideal site for a colony was on the coast. There, the settlers could anchor their ships. They could also set up a port for trading with other ports. The best spot would have good land for farming. It needed to be near important resources such as timber or minerals that could be exported. Homer described the founding of a fictional colony:

Recall How did most enslaved people in Greece become slaves? *(They were prisoners of war.)*

Draw Conclusions What does this suggest about how the ancient Greeks regarded their defeated enemies? *(They were the spoils of war and were considered to be the property of the victor.)*

The Greek Economy

Discuss the Greek economy. How did economic issues spur the establishment of new colonies? How did colonization affect Greek culture?

Identify Cause and Effect What was a major factor that drove the Greeks to establish new colonies? *(the need to feed increasing populations)*

Identify Implied Ideas What was one reason Sparta did not turn to trade for growth? *(It was inland, and so was unable to use the sea for trading.)*

Synthesize Information Aside from danger and the possibility of faiure, what aspect of Greek culture might have kept potential colonists from seeking a new place to live? *(Greeks were very tied to their polis. Not wanting to leave their city-state might have been reason enough to remain home.)*

ELD.PI.B.6.c

parts of the root word (such as the *y* in *colony*) are cut off before the suffix is added on.

Bridging Have students read the entire section The Greek Economy silently. Tell them to look for words with affixes, such as *overpopulation*. Help them identify the affix *over*. Then ask them to tell you what the sentences around *overpopulation* tell them about the meaning of the word.

WORKSHEET **TEACHER RESOURCES**

For additional IELD support addressing the standard, have students complete the Lesson ELD activity from the Teacher Resources found on the course.

ANSWERS

Use Visual Information *They assisted in the task of spinning as well as other domestic activities, such as fetching water..*

Identify Supporting Details *Greek society included landowners, tenant farmers, metics, and slaves; men and women; citizens and noncitizens.*

INTERACTIVE **INTERACTIVE MAP**

Expansion and Trade in the Greek World

Interactive Instruction Display the Interactive Map: Expansion and Trade in the Greek World. Work through the interactive to learn more about Greek trade. Have volunteers read the text. Discuss ways that trade influenced Greek civilization. *(Trade exposed Greeks to different cultures from which they learned, such as the Minoans and the Egyptians. It also served as motivation to extend Greek settlement in the Mediterranean.)*

ACTIVE CLASSROOM

Use the Connect Two strategy. Select 10 to 12 words or phrases related to the information in the interactive. List the words on the board for students to copy on small pieces of paper. Read the list of words with students. Ask students to "connect two" or choose two words or phrases they think belong together, and state the reason. ("I connect ______ and ______ because.")

Primary Source

"So [the founder] led them away, settling them in [a place called] Scheria, far from the bustle of men. He had a wall constructed around the town center, built houses, erected temples for the gods, and divided the land."

—Homer, the *Odyssey*

Academic Vocabulary
symbolized • *v.*, represented

Greek colonists brought a flame from home to light fires in the new colony. This flame **symbolized** their ties to their old city-state. They often traded with the home city. But most colonists never returned home. They made new lives in their new city-state.

By the 500s BCE, there were hundreds of Greek colonies around the Mediterranean Sea and the Black Sea. They stretched from the shores of what is now Russia all the way west to Spain.

Currency Trade led to an important new development. Around 650 BCE, the kings of Lydia began making the world's first gold and silver coins. Lydia was in Anatolia (also called Asia Minor, in present-day Turkey), near the city-states of Ionia. Using coins led to a kind of economic revolution. Coins of standard size and value gradually replaced the old bartering system, in which some goods would

GEOGRAPHY SKILLS

Greeks took advantage of their location on the water to trade with other lands.

1. **Interaction** How did Greek traders interact with the people who lived along the Black Sea?
2. **Draw Conclusions** How might the city-states of Athens and Sparta have focused on different regions when trading?

Trade Routes of Ancient Greece

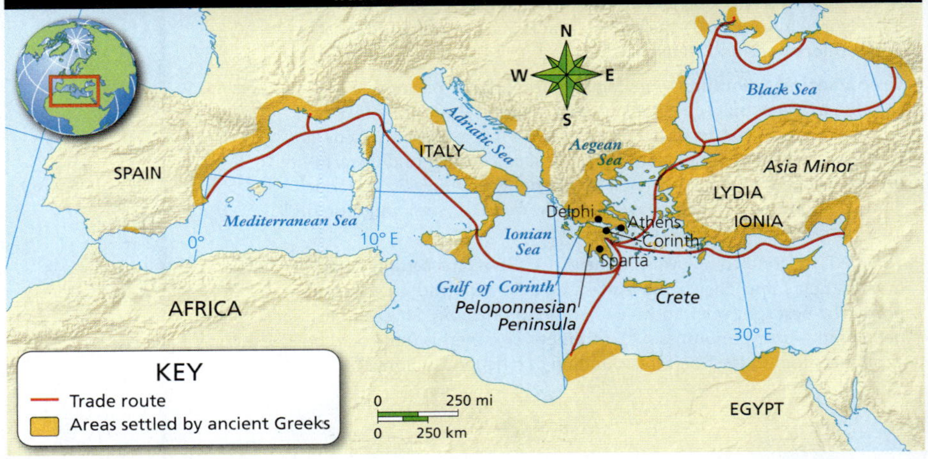

HISTORY BACKGROUND

Colonization and Trade Greek colonies served as trading outposts for their city-states. Colonists looked for locations where traders could easily come and go. Many early colonies were established near the end of an inland trade route. Desirable areas also had metals, fish, or game for trading. The Greeks' armor and organization gave Greek colonists an advantage over native people who might already be living in an area they wished to colonize. Greek colonies traded local goods for products from their original homeland. The ceramic arts flourished as a result of growing trade. Trade also spread Greek culture.

ANSWERS

Interaction *Athenians came to rely on grain shipped from Black Sea ports. To pay for the grain, they traded silver, pottery, jewelry, and other goods.*

Draw Conclusions *Athens would have traded with regions it could reach by ship; Sparta would have traded with regions its traders could reach by land routes.*

be traded for other goods. These coins were used as currency, a way of exchanging value. Thanks to the use of coins, trade became easier.

Greeks learned about coins from trading with Lydia. Several city-states set up their own mints, or places where coins are made. Each city-state stamped its coins with symbols of the city or an image of the god or goddess who protected the city. The coins of Athens, for instance, were marked with an owl. This bird was associated with Athena, the goddess for whom Athens was named.

▲ Athenian coins

Trade in Athens Trade made the city-state of Athens rich. Athens had very little farmland, so it relied on commerce to meet the need for food and other resources. Athenians founded colonies around the Black Sea, on the coast of North Africa, and in other regions. They came to rely on grain that was shipped from ports on the Black Sea. They traded silver for much-needed food.

To pay for the grain, Athenian workshops also produced pottery, jewelry, and other trade goods. These products, along with olive oil and wine, were also shipped to other lands. Ships returned to Athens with timber, minerals, and luxury goods such as ivory, glass, and perfume. Streets and markets bustled with activity.

The Effects of Expansion Greek colonization affected both trade and culture. Just as colonization spread Greek culture and goods across the Mediterranean world, it also drew new customs and ideas back to Greece. As a result, cultural borrowing increased throughout the Mediterranean region. The Greek alphabet was likely influenced by the Phoenician alphabet. Stories of Egyptian gods and goddesses mingled with the stories of Greek mythology, with some Greeks choosing to worship Egypt's deities as well.

The establishment of colonies had economic effects on Greece. Many colonies became successful through active trade with Greece. They also introduced Greeks to new goods from foreign lands.

INTERACTIVE

Expansion and Trade in the Greek World

READING CHECK **Identify Supporting Details** How did Greek city-states gain needed resources when their populations grew?

Lesson Check

HSS 6.4.1; ELA RI.6.1; ELD.PI.C.10.a

Practice Vocabulary

1. How would a **tenant farmer** earn his living?
2. What was the difference between a citizen, a **metic**, and a slave?

Critical Thinking and Writing

3. **Make Inferences** Why did the physical geography of Greece encourage colonization?
4. **Draw Conclusions** How did the adoption of coins help increase Greek wealth?
5. **Writing Workshop: Support Thesis with Details** How did ancient Greece's society and economy affect the rise and peak of the independent city-states? Collect details to support your thesis in your Active Journal.

LESSON CHECK

1. A tenant farmer would work on a landowner's estate. **DOK1**
2. A slave was not free. Citizens and metics were both free, but a metic did not have as many rights as a citizen. **DOK1**
3. Because mainland Greeks could not grow enough food, they searched for other places to trade for or grow food. Many early colonies were established near the end of inland trade routes. Colonies were often founded on a coast where ships could be easily anchored. **DOK2**
4. Silver and gold coins replaced the old bartering systems. As a result, trade became easier and wealth increased. **DOK3**
5. Students will use content from the lesson to support their thesis statements. **DOK3**

HSS 6.4.1; ELA RI.6.1; ELD P1.C.10.a

SYNTHESIZE

Assess and Reteach Have students use a Give One, Get One strategy to complete Lesson Check questions 1–4. Remind students to use details from the text to support their answers. Ask volunteers to share their answers with the class.

If responses are incorrect, use the Guiding Questions to revisit the lesson's main ideas, focusing on ideas that are causing difficulty.

ACTIVE JOURNAL

Writing Workshop Have students complete the Lesson 4 Writing Task in their Active Journals. Students will collect details from the lesson to support their thesis statements about how ancient Greece's society and economy affected the rise and peak of the city-states.

DEMONSTRATE

ASSESSMENT **ONLINE LESSON QUIZ**

Assign the Online Lesson Quiz for this lesson if you haven't already done so. Students will be offered automatic remediation or enrichment based on their score.

DISCUSSION **DISCUSSION BOARD**

Post this question to the class on the Discussion Board:

Synthesize Do you think the cultures and values of ancient Greece served it well? Why or why not? *(Possible response: Greek culture and values enabled them to face challenges imposed by the geography of the region. They responded to those challenges in ways that allowed their culture to thrive and influence the world for thousands of years.)*

ANSWERS

Identify Supporting Details *They gained resources through conquest and colonization or through trade.*

HSS 6.4.2, 6.4.6

Warfare in Ancient Greece

CONNECT

GET READY TO READ

ETEXT **START UP**

Project the Start Up Activity. As students enter the classroom and get settled, have them study the photograph. Explain that this is a model of an ancient Greek warship.

Synthesize Visual Information Why would the ancient Greeks have needed to develop a strong navy in order to fight with other nations? *(Crossing large bodies of water was the most direct way to attack other nations. If they did not have a strong navy, they would be unable to wage war as successfully.)*

Draw Conclusions What features of this ship suggest that the Greek navy was a powerful one? *(It is large and apparently carries a large number of people. By using both oars and wind power, it would be able to sail swiftly.)*

After completing the Start Up activity, project the Lesson Opener or direct students to their textbooks. Preview the lesson by working through the Get Ready to Read items with the class. Remind students to pay close attention to the Guiding Questions as they read the lesson.

ACTIVE JOURNAL

Take Notes Have students use the lesson literacy skill graphic organizer in their Active Journals to take notes as the read the lesson.

Practice Vocabulary Have students complete the activity in their Active Journals to build their vocabulary.

VIDEO **VIDEO**

Assign the lesson video as homework.

HSS 6.4.2, 6.4.6

Warfare in Ancient Greece

BOUNCE TO ACTIVATE VIDEO

GET READY TO READ

START UP

The boat pictured is a model of an ancient Greek warship. Why would the ancient Greeks have needed to develop a strong navy in order to fight with other nations?

GUIDING QUESTIONS

- How did the Greek city-states defeat the mighty Persian empire?
- What role did Athens take after the Persian Wars?
- What were the causes and effects of the Peloponnesian War?

TAKE NOTES

Literacy Skills: Compare and Contrast

Use the graphic organizer in your Active Journal to take notes as you read the lesson.

PRACTICE VOCABULARY

Use the vocabulary activity in your Active Journal to practice the vocabulary words.

Vocabulary	Academic Vocabulary
Battle of Marathon	pursue
Battle of Salamis	ally
Delian League	
Peloponnesian League	

Warfare was frequent in ancient Greece. The quarrelsome city-states battled one another over land and resources. In addition to all their minor conflicts, the Greeks fought three major wars in the 400s BCE. Twice they united long enough to defeat the Persian empire.

The Persian Wars

After 546 BCE., Persia conquered the Greek city-states of Ionia in western Asia. The Ionian city-states were used to governing themselves, so they rebelled in 500 BCE. To help them, Athenian soldiers burned the Persian city of Sardis. This enraged Darius, the Persian king. After his troops recaptured the Ionian cities, Darius set out to conquer the rest of Greece.

War and conquest were second nature to the Persians. They established a vast empire after defeating Babylon in 539 BCE. The Persians eventually controlled a vast territory from Anatolia to India. Although it was the greatest empire of its time, Persia's rulers had a difficult time defeating the Greeks on their home soil.

PRACTICE VOCABULARY

To help students integrate new vocabulary, group the terms and introduce them. Explain that the *Battle of Marathon* and the *Battle of Salamis* are related in two ways. They are both important battles fought by the ancient Greeks. Explain that *Delian League* and *Peloponnesian League* are related because they were both military alliances of Greek city-states. Ask students to explain what a military alliance is. *(An agreement among nations to help one another in times of war.)*

Have students locate and pronounce the academic vocabulary in the lesson margins. Provide sample sentences that clarify meaning.

pursue: Xerxes ordered his navy to pursue the Greek ships in an effort to catch them.

ally: A nation might need an ally to help fight a war.

The Battle of Marathon In 490 BCE, about 20,000 Persian soldiers sailed for Greece. They landed by the plain of Marathon, near Athens. Athenian soldiers rushed to Marathon, but they were outnumbered by about two to one. Also, unlike the Persians, they had no archers or soldiers on horseback.

Despite these disadvantages, the Athenians attacked the day after the Persian landing. At dawn, Greek phalanxes raced across the plain, taking the Persians by surprise. In panic, the Persians fled to their ships. The unexpected Greek victory at the **Battle of Marathon** ended the First Persian War. In ancient times, a legend told of a messenger who died after running 26 miles to carry the news of the victory back to Athens. Ever since then, the word "marathon" has been used to describe a challenging footrace.

The Second Persian War Darius died before he could launch another attack. But his son, Xerxes (ZURK seez), was determined to defeat the Greeks and began the Second Persian War.

In 480 BCE, Xerxes assembled an invasion force of about 100,000 men. The Persian empire was the superpower of its day. Because it controlled Egypt, Persia was able to add the Egyptian army to its ranks. Although the Persians did not have a navy, they used the ships of the Phoenicians, who were part of their empire.

The Spartans moved north to block the huge army. Led by King Leonidas, a small Spartan force stopped the Persians at a narrow mountain pass called Thermopylae (thur MAHP uh lee). The Spartans held off the invaders for days. Then, a Greek traitor showed the Persians another path through the mountains. Attacked from both sides, the Spartans died heroically, in defense of Greece.

Analyze Images Athenians and Persians do battle at the Battle of Marathon. **Use Visual Information** What mood was the artist trying to convey about this battle?

WORKSHEET **TEACHER RESOURCES**

Have students who need additional support use the following worksheets from the Teacher Resources on the course:

- **Reading Support**
- **English Language Development**
- **Lesson Summary**

INVESTIGATE

The Persian Wars

Discuss the origin of the Persian Wars. How did the Greeks defeat the Persians in both wars?

Identify Cause and Effect What was the cause of the first Persian War? *(The Persian king, Darius, decided to conquer Greece because Athens had burned the Persian city of Sardis.)*

Identify Main Ideas How were the Greeks able to defeat the superior Persian force at the Battle of Marathon? *(They caught the Persians by surprise.)*

Identify Cause and Effect What was the cause of the second Persian War? *(Darius's invasion of Greece had failed, but his son, Xerxes, who became king, was still determined to conquer Greece.)*

INTERACTIVE **PRIMARY SOURCE**

Have students go online to analyze the Interactive Primary Source Herodotus, *The Persian Wars*. Then ask: How does Herodotus' account add to your picture of the Battle of Thermopylae? *(Possible answer: It adds more detail and drama to the story told in the student text.)*

DIFFERENTIATED INSTRUCTION

Special Education Discuss the word *marathon* with students. Ask if they have ever heard of a modern footrace called a marathon. Point out the section of text that mentions where this is mentioned. Explain that modern marathons in which people compete in 26.2-mile races are held in many cities.

Below Level Have students discuss the image of the battle on this page. What conclusions can they draw about war in ancient Greece. Ask how they think a soldier in such a battle might feel about his experience.

Advanced Have students research online or in a library for the account by Herodotus of the Battle of Marathon. Have them share parts Herodotus' account with the class.

ANSWERS

Use Visual Information *chaos, fury, desperation, intense destruction*

Identify Main Ideas How were the Greeks able to defeat the superior Persian naval force at the Battle of Salamis? *(They kept their ships hidden until the huge Persian navy filled a narrow body of water; then they rammed the Persian ships, breaking them up.)*

Compare and Contrast What was similar about Greek military strategy at Thermopylae and Salamis? *(Facing overwhelming numbers, they used geography—a narrow mountain pass; a narrow body of water—to their advantage.)*

INTERACTIVE **INTERACTIVE MAP**

Persian Wars

Display the Interactive Map: Persian Wars, 490 BCE–479 BCE for the class.

Interactive Instruction Display the Interactive Map: Persian Wars, 490 BCE–479 BCE for the class. Have a volunteer read the drop down text. Click through the interactive in this order: Sardis, Sparta, Marathon, Thermopylae, Athens, Salamis. Ask: What was different about how the Greek city-states acted during the war? *(Instead of fighting with one another, they formed an alliance to resist the Persians.)*

ACTIVE CLASSROOM

Use the Make Headlines strategy. Have students choose one of the hotspots and write a newspaper headline about that event. Ask volunteers to share their headlines with the class.

ANSWERS

Movement *Salamis*

Draw Conclusions *He had to defeat both Sparta and Athens, and their forces were in two different places.*

Identify Cause and Effect *He failed to spot the trap and allowed his ships to fall into it.*

Persian Wars, 490 BCE–479 BCE

GEOGRAPHY SKILLS

Xerxes sent his army and navy to attack Greece after Athenians burned down the city of Sardis.

1. **Movement** Where was the last battle for the Persians?
2. **Draw Conclusions** Why did it make sense for Xerxes to send his army and navy in two different directions?

The Greek historian Herodotus recorded the events:

Primary Source

"King Xerxes pitched his camp in the region of Malis called Trachinia, while on their side the Greeks occupied the straits . . . . [T]he Greeks in general call Thermopylae (the Hot Gates) . . . . Here then the two armies took their stand. . . ."

—Herodotus, *The Histories*

Victory for Athens The Persians advanced on Athens. The Athenian leader Themistocles (thuh MIS tuh kleez) convinced Athenians to flee to nearby islands. When the Persians reached Athens, they found the city almost empty.

Xerxes burned Athens and sent his ships to **pursue** the Greek navy. Confident of victory, Xerxes had his throne placed on a hill to watch the naval battle in the Strait of Salamis.

Academic Vocabulary
pursue • *v.*, to chase

But Themistocles had set a trap. He kept his Greek ships hidden until Persian ships filled the narrow strait. Suddenly, the Greeks attacked. They rammed the crowded Persian ships, splintering their hulls. By nightfall, the strait was clogged with more than 200 broken Persian ships. The Greeks lost only about 40 ships. The **Battle of Salamis** broke Persian naval power. After another defeat for Xerxes on land, the Persians returned home.

INTERACTIVE
Persian Wars

READING CHECK **Identify Cause and Effect** How did Xerxes' over-confidence lead to a Persian defeat?

INTEGRATED ENGLISH LANGUAGE DEVELOPMENT

Interpretive Explain that writers use specific language to support their ideas and arguments in a text. Read aloud the section "Why Were Athens and Sparta Rivals?" Ask students to listen carefully for vocabulary words that they believe helped the author answer this question.

Emerging Reread the section Why Were Athens and Sparta Rivals? Have students raise their hands when you come to a sentence that gives a reason why the two city-states were rivals. Make sure that students understand the meaning of the words *rivals*, *allies*, and *league*. Discuss how these words affect their understanding of the conflict between Athens and Sparta.

Expanding Have students work in pairs to ask and answer questions about the role of both city-states in the rivalry.

Why Were Athens and Sparta Rivals?

After defeating the Persians at Salamis, Athens enjoyed a "golden age." The Athenian leader Pericles began rebuilding the city, which became famous for its art and learning. The wealth and power of the city grew.

However, trouble was brewing. Greece now had two rival powers—Athens, with the strongest navy, and Sparta, with the strongest army. Each wanted to be the supreme power in Greece. Their rivalry would lead to deadly conflict.

Athens's Alliance Soon after the Persian wars, Athens formed an alliance with other city-states. An alliance is an association of nations formed to achieve a goal. Because Athens and its **allies** met together on the island of Delos, their alliance was called the **Delian League**. Members promised to protect one another from Persia and provide ships or money for defense. This money was kept in the League's treasury on Delos.

Academic Vocabulary
ally • *n.*, member of an alliance

The Delian League had about 150 members. All of the allies were supposed to be equal. However, Athens was by far the most powerful member. Athenian ships protected Greek traders and travelers. By building an alliance of city-states that bordered the Aegean Sea, Athens was able to protect its grain supply.

Athens ran the Delian League as if it were its own empire rather than an alliance of equals. The Athenians brought some cities into the League by force and blocked others from leaving. When Naxos tried to leave, Athens attacked the city-state and forced it to stay.

▼ A Greek military helmet

The arrogant behavior of the Athenians angered other League members. Rather than asking city-states to contribute ships, Athens requested money. Athens used the money to build its navy. It continued to collect these funds even when there was no fighting with Persia. Athens also forced League members to use Athenian currency instead of their own.

In 454 BCE, Athenian leaders moved the League's treasury from Delos to Athens. Soon after, money from League members was used to rebuild Athens. Some of this money went to constructing the Parthenon, the great temple to Athena that stood on the Acropolis. Other members of the Delian League came to resent this use of the League's funds.

Sparta's Alliance The Spartans had already formed their own alliance on the Peloponnesian Peninsula. It is known today as the **Peloponnesian League**. Like Sparta, other members of the Peloponnesian League feared the power of Athens and its style of government. In contrast to democratic Athens, Sparta and most of its allies were oligarchies.

In 433 BCE, Sparta's Peloponnesian League and Athens's Delian League came into conflict. That year, Athens placed a ban on trade with Megara, a member of the

Why Were Athens and Sparta Rivals?

Discuss the rivalry between Athens and Sparta. Why were they rivals? How did each city-state respond to the threat it felt from the other?

Compare and Contrast What was the main difference between the military power of Athens and the military power of Sparta? *(Athens had the stronger navy; Sparta had the stronger army.)*

Identify Main Ideas Why was the **Delian League** an alliance more in name than in practice? *(Athens dominated the league and ran it more like an empire than a true alliance among equals).*

Use Evidence Give two examples that support this response. *(Possible responses: Athens forced cities to join or remain in the league; it forced league members to use Athenian currency; it made city-states contribute money to the league and used that money to increase its own navy and to rebuild Athens.)*

ELD TIP English learners may struggle with pronunciation of words that have more syllables or different concentrations or clusters of consonants than are present in their language of origin. Check in with ELL students to make sure they can pronounce proper names such as *Peloponnesian* and *Xerxes*.

ELD.PI.B.7

Bridging Ask students why the words *allies, rivals,* and *league* are important in discussing a war. Discuss whether the writer of this section could have explained the conflict between Athens and Sparta without using these words.

WORKSHEET **TEACHER RESOURCES**

For additional IELD support addressing the standard, have students complete the Lesson ELD activity from the Teacher Resources found on the course.

Compare What was similar about the reasons why the **Delian League** and the **Peloponnesian League** were formed? *(They were formed for the same reason: Athens and Sparta feared each other.)*

The Peloponnesian War

Discuss the Peloponnesian War. Why was it fought? What factors led to Athens' eventual defeat?

Identify Cause and Effect Why did the Peloponnesian War last so long? *(Because of Athens' strong navy and Sparta's strong army, neither side could defeat the other.)*

Identify Cause and Effect What action by Athens laid the groundwork for its eventual defeat? *(Athens invaded Sicily and lost a large part of its fleet.)*

Recognize Multiple Causes What other factor led to Athens' defeat? *(Persia helped Sparta rebuild its navy, making Sparta stronger than Athens at sea.)*

Understand Effects What finally led to the downfall of Greece? *(The Greek city-states grew weaker because they kept fighting one another; this enabled Macedonia to conquer Greece.)*

Peloponnesian League. This angered Sparta and its allies, who prepared for war. Athens and its allies did the same. Both sides were confident of a quick and easy victory.

READING CHECK **Identify Cause and Effect** Why did Athens form the Delian League?

The Peloponnesian War

War between the two Greek alliances broke out in 431 BCE. Known as the Peloponnesian War, the conflict lasted on and off for 27 years.

Sparta's Siege of Athens The Peloponnesian War began when an army led by Sparta marched into Athenian territory. Pericles, the leader of Athens, instructed farmers living in the Athenian countryside to move inside the walled city for safety.

The Spartans settled down around Athens for a long siege. The goal of a siege is to force the enemy to surrender by cutting off its food and other supplies. Athenians had prepared for just such an event, however. They had built two long walls to line the four-mile road that connected Athens to its port city. While these long walls stood, Athenians could receive supplies by sea.

Supplied with food by ship, the Athenians held out for more than a year. Then, a plague, or contagious disease, broke out in the overcrowded city. Thousands of people died in Athens.

However, the war dragged on. Sparta, with its powerful army, and Athens, with its strong navy, found it difficult

GEOGRAPHY SKILLS

The Peloponnesian War was fought between Athens and Sparta.

1. **Place** Where were Sparta and its allies located? Where was the Athenian empire located?
2. **Draw Conclusions** Why would a defeat in a location like Aegospotami be so damaging to the Athenian economy?

ANSWERS

Identify Cause and Effect *The original purpose was to help prevent or stop another Persian invasion of Greece; Athens gradually began to impose its will on other members and to use league funds for Athens's own end.*

Place *Sparta and its allies were located mostly in Macedonia and the Peloponnesian Peninsula. The Athenian empire was located mostly along the coasts and islands of the Aegean.*

Draw Conclusions *Aegospotami was an important port on Athens's grain-supply route.*

HISTORY BACKGROUND

The Sacred Band of Thebes Although Sparta had won the Peloponnesian War, its dominant position among the city-states did not last. A few decades later, in 375 BCE, a Spartan army was defeated by a Theban force that included the Sacred Band of Thebes—an elite fighting unit of 150 same-sex couples. Then in 371 BCE, the Sacred Band helped Thebes administer a crushing defeat to Sparta in the Battle of Leuctra, which ended two centuries of Spartan military supremacy. The concept of a fighting force of same-sex couples was much discussed by ancient writers, including Plato, who speculated in his *Symposium* about an army of lovers whose loyalty to one another would make them invincible as fighters.

254 Lesson 6.5 • Warfare in Ancient Greece

to defeat each other. In 421 BCE, both sides agreed to a truce, or an agreement to stop fighting, while they discussed peace terms.

Athens Surrenders Within a few years, however, the truce was broken. Athens launched an invasion of Sicily. With help from Sparta, the Greeks of Sicily destroyed the Athenian forces. Athens lost a large part of its navy at Syracuse.

Athens was now desperately weakened. The Persians saw a chance to deal Athens a fatal blow. They gave money to Sparta so it could build its own powerful navy. With this new fleet, Sparta defeated the Athenian navy at the Battle of Aegospotami in 404 BCE. After that, the Spartans attacked Athens itself.

Once again, the Athenians resisted. But with its new navy, Sparta was able to keep food from reaching Athens by sea. The following year, Athens was forced to surrender.

The peace terms were harsh. Sparta even made the Athenians give up their democratic government. Although democracy was soon restored, Athens had lost its power.

Analyze Images The Spartans settle around Athens for a siege. **Identify Main Ideas** How does surrounding a city like this weaken an opponent?

The Peloponnesian War hurt all the city-states, bringing Athens to its knees and ending the golden age of Greece. Throughout the 300s, the Greeks persisted in fighting amongst themselves. The constant fighting among city-states opened the door to the military conquest of Greece by Macedonia, a powerful kingdom to the north. As you will read, Macedonian rulers united the Greek city-states by force. After a rich period of democracy, Athenians were back to living under one powerful ruler.

READING CHECK **Identify Cause and Effect** Why did Athens lose the Peloponnesian War?

Lesson Check

HSS 6.4.2, 6.4.6; ELD.PI.C.10.a

Practice Vocabulary

1. Who fought at the **Battle of Marathon** and the **Battle of Salamis**?
2. What groups made up the **Delian League** and the **Peloponnesian League**?

Critical Thinking and Writing

3. **Compare Viewpoints** Why did other Greek city-states resent Athens's power?
4. **Draw Conclusions** Why was it so difficult for Athens and Sparta to defeat each other?
5. **Writing Workshop: Update Your Thesis** What does the information about conflict in ancient Greece tell you about the downfall of the independent Greek city-states? Update your thesis with new information in your Active Journal.

LESSON CHECK

1. The Greeks and the Persians fought the Battles of Marathon and Salamis. **DOK1**
2. Athens and its allies made up the Delian League; Sparta and its allies made up the Peloponnesian League. **DOK1**
3. Athens used the Delian League and its great power for its own purposes. **DOK3**
4. They were evenly matched, but strong in different ways. **DOK3**
5. Students will update their thesis on the basis of content in the lesson. **DOK3**

HSS 6.4.2, 6.4.6; ELD.P1.C.10.a

SYNTHESIZE

Assess and Reteach Have students use a Think-Pair-Share strategy to complete Lesson Check questions 1–4. Ask volunteers to share their answers with the class.

If responses are incorrect, use the Guiding Questions to revisit the lesson's main ideas, focusing on ideas that are causing difficulty.

ACTIVE JOURNAL

Writing Workshop Have students complete the Lesson 5 Writing Task in their Active Journals. Students will add details about the decline of the independent Greek city-states from the lesson to support their thesis statement, and consider the best way to write their essays.

DEMONSTRATE

ASSESSMENT **ONLINE LESSON QUIZ**

Assign the Online Lesson Quiz for this lesson if you haven't already done so. Students will be offered automatic remediation or enrichment based on their score.

DISCUSSION **DISCUSSION BOARD**

Post this question to the class on the Discussion Board:

Synthesize Do you think ancient Greek civilization could have lasted longer if the Greeks had behaved differently? *(Possible response: Ancient Greece could have lasted longer if the Greeks had not weakened themselves by fighting each other.)*

ANSWERS

Identify Main Ideas *The people in the city are unable to get food, water, and other supplies.*

Identify Cause and Effect *Persia outfitted Sparta with a new navy that defeated the navy of Athens.*

Analysis RE.5, ELA RI.6.9

Analysis Skills
Compare Different Points of View

LEARN

Preview the steps in the student text with students, and then play the video.

VIDEO **21ST CENTURY SKILLS**

Project the Compare Viewpoints video in the 21st Century Skills Tutorial. Use the Quick Reference and Assessment to provide additional instruction in this skill.

PRACTICE

Have students practice the skill of comparing viewpoints by reading the two primary source excerpts on the student page. Follow the steps on the student page and provide instruction. Ask students to answer the questions.

As an alternative, you might wish to form students into pairs or small groups to discuss the points of view in the inscription and in Herodotus' history. Suggest that students list and compare the words used to describe Darius.

ASSESS

To assess this skill, have students reread The Unification of China in the previous topic. Ask them to compare Shi Huangdi's view of himself and the viewpoint of history.

ANSWERS

1. *The first passage proclaims Darius I's greatness. The second is an evaluation of Darius by a Greek historian.*
2. The first source describes Darius as a great kings. The second views him as a petty, greedy ruler.
3. The first came from an inscription in Darius' palace. The second came from a Greek historian.
4. Herodotus was from Greece, Persia's enemy. The person who wrote the inscription was a most likely a subject of Darius'.

Analysis RE.5, ELA RI.6.9

Compare Different Points of View

Follow these steps to detect historical points of view.

INTERACTIVE
Compare Viewpoints

1 Identify the topic or issue. The first source is an inscription on a monument in Persepolis, one of Persia's ancient capitals. The monument shows tribute bearers bringing tribute to Persian king Darius I. The second source was written by Greek historian Herodotus. He wrote about how he viewed Darius I. What is the main idea of each passage?

2 Determine the author's position on the topic or issue. What is each author's position on the subject? Sometimes an author will state his or her overall point of view in a topic sentence. Other times the point of view is expressed over a whole passage or work. How do the two sources describe Darius I differently?

3 Identify important background information about the passage. Identifying facts such as the author's background and the time and place in which the author lived can prove valuable when analyzing a historical point of view. Where did the authors of the following pieces of text come from?

4 Analyze possible impact of historical background on the author's beliefs. People's beliefs and opinions may be influenced by what is happening in the world around them—the context.

a. How does the inscription show the Persian point of view?

b. How did Herodotus' background as a affect his point of view of Darius I?

Primary Source

"I am Darius the great king, king of kings, king of countries containing all kinds of men, king on this great earth far and wide. . . . If now you shall think that 'How many are the countries which King Darius held?' look at the sculptures (of those) who bear the throne. . . ."

—Inscription on the stairs of Apandana at Persepolis

Primary Source

"[Darius I] divided his dominions into twenty provinces, which they call satrapies; and having divided his dominions and appointed governors, he instructed each people to pay him tribute....It is because of this fixing of tribute, and other similar ordinances, that the Persians called Darius the merchant, Cambyses the master, and Cyrus the father; for Darius made petty profit out of everything, Cambyses was harsh and arrogant, Cyrus was merciful and always worked for their well-being."

—Herodotus, Greek historian

DIFFERENTIATED INSTRUCTION

Advanced Have students do research in the library or online to find examples of the way Herodotus described other leaders, both Greek and non-Greek. Have students evaluate Herodotus' impartiality. Ask students to share their conclusions with the class.

INTEGRATED ENGLISH LANGUAGE DEVELOPMENT

Bridging Have students turn to a partner to determine the relationship between the two primary source quotes. What does each quote tell them about King Darius? Which quote seems more honest, and why?

HSS 6.4.4, 6.4.8; ELA RI.6.7

Ancient Greek Beliefs and Arts

BOUNCE TO ACTIVATE

VIDEO

GET READY TO READ

START UP

The image shows a scene from a Greek myth in which dangerous creatures called sirens tempted sailors into shipwrecks with their loud singing. What myths have you learned in school?

GUIDING QUESTIONS

- What effect did religion and mythology have on Greek people and their society?
- In what ways have Greek art and architecture remained influential today?
- How does Greek literature continue to influence our literature and language today?

TAKE NOTES

Literacy Skills: Synthesize Visual Information

Use the graphic organizer in your Active Journal to take notes as you read the lesson.

PRACTICE VOCABULARY

Use the vocabulary activity in your Active Journal to practice the vocabulary words.

Vocabulary		Academic Vocabulary
polytheism	lyric poetry	cease
mythology	chorus	submission
Olympic games		

Greek children grew up hearing many stories about their gods. In one tale, a proud girl named Arachne boasts that her weaving skills are better than those of the goddess Athena. Athena challenges Arachne to a weaving competition. When Arachne creates a tapestry, or cloth with pictures, that mocks the gods, Athena is furious. The goddess changes the girl into a spider, condemned to weave webs forever. The Greeks told the story of Arachne as a warning against the sin of excessive pride.

Greek Religion and Mythology

The ancient Greeks practiced **polytheism**, the worship of many gods, or deities. A deity is a being with supernatural powers. Unlike the gods of Egypt, however, Greek gods were believed to look and behave like human beings. They were portrayed as human-like in art and literature.

What Was Greek Mythology? Greeks expressed their religious beliefs in their mythology. **Mythology** is the collection of myths or stories that people tell about their gods and heroes. These rich and powerful tales influenced all forms of literature and art.

PRACTICE VOCABULARY

To help students integrate new vocabulary, group the terms and introduce them. Explain that *polytheism* and *mythology* are related because *polytheism* refers to religion of the ancient Greeks and *mythology* refers to the stories they told about their gods. Explain that *lyric poetry* and *chorus* are related because they both have to do with the arts of the ancient Greeks. Reinforce the terms during the lesson using the teaching notes.

Have students locate and pronounce the academic vocabulary in the lesson margins. Provide sample sentences that clarify meaning.

cease: All fighting between the city-states would cease during the Olympic games.

submission: Submission to the gods was a part of Greek religion.

HSS 6.4.4, 6.4.8; ELA RI.6.7

Ancient Greeks Beliefs and Arts

CONNECT

GET READY TO READ

ETEXT START UP

Project the Start Up Activity. As students enter the classroom and get settled, have them study the image. Explain that it shows a scene from Greek myth in which the songs of creatures called sirens lured sailors to wreck their ships on the rocks.

Describe What myths have you learned in school? *(Students may recall myths from other cultures they have studied, such as from Mesopotamia or Native American groups.)*

Draw Conclusions How do you think this myth might have inspired the English word *siren*? *(Sample response: A siren is very loud and acts to warn people to get out of the way or call them people to act.)*

After completing the Start Up activity, project the Lesson Opener or direct students to their textbooks. Preview the lesson by working through the Get Ready to Read items with the class. Remind students to pay close attention to the Guiding Questions as they read the lesson.

ACTIVE JOURNAL

Take Notes Have students use the lesson literacy skill graphic organizer in their Active Journals to take notes as they read the lesson.

Practice Vocabulary Have students complete the activity in their Active Journals to build their vocabulary.

VIDEO VIDEO

Assign the lesson video as homework.

WORKSHEET **TEACHER RESOURCES**

Have students who need additional support use the following worksheets from the Teacher Resources on the course:

- **Reading Support**
- **English Language Development**
- **Lesson Summary**

INVESTIGATE

Greek Religion and Mythology

Discuss Greek religion and **mythology**. Why do people have **mythology**? How did the Greek view their gods? What was the place of the **Olympic games** in Greek culture?

Identify Central Ideas Why do people have myths? *(to explain how things came to be; to teach the values of a culture; to remember and celebrate heroes of the past.)*

Identify Main Ideas In the primary source, Homer is using the words of a god. What point is being made here? *(When people have troubles they blame the gods, but humans, through their own bad judgment, bring trouble on themselves.)*

Find Evidence What evidence in the text shows that the Greeks thought the gods sometimes caused natural events? *(Poseidon was god of the sea. His anger made the earth shake and the seas churn.)*

ELD TIP English learners can absorb information in a text more easily with the help of a chart or graph. Look at the chart in the lesson about the Olympian gods and their characteristics together with ELL students. Ask them if the descriptions of the gods in the chart are mostly negative or positive, and ask why they think that.

ANSWERS

Identify Central Ideas *Their roles suggest that the Greeks turned to their gods for protection and well-being in day-to-day life.*

Some myths explained the changing of the seasons. Others revealed why so much suffering exists in the world. Many myths explained human behavior or taught moral lessons. Some told the stories of heroes, such as Hercules, who was described as having amazing strength. Homer's *Odyssey* tells the story of Odysseus' decade-long struggle to return to Ithaca from the Trojan War. Written in the late 700s BCE, the *Odyssey* was an epic poem that was recited to a listening audience.

Greek myths and stories are still read and retold today. Some of the ancient stories describe entertaining adventures. They also reveal important truths about human nature and why people act in certain ways.

Primary Source

"Look you now, how ready mortals are to blame the gods. It is from us, they say, that evils come, but they even of themselves, through their own blind folly, have sorrows beyond that which is ordained."

—Homer, the *Odyssey*, Book 1

Greek Gods and Goddesses In Greek mythology, Zeus was the supreme ruler of the gods, as well as the lord of the sky and the god of rain. He lived on Mount Olympus and threw thunderbolts at those who displeased him. His wife, Hera, protected married women and their households.

Zeus had two brothers. The first, Poseidon, was god of the sea. Zeus' other brother, Hades, ruled and lived in the underworld, which was inhabited by the souls of the dead.

Analyze Charts This chart shows eight of the most important gods and goddesses in Greek mythology. **Determine Relevance** What do their roles tell you about what was important to the ancient Greeks?

Olympian Gods

Name	Characteristics
Zeus	Father of many of the other gods; conjurer of storms and god of justice
Hera	Wife of Zeus and queen of the gods; goddess of marriage
Athena	Daughter of Zeus; goddess of wisdom and protector of cities
Apollo	God of prophecy, music, poetry, and god of light
Artemis	Twin sister of Apollo; goddess of hunting and childbirth
Poseidon	Brother of Zeus; god of the sea
Ares	God of war
Aphrodite	Goddess of love and beauty

INTEGRATED ENGLISH LANGUAGE DEVELOPMENT

Interpretive Tell students that words that are similar in meaning can convey different impressions. For example, calling a person silly or funny both mean that the person is amusing. However, *silly* is negative. It implies that the person is foolish. *Funny* is positive. A funny person is entertaining.

Emerging Read the subsection Greek Gods and Goddesses aloud with the group. Note the word *displeased* in the first paragraph. Explain that *displeased, enraged* and *infuriated* all mean "angered." Yet *enraged* and *infuriated* mean "intensely angry." The word *displeased* seems very mild. Ask students what this tells about Zeus' temperament.

Expanding Point out that Poseidon made the seas *churn* when he was angry. *Churn* can mean "move violently," "agitate" or "tumble." Discuss

Other major gods included Apollo, god of the arts, prophecy, and healing, and Ares, god of war. Aphrodite was goddess of love and beauty, and the goddess Artemis oversaw hunting and childbirth.

Athena was a popular goddess because, according to one myth, she had given the Greeks the gift of the olive tree. Athena was also the guardian of the city of Athens. When the Greeks fought against other peoples, they believed Athena would appear to help them.

Greeks believed that their gods and goddesses behaved like human beings. The deities fell in love, got married, and had children. They liked to celebrate and play tricks. They also felt jealousy and rage.

What was Greek Religion's Role in Everyday Life? The Greeks honored their gods with public and private religious rituals. Public meetings began with prayers and animal sacrifices. Women played important roles in some of these public ceremonies. In private homes, families maintained household shrines.

Academic Vocabulary
ceased • *v.,* stopped

Each city-state built temples to its patron deity. On holy days, citizens made sacrifices in front of the gods' temples. They asked the gods for favors, such as good crops or good health.

The Olympic Games Some religious festivals included athletic contests. Athletes competed in sports such as boxing, wrestling, and running. They displayed their skill to honor the gods.

The leading competitions brought together athletes from many city-states. The most famous sports event was the **Olympic games**, which honored Zeus. These games took place every four years. During the games, all conflicts between city-states **ceased**. Travelers came from all over the Mediterranean to attend the games. The festival site at Olympia was crowded with merchants, food sellers, and artisans. Successful athletes were rewarded not with money, but with privileges and fame.

▼ A statue of a Greek discus thrower

Sacred Sites The Greeks considered groves of trees, springs, and other places to be sacred because they were home to a god or spirit. Mount Olympus, in northern Greece, was an important sacred spot. The Greeks believed it was home to the major gods.

Another sacred site was Delphi, on the slopes of Mount Parnassus. Delphi contained many shrines, but the most important building was the holy temple of the god Apollo. The temple of Apollo housed Apollo's priestess, who was known as the Delphic oracle. An oracle is someone who predicts what will happen in the future. People traveled to Delphi from all over Greece and other lands to ask the priestess questions about the future.

READING CHECK **Draw Conclusions** Why are the stories of ancient Greece still influential today?

Identify Implied Ideas During the **Olympic games** all conflicts between city-states **ceased**. What does that say about how the Greeks viewed the **Olympic games**? *(The Greeks felt the **Olympic games** were sacred.)*

Synthesize Information What is another indication of the Greeks' high regard for the **Olympic games**? *(The games honored Zeus, who was the supreme ruler of the gods.)*

Integrate Information Why would the Delphic oracle be housed in a temple dedicated to Apollo? *(The Delphic oracle predicted the future, and Apollo was the god of prophecy.)*

ELD.PI.B.8

with students which meaning applies to what Poseidon did to the sea when he was angry.

Bridging Divide students into two groups. Have one group make up sentences for the synonyms for *displeased*. Have the other group do the same for the word *churn*. Remind students to pay attention to the different shades of meaning.

WORKSHEET **TEACHER RESOURCES**

For additional IELD support addressing the standard, have students complete the Lesson ELD activity from the Teacher Resources found on the course.

ANSWERS

Draw Conclusions *The entertaining stories reveal insights into human nature and human activity that are still meaningful today.*

Arts in Ancient Greece

Discuss the arts of the ancient Greeks. What were important guiding ideas in sculpture and architecture?

Identify Implied Ideas Why was the Parthenon created as such a magnificent building? *(It was built to honor Athena, the guardian of Athens.)*

INTERACTIVE **INTERACTIVE GALLERY**

Art and Architecture in Ancient Greece

Interactive Instruction Display the Interactive Gallery: Art and Architecture in Ancient Greece for the class. Click through the interactive to learn more about the art and architecture of the Greeks.

Ask a volunteer to read the text on the right. Discuss and clarify the terms *realism*, *heroic idealism*, *balance*, and *proportion* as they relate to Greek art. Discuss each image and how it relates to or reflects the Greek ideals of realism, heroic idealism, balance, and proportion.

ACTIVE CLASSROOM

Use the See-Think-Wonder strategy. Have students working with a partner select one of the images in the gallery. Students should ask their partner these questions: What do you see? What does that make you think? What are you wondering about now that you've seen this? Ask students to share their responses with the class.

ANSWERS

Cite Evidence *Greek architects created buildings that gave a sense of balance and harmony of parts.*

Identify Main Ideas *It is balanced, and it also conveys peacefulness and calm.*

Arts in Ancient Greece

The Greeks had a strong appreciation of beauty. They expressed this in their painting, sculpture, and architecture. Even ordinary objects such as vases and jugs were carefully designed. Although most of their paintings have not survived, Greek statues and buildings have been admired for generations.

INTERACTIVE

Art and Architecture in Ancient Greece

Painting and Sculpture From the descriptions of ancient writers, we know that ancient painting was realistic. Painters created an impression of depth and perspective in their work.

Early Greek sculpture shows strong Egyptian influence. However, Greek sculptors gradually developed a style that was much more realistic than any other sculpture in the ancient world. At the same time, Greek sculptors created images of humans and deities that seemed to inhabit an ideal world of calm and peace. They often used this ideal style to decorate their temples and gravestones.

The Greeks honored their deities by creating huge statues of gods and goddesses for shrines and temples. They also carved scenes to decorate temple walls.

Architecture Like Greek sculpture, Greek architecture was inspired by the proportions of the human body. Architects also tried to achieve perfection in their work. They created buildings that gave a sense of balance and harmony of parts. The finest example of classical Greek architecture is the temple known as the Parthenon, built to honor Athena. The architects Ictinus and Callicrates designed graceful marble columns to support the roof. Above the columns, bands of sculptures showed images of gods and humans. Inside the temple stood a giant statue of the goddess Athena, designed by the sculptor Phidias.

People today think of Greek buildings and statues as dazzling white marble. In ancient times, however, these works would have been painted. Statues would have had colored eyes, skin, and hair, making them appear startlingly real. Over time, however, the ancient colors have faded.

Analyze Images These ruins once belonged to the Temple of Apollo at Delphi. **Cite Evidence** What considerations would the architects of this temple have taken into account? Find evidence in the text to support your answer.

READING CHECK **Identify Main Ideas** What makes Greek sculpture unique?

Greek Literature

Like the other arts, Greek literature was linked with religion. Religious festivals often included contests between poets. Others included plays based on myths. The *Iliad* and the *Odyssey,* Homer's great epic poems, reflected the Greeks' belief that the gods controlled human lives.

HISTORY BACKGROUND

The Poet Sappho Although Sappho is considered one of the greatest poets of all time, only one of her poems survives in its entirety. In that poem, Sappho asks Aphrodite, the goddess of love, for her help in winning the love of another woman. Sappho's romantic relationships with other women inspired the modern term *lesbian* after her home on the Isle of Lesbos in the Aegean Sea. Sappho's reputation as a lesbian caused her works to be targeted by the early and medieval Catholic Church, which is one reason why so few of her poems have survived. However, there are 250 fragments of Sappho's poems, some found recently on scraps of ancient papyrus. Scholars hope that more will be found in the future.

Analyze Images The ruins of the Parthenon in Athens are on the left. On the right is pictured the Lincoln Memorial in Washington, D.C. **Compare** What similarities do you see between the structures?

Lyric Poetry Some Greek poets who came after Homer wrote shorter poems. Performers often sang these poems while playing a stringed instrument known as a lyre. As a result, these poetic songs became known as **lyric poetry**.

Greeks wrote lyric poetry on many different subjects. Pindar praised victorious athletes while Alcaeus wrote about politics and war. In contrast, Sappho wrote about human emotions. Although most of her poetry has been lost, she was greatly admired in ancient times.

Greek Drama The roots of modern Western theater reach back to ancient Greece. The word *drama*, which means a play or performance on stage, is a Greek word. The words *theater, tragedy, comedy,* and *scene* also come from Greek.

Greek drama developed from performances honoring the god Dionysus. In the earliest plays, a few individual actors performed the character roles. The **chorus** commented on the action and advised the characters. In time, plays became a central feature at festivals. Prizes were awarded for the best play, the best chorus, and the best actor.

Greek dramatists wrote two types of plays: tragedy and comedy. The plot of a tragedy often came from mythology or Homer's epics. Tragedies often traced the downfall of heroic figures caught in violent conflict with their family, their city, or the gods. In the tragedy *Antigone* by Sophocles, the chorus offers the audience this advice:

Quest CONNECTIONS

Study the photographs of the two buildings. How has ancient Greek architecture endured in the modern age? Record your observations in your Active Journal.

Primary Source

"There is no happiness where there is no wisdom;
No wisdom but in submission to the gods. Big
words are always punished, And proud men in old
age learn to be wise."

—Sophocles, *Antigone*

Academic Vocabulary

submission • *n.*, obedience

Integrate Information Greek sculpture was realistic, yet it sought to depict an ideal world. How might those two seemingly contradictory concepts—the real and the ideal—work together? *(Accept reasonable responses. Sample answer: Greek sculptures could be painted to look like people, but the people were depicted as perfect beings.)*

ACTIVE JOURNAL

Quest Connections Direct students to the Quest Connections pages in their Active Journals. After students complete this activity, tell them to consider how they can use their response when they complete their Quest.

Greek Literature

Greek literature was often linked to religion and religious celebrations. Ancient Greeks pioneered drama.

Connect Why do you think Homer's epics were often the source of the plots for tragedies? *(Tragedies trace the downfall of heroic figures, and Homer's epics are full of heroes.)*

Identify Main Ideas What is the main point in the primary source passage from Sophocles? *(People must not be overly proud. They must learn to be wise, which means learning to submit to the gods.)*

CURRICULUM CONNECTION: PERFORMING ARTS

The word *theater* comes from the Greek *theatron*, which means "a place of seeing." The first theatrical performances took place in the agora. Later, actual theaters were built. In early Greek theaters, the center of the theater was an area for dancing called the orchestra. In the earliest plays, the actors dressed in a small tent called the *skēnē* (from which we get our modern word *scene*). Performances were like religious rituals, and people were expected to attend them.

Theater was not unique to ancient Greece. Archeological evidence of what we today call theater has been found in Asia, Egypt, and Mesoamerica.

ANSWERS

Use Visual Information *Steps lead up to a building with tall thick round columns.*

HSS 6.4.4, 6.4.8; ELA RI.6.7; ELD.P1.A2, ELD.P1.C.10.a

ACTIVE JOURNAL

Quick Activity Divide students into pairs, and have them work on the Quick Activity in their Active Journals. Students should state the moral of the fable, explain how the fable teaches this lesson, and then brainstorm ways to illustrate it. Have volunteers share their work.

SYNTHESIZE

Assess and Reteach Have students use a Numbered Heads strategy to complete Lesson Check questions 1–4. Ask volunteers to share their answers with the class.

If responses are incorrect, use the Guiding Questions to discuss the lesson's main ideas, focusing on the ideas that are causing difficulty.

ACTIVE JOURNAL

Writing Workshop Have students complete the Lesson 6 Writing Task in their Active Journals. Students will collect details from the lesson to support their response to the question: How did ancient Greece's artistic achievements show its society was at its peak?

DEMONSTRATE

ASSESSMENT **ONLINE LESSON QUIZ**

Assign the Online Lesson Quiz for this lesson if you haven't done so. Students will be offered automatic remediation or enrichment based on their score.

DISCUSSION **DISCUSSION BOARD**

Post this question to the class on the Discussion Board:

Synthesize What element in Greek culture do you find the most interesting? Why? *(Sample response: Greek mythology is interesting because it's full of exciting stories about gods and heroes.)*

▲ In this scene from one of Aesop's fables, a fox tries to trick a rooster into leaving a tree.

Two other famous authors of Greek tragedies are Aeschylus and Euripides.Theater groups still stage some of the tragedies of these dramatists. In addition, modern playwrights continue to draw inspiration from the plots and themes of ancient Greek tragedies.

Greek comedies ended happily. They dealt with current events and made amusing observations about Greek culture, society, and politicians. Aristophanes was perhaps the most famous comic playwright. Two of his comedies are still performed today.

What did Aesop's Fables Teach? Another lasting form of Greek literature is the fable, a story that teaches a moral lesson. The most famous of these fables are by Aesop. According to some legends, Aesop was a slave who lived on the Greek island of Samos during the 500s BCE. Freed as a reward for his learning, Aesop traveled widely, collecting and retelling his fables.

Many of Aesop's fables are still familiar. A tale about a tortoise and a hare shows the Greeks' love of athletic competition. In this fable, a hare mocked the slow speed of a tortoise, so the tortoise challenged the hare to a race. The hare was so confident of winning that he took a nap. When he awoke, the tortoise had won. The moral: "Slow and steady wins the race!"

Quick Activity

Explore the moral lesson of Aesop's fable "The Fox and the Crow" in your Active Journal.

READING CHECK **Compare and Contrast** Compare the two main types of Greek drama.

Lesson Check

HSS 6.4.4, 6.4.8, ELD.PI.C.10.a

Practice Vocabulary

1. How was Greek **mythology** a form of **polytheism**?
2. What role did a **chorus** have in Greek drama?

Critical Thinking and Writing

3. **Synthesize** What were some qualities that the Greeks admired?
4. **Draw Conclusions** Why are Greek myths and dramas still important to us today?
5. **Writing Workshop: Support Thesis with Details** How do ancient Greece's achievements in literature and the arts show a society at its peak? Collect details to support your claims in your Active Journal.

ANSWERS

Compare and Contrast *Tragedies told about the downfall of heroes; comedies told stories of everyday life and ended happily.*

LESSON CHECK

1. Greek myths featured many gods. **DOK1**
2. The chorus commented on the action and advised the characters. **DOK1**
3. The Greeks admired athletic and military prowess and literary and artistic talent. **DOK3**
4. Greek myths and dramas, which are still read and produced, have exercised a huge influence on our literature, theater, and film. **DOK3**
5. Students should use the content of the lesson to support their thesis statements. **DOK3**

Primary Source

HSS 6.4.4; ELA RH.6.1, 6.3

Homer, the *Odyssey*

The *Odyssey* is one of the first great works of Western literature, alongside the *Iliad.* According to tradition, both were written by the Greek poet Homer. The *Odyssey* is a tale of the Greek hero Odysseus, also called Ulysses, and his epic journey home after the fall of Troy. Homer's works provided the foundations of Greek education and culture. They still impact Western ideas today.

▶ This mosaic shows Odysseus with his men.

Tell me, O muse ①, of that ingenious hero who travelled far and wide after he had sacked the famous town of Troy. Many cities did he visit, and many were the nations with whose manners and customs he was acquainted; moreover he suffered much by sea while trying to save his own life and bring his men safely home; but do what he might he could not save his men, for they perished through their own sheer folly in eating the cattle of the Sun-god Hyperion; so the god prevented them from ever reaching home. Tell me, too, about all these things, O daughter of Jove ②, from whatsoever source you may know them.

So now all who escaped death in battle or by shipwreck had got safely home except Ulysses, and he, though he was longing to return to his wife and country, was detained by the goddess Calypso, who had got him into a large cave and wanted to marry him ③. But as years went by, there came a time when the gods settled that he should go back to Ithaca; even then, however, when he was among his own people, his troubles were not yet over; nevertheless all the gods had now begun to pity him except Neptune ④, who still persecuted him without ceasing and would not let him get home.

—Homer, the *Odyssey*, Book 1

Reading and Vocabulary Help

① The narrator of the story asks the muse for inspiration as he prepares to tell the story.

② In this context, Jove is the Greek god Zeus and his daughter is Athena.

③ Why does Calypso detain Odysseus?

④ Neptune is the Roman god of the sea; however, in Greek mythology his name is Poseidon.

Analyzing Primary Sources

Cite specific evidence from the document to support your answers.

1. **Determine Author's Point of View** How does Homer use the second paragraph to foreshadow the rest of the poem?
2. **Use Evidence** From the reading, which god do you suppose will give Odysseus the most trouble on his journey?
3. **Analyze Style** This text is the very beginning of the *Odyssey*. How does the author introduce the hero of the story?

ANALYZING PRIMARY SOURCES

1. It hints that Ulysses, who has yet to return home, will face many trials on his journey. **DOK2**
2. Neptune **DOK2**
3. Homer introduces Odysseus (Ulysses) as an "ingenious" hero who did his best to get all his men home and wants to return home himself. **DOK2**

INTEGRATED ENGLISH LANGUAGE DEVELOPMENT

Bridging Have students turn to a partner to determine the meaning of the primary source quotation. Students may be confused by the use of the name Ulysses in the text. Explain Odysseus is the hero's Greek name, and Ulysses is his name in Latin. Ask students to discuss why the gods had begun to pity Odysseus/Ulysses.

HSS 6.4.4; ELA RH.6.1, 6.3

Primary Sources

Homer's *The Odyssey*

Read aloud the explanatory note about the source. Direct students' attention to the illustration on the page. Tell them that this mosaic is another illustration of Odysseus and his men sailing near the sirens. The men's ears are plugged, and Odysseus is tied to the mast to prevent him from following the sirens' fatal song. Ask: What do you see in the picture that suggests the conditions under which the ship is sailing? *(The sails are bending and twisting in the wind.)* What does this suggest? *(The ship is sailing in a storm or other dangerous conditions.)*

GUIDED READING

Read aloud or ask volunteers to read aloud the text. Use the Reading and Vocabulary Support notes to deepen students' understanding of the primary source.

Reading and Vocabulary Help Answers

3. *She wants to marry him.*

GUIDED ANALYSIS

After completing the text, discuss what this primary source reveals about Ulysses' journey home and the Greeks' view of the roles of the gods in this journey.

Interpret Sources What did Ulysses' men do that led to their doom? *(They angered the sun-god Hyperion by eating his cattle.)* Why does Homer call this "folly"? *(The sailors should have known better than to do anything that would make a god angry.)* How is Ulysses finally able to leave Calypso? *(The gods decide he should go back to Ithaca.)* Why will Ulysses continue to have problems after he leaves Calypso? *(One god is still angry at him.)*

To assess understanding, have students respond to the Analyze Primary Sources questions in writing.

HSS 6.4.8

Ancient Greek Learning

CONNECT

GET READY TO READ

ETEXT **START UP**

Project the Start Up Activity. As students enter the classroom and get settled, have them study the image. Explain that it shows Greek philosophers exchanging ideas and sharing their teachings.

Discuss Ask students: Why is education so important to a society? *(Sample response: It helps people to be good citizens; it helps promote shared values and ideas.)*

Synthesize Visual Information What do you see in the image that might be considered unusual for this time and place? Why is it unusual? *(There is a woman in the image; in ancient Greece philosophers were usually men.)*

After completing the Start Up activity, project the Lesson Opener or direct students to their textbooks. Preview the lesson by working through the Get Ready to Read items with the class. Remind students to pay close attention to the Guiding Questions as they read the lesson.

ACTIVE JOURNAL

Take Notes Have students use the lesson literacy skill graphic organizer in their Active Journals to take notes as the read the lesson.

Practice Vocabulary Have students complete the activity in their Active Journals to build their vocabulary.

VIDEO **VIDEO**

Assign the lesson video as homework.

LESSON 7

HSS 6.4.8

Ancient Greek Learning

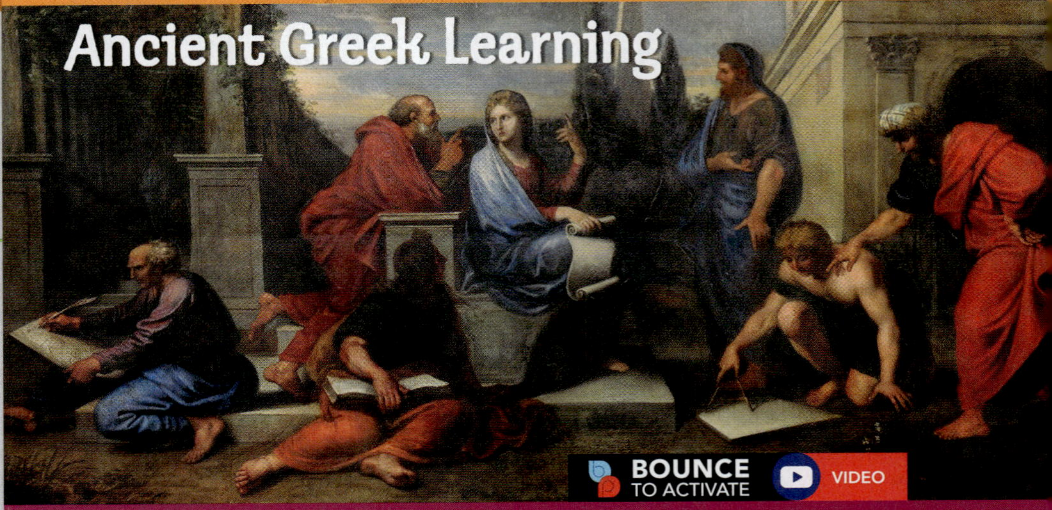

BOUNCE TO ACTIVATE VIDEO

GET READY TO READ

START UP

In the image, Greek philosophers exchange ideas and share their teachings. List several reasons why education is important to a society.

GUIDING QUESTIONS

- What enduring contributions did Greek scholars make to philosophy and history?
- What scientific and medical discoveries did the ancient Greeks make?
- How did Greek thought affect individuals, states, and societies?

TAKE NOTES

Literacy Skill: Summarize
Use the graphic organizer in your Active Journal to take notes as you read the lesson.

PRACTICE VOCABULARY

Use the vocabulary activity in your Active Journal to practice the vocabulary words.

Vocabulary		Academic Vocabulary
Socratic method	Hippocratic oath	reason
Academy		concept
hypothesis		

Just as the Greeks appreciated beauty and the arts, they saw the value of learning about the world. Scholars, scientists, and great thinkers were honored members of society. Some of their scientific findings lay the foundation for future discoveries. Greek philosophers, thinkers who explored the nature of knowledge, came up with ideas that we still use to understand our world.

Greek Philosophy

As you read earlier, Chinese thinkers were among the world's first philosophers. Their goal was to pursue wisdom. Greek philosophers had the same goal. In fact, the word *philosophy* comes from Greek words meaning "love of wisdom."

The Importance of Reason The Greeks began their search for wisdom by asking questions similar to those the Chinese asked, such as: "What is the nature of the universe? What is a good life?" The Greeks, however, took their search a step further. They also asked: "How do we know what is real? How can we determine what is true?"

264 Lesson 6.7 • Ancient Greek Learning

PRACTICE VOCABULARY

To help students integrate new vocabulary, group the terms and introduce them. Explain that *Socratic method* and *Hippocratic oath* are related because they both refer to ideas put forth by leading Greek thinkers. Ask students: What is a method? *(an organized way of doing something.)* What is an oath? *(a promise)* Explain that academy (a place where people are educated) and *hypothesis* (a starting point for an investigation) both have to do with learning.

Have students locate and pronounce the academic vocabulary in the lesson margins. Provide sample sentences that clarify meaning.

reason: One must use reason to solve math problems.

concept: Children have to be taught the concept of sharing.

The Greeks believed that they could answer these questions by using the human power of **reason**. Reason is the power to think clearly. To increase their thinking power, the Greeks developed a system of reasoning known as logic. Logic involves a step-by-step method of thinking through a problem or question.

Academic Vocabulary
reason • *n.*, the power to think clearly

Socrates and Plato Several important philosophers lived in Athens. One of them, Socrates, wandered around the city, drawing other Athenians into discussion. In these discussions, Socrates asked question after question to force his listeners to think more clearly. Today, this question-and-answer method of teaching is called the **Socratic method** and is used to instruct students in a variety of subjects.

Socrates' discussions challenged accepted beliefs. Eventually, this got him into trouble with the leaders of Athens. They charged him with corrupting the young. Socrates was also accused of not believing in the gods that the city recognized. In the trial that followed, Socrates defended himself:

Primary Source

"I have never set up as any man's teacher. But if anyone, young or old, is eager to hear me . . . I never grudge [deny] him the opportunity. . . . If any given one of these people becomes a good citizen or a bad one, I cannot fairly be held responsible."

—Socrates, quoted in Plato's *Apology*

Plato, a student of Socrates, recorded his teacher's ideas in a series of conversations called dialogues. Plato went on to found a school of

Analyze Images In 399 BCE, Socrates was sentenced to death for teaching his beliefs to his students. In this painting, he takes the poison that will kill him, as his students look on. **Analyze Images** How would you describe Socrates' attitude as he faces his death? How did the artist portray the reaction of his followers?

DIFFERENTIATED INSTRUCTION

Special Education Teach students the elements of Socratic dialogue. Tell them that Socrates did not let his students get away with giving an answer without asking them a question. Ask them: What is honesty? Challenge their responses with probing questions. Question their assumptions. Explain that that was how Socrates taught his students.

Below Level Have students study the picture of Socrates in the 5 Things To Know box later in the lesson or in the painting on this page and then write a sentence about him based on what they see.

Advanced Have students learn more about the death of Socrates by doing research online or at the library. Ask students to share their findings with the class. Suggest that they quote from Plato's account of Socrates' last hour.

WORKSHEET **TEACHER RESOURCES**

Have students who need additional support use the following worksheets from the Teacher Resources on the course:

- **Reading Support**
- **English Language Development**
- **Lesson Summary**

INVESTIGATE

Greek Philosophy

Discuss Greek philosophy. How did the Greeks view reason and logic? Who were Socrates, Plato, and Zeno?

Apply Concepts The Greeks asked questions like "How do we know what is real?" How would you answer this question? *(Possible answers: Something is real if more than one person experiences it. Something is real if you can take a picture of it.)*

Compare and Contrast How did Athens's treatment of Socrates contradict other aspects of the city's behavior? *(Athens was an innovative city that introduced democracy and prided itself on letting its citizens behave as they wanted to. Yet it put Socrates on trial for his ideas.)*

Identify Implied Ideas What is Socrates' main point in his defense of himself as expressed in the primary source? *(He is not responsible for what people do with what they learn from him.)*

ELD TIP Illustrations can help English learners absorb a story better. Have ELL students look at the image of the painting of Socrates on his deathbed. Have them discuss what they think is going on in the picture and the feelings of each of the people depicted in the painting.

ANSWERS

Use Visual Information *Socrates appears to be defiant. Perhaps he is still teaching. His followers appear to be extremely upset or sad.*

How Did History and Politics Shape Greece?

Discuss how history and politics shaped Greece. Who were the great historians, political thinkers, orators, and scientists?

Summarize What did the stoics believe? *(Reason governed the universe, and people should live in harmony with nature. Stoics tried to master their emotions through self-control.)*

INTERACTIVE **INTERACTIVE CHART**

Understanding Greek Philosophers

Interactive Instruction Display the Interactive Chart: Understanding Greek Philosophers for the class. Click through the interactive to learn more about the ideas of these ancient Greeks thinkers.

Have volunteers place the eight balls in the proper places on the chart. Discuss each one and how it relates to or reflects Greek ideas and culture. Ask: How did philosophy shape Greek life? *(Sample response: It encouraged people to think about and solve problems facing society.)*

ACTIVE CLASSROOM

Use the Conversation With ______ strategy. Have students imagine they are having a conversation with one of the people on the chart. Students should write down a question they'd like to ask, and then write what that person would say in response.

ANSWERS

Infer *Socrates meant that people should think about what they do and how they live, not go through life unware of their decisions or the effects of their actions.*

Identify Main Ideas *He introduced a question-and-answer method of teaching.*

BIOGRAPHY

5 Things to Know About SOCRATES

Philosopher (469 BCE–399 BCE)

- He was the son of a stonemason and a midwife, not an aristocrat.
- Many people considered him annoying.
- Plato said he was the "wisest, justest, and best of all I have ever known."
- He said "an unexamined life is not worth living."
- Fairly or not, Socrates was found guilty and sentenced to death in 399 BCE.

Critical Thinking What do you think Socrates meant by saying that "an unexamined life is not worth living"?

philosophy called the **Academy**. Today, the word *academy* often means a school of higher learning. Plato was interested in the nature of reality. He remains one of the most influential thinkers in history.

INTERACTIVE
Greek Philosophers

What did the Stoics Believe? During the Hellenistic period, new philosophies arose. One group, founded by Zeno, was called the Stoics.

To the Stoics, divine reason governed the universe so people needed to live in harmony with nature. Stoics tried to master their emotions through self-control.

READING CHECK **Identify Main Ideas** How did Socrates change how teachers and students interacted?

How did History and Politics Shape Greece?

The Greeks' search for wisdom also led them to study the past. Greek historians did more than record events, however. Most importantly, they examined why these events took place.

Three Great Historians The Greek writer Herodotus is often called "the father of history" because he asked why certain events happened. Born about 484 BCE, Herodotus lived during the Second Persian War. The Persian Wars, and the cultures of both peoples, are carefully described in his masterwork, *The Histories*. In this work, he investigates the causes of the conflict between the Greeks and the Persians.

Thucydides, of Athens, was another important Greek historian, whose contributions still endure. Born in 460 BCE, Thucydides lived during the Peloponnesian War. He began writing his history of the war while the events were fresh in people's memories. Before writing about a battle, he would visit the battle site. He would also interview people who had participated in the event. He hoped that his history would be accurate—and that it would help people avoid repeating the mistakes of the past.

INTEGRATED ENGLISH LANGUAGE DEVELOPMENT

Productive Explain to students that reading is often the first step in planning an oral presentation. Read How Did History and Politics Shape Greece? with students. Tell them that they will be making an oral presentation about a famous person in ancient Greece. As they read the section, tell them to choose an historian, a political thinker, or an orator.

Emerging Have students plan their presentation. Tell them to look for more information about their subject in the library or online. Point out that the people mentioned in the text had a great effect on western culture. Remind students to mention why the person they have chosen to talk about is important.

Xenophon lived from about 427 to around 355 BCE. He traveled widely in the Persian empire and Greece. He wrote the first known autobiography in world history. An autobiography is a book about a person's life written by the subject of the book. Xenophon believed that the study of history could teach people how to live moral lives.

Political Thinkers Greek writers also discussed politics and government. For example, Plato wrote a book called *The Republic*, which presented his views about the ideal government. Plato did not approve of the way democracy functioned in Athens. He thought that the ideal city-state would be led by philosopher-kings, who had the wisdom to make the right decisions. Such leaders would not be elected by the people.

The philosopher Aristotle also wrote a book about government, called *Politics*. In this book, Aristotle compared existing governments. He argued that the best government would be a balanced one that avoided extremes. Aristotle also believed that citizens must participate in politics in order to be happy.

Great Orators Greece was also brimming with great orators, or gifted public speakers. These orators included Demosthenes, and Pericles, who was discussed in earlier lessons. Demosthenes was an Athenian statesmen who overcame a stammer to become one of the greatest orator of his day. Many of his speeches, especially those against Philip II of Macedonia, still survive.

READING CHECK **Identify Main Ideas** Why did the Greeks study the past?

Science and Technology

Most ancient peoples associated everyday occurences, like the rising of the sun or common illnesses, with the activities of various gods or spirits. While most Greeks shared these beliefs, some began to look for natural causes of such events.

The Power of Observation Like modern scientists, the Greeks first made observations of nature. They then formed a **hypothesis**, or logical guess, to explain their observations. This way of thinking represented something new in the ancient world. It laid the foundations of modern science, mathematics, and medicine.

The Study of Nature Greek philosophers began the scientific study of nature. These early scientists believed that natural laws governed the universe. They set out to identify and explain those laws.

One of the first scientific thinkers was a philosopher named Thales of Miletus. Thales was born around 624 BCE. Thales asked questions such as: How big is the Earth? What is its shape? What holds it up in space? In each case, he based his answer on his observations of nature.

▲ Demosthenes practices a speech by speaking to the sea.

Synthesize Information Do you agree with Plato that the ideal city-state would be one led by wise philosopher-kings who would not be elected by the people? Why or why not? *(Sample answer: I do not agree, because that isn't democracy. I think democracy is the best form of government.)*

Apply Concepts Aristotle claimed that the best government avoided extremes. Does this make sense to you? Why or why not? *(Possible response: This makes sense because avoiding extremes can prevent actions like engaging in an unnecessary war or taking away people's freedoms.)*

Science and Technology

Discuss the science and technology of the ancient Greeks. How was their approach to science and technology different from earlier times?

Compare and Contrast What change did the Greeks bring to science? *(They began to look for logical, natural causes of events rather than always believing natural events were caused by gods or spirits.)*

Integrate Information Thales of Miletus asked questions like "What holds Earth up in space?" and based his answer on his observations of nature. What observation might have helped him answer this question? *(Sample responses: He might have studied the stars; he might have studied the changing positions of the sun or moon in the sky.)*

ELD.PI.C.9

Expanding Have each student tell some interesting details that they have learned about their subject during their research. Encourage students to speak in complete sentences.

Bridging Have students deliver a brief oral presentation about the subject they have chosen. Remind them to use the facts they learned during their research as well as any new words they have acquired.

WORKSHEET **TEACHER RESOURCES**

For additional IELD support addressing these standards, have students complete the Lesson ELD activity from the Teacher Resources found on the course.

ANSWERS

Identify Main Ideas *They wanted to examine reasons for events and prevent mistakes from happening again.*

Find Evidence What evidence in the text is an example of incorrect thinking by some Greek scientists? *(Thales believed that all things are made of water and that Earth was a disk that floated on water.)*

Find Evidence What evidence in the text is an example of extremely advanced thinking by some Greek scientists? *(Democritus said that the universe was made up of tiny particles that could not be split. He called them "atoms.")*

ACTIVE JOURNAL

Quest Connections Direct students to the Quest Connections pages in their Active Journals. After students complete this activity, tell them to consider how they can use these ideas when they complete their Quest.

Analyze Images This artwork, *The School of Athens* by Raphael, shows Plato and Aristotle surrounded by other philosophers. Raphael painted this between 1509 and 1511 CE. **Draw Conclusions** What does the large gap in time between these philosophers' time and Raphael's painting say about Plato and Aristotle's importance?

These early Greek scientists were not always correct. For example, Thales believed that all things are made of water. Thales also believed that Earth was a disk that floated on water. Even though Thales's ideas were incorrect, he inspired other thinkers to use logic to develop answers. For example, the philosopher Democritus said that the universe was made up of tiny particles that could not be split. He called them "atoms."

Aristotle The most famous natural philosopher was the scholar Aristotle. He was born in 384 BCE and studied at Plato's Academy. Later, he set up his own school, called the Lyceum.

Unlike Plato, who distrusted the senses, Aristotle sought knowledge through observation. He analyzed data about plants, animals, and rocks. He studied mathematics and logic. He analyzed government and the arts. A modern historian summarized Aristotle's work:

Primary Source

> "He was a great collector and classifier of data. . . . What he wrote provided the framework for the discussion of biology, physics, mathematics, logic, literary criticism, aesthetics, psychology, ethics, and politics for two thousand years."
>
> —J. M. Roberts, *History of the World*

Quest CONNECTIONS

Read the information about Thales and the quote about Aristotle. How did these scientists influence how we study science today? Record your findings in your Active Journal.

How Did the Greeks Improve of Technology? The Greeks put their powers of observation to practical use as they developed sophisticated technology. From the 400s on, the Greeks invented all kinds of mechanisms, including water clocks, watermills, and locks. They understood the principle of steam power, which they used to operate mechanical statues, gadgets, and toys. The inventor Archimedes is said to have created a weapon that used mirrors to redirect the sun's light to set fire to enemy ships—an early laser!

READING CHECK **Identify Main Ideas** How did Greek science develop?

HISTORY BACKGROUND

Demosthenes One of the best orators in ancient Greece, Demosthenes started out facing many obstacles. According to the Greek historian Plutarch, as a young man Demosthenes stuttered and did not speak clearly. To overcome this, he put pebbles in his mouth when he practiced speaking and also gave speeches before a large mirror. In addition, he built an underground room where he strengthened his voice, and even shaved half his head to prevent himself from going out in public so he could concentrate on his speaking.

ANSWERS

Draw Conclusions *Plato and Aristotle continued to inspire people for many centuries after their deaths.*

Identify Main Ideas *Greek science developed from a new way of thinking: first observing nature and then making hypotheses based on observation.*

268 Lesson 6.7 • Ancient Greek Learning

A Golden Age for Mathematics and Medicine

Greek thinkers often excelled in many different fields. For example, Thales, the philosopher, was also a leading mathematician. The Greeks also believed that Thales had studied geometry in Egypt. Later, in the Hellenistic period, this kind of cultural exchange helped produce a golden age of Greek mathematics and medicine.

Mathematics The Greeks first discovered many basic **concepts** in mathematics. Pythagoras of Samos was an early Greek mathematician. Pythagoras thought that numbers were the key to understanding the universe. He developed the idea of "square numbers." Today students of geometry still learn the Pythagorean theorem, which bears his name. A theorem is a statement in mathematics that can be proved to be true.

Academic Vocabulary
concept • *n.,* idea

Hypatia was one of the world's leading mathematicians and astronomers. She was the daughter of Theon of Alexandria, himself a leading mathematician. She carried on his work and even became a popular philosopher. Another mathematician, Euclid, has endured as the "father of geometry." He taught in Alexandria and compiled a number of works including *The Elements*, a textbook that became the basis for modern geometry.

Medicine The Greeks also made contributions in the field of medicine. Greek doctors looked for natural causes of illnesses instead of blaming them on the gods. Their success at treating patients brought them fame throughout the Mediterranean world. Greek doctors practiced surgery and dentistry.

Hippocrates became the best-known Greek doctor. He also wrote many medical books and ran a school that trained new doctors. Hippocrates taught his students to diagnose patients by asking them questions and making observations so they could learn about their symptoms.

Hippocrates also had his students swear an oath. In this oath, medical students promised to use their knowledge only in ethical ways. The **Hippocratic oath** still guides doctors today.

▶ Hypatia, a leading mathematician and astronomer

A Golden Age for Mathematics and Medicine

Discuss Greece's golden age of math and medicine. What breakthroughs in mathematics and medicine did the Greeks make?

Draw Conclusions Direct students' attention to the image in the Start Up activity. Ask: Who is the woman in this image most likely to be? *(Hypatia.)*

Evaluate If Hypatia had not been the daughter of a leading mathematician, would it have been likely that she could have used her abilities to become a renowned mathematician, astronomer, and philosopher? Why or why not? *(Possible responses: She would probably have been denied an education because she was a woman; she may have achieved notoriety eventually because of her great ability.)*

Compare and Contrast How did the Greeks change the way medicine was practiced? *(They looked for natural causes of illnesses instead of blaming them on the gods.)*

Compare and Contrast What was similar about Socrates' and Hippocrates' methods? *(They both asked questions.)*

Integrate Information Hippocrates had his students swear what is called the **Hippocratic oath**, promising to use their knowledge only in ethical ways. Why is such an oath a good idea for doctors? *(Doctors can hurt people, make them ill, or kill them if they don't act ethically.)*

CURRICULUM CONNECTION: MATHEMATICS

Pythagoras was a philosopher and mathematician from the island of Samos. He founded a religious sect that explored mathematical theory as well as religious ideas. It is generally believed that the basic mathematical formula that bears his name was created by one of his disciples. The Pythagorean theorem (written as $a^2 + b^2 = c^2$) postulates that the sum of the squares of the legs of a right triangle is equal to the square of the hypotenuse. Thus, if a right triangle has one side (a) that is 3 feet long and another side (b) that is 4 feet, the hypotenuse will be 5 feet. The sum of the squares of side *a* (3 x 3, or 9) and side *b* (4 x 4, or 16) is 25. The square root of 25 is 5. So, the hypotenuse is 5 feet.

HSS 6.4.8; ELD.PI.C.10.a

SYNTHESIZE

Assess and Reteach Have students use a Think-Pair-Share strategy to complete Lesson Check questions 1–5. Ask volunteers to share their answers with the class.

If responses are incorrect, use the Guiding Questions to discuss the lesson's main ideas, focusing on the ideas that are causing difficulty.

ACTIVE JOURNAL

Writing Workshop Have students complete the Lesson 7 Writing Task in their Active Journals. Students will use their theses and supporting details as they draft their essays.

DEMONSTRATE

ASSESSMENT **ONLINE LESSON QUIZ**

Assign the Online Lesson Quiz for this lesson if you haven't already done so. Students will be offered automatic remediation or enrichment based on their score.

DISCUSSION **DISCUSSION BOARD**

Post this question to the class on the Discussion Board:

Synthesize What Greek accomplishment in science or technology did you find the most surprising or interesting? Why? *(Sample response: Democritus said the universe was made up of atoms. I thought this was a modern discovery.)*

▲ This carved sculpture shows a Greek doctor and his patients.

Primary Source

"I will prescribe treatment for the good of my patients according to my ability . . . and never do harm to anyone. To please no one will I prescribe a deadly drug nor give advice which may cause his death. . . . In every house where I come I will enter only for the good of my patients. . . . All that I learn from my patients . . . I will keep secret. If I keep this oath faithfully, may I enjoy my life and practice my art, respected by all men and in all times."

—Hippocrates, from *The Hippocratic Oath*

Medicine in Alexandria The city of Alexandria, Egypt, became an important center for the study of medicine. The Greeks benefited from the medical knowledge of the Egyptians. Egyptian doctors carefully examined patients and recorded their symptoms. But the Greeks went further and sought to understand the reasons for a patient's illness.

Although Greek societies frowned on dissection of the human body, two scientists working in Alexandria, Herophilus and Erasistratus, studied human anatomy. It was in Alexandria that doctors realized that the optic nerve linked the eye to the brain. Ancient Greek doctors also discovered that the brain was the center of thought, and that the pulse sent blood through the arteries.

READING CHECK **Identify Supporting Details** Why were medical students required to take an oath?

Lesson Check

HSS 6.4.8; ELD.PI.C.10.a

Practice Vocabulary

1. What does a teacher do when using the **Socratic method**?
2. What do scientists need to do to form a **hypothesis**?
3. What do doctors promise by taking the **Hippocratic oath**?

Critical Thinking and Writing

4. **Evaluate Explanations** Why is learning about a scholar like Thales still valuable, even though some of his ideas were later proved to be incorrect?
5. **Synthesize** What methods of the early Greek historians might be useful to historians today?
6. **Writing Workshop: Draft your Essay** Review your thesis and supporting details, then begin drafting your essay. Consult your Active Journal.

LESSON CHECK

1. The teacher asks the student questions to clarify responses and probe assumptions. **DOK1**
2. make observations **DOK1**
3. to do no harm and protect patients' privacy **DOK1**
4. Thales's theories were wrong, but he arrived at them using logic and reason, a way of thinking that influenced thinkers after him. Some scholars who used this way of thinking did come up with proven ideas. **DOK3**
5. Early Greek historians visited battle sites, interviewed participants, and traveled widely. **DOK4**
6. Responses will be students' first draft of their essays. **DOK3**

ANSWERS

Identify Supporting Details *Hippocrates wanted to be sure they would use their studies ethically.*

Analysis HI.5

Update an Interpretation

Using the secondary source, follow these steps to learn ways to update interpretations of history as new information is uncovered.

INTERACTIVE
Synthesize

1 **Identify the interpretation that may need to change.** For a long time, scholars believed the ancient city of Troy as described by Homer in the *Iliad* was a Greek settlement.

2 **Study new information about the subject.** Read about the evidence found by archaeologists in the article below.

a. What question of history is the source discussing?

b. Does the source suggest new information that may require a new interpretation of events?

3 **Revise the interpretation, if needed, to reflect the new information.** Remember that the original interpretation was that Troy was a Greek settlement. What does the new evidence suggest about Troy?

Secondary Source

"We know today, from our own excavations and even from earlier ones, that in all main respects, Bronze Age Troy had stronger ties with Anatolia than with the Aegean. We've learned this from the tons of local pottery and small finds, such as a seal with a local hieroglyphic inscription, as well as the overall settlement picture, mud-brick architecture, and cremation burials. . . .

. . . [I]t is now more likely than not that there were several armed conflicts in and around Troy at the end of the Late Bronze Age. At present we do not know whether all or some of these conflicts were distilled in later memory into the "Trojan War" or whether among them there was an especially memorable, single "Trojan War." However, everything currently suggests that Homer should be taken seriously, that his story of a military conflict between Greeks and the inhabitants of Troy is based on a memory of historical events—whatever these may have been. If someone came up to me at the excavation one day and expressed his or her belief that the Trojan War did indeed happen here, my response as an archaeologist working at Troy would be: Why not?"

—Manfred Korfmann, *Archaeology*, May/June 2004

Analysis HI.5

Analysis Skills
Update an Interpretation

LEARN

Preview the steps in the student text with students, and then play the video.

VIDEO **21ST CENTURY SKILLS**

Project the Synthesize video in the 21st Century Skills Tutorial. Use the Quick Reference and Assessment to provide additional instruction in the skill.

PRACTICE

Have students practice the skill using the text on the student page. When students are finished, discuss their responses as a class. Have students describe the revisions they made, explain why they made them, and cite evidence in the text that supports these changes.

As an alternative, you could form students into pairs or groups to perform the activity. Then, invite the groups to share their responses with the class. Discuss the revisions and have students explain why they made them. Also have students cite evidence in the text that supports these changes.

APPLY

To apply this skill, have students revisit the text in the Science and Technology section of Lesson 7 that discusses Thales' belief that all things are made of water and Earth was a disk that floated on water. Have students do online research to find information that updates Thales' beliefs to align with what we know now. Ask students to share their findings with the class.

DIFFERENTIATED INSTRUCTION

Below Level To help students understand the idea of updating an interpretation, draw their attention to the image of Hypatia in Lesson 7. Make an incorrect statement about the image (This is a man; this person is sitting.) and have students "update" your "interpretation" by correcting it.

INTEGRATED ENGLISH LANGUAGE DEVELOPMENT

Bridging Have students turn to a partner to discuss the relationship between the secondary source quotation and what they have learned about Homer's account of the Trojan war. Does the source confirm or deny that a war took place in Troy? Why does the author say that Troy was not a Greek settlement?

ANSWERS

2. (a) Was there really a Trojan War? (b) Yes.
3. Evidence suggests that Troy was not a Greek settlement. Rather, it was more oriented to Anatolia than the Aegean. However, the evidence of several battles on the site of Troy suggests there is quite possibly truth in Homer's stories.

HSS 6.4.7, 6.4.8

Alexander and the Hellenistic World

CONNECT

GET READY TO READ

ETEXT **START UP**

Project the Start Up Activity. As students enter the classroom and get settled, have them study the image. Explain that the image shows Alexander the Great, who conquered many lands.

Identify Cause and Effect In what way can military conquest spread the culture of one nation? *(A country that conquers others often brings it culture to the newly won territory and sometimes even forces it on the vanquished.)*

Synthesize Visual Information What element in this image might have appeared in nations conquered by Alexander the Great? *(Alexander's face might have appeared on coins.)*

After completing the Start Up activity, project the Lesson Opener or direct students to their textbooks. Preview the lesson by working through the Get Ready to Read items with the class. Remind students to pay close attention to the Guiding Questions as they read the lesson.

ACTIVE JOURNAL

Take Notes Have students use the lesson literacy skill graphic organizer in their Active Journals to take notes as the read the lesson.

Practice Vocabulary Have students complete the activity in their Active Journals to build their vocabulary.

VIDEO **VIDEO**

Assign the lesson video as homework.

LESSON 8

HSS 6.4.7, 6.4.8

Alexander and the Hellenistic World

BOUNCE TO ACTIVATE VIDEO

GET READY TO READ

START UP

Look at the image of the leader Alexander the Great, who conquered many lands. In what way can military conquest spread the culture of one civilization?

GUIDING QUESTIONS

- How did Macedonian rulers defeat the Greek city-states?
- In what ways did Alexander's conquests affect connections between cultures in the ancient world?
- How did Hellenistic learning expand the impact of Greek culture?

TAKE NOTES

Literacy Skills: Sequence

Use the vocabulary activity in your Active Journal to take notes as you read the lesson.

PRACTICE VOCABULARY

Use the graphic organizer in your Active Journal to practice the vocabulary words.

Vocabulary	Academic Vocabulary
sarissa	period
Hellenistic	acquire
classical civilization	

The Greeks told a story about Alexander the Great, the young man who set out to conquer the world. The story begins one afternoon as 12-year-old Alexander, the prince of Macedonia, watched his father, King Philip II, barter over a horse. It was a fine black stallion, but it was also angry and unruly. The king decided that the horse could not be tamed. As the king turned away, Alexander grabbed the reins. Alexander sensed that the horse's wildness was caused by fear. He turned the horse to face the sun so that it would no longer be frightened by its own shadow. Alexander quickly calmed and mounted the horse, to everyone's astonishment. The king bought the horse for Alexander, who named him Bucephalus. Bucephalus never allowed anyone else to ride him. He carried Alexander into many battles as the young Macedonian fought for world conquest.

What Fueled Macedonia's Rise?

Macedonia was a land in the north of the Greek peninsula. The Macedonians had their own traditions, which the Greeks considered

PRACTICE VOCABULARY

To help students integrate new vocabulary, group the terms and introduce them. Explain that *Hellenistic* and *classical civilization* are related because they both refer to ancient culture. Ask students if they can think of a word that is similar to *civilization. (society)* Ask students if they can think of a word that is similar to *Hellenistic*, which is an adjective describing a culture. *(Greek, Roman, African, American)*

Have students locate and pronounce the academic vocabulary in the lesson margins. Provide sample sentences that clarify meaning.

period: The Hellenistic period refers to the time of Alexander the Great's empire.

acquire: Alexander wanted to acquire as much territory as possible through conquest.

old-fashioned. Unlike most Greek city-states, the Macedonians were still governed by kings. Despite their different customs, the Macedonians were influenced by Greek culture.

Philip of Macedonia Macedonia was briefly part of the Persian empire. But after Persia's defeat during Xerxes' invasion of Greece, the Macedonians regained their independence. Their kingdom expanded over the lands north of Greece.

One of the rulers of Macedonia was a brilliant and ambitious leader named Philip. Philip gained power after his brother, the Macedonian king, was killed in battle in 359 BCE. The king's son, who was heir to the throne, was only an infant, so the nobles of Macedonia elected Philip as king.

To strengthen his power, Philip built up a powerful army and developed new tactics. Like the Greeks, Philip organized his infantry into phalanxes. Then he armed each man with an 18-foot-long pike. The Macedonian pike, or **sarissa**, was much longer than the spears used by the Greeks. It gave the Macedonians an advantage in battle, as the Macedonian pikes could be used to keep enemies at a greater distance. Philip also trained his men to change directions in battle without losing formation. Armed with long pikes and fighting with greater discipline, Philip's soldiers were a powerful force.

Philip proved the value of his ideas soon after becoming king. His powerful army defeated the Illyrians, who had won a victory over the Macedonians just a few months before.

Philip Conquers Greece Philip then turned to conquer Greece. First, he tried to win the loyalty of each city-state with diplomacy. When these tactics failed, he went to war.

Analyze Images
Macedonians use sarissas in battle. **Use Visual Information** How would these long pikes be an advantage in a battle like this?

DIFFERENTIATED INSTRUCTION

Special Education Tell students that Philip defeated the Illyrians. Then he wanted to defeat Greece. Ask students what reason a king might have to want to conquer other countries. Guide them to consider such motives as the desire for territory, wealth, and enslaved laborers. Discuss the cost of conquest in terms of people's lives. Ask if they think acquiring new territory was worth the cost.

Below Level Have students look at the image on the page. Ask them what they thought the battle was like. Ask them what they would think about war if they survived a battle like that.

Advanced Have students research what it might have been like to be a soldier in Philip's army. Tell them to find out more about the weapons soldiers used and how the army was organized. Ask them to share their knowledge with the class.

WORKSHEET **TEACHER RESOURCES**

Have students who need additional support use the following worksheets from the Teacher Resources on the course:

- **Reading Support**
- **English Language Development**
- **Lesson Summary**

INVESTIGATE

What Fueled Macedonia's Rise?

Discuss the rise of Macedonia. How did Philip make Macedonia a dominant power?

Draw Conclusions How did Xerxes' invasion of Greece help Macedonia regain its independence? *(Macedonians were able to regain their independence because Persia was greatly weakened by its defeat in Greece.)*

Compare and Contrast In what way was Philip's success in war similar to the past successes of Athens and Sparta? *(Athens had the advantage of a powerful navy; Sparta had the advantage of a powerful army; Philip had the advantage of a well-disciplined army that fought with new tactics and a new weapon—the sarissa.)*

ELD TIP English learners can practice language skills by talking about illustrations. Look at the illustration of Macedonians in battle. Have students work as a group to list words describing the scene.

ANSWERS

Use Visual Information *Macedonian soldiers could strike at the enemy before enemy soldiers could reach them. They could also use the sarissa to stop enemy soldiers from reaching them.*

Alexander on the March

Discuss the ascendancy of Alexander. How did Alexander spread Greek culture throughout the world? How did his empire end?

Apply Concepts How would leading his army into battle have inspired great loyalty among Alexander's soldiers? *(They saw that he was willing to take the same risks they were taking; they respected a commander who was willing to fight and could fight well.)*

Draw Conclusions After putting down a rebellion against him, Alexander burned Thebes to the ground. What does that say about him? *(He was sometimes ruthless.)*

In 338, Philip, along with his son Alexander, who led the cavalry, won a decisive battle in central Greece over the combined armies of Thebes and Athens. Philip gained control of all of Greece. The city-states were allowed to keep their governments. However, they were expected to support Philip in his next goal—a war against Persia. But as preparations were being made for the invasion of Asia, Philip was assassinated, or murdered, during his daughter's wedding.

READING CHECK **Identify Supporting Details** How did Philip strengthen his power?

Alexander on the March

Alexander, Philip's 20-year-old son, now gained the throne. Alexander was already a military leader. His brilliant mind had been shaped by the famous scientist and philosopher, Aristotle. Alexander was filled with dreams of glory. As a boy, Alexander's favorite book was a copy of the *Iliad* that Aristotle had given to him. Alexander wanted to be like the book's hero, Achilles. This ambition would inspire his spectacular conquests.

Alexander would lead his armies through Persia, central Asia, and Europe. His conquests would spread Greek culture well beyond Greece, but his first task was to secure its control.

Did you know?
Alexander was the first Greek ruler to shave his beard—a fashion that lasted 500 years!

Conquering Greece After Philip's death, some city-states in Greece tried to regain their independence. Alexander quickly crushed these revolts. To discourage future rebellions, he burned Thebes to the ground.

With Greece secure, Alexander turned eastward. In 334, he took his army of 30,000 foot soldiers and 5,500 cavalry troops into Asia. Alexander inspired fierce loyalty among his soldiers by personally leading them in battle.

BIOGRAPHY
5 Things to Know About
ALEXANDER THE GREAT
King and Conquerer (356 BCE–323 BCE)

- His mother, Olympias, was the daughter of King Neoptolemus of Epirus, a region in northwest Greece and southern Albania.
- He left with his mother on the day his father married a new wife.
- He won his first victory against the Persians at the Granicus River in 334 BCE.
- After conquering Egypt, Alexander let Egyptians practice their own religion.
- Although he named many cities for himself, he also named one for his horse.

Critical Thinking Looking at Alexander's lifespan, what was so remarkable about his many victories?

INTEGRATED ENGLISH LANGUAGE DEVELOPMENT

Productive Explain to students that writing about one's beliefs is called argumentative writing. Ask what it means to argue. Discuss the idea that a good argument is a point of view that is supported by facts.

Emerging Read aloud the section Alexander on the March with the class. Then ask them to read the section again independently. Tell them to write down three reasons why Alexander deserves to be called "great" and three reasons why he might not be "great."

Expanding Arrange students in pairs. Have each pair choose a position for or against Alexander's "greatness." Tell them to work on a statement of their belief about him. Then have them use their notes to list all the reasons for their point of view.

ANSWERS

Identify Supporting Details *He developed his army by organizing the men into phalanxes, arming them with long pikes, and training them to change direction in battle without losing formation.*

Integrate Information *Alexander died when in his early 30s, having built a huge empire in only 11 years. He proved himself to be a superb leader while he was still young.*

274 Lesson 6.8 • Alexander and the Hellenistic World

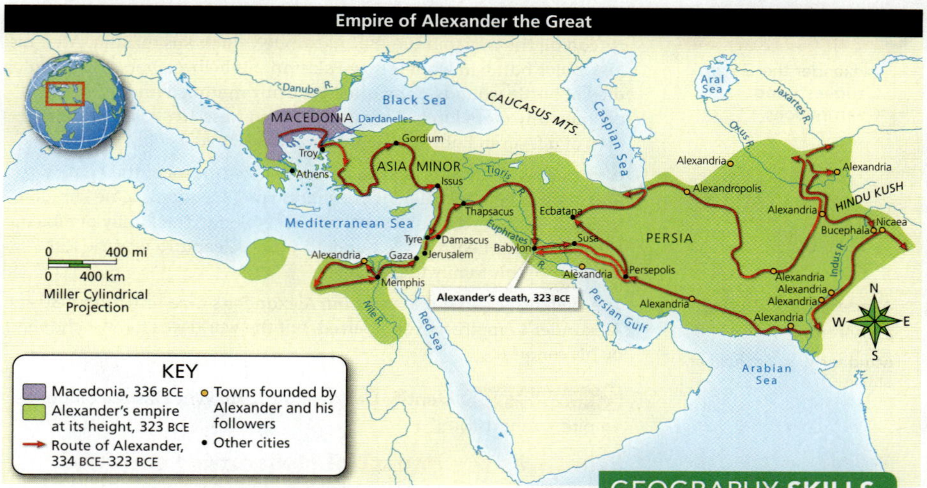

GEOGRAPHY SKILLS

Alexander built a vast empire in only 11 years.

1. **Location** How far south did Alexander's empire extend?
2. **Identify Cause and Effect** Across which three continents did Alexander's empire stretch? What effect did this conquest have on these lands?

Hoping for World Conquest In Asia, Alexander freed the Ionian city-states from Persian rule. He marched south to capture the cities along the Mediterranean coast. Then the army marched to Egypt. The Egyptians welcomed Alexander for liberating them from the Persians. Before leaving Egypt, he founded the city of Alexandria on the edge of the Nile delta.

From Egypt, Alexander headed back toward Persia. By the end of 330, he had defeated the Persian king.

Alexander was not satisfied with the defeat of the Persian empire. His eyes were fixed on a greater goal—world conquest. He led his army farther east, into Afghanistan and India. These were lands no Greek had ever seen. Because he built a vast empire in only 11 years, people called him "Alexander the Great."

The Hellenistic Period Alexander founded Greek-style cities everywhere he went. In these cities, Greek customs mingled with the ideas and art of other lands. Greek soldiers, traders, and artisans settled in these new areas. From Egypt to India, the Greeks built temples and filled them with Greek statues. Those already living in these lands absorbed Greek ideas and customs. Out of this exchange emerged a new form of Greek culture called **Hellenistic**, or Greek-like. The word *Hellenistic* comes from the Greeks' word for themselves: Hellenes.

Greek culture mixed with local cultures in Egypt, Persia, and India. For example, the Egyptian goddess Isis was given a place in Greek mythology and was honored across the Hellenistic region.

Draw Conclusions The Egyptians welcomed Alexander because he freed them from the Persians. What does this suggest about how Alexander might have been regarded in other places? *(He might have been seen as a liberator instead of a conqueror.)*

Apply Concepts The culture that Alexander spread across the world was called **Hellenistic**, or Greek-like. Why wasn't it called Greek? *(It wasn't a purely Greek culture. Alexander was inspired by Greek culture, but he was Macedonian.)*

Integrate Information Do you think it was good that Greek culture spread throughout Alexander's empire? Why or why not? *(Accept all reasonable responses. Sample response: I think it good because Greek culture valued things like education, so there was probably more education in some places that became part of Alexander's empire.)*

Integrate Information Do you think Alexander was a good ruler? Why or why not? *(He allowed conquered people to go on living as they had before. He also allowed women to be educated.)*

ELD.PI.A.1

Bridging Have students work together to write a paragraph arguing their case. Remind them to include a statement of their belief, supported by facts from the text. Tell them to end their paragraph with a sentence that restates their opening statement.

WORKSHEET **TEACHER RESOURCES**

For additional IELD support addressing these standards, have students complete the Lesson ELD activity from the Teacher Resources found on the course.

ANSWERS

Location *His empire extended into India and Egypt*

Identify Cause and Effect *Alexander's empire stretched from Europe into Asia and Africa; His conquests spread Greek culture.*

INTERACTIVE **INTERACTIVE GALLERY**

Alexander the Great's Conquests and Contributions

Interactive Instruction Display the Interactive Gallery: Alexander the Great's Conquests and Contributions for the class. Click through the gallery to learn more about Alexander. Ask: What qualities did Alexander display in his life? *(Sample responses: courage, ambition, ego, ruthlessness, openmindedness)*

ACTIVE CLASSROOM

Use the Wallpaper strategy. Have each student design a piece of "wallpaper" on which they complete the following sentence: Alexander was __________. Encourage students to design their wallpaper creatively. Then, post the wallpaper. Have students take a gallery walk and note what others have written.

What Was the Impact of Hellenistic Learning?

Discuss **Hellenistic** Egypt. How did **Hellenistic** Egypt influence its own world and today's world?

Find Evidence What detail in the text shows how Aristotle's constant search for knowledge influenced Alexander? *(When Alexander led his army into Asia, he brought scientists to study local plants and animals.)*

ANSWERS

Identify Cause and Effect *Alexander died young, before solidifying his empire.*

Use Visual Information *The city was planned carefully and thoughtfully laid out.*

INTERACTIVE

Alexander the Great's Conquests and Contributions

The Fall of the Greek Empire Because of Alexander, Greek culture spread all the way to India. But Alexander's luck was turning. After his last major battle in what is now Pakistan, his beloved horse Bucephalus died of battle wounds. Soon after, his army mutinied and refused to conquer any more lands. The army headed west. In 323, Alexander died of a fever in Babylon. He was not quite 33 years old.

Alexander's infant son was too young to take control of the empire, so Alexander's generals divided the empire into kingdoms. One kingdom, in Egypt, was ruled by a general named Ptolemy. The family of Ptolemy ruled Egypt for nearly three hundred years. Cleopatra was the last member of this family to rule Egypt.

Academic Vocabulary
period • *n.*, a span of time
acquire • *v.*, to get hold of, obtain

The Hellenistic **period** lasted from Alexander's time until about 30 BCE. Alexander's empire was short-lived, but the world was forever changed by his conquests.

READING CHECK **Identify Cause and Effect** Why was Alexander's empire so short-lived?

What was the Impact of Hellenistic Learning?

Alexander the Great had been deeply impressed by his teacher Aristotle's interest in the world. When Alexander led his army into Asia, he brought scientists to study local plants and animals. Alexander's support for research flourished in one of the cities that he founded—Alexandria, the Greek capital of Egypt.

Hellenistic Egypt Alexandria became an important site of encounter as the city grew rich from handling the trade between peoples of Europe, Africa, and Asia. The wealth of the city helped fund projects like the Great Library. The Library was founded by the Ptolemies, the Hellenistic rulers of Egypt. Their goal was to **acquire** a copy of every book in the world. Over the years, the collection grew to about 500,000 book rolls, or scrolls.

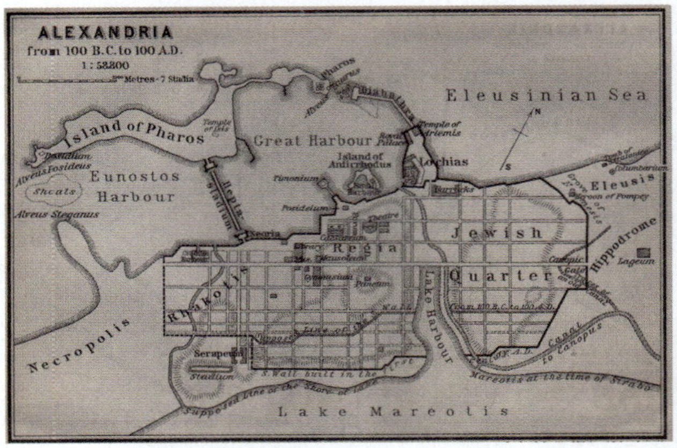

Analyze Images This map of Alexandria shows the grids created by the layout of its main streets. **Draw Conclusions** What does the street grid tell you about how the city was planned and built?

HISTORY BACKGROUND

The Great Library at Alexandria The Ptolemies did everything they could to acquire books for Alexandria's library. It is said that they searched every ship entering the city's harbor. Books that were found were taken to the library, where it was decided if the book would be returned. Sometimes a copy of the book was made. The original remained in the library and the copy was returned to the ship. In the library, these books were labeled "from the ships."

City of Scholars Alexandria's library and museum attracted some of the most important scholars in history. It was here that Jewish scholars created the Septuagint, a translation of the Hebrew Bible into Greek. Euclid, Theon, and Hypatia, who you read about in the last lesson, all lived and worked in Alexandria.

Although the inventor and mathematician Archimedes spent most of his life in Syracuse, he may have studied in Alexandria. Archimedes created many useful inventions. One of them, the Archimedean screw, is still used to lift water for irrigation or to drain swamps. Archimedes also made important contributions to mathematics.

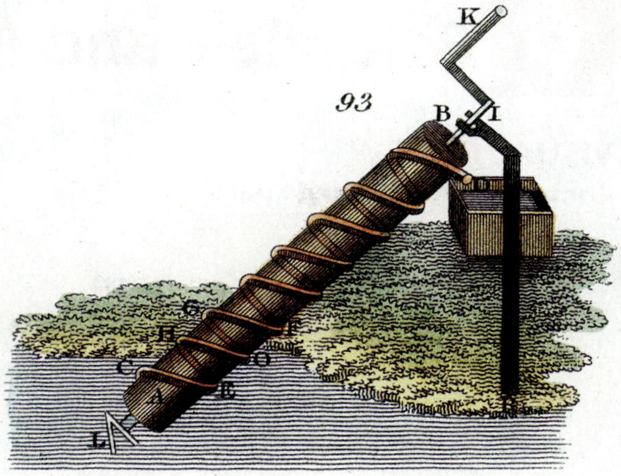

▲ A diagram of an Archimedean screw shows a method of draining water.

Greek Culture Spreads Greek culture spread during Alexander's conquests. In Italy, Greek culture influenced the Romans, long before they conquered Greek lands. The union of Greek and Roman culture created what we call Greco-Roman or **classical civilization**. As you will read later, the Romans spread this civilization across even larger parts of the world.

Exchange Between Continents During the Hellenistic period, many cities along the Silk Road became sites of encounter for people of different religions, cultures, and regions across Europe, Africa, and Asia. The Silk Road connected people from the Mediterranean Sea to China. As a result, cities from Athens to Alexandria to Luoyang in China became great gathering places for traders, artisans, and merchants of different cultures. Each brought new ideas and new ways of life.

READING CHECK **Identify Cause and Effect** How did Alexandria become so rich?

Lesson Check

HSS 6.4.7, 6.4.8; ELD.PI.A.2

Practice Vocabulary

1. How did Alexander's men use the **sarissa**?
2. What cultures influenced **Hellenistic** culture?

Critical Thinking and Writing

3. **Draw Inferences** Why did Alexander burn Thebes to the ground?
4. **Draw Conclusions** How was Alexandria a site of encounter?
5. **Writing Workshop: Revise** Now that you have read about the fall of the independent Greek city-states, make revisions to your essay to include these new details. If possible, exchange drafts with a partner and comment respectfully on one another's work.

LESSON CHECK

1. Alexander's men carried sarissas, which were long spears, into battle. **DOK1**
2. Greek, Egyptian, Persian, and Indian cultures all influenced Hellenistic culture. **DOK1**
3. He burned it as a warning to other city-states not to rebel. **DOK2**
4. Alexandria was a center of trade between Europe, Africa, and Asia. It attracted important scholars and became a center of learning and a source of wealth. **DOK3**
5. Responses will be students' revisions to their essays. **DOK3**

HSS 6.4.7, 6.4.8; ELD.PI.C.10.a

SYNTHESIZE

Assess and Reteach Have students use a Give One, Get One strategy to complete Lesson Check questions 1–4. Ask volunteers to share their answers with the class.

If responses are incorrect, use the Guiding Questions to discuss the lesson's main ideas, focusing on the ideas that are causing difficulty.

ACTIVE JOURNAL

Writing Workshop Have students complete the Lesson 8 Writing Task in their Active Journals. Students will revise their essays to include details about the fall of Greece.

DEMONSTRATE

ASSESSMENT **ONLINE LESSON QUIZ**

Assign the Online Lesson Quiz for this lesson if you haven't already done so. Students will be offered automatic remediation or enrichment based on their score.

DISCUSSION **DISCUSSION BOARD**

Post this question to the class on the Discussion Board:

Synthesize Which person that you read about would you most like to learn more about? Why? *(Sample response: I would like to learn more about Alexander the Great because he accomplished amazing things at a young age.)*

ANSWERS

Identify Cause and Effect *Its location brought traders from three continents, which made it wealthy.*

Lesson 6.8 • Alexander and the Hellenistic World 277

HSS 6.4.1, 6.4.2, 6.4.3, 6.4.4, 6.4.6, 6.4.7, 6.4.8; ELA W.6.2, WHST.6.2; ELD.PI.C.10.a

Review and Assessment

VISUAL REVIEW

Direct students' attention to the "Comparing Athens and Sparta" Venn diagram. Review the differences between these two city-states, and discuss the reasons for the differences.

Direct students' attention to the "Notable Greek Achievements" table. Ask volunteers to describe how these achievements influenced the world we live in today.

READING REVIEW

WORKSHEET **TEACHER RESOURCES**

Have students who need additional support read the Lesson Summary, available in Teacher Resources on the Realize course.

GAMES **TOPIC MINI-GAMES**

For additional vocabulary practice, students can go online to access the Topic Mini-Games in Realize.

Quest FINDINGS

Create a News Magazine

Have students complete their Topic Quests by writing their segment for their news magazine in their Active Journals. Each student should research and write one segment. Student groups should then present their news magazine, either recorded or performed live, to the class.

TOPIC 6

Review and Assessment

VISUAL REVIEW

Comparing Athens and Sparta

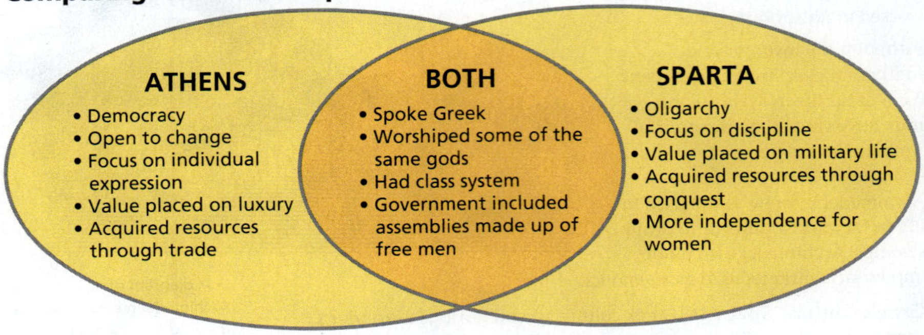

Notable Greek Achievements

Field	Achievement
art	realistic depictions
architecture	details such as columns and sculptures
sports	founding of the Olympic games
literature	lyric poetry, comedy and drama, Aesop's fables
philosophy	Socratic method, focus on reason, Stoicism
science and technology	the use of observation and hypothesis
mathematics	Pythagorean theorem
medicine	Hippocratic oath

READING REVIEW

Use the Take Notes and Practice Vocabulary activities in your Active Journal to review the topic.

INTERACTIVE

Practice vocabulary using the Topic Mini-Games.

Quest FINDINGS

Present Your News Magazine

Get help for writing your news magazine in your Active Journal.

278 Topic 6 • Ancient Greece

ANSWERS

1. Greece's mountains isolated communities. As a result, city-states developed separately and differently. City-states near the sea grew as centers of commerce, bringing them into contact with the wider world. **DOK2**
2. the main political unit in ancient Greece **DOK1**
3. Coastal areas allowed settlers to anchor their ships and set up trading ports. **DOK2**
4. An oligarchy is a government run by a small group of people. **DOK1**
5. Lyric poems were short poems often performed by singers accompanied by musicians. Epic poems were long tales that reflected the Greeks' belief that the gods controlled their lives. **DOK2**
6. Greece, Asia Minor, Egypt, Persia, Afghanistan, India **DOK2**
7. Sea trade resulted in the Minoan and Myccenean people traveling widely and acquiring new ideas. **DOK2**

HSS 6.4.1, 6.4.2, 6.4.3, 6.4.4, 6.4.6, 6.4.7, 6.4.8; ELA W.6.2, WHST.6.2; ELD.PI.C.10.a

ASSESSMENT

Vocabulary and Key Ideas

1. **Trace** How did the geography of Greece give rise to city-states?
2. **Define** What is a **polis**?
3. **Describe** Why did Greek colonists settle along coastal areas?
4. **Define** What is an oligarchy?
5. **Describe** What is the difference between a lyric poem and epic poem?
6. **Recall** What regions became part of Hellenistic Greece?

Critical Thinking and Writing

7. **Determine Relevance** How did trade contribute to the development of the Minoan and Mycenaean cultures?
8. **Compare and Contrast** What were the key differences between Athens and Sparta?
9. **Draw Conclusions** What caused the Greek city-states to become part of the Macedonian empire?
10. **Revisit the Essential Question** Of the forms of government you learned about in this topic, which do you think was the best form? Explain your reasoning.
11. **Writing Workshop: Write an Explanatory Essay** Using the thesis statement and details you recorded in your Active Journal, complete an essay on this question: Why did the power of the independent Greek city-states rise, peak, and fall?

Analyze Primary Sources

12. In the view of Aristotle in the selection below, what is the role of government?
    - **A.** to conquer other governments
    - **B.** to do the least for their citizens
    - **C.** to do the greatest amount of good
    - **D.** to rule only for the aristocracy

"Every state is a community of some kind, and every community is established with a view to some good; for mankind always act in order to obtain that which they think good. But, if all communities aim at some good, the state or political community, which is the highest of all, and which embraces all the rest, aims at good in a greater degree than any other, and at the highest good."

—Aristotle, *Politics*

Analyze Maps

Use the map at the right to answer the following questions.

13. Locate Athens and Sparta on the map.
14. Which body of water is west of the Peloponnesian Peninsula?
15. What body of water does the letter D mark?

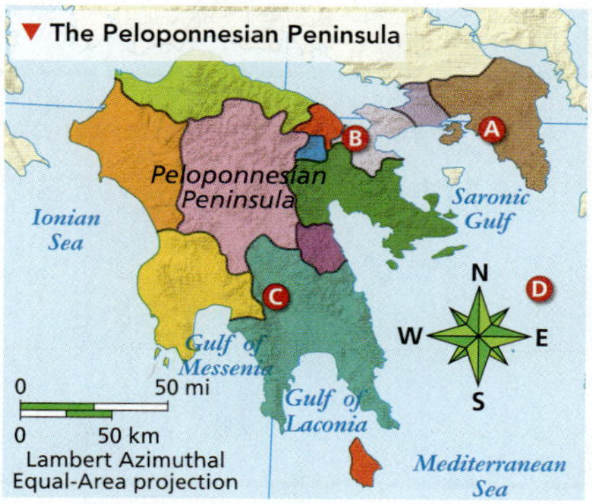

The Peloponnesian Peninsula

8. Athens was a democracy, with an emphasis on new ideas and the pursuit of luxury. Sparta was an oligarchy, with an emphasis on discipline and the military. Women in Sparta had more freedom then women in Athens. **DOK2**

9. Phillip and Alexander of Macedonia conquered them. Even though they kept their independence, they needed to support Macedonia in its fight against Persia in order to avoid future war. Eventually, as Macedonia became stronger, the city-states were absorbed into the empire. **DOK3**

10. Students should choose one of the forms of government, such as Athenian democracy, and give examples from the text explaining its benefits. **DOK3**

11. Students' essays should be well-constructed explanations that reflect a knowledge of the reasons behind the rise and later fall of the independent Greek city-states. **DOK4**

12. C. to do the greatest amount of good **DOK3**

13. A; C **DOK1**

14. Ionian Sea **DOK1**

15. different city-states **DOK2**

ASSESSMENT **TOPIC SYNTHESIZE**

Use the Topic Synthesize to help students revisit and reflect on the Essential Question for this Topic.

ASSESSMENT **TOPIC TEST**

For summative assessment, assign the Topic Test in Realize

TOPIC 7

Topic-at-a-Glance

The Roman Republic

Pacing: Approximately 15 periods, 7.5 blocks	Resources: Student Edition	Resources: Active Journal	Resources: Online	Pacing	California Standards
CONNECT					
NBC LEARN VIDEO Cicero and the Roman Republic			●	10 min.	HSS 6.7.1, 6.7.2
ESSENTIAL QUESTION ACTIVITY What is the best form of government?		✓	●	10 min.	HSS 6.7.2
OVERVIEW ACTIVITY: TIMELINE & MAP The Roman Republic		✓	●	10 min.	HSS 6.7.1, 6.7.2
Quest KICK OFF: Ask Questions	✓	✓		20 min.	Analysis HI.1; ELA RI.6.1, RH.6.1, W.62, WHST.6.2; ELD.P1.A.2
INVESTIGATE					
LESSONS 1–4	See Lesson-at-a-Glance pages				
Quest INVESTIGATE: Quest Connections	✓	✓		20 min.	HSS 6.7.2, 6.7.4; Analysis HI.1; ELA RI.6.1, RH.6.1, W.6.2, WHST.6.2; ELD.P1.A.2
SYNTHESIZE					
WRITER'S WORKSHOP Write an Explanatory Essay		✓	●	30 min.	HSS 6.7.2; ELA W.6.2, WHST.6.2
TOPIC MINI-GAMES The Roman Republic			●	10 min.	Analysis HI.1; ELA RI.6.1, RH.6.1, W.62, WHST.6.2; ELD.P1.A.2
Quest SOURCES: Examine Primary Sources			●	30 min.	Analysis HI.1; ELA RI.6.1, RH.6.1, W.62, WHST.6.2; ELD.P1.A.2
DEMONSTRATE					
TOPIC REVIEW AND ASSESSMENT The Roman Republic	✓		●	20 min.	
TOPIC TEST The Roman Republic	✓		●	30 min.	
Quest FINDINGS: Write Your Explanatory Essay	✓	✓	●	30 min.	Analysis HI.1; ELA RI.6.1, RH.6.1, W.62, WHST.6.2; ELD.P1.A.2

Quest

Each Quest is designed to reinforce the topic content through an inquiry arc that students work on throughout the topic. This topic's Quest, The Roman Influence, is a document-based writing inquiry in which students write an explanatory essay that explains how the Roman republic's government influenced later governments.

Active Journal Resources

- Ask Questions
- Quest Connections
- Examine Primary Sources
- Write Your Explanatory Essay

Quest Sources Online

- Preamble to the U.S. Constitution
- Law of the Twelve Tables
- Separation of Powers in Practice
- U.S. Capitol Building and Roman Pantheon
- The Founders of the United States' Classical Education
- Rubric for an Explanatory Essay

Additional Resources

Support for Struggling Readers

- Reading Support, Teacher Resources
- Lesson Summaries, Teacher Resources
- English Language Development Teacher Resources

Suggested Resources

- *Ancient Civilization: Rome* by Valerie Bodden
- *Art and Culture of Ancient Rome* by Nicholas Pistone, Giovanni Di Pasquale, and Matilde Bardi
- *DK Eyewitness Books: Ancient Rome* by Simon James
- *City: A Story of Roman Planning and Construction* by David Macaulay
- *When Rome Ruled*, a six-part video series by National Geographic

Beyond the Classroom

Support Parent Involvement

For their Quest writing project, students will need to read and understand informational texts about the influence that Rome had on other governments. Parents can use the tips for sixth graders on parenttoolkit.com to help their students learn how to identify essential information while reading.

The Roman Republic Rises

Objectives

Objective 1: Describe how geography affected Rome's growth.

Objective 2: Analyze how the Etruscans and Greeks influenced Roman culture.

Objective 3: Identify the form of government the Romans founded.

Objective 4: Explain how the Romans gained control of the Italian Peninsula.

	Resources			Pacing	
	Student Edition	Active Journal	Online	approx. 3 periods, 1.5 blocks	California Standards
CONNECT					
VIDEO Rome's Founding and Early Days			●	5 min.	HSS 6.7.1
START UP ACTIVITY Get Ready to Read	✓	✓	●	5 min.	HSS 6.7.1
TAKE NOTES AND PRACTICE VOCABULARY		✓			
INVESTIGATE					
READ Lesson 1: The Roman Republic Rises	✓	✓	●	40 min.	HSS 6.7.1
INTERACTIVE MAP Growth of the Roman Republic, 500 BCE to 44 BCE			●	10 min.	HSS 6.7.1
PRIMARY SOURCES Livy, *History of Rome*	✓		●	40 min.	HSS 6.7.1; ELA RI.6.2; RH.6.2
READING SUPPORT			●		
SYNTHESIZE					
WRITING WORKSHOP Develop a Clear Thesis	✓	✓	●	10 min.	ELA W.6.2, WHST.6.2
LESSON SUMMARY			●		
DEMONSTRATE					
LESSON QUIZ			●	10 min.	HSS 6.7.1

Objectives

Objective 1: Analyze why and how power was divided among different groups in the Roman republic.

Objective 2: Describe how the Romans viewed the concept of citizenship.

Objective 3: Explain how the Roman republic functioned.

Objective 4: Analyze the influence the Roman republic had on later governments.

Government of the Republic

	Resources			Pacing	California Standards
	Student Edition	Active Journal	Online	approx. 2 periods, 1 blocks	
CONNECT					
VIDEO Citizenship in Rome			Video	5 min.	HSS 6.7.2
START UP ACTIVITY Get Ready to Read	✓	✓	Online book	5 min.	HSS 6.7.2
TAKE NOTES AND PRACTICE VOCABULARY		✓			
INVESTIGATE					
READ Lesson 2: Government of the Republic	✓	✓	Online book	40 min.	HSS 6.7.1, 6.7.2
QUICK ACTIVITY Explore Roman Numerals		✓			
INTERACTIVE SIMULATION The Race of Honors			Interactive	10 min.	HSS 6.7
READING SUPPORT			Document		
SYNTHESIZE					
WRITING WORKSHOP Support Thesis With Details	✓	✓	Online book	10 min.	ELA W.6.2, WHST.6.2
LESSON SUMMARY			Document		
DEMONSTRATE					
LESSON QUIZ			Quiz	10 min.	HSS 6.7.1, 6.7.2

Society in the Republic

Objectives

Objective 1: Describe the roles men and women held in Roman society.

Objective 2: Understand how life differed for different classes of Romans.

Objective 3: Explain how religion and citizenship were connected in Romans' lives.

	Resources: Student Edition	Resources: Active Journal	Resources: Online	Pacing (approx. 3 periods, 1.5 blocks)	California Standards
CONNECT					
VIDEO Roman Society			▶	5 min.	HSS 6.7
START UP ACTIVITY Get Ready to Read	✓	✓	📖	5 min.	HSS 6.7
TAKE NOTES AND PRACTICE VOCABULARY		✓			
INVESTIGATE					
READ Lesson 3: Society in the Republic	✓	✓	📖	40 min.	HSS 6.7
QUICK ACTIVITY How Does Roman Society Compare?		✓			HSS 6.7
INTERACTIVE 3D Model Roman Villa			👆	10 min.	HSS 6.7
ANALYSIS SKILLS Identify Central Issues and Problems	✓		📖	30 min.	Analysis HI.1
21ST CENTURY SKILLS TUTORIAL Solve Problems			▶	10 min.	Analysis HI.1
READING SUPPORT			📄		
SYNTHESIZE					
WRITING WORKSHOP Draft Your Essay	✓	✓	📖	10 min.	ELA W.6.2, WHST.6.2
LESSON SUMMARY			📄		
DEMONSTRATE					
LESSON QUIZ			☑	10 min.	HSS 6.7

The Republic Struggles

Objectives

Objective 1: Describe how Rome changed after the Punic Wars.

Objective 2: Identify the strengths and weaknesses of the Roman republic.

Objective 3: Explain why the Roman republic fell.

	Resources: Student Edition	Resources: Active Journal	Resources: Online	Pacing (approx. 3 periods, 1.5 blocks)	California Standards
CONNECT					
VIDEO Why Did the Roman Republic End?			✓	5 min.	HSS 6.7.1, 6.7.4
START UP ACTIVITY Get Ready to Read	✓	✓	✓	5 min.	HSS 6.7
TAKE NOTES AND PRACTICE VOCABULARY		✓			
INVESTIGATE					
READ Lesson 4: The Republic Struggles	✓	✓	✓	30 min.	HSS 6.7.1, 6.7.3, 6.7.4
INTERACTIVE GALLERY Who Was Julius Caesar?			✓	10 min.	HSS 6.7.1, 6.7.4
ANALYSIS SKILLS Analyze Sequence, Causation, and Correlation	✓		✓	30 min.	Analysis HI.2
21ST CENTURY SKILLS TUTORIAL Analyze Cause and Effect			✓	10 min.	Analysis HI.2
INTERACTIVE BIOGRAPHY Julius Caesar			✓	10 min.	HSS 6.7.1
READING SUPPORT			✓		
SYNTHESIZE					
WRITING WORKSHOP Write a Conclusion	✓	✓	✓	10 min.	ELA W.6.2, WHST.6.2
LESSON SUMMARY			✓		
DEMONSTRATE					
LESSON QUIZ			✓	10 min.	HSS 6.7.1, 6.7.3, 6.7.4

TOPIC 7 The Roman Republic

800 BCE–30 BCE

HSS 6.7, 6.7.1, 6.7.2, 6.7.3, 6.7.4; Analysis HI.1, HI.3

CONNECT

Introduction

At about the same time that the ancient Greeks held the first Olympic games, a small city called Rome was founded on the Italian Peninsula. Rome went on to develop a republic and to conquer many of the surrounding lands. Roman government had a strong influence on later governments, including that of the United States. Over time, however, the Roman republic weakened and fell.

Activate Prior Knowledge

Have students describe what they know of the way the U.S. government works. Ask: Do citizens vote directly on most laws? *(No, citizens vote for legislators who propose and vote on laws.)* Explain that government by representatives is one of the primary differences between a direct democracy and a republic.

Explore the Essential Question

Project the Essential Question activity from the course. Have a volunteer read the question. As students consider the Essential Question, remind them that even today people debate about how big government should be and how much power it should have to regulate citizens.

ACTIVE JOURNAL

Essential Question Have students begin to explore the Essential Question in their Active Journals.

Classify Ask students to name as many different types of government as they can think of and make a class list of their answers. *(Sample Answers: democracy, republic, monarchy, empire, dictatorship)* Then ask students to predict which of those forms of government they will read about in this topic.

TOPIC 7 The Roman Republic

800 BCE–30 BCE

GO ONLINE to access your digital course

- VIDEO
- AUDIO
- ETEXT
- INTERACTIVE
- WRITING
- GAMES
- WORKSHEET
- ASSESSMENT

Go back 2,500 years

to THE ROMAN REPUBLIC to discover the beginnings of one of the ancient world's greatest civilizations. You won't be surprised to find that its government, with a senate, judges, and a strong executive, had a major influence in shaping our own.

Explore The Essential Question

What is the best form of government?

Rome developed a new way of governing. How was the Roman republic different from the monarchies that came before it?

Unlock the Essential Question in your Active Journal.

280

ANALYZE VISUALS

Ask students to closely examine the photograph of Roman ruins. What details do they notice? *(Sample answers: There are arches and ornate columns. Some of the structures are very high. There is also a lot of rubble.)* Ask: What types of buildings do you think these might have been? Explain. *(Sample answers: Some of the ruins are very large, so they were probably public buildings. These may have been government or religious buildings.)*

HSS 6.7, 6.7.1, 6.7.2, 6.7.3, 6.7.4; Analysis HI.2, HI.6

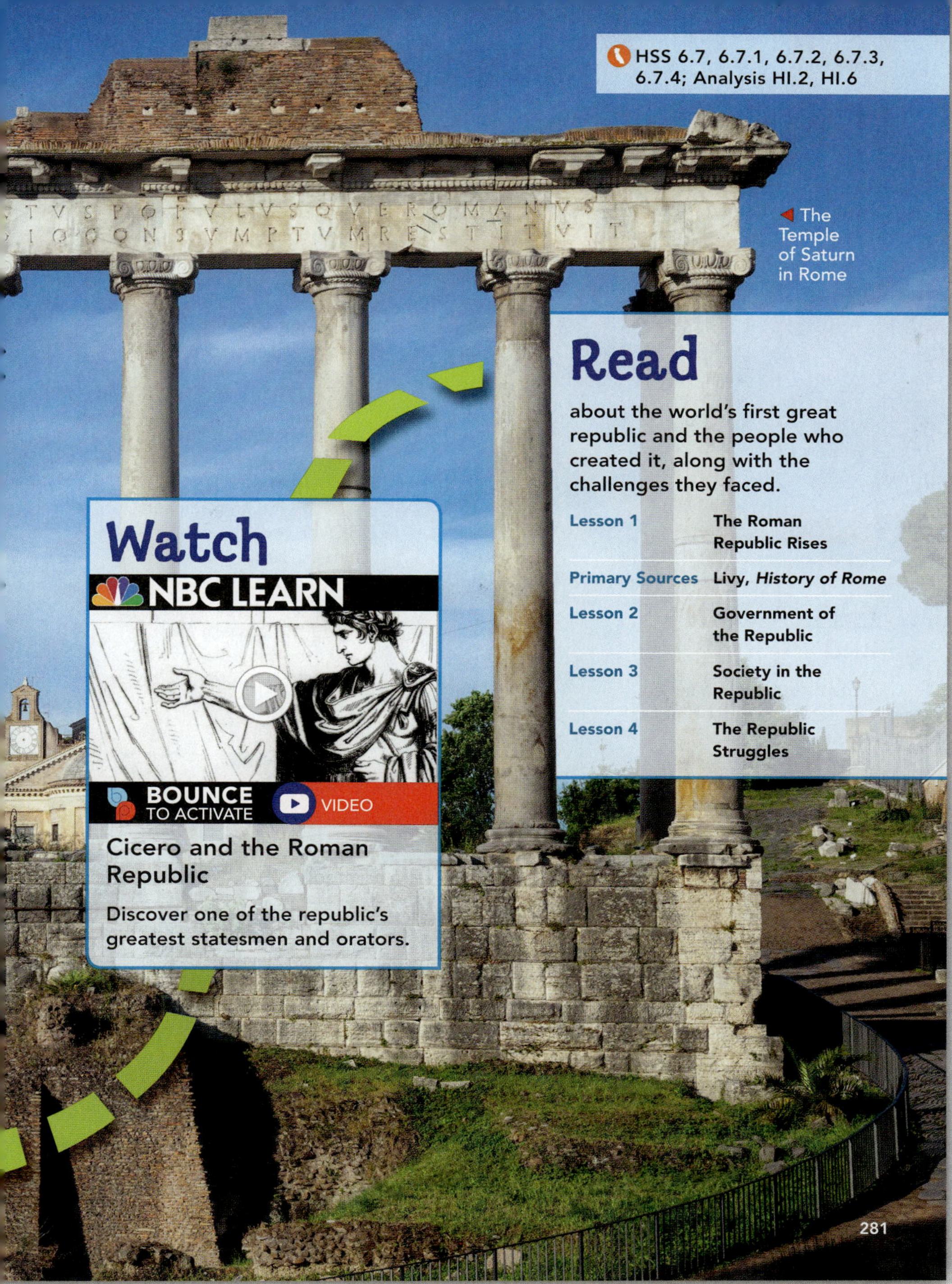

The Temple of Saturn in Rome

Read

about the world's first great republic and the people who created it, along with the challenges they faced.

Watch

NBC LEARN

BOUNCE TO ACTIVATE VIDEO

Cicero and the Roman Republic

Discover one of the republic's greatest statesmen and orators.

RECOGNIZE CULTURAL AND EXPERIENTIAL BACKGROUNDS

Make use of your knowledge of students' lives to make connections between their own experiences, backgrounds, and interests and the content of this topic. If you have students whose ethnic heritage is related to the content of this topic, make an effort to emphasize the contributions and achievements of this society and how it has enriched the world.

If appropriate, allow the students the opportunity to share cultural, ethnic, or linguistic traditions and knowledge from their experiences.

If students have family experiences (such as travel to or family members who have lived in the region being studied), allow them to share relevant stories.

Watch

VIDEO NBC LEARN VIDEO

Project the Topic video about Cicero and the Roman republic. After viewing the video, ask students to respond to the following questions:

Paraphrase In your own words, restate what Cicero believed was important about a republic. *(Sample answers: Civilians need to control the military. The government belongs to the people. The important values of a republic are patriotic duty, honesty, and justice, with justice being the most important.)*

Summarize What actions did Cicero take to try to protect the republic? *(He stopped a conspiracy to overthrow the republic; he spoke out against the rise of dictators, attacking both Julius Caesar and Mark Antony.)*

Read

Share these lesson previews with students.

Lesson 1: Geographic advantages helped Rome grow. Rome changed from a monarchy to a republic.

Primary Sources: Roman historian Livy recounts the legendary founding of Rome.

Lesson 2: Rome had an unwritten constitution and a government with separation of powers. Two main orders of citizens called patricians and plebeians existed.

Lesson 3: Roman society was dominated by men, who ruled their families. It was also divided into classes—the wealthy, the poor, and those who were enslaved. Religion was a part of daily life.

Lesson 4: Rome came into conflict with Carthage, a North African city-state, for control of the Mediterranean. As Rome grew, the republic experienced conflicts that led to its overthrow and the founding of an empire.

TOPIC 7

HSS 6.7, 6.7.1, 6.7.2, 6.7.3, 6.7.4

What Happened and When?

Have students examine the timeline. Ask: How many years are shown on the timeline? *(1,000 years)* Ask: How much time occurred between the first settlement of Rome and the founding of the republic? *(about 291 years)* Who was Rome's first emperor, and when did his rule begin? *(Augustus became emperor in 30 BCE.)*

ACTIVE JOURNAL

Timeline Skills Students can also use the Timeline Skills activity in their Active Journals to record information about the history of the Roman republic as they read the topic. During their reading, they should add the dates of at least three events they think are important. After completing the topic, have students write a paragraph identifying the dates they added and explaining why each is significant.

INTERACTIVE — INTERACTIVE TIMELINE

Display the Interactive Topic Timeline for the class. Have volunteers read entries.

Discuss Ask students: Which event on this interactive timeline is an example of someone trying to conquer the Roman republic? *(Hannibal and his army tried, but failed to conquer the Roman republic.)*

TOPIC 7

The Roman Republic

800–30 BCE

Learn more about the Roman republic by making your own map and timeline in your Active Journal.

INTERACTIVE

Topic Map

Where was the Roman republic?

The ancient city of Rome was located on the Tiber River on the west coast of the Italian peninsula. Over several centuries, the republic expanded into much of western and southeastern Europe and the eastern and southern shores of the Mediterranean Sea. Locate the city of Rome on the larger map.

INTERACTIVE

Topic Timeline

What happened and when?

A town founded on seven hills grows into the biggest city in the world...epic power struggles...Explore the timeline to learn what was happening in Rome and the rest of the world during this period.

TOPIC EVENTS

800 BCE People first settle in Rome.

509 BCE The Roman republic is founded.

900 BCE | 700 BCE | 500 BCE

WORLD EVENTS

586 BCE Nebuchadnezzar II destroys the Temple in Jerusalem.

400 BCE Olmec civilization disappears in Central America.

DIFFERENTIATED INSTRUCTION

Special Education Explain that several of the entries on this timeline relate to government. Allow students to work in pairs to identify which entries those are and then compare their answers with those of another pair.

Below Level Make sure that students do not confuse Rome's republican government with today's Republican party. A republican form of government is one in which power rests with citizens, who elect representatives to make their laws.

Advanced Suggest that students research Caesar's appointment as dictator for life and write a speech supporting or criticizing it.

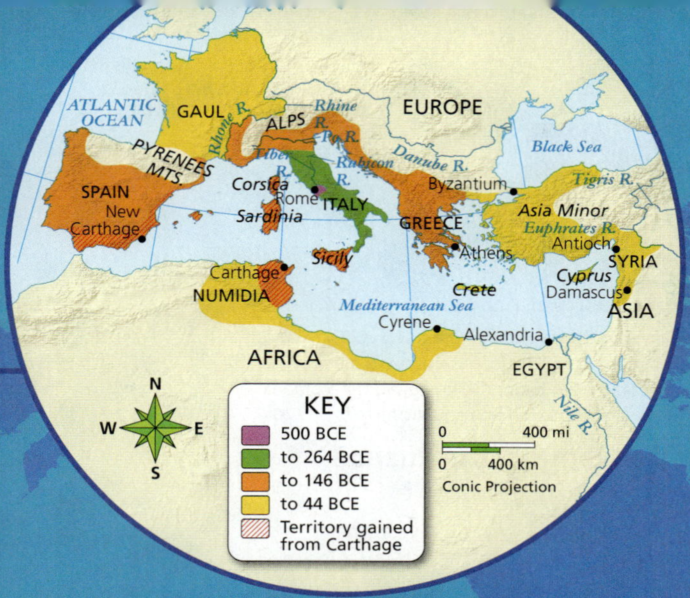

HSS 6.7, 6.7.1, 6.7.2, 6.7.3, 6.7.4

Who will you meet?

Aeneas, Trojan prince and legendary founder of Rome

Cicero, scholar, writer, and defender of the Roman republic's ideals

Julius Caesar, soldier-politician who dealt a final blow to the republic

218 BCE Hannibal's army invades Italy and threatens Rome.

146 BCE Rome destroys Carthage.

44 BCE Julius Caesar becomes dictator for life.

30 BCE Augustus becomes Rome's first emperor.

300 BCE | 100 BCE | 100 CE

221 BCE Shi Huangdi founds Qin Dynasty in China

185 BCE Last Maurya emperor dies in India

283

Where Was the Roman Republic?

Direct students' attention to the map of Europe in the student text. Make sure they identify the Italian Peninsula. Ask: How would you describe the position of the Italian Peninsula in relation to the Mediterranean Sea? *(It is on the north coast and extends into the central part of the sea.)* Ask: Where is Rome located on the Italian Peninsula? *(about halfway up the west coast)*

ACTIVE JOURNAL

Map Skills Have students use the Map Skills activity in their Active Journals to fill in an outline map of Europe with the labels of key geographic and political features.

Analyze Maps Was Italy's position advantageous for trade? Explain. *(Sample answer: Its central position in the Mediterranean is an advantage because traders going between the eastern and western ends of the sea would pass by Italy and probably stop there for supplies or trade.)*

INTERACTIVE — INTERACTIVE MAP

Display the Interactive Topic Map for the class. Work through the map with students to learn more about the culture of the Roman republic.

Have volunteers read the captions associated with the images. Ask: What other places were influenced by Roman culture? *(Sample answer: France, the lands along the Mediterranean, Carthage)*

Who Will You Meet?

Many students access historical materials best through the stories of the people who made them. Preview these key people that students will encounter in the topic. Read the short description of each, and then conduct a poll asking students which figure they are most interested in. Record the results on the board. Then ask volunteers why they are interested in a particular figure. *(Accept reasonable responses. Students may say that they are curious why a legendary figure such as Aeneas is included; that they want to know why Cicero believed so strongly in the republic; or that they wonder how Julius Caesar gained so much power.)*

COMMON MISCONCEPTIONS

Students may think that Roman names worked the way our names do, so that Julius was a first name and Caesar was a surname. In fact, male patricians usually had three names: the famous dictator's full name was Gaius Julius Caesar. Gaius was his personal name. Julius, the second name, was a clan name. (An individual in that clan was called Julius; the clan as a whole went by the plural form, the Julii.) Caesar, the third name, was used to distinguish which branch of the clan was meant. Some scholars believe that the name Caesar originally meant "hairy," which is ironic since statues of Julius Caesar indicate that he was losing his hair.

TOPIC 7

HSS 6.7.2, 6.7.4; Analysis HI.2; ELA RI.6.1, RH.6.1, W.6.2, WHST.6.2; ELD P1.A.2

Quest

Document-Based Writing Inquiry

The Roman Influence

Quest Kick Off

In this Quest, students will use the student text, other sources, and the Active Journal to write an explanatory essay about how Rome's government influenced later governments.

1 Ask Questions

Launch the Quest by discussing the Guiding Question as a class. Have students generate the questions they will need to have answered to accomplish the Quest in their Journals.

2 Investigate

As they read the lessons, remind students to look for and respond to the three Quest Connections in the student text that provide clues to their Quest. They should also identify and record two connections of their own. **Suggestion:** If students are struggling to identify their own connections, refer them to the Analysis Skills feature following Lesson 4, Analyze Sequence, Causation, and Correlation.

3 Examine Primary Sources

As students complete the topic, distribute the Quest Primary Sources for this topic.

Analyze Documents Have students process the primary sources in their Active Journals, focusing on identifying information related to the Guiding Question in preparation for writing their explanatory essays about the influence of Rome's government on later governments.

4 Write Your Explanatory Essay

When students complete the topic, have them return to the Quest, which can be used as a performance-based authentic assessment. To complete their Quests, they should follow the steps of (1) prewriting, (2) drafting their essays, (3) sharing with a partner, (4) revising the draft based on feedback, and (5) presenting the final product. **DOK4**

HSS 6.7.2, 6.7.4; Analysis HI.1; ELA RI.6.1, RH.6.1, W.6.2, WHST.6.2; ELD P1.C.10.a

Quest

Document-Based Writing Inquiry

The Roman Influence

Quest KICK OFF

In **509 BCE**, ancient Romans overthrew their king and established a republic, a form of government in which citizens vote and elect officials. In fact, the word *republic* come from Latin, the language the Romans spoke. What other influences did the Roman republic have?

How did Rome's government influence later governments?

Explore the Essential Question "What is the best form of government?" in this Quest.

▼ Statue of a Roman Senator

1 Ask Questions

First, you'll need to review the elements of Rome's government discussed in the topic. Then think about past and current governments in Europe, the Americas, Africa, and Asia to focus on in your explanatory essay. How do their governments compare to Rome's? Make a list of the questions you need to answer in your essay in your Active Journal.

2 Investigate

As you study the topic, look for Quest CONNECTIONS that indicate elements of Rome's government that have influenced the United States government or governments of other countries. Record your notes in your Active Journal.

3 Examine Primary Sources

Next explore a set of sources of information that reveal the influence of Rome's government on later governments. Capture your thoughts in your Active Journal.

Quest FINDINGS

4 Write Your Explanatory Essay

Next, develop an answer to the Guiding Question, and shape it into an essay explaining how Rome's government influenced later governments. Get help for this task in your Active Journal.

DIFFERENTIATED INSTRUCTION

Below Level Remind students that the term *influence* does not mean that every feature of the later government has to be the same as Rome's. For example, a government might have an elected leader that is called something other than a consul.

Special Education Allow students to draw a poster comparing the Roman government to a later government rather than writing a formal essay.

ENGLISH LANGUAGE DEVELOPMENT

Emerging Instead of writing an essay, encourage English learners to write a paragraph about one Roman influence on later governments or draw pictures showing Roman government and its influence.

LESSON 1

HSS 6.7.1

The Roman Republic Rises

BOUNCE TO ACTIVATE

VIDEO

GET READY TO READ

START UP

Study the photograph of the Tiber River valley and quickly preview the headings and images in the lesson. What do these images add to what you already know about Rome? Write down two facts you already know.

GUIDING QUESTIONS

- In what ways did geography affect Rome's growth?
- How did the Etruscans and Greeks influence Roman culture?
- What form of government did the Romans found?
- How did the Romans gain control of the Italian peninsula?

TAKE NOTES

Literacy Skills: Analyze Cause and Effect

Use the graphic organizer in your Active Journal to take notes as you read the lesson.

PRACTICE VOCABULARY

Use the vocabulary activity in your Active Journal to practice the vocabulary words.

Vocabulary		Academic Vocabulary
forum	legion	identify
republic	maniple	diplomacy

You have learned how civilizations developed in the eastern Mediterranean in Mesopotamia, Egypt, and Greece. Around 800 BCE, along the Tiber River in present-day Italy, a village called Rome was built. This settlement became the world's largest city and center of a mighty empire.

Italy's Varied Geography

Rome lies near the center of the Italian Peninsula. A high mountain range called the Alps separates Italy from the rest of Europe. The Apennines run down the center.

Despite its many mountains, Italy has a less rugged landscape than Greece. Soldiers could march from one place to another relatively easily. This made it easier for Rome to unite the peninsula. In addition, Italy has several rivers that ships can use. Since ancient times these rivers have provided water and transportation routes.

Italy has large, fertile, flat plains. These gave it plenty of land suited for farming. Roman farmers produced such products as olive oil, wheat, grapes and wine. They raised sheep and goats for milk and wool.

Lesson 7.1 • The Roman Republic Rises 285

PRACTICE VOCABULARY

To help students integrate new vocabulary, explain that a *forum* is an open area in a city that is surrounded by public buildings. Rome developed a *republic*, which is a representative form of government. The terms *legion* and *maniple* both refer to units of an army. A legion had from 4,500 to 5,000 soldiers, while a maniple had between 60 and 160. Reinforce the terms during the lesson using the teaching notes.

Point out the academic vocabulary in the lesson margins. Provide sample sentences that clarify meaning.

identifying: Rey wears a Chicago Bears jersey as a way of identifying with the team.

diplomacy: The ambassador used diplomacy to end the war.

HSS 6.7.1

The Roman Republic Rises

CONNECT

GET READY TO READ

ETEXT — START UP

Project the Start Up Activity. As students enter the classroom and get settled, ask them to examine the photograph of the Tiber Valley. Have students pay close attention to the details of topography and human activity that are evident.

Recall Have students record two facts that they already know about Rome. *(Sample answers: The Romans had a large army. They built an empire. Rome is in Italy. They watched fighters called gladiators.)* Then have them share their facts with another student, either in class or through a chat or blog.

Discuss Remind students of the important roles that agriculture and transportation played in other ancient civilizations.

After completing the Start Up Activity, project the Lesson Opener or direct students to their textbooks. Preview the lesson by working through the Get Ready to Read items with the class. Remind students to pay close attention to the Guiding Questions as they read the lesson.

ACTIVE JOURNAL

Take Notes Have students use the lesson literacy skills graphic organizer in their Active Journals to take notes as they read the lesson.

Practice Vocabulary Have students complete the activity in their Active Journals to build their vocabulary.

VIDEO — VIDEO

Assign the lesson video as homework.

WORKSHEET **TEACHER RESOURCES**

Have students who need additional support use the following worksheets from the Teacher Resources on the course:

- **Reading Support**
- **English Language Development**
- **Lesson Summary**

INVESTIGATE

Italy's Varied Geography

Discuss how Italy's mountains, plains, and rivers affected Rome's economy.

Summarize Describe the physical geography of Italy. *(Italy is on the Italian Peninsula, which extends into the Mediterranean Sea. It has mountains across its base and another mountain chain down its length. It has large, flat plains with fertile soil.)*

Compare and Contrast How is Italy's geography similar to and different from that of Greece? *(Both Greece and Italy are mountainous; however, Italy's landscape is less rugged than that of Greece. It also has rivers that work well for shipping.)*

The Earliest Days of Rome

Discuss how seven villages grew into the city of Rome, which developed a republic.

Make Generalizations Why are Roman beliefs about the founding of their city important? *(Sample answer: Those beliefs tell us that Romans thought their city had a connection to the gods. This might cause Romans to feel superior to other people.)*

ANSWERS

Identify Main Ideas *Italy's plains provided land suitable for farming.*

Location *Rome's location near bodies of water was an advantage for shipping goods.*

Infer *Sample answer: The Tiber's swift current might have overflowed the river's banks, destroying bridges and flooding Rome.*

INTERACTIVE
Growth of the Roman Republic

Ancient Rome was part of a region called Latium. This region gave its name to the Latin people and their language, also called Latin.

READING CHECK **Identify Main Ideas** What advantages did Italy's plains give Rome?

The Earliest Days of Rome

Archaeologists have discovered that people first settled in Rome around 800 BCE. They built villages on the tops of seven hills overlooking the Tiber River, near where the river flows into the sea. Over time these villages formed a single town that grew into a small city.

Historians do not know exactly *how* Rome was founded, or established. The Romans themselves told a legend about the beginning of their city.

According to the legend, Rome was founded by twins named Romulus and Remus. Their mother was a Latin princess. The twins' father was Mars, the god of war. The king, their uncle, was jealous of the twins. He had the babies placed in a basket and thrown into the Tiber. They were saved from death by a she-wolf and raised by a shepherd.

As adults, the twins gathered a group of men to found a new city. However, they quarreled and Romulus killed Remus. Romulus lived and gave his name to the city he built—Rome.

Historians do not believe this legend. However, we can learn from the story that the Romans believed their city had a special origin and a connection to the gods.

GEOGRAPHY **SKILLS**

Roman civilization began by the Tiber River, close to the center of the Italian Peninsula and the Mediterranean Sea.

1. **Location** How was Rome's location relative to bodies of water an advantage?
2. **Infer** How might the Tiber have interfered with the development of Rome?

Italy: Physical

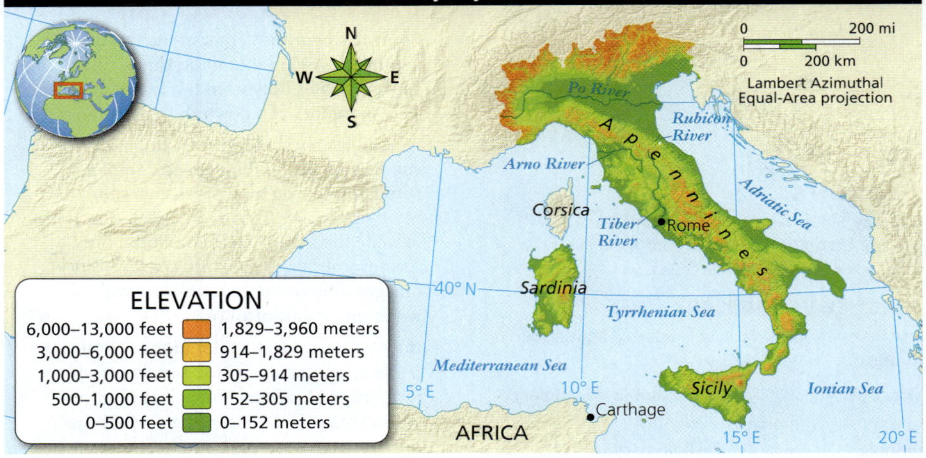

DIFFERENTIATED INSTRUCTION

Special Education Review the idea of what a legend is by mentioning some of the legends in our own culture: Paul Bunyan, the giant lumberjack whose footprints made the lakes of Minnesota; John Henry, who proved he was better at digging tunnels than a machine; and Johnny Appleseed, who walked from coast to coast scattering apple seeds to start fruit orchards.

Below Level Suggest that students work with partners to identify details that mark the story of Romulus and Remus as legend rather than fact. When they finish, they should exchange ideas with another pair.

Advanced Ask students to research the founding myth of another culture and then prepare an oral retelling of it to share with the class.

Rome began in the 800s BCE as a group of villages on top of hills overlooking the Tiber River, like the one shown here.

By the 300s CE, Rome was the largest city in the world.

Analyze Diagrams The two diagrams show Rome's growth over hundreds of years. **Make Predictions** What factors caused Rome to grow?

A Roman writer made this point.

Primary Source

Now, if any nation ought to be allowed to claim a sacred origin. . . that nation is Rome.

—Livy, *History of Rome*

What Was the Forum? The early Romans drained a swampy area between two of the town's hills. This became the Roman Forum. A **forum** is an open area in a city filled with public buildings, temples, and markets. The Roman Forum was the center of Rome's government, religion, and economy. When the Romans founded new cities in later years, they usually built a forum at the center.

What Were Rome's Natural Advantages? Several factors in Rome's geography helped the city grow and prosper. The city's hills gave the Romans a natural defense. Because Rome was located on the Tiber River, it had access to a nearby port. Although the river was shallow, small boats could reach the city. However, the river was too fast and dangerous for large boats. Seagoing sips could not attack Rome.

Rome was also located on key trade routes. The Tiber Valley was a natural east–west route for trade. In addition, several north–south trade routes crossed the Tiber just south of Rome.

READING CHECK **Summarize** What were Rome's natural advantages?

▼ Romans built aqueducts, like this one in Spain, in Rome and in many other places under their control.

Rome Becomes a Republic

Like Athens and Sparta, Rome began as an independent city-state. Its first form of government was a monarchy.

The Roman Kings Rome's early kings had broad powers. They served as head of the army, chief priest, and supreme judge. The Roman kings helped the city grow. They built the first buildings in the Forum and led wars against nearby villages.

Infer How was the Roman **Forum** important to Roman culture? *(It provided a center for all main Roman activities.)*

Identify Cause and Effect How did Rome's geography help it grow? *(Rome's hills protected the city from attack. Its location on the Tiber gave it access to a Mediterranean port. The Tiber was too shallow to allow large enemy warships to reach the city. Finally, Rome was located on key trade routes.)*

INTERACTIVE **INTERACTIVE MAP**

Growth of the Roman Republic, 500 BCE to 44 BCE

Display the Interactive Map: Growth of the Roman Republic, 500 BCE to 44 BCE. Click through the layers. Point out that by 44 BCE, Rome controlled most of the Mediterranean coastline. Discuss the impact that this would have on trade and culture. Ask: Judging from the map, why were Rome and Carthage rivals? *(Sample answer: Both were located on the Mediterranean, and each would have wanted to control trade.)*

ACTIVE CLASSROOM

Use the See-Think-Wonder strategy. With the final layer of the map visible, have student pairs answer the following questions: *What do you see? What does that make you think? What are you wondering about now that you've seen this?* Allow pairs to share their insights in class.

INTEGRATED ENGLISH LANGUAGE DEVELOPMENT

Productive Use Rome Becomes a Republic to help students understand Rome's monarchy and republic.

Emerging Write or display the following words: king, republic. Work together to write a two-sentence summary with one sentence about Rome's king and one about Rome's republic.

Expanding Together, identify important words from the text. Then have students write a summary of Rome Becomes a Republic.

(Continued on the next page.)

ANSWERS

Make Predictions *River trade and access to a seaport via the river helped it to grow.*

Summarize *It was protected by hills. It had access to a port via the Tiber River.*

Rome Becomes a Republic

Discuss how Rome changed from a monarchy to a republic.

Compare How was early Rome similar to Athens and Sparta? *(It was an independent city-state.)*

Contrast How is a monarchy different from a **republic**? *(In a monarchy, a king or queen holds governmental power. In a republic, citizens vote to elect officials who hold governmental power.)*

ACTIVE JOURNAL

Quest Connection Have students respond to the Quest Connection questions in their Active Journals.

The People of Italy

Discuss how Greeks and Etruscans contributed to Roman culture.

Identify Cause and Effect Which aspects of Roman life were shaped by contact with Greek culture? *(The Romans were influenced by Greek ideas about government, Greek mythology, and Greek religion.)*

How Did Rome Expand?

Discuss how Rome used conquest and diplomacy to extend its territory.

Draw Conclusions What was one way that Roman armies improved the lands they conquered? *(They built roads and bridges.)*

ANSWERS

Identify Supporting Details *It means "public thing" or "public business."*

Identify Cause and Effect *Greeks influenced Roman mythology and literature.*

Analyze Images *Latin and Roman letters*

Quest CONNECTIONS

How did the government of the Roman republic resemble ours? How was it different? Record your findings in your Active Journal.

The kings ruled with the consent of Rome's wealthy aristocrats. Older male aristocrats formed a body called the senate. The senate advised the king on important matters. The word *senate* comes from the Latin word *senex*, which means "old man."

Founding the Republic Over time, Roman aristocrats grew tired of royal rule. The seventh king of Rome, Tarquin the Proud, mistreated his people. In 509 BCE, leading Romans overthrew the king and formed a **republic**. A republic is a government in which citizens have the right to vote and elect officials. As in other spheres, Romans were strongly influenced by Greek forms of government, particularly Athens' democracy.

The word *republic* comes from the Latin term *res publica*, which means "public thing" or "public business." In the Roman republic, all free adult male citizens could play a role in the city's government.

READING CHECK **Identify Supporting Details** What does *res publica* mean?

The People of Italy

As Roman power grew, the Romans came into contact with different Italian peoples and borrowed from their cultures.

Greek Colonies Greeks settled in Italy starting around the 700s BCE. They founded cities in southern Italy. Rome came into contact with these cities and learned about Greek culture. The example of Athens inspired the Roman form of democracy. Many Hellenistic traditions also were adopted by the Romans.

Academic Vocabulary
identify • *v.*, consider or treat as the same

The Greeks of Italy had a strong influence on Roman culture. Romans made Greek mythology their own by **identifying** their gods with those of the Greeks. For example, the Greek Zeus was identified with Roman Jupiter, Hera with Juno, and Athena with Minerva.

The Romans also adopted Greek legends. According to legend, Romulus and Remus were Aeneas's descendants. Aeneas was a Trojan hero in the *Iliad*, a Greek poem. His story was written down during the first century CE by the Roman writer Virgil in a poem called the *Aeneid*.

Analyze Images Early writing systems had both similarities and differences. **Compare and Contrast** Which are more similar, Etruscan and Latin letters or Latin and Roman letters?

Early Alphabets

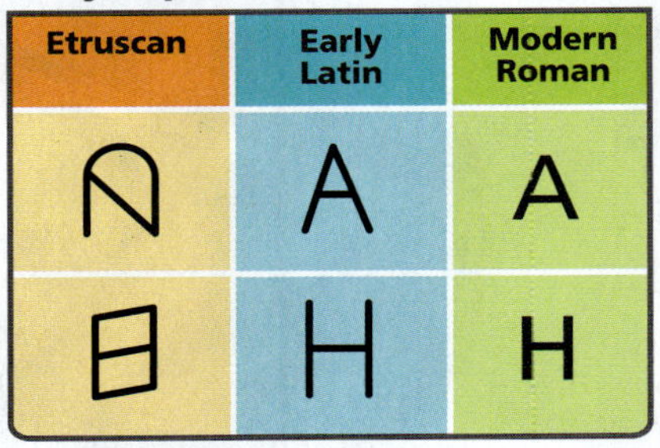

SOURCE: *Blackwell Encyclopedia of Writing Systems*

Who Were the Etruscans? The Etruscans were the most powerful people in central Italy when Rome was founded. They lived in Etruria, just north of Latium. The Etruscans were skilled artists and builders. They sailed around the Mediterranean as traders. They learned from the Greeks and the Phoenicians. The Etruscans developed their own alphabet based on Greek. From this, the Romans developed an alphabet. Today we use Roman letters in English and many other languages. The Etruscans also influenced Roman religion and architecture.

READING CHECK **Identify Cause and Effect** How did the Greeks influence the Romans?

INTEGRATED ENGLISH LANGUAGE DEVELOPMENT continued ELD.PI.C.10.b

Bridging Have students work in groups to summarize the sections The Roman Kings and Founding the Republic.

WORKSHEET **TEACHER RESOURCES**

For additional IELD support addressing the standard, have students complete the Lesson ELD activity from the Teacher Resources found on the course.

How Did Rome Expand?

The Roman people were feared conquerors. They also made skillful use of **diplomacy**. By using both force and diplomacy, the Romans ruled all of Italy by the late 200s BCE.

Rome's Army The basic unit of the Roman army was the **legion** (LEE jun). Each legion had from 4,500 to 5,000 heavily armed soldiers. Most served as infantry, or foot soldiers.

Each legion was broken up into manipes. A **manipe** was a unit of between 60 and 160 soldiers. On flat plains, all the manipes in a legion formed a solid battle line. But in rough country, each manipe could move and fight on its own. This flexibility gave the Roman legions a great advantage over enemies who fought in a single square block, including Greek phalanxes. Phalanxes were less flexible.

The Roman military did not just use Roman innovations. It was open to good ideas wherever they came from. For example, manipes were first used by the Samnites, a mountain people who lived in the Apennines in central Italy.

Roman soldiers were builders as well as fighters. When a Roman army was on the move, its soldiers would build a temporary fort every night. Soldiers also built roads and bridges. These helped armies move faster.

Rome's Friends and Allies Rome gained power with the help of its allies. The Romans signed treaties with other peoples, often defeated enemies. The treaties required allies to send troops to fight alongside the Romans in their campaigns. Eventually, many loyal allies were given Roman citizenship and the right to vote.

READING CHECK What methods did Roman leaders use to expand their territory?

Academic Vocabulary
diplomacy • *n.*, managing relationships with other countries through negotiation

▲ Roman legions, clad in armor and helmets, were feared all over the Mediterranean.

Lesson Check

HSS 6.7.1; ELD.P1.C.10.a

Practice Vocabulary

1. What is a **republic**?
2. What was the role of the Roman **Forum**?
3. What was the basic unit of the Roman army?

Critical Thinking and Writing

4. **Compare and Contrast** How was a Roman legion different from a Greek phalanx?
5. **Draw Conclusions** Find evidence to support the idea that the Romans were open to the influences of foreign cultures.
6. **Identify Cause and Effect** In what ways did Rome's geography help it grow?
7. **Writing Workshop: Develop a Clear Thesis** Recall what you know or have learned about Rome and other earlier or contemporary societies, such as Egypt, Persia, Greece, and China. Write a thesis statement that compares Rome to one of these societies in terms of the environment, political system, citizenship, or cultural connections in your Active Journal.

LESSON CHECK

1. a government in which citizens vote to elect their leaders **DOK1**
2. It was the center of Roman government, religion, economy, and social life. **DOK1**
3. the legion **DOK1**
4. A Roman legion fought in flexible groups of 100 soldiers, while a phalanx fought in a single large square. **DOK3**
5. Sample: Romans absorbed Greek mythology and Etruscan architecture. **DOK3**
6. Rome's hills and the shallow nature of the Tiber protected the city from attack. The Tiber gave shallow boats access to the Mediterranean. **DOK2**
7. Sample answer: Rome and Egypt both developed centralized governments, but their political systems differed substantially. **DOK4**

HSS 6.7.1; ELD.P1.C.10.a

SYNTHESIZE

Assess and Reteach Have students use a Think-Pair-Share strategy to complete Lesson Check questions 1–6. Review their responses. If they had any incorrect answers, use the guiding questions to discuss the lesson's main ideas, focusing on the ideas they struggled with.

ACTIVE JOURNAL

Writing Workshop Have students complete the Lesson 1 Writing Task in their Active Journals. Students will write a thesis statement that compares Rome to an earlier society they studied. As they move through the topic, students will revisit their thesis, revising it as needed.

ELD TIP For the Writing Workshop, offer students a word box of key vocabulary terms to use in creating their thesis statement.

DEMONSTRATE

ASSESSMENT **ONLINE LESSON QUIZ**

Assign the Online Lesson Quiz for this lesson if you haven't already done so. Students will be offered automatic remediation or enrichment based on their score.

DISCUSSION **DISCUSSION BOARD**

Post this question to the class on the Discussion Board:

Summarize How did geography affect Rome's growth? *(Rome's hills protected the city from attack. In addition, the Tiber was not deep enough for warships to sail up it and attack the city. Rome's location on the Tiber gave it access to a Mediterranean port, and the river was deep enough for shallow boats to travel between the city and the sea. Finally, Rome was located on key trade routes.)*

ANSWERS

Identify Cause and Effect *Roman leaders used conquest and diplomacy to expand their territory.*

HSS 6.7.1; ELA RI.6.2; RH.6.2

Primary Sources

Livy, *History of Rome*

Read aloud the explanatory note about the source. Direct students' attention to the art on the page. Ask: What part of the Romulus and Remus legend does this show? *(It shows them being raised by a shepherd and his wife.)*

GUIDED READING

Read aloud the excerpt without stopping. Then reread the passage, pausing after each sentence to let students answer the numbered questions. Use the questions in the text to prompt students' analysis of the primary source.

Reading and Vocabulary Support Answers

1. *Romulus is a legendary founder of Rome. Sample answer: He is trying to unite people into a political body.*

2. *He feels they are "rude and uncivilized."*

5. *from the lictors of the Etruscans' twelve cities*

6. *in religious practices, architecture, and the alphabet*

GUIDED ANALYSIS

After completing the reading, discuss what this primary source reveals about the early government of Rome.

Use Context Clues What does Livy mean when he says that Romulus "surrounded himself with greater state"? What context clues helped you to understand the phrase? *(Sample answer: It means he surrounded himself with things to show he had higher status than his subjects. The phrase "outward symbols of power" provides a context clue.)*

Infer What do you learn about the Romans from the fact that they believed birds foretold that Romulus should rule? *(Sample answer: They were superstitious.)*

To assess understanding, have students respond to the Analyzing Primary Sources questions in writing.

Primary Sources

HSS 6.7.1; ELA RI.6.2, RH.6.2

Livy, *History of Rome*

Titus Livius, known as Livy, wrote a history of the Roman republic in the early days of the Roman empire. His work was huge—142 volumes long! However, only about a quarter of the work survives. Livy started his history at the beginning, with the legendary founders Romulus and Remus.

◀ Romulus and Remus were the legendary founders of Rome.

Reading and Vocabulary Support

(1) Recall what you have learned about early Roman history. Who is Romulus? Why do you think he is calling people together?

(2) What is Romulus's attitude toward the people he is leading?

(3) Lictors were Roman officials who cleared the way for chief magistrates in public and caught and punished criminals.

(4) Sovereignty is supreme power and authority, especially political authority.

(5) Where does Livy think Romulus got the idea to have twelve lictors?

(6) How did the Etruscans influence the early Romans?

After the claims of religion had been duly acknowledged, Romulus (1) called his people to a council. As nothing could unite them into one political body but the observance of common laws and customs, he gave them . . . a body of laws which he thought would only be respected by a rude and uncivilised race (2) of men if he inspired them with awe by assuming the outward symbols of power. He surrounded himself with greater state, and in particular he called into his service twelve (3) lictors. Some think that he fixed upon this number from the number of the birds who foretold his sovereignty; (4) but I am inclined (5) to agree with those who think that as this class of public officers was borrowed from . . . their neighbours, the Etruscans (6) . . . . Its use amongst the Etruscans is traced to the custom of the twelve sovereign cities of Etruria when jointly electing a king furnishing him each with one lictor.

—Livy's *History of Rome*, Book I, Chapter 8

Analyzing Primary Sources

Reread the excerpt to find evidence to support your answers.

1. **Determine Author's Purpose** Why does Livy discuss the origin of lictors?
2. **Identify Main Ideas** Why does Romulus give a body of laws to his people?
3. **Write a Summary** In your own words, summarize the main ideas of this passage. Avoid letting your own opinions influence the summary.

290 Primary Sources • Livy, *History of Rome*

ANALYZING PRIMARY SOURCES

1. Livy wants to explain the origin of an important Roman official. **DOK3**

2. He thinks only the observance of common laws and customs will bring the people together into a political body. **DOK1**

3. Sample answer: Romulus gathered people together and gave them laws to unify them. To inspire people with awe, he assumed symbols of power and took twelve officials, called lictors, into his service. Livy thinks Romulus got the idea of lictors from the Etruscans, neighbors of the Romans. **DOK2**

LESSON 2

HSS 6.7.1, 6.7.2

Government of the Republic

BOUNCE TO ACTIVATE

VIDEO

GET READY TO READ

START UP

Examine the painting of Cicero addressing Roman senators. Write one prediction about how the Roman Senate may be similar to the United States Senate and one prediction of how it was different.

GUIDING QUESTIONS

- Why and how was power divided among different groups in the Roman republic?
- How did the Romans view of the concept of citizenship?
- How did the Roman republic function?
- What influence did the Roman republic have on later governments?

TAKE NOTES

Literacy Skills: Identify Main Ideas

Use the graphic organizer in your Active Journal to take notes as you read the lesson.

PRACTICE VOCABULARY

Use the vocabulary activity in your Active Journal to practice the vocabulary words.

Vocabulary		Academic Vocabulary
constitution	toga	violate
veto	consul	policy
magistrate		

The Roman republic was a unique system of government that lasted for 500 years. It led the Roman people from humble origins to conquest of the Mediterranean world.

What Were the Principles of Roman Government?

The ancient historian Polybius said about the Roman republic that "it was impossible even for a native to pronounce with certainty whether the whole system was aristocratic, democratic, or monarchical." Rome's system combined all three forms of government. Strong leaders, wealthy aristocrats, and average citizens all had a role to play.

Rome's Constitution Roman government was structured by a **constitution**. This is a system of rules by which a government is organized. Unlike the United States' constitution, the Roman constitution was unwritten. It was based on tradition, custom, and a collection of laws.

PRACTICE VOCABULARY

To help students integrate new vocabulary, explain that most of these terms relate to government. A *constitution* is a system of rules by which a government is organized. A *veto* stops a specific government action. A *magistrate* is an elected official who enforces the law, while *consuls* were the top officials in the Roman government. Reinforce the terms during the lesson using the teaching notes.

Point out the academic vocabulary in the lesson margins. Provide sample sentences that clarify meaning.

violate: If you violate the school's rules, you will face consequences.

policy: In the election, people voted for a new policy about national parks.

HSS 6.7.1, 6.7.2

Government of the Republic

CONNECT

GET READY TO READ

ETEXT **START UP**

Project the Start Up Activity. As students enter the classroom and get settled, ask them to examine the painting of Cicero addressing the Roman Senate.

Make Predictions Have students record two predictions about how the Roman Senate and the U.S. Senate were alike and different. *(Sample answers: The U.S. Senate is more diverse than the Roman senate was. In both senates, lawmakers make speeches to each other.)* Then have them share their predictions with another student, either in class or through a chat or blog.

Discuss Remind students that in the United States, senators are elected. Explain that in Rome, senators were appointed, usually for life.

After completing the Start Up Activity, project the Lesson Opener or direct students to their textbooks. Preview the lesson by working through the Get Ready to Read items with the class. Remind students to pay close attention to the Guiding Questions as they read the lesson.

ACTIVE JOURNAL

Take Notes Have students use the lesson literacy skills graphic organizer in their Active Journals to take notes as they read the lesson.

Practice Vocabulary Have students complete the activity in their Active Journals to build their vocabulary.

VIDEO **VIDEO**

Assign the lesson video as homework.

WORKSHEET **TEACHER RESOURCES**

Have students who need additional support use the following worksheets from the Teacher Resources on the course:

- **Reading Support**
- **English Language Development**
- **Lesson Summary**

INVESTIGATE

What Were the Principles of Roman Government?

Discuss how Roman government incorporated separation of powers and checks and balances.

Compare and Contrast How was the Roman constitution different from modern constitutions such as that of the United States? *(It was not a formal, written document.)*

Draw Conclusions What problems might be caused by spreading power out among many officials? *(Sample answer: It might make it harder to achieve change because someone will always disagree with it.)*

ACTIVE JOURNAL

Quest Connection Direct students to respond to the diagram and Quest Connection questions in their Active Journals.

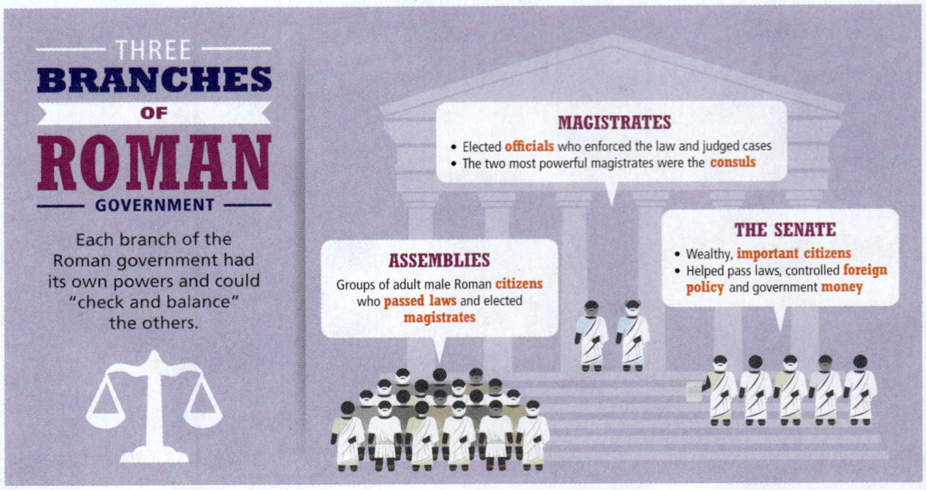

Analyze Charts The Roman government was made up of three different parts. **Apply Concepts** How could the assemblies check the magistrates?

What Was the Separation of Powers? The main idea in Rome's system of government was the separation of powers. Power was shared among different people with set roles. After overthrowing the last king, Romans did not want to be ruled by a single man. They built their new system of government to make sure no one person could become too powerful. For centuries, it worked.

One way in which the Romans limited officials' power was by splitting offices between two or more men. The Romans did not elect one top leader. Instead, they elected two leaders called consuls. They held equal powers. Each could veto the action of the other. To **veto** means to stop or cancel the action of a government official or body. In Latin, *veto* means "I forbid."

The Romans also limited an official's by time in office to one year. Even a powerful official could not do much harm in that short time.

Quest CONNECTIONS

Look at the diagram. What influence on modern government do you see? Capture your notes in your Active Journal.

How Do Checks and Balances Work? Power was also divided among the three branches of government. They were the assemblies, the senate, and the **magistrates**, or elected officials who enforce the law. A government with three parts is called a tripartite government.

Each branch had its own set of powers. One branch could check, or stop, another branch from misusing its power. No branch could hold total power, though the senate was often the most powerful branch.

The Roman Rule of Law Another key principle was the rule of law. This means the law applied to everyone. Even elected officials could be tried for **violating** the law after their term of office was over.

Academic Vocabulary
violate • *v.*, break a rule or agreement

READING CHECK **Identify Main Ideas** What are checks and balances?

HISTORY BACKGROUND

Assemblies of the Republic The Roman republic had three types of assemblies. In the *comitia centuriata* (Assembly of the Centuries), citizens were organized into groups called centuries according to their class. Votes of the wealthy centuries counted for more than those of poorer centuries. This assembly elected important officials like the consuls and passed laws. The *comitia tributa* (Assembly of the Tribes) organized citizens into tribes by where they lived. This assembly elected minor officials and judged cases. In the *concilium plebis* (Plebeian Assembly), only plebeians could vote. It elected tribunes and could pass laws called plebiscites, which were binding on patricians and plebeians alike.

ANSWERS

Apply Concepts *They elected the magistrates.*

Identify Main Ideas *Checks and balances are divisions of power in a multipart government. Each part of government has powers that control or limit the powers of other parts of government. This keeps any one part from getting more power than the others.*

292 Lesson 7.2 • Government of the Republic

Who Were the Citizens of Rome?

Free Roman men were citizens of the Roman republic. If both his parents were Roman citizens, males could be Roman citizens at birth. Women and slaves were not citizens and had no direct role in government. The symbol of Roman citizenship was the **toga**, a garment that adult men wore wrapped around their bodies. Only citizens could wear togas. Citizenship could also be granted by the Roman people and later on by generals and emperors.

Rights and Responsibilities Roman citizens had the right to a trial. Any adult male citizen had the right to vote. He had to pay taxes. Citizen also were obligated to serve in the military and in Roman courts as legal guardians, witnesses, jurors, or judges, both at their own expense. Roman culture stressed civic duty, meaning the responsibility of a citizen.

Patricians and Plebeians Roman citizens were divided into two orders. One was the patricians, members of the oldest families in Rome. They were usually wealthy. In the early days of the republic, they may have controlled all government offices.

The other order was made up of the plebeians, who were a majority of Romans. They did not come from famous old families like the patricians. Most were common farmers or artisans. However, some plebeians were wealthy.

The plebeians forced patricians to open up political offices to them. According to Roman tradition, they did so by going on strike. During a war, the plebeians walked out of the city and sat down on a nearby hill. Rome could not fight on without them, so the patricians had to give in.

Quick Activity

Discover how the Romans used numerals in your Active Journal.

READING CHECK **Summarize** Who had the right to vote during the Roman republic?

What did the Assemblies and the Senate Do?

Patricians and plebeians alike had a role to play in Roman government.

The Assemblies Assemblies of Roman citizens were the democratic part of Roman government. All adult male citizens could participate in assemblies, though the votes of the wealthy usually counted for more than those of the poor.

At assemblies, Roman citizens elected officials and passed laws. This was a form of direct democracy, like the assembly in Athens. However, the power of the assemblies was checked by the powers of the senate and of elected officials.

The Senate The senate was the part of Roman government that worked like an oligarchy. It was made up of the wealthiest and best-known older Roman men, often former magistrates. Senators were chosen by an official called the censor. They did not represent the people. They were supposed to guide the state. Rich, older senators were thought to be wiser than other citizens.

▼ This silver coin from around 100 BCE shows Romans voting.

Who Were the Citizens of Rome?

Discuss who held Roman citizenship and what the rights and responsibilities of citizens were.

Categorize What were some rights and responsibilities adult male citizens had? *(They could vote and had the right to a trial. They had to pay taxes and serve in the army and the courts.)*

Compare and Contrast How were patricians and plebeians the same and different? *(Both were citizens. Patricians came from wealthy, older families; in the early republic, they may have controlled all government offices. Plebeians were common farmers or artisans, though some were wealthy. At first plebeians could not hold political office, but they gained this right after going on strike.)*

What Did the Assemblies and the Senate Do?

Discuss the structures and duties of the branches of Roman government.

Contrast How did the assemblies and the senate differ? *(The assemblies functioned more like direct democracy by allowing all adult male citizens to vote on laws. The senate worked more like an oligarchy; it did not represent the people.)*

ACTIVE JOURNAL

Quick Activity Divide the students into pairs and have them complete the Roman numeral activity in their Active Journals. Have students share their answers with another pair.

ELD TIP For the Quick Activity, pair emerging and expanding students with fluent speakers to complete the Roman numeral activity.

ANSWERS

Summarize *Adult male citizens could vote.*

INTEGRATED ENGLISH LANGUAGE DEVELOPMENT

Productive Use Who Were the Citizens of Rome? to help students express opinions about the rules of citizenship for the Roman republic.

Emerging Ask students to answer the following question with a yes or no answer: *Were Roman rules on who could be a citizen fair?* Have the student explain why they answered yes or no in a short sentence.

Expanding Ask students to explain whether Roman rules on who could be a citizen were fair or not, using information from the text to support their position.

Bridging Divide students into two groups and have them debate whether Roman rules on who could be a citizen were fair. Give each side a chance to make an argument and a

(Continued on the next page.)

Who Were the Magistrates?

Discuss the duties of various Roman officials and the path of advancement.

Compare In what way were Roman **magistrates** like monarchs? *(They had a lot of power.)*

Infer Why do you think the office of Tribune of the Plebs developed? Explain. *(Sample answer: It developed in response to abuse of the lower classes by patricians; tribunes acted as protectors of the plebeians.)*

INTERACTIVE **INTERACTIVE SIMULATION**

The Race of Honors

Display the opening screen of the Interactive Simulation: The Race of Honors. Ask a volunteer to read the text and then click "Start." Read the description of the first decision. Ask volunteers to share ideas about what to do. Take a class vote and click on the majority's choice. If it turns out to be a bad decision, ask a volunteer to read the reason why and then try again. Ask: What actions helped Roman politicians advance? *(Sample answers: pleasing the rich; conquering territory; capturing wealth and slaves)*

ACTIVE CLASSROOM

Use the Wallpaper strategy. Have each student design a piece of "wallpaper" about key learnings from the simulation. Post the wallpaper around the classroom and note what others created about the Race of Honors.

ANSWERS

Cite Evidence *The senate controlled foreign policy and spending.*

Draw Conclusions *Sample answer: No. It wasted energy better used on civil affairs.*

Academic Vocabulary
policy • *n.*, course of action taken by a government

The senate advised the assemblies and magistrates. Its advice was almost always followed. It also ran foreign **policy** and decided how to spend the state's money. It was the most powerful part of the Roman government.

READING CHECK **Cite Evidence** What did the senate control directly?

INTERACTIVE
The Race of Honors

Who Were the Magistrates?

The Romans elected a number of powerful magistrates. The power of these high officials made them almost like monarchs. Magistrates were wealthy men. Their ancestors had usually held high offices. For men from elite families, politics was a key part of life.

Politicians usually moved from lower offices to higher offices. This path was called the Race of Honors. It changed over time, but by the later years of the republic, it followed a standard form.

What Were the Lower Offices? The Race of Honors started with the lowest office, the quaestor (KWY stor). Quaestors were accountants who kept track of the state's money. They also served as assistants to higher officials. If a citizen did well as a quaestor, he might seek election as an aedile (ee dile). Aediles were in charge of holding festivals and maintaining public buildings. These lower offices were stepping-stones to greater power.

Tribunes of the Plebs Plebeians could run for the powerful office of tribune of the plebs before moving on to higher offices. Tribunes acted as the protectors of the plebeians. Sometimes they took radical or even revolutionary positions.

Analyze Charts During the Roman republic, citizens could rise through a variety of roles to become consul. **Draw Conclusions** Do you think this competitive set-up was an effective way of training government officials? Use evidence to support your answer.

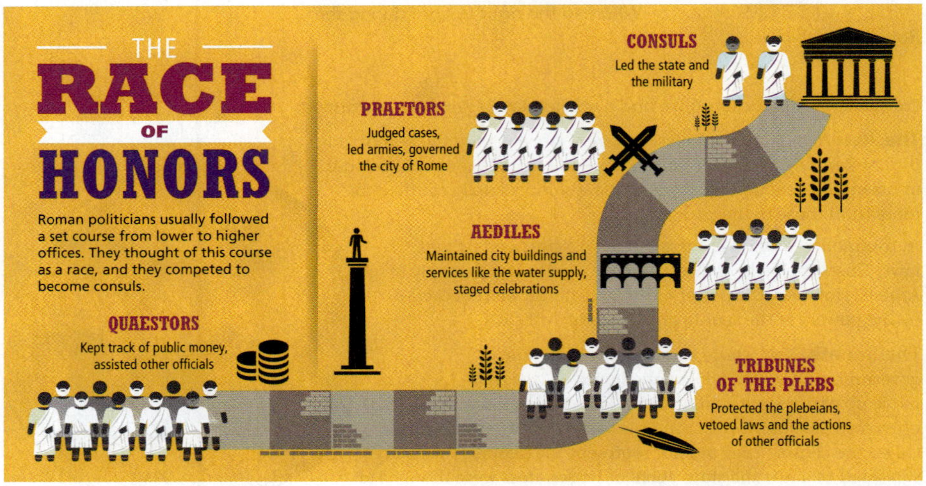

INTEGRATED ENGLISH LANGUAGE DEVELOPMENT continued ELD.PI.C.11.a

counter-argument. Groups should cite information from the text to support their positions.

WORKSHEET **TEACHER RESOURCES**

For additional IELD support addressing the standard, have students complete the Lesson ELD activity from the Teacher Resources found on the course.

BIOGRAPHY 5 Things to Know About

LUCIUS QUINCTIUS CINCINNATUS

Roman Statesman (Born c. 519? BCE)

- Cincinnatus was a historical figure who became a Roman legend for his devotion to his country.
- According to tradition, in 468 BCE, the Roman senate called on Cincinnatus to save a surrounded Roman army. He left his plow standing in the field, said good-bye to his wife, and went to war.
- He defeated the enemy in one day, legend says, and held power only as long as the emergency lasted, then returned to his farm.
- George Washington's contemporaries thought of him as an American Cincinnatus. He left retirement to lead the Continental Army. In 1783, with the war won, he returned to his farm.
- To Romans and Americans, the story of Cincinnatus demonstrated an ideal of republican patriotism.

Critical Thinking Why was George Washington thought of as an American Cincinnatus?

Tribunes had the right to veto any law, or the action of any magistrate. The veto gave the tribunes great power over all other parts of the government. It was also strictly forbidden to harm a tribune or stop him from doing his job.

Praetors and Consuls After serving as an aedile or tribune, men could try to be elected as a praetor (PRY tor). Praetors judged cases, managed the city of Rome, and led armies in times of war.

After serving as a praetor, a politician could be elected consul. The **consuls** were the top officials in the Roman republic. Their most important job was to lead the army. They also presided over the senate and assemblies and were the highest judges.

Consuls and praetors had visible symbols that showed their authority. They wore special togas and sat on ivory chairs. They were followed around by bodyguards called lictors. The lictors carried the consul's or praetor's fasces, a symbol of power.

Dictators In the modern world, when we call someone a dictator we usually mean that he is a cruel tyrant. But in ancient Rome, a dictator was an important public official. The senate could vote to name a dictator in times of great emergency. Dictators held complete power, but only for a limited time. They served for a maximum of six months.

A man named Cincinnatus was one famous dictator. Cincinnatus was working his farm when he heard that he had been chosen dictator. He quickly defeated Rome's enemies, resigned his office, and went back to his fields. He was thought of as a model citizen.

READING CHECK **Infer** Why did Cincinnatus become famous?

Distinguish What were the main roles of praetors and **consuls**? *(Praetors judged cases, managed the city of Rome, and led armies in war. Consuls were the most senior officials; they led the army, presided over the senate and assemblies, and were the highest judges.)*

Connect How were Roman dictators different from modern dictators? *(A modern dictator is usually a cruel tyrant. In ancient Rome, a dictator was an important official appointed to handle an emergency.)*

Draw Conclusions After students have read 5 Things to Know About Lucius Quinctius Cincinnatus, ask: What characteristic do you most admire Cincinnatus for? Why? *(Sample answer: He sacrificed for his country. He left his farm when they asked him to save an army.)*

How Did the Romans Set an Example?

Discuss how the Roman republic set an example for later societies.

Compare and Contrast List three ways the U.S. government today differs from the Roman republic. *(Sample answer: The U.S. government has a written constitution, representative democracy, and women participating in politics.)*

DIFFERENTIATED INSTRUCTION

Special Education To help students learn the different political offices in Rome, suggest that they work in groups to organize them on a graphic organizer such as a pyramid or staircase. Help them practice how to say the unfamiliar Latin terms.

Below Level Students who are used to the U.S. political system may not understand that all upper-class Roman men were expected to take part in politics. Have pairs of students reread the first paragraph under the heading *Who Were the Magistrates?* Ask them to write an explanation of how political service in Roman related to family and economic class.

Advanced Suggest that students choose a well-known Roman statesman to research. They can either write a biographical essay or create a brief comic book about his life.

ANSWERS

Critical Thinking *Like Cincinnatus, George Washington left retirement at his farm to successfully lead his country's army in an emergency. When the war was over, he returned to his farm. He did not seek to hold on to political power or use his position for personal gain.*

Infer *Cincinnatus became famous because he did his job as a Roman dictator and left office as soon as his work was completed.*

HSS 6.7.1, 6.7.2; ELD.P1.A.2

SYNTHESIZE

Assess and Reteach Have students use a Jigsaw strategy to complete Lesson Check questions 1–6. Review their responses. If they had any incorrect answers, use the Guiding Questions to discuss the lesson's main ideas, focusing on the ideas they struggled with.

ACTIVE JOURNAL

Writing Workshop Have students complete the Lesson 2 Writing Task in their Active Journals. Students will choose details to support their thesis. As they move through the topic, students will revisit the details, adding to them as needed.

DEMONSTRATE

ASSESSMENT ONLINE LESSON QUIZ

Assign the Online Lesson Quiz for this lesson if you haven't already done so. Students will be offered automatic remediation or enrichment based on their score.

DISCUSSION DISCUSSION BOARD

Post this question to the class on the Discussion Board:

Summarize How did Romans view the concept of citizenship? *(Roman culture emphasized civic duty, or the responsibility of a citizen. Responsibilities included paying taxes, serving in the military, and serving in the courts.)*

ANSWERS

Compare and Contrast *Both have the power to veto laws.*

Did you know?

The Roman Senate had as many as **900** members, all men. The United States Senate has only **100**, both men and women.

▼ Elected in 2016, Tammy Duckworth of Illinois is one of the U.S. Senate's 21 female Senators.

How Did the Romans Set an Example?

The Roman republic was the most successful and long-lasting republic until modern times. The writers of the American constitution knew a great deal about Roman history and government. They followed the Roman example in many areas.

For instance, like Roman citizens, American citizens have the right to vote and stand for office. The United States government has three branches with separate powers, like the Roman republic had. Checks and balances limit the power of each branch. The rule of law applies equally to every American, as it did to every Roman citizen. Like tribunes of the plebs, presidents have the power to veto laws. The United States has a senate, as ancient Rome did.

Still, many parts of American government are different. As you read, the Roman republic did not have a written constitution, while the United States does. Ancient Rome also practiced forms of direct democracy. In contrast, the United States practices representative democracy. Roman citizens voted directly on laws. In the United States, laws are usually passed by representatives elected by the citizens.

In the United States today, women participate equally in the government. In ancient Rome, women did not have a role in politics. While slavery has been illegal in the United States since the 1860s, many people in ancient Rome were slaves who had no political rights.

READING CHECK **Compare and Contrast** How was a tribune of the plebs like an American president?

Lesson Check

HSS 6.7.1, 6.7.2; ELD.P1.A.2

Practice Vocabulary

1. What is a **constitution**? Did the Romans write theirs down?
2. What was a **toga** a symbol of?
3. What do **magistrates** do?

Critical Thinking and Writing

4. **Identify Main Ideas** In what ways were the tribunes of the plebs especially powerful?
5. **Compare and Contrast** How is direct democracy in the Roman republic different from representative democracy in the United States?
6. **Draw Conclusions** What do you think America's founders thought of the Roman republic? Explain.
7. **Writing Workshop: Support Thesis with Details** Compare Rome's government with those of other societies, such as Egypt, Persia, Greece, or China. Gather details to support the thesis for your essay. Write these supporting details in your Active Journal.

LESSON CHECK

1. A constitution gives rules to organize a government; no, the Roman constitution was not written. **DOK1**
2. Roman citizenship **DOK1**
3. Magistrates enforce laws. **DOK1**
4. The tribunes could veto any law or action of a magistrate. **DOK1**
5. In ancient Roman direct democracy, citizens voted directly on laws. In American representative democracy, citizens elect representatives who vote on laws. **DOK3**
6. They admired it and modeled their government on it. **DOK3**
7. Answers will vary. Students should choose details about Rome and the other ancient society they have chosen. The details should address themes of environment, politics or cultural connections for both societies. **DOK3**

296 Lesson 7.2 • Government of the Republic

LESSON 3

HSS 6.7

Society in the Republic

BOUNCE TO ACTIVATE

VIDEO

GET READY TO READ

START UP

Look at the photo. Think about the different groups in your school, such as students, teachers, and staff members. How do they work together? Predict how groups of people in ancient Rome worked together.

GUIDING QUESTIONS

- What roles did men and women hold in Roman society?
- How did life differ for different classes of Romans?
- In what ways were religion and citizenship connected in Romans' lives?

TAKE NOTES

Literacy Skills: Classify and Categorize

Use the graphic organizer in your Active Journal to take notes as you read the lesson.

PRACTICE VOCABULARY

Use the vocabulary activity in your Active Journal to practice the vocabulary words.

Vocabulary		Academic Vocabulary
patriarchal society	villa	minority
paterfamilias	established religion	tenant

Like other ancient societies, Rome was divided by gender and class. Men and women had their own social roles. The lives of wealthy Romans were very different from the lives of poor Romans and slaves.

Roman Men and Women

Rome was a **patriarchal society**. This means that men ruled their families and that people traced their origins through male ancestors.

What Power Did Fathers Have? The oldest man in a Roman family was called the **paterfamilias**, or head of the household. He owned all the family's property. In theory, a father had absolute, or unlimited, power over his wife, children, slaves, and underage siblings. He could sell his children into slavery. He could even kill them if he chose. In practice, however, a father's power was limited by custom. In fact, many fathers felt that doing one's duty to their families was one of the highest Roman virtues. This duty also included honoring ancestors and continuing the family name through sons.

Lesson 7.3 • Society in the Republic 297

HSS 6.7

Society in the Republic

CONNECT

GET READY TO READ

ETEXT START UP

Project the Start Up Activity. As students enter the classroom and get settled, ask them to examine the photograph of the mosaic showing Roman society.

Make Predictions Have students record three predictions about how the people in ancient Rome worked together. *(Sample answers: Politicians probably had to have many discussions to get laws passed. Wealthy Romans had slaves to do their household tasks. Lower-class Romans may have worked cooperatively as farmers or artisans.)* Then have them share their predictions with another student, either in class or through a chat or blog.

Discuss Remind students that the ancient societies they have studied so far had clearly defined gender roles. This was also the case of Rome.

After completing the Start Up Activity, project the Lesson Opener or direct students to their textbooks. Preview the lesson by working through the Get Ready to Read items with the class. Remind students to pay close attention to the Guiding Questions as they read the lesson.

ACTIVE JOURNAL

Take Notes Have students use the lesson literacy skills graphic organizer in their Active Journals to take notes as they read the lesson.

Practice Vocabulary Have students complete the activity in their Active Journals to build their vocabulary.

VIDEO VIDEO

Assign the lesson video as homework.

PRACTICE VOCABULARY

To help students integrate new vocabulary, preview how the following terms relate to family: In a *patriarchal society,* men ruled their families. The oldest man in the family was the *paterfamilias*. Many upper-class families owned *villas*, or large country homes. The *established religion*, or official religion, included both public and private family ceremonies. Reinforce the terms during the lesson using the teaching notes.

Point out the academic vocabulary in the lesson margins. Provide sample sentences that clarify meaning.

minority: Spanish speakers are a large minority group in the United States.

tenant: My grandmother has been a tenant in her apartment building for 20 years.

INVESTIGATE

Roman Men and Women

Discuss the different roles that men and women held in Roman society.

Cite Evidence Describe the power balance between men and women in Rome's **patriarchal society**. Give examples. *(Men had vastly more power than women. Fathers ruled families. Male citizens took part in politics. Women could not vote, attend assemblies, or hold office.)*

How Did the Rich and Poor Live?

Discuss what daily life was like for rich and poor Romans.

Contrast How did life differ for wealthy Romans and poor Romans? *(Wealthy Romans earned fortunes from their estates. They lived in large, lavish houses. Poor city people lived in crowded apartments, in danger of crime, disease, and fire. They worked at jobs.)*

INTERACTIVE **INTERACTIVE 3-D MODEL**

Roman Villa

Display the Roman villa 3-D model. Click on hotspots. Ask volunteers to read captions. Ask: Which details showed the owner's wealth? *(Sample answers: its size, artwork)*

ACTIVE CLASSROOM

Use the Quick Write strategy. Have students take a minute to jot down what they learned about Roman life from the 3-D villa model.

ANSWERS

Identify Supporting Details *yes*

Identify Main Ideas *poor*

▲ A Roman husband and wife

What Was the Role of Women? Roman women enjoyed more freedom than Greek women. Unlike most Greek women, they could own personal property. Also unlike many Greek women, Roman women took an active role in social life. Women went to parties, enjoyed the theater, and participated in religious rituals. They could make wills, divorce their husbands, and go out in public. In addition, rich wives and mothers could sometimes influence public decisions through their husbands and sons But, as you have read, women could not vote, attend assemblies, or hold public office.

According to the Romans, the most important role of a Roman woman was to bear children and raise them to follow traditions. The ideal woman was a faithful wife and mother, devoted to her family.

READING CHECK **Identify Supporting Details** Could Roman women own property?

How Did the Rich and Poor Live?

Most Romans were poor free people or people who were enslaved. A tiny **minority** were wealthy.

Living the Good Life Most wealthy Romans earned their money from agriculture. They owned huge farms worked by poor Romans or slaves. The landowners grew rich from what these people produced. Other wealthy Romans earned their fortunes through business.

INTERACTIVE
Roman Villa

Upper-class Romans lived in one- or two-story houses as large as a city block. These homes had courtyards, gardens, private baths, beautiful decorations, and even running water. Many elite families also owned **villas**, or large country homes.

What Was Life Like for the Common People? Life was different for poor Romans. In the city, most poor people lived in cramped apartments without running water. Crime, disease, and fire were serious dangers. Apartment buildings were often badly built, and sometimes collapsed.

Academic Vocabulary
minority • *n.*, a group that is less than half the population
tenant • *n.*, person who rents land or a home

Common men and women worked at a variety of jobs. Many were **tenant** farmers who rented land from wealthy landlords. Others worked as day laborers in construction or at the city docks. Some ran stores, taverns, or restaurants.

READING CHECK **Identify Main Ideas** Were the majority of Romans rich or poor?

INTEGRATED ENGLISH LANGUAGE DEVELOPMENT

Productive Use How Did the Rich and Poor Live? to help students express opinions about the different conditions for rich and poor Romans.

Emerging Ask students to describe the lives of rich and poor Romans in short sentences.

Expanding Have students use a Venn Diagram to compare and contrast the lives of rich and poor Romans, being sure to note differences within each group.

Roman Slavery

Slavery was very common in ancient Rome. As Rome became richer and more powerful, Romans bought or captured more and more slaves. As many as 40 percent of people in Rome in the year 1 BCE may have been enslaved.

How did Enslaved People Live? For most of Roman history, enslaved people had no rights. They were bought and sold as property. They could be beaten or killed by their masters for any reason. Children born to slaves were also slaves. Many slaves worked in mines or on large farms. These enslaved people often died quickly due to brutal treatment.

Other slaves led easier lives. Some enslaved people worked in the homes of their wealthy masters. They lived like typical poor Romans or even better, performing housework for their masters.

Some educated slaves worked as secretaries or teachers. These slaves were usually Greeks. Although they lived in much better conditions than other enslaved people, they could still be treated very cruelly.

Enslaved people who served loyally could be freed as a reward. They could also save up to buy their freedom. Freed slaves became citizens and had the right to vote.

Did Enslaved People Fight Back? Some slaves fought back against their masters. One famous fighter was Spartacus, who led an army of rebel slaves in the 70s BCE. They fought the Roman army and threatened to capture Rome before the Romans defeated them.

READING CHECK **Summarize** Could slaves become free? If so, how?

Quick Activity

This painting shows a Roman slave who worked in a kitchen. Compare the social hierarchy of Roman society with other civilizations in your Active Journal.

Analyze Diagrams Like other early societies, Rome had a strict social order. **Compare** What roles did both poor citizens and enslaved people fulfill?

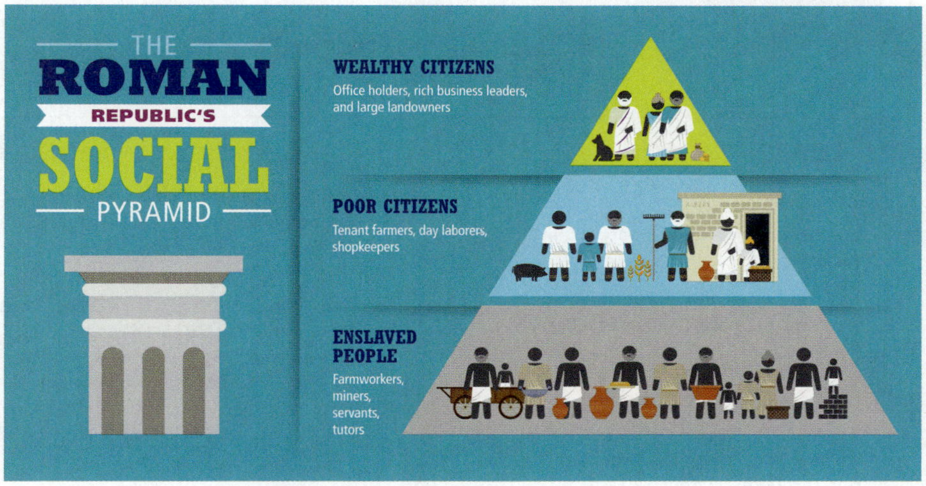

Roman Slavery

Discuss how enslaved people in Rome lived.

Draw Conclusions Why do you think the number of slaves in Rome grew over time? *(Sample answer: Romans won wars and captured slaves. They also became rich and bought more slaves.)*

Summarize Describe the life of typical Roman slaves. *(Enslaved people had no rights and were bought and sold as property. Many worked in mines or on farms. Others worked in people's homes or on the staff of the wealthy. All enslaved people could be treated cruelly and even killed by their masters.)*

ACTIVE JOURNAL

Quick Activity Divide students into pairs and have them conduct the Quick Activity exercise comparing Roman society to that of other ancient cultures. Have volunteers share their comparisons with the class.

ELD TIP For the Quick Activity, pair emerging and expanding students with fluent speakers to compare Roman society to that of other cultures.

Roman Religion

Discuss the role that religion played in Roman life.

Interpret Have students read the quotation by Cicero. Ask: Does Cicero believe that it is an important part of the **established religion** to please the gods? Explain your answer. *(Sample answer: He believed it was very important. He thought that it was the reason Rome was successful.)*

ANSWERS

Summarize *Yes, they could be freed as a reward or save up to buy their freedom.*

Compare *They could be farmworkers or laborers.*

ELD.PI.C.11.b

Bridging Have students compare and contrast the lives of rich and poor Romans, being sure to note differences within each group.

WORKSHEET **TEACHER RESOURCES**

For additional IELD support addressing the standard, have students complete the Lesson ELD activity from the Teacher Resources found on the course.

HSS 6.7; ELD.P1.C.10.a

SYNTHESIZE

Assess and Reteach Have students work in teams of five to answer questions 1–5 of the Lesson Check. Then use a Numbered Heads Together strategy to have students share answers with the class. Review their responses. If they had any incorrect answers, use the guiding questions to discuss the lesson's main ideas, focusing on the ideas they struggled with.

ACTIVE JOURNAL

Writing Workshop Have students complete the Lesson 3 Writing Task in their Active Journals. Students will write a draft of their explanatory essays. As they complete the topic, students will revisit their drafts, revising them as needed.

DEMONSTRATE

ASSESSMENT **ONLINE LESSON QUIZ**

Assign the Online Lesson Quiz for this lesson if you haven't already done so. Students will be offered automatic remediation or enrichment based on their score.

DISCUSSION **DISCUSSION BOARD**

Post this question to the class on the Discussion Board:

Synthesize How was religion connected to civic life in Rome? *(Top government officials served as priests. They often consulted religious experts before they made decisions. Romans believed that it was part of the government's job to maintain good relations with the gods.)*

▼ Minerva, the goddess of wisdom.

Roman Religion

Religion was an important part of everyday life in ancient Rome. Religious practices were at the center of the lives of Roman citizens, both with their families at home altars, where they offered sacrifices, and at many public events.

Origins of the Gods The Romans worshipped hundreds of gods. Many were adapted from the Greeks or Etruscans. Others came from Latin traditions. Some came from people the Romans conquered.

What Was Government's Role in Religion? Rome had an **established religion**, an official religion supported by a government. Government officials also served as priests. They often consulted religious experts before making decisions. Romans believed that maintaining good relations with the gods was part of the government's job. Rome was also home to thousands of Jews, and Judaism was recognized by Julius Caesar as an officially permitted religion.

The Romans tried to placate their gods, or keep them happy. They believed that if they did certain things, the gods would give them what they asked for. They prayed, worshiped at home, built temples, offered animal sacrifices, and held games in the gods' honor. Romans like Cicero believed that their success was due to their attention to the gods.

Primary Source

I am quite certain that . . . [Rome] would never have been able to be so great had not the immortal gods been placated.

—Cicero, from *The Nature of the Gods*

READING CHECK **Identify Cause and Effect** Why did the Romans sacrifice to their gods?

Lesson Check

HSS 6.7; ELD.P1.C.10.a

Practice Vocabulary

1. In what way was Rome a **patriarchal society**?
2. What class of people owned **villas**?
3. Who was the **paterfamilias** of a Roman family?

Critical Thinking and Writing

4. **Compare Viewpoints** How might a wealthy Roman view the growth of Roman power differently from a slave?
5. **Identify Main Ideas** What were three important influences on Roman religion? Which do you feel was the most powerful? Why?
6. **Writing Workshop: Draft Your Essay** Draft your explanatory essay comparing Rome to other societies. Start your essay with an introduction and develop your strongest points in the body paragraphs. Get help in your Active Journal.

LESSON CHECK

1. Rome was a patriarchal society in that men ruled their families and inheritance was passed down through the male line. **DOK1**
2. The wealthy class owned villas. **DOK1**
3. the oldest man in a Roman family **DOK1**
4. A wealthy Roman likely viewed the growth of Roman power as positive, while a slave might expect it to lead to more slavery. **DOK3**
5. Greek culture, Etruscan culture, local Latin tradition; many students will point to the influence of Greece on Roman religion. **DOK1**
6. Answers will vary. Students should draft an essay that has an introduction with a clear thesis statement, a body with key ideas and supporting details, and a strong conclusion. **DOK3**

ANSWERS

Identify Cause and Effect *They believed that sacrifices would make the gods happy.*

Interpret Economic Performance

Follow these steps to learn how to interpret economic performance using the information in a source.

INTERACTIVE

Analyze Data and Models

1 Identify the type of economic information being presented. Economists often refer to different kinds of statistics or theories to explain economic performance. For example, they may use a graph showing the rate of unemployment, tables about the standard of living, or statements about levels of income inequality.

a. In the passage below, what kinds of economic information are presented?

b. Could any of the information be presented in a chart, graph, or diagram?

2 Summarize the main points of your source. Try to identify the key economic points that the source is presenting. If there are graphs or tables, you can often find key information there. In discussions like the one below, pay close attention to the first and last sentences of the paragraphs. What do you consider the key points of this passage to be?

3 Interpret the information presented in your source. Using your source, formulate a conclusion about the economic information presented.

a. Is the author noting positive or negative economic performance?

b. Based on this passage, what conclusions about the state of Rome's farmers can you draw?

c. What effect might the economic situation described have on the stability of the Roman republic?

Secondary Source

The growth of Rome's territory through the conquest of lands outside of Italy affected the republic's poorer classes in surprising ways. As the republic grew, food was brought into the city from distant provinces. For example, grain was imported from Egypt. As the food supply increased, prices fell. Low prices were disastrous for Italian farmers, many of whom were not able to make a living off their small plots and land. They had little choice but to sell their property to rich landowners.

At the same time, large numbers of prisoners-of-war, now slaves, came to Italy. Rather than hire landless farmers to work their growing estates, wealthy landowners bought slaves. Therefore, farmers ended up with no land and no jobs. As a result, these farmers joined a growing class of poor, jobless Romans.

DIFFERENTIATED INSTRUCTION

Below Level Remind students that multiple causes often work together to bring about a trend. Have them work with a partner to create a cause-effect chart to organize the information in the secondary source. You may want to provide examples of several styles of cause-and-effect charts that they can choose from.

INTEGRATED ENGLISH LANGUAGE DEVELOPMENT

Bridging Help students connect their own experiences to the text by asking the following questions: *Are people usually happy or unhappy when food prices go down? Why? Are people usually happy or unhappy when their income goes down? Why*

Analysis HI.6

Analysis Skills
Interpret Economic Performance

LEARN

Preview the steps in the student text with students, and then play the video.

VIDEO **21ST CENTURY SKILLS**

Project the Identify Trends video in the 21st Century Skills Tutorial. Use the Quick Reference and Assessment to provide additional instruction on this skill.

PRACTICE

Have students practice the skill using the secondary source on the student page, providing the instruction and then asking students the questions.

ASSESS

To assess this skill, have students read the section titled "The Greek Economy" in Lesson 4 of the topic Ancient Greece and then write a summary of the economic performance of ancient Greece.

ANSWERS

1. a. The passage presents information about how dropping food prices affected Italian farmers and how the use of slaves took away the jobs landless farmers used to do.
b. Sample answer: The information about falling food prices could be presented in a graph if statistics were available.

2. The key points are that the conquest of lands outside Italy led to cheaper food supplies and the increased use of slave labor, both of which hurt small farmers.

3. a. Sample answer: Positive economic performances, such as the increase in food supplies; negative economic performances such as farmers losing their land and not being able or to find work.
b. Sample answer: The farmers lost their means of livelihood through economic forces that were beyond their control.
c. Sample answer: The situation would make the republic less stable because the farmers who had lost their land and their jobs would be angry and desperate.

HSS 6.7.1, 6.7.3, 6.7.4; ELD.P1.C.10.a

The Republic Struggles

CONNECT

GET READY TO READ

ETEXT START UP

Project the Start Up Activity. As students enter the classroom and get settled, ask them to examine the painting of Carthaginians on elephants attacking a Roman army.

Infer Have students write down what they think went through the Roman soldiers' minds when they saw war elephants. *(Sample answers: What are those animals? They are as big as a temple, they have snakes for noses, and they trumpet loudly. How can we defeat them?)* Then have them share their thoughts with another student, either in class or through a chat or blog.

Discuss Remind students that trade was often the basis for an empire's wealth. Both Carthage and Rome wanted to control trade on the Mediterranean.

After completing the Start Up Activity, project the Lesson Opener or direct students to their textbooks. Preview the lesson by working through the Get Ready to Read items with the class. Remind students to pay close attention to the Guiding Questions as they read the lesson.

ACTIVE JOURNAL

Take Notes Have students use the lesson literacy skills graphic organizer in their Active Journals to take notes as they read the lesson.

Practice Vocabulary Have students complete the activity in their Active Journals to build their vocabulary.

VIDEO

Assign the lesson video as homework.

LESSON 4

HSS 6.7.1, 6.7.3, 6.7.4; ELD.P1.C.10.a

The Republic Struggles

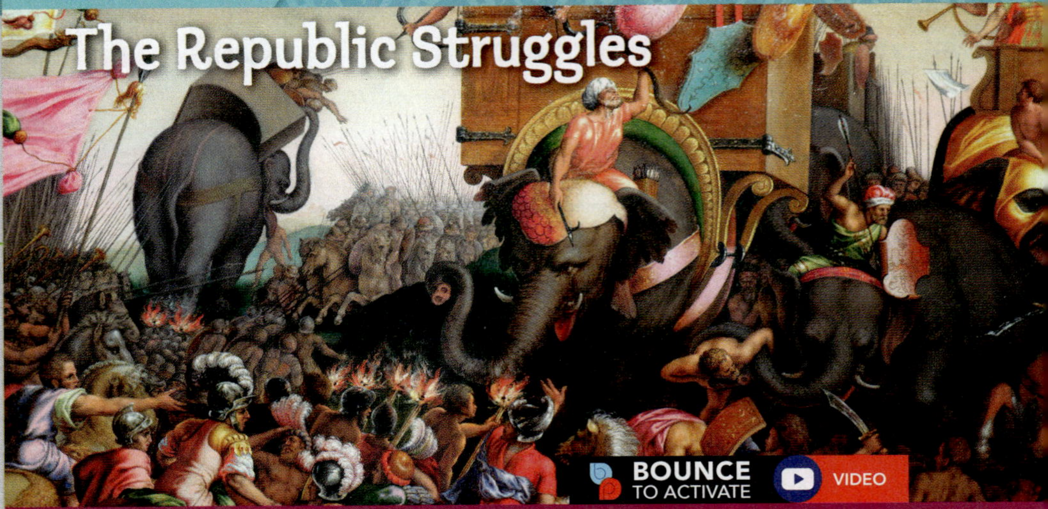

BOUNCE TO ACTIVATE

VIDEO

GET READY TO READ

START UP

Look closely at the illustration of one of Rome's enemies attacking Roman soldiers at the Battle of Zama. How do you think the Roman legions felt to be confronted with these strange African animals?

GUIDING QUESTIONS

- What changes resulted in Rome after the Punic Wars?
- What were the strengths and weaknesses of the Roman republic?
- Why did the Roman republic fall?

TAKE NOTES

Literacy Skills: Summarize

Use the graphic organizer in your Active Journal to take notes as you read the lesson.

PRACTICE VOCABULARY

Use the vocabulary activity in your Active Journal to practice the vocabulary words.

Vocabulary	Academic Vocabulary
empire	equipment
province	professional
civil war	
Augustus	

Rome began as a small city-state. It conquered a large area around the Mediterranean Sea, but its system of government did not survive this change.

Conflict with Carthage

Rome fought Carthage for control of the western Mediterranean in a series of three wars. These are known as the Punic Wars.

How Did Hannibal Invade Italy?

Carthage was a city in North Africa that also controlled parts of Spain and Sicily. The second of Rome's wars with Carthage nearly destroyed the Roman republic. Hannibal, Carthage's greatest general, led his city's troops. In 218 BCE he marched from Spain into Italy over the Alps mountains with 40,000 soldiers and about 40 war elephants. Despite the long, difficult, and dangerous trip, his army reached Italy.

Through clever tactics, Hannibal defeated three Roman armies. He probably expected Rome to give up after these crushing defeats, but the Romans kept up the fight. They wore down Hannibal's men.

PRACTICE VOCABULARY

To help students integrate new vocabulary, explain how the words *empire* and *province* are related. An empire is a state containing several countries; empires can also be divided into provinces. A *civil war* is a war between groups in the same country. *Augustus* was the title taken by Octavian when he became the first Roman emperor. Reinforce the terms during the lesson using the teaching notes.

Point out the academic vocabulary in the lesson margins. Provide sample sentences that clarify meaning.

equipment: Equipment for playing baseball includes a ball, bat, and gloves.

professional: A doctor is a professional healer trained in medical school.

In 204 BCE, the Roman general Scipio crossed the sea into Africa. His army attacked Carthage. Hannibal had to sail home from Italy to protect his city. In Africa, Scipio defeated Hannibal and won the war.

The End of Carthage Although Rome had defeated Hannibal, many Romans still feared Carthage. One senator ended every speech with the words, "Carthage must be destroyed." Rome attacked Carthage in 146 BCE, and Roman troops burned and looted the city. They sold its people into slavery. From Carthage, Rome gained fertile land for growing wheat in Sicily and North Africa, as well as silver deposits in Spain.

Rome now controlled most of the lands along the western half of the Mediterranean Sea. Rome also sent armies to the east. They conquered Greece and parts of southwest Asia. Rome did not yet have an emperor, but it ruled an **empire**, or a state containing several countries or territories. It was divided into **provinces**, or areas within a country or empire. Roman magistrates were sent out to govern these provinces. Many governors were corrupt and cruel.

READING CHECK **Identify Main Ideas** Who was Hannibal?

What Were Rome's Growing Pains?

Conquest brought Rome power and wealth, but the vast riches from trade and the conquest of new territories also caused problems. As the Romans conquered more land, huge numbers of slaves were brought to Italy. The gap between the rich and powerful senators, patricians, and some plebeians and poor plebeians, conquered foreigners, and enslaved people grew. This tension began to affect the Roman political system.

GEOGRAPHY SKILLS

During the republic, Rome grew from a city to a power controlling nearly the whole Mediterranean.

1. **Location** Use the compass rose to describe Carthage's location relative to Rome.
2. **Sequence** When did Rome unite Italy?

The Punic Wars: 218–146 BCE

WORKSHEET **TEACHER RESOURCES**

Have students who need additional support use the following worksheets from the Teacher Resources on the course:

- **Reading Support**
- **English Language Development**
- **Lesson Summary**

INVESTIGATE

Conflict With Carthage

Discuss how Rome and Carthage fought to control the western Mediterranean.

Summarize How did Hannibal attack Rome? *(He led his army from Spain over the Alps into Italy.)*

Identify Cause and Effect What were the results of the second Punic War? *(Rome was nearly destroyed, but eventually it triumphed.)*

Summarize Describe the extent of Rome's **empire** after the Punic Wars. *(Rome controlled most of the western Mediterranean, Greece, and parts of Southwest Asia.)*

What Were Rome's Growing Pains?

Discuss how Rome's growing power and wealth created problems.

Identify Cause and Effect How did the wealth created by conquest and trade affect Rome's class system and political system? *(The gap between rich and poor grew, which created tensions in the political system.)*

INTEGRATED ENGLISH LANGUAGE DEVELOPMENT

Productive Use What were Rome's Growing Pains? to help students understand and use the academic words *equipment* and *professional*.

Emerging Have students give examples of equipment and examples of people who are professional.

Expanding Have students write a paragraph that uses the words *equipment* and *professional* correctly.

(Continued on the next page.)

ANSWERS

Identify Main Ideas *Hannibal was a general from Carthage who attacked and nearly defeated Rome.*

Location *southwest*

Sequence *by 264 BCE*

Express Problems Clearly How did the methods the wealthy used to increase their power cause problems? *(They stole, looted, broke rules, and used violence to increase and keep power. As a result, Rome's government stopped working.)*

Contrast What two views about reform arose in the later years of the republic? *(Some favored reform that would help the poor, such as giving out land, while others opposed that.)*

Identify Cause and Effect How did changes to the military affect the poor in Rome? *(They helped the poor by offering them military careers. When they retired from the military, they were given land.)*

How Did Rome Change From Republic to Empire?

Discuss how the increasing power of military leaders and a civil war brought about the end of the republic.

Hypothesize What change in Roman life led to the **civil war** between Marius and Sulla? *(Sample answer: Military commanders gained too much power and could not be controlled.)*

Analyze Images Mobs rioted in Rome as the gap between rich and poor widened. **Infer** What kinds of pressures would lead poor people to respond by rioting?

Breaking the Rules In the later years of the republic, magistrates often became very wealthy by stealing from people in the provinces and looting from rich foreign enemies they fought overseas. Wealth made them more powerful at home. Because politicians could become so powerful in this way, they became willing to break the rules of politics or use violence to win elections. Government slowly stopped working.

The Urban Poor Although Rome was growing richer, many Romans were getting poorer. Landowners and employers bought slaves to do work that used to be done by poor Romans. Tenant farmers lost their livelihood. Poor people came to the city in search of work.

The government feared that Rome's poor could riot or start a revolution. It gave out free grain to keep the peace. Some politicians supported reforms. They appealed to the poor to win office. More traditional elite politicians opposed them. Politicians supported gangs that fought one another. In the 120s BCE, Tiberius and Gaius Gracchus tried to give land to the poor. Their opponents killed them.

The Power of the Army Gaius Marius was a powerful consul. He reformed, or changed and improved, the Roman army. Until around 100 BCE, only citizens who could afford their own armor served in the military. But Marius allowed even the poorest citizens to join. The government paid for their **equipment**. This made the army larger and more **professional**. It also helped the poor.

Academic Vocabulary
equipment • *n.*, things used for a specific purpose
professional • *adj.*, trained, expert

These soldiers stayed in the army for years. When they retired, they needed land. They relied on their commander to make the government give it to them. As a result, soldiers became more loyal to their commander than to the government.

READING CHECK **Identify Main Ideas** What did Tiberius and Gaius Gracchus try to do?

How Did Rome Change From Republic to Empire?

The republic's military commanders used their new power. They turned their armies against their rivals and the senate. Rome had its first **civil war**, or war between groups from the same country.

Who Were Marius and Sulla? In 87 BCE, an assembly voted to strip a general named Sulla of his power and give it to Marius. Sulla marched his troops to Rome to get his job back. He won a civil war against Marius and his supporters. Sulla ruled as dictator for more than a year.

INTEGRATED ENGLISH LANGUAGE DEVELOPMENT continued ELD.PI.C.12.a

Bridging Have students write a paragraph explaining how Gaius Marius improved the army. Students should use the words *equipment* and *professional* in their explanations.

WORKSHEET **TEACHER RESOURCES**

For additional IELD support addressing these standards, have students complete the Lesson ELD activity from the Teacher Resources found on the course.

ANSWERS

Infer *Sample answer: Lack of food, money to buy food, and jobs to earn money are among the kinds of pressures that could lead poor people to respond by rioting.*

Identify Main Ideas *They tried to give land to the poor.*

Why Did Pompey and Caesar Fight? New commanders rose up to take Sulla's place. Gnaeus Pompey conquered parts of southwest Asia. Gaius Julius Caesar conquered Gaul. The two men teamed up and used their influence to run the government together, ignoring laws and customs. Caesar invited the brilliant lawyer, scholar, and famous speaker, Marcus Tullius Cicero, to join his political alliance with Pompey. Cicero thought the alliance was unconstitutional, so he turned Caesar down. He chose instead to support the senate and to hold fast to the principles of the republic. In Cicero's *The Republic*, he describes the traditional authority and role of the senate:

Primary Source

... the senate governed the commonwealth [community] in those days.... Public affairs were principally managed under the authority, and by the rules and customs of the senate. And although the consuls possessed their power only for a year, it was royal in its nature and effect. And this was strenuously preserved, as necessary to the preservation of the influence of the nobles and principal chiefs....

—Cicero, *The Republic*, Chapter XXXII

Quest CONNECTIONS

Cicero made many great speeches in the Senate. Do leaders today still use speeches as a way of communicating? Record your answer in your Active Journal.

BIOGRAPHY 5 Things to Know About

CICERO

Roman Statesman, Scholar, Writer (106 BCE–43 BCE)

- Marcus Tullius Cicero was a famous Roman lawyer, speaker, and writer. Much of what we know of the decline and fall of the Roman republic comes from his writings about events he observed or participated in.
- Cicero won fame for his warnings against armed uprisings planned by his rival Catiline.
- He made his way along the *cursus honorum*, becoming a consul in 63 BCE and later governor of the province of Cilicia.
- During the civil war, when Pompey, Caesar, and Crassus seized the Roman government, Cicero refused to take sides. He remained loyal to the senate and the idea of the republic.
- Later, when Cicero was exiled, he studied philosophy. Eventually, he was allowed to return. He was assassinated in 43 BCE.

Critical Thinking Why might Romans hungry for power consider Cicero an enemy?

DIFFERENTIATED INSTRUCTION

Special Education Ask students to name some of the rules that help your school to run smoothly. Ask: What would happen if many students broke the rules? *(Sample answer: Bad behavior would disrupt school.)*

Below Level Have students work with a partner to create a cause-and-effect chart based on one of the two sections, Breaking the Rules or The Urban Poor. After they finish, have them exchange work with a pair who made a chart on the other section.

Advanced Suggest that students choose an issue discussed in this lesson, such as the wealthy breaking rules to gain political power or poor people losing jobs because of economic changes. Have them ask at least three adults whether they think those problems exist today, then summarize their findings.

Categorize Which side did the senate take in the civil war between Caesar and Pompey? *(It took Pompey's side.)*

Draw Conclusions After students read 5 Things to Know About Cicero, ask: Do you think Cicero was a good citizen? Explain. *(Sample answer: Yes, he cared about preserving the republic more than about power for himself.)*

ACTIVE JOURNAL

Quest Connections Divide students into groups to discuss whether leaders still use speeches as a main way to communicate. Have students record their answers in their Active Journals.

ELD TIP For the Quest Connection, ensure groups contain emerging and expanding students, and fluent speakers. Have emerging and expanding students answer questions first. Fluent speakers build on their answers.

INTERACTIVE **INTERACTIVE GALLERY**

Who Was Julius Caesar?

Display the Interactive Gallery: Who Was Julius Caesar? Click on each image and ask volunteers to read the captions. Ask: Why did it matter that he crossed the Rubicon? *(That action started a civil war.)*

ACTIVE CLASSROOM

Use the Take a Stand strategy. Ask students: Was Julius Caesar a good leader or not? Divide students by their answers into two groups and move them to separate areas. Have groups list reasons for their viewpoints. Appoint students to share group views with the class.

ANSWERS

Critical Thinking *Cicero wanted to hold fast to the principles of the republic and strongly opposed Romans who were hungry for power.*

Lesson 7.4 • The Republic Struggles 305

HSS 6.7.1, 6.7.3, 6.7.4; ELD.P1.C.10.a

SYNTHESIZE

Assess and Reteach Have students use a Think-Pair-Share strategy to complete Lesson Check questions 1–5. Review their responses. If they had any incorrect answers, use the guiding questions to discuss the lesson's main ideas, focusing on the ideas they struggled with.

ACTIVE JOURNAL

Writing Workshop Have students complete the Lesson 4 Writing Task in their Active Journals. Students will write a conclusion to their explanatory essay. As they finish the topic, they will revise and refine their essays.

DEMONSTRATE

ASSESSMENT **ONLINE LESSON QUIZ**

Assign the Online Lesson Quiz for this lesson if you haven't already done so. Students will be offered automatic remediation or enrichment based on their score.

DISCUSSION **DISCUSSION BOARD**

Post this question to the class on the Discussion Board:

Summarize How did Rome change after the Punic Wars? *(The victory over Carthage brought Rome power and wealth. Huge numbers of slaves were brought to Italy. The gap between rich and poor grew, and some lower-class people lost jobs because of the increase of slavery. The wealthy began to do unethical things to gain power. Tensions between rich and poor grew, and politicians could not agree on how to respond, creating divisions in the republic.)*

▲ Julius Caesar was a brilliant military commander. His numerous victories allowed Caesar to force the senate to make him dictator. This painting shows Caesar receiving the surrender of a Gallic tribal leader.

But later the two commanders fought. The senate sided with Pompey. It ordered Caesar to give up his legions. Caesar marched his army across the Rubicon River into Italy. This began a civil war. Caesar defeated Pompey and the senate.

Caesar took control of Rome. He used his power to help the poor, but he also made himself dictator for life. This angered many senators who wanted to keep the republic as it was. A group of senators murdered Caesar in 44 BCE.

The End of the Republic Caesar's death did not save the republic. In his will, Caesar made his teenage relative Octavian his heir. Octavian became a leader of Caesar's many followers. He swore to avenge Caesar's death. He defeated Caesar's murderers in a civil war.

Octavian defeated Mark Antony and Antony's ally Cleopatra, the queen of Egypt. By 30 BCE, he ruled Rome. The republic became a monarchy, the Roman empire. Octavian became the first emperor. He took the title **Augustus**, meaning honored one.

Augustus made new rules for senate membership. He increased the property requirement and prohibited senators from being directly involved in business. The emperor could call for and lead senate discussions, introduce laws, and appoint new senators. Augustus pretended to respect republican traditions, but as emperor he held all the real power. The senate became merely a group of advisors.

Why did the Roman republic fall? And why were Julius Caesar and Augustus allowed to take control of Rome? The empire's swift expansion, with its increasing wealth and the growing gap between rich and poor, put pressure on the republic's government and society. As the military's power grew, commanders were tempted to seize power for themselves. These conflicts led to a long civil war. Augustus ended the civil wars, but at the cost of the republic's freedom.

INTERACTIVE
Who Was Julius Caesar?

READING CHECK **Identify Cause and Effect** What was decided when Caesar crossed the Rubicon?

Lesson Check

HSS 6.7.1, 6.7.3, 6.7.4; ELD.P1.C.10.a

Practice Vocabulary

1. Who is involved in a **civil war**?
2. Who first led the Roman **empire**?

Critical Thinking and Writing

3. **Summarize** How did Rome defeat Hannibal?
4. **Compare and Contrast** Compare and contrast the Roman army before and after Marius's reforms.
5. **Identify Main Ideas** What was the main reason why the Roman republic fell?
6. **Writing Workshop: Write a Conclusion** Review what you've written already for your explanatory essay that compares Rome to earlier and contemporary societies. Write a strong conclusion that sums up your ideas. Consult your Active Journal for help.

LESSON CHECK

1. Two or more groups from the same country fight in a civil war. **DOK1**
2. Octavian, the heir of Julius Caesar, later known as Augustus **DOK1**
3. Rome refused to give up and eventually wore out Hannibal's army. It then attacked Carthage itself. **DOK2**
4. After the reforms, the army was larger, was more professional, included poor Romans, and had greater loyalty to generals. **DOK3**
5. Sample: The republic fell because it grew too large and the gap between rich and poor was too great. Also, its leaders focused on personal power and gain, not governing effectively. **DOK1**
6. Answers will vary. Student conclusions should review their thesis statement and their main ideas that compare Rome to another ancient society. **DOK4**

ANSWERS

Identify Cause and Effect *Two opposing sides decided to start a civil war.*

Analyze Sequence, Causation, and Correlation

INTERACTIVE
Analyze Cause and Effect

Read the passage and then follow these steps to help you identify sequence and to distinguish between causation and correlation.

1 **Choose an event or a condition as a starting point.** You might want to choose an event at the beginning of the passage.

2 **Identify sequence.** Look for clue words or phrases like *first, next,* and *then.* These terms signal sequence. Make a rough timeline of events that led up to that event and events that occurred after that event. Note that all the events in the passage took place in BCE. This means that more recent years have *smaller* numbers than earlier years.

3 **Identify cause-and-effect relationships.** Look for clue words or phrases that signal cause-and-effect like *because, for this reason, brought about, led to, as a result,* and *therefore.* Which cause-and-effect clues do you see in the passage?

4 **Look at other events or conditions for possible correlations.** Look for clue words or phrases like *meanwhile, at the same time,* and *also.* Terms like these suggest that although events and conditions may have something in common, one thing has not *caused* the other. Which correlation clue words or phrases do you see in the passage?

5 **Summarize the cause-and-effect relationships and correlations.** Make a table or chart of the events. Indicate which events were causes of another event and which were correlations, or events happening at the same time.

Secondary Source

The Roman republic faced many conflicts as it gained territory and power. Beginning in 264 BCE, Rome fought three Punic wars against Carthage, a rival city-state in North Africa. The Romans won the First Punic War in 241 BCE and as a result gained control of Sicily, Corsica, and Sardinia.

For revenge, the Carthaginian general Hannibal started the Second Punic War in 218 BCE and won battles in Italy for the next 15 years, but the Romans wore his army down and eventually captured Carthage. Then, in 149 BCE, the Third Punic War erupted, and the Romans burned and looted Carthage in 146 BCE. Survivors were killed or sold into slavery.

Meanwhile, Roman armies also conquered Greece and parts of southwest Asia. The magistrates who governed these new Roman territories were often corrupt and brutal. At home, the growing gap between rich and poor led to gang wars in Rome's streets. In 123 BCE, when the tribune Tiberius Gracchus tried to give land to the poor, his enemies killed him and his brother.

Analysis HI.2

Analysis Skills

Analyze Sequence, Causation, and Correlation

LEARN

Preview the steps in the student text with students, and then play the video.

VIDEO **21ST CENTURY SKILLS**

Project the Analyze Cause and Effect video in the 21st Century Skills Tutorial. Use the Quick Reference and Assessment to provide additional instruction on this skill.

PRACTICE

Have students practice the skill using the secondary source on the student page, providing the instructions and then asking students the questions.

As an alternative, you could form students into pairs or groups to perform the activity. Then invite the groups to state their conclusions to the class. Discuss the different opinions that students formed about cause-and-effect relationships and correlation in the excerpt.

ASSESS

To assess this skill, have students reread the section What Were Rome's Growing Pains? in Lesson 4 of this topic. Ask them to list the effects of Rome's expansion through conquest.

DIFFERENTIATED INSTRUCTION

Below Level Remind students of the difference between correlation and causation. Just because two events occur in sequence does not make the first event a cause of the second. Rather, the first event has to directly or indirectly bring about the second event to be a cause.

ENGLISH LANGUAGE LEARNERS

Emerging Support emerging students by writing key events on sentence strips. Then, as a class, organize the events into their proper order.

ANSWERS

1. Sample answer: the Second Punic War.
2. Sample answer: The Romans won the First Punic War in 241 BCE, began the Third Punic War in 149 BCE, then burned and looted Carthage in 146 BCE.
3. as a result, led to
4. Then, also, Meanwhile
5. Sample answer (table entries): Victory in First Punic War causes Romans to gain control of Sicily, Corsica, and Sardinia (effect); For revenge (cause), Hannibal starts Second Punic War (effect). He wins battles in Italy for 15 years (correlation). Romans wear his army down (cause), capture Carthage (effect).

HSS 6.7, 6.7.1, 6.7.2, 6.7.3, 6.7.4; ELA W.6.2, WHST.6.2; ELD.P1.A.2, ELD.P1.C.10.a

Review and Assessment

VISUAL REVIEW

Direct students' attention to the "Rome: Comparing Monarchy and Republic" chart. Ask volunteers to read the characteristics that were specific to each type of government and the characteristics shared by both.

Direct students' attention to the "Roman Citizenship" chart. As a class, review the rights and responsibilities of Roman citizenship.

READING REVIEW

WORKSHEET **TEACHER RESOURCES**

Have students who need additional support read the Lesson Summaries available in Teacher Resources on the Realize course.

GAMES **TOPIC MINI-GAMES**

For additional vocabulary practice, students can go online to access the Topic Mini-Games in Realize.

Quest FINDINGS

Write an Explanatory Essay

Have students complete their Topic Quests by writing an explanatory essay in their Active Journals. Remind students to follow the writing process steps: (1) prewrite, (2) draft, (3) share, (4) revise, and (5) present. **DOK4**

TOPIC 7

Review and Assessment

VISUAL REVIEW

Rome: Comparing Monarchy and Republic

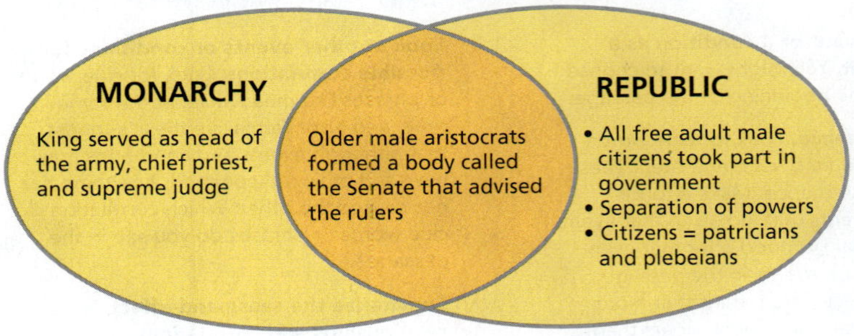

Roman Citizenship

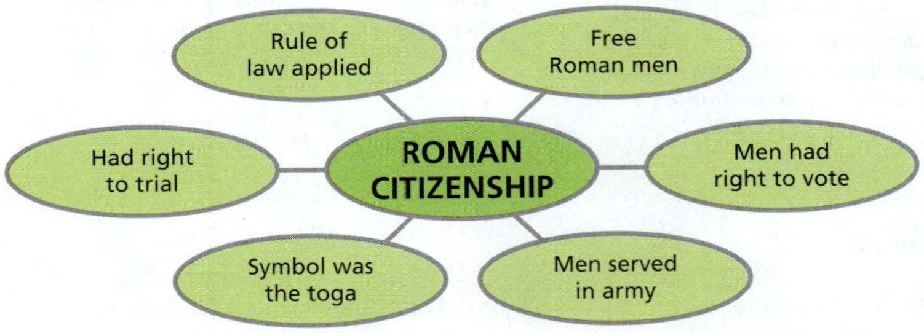

READING REVIEW

Use the Take Notes and Practice Vocabulary in your Active Journal to review the topic.

- Reading Skill Graphic Organizers
- Practice Vocabulary Activities

Complete an interactivity to help you practice vocabulary.

INTERACTIVE

Practice vocabulary using the Topic Mini-Games

Quest FINDINGS

Write Your Explanatory Essay

Get help for writing your essay explaining the Roman republic's influence on later governments in your Active Journal.

ANSWERS

1. Geography allowed Roman soldiers to move easily and conquer peoples throughout the peninsula. **DOK1**
2. The Romans adapted many of their gods and heroes from the Greeks. **DOK1**
3. Male Roman citizens could wear a toga. **DOK1**
4. Rome signed treaties making those it conquered into allies. These allies then fought for and with Rome to conquer additional lands. **DOK1**
5. Roman armies frequently took as slaves those they captured. Also, conquest brought Rome wealth, which Romans used to buy more slaves. **DOK1**
6. Rome had an official religion supported by the government. **DOK1**

HSS 6.7, 6.7.1, 6.7.2, 6.7.3, 6.7.4; ELA W.6.2, WHST.6.2; ELD.P1.A.2, ELD.P1.C.10.a

ASSESSMENT

Vocabulary and Key Ideas

1. **Describe** How did Italy's geography help Rome unite the peninsula?
2. **Identify Main Ideas** How did the Greeks influence Roman religion?
3. **Recall** Who could wear a **toga**?
4. **Check Understanding** How did Rome's allies help it expand?
5. **Check Understanding** How did Rome's expansion lead to a rise in the number of enslaved people in Rome?
6. **Define** What does it mean to say that ancient Rome had an **established religion**?

Critical Thinking and Writing

7. **Identify Implied Main Ideas** Why are Roman beliefs about the founding of their city, such as those about Romulus and Remus and Aeneas, important?
8. **Compare and Contrast** List one similarity and one difference between the governments of the Roman republic and the United States.
9. **Identify Central Issues** Suppose that you could travel back in time to ancient Rome. List one question you would ask each of the following: a man, a woman, a rich person, a poor person, and an enslaved person.
10. **Revisit the Essential Question** Defend the statement that the Roman republic was structured to keep a single person from holding too much power. Support your answer with evidence from this lesson.
11. **Writing Workshop: Write a Research Paper** Using the preparatory work you've done in your Active Journal, conduct research in order to answer the following question in a research essay: How did other societies influence and affect the Romans? Consider the Greek, Hellenistic, Chinese, and Persian civilizations you've already studied in this course in your essay.

Analyze Primary Sources

12. Why does Polybius believe the Roman constitution worked so well?
    - A. because it gave all power to a single ruler
    - B. because different parts of the government balanced one another
    - C. because it was a pure democracy
    - D. because one part of the government had total power over all other parts

"The three kinds of government, monarchy, aristocracy and democracy, were all found united in the common wealth [government] of Rome. . . . Such being the power that each part has of hampering the others or co-operating with them... it is impossible to find a better political system than this."

—Polybius *Histories*, 200s BCE

Analyze Maps

Use the map to answer the following questions.

13. Which letter represents the eastern Mediterranean? How did Rome's location near this area help it develop?
14. Which letter represents Carthage?
15. Which letter represents Rome? Which part of Europe did the Romans conquer after Italy?

▼ Roman Republic

Review and Assessment 309

7. They tell us that Romans believed their city had a connection to the gods and to heroes of ancient Greece. **DOK2**

8. Sample answer: Both the Roman and U.S. governments include checks and balances. The Roman government had no written constitution, while the U.S. government does. **DOK3**

9. Sample questions: (man) What role do you want to play in Roman government? (woman) How do you feel about the restrictions on your participation in Roman society? (rich) What can you do to give back to the Roman society that has made you wealthy? (poor) What would you like to change about Roman society? (enslaved person) If Rome were threatened in a war, would you fight for it or against it? Explain. **DOK1**

10. No one man in the Roman republic could have too much power because power was divided up among several branches of government and within those branches among different roles. There were many checks and balances within and between branches. **DOK4**

11. Student answers will vary. They should choose one of the societies named and use reliable sources such as history books or museum websites to find information about how it influenced the Romans.

12. B **DOK4**

13. C; Rome's location on the edge of this region allowed it to build on the economic prosperity of earlier civilizations. **DOK3**

14. A **DOK1**

15. B; modern-day Spain, parts of Greece **DOK3**

ASSESSMENT **TOPIC TEST**

For summative assessment, assign the Topic Test in Realize.

TOPIC 8

The Roman and Byzantine Empires

Pacing: Approximately 26.5 periods, 12.25 blocks	Resources: Student Edition	Resources: Active Journal	Resources: Online	Pacing	California Standards
CONNECT					
NBC LEARN VIDEO Augustus and the Pax Romana			video	10 min.	HSS 6.7.4
ESSENTIAL QUESTION ACTIVITY What Forces Can Cause a Society to Change?		✓	interactive	10 min.	HSS 6.7.3, 6.7.4
OVERVIEW ACTIVITY: TIMELINE & MAP The Roman and Byzantine Empires, 30 BCE–1453 CE		✓	interactive	10 min.	HSS 6.7.3, 6.7.4, 6.7.5, 6.7.6, 6.7.7, 6.7.8
Quest KICK OFF: Ask Questions	✓	✓		20 min.	HSS 7.1.1; ELA SL.6.1, 6.3, RI.6.6, 6.9; ELD P1.A.3 ELD P1.C.11.a
INVESTIGATE					
LESSONS 1–7	See Lesson-at-a-Glance pages				
Quest INVESTIGATE: Quest Connections	✓	✓		20 min.	HSS 7.1.1; ELA SL.6.1, 6.3, RI.6.6, 6.9; ELD P1.A.3 ELD P1.C.11.a
SYNTHESIZE					
WRITING WORKSHOP Write an Argumentative Essay		✓	interactive	30 min.	ELD P1.C.10.a
TOPIC MINI-GAMES The Roman and Byzantine Empires			game	10 min.	
Quest SOURCES: Examine Primary Sources	✓		book	30 min.	HSS 7.1.1; ELA SL.6.1, 6.3, RI.6.6, 6.9; ELD P1.A.3 ELD P1.C.11.a
DEMONSTRATE					
TOPIC REVIEW AND ASSESSMENT The Roman and Byzantine Empires	✓		book	20 min.	
TOPIC TEST			test	30 min.	
Quest FINDINGS: Prepare Your Position	✓	✓	book	30 min.	HSS 7.1.1; ELA SL.6.1, 6.3, RI.6.6, 6.9; ELD P1.A.3 ELD P1.C.11.a

Quest

Each Quest is designed to reinforce the topic content through an inquiry arc that students work on throughout the topic. This topic's Quest, The Fall of Rome, is a Discussion Inquiry in which students debate whether the fall of Rome could have been prevented.

Active Journal Resources

- Ask Questions
- Quest Connections
- Examine Primary Sources
- Prepare Your Position

Quest Sources Online

- *The Decline and Fall of the Roman Empire* by Edward Gibbon
- *The Day of the Barbarians* by Alessandro Barbero
- *The History of the Later Roman Empire* by J.B. Bury
- *The Fall of the Roman Empire* by Michael Grant
- Rules for Civic Discussion
- Rubrics for Civic Discussion

Additional Resources

Support for Struggling Readers

- Reading Support, Teacher Resources
- Lesson Summaries, Teacher Resources
- English Language Development Teacher Resources

Suggested Resources

- *History and Activities of the Roman Empire* by Alexandra Fix
- *Life in Ancient Rome* by Shilpa Mehta-Jones
- *The Fall of the Roman Empire* by Rita J. Markel
- *Rome Falls (video),* History.com

Beyond the Classroom

Use Online and Library Media Centers

Use a media center to gain online access to the resources of distant museums, such as the Metropolitan Museum of Art, the Louvre, or the British Museum, or educational institutions that specialize in the region, such as the University of Pennsylvania. Virtual tours are available of imperial Rome, such as the virtual tour Visualizing Imperial Rome available on the Khan Academy website. These experiences can help students grasp the cultural achievements of imperial Rome.

The Roman Empire Begins

Objectives

Objective 1: Explain what the Pax Romana was and how it affected Rome.

Objective 2: Describe how the Roman Empire gained and maintained power over people and territories.

Objective 3: Identify how Rome's achievements in architecture and technology encouraged its growth.

Objective 4: Summarize how Rome's environment affected its growing economy and trade networks.

	Resources: Student Edition	Resources: Active Journal	Resources: Online	Pacing (approx. 5 periods, 2.5 blocks)	California Standards
CONNECT					
VIDEO Trade in the Roman Empire			●	5 min.	HSS 6.7.3, 6.7.4, 6.7.8, 7.1.1, 7.1.2
START UP ACTIVITY Get Ready to Read	✓	✓	●	5 min.	HSS 6.7.3
TAKE NOTES AND PRACTICE VOCABULARY		✓			
INVESTIGATE					
READ Lesson 1: The Roman Empire Begins	✓	✓	●	80 min.	HSS 6.7.3, 6.7.4, 6.7.8, 7.1.1, 7.1.2
QUICK ACTIVITY Where Do They Go Next?		✓			
INTERACTIVE TIMELINE Roman Rulers Who Made History			●	10 min.	HSS 6.7.4
PRIMARY SOURCES Augustus, *The Deeds of the Divine Augustus*	✓		●	40 min.	HSS 6.7.4; ELA RI.6.6
ANALYSIS SKILLS Identify Central Issues and Problems	✓		●	30 min.	Analysis HI.1
21ST CENTURY SKILLS TUTORIAL Solve Problems			●	10 min.	Analysis HI.1
READING SUPPORT			●		
SYNTHESIZE					
WRITING WORKSHOP Gather Details	✓	✓	●	10 min.	HSS 6.7.2, 6.7.8, 7.1.1; ELD.P1.C.10.a
LESSON SUMMARY			●		
DEMONSTRATE					
LESSON QUIZ			●	10 min.	HSS 6.7.3, 6.7.4, 6.7.8, 7.1.1, 7.1.2

Objectives

Objective 1: Discuss the relationship between Rome and Judea.

Objective 2: Explain who Jesus was and what he taught.

Objective 3: Describe how the religion of Christianity developed and changed.

Objective 4: Analyze how Christianity spread.

Origins of Christianity

	Resources			Pacing	
	Student Edition	Active Journal	Online	approx. 3 periods, 1.5 blocks	California Standards
CONNECT					
VIDEO Reasons for the Spread of Christianity			✓	5 min.	HSS 6.7.5, 6.7.6, 6.7.7, 7.1.1
START UP ACTIVITY Get Ready to Read	✓	✓	✓	5 min.	HSS 6.7.5, 6.7.6, 6.7.7
TAKE NOTES AND PRACTICE VOCABULARY		✓			
INVESTIGATE					
READ Lesson 2: Origins of Christianity	✓	✓	✓	40 min.	HSS 6.7.5, 6.7.6, 6.7.7, 7.1.1
INTERACTIVE GALLERY Early Christian Symbols			✓	10 min.	HSS 6.7.6
ANALYSIS SKILLS Detect Changing Patterns	✓		✓	30 min.	HSS 6.7.6, 6.7.7, 7.1.1; Analysis HI.3
21ST CENTURY SKILLS TUTORIAL Identify Trends			✓	10 min.	Analysis HI.3
READING SUPPORT			✓		
SYNTHESIZE					
WRITING WORKSHOP Gather Details	✓	✓	✓	10 min.	HSS 6.7.2, 6.7.3, 6.7.8, 7.1.1; ELD P1.A.2, P1.C.10.a
LESSON SUMMARY			✓		
DEMONSTRATE					
LESSON QUIZ			✓	10 min.	HSS 6.7.5, 6.7.6, 6.7.7, 7.1.1

Beliefs of Christianity

Objectives

Objective 1: Describe the writings that form Christianity's scripture.

Objective 2: Explain the core beliefs that most Christians share.

Objective 3: Discuss how Christians practice their religion.

Objective 4: Identify what Christians believe about atonement, or making up for one's sins.

	Resources: Student Edition	Resources: Active Journal	Resources: Online	Pacing (approx. 3 periods, 1.5 blocks)	California Standards
CONNECT					
VIDEO The New Testament			Video	5 min.	HSS 6.7.6, 6.7.8; ELA RI.6.5
START UP ACTIVITY Get Ready to Read	✓	✓	Book	5 min.	HSS 6.7.7
TAKE NOTES AND PRACTICE VOCABULARY		✓			
INVESTIGATE					
READ Lesson 3: Beliefs of Christianity	✓	✓	Book	35 min.	HSS 6.7.6, 6.7.8; ELA RI.6.5
INTERACTIVE GALLERY Christianity Today			Interactive	10 min.	HSS 6.7.6
PRIMARY SOURCES The Gospel of Matthew, The Sermon on the Mount	✓		Book	40 min.	HSS 6.7.6; ELA RH.6.1
INTERACTIVE PRIMARY SOURCE First Letter to the Corinthians			Video	5 min.	HSS 6.7.6
READING SUPPORT			Document		
SYNTHESIZE					
WRITING WORKSHOP Use Credible Sources	✓	✓	Book	10 min.	HSS 6.7.6, 6.7.8
LESSON SUMMARY			Document		
DEMONSTRATE					
LESSON QUIZ			Quiz	10 min.	HSS 6.7.6, 6.7.8; ELA RI.6.5

Roman Culture and Its Legacy

	Resources: Student Edition	Resources: Active Journal	Resources: Online	Pacing (approx. 4 periods, 2 blocks)	California Standards
CONNECT					
VIDEO Rome's Cultural Gifts			✓	5 min.	HSS 6.7.7, 6.7.8
START UP ACTIVITY Get Ready to Read	✓	✓	✓	5 min.	HSS 6.7.8
TAKE NOTES AND PRACTICE VOCABULARY		✓			
INVESTIGATE					
READ Lesson 4: Roman Culture and Its Legacy	✓	✓	✓	120 min.	HSS 6.7.7, 6.7.8, 7.1.1, 7.1.2; ELA RI.6.2
3D MODEL The Pantheon			✓	10 min.	HSS 6.7.8, 7.1.1
READING SUPPORT			✓		
SYNTHESIZE					
WRITING WORKSHOP Introduce a Claim	✓	✓	✓	10 min.	HSS 6.7.2, 6.7.8, 7.1.1; ELD.P1.C.10.a
LESSON SUMMARY			✓		
DEMONSTRATE					
LESSON QUIZ			✓	10 min.	HSS 6.7.7, 6.7.8

Objectives

Objective 1: Summarize the cultural exchanges that took place between Rome and other ancient civilizations.

Objective 2: Identify the Roman achievements in art, literature, and science.

Objective 3: Explain how ancient Rome influenced language and popular culture.

Objective 4: Describe the legacies left by Rome's government and concept of citizenship.

Decline of the Roman Empire

Objectives

Objective 1: Discuss the factors that led to the Roman empire's decline.

Objective 2: Identify the attempts that Rome's leaders made to hold the empire together.

Objective 3: Explain what happened to the two halves of the Roman empire.

Objective 4: Describe which parts of society challenged Roman emperors.

	Resources: Student Edition	Resources: Active Journal	Resources: Online	Pacing (approx. 2 periods, 1 block)	California Standards
CONNECT					
VIDEO Why Did the Roman Empire End?			✓	5 min.	HSS 7.1.3; ELA RH.6.5
START UP ACTIVITY Get Ready to Read	✓	✓	✓	5 min.	HSS 6.7.8, 7.1.1
TAKE NOTES AND PRACTICE VOCABULARY		✓			
INVESTIGATE					
READ Lesson 5: Decline of the Roman Empire	✓	✓	✓	40 min.	HSS 7.1.1, 7.1.2, 7.1.3
QUICK ACTIVITY Did the Roman Empire Fall?		✓			
INTERACTIVE MAP Invasions of the Roman Empire, 378–533 CE			✓	10 min.	HSS 7.1.2; ELA RH.6.5
READING SUPPORT			✓		
SYNTHESIZE					
WRITING WORKSHOP Support a Claim	✓	✓	✓	10 min.	HSS 6.7.8, 7.1.1, 7.1.2, 7.1.3
LESSON SUMMARY			✓		
DEMONSTRATE					
LESSON QUIZ			✓	10 min.	ELA RH.6.5

The Byzantine Empire Rises

	Resources: Student Edition	Resources: Active Journal	Resources: Online	Pacing (approx. 3 periods, 1.5 blocks)	California Standards
CONNECT					
VIDEO The Byzantine Empire's Place in History			✓ (video)	5 min.	HSS 7.1.3; ELA RI.6.1, RH.6.1
START UP ACTIVITY Get Ready to Read	✓	✓	✓ (book)	5 min.	HSS 7.1.3
TAKE NOTES AND PRACTICE VOCABULARY		✓			
INVESTIGATE					
READ Lesson 6: The Byzantine Empire Rises	✓	✓	✓ (book)	30 min.	HSS 7.1.3; ELA RI.6.1, RH.6.1
INTERACTIVE MAP The Byzantine Empire			✓ (interactive)	10 min.	HSS 7.1.3
ANALYSIS SKILLS Conduct a Cost-Benefit Analysis	✓		✓ (book)	30 min.	HSS 7.1.2, 7.1.3; Analysis HI.6
21ST CENTURY SKILLS TUTORIAL Make Decisions			✓ (video)	10 min.	Analysis HI.6
READING SUPPORT			✓ (document)		
SYNTHESIZE					
WRITING WORKSHOP Distinguish Claims from Opposing Claims	✓	✓	✓ (book)	10 min.	ELD P1.A.2
LESSON SUMMARY			✓ (document)		
DEMONSTRATE					
LESSON QUIZ			✓ (quiz)	10 min.	HSS 7.1.3; ELA RI.6.1, RH.6.1

Objectives

Objective 1: Analyze the ways in which the Byzantine empire differed from the Roman empire.

Objective 2: Discuss Justinian's achievements.

Objective 3: Identify what caused the Byzantine empire to decline.

Objective 4: Describe how the Byzantine empire influenced the cultures around it, including early Russia.

TOPIC 8

Byzantine Religion and Culture

	Resources: Student Edition	Resources: Active Journal	Resources: Online	Pacing (approx. 2 periods, 1 block)	California Standards
CONNECT					
VIDEO Byzantine Culture			●	5 min.	HSS 7.1.3
START UP ACTIVITY Get Ready to Read	✓	✓	●	5 min.	HSS 7.1.3
TAKE NOTES AND PRACTICE VOCABULARY		✓			
INVESTIGATE					
READ Lesson 7: Byzantine Religion and Culture	✓	✓	●	40 min.	HSS 7.1.3
INTERACTIVE IMAGE Hagia Sophia			●	10 min.	HSS 7.1.3
READING SUPPORT			●		
SYNTHESIZE					
WRITING WORKSHOP Shape Tone	✓	✓	●	10 min.	ELD P1.A.2
LESSON SUMMARY			●		
DEMONSTRATE					
LESSON QUIZ			●	10 min.	HSS 7.1.3

Objectives

Objective 1: Summarize the differences that arose between Christians during this period.

Objective 2: Analyze the ways the Eastern Orthodox Church and the Roman Catholic Church differ.

Objective 3: Discuss the ways in which the culture of the Byzantines was unique.

Objective 4: Describe the difference in leadership between the Eastern and Western churches.

PEARSON realize™

Use the suite of online resources to

Enrich your instruction with topic and lesson videos and interactivities.

VIDEO

Assess and monitor student progress with automatic answer reporting for lesson prompts, lesson quizzes with remediation, and topic-level assessments.

ETEXT

ASSESSMENT

GAMES

Help struggling learners with tools built into the eText, reading support worksheets, lesson summaries, English Language Development exercises, and more.

ETEXT

WORKSHEET

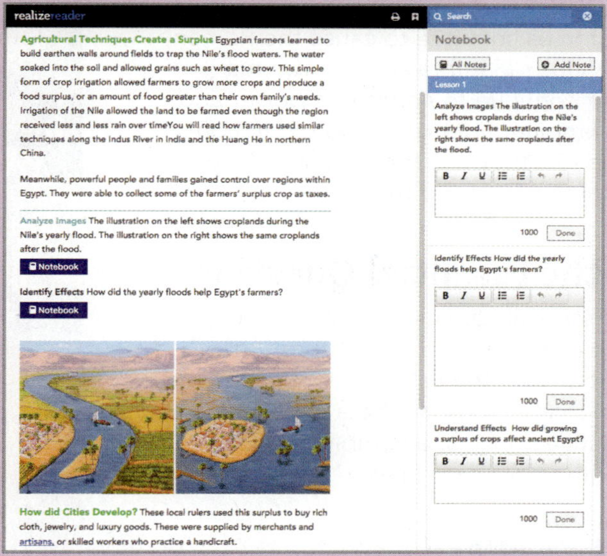

TOPIC 8 The Roman and Byzantine Empires (30 BCE–1453 CE)

HSS 6.7.3, 6.7.4, 6.7.5, 6.7.6, 6.7.7, 6.7.8, 7.1.1, 7.1.2, 7.1.3; Analysis HI.1, HI.3, HI.6

CONNECT

Introduction

The Roman empire dominated the world for about five centuries. After the Western Roman empire collapsed, the eastern half—the Byzantine empire—continued for another thousand years. This topic will explore the rise and decline of these famous empires.

Activate Prior Knowledge

Remind students that before becoming an empire, the Roman republic experienced great changes because of political strife, increasing diversity, and economic tensions. Ask: How might these forces continue to cause the Roman empire to change? *(Sample answer: Various groups might continue to agitate for power and wealth. The empire might grow too big to control.)* Tell students they are about to study the forces that caused Rome to decline.

Explore the Essential Question

Project the Essential Question activity from the course. Have a volunteer read the question. As students consider the Essential Question, remind them that change can be a positive thing, a negative thing, or a combination of the two. Ask them for examples.

ACTIVE JOURNAL

Essential Question Have students begin to explore the Essential Question in their Active Journals.

Draw Conclusions Ask students to think of forces that cause change in today's world. *(Sample answers: technological change, changes in values that not everyone shares)* Have them record their ideas in their journals to refer to as they read the topic.

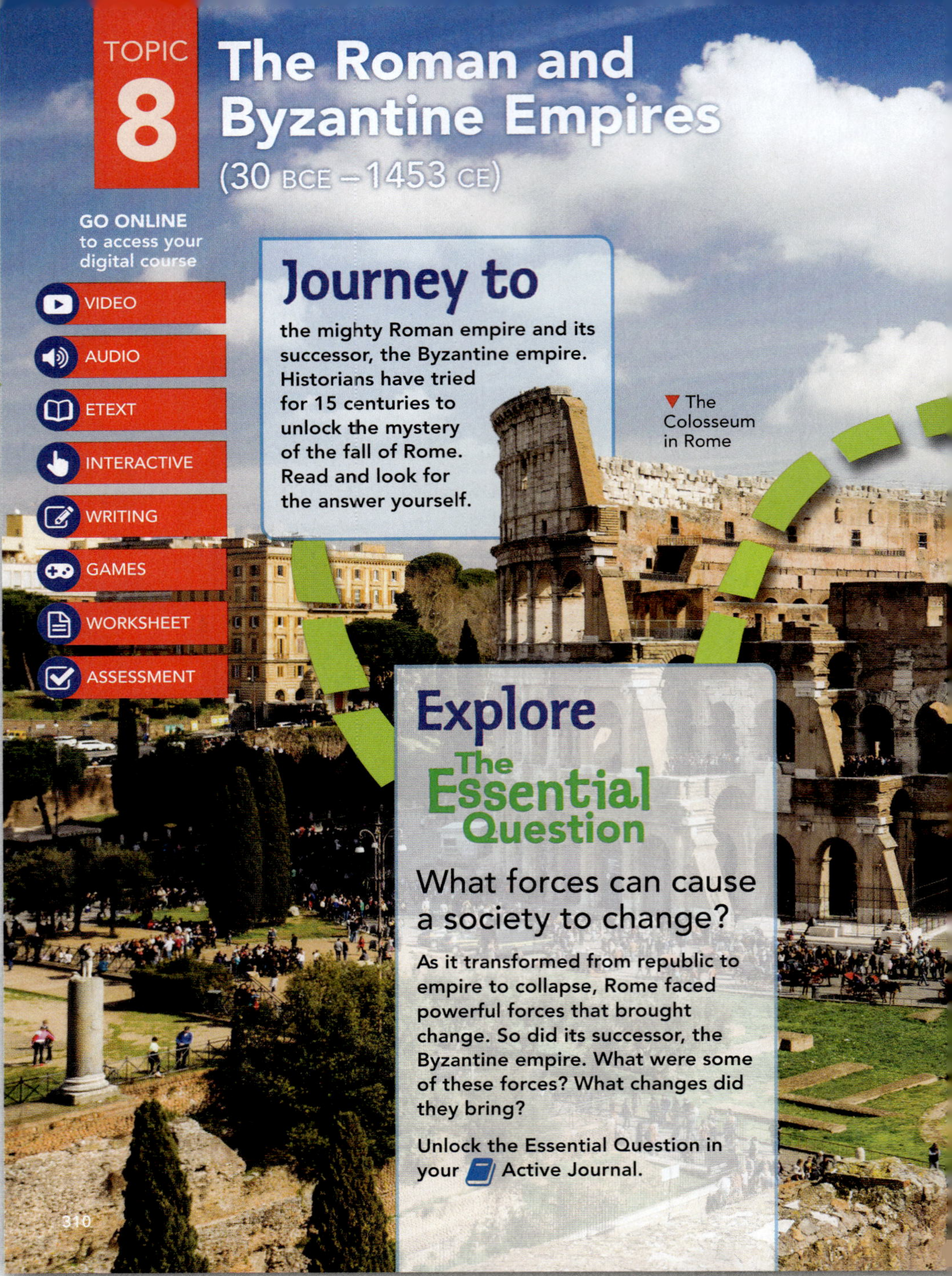
TOPIC 8 The Roman and Byzantine Empires (30 BCE – 1453 CE)

GO ONLINE to access your digital course

VIDEO
AUDIO
ETEXT
INTERACTIVE
WRITING
GAMES
WORKSHEET
ASSESSMENT

Journey to the mighty Roman empire and its successor, the Byzantine empire. Historians have tried for 15 centuries to unlock the mystery of the fall of Rome. Read and look for the answer yourself.

▼ The Colosseum in Rome

Explore The Essential Question

What forces can cause a society to change?

As it transformed from republic to empire to collapse, Rome faced powerful forces that brought change. So did its successor, the Byzantine empire. What were some of these forces? What changes did they bring?

Unlock the Essential Question in your Active Journal.

310

ANALYZE VISUALS

Ask students to closely examine the photograph of ruins. What kind of modern structure does this resemble? *(Sample answer: It looks like a sports stadium.)* Ask: What type of events do you think occurred here? *(Sample answers: sporting events, entertainment, political gatherings)*

HSS 6.7.3, 6.7.4, 6.7.5, 6.7.6, 6.7.7, 6.7.8, 7.1.1, 7.1.2, 7.1.3; Analysis HI.1, HI.3, HI.6

Watch

NBC LEARN

BOUNCE TO ACTIVATE VIDEO

Augustus and the Pax Romana

Learn about the glorious period of peace and prosperity that began with Rome's first emperor.

Read

about the rise of the Roman empire, its glory years, and its decline and transformation into the Byzantine empire.

Lesson 1	The Roman Empire Begins
Primary Sources	Augustus, *The Deeds of the Divine Augustus*
Lesson 2	Origins of Christianity
Lesson 3	Beliefs of Christianity
Primary Sources	The Gospel of Matthew, The Sermon on the Mount
Lesson 4	Roman Culture and Its Legacy
Lesson 5	The Decline of the Roman Empire
Lesson 6	The Byzantine Empire Rises
Lesson 7	Byzantine Religion and Culture

311

RECOGNIZE CULTURAL AND EXPERIENTIAL BACKGROUNDS

Make use of your knowledge of students' lives to make connections between their own experiences, backgrounds, and interests and the content of this topic. If you have students whose ethnic heritage is related to the content of this topic, make an effort to emphasize the contributions and achievements of this society and how it has enriched the world.

If appropriate, allow the students the opportunity to share cultural, ethnic, or linguistic traditions and knowledge from their experiences.

If students have family experiences (such as travel to or family members who have lived in the region being studied), allow them to share relevant stories.

Watch

VIDEO NBC LEARN VIDEO

Project the Topic Opener video about Augustus and the Pax Romana. After viewing the video, ask students to respond to the following questions.

Identify Main Ideas What was the Pax Romana? *(a period of peace and prosperity)*

Identify Cause and Effect What was the motive behind Augustus' reforms? *(Sample answer: to create a stable government)*

Read

Share these lesson previews with students.

Lesson 1: During the Pax Romana, the Roman empire achieved many things.

Primary Sources: Augustus recounts many of his accomplishments.

Lesson 2: The teachings of a Jew named Jesus led to a new religion, Christianity, which spread across the Roman empire.

Lesson 3: Christians developed a set of beliefs and practices based on Jesus' teachings and the Christian Bible.

Primary Sources: In the Sermon on the Mount, Jesus pronounces blessings.

Lesson 4: Rome left a legacy of art, language, literature, science, government, and law.

Lesson 5: The Roman empire experienced conflict over imperial succession, economic problems, and foreign invaders. The western Roman empire eventually fell.

Lesson 6: The Byzantine empire carried on the traditions of Rome and influenced other countries such as Russia.

Lesson 7: The Eastern Orthodox and Roman Catholic churches developed in different ways. Byzantine civilization left a distinct cultural legacy.

TOPIC 8

HSS 6.7.3, 6.7.4, 6.7.5, 6.7.6, 6.7.7, 6.7.8, 7.1.1, 7.1.2, 7.1.3

What Happened and When?

Have students examine the timeline. Ask: When did the Roman empire reach its greatest size? *(117 CE)* How many years passed between the collapse of the western Roman empire and the fall of Constantinople? *(977 years)*

ACTIVE JOURNAL

Timeline Skills Students can also use the Timeline Skills activity in their Active Journals to record information about the history of the Roman and Byzantine empires as they read the topic. During their reading, they should add the dates of at least three events they think are important. After completing the topic, have students write a paragraph identifying the dates they added and explaining why each is significant.

INTERACTIVE

INTERACTIVE TIMELINE

Display the Interactive Topic Timeline for the class. Click through the interactive to learn more about the Roman and Byzantine empires. Have volunteers read entries.

Discuss Ask students: What is the sequence of the Roman and Byzantine empires? *(The Roman empire came first, then the Byzantine empire.)*

TOPIC 8

The Roman and Byzantine Empires (30 BCE – 1453 CE)

Learn more about the Roman and Byzantine empires by making your own map and timeline in your Active Journal.

INTERACTIVE
Topic Map

Where were the Roman and Byzantine empires?

These empires covered much of western and southeastern Europe and the eastern and southern shores of the Mediterranean Sea. In the detailed map, yellow shading shows Rome at the end of the republic; other colors show the empire's later growth. Locate Rome and Constantinople on the larger map.

INTERACTIVE
Topic Timeline

What happened and when?

The Roman republic gave way to an even mightier empire. But even a great empire declines. Explore the timeline to see what was happening in the Roman empire and its successor, the Byzantine empire, along with the rest of the world.

27 BCE Augustus becomes the first Roman emperor.

c. 1 BCE According to Christian tradition, Jesus is born.

117 CE The Roman empire reaches its largest extent.

313 Emperor Constantine ends the persecution of Christians in the empire.

476 The western Roman empire collapses.

TOPIC EVENTS

250 BCE | 1 CE | 250

WORLD EVENTS

87 BCE Long reign of Chinese emperor Wu Di ends.

320 CE Gupta emperors create a Golden Age in India.

DIFFERENTIATED INSTRUCTION

Special Education Point out that this timeline includes events both before and during the Common Era. Remind students that there is no zero year. 1 BCE was followed directly by 1 CE.

Below Level Make sure that students understand that the Byzantine empire was originally the eastern part of the Roman empire. It continued after the western Roman empire fell.

Advanced Suggest that students research the Chinese Emperor Wu Di and write a paragraph comparing him to either Augustus or Constantine.

HSS 6.7.3, 6.7.4, 6.7.5, 6.7.6, 6.7.7, 6.7.8, 7.1.1, 7.1.2, 7.1.3

Who will you meet?

Paul helped spread Christianity throughout the Roman empire.

Constantine transformed the Roman empire.

Theodora ruled with her husband Justinian at the height of the Byzantine empire.

527
Justinian becomes Byzantine emperor.

1054
Great Schism divides Eastern Orthodox and Roman Catholic churches.

1453
Constantinople falls to the Ottoman Turks. Byzantine empire ends.

500 | 1000 | 1250 | 1500

1325 CE
Aztecs found their capital at Tenochtitlan in Mexico.

313

COMMON MISCONCEPTIONS

Byzantium, Constantinople, or Istanbul? Students probably don't realize that Byzantium, Constantinople, and Istanbul are all names for the same city. It was originally a Greek city, built around 660 BCE. Constantine the Great made the city his capital in 330 CE and called it New Rome at first and later Constantinople, after himself. The city fell to Muslims in 1453. After that, it became known as Istanbul, which remains its name today.

Where Were the Roman and Byzantine Empires?

Direct students' attention to the map of the Roman and Byzantine empires in the student text. Ask: What did the cities of Rome and Byzantium have in common? *(Sample answers: Both were on the northern side of the Mediterranean. Both had been in the Roman empire since the earliest times.)* Ask: What would be the easiest way to travel between Rome and Byzantium? Explain. *(Sample answer: by ship because both had access to the Mediterranean Sea)*

ACTIVE JOURNAL

Map Skills Have students use the Map Skills activity in their Active Journals to fill in an outline map of the region with the labels of key geographic and political features.

Analyze Maps Byzantium was located at the meeting place of which two continents? *(Europe and Asia)*

INTERACTIVE | INTERACTIVE MAP

Display the Interactive Topic Map for the class. Ask the class to direct where to place the draggable labels. Then have volunteers read the text that pops up for each one. Ask: What were the capital cities of the Roman and Byzantine empires? *(Rome and Constantinople)*

Who Will You Meet?

Many students access historical materials best through the stories of the people who made them. Preview these key people that students will encounter in the topic. Read the short description of each, and then ask volunteers to say what more they would like to know about them. *(Accept reasonable responses. Students may say that they wonder how Paul spread Christianity; that they are curious about the ways Constantine transformed the Roman empire; or that they wonder how much power Theodora had.)*

TOPIC 8

HSS 7.1.1; ELA SL.6.1, SL.6.3, RI.6.6, RI.6.9; ELD.P1.A.3, ELD.P1.C.11.a

Quest

Discussion Inquiry

The Fall of Rome

Quest Kick Off

In this Quest, students will use the student text, other sources, and the Active Journal to hold a discussion about whether the fall of Rome could have been prevented.

1 Ask Questions

Launch the Quest by discussing the Guiding Question as a class. Have students generate the questions they will need to have answered to accomplish the Quest in their Journals. **Suggestion:** If students need help with the Ask Questions step, refer them to the Analysis Skills feature following Lesson 2, Detect Changing Patterns. Have them consider how to pose questions that focus on the changes in the empire that might make it less stable.

2 Investigate

As they read the lessons, remind students to look for and respond to the three Quest Connections in the student text that provide clues to their Quest. They should also identify and record two connections of their own. **Suggestion:** If students are struggling to identify their own connections, suggest that they look for words and phrases that indicate passages where political, economic, or social changes are being discussed.

3 Examine Primary Sources

As students complete the topic, distribute the Quest Sources for this topic.

Analyze Documents Have students process the sources in their Active Journals, focusing on identifying information related to the Guiding Question in preparation for holding a discussion on the fall of Rome.

4 Prepare Your Position

When students complete the topic, have them return to the Quest, which can be used as a performance-based authentic assessment. To complete their Quests, they should use their knowledge of issues during the late empire to make convincing arguments. **DOK4**

HSS 7.1.1; ELA SL.6.1, SL.6.3, RI.6.6, RI.6.9; ELD. P1.A.3, ELD.P1.C.11.a

Quest

Discussion Inquiry

The Fall of Rome

Quest KICK OFF

As the Roman empire continued, political, social, and economic conflicts built up over time within and along its borders. These conflicts eventually led to important changes in the empire.

Your quest is to study these conflicts to understand their consequences, and prepare to take a position in one-on-one discussions based on the question:

Could the fall of Rome have been prevented?

How did different events and forces affect the empire? Consider the Essential Question, What forces can cause a society to change? in this Quest.

▼ Julian, emperor of Rome for less than two years in the late 300s

1 Ask Questions

Recall what you know about the Roman empire. List questions you need to answer to understand why the empire fell. Write down these questions in your Active Journal.

2 Investigate

As you read the topic, look for **Quest CONNECTIONS** that reveal major conflicts that over time had an effect on the Roman empire.

3 Examine Primary Sources

Next, closely study the positions of historians on this question in sources provided to you online.

Quest FINDINGS

4 Prepare Your Position

After reading the sources, discuss the strongest arguments with your partner or small group. Discuss first taking one side of the question, then taking the other side. Get help for this task in your Active Journal.

DIFFERENTIATED INSTRUCTION

Below Level: Suggest students consider the discussion question by brainstorming the consequences of policy decisions Roman leaders could have made. They should try to think of different possible outcomes.
Advanced: Suggest students examine factors that made the Eastern empire different. This analysis might suggest how the western Roman empire could have avoided its fall.

INTEGRATED ENGLISH LANGUAGE DEVELOPMENT

Expanding Students can work in pairs to have a dialogue about whether or not the fall of Rome could have been prevented. Students listen to each other and ask questions to clarify the reasons for their positions.

LESSON 1

HSS 6.7.3, 6.7.4, 6.7.8, 7.1.1, 7.1.2

The Roman Empire Begins

BOUNCE TO ACTIVATE | VIDEO

GET READY TO READ

START UP

Look at the carving of elite Roman troops known as Praetorian Guards. Why might an emperor need elite guards?

GUIDING QUESTIONS

- What was the Pax Romana and how did it affect Rome?
- How did the Roman empire gain and maintain power over people and territories?
- How did Rome's achievements in architecture and technology encourage its growth?
- How did Rome's environment affect its growing economy and trade networks?

TAKE NOTES

Literacy Skills: Analyze Cause and Effect

Use the graphic organizer in your Active Journal to take notes as you read the lesson.

PRACTICE VOCABULARY

Use the vocabulary activity in your Active Journal to practice the vocabulary words.

Vocabulary		Academic Vocabulary
deify	concrete	succession
Pax Romana	aqueduct	structure

Rome began as small settlements along the Tiber River. Mediterranean Europe has mild, rainy winters and hot, dry summers. Early farmers transformed southern Europe's forests into wheat fields, olive orchards, and vineyards. Italy's geography included mountains, rivers that supplied water and offered transportation routes, and plains that provided farmland. The early settlements joined together and became a city. The city's soldiers conquered its neighbors, and in time Rome ruled all of Italy.

The Rise of the Roman Empire

Free adult male citizens of the Roman republic had the right to vote to elect their officials. Through war and diplomacy, Rome's power and wealth grew rapidly. The republic, however, did not survive the new challenges brought by its armies' successes. After the fall of the Roman republic, Rome was ruled by all-powerful individuals—emperors. They helped bring about two centuries of peace.

In 30 BCE Octavian took control of the Roman world. He became Augustus, the first and one of the greatest Roman emperors.

PRACTICE VOCABULARY

To help students integrate new vocabulary, explain that *deify* means to declare that someone is a god. The *Pax Romana*, or "Roman Peace," was a long period of peace and prosperity. The remaining two words are related to Roman technology: *concrete* is a strong building material, while an *aqueduct* is a channel that moves water over land. Reinforce the terms during the lesson using the teaching notes.

Point out the academic vocabulary in the lesson margins. Provide sample sentences that clarify meaning.

succession: The rules of inheritance determine the succession from one monarch to the next.

structure: Homes, schools, and office buildings are all structures.

HSS 6.7.3, 6.74, 6.7.8, 7.1.1, 7.1.2

The Roman Empire Begins

CONNECT

GET READY TO READ

ETEXT — START UP

Project the Start Up Activity. As students enter the classroom and get settled, ask them to examine the carving of the elite Praetorian Guards.

Infer Have students record their ideas about why an emperor might need elite guards. *(Sample answer: Like the U.S. President, a Roman emperor would need protection from assassination attempts. Therefore, he needed the best possible guards.)* Then have them share their thoughts with another student, either in class or through a chat or blog.

Discuss Remind students that the Roman republic was ruled by elected officials. In contrast, the Roman empire was ruled by powerful rulers called emperors who were not elected officials.

After completing the Start Up activity, project the Lesson Opener or direct students to their textbooks. Preview the lesson by working through the Get Ready to Read items with the class. Remind students to pay close attention to the Guiding Questions as they read the lesson.

ACTIVE JOURNAL

Take Notes Have students use the lesson literacy skills graphic organizer in their Active Journals to take notes as they read the lesson.

Practice Vocabulary Have students complete the activity in their Active Journals to build their vocabulary.

VIDEO — VIDEO

Assign the lesson video as homework.

INVESTIGATE

The Rise of the Roman Empire

Discuss how Augustus's rule launched a period of peace and prosperity.

Summarize Describe the overall results of Augustus's reign as emperor. *(Ordinary people's lives improved. There was peace and stability.)*

Analyze Information In what way was Rome's government a monarchy? *(Rome was ruled by a single emperor. When he died, power passed to another emperor.)*

INTERACTIVE **INTERACTIVE TIMELINE**

Roman Rulers Who Made History

Display the Interactive Timeline: Romans Rulers Who Made History. Click on each image. Ask: Which emperors were known for their building projects? *(Sample answers: Augustus, Trajan, Hadrian)*

ACTIVE CLASSROOM

Use the Cartoon It strategy. Have students copy a timeline image, turning it into a political cartoon about an emperor.

ANSWERS

Critical Thinking *He formed alliances, fought battles, and convinced the senate that he ruled by the republic's traditions.*

Who Was Augustus? After Augustus won the civil wars that had torn apart the Roman republic, he brought peace to the Roman world. He held nearly total power over the empire, although Rome still had a senate. Augustus made the empire more stable. He shrank the size of the army and raised soldiers' pay. By bringing peace, Augustus gave the economy a boost, improving life for ordinary people. He also fought corruption. He was considered an ideal emperor. After his death he was **deified**, or officially declared to be a god, and worshiped. Most later emperors were also deified, some while they were still alive.

INTERACTIVE
Roman Rulers Who Made History

Who Were the Other Emperors? When Augustus died, his stepson Tiberius became emperor. Rome was now clearly a monarchy. The republic was not coming back. Later, a law was passed stating that the emperor had nearly total power, though in fact this had already been the case.

Primary Source

"Whatever he considers to be in accordance with the public advantage and . . . public and private interests he shall have the right and the power to do and to execute, just as had the deified Augustus."

—Law concerning the power of Vespasian, from *Ancient Roman Statutes*

Academic Vocabulary
succession • *n.*, one person or thing following another

Rome had no formal or set way to choose a new emperor. **Succession** was a serious problem. Members of the imperial family and other powerful Romans schemed and even killed to become emperor. Sometimes the Roman army made the final decision.

BIOGRAPHY 5 Things to Know About AUGUSTUS

Roman Emperor (c. 62 BCE–14 CE)

- He founded the Roman empire and became its first, and one of its greatest, emperors.
- His great-uncle, Julius Caesar, won a civil war and was named Rome's dictator in 46 BCE. Without a son and needing an heir, Caesar adopted Octavian.
- Augustus was named Octavius at birth. When Julius Caesar adopted him, his name changed to Octavian. In 26 BCE, the Roman Senate renamed him Augustus.
- After Caesar was murdered in 44 BCE, Augustus formed alliances and fought bloody battles to win control of the empire.
- He persuaded the senate that he ruled according to the traditions of the republic. In fact, he held all power. His long reign as emperor was prosperous and peaceful.

Critical Thinking What methods did Augustus use to gain total power over Rome?

INTEGRATED ENGLISH LANGUAGE DEVELOPMENT

Productive Use the subsection Aqueducts Transport Water later in this lesson. Explain that affixes are word parts attached to root (base) words that can be used to change their meanings. A prefix is attached to the front of the root word. A suffix is attached to the end of the root word.

Emerging Read the subsection aloud to students. Point out the term *aqueduct*. Tell students that *aqua* means water in Latin. Ask them to guess the meaning of *duct*.

Expanding Read the subsection aloud to students. Point out the term *aqueduct*. Ask them to identify the prefix. Tell students that *aqua* means water in Latin. Ask them to guess the meaning of *duct*. Write the word *aquarium* on the board. Ask students to tell how the prefix *aqua* works.

Roman Empire in 118 CE

Some of the emperors after Augustus were successful. Trajan conquered new territory for Rome. Hadrian travelled around the empire. He also built walls that separated Roman provinces from non-Roman lands. Marcus Aurelius wrote a famous book of philosophy. Many emperors built aqueducts, public baths, temples, stadiums, and other large buildings in Rome and across the empire.

Other emperors were considered failures. Some are still known for their cruelty. For example, Nero was accused of killing Roman citizens without cause, even his close relatives. He was also the first emperor to persecute Christians.

What Was the Pax Romana? Still, Augustus's rule began a long period of peace and prosperity known as the **Pax Romana**, or the "Roman Peace." It lasted from 30 BCE to around 180 CE. During that time as many as 65 million people were able to go about their lives in relative peace. No major wars threatened most of the people of the empire.

The Empire at Its Height During the Pax Romana, at its farthest expansion, the Roman empire reached from Britain in the north to Egypt in the south and from the Atlantic in the west to present-day Iraq in the east. The Romans were the first (and only) empire to unite all the territories that border the Mediterranean. However, dense forests to the north, deserts to the south and southwest, and the Atlantic Ocean to the west blocked further Roman conquests.

That left only Rome's eastern border available for the empire's further growth. In the east, however, the Romans faced continuing conflict,

GEOGRAPHY SKILLS

The Roman empire eventually controlled territories that extended from the Mediterranean into Europe, Africa, and Asia.

1. **Region** Which was added to the empire first, Britain or Spain?
2. **Use Visual Information** Name two rivers that formed borders of the Roman empire.

Quick Activity

Trace how the Roman Empire expanded in your Active Journal.

Infer What problems resulted from Rome's methods for succession? *(Without a clear method for succession, Rome suffered from political scheming and decisions imposed by the military. Some of the emperors were failures.)*

Contrast How was the **Pax Romana** different from other periods in Rome's history? *(It was a long period of peace and prosperity, where other times had political infighting and tumult.)*

Predict What problems might the inability to continue expanding cause for the Roman empire? *(No new income or products from newly conquered lands might cause economic problems.)*

ACTIVE JOURNAL

Quick Activity Divide students into pairs and have them conduct the Quick Activity map analysis in their Active Journals. Make sure students understand how the Roman empire expanded.

ELD TIP English learners have trouble remembering Latin vocabulary in addition to English, especially if their language of origin is not Latin-based. Make sure ELL students understand the meaning of Latin terms in a text, such as Pax Romana. Ask if they can think of any other Latin terms.

ELD. P1.C.12.b

Bridging Read the subsection aloud to students. Point out the term *aqueduct*. Ask them to identify the prefix. Tell students that *aqua* means water in Latin. Ask them to guess the meaning of *duct*. Write the word *aquarium* on the board. Ask students to tell how the prefix *aqua* works. Ask students to find other words with the prefix *aqua*.

WORKSHEET **TEACHER RESOURCES**

For additional IELD support addressing these standards, have students complete the Lesson ELD activity from the Teacher Resources found on the course.

ANSWERS

Region *Spain*

Use Visual Information *Sample answers: Euphrates, Danube, Rhine*

What Were Rome's Practical Achievements?

Discuss how Romans built lasting roads and structures using concrete, arches, and domes.

Draw Conclusions Why do you think most roads in Italy led to Rome? *(Sample answer: It was the capital of the empire.)*

Distinguish Cause and Effect What were the intended and unintended effects of building the Roman roads? *(Sample answer: The intended effect was to help the army move quickly. The unintended effect was that it helped communication, government, and trade.)*

Connect What do we use **concrete** for today? *(Sample answers: driveways, sidewalks, curbs, walls, foundations)*

Analyze Images About 73 miles long, Hadrian's Wall was designed to protect Roman Britain from attacks. **Use Visual Information** How effective do you think this wall would have been in the 100s CE?

although not a major war, with the Persian empire, first under the Parthians and later under the Sasanians. Near the end of the Roman republic period, the Parthians defeated the Roman army at Carrhae. The emperors Trajan and Severus had minor battles with them during and after the Pax Romana. The Romans could not secure their empire's eastern border against the Persian threat.

READING CHECK **Identify Main Ideas** What was the Pax Romana and why was it important?

What Were Rome's Practical Achievements?

The Romans were a practical people. They excelled at using technology to improve daily life.

Roman Roads Link the Empire "All roads lead to Rome" is an old saying. In ancient Italy, it was true. Major roads extended out from the city like the spokes of a wheel. More than 50,000 miles (80,467 km) of paved roads crisscrossed the Roman empire, linking cities and forts. Roman roads were built to last. Some are still used today.

Roman roads were built mainly so that soldiers could march quickly from place to place. Military engineers traveled with the army. So did architects, stonemasons, and surveyors. Roman soldiers often worked on the roads when not fighting.

Roman roads were superbly engineered. Main roads were hard-paved and well drained. Smooth, all-weather roads were a considerable improvement over dirt paths. They sped up communication throughout the empire. This made government and trade more efficient. Good roads from ports to large inland cities also helped supply food.

Roman Architecture Roman architects devised new building methods and materials, such as concrete. **Concrete** is a building

ANSWERS

Use Visual Information *Sample answer: It might not have been very effective because it was too long to defend.*

Identify Main Ideas *The Pax Romana was a period of peace and prosperity for the Roman empire. Millions of people lived without major wars for about two hundred years.*

DIFFERENTIATED INSTRUCTION

Special Education Allow students to make flash cards with drawings of Roman achievements, such as concrete, roads, domes, arches, and aqueducts. If necessary, bring in photographs for them to use for reference.

Below Level Have students work in pairs to make a T-chart of Roman achievement. In the left-hand column, they should list the achievement. In the right-hand column, they should explain why it was important or how it improved the previous way of doing things.

Advanced Have students create a poster showing modern examples of how Roman innovations, such as concrete, rounded arches, and domes, are still used today. Each image should have an explanatory caption. Ask them to display their posters in class.

material made by mixing cement (a gray powder made from different materials) with small stones, sand, and water. The thick, soupy mixture is then poured into molds, where it hardens. Many Roman concrete harbors have survived for more than 2,000 years.

Concrete was lighter and easier to work with than stone. Workers needed less skill to pour concrete than to carve stone. Using this new material, workers built large **structures** covered with domes. The largest dome covered the Pantheon.

Academic Vocabulary
structure • *n.*, building

In addition to domes, Roman engineers and soldiers also built large, sturdy bridges, supported by rounded, semi-circular arches. Such arches allowed for longer bridge spans. In fact, a rounded arch is the most typical feature of Roman architecture.

Aqueducts Transport Water A good water supply is as important to city life as are bridges and roads. Roman engineers designed water systems to supply towns with clean water. They built hundreds of miles of aqueducts. An **aqueduct** is a channel that moves water over land.

Roman aqueducts were usually made of stone or concrete channels. They flowed mostly underground. When aqueducts needed to cross valleys, the Romans built long arched bridges to pipe the water along. Some of these bridges still stand today.

In the city, water flowed into public fountains. Some wealthy people had water piped directly into their homes. Aqueducts also supplied public baths. The baths were an important part of the Roman lifestyle. Many Romans went to the baths every day to bathe, exercise, see friends, and even conduct business.

Analyze Charts Human activity increased methane levels, which raised temperatures slightly during the Roman empire. **Draw Conclusions** What connections might this chart have to today's environment?

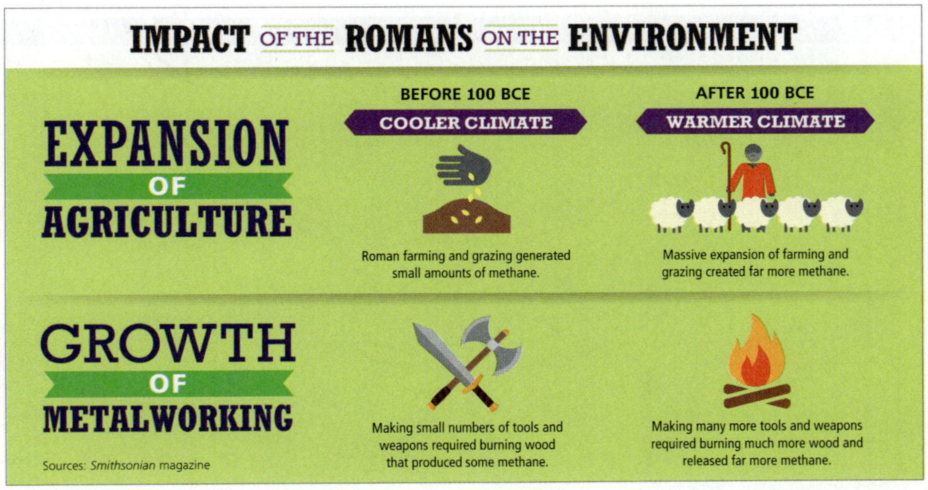

Identify Cause and Effect What made the building of large domed structures possible? Explain. *(The invention of concrete, which is lighter than stone, made it possible to build large domes that did not collapse on themselves.)*

Draw Conclusions Why is a water supply as important to city life as bridges and roads? *(Sample answers: People must drink water or die. Water is also used for cleaning and sanitation. Water is needed to put out fires.)*

Infer What can you infer about the Romans from the fact that some of their roads and aqueducts are still in use today? *(Sample answer: They were very skillful engineers, architects, and builders.)*

CURRICULUM CONNECTION: ENVIRONMENTAL EDUCATION

Nature's Bounty The California EEI Curriculum Unit, "Managing Nature's Bounty," provides a map of the physical features and natural regions of Europe, and Lesson 4 explores the products of different European regions. Students analyze what effect geographic location had on the Roman empire and on the Germanic peoples who lived in the northern forests beyond the Danube and Rhine rivers. Students map the extent of the empire and label the most important provinces (Egypt, Spain, Gaul, Greece, Syria) and bodies of water. They also examine Roman buildings and roads to see the application of the two most important Roman technological innovations: the arch and cement.

ANSWERS

Draw Conclusions *This process is related to the increase in greenhouse gases that is one factor causing climate change today.*

Trade and the Roman Economy

Discuss how farming was the basis of the Roman economy, but Rome also depended on trade across the empire.

Categorize By what methods did goods travel in the Roman empire? *(Goods traveled over roads and by sea.)*

Synthesize How did Roman practical achievements affect trade in the empire? *(Traders could easily and safely move goods on Roman roads and ships, so trade expanded.)*

Identify Cause and Effect How did farming help Roman provinces develop? *(Provincial farmers grew wealthy from sales to Rome, then spent money to build temples, theaters, and so on in the provinces.)*

Draw Conclusions Why is stable currency important? *(Stable currency gives people trading at great distance confidence about the price they are paying and the value of what they are buying.)*

Aqueducts were only part of the water system. Sewers carried waste away from the cities. Roman water and sewer systems were not equaled until modern times.

READING CHECK **Draw Conclusions** What were some of Rome's greatest engineering achievements?

Trade and the Roman Economy

Roman roads were usually built for military purposes, but goods also moved across the empire by road. Merchants also traveled by sea. Trade increased across the empire. Cities became centers of industry and commerce. The Roman empire was based on a network of such cities that depended on trade with the empire's other regions. This network of cities was unusual in the ancient world.

GEOGRAPHY SKILLS

By 117 CE, the Roman trade network extended throughout most of Europe and into parts of Asia and North Africa.

1. **Location** How far to the east did the Roman trade routes extend by sea? How far to the west?
2. **Draw Conclusions** What advantages did such wide-ranging trade routes bring to Rome?

Trade Grows Before the Romans built a navy, piracy was a problem. It made shipping dangerous and expensive. But the Romans cleared the sea of most pirates. This made trade by sea safer, faster, and cheaper than travel by land. Ships carried grain, wine, olive oil, and pottery across the empire.

At the empire's height, imported grain and olive oil fed Rome's population of between one and two million people. A web of land and sea trade routes served the city. Romans had access to the varied resources and products of Europe, Greece, Anatolia, Syria, Egypt, and North Africa. Roman roads linked the empire's regions.

Merchants brought goods from other civilizations along trade routes across Afroeurasia on land, like the Silk Road between Central Asia and China, and over the

Roman Trade Routes

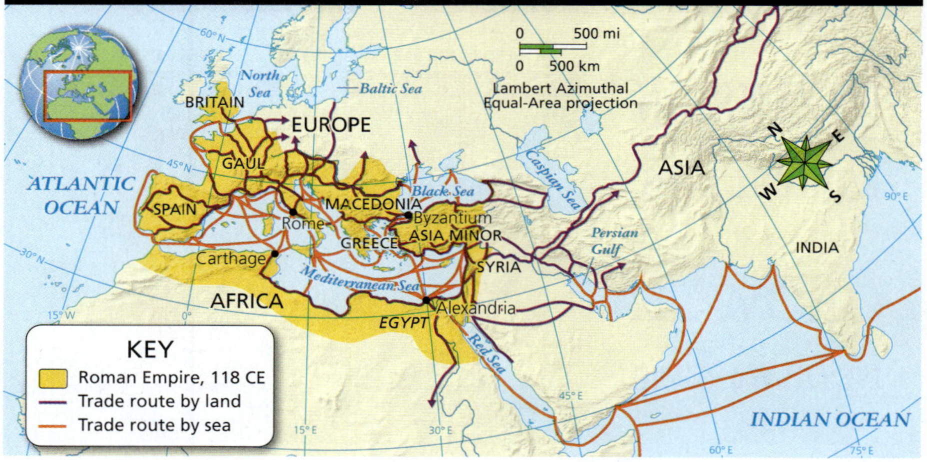

320 Lesson 8.1 • The Roman Empire Begins

ANSWERS

Draw Conclusions *Sample answer: Developing concrete, using the arch in architecture, and building aqueducts were three great Roman engineering achievements.*

Location *to the eastern Mediterranean coast near Syria and to the northern and southeastern Black Sea coast; to Africa at Gibraltar and the Atlantic coasts of Spain, Gaul, and southern Britain*

Draw Conclusions *Romans could import needed grain, wine, olive oil, and a great variety of goods they did not have at home.*

HISTORY BACKGROUND

Hadrian and Antinoüs Born in 76 CE, Hadrian came to power in 117 when the Roman empire was at its height. During his 21-year reign, Hadrian traveled around his empire extensively. He spent less than half his time as ruler in Rome itself. During one of these travels, he began construction on the wall that bears his name in the province of Britain. On another journey, this time in northwestern Anatolia, he met a young man named Antinoüs, and the two formed a deeply emotional romantic relationship. When Antinoüs drowned in 130, Hadrian's grief was so great that he deified Antinoüs and founded the city of Antinoöpolis in Egypt to honor his memory.

Mediterranean Sea and the Indian Ocean. These goods included medicine and jewels from India, silk from China, and frankincense and animals from Africa. Small groups of wealthy people purchased these imported luxury items. As travelers journeyed between cultures, they also brought along various ideas and technologies.

Agriculture and Crafts Farming was the base of the Roman economy. Grains like wheat were key. Grain was shipped to Rome to feed its massive population. Imported grain also fed Rome's armies. By the time of the Pax Romana, food for Roman cities depended on the work of enslaved or poor laborers on vast agricultural estates.

In return, money flowed from Rome to the provinces. The owners of provincial farms grew rich. Many used their new wealth to develop their provinces. They built temples, theaters, and baths. Some wealthy provincial people joined the Roman elite. They became senators and even emperors.

Craft industries were also part of the economy. Skilled workers produced cloth, glass, pottery, metalwork, and ships. The construction industry supplied building projects with marble, terracotta tiles, and lead plumbing pipes.

Currency Aids Trade Economic growth in the empire was helped by a stable currency. A stable currency is a system of money that does not change much in value over time. It is more quickly and widely accepted in trade and commerce. Rome's stable currency made it easier to conduct long-distance trade than in the past.

Analyze Images Roman glassware in the 200s and 300s CE included bottles and amphoras, two-handled storage jars. **Infer** What do you think the Romans stored in vessels like these?

READING CHECK **Identify Cause and Effect** Why was it important for Rome's government to import grain to feed its population and armies?

Lesson Check

HSS 6.7.3, 6.7.4, 6.7.8, 7.1.1, 7.1.2; ELD.P1.C.10.a

Practice Vocabulary

1. How were **aqueducts** used?
2. What is **concrete** made from?

Critical Thinking and Writing

3. **Infer** How did the Pax Romana spur economic growth?
4. **Summarize** How did roads, aqueducts, and concrete affect city life?
5. **Summarize** What was the role of farming in the Roman economy?
6. **Writing Workshop: Gather Details** In this topic, you will write an argument on the question: Which was greater, the Greek city-states or the Roman empire? Consider the following factors: size, longevity, economic power, cultural achievements, and influence. Begin to record details about Greece and Rome in your Active Journal.

LESSON CHECK

1. Aqueducts brought fresh water to Roman cities. **DOK1**
2. Concrete is a mix of stones, sand, limestone, clay, and water. **DOK1**
3. Peace during the Pax Romana allowed Rome and its people to focus on the economy instead of on political or military conflict. **DOK2**
4. Roads enabled people and goods to move efficiently. Aqueducts brought fresh water to the cities. Concrete enabled Romans to build great temples, baths, and public buildings. **DOK2**
5. Farming was the foundation of the Roman economy. **DOK2**
6. Student answers will vary. They should include specific, verifiable details about Greece's size, longevity, economic power, cultural achievements, and influence. **DOK4**

HSS 6.7.3, 6.7.4, 6.7.8, 7.1.1, 7.1.2; ELD.P1.C.10.a

SYNTHESIZE

Assess and Reteach Have students work with a partner to complete Lesson Check questions 1–5. Review their responses. If they had any incorrect answers, use the Guiding Questions to discuss the lesson's main ideas, focusing on the ideas they struggled with.

ACTIVE JOURNAL

Writing Workshop Have students complete the Lesson 1 Writing Task in their Active Journals. Students will gather details about Greece's size, longevity, economic power, cultural achievements, and influence. As they move through the topic, students will revisit these details, adding to them as needed.

DEMONSTRATE

ASSESSMENT **ONLINE LESSON QUIZ**

Assign the Online Lesson Quiz for this lesson if you haven't already done so. Students will be offered automatic remediation or enrichment based on their score.

DISCUSSION **DISCUSSION BOARD**

Post this question to the class on the Discussion Board:

Summarize How did Roman achievements in architecture and technology encourage its growth? *(The Romans were able to build good roads, which unified the empire and encouraged trade and communication. Their building achievements allowed them to build aqueducts to transport water, a necessity of life. They also used concrete to build large buildings, which were used for government and other public purposes.)*

ANSWERS

Infer *Sample answers: wine or oil*

Identify Cause and Effect *Without food, the huge population of the city and the many soldiers could become angry and rebellious against the government.*

HSS 6.7.4; ELA RI.6.6

Primary Sources

Augustus, *The Deeds of the Divine Augustus*

Read aloud the explanatory note about the source. Direct students' attention to the image of the coin with the bust of Augustus on it. Ask: In what way is this like and unlike our money? *(Sample answer: Our coins have past presidents on them, but they do not feature current leaders.)*

GUIDED READING

Read aloud the excerpt without stopping. Then reread the passage, pausing after each section to let students answer the numbered questions. Use the questions in the text to prompt students' analysis of the primary source.

Reading and Vocabulary Support Answers

1. *Sample answer: Yes, people often feel forced by peer pressure or by officials to do things that they don't believe in.*

3. *Sample answer: In this case, Augustus is deciding that his own actions were just.*

GUIDED ANALYSIS

After completing the reading, discuss what this primary source reveals about Augustus.

Draw Conclusions Why do you think Augustus wanted people to know that he paid for the army he raised? *(Sample answers: It showed his generosity to the state and the people. He wanted Romans to feel they owed him.)*

Analyze Information According to Augustus, what did he do for all the territories he brought under Roman control? What detail in the text supports your answer? *(Sample answer: He brought peace to every region. He uses the phrase* restored peace *or* brought peace *three times.)*

To assess understanding, have students respond to the Analyzing Primary Source questions in writing.

ACTIVE JOURNAL

Quest Connection After answering the questions, have students respond to the Quest Connection question in their Active Journals.

Primary Sources

HSS 6.7.4; ELA RI.6.6

Augustus, *The Deeds of the Divine Augustus*

Augustus, also known as Octavian, ruled the Roman empire for 40 years. Under Augustus's leadership, the size of the Roman empire doubled. *The Deeds of the Divine Augustus* is a document that Augustus wrote about his accomplishments.

◀ Roman coin showing the head of Augustus

1. In my nineteenth year, on my own initiative and at my own expense, I raised an army with which I set free the state...

25. I restored peace to the sea from pirates.... All Italy swore allegiance to me voluntarily ①, and demanded me as leader of the war which I won at Actium; the provinces of Gaul, Spain, Africa, Sicily, and Sardinia swore the same allegiance. And those who then fought under my standard ② were more than 700 senators, among whom 83 were made consuls either before or after, up to the day this was written, and about 170 were made priests.

26. I extended the borders of all the provinces of the Roman people which neighbored nations not subject to our rule. I restored peace to the provinces of Gaul and Spain, likewise Germany, which includes the ocean from Cadiz to the mouth of the river Elbe. I brought peace to the Alps from the region which is near the Adriatic Sea to the Tuscan, with no unjust war ③ waged against any nation. I sailed my ships on the ocean from the mouth of the Rhine to the east region up to the borders of the Cimbri, where no Roman had gone before that time by land or sea, and the Cimbri and the Charydes and the Semnones ④ and the other Germans of the same territory sought by envoys ⑤ the friendship of me and of the Roman people. [3]

—Caesar Augustus, *The Deeds of the Divine Augustus*

Reading and Vocabulary Support

① Do you think it is possible to swear allegiance to someone involuntarily?

② A standard in this sense is a flag carried by a military unit.

③ Augustus says he waged no unjust war. Who determined whether his wars were just or unjust?

④ The Cimbri, Charydes, and the Semnones were Germanic groups living in Europe at the time of Augustus.

⑤ An envoy is a person who represents one government in dealings with another.

Quest CONNECTIONS

What evidence can you find in the reading that Augustus was concerned about maintaining the strength of the empire? Record your findings in your Active Journal.

Analyzing Primary Sources

Cite specific evidence from the document to support your answers.

1. **Draw Conclusions** What does Augustus mean when he says "All Italy swore allegiance to me voluntarily, and demanded me as leader"?
2. **Support Ideas with Examples** Review the passage and identify an example of propaganda.
3. **Analyze Information** What does Augustus suggest are key accomplishments necessary for an emperor to be successful?

322 Primary Sources • Augustus, *The Deeds of the Divine Augustus*

ANALYZING PRIMARY SOURCES

1. Sample answer: He uses that phrase to demonstrate that he was not a dictator who imposed his rule on the people. **DOK3**

2. Sample answer: His claim that he went where no Roman had gone before is propaganda meant to demonstrate his greatness. **DOK3**

3. Sample answers: raising an army, freeing the state from oppression, restoring peace, extending the borders, establishing friendship with other peoples. **DOK3**

Analysis Skill

Analysis HI.1

Identify Central Issues and Problems

INTERACTIVE
Solve Problems

Follow these steps to learn ways to identify central issues and problems.

1 Identify the subject of the passage. Read the passage to find out what it is about.

a. What is the subject of the passage?

b. Which sentence or sentences identify the subject?

2 Identify the people, time, and place discussed in the passage. Look for clues telling you what people and time period are being discussed.

a. Who is being discussed in the passage? What is the time period?

b. Where are the events in the passage taking place?

3 Determine the central issue or problem. Read the details of the passage.

a. What problem or issue is the main focus of the passage?

b. What facts or details support your answer?

4 Explain why this issue was important. Look for information that suggests why this issue was important at that time.

a. Why was this issue important at that time and place?

b. Have people at other times and places faced similar issues? Explain.

Secondary Source

After the end of the Pax Romana, the Roman empire began to struggle with many problems. One of the biggest problems was the transition from one emperor to another, which was rarely smooth. Civil war broke out multiple times. War and instability hurt the economy and allowed foreigners to threaten Rome's borders.

How could emperors make the empire more stable? In 284 CE, a solider named Diocletian became emperor of Rome. Diocletian faced serious challenges. After years of civil war, the army was divided. The machinery of government barely worked. Prices were rising. Taxes were no longer being paid. The frontiers were not well guarded. The emperor believed harsh measures were necessary to meet these challenges. He knew that reforms he had in mind would not be popular. But he believed only strong action on his part would be the empire back under control.

Analysis HI.1

Analysis Skills
Identify Central Issues and Problems

LEARN

Preview the steps in the student text with students, and then play the video.

VIDEO **21ST CENTURY SKILLS**

Project the Solve Problems video in the 21st Century Skills Tutorial. Use the Quick Reference and Assessment to provide additional instruction on this skills.

PRACTICE

Have students practice the skill using the secondary source on the student page, providing the instruction and then asking students the questions.

As an alternative, you could form students into pairs or groups to perform the activity. Then invite the groups to share their conclusions with the class. Discuss students' different ideas.

ASSESS

To assess this skill, have students read the excerpt from Livy's *History of Rome* in the Primary Sources feature after Lesson 1 in the topic The Roman Republic. Ask them to summarize the main issue described in the passage.

DIFFERENTIATED INSTRUCTION

Special Education Point out that the phrase *machinery of government* does not literally mean a machine. Rather, it refers to the organization of the government and the way all the parts work together. Ask students what would happen if the different parts of a machine stopped running at the same pace as the others. *(Sample answer: The machine would break or get jammed.)* Similarly, the Roman government no longer ran smoothly.

INTEGRATED ENGLISH LANGUAGE DEVELOPMENT

Emerging Support emerging students by asking yes or no questions, such as, *Were there conflicts within the empire? Was the empire in danger from foreigners? Did the government work well? Did Diocletian have a plan to improve things?*

ANSWERS

1. a. Diocletian's efforts to fix instability
b. first sentence of each paragraph

2. a. emperor Diocletian; 284 CE
b. the Roman empire

3. a. instability in the empire
b. the details in the first paragraph.

4. a. Sample answer: The empire was hurting from civil wars and economic problems.
b. Sample answer: Yes, many peoples have faced economic problems, wars, and weak government.

HSS 6.7.5, 6.7.6, 6.7.7, 7.1.1

Origins of Christianity

CONNECT

GET READY TO READ

ETEXT

START UP

Project the Start Up Activity. As students enter the classroom and get settled, ask them to examine the painting of Jesus and his disciples eating their last meal together. Point out the faint outlines of haloes over their heads.

Make Predictions Remind students that the Romans deified many of their emperors. Have students write down a prediction about how the Romans will react to the new religion of Christianity. *(Sample answer: They will be angry at a religion that doesn't honor the Roman gods and emperors.)* Then have them share their prediction with another student, either in class or through a chat or blog.

Discuss Remind students of the Jews' belief that God gave them their land as part of his covenant with Abraham. Explain that many Jews resented Roman rule.

After completing the Start Up activity, project the Lesson Opener or direct students to their textbooks. Preview the lesson by working through the Get Ready to Read items with the class. Remind students to pay close attention to the Guiding Questions as they read the lesson.

ACTIVE JOURNAL

Take Notes Have students use the lesson literacy skills graphic organizer in their Active Journals to take notes as they read the lesson.

Practice Vocabulary Have students complete the activity in their Active Journals to build their vocabulary.

VIDEO

VIDEO

Assign the lesson video as homework.

LESSON 2

HSS 6.7.5, 6.7.6, 6.7.7, 7.1.1

Origins of Christianity

GET READY TO READ

START UP

Look at the painting of Jesus and his disciples at their last meal together. Write a prediction on how the Roman authorities will respond to the new religion of Christianity.

GUIDING QUESTIONS

- What was the relationship between Rome and Judea like?
- Who was Jesus and what did he teach?
- How did the religion of Christianity develop and change?
- How did Christianity spread?

TAKE NOTES

Literacy Skills: Sequence

Use the graphic organizer in your Active Journal to take notes as you read the lesson.

PRACTICE VOCABULARY

Use the vocabulary activity in your Active Journal to practice the vocabulary words.

Vocabulary		Academic Vocabulary
resurrection	conversion	isolated
baptism	martyr	authorities
crucifixion		

Despite Rome's power and influence, many people in the empire opposed Roman rule. A Jewish spiritual leader named Jesus arose during the Pax Romana. He was executed by the Romans. A new religion soon emerged based on his teachings and the writings of his early followers.

What Was Judea Like Under Roman Rule?

Although centered in the Jewish kingdom of Judea, Jewish people had migrated throughout the Greek and Roman world since the third century BCE. By the late first century BCE, large Jewish communities existed in Egypt, Syria, Anatolia, Greece, Italy (including Rome), and southern France.

In 63 BCE, the Romans took control of Judea, including the city of Jerusalem. A large number of Jews opposed Roman rule.

Zealots Many Jews saw the Romans as foreigners who occupied their land and treated them cruelly. They hoped that God would send a Messiah, or specially chosen

PRACTICE VOCABULARY

To help students integrate new vocabulary, explain that all these terms are related to religion. *Crucifixion* was a method of execution by nailing or tying a person to a cross. *Resurrection* is coming back to life after death. A *martyr* is someone who is killed for his or her beliefs. *Conversion* is a heartfelt change in one's beliefs. *Baptism* is a ritual cleansing by plunging into water.

Reinforce the terms during the lesson using the teaching notes.

Point out the academic vocabulary in the lesson margins. Provide sample sentences that clarify meaning.

isolated: The goalie is often isolated from other players in a hockey game.

authorities: The principal and teachers are authorities in your school.

king, who would save the Jews from oppression. The Messiah would drive the Romans from their homeland. One group of Jews called the Zealots resisted the Romans by force. They refused to pay taxes and killed Roman officials.

Jewish Groups in Judea Different religious groups existed among Jews during this time. The Pharisees (FARuh seez) were educated people who observed Jewish law. They believed that good people could be resurrected after the Messiah came. **Resurrection** means coming back to life. The Sadducees, another large group, came from the elite and supported the traditions of the Temple in Jerusalem. They generally cooperated with Roman rule.

Other, smaller, groups of Jews withdrew from society and lived in **isolated** communities in the desert. Many of these groups practiced ritual cleansing by plunging into water. Christianity later adopted this ritual as **baptism**.

Academic Vocabulary
isolated • *adj.*, set away from other people or places

READING CHECK **Identify Supporting Details** Who were the Sadducees? Did they support the Zealots?

Jesus' Life and Teachings

During this time, a Jewish man named Jesus of Nazareth lived and taught. He gained a large following.

Early Life of Jesus Most of what we know about Jesus comes from early Christian writings known as the Gospels. According to the Gospels, Jesus was a descendant of the great Jewish king, David, and his birth was miraculous. According to tradition, Jesus was a carpenter, like his father.

Jesus the Teacher The Gospels tell us that as an adult, Jesus was baptized by a prophet named John in the Jordan River. Afterward, he began teaching from the Hebrew scriptures. For three years, Jesus traveled throughout Judea, telling people that God would soon come to establish his kingdom.

Jesus became known as a champion of the poor and the outcasts of society. Word spread that he could heal sick people. His closest followers began to wonder whether Jesus was the Messiah.

Jesus preached about how to live a good life. In one famous passage in the Gospels, Jesus lists what he considered the two most important commandments from the Hebrew Bible.

▲ This painting shows Jesus as an infant.

WORKSHEET **TEACHER RESOURCES**

Have students who need additional support use the following worksheets from the Teacher Resources on the course:

- **Reading Support**
- **English Language Development**
- **Lesson Summary**

INVESTIGATE

What Was Judea Like Under Roman Rule?

Discuss that many Jews opposed Roman rule, and that Jews were divided into several different groups.

Summarize What were the Zealots' views about Roman rule? *(They opposed it and believed Jews should resist it by refusing to pay taxes and through armed rebellion.)*

Contrast How were the Pharisees and Sadducees different? *(Sample answer: The Pharisees believed in observing Jewish law in the hope of resurrection. Sadducees supported Temple traditions and cooperated with Romans.)*

Jesus' Life and Teachings

Discuss how a Jewish teacher named Jesus attracted a large following, but was executed by the Romans.

Support a Point of View with Evidence Why did Jesus' followers begin to think he was the Messiah? *(He taught that God would soon establish his kingdom. He spoke out for the poor and outcast. They believed he could heal the sick.)*

DIFFERENTIATED INSTRUCTION

Special Education Ask students to think of reasons someone might be highly honored after his or her death. Point out that Jesus was a Jew who originally taught his followers how to improve Judaism. Christianity did not become a separate religion until after Jesus' death. As time passed, the two religions became increasingly different.

Below Level Ask students to create a Venn diagram that compares what the Zealots expected a Messiah to do with the things Jesus did. Have them write a conclusion about whether the Zealots were likely to be among the people who considered Jesus the Messiah.

Advanced Have students research when scholars believe that Jesus lived and when the four Gospels (Matthew, Mark, Luke, and John) were written. Have them create a timeline to share their findings with the class.

ANSWERS

Identify Supporting Details *The Sadducees were an elite group who supported Temple traditions and generally cooperated with Roman rule. They would not have supported the Zealots, who resisted the Romans by force.*

Paraphrase Have students read the Primary Source. Ask: How would you restate this in your own words? *(Sample answer: Love God more than anyone else. Love your neighbor as much as you love yourself.)*

Summarize Why was Jesus executed? *(Sample answer: Local leaders feared that his followers might cause trouble during Passover. If a riot broke out, the Romans might punish the whole city. The Roman government had Jesus arrested, beaten, and executed.)*

Analyze Images Pontius Pilate presided over the trial of Jesus and ordered his crucifixion. **Infer** Why might the Roman authorities have considered Jesus a threat?

Jesus told his followers:

Primary Source

"'You shall love the Lord your God with all your heart, and with all your soul, and with all your mind.' This is the greatest and first commandment. And a second is like it: 'You shall love your neighbor as yourself.'"

—Matthew 22:37–39

Academic Vocabulary
authorities • *n.*, people who have the right to give orders

Opposition, Arrest, and Death The Gospels say that Jesus went to Jerusalem around 33 CE to celebrate the Jewish holiday of Passover. Roman **authorities** in Jerusalem worried about the large holiday crowds. Local leaders also feared trouble. A riot might provoke the Romans into destroying the city.

In response to these concerns, the Roman governor Pontius Pilate acted. He had Jesus arrested, beaten, and executed by being crucified. **Crucifixion** was a slow and painful Roman method of execution. The victim was nailed or tied to a large wooden cross and left to hang until dead.

The Resurrection After Jesus died, his body was taken down from the cross and laid in a tomb. The Romans sealed the tomb and posted guards around it. According to the Gospels, some of Jesus' followers visited the tomb three days later. They found the guards gone and the tomb empty. They ran to tell the other disciples. Many claimed to have seen him after his death. They believed that God had resurrected Jesus and that he was indeed the Messiah. The Greek word for *Messiah* is "Christ."

READING CHECK **Identify Main Ideas** Which groups did Jesus champion in his teachings?

INTEGRATED ENGLISH LANGUAGE DEVELOPMENT

Structuring Cohesive Texts Explain that authors can express ideas in writing with the help of different types of structure or organization of text. A narrative or account of events is organized into stages, with descriptions of things happening in order. An argument text is organized around the ideas the writer uses to support that argument.

Emerging Read the section Jesus' Life and Teachings to the students. Ask them if this text is organized into predictable stages or constructed to defend an argument or point of view. Ask students to say what occurs, as described by the events in the text.

Expanding Read the section Jesus' Life and Teachings to the students. Ask them if this text is organized into predictable stages or constructed to defend an argument or point of view. Ask students what stage in Jesus' life

ANSWERS

Infer *Some people thought Jesus was the Messiah, which was believed to be a king who would drive the Romans from Judea. That was a threat to Roman rule.*

Identify Main Ideas *Jesus championed the poor and outcasts.*

How Did Christianity Spread?

Jesus and his early followers were Jews. But those who believed Jesus was the Messiah eventually formed a new religion known as Christianity. During his life, Jesus chose twelve trusted followers, called disciples or apostles. After his death, they spread his teachings.

The Early Church When Jesus died, Peter, a key apostle, became a leader of the new church. The word *church* can refer to the community of all Christians, a specific group of Christians, or a building Christians worship in. Peter and other apostles such as James and, a few years later, Paul spread belief in Jesus as the Messiah. They carried their faith to many parts of the world. They visited Europe, Asia, and North Africa.

Christians and Jews The first followers of the new faith considered themselves Jews. They respected Jewish laws and traditions, read the Hebrew Bible, and prayed in Jewish synagogues.

But differences grew between Jewish followers of Christianity and other Jews. Christians began sharing their beliefs with non-Jews outside of Judea. The apostle Peter even traveled to Rome itself. People from different backgrounds heard the apostles' message. More and more gentiles, or non-Jews, became Christians.

In 66 CE, the Zealots you have already read about led a huge rebellion against Rome. With difficulty, the Romans defeated them and destroyed the Temple in Jerusalem. After a later rebellion, Jews were forbidden to live in Jerusalem. Many left Judea as migrants or were taken away as slaves. They settled around the empire.

Travels of the Apostle Paul A man named Paul helped spread Christianity around the Roman empire. Early in

GEOGRAPHY SKILLS

Christianity spread throughout most of the Roman empire.

1. **Interaction** Did Christianity spread first in Asia Minor or Britain? Why do you think this might be so?
2. **Region** What Christian areas were outside of the Roman empire in 476?

Spread of Christianity to 476 CE

How Did Christianity Spread?

Discuss how Christianity spread as Jesus' followers began to tell others, including those in new lands, of their beliefs.

Use Context Clues Direct students to reread the paragraph under the head The Early Church. Ask: Which of the three meanings of the word *church* is used in the sentence, "Peter . . . became a leader of the new church." Explain. *(Sample answer: This use of the term* church *refers to the community of all Christians here because the sentence is talking about the entire group of believers.)*

Draw Conclusions Why did the new faith of Christianity become increasingly different from Judaism? *(Sample answers: It had a different view of Jesus than most Jews held. More and more non-Jews became Christians.)*

Identify Cause and Effect How did Roman rule contribute to the spread of Judaism? *(Under Roman rule, many Jews left Judea, both by choice and under Roman force or pressure. This spread Judaism outside Judea.)*

Identify Cause and Effect How did Paul change after his **conversion**? *(He changed from opposing Christians to believing in Jesus and spreading the new faith.)*

ELD TIP Maps can help English learners absorb concepts they read in a text. Have English learners look at the map titled Spread of Christianity to 476 CE. Ask students to study the key, and think about how Paul helped to spread Christianity in such a large part of the Mediterranean world. How do they think he was helped to do this by the people he met?

ELD PII.A.1

first made people around him think he might be the Messiah they had been looking for.

Bridging Ask pairs of students to read Jesus' Life and Teachings aloud. Ask them if this text is organized into predictable stages or constructed to defend an argument or point of view. Ask students what sequence of events in the story made some people believe that Jesus had been resurrected, and in what part of the story (beginning, middle, or end) this happened.

WORKSHEET **TEACHER RESOURCES**

For additional IELD support addressing these standards, have students complete the Lesson ELD activity from the Teacher Resources found on the course.

ANSWERS

Interaction *Asia Minor; it was much closer to Judea than Britain was.*

Region *By 476, Christianity had spread east of the easternmost border of the empire, and it had spread outside the empire to the north of Philippi.*

INTERACTIVE **INTERACTIVE GALLERY**

Early Christian Symbols

Display the Interactive Gallery: Early Christian Symbols. Click on each image, and ask for volunteers to read the captions. Ask: Which symbol was used as a secret code? *(the fish)*

ACTIVE CLASSROOM

Use the Quick Write strategy. Have students write a tweet about one symbol. Suggest that they create an appropriate hashtag.

Christianity and the Empire

Discuss how Christianity went from a persecuted religion to Rome's official religion.

Identify Cause and Effect Why did the Roman government oppose Christianity at first? *(People who converted stopped worshiping Roman gods. Officials feared the gods' anger.)*

Summarize What events finally gave Christianity an official place in the Roman empire? *(Emperor Constantine became committed to Christianity and ended the persecutions. Later, Christianity became the official religion of the empire.)*

Analyze Images This dramatic painting by Italian Renaissance artist Caravaggio shows Paul's conversion to Christianity. **Synthesize Visual Information** How does Caravaggio communicate the power of Paul's experience?

his life he was opposed to Christians. He had an experience that led to his conversion to Christianity. A **conversion** is a heartfelt change in one's opinions or beliefs. Paul believed that Jesus had appeared to him and told him to spread the new faith. Paul is called an apostle, even though he was not one of the original twelve.

Paul helped both to spread and define Christianity. Paul traveled to Greece and other areas. He founded churches and preached. Paul also wrote letters called epistles to various Christians. He helped spread the belief that non-Jews did not need to follow all Jewish laws to become Christians. They still needed to live moral lives and could not worship other gods. He taught many basic Christian beliefs, including the resurrection of Jesus. He also preached that Jesus' death saved believers from sin and guilt. Almost half of the text of the New Testament comes from Paul's epistles or writings of those he influenced.

As more non-Jews came into the church, Christianity became a separate religion and no longer a part of Judaism. Christian communities soon arose around the Mediterranean as well as in Persia and Central Asia.

Why Did Christianity Grow Rapidly? Christianity spread rapidly during the Pax Romana, although it remained a minority faith in the empire for centuries. Several factors helped the new faith grow quickly.

As you read, the Roman government built roads and kept the seas free of pirates. This made travel safer. It allowed Christians to move more easily from place to place, spreading their beliefs. Paul's journeys, for example, might not have been possible in an earlier period.

As well, Greek was widely spoken in the eastern half of the empire, and by educated people everywhere. Christian scriptures were in Greek, so a large number of people could understand them. Later, the scriptures were translated into Latin.

The ideas of Christianity also appealed to many people. Many appreciated Christianity's moral teachings and its monotheism, or belief in one God. Some were also attracted by the Christian belief that all people are equal in God's sight, including poor and enslaved people. Women were drawn to the new religion and may have led some of the growing Christian communities.

INTERACTIVE
The Spread of Christianity

READING CHECK **Summarize** How did Paul help develop and contribute to the growth of Christianity?

HISTORY BACKGROUND

Crucifixion The crucifixion of Jesus is well-known, but this method of execution was not specific to Jesus, nor did it have any relation to his religious ideas. The Romans used crucifixion as a common method of execution. Because they viewed crucifixion as shameful and cruel, it was not used on Roman citizens but instead was reserved for slaves, foreigners, and prisoners. For example, according to historians and ancient texts, one Roman general ordered as many as 6,000 prisoners crucified. Some people condemned by the Romans had to carry part of their cross to the site of execution outside the city walls, as Jesus did according to the Gospels.

ANSWERS

Synthesize Visual Information *Sample answer: The painting shows Paul lying on the ground, reaching up as though stunned.*

Summarize *Paul traveled widely, founding churches and preaching. He wrote letters to Christians; he defined basic Christian beliefs.*

Christianity and the Empire

The growth of Christianity worried Roman officials. They sometimes persecuted, or mistreated, Christians.

A New Faith Faces Opposition The Romans generally allowed people to worship their own gods, so long as they also worshiped Roman gods and emperors as a sign of loyalty. Jews did not worship Roman gods, but this did not greatly bother the Romans. They respected the Jewish traditions that forbade worshiping more than one God.

Christianity, however, was a new religion. The government opposed it because when non-Jews became Christians they stopped worshiping the old gods. Officials feared that Christians were disloyal and that the gods would be angry if people who became Christians stopped worshiping them. It was considered the government's job to keep the gods happy.

Christians Are Persecuted A fire destroyed much of Rome in 64 CE. Emperor Nero falsely blamed Christians. Many Christians were killed. After 250 CE, emperors persecuted Christians. Persecution scared some away from Christianity. However, it caused others to bond to their faith. Persecution produced **martyrs**, or people who die for their beliefs. Their courage strengthened many Christians' faith.

Persecution continued, on and off, until the reign of Emperor Constantine. According to tradition, he had a dream just before a battle that told him to fight under the sign of the cross. He won the battle. In 313, he ended persecution of Christians and eventually became a Christian himself.

Constantine thought the Christian Church could help hold together the divided Roman empire. A later emperor made Christianity Rome's official religion around 380. Church leaders chose a Roman structure to organize the Church. They also chose the gospels and letters to be included in the Christian Bible. As the western Roman empire declined, Roman cities were often led by Christian bishops.

READING CHECK **Draw Conclusions** Which emperor ended the persecution of Christians? Why?

Did you know?

Early Christians used a simple fish drawing as a secret code to other Christians.

Lesson Check

HSS 6.7.5, 6.7.6, 6.7.7, 7.1.1; ELD.P1.A.2, P1.C.10.a

Practice Vocabulary

1. What is **baptism?**
2. What does it mean to be **resurrected?**
3. How did Christian **martyrs** help strengthen the faith of other Christians?

Critical Thinking and Writing

4. **Identify Main Ideas** Why did the Romans persecute Christians?
5. **Summarize** Summarize the events of Jesus' life according to the Gospels.
6. **Analyze Cause and Effect** According to tradition, how did Constantine's dream change the course of Roman history?
7. **Writing Workshop: Gather Details** In your Active Journal, add details about Rome's size, longevity, economic power, cultural achievements, influence, expansion, and trade.

LESSON CHECK

1. ritual cleansing by plunging into water **DOK1**
2. to come back to life after death **DOK1**
3. The courage of martyrs inspired Christians to hold to their beliefs. **DOK2**
4. The Romans feared the gods would be angered because Christians didn't worship them. **DOK1**
5. He was born, was baptized, taught, was arrested and crucified, and was resurrected. **DOK2**
6. Constantine's dream led him to end the persecution of Christians. **DOK2**
7. Student answers will vary. They should include specific, verifiable details about Rome's size, longevity, economic power, cultural achievements, and influence. **DOK4**

HSS 6.7.5, 6.7.6, 6.7.7, 7.1.1; ELD P1.A.2, P1.C.10.a

SYNTHESIZE

Assess and Reteach Have students use a Jigsaw strategy to complete Lesson Check questions 1–6. Review their responses. If they had any incorrect answers, use the Guiding Questions to discuss the lesson's main ideas, focusing on the ideas they struggled with.

ACTIVE JOURNAL

Writing Workshop Have students complete the Lesson 2 Writing Task in their Active Journals. Students will gather details about Rome's size, longevity, economic power, cultural achievements, and influence. As they move through the topic, students will revisit these details, adding to them as needed.

DEMONSTRATE

ASSESSMENT — ONLINE LESSON QUIZ

Assign the Online Lesson Quiz for this lesson if you haven't already done so. Students will be offered automatic remediation or enrichment based on their score.

DISCUSSION — DISCUSSION BOARD

Post this question to the class on the Discussion Board:

Summarize What did Jesus teach? *(Jesus taught that God would soon establish his kingdom on earth. He spoke up for the poor and the outcast. He was said to be able to heal people. His two most important commandments were to love God with all your heart, soul, and mind, and to love your neighbor as yourself.)*

ANSWERS

Draw Conclusions *Constantine; he felt the Christian Church might help hold the empire together, and he won a battle while fighting beneath a cross.*

HSS 6.7.6, 6.7.7, 7.1.1; Analysis HI.3

Analysis Skills
Detect Changing Patterns

LEARN

Preview the steps in the student text with students, and then play the video.

VIDEO **21ST CENTURY SKILLS**

Project the Identify Trends video in the 21st Century Skills Tutorial. Use the Quick Reference and Assessment to provide additional instruction on this skill.

PRACTICE

Have students practice the skill using the secondary source on the student page, providing the instruction and then asking students the questions.

As an alternative, you could form students into pairs or groups to perform the activity. Then invite the groups to describe the patterns they identified to the class.

ASSESS

To assess this skill, have students read the section The Shrinking Empire in Lesson 6 of this topic. Have them identify the factors that caused the Byzantine empire to decline.

ANSWERS

1. Sample answers: It became easier for people to travel. Members of the Roman empire shared a common language. The empire was wealthy, but many people remained poor or enslaved.
2. a. Paul of Tarsus and Constantine contributed to the spread of Christianity.
   b. trade and having a common language
3. a. Paul spread the Christian faith through his preaching and gave poor people hope. Constantine's conversion set an example for Romans.
   b. Trade made travel easy; a common language made it easier to share ideas and beliefs; and Rome's social system encouraged poor or enslaved people to seek hope and change.
4. Sample answers: Improvements in travel and communication enable cultures to spread. New ideas will spread quickly if they offer poor people hope.

HSS 6.7.6, 6.7.7, 7.1.1; Analysis HI.3

Detect Changing Patterns

INTERACTIVE
Identify Trends

Follow these steps and use the source to identify a changing pattern in Roman society.

1 **Gather information about the society.** Carefully read the source provided here. What are some details that describe Roman society during the time of the Roman empire?

2 **Identify possible sources of change in the society.** Consider the sources of change described in the passage.

a. Which individuals contributed to the rise and spread of Christianity during the Roman empire?

b. What specific factors helped make this change happen?

3 **Determine how the sources of change led to new patterns of living.** Using the people and factors you identified in step 2, analyze how a new pattern of living emerged during the Roman empire.

a. How did Paul and Constantine change Romans' lives?

b. How did trade, language, and Rome's social system encourage this new pattern?

4 **Summarize what you discover.** Use the information you have learned to identify trends. What general statement can you make about the rise and spread of Christianity during the Roman empire?

Secondary Source

During the time of the Roman empire, several factors contributed to the rise and spread of Christianity throughout the region. In the early years of Christianity, one of Jesus' apostles, Paul of Tarsus, spread the Christian faith through his preaching and leadership.

As the Roman empire grew larger and more powerful, established trade routes made it easier for people to travel. Because the members of the Roman empire often shared a common language, communication among strangers was possible, furthering the spread of ideas and beliefs. Additionally, despite the wealth of the Roman empire, many people remained poor or enslaved. The message of Christianity brought hope to those whose lives were burdened by a lack of freedom or poverty.

Finally, important leaders of the Roman empire embraced Christianity. In 312 CE, Emperor Constantine converted to Christianity. Within 70 years, Christianity had become the official religion of the Roman empire.

DIFFERENTIATED INSTRUCTION

Below Level Have students work in pairs to identify words that signal when a change is being described. First, they should identify words such as *rise*, *spread*, *grew*, and *converted* in the passage on the student page. Then suggest that they brainstorm a list of additional words that signal change, such as *transformation* or *reform*.

INTEGRATED ENGLISH LANGUAGE DEVELOPMENT

Bridging Have students turn to a partner to talk about the secondary source quote. Why were so many people in Rome still poor, even though the Roman empire had great wealth? Why would poor people be attracted to Christianity?

Beliefs of Christianity

GET READY TO READ

START UP

The photograph shows a Catholic church in France. What can you infer about Christianity today from this photograph?

GUIDING QUESTIONS

- What writings form Christianity's scripture?
- What core set of beliefs do most Christians share?
- How do Christians practice their religion?

TAKE NOTES

Literacy Skills: Analyze Text Structure
Use the graphic organizer in your Active Journal to take notes as you read the lesson.

PRACTICE VOCABULARY

Use the vocabulary activity in your Active Journal to practice the vocabulary words.

Vocabulary		Academic Vocabulary
New Testament	Trinity	controversial
Gospel	ethics	element
parable	denomination	
epistle		

In the centuries after the death of Jesus, Christians gathered their sacred writings and developed their faith. Their writings centered on the life of Jesus and the Christian belief in Jesus as the son of God.

The Christian Bible

You have already read about the Hebrew Bible, which contains Jewish history, religious laws, and many other writings. Like Jews, early Christians read the Hebrew Bible as their scripture, or holy writings.

The Old and New Testaments At first, the Hebrew Bible was the Christians' only sacred text. Then they began to add their own body of writings. Jews did not and still do not accept these as scripture. Christians called the Hebrew Bible the Old Testament, and this new body of work the **New Testament**. They read both together as their holy text.

The works that became the New Testament were written down between 50 CE and 150. By the 300s they were collected and began circulating in the form that Christians

PRACTICE VOCABULARY

To help students integrate new vocabulary, explain that the *New Testament* is a set of writings that Christians added to the Hebrew Bible. It contains the *Gospels*, which recount Jesus' life and teachings, and *epistles*, which are formal letters. Jesus often taught in *parables*, stories with a moral. Many of his teachings concerned *ethics*, issues of right and wrong. Christians believe that God exists in three forms, known collectively as the *Trinity*. A *denomination* is a particular group of Christians. Reinforce the terms during the lesson using the teaching notes.

Point out the academic vocabulary in the lesson margins. Provide sample sentences that clarify meaning.

controversial: Politics is often a controversial topic.

element: Practice, lessons, and performances are all elements of a musician's work.

HSS 6.7.6, 6.7.8; ELA RI.6.5

Beliefs of Christianity

CONNECT

GET READY TO READ

ETEXT START UP

Project the Start Up Activity. As students enter the classroom and get settled, ask them to examine the procession at a Catholic church in France.

Formulate Questions Have students record an inference that they can draw about Christianity from this photograph. *(Sample answers: The cross is still an important symbol. Christians are ethnically diverse.)* Then have them share their inferences with another student, either in class or through a chat or blog.

Discuss Remind students that Christianity became the official religion of the Roman empire. Ask them whether they think the church became more or less formal as a result, and why.

After completing the Start Up activity, project the Lesson Opener or direct students to their textbooks. Preview the lesson by working through the Get Ready to Read items with the class. Remind students to pay close attention to the Guiding Questions as they read the lesson.

ACTIVE JOURNAL

Take Notes Have students use the lesson literacy skills graphic organizer in their Active Journals to take notes as they read the lesson.

Practice Vocabulary Have students complete the activity in their Active Journals to build their vocabulary.

VIDEO

Assign the lesson video as homework.

WORKSHEET **TEACHER RESOURCES**

Have students who need additional support use the following worksheets from the Teacher Resources on the course:

- **Reading Support**
- **English Language Development**
- **Lesson Summary**

INVESTIGATE

The Christian Bible

Discuss how the Christian Bible contains the Hebrew Bible, known as the Old Testament, and additional writings in the New Testament.

Connect How do Christians view the Hebrew Bible? *(They include it as part of their sacred text. They call it the Old Testament.)*

Infer Why do you think the early Christians wrote the documents that became the **New Testament** in Greek? *(Sample answer: It was the most widely spoken language in the eastern part of the Roman empire.)*

Identify Cause and Effect Why were the **epistles** written? *(They were written to explain Christian teachings or to solve problems in the early church.)*

Draw Conclusions Have students read 5 Things to Know About Paul the Apostle. Ask: Why do you think Paul traveled widely? *(He hoped to spread Christianity to as many places as possible.)*

ELD TIP Academic vocabulary and subject matter vocabulary can be particularly challenging for English learners. Review terms in the topic such as *parable, epistle, denomination,* and *controversial* to assess their comprehension.

ANSWERS

Compare and Contrast *the Gospels; they describe the life and teachings of Jesus from four different points of view.*

Critical Thinking *Sample answer: He himself was a convert.*

Did you know?

Our word *Gospel* comes from an Old English word meaning "good spell." The Old English word is a translation of a Greek word meaning "good news."

recognize today. Jesus and his early followers probably spoke Aramaic. But the New Testament was written in Greek. Greek was the most widely spoken language in the eastern part of the Roman empire. The New Testament contains 27 separate documents, called books.

What Are the Gospels? The first four books of the New Testament are the **Gospels**. They describe the life and teachings of Jesus from four different points of view. The Gospels do not all describe the same events in exactly the same way. Together, however, they create a powerful portrayal of Jesus and his teachings.

Many of Jesus' teachings are presented in the form of **parables**, or stories with a moral. Jesus often used parables to explain important lessons.

Teachings in Other Books After the Gospels come a number of other books. Most of them are **epistles**, or formal letters. These are letters that apostles and other early leaders wrote to the newly established churches.

Most epistles were written to explain Christian teachings or to solve problems in the church. Paul wrote many of these epistles to churches he had started himself. His letters explained many Christian beliefs—such as the Trinity, resurrection, and salvation—in great detail. Paul's life and the lives of other early Christians are described in another book in the New Testament, the Acts of the Apostles.

The last book of the New Testament is the Book of Revelation. It is written like an epistle, but makes predictions about future events. It uses complicated images to predict Jesus' return to Earth and a final battle between good and evil.

READING CHECK **Compare and Contrast** What are the first four books of the New Testament called? How do they differ in describing their subject?

BIOGRAPHY
5 Things to Know About
PAUL THE APOSTLE
Missionary, Saint (4 BCE?–c. 62–64 CE)

- He spoke Greek.
- His Hebrew name was Saul. He changed it to Paul when he converted to Christianity about 33 CE.
- He learned, as he says, to "work with [his] own hands" as a tent maker.
- He traveled widely by ship and by foot as a missionary in the 40s and 50s CE, aiming to convert non-Jews.
- He emphasized belief in the resurrection of Jesus.

Critical Thinking Why might Paul have been a particularly effective spokesperson for the new religion of Christianity?

INTEGRATED ENGLISH LANGUAGE DEVELOPMENT

Structuring Cohesive Texts Remind students about what a pronoun is; a word that can take the place of a noun in a sentence to refer back to it. List pronouns for students: *I, me, we, us, you, she, her, he, him, it, they, them.* Point out the object pronouns and the subject pronouns and explain the difference. Model using a noun in a sentence and then a pronoun to refer back to it.

Emerging Read the subsection of text, The Son of God, with students. Ask students to tell who the words *he* and *they* refer to in each place they are found in the paragraph.

Expanding Read the subsections of text, The Son of God, The Soul and Salvation, and The Trinity, with students. Ask students to tell who the words *he* and *they* refer to in each occurrence.

What Do Christians Believe About God?

Christians use the New Testament as a source for their teachings. Throughout the centuries, Christians have disagreed about some parts of their faith. But most Christians today share many basic beliefs in common.

The Son of God The Gospels refer to Jesus not only as the Messiah, but also as the Son of God. Christian belief holds that Jesus was God in human form. To the early Christians, Jesus' death proved he was human. His resurrection proved that he was divine, or godlike. For some, the idea of Jesus as both human and divine was puzzling or **controversial**. But Christians could have faith that they, too, would be resurrected after death. Christians believe that by believing in Jesus, they will be rewarded with eternal, or endless, life in the presence of God.

Analyze Images This is a page from the Book of Kells, an illuminated manuscript created in the British Isles around 800. It contains the gospels and other material. **Use Visual Information** How did creations like this help keep Christianity alive during the Middle Ages?

The Soul and Salvation Christians believe that everyone has a soul, or spirit. To a Christian, what happens to the soul after death depends on how that person has lived and whether that person believes in Jesus. Christians believe that people need God to forgive their sins, or wrongdoings, so that their souls can live on in the presence of God after death. They have faith that God may forgive people who are truly sorry for their sins and choose to follow Jesus. They believe Jesus promised eternal salvation to those who believe in him as their savior.

Many Christians view Jesus' death and resurrection as key to forgiveness. In the ancient world, some peoples atoned, or made up for sins, by offering animal sacrifices to their gods. Many Christians believe that Jesus, by being crucified, became the sacrifice for everyone's sins.

The Trinity Like Jews, Christians are monotheists. As you have read, this means that they worship one God. Most Christians, however, believe that God exists as three forms, called persons. Together, these three forms are known as the **Trinity**. The Trinity includes God the Father, Jesus the Son, and the Holy Spirit.

Christians believe that God the Father created the universe. They believe that Jesus is God's son. He is God in human form. The Holy Spirit, also called the Holy Ghost, is described as the power of God as experienced on Earth. To early Christians, the Holy Spirit allowed them to sense the presence of God after Jesus was no longer with them.

Academic Vocabulary
controversial • *adj.*, subject to disagreement or argument

READING CHECK What do Christians believe about Jesus' death and resurrection?

What Do Christians Believe About God?

Discuss what Christians believe about Jesus, the soul, salvation, and the Trinity.

Compare and Contrast In what ways do Christians agree and disagree with each other about their beliefs? *(Most Christians share the same basic beliefs but some groups disagree about elements of the faith.)*

Identify Cause and Effect According to Christian belief, what determines what happens to a soul after death? *(According to Christian belief, what happens to a soul after death is determined by how the person has lived and whether he or she believes in Jesus.)*

Synthesize What are some of the most difficult or **controversial** Christian beliefs? *(Sample answers: the belief that Jesus is both human and divine; the belief that there is one God who exists in three forms)*

INTERACTIVE **PRIMARY SOURCE**

Have students go online to analyze the First Letter to the Corinthians Primary Source.

Then ask what virtue the apostle Paul is describing in this letter. (*love*)

ELD.PII.A.2.a

Ask students why they think the author used the pronouns *he* and *they* in those sentences, instead of repeating the names of the people being discussed.

Bridging Ask pairs of students to work together. Have students read the subsections The Son of God, The Soul and Salvation, and The Trinity. Ask students to talk about who *he* and *they* refer to in each place in the paragraph. Have students create sentences about this subject using a proper noun, then with a pronoun.

WORKSHEET **TEACHER RESOURCES**

For additional IELD support addressing these standards, have students complete the Lesson ELD activity from the Teacher Resources found on the course.

ANSWERS

Use Visual Information *Sample answer: They recorded Christian teachings in both writing and images.*

Identify Main Ideas *They believe that, because Jesus was resurrected after death they will also be resurrected and rewarded with eternal life.*

Practicing Christianity

Discuss how Christians follow Christianity's teachings and observe its rituals and holidays.

Connect Consider the structure of Roman society. Why might Christianity appeal to people of low social standing? *(Sample answer: In Roman society, people of low social standing had little power or status. Christianity offered equality with those of greater wealth and power.)*

INTERACTIVE **INTERACTIVE GALLERY**

Christianity Today

Display the Interactive Gallery: Click on each image, and have volunteers read the captions. Ask: What activities are part of living as a Christian? *(worship at church, helping those in need, prayer)*

ACTIVE CLASSROOM

Use the Imagine strategy to talk with Paul the Apostle. Write a question you'd like to ask him about Christianity, what he would say, and your response.

What Is the Judeo-Christian Tradition?

Discuss how the common elements of Judaism and Christianity have affected many cultures.

Identify Cause and Effect How does the Judeo-Christian tradition influence society today? (*It shapes art, literature, and law.*)

ANSWERS

Analyze Graphs *North and South America; Middle East and North Africa*

INTERACTIVE
Christianity Today

Practicing Christianity

In daily life, Christians try to follow Jesus' teachings. Most Christians also observe similar rituals and holidays.

Following Jesus' Teachings Much of Jesus' teaching has to do with **ethics**, or issues of right and wrong, and how to treat people. Jesus taught that God loved all his creations no matter who they were or what they did... Jesus urged his followers to reflect that love in their relationships with others and to treat others as they would like to be treated. This is called the "Golden Rule."

Primary Source

> **"In everything, do to others as you would have them do to you."**
>
> —Matthew 7:12

Jesus also showed great concern for poor and humble people. He accepted even those with the lowest social standing among his followers.

As well as following Jesus' teachings, most Christians believe religious faith is also important. To most Christians, Christianity means believing in Jesus, in his sacrifice for other people's sins, and in his resurrection.

Christianity Today Today, Christianity is the world's largest religion. There are about 2 billion Christians in the world. They are divided into thousands of **denominations**, or religious groups. Different groups share some beliefs and rituals but disagree about others. The largest single groups are Roman Catholicism and Eastern Orthodoxy. Protestantism is a large family of groups. Some Protestant

Christianity in the World Today

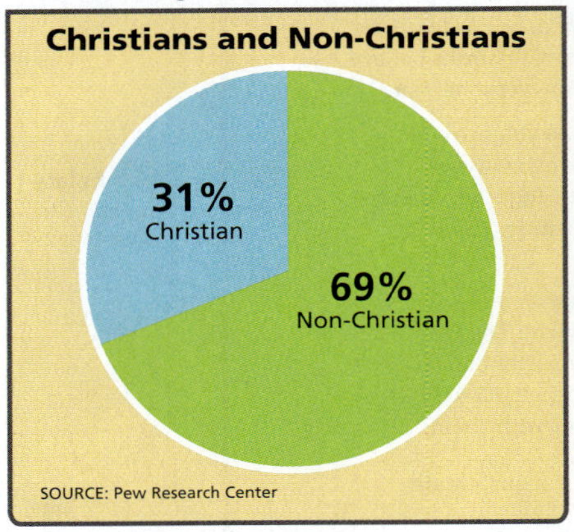

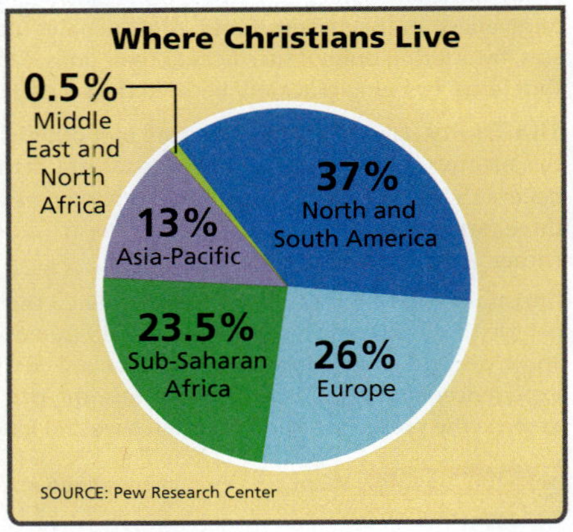

Analyze Diagrams These graphs illustrate facts about Christians in the world today.
Analyze Graphs Which region of the world has the most Christians? The fewest?

DIFFERENTIATED INSTRUCTION

Special Education Ask students to share examples of how they like to be treated by other people. Then explain that the "Golden Rule" says that we should treat others the way we want to be treated.

Below Level Have students work with partners to answer the following question: How do you think the "Golden Rule" relates to the idea of accepting people no matter what their social standing? If time allows, ask pairs to share their answers in class.

Advanced Ask students to research whether non-Christian religions have teachings that are similar to the "Golden Rule." They can make a poster or write a brief editorial to share their findings with the class.

334 Lesson 8.3 • Beliefs of Christianity

denominations are the Baptist, Methodist, Lutheran, Presbyterian, Pentecostal, and Episcopalian churches.

Christian Rituals and Holidays

Many practices are shared by nearly all groups of Christians. Most Christians observe Sunday as the special day of rest and prayer. At worship services, many Christians participate in a ritual meal called a Holy Communion or Eucharist. This usually includes bread and wine or grape juice. Many Christians are baptized.

Christmas and Easter are two important holidays for most Christians. Christmas celebrates the birth of Jesus, a miracle according to Christian tradition. Easter celebrates Jesus' resurrection.

READING CHECK **Draw Conclusions** Why is ethics important to a religion?

▲ These Christians in Honduras celebrate Palm Sunday, the Sunday before Easter.

What Is the Judeo-Christian Tradition?

Judaism and Christianity are separate religions. They have many important differences, but the two faiths also have much in common. Both Jews and Christians worship one God. Both read the Hebrew Bible (Old Testament) as scripture. They share a similar ethical tradition. Members of both groups respect the Ten Commandments.

The common **elements** of Judaism and Christianity are called the Judeo-Christian tradition. It has helped shaped much about life in Europe, the Americas, and other areas. It has contributed to art and literature. For example, stories from parts of the Bible read by members of both faiths are common themes in art. The tradition also helps shape law. For example, it teaches the equality of all people before the law.

Academic Vocabulary
element • *n.*, part

READING CHECK **Compare and Contrast** What is one element that Judaism and Christianity have in common?

Lesson Check

HSS 6.7.6, 6.7.8

Practice Vocabulary

1. When was the **New Testament** written down?
2. Who do Christians believe are the members of the **Trinity**?

Critical Thinking and Writing

3. **Summarize** What is the relationship between the Hebrew Bible and the Christian scriptures?
4. **Identify Main Ideas** What do Christians believe about atonement, or making up for sins?
5. **Infer** What is the "Golden Rule"? Why do you think it is called "golden"?
6. **Writing Workshop: Use Credible Sources** You might need more information to make a decision for your essay. List three credible sources of information you could use to compare the Greek city-states and the Roman empire in your Active Journal.

HSS 6.7.6, 6.7.8

SYNTHESIZE

Assess and Reteach Have students use a Think-Pair-Share strategy to complete Lesson Check questions 1–5. Review their responses. If they had any incorrect answers, use the Guiding Questions to discuss the lesson's main ideas, focusing on the ideas they struggled with.

ACTIVE JOURNAL

Writing Workshop Have students complete the Lesson 3 Writing Task in their Active Journals. Students will list three credible sources of information they could use to compare Greece and Rome. As they move through the topic, students will revisit their lists, revising them as needed.

DEMONSTRATE

ASSESSMENT **ONLINE LESSON QUIZ**

Assign the Online Lesson Quiz for this lesson if you haven't already done so. Students will be offered automatic remediation or enrichment based on their score.

DISCUSSION **DISCUSSION BOARD**

Post this question to the class on the Discussion Board:

Categorize What writings form Christianity's scripture? *(The Old Testament is the same as the Hebrew Bible. The New Testament contains the Gospels, epistles, and the Book of Revelation.)*

LESSON CHECK

1. between 50 and 150 CE. **DOK1**
2. God the Father, Jesus, the Holy Spirit **DOK1**
3. Christians accept the Hebrew Bible as scripture and call it the Old Testament, but have added writings, called the New Testament, about the life and teachings of Jesus and his followers. **DOK2**
4. Christians believe that those who feel sorry for their sins and follow Jesus can be forgiven by God. **DOK1**
5. The "Golden Rule" is: Treat others as you would like to be treated. Sample: It is called "golden" because it summarizes a very valuable ethical teaching. **DOK2**
6. Students should list sources like history books, museums, and reputable encyclopedias. **DOK3**

ANSWERS

Draw Conclusions *Ethics help people know what is right in the eyes of their religion.*

Compare and Contrast *Sample answers: monotheism; the Hebrew Bible; ethical teachings*

HSS 6.7.6; ELA RH.6.1

Primary Sources

The Gospel of Matthew, The Sermon on the Mount

Read aloud the explanatory note about the source. Direct students' attention to the image of Jesus speaking to his disciples. Ask: What details in the image hint that Jesus is teaching about spiritual things? *(Sample answer: He has a halo, and his hands are clasped as if in prayer. The disciples' hands are also clasped as if praying.)*

GUIDED READING

Read aloud the excerpt without stopping. Then reread the passage, pausing after each verse to let students answer the numbered questions. Use the questions in the text to prompt students' analysis of the primary source.

Reading and Vocabulary Support Answers

4. *Sample answer: He knows that he and his disciples will be persecuted, and he wants to prepare them to carry on in spite of that.*

5. *Sample answer: He mentions the fate of past prophets to emphasize the importance and danger of the disciples' mission.*

GUIDED ANALYSIS

After completing the reading, discuss what this primary source reveals about the teachings of Jesus.

Cite Evidence Which of these Beatitudes do you think would be comforting to those who have a low place in society? Explain why using details from the text. *(Sample answer: The one that says, "Blessed are the meek, for they will inherit the land." It seems to promise that the poor will be provided for by God.)*

Infer What do you think Jesus means by "the clean of heart"? *(Sample answer: He means people who are pure, who don't hate, who aren't greedy, and who don't lie.)*

To assess understanding, have students respond to the Analyzing Primary Sources questions in writing.

Primary Sources

HSS 6.7.6; ELA RH.6.1

The Gospel of Matthew, The Sermon on the Mount

The Sermon on the Mount is a collection of teachings that Jesus gave in a speech on a mountain. The teachings, recorded in the New Testament, emphasized that Jesus' followers should love one another and welcome even the most humble of believers.

◀ Jesus speaks to his disciples.

Reading and Vocabulary Support

① Jesus' disciples were twelve of his closest followers.

② To be meek is to be humble and not boastful or loud.

③ Righteousness is being good and moral.

④ Why might Jesus specifically mention people who are persecuted?

⑤ Why do you think Jesus mentions the fate of the prophets who came before him?

When he saw the crowds, he went up the mountain, and after he had sat down, his disciples ① came to him. He began to teach them, saying:

"Blessed are the poor in spirit, for theirs is the kingdom of heaven.

Blessed are they who mourn, for they will be comforted.

Blessed are the meek ②, for they will inherit the land.

Blessed are they who hunger and thirst for righteousness ③, for they will be satisfied.

Blessed are the merciful, for they will be shown mercy.

Blessed are the clean of heart, for they will see God.

Blessed are the peacemakers, for they will be called children of God.

Blessed are they who are persecuted ④, for the sake of righteousness, for theirs is the kingdom of heaven.

Blessed are you when they insult you and persecute you and utter every kind of evil against you [falsely] because of me.

Rejoice and be glad, for your reward will be great in heaven. Thus they persecuted the prophets who were before you ⑤.

—Matthew 5:1-12, *New American Bible*

Analyzing Primary Sources

Cite specific evidence from the document to support your answers.

1. **Analyze Information** What encouragement does Jesus give his followers when he says, "Blessed are you when they insult you and persecute you and utter every kind of evil against you [falsely] because of me./ Rejoice and be glad, for your reward will be great in heaven"?
2. **Draw Conclusions** Which of these statements do you think would have been most threatening to the Roman authorities of Jesus' time? Why?

336 Primary Sources • The Gospel of Matthew, The Sermon on the Mount

---

ANALYZING PRIMARY SOURCES

1. Sample answer: He tells them that though they may suffer when they are persecuted, they will receive a reward in heaven. **DOK2**

2. Sample answer: The Beatitude about being a peacemaker would threaten the Romans because their empire was built on war and conquest. **DOK3**

HSS 6.7.7, 6.7.8, 7.1.1, 7.1.2; ELA RI.6.2

Roman Culture and Its Legacy

GET READY TO READ

START UP

Tourists visit a Roman ruin in present-day Turkey. Why do you think Roman civilization continues to fascinate people?

GUIDING QUESTIONS

- What cultural exchanges took place between Rome and other ancient civilizations?
- What were Roman achievements in art, literature, and science?
- How did ancient Rome influence language, government, and ideas of citizenship?

TAKE NOTES

Literacy Skills: Identify Main Ideas

Use the graphic organizer in your Active Journal to take notes as you read the lesson.

PRACTICE VOCABULARY

Use the vocabulary activity in your Active Journal to practice the vocabulary words.

Vocabulary		Academic Vocabulary
site of encounter	Romance language	achievement
Greco-Roman	oratory	tradition
mosaic	satire	
	gladiator	

The Roman empire may be ancient history, but Roman culture is still with us in many ways. Rome's art, language, entertainment, and law continue to influence the modern world. Also, in the city of Rome, people from different cultures mixed and interacted creatively, adding to Rome's cultural legacy.

Rome as a Site of Encounter

Ancient Rome was a **site of encounter**. Sites of encounter are places where people from different cultures meet and exchange products, ideas, and technologies.

A Multicultural Empire The Roman empire contained many different cultures. The Latin-speaking Romans had conquered Egyptians, Greeks, Syrians, Jews, Celts, and Gauls. These peoples had dozens of religions and spoke hundreds of languages, including Greek, Aramaic, and Hebrew. Roman emperors brought to Rome the best of everything they could find from their empire and the world. The emperors used what they found to enrich Rome and their empire.

PRACTICE VOCABULARY

To help students integrate new vocabulary, explain that a *site of encounter* is a place where people from different cultures meet and exchange products and ideas. Some aspects of Roman culture include *mosaics*, designs formed from small tiles; *satires*, works of literature that make fun of their subject; *oratory*, or the art of speechmaking; and *gladiators*, people who fought as part of public entertainment. *Greco-Roman* culture included elements from both Greece and Rome. Over time, Latin developed into several related languages called Romance languages.

Point out the academic vocabulary in the lesson margins. Provide sample sentences that clarify meaning.

achievement: Winning the game was a great achievement for the team.

tradition: Our family's Sunday meal is a tradition everyone enjoys.

HSS 6.7.7, 6.7.8, 7.1.1, 7.1.2; ELA RI.6.2

Roman Culture and Its Legacy

CONNECT

GET READY TO READ

ETEXT — START UP

Project the Start Up Activity. As students enter the classroom and get settled, ask them to examine the photograph of tourists visiting a Roman ruin in Turkey.

Draw Conclusions Have students record their conclusions about why people remain so fascinated with Roman civilization. *(Sample answers: People are fascinated with Rome because of stories of emperors and gladiators.)* Then have them share their ideas with another student, either in class or through a chat or blog.

Discuss Remind students that cultural diffusion is the spreading of cultural traits. Explain that Rome was a place where many diverse cultures met. Have students discuss how that would affect cultural diffusion.

After completing the Start Up activity, project the Lesson Opener or direct students to their textbooks. Preview the lesson by working through the Get Ready to Read items with the class. Remind students to pay close attention to the Guiding Questions as they read the lesson.

ACTIVE JOURNAL

Take Notes Have students use the lesson literacy skills graphic organizer in their Active Journals to take notes as they read the lesson.

Practice Vocabulary Have students complete the activity in their Active Journals to build their vocabulary.

VIDEO — VIDEO

Assign the lesson video as homework.

WORKSHEET **TEACHER RESOURCES**

Have students who need additional support use the following worksheets from the Teacher Resources on the course:

- **Reading Support**
- **English Language Development**
- **Lesson Summary**

INVESTIGATE

Rome as a Site of Encounter

Discuss how ancient Rome had a multicultural empire.

Synthesize Judging from what you have already learned about Rome, why was it a **site of encounter**? *(Sample answer: People from many conquered lands and traders from around the empire came there.)*

Categorize Which aspects of culture were affected by the diversity of the Roman empire? *(languages, religion)*

Identify Cause and Effect Why did Roman emperors like the religion of Mithraism? *(It encouraged loyalty to the ruler.)*

What Was Greco-Roman Culture?

Discuss how Greek and Roman culture blended into Greco-Roman culture.

Categorize What were some of the Greek elements of **Greco-Roman** culture? *(They included seeing plays by Greek authors and studying Greek philosophy.)*

ANSWERS

Identify Main Ideas *a place where people from different cultures meet and exchange products, ideas, and technologies*

▲ This painting from the 1800s shows Rome at its height.

International Influences International trade both spread Rome's influence and brought influences to Rome from other cultures. By the end of the first century BCE, a major expansion of international trade brought Rome into contact with the Parthian Persian, Kushan, Xiongnu (Central Asia), and Han empires. Ideas, customs, and beliefs spread as valuable goods moved long distances between empires.

Arab merchants brought frankincense, myrrh, spices, gold, ivory, pearls, precious stones, and textiles from Africa, India, and East Asia by camel caravan. Chinese silk, much desired by wealthy Romans, traveled to Rome along sea routes and the Silk Road. In return, the Chinese traded for Roman metalwork and glassware. Mithraism, a religion from Persia and the east, attracted many Romans. Roman emperors encouraged this religion's idea of loyalty to the king. In turn, Christianity spread into Persia and parts of Africa.

READING CHECK **Identify Main Ideas** What is a site of encounter?

What Was Greco-Roman Culture?

You have read that the Romans borrowed from Greek civilization. They adopted Greek cultural practices and spread their own as well. A combined **Greco-Roman** culture emerged that included Greek and Roman elements. Many people in the empire combined Greco-Roman culture with other local traditions.

Some Roman practices in this joint culture were visiting public baths and worshiping the emperors. Greek traditions included seeing plays by Greek authors and studying Greek philosophy.

Government Spreads Culture Some actions of the Roman government helped spread Greco-Roman culture. For military purposes, it built roads and founded cities called colonies in the provinces. Roads made it easier to travel and spread ideas. Colonies looked like Rome in many ways. Each had a forum, amphitheater, and baths. Roman culture spread from colonies to nearby lands.

338 Lesson 8.4 • Roman Culture and Its Legacy

INTEGRATED ENGLISH LANGUAGE DEVELOPMENT

Structuring Cohesive Texts Explain that we can understand better how ideas and events described in a text are linked by keeping an eye out for certain sets of words and phrases, e.g., *first/next* or *first/then*, which show an order of events, or *as a result*, which shows that something was caused by something else. Encourage students to think of phrases that point out connected events.

Emerging Read the subsection Gladiatorial Games later in the lesson with students aloud. Point out the words *first, originally, later,* and *sometimes*. Talk to students about the meaning of these words and what they tell us about what is going on in the text.

Expanding Have students read the subsection Gladiatorial Games aloud. Point out the words *first, originally, later,* and *sometimes.*

The government also spread Roman culture when it allowed more people to become Roman citizens. By 212 CE, almost every free person in the empire was a citizen. As citizens, they lived under Roman law. They used Roman courts to settle disputes. Male citizens could serve in the Roman army.

The Army Shares Culture Roman soldiers helped spread Greco-Roman culture as well. Many soldiers were sent to the far reaches of the empire. They often married local women and settled where they had served. Military outposts on the frontiers grew into towns and cities, which introduced the local people to Greco-Roman culture.

READING CHECK **Identify Implied Main Ideas** How did colonies help spread Greco-Roman culture?

Roman Art and Language

The arts flourished in the Roman empire. Roman art is still widely admired. The Latin language also remains important.

The Arts of the Empire In Roman towns, art filled public buildings and the homes of the wealthy. Colorful mosaics brightened up floors. A **mosaic** is a design formed with small tiles of glass, stone, or pottery. Public buildings and the homes of the wealthy boasted colorful painted murals on the walls and ceilings. These showed beautiful landscapes, events from mythology and history, and scenes from daily life.

The Romans built statues of their gods, great heroes, and important people. They stood in markets, temples, and other public places. Many were copies of Greek originals. But the Romans also developed their own style. Greek sculptors usually idealized their subjects, or made them look like ideal people. In contrast, earlier Roman sculptors usually showed their subjects as they were in real life.

Analyze Images Roman art, as in this painting from near Pompeii, often showed scenes of daily life. **Synthesize Visual Information** What are some words you would use to describe the lives of upper-class Romans?

Sumarize How did the government spread Roman culture? *(It built roads that made travel and the spread of ideas easier. It built characteristically Roman facilities like a forum, an amphitheater, and baths in colonies. It allowed more people to become citizens, which brought more people under Roman law.)*

Draw Conclusions How did Roman soldiers spread culture by getting married to local women? *(Sample answer: As the head of the family, the married soldier would teach Roman culture to any children he had with his wife.)*

Roman Art and Language

Discuss what art the Romans created and how Latin influenced other languages.

Contrast How were **mosaics** and murals different? *(A mosaic is a design formed with small tiles; they were usually on floors. Murals were painted on walls and ceilings.)*

Identify Cause and Effect How did Roman religion affect Roman art? *(Roman murals showed scenes from mythology, and Roman statues often depicted their gods.)*

ELD.PII.A.2.b

Talk to students about what they tell us about what is going on in the text. Explain the meaning of the phrase *in the first place*. Ask how the phrase could be used in a rewrite of one of the sentences in this section.

Bridging Have students read the subsection Gladiatorial Games aloud. Point out the words *first*, *originally*, *later*, and *sometimes*. Explain what they tell us about what is going on in the text. Explain the meaning of *consequently* and *however*. Ask how either word could be used to rewrite a sentence in this section.

WORKSHEET **TEACHER RESOURCES**

For additional IELD support addressing these standards, have students complete the Lesson ELD activity from Teacher Resources.

ANSWERS

Identify Implied Main Ideas *Colonies helped spread Greco-Roman culture because they were built on the pattern of Rome, and Romans living in the colonies shared their ideas and ways of life.*

Synthesize Visual Information *Sample answer: easy, luxurious, lazy*

Compare and Contrast How was Roman art initially similar to and different from Greek art? *(Roman art often copied Greek art in subject, but Roman artists showed subjects realistically while Greek artists made subjects look ideal.)*

Infer What would you expect to find if you compared Spanish and Latin? Explain. *(They would have many similarities; Spanish developed from Latin.)*

Connect What are some ways that Latin appears in English today? *(Many English words have Latin roots. Latin was used in European education and in Roman Catholic Church services, and is still used in science.)*

Literature and Science in Ancient Rome

Discuss how Rome developed certain forms of literature and made advances in science and medicine.

Identify Cause and Effect How did Cicero's skill at oratory help him? *(It helped him get elected.)*

▲ The Roman poet Virgil whose epic poem the *Aeneid* influenced many later writers

Skillful Roman artisans used various materials to make beautiful objects. They crafted vases and jars of blue glass and mirrors of polished silver. Romans wore jewelry made of silver, gold, and gems.

The Influence of Latin Roman soldiers, colonists, and merchants took their language to many parts of Europe. Latin, the Roman language, became the spoken language across much of the western part of the empire. Over centuries, local ways of speaking of Latin changed into new languages, including Spanish, Italian, French, and Portuguese. These are called **Romance languages**, or languages that developed from Latin. Millions of people speak Romance languages today.

English is not a Romance language, but as many as half of all English words may come from Latin. For example, the word *educate* comes directly from Latin, while *labor* comes indirectly from Latin by way of French.

Latin was the language of education in Europe for many centuries. Scientists still use it to name plants and animals. Latin also served as the language of the Roman Catholic Church. All Catholic services were held in Latin into the 1900s.

READING CHECK **Understand Effects** In what ways does the Latin language continue to influence English speakers today?

Literature and Science in Ancient Rome

The Romans prized literature and science. They built on Greek **achievements**.

Academic Vocabulary
achievement • *n.*, accomplishment that requires effort or skill

Oratory and Poetry Flourish The Romans developed **oratory**, the art of giving speeches. Rome's most famous orator was Cicero, a politician during the last days of the Roman republic. Cicero spoke about the great political issues of his time. He used his powers of persuasion to win election to high office. Many of his speeches were written down and used as models by later orators.

The poet Virgil lived around the same time as Cicero. He wrote the *Aeneid*, an epic poem. It was modeled on Homer's Greek epics, the *Iliad* and the *Odyssey*.

Horace was another famous Roman poet. He is best known for a collection of poems called *Odes*. Some are about friendship and love. Others give advice, which is still relevant today.

The poet Ovid wrote witty verses. Many of his poems explored the theme of love. Some retold stories from Greek and Roman myths.

DIFFERENTIATED INSTRUCTION

Special Education Ask students what the word *romance* means. *(Sample answer: related to love)* Explain that a Romance language is one developed from the Roman language of Latin.

Below Level Have students complete the outline map of the Roman empire in their Active Journals. Then have them refer to a modern map to determine where the modern Spain, Italy, France, and Portugal are. Have them label those regions on their outline maps with the Romance languages spoken there.

Advanced Have students research some basic Latin words and their counterparts in modern Romance languages, such as the words for *mother: mater* (Latin), *mère* (French), *madre* (Spanish and Italian), and *matriz* (Portuguese). Have them make a poster showing at least six groups of terms.

ANSWERS

Understand Effects *As many as half of English words come from Latin directly or indirectly.*

Satire and Biography The author Juvenal wrote **satires**, works of literature that make fun of their subject. Juvenal mocked Roman life. For example, he complained that the Roman people accepted the rule of the emperors instead of having a republic. He wrote that in his day Roman citizens only wanted free food and entertainment.

Primary Source

"The people that once bestowed [gave out] commands, consulships, legions, and all else, now . . . longs eagerly for just two things—bread and circuses!"

—Juvenal, *Satire 10*

Quest CONNECTIONS

Read the quote from Juvenal's *Satire 10* again. How do you think the Roman citizenry's attitude towards the government affected the empire's stability? Record your thoughts in your Active Journal.

The biographer and essayist Plutarch wrote about 227 works. *Parallel Lives* is his most famous book. He compares the characters and lives of pairs of Greek and Roman soldiers, orators, and politicians. These popular biographies provided models for good behavior. Plutarch also wrote many essays on political, religious, ethical, philosophical, and literary subjects. His works were a major influence on the development of essays and biographies.

Philosophy Develops The Romans also continued developing philosophy, inspired by the Greeks. One famous Roman philosopher was Seneca. He wrote about Stoic philosophy. Stoicism urges people to accept suffering and practice self-control.

Roman Advances in Science and Medicine Like philosophy, the Romans also contributed to science and medicine. One important scientist during this period was an astronomer and mathematician named Claudius Ptolemy (KLAWdee uhs TAHLuh mee). He lived in Egypt, which was part of the Roman empire.

Ptolemy wrote a famous book called the *Almagest*. It shaped the way astronomers viewed the universe until the 1400s, although its main idea was wrong. Ptolemy also wrote important works on geography and optics, or the study of light.

The scholar and writer Pliny the Elder wrote the famous *Natural History*, an encyclopedia of scientific matters. Although not always accurate, it was accepted as an authority until the Middle Ages. Pliny carefully names his more than 100 sources, an unusual feature. *Natural History* also provides much valuable information about Roman life for modern scholars.

Analyze Images This drawing illustrates Ptolemy's idea that the earth is at the center of the solar system. **Compare and Contrast** How has Ptolemy's theory been disproved today?

HISTORY BACKGROUND

Ptolemy In addition to astronomy and mathematics, Ptolemy is important because of his work in geography. Using data from an earlier geographer, Marinus of Tyre, Ptolemy developed methods that allowed for mapping the world of his time. For example, he noted the latitude and longitude of about 8,000 places. This allowed others to reproduce his map with locations correctly positioned. Ptolemy also developed early map projection techniques for showing the round Earth on a flat map. Some modern map projections build on Ptolemy's methods. Ptolemy's *Guide to Geography* was reprinted and translated many times during the European Renaissance period, when it became a strong influence on thinkers of that time.

Categorize What is each of these writers known for: Ovid, Seneca, Plutarch? *(Ovid, witty poems of love and mythology; Seneca, the philosophy of Stoicism; Plutarch, biographies)*

Identify Cause and Effect What field of science did Ptolemy influence? *(astronomy)*

ACTIVE JOURNAL

Quest Connection After students reread the Primary Source, direct them to the Quest Connections pages in their Active Journals. Make sure that they address the question of how the attitude described by Juvenal affected the empire's stability.

ANSWERS

Compare and Contrast *Today, scientists know that the sun is at the center of the solar system and the earth revolves around it.*

Popular Entertainment on a Massive Scale

Discuss how the Romans entertained the public with fights and races.

Identify Cause and Effect What was the purpose of the gladiatorial games? *(entertainment)*

Draw Conclusions How did gladiatorial games enter Roman culture? *(Romans adopted the tradition from people living in southern Italy.)*

Compare and Contrast How were chariot races different from gladiatorial games? *(They were held more often. They were not focused on violence.)*

ELD TIP Have English learners look at the image of art of gladiator races. Ask them yes/no questions to see if they recall key facts about these races.

The best-known physician in the Roman empire was a Greek named Claudius Galen. Galen carefully dissected, or cut open, animals such as monkeys. He did this to study how bodies work. Galen was the first to discover that arteries and veins carry blood. Earlier, people believed that they carried air. Doctors used Galen's writings for more than a thousand years.

READING CHECK **Classify and Categorize** What is each of these writers known for: Horace, Ovid, Juvenal?

Popular Entertainment on a Massive Scale

The Greeks staged public entertainments, including plays and athletic events. But the Romans developed a taste for public entertainment on a massive scale. They invented the round amphitheater and built stadiums across the empire.

Gladiatorial Games The Romans enjoyed fights between **gladiators**, or men and sometimes women who fought one another and wild animals as part of a public entertainment. Fights were held in the arenas such as the Colosseum in Rome.

Gladiatorial matches were first held in southern Italy before Rome existed. Originally, these games were staged at funerals. The death of a gladiator was meant as a sacrifice to the spirit of the person whose death was being mourned. Later, the games lost this connection with funerals and were held just to entertain.

The word *gladiator* means swordsman in Latin, though gladiators used a variety of weapons. Gladiators were usually slaves or criminals. They

Analyze Images This drawing shows the Colosseum in cutaway. **Synthesize Visual Information** In what ways does this building resemble modern ones?

HISTORY BACKGROUND

Bread and Circuses The phrase "bread and circuses," coined by Juvenal in his Satire 10, describes a deliberate attempt by Rome's leaders to keep the lower classes from rioting in two ways. The first was by giving Rome's poorer plebeians grain or subsidizing the cost of other foodstuffs. The second was by distracting them with public spectacles. These practices began in the Roman republic era and continued into the empire. The two most popular spectacles were gladiatorial games and chariot racing. Both were highly dangerous for the main participants, especially gladiators. The drama was heightened by the audience's participation on occasion in deciding whether or not a fallen gladiator should be spared.

ANSWERS

Classify and Categorize *Horace wrote odes; Ovid wrote witty verses, often about love, and Juvenal wrote satires.*

Synthesize Visual Information *Sample answer: The different levels, the tiers of seats, the round shape, and the many entrances are similar to modern buildings.*

were trained both to fight and to entertain a crowd. Skilled or lucky gladiators who survived many matches could win their freedom. They could even become celebrities.

Sometimes, huge battles between teams of gladiators were staged. Special arenas were flooded so that gladiators could fight one another on boats, recreating famous naval battles from history. Exotic animals like lions and elephants were brought to Rome. Special fighters, condemned criminals, and prisoners of war were made to fight these wild animals.

▲ Events like this chariot race thrilled Roman spectators.

Emperors or wealthy aristocrats paid for these extravagant games. Expensive events showed off the wealth and power of the person who sponsored them.

Chariot Races One of the most popular events in ancient times was chariot racing. In Rome, chariot races took place at the Circus Maximus. The Circus Maximus was a huge racecourse that could seat as many as 270,000 people.

Races were held far more often than gladiatorial games. Horses pulled charioteers seven times around the course. Cheering fans encouraged their favorite team of charioteers.

READING CHECK **Compare and Contrast** How did Roman entertainments differ from Greek ones?

Roman Government and Law

You have read that the government of the Roman republic influences governments today. Similarly, Roman law shapes the laws of many modern countries.

Government by Citizens The Roman republic's innovative system of government provided its citizens with roles to play. Power was shared by different people with set roles. Officials' time in office was limited to one year to prevent anyone from gaining too much power. The government had three parts—the assemblies, the senate, and the magistrates. Each part had powers that limited the powers of other parts. These ideas were adapted by many later governments.

Roman culture emphasized civic duty. During the republic, free adult Roman men were citizens. Free Roman women were considered citizens, but could not vote or take part in the government. Slaves were not citizens. Male citizens had the right to vote and to a trial. Male citizens had a responsibility to take part in the life of the Roman community.

COMMON MISCONCEPTIONS

Circus The modern word *circus* refers to entertainment by trained acrobats and animals. *Circus* troupes often travel from city to city with their shows. The modern circus has roots in ancient Rome, where *circus* referred to the building in which certain kinds of entertainment took place. Romans used this word because the buildings were round or circular—*circus* means "round" in Latin. Although the entertainment at a Roman *circus* was mainly racing and combat, there were trained animal acts and a parade either before or between the main events.

Roman Government and Law

Discuss Roman ideas about government and law and how they influenced later governments.

Identify Main Ideas? What was the Roman idea of citizenship? *(Citizens had a responsibility to take part in the life of the community.)*

Infer Why might Roman law influence legal systems today in some European countries more than others? *(Sample answer: Roman culture was firmly established in places that were once provinces of Rome and left a legal legacy for later societies there.)*

INTERACTIVE — INTERACTIVE 3-D MODEL

The Pantheon

Display the Interactive 3-D Model: The Pantheon. Slide the cursor to rotate the initial image. Then go to the second screen. Click on each hotspot, and ask for volunteers to read the captions. Ask: Why would the heavier materials be used toward the base? *(Sample answers: to provide stability, to prevent the dome from being too heavy)* Conclude by asking students to answer the questions on the third and fourth screens.

ACTIVE CLASSROOM

Use the Audio Tour strategy. Pair students. Have the first student give the second a verbal "tour" of the Pantheon. Have the second student explain its importance.

ANSWERS

Compare and Contrast *Roman entertainments took place on a more massive scale than Greek entertainments and included violence.*

HSS 6.7.7, 6.7.8, 7.1.1, 7.1.2; ELD.P1.C.10.a

SYNTHESIZE

Assess and Reteach Have students work in discussion groups to complete Lesson Check questions 1–6. Review their responses. If they had any incorrect answers, use the Guiding Questions to discuss the lesson's main ideas, focusing on the ideas they struggled with.

ACTIVE JOURNAL

Writing Workshop Have students complete the Lesson 4 Writing Task in their Active Journals. Students will make a claim about whether Greek city-states or the Roman empire was a greater civilization. As they move through the topic, students will revisit their claim, revising it as needed.

DEMONSTRATE

ASSESSMENT **ONLINE LESSON QUIZ**

Assign the Online Lesson Quiz for this lesson if you haven't already done so. Students will be offered automatic remediation or enrichment based on their score.

DISCUSSION **DISCUSSION BOARD**

Post this question to the class on the Discussion Board:

Categorize List Roman achievements in art, literature, and science. *(Roman artists created mosaics, painted murals, and sculpture. Roman writers produced epics, odes, verses, satire, and biographies. Roman scientists developed ideas about astronomy, geography, optics, natural history, and medicine.)*

▲ Roman laws, like those inscribed on these tablets, influenced later societies.

This included serving in the military (paying their own way) and in Roman courts. Much changed after Rome became an empire. The Roman idea of citizenship, however, remained strong. Many wealthy Romans acted to improve city life. They often paid for the construction of buildings or funded public events out of their own money to improve their city.

What Were the Twelve Tables? In the early years of the Roman republic, there were no written laws. Judges decided what the law was in each case. They based decisions on custom and **tradition**. In the 400s BCE, the Romans wrote down a law code called the Twelve Tables. It set down laws relating to family relations, property, inheritance, and other important issues.

Academic Vocabulary
tradition • *n.*, a custom or practice that is handed down over generations

INTERACTIVE
Influence of Roman Laws

What Was the Influence of Roman Law? Roman law lasted longer than the empire itself. It changed a great deal over the centuries. Over time it developed into a system called civil law. Today, civil law is used in many parts of the world. For example, it is used in some countries that were once Roman provinces, such as France, Spain, and Portugal. It is also used in nations that were once colonies of these countries, including Algeria, Mexico, and Brazil. Even today, one American state uses a legal system partly based on civil law. This is Louisiana, which was founded as a French colony.

READING CHECK **Identify Cause and Effect** How did the Twelve Tables change the Roman legal system?

Lesson Check

HSS 6.7.7, 6.7.8, 7.1.1, 7.1.2; ELD.P1.C.10.a

Practice Vocabulary

1. What are **mosaics** made from?
2. Were Roman **gladiators** usually slaves or usually free men?
3. What is a **Romance language**? Is English one of these?

Critical Thinking and Writing

4. **Compare and Contrast** How are Cicero's writings different from Juvenal's?
5. **Identify Main Ideas** In what ways is the legacy of the Latin language important to scientists today?
6. **Classify and Categorize** In what ways were gladiatorial games entertainment and in what ways were they combat?
7. **Writing Workshop: Introduce a Claim** As you continue to add information to your chart, start to think about which civilization you feel was greater, Greece or Rome. Form your thoughts into a claim, or thesis statement for your argument. Make a list in your Active Journal.

LESSON CHECK

1. small tiles of glass, stone, or pottery **DOK1**
2. They were usually slaves. **DOK1**
3. A Romance language is based on Latin; no, it isn't. **DOK1**
4. Cicero wrote about political issues, while Juvenal wrote satires about Roman life. **DOK3**
5. Scientists today use Latin to name plants and animals. **DOK1**
6. The gladiators were trained both to entertain and to fight. The battles were staged like entertainment, but once they began were still combat. Some gladiators were prisoners of war, which made the games like a battle. **DOK2**
7. Sample answer: The Roman empire was greater because it influenced a wider territory and had greater economic power. **DOK4**

ANSWERS

Identify Cause and Effect *They made it more reliable by writing down the law.*

HSS 7.1.1, 7.1.2, 7.1.3

The Decline of the Roman Empire

GET READY TO READ

START UP

Look at the photograph of the ruins of the Roman Forum. Do you think all civilizations must eventually decline? Why or why not?

GUIDING QUESTIONS

- What factors led to the Roman empire's decline?
- How did Rome's leaders attempt to hold the empire together?
- What happened to the two halves of the empire?

TAKE NOTES

Literacy Skills: Analyze Cause and Effect

Use the graphic organizer in your Active Journal to take notes as you read the lesson.

PRACTICE VOCABULARY

Use the vocabulary activity in your Active Journal to practice the vocabulary words.

Vocabulary		Academic Vocabulary
inflation	mercenary	communication
barbarian	orthodoxy	collapse

For centuries, the Roman empire ruled the Mediterranean region. In the 200s CE, however, Rome began to decline.

Why Did the Pax Romana End?

In 180 CE, the emperor Marcus Aurelius died. He was the last of five powerful emperors who had kept the empire strong and united for many years. His death marks the end of the Pax Romana. Over the next 300 years, the empire slowly declined and finally collapsed.

After 200 CE, the empire began to struggle with continuing problems from outside and within its long borders. The Romans came face to face with the limits of their empire. Without conquering new territories, Rome did not receive the large streams of income it had come to depend upon. Other internal weaknesses included widespread corruption, depending too heavily on slave labor, a general lack of education, and the restless poor in the cities. The divide between rich and poor undermined the Roman traditions of citizenship. Depopulation from epidemics also contributed to the empire's decline.

PRACTICE VOCABULARY

To help students integrate new vocabulary, explain that *inflation* is an overall rise in prices. *Barbarian* is a term the Romans and Greeks used for people they thought were uncivilized. *Mercenaries* are soldiers who fight for pay rather than for their own country. *Orthodoxy* means traditionally accepted religious beliefs. Reinforce the terms during the lesson using the teaching notes.

Point out the academic vocabulary in the lesson margins. Provide sample sentences that clarify meaning.

communication: The Internet is a very fast method of communication.

collapse: As the waves crashed over the sand castle, it collapsed.

HSS 7.1.1, 7.1.2, 7.1.3

The Decline of the Roman Empire

CONNECT

GET READY TO READ

ETEXT — START UP

Project the Start Up Activity. As students enter the classroom and get settled, ask them to examine the photograph of the ruins of the Roman Forum.

Make Generalizations Have students record their answer to the following question: Do you think all civilizations must eventually decline? Why or why not? *(Sample answer: Yes, they all must decline because individual desires for power or wealth cause people to act against the common good.)* Then have them share their generalizations with another student.

Discuss Ask students to volunteer some of the reasons that wars start. *(Sample answers: for control of land, over religious differences, for economic reasons, to overthrow a government)* Explain that in this lesson they will learn about the forces that ended the Pax Romana.

After completing the Start Up activity, project the Lesson Opener or direct students to their textbooks. Preview the lesson by working through the Get Ready to Read items with the class. Remind students to pay close attention to the Guiding Questions as they read the lesson.

ACTIVE JOURNAL

Take Notes Have students use the lesson literacy skills graphic organizer in their Active Journals to take notes as they read the lesson.

Practice Vocabulary Have students complete the activity in their Active Journals to build their vocabulary.

VIDEO — VIDEO

Assign the lesson video as homework.

WORKSHEET **TEACHER RESOURCES**

Have students who need additional support use the following worksheets from the Teacher Resources on the course:

- **Reading Support**
- **English Language Development**
- **Lesson Summary**

INVESTIGATE

Why Did the Pax Romana End?

Discuss how problems such as corruption, lack of education, and the gap between the rich and poor weakened the empire.

Cause and Effect What effect did the death of Marcus Aurelius have on the Roman empire? *(He had kept the empire stable, so his death contributed to the end of the Pax Romana.)*

Draw Conclusions Why was peaceful succession between emperors so important to the empire? *(Without peaceful succession, civil wars broke out.)*

What Was the Imperial Crisis?

Discuss how conflicts over the succession, economic problems, and foreign threats continued to weaken the empire.

Sequence What was the sequence of events during the Imperial Crisis? *(Military leaders fought for power and took and lost control of the empire one after another.)*

ACTIVE JOURNAL

Quest Connection As students read the text, direct them to the Quest Connections pages in their Active Journals. Make sure they understand how economic problems contributed to the empire's decline.

ANSWERS

Identify Main Ideas *Military commanders increasingly challenged emperors for power.*

▲ This eagle clasp was made by Visigoths, or West Goths, around 500 CE. The Visigoths were one group who began to invade the Roman empire during the Imperial Crisis.

The peace of the Roman empire depended on one emperor following another without violence. Starting in the late 100s CE, military commanders, supported by their armies, began to challenge emperors, hoping to become emperor themselves. Civil wars broke out more frequently.

A general named Septimius Severus briefly restored peace. Severus became emperor after winning a civil war. He understood he was emperor because the army supported him, not because the people liked him. His strategy for holding on to power was simple. He said, "Enrich the soldiers, scorn all other men." While many earlier emperors had tried to win over the people and the senate, later emperors cared less for their opinions and focused on the military.

READING CHECK **Identify Main Ideas** By what part of society were many emperors after Marcus Aurelius challenged? Explain.

What Was the Imperial Crisis?

Severus's successors lost power. The empire soon fell again into civil wars. The years 235 to 284 are called the Imperial Crisis. During the crisis, Rome was torn apart by civil wars and even split into pieces. Generals quickly became emperor one after another. Each killed or defected the previous emperor.

Economic Problems Worsen Civil wars created massive economic problems. Wars were expensive. Men who wanted to be emperor needed to convince soldiers to support them. They increased soldiers' pay or gave them bribes. Emperors raised taxes to support these expenses. That hurt common people and the economy.

Emperors also tried to get the money they needed by making coins with less gold or silver and more copper or other less valuable metals. When merchants realized that coins had less precious metal than before, they raised their prices. This caused **inflation**, or a general rise in the cost of goods.

Wars also hurt the economy by making trade dangerous. The trade networks that had made Rome wealthy were disrupted.

Foreign Invaders Threaten the Empire During this period, Rome's foreign enemies became more dangerous. Roman armies were often tied up fighting civil wars. Troops were pulled away from the borders.

As Romans fought other Romans, people from outside the empire took advantage of the bad situation. They raided Roman lands more often.

The empire's size made it hard to defend the borders. Despite good roads, **communication** and travel were much slower than they are

Quest CONNECTIONS

How do you think the economic problems described here contributed to the empire's decline? Record your findings in your Active Journal.

Academic Vocabulary
communication • *n.*, way of passing on information

INTEGRATED ENGLISH LANGUAGE DEVELOPMENT

Expanding and Enriching Ideas
Explain that writers use a variety of verb types and tenses to tell a story, especially one about history. Students should be able to manipulate a verb in simple present, past, and future tenses to describe a onetime event; as well as progressive tenses to describe ongoing, continual happenings; and perfect tenses to talk about things that went on for a while and then ended. Model some verbs in sentences for the class (e.g., *do, did, doing,* or *think, thought, thinking, had thought,* etc.).

Emerging Read the first two paragraphs of the section Why Did the Pax Romana End? Ask students to identify various tenses of verbs in the text, i.e., simple past: "...Marcus Aurelius died."; present: "His death marks..."; and verbs in the progressive tense, such as *continuing* and *conquering*. Point out that the author uses a present tense verb, *marks*, today. Troops could not be moved quickly to fight invaders. It took a long time to bring word of an invasion to the emperor.

In the 200s, the Sassanian empire rose up in Persia. The Sassanian Persians took advantage of Roman civil wars to raid Roman lands. In 260, they captured and executed the Roman emperor Valerian. The Romans could not defeat the Sassanian Persians in the east.

The Germanic Tribes The Romans called the people who lived across the empire's northern borders Germans. They were made up of many different groups. Some were the Franks, Vandals, and Goths.

Like the Persians, the Germans also raided Roman territory more often during the Imperial Crisis. They saw Rome as a rich, easy target. Many Germans also wanted to settle in the empire. Living conditions were often better there.

Romans called the Germans **barbarians**. This is the word Greeks and Romans used for all people who did not share their cultures. They believed that barbarians were savage or uncivilized.

In fact, many Germans adopted parts of Greco-Roman culture. They lived in or near the empire for generations. After Rome became Christian, many Germans converted as well. During and after the Imperial Crisis, tens of thousands of Germans joined the Roman army. By the end of the empire, Germans had become leading Roman generals.

READING CHECK **Identify Cause and Effect** What were some of the factors that made it difficult to defend the Roman empire against foreign invasion?

The Late Empire

The Roman empire did not recover from the Imperial crisis until the late 200s. Diocletian (dy uh KLEE shun), a military leader, became emperor in 284. For the first time in decades, a single man ruled the whole empire. He held on to power for many years.

Diocletian Divides the Empire During his rule, Diocletian tried to make Rome more stable. He reorganized the imperial government. He sent troops to restore peace to frontier regions. Diocletian also persecuted Christians, since many Romans believed that Christians had made the gods angry and that this had caused Rome's problems.

Diocletian's most important contribution was to divide the empire into two halves. He chose a co-emperor to help him manage the empire. Diocletian ruled over the eastern part of the empire, while Maximian ruled in the west.

Constantine Builds a "New Rome" But Diocletian's reforms failed. After his death, military leaders again fought for power. In time, Constantine

▼ Diocletian and his co-emperor Maximian ruled over the two halves of the Roman empire.

Distinguish Which group threatened the eastern part of the empire? *(the Sassanian Persians)*

Distinguish Fact from Opinion What was the Roman opinion of Germans, and was it accurate? *(They viewed Germans as barbarians because they did not adopt Greco-Roman culture. However, many Germans did adopt parts of Greco-Roman culture.)*

The Late Empire

Discuss how Diocletian and Constantine made reforms to try to save the empire.

Infer What can you infer about Diocletian as a leader? Explain. *(Sample: He was focused on results. He took practical steps, such as dividing the empire, to solve pressing problems.)*

Cause and Effect What were the results of the Huns' attack on the empire? *(Romans resisted the Huns in battle, but the Huns pushed more Germanic people into Roman territory.)*

ELD TIP English learners may struggle with mechanics of grammar like verb tenses, particularly if their language of origin has a very different structure for grammar and syntax. Make sure ELL students understand nomenclature for all grammatical terms in an exercise before teaching it.

ANSWERS

Identify Cause and Effect *civil wars, difficulty of defending extensive borders, slow communication and transportation*

ELD.PII.B.3

to describe a past event. Explain that is done in historical texts sometimes.

Expanding Read the first three paragraphs of the section The Late Empire. Point out one simple past verb and one past perfect verb phrase in sentences there. (The sentence that starts with "Diocletian" has two.) Ask students to pick out one simple past verb and another past perfect verb phrase. Have each student write a sentence with a simple past verb and a sentence with a past perfect verb.

Bridging Have student pairs read The Late Empire's first three paragraphs. Ask students to pick out a simple past verb and a past perfect verb phrase. Have students write a sentence with a simple past verb, a sentence with a past perfect verb, and a sentence with a past progressive verb. Give support as needed.

WORKSHEET **TEACHER RESOURCES**

For additional IELD support addressing these standards, have students complete the Lesson ELD activity from the Teacher Resources found on the course.

The West Collapses

Discuss the events that led to the collapse of the Western Roman empire.

Infer Why might the Roman strategy of hiring **mercenaries** to fight German soldiers have failed? *(Sample answer: People who fight for pay might not be as loyal as soldiers who fight for their country.)*

INTERACTIVE **INTERACTVE MAP**

Invasions of the Roman Empire, 378–533 CE

Display the Interactive Map: Invasions of the Roman Empire, 378–533 CE. Read the introduction to the class. Click on each layer, and ask volunteers to read the captions. Ask: In what way were the invasions a chain of related events? *(Sample answer: The migration of the Huns led other Germanic tribes to enter Roman lands for safety.)*

ACTIVE CLASSROOM

Use the Take a Stand strategy. Ask students which most damaged the Roman empire. Have students discuss their reasons.

INTERACTIVE

Invasions of the Roman Empire, 378–533 CE

became emperor. As you read, Constantine converted to Christianity and made it a legal religion in the empire.

In 324, Constantine began work on an impressive new capital for the eastern half of the empire. He built his "New Rome" in what is now Turkey. It was on the site of an old Greek city called Byzantium. After his death, the city was called Constantinople, city of Constantine.

READING CHECK **Sequence** What key emperor ruled soon after Diocletian, and what changes did he make to the empire?

Academic Vocabulary
collapse • *v.*, fall apart, break into pieces

The West Collapses

Rome declined after Constantine's death. Its enemies took advantage of its weakness and caused it to **collapse**.

The Huns Arrive Nomads from the plains of Central Eurasia, known to the Romans as the Huns, triggered a crisis along the empire's northern borders. These fierce mounted warriors attacked Rome and other large empires of the time, such as those in China, Persia, and India.

The Huns' attacks helped cause a decline in trade on the silk roads and other land routes across Eurasia between 300 and 600. The Huns moved into Europe in the 300s. Later, in the 400s, they attacked Rome under their leader Attila. The Romans defeated that invasion at the battle of Châlons. But the arrival of the Huns was still dangerous. Germans fled ahead of them into Roman lands.

The Germans Invade By 376, some Germans had reached the Danube River, the border of the empire. The German Goths crossed the river. They entered the empire, looking for refuge.

GEOGRAPHY SKILLS

The empire's weakened borders made it vulnerable to invasions by tribal groups from across Europe.

1. **Movement** In what direction did most tribes flee from the Huns?
2. **Draw Conclusions** What appears to be the common goal of all the tribes' invasions?

Invasions of the Roman Empire, 378–533 CE

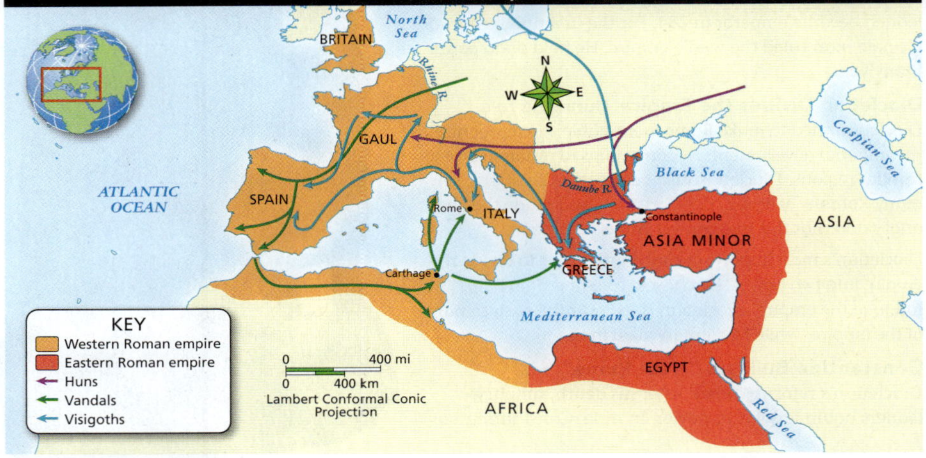

DIFFERENTIATED INSTRUCTION

Special Education Students who are colorblind may have difficulty distinguishing the regions and routes on the map. For these students, provide a grayscale copy of the map they can use.

Below Level Explain to students that the Visigoths shown on the map were a division of the Goths mentioned in the text. The Vandals, Visigoths, and Goths were all Germanic peoples. In contrast, the Huns were from the plains of Central Eurasia.

Advanced Suggest that students research Attila the Hun and then write a rap song or create a comic strip about his life. Allow them to share their work in class.

ANSWERS

Sequence *Constantine; built a capital for eastern empire, made Christianity legal*

Movement *west*

Draw Conclusions *entering Roman lands*

The Romans attacked the Goths and tried to control them, but the Goths defeated them at the battle of Adrianople. Gothic invasions followed. Goths and other Germans crossed into the empire.

Romans tried to pay some tribes of Germans to fight others. They hired **mercenaries**, or soldiers who fight for pay rather than for their country. But these mercenaries were not always loyal. They sometimes turned against the empire. Rome failed to stop the invasions.

The emperor Theodosius took over after the disaster at Adrianople. He was the last person to rule both the eastern and western halves of the Roman empire. Theodosius became a strong supporter of Christian **orthodoxy**, meaning traditional or established religious beliefs. He made Christianity the official Roman religion.

After Theodosius's death, German tribes began to seize whole provinces. In 410, Roman troops pulled out of Britain. They abandoned the province to German invaders. As the western empire fell apart, German generals dominated western Roman emperors from behind the scenes. The emperors lost power.

The Fall of Rome In time, the city of Rome itself was attacked. Goths captured Rome in 410 and looted the city. In 455, the Vandals plundered Rome. Rome never recovered from these attacks. The western Roman empire ended in 476. In that year, a German general named Odoacer deposed, or removed from power, Romulus Augustus, the last western Roman emperor. Odoacer became king of Italy.

As the government of the western Roman empire collapsed, cities came under attack. People moved from the cities to the country for safety. Trade and learning declined. For 500 years in Europe few except the clergy, or church workers, could understand Latin.

The Roman empire survived in a smaller form in the east, however. The eastern Roman empire, called the Byzantine empire, survived for almost 1,000 years after the western empire fell.

READING CHECK **Compare and Contrast** How did the result of foreign invasions differ between the two halves of the empire?

Quick Activity

Odoacer became king of Italy in 476. Did Rome "fall"? Gather evidence in your Active Journal and decide for yourself.

Lesson Check

HSS 7.1.1, 7.1.2, 7.1.3

Practice Vocabulary

1. When **inflation** occurs, do prices rise or fall?
2. Why do **mercenaries** fight?

Critical Thinking and Writing

3. **Identify Cause and Effect** How did civil wars lead to economic problems?
4. **Identify Main Ideas** What changes did Diocletian make to try to solve the Roman empire's succession problem?
5. **Understand Effects** How did the Huns' movement affect the Roman empire?
6. **Writing Workshop: Support a Claim** To be persuasive, you must support your claim with evidence. Record the three best examples of your chosen society's greatness in your Active Journal.

LESSON CHECK

1. Prices rise. **DOK1**
2. Mercenaries are employed to fight and paid for their services. **DOK1**
3. Civil wars forced emperors to raise taxes and devalue currency so that they could pay soldiers. **DOK2**
4. Diocletian split the empire into two halves ruled by senior emperors, and he appointed junior emperors who were supposed to succeed their senior emperors smoothly. **DOK2**
5. As they advanced into Europe, the Huns pushed Germanic people into Roman territory, where they influenced the empire's fate. **DOK2**
6. Answers will vary. Students should choose examples that show the greatness of either Greece or Rome and relate to the categories of size, longevity, economic power, cultural achievements, or influence. **DOK3**

HSS 7.1.1, 7.1.2, 7.1.3

ACTIVE JOURNAL

Quick Activity Divide students into pairs to conduct the Quick Activity in their Active Journals. Students should gather evidence that both supports and contradicts the idea that Rome fell, and then decide.

SYNTHESIZE

Assess and Reteach Have students work in groups and then use a Numbered Heads Together strategy to complete Lesson Check questions 1–5. Review their responses. If they had any incorrect answers, use the Guiding Questions to discuss the lesson's main ideas, focusing on the ideas they struggled with.

ACTIVE JOURNAL

Writing Workshop Have students complete the Lesson 5 Writing Task in their Active Journals. Students will record supporting evidence in their journals. As they move through the topic, students will revisit their evidence, revising or adding to it as needed.

DEMONSTRATE

ASSESSMENT **ONLINE LESSON QUIZ**

Assign the Online Lesson Quiz for this lesson if you haven't done so. Students will be offered automatic remediation or enrichment based on their score.

DISCUSSION **DISCUSSION BOARD**

Post this question to the class on the Discussion Board:

Summarize What factors led to the Roman empire's decline? *(Factors included a decrease in income, corruption, overreliance on slave labor, lack of education, struggles over succession, civil wars, inflation, and foreign threats.)*

ANSWERS

Compare and Contrast *The government of the western Roman empire collapsed. The eastern Roman empire survived the attacks and lasted almost 1,000 years longer.*

HSS 7.1.3; ELA RI.6.1, RH.6.1

The Byzantine Empire Rises

CONNECT

GET READY TO READ

ETEXT **START UP**

Project the Start Up Activity. As students enter the classroom and get settled, ask them to examine the photograph of the Byzantine mosaic. Have them pay special attention to the people in the image.

Infer Have students record their ideas about who the woman in the center of the mosaic might be. Ask them to list the visual details that might be clues to her identity. *(Sample answers: She is an empress or a high noble-woman. She is wearing an elaborate head-dress and jewelry.)* Then have them share their inferences with another student, either in class or through a chat or blog.

Discuss Remind students that in Lesson 4 they learned about Rome being a site of encounter; review what the term means. Explain that Constantinople was also a site of encounter.

After completing the Start Up activity, project the Lesson Opener or direct students to their textbooks. Preview the lesson by working through the Get Ready to Read items with the class. Remind students to pay close attention to the Guiding Questions as they read the lesson.

ACTIVE JOURNAL

Take Notes Have students use the lesson literacy skills graphic organizer in their Active Journals to take notes as they read the lesson.

Practice Vocabulary Have students complete the activity in their Active Journals to build their vocabulary.

VIDEO **VIDEO**

Assign the lesson video as homework.

LESSON 6

HSS 7.1.3; ELA RI.6.1, RH.6.1

The Byzantine Empire Rises

GET READY TO READ

START UP

Examine the image. Who might the woman in the center be? What details give you clues about her identity?

GUIDING QUESTIONS

- In what ways did the Byzantine empire differ from the Roman empire?
- What were Justinian's achievements?
- What caused the Byzantine empire to decline?
- How did the Byzantine empire influence the cultures around it, including early Russia?

TAKE NOTES

Literacy Skills: Use Evidence

Use the graphic organizer in your Active Journal to take notes as you read the lesson.

PRACTICE VOCABULARY

Use the vocabulary activity in your Active Journal to practice the vocabulary words.

Vocabulary		Academic Vocabulary
Byzantine	missionary	successor
strait	Cyrillic alphabet	core
moat		
Greek fire		

By the year 500 CE, the western Roman empire had collapsed, but the eastern Roman empire lasted nearly 1,000 years more.

What Was the New Rome?

During the later years of the Roman empire, power shifted from the western part of the empire to its east and the empire changed. Emperor Constantine built Constantinople as a new capital for the empire.

Who Were the Byzantines? The people of this empire did not call themselves "Byzantines" (BIZ un teens). They thought of themselves as Romans. But their empire was different from the ancient Roman empire. Most of the time, it did not control the city of Rome. Most of the empire's people were Christians, unlike people in the early Roman empire. They also spoke Greek, not Latin.

Because of these and other differences, historians needed a separate name for this empire. They called it the **Byzantine** empire because its capital, Constantinople, was built at a place called Byzantium.

350 Lesson 8.6 • The Byzantine Empire Rises

PRACTICE VOCABULARY

To help students integrate new vocabulary, explain that the *Byzantine* empire was the eastern half of the Roman empire, whose capital was originally called Byzantium. A *strait* is a narrow body of water that cuts through land, while a *moat* is a defensive trench filled with water. *Greek fire* was a chemical mixture that burned and was used as a weapon. A *missionary* tries to convert others to his or her religion. The *Cyrillic alphabet* is used to write Slavic languages. Reinforce the terms during the lesson using the teaching notes.

Point out the academic vocabulary in the lesson margins. Provide sample sentences that clarify meaning.

successor: Harry will take over as successor when the current student body president graduates.

core: Most large groups have a small core of people who do most of the work.

The City's Location Constantine built his new capital on the Bosporus Strait. A **strait** is a narrow body of water that cuts through land, connecting two larger bodies of water. The Bosporus and other waterways link the Black and Mediterranean seas. On one side of the Bosporus is Asia. On the other side is Europe.

Defense and Trade Because of its location, Constantinople was easier to defend than Rome. It was built on a peninsula. The city was surrounded on three sides by water. Two rings of thick walls and a **moat**, or trench filled with water, protected the city on land.

Constantinople's strategic location and good harbors made it an ideal trading center. Merchants brought spices from India, furs from Russia, silk from China, and grain from Egypt. Traders from Western Europe came to Constantinople to buy products from Asia. Trade made Constantinople rich.

READING CHECK **Compare and Contrast** How did the Byzantine empire differ from the western Roman empire?

Who Were Justinian and Theodora?

One great Byzantine emperor was Justinian, who ruled for nearly 40 years, from 527 to 565. He and his wife, Theodora, who is portrayed on the previous page, were a colorful and unusual royal couple.

Justinian was born to a family of peasants. His uncle Justin began his career as an impoverished soldier. He worked his way up through the army to the throne. Justinian was his **successor**. Theodora also came from a lower-class family. Her father worked

Academic Vocabulary

successor • *n.*, person who follows another in an office or role

GEOGRAPHY SKILLS

Constantinople's location made it the political and economic center of the Byzantine empire.

1. **Location** On what continent was Constantinople located?
2. **Synthesize Visual Information** Summarize how Constantinople's location helped protect it.

The Byzantine Empire

WORKSHEET **TEACHER RESOURCES**

Have students who need additional support use the following worksheets from the Teacher Resources on the course:

- **Reading Support**
- **English Language Development**
- **Lesson Summary**

INVESTIGATE

What Was the New Rome?

Discuss how the Byzantine empire prospered because of its location.

Summarize How did power shift during the later years of the Roman empire? *(Power shifted to the eastern part of the empire, and after Rome fell, the Byzantine empire continued.)*

Identify Cause and Effect What might be some geographic reasons that Constantine chose this location for his capital city? *(Constantinople sat on the Bosporus Strait, with access to Europe and Asia, and the ability to control travel between the Black Sea and Mediterranean Sea by water.)*

Who Were Justinian and Theodora?

Discuss how the Byzantine empire changed under the rule of Justinian and Theodora.

Cite Evidence What made Justinian and Theodora unusual rulers? *(They came from families with little wealth or status.)*

DIFFERENTIATED INSTRUCTION

Special Education Read the section Defense and Trade aloud. Allow students to make a diagram or draw a picture of what they think Constantinople's defenses looked like.

Below Level Suggest that students make a T-chart with the headings *Defense* and *Trade*. Have them record details about what gave Constantinople an advantage in each category.

Advanced Suggest that students learn more about the advantages of Constantinople's location and then write a guidebook entry that summarizes those advantages in a paragraph.

ANSWERS

Compare and Contrast *Most of the Byzantine empire's people were Christians, and they spoke Greek, not Latin.*

Location *Europe*

Synthesize Visual Information *Sample: Constantinople was guarded on three sides by water and protected by a system of defensive land and sea walls.*

Distinguish Fact from Opinion Have students read the Primary Source. Ask: Is Justinian's belief that God will help him a fact or an opinion? Explain. *(It is an opinion because it cannot be proven by evidence.)*

Express Problems Clearly What problems were caused by Justinian's wars? *(They left the empire with money problems. After his death, the empire was unable to hold on to all his conquests.)*

Identify Cause and Effect What were some important legacies of Justinian's rule? *(He rebuilt Hagia Sophia. He collected a law code.)*

ELD TIP English learners may struggle with idioms and nicknames that are not literal. Make sure they understand the meaning of the phrase *Greek fire* described in the text.

Analyze Images Stout walls like these protected the Byzantine capital. **Identify Main Ideas** What other natural and constructed features helped defend Constantinople?

as a bear trainer at the circus. When she grew up, she became an actress. Both Justinian and Theodora were intelligent, bold, and ruthless.

Justinian's Conquests Justinian dreamed of restoring Rome's lost empire. He wrote:

Primary Source

"We have good hopes that [God will help us to establish] our empire over the rest of those whom the Romans of old ruled from the boundaries of one ocean to another and then lost by their negligence."

—Justinian

He worked for more than 30 years trying to do just that. Justinian's generals won back lands around the Mediterranean, such as Spain, Italy, and North Africa. He even recaptured the city of Rome. During Justinian's reign, the Byzantine empire reached its greatest size.

Justinian's many wars, however, left the empire with money problems. Disease broke out across the empire as he was trying to complete his conquests. After his death, invaders chipped away at the territory he had gained. The Byzantine empire lost the areas he conquered.

Justinian's Legacy Although Justinian could not restore the Roman empire, he did leave an important legacy. He rebuilt Hagia Sophia, the empire's central church. He also collected a law code. You will read more about Justinian's accomplishments later in this topic.

READING CHECK **Identify Main Ideas** What was Justinian's goal for the Byzantine empire? How did he try to achieve it?

INTEGRATED ENGLISH LANGUAGE DEVELOPMENT

Expanding and Enriching Ideas Tell students that writing can be improved by describing nouns using sensory adjectives (those noting things perceived by the senses, e.g., *hot, cold, bitter, sweet*) or comparative or superlative adjectives (e.g., *better, best brighter, brightest*).

Emerging Read the section Who Were Justinian and Theodora? aloud. Point out adjectives about the two, such as *colorful, intelligent, unusual, bold,* and *ruthless*. Ask students how the words make them feel about Justinian and Theodora.

Expanding Read the section Who Were Justinian and Theodora? aloud. Point out adjectives about the two noted in the Emerging activity. Talk about comparative and superlative adjectives. Have students write sentences describing Justinian and stating

ANSWERS

Identify Main Ideas *Being surrounded by water on three sides helped protect Constantinople as did the construction of two rings of walls and a moat.*

Identify Main Ideas *He wanted to restore Rome's lost empire; he used his armies to conquer land.*

The Shrinking Empire

After the death of Justinian, the Byzantine empire slowly shrank. Over the next 800 years, it declined and fell.

Foreign Invaders Many outside groups took parts of the empire. Germans took back lands in the west that Justinian had conquered. Slavic peoples invaded from the north. The Roman empire's conflicts with the Persians on its eastern frontier continued under the Byzantines. Weakened from the long conflict, the Byzantine and Persian empires were open to attack by Muslim armies in the mid-600s.

Arab Muslim invaders conquered the Sassanian Persian empire, and the Byzantines lost huge territories in Syria, Egypt, and North Africa. The Turks, a Muslim Central Asian people, seized much of modern-day Turkey and other areas from the Byzantines.

However, the Byzantine emperors kept control of the **core** of their empire, modern-day Greece and western Turkey. They also continued to rule Constantinople. Toward the end, they controlled little else. The empire was more like a city-state. The once powerful emperors had to hire Italian ships and soldiers to help defend their capital.

Constantinople's Defenses Invaders often tried to capture the city of Constantinople. Nearly all failed. Those who attacked by land could not get past the city's strong walls. Those who came by sea were stopped by a heavy chain across the city's harbor. The Byzantines also used a secret weapon against ships. This was **Greek fire**, a chemical mixture that burned furiously, even in water. The Byzantines shot Greek fire at enemy ships or against troops attacking the city walls. The result was terrible to see.

The Defenses Fail Still, Constantinople could not hold out forever. In 1204, soldiers from Western Europe called *crusaders* took the city. They looted it and did great damage. You will read more about the crusaders later. The Byzantine empire eventually retook its capital.

The final attack came from the Turkish Ottoman empire. Constantinople's walls were built in an age before gunpowder. The Ottomans used cannons that helped them break down the walls. In 1453, Constantinople fell to the Ottomans. The Byzantine empire was no more.

READING CHECK Compare and Contrast How was the fall of the Byzantine empire similar to the end of Rome?

INTERACTIVE
Interactive Map
The Byzantine Empire

Academic Vocabulary
core • *n.*, center, most important part

▼ The Ottomans used cannons like this one in the siege of Constantinople.

The Shrinking Empire

Discuss how the Byzantine empire lost territory after it reached its greatest expanse under Justinian's rule.

Identify Cause and Effect How did the Byzantine empire change after Justinian's death? *(It got smaller piece by piece.)*

Categorize As the empire lost land over time, who controlled Constantinople? *(Byzantine emperors)*

Contrast How were the people who finally conquered Constantinople different from Byzantines? *(They were Turks, and they were Muslim. Most people in the Byzantine empire were Christians and spoke Greek.)*

INTERACTIVE INTERACTIVE MAP

The Byzantine Empire

Display the Interactive Map: The Byzantine Empire. Click through the map to show the different layers, and ask volunteers to read the captions. Ask: What happened to the Byzantine empire over time? *(It shrank.)* Ask: Which city remained part of the Byzantine empire throughout its changes? *(Constantinople)*

ELD.PII.B.4

whether they think he was a better ruler than his uncle.

Bridging Ask pairs of students to read the section Who Were Justinian and Theodora? together. Have students find all adjectives that describe them. Have them write sentenced about Justinian and Theodora using comparative and superlative adjectives.

WORKSHEET TEACHER RESOURCES

For additional IELD support addressing these standards, have students complete the Lesson ELD activity from the Teacher Resources found on the course.

ACTIVE CLASSROOM

Use the Make Headlines strategy. Have students write a headline that captures the action in the map. Ask: What is the most important thing that you want people to remember about the Byzantine empire? Have students share their headlines with a partner to get feedback.

ANSWERS

Compare and Contrast *Sample answer: Both empires gradually weakened and then fell to foreign invaders.*

The Empire's Influence

Discuss how Byzantine culture spread beyond the empire's borders.

Support Ideas with Evidence Have students read the Primary Source. Ask: How does this quotation support the idea that Byzantine culture was attractive to others? *(Sample answer: The quotation states that visitors thought it had more splendor and beauty than any other culture on earth.)*

Draw Conclusions Considering that Cyril and Methodius were **missionaries**, what might their purpose have been for inventing the **Cyrillic alphabet**? *(Sample answer: They may have wanted to translate the Bible into Slavic languages.)*

Early Russia

Discuss how Byzantine culture influenced early Russia.

Identify Cause and Effect What brought the Kievan Rus into contact with the Byzantines? *(trade)*

Categorize What categories of Russian culture were affected by **Byzantine** culture? *(religion, architecture)*

The Empire's Influence

The politics of the Byzantine empire were often violent. The imperial court was known for its plots and power struggles. Some rulers were blinded or poisoned by rivals. Even so, the Byzantine empire was so wealthy and its culture was so attractive that its influence spread far beyond the empire's borders.

The Lure of Constantinople Byzantine culture spread in two ways. One was by attracting visitors to Constantinople. Merchants came to trade. Scholars came to study. Artists came to work. Visitors were amazed. Byzantine leaders impressed their visitors with elaborate ceremonies, glittering jewels, and rich clothing. One visitor was impressed by Byzantine religious practices.

Primary Source

"We knew not whether we were in heaven or on earth. For on earth there is no such splendour or such beauty . . . We know only that God dwells there among men."

—The Russian Primary Chronicle

The visitors took ideas home with them. Many Eastern Europeans adopted parts of Byzantine culture.

▼ This sample of the Cyrillic alphabet, developed by Byzantine missionaries, is written on birch bark, a tree common in the cold climate of Russia.

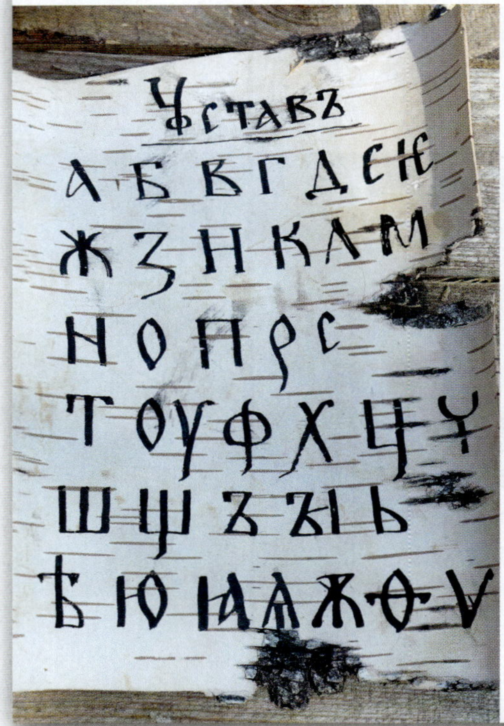

Spreading the Faith Byzantine culture was also spread by Eastern Orthodox missionaries. A **missionary** is someone who tries to convert others to a particular religion. Beginning in the late 800s, Eastern Orthodox missionaries began to travel among non-Christians in southeastern Europe, the home of people called Slavs.

Byzantine missionaries converted many Slavs to Christianity. Many Eastern Europeans practice Eastern Orthodox Christianity today.

The best-known Eastern Orthodox missionaries were two brothers named Cyril and Methodius. They came from a noble family, but gave up their wealth to become priests. They made a major contribution to Slavic culture. Cyril and Methodius invented the **Cyrillic alphabet** (suh RIL ik), which allowed the Slavs to write down their language. It was based on the letters of the Greek alphabet. Today it is used mostly for Slavic languages such as Russian and Bulgarian.

READING CHECK **Classify and Categorize** What are two ways that Byzantine culture spread?

CURRICULUM CONNECTION: VISUAL AND PERFORMING ARTS

Icons In the Eastern Orthodox Church, an icon is an image of a sacred person or event. Some icons are painted; others are mosaics. Icons are not intended to be idols; they are not worshiped as gods. Rather, they are symbolic images that help convey church teaching. Because of this, the artist does not attempt to make a realistic picture. Instead, the artist seeks to portray some theological truth about the person or event being shown. For example, an icon of Mary and the baby Jesus might seek to convey Mary's perfect maternal love for her son.

Early Russia

The early history of Russia was strongly influenced by the Byzantine empire. The first large state in what would become Russia and Ukraine was the Kievan Rus (KEEehvun ROOS). It was based in the city of Kiev and founded by a people called the Rus. The Rus were Vikings, a people from northern Europe. The Rus joined with local Slavs to form a powerful state. They controlled trade routes along Russia's rivers south to Constantinople.

Trade made the Kievan Rus rich. It also brought Russians into contact with the Byzantines. Eventually the rulers of the Rus converted to Eastern Orthodox Christianity.

As in the Byzantine empire, icons were very important to Russian Christians. In addition, Russian architecture was influenced by Byzantine building styles.

Over time, the power of Kiev declined just as the Byzantine empire was also declining. Although the Byzantine empire fell in 1453, in time a new Russian empire developed. The Russian empire considered itself the "third Rome," taking up the legacy of ancient Rome and the Byzantine empire. Russian emperors even took the title *tsar*, the Russian version of *caesar*, a title used by both Roman and Byzantine emperors.

▼ The Golden Gate of Kiev greeted visitors to the city.

READING CHECK **Identify Main Ideas** Who were the Kievan Rus and where did they live?

Lesson Check

HSS 7.1.3; ELD.P1.A.2

Practice Vocabulary

1. What is a **strait**?
2. What was the **Cyrillic alphabet** based on?

Critical Thinking and Writing

3. **Identify Evidence** Why might Justinian be considered a successful emperor? Why might he be considered a failure?
4. **Identify Main Ideas** Which two influences helped shape Byzantine culture?
5. **Infer** What are some ways that a written language helps cultures develop?
6. **Writing Workshop: Distinguish Claims from Opposing Claims** Part of a good argument is countering an opposing claim. Plan out how you will do so in your essay in your Active Journal.

LESSON CHECK

1. A strait is a narrow body of water that connects two large bodies of water and separates two areas of land. **DOK1**
2. the letters of the Greek alphabet **DOK1**
3. Justinian enlarged the empire, rebuilt Hagia Sophia, and wrote important laws. However, he weakened the empire by spending too much money. **DOK3**
4. Byzantine culture blended Greco-Roman traditions with those of Eastern Orthodox Christianity. **DOK2**
5. People can share cultural ideas and traditions across distance and over time more easily. **DOK2**
6. Student answers will vary. Students who have chosen Greece should plan how to refute the idea that the Roman empire was superior and vice versa. **DOK4**

HSS 7.1.3; ELD.P1.A.2

SYNTHESIZE

Assess and Reteach Have students work with a partner to complete Lesson Check questions 1–5. Review their responses. If they had any incorrect answers, use the Guiding Questions to discuss the lesson's main ideas, focusing on the ideas they struggled with.

ACTIVE JOURNAL

Writing Workshop Have students complete the Lesson 6 Writing Task in their Active Journals. Students will identify opposing claims and plan how to counter them. As they move through the topic, students will revisit their ideas, revising them as needed.

DEMONSTRATE

ASSESSMENT **ONLINE LESSON QUIZ**

Assign the Online Lesson Quiz for this lesson if you haven't already done so. Students will be offered automatic remediation or enrichment based on their score.

DISCUSSION **DISCUSSION BOARD**

Post this question to the class on the Discussion Board:

Contrast How did the **Byzantine** empire differ from the Roman empire? *(Its capital was Constantinople, not Rome. It was Christian from the beginning. Its people spoke Greek.)*

ANSWERS

Classify and Categorize *Visitors came to Constantinople and took its culture back with them. Missionaries traveled to spread Byzantine ideas.*

Identify Main Ideas *They were people of Viking and Slavic ancestry who lived in and near the city of Kiev.*

HSS 7.1.2, 7.1.3; Analysis HI.6

Analysis Skills

Conduct a Cost-Benefit Analysis

LEARN

Preview the steps in the student text with students, and then play the video.

VIDEO **21ST CENTURY SKILLS**

Project the Make Decisions video in the 21st Century Skills Tutorial. Use the Quick Reference and Assessment to provide additional instruction on this skill.

PRACTICE

Have students practice the skill using the secondary source on the student page, providing the instruction and then asking students the questions.

As an alternative, you could form students into pairs or groups to perform the activity. Then invite the groups to share their conclusions about economic performance with the class.

ASSESS

To assess this skill, have students reread the subsection titled Economic Problems Worsen in Lesson 5 of this topic. Have them work with a partner to do a cost-benefit analysis on the economic decisions made by the men who wanted to be the emperor.

ANSWERS

1. Constantine had to decide whether to build a new capital in Byzantium.
2. He decided to build a new capital.
3. a. The costs were the expense of new buildings, the need for higher taxes, and the harm such a move might do to the West.
   b. The benefits were that Constantine could fill Byzantium with Christian churches, establish a new senate, and make other changes to government. In addition, the location was good for military defense and trade.
4. Sample answers: Yes, the benefits outweigh the costs because the new capital offers a fresh start. No, the costs outweigh the benefits because Constantinople is too far from the center of the empire and the move will put the western half in too much danger.

HSS 7.1.2, 7.1.3; Analysis HI.6

Conduct a Cost-Benefit Analysis

INTERACTIVE
Make Decisions

Follow these steps to conduct a cost-benefit analysis on the question: Should Emperor Constantine move the capital of the Roman empire?

1. **Identify the decision that has to be made.** A decision often starts with a problem. For example: How can I make my government stronger? How can I improve the economy? In the early 300s, Constantine needed to strengthen the eastern empire. What decision did Constantine have to make?

2. **Identify a possible solution.** Next, consider what steps you could take that might solve your problem. What did Constantine do to solve his problem?

3. **Identify the costs and benefits of your solution.** Ask, "What might this solution cost to put into place?" Then ask, "What are the benefits that might occur?" Be thorough in listing costs and benefits. Review the passage.
   - **a.** What are the costs of moving the capital of the Roman empire from Rome to Byzantium?
   - **b.** What are the benefits of the move?

4. **Compare the benefits to the costs.** A good solution offers benefits that are far greater than the costs. Compare the list of costs to the list of benefits you identified from Step 3. Do the costs of building the new capital outweigh the benefits?

Secondary Source

Constantine was emperor of both the eastern and western Roman empires. At the time, Rome was the capital. Constantine had an important decision to make: should he build a new capital in Byzantium? There were many benefits to doing this. For one thing, Constantine was a Christian. If he built a new city, he could fill it with Christian churches. He could establish a new senate, and make other changes in government. Byzantium was in a good location for military defense and was also an established trade center. There would be costs in moving to Byzantium, though. Constantine would have to impose high taxes to pay for all the new buildings. Moving the center of power to the East would impact the West because it could hurt its economy and weaken its government and defenses.

Constantine decided to build a new capital in Byzantium. This important decision would affect the history of the world.

DIFFERENTIATED INSTRUCTION

Below Level Explain that, generally, a cost-benefit analysis is not a clear-cut mathematical formula. People can examine the same costs and benefits and still come up with different conclusions. One reason for this is that they might have different values. For example, in the case of Constantine's decision, an emperor who valued tradition and low taxes more than he valued government reorganization might have made the decision to keep the capital in Rome.

INTEGRATED ENGLISH LANGUAGE DEVELOPMENT

Expanding Read the secondary source quote. Have students turn to a partner to talk about whether Constantine made a good decision in building a new capital in Byzantium. Ask them to discuss what additional information they would need to create an oral report about Constantine's decision.

LESSON 7

HSS 7.1.3

Byzantine Religion and Culture

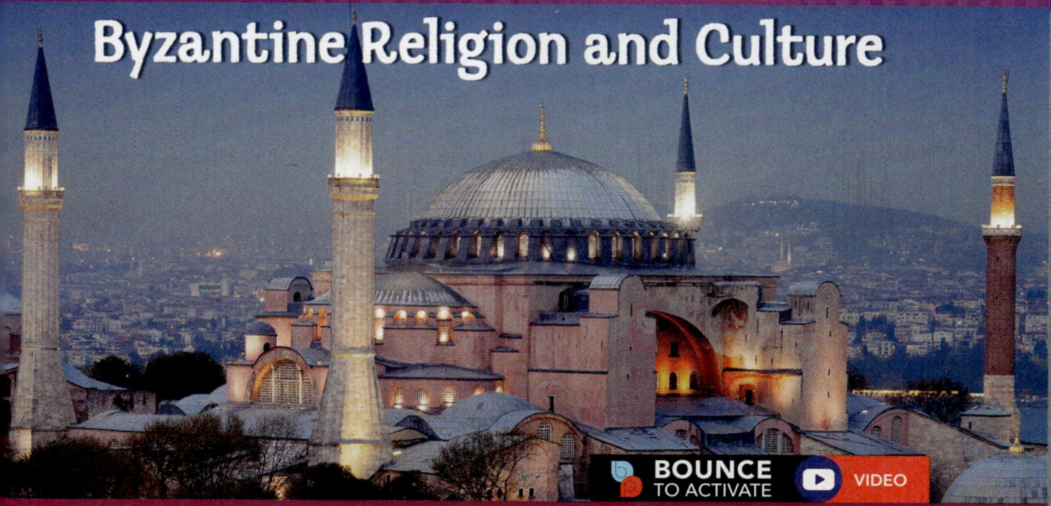

GET READY TO READ

START UP

Look at the photograph of Hagia Sophia in Istanbul (formerly Constantinople), Turkey. What conclusions can you draw about the Byzantine empire based on this building?

GUIDING QUESTIONS

- What differences arose between Christians during this period?
- In what ways did the Eastern Orthodox Church and the Roman Catholic Church differ?
- How was Byzantine culture unique?

TAKE NOTES

Literacy Skills: Compare and Contrast

Use the graphic organizer in your Active Journal to take notes as you read the lesson.

PRACTICE VOCABULARY

Use the vocabulary activity in your Active Journal to practice the vocabulary words.

Vocabulary		Academic Vocabulary
creed	Great Schism	unified
icon	Justinian's Code	discriminated
iconoclast		
pope		

By the late 300s, Christianity was the official religion of the Roman empire. However, various groups of Christians held different religious beliefs and views about important issues. Christianity split into two churches, Roman Catholic and Eastern Orthodox.

Religious Differences

As Christianity grew, Christians began to argue about the beliefs of their faith. These arguments divided Christians into different groups.

The Nicene Creed Early Christians disagreed over exactly who Jesus was. Some argued that he was fully human. Others believed that he was fully divine, or that he was both human and divine. The emperor Constantine called a council of bishops in 325. They met in the city of Nicea (nySEEuh) and adopted a statement of beliefs, or a **creed**, called the Nicene Creed. It said that Jesus was both human and divine. Most Christian groups accepted it. But over time, Eastern and Western Christians came to disagree over the creed's exact wording.

PRACTICE VOCABULARY

To help students integrate new vocabulary, explain that most of these terms are related to religion. A *creed* is a statement of beliefs. An *icon* is a holy image, while an *iconoclast* is someone who opposed and smashed icons. The *pope* is the head of the Roman Catholic Church. The *Great Schism* was the split between the Eastern and Western churches. *Justinian's Code* was a body of law. Reinforce the terms during the lesson using the teaching notes.

Point out the academic vocabulary in the lesson margins. Provide sample sentences that clarify meaning.

unified: Everyone in our school contributed to a unified effort to reduce electricity use.

discriminated: The employer discriminated against women by refusing to promote them to management jobs.

HSS 7.1.3

Byzantine Religion and Culture

CONNECT

GET READY TO READ

ETEXT START UP

Project the Start Up Activity. As students enter the classroom and get settled, ask them to examine the Hagia Sophia, a building that has been a Christian church, a Muslim mosque, and a museum.

Draw Conclusions Have students record a conclusion they can draw about Byzantine culture based on this building. *(Sample answers: It was a sophisticated culture with skilled engineers and sufficient wealth for such large construction projects.)* Then have them share their conclusions with another student.

Discuss Ask students to name some of the different types of Christian denominations they have heard of. Remind them that originally, there was only one church—the Roman Catholic Church. This lesson will explain the first split in the Church.

After completing the Start Up activity, project the Lesson Opener or direct students to their textbooks. Preview the lesson by working through the Get Ready to Read items with the class. Remind students to pay close attention to the Guiding Questions as they read the lesson.

ACTIVE JOURNAL

Take Notes Have students use the lesson literacy skills graphic organizer in their Active Journals to take notes as they read the lesson.

Practice Vocabulary Have students complete the activity in their Active Journals to build their vocabulary.

VIDEO VIDEO

Assign the lesson video as homework.

WORKSHEET **TEACHER RESOURCES**

Have students who need additional support use the following worksheets from the Teacher Resources on the course:

- **Reading Support**
- **English Language Development**
- **Lesson Summary**

INVESTIGATE

Religious Differences

Discuss why Eastern and Western Christians began to have disagreements.

Identify Cause and Effect What was the purpose of adopting the Nicene **Creed**? *(to end the arguments about the nature of Jesus)*

Determine Point of View Which viewpoint about **icons** was held by the **iconoclasts**? Explain. *(They destroyed icons, so they most likely held the view that praying to icons was a form of worshiping objects.)*

Church Organization

Discuss how the early Christian church was organized.

Contrast What was the difference between bishops and patriarchs? *(A bishop oversees all churches in a city; the bishops of the five most important cities were the patriarchs.)*

Distinguish What made the **pope** different from other patriarchs? *(At first he was equal to the other patriarchs; in time, he claimed authority over Christians everywhere.)*

ANSWERS

Identify Implied Main Ideas *Attacks on icons created bitterness between Eastern and Western Christians that lasted even after the issue was resolved.*

Compare and Contrast *Some Christians believe that honoring an icon is a pathway to God. Others believe it is worship of an object, which the Bible forbids.*

Analyze Images This Byzantine icon shows St. Michael holding a sword. **Identify Implied Main Ideas** What role did icons play in creating tension between Eastern and Western Christians?

The Controversy Over Icons

Christians also argued over the use of icons. An **icon** is a holy image, usually a portrait of Jesus or a saint. Many Christians displayed icons in their homes and churches. For them, honoring an icon was a pathway to God. But to others, praying to icons seemed like worshiping objects, which is forbidden in the Bible.

In the 700s, several Byzantine emperors tried to stop icon use. People who opposed icons were called **iconoclasts**, meaning "image-breakers." They went into churches and smashed icons. Violence broke out between iconoclasts and their opponents.

Attacks on icons angered Christians in Western Europe. There, Church leaders saw holy images as a way to teach people about God, not as objects of worship. Eventually, Byzantine emperors who opposed the iconoclasts took power. Today, icons are an important part of worship in Eastern Orthodox churches. But the issue left bitterness between Eastern and Western Christians.

READING CHECK **Compare and Contrast** Describe two important views about the use of icons.

Church Organization

Christianity spread and grew in part because of its strong organization. But Christians came to disagree about who should lead the Church.

Bishops and Patriarchs The most important Christian leaders were called bishops. In early days each church was led by its own bishop. Later, a single bishop took charge of all the churches in a city, aided by members of the community. Eventually, bishops gained authority, or power,over all the churches in a region. The bishops of the five most important cities were known as patriarchs. These cities were Constantinople, Rome, Alexandria, Antioch, and Jerusalem.

The bishops' authority was based on a tradition known as apostolic succession. According to this tradition, Jesus gave authority over his Church to the original apostles. They then passed this authority down to each generation of bishops.

The Power of the Pope At first, the five patriarchs were equal in authority. Over time, however, the bishop of Rome claimed authority over Christians everywhere. He began to be called **pope**, which means father, or head, of the Church.

INTEGRATED ENGLISH LANGUAGE DEVELOPMENT

Expanding and Enriching Ideas Explain that an adverb tells when, where, how, in what manner, or how much an action is performed. An adverb describes a verb, an adjective, or another adverb: "She ran *today*." "She ran *very* quickly." An adverb can also be made up of more than one word: "She ran *while I was sitting down*"; or "She ran *more swiftly than I could*."

Emerging Read the first two sentences in the section A Unique Culture. Point out the adverbs in the first two sentences: *previously* and *strongly*. Have students write original sentences with both of those two words.

Expanding Read the section A Unique Culture. Ask students to look for adverbs in the text. Have them write original sentences with one of the adverbs or an adverbial phrase using

The popes based their claim on the idea that they were the successors to the apostle Peter. They argued that Jesus had made Peter head of the Church. According to tradition, Peter had traveled to Rome to become its first bishop. After his death, his authority as head of the Church passed on to the bishops who followed him. The popes pointed to a passage in the Bible to back up their case. Here, Jesus spoke to Peter, whose name means "rock" in Greek.

Primary Source

"You are Peter, and on this rock I will build my church. . . . I will give you the keys of the kingdom of heaven, and whatever you bind on earth shall be bound in heaven."

—Matthew 16:18–19

Did you know?

There are at least 233 million Eastern Orthodox Christians in the world.

Eastern patriarchs and the Byzantine emperors rejected this view of the pope. Eastern emperors wanted to be in charge of the church in their empire. If the pope was the head of the Church, this would take away from their authority.

READING CHECK **Identify Main Ideas** How did Eastern and Western Christians feel about who should lead the Church?

What Was the Great Schism?

Over time, differences between the Eastern and Western churches grew. Two religious traditions developed. In 1054, these two traditions formally split. The split is known as the **Great Schism** (SIZ um). The word *schism* comes from a Greek word meaning split, or division.

Two Christian Churches The Eastern branch of the church came to be called the Eastern Orthodox Church. *Orthodox* means following established beliefs.

In the Eastern Orthodox tradition, the Byzantine emperor was head of the Church. Patriarchs handled the churches' day-to-day affairs. They were all equals, though the Patriarch of Constantinople was considered first among equals. The Byzantine emperor had the power to remove a patriarch if he chose to.

Analyze Charts The chart shows key differences between two branches of Christianity. **Understand Effects** Which church has divided authority? What effects might this fact have on church policies?

The Christian Church Splits

Roman Catholic Church	Eastern Orthodox Church
• The pope headed the Church.	• The Byzantine emperor headed the Church.
• The pope was the highest Church official.	• All patriarchs had equal authority in their regions.
• Rituals and teaching were in Latin.	• Rituals and teaching were in Greek.
• Priests could not marry.	• Priests could marry.

Cite Evidence What evidence did the popes use to support their claim to be the head of all the Church? *(They used a Bible verse in which Jesus said Peter was the rock on which he would build the church and the fact that Peter had been the first bishop of Rome.)*

Categorize Do you think the Byzantine emperors' objection to the authority of the pope was mostly religious or political? Explain. *(Sample answer: They wanted to be in charge of the church in their empire so they would not have to share authority with anyone. That is a political motivation.)*

ELD TIP Illustrations can help English learners absorb a story better. Have ELL students look at the image of religious icon next to the section The Controversy Over Icons, to help them understand the idea of an icon better.

What Was the Great Schism?

Discuss how the Eastern and Western churches formally split in 1054.

Identify Central Ideas After the Great Schism, who was the head of the Eastern Orthodox Church? *(the Byzantine emperor)*

Support Ideas with Evidence Point out that the term *Catholic* means "universal." Ask: Was the Roman Catholic Church universal? Support your answer with evidence. *(Sample answer: No, it was not because many Christians belonged to the Eastern Orthodox Church.)*

ELD.PII.B.5

one of those words. Provide support as necessary.

Bridging Have students work in pairs. Have them read the section A Unique Culture. Tell them to look for adverbs in the text. Have them write original sentences with adverbial phrases using one of those words. Provide support as necessary.

WORKSHEET **TEACHER RESOURCES**

For additional IELD support addressing these standards, have students complete the Lesson ELD activity from the Teacher Resources found on the course.

ANSWERS

Identify Main Ideas *Western Christians accepted the idea that the bishop or patriarch of Rome would be pope. Eastern Christians believed all patriarchs were equal.*

Understand Effects *The Eastern Orthodox Church has divided authority because all the patriarchs are equal. This might make it harder to decide on uniform church policies or to make sure they are applied equally in all regions.*

A Unique Culture

Discuss how the Byzantines developed a culture that differed from Western culture.

Identify Cause and Effect How did Byzantine architecture influence houses of worship in Europe and the Middle East? *(Many houses of worship copied the dome on the Hagia Sophia.)*

Express Problems Clearly What problem was Justinian trying to solve by compiling **Justinian's Code**? *(He inherited a jumble of local laws, imperial decrees, and judge's decisions. He wanted an orderly system of law.)*

INTERACTIVE **INTERACTIVE GALLERY**

Hagia Sophia

Display the Interactive Gallery: Hagia Sophia. Click on the instructions and read them aloud. Ask: What are Muslim features of the Hagia Sophia? *(Sample answer: the calligraphy and the minarets)* Ask: What are Christian features? *(Sample answer: the mosaic of the Virgin and Child)*

ACTIVE CLASSROOM

Use the Quickdraw strategy. Allow students a minute to share what they learned about the Hagia Sophia through drawings.

ANSWERS

Identify Main Ideas *The biggest issue was disagreement over whether the pope or the emperor had the highest authority.*

Cite Evidence *Sample answers: Islamic calligraphy, Christian images*

The Western tradition became known as the Roman Catholic Church. *Roman* refers to the fact that it was based in Rome. *Catholic* means universal, or concerned with all people. This church shaped the culture of Western Europe.

The pope was the head of the Roman Catholic Church. As the spiritual leader of the Church, the pope claimed authority over all secular, or nonreligious, rulers. He did not take orders from any secular ruler, including the Byzantine emperor. This was the most important issue dividing the Eastern Orthodox and Roman Catholic churches.

Different Traditions There were other differences between the two churches. The language of the Eastern Orthodox Church was Greek. The language of the Roman Catholic Church was Latin. Orthodox priests were allowed to be married. Catholic priests were not. The churches also differed in some rituals.

INTERACTIVE
Hagia Sophia

Today there is no Byzantine emperor. Eastern Orthodox churches in different countries are led by their own patriarchs. Eastern Orthodox Christians still do not recognize the pope's power. Since 1054, the two churches have been separate. Recently, relations between the churches have improved, but the division remains.

READING CHECK **Identify Main Ideas** What was the most important issue contributing to the Great Schism?

A Unique Culture

The people of the Byzantine empire maintained some of the Greco-Roman traditions you read about previously. But their society was also strongly shaped by Eastern Orthodox Christianity. The result was a cultural blend that was unique, or distinct from other cultures.

Architecture and Literature Byzantine civilization produced its own styles of architecture. The most famous example is Justinian's church, Hagia Sophia. Similar domes can be seen on churches and other houses of worship in southern Europe and the Middle East.

Analyze Images In its almost 1,500-year history, Hagia Sophia has been a Christian church, a mosque, and, today, a museum. **Cite Evidence** What details can you find in the photograph of Hagia Sophia's changing roles in the past?

DIFFERENTIATED INSTRUCTION

Special Education Review that a tradition is a customary action or behavior. Allow students to describe traditions they share with their family or friends before moving on to the section Different Traditions in the text.

Below Level Suggest that students work with a partner to create a Venn diagram comparing the Roman Catholic and Eastern Orthodox churches. Because the text focuses on differences, you may need to conduct a class discussion to highlight similarities between the churches; for example, they are both Christian, they both have priests, and they both use the Bible.

Advanced Suggest that students research the difference between the Roman Catholic Church's calendar of religious holidays and that of the Eastern Orthodox Church. They may present their findings to the class in a poster or a brief oral presentation.

Byzantine librarians and monks copied and preserved the manuscripts, or handwritten documents, of ancient Greece and Rome. Many of these works would have been lost if Byzantine librarians and monks had not preserved them.

Organizing Roman Law You have read about Roman law and its later influence. It was preserved and updated in the Byzantine empire. This effort was largely the work of the emperor Justinian.

▲ A page of Justinian's Code from the 1400s

Justinian found the vast legal legacy he inherited from Rome to be a confusing jumble of local laws, imperial decrees, and judges' decisions. He ordered a group of lawyers to organize this material. He had them produce a **unified** code, or systematic body of law. His code brought order to the system of Roman law. **Justinian's Code** was published in 529. It gave great power to the emperor. The code said "that which seems good to the emperor has the force of law."

The code reveals ways people were treated in the empire. For example, the code **discriminated** against Jews and other non-Christians. On the other hand, it allowed women to inherit property and protected some individual rights.

Academic Vocabulary
unified • *adj.*, joined together as a single whole
discriminate • *v.*, treat some people differently or worse

READING CHECK **Analyze Cause and Effect** Why did Byzantine lawyers try to organize a new system of laws?

Lesson Check

HSS 7.1.3; ELD.P1.A.2

Practice Vocabulary

1. Why did **iconoclasts** oppose the use of icons?
2. Which city has the **pope** for its bishop?

Critical Thinking and Writing

3. **Compare and Contrast** List three differences between the Roman Catholic and Eastern Orthodox churches.
4. **Summarize** the difference in leadership between the Eastern and Western churches.
5. **Identify Main Ideas** Which two influences helped shape Byzantine culture?
6. **Writing Workshop: Shape Tone** In your essay, take a firm but tactful tone. Answer opposing arguments effectively and respectfully.

HSS 7.1.3; ELD.P1.A.2

SYNTHESIZE

Assess and Reteach Have students use a Think-Pair-Share strategy to complete Lesson Check questions 1–5. Review their responses. If they had any incorrect answers, use the Guiding Questions to discuss the lesson's main ideas, focusing on the ideas they struggled with.

ACTIVE JOURNAL

Writing Workshop Have students complete the Lesson 7 Writing Task in their Active Journals working on tone.

DEMONSTRATE

ASSESSMENT **ONLINE LESSON QUIZ**

Assign the Online Lesson Quiz. Students will be offered automatic remediation or enrichment based on their score.

DISCUSSION **DISCUSSION BOARD**

Post this question to the class on the Discussion Board:

Summarize What differences arose between Christians during this period? *(Christians disagreed about the exact nature of Jesus, about whether it was appropriate to use icons, and over which leaders had the most authority over Christians and other Church officials.)*

ANSWERS

Analyze Cause and Effect *to increase order in the legal system*

LESSON CHECK

1. They believed that prayer to icons was forbidden by the Bible as worship of objects. **DOK1**
2. Rome **DOK1**
3. Sample answer: language of worship, ability for priests to marry, acceptance of icon worship, who is head of church and is highest church official, equality of patriarchs and the pope **DOK3**
4. In the Eastern Orthodox tradition, the Byzantine emperor was head of the church and the patriarch of Constantinople was the highest church official. In the Western tradition, both of these roles belonged to the pope. **DOK2**
5. Byzantine culture blended Greco-Roman traditions with those of Eastern Orthodox. **DOK1**
6. Student answers will vary. Their essays should display a firm tone by stating their conclusions using positive, definitive language. However, they should be tactful and avoid using overly critical or disrespectful descriptions of the opposing view. **DOK4**

HSS 6.7.3, 6.7.4, 6.7.5, 6.7.6, 6.7.7, 6.7.8, 7.1.1, 7.1.2, 7.1.3; ELA W.6.1, WHST.6.1; ELD P1.A.2

Review and Assessment

VISUAL REVIEW

Direct students' attention to the "Pressures on the Roman Empire" cause-and-effect chart. Ask volunteers to read the entries for the cause boxes.

Direct students' attention to the Venn diagram comparing the Roman and Byzantine empires. As a class, review the two empires' similarities and differences.

READING REVIEW

WORKSHEET **TEACHER RESOURCES**

Have students who need additional support read the Lesson Summaries available in Teacher Resources on the Realize course.

GAMES **TOPIC MINI-GAMES**

For additional vocabulary practice, students can go online to access the Topic Mini-Games in Realize.

TOPIC 8

Review and Assessment

VISUAL REVIEW

Pressures on the Roman Empire

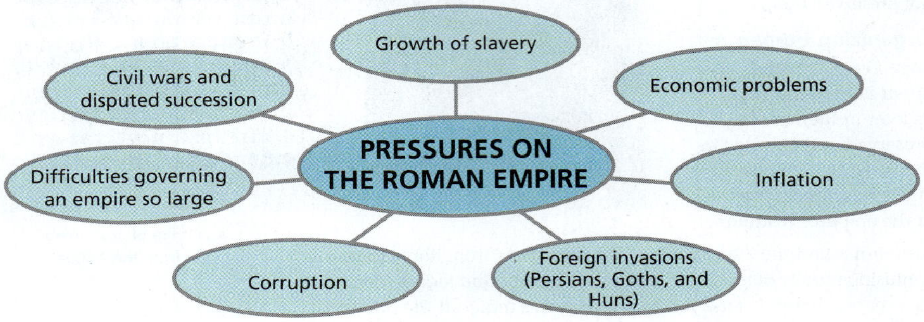

Comparing the Roman and Byzantine Empires

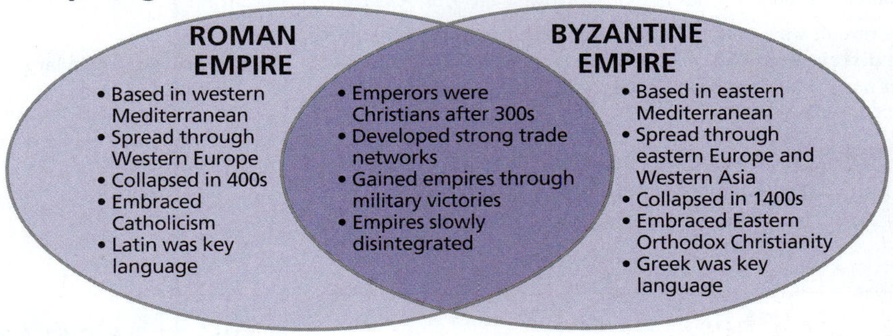

READING REVIEW

Use the Take Notes and Practice Vocabulary activities in your Active Journal to review the topic.

INTERACTIVE

Practice vocabulary using the Topic Mini-Games.

Quest FINDINGS

Hold your discussion on Rome's fall and whether it could have been prevented. Get help for your discussion by using the evidence you collected in your Active Journal.

Quest FINDINGS

Prepare Your Position

Have students complete their Topic Quests by using the notes in their Active Journals to prepare for and participate in a discussion of the question, Could the fall of Rome have been prevented? Remind students to use their knowledge of forces that weakened the empire and attempts to strengthen the empire to make convincing arguments. **DOK4**

ANSWERS

1. the Roman Peace **DOK1**
2. Satire ridicules its subject. **DOK2**
3. Sample answer: Ethics would be useful in knowing not to lie to friends and choosing to finish a job without taking shortcuts. **DOK3**
4. Emperors devalued the currency to get money for fighting wars. This meant the money was worth less, which led merchants to raise prices. **DOK2**
5. Constantine made Christianity legal in the Roman empire and founded a new capital for the eastern empire in Constantinople. **DOK2**
6. Constantinople was at a crossroads for traders traveling by land to and from Asia and Europe, and for traders traveling by sea between the Black Sea and the Mediterranean Sea. **DOK1**

HSS 6.7.3, 6.7.4, 6.7.5, 6.7.6, 6.7.7, 6.7.8, 7.1.1, 7.1.2, 7.1.3; ELA W.6.1, WHST.6.1; ELD.P1.A.2

ASSESSMENT

Vocabulary and Key Ideas

1. **Recall** What do the words **"Pax Romana"** mean in Latin?
2. **Check Understanding** What is the purpose of **satire**?
3. **Identify** List two everyday situations in which a person would have to think about **ethics**.
4. **Describe** What caused **inflation** in the Roman empire?
5. **Recall** What are two important ways in which Constantine changed the Roman empire?
6. **Identify Main Ideas** What made Constantinople a good location for a new city?
7. **Check Understanding** What were the most important accomplishments of Emperor Justinian?
8. **Identify Supporting Details** In Byzantine times, what aspects of the pope's powers did Roman Catholic and Eastern Orthodox Christians disagree about?

Critical Thinking and Writing

9. **Compare and Contrast** How did the government of the Roman empire differ from that of the republic?
10. **Infer** In what ways did the Roman government help the spread of Christianity, despite its persecution of Christians?
11. **Identify Cause and Effect** In what way did civil wars lead to economic problems?
12. **Infer** How did the appeal of Constantinople help spread Byzantine culture?
13. **Revisit the Essential Question** What forces brought about changes in the Roman empire?
14. **Writer's Workshop: Write Arguments** Using the notes you made in your Active Journal, write an essay that presents and supports your argument on this question: Which was greater, the Greek city-states or the Roman empire? Keep in mind the following factors: size, longevity, economic power, cultural achievements, and influence.

Analyze Primary Sources

15. Use your knowledge of the Byzantine empire to answer the question.
Why did Justinian create his law code?
    A. to gain more power
    B. to make Roman law less confusing
    C. to help him recapture the western Roman empire
    D. to support Eastern Orthodox Christianity

"We have found the entire arrangement of the law which has come down to us ... to be so confused that it ... is not within the grasp of human capacity; and hence We [worked to] make them more easily understood."
—*Justinian's Code*

Analyze Maps

Use the map at right to answer the following questions.

16. Which letter represents Constantinople? Who made this the capital of an empire? Why?
17. Which letter represents Jerusalem? This city was the capital of which Roman province?
18. Which letter represents Rome? What was the Pax Romana?

▼ **Roman and Byzantine Empires**

7. Justinian rebuilt Hagia Sophia and organized Byzantine law into Justinian's Code. **DOK2**
8. Roman Catholics believed that the pope had authority over all Christians and was not subject to political authority. Eastern Orthodox Christians believed that the pope was equal in authority to other patriarchs and that the church was subject to the political authority of the Byzantine emperor. **DOK2**
9. During the empire, the senate lost most of the power it had under the republic, and the empire was ruled by one powerful individual, the emperor. **DOK3**
10. The Roman government helped spread Christianity by making travel easier on land by building good roads, and on sea by fighting piracy. This made it easier for Christians to move about and spread their message. **DOK3**
11. Civil wars forced emperors to raise taxes and devalue currency so that they could pay soldiers. **DOK2**
12. Visitors traveled to see the wonders of Constantinople. They carried ideas and cultural features with them back to their home cultures. **DOK2**
13. Sample answer: Civil and political unrest and economic instability often lead to governmental upheaval and change. Military pressure on the empire's borders led to instability in the provinces and eventually, in Italy itself. This instability led to the division of the empire to make it easier to govern and maintain stability. Declining financial resources and political corruption undermined citizenship and brought about a decline in civic life and ethics. **DOK2**
14. Answers will vary. Student essays should make a clear argument that either Greek or Roman civilization was greater, and the argument should be supported with evidence that pertains to size, longevity, economic power, cultural achievements, and influence. The essay should be written with a firm but tactful tone, and it should have an effective conclusion that sums up the main ideas. **DOK4**
15. B **DOK2**
16. B; the emperor Constantine founded the city to be the new capital of the Eastern Roman Empire. **DOK1**
17. C; Judea **DOK1**
18. A; a 200-year period of peace and prosperity **DOK1**

ASSESSMENT **TOPIC TEST**

For summative assessment, assign the Topic Test in Realize.

California: Political

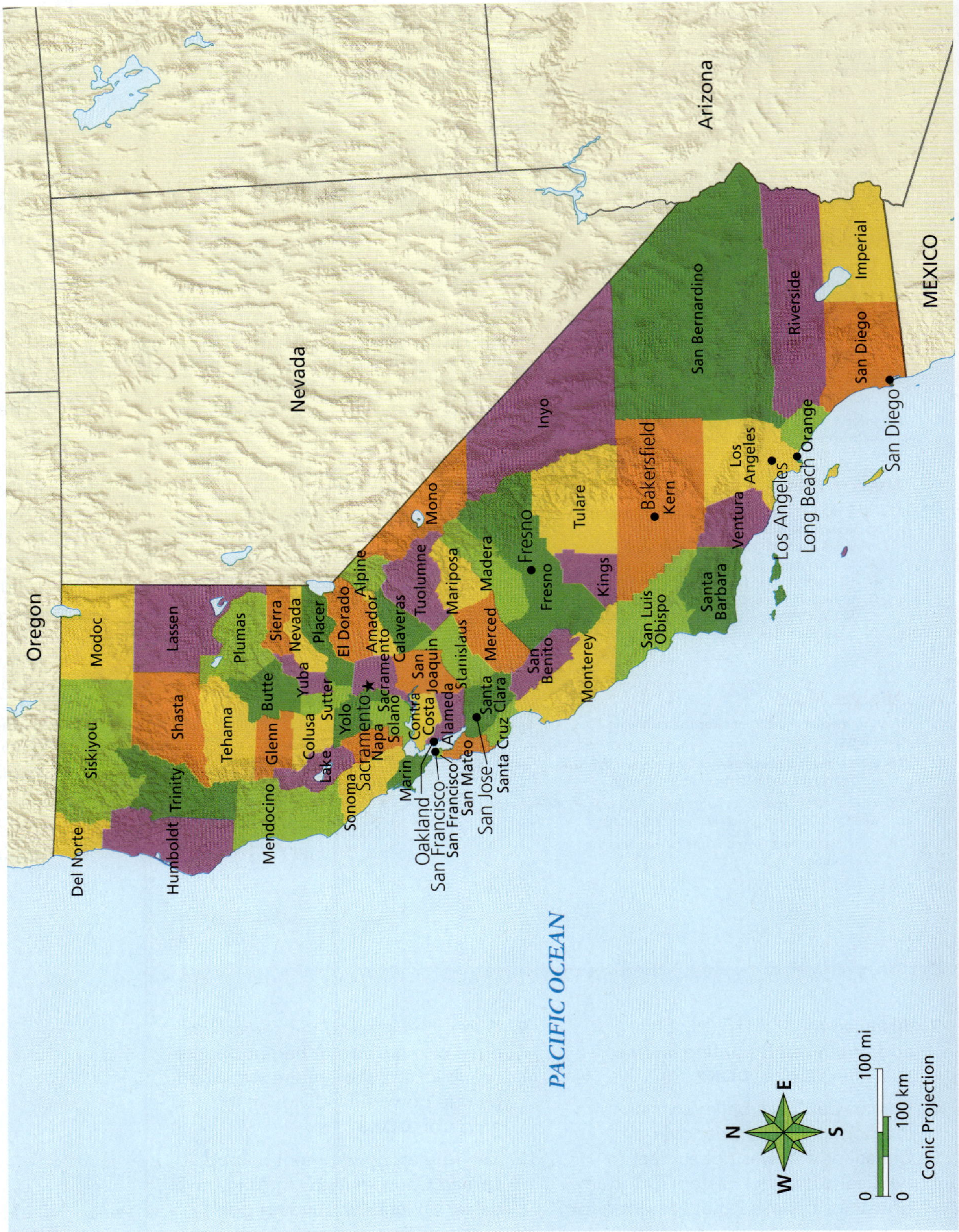

364 Atlas

California: Physical

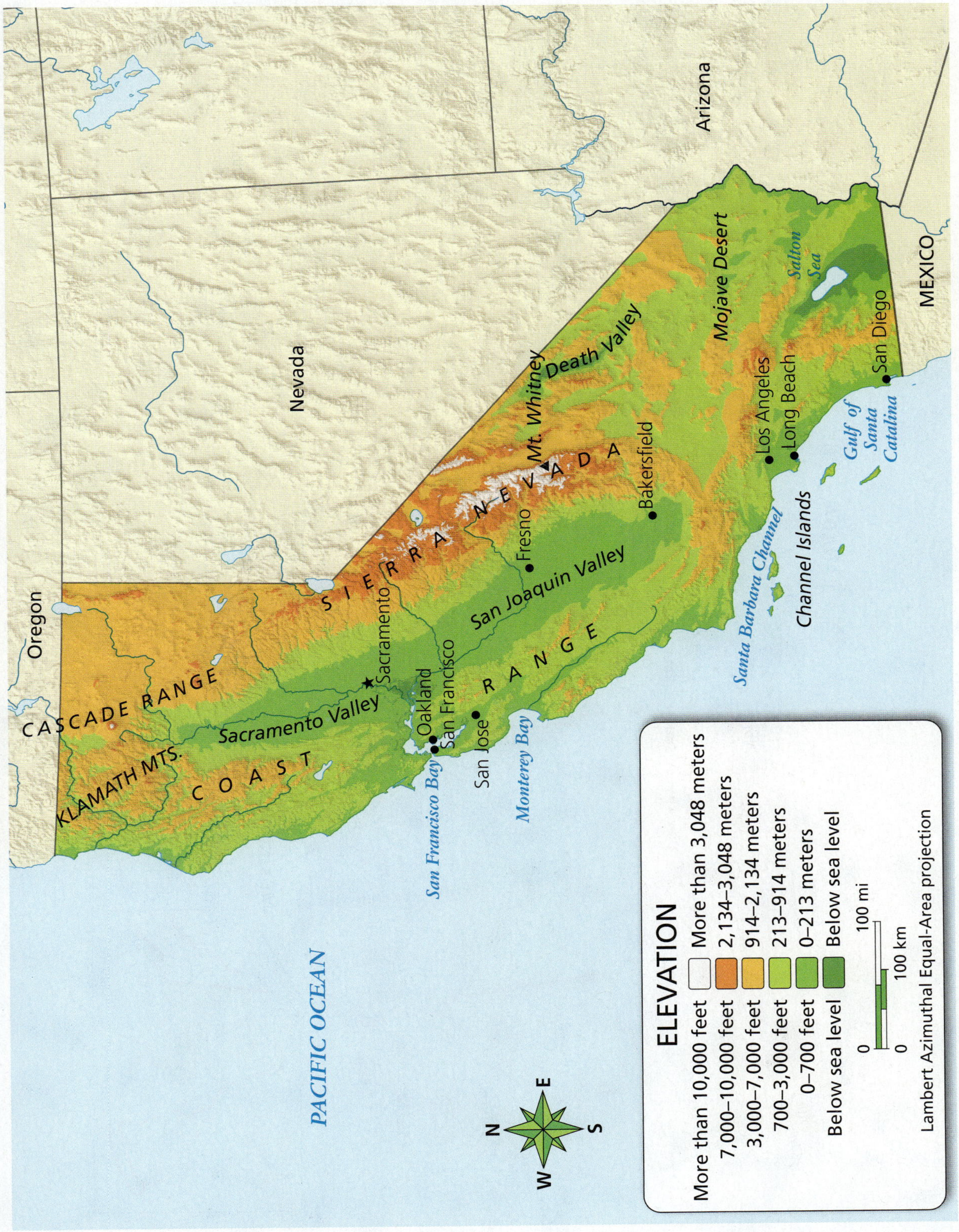

Atlas 365

US: Political

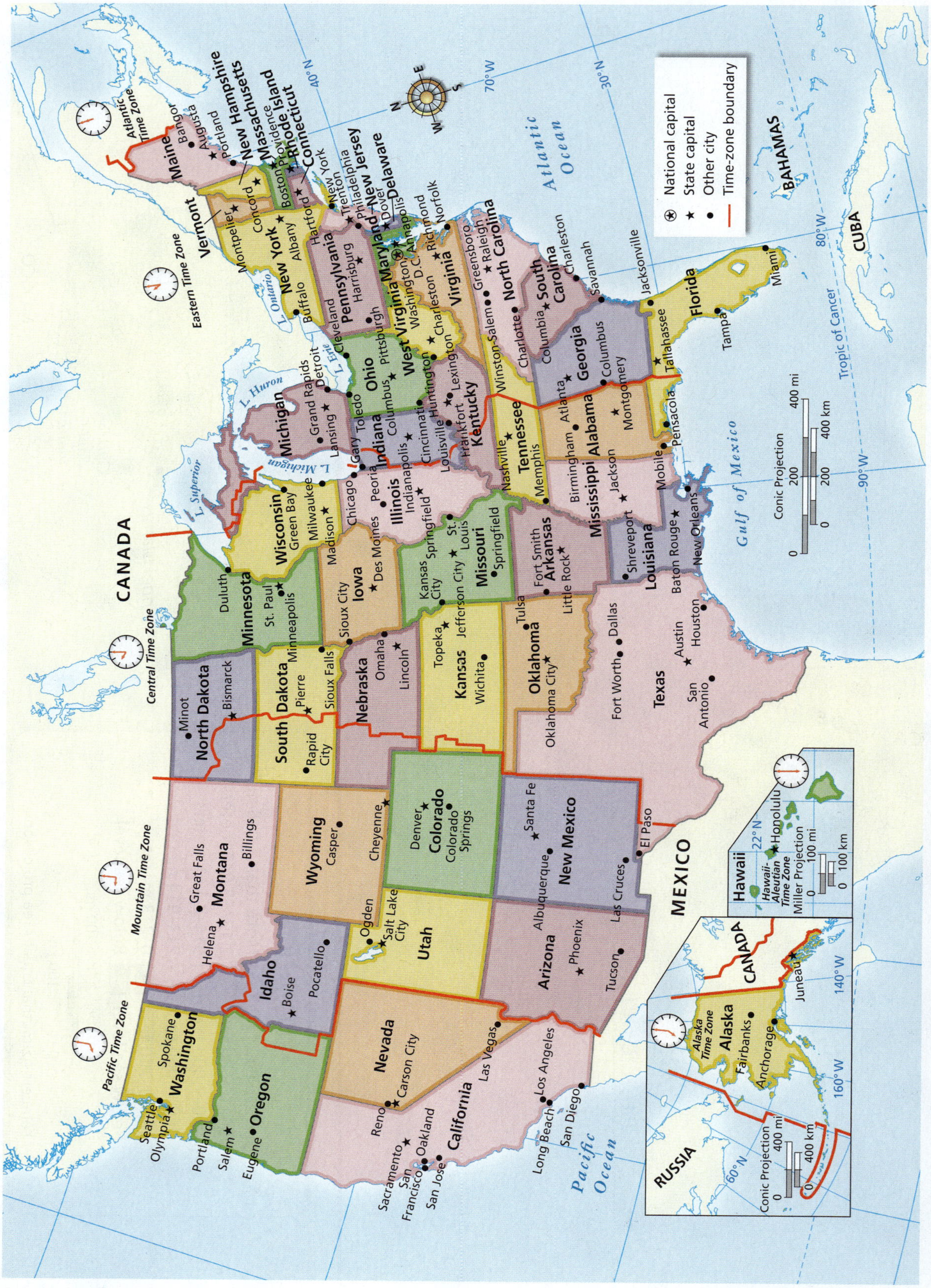

366 Atlas

US: Physical

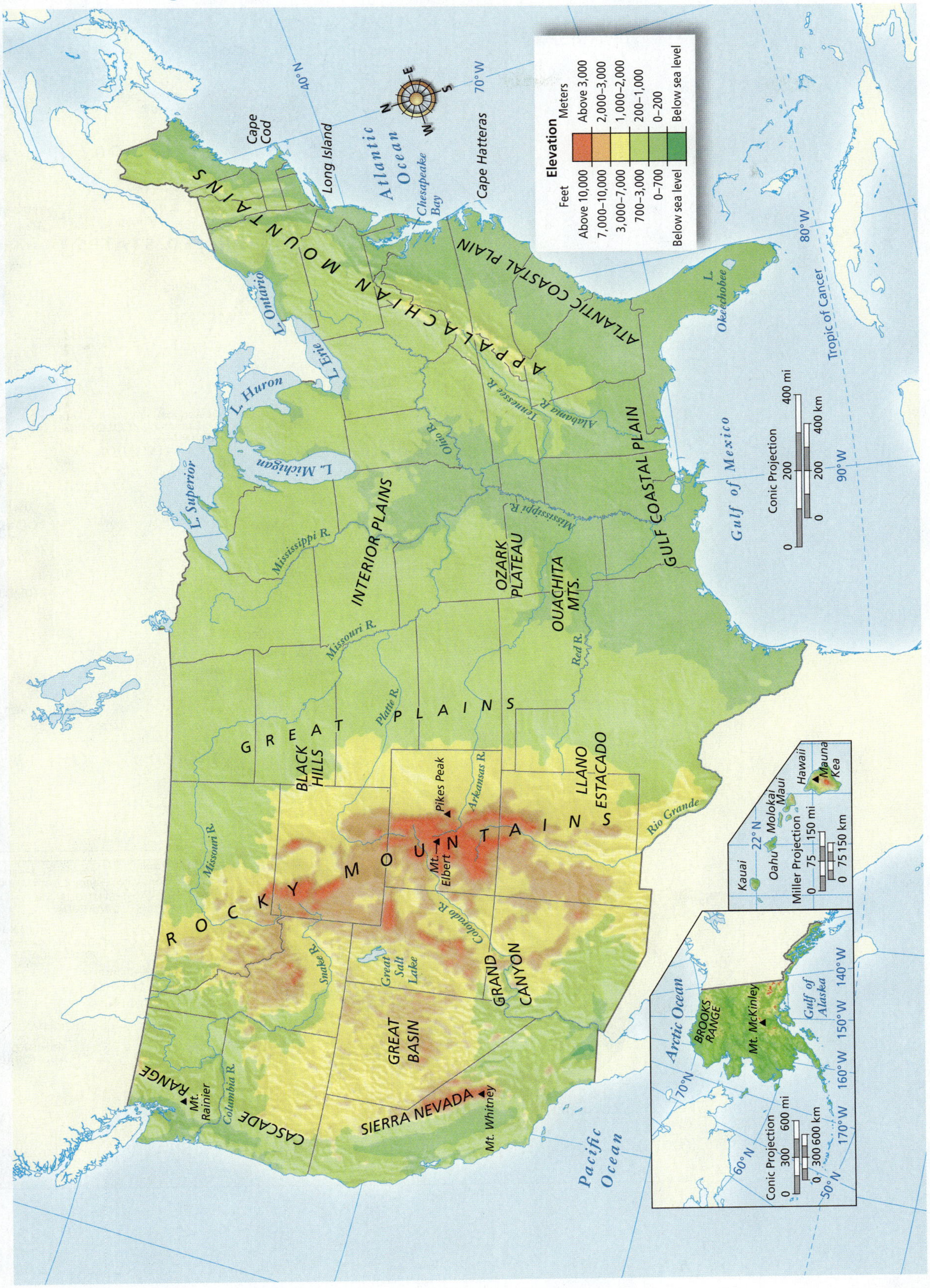

Atlas 367

The World: Political

368 Atlas

Arctic Ocean
Arctic Circle
RUSSIA
EUROPE
ASIA
KAZAKHSTAN
MONGOLIA
GEORGIA
AZER.
ARMENIA
UZBEK.
TURKMEN.
KYRGYZSTAN
TAJIKISTAN
Tehran
IRAQ
IRAN
AFGHAN.
ISRAEL
JORDAN
KUWAIT
BAHRAIN
QATAR
PAKISTAN
Karachi
U.A.E.
OMAN
SAUDI ARABIA
YEMEN
Cairo
EGYPT
LIBYA
ALGERIA
AFRICA
CHAD
SUDAN
ERITREA
DJIBOUTI
Addis Ababa
ETHIOPIA
SOMALIA
SOUTH SUDAN
CEN. AFR. REP.
CAMEROON
GABON
CONGO
DEM. REP. OF THE CONGO
UGANDA
KENYA
RWANDA
BURUNDI
TANZANIA
SÃO TOMÉ AND PRÍNCIPE
ANGOLA
MALAWI
ZAMBIA
MOZAMBIQUE
ZIMBABWE
BOTSWANA
NAMIBIA
SWAZILAND
SOUTH AFRICA
LESOTHO
Cape Town
SEYCHELLES
COMOROS
MADAGASCAR
MAURITIUS
MALDIVES
NEPAL
BHUTAN
New Delhi
INDIA
BANGLADESH
Mumbai
SRI LANKA
CHINA
Beijing
NORTH KOREA
Seoul
SOUTH KOREA
Shanghai
JAPAN
Tokyo
MYANMAR (BURMA)
LAOS
TAIWAN (Claimed by China)
Hong Kong
THAILAND
Bangkok
VIETNAM
CAMBODIA
PHILIPPINES
BRUNEI
MALAYSIA
SINGAPORE
INDONESIA
Jakarta
TIMOR-LESTE
PAPUA NEW GUINEA
SOLOMON ISLANDS
TUVALU
NAURU
KIRIBATI
MARSHALL ISLANDS
FEDERATED STATES OF MICRONESIA
OCEANIA
FIJI ISLANDS
VANUATU
New Caledonia (France)
AUSTRALIA
Sydney
NEW ZEALAND
Pacific Ocean
Indian Ocean
Atlantic Ocean
Southern Ocean
ANTARCTICA
N
E
S
W
Robinson Projection
1,000
2,000 mi
1,000
2,000 km
0°
20°E
40°E
60°E
80°E
100°E
120°E
140°E
160°E
80°N
60°N
40°N
20°N
0°
20°S
40°S
60°S

Western Sahara (Morocco)
ALGERIA
MAURITANIA
MALI
NIGER
SENEGAL
GAMBIA
GUINEA-BISSAU
GUINEA
BURKINA FASO
BENIN
SIERRA LEONE
TOGO
CÔTE D'IVOIRE
GHANA
NIGERIA
LIBERIA
Lagos
Atlantic Ocean
Gulf of Guinea
EQUATORIAL GUINEA
20°W
0°
N
E
S
W
Azimuthal Equidistant Projection
0
200
400 mi
0
200
400 km

Barents Sea
SWEDEN
FINLAND
NORWAY
ESTONIA
LATVIA
LITHUANIA
RUSSIA
North Sea
DENMARK
Baltic Sea
IRELAND
UNITED KINGDOM
NETHERLANDS
London
Berlin
BELARUS
POLAND
GERMANY
BELGIUM
LUX.
Moscow
RUSSIA
Kiev
UKRAINE
Atlantic Ocean
Paris
FRANCE
LIECH.
SWITZ.
CZECH REP.
SLOVAKIA
AUSTRIA
HUNGARY
MOLDOVA
ROMANIA
SLOVENIA
CROATIA
BOS. AND HERZ.
SERBIA
MONT.
BULGARIA
Bay of Biscay
PORTUGAL
ANDORRA
MONACO
ITALY
SAN MARINO
Madrid
SPAIN
Corsica (France)
Rome
VATICAN CITY
MAC.
ALBANIA
Black Sea
Istanbul
TURKEY
Sardinia (Italy)
Balearic Isands (Spain)
Gibraltar (U.K.)
Ceuta (Spain)
Melilla (Spain)
Sicily (Italy)
GREECE
MOROCCO
ALGERIA
TUNISIA
MALTA
Mediterranean Sea
Crete (Greece)
CYPRUS
LEBANON
SYRIA
N
E
S
W
Conic Projection
0
200
400 mi
0
200
400 km

Atlas 369

Africa: Political

370 Atlas

Africa: Physical

Atlas 371

Asia: Political

372 Atlas

Asia: Physical

Atlas 373

Europe: Political

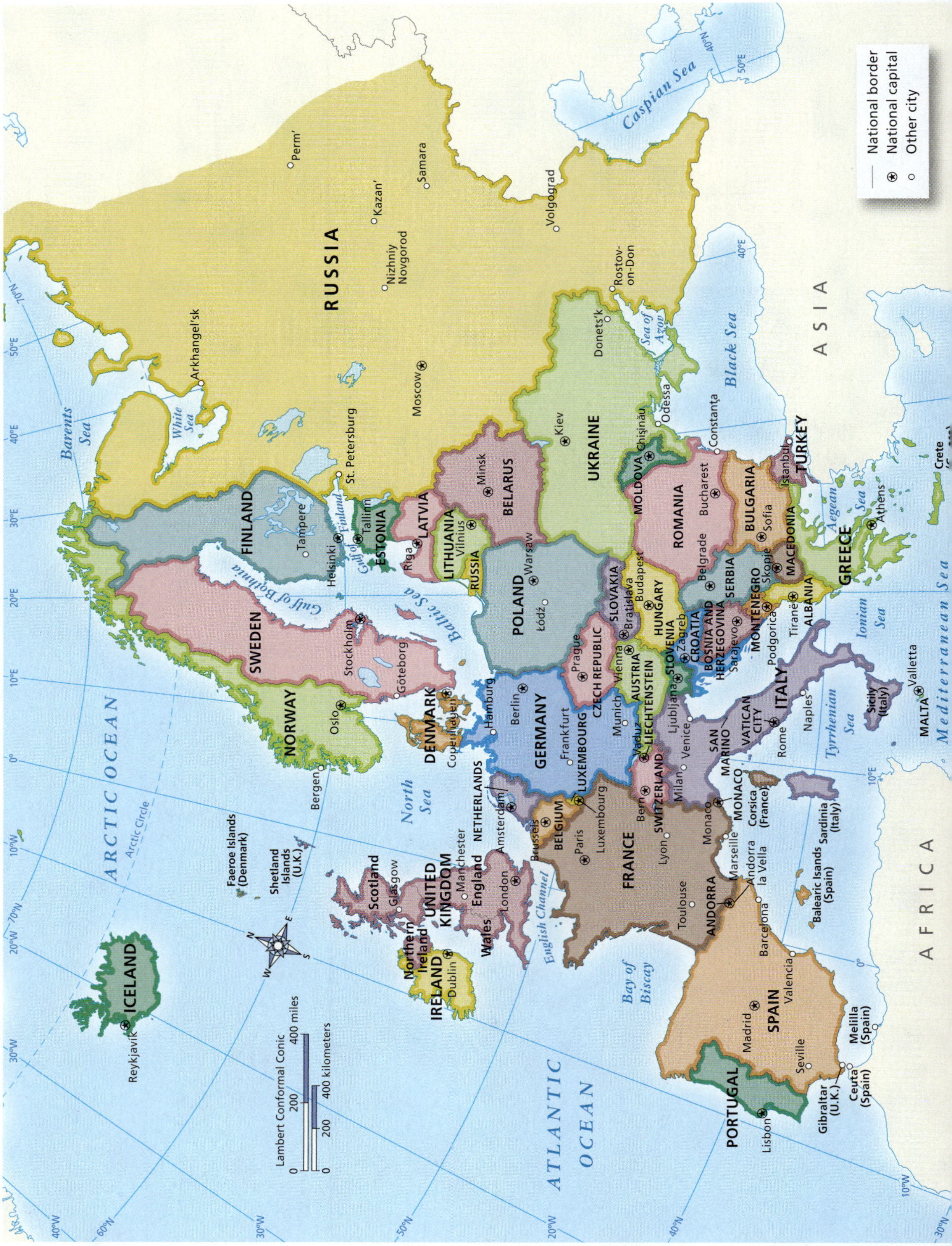

374 Atlas

Europe: Physical

Atlas 375

North & South America: Political

North & South America: Physical

Atlas 377

Australia, New Zealand & Oceania: Political-Physical

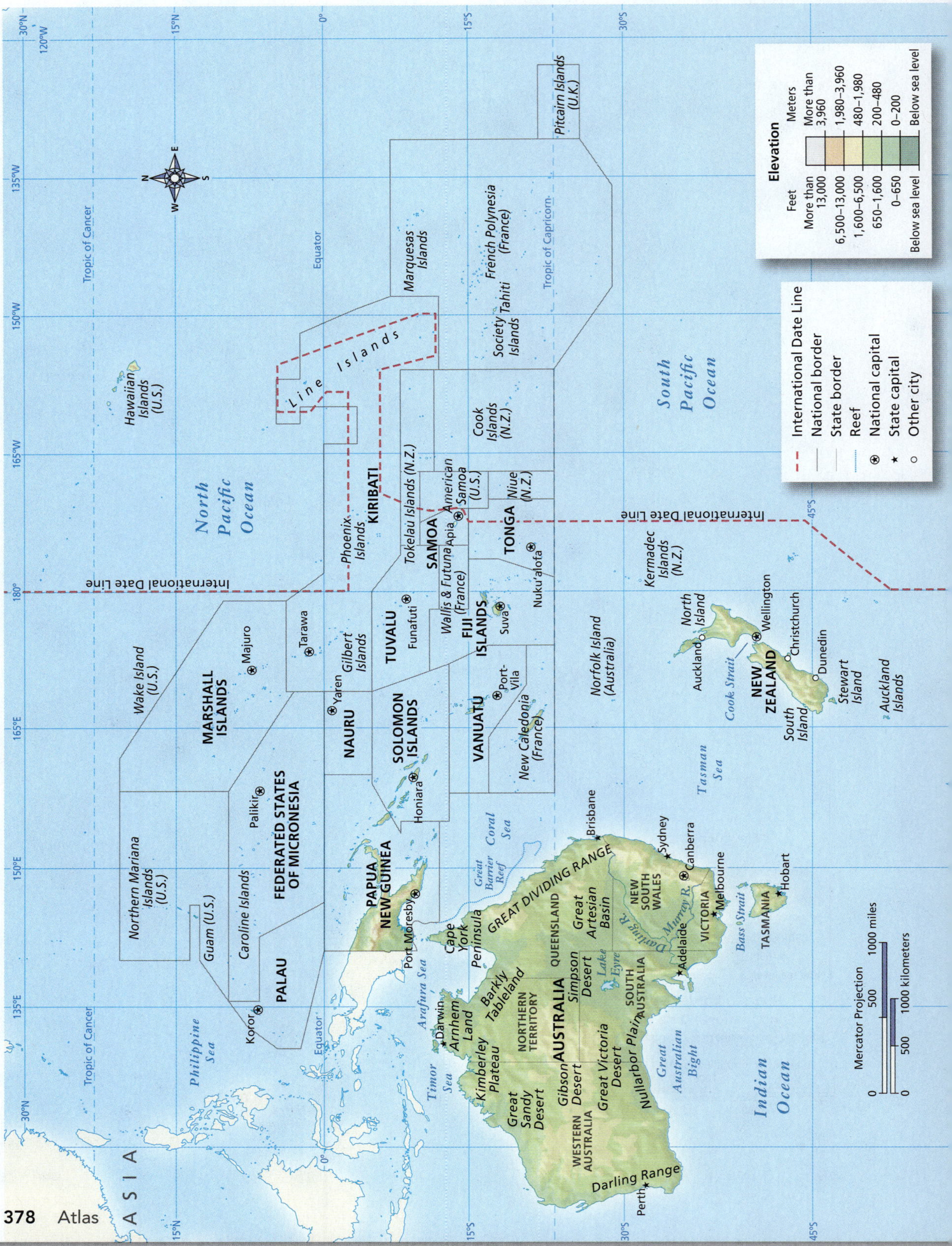

The Arctic: Physical

Elevation

Feet	Meters
More than 13,000	More than 3,960
6,500–13,000	1,980–3,960
1,600–6,500	480–1,980
650–1,600	200–400
0–650	0–200
Below sea level	Below sea level

National border
International Date Line

Atlas 379

Antarctica: Physical

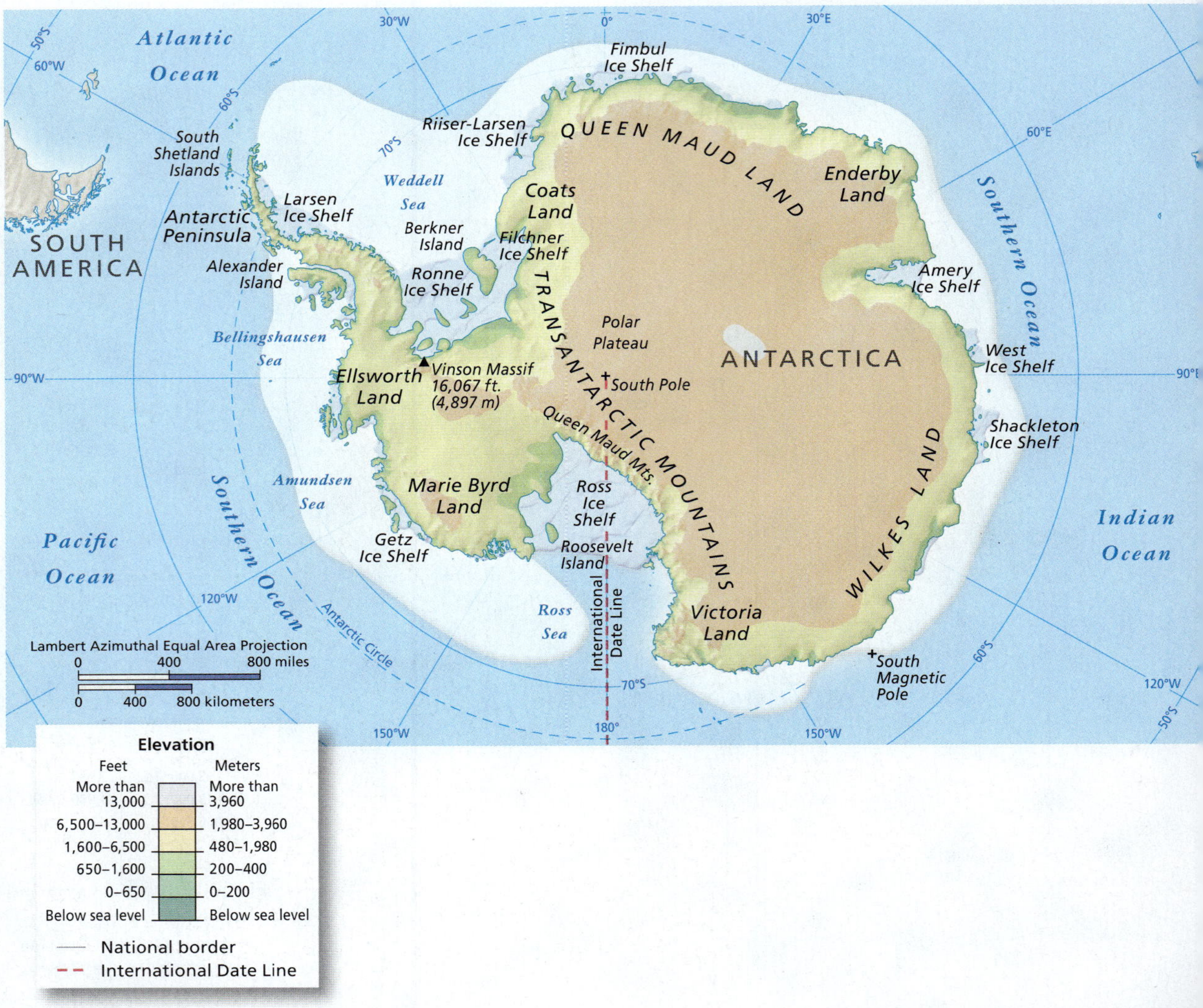

380 Atlas

Glossary

A

abundant *adj.,* existing in a large amount
Academy school of philosophy founded by Plato
accumulate collect or attain a large amount of something
achievement *n.,* accomplishment that requires effort or skill
acquire *v.,* to get hold of; obtain
acropolis "high city" in Greek; the upper part of an ancient Greek city, where public buildings and the city's defenses were located
acupuncture therapy that uses needles to cure sickness and stop pain
adapt change
ahimsa avoiding doing harm to any living thing
ally independent state that works with other states to achieve a shared military or political goal
alphabet small set of letters or symbols, each of which stands for a single sound
anatomy study of the structure of the body and its organs
animism belief that the natural world is full of spirits
anthropology study of humankind in all aspects, especially development and culture
aqueduct: channel that moves water over a long distance
artifact: object made by a human being
archaeologist scientist who studies human life in the past by examining the things that people left behind
aristocracy hereditary class of rulers, Greek for "rule by the best people"
artisan skilled worker who practices a handicraft
assembly *n.,* a company of persons gathered for deliberation and legislation, worship, or entertainment
Augustus title used by Roman emperors meaning venerable or greatly honored person
authorities *n.,* people who have the right to give orders
available *adj.,* able to be reached

B

baptism ritual cleansing by plunging into water
barbarian word used by Greeks and Romans for all people who did not share their cultures
barracks military housing
barter trading system in which people exchange goods directly without using money
Battle of Marathon Greek victory over the Persian army that ended the First Persian War
Battle of Salamis Greek victory over the Persian navy during the Second Persian War
benefit *n.,* gain; favorable result
benefits *n.,* things that produce good or helpful results or effects or that promote well-being
Brahman in Hinduism, the supreme cosmic consciousness, spiritual force, or God
Brahmanism religion of Vedic India, based on priests and rituals, particularly sacrifices to the gods
Brahmin member of the highest Indian caste grouping made up of priests
bureaucracy system of many government officials who carry out government rules and regulations
Byzantine word used by historians to describe the eastern Roman empire after the fall of the western Roman empire

C

calligraphy art of beautiful writing
caste fixed social class into which a person is born
cataract group of rocky rapids
cavalry soldiers who fight while riding horses
cease *v.,* to stop
censor *v.,* to keep objectionable material from being revealed
challenge *n.,* something that is difficult or demanding to do
chaos total disorder and confusion
chorus in ancient Greek drama, a group of people who commented on the action of a play and advised the characters
citadel fortified area
citizen legal member of a country or city-state
citizenship membership in a state or community which gives a person civil and political rights and obligations
city-state independent state consisting of a city and its surrounding territory
civil service the people who work for a government
civil war war between groups from the same country
civilization complex society that has cities, a well-organized government, and workers with specialized job skills
classical civilization the civilization of the ancient Greeks and Romans
collapse *v.,* to break down or fall down
colony group of people living in a new territory with ties to a distant state
commandment an order to do something
commentary *n.,* a set of comments or a recorded discussion about something
commerce buying and selling of goods and services
commission *v.,* order the creation of
communication *n.,* way of passing on information
complex *adj.,* having many related parts; not simple
concept *n.,* idea
conclude *v.,* to decide as a result of thinking or reasoning
concrete building material made by mixing small stones and sand with limestone, clay, and water
consequence *n.,* result of an action, effect
construct *v.,* to build or put together
constitution system of basic rules and principles by which a government is organized
consul one of two top officials and military leaders in the Roman republic
controversial *adj.,* subject to disagreement or argument
conversion heartfelt change in one's opinions or beliefs, especially in religion
core *n.,* center, most important part

Glossary 381

covenant binding agreement
credit arrangement in which a buyer can purchase something and pay for it over time
creed statement of beliefs
crucifixion Roman method of execution by nailing a person to a wooden cross
cuisine style of food
cultural diffusion spread of cultural traits from one culture to another
cultural trait idea or way of doing things that is common in a certain culture
culture beliefs, customs, practices, and behavior of a particular nation or group of people
cuneiform Mesopotamian system of writing that uses triangular-shaped symbols to stand for ideas or things
currency money that is used as a medium of exchange, usually bills or coins
Cyrillic alphabet alphabet used mostly for Slavic languages such as Russian and Bulgarian, as well as for other languages

D

decimal system counting system based on units of ten
deify officially declare a person to be a god
Delian League military alliance led by Athens
delta a flat plain formed on the seabed where a river deposits material over many years
democracy form of government in which citizens hold political power
denomination religious group
dense *adj.*, tightly packed; very thick
devote *v.*, to set aside for a purpose
devotion *n.*, dedication, loyalty
dharma a person's duty or what is right for him or her
Diaspora Jewish communities outside the ancient Jewish homeland, from a Greek word meaning dispersion, or scattering
dike wall to hold back water
diplomacy *n.*, the ability to handle relationships without increasing hostility
distinct *adj.*, separate, different
direct democracy government in which citizens take part directly in the day-to-day affairs of government
discriminate *v.*, treat some people differently or worse
drama *n.*, plays or performances that tell stories
drought long period of extremely dry weather
dynasty a series of rulers from the same family

E

ebony black wood from West Africa
economy system that a community uses to produce and distribute goods and services
element *n.*, part
elite *adj.*, representing the best
empire state containing several countries or territories
enlightenment in Buddhism, a state of perfect wisdom
environment surroundings
environmental *adj.*, having to do with natural surroundings
envoy representative of a government sent to another country
ephor man responsible for the day-to-day operation of the government in Sparta
epistle formal letter, several of which form part of the New Testament
equipment *n.*, things used for a specific purpose
established religion official religion supported by the government
ethics beliefs about what is right and wrong
eventual *adj.*, final
eventually *adv.*, after a time
evidence *n.*, information used to prove something
exclude *v.*, to shut out, keep from participating
exempt *adj.*, to be free from a punishment or duty
exile separation from one's homeland
Exodus escape of the Israelites from slavery in Egypt
export good or service produced within a country and sold outside the country's borders
extract *v.*, remove, draw out

F

Fertile Crescent a region with good conditions for growing crops that stretches from the Mediterranean coast east through Mesopotamia (modern Iraq) to the Persian Gulf
filial piety devotion of children to their parents
forum open area in a Roman city filled with public buildings, temples, and markets
fossil preserved remains of ancient human, animal, or plant

G

generate *v.*, to produce, create
geologist scientist who studies the physical materials of the Earth itself, such as soil and rocks
gladiator man who fought as part of public entertainment in ancient Rome
Gospel one of the first four books of the New Testament that describe the life and teachings of Jesus
govern *v.*, to control or strongly influence
granary special building used to hold grain
Great Schism split between the Eastern Orthodox and Roman Catholic churches in 1054
Great Wall long wall running east and west along the Chinese empire's northern border
Greek fire a chemical mixture that burned in water which was used by the Byzantine empire against enemy ships
Greco-Roman something that combines elements of Greek and Roman culture and traditions
guru thinker or teacher

H

Hammurabi's Code a set of laws that governed life in the Babylonian empire
Hellenistic the form of Greek culture that emerged after Alexander's conquests

382 Glossary

helot Messenian person forced to work as a lowly farmer by Sparta
hieroglyphic symbol that stands for a word, idea, or sound
Hippocratic oath oath taken by medical students swearing to practice medicine in an ethical way
hunter-gatherer person who lives by hunting animals and gathering plants
hypothesis logical guess

I

icon a holy image, usually a portrait of Jesus or a saint
iconoclast "image-breaker," person who opposed the use of icons in Christian worship
identify *v.*, consider or treat as the same
import good or service sold within a country that is produced in another country
income *n.*, payments of money
individual *adj.*, having to do with a single person or thing
inflation general increase in prices
innovation *n.*, new ways of doing things
interdependence dependence by each country or group on the other
interpret *v.*, to explain, give the meaning of
irrigate to supply water to
isolated *adj.*, set away from other people or places
ivory hard white material made from elephant tusks
issue *n.*, problem or subject to be discussed or decided

J

jati: occupation-based caste
judge in the Hebrew Bible, a leader who could rally the Israelites to defend their land
justice fairness or fair treatment
Justinian's Code a law code published by the Byzantine emperor Justinian

K

karma in Hinduism, the effect of a person's actions in this and in previous lives

L

lacquer a protective coating made from the sap of a special tree
lecturer *n.*, person who gives an informative talk to students
Legalism an ancient Chinese philosophy stating that a strong leader and a strong legal system, not moral values, are needed to create social order
legion basic unit of the Roman army, consisting of 4,500 to 5,000 heavily armed soldiers
loess a dustlike material that can form soil
logograph *n.*, a symbol that represents a word or group of words
lyric poetry poetic songs

M

magistrate government official who enforces the law
Mahayana Buddhism Buddhist sect that focuses on the compassion of the Buddha
maintain *v.*, to keep and support
manage *v.*, to direct; have control over
Mandate of Heaven in ancient China, the presumed right to rule given to a dynasty by heaven, the highest force of nature
maniple unit of 60 to 120 soldiers within a Roman legion that could act independently in battle
martyr person who dies for his or her beliefs
meditate calm or clear the mind, often by focusing on a single object
mercenary soldier who fights for pay rather than for his or her country
Meroitic script one of the world's first alphabets, invented in ancient Nubia
Mesopotamia wide, flat plain in between the Tigris and Euphrates rivers in present-day Iraq
metallurgy science that deals with extracting metal from ore and using it to create useful objects
metic foreigner in a Greek city-state, often a merchant or artisan
migrate *v.*, to move from one region to another in order to live there
migration movement of people from one place to another
military state society organized for the purpose of waging war
minor *adj.*, not serious, not important
minority *n.*, a group that is less than half of a population
mission *n.*, journey with a purpose
missionary someone who tries to convert others to a particular religion
moat trench filled with water as part of a fortification
moksha liberation from reincarnation
monopoly single person or group who controls the production of a good or service
monotheism belief in a single God
monastery secluded religious community
monsoon seasonal wind that brings rain to the Indian subcontinent during parts of the year
mosaic design formed with small tiles of glass, stone, or pottery
mummy a body that has been preserved so it will not decompose
mythology collection of myths or stories that people tell about their gods and heroes

N

navigation art of steering a ship from place to place
network *n.*, a closely interconnected group of people or things
New Testament writings that form part of the Christian Bible which tell the story of Jesus and his early followers
nirvana a state of blissful peace without desire or suffering
nomad person who moves often in search of food
numeral symbol used to represent a number

Glossary 383

O

observatory building for observing the sky
obsidian natural volcanic glass used to make very sharp blades for spears and arrows
official person who holds a government job
oligarchy government in which a small group of people rule
Olympic games in ancient Greece, an athletic competition held every four years in honor of Zeus
oracle bone animal bone or shell carved with written characters that was used to predict the future in ancient China
oratory art of giving speeches
orthodoxy traditional or established religious beliefs

P

papyrus a writing surface similar to paper named after the papyrus reed that grew along the Nile River in ancient Egypt
parable story with a religious moral
paterfamilias oldest man in a Roman family who had absolute power over his family
patriarchal society society in which men rule their families, and people trace their origins through male ancestors
Pax Romana period of stability in the Roman empire
Peloponnesian League military alliance led by Sparta
period *n.,* a span of time
phalanx Greek military formation of heavily armed foot soldiers who moved together as a unit
pharaoh king of ancient Egypt
philosophy general study of knowledge and the world; Greek for "love of wisdom"
pictograph a picture that represents a word or idea
policy *n.,* course of action taken by a government
polis Greek city-state
politics art and practice of government
polytheism worship of many gods or deities
pope leader of the Roman Catholic Church
populate to become an inhabitant of a place
potential *n.,* possibility to grow or change in the future
prehistory time before humans invented writing
professional *adj.,* trained, expert
profit *v.,* to make a gain
prophet person believed to be chosen by God to bring truth to the people
prosper *v.,* gain in wealth
province territory that is under the control of a larger country
pursue *v.,* to chase
pyramid structure with triangular sides

Q

quetzal colorful tropical bird

R

rabbi Jewish religious teacher
reason *n.,* the power to think clearly
reform *v.,* to improve
reincarnation rebirth of a soul in a new body
reject *v.,* decide against, turn away
reliable *adj.,* dependable; steady; not risky
religion people's beliefs and practices about the existence, nature, and worship of a god or gods
rely *v.,* to depend, trust
representative democracy democracy in which people elect representatives to make the nation's laws
republic form of government in which citizens have the right to vote and elect officials
resource supply of something that can be used as needed
resurrection coming back to life
revolution a complete change in ways of thinking, working, or living
righteousness acting or living in a way that is ethically right and obeys God's laws
river system main river and all of the other rivers and streams that drain into it
Romance language language that developed from Latin, such as French, Spanish, Portuguese, or Italian
rule of law idea that all members of a society—even the rich and powerful—must obey the law

S

Sabbath weekly day of rest
sarissa 18-foot-long Macedonian pike
satire work of literature that makes fun of its subject, often mocking vice or folly site of encounter place where people from different cultures meet and exchange products, ideas, and technologies
Scripture sacred writing
sculpture statue or other free-standing piece of art made of clay, stone, or other materials
seismometer a tool to measure earthquakes
Silk Road series of trade routes that crossed Asia
slavery ownership and control of other people as property
social class group of people living in similar economic conditions
Socratic method form of teaching in which the teacher asks students question after question to force them to think more clearly
specialization *n.,* act of concentrating on production of limited number of of goods or services
status
stable *adj.,* able to last, not likely to fall apart
standardize to set rules to make things more similar
standing army a permanent army of professional soldiers
stele grand stone pillar
strait narrow body of water that cuts through land, connecting two larger bodies of water
strategy a long-term plan for achieving a goal
stupa Buddhist commemorative burial mound
structure *n.,* building
subcontinent a large landmass that is set apart from the rest of the continent
subject person under the rule of a monarch
submission *n.,* obedience

384 Glossary

succession *n.,* one person or thing following another
successor *n.,* person who follows another in an office or role
surplus extra
survive *v.,* to last, to continue to live
symbolize *v.,* to represent
synagogue Jewish house of worship

T

Talmud collection of oral teachings and commentaries about the Hebrew Bible and Jewish law
tenant *n.,* person who rents land or a home
tenant farmer person who pays rent, either in money or crops, to grow crops on another person's land
Theravada Buddhism Buddhist sect that focuses on the wisdom of the Buddha
toga garment that adult men wore wrapped around their bodies as a symbol of Roman citizenship
tolerance willingness to respect different beliefs and customs
Torah first five books of the Hebrew Bible
tradition *n.,* a custom or practice that is handed down over generations
tribute payment or gift to a stronger power
Trinity the three persons, or forms, of God according to Christian belief: God the Father, Jesus the Son, and the Holy Spirit
tyranny unjust use of power, or in ancient Greece a government run by a strong ruler

U

unified *adj.,* joined together as a single whole
uniform

V

Veda collection of hundreds of sacred hymns composed by the Aryans of ancient India
varna: grouping based on one's skill
veto stop or cancel the action of a government official or body
villa large country home
violate *v.,* break a rule or agreement

W

warlord military ruler
welfare *n.,* well-being, comfort, prosperity
widespread: adj., common, spread across a large area

Z

ziggurat brick, pyramid-shaped Mesopotamian temple

Glossary 385

Glosario

A

abundant > abundante que existe en gran cantidad
Academy > Academia escuela de filosofía fundada por Platón
accumulate > acumular reunir u obtener una gran cantidad de algo
achievement > logro resultado que requiere esfuerzo o habilidad
acquire > adquirir conseguir algo; obtener
acropolis > acrópolis "ciudad alta" en griego; la parte elevada de una ciudad griega de la antigüedad, donde se ubicaban los edificios públicos y las defensas
acupuncture > acupuntura terapia que utiliza agujas para curar enfermedades y aliviar el dolor
adapt > adaptarse cambiar
ahimsa > ahimsa evitar hacerle daño a un ser viviente
ally > aliado estado independiente que colabora con otros estados para lograr un objetivo militar o político común
alphabet > alfabeto conjunto limitado de letras o símbolos, cada uno de los cuales representa un sonido
anatomy > anatomía estudio de la estructura del cuerpo y sus órganos
animism > animismo la creencia de que la naturaleza está llena de espíritus
anthropology > antropología estudio de todos los aspectos de la humanidad, especialmente el desarrollo y la cultura
aqueduct > acueducto canal que transporta agua a grandes distancias
archaeologist > arqueólogo científico que estudia la vida humana del pasado mediante el estudio de los objetos que las personas dejaron
aristocracy > aristocracia clase hereditaria de gobernantes, "gobierno ejercido por los mejores" en griego
artifact > artefacto objeto hecho por un ser humano
artisan > artesano trabajador especializado que ejerce un oficio manual
assembly > asamblea grupo de personas que se reúnen para deliberar, legislar, practicar una religión o entretenerse
Augustus > Augusto título usado por los emperadores romanos, significa persona venerable o con muchos honores
authorities > autoridades personas que tienen el derecho de dar órdenes
available > disponible que puede ser alcanzado

B

baptism > bautismo limpieza ritual que se realiza sumergiéndose en agua
barbarian > bárbaro término usado por los griegos y romanos para referirse a los pueblos que no compartían sus culturas
barracks > barracas alojamientos militares
barter > trueque sistema de comercio en el cual las personas intercambian bienes directamente, sin usar dinero
Battle of Marathon > Batalla de Maratón victoria griega sobre el ejército persa que terminó la Primera Guerra Médica
Battle of Salamis > Batalla de Salamina victoria griega sobre la armada persa durante la Segunda Guerra Médica
benefit > beneficio ganancia, resultado favorable
benefits > beneficios cosas que producen resultados o efectos buenos o útiles, o que contribuyen al bienestar
Brahman > Brahman en la religión hindú, la conciencia cósmica suprema, fuerza espiritual, o Dios
Brahmanism > brahmanismo religión de la India védica, basada en sacerdotes y rituales, especialmente sacrificios a los dioses
Brahmin > brahmán miembro de la casta más alta en la India, compuesta de sacerdotes
bureaucracy > burocracia sistema de numerosos funcionarios que ejecutan las normas y reglamentos del gobierno
Byzantine > bizantino término usado por los historiadores para describir el Imperio Romano oriental después de la caída del Imperio Romano occidental

C

calligraphy > caligrafía arte de escribir con letra bella
caste > casta clase social fija en la que nace una persona
cataract > catarata formación de rápidos rocosos
cavalry > caballería soldados que combaten montados a caballo
cease > cesar parar
censor > censurar impedir que un material cuestionable sea difundido
challenge > desafío algo que es difícil de hacer o exigente
chaos > caos desorden y confusión totales
chorus > coro en el teatro griego de la antigüedad, grupo de personas que comentaban sobre la acción de la obra y aconsejaban a los personajes
citadel > ciudadela área fortificada
citizen > ciudadano miembro legal de un país o ciudad estado
citizenship > ciudadanía membresía en un estado o una comunidad que confiere derechos y obligaciones civiles y políticos a las personas
city-state > ciudad-estado estado independiente que consiste en una ciudad y el territorio aledaño
civil service > servicio civil las personas que trabajan para un gobierno
civil war > guerra civil guerra entre grupos de un mismo país
civilization > civilización sociedad compleja con ciudades, un gobierno organizado y trabajadores con destrezas especializadas
classical civilization > civilización clásica la civilización de los griegos y romanos antiguos
colony > colonia grupo de personas que viven en un nuevo territorio que tiene vínculos con un estado distante
collapse > colapsar desmoronarse, venirse abajo

386 Glosario

commandment > mandamiento una orden de hacer algo
commentary > comentarios una serie de explicaciones o el registro de una discusión sobre algo
commerce > comercio compra y venta de bienes y servicios
commission > encargar ordenar la creación de algo
communication > comunicación manera de transmitir información
complex > complejo que tiene muchas partes relacionadas; que no es simple
concept > concepto idea
conclude > concluir decidir algo como resultado de pensar o razonar
concrete > concreto material de construcción fabricado mediante la mezcla de piedras pequeñas y arena con piedra caliza, arcilla y agua
consequence > consecuencia resultado de una acción, efecto
constitution > constitución sistema de reglas y principios básicos que establece la organización de un gobierno
construct > construir fabricar o armar
consul > cónsul uno de los dos altos funcionarios y líderes militares en la República romana
controversial > controvertido que tiende a causar disputa o desacuerdo
conversion > conversión cambio sincero de opiniones o creencias, especialmente en el campo religioso
core > núcleo centro, parte más importante
covenant > alianza pacto vinculante
credit > crédito arreglo que permite al consumidor comprar algo y pagarlo durante un plazo de tiempo
creed > credo afirmación de creencias
crucifixion > crucifixión método romano de ejecución clavando a una persona a una cruz de madera
cuisine > cocina estilo de comida
cultural diffusion > difusión cultural propagación de los rasgos culturales de una cultura a otra
cultural trait > rasgo cultural idea o manera de hacer las cosas que es común en una cultura determinada
culture > cultura creencias, costumbres, prácticas y comportamientos de una nación o un grupo de personas determinado
cuneiform > cuneiforme sistema de escritura usado en Mesopotamia que emplea símbolos de forma triangular para representar ideas y objetos
currency > moneda corriente dinero que se usa como medio de intercambio, usualmente en forma de billetes y monedas
Cyrillic alphabet > alfabeto cirílico alfabeto utilizado sobre todo para las lenguas eslavas, como el ruso, el búlgaro y otras

D

decimal system > sistema decimal sistema para contar basado en unidades de diez
deify > deificar declarar oficialmente dios a una persona
Delian League > Liga de Delos alianza militar liderada por Atenas
delta > delta llanura plana que se forma en el lecho marino donde un río deposita sedimento a través de los años
democracy > democracia tipo de gobierno en el que los ciudadanos tienen el poder político
denomination > denominación grupo religioso
dense > denso agrupado en forma compacta; espeso
devote > dedicar reservar para un propósito
devotion > devoción dedicación, lealtad
dharma > dharma el deber de una persona o lo que es correcto para él o ella
Diaspora > Diáspora conjunto de comunidades judías que viven fuera de la antigua patria judía; viene de una palabra griega que significa dispersión
dike > dique muro construido para contener el agua
diplomacy > diplomacia la capacidad de manejar relaciones sin aumentar la hostilidad
direct democracy > democracia directa tipo de gobierno en el que los ciudadanos participan directamente en los asuntos diarios del gobierno
discriminate > discriminar tratar peor o de forma diferente a ciertas personas
distinct > distinto separado, diferente
drama > drama obras o representaciones que cuentan
drought > sequía largo período de tiempo extremadamente seco historias
dynasty > dinastía serie de monarcas pertenecientes a la misma familia

E

ebony > ébano madera negra del África occidental
economy > economía sistema usado por una comunidad para producir y distribuir bienes y servicios
element > elemento parte
elite > élite que representa lo mejor
empire > imperio estado que incluye a varios países o territorios
enlightenment > iluminación en el budismo, un estado de sabiduría perfecta
environment > medio ambiente lo que hay en los alrededores
environmental > medioambiental relacionado con los entornos naturales
envoy > enviado representante de un gobierno ante otro gobierno
ephor > éforo hombre encargado de las operaciones cotidianas del gobierno en Esparta
epistle > epístola carta formal; escritos que forman parte del Nuevo Testamento
equipment > equipo cosas usadas con un propósito específico
established religion > religión establecida religión oficial apoyada por el gobierno
ethics > ética creencias sobre el bien y el mal
eventual > eventual final
eventually > eventualmente después de un tiempo
eventually > con el tiempo después de un tiempo

Glosario 387

evidence > evidencia información que se usa para probar algo
exclude > excluir apartar, evitar la participación de alguien
exempt > exento libre de un castigo o una obligación
exile > exilio separación de la patria
Exodus > Éxodo huida de los israelitas de la esclavitud en Egipto
export > exportación bien o servicio que se produce en un país y se vende fuera de los límites del país
extract > extraer quitar, sacar

F

Fertile Crescent > Creciente Fértil región con buenas condiciones para cultivos que se extiende desde las áreas de la costa del Mediterráneo, hacia el este por Mesopotamia (que hoy se conoce como Iraq) hasta el golfo Pérsico
filial piety > amor filial devoción de los hijos hacia sus padres
forum > foro área abierta en una ciudad romana llena de edificios públicos, templos y mercados
fossil > fósil restos conservados de personas, animales o plantas de la antigüedad

G

generate > generar producir, crear
geologist > geólogo científico que estudia los materiales físicos de la Tierra, como el suelo y las rocas
gladiator > gladiador hombre que combatía en espectáculos públicos en la antigua Roma
Gospel > Evangelio cada uno de los primeros cuatro libros del Nuevo Testamento, que describen la vida y las enseñanzas de Jesús
govern > gobernar controlar o influir fuertemente
granary > granero edificio especial usado para almacenar granos
Great Schism > Gran Cisma separación de la Iglesia ortodoxa oriental y la Iglesia católica romana en 1054
Great Wall > Gran Muralla China largo muro que recorre lo que fue la frontera norte del imperio Chino en dirección este-oeste
Greek fire > fuego griego una mezcla química que ardía en el agua y era usada por el Imperio Bizantino contra los barcos enemigos
Greco-Roman > greco-romano que combina elementos de las culturas y tradiciones griega y romana
guru > gurú pensador o maestro

H

Hammurabi's Code > Código de Hammurabi conjunto de leyes que regían la vida en Babilonia
Hellenistic > helenística la forma de cultura griega que surgió después de las conquistas de Alejandro
helot > ilota persona originaria de Mesenia forzada a trabajar como siervo agrícola en Esparta
Hippocratic oath > juramento hipocrático juramento hecho por los estudiantes de medicina en el que prometen practicar su profesión de una manera ética
hieroglyphic > jeroglífico símbolo usado para representar una palabra, idea o sonido
hunter-gatherer > cazador-recolector persona que vive de la caza de animales y la recolección de plantas
hypothesis > hipótesis suposición lógica

I

icon > ícono imagen sagrada, usualmente un retrato de Jesús o de un santo
iconoclast > iconoclasta "destructor de imágenes", persona que se oponía al uso de íconos en el rito cristiano
identify > identificar considerar o tratar como una misma cosa
import > importación bien o servicio que se vende en un país pero se produce en otro
income > ingreso pagos de dinero
individual > individual relacionado con una sola persona o cosa
inflation > inflación alza general de los precios
innovation > innovación nuevas formas de hacer las cosas
interpret > interpretar explicar, dar un significado
interdependence > interdependencia dependencia de cada país o grupo respecto de otro
irrigate > irrigar suministrar agua
isolated > aislado alejado de otras personas o lugares
issue > cuestión problema o tema que debe ser discutido o decidido
ivory > marfil material blanco duro hecho de colmillos de elefante

J

jati > jati casta definida por la ocupación
judge > juez en la Biblia hebrea, se refiere a un líder que podía organizar a los israelitas para defender su tierra
justice > justicia equidad o trato equitativo
Justinian's Code > Código de Justiniano un código de leyes publicado por el emperador bizantino Justiniano

K

karma > karma en el hinduismo, el efecto de las acciones de una persona en su vida actual y en las anteriores

L

lacquer > barniz capa protectora hecha de la savia de un árbol especial
lecturer > profesor disertante persona que da una charla informativa a estudiantes
Legalism > legismo antigua filosofía china según la cual se requiere de un líder y de un sistema legal fuertes, y no de valores morales, para mantener el orden social
legion > legión unidad básica del ejército romano, formada por 4,500 a 5,000 soldados fuertemente armados
loess > loes material en forma de polvo que puede formar tierra

388 Glosario

logograph > logograma símbolo que representa una palabra o un grupo de palabras
lyric poetry > poesía lírica canciones poéticas

M

manage > administrar dirigir; tener control sobre algo
magistrate > magistrado funcionario de gobierno encargado de hacer cumplir las leyes
Mahayana Buddhism > budismo mahayana secta budista que se concentra en la compasión de Buda
maintain > mantener sostener y apoyar
Mandate of Heaven > Mandato Celestial en la antigua China, el supuesto derecho a gobernar concedido a una dinastía por el Cielo, la más alta fuerza de la naturaleza
maniple > manípulo unidad de 60 a 120 soldados en una legión romana que podía actuar con independencia en la batalla
martyr > mártir persona que muere por sus creencias
meditate > meditar calmar o aclarar la mente, generalmente mediante la concentración en un único objeto
mercenary > mercenario soldado que combate a cambio de dinero, en lugar de hacerlo por su país
Meroitic script > escritura meroítica uno de los alfabetos más antiguos del mundo, inventado en la antigua Nubia
Mesopotamia > Mesopotamia planicie ancha situada entre los ríos Tigris y Éufrates en el Iraq actual
metallurgy > metalurgia ciencia que se ocupa de la extracción de metales y su uso en la creación de objetos útiles
metic > meteco extranjero en una ciudad estado griega, con frecuencia un mercader o artesano
migrate > migrar pasar de una región a otra para vivir allí
migration > migración desplazamiento de personas de un lugar a otro
military state > estado militarista sociedad organizada con el propósito de hacer la guerra
minor > menor no serio, no importante
minority > minoría grupo que representa menos de la mitad de una población
mission > misión viaje con un objetivo
missionary > misionero alguien que intenta convertir a otras personas a una religión en particular
moat > foso trinchera llena de agua usada como parte de una fortificación
moksha > moksha liberación de la reencarnación
monastery > monasterio comunidad religiosa retirada
monopoly > monopolio control de la producción de un bien o servicio por parte de una sola persona o grupo
monotheism > monoteísmo creencia en un solo Dios
monsoon > monzón viento de estación que trae lluvia al subcontinente índico durante partes del año
mosaic > mosaico diseño formado usando pequeñas tejas de vidrio, piedra o cerámica
mummy > momia cadáver preservado para evitar su descomposición
mythology > mitología colección de mitos o historias que la gente cuenta sobre sus dioses o héroes

N

network > red un grupo de personas o cosas conectadas entre sí
nomad > nómada persona que se traslada a menudo en busca de alimento
navigation > navegación arte de conducir un barco de un lugar a otro
New Testament > Nuevo Testamento escritos incluidos en la Biblia cristiana que cuentan la historia de Jesús y sus primeros seguidores
nirvana > nirvana estado de paz beatífica sin deseo ni sufrimiento
numeral > número símbolo usado para representar una cantidad

O

observatory > observatorio edificio usado para observar el cielo
obsidian > obsidiana cristal volcánico natural que se usaba para hacer cuchillos muy afilados y puntas de lanzas y flechas
official > funcionario persona que trabaja para el gobierno
oligarchy > oligarquía tipo de gobierno en el que un grupo pequeño de personas tienen el poder
Olympic games > Juegos Olímpicos en la antigua Grecia, competición atlética celebrada cada cuatro años en honor a Zeus
oracle bone > hueso oracular hueso animal o caparazón tallado con caracteres escritos que se usaba para predecir el futuro en la antigua China
oratory > oratoria arte de dar discursos
orthodoxy > ortodoxia creencias religiosas establecidas o tradicionales

P

papyrus > papiro superficie para escribir similar al papel, nombrada así por los papiros, juncos que crecían en la ribera del río Nilo en el antiguo Egipto
parable > parábola historia con una moraleja religiosa
paterfamilias > paterfamilias el hombre de más edad en una familia romana, que tenía poder absoluto sobre su familia
patriarchal society > sociedad patriarcal sociedad en la cual los hombres rigen las familias y las personas establecen sus orígenes a través de ancestros masculinos
Pax Romana > Paz Romana período de estabilidad del Imperio Romano
Peloponnesian League > Liga del Peloponeso alianza militar liderada por Esparta
period > período un lapso de tiempo
phalanx > falange formación militar griega compuesta por soldados a pie fuertemente armados que se movían juntos como una unidad
pharaoh > faraón rey del antiguo Egipto
philosophy > filosofía estudio general sobre el conocimiento y el mundo; en griego significa "amor por la sabiduría"

Glosario 389

pictograph > pictografía imagen que representa una palabra o idea
prophet > profeta persona de quien se cree que ha sido elegida por Dios para enseñar la verdad a la gente
policy > política curso de acción que toma un gobierno
polis > polis ciudad estado en Grecia
politics > política arte y práctica de gobernar
polytheism > politeísmo adoración de muchos dioses o deidades
pope > papa líder de la Iglesia católica romana
populate > poblar habitar un lugar
potential > potencial posibilidad de crecimiento o cambio en el futuro
prehistory > prehistoria época anterior a la invención de la escritura
professional > profesional entrenado, experto
profit > obtener ganancias obtener un beneficio económico
prosper > prosperar mejorar en lo económico
province > provincia territorio que se encuentra bajo la administración de un país más grande
pursue > perseguir seguir
pyramid > pirámide estructura con lados triangulares

Q

quetzal > quetzal ave tropical colorida

R

rabbi > rabino maestro espiritual de la religión judía
reason > razón capacidad de pensar claramente
reform > reformar mejorar
reincarnation > reencarnación renacimiento del alma en un nuevo cuerpo
reject > rechazar negarse, alejar algo
reliable > confiable digno de confianza, estable, no riesgoso
religion > religión creencias y prácticas de los seres humanos acerca de la existencia, la naturaleza y la adoración de un dios o dioses
rely > confiar depender de algo, tener confianza
representative democracy > democracia representativa democracia en la que el pueblo elige representantes que redactan las leyes de la nación
republic > república forma de gobierno en la que los ciudadanos tienen el derecho a votar y elegir funcionarios
resource > recurso existencia de algo que puede usarse según se necesite
resurrection > resurrección retorno a la vida
revolution > revolución cambio completo en la forma de pensar, trabajar o vivir
righteousness > rectitud cualidad de comportarse o vivir de una forma éticamente correcta y obedecer la ley de Dios
river system > sistema fluvial río principal y los ríos y arroyos que desembocan en él
Romance language > lengua romance idioma que derivó del latín, como el francés, el español, el portugués o el italiano
rule of law > imperio de la ley la idea de que todos los miembros de una sociedad, incluso los ricos y poderosos, deben obedecer la ley

S

Sabbath > sabbat día de la semana establecido para el descanso
sarissa > sarissa pica macedonia de 18 pies de largo
satire > sátira obra literaria que se burla de su tema, con frecuencia los vicios o los absurdos de la vida
Scripture > Escritura texto sagrado
sculpture > escultura estatua u otra pieza de arte hecha de arcilla, piedra o materiales similares
seismometer > sismómetro instrumento para medir terremotos
Silk Road > Ruta de la Seda red de rutas comerciales que atravesaban Asia
site of encounter > lugar de encuentro lugar donde las personas de diferentes culturas se encuentran e intercambian productos, ideas y tecnologías
slavery > esclavitud control y propiedad de algunas personas por otras
social class > clase social grupo de personas que tienen una condición económica similar
Socratic method > método socrático forma de enseñanza en la que el maestro hace preguntas a los estudiantes continuamente para hacerlos pensar con más claridad
specialization > especialización concentración en una cantidad limitada de bienes o actividades
stable > estable capaz de durar, con pocas posibilidades de deteriorarse
standardize > estandarizar establecer normas para hacer las cosas más similares
standing army > ejército regular un ejército permanente compuesto por soldados profesionales
status > estatus
stele > estela gran pilar de piedra
strait > estrecho masa de agua angosta que atraviesa la tierra y conecta dos masas de agua mayores
strategy > estrategia plan de largo plazo para obtener un objetivo
structure > estructura edificio
stupa > estupa montículo funerario conmemorativo de la religión budista
subcontinent > subcontinente masa continental separada del resto del continente
subject > súbdito persona gobernada por un monarca
submission > sumisión obediencia
succession > sucesión una persona o cosa que sigue a otra
successor > sucesor persona que sigue a otra en un puesto o función
surplus > superávit excedente
survive > sobrevivir persistir, seguir viviendo
symbolize > simbolizar representar
synagogue > sinagoga casa de reunión y culto de las comunidades judías

390 Glosario

T

Talmud > Talmud colección de enseñanzas orales y comentarios sobre la Biblia hebrea y la ley judía

tenant > arrendatario persona que alquila tierra o un hogar

tenant farmer > granjero arrendatario persona que paga renta, ya sea en dinero o cosecha, para poder cultivar en la tierra de otra persona

Theravada Buddhism > budismo teravada secta budista que se concentra en la sabiduría de Buda

tolerance > tolerancia voluntad de respetar costumbres y creencias diferentes

tradition > tradición costumbre o práctica que es transmitida a través de las generaciones

tribute > tributo pago u obsequio a un poder mayor

toga > toga vestimenta que los hombres adultos usaban, envolviéndose en ella, como símbolo de ciudadanía romana

Torah > Torá primeros cinco libros de la Biblia hebrea

Trinity > Trinidad las tres personas o formas de Dios según las creencias cristianas: Dios padre, Dios hijo y Espíritu Santo

tyranny > tiranía uso injusto del poder; en la antigua Grecia, el gobierno controlado por un gobernante firme

U

unified > unificado unido de modo que forma una totalidad

uniform > uniforme

V

varna > varna forma de agrupar a las personas según sus habilidades

Veda > Vedas colección de cientos de himnos sagrados compuestos por los arios de la antigua India

veto > vetar detener o cancelar las acciones de un funcionario o agencia de gobierno

villa > villa casa de campo grande

violate > violar no cumplir una regla o acuerdo

W

warlord > señor de la guerra gobernante militar

welfare > bienestar buena situación, comodidad,

widespread > extendido común, difundido a través de una gran área

Z

ziggurat > zigurat templo de Mesopotamia de forma piramidal, hecho de ladrillo

Glosario 391

Index

The letters after some page numbers refer to the following: *c* = chart; *g* = graph; *m* = map; *p* = picture; *q* = quotation.

A

392 Index

Index **393**

D

394 Index

Index **397**

398 Index

Index 399

400 Index

Index **401**

T

402 Index

Index 403

404 Index

Acknowledgments

Photography

i Hero Images/Getty Images; **iv** 123RF; **viB** Peter Horree/Alamy Stock Photo; **viT** Ursula Gahwiler/Robertharding/Alamy Stock Photo; **vii** Sylvain Grandadam/Age Fotostock; **viiiB** Catherine Leblanc/Godong/Getty Images; **viiiT** Ephotocorp/Alamy Stock Photo; **ix** Lambros Kazan/Shutterstock; **xB** Scaliger/IStock/Getty Images; **xT** Dmitry Naumov/123RF; **xxx** The Irish ImAge Collection/Design Pics Inc/Alamy Stock Photo; **xxxi** Fabian von Poser/ImageBROKER/Age Fotostock; **xxxii** Debu55y/Fotolia; **xxxiii** View of Ancient Babylon showing the Hanging Gardens and the Temple of Jupiter Belus, plate 3 from 'Entwurf einer historischen Architektur', engraved by Johann Adam Delsenbach (1687–1765) 1721 (engraving) (later colouration), Fischer von Erlach, Johann Bernhard (1656–1723) (after)/Private Collection/The Stapleton Collection/Bridgeman Art Library; **xxxiv** De Agostini/G. Dagli Orti/UIG Universal Images Group/Newscom; **xxxvB** Zhuhe2343603/Shutterstock; **xxxvi** Mary Evans Picture Library/Alamy Stock Photo; **xxxviiB** Interfoto/Personalities/Alamy Stock Photo; **xxxviiT** Transporting ceramics (painted silk),Chinese School, (15th century)/Topkapi Palace Museum, Istanbul, Turkey/Bridgeman Art Library; **xxxvT** Erich Lessing/Art Resource, NY; **xxxviii** Hero Images Inc./Alamy Stock Photo; **xlvii** Chassenet/BSIP SA/Alamy Stock Photo; **002–003** Ursula Gahwiler/Robertharding/Alamy Stock Photo; **005BR** Interfoto/Fine Arts/Alamy Stock Photo; **005CR** Marion Bull/Alamy Stock Photo; **005L** Ann Ronan Picture Library HeritAge Images/Newscom; **005TR** John Reader/Science Source; **006** E&E ImAge Library HeritAge Images/Newscom; **007** Eric Cabanis/Staff/AFP/Getty Images; **009** John Reader/Science Source; **010** Julian Stratenschulte/Dpa picture alliance/Alamy Stock Photo; **011B** Werner Forman Archive/HeritAge ImAge Partnership Ltd/Alamy Stock Photo; **011T** World History Archive/Alamy Stock Photo; **012** Eyal Bartov/Alamy Stock Photo; **013** Zev Radovan/BibleLandPictures/Alamy Stock Photo; **015** Clement Philippe/Arterra Picture Library/Alamy Stock Photo; **016** John Reader/Science Source; **019** Steppenwolf/Alamy Stock Photo; **021** Pierre Andrieu/Staff/AFP/Getty Images; **022** lorenzo rossi/Alamy Stock Photo; **023** Marion Bull/Alamy Stock Photo; **024** The Irish ImAge Collection/Design Pics Inc/Alamy Stock Photo; **025L** Critterbiz/Shutterstock; **025R** Mikkel Bigandt/Shutterstock; **026** Zev Radovan/BibleLandPictures/Alamy Stock Photo; **027** Ancient Art & Architecture Collection Ltd/Alamy Stock Photo; **030** Will Steeley/Alamy Stock Photo; **031** Ann Ronan Picture Library HeritAge Images/Newscom; **032** Debu55y/Fotolia; **033** Essam Al-Sudani/Stringer/AFP/Getty Images; **034** Interfoto/Fine Arts/Alamy Stock Photo; **036** Werner Forman Archive/HeritAge ImAge Partnership Ltd/Alamy Stock Photo; **037** Werner Forman/Universal Images Group/Getty Images; **038** Gary718/Shutterstock; **040** Carver Mostardi/Alamy Stock Photo; **041** Werner Forman Archive HeritAge Images/British Museum, London/Newscom; **042** Peter Horree/Alamy Stock Photo; **043** Jo Ann Snover/Shutterstock; **046–047** Peter Horree/Alamy Stock Photo; **048** Interfoto/Personalities/Alamy Stock Photo; **049BR** Fine Art Images/HeritAge ImAge Partnership Ltd/Alamy Stock Photo; **049CR** Pictures From History/The ImAge Works; **049TR** ImAge Asset Management/World History Archive/Age Fotostock; **050** ImAge Asset Management/World History Archive/Age Fotostock; **051** CM Dixon HeritAge Images/Newscom; **053** Mediacolor's/Alamy Stock Photo; **055** ZUMA Press, Inc./Alamy Stock Photo; **057** M. Seemuller/DEA/Getty Images; **058** Photo Researchers, Inc/Alamy Stock Photo; **060** View of Ancient Babylon showing the Hanging Gardens and the Temple of Jupiter Belus, plate 3 from 'Entwurf einer historischen Architektur', engraved by Johann Adam Delsenbach (1687–1765) 1721 (engraving) (later colouration), Fischer von Erlach, Johann Bernhard (1656–1723) (after)/Private Collection/The Stapleton Collection/Bridgeman Art Library; **061** Interfoto/Personalities/Alamy Stock Photo; **062** Josse Christophel/Alamy Stock Photo; **064** Peter Horree/Alamy Stock Photo; **065** Zev Radovan/www.BibleLandPictures.com/Alamy Stock Photo; **066** Adam Eastland Art + Architecture/Alamy Stock Photo; **068** Pictures From History/The ImAge Works; **069** W. BUSS/De Agostini/DEA/Getty Images; **070** Pictures From History/Newscom; **072** Fabian von Poser/ImageBROKER/Age Fotostock; **074** Nicholas Pitt/Alamy Stock Photo; **076** Goir/Shutterstock; **077** Eddie Gerald/Alamy Stock Photo; **078** ArtPix/Alamy; **081** Lawrence Migdale/Science Source; **082** www.BibleLandPictures.com/Alamy Stock Photo; **083** Ira Berger/Alamy Stock Photo; **084** Israel Images/Alamy Stock Photo; **085** Prisma Archivo/Alamy Stock Photo; **087** Dpa picture alliance archive/Alamy Stock Photo; **088** Nir Elias/Reuters; **089** Corey Weiner/Alamy Stock Photo; **090** Fine Art Images/HeritAge ImAge Partnership Ltd/Alamy Stock Photo; **093** Sebastian Scheiner/AP Images; **094** Flik47/iStock/Getty Images; **096** Jack Guz/Staff/AFP/Getty Images; **105** The Print Collector/Alamy Stock Photo; **100–101** Sylvain Grandadam/Age Fotostock; **102** Catherine Leblanc/Godong/Getty Images; **103B** Prisma Archivo/Alamy Stock Photo; **103C** David Keith Jones/Images of Africa Photobank/Alamy Stock Photo; **103T** Peter Horree/Alamy Stock Photo; **104** Efesenko/Fotolia; **108** David Keith Jones/Images of Africa Photobank/Alamy Stock Photo; **110** DEA/S. Vannini/De Agostin/Getty Images; **112** Peter Horree/Alamy Stock Photo; **113** Franois Gunet/Akg Images/Newscom; **114** Kostin SS/Shutterstock; **115** Brian_Kinney/Fotolia; **116** Michael DeFreitas Middle East/Alamy Stock Photo; **117** Fatih Kocyildir/Shutterstock; **118** Cultnat, Dist. RMN-GP/Art Resource, NY; **119** Tor Eigeland/Alamy Stock Photo; **120** Mickael David/Invictus SARL/Alamy Stock Photo; **121** Urosr/Fotolia; **123** Mary Evans Picture Library/Alamy Stock Photo; **124** Interfoto/Fine Arts/Alamy Stock Photo; **125C** Peter Horree/Alamy Stock Photo; **125L** Kokhanchikov/Shutterstock; **125R** Jim Batty/Alamy Stock Photo; **126** Werner Forman Archive/HeritAge ImAge Partnership Ltd/Alamy Stock Photo; **127** Natasha Owen/Fotolia; **130–131** Ephotocorp/Alamy Stock Photo; **132** De Agostini/G. Dagli Orti/UIG Universal Images Group/Newscom; **133B** Mary Evans Picture Library/Alamy Stock Photo; **133C** Coins depicting the King Chandragupta and Queen Durdhara, Mauyra Dynasty (gold), Indian School/Dinodia/Bridgeman Art Library; **133T** Godong/Alamy Stock Photo; **134** Pjhpix/Alamy Stock Photo; **135** Arnim Schulz/Moment Open/Getty Images; **137B** G Nimatallah/Dea/De Agostini Editore/Age Fotostock; **137T** Peter Horree/Alamy Stock Photo; **139** Robert Harding Productions/Alamy Stock Photo; **140** Twinsterphoto/Fotolia; **141** Anders Blomqvist/Lonely Planet Images/Getty Images; **143** Dea Picture Library/De Agostini Editore/Age Fotostock; **144** Yasir Nisar/Getty Images; **146** STR/EPA/Newscom; **148** Dbrnjhrj/Fotolia; **149** De Agostini/G. Dagli Orti/UIG Universal Images Group/Newscom; **150B** Bl/Robana/Robana Picture Library/Age Fotostock; **150T** Dinodia Photos/Alamy Stock Photo; **151** Fedyaeva Maria/Shutterstock; **152** K.Decha/Shutterstock; **153** Michael Runkel/robertharding/Alamy Stock Photo; **155** Gunnar Kullenberg/RGB Ventures/SuperStock/Alamy Stock Photo; **156** Bl/Robana/Robana Picture Library/Age Fotostock; **157** Davidevison/Fotolia; **158** Godong/Alamy Stock Photo; **159** Godong/Alamy Stock Photo; **160** Marc Bruxelle/Alamy Stock Photo; **162** Kaitune/Fotolia; **163** Roger Bacon/Reuters/Alamy Stock Photo; **164** Peter Horree/Alamy Stock Photo; **165** Ashish Bhatnagar; **167** Coins depicting the King Chandragupta and Queen Durdhara, Mauyra Dynasty (gold), Indian School/Dinodia/Bridgeman Art Library; **168** Chandragupta (w/c on paper)/Indian School/Dinodia/Bridgeman Art Library; **170** Mary Evans Picture Library/Alamy Stock Photo; **171** Saiko3p/iStock/Getty Images; **172** M.A.Pushpa Kumara/EPA/Newscom; **173** Rafal Cichawa/Fotolia; **174** Roger Bacon/Reuters/Alamy Stock Photo; **176** Paul Kim/DBImages/Alamy Stock Photo; **178** Angelo Giampiccolo/Shutterstock; **182–183** Jean-Pierre De Mann/Robertharding/Alamy Stock Photo; **190** V&A Images, London/Art Resource, NY; **184** V&A Images, London/Art Resource, NY; **185B** Robana/BL/Robana Picture Library/Age Fotostock; **185C** BnF, Dist. RMN-Grand Palais/Art Resource, NY; **185T** Pictures From History/Newscom; **186** 360b/Alamy Stock Photo; **187** Paul Springett 10/Alamy Stock Photo; **189** Zens photo/Moment Open/Getty Images; **191** The Emperor Mu Wang (c.985–c.907 BC) of the Chou Dynasty in his chariot, from a history of Chinese emperors (colour on silk), Chinese School, (17th century)/Bibliotheque Nationale, Paris, France/Bridgeman Art Library; **193** Chronicle/Alamy Stock Photo; **194** SSPL/The ImAge Works; **195** Pictures From History/Newscom; **197** Christopher Pillitz/Corbis Historical/Getty Images; **198** Ivy Close Images/Alamy Stock Photo; **200** BnF, Dist. RMN-Grand Palais/Art Resource, NY; **201** Weerapong Pumpradit/Shutterstock; **202** Zhuhe2343603/Shutterstock; **203** Danita Delimont/Gallo Images/

Acknowledgments 405

Getty Images; **204** Hung Chung Chih/Shutterstock; **206** Robana/BL/Robana Picture Library/Age Fotostock; **207** Snark/Art Resource, NY; **209** Transporting ceramics (painted silk), Chinese School, (15th century)/Topkapi Palace Museum, Istanbul, Turkey/Bridgeman Art Library; **210** Emperor Wu Ti (156–87, r.141–87 BC), leaving his palace, from a history of Chinese emperors (colour on silk), Chinese School, (17th century)/Bibliotheque Nationale, Paris, France/Archives Charmet/Bridgeman Art Library; **213** Dorling Kindersley ltd/Alamy Stock Photo; **214** Manfred Gottschalk/Lonely Planet Images/Getty Images; **215** Burt Silverman/National Geographic Creative/Alamy Stock Photo; **216** Prisma Bildagentur AG/Snyder Collection/Alamy Stock Photo; **217** Martha Avery/Corbis Historical/Getty Images; **218** SSPL/The ImAge Works; **222–223** Lambros Kazan/Shutterstock; **224** The Print Collector/Alamy Stock Photo; **225BR** Ancient Art & Architecture Collection Ltd/Alamy Stock Photo; **225CR** Stefanos Kyriazis/Fotolia; **225L** Akg Images/Newscom; **225TR** Martin Beddall/Alamy Stock Photo; **226** Dimitrios/Shutterstock; **227** Andrei Nekrassov/Fotolia; **229** Leonid Serebrennikov/Alamy Stock Photo; **230** AF archive/Alamy Stock Photo; **231** Starush/Fotolia; **232** John Hios/Akg Images/Newscom; **233** North Wind Picture Archives/Alamy Stock Photo; **234** Chigi vase, 650–640 BC (ceramic), Greek, (7th century BC)/Museo Nazionale Etrusco di Villa Giulia, Rome, Italy/De Agostini Picture Library/Bridgeman Images; **235** Lanmas/Alamy Stock Photo; **237** Erich Lessing/Art Resource, NY; **238** Martin Beddall/Alamy Stock Photo; **240** Tatiana Popova/Shutterstock; **242** Illustration Art/Alamy Stock Photo; **244** H.M. Herget/National Geographic Creative/Alamy Stock Photo; **245** World History Archive/Alamy Stock Photo; **247** Stefano Bianchetti/Corbis Historical/Getty Images; **249** Glevalex/Fotolia; **250** Mike Andrews/Ancient Art & Architecture Collection Ltd/Alamy Stock Photo; **251** Akg Images/Newscom; **253** Anatoly Vartanov/Fotolia; **255** Historical Picture Archive/Corbis Historical/Getty Images; **257** AF Fotografie/Alamy Stock Photo; **259** Vvasiliki/E+/Getty Images; **260** George Papapostolou/Moment Open/Getty Images; **261L** Olga Drabovich/Shutterstock; **261R** Zack Frank/Fotolia; **262** Ivy Close Images/Alamy Stock Photo; **263** Kpzfoto/Alamy Stock Photo; **264** Fine Art Images/HeritAge ImAge Partnership Ltd/Alamy Stock Photo; **265** Tomas Abad/Alamy Stock Photo; **266** Stefanos Kyriazis/Fotolia; **267** North Wind Picture Archives/Alamy Stock Photo; **268** Richard Osbourne/Alamy Stock Photo; **269** Ancient Art & Architecture Collection Ltd/Alamy Stock Photo; **270** Ancient Art & Architecture Collection Ltd/Alamy Stock Photo; **272** Peter Horree/Alamy Stock Photo; **273** Ivy Close Images/Alamy Stock Photo; **274** M.Coudert/Fotolia; **276** Antiqua Print Gallery/Alamy Stock Photo; **277** World History Archive/Alamy Stock Photo; **280–281** Dmitry Naumov/123RF; **283BR** Caesar Dictating his Commentaries (oil on canvas), Palagi, Pelagio (1775–1860)/Palazzo del Quirinale, Rome, Italy/Bridgeman Art Library; **283CR** Rabatti-Domingie/Akg Images/Newscom; **283L** Niday Picture Library/Alamy Stock Photo; **283TR** HeritAge ImAge Partnership Ltd/Alamy Stock Photo; **284** Alessandro0770/123RF; **285** Laura Zulian Photography/Getty Images; **287B** Nito/Shutterstock; **289** Album/Prisma/Newscom; **290** HeritAge ImAge Partnership Ltd/Alamy Stock Photo; **291** Atlaspix/Alamy Stock Photo; **293B** De Agostini Picture Library Universal Images Group/Newscom; **293T** Yullishi/Shutterstock; **295** Le Pictorium/Active Museum/Alamy Stock Photo; **296** Cliff Owen/AP Images; **297** Christine Osborne Pictures/Alamy Stock Photo; **298** Paco Gómez García/Age Fotostock/Alamy Stock Photo; **299** Fine Art/Getty Images; **300** World History Archive/Alamy Stock Photo; **302** Niday Picture Library/Alamy Stock Photo; **304** The Turmoils in Rome after the Death of Caesar (oil on panel), Roore, Jacques Ignatius de (1686–1747)/Private Collection/Photo Christie's Images/Bridgeman Art Library; **305** Rabatti-Domingie/Akg Images/Newscom; **306** Caesar Dictating his Commentaries (oil on canvas), Palagi, Pelagio (1775–1860)/Palazzo del Quirinale, Rome, Italy/Bridgeman Art Library; **310–311** David Soanes Photography/Moment Open/Getty Images; **313BR** JT Vintage/Glasshouse Images/Alamy Stock Photo; **313CR** Vicspacewalker/Fotolia; **313L** Bible Land Pictures/Akg Images; **313TR** FineArt/Alamy Stock Photo; **314** C M Dixon/AAA Collection/Ancient Art & Architecture Collection Ltd/Alamy Stock Photo; **315** RMN-Grand Palais/Art Resource, NY; **316** Peter Horree/Alamy Stock Photo; **318** David Ball/Alamy Stock Photo; **321** Ilan Amihai/PhotoStock-Israel/Alamy Stock Photo; **322** Interfoto/Personalities/Alamy Stock Photo; **324** Mattes Rene/Hemis/Alamy Stock Photo; **325** The Artchives/Alamy Stock Photo; **326** PjrTravel/Alamy Stock Photo; **328** Niday Picture Library/Alamy Stock Photo; **329** Prisma Archivo/Alamy Stock Photo; **331** Melvyn Longhurst/Alamy Stock Photo; **332** FineArt/Alamy Stock Photo; **333** Walker Art Library/Alamy Stock Photo; **335** EPA/EPA European Pressphoto Agency b.v./Alamy Stock Photo; **336** Zvonimir Atletic/Alamy Stock Photo; **337** Vasily Kovalev/Alamy Stock Photo; **338** Peter Horree/Alamy Stock Photo; **339** Adam Eastland Art + Architecture/Alamy Stock Photo; **340** Gabriel Jules Thomas/Getty Images; **341** Ann Ronan Picture Library HeritAge Images/Newscom; **342** Reconstruction of the Colosseum, Rome (w/c on paper), French School, (20th century)/Archives Larousse, Paris, France/Bridgeman Art Library; **343** Chariot race at the Circus Maximus,Baraldi, Severino (b.1930)/Private Collection/Look and Learn/Bridgeman Art Library; **344** Ivy Close Images/Alamy Stock Photo; **345** Viacheslav Lopatin/Shutterstock; **346** Akg Images/Newscom; **347** Erich Lessing/Art Resource, NY; **349** Universal Images Group/Superstock; **350** Realy Easy Star/Alamy Stock Photo; **352** Hackenberg/F1online digitale Bildagentur GmbH/Alamy Stock Photo; **353** Sadikgulec/IStock/Getty Images; **354** Popovariel/Shutterstock; **355** Verkhovynets Taras/Shutterstock; **357** Ig0rZh/Fotolia; **358** Erich Lessing/Art Resource, NY; **360** EpicStockMedia/Fotolia; **361** Interfoto/History/Alamy Stock Photo;

Text

Archaeological Institute of America "Was There a Trojan War?" from Archaeology, Vol 57, No. 03 by Manfred Korfmann. Copyright © 2004 by Archaeological Institute of America. **Archaeology Online** Harappan Horse: Polemics and Propaganda by Michael Witzel. Copyright © Archaeology Online. **Archaeology Online** The Horse and the Aryan Debate by Michel Danino. Copyright © Archaeology Online. **London, Methuen & Co. Ltd** The Literature of the Ancient Egyptians; Poems, Narratives, and Manuals of Instruction, from the Third and Second Millennia B. C. by Adolf Erman. Copyright © London, Methuen & Co. Ltd. **Ministry of Culture and Communication** The Cave of Chauvet-Point-D'Arc by Robert Begouen. Copyright © Ministry of Culture and Communication. **Nature Publishing Group** "Evolution, Consequences and Future of Plant and Animal Domestication" from Nature, August 8, 2002, Vol. 418, pp. 700–707 by Jared Diamond. Copyright © Nature Publishing Group 2002. **The Jewish Publication Society** The Tanakh: The Holy Scriptures by The Jewish Publication Society. Copyright © 1985 by The Jewish Publication Society. Used by permission. **Oxford University Press** The Oxford History of Ancient Egypt by Betsy M Bryan. Copyright © Oxford University Press 2000. **Oxford University Press** The Tale of Sinuhe and Other Ancient Egyptian Poems, 1940–1640 BC translated by R B Parkinson. Copyright © 1997 by Oxford University Press. Used by permission.

406 Acknowledgments